P9-EDN-759

When should I travel to get the best airfare?
Where do I go for answers to my travel questions?
What's the best and easiest way to plan and book my trip?

www.frommers.travelocity.com

Frommer's, the travel guide leader, has teamed up with **Travelocity.com**, the leader in online travel, to bring you an in-depth, easy-to-use resource designed to help you plan and book your trip online.

At **www.frommers.travelocity.com**, you'll find free online updates about your destination from the experts at Frommer's plus the outstanding travel planning and purchasing features of Travelocity.com. Travelocity.com provides reservations capabilities for 95 percent of all airline seats sold, more than 47,000 hotels, and over 50 car rental companies. In addition, Travelocity.com offers more than 2,000 exciting vacation and cruise packages. Travelocity.com puts you in complete control of your travel planning with these and other great features:

> **Expert travel guidance from Frommer's** - over 150 writers reporting from around the world!

> **Best Fare Finder** - an interactive calendar tells you when to travel to get the best airfare

> **Fare Watcher** - we'll track airfare changes to your favorite destinations

> **Dream Maps** - a mapping feature that suggests travel opportunities based on your budget

> **Shop Safe Guarantee** - 24 hours a day / 7 days a week live customer service, and more!

Whether traveling on a tight budget, looking for a quick weekend getaway, or planning the trip of a lifetime, Frommer's guides and Travelocity.com will make your travel dreams a reality. You've bought the book, now book the trip!

Travelocity.com
A Sabre Company

Frommer's

Here's what the critics say about Frommer's:

"Amazingly easy to use. Very portable, very complete."
—Booklist

♦

"The only mainstream guide to list specific prices. The Walter Cronkite of guidebooks—with all that implies."
—Travel & Leisure

♦

"Complete, concise, and filled with useful information."
—New York Daily News

♦

"The best series for travelers who want one easy-to-use guidebook."
—U.S. Air Magazine

Other Great Guides for Your Trip:

Frommer's Bahamas

Frommer's Bermuda

Frommer's Cancún, Cozumel & the Yucatan

Frommer's Caribbean

Frommer's Caribbean from $70 a Day

Frommer's Costa Rica

Frommer's Florida

Frommer's Jamaica & Barbados

Frommer's Mexico

Frommer's Miami & the Keys

Frommer's Puerto Rico

Frommer's Virgin Islands

Frommer's Walt Disney World & Orlando

Other Great Cruise Guides:

Frommer's Alaska Cruises

Frommer's European Cruises

Cruise Vacations for Dummies

Frommer's® 2001

CARIBBEAN CRUISES
AND PORTS OF CALL

by Heidi Sarna

IDG Books Worldwide, Inc.
An International Data Group Company
Foster City, CA • Chicago, IL • Indianapolis, IN • New York, NY

ABOUT THE AUTHOR

Heidi Sarna has cruised on some 70 ships of all shapes and sizes, from 100-passenger sailing ships to 3,000-passenger megas, and she loves them all (well, OK, some more than others). She's a contributing editor to *Travel Holiday* magazine and over the past 10 years has contributed articles on cruising and travel to *Bride's, New Choices, Cigar Aficionado, Diversion, Frommer's Budget Travel On-Line, Travel Weekly, Travel Counselor, Leisure Travel News, Travel Agent, Cruise & Vacation Views,* and *Porthole*, as well as to other major guidebooks and the *Boston Herald, Star Ledger,* and *Washington Times* newspapers. When she's not cruising, you're bound to find her at Manhattan's West Side docks, touring and inspecting the many ships that pass through New York.

IDG BOOKS WORLDWIDE, INC.

An International Data Group Company
919 E. Hillsdale Blvd.
Suite 400
Foster City, CA 94404

Find us online at **www.frommers.com**.

Copyright © 2000 by IDG Books Worldwide, Inc.
Maps copyright © 2000 by IDG Books Worldwide, Inc.

All rights reserved. No part of this book may be reproduced or transmitted in any form or by any means, electronic or mechanical, including photocopying, recording, or by any information storage and retrieval system, without permission in writing from the Publisher.

FROMMER'S is a registered trademark of Arthur Frommer. Used under license.

ISBN 0-02-863776-3
ISSN 1090-2600

Editor: Matt Hannafin
Production Editor: Carol Sheehan
Photo Editor: Richard Fox
Design by Michele Laseau, Holly Wittenberg
Staff cartographers: John Decamillis, Elizabeth Puhl, Roberta Stockwell
Additional Cartography by Nicholas Trotter
Page creation by IDG Books Indianapolis Production Department

SPECIAL SALES

For general information on IDG Books Worldwide's books in the U.S., please call our Consumer Customer Service department at 1-800-762-2974. For reseller information, including discounts, bulk sales, customized editions, and premium sales, please call our Reseller Customer Service department at 1-800-434-3422.

Manufactured in the United States of America

5 4 3 2 1

Contents

Part 1: Planning, Booking & Preparing for Your Cruise

3 Things to Know Before You Go 66

4 The Cruise Experience 70

Part 2: The Cruise Lines & Their Ships

5 The Ratings (and How to Read Them) 89

6 The Mainstream Lines 100

7   Cheap Cruises, Older Ships: The Budget Lines   227

8   The Ultra-Luxury Lines   260

9   Soft-Adventure Lines & Sailing Ships   312

Part 3: The Ports

Part 4: Appendixes

List of Maps

ACKNOWLEDGMENTS

A select group of experienced travel journalists and experts contributed to this book.

Kenneth Lindley, a Brooklyn-based freelance writer and a passionate, curious and devoted traveler, didn't leave a palm tree or conch shell unturned when he explored the Caribbean islands of Bonaire, Guadeloupe, Les Saintes, and Dominica and reviewed them for this book. **Arline and Sam Bleecker,** everyone's favorite husband-and-wife travel-writing team, contributed their valuable two cents to the *Radisson Diamond, Voyager of the Seas, Volendam,* Barbados, Cozumel, Jamaica, and St. Lucia reviews. **Brian Major,** a respected (not to mention cool) travel writer and cruise editor at *Travel Weekly,* contributed his point of view to the Martinique, Trinidad and Tobago, and BVI reviews. **Laura Dennis,** a former editor at *Travel Weekly,* has been to the Caribbean a zillion times and contributed her experiences to the Dominican Republic and Antigua reviews. **Lesley Abravanal,** a writer and editor living in Miami, provided the real scoop on that wild and crazy Pez-colored city by the sea. **Jonathan Siskin,** seasoned travel writer, broadcaster, and poet-artist, contributed to the NCL, Crown, and St. Croix reviews. **Ted Scull,** a well-respected ship authority and travel writer, contributed to the ACCL review in this edition as well as his input to past editions of this book. Freelancers **Rich Steck** and **Judi Janofsky,** avid cruisers for 20 years, contributed to the *Seabourn Sun* review. **Alan Zamchick,** ship lover since the age of 7 and Steamship Historical Society and World Ship Society member, was the history guru for the book. Thanks to **Dr. Christina Colon** for her help researching and verifying some of the more esoteric tidbits in the book. **Ronald I. Framson,** Certified Travel Counselor (CTC) and travel industry consultant, along with his wife, **Dee L. Framson,** CTC, Master Cruise Counselor (MCC), and active agent, contributed their years of industry experience to the "Booking Your Cruise & Getting the Best Price" chapter. **Mark Chapman,** travel editor at the *Boston Herald* and cabaret star in the making, contributed to past editions of this book. Special thanks to **Matt Hannafin,** the most thorough, patient, and good-hearted editorial bodhisattva in New York (who also wrote the Clipper, Bequia, and Nevis reviews and contributed to the Celebrity, Royal Olympic, HAL, Commodore, and St. Kitts reviews).

Many thanks also to all the helpful public-relations staff at the cruise lines.

And most importantly, to my wonderful husband, **Arun,** for his support, insight, and much-appreciated daily dose of "go do your work."

AN INVITATION TO THE READER

In researching this book, we discovered many wonderful places—hotels, restaurants, shops, and more. We're sure you'll find others. Please tell us about them, so we can share the information with your fellow travelers in upcoming editions. If you were disappointed with a recommendation, we'd love to know that, too. Please write to:

Frommer's Caribbean Cruises and Ports of Call 2001
IDG Books Worldwide, Inc.
909 Third Ave.
New York, NY 10022

AN ADDITIONAL NOTE

Please be advised that travel information is subject to change at any time—and this is especially true of prices. We therefore suggest that you write or call ahead for confirmation when making your travel plans. The authors, editors, and publisher cannot be held responsible for the experiences of readers while traveling. Your safety is important to us, however, so we encourage you to stay alert and be aware of your surroundings. Keep a close eye on cameras, purses, and wallets, all favorite targets of thieves and pickpockets.

WHAT THE SYMBOLS MEAN

✪ Frommer's Favorites

Our favorite places and experiences—outstanding for quality, value, or both.

The following abbreviations are used for credit cards:

AE	American Express	EC	Eurocard
CB	Carte Blanche	JCB	Japan Credit Bank
DC	Diners Club	MC	MasterCard
DISC	Discover	V	Visa
ER	EnRoute		

FIND FROMMER'S ONLINE

www.frommers.com offers up-to-the-minute listings on almost 200 cities around the globe—including the latest bargains and candid, personal articles updated daily by Arthur Frommer himself. No other Web site offers such comprehensive and timely coverage of the world of travel.

The Gulf of Mexico & the Caribbean

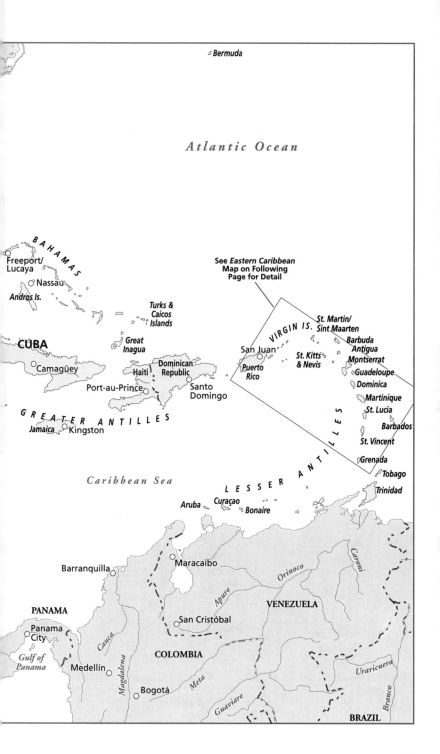

Bermuda

Atlantic Ocean

B A H A M A S

Freeport/
Lucaya

Nassau

Andros Is.

Turks &
Caicos
Islands

See *Eastern Caribbean*
Map on Following
Page for Detail

VIRGIN IS.

St. Martin/
Sint Maarten

Great
Inagua

CUBA

Camagüey

Haiti

Dominican
Republic

San Juan

Puerto
Rico

*St. Kitts
& Nevis*

Barbuda
Antigua
Montserrat

Guadeloupe

Dominica

Port-au-Prince

Santo
Domingo

Martinique

St. Lucia

G R E A T E R   A N T I L L E S

Barbados

Jamaica   Kingston

St. Vincent

Grenada

L E S S E R   A N T I L L E S

Tobago

Trinidad

Caribbean Sea

Aruba

Curaçao

Bonaire

Barranquilla

Maracaibo

Orinoco

Caroni

Apure

PANAMA

VENEZUELA

Panama
City

San Cristóbal

*Gulf of
Panama*

Cauca

COLOMBIA

Magdalena

Medellín

Meta

Uraricuera

Bogotá

Guaviare

Branco

BRAZIL

The Eastern Caribbean

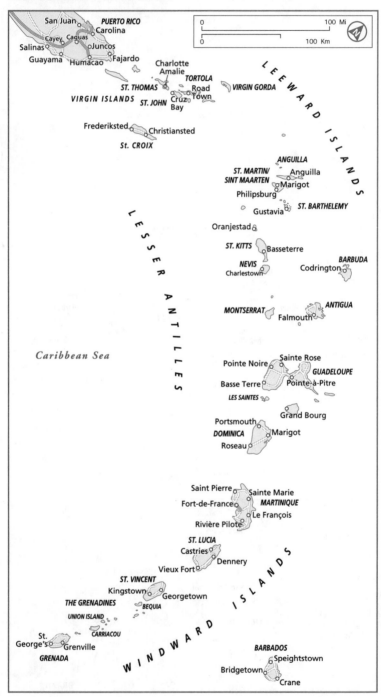

Cruising Into the 21st Century

Strangely enough, I didn't always love cruising. In fact, before I took my first one nearly a decade ago, I, like many nonbelievers, assumed cruises were pretty much all the same and not something I'd like. I assumed they were either weigh stations for the nursing-home set or cheesy floating frat parties. That they'd be confining and dull.

Well, first impressions were made to be broken. After cruising on more ships than I can count, I have a different attitude, and I'm hooked. A vacation at sea is intoxicating. Nowhere else can you be so isolated and away from it all, yet so immersed in and connected to the community of cruisers and crew on board. No matter what size or style of ship—and believe me, there are lots of choices—there's just so much to love. I love socializing with people of all ages and walks of life, the ritual of dining, and the chance to explore the islands. And who knew that the romance and nostalgia of being at sea, even on the newest, flashiest megaships, is so alluring? If you can break away from the disco and the conga lines long enough to wander out to some quiet corner of the deck, you'll see what I mean. The sea is a mesmerizing, powerful, and magical place to call home for a week. Just you and your shipmates alone at sea, with not another thing in sight.

HELPING YOU FIND YOUR IDEAL CRUISE

I've got a mission. Above all else, with this guide I want to show you that all cruises are not created equal. They're not all glitzy cities at sea by any means, and the truth is you've got choices galore. I'll help you wade through the options and illustrate the vast differences between ships and cruise experiences. To do this, I've done something no other guidebook has attempted: I've divided the 24 cruise lines covered in this book into four categories—mainstream lines, ultra-luxury lines, older-ship budget lines, and soft-adventure lines—and developed a **new rating system** that judges them against only other ships in the same category, so as to offer comparisons between comparable lines and ships. It's important to compare apples with apples, and not draw irrelevant comparisons between wildly different cruises (say, between ultra-luxurious Seabourn and adventurous Star Clippers, or riotous mainstream Carnival and genteel, upscale Cunard). You wouldn't compare a two-seater sports car with a hulking sport utility vehicle or a notepad with a Palm Pilot, would you? Same idea applies here.

HELPING YOU REALISTICALLY BUDGET YOUR TRIP

This book offers something else you'll find in no other cruise guide: the ability to see how much you can *realistically* expect to pay for your cruise.

Just like new-car prices, cruise line brochure prices are notoriously misleading. It's a matter of supply and demand: Cruise lines may ask $2,000 for a cabin, but they're more than willing to book you into that same cabin for a fraction of that amount if it looks like they won't be able to get the asking price. Cruises hardly ever sell for the brochure price, but other guidebooks print those prices anyway, leaving it up to you to take a guess at what the real price might be.

I took a different approach, partnering with Icruise.com, a Web-based cruise agent, to provide you with the **actual prices** consumers were paying for cruises aboard all the ships reviewed in this book. Each review shows you approximately how much you can expect to pay for an inside cabin (one without windows), an outside cabin (with windows), and a suite, and in chapter 2 I've provided a chart that shows how these prices compare with the published brochure rates. How much of a difference could it be, you ask? Think about this: The brochure rate for a 7-night eastern Caribbean cruise aboard Princess's beautiful *Grand Princess* is $2,553 for a low-end outside cabin. In reality, however, people who booked during our sampling period (approximately 8 months ahead of time) for an early 2001 sailing were able to get that same cabin for $1,372. If that ain't a big difference, I don't know what is.

CRUISING TODAY: SO MANY NEW SHIPS!

It's mind-boggling just how many ships are being built and introduced these days to accommodate an ever-growing number of cruisers (industry gurus predict that by year-end some 6.5 million people will have taken a cruise in 2000). More ships equals more choice, as never before—and, incidentally, it also means more deals for you as competition between the lines becomes fierce. There's a head-spinning variety of Caribbean-bound ships to choose from—sailing mostly 7-night cruises, but also more short 3-, 4-, and 5-nighters than ever—and lots more on the way. Joining the nearly 100 ships already plying Caribbean routes, 10 new Caribbean-bound vessels were launched in 2000 alone, including Princess Cruises' 1,950-passenger *Ocean Princess,* which debuted in February; Holland America's 1,440-passenger *Zaandam,* which debuted in May, and 1,380-passenger *Amsterdam,* expected to hit the high seas by year-end; Star Clippers' 228-passenger, five-masted, fully-rigged *Royal Clipper,* which became one of the biggest sailing ships ever built when it debuted in May; and Celebrity's 1,950-passenger *Millennium,* which entered service in June as a modern tribute to the classic liners of yesteryear. Carnival also popped out another mega with the 2,758-passenger *Carnival Victory* debuting in August; Costa Cruises' 2,100-passenger *CostaAtlantica* debuted in July, became the line's first new build since the *Victoria* in 1996 and the first to have verandas in over 75% of the cabins; and Royal Olympic's new high-speed, 840-passenger ship, the *Olympic Voyager,* hit the seas running in June. As if that's not enough, two more ships are slated to be introduced right after this book goes to press: In September Silversea Cruises' 396-passenger *Silver Shadow* sails its first cruise, and in October *Explorer of the Seas,* a sister to Royal Caribbean's behemoth 3,114-passenger *Voyager* (the largest passenger ship ever) is slated to debut.

No less impressive, at last count it appeared 2001 will see yet another 10 ships launched. Radisson Seven Seas' largest ship to date, the 708-passenger *Mariner,* and a second 840-passenger ship for Royal Olympic, the *Olympic Explorer,* are both due in March 2001; and a second 396-passenger Silversea ship, the *Silver Mirage,* is scheduled for delivery in June. On the megaship front, two more 1,950-passenger

Millennium-class ships are due for Celebrity in January and August; a 2,600-passenger sister to Princess's *Grand Princess* is scheduled for April; a second 2,004-passenger *Norwegian Cruise Line* ship, sister to the *Sky,* is due in June; a pair of 2,112-passenger Carnival ships, the *Carnival Spirit* and *Carnival Pride,* are due in early and late 2001; and Royal Caribbean's 2,100-passenger *Radiance of the Seas,* first of the line's Vantage-class ships, is to enter service in spring of 2001. Industry sources even say Caribbean resort operator Sandals is interested in getting into the cruise business with a ship perhaps as early as 2001. And don't look for the building frenzy to slow down anytime soon—with dozens of ships on order as of early 2000, the next few years will be just as busy. In fact, I'm not the only one to wonder if the cruise lines haven't gone too far, building more ships than there are passengers. If so, it will only mean one thing for you: cutthroat competition and good bargains!

TODAY'S ONBOARD OFFERINGS, FROM E-MAIL TO ICE-SKATING

Although there are a handful of new small ships, the majority of the new ships are massive, carrying upward of 2,500 passengers (plus about half again that number in crew), weighing from 80,000 to 142,000 gross registered tons, and measuring nearly 1,000 feet long. The biggest cruise ships in the world (at least for now), Royal Caribbean's new *Voyager* and *Explorer of the Seas,* are nearly as long as the Empire State Building is tall. The *Norway, QE2, Disney Magic* and *Disney Wonder,* and *Grand Princess* are all about twice as long as the Washington Monument is tall. Get the picture? Floating hotels, floating cities, floating galaxies—whatever you want to call them—these babies are *big.*

So what's one of these hot new $300 million to $500 million cruise ships come loaded with? Like the race to build the tallest skyscraper, lines are forever trying to outdo each other in the size and gimmick department. Not only do their megaships have three or four (or more) sprawling dining rooms, easily a dozen bars and entertainment lounges, several pools, cavernous gyms and spas, and a mall-like string of shops, they have things you'd never imagine finding on a ship, much less at some resort or hotel. The *Voyager* and *Explorer of the Seas* have—no kidding—**rock-climbing walls** and **ice-skating rinks** (you know, in case the four pools and regulation-size basketball courts aren't enough for you). The Carnival *Elation, Paradise, Imagination, Inspiration,* and *Jubilee* have **sushi bars.** The *Grand Princess* sports a nine-hole **miniature golf course** and a sprawling **virtual-reality video arcade** with dozens of machines you can climb onto and do things like hang-gliding, fly-fishing, and skiing.

On ships large and small, a few must-have accessories are private balconies, casual dining venues, specialty coffee cafes, well-equipped spas, cigar bars, and computer rooms with **E-mail and Internet access,** giving passengers more onboard choices than ever. Crystal, a pioneer in bringing computers to sea, as well as the newest ships of Holland America, NCL, Royal Caribbean, Radisson, Carnival, Princess, and Seabourn, already provide passengers with the ability to send and receive E-mail while on board, and even budget line Regal Cruises is planning on adding a computer with E-mail access before year-end 2000. It's only a matter of time—a very short time—before every ship in town is plugged in (see chapter 4 for a round-up on who's currently got what).

So whatever happened to deck chairs, piña coladas, and afternoon naps? Well, for you Luddites out there, you can still choose to do nothing more than laze by the pool all day with a cold beer and a bestseller. It's up to you. There's that word again: choice.

There is a caveat to all of this choice, though: The more you choose to do, the more it may cost you. As there's more and more to do on board, there are more and more opportunities for you to spend more money. Golf costs extra, and cappuccinos, Häagen-

---

Tell Us About Your Cruise!

While I, my editor, and my cronies can cover the cruise waterfront pretty well, we aren't privy to *every* great cruise moment. Let us know about your cruise. What did you like best? What did you like least? What nice little touch really made your trip special? And what was your favorite experience in port? Let us know! The more opinions we hear, the better. And we may even include your impressions in future editions of this book. E-mail your thoughts to **CRUZHMS@aol.com**, or snail-mail them to Heidi Sarna, *Frommer's Caribbean Cruises & Ports of Call,* IDG Books Worldwide, Inc., 909 Third Ave., New York, NY 10022.

Dazs ice cream, and chocolate-covered strawberries all vie for your discretionary dollars, along with the bars, shops, casinos, bingo games, florists, and spas. Three dollars here, 10 or more there—it adds up, and can easily add a few hundred dollars (or more) to what seemed initially like a bargain cruise.

DIFFERENT SHIPS FOR DIFFERENT TASTES

While the mondo-megas attract most of the attention these days, they're not the only fish in the sea. Just like there are five-star hotels, cozy B&Bs, and roadside motels, cruise ships come in all shapes and sizes to please all different walks of life. There are **adventurous sailing ships** and **small expeditionlike vessels** navigating off-the-beaten-track ports, 40-year-old **ocean liners** reeking of the past, and **ultra-deluxe ships** serving oceans of caviar and champagne. You can sail on ships that require you pack nothing more than flip-flops, bathing suits, T-shirts, and a pass-me-another-cup-of-that-rum-punch attitude. Or you can fill your suitcase with sequins and silk and enough dinner conversation for a week's worth of elegant soirées. It all depends on what you like, how much you want to spend, and where you want to go.

I COVER THE WATERFRONT: THE PORTS OF CALL TODAY

The **Caribbean** is a time-tested favorite, your classic picture-perfect island-vacation destination. It's warm and sunny all year round and the major ports of embarkation are easily accessible (and relatively cheap by air, when you compare it to flying to Europe or Asia). Better yet, it's hassle-free because American, Canadian, and British citizens don't need visas to go there.

Even as cruise destinations continue to expand into the far corners of the world, the Caribbean has never been more popular. With all the new ships coming on the scene, lines like Princess, Carnival, Royal Caribbean, Norwegian, Holland America, and Star Clippers are increasing their presence in the Caribbean, deploying more and bigger ships there. It's an exciting time. And just like the new ships, **new and improved facilities** are being introduced at the ports of call, as island nations recognize how lucrative cruise ship arrivals can be. **Shore excursions,** too, are getting more interesting and more active, with biking, horseback riding, golfing, and river-tubing trips exposing cruisers to the more natural parts of the islands.

While the Caribbean remains hot, hot, hot (and increasingly packed, packed, packed), you may notice that some of the huge ships in the Carnival, Princess, Royal Caribbean, and Norwegian fleets are visiting only three ports during a typical weeklong western or eastern Caribbean cruise instead of four or five ports. Ships too big? Ports too crowded? Cruise lines wanting to keep passengers on board to spend more money in the shops, bars, and casinos? A bit of all three if you ask me. First-time cruisers who want to see

In the News

The cruise industry has had its share of bad press over the past few years. For example, several major investigative reports in the *New York Times* have criticized the industry's foreign-flag status, which allows them to register ships in foreign countries to avoid paying income tax in the United States and at least minimum wage to employees. Major articles have also looked at onboard medical care, illegal ocean dumping, and personal safety. A series of dramatic (but not fatal) fires on Carnival ships in the last few years (most notably on the *Ecstasy* in July 1998, *Tropicale* in September 1999, and *Celebration* in January 2000) were broadcast live on major networks, including CNN, and during that same time frame a much-hyped report came out stating there had been 108 accusations of sexual assaults by crew members against fellow crew or passengers on Carnival ships during a 5-year period. Carnival also made waves when it had electrical power failures in late 1999 and early 2000 on the *Paradise* and *Destiny,* which caused the ships to float listlessly for as long as 27 hours before making it back to land. In 1998 and 1999, Royal Caribbean pleaded guilty to illegally dumping contaminated water (namely, waste oil and chemicals) into the sea in the mid-1990s from New York to Alaska, and had to ante over some $30 million in fines.

Should all of this scare you away? Are more bad things happening, or is the press just paying closer attention? As cruising continues to become more and more popular, and the industry becomes a bigger and bigger business, it will be scrutinized that much more. In some cases, media attention is good and acts as a watchdog, shedding light and attention on issues in the cruise industry that need to be changed, like ocean dumping and reporting crimes. On the other hand, as we all know, the media is also deft at blowing things out of proportion and taking things out of context. When looked at objectively, the number of sexual assaults alleged on Carnival's ships, for instance, isn't nearly as scary as some would like the public to believe—in a 5-year period, 108 assaults breaks down to about 1.8 a month for every 130,000 people (100,000 passengers and 30,000 crew or so, based on the line having about 11 ships in the 1993-to-1998 time period, sailing at least four cruises a month). Of course, that's still too much, but there's no question that more assaults, fires, and breakdowns occur on land than they do at sea.

Naturally, I don't mean to suggest that you shouldn't pay attention and exercise caution and common sense, but it's like the old saw about air travel: You have a better chance of being hit by a bus while crossing the street than you do of being in a plane crash. Same thing for cruising. Be alert, be aware, but overall my advice is, *relax.*

as many islands as possible may be disappointed, but if you've been there, done that, the big ships have so much happening on board, you'll barely have time to think about going ashore.

That said, small-ship lines like Windstar, Star Clippers, Club Med, Windjammer, Clipper, American Canadian Caribbean, and Seabourn really pack in the ports of call, visiting a different island nearly every single day, and sometimes even making two stops, one in the morning and another after lunch. Even some of the big ships, like Celebrity's *Galaxy,* Princess's *Ocean Princess* and *Dawn Princess,* and NCL's *Norwegian Dream,* visit five ports on their 7-night southern Caribbean itineraries.

Late-Breaking News: Cruise Ship to Visit Cuba in 2001

Beginning in November 2000, Canada's Blyth & Co. Travel Ltd. and The Cuba Cruise Corporation will begin offering Americans a totally legal way to visit Cuba, which for the past several decades has been effectively closed to American visitors because of the U.S. embargo. The crux of the travel problem has been that American citizens are barred from contributing to the Cuban economy—i.e., they can't spend any money there—and since we all know travel isn't free, that's put the kibosh on that. The Cuba Cruise Corporation has gotten around these restrictions by partnering with an organization founded to promote international peace through facilitating people-to-people contact. This organization will "host" all U.S. citizens participating in the program, covering all their expenses (food, transportation, and guides) while they're on Cuban soil.

Sailing on 3- and 4-night itineraries year-round out of Nassau, the company's 400-passenger, 1960s-era *La Habana* is decorated in 1940s Cuban style and will offer a Cuban saturation from the moment passengers board, with an onboard cigar factory and experts on Cuban history, culture, plants, and animals, who will give informal lectures aboard the ship and provide information on shore. The ship will spend 2 or 3 nights docked in Havana (depending on itinerary length), where passengers will be able to explore on their own or participate in various shore excursions. One program operated through the University of Havana will allow guests to meet with Cuban students, professors, professional groups, and artists. On the 4-night itinerary, passengers may take an excursion that visits the Bay of Pigs. Bicycles will be available to rent on the ship for those who want to explore independently.

Prices for the 3-night itinerary begin at $535 per person double occupancy and go up to $795. You can also book in a quad for as low as $335, or in a suite for $1,795. Four-night cruises start at $615 double. You can book air arrangements to and from Nassau through The Cuba Cruise Corporation, which will also provide U.S. citizens with all the information they need to avoid problems with Immigration upon reentry to the United States (note that U.S. citizens are not permitted to purchase goods on Cuban soil). These cruises will not be for sale through travel agents, so contact the company directly at ☎ **800/387-1387** or www.cubacruising.com.

To give you an even more well-rounded look at Caribbean cruises, this book includes coverage of **Panama Canal itineraries** and **Bermuda** cruises. Sure, I know Bermuda's not in the Caribbean, but the British-flavored island is a unique cruise destination; unlike other ports where visits rarely exceed 1 day, the five ships that do regularly scheduled weeklong cruises to Bermuda spend three of those days tied up at Hamilton or St. George's.

BON VOYAGE!

Just the fact that you've bought this book means you've got a hankering to cruise; now it's our job to find the cruise that's just right for you from among the huge selection of ships and cruise experiences in the market. I've made the reviews candid and provided lots of tips and firsthand experience to help you navigate the vast sea of choices. Together, we'll get you hooked up with the vacation of your dreams.

Bon Voyage!

Frommer's Favorites

To make it easier for you to select your cruise, I've compiled these "Frommer's Favorites," my picks of the best lines, ships, and ports of call for different types of cruise experiences. You'll find detailed reviews of all the lines and ships in part 2, "The Cruise Lines & Their Ships," and all the ports in part 3, "The Ports."

1 My Favorite Ships

Now, this is subjective, mind you, but that's the point—even two ships that are equally well designed and equally well run will appeal differently to different people. While I love lots of ships, here are my two personal favorites in each of the four categories into which I've divided the reviews in this book.

- **Mainstream Ships.** Mainstream ships are the big boys of the industry, carrying the most passengers and providing the most diverse cruise experiences to suit many different tastes, from party-hearty to elegant and refined. Among them, my picks are Princess's huge but cozy *Grand Princess* and Celebrity's 100% classy *Mercury*.
- **Budget/Old-Timer Ships.** The budget lines and their older, midsize ships offer some great bargains, particularly on shorter sailings of 2, 3, and 4 nights. And for the price, these lines tend to pack in plenty of good times. Among them, my picks are Premier's *Rembrandt* (formerly Holland America's *Rotterdam V,* a veritable icon among ship buffs), and, on the other end of the scale, Regal's *Regal Empress,* a ship that's seen more use than almost any other afloat but still manages to retain some of its old ocean-liner style.
- **Ultra-Luxury Ships.** Got some big bucks to spend on a superluxurious cruise? These are the ships for you. Offering elegant, refined, and doting service, extraordinary dining, spacious cabins, and high-toned entertainment aboard intimately sized, finely appointed vessels, they're the Dom Perignon of cruises. My picks overall are Windstar's luxurious sailing ships *Wind Song, Wind Spirit,* and *Wind Star,* and Radisson's lovely *Seven Seas Navigator.*
- **Soft-Adventure & Sailing Ships.** Maybe you want to sail on a ship that *really* sails. If so, several lines offer cruises aboard vessels that, while they do use engines to assure maintenance of schedules, are fully capable of going it under sail alone. Among them, Star Clipper's *Star Clipper* offers an experience that's incredibly romantic, while

Windjammer Barefoot Cruises' *Mandalay* offers an experience that'll bring out the rum-swilling buccaneer in you.

2 Best Luxury Cruises

Here's the very best for the Caribbean cruiser who's used to traveling deluxe and who doesn't mind paying for the privilege. These ships have the best cuisine, accommodations, and service at sea.

- **Seabourn.** Best overall high-brow, small-ship cruise line. With their cuisine, service, and luxurious suites, the 200-passenger *Pride* and *Legend* and the 116-passenger *Seabourn Goddesses* are the crème de la crème of cruises.
- **Cunard.** Cunard's 30-year-old *QE2* wins in the best traditional, old-time ocean liner category.
- **Celebrity Cruises.** The 1,880-passenger *Galaxy* and *Mercury* and 1450-passenger *Millennium* are the best luxury megaships, featuring wonderful spas, cigar bars, and entertainment lounges, and prices that are far lower than you'd expect.
- **Crystal Cruises.** The 960-passenger *Crystal Harmony* and *Crystal Symphony* are the best midsize ships out there, big enough to offer lots of dining, entertainment, and fitness options and small enough to bathe passengers in luxury.
- **Radisson Seven Seas.** The 490-passenger *Seven Seas Navigator* has the best cabins. At 301 square feet, they're roomy, most have balconies, and those huge bathrooms—ooh la la!
- **Windstar Cruises.** The *Wind Spirit* and its larger sibling *Wind Surf* are the best casual luxury ships at sea. No need for a jacket and tie; these casually elegant sailing ships offer a pampered adventure.

3 Best Cruises for First-Timers

Short 3- and 4-night cruises are one of the best ways to test the waters. Here are my favorite shorties as well as one particularly good weeklong cruise, any of which would be a good choice for first-timers.

- **Carnival Cruise Lines.** The 3- and 4-night Bahamas cruises on the *Ecstasy,* sailing from Miami, or *Fantasy,* sailing from Port Canaveral, are great choices. These flashy megas offers lots to do all day long, and their standard cabins are among the largest at sea.
- **Premier Cruise Lines.** The *Big Red Boat*'s 3- and 4-night Bahamas cruises out of Port Canaveral are a good, affordable choice for families, with extensive kids' programs and facilities and lots to do for adults, too.
- **Regal Cruises.** The *Regal Empress* may be nearly 50 years old and not so regal, but its 1-, 2-, and 3-night cruises to nowhere from New York City and its 4- and 5-night western Caribbean cruises from Port Manatee, Florida, are a cheap and fun way to test the waters.
- **Royal Caribbean International.** Its ships offer a healthy dose of razzle-dazzle, but they don't go overboard. The *Nordic Empress,* although one of Royal Caribbean's older ships, is a great vessel with lots to do on board and a great 3- and 4-night itinerary round-trip from San Juan, visiting St. Thomas and Sint Maarten, and also St. Croix on the 4-nighter.
- **Disney Cruise Line.** For Disney fanatics, a 3- or 4-night Bahamas cruise on the *Wonder* is the closest you'll get to a Disney park at sea. Half cruise, half theme park, the Disney ships are a great segue into cruising for first-timers.

- **Commodore Cruise Line.** The line's *Enchanted Capri* offers fun, 2-night "cruises to nowhere" that depart from New Orleans and head down the Mississippi into the Gulf of Mexico. Prices are ridiculously low, the casino is open 24 hours, food and entertainment are decent, and the ship's staff goes all out to make sure everyone has a good time.
- **Crystal Cruises.** If you're a glutton for the best of everything, unlike the other high-end ships, the 960-passenger *Crystal Harmony* and *Symphony* are big enough to keep first-timers busy (even considering the typical Crystal itinerary is 10 nights) with lots of outdoor deck space, generous fitness facilities, and over a half dozen bars and entertainment venues as well as pampering service and scrumptious cuisine.

4 The Most Romantic Cruises

The majority of all cruise passengers are couples, romantic or otherwise, and more of those romantic couples than ever are getting married on board or in port, renewing their vows, or celebrating anniversaries. (For how to get married on board, see chapter 1, "Choosing Your Ideal Cruise.")

- **Windstar Cruises.** Pure romance. Spend the day with your loved one in a private cove with the *Wind Surf* or *Wind Spirit* anchored offshore, bobbing calmly on the waves, their sails furled. Windstar offers a truly unique cruise experience, giving passengers the delicious illusion of adventure and the ever-pleasant reality of first-class cuisine, service, and itineraries.
- **Holland America Line.** This line attracts lots of 50-plus couples celebrating anniversaries and/or renewing vows (HAL has several goodie packages you can buy to sweeten the moment). The midsize **Statendam-class ships** as well as the *Volendam* and *Zaandam* twins will put you in the mood with their elegant Crow's Nest observation lounges/nightclubs, with floor-to-ceiling windows, dim lighting, and cozy seating. The private cabin balconies and glamorous two-story dining rooms will help, too.
- **Seabourn Cruise Line.** If you crave small and intimate, the *Seabourn Goddess I* and *II* are good choices and are nothing short of pampering private yachts. Of course, the champagne and caviar served to you poolside whenever you want it is a nice touch, too.
- **Carnival Cruise Lines.** Any line that names its vessels after moments of high passion has to take romance seriously—how could the *Paradise, Ecstasy,* or *Fantasy* not conjure up naughty thoughts? If your idea of romance is a date with Vegas-style glamour and excitement, Carnival is a sure thing.
- **Windjammer.** If foot loose and fancy free describes you and your betrothed, then the rum-swigging, T-shirts-and-shorts-wearing ambiance of the *Mandalay,* the *Legacy,* and their sister ships will be your ideal of romance. Ultra-casual and ultra-free, these eclectic sailing ships are a trip, and their itineraries are offbeat, too.

5 Best Cruises for Singles

A cruise can be a great social vacation for solo travelers, *if* you choose the right one.

- **Windjammer Barefoot Cruises.** If you're under 40 and have an informal attitude, these cruises—especially those aboard the *Polynesia*—are your best bet. Extremely dress-down and casual, things can get very, very intimate aboard these small wind-driven ships. It's amazing what a little wind, waves, stars, and moonlight can do. There are a handful of singles-only cruises on the *Polynesia* annually.

- **Carnival Cruise Lines.** Single women under 35 seek out Carnival's fun and casual ships, in part because they attract more men under 40 than just about any other cruise line. The ships are big, offering many places to meet and mingle. Who knows who you might meet in that aerobics class, on that shore excursion, or even at your dining table?
- **Premier Cruise Lines.** Aboard its *Big Red Boat,* reasonable single-parent rates attract single moms and dads and their children. Cartoon characters like Bugs Bunny and Sylvester can entertain the offspring while unattached moms and dads enjoy the company of other single parents.
- **Royal Caribbean International.** This line draws a good cross section of men and women from all walks of life. Like Carnival, a decent number of passengers are singles in their twenties, thirties, and forties. Hey, you never know!
- **Crystal Cruises.** This line's pair of elegant 960-passenger ships, the *Harmony* and *Symphony,* are good choices for single ladies and men over 50. Since there tend to be more older single women cruising than older single men, "gentleman hosts"—men in their fifties and sixties, semi-employed by the line (at least for one trip)—sail on board all Panama Canal cruises and act as dancing and dinner hosts for unattached ladies.

6 Best Cruises for Families with Kids

More families are cruising than ever before and lines are beefing up their family programs to keep the kids happy and content. All the lines included here offer supervised activities for three to five age groups for kids between ages 3 and 17, and have well-stocked playrooms, wading pools, kids' menus, and cabins that can accommodate three to five people. See "Family Cruising Tips" in chapter 1 and the cruise line reviews in chapters 6 through 9, which describe children's activities in detail.

- **Disney Cruise Lines.** This family magnet offers a seagoing children's program that's the most sophisticated and high-tech in the world. Huge play areas, family-friendly cabins, and, of course, the ubiquitous Mickey all spell success. Plus, its 3- and 4-night Bahamas cruises are marketed in tandem with stays at Disney World, so you can have your ocean voyage and your Space Mountain, too.
- **Premier Cruise Lines.** On Premier's old but still lively *Big Red Boat I* and newly acquired *Big Red Boat II,* children are entertained all day long with supervised activities for five age groups. The *Big Red Boat I*'s 3- and 4-day cruises to the Bahamas are particularly good for families on their first cruise, and although they're a bit less well accessorized than the Disney vessels, they make up for it by being cheaper.
- **Carnival Cruise Lines.** Despite a let-the-good-times-roll allure that appeals to adults, Carnival goes out of its way to amuse people of all ages, and does a particularly fine job with kids 2 to 15 years old. In 1998, some 200,000 kids sailed with Carnival— a few hundred per cruise is pretty normal, and there are as many as 700 to 800 on Christmas and New Year's cruises. On Carnival's post-1990 ships, the kids' facilities are the most extensive, with the *Triumph, Destiny, Elation,* and *Paradise* offering the biggest and brightest playrooms in the fleet, stocked with computer stations, a climbing maze, a 16-monitor video wall showing movies and cartoons, arts and crafts, and oodles of toys and games.
- **Royal Caribbean.** The huge *Voyager* and *Explorer of the Seas* are truly theme parks at sea, with such totally bizarro features as an onboard rock-climbing wall, ice-skating rink, in-line skate rink, a Disneyesque Main Street running down the center of each vessel, with parades and other entertainment throughout the day. All this in addition to the usual (though bigger-than-normal) features like kids' centers and video-game rooms, plus regulation-size basketball, paddleball, and volleyball courts.

- **Princess Cruises.** The *Grand Princess* and *Ocean, Sea, Sun,* and *Dawn Princesses* each have a spacious children's playroom and a sizable piece of outside fenced-in deck dedicated to kids only, with a shallow pool and tricycles. Teen centers have computers, video games, and a sound system (and the one on the *Grand* even has a teen's hot tub and private sunbathing deck). Children and their activities are kept separate from adults and theirs, which suits both groups just fine.

7 Best Party Cruises

With the right mix of passengers, nights aboard any ship can be a party, but many passengers still appreciate the efforts of cruise directors to make partying come alive. Some hard-partying fans opt for a cruise set up around a specific theme, such as country-western or big-band music. Others like to book shorter 3- or 4-day cruises, where some passengers come on board dead-set on packing as much party into a half week as possible.

- **Carnival Cruise Lines.** Carnival calls them "fun ships" for good reason, and their names—*Celebration, Fantasy, Imagination,* et al—couldn't be more appropriate. By day, the Pool Deck is bustling, with music playing so loud you'll have to go back to your cabin to think. And the fun keeps going after the sun goes down, with some of the best entertainment afloat. Usually three different live bands and orchestras play aboard each Carnival ship, and the discos rock until the early morning hours. Casino action is big on Carnival ships, as are Las Vegas–style revues.
- **Princess Cruises.** The *Grand, Ocean, Sea, Sun,* and *Dawn Princesses,* while not as wild and crazy as Carnival, can throw a good party with their flashy discos (the multilevel, observatorylike one on *Grand Princess* is the best) and endless activities.
- **Norwegian Cruise Line.** This line is a heavy contender in the party-and-entertainment sweepstakes. The ships also provide the best and most elaborate theme cruises in the industry, with options that include big bands, country music, jazz, blues, and sports. When the sun goes down, NCL's ships shine with outstanding entertainment. Fully equipped theaters have stages big enough to present Broadway hits, or you could opt for NCL's own extravagant cabaret production, *Sea Legs Review.*
- **Royal Caribbean International.** You'll definitely find a party aboard any of the vessels whose names end with the phrase **"of the Seas."** From dancing to singing to comedy to elaborately costumed revues and glittery casinos, Royal Caribbean's got it all. For an exciting Saturday-night-out-on-the-town kind of thing, the new *Voyager* and *Explorer of the Seas* feature a truly unique multideck boulevardlike promenade running down the center of each ship, with its ground floor lined with shops, bars, restaurants, and entertainment outlets, and multistory atria at either end.
- **Windjammer Barefoot Cruises.** Yo ho ho and a barrel of rum—no kidding, a real barrel, from which the bartenders siphon off the fixings for free Rum Swizzles as the sun goes down. On these sailing ships you get to pretend you're a freewheeling pirate sailing over the bounding main, grog in hand. Ships often anchor late in port, allowing you to enjoy some of the Caribbean's legendary nightspots, like Foxy's on Jost Van Dyke.

8 Best Soft-Adventure & Learning Cruises

If you want to explore more remote areas of the Caribbean where the megaships can't venture (and maybe even learn something in the process) or be aboard a vessel that recalls the sailing days of yore, here are your best bets:

- **American Canadian Caribbean Line.** One or more of this line's small-scale, shallow-draft, no-frills vessels heads every winter for the remote waters of the Caribbean, especially offshore Panama, Belize, and Honduras. This fascinating and little-visited part of Central America opens onto one of the world's greatest barrier reefs, which you may glimpse on a ride in the glass-bottom boats ACCL carries aboard ship. The *Grande Caribe, Grande Mariner,* and *Niagara Prince* are tiny and spartan, but they'll get you to parts of the Caribbean that few other travelers see.

- **Windstar Cruises.** *Wind Spirit* and its larger sibling *Wind Surf* are the most high-end of the motorized sailing ships, and make stops in some of the most intriguing off-the-beaten-path ports in the Caribbean, such as Dominica and Bequia, one of the jewels of the Grenadines but a place where the megaships don't go. Other stops include the remote, little-visited Carriacou and, in some cases, the Tobago Cays. The ships don't just "do" Guadeloupe, but take you to the even more exotic Iles des Saintes.

- **Clipper Cruise Line.** Despite their names, the *Nantucket Clipper* and *Yorktown Clipper* don't have sails, but they're the perfect ships for people who like the Holland America or Princess experience but want to see what a small, more exploration- and education-oriented vessel can do. Some cruises will introduce you to history and culture, but others are oriented toward pure adventure, concentrating on ports of call with rugged scenic beauty and opportunities for wildlife viewing. The company's ships call at remote islands in the British Virgins, such as Jost Van Dyke, Salt Island, and Norman Island, which, according to legend, inspired Robert Louis Stevenson's *Treasure Island.*

- **Star Clippers.** Clipper's biggest and plushest ship to date, the 5,000-ton, 228-passenger *Royal Clipper,* is scheduled to be launched just as this book goes to press. At 439 feet in length and with five masts flying 42 sails that together stretch to 56,000 square feet, it will be one of the largest sailing ships ever built, and will visit small ports including Martinique, Iles des Saintes, Antigua, St. Kitts, Dominica, St. Lucia, Bequia, Tobago Cays, and Grenada.

- **Windjammer Barefoot Cruises.** This eclectic fleet of piratelike sailing ships feels more adventurous then any of the others, and the ships will take you to some of the Caribbean's lesser frequented islands. The typical itinerary round-trip from Grenada is Carriacou, Palm Island, Bequia, St. Vincent, and Mayreau. Two of the line's ships—the passenger/cargo ship *Amazing Grace* and the sailing ship *Mandalay*—sail 13-day itineraries that stop at a whole bundle of off-the-beaten-track islands.

- **Royal Olympic Cruises:** The line's *Stella Solaris,* though much larger than the other ships in this faves list (carrying 620 passengers), offers some fascinating and adventurous itineraries, including a "Land of the Maya" cruise that visits Mexico's Yucatán Peninsula and Central America and carries aboard a panel of archaeologists, anthropologists, and astronomers to help you understand the Mayan civilization.

9 Best Theme Cruises

Theme cruises combine a Caribbean cruise with a particular entertainment-related interest—everything from solar-eclipse viewing to an Oktoberfest celebration, from a jazz festival to golfing, from basketball legends to Elvis. Check with a travel agent or cruise specialist for current offerings and options.

- **Norwegian Cruise Line.** When it comes to theme cruises, NCL, which pioneered the concept of theme cruises in the early 1980s, is tops. The *Norway* hosts about seven or eight music cruises a year, from country to blues, big band, fifties, and country, including its annual 2-week Jazz Festival cruise. On the *Norwegian Sea*'s popular

"Sports Afloat" cruises, professional players and Hall-of-Famers from pro basketball, football, hockey, and baseball sail on board, signing autographs, conducting demonstrations and contests, and mingling with passengers.

- **Holland America Line.** Big-band cruises with the Glenn Miller Orchestra, Guy Lombardo's Royal Canadians, and the Tommy Dorsey Orchestra are always a hit on board the 1,494-passenger *Westerdam* in the eastern Caribbean. Other themes include some 1950s "Sock Hop" cruises featuring performers like the Platters and the Shirelles; a series of Broadway-theme sailings, featuring greats like Joel Grey (from *Cabaret* and *Chicago*); and a cruise paying tribute to Frank Sinatra.
- **Disney Cruise Line.** Disney is basically a theme in and of itself, and the company's cruise ships are no different. The Disney theme is woven through virtually every aspect of shipboard life—restaurants, entertainment, cabins, the Pool Deck, even the artwork that hangs on the wall.
- **Royal Olympic Cruises.** Believing that cruising can be both fun and educational, this line has offered special cruises to view Halley's Comet, the May Equinox at Chichén-Itzá, and the Perseid meteor shower, and brought guest lecturers aboard its *Stella Solaris* who are among the best in the industry. After visiting major ports in the Caribbean, the ship often heads for the Amazon on its "Sail with the Stars" program, which celebrates theater at sea with theatrical icons such as Anne Jackson and Eli Wallach.

10 Best Cuisine

Here's where you'll find the best floating restaurants, rivaling what you'd find at the best restaurants in the world's major cities.

- **Seabourn Cruise Line.** The sophisticated and contemporary cuisine on board this line's fleet of 100- to 200-passenger ships is flavorful and artfully presented, and if there's anything you want specially prepared, just ask. The dining-room service is the finest of any vessel afloat.
- **Windstar Cruises.** While the fare aboard the *Wind Spirit* and *Wind Surf* doesn't equal that aboard Seabourn, it's still darn good. In 1995, this fleet upgraded its cuisine by hiring renowned Los Angeles–based restaurateur Joachim Splichal as consultant. Mealtime is a definite highlight of a Windstar cruise.
- **Radisson Seven Seas Cruises.** The award-winning chefs aboard the *Radisson Diamond* and *Seven Seas Navigator* produce artful culinary presentations that compare favorably to those of New York's or San Francisco's top restaurants, and the waiters are some of the industry's best. An excellent selection of vintage wines is also available.
- **Celebrity Cruise Line.** You'll find the best megaship cuisine and service on the *Century, Galaxy, Mercury,* and *Millennium.* Designed by Michel Roux, Britain's most famous and celebrated French chef, who sometimes cooks for Queen Elizabeth when she "drops in" to his place on the Thames, seagoing menus are to die for. (The line's midsize ships, *Horizon* and *Zenith,* have the same cuisine and service.)
- **Crystal Cruises.** While all the food you'll get on these ships is first-class, the ships' reservations-only Asian specialty restaurants are the best at sea. The one on the *Harmony,* for instance, serves up utterly delicious, authentic, fresh Japanese food, including sushi. The accoutrements help set the tone, too—chopsticks (and little chopstick rests), sake served in tiny sake cups and decanters, and sushi served on thick blocky square glass platters. An Asian-theme buffet lunch, offered at least once per cruise, gives passengers an awesome spread, from jumbo shrimp to chicken and beef satays to stir dry dishes.

- **Carnival Cruise Line.** It's nowhere near the league of the other lines in this category, but Carnival racks up points for at least having lots of it, and its 24-hour pizza and Caesar salad service is a big hit fleet-wide, as is the sushi bar (open for a few hours every afternoon) on the *Elation, Paradise, Imagination, Inspiration,* and *Jubilee.*

11 Best Port-Packed Itineraries

If you want to see as much of the Caribbean as possible, consider one of the following cruises for their one-port-every-day itineraries.

- **American Canadian Caribbean Line.** The small, spartan *Grande Mariner* and *Grande Caribe* have no equal in the remote Caribbean and Central American hinterlands they visit. On 12-night itineraries, you'll explore cays and islets you've never heard of, including Laughingbird Cay, Ambergris Cay, and Man-of-War Cay, plus Mayan ruins and even remote territories in Panama, Costa Rica, and Honduras.
- **Windjammer Cruises.** In its role as supply ship for the Windjammer Fleet, *Amazing Grace* is the ultimate island hopper, with stops at more Caribbean islands within the span of its 13-day itineraries than virtually any other cruise ship afloat. Beginning in Freeport and ending in Trinidad, its port stops include St. Kitts, Nevis, Montserrat, Iles des Saintes, Guadeloupe, Dominica, Jost Van Dyke, Beef Island, Virgin Gorda, Norman Island, Peter Island, and possibly others as well. The line's *Mandalay* also sails a 13-day route, this one between Granada and Antigua, visiting Bequia, Carriacou, Canouan, Dominica, Guadeloupe, Iles des Saintes, Martinique, Mayreau, Nevis, Palm Island, St. Lucia, St. Vincent, and Tobago Cays.
- **Clipper Cruise Lines.** Sailing itineraries roughly similar to American Canadian Caribbean's, though shorter, Clipper's small, comfortable vessels concentrate on similarly small and less-visited ports, such as Bequia, Dominica, Union Island, and Nevis. Their onboard naturalists and historians do a great job, giving passengers a real understanding of the places they're seeing.

12 Best Beaches

If time logged on the beach is just as important to you as days spent at sea, you'll want to consider cruises that stop in the following ports.

- **In the Western Caribbean.** Grand Cayman and Jamaica are two of the Caribbean's best. Grand Cayman's **Seven Mile Beach** is a stretch of pristine sand easily accessible via a short taxi ride from George Town. Jamaica's **Negril** is also accessible via taxi, and is closer to Montego Bay than to Ocho Rios.
- **In the Eastern and Southern Caribbean.** Beach bums should head to **Trunk Bay** in St. John (protected by the U.S. National Park Service), **Grand Anse Beach** in Grenada, **Shoal Bay** in Anguilla (topless and sometimes bottomless, too), **Orient Beach** in St. Martin, and Aruba's 7 miles of beach—all excellent stretches of white sand. All are easily accessible via taxi.

13 Best Cruises for Snorkelers & Scuba Divers

Virtually any cruise you take in the Caribbean will allow you an opportunity to snorkel at one of the island ports. Scuba-diving excursions are fairly common, too. Grand Cayman, Bonaire, Virgin Gorda, St. Croix, and Belize offer the best waters.

- **American Canadian Caribbean Line.** For getting to the Caribbean's most natural, unspoiled spots known for superb snorkeling and a wealth of marine life, this line is unbeatable. Few major cruise lines ever call at Belize, which has the world's second-largest barrier reef, but ACCL's *Grande Caribe* does.

- **Princess Cruises.** Princess features "New Waves," a PADI-certified diving program available aboard ships sailing the Caribbean on 7-day itineraries. Endorsed by Scuba Schools International, this program offers introductory scuba tours, dive trips, and demonstrations, and employs fully certified instructors who are some of the best in the business.
- **Star Clippers.** This line's owner, Mikael Krafft, is a dedicated scuba diver, and he selects his sailing ships' itineraries through the Caribbean based in part on the accessibility of superior, intriguing, and often offbeat dive sites, including small ports that many big cruise ships can't even approach. The line's *Star Clipper* is the largest sailing vessel to feature onboard PADI dive centers.
- **Windjammer Barefoot Cruises.** Windjammer's ships offer year-round diving possibilities on 6- to 13-day cruises to some 50 ports, including the rarely visited Grenadines. For divers, the best ship in this fleet is the *Flying Cloud,* which departs from Tortola, capital of the British Virgin Islands.

14 Best Cruises for Golfers

Many lines sell **golfing shore excursions** with tee times and transportation between the ship and the course, and on some ships a golf pro sails on board, offering onboard lessons ($60 to $70 per hr.) and escorting players to the island courses. The best courses are in Bermuda, St. Thomas, Puerto Rico, and Jamaica.

Some Royal Caribbean, Princess, and Crystal ships have actual **putting greens** on board, while others, including the new, technologically advanced ships like Celebrity's *Century, Galaxy,* and *Mercury,* Royal Caribbean's *Voyager,* and Princess's *Grand, Sea, Sun,* and *Dawn Princess* have **golf simulators.** These state-of-the-art virtual-reality machines allow you to play the great courses of the world without ever leaving the ship (for about $20 per half hour). Full-size clubs are used and a virtual-reality video screen allows players to watch the electronic path of a ball they've actually hit soar high over the greens or land flat in a sand trap.

- **Royal Caribbean International.** This line is the golfer's favorite, as four of its ships—*Legend of the Seas, Splendour of the Seas, Voyager of the Seas,* and *Explorer of the Seas*—feature a real live 18-hole putting green on board. The *Voyager* and *Explorer* also have golf simulators. The ships are so huge and well stabilized that golfers are seldom bothered by motion.
- **Crystal Cruises.** Both the *Harmony* and *Symphony* have two golf driving nets and a large putting green, so golfing fanatics can hit balls virtually all day long. There's often an instructor on board giving group instruction throughout the week.
- **Celebrity Cruises.** On every one of its Bermuda cruises, the *Zenith* features a PGA-certified pro who gives lessons at the ship's driving net. In port, the pro takes golfers to the courses for hands-on instruction ($200 for 5-hr. playing lessons). The *Century, Galaxy, Mercury* and *Millennium* have golf simulators.
- **Princess Cruises.** The *Grand Princess* has a nine-hole miniature-golf course right on board. The *Grand, Ocean, Sea, Sun,* and *Dawn* also have one of those neat golf simulators.
- **Radisson Seven Seas.** As the official cruise line of the PGA of America, Radisson offers lots of golf excursions on *Radisson Diamond* and *Seven Seas Navigator* Caribbean itineraries. Both ships have golf cages, and on some sailings a certified pro offers videotaped lessons.

15 Best Islands for Serious Shoppers

There are few islands that don't have at least some shops, and most have a sprawling market or complex of stores near the cruise ship docks. Even the smaller, less touristed ports have a few stores and a market. Believe me, if a ship is coming to an island, the locals will be prepared.

The following are the absolute best spots for dedicated shoppers. All offer duty-free shopping and stores bursting with jewelry, perfume and cosmetics, clothing, accessories, arts and crafts, liquor, and souvenirs. Ubiquitous chains like Little Switzerland, Colombian Emeralds, and Diamonds International sell a wide variety of duty-free gold and silver jewelry with diamonds as well as precious and semiprecious gems. In outdoor markets and craft shops, look for local specialties, such as straw hats and purses, beaded necklaces, and brightly painted folk art and carved-wood boxes, as well as your typical souvenirs: T-shirts and beach towels.

- **St. Thomas.** Close to the cruise ship docks, lovely Charlotte Amalie is the island's shopping mecca.
- **St. Croix.** Christiansted has shopping galore, and since it's part of the U.S. Virgin Islands, you get a bigger customs allowance than you do coming from non-U.S. ports.
- **Puerto Rico.** The capital, San Juan, is historic and a great shopping spot, and the same customs deal applies here as at St. Croix.
- **Grand Cayman.** George Town has numerous shops clustered right around its port facilities.
- **St. Martin/Sint Maarten.** French Marigot and Dutch Philipsburg are particularly good for European luxury items.
- **Aruba.** Oranjestad's Caya G. F. Betico Croes compresses six continents into one main, theme-park–like shopping street.
- **The Bahamas.** Nassau and Freeport are veritable shopping free-for-alls. Go wild.

16 Best Ships for Gamblers

Gamblers are in luck. Most cruise ships, with the exception of the small ships in the Soft-Adventure category (see chapter 9, "Soft-Adventure Lines & Sailing Ships"), have casinos. The megaships have sprawling Vegas-style operations with dozens of gaming tables and hundreds of slots as well as roulette and craps. Some of the midsize ships are more modest, with just a couple of blackjack and poker tables and a handful of slots. The following lines have the biggest and best in the size and flashiness departments.

- **Carnival Cruise Lines.** Fleet-wide, Carnival's casinos are the best at sea: bold, bright, and glowing with neon.
- **Royal Caribbean International.** Fleet-wide, the casinos are exciting places to play. The three-level casino on the *Nordic Empress* is particularly appealing, and the ones on the new *Voyager* and *Explorer of the Seas* are mind-blowing.
- **Princess Cruises.** All of the line's megas attract gamblers, and the huge casino on the *Grand Princess* is the best of the lot.
- **Holland America Line.** This line's casinos are more low-key and less flashy than those on Carnival, but there always seems to be a lot of action going on.
- **Celebrity Cruises.** Some of the Caribbean's best casinos are aboard Celebrity's three megas, the *Century, Galaxy,* and *Mercury.* They're large and dazzling, but in a more subdued way than their neon competition.

17 Best Islands for Gamblers

If gambling on board ship isn't enough for you, a handful of the islands have casinos to tide you over (ships' casinos must remain closed while a ship is in port).

- **Bahamas.** In Nassau, the casinos on Cable Beach and Paradise Island are dazzling and Vegas-style, and along with those in Puerto Rico are the biggest and flashiest you'll find in the Caribbean. The two best in Nassau are the Paradise Island Casino and the Crystal Palace Casino, both huge, glittery extravaganzas.
- **Puerto Rico.** The island's gambling strip lies along the Condado in San Juan, where the casinos are Vegas-style and exciting and the locals dress for a night out. In addition to cards and slots, there are entertainment lounges and restaurants in the casino complexes.
- **Aruba.** There are about 10 casinos on this island, all near Oranjestad or along the nearby hotel strip on Palm Beach. Some of the best are at the Americana Aruba Beach Resort, the Aruba Palm Beach Resort and Casino, the Aruba Sonesta Resort & Casino at Seaport Village, and the Holiday Inn Aruba Beach Resort.
- **Curaçao.** Here, too, there are about a dozen casinos, many in Willemstad. You'll find casinos in the Sonesta Beach Hotel & Casino, Four Points Resorts, the Holiday Beach Hotel & Casino, and the Princess Beach Resort & Casino. The atmosphere is casual.
- **Sint Maarten.** While gambling is illegal on the French side of this island, it's not on the Dutch side, where there are about six or seven casinos, mostly in the major hotels, like the Maho Beach Hotel and the Pelican Resort and Casino. Also check out the Roman-themed Coliseum Casino on Front Street in Philipsburg.

18 Best Gyms

If you can't bear to miss a workout, even while on a cruise, you're in luck. Most ships, especially those built within the past few years, have excellent fitness facilities.

- **Carnival Cruise Lines.** The gyms on the *Destiny, Triumph,* and *Victory* are cavernous, with more than 40 state-of-the-art exercise machines, including virtual-reality stationary bikes. The huge spaces are framed in floor-to-ceiling windows and the workout machines are spaced far apart so you you'll never feel cramped. There's a juice bar, men's and women's sauna and steam rooms, and a whirlpool-like hydrotherapy tub whose bubbling waters are loaded with extracts of seaweed and rejuvenating oils.
- **Holland America.** The gyms aboard the line's new *Volendam* and *Zaandam* are downright palatial, and you might wonder, as I did on a recent sailing, if there was more equipment on back order coming to fill all the space. Hey, no complaints here. Because of its size, it's one of the best gyms at sea. Dozens of state-of-the-art machines are surrounded by floor-to-ceiling windows. The adjacent aerobics room is huge, too—nearly as big the one I go to at home.

19 Best Spas

If a massage is your idea of nirvana, you're in luck. Most ships, especially those built within the past few years, have excellent spa facilities.

- **Celebrity Cruises.** No contest: *Century, Galaxy, Mercury,* and especially the line's new *Millennium* have the best spas at sea. The 10,000-square-foot AquaSpas (25,000 square feet on *Millennium!*) manage to combine the best health, beauty, and fitness regimens with striking aesthetics inspired by Japanese gardens and bathhouses and Moorish and Turkish spas. Facilities include saunas, mud baths, massage rooms, and Turkish baths. Each also offers the Rasul, an Oriental therapy that includes applying medicinal mud, a seaweed soap shower, an herbal steam bath and massage, and a dip in the 15,000-gallon thalassotherapy pool (an oversize, souped-up hot tub). Special features include deep-cleansing facials and newfangled slimming treatments, too.

- **Windstar Cruises.** How wonderful to sail on such an intimate ship like the 312-passenger *Wind Surf* and be treated to extensive spa facilities. It's unheard of!
- **Radisson Seven Seas.** The spa aboard the 490-passenger *Seven Seas Navigator* might not look all that different, but venture further and you'll learn it is, since it's not run by Steiner Leisure, which controls the spa concession on virtually every other ship in the sea. Instead, it's got the Judith Jackson spa that provides quality, first-rate treatments and, thankfully, doesn't go the Steiner route of hawking its skin-care products just as clients are coming out of a massage-induced trance. Some 17 different treatments are doled out by a staff of five in six rooms and include innovative ones you won't find on other ships, like a relaxing 20-minute hair and scalp oil massage for $25 and a 1-hour four-hand massage (two therapists work simultaneously) for $165.
- **Royal Caribbean.** The two-level spa complexes aboard the line's new *Voyager* and *Explorer of the Seas* are two of the largest and best accoutred out there. There's a peaceful waiting area with New Agey tropical birdsong music piped in overhead. Ahhhh, relaxation—until you get your bill.
- **Norwegian Cruise Line.** Deep down in the lowest decks of the line's *Norway* you'll find the memorable Roman Spa, which features an indoor pool, 16 treatment rooms, exercise equipment, two steam rooms, and two saunas, plus body-jet showers and a whirlpool.
- **Costa Cruises.** Done with richly colored mosaic tiles and Roman columns, the soothing Pompeii Spa on the *Costa Victoria* isn't huge, but so attractively designed. It includes a pool, therapy rooms, and a Turkish bath. The attractive but smallish workout room shares a glass wall with the spa and pool area, and features over a dozen pieces of equipment.

20   Best Bathrooms at Sea

OK, so you don't want to spend all day in them (people will start to talk), but bathrooms are important places, let's all admit it. Here's my pick of the best.

- **Radisson Seven Seas.** Bigger and better than those on the other high-end Seabourn, Silversea, and Crystal ships, every single bathroom on the *Seven Seas Navigator* has a separate shower stall and a full-size bathtub long enough for a normal-size human to actual recline in (and for two to get real cozy!), as well as a long marble counter flanked by two sets of tall shelves, and a generous collection of chichi lemon-scented soaps and shampoos by spa-guru Judith Jackson.
- **Disney.** They don't come any family-friendlier than this! The majority of the *Wonder* and *Magic's* 875 cabins are equipped with *two bathrooms*—a sink and toilet in one and a shower/tub combo and a sink in the other. Both, while compact, have ample shelf space. This will cut down on family squabbles for sure!
- **Windstar.** The *Wind Surf's* 30 suites also have two full bathrooms, his and hers, each with its own shower and toilet.

Part 1

Planning, Booking & Preparing for Your Cruise

With advice on choosing and booking your ideal cruise and tips on getting ready for the cruise experience.

Choosing Your Ideal Cruise

1

There are many things you should consider before plunking down your cash for the perfect cruise—oh, you know, like should you pack a bikini or a one-piece? John Grisham or Ken Follett? The new Nikon or a disposable? But way before you deal with these vital decisions, you really do need to consider some important issues. What kind of itinerary are you looking for and when do you want to go? What size ship will make you most comfortable, and will its age matter? Which are family-friendly or accessible to travelers with disabilities? Is a particular cruise active enough for you? In this chapter I'll address all of these issues and more.

1 When to Go

THE CARIBBEAN   With temperatures in the balmy 80s almost year-round, dozens of ships stay in the Caribbean the entire year, and a bunch more spend the winters there after summering in Alaska or Europe. It's great: The Caribbean is the only major cruise destination that never closes; it's the sea that never sleeps. But (there's always a but) the only caveat to this ideal climate is **hurricane season,** which officially runs June 1 to November 30 but rarely causes cruisers anything more than a few days of rain and a bit of rocking and rolling. I've taken many cruises in the Caribbean during this period and have only occasionally run into stormy weather; it's rare, but it's a risk you take. With today's modern navigational equipment, though, it's next-to-impossible to actually get caught in a hurricane, as ships change course as soon as they get wind of a storm.

Defining seasons as "low" and "high" is hardly a science, since most lines seem to come up with their own unique pricing schemes. It is generally accepted, though, that the **high season** in the Caribbean is mid-December through mid-April. During this time, weather will most likely be perfect, the islands and ships jam-packed, and prices the highest. The holiday weeks of Christmas, New Year's, Presidents' Day, and Easter are the absolute busiest and most expensive, especially on the family-oriented megas—it's one of the few times in the year when brochure rates are often not discounted.

Despite it being hurricane season, the summer months of **June, July, and August** are the next busiest time of the year (to many lines, these months are also considered high season along with Dec through Apr) because families traditionally vacation during the summer and because many ships migrate to Alaska and Europe for the season, leaving fewer vessels in the Caribbean. Temperatures may be a bit hotter in summer, but the islands' lush and colorful flowering trees are at their height and the winds are mildest.

September, October, and early November are considered **low-season** (often referred to as "value season"), and are the time when you encounter the fewest crowds onshore and onboard, and some of the lowest rates—sometimes hundreds of dollars less than other times of the year. There can also sometimes be a lull during the first 2 weeks of January, just after the rush of the holidays, and sometimes in late April and May, so look for good prices then.

PANAMA CANAL The Panama Canal cruise season is roughly the same as the Caribbean's, generally between about November and April. A few lines, like Holland America, have a ship doing Panama Canal cruises in September and October, too. Many ships do only two Panama Canal cruises annually, when repositioning between the summer season in Alaska and the fall/winter season in the Caribbean.

BERMUDA The Bermuda cruise season extends from late April to early October, with the peak between late June and late August, when the average temperature is 80°— 10° to 15° higher than the rest of the year.

2 Choosing the Itinerary That's Best for You

If you count every little rocky outcropping or sand bar, there are hundreds of islands in the Caribbean. Of the 40 or 50 islands that make it onto the map, though, cruise ships regularly visit about 25 of them. Most Caribbean cruises are 7 nights long and visit anywhere from three to six different ports of call, the trend for the megas being to visit fewer rather than more ports. There are a handful of 3- and 4-night cruises out of Florida visiting the Bahamas or Cozumel; 4- and 5-night cruises out of Tampa, New Orleans, and Galveston, Texas, doing western Caribbean itineraries; and 10- to 14-night Caribbean cruises that transit the Panama Canal, typically sailing between Florida and Acapulco, Mexico, visiting three to seven ports.

While they're all pretty darned appealing in some way, the Caribbean islands are not all created equal. Some islands are better for shopping, others are better for beaches or scenic drives. Some are quite developed, others remain natural. Some have piers that ships can conveniently tie right up to, while others require that ships anchor up to a mile or so offshore and shuttle passengers back and forth in small motorized launches called *tenders*. Big ships tend to visit the more commercialized, developed islands that can see visits by as many as 10 ships in a day, while the small ships are able to access off-the-beaten-track, more-natural islands. Typically, the big lines divide Caribbean itineraries into **eastern, western,** and **southern,** but smaller ship lines rarely adhere to such rigid labels.

MEGASHIP ITINERARIES

WESTERN CARIBBEAN Most western Caribbean itineraries depart from Miami, Fort Lauderdale, Port Canaveral, or Tampa, Florida (a few depart from New Orleans and one even from Galveston, Texas), and typically visit Grand Cayman, Jamaica, and Cozumel, on Mexico's Yucatán Peninsula. This is a popular itinerary for many lines, and you'll certainly notice the throngs of other cruise passengers in each port—often three or four (or more) ships will be visiting at a time.

EASTERN CARIBBEAN Eastern Caribbean itineraries also typically sail out of Florida, and may include Puerto Rico, St. Thomas, St. Croix, St. Maarten, and the

Bahamas—all very popular and busy ports of call, especially St. Thomas and Puerto Rico.

SOUTHERN CARIBBEAN A southern itinerary is typically round-trip out of San Juan, Puerto Rico, or sometimes Aruba. Southern routes, which often overlap with eastern Caribbean itineraries, are bound to visit islands including St. Thomas, St. Maarten, Barbados, St. Lucia, Martinique, Antigua, and maybe Dominica, Guadeloupe, Aruba, and Grenada.

SMALL-SHIP ITINERARIES

Most small ships cruise in the eastern and southern Caribbean, where distances between islands are shorter. Instead of Florida, they may sail out of Barbados, Grenada, St. Kitts, or San Juan (Puerto Rico), and visit more-remote islands.

EASTERN CARIBBEAN An eastern Caribbean itinerary might include visits to St. Barts, Virgin Gorda, Jost Van Dyke, Tortola, and St. John, as well as one or two more touristy islands, like St. Thomas.

SOUTHERN CARIBBEAN Southern Caribbean cruises may visit Guadeloupe, Dominica, Martinique, St. Lucia, St. Vincent, Grenada, and Bequia, and maybe the truly unspoiled and remote Palm, Canouan, Mayreau, and Carriacou islands.

SHORTER ITINERARIES

Short, sweet, affordable, and generally more wild and crazy, **3- and 4-night cruises** offer a more action-packed, nonstop party ambiance than longer 7-night Caribbean itineraries. It's obvious why: The 3-nighters and some of the 4-nighters are weekend cruises departing Thursday or Friday afternoons, so people are ready to squeeze in as much fun, relaxation, drinking, gambling, dancing, eating, or whatever as they can. You'll still see a wide range of ages on these shorties, but all are young-at-heart types and you definitely will find more 20- and 30-somethings than on any other type of cruise. The ships that ply these mini–fun fests tend to be the oldest ships in a fleet and are a bit beat up in comparison to the newest megas—not a shock considering the wear and tear they get doing two cruises a week instead of one. I've also noticed service is not as good on the weekend party cruises compared to longer itineraries; the crew's overworked and probably a tad fed-up with the throngs of rowdies week after week.

On the other hand, the **4- and 5-night itineraries** that depart on Sunday or Monday afternoons tend to attract an older and less party-oriented type of crowd.

Aside from the fun-factor, 3-, 4-, and 5-night cruises are a great way to test the waters before committing to a full week. They're also a good idea if you're short on time or moolah. The majority of the mini-cruises sail round-trip from Miami and Port Canaveral in southern Florida and visit the Bahamas and/or Key West and Cozumel, on Mexico's Yucatán Peninsula. Others depart from New Orleans and San Juan. Short cruises include the same fun and games, five-course meals, and entertainment featured on weeklong cruises, and there's usually one formal night per cruise as well as the traditional captain's cocktail party. If you want, many cruise lines will pair a cruise with a stay on land, either before or after your cruise. For instance, Disney and Premier Cruise Lines will combine a 3- or 4-night cruise out of Port Canaveral with a 4- or 3-night visit to one of central Florida's theme parks, like Walt Disney World, Universal Studios, Sea World, or Busch Gardens.

MATCHING YOUR HABITS TO YOUR DESTINATION

Some ports are better for certain things than others. Here's a short run-down (see part 3, "The Ports," for more detailed information).

PORTS FOR SHOPPERS

Eastern Caribbean: St. Croix, St. Martin/St. Maarten, St. Thomas, Puerto Rico. **Western Caribbean:** Grand Cayman, Cozumel. **Southern Caribbean:** Aruba, Barbados. **Bermuda.**

PORTS FOR BEACH LOVERS

Eastern Caribbean: Anguilla, British Virgin Islands, St. John, St. Martin. **Western Caribbean:** Grand Cayman, Jamaica. **Southern Caribbean:** Aruba, Grenada. **Bermuda.**

PORTS FOR SNORKELERS

Eastern Caribbean: St. Croix, St. John, St. Thomas. **Western Caribbean:** Grand Cayman. **Southern Caribbean:** Bonaire, Curaçao.

PORTS FOR HISTORY & ARCHAEOLOGY BUFFS

Eastern Caribbean: Puerto Rico, Dominican Republic. **Western Caribbean:** Cozumel/Playa del Carmen/Calica. **Southern Caribbean:** Barbados, Curaçao. **Bermuda.**

PORTS FOR NATURE BUFFS

Eastern Caribbean: St. John, Puerto Rico. **Southern Caribbean:** Aruba, Dominica, Grenada, Trinidad.

PORTS FOR FRANCHOPHILES

Eastern Caribbean: Guadeloupe, Iles des Saintes, French St. Martin, St. Barts.

SHORE EXCURSIONS: THE WHAT, WHY & HOW

No matter what size ship you're on or what its itinerary, you can choose from 4 to over 40 tours in any given port, ranging in price from $20 to $200 per person. The tried-and-true standards are walking tours, bus trips, snorkeling and diving excursions, booze cruises on catamarans, glass-bottomed boat rides, and helicopter tours. In the past few years a slew of more active, unique excursions have been introduced as well, such as biking, hiking, horseback riding, golfing, kayaking, and river tubing.

On the megaships, excursions can sell out real fast, so don't dawdle if you know what you want; sign up on the first or second day of the cruise. Because of the large numbers of passengers on a megaship, be prepared for some waiting around as each jumbo-size tour group is herded from the ship to the awaiting army of buses or minivans.

On smaller ships, tours might never get sold out because there's room to accommodate all passengers on board. The whole process is saner, and group sizes are most likely smaller. That said, big ship or small, the attraction itself, quality of the tour guide, and execution of the tour are what determine whether you have an enjoyable time.

Although many tours are wonderful complements to your cruise and leave lasting, fond memories—especially if you're a first-time visitor or want to leave the planning to someone else—others are overcrowded, disappointing, and not worth the money. Choose wisely, and remember, sometimes it's best to skip the organized tour and go off exploring on your own. Much of Aruba, Curaçao, St. Thomas, St. Martin, Puerto Rico, Grand Cayman, Grenada, and Bermuda, for instance, are easily explored independently—all you need is a good guidebook (this one!) and a sense of adventure and you'll have a great time. In the port chapters of this book, I list both the best shore excursions and the best sights you can see on your own.

Indulging Your Obsessions at Sea: Theme Cruises

Theme cruises are becoming more and more popular as lines look for more ways to attract passengers with unique onboard activities. There are jazz, big-band, opera, and country-music cruises; sailings focused on French cooking and wine; and cruises whose activities are based around international affairs, history, or investing. Crystal and Windstar, for instance, feature an annual series of **food-and-wine cruises,** where well-known chefs and sommeliers are on board to conduct demonstrations and tastings. Holland America, Cunard, NCL, and Crystal do quite a few **music-theme cruises** every year, paying tribute to jazz, big band, fifties, or Broadway, with live bands and lots of dancing.

---

3 Choosing the Ship of Your Dreams

News flash: All ships are not the same. Even before getting to the kind of experience offered by the cruise lines, physical factors such as the size and age of the ship figure into whether it can offer you the vacation experience you want.

BIG SHIP OR SMALL?

A cruise on a big ship with 2,000-plus passengers versus a small one with only 200 is like night and day—like spending a week in a 500-room high-rise hotel in Cancún versus hiding out in a cozy New England bed-and-breakfast. As much as anything else, a ship's size greatly determines its personality and the kind of vacation you'll have. Big ships tend to be busy, exciting affairs, while the smaller ones are most often low-key retreats with unique personalities. Big ships normally spend 2 or 3 days at sea on a weeklong cruise because they travel great distances between ports and because there's so much to do on board; small ships are more destination-oriented, visiting a different port nearly every day.

BIG SHIPS

Attention type A's: If you seek nonstop fun and games set among twinkling lights and splashes of neon, flamboyant art and towering atriums, and sweeping staircases pouring into grand two-story dining rooms, then the 1,800-passenger-plus megaliners of the Carnival, Royal Caribbean, Princess, Celebrity, and Disney cruise lines will appeal to you big-time. Slightly smaller big ships, like those of the Norwegian, Holland America, Crystal, Royal Olympic, and Premier fleets, are not quite megas, but with 800 to 1,500 passengers are big enough to offer a similarly exciting and active experience. All of these ships are so large, in fact, that they are limited to where they can tie up—certain islands and ports simply cannot handle them.

The onboard atmosphere is carefree and casual by day—with passengers decked out in bathing suits, shorts, sarongs, and sandals—and more elegant by evening, with sport jackets and decent dresses or pantsuits the norm on most nights and the occasional formal night calling for a tuxedo or suit for men and a cocktail dress or fancy pantsuit for women. Granted, the megas are buzzing social meccas, but, just as you would if you live in a metropolis such as New York City, you'll be able to blend in with the crowd and become an anonymous passenger among the throngs. Chances are you won't run into the same person twice (except your dinner mates, of course). In fact, if you don't plan specific times and places to meet up with your spouse, lover, or friend, you can

Ship Size Comparisons

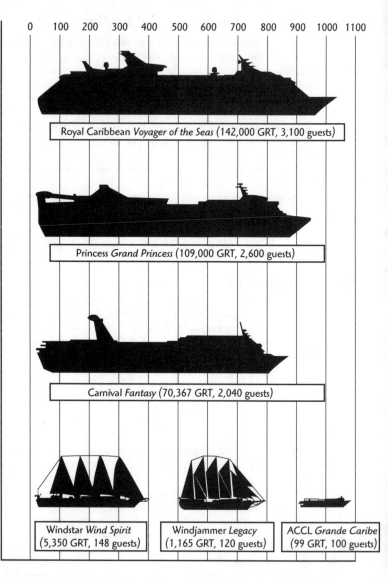

0 100 200 300 400 500 600 700 800 900 1000 1100

Royal Caribbean *Voyager of the Seas* (142,000 GRT, 3,100 guests)

Princess *Grand Princess* (109,000 GRT, 2,600 guests)

Carnival *Fantasy* (70,367 GRT, 2,040 guests)

Windstar *Wind Spirit*
(5,350 GRT, 148 guests)

Windjammer *Legacy*
(1,165 GRT, 120 guests)

ACCL *Grande Caribe*
(99 GRT, 100 guests)

Ships selected for this chart are representative of the various size vessels sailing in the cruise market today. See the specifications tables accompanying every ship review in chapters 6-9 to see the approximate comparative size of all the ships not shown here. (**GRT** = gross register tons, a measure that takes into account interior space used to produce revenue on a vessel. One GRT = 100 cubic feet of enclosed, revenue-generating space.)

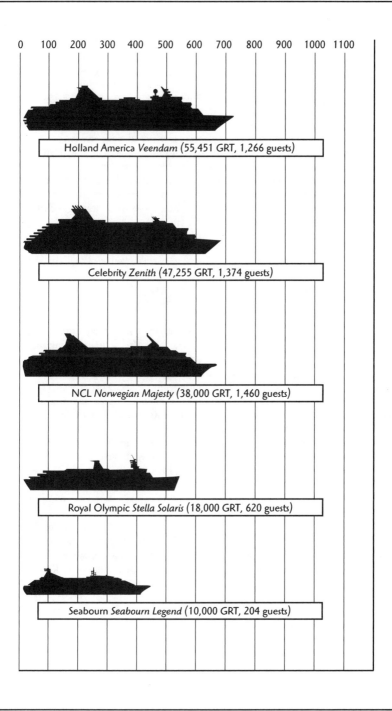

0   100   200   300   400   500   600   700   800   900   1000   1100

Holland America *Veendam* (55,451 GRT, 1,266 guests)

Celebrity *Zenith* (47,255 GRT, 1,374 guests)

NCL *Norwegian Majesty* (38,000 GRT, 1,460 guests)

Royal Olympic *Stella Solaris* (18,000 GRT, 620 guests)

Seabourn *Seabourn Legend* (10,000 GRT, 204 guests)

sometimes roam the decks for what seems like hours looking for them. (I know, it's happened to me. Then again, a few hours of freedom might be a blessing.)

The megas have as many as 12 or 14 decks of shops, restaurants, bars, and lounges, plus cabins of all shapes and sizes (and there are even more decks for the crew, decks you'll never see). Most of these ships have a multistory atrium, three or four swimming pools and hot tubs, casinos with hundreds of slot machines and dozens of card tables, three or four restaurants, a jogging track, movie theater, pizzeria, and patisserie. Mammoth spas and gyms boast dozens of exercise machines and treatment rooms. Vast areas dedicated to children include splash pools, play rooms, and video arcades.

As you'd expect, the largest ships offer the greatest variety of **activities,** with an emphasis on choice. Countless activities are offered all day long, from dance lessons to wine tastings, fashion shows, art auctions, aerobics classes, bingo, bridge, ship tours, cooking demonstrations, pool games, and trivia contests. There are more entertainment options—piano bars, discos, martini bars, champagne bars, sports bars, theaters, and show lounges—than you could ever sample in one evening.

SMALL SHIPS

If the thought of a ship carrying thousands of passengers makes you want to jump overboard, a smaller ship may be more up your alley. Small ships are ideal if you're the type who craves a calm, intimate experience in a clublike atmosphere where conversation is king. As in a tiny town, you'll quickly get to know your neighbors on a smaller ship, as you'll see the same faces at meals and on deck throughout the week.

Unlike the more homogenous, cookie-cutter megas, there is a variety of small-ship styles. The Windjammer, Star Clippers, Windstar, and Club Med fleets are **sailing ships** relying on both sail and engine power, and attracting passengers in their thirties through seventies who are looking for something a little different. Windstar is the most upscale version, emphasizing fine cuisine and plush cabin amenities like CD players and VCRs. Windjammer is the most casual and adventurous, maintaining an anything-goes onboard atmosphere where shorts and T-shirts can be worn to dinner. Star Clippers and Club Med offer an experience midway between these two.

The Clipper and American Canadian Caribbean lines have **simple, cozy, motorized ships,** with a more sedate ambiance for a generally older (over 50) clientele. The **small luxury ships** of high-end lines such as Seabourn and Radisson Seven Seas cruise lines offer a refined, ultra-elegant ambiance. Cabins are spacious with large marble bathrooms, gourmet meals are served on fine china by gracious waiters, and guests dress to impress in sequins and tuxedos.

A small ship might have only one restaurant and one or two bars; a pianist or duo will entertain before dinner, and perhaps there will be a crew or passenger talent show afterward. Small ships have fewer activities options, but are no less appealing. There's usually one all-purpose lounge, or maybe a bar or central patch of outdoor deck where passengers can congregate to chat, read, have a drink, or listen to a presentation about their next port destination. There's often a library of books and videos nearby, either in a separate room or tucked into the corner of a lounge. Generally, there's a focus on learning. On Windstar, Star Clippers, Windjammer, and ACCL, for instance, the cruise director or captain will discuss the native wildlife or history of the next port of call (on the megas, port talks are mostly about shopping opportunities). Sometimes a naturalist, author, or celebrity joins the cruise to present informal lectures on a wide variety of topics (and in fact, Clipper Cruise Line carries naturalists and historians as part of the crew, offering passengers full-time learning opportunities). Small ships generally visit a port nearly every single day, and they're able to easily slip in and out of more off-the-beaten-track, less spoiled ports, such as Iles des Saintes, Virgin Gorda, and St. Barts.

Old Ships, Aging Gracefully

Like people, some older ships have aged gracefully, others have not. At press time, Premier's 42-year-old **Rembrandt,** formerly the *Rotterdam V* of Holland America Line, was the most beautiful and intact relic left, with much of her original furniture, wall finishings, and artwork. The two-level Ritz-Carlton Lounge is one of the most stunning rooms, with its undulating lines, mosaic cocktail tables, chunky velvet chairs, and enormous wraparound mural. You won't forget the funky, circular Ambassadors Lounge with its leather padded bar, red Formica cocktail tables, wavy-backed chairs, and bronzy headlightlike wall panels. Sadly, the *Rembrandt* was scheduled to be painted red (do you believe this?) in late 2000 and be renamed the *Big Red Boat IV,* as Premier continues to try and reinvent itself. It was unclear how much (or even if) the interior would be altered; let's keep our fingers crossed that its beauty won't be utterly sacrificed for easy profit.

There are several other wonderful old ships out there. Cunard's 32-year-old **QE2,** while having undergone many more face-lifts, manages to hold on to the past with dignity and her long body and razor-sharp bow still turn heads. The *QE2*'s running mate, Cunard's **Caronia,** is extremely well maintained and boasts gorgeous and expansive tiered aft decks that are as inviting as they were in 1973, when the ship was built. Norwegian Cruise Line's 39-year-old **Norway** shares the *QE2*'s stunning lines, but her interior has been mostly stripped of it original grandeur over the years, though some stunning rooms remain, like the elegant Club Internationale. On a lesser scale, ships like the 48-year-old **Regal Empress** of Regal Cruises have managed to retain some of their original charm, although you have to look harder to find it.

See the cruise line reviews in chapters 6, 7, and 8 for complete descriptions of these vessels.

OLD SHIP OR NEW?

Depending on what you like, the age of a ship can be a plus or a minus. **New ships** come stocked with all the bells and whistles. Aside from fresh new carpeting and upholstery, the newest ships have computer rooms for sending E-mail, big gyms and spas, cabin balconies, TVs and VCRs, several restaurants, pizza and ice-cream shops, uncluttered open expanses of deck and wide promenades, and big windows everywhere.

Now, if you appreciate relics of the past—prewar apartments over modern ones, antiques instead of IKEA—then you'll like the handful of 30-year-old-plus **classic ocean liners** still plying the Caribbean. With long, sweeping hulls and tiered decks, wood paneling, and chunky portholes, these shippy ships offer a nostalgic glimpse back to a lost age of passenger shipping. Decks, doors, railings, and bar tops are made of solid varnished wood, and you may notice cabin corridors are sheered or bowed, matching the line of the ship. On the bridge, an oversize wooden wheel and heavy brass compasses may sit alongside modern radar devices. Cabin doors may still operate with a lock and key rather than a computerized key-card. Tall sills in most doorways will require some high stepping to avoid tripping (old ships are not for wheelchair users), and there's no shortage of exposed cables, fire doors, pipes, ropes, winches, and all manner of hardware. These are ships that look like ships, and for maritime buffs they're charming (and for bargain hunters, they're often the best deal in town).

That said, most of the old-timers can't hide the wear and tear accumulated from logging thousands of miles at sea. If you're a lover of all things fresh, new, and modern, don't even consider a cruise on one of the oldies. Repeatedly refurbished and restored through the years (often haphazardly and in the least expensive ways), many are a hodge-podge of design schemes and awkward spaces. Discos, spas, and gyms are often small, dark spaces in lower decks, and carpeting, wall finishes, and outside decks are often worn. You won't find two-story dining rooms, Vegas-style casinos (they do have casinos, but they're often small and dark), and long stretches of uninterrupted deck space.

The future of some of these old-timers depends on compliance with a set of international safety regulations known as the **Safety of Life at Sea (SOLAS),** which are predominately concerned with issues like fire prevention. Ships built after 1994 automatically incorporate SOLAS safety features; ships built before 1994 have been required to add them by a progressive set of deadlines. The most sweeping changes were completed by a 1997 deadline, a further series had to be implemented by October of 2000, and the next are scheduled for 2005 and 2010. These last, especially, may prove too costly for many of these old-timers and seal their fate forever. We'll see.

4 Matching the Cruise to Your Needs

CRUISES FOR FAMILIES

The right cruise can be the perfect family vacation—safe, fun, and oh-so-relaxing for the whole brood. Cruise lines have been going to great lengths to please parents and kids alike, as families continue to become a large and influential segment of the cruising public.

It's the **megaships** that cater most to families and attract the largest numbers of them, with playrooms, video arcades, and supervised activities generally provided for children who are potty trained, generally ages 3 through 17 (although the trend is to go younger, with Disney now offering a supervised nursery for ages 3 months and up), with programs broken down into several age categories.

The most family-friendly ships at sea are Disney's *Magic* and *Wonder* and Premier's *Big Red Boat.* Carnival's post-1990 ships do a great job, too, and the newer ships (those built after 1993, when family cruising was becoming more mainstream) in the Princess, Norwegian, Celebrity, and Royal Caribbean fleets are also well equipped to cater to families (Royal Caribbean's giant new *Voyager* in particular is awesome for families). Even lines traditionally geared to older folks are getting in on the kid craze. Holland America's new *Volendam,* for instance, has a sizable playroom. (See the section "Best Cruises for Families with Kids" in the "Frommer's Favorites" chapter for more on the best family ships.)

ACTIVITIES With dedicated camp-counselor-like supervisors, playrooms, computer stations, state-of-the-art video arcades, and pools, your kids will have so much fun you may have to drag them away kicking and screaming at the end of the cruise. Chances are, even too-cool, nonchalant teens will be worn down by the endless activities and the chance to make new friends.

The youngest kids frolic in toy- and game-stocked playrooms, listen to stories, and go on treasure hunts; older kids keep busy with arts and crafts, computer games, lip-sync competitions, pool games, and volleyball; and teenagers go snorkeling, mingle at teen parties, or hang out at the video arcade. The megas have large playrooms with computer stations and video games as well as shelves of toys. There's usually a TV showing movies throughout the day and, for the younger ones, there are ball bins and plastic jungle gyms to crawl around in. Many megaships have shallow kiddie pools, sometimes sequestered on an isolated patch of deck.

BABY-SITTING   To ensure that parents have a good time, too, there are adults-only discos and lounges, and baby-sitting from about 8pm to 2am on many ships (though not all). **Group baby-sitting,** slumber-party style in the playroom, is about $4 to $5 per hour per child, and **private in-cabin baby-sitting** by a crew member, if available, is a steep $8 to $10 per hour for the first child, plus generally a dollar or two more for a sibling. Using a private baby-sitter every night could put a serious dent in your budget, but it's a nice option.

FAMILY-FRIENDLY CABINS   Worried about spending a whole week with the family in some cramped cabin? Well, depending on your budget, you don't have to.

Now, a family of four *can* share a cabin that has **bunk-style third and fourth berths,** which pull out of the walls just above the pair of regular beds (some even have a fifth berth), but there's no two ways to slice it: A standard cabin with four people in it will be cramped, and with one bathroom . . . well, you can imagine. However, when you consider how little time you'll spend in the cabin, it's doable and many families take this option. The incentive to share one cabin is the price—whether children or adults, the rates for third and fourth people sharing a cabin with two full-fare (or even heavily discounted) passengers are usually about half of the lowest regular rates. On occasion there are special deals and further discounts. Norwegian Cruise Line, Premier Cruise Lines, and Royal Olympic Cruises allow children under 2 to sail for free (excluding port charges, which will run about $100 to $200 per person). Disney offers a reduced rate of $80 per cruise for children under 3. If you're a single parent sailing with children, Premier offers some of the best single-person rates, as low as the normal per-person rate (on most lines, singles have to pay 50% to 100% more than the regular per-person rate, since rates are based on double adult occupancy of cabins).

If you can afford it, and if space equals sanity in your book, **consider booking a suite.** Many have a pull-out couch in the living room—or, better yet, two separate bedrooms—and accommodate up to three or four children. The *Disney Magic* and *Wonder* boast the family-friendliest cabins at sea (and you'll pay more for them, too). The majority of the ships' 875 cabins are equipped with two bathrooms and a sitting area and are like mini-suites, about 25% larger than the industry standard, comfortably sleeping families of three or four. The ships' bona fide suites accommodate families of five, and nearly half of all cabins have private verandas.

Families with older kids can always consider booking **two separate cabins with interconnecting doors.** Lots of ships, big and small, have them. You'll be close to each other, but separate.

TAKING THE KIDS ON SMALL SHIPS   While there's no doubt the big new ships are best prepared for families, if your children are at least 10 or 12, some of the casual, off-beat cruises (for example, Windjammer's *Legacy* and Star Clippers' *Star Clipper*) can be loads of fun and educational to boot—if you and your kids come armed with the right attitude, of course. While you won't find a kids' playroom stuffed with toys (or many other kids on board for that matter), the experience of visiting a remote port of call every day will help keep you and the kids from going stir crazy on board. If your child is inquisitive and somewhat of an extrovert, these ships offer him or her a chance to talk with the crew and learn something about how a sailing ship operates. That said, if your kids are attached at the hip to video games, computers, and big-screen TVs, the megaships are the route to take.

CRUISES FOR HONEYMOONERS & ANNIVERSARY COUPLES

You want romance? You're in luck: All cruises are romantic. All the elements are there to make your honeymoon or anniversary cuddly and cozy: moonlit nights on deck, the

---

Family Cruising Tips

Here are some suggestions for better sailing and smoother seas on your family cruise.

- **Ask about children's amenities.** If you'd like a crib, for instance, check in advance with the cruise line to see if they can provide it.

- **Pack some basic first-aid supplies,** and even a thermometer. Cruise lines have limited supplies of these items (and charge for them, too) and can quickly run out if the ship has many families aboard. If an accident should happen aboard, virtually every ship afloat (except for the smallest ones) has its own infirmary staffed by doctors and/or nurses. Keep in mind, first aid can usually be summoned more readily aboard ship than in port.

- **Warn younger children about the danger of falling overboard** and make sure they know not to play on the railings.

- **When in port, prearrange a meeting spot on board.** If your child is old enough to go off on his or her own, prearrange a meeting spot onboard and a time (well before the ship is scheduled to depart) and meet there just after boarding to make sure no one is still ashore.

- **Make sure your kids know their cabin's number and what deck it's on.** The endless corridors and doors on the megas often look exactly alike (though some are color-coded).

- **Prepare kids for TV letdown.** Televisions on ships just don't have 200 channels of cable—you'll be lucky to get five or eight channels. On the brighter side, your ship is likely to have nightly movies and a video arcade.

---

undulating sea all around you, dining in dimly-lit restaurants, silky beaches and exotic ports of call, maybe even a private balcony for your cabin.

Of course, different ships are romantic to different kinds of people. The megas offer glamorous, Vegas-style romance; the small, casual ships, an intimate and Sunday-drive-in-the-country kind of romance; the ultra-luxury lines, epicurean romance with gourmet cuisine, fine wine, and plush surroundings; and older ships, a nostalgic brand of romance (think Cary Grant and Deborah Kerr in *An Affair to Remember*).

Besides their inherent romantic qualities, cruises are honeymoon havens for lots of reasons—like **Sunday departures,** which mean that couples who marry on Saturday can leave on a cruise the next day. Other **romantic ship features** include private balconies, 24-hour room service, hot tubs, spas, and, of course, the balmy island ports of call.

SPECIAL HONEYMOON FREEBIES Most lines will serve honeymooners a special cake in the dining room one night, and some lines—Carnival, Royal Caribbean, Premier, and NCL—even go one step further and invite honeymooners to a **private cocktail party** for complimentary drinks and hors d'oeuvres (couples celebrating anniversaries are often invited as well). Norwegian Cruise Line treats honeymooners to breakfast in bed one morning, hors d'oeuvres delivered to the cabin one evening, a free photograph, the choice of dining at a special newlyweds-only table or a private table for two, and a $100 onboard credit per 7-night cruise or a $50 credit for 3- and 4-nighters (to claim these goodies, you need to have been married 90 days or less and bring along a copy of your marriage certificate). Premier gives honeymooners and couples celebrating anniversaries a complimentary bottle of champagne, an 8-by-10 photo, and special commemorative dinner menus one night.

To get your share of honeymoon and anniversary freebies, be sure to tell your travel agent or the cruise line reservation agent that you'll be celebrating your honeymoon or anniversary on the cruise.

HONEYMOON & ANNIVERSARY PACKAGES   If you want even more romantic stuff to enhance your cruise, the lines aren't shy about selling a variety of goodies and packages geared to honeymooners and couples celebrating anniversaries and vow renewals. You'll get a pamphlet describing the available packages when you receive your cruise tickets in the mail. These packages, which need to be ordered before the cruise, start at around $30 per couple and can run into the thousands of dollars, with **wedding ceremony packages** being the most costly.

Celebrity Cruises' $134 package is typical; it includes breakfast in bed served with champagne, engraved champagne flutes, fresh floral arrangement, a red rose placed on the pillow, a pair of bathrobes, Cova pralines, and a personalized honeymoon or anniversary certificate. Costa's $99 package includes a chilled bottle of sparkling wine in the cabin, fresh flowers, a portrait taken by the ship's photographer and a frame to go with it, his and hers bathrobes, and an invite to a cocktail party hosted by the captain. For a more gourmet palate, Windstar offers a box of Swiss truffles in your cabin for $24.50, a tray of French cheeses for $24, and/or a bottle of Dom Perignon and caviar at $195 a pop. Other packages may include a photograph and wedding album, chocolate-covered strawberries, limousine service between the ship and airport, shore excursions, and even a pair of massages at the spa.

Some lines offer **vow-renewal packages** for couples who'd like to celebrate their marriage all over again. On Holland America ships, for example, couples can renew their vows at a special ceremony while at sea or in port; the $95 package includes a floral arrangement in the cabin, a photo and photo album, music, wine or champagne, and hors d'oeuvres. Princess offers similar (but souped-up) vow-renewal packages for $149 and $349 per couple, which include a bottle of Moët et Chandon champagne, engraved champagne flutes, a pair of terry robes, and a massage or facial in the spa.

To ensure a dapper appearance on formal nights, **tuxedo rentals** can even be ordered for about $75, complete with shirt and shoes. Your tux will be pressed and waiting in your cabin. All these extras are usually purchased for a couple before a cruise by the couple themselves or by parents, friends, or their travel agent.

HONEYMOON LUXURY   High-end lines, such as Windstar, Radisson Seven Seas, Seabourn, Cunard, and Crystal, don't offer special cocktail parties and the like, but their ultra-deluxe amenities are especially pleasing to honeymooners. From terry-cloth bathrobes and slippers that await in walk-in closets, to whirlpool bathtubs, five-course dinners served in your cabin, stocked minibars, and high crew-to-passenger ratios (meaning more personalized service), extra-special touches are business as usual on these upscale lines.

GETTING MARRIED AT SEA

If you'd like to have your marriage and honeymoon all in one, you can legally get hitched on board many ships—though not, as you might think, by the skipper (with the exception of Princess's *Grand Princess,* captains are rarely qualified—much less have the time or inclination—to legally do the officiating). The *Grand Princess* and Royal Caribbean's *Voyager of the Seas* both have wedding chapels on board. Other ships hold ceremonies in lounges, which are decorated with flowers and ribbons and other frilly wedding accoutrements.

CIVIL CEREMONIES IN U.S. PORTS   Passengers can have a civil marriage ceremony performed by a local justice of the peace or church official on board the ship before a cruise departs from any U.S. port—for example, in **Florida, New York,** or **Puerto Rico.** This way, friends and family can come aboard for a few hours for a ceremony and a reception before the ship departs.

CEREMONIES IN BERMUDA   Couples can also tie the knot while in port in Bermuda and several Caribbean islands, either on the ship or on shore. Sometimes, where permitted, you can request or arrange to have a priest, rabbi, or other official of your choice. Ceremony and reception packages include not only the services of the officiant, but also things such as floral arrangements, tuxedo/gown rental, wedding cake, photography, music, and hors d'oeuvres, and generally start at about $500 per couple, and like weddings shore-side, can run into the thousands of dollars.

IN THE U.S. VIRGIN ISLANDS, THE BAHAMAS & JAMAICA   The U.S. Virgin Islands (USVI)—**St. Croix, St. Thomas,** and **St. John**—as well as the Bahamas and Jamaica, are some of the most popular wedding spots. Carnival may be the biggest wedding factory at sea, offering packages in San Juan, St. Thomas, Ocho Rios, Jamaica, Key West, and Nassau, and on board while anchored in Grand Cayman or Barbados.

HAVING THE CAPTAIN OFFICIATE   Have your heart set on the big boss performing your marriage rites at sea? If, so, you've only got one choice. Princess Cruises' *Grand Princess* is currently the only ship where the captain himself performs about four or five bona fide, 100% legal civil ceremonies a week (don't wait till the last minute to decide, since there's often a waiting list for these onboard marriages). He performs the wedding ceremonies in the ship's charming wedding chapel. Adorned with fresh flower arrangements (there are two full-time florists on board) as well as ribbons strung along the aisle, the room is tastefully designed in warm caramel-colored wood tones and stained glass, and there is seating for a few dozen friends and family members. Assistant pursers, decked out in their handsome dress blues, are available to escort a bride down the mini-aisle. Three different ceremony packages are offered on the ship, ranging from $1,400 to $2,400 per couple, and depending which you choose, they include photography, video, music, and salon treatments for the bride. And if you've got friends and family on board, reception packages start at $70 per person, and include hors d'oeuvres, champagne, and wedding cake.

THE DETAILS   No matter where you choose to wed, U.S. or foreign port, a **wedding license** must be obtained (or an application filed) in advance of the cruise and specific arrangements must be made for the wedding ceremony itself. Policies vary from country to country, and you need to find out what the rules are well in advance of your sailing date. At the time of booking, the cruise line or your travel agent can fill you in on the rules and regulations of the ports visited and assist you with the paperwork—for example, by sending you a license application form or telling you where to get one. To help you with the details, Carnival and Princess have **wedding departments;** other lines handle wedding planning through the guest-relations office or refer you to a wedding consultant.

To get married in the USVI, for example, license applications must be received by the Territorial Court in the USVI at least 8 days before your wedding day (the license application fee is $50; contact the **USVI Territorial Court** in St. Thomas at ☎ **340/ 774-6680** for an application). In Bermuda, couples are required to file a Notice of Intended Marriage with the office of the registrar general in Bermuda at least 3 weeks in advance (the fee is $176 and you can get a form from the **Bermuda Department of Tourism** at ☎ **800/223-6106**). You must be in the Bahamas for at least 24 hours before marrying there (the fee for a marriage license is $40; contact the **Bahamas Tourist Office** at ☎ **800/422-4262** for more information).

Remember, the cruise itinerary limits where and when you can tie the knot; time spent in a given port generally ranges from 3 to 10 hours.

CRUISES FOR 20- AND 30-SOMETHINGS

So, what is young? I know a few 60-year-olds who act a lot younger than people who haven't even hit 30, so who's to say. But still, I am often asked to recommend ships geared to folks in their 20s and 30s. Here's the deal: There aren't any. What I mean is that there aren't any that attract *only* young people. While the age of the average cruiser continues to sail downward (it's now somewhere around 50 years old), the majority of cruisers are people in their fifties and sixties. No ships attract *only* 20- and 30-somethings, just like you'd be hard-pressed to find a hotel that does, or even a resort. Most ships are a mixed bag of ages, and more so in the Caribbean, which tends to attract a sizable young crowd as well as retirees. Alaska, Europe, and Asia itineraries, on the other hand, draw mostly an older, 50-plus mix.

That said, here are some general guidelines about ships and the ages of the people you'll find on them.

The **youngest crowds,** in the twenties-to-forties range, are typically found on 3- and 4-night cruises (and next on the 7-night cruises) on the mainstream lines like Carnival, Royal Caribbean, and NCL, and on soft-adventure lines like Windjammer, Star Clippers, and Club Med.

The **oldest folks,** upwards of 65, will be the vast majority on the luxury lines like Seabourn, Cunard, and Radisson, and on the budget lines Commodore and Premier (although the shortest itineraries these lines offer tend to draw a somewhat younger crowd). Holland America, a mainstream line, has traditionally attracted a mature crowd, and the soft-adventure lines American Canadian Caribbean and Clipper draw an older group, too.

Young-at-heart types, who may be 54 or 67 or 72 but who wear bikinis and short-shorts and drink piña coladas for lunch, will be found on the fun-loving lines like Carnival, Royal Caribbean, NCL, Windjammer, and Star Clippers.

CRUISES FOR GAY MEN & LESBIANS

There are a number of particularly gay-friendly cruises and special chartered sailings for gay men and lesbians. For details, contact these specialists: **RSVP Vacations,** 2800 University Ave. SE, Minneapolis, MN 55414 (☎ **800/328-7787** or 612/379-4697); **Pied Piper Travel,** 330 W. 42nd St., Suite 1804, New York, NY 10036 (☎ **800/TRIP-312** or 212/239-2412); and **Olivia Cruises and Resorts,** 4400 Market St., Oakland, CA 94608 (☎ **800/631-6277** or 510/655-0364), which caters specifically to lesbians.

You can also contact the **International Gay and Lesbian Travel Association,** 4331 N. Federal Hwy., Suite 304, Fort Lauderdale, FL 33308 (☎ **800/448-8550**), which has over 1,000 travel industry members. You might want to check out the well-known *Out & About* travel newsletter ($49 a year for 10 issues; to subscribe, call ☎ **212/645-6922** or 800/929-2268) or *Our World* travel magazine ($35 a year for 10 issues; call ☎ **904/441-5367** to subscribe) for articles, tips, and listings on gay and lesbian travel.

CRUISES FOR ACTIVE PEOPLE

Sure, there are lots of activities offered on cruises—bingo, dancing lessons, wine tasting, napkin-folding, makeup demonstrations, and lots more. But what about people who like to be physically active? Well, on the megas, and even on the small ships, there's quite a bit to do to keep your heart pumping and muscles moving (see individual ship descriptions in chapters 6 through 9).

The newer megaships (built after 1990) in the Carnival, Royal Caribbean, Princess, Celebrity, and Holland America fleets have **jogging tracks** and **well-equipped gyms** that rival those on shore (the biggest exceed 10,000 sq. ft., and all have dozens of exercise machines). Smaller ships, like Radisson's *Seven Seas Navigator* and Seabourn's *Seabourn Legend, Pride,* and *Spirit,* have decent gyms, too, they're just more compact versions of those on the megas. Some ships—Royal Caribbean's *Voyager of the Seas,* Princess's *Ocean, Grand, Sea, Sun,* and *Dawn Princess,* Holland America's *Maasdam, Ryndam, Veendam, Volendam,* and *Zaandam,* NCL's *Norwegian Dream, Wind,* and *Sky,* the entire Carnival fleet, Disney's *Magic* and *Wonder,* and Crystal's *Symphony*—have **basketball, volleyball,** and/or **paddle-tennis courts.** Princess's *Grand Princess* and Royal Caribbean's *Voyager, Splendour,* and *Legend of the Seas* even have **miniature-golf courses** on board. The enormous *Voyager of the Seas* takes the cake, though, boasting an **ice-skating rink,** outdoor **rock-climbing wall,** and **in-line-skating track.**

Celebrity, Norwegian, Crystal, Princess, Radisson Seven Seas, and Cunard have **outdoor golf cages**—areas enclosed in netting where you can swing, putt, and whack at real golf balls (sometimes, though, these nets are monopolized by the onboard golf pro and his students). Celebrity's and Cunard's golf cages are pretty much only for the golf pro.

A handful of smaller ships—those in the Windstar and Seabourn fleets, plus the *Radisson Diamond* and the *Club Med II*—have **retractable water-sports platforms** that unfold from the stern for easy access to the water. Weather and conditions permitting, you can swim, be taken waterskiing or on banana-boat rides, or use the kayaks, sailboats, and Windsurfers provided—all free of charge, and all just a few steps from your cabin. Star Clippers' *Star Clipper* and *Royal Clipper* both carry a fleet of Zodiac boats on board, so passengers can be taken waterskiing or on banana-boat rides.

On shore, there are more and more **active excursions** being offered. No need to sit on a bus for 3 hours sweating if you'd rather be working up a sweat the natural way. Along with snorkeling and diving, options like biking, hiking, and horseback riding have become popular tours in many ports. (For more details, see chapter 11, "Caribbean Ports of Call.")

CRUISES FOR PEOPLE WITH DISABILITIES

The newest ships have been built with accessibility for disabled passengers in mind, and some of the older ships have been refitted to accommodate travelers with disabilities. Like hotels, restaurants, movie theaters, and other public places, cruise ships are catering more and more to the needs of all potential travelers. Technically, though, as foreign-flagged vessels, cruise ships are not subject to U.S. laws governing construction and design, nor are they required to obey the Americans with Disabilities Act.

For those ships that can accommodate passengers with disabilities, most require wheelchair-bound passengers to be accompanied by a fully mobile companion. The vast majority of ships travel with a nurse on board at all times and often there is a doctor, too; I've listed which ships have infirmaries in the "Ships at a Glance" chart in chapter 5, but if you've got special needs, check with the line to see exactly what medical services are provided.

In the ship reviews in part 2, I've provided information about which ships provide the best access and facilities for passengers with disabilities, but be sure to discuss your needs fully with your travel agent prior to booking, to be sure all your needs are met.

ACCESSIBLE CABINS & PUBLIC ROOMS On newer ships, most public rooms—dining rooms, lounges, discos, and casinos, for example—have ramps. Keep in mind that older ships, though, (generally those more than 20 years old) may have raised doorways (known as *sills* or *lips,* originally created to contain water) in bathrooms, hallways, and other public rooms, which can protrude as high as 6 to 8 inches. New ships have no or very low sills; those that do may be able to install temporary ramps to accommodate wheelchair users, which must be arranged in advance.

Many ships have a handful of cabins specifically designed for travelers with disabilities, with extra-wide doorways, large bathrooms with grab bars and roll-in showers, and furniture built to a lower height (the "Cabins" section in each of my ship reviews indicates if and how many are accessible, as does the "Ships at a Glance" chart in chapter 5). All of the ships reviewed in the mainstream category (chapter 6) have accessible cabins, while most of the ships in the luxury category also do (chapter 8). The budget lines (chapter 7) have few or no accessible cabins and none of the soft-adventure ships (chapter 9) are accessible.

ELEVATORS All of today's newest megaships are built with elevators and most are wide enough to accommodate wheelchairs; however, make sure you're certain of this before booking. Sailing ships and small vessels do not have elevators. Even if a ship does have elevators, the size of today's huge megaships means your cabin could be quite a distance from the elevators and stairs, unless you specify otherwise. Cabins designed specifically for wheelchair users are intentionally located near elevators. If you don't use a wheelchair but have trouble walking, you'll want to choose a cabin close to an elevator to avoid a long hike down the corridor.

TENDERING INTO PORT If your ship is too large to dock or if a port's docks are already taken by other vessels, your ship might anchor offshore and shuttle passengers to land via tenders (small boats). Some tenders are large and stable, others are not. Keep in mind that if you have trouble walking or use a wheelchair, it might be difficult or impossible to get into certain tenders; even calm seas can rock the boats enough to make climbing inside a tricky maneuver. For liability reasons, many lines forbid wheelchairs to be carried onto tenders, meaning you might have to forgo a trip ashore and stay on board when in these ports. Check with your travel agent to find out if itineraries you're interested in allow your ship to dock at a pier. Note, though, that once on the cruise, weather conditions and heavy traffic may necessitate last-minute changes in the way your ship reaches a port of call. Generally, though, ships do pull alongside the piers in Nassau, Key West, Ocho Rios (Jamaica), Cozumel, San Juan, St. Thomas, St. Croix, Grenada, Barbados, Aruba, and Curaçao. All ships calling on Grand Cayman, on the other hand, always anchor offshore and tender passengers in.

TRAVEL-AGENT SPECIALISTS A handful of experienced travel agencies specialize in booking cruises and tours for travelers with disabilities. **Accessible Journeys,** 35 W. Sellers Ave., Ridley Park, PA 19078 (☎ **800/846-4537;** www.disabilitytravel.com), can even provide licensed health-care professionals to accompany those who require aid. **Flying Wheels Travel,** 143 W. Bridge St., Owatonna, MN 55060 (☎ **800/535-6790**), is another option.

2

Booking Your Cruise & Getting the Best Price

Sure, cruises cost money, but the educated consumer can often slice hundreds or thousands off the brochure rate. In this chapter I'll show you how to get a good price, keep costs down, and find a reputable travel agent or a good online cruise site. After that, I'll tip you off on how to choose your cabin once you've hunted down the (affordable) ship of your dreams.

1 Booking a Cruise: The Short Explanation

Every cruise line has a brochure, or sometimes many different brochures, full of beautiful glossy photos of beautiful glossy people enjoying beautiful glossy vacations. They're colorful! They're gorgeous! They're enticing!

They're also about as believable as a cow in lederhosen, particularly when it comes to prices.

But that doesn't mean what you think it does. Instead of publishing rates that say something like "from $500" when in fact most of the cabins sell for much more, cruise lines actually publish rates that are *higher* than almost anyone will ever pay. What these published rates are are the cruise line's pie-in-the-sky wish for how much they'd like to sell the cruise for in an ideal world. In reality, especially as a sailing gets close and it looks as if they'll get stuck with unsold space, cruise lines are almost universally willing to sell their cruises for much, much less.

Here's the rule to follow: Except for peak-season cruises between Christmas and New Year's (plus Presidents' week, Thanksgiving, and Fourth of July week), when prices are often higher than those listed in these cruise line brochures, **forget the brochure prices**—you'll always pay less (except with a tiny minority of lines, like American Canadian Caribbean Line, which do stick to their brochure rates). Overcapacity and fierce competition have ushered in the age of the discounted fare, and rates continue to stay relatively low. In addition to last-minute deals, there are early-booking discounts and all sorts of other bargains.

So how do you find them? Traditionally (meaning over the past 30 years or so) people have booked their cruises through **travel agents.** But, you may be wondering, hasn't the traditional travel agent been replaced by the **Internet,** and gone the way of typewriters and eight-track tapes? Well, not exactly. Travel agents are alive and kicking, though the Internet has indeed staked its claim alongside them and knocked some out of business. Some traditional agencies have also created their own Web sites to try to keep pace.

So which is the better way to book a cruise these days? Good question. The answer can be "both." If you're computer savvy and have a good idea of the cruise you're looking for (which you probably will after reading this book), Web sites are a great way to trawl the seas at your own pace and check out last-minute deals, which can be dramatic. On the other hand, you'll barely get a stitch of personalized service searching for and booking a cruise online. If something goes wrong or you need help getting a refund or arranging special meals or other matters, you're on your own.

For a more in-depth discussion of this topic, see "Using Travel Agents & Internet Sites" later in this chapter.

However you arrange to buy your cruise, what you basically have in hand at the end is a contract for transportation, lodging, dining, entertainment, housekeeping, and assorted other miscellaneous services that will be provided to you over the course of your vacation. That's a lot of services, involving a lot of people. It's complex, and like any complex thing, it pays (and saves) to study up. That's why it's important you read the rest of this chapter.

2 The Prices in This Guide

Cruise guides have struggled for years to adequately drive home the point that cruise-line brochure prices are almost always much, much higher than you'll actually pay. Trouble is, when all was said and done, they still would generally print the brochure rates, and rely on admonitions like "See the travel specials advertised in your Sunday newspaper" to get people the scoop on how much they'll really save.

In this guide, however, I've come up with a new approach, working with Icruise.com, a Web-based cruise seller, to present to you a sample of the **actual prices** cruises aboard all the ships in this book sell for. You can see the difference for yourself. For example, the brochure rate for a 7-night eastern Caribbean cruise aboard Princess's beautiful *Grand Princess* is $2,553 for a low-end outside cabin. In reality, however, people who booked during our sampling period (approximately 8 months ahead of time) for an early 2001 sailing got that same cabin for $1,372. What a difference!

In the ship-review chapters, I've listed these realistic prices for every ship, and in the "Cruise Price Comparisons" table in this section I've shown how the brochure prices for every ship stack up against what consumers actually pay. See chapter 5, "The Ratings (and How to Read Them)," for a detailed explanation of how we arrived at these prices. Remember that rates are always subject to the basic principles of supply and demand, so those listed here are meant as a guide only and are in no way etched in stone—the price you pay may be higher or even lower, depending on how far ahead you book, when you choose to travel, whether there are any special discounts being offered by the lines, and a slew of other factors. All rates are cruise only; per person and based on double occupancy, and include port charges; government fees and taxes are additional.

Both the table in this section and the ship reviews in chapters 6 through 9 offer prices for the following three basic types of accommodations:

- Lowest-category inside cabins (i.e., without windows)
- Lowest-category outside cabins (i.e., with windows)
- Lowest-category suites

Remember that cruise ships generally have several different categories of cabins within each of these three basic divisions, all priced differently, and that the prices I've listed represent the *lowest* categories for inside and outside cabins and suites. If you're interested in booking a roomier, higher-level cabin in any category, you'll find the price will be higher. In general, the cost of a top-level inside cabin will probably be very close to the rate for a low-level outside cabin, and the cost of a top-level outside may be very

Price Comparisons: Discounted Rates vs. Brochure Rates

Line	Ship	Itinerary (number of nights/region)	Lowest Inside (cruise vs. brochure)	Lowest Outside (cruise vs. brochure)	Lowest Suite (cruise vs. brochure)
ACCL	Grande Caribe	11/Carib/Canal	$2,657/$2,785	$2,871/$3,010	N/A
	Grande Mariner	11/Carib/Canal	$2,274/$2,385	$2,449/$2,570	N/A
	Niagara Prince	11/Carib/Canal	$1,939/$2,030	$2,449/$2,620	N/A
Carnival	Carnival Destiny	7/S. Carib	$611/$1,635	$786/$1,835	$1,711/$2,785
	Carnival Triumph	7/E. Carib	$694/$1,635	$844/$1,835	$1,794/$2,785
	Carnival Victory	7/W. Carib	$694/$1,635	$844/$1,835	$1,744/$2,785
	Celebration	4/W. Carib	$375/$853	$445/$953	$1,313/$1,383
	Ecstasy	3/Bahamas	$310/$693	$360/$763	$635/$1,043
	Fantasy	4/Bahamas	$314/$853	$384/$953	$709/$1,283
	Fascination	7/S. Carib	$601/$1,339	$741/$1,539	$1,566/$2,389
	Imagination	5/W. Carib	$520/$1,013	$600/$1,123	$995/$1,563
	Inspiration	7/W. Carib	$574/$1339	$724/$1,539	$1,549/$2,389
	Jubilee	4/W. Carib	$375/$853	$445/$953	$850/$1,383
	Paradise	7/W. Carib	$664/$1,339	$814/$1,539	$1,639/$2,389
	Sensation	7/W. Carib	$574/$1,339	$724/$1,539	$1,549/$2,389
	Tropicale	10/Canal	$763/$1,649	$1,013/$1,899	$2,138/$3,049
Celebrity	Century	7/E. Carib	$913/$1,795	$1,163/$2,225	$2,393/$3,825
	Galaxy	7/S. Carib	$913/$1,795	$1,113/$2,225	$2,390/$3,825
	Horizon	7/S. Carib	$649/$2,149	$849/$2,349	$3,663/$5,049
	Infinity	14/Canal	$1,554/$2,212	$2,184/$3,248	$2,954/$4,522
	Mercury	12/S. Amer	$1,809/$3,360	$2,309/$4,150	$2,939/$6,385
	Millennium	7/W. Carib	$1,013/$1,795	$1,213/$2,245	$2,313/$3,695
	Zenith	10/E. Carib	$1,299/$2,345	$1,449/$2,745	$2,554/$4,345
Clipper	Nantucket Clipper	7/Carib	N/A	$1,889/$1,980	$3,333/$3,500
	Yorktown Clipper	7/Carib	N/A	$1,889/$1,980	$3,333/$3,500
Commodore	Enchanted Capri	5/Carib	$515/$935	$595/$1,095	$765/$1,435
	Enchanted Isle	7/Carib	$656/$1,185	$771/$1,415	$911/$1,695
Costa	CostaAtlantica	7/E. Carib	$820/1,299	$964/$1,449	$2,068/$2,599
	CostaVictoria	7/W. Carib	$724/$1,199	$916/$1,399	$2,068/$2,599
Crown	Crown Dynasty	7/Bermuda	$962/$1,162	$1,162/$1,362	$1,462/$1,662

The right-hand price in each column is the cruise line's brochure price, while the left-hand price represents the actual rate consumers were paying through the online booking site icruise.com for the lowest-priced inside cabin, outside cabin, and suite aboard each ship for January 2001 sailings booked 8 months ahead. These prices are shown only as an example of the kinds of discounts available. Discounts shown may not apply when you book—or you may even get a larger discount. It's all a matter of supply and demand (and timing).

Line	Ship	Itinerary (number of nights/region)	Lowest Inside (cruise vs. brochure)	Lowest Outside (cruise vs. brochure)	Lowest Suite (cruise vs. brochure)
Crystal	Crystal Harmony	12/S. Amer	$3,525/$5,105	$4,380/$6,430	$5,770/$8,025
	Crystal Symphony	10/Canal	$2,280/$5,145	$3,490/$6,210	$6,970/$11,505
Cunard	Caronia	18/Canal	$3,265/$4,540	$3,545/$4,940	$6,842/$9,650
	QE2	10/Bermuda	$2,290/$3,540	$3,116/$4,720	$6,154/$9,060
Disney	Disney Magic	7/E. Carib	$680/$1,380	$880/$1,680	$1,080/$2,080
	Disney Wonder	4/Bahamas	$589/$769	$749/$1,004	$1,143/$1,684
Holland America	Amsterdam	10/Canal	$1,752/$2,939	$1,975/$3,739	$2,842/$5,439
	Maasdam	7/W. Carib	$909/$1,802	$1,101/$2,219	$1,450/$2,978
	Noordam	14/S. Carib	$1,731/$2,888	$2,125/$3,579	$2,380/$4,026
	Ryndam	17/S. Amer	$2,665/$4,756	$3,136/$5,644	$4,433/$8,092
	Veendam	7/S. Carib	$958/$1,039	$1,163/$2,219	$1,535/$2,978
	Volendam	9/E. Carib	$1,446/$2,617	$1,752/$3,205	$2,358/$4,370
	Westerdam	8/E. Carib	$954/$1,688	$1,142/$2,051	$2,252/$4,185
	Zaandam	9/E. Carib	$1,593/$2,617	$1,934/$3,205	$2,609/$4,370
Mediterranean Shipping	Melody	11/W. Carib	$885/$1,185	$1,235/$1,735	$1,895/$2,385
Norwegian	Norway	7/E. Carib	$804/$1,634	$1,004/$2,004	$1,254/$2,254
	Norwegian Dream	15/S. Amer	$1,999/$4,799	$2,299/$5,399	$2,949/$6,699
	Norwegian Majesty	7/S. Carib	$901/$2,201	$1,051/$2,501	$1,451/$3,301
	Norwegian Sea	3/Bahamas	$384/$964	$434/$1,064	$704/$1,604
	Norwegian Sky	7/W. Carib	$1,054/$2,704	$1,114/$2,824	$1,614/$3,704
	Norwegian Wind	7/W. Carib	$957/$2,307	$1,107/$2,607	$1,357/$3,107
Premier	Big Red Boat I	3/Bahamas	$388/$578	$478/$758	$1,048/$1,048
	Big Red Boat II	7/W. Carib	$638/$1,038	$988/$1,388	$1,488/$1,888
	Big Red Boat III	7/W. Carib	$788/$1,088	$988/$1,288	$1,588/$1,888
	Rembrandt	7/E. Carib	$668/$1,498	$1,018/$1,998	$1,518/$2,898
	SeaBreeze	7/W. Carib	$538/$1,198	$888/$1,498	$1,388/$2,298
Princess	Crown Princess	10/Canal	$1,516/$2,833	$1,659/$3,133	$3,511/$5,922
	Dawn Princess	7/S. Carib	$991/$1,813	$1,276/$2,363	$1,941/$3,052
	Golden Princess	7/Carib	$2,940/$3,565	$3,640/$4,340	$4,540/$5,415
	Grand Princess	7/E. Carib	$1,182/$2,203	$1,372/$2,553	$1,744/$3,681

Price Comparisons: Discounted Rates vs. Brochure Rates (continued)					
Line	Ship	Itinerary (number of nights/region)	Lowest Inside (cruise vs. brochure)	Lowest Outside (cruise vs. brochure)	Lowest Suite (cruise vs. brochure)
Princess *(continued)*	Ocean Princess	7/S. Carib	$988/$1,813	$1,273/$2,363	$1,938/$3,052
	Pacific Princess	7/Bermuda	$599/$1,473	$799/$1,773	$1,917/$3,113
	Sea Princess	7/W. Carib	$963/$1,693	$1,248/$2,243	$1,509/$2,783
	Sun Princess	10/Canal	$1,475/$2,733	$1,893/$3,633	$3,508/$5,922
Radisson Seven Seas	Radisson Diamond	4/E. Carib	$1,895/$2,095	$2,095/$2,295	$3,695/$3,995
	Seven Seas Mariner	9/W. Carib	$2,921/$3,820	$4,796/$6,320	$6,521/$7,420
	Seven Seas Navigator	9/W. Carib	$2,831/$3,865	$3,971/$5,465	$7,331/$8,765
Regal	Regal Empress	4/W. Carib	$339/$489	$509/$689	$789/$999
Royal Caribbean	Enchantment of the Seas	7/E. Carib	$933/$1,413	$1,163/$1,863	$1,913/$3,213
	Explorer of the Seas	7/E. Carib	$1,113/$1,963	$1,413/$2,263	$1,963/$3,913
	Grandeur of the Seas	7/S. Carib	$1,013/$1,413	$1,263/$1,863	$2,463/$3,213
	Majesty of the Seas	3/Bahamas	$333/$513	$423/$863	$1,433/$1,913
	Monarch of the Seas	7/S. Carib	$883/$1,313	$1,113/$1,713	$3,063/$4,063
	Nordic Empress	7/Bermuda	$772/$1,504	$1,104/$1,904	$3,038/$4,554
	Radiance of the Seas	7/Carib	$1,149/$1,699	$1,449/$2,099	$2,099/$3,059
	Sovereign of the Seas	4/Bahamas	$443/$713	$543/$963	$1,363/$1,813
	Splendour of the Seas	7/S. Amer	$949/$1,658	$1,149/$2,058	$2,149/$4,058
	Vision of the Seas	14/Canal	$1,449/$3,208	$2,108/$3,758	$3,608/$5,308
	Voyager of the Seas	7/W. Carib	$1,163/$2,013	$1,463/$2,513	$2,013/$3,213
Royal Olympic	Olympic Voyager	17/S. Amer	$2,315/$4,210	$2,945/$5,355	$3,786/$6,885
	Stella Solaris	14/Canal	$1,745/$3,265	$1,975/$3,725	$2,445/$4,665
Seabourne	Seabourn Goddess I	7/E. Carib	N/A	$2,587/$3,410	$3,028/$4,240
	Seabourn Goddess II	7/S. Carib	N/A	$2,587/$3,610	$3,028/$4,240
	Seabourn Legend	14/S. Amer	N/A	$6,993/$9,870	$8,155/$11,530
	Seabourn Pride	22/—	N/A	$7,433/$10,490	$8,791/$12,430
	Seabourn Sun	22/—	$6,700/$7,400	$8,162/$9,020	$19,894/$22,020
Star Clippers	Royal Clipper	7/Carib	$1,300/$1,600	$1,400/$1,700	$3,497/$3,620
	Star Clipper	7/Carib	$1,100/$1,500	$1,300/$1,700	$2,497/$2,620
Windjammer	Amazing Grace	13/S. Carib	N/A	$1,741/$1,825	$2,771/3,225
	Flying Cloud	6/E. Carib	N/A	$1,110/$1,165	$1,300/1,365
	Legacy	6/E. Carib	N/A	$1,277/$1,340	$1,372/1,440
	Mandalay	13/S. Carib	N/A	$2,106/$2,210	$2,248/$2,360

Line	Ship	Itinerary (number of nights/region)	Lowest Inside (/cruise vs. brochure)	Lowest Outside (/cruise vs. brochure)	Lowest Suite (/cruise vs. brochure)
Windjammer *(continued)*	Polynesia	5/S. Carib	N/A	$855/$900	$1,045/$1,100
	Yankee Clipper	6/S. Carib	N/A	$1,110/$1,165	$1,110/$1,165
Windstar	Wind Spirit	7/E. Carib	N/A	$2,482/$3,000	$2,602/$4,200
	Wind Star	7/W. Carib	N/A	$2,672/$3,000	$2,802/$4,200
	Wind Surf	7/E. Carib	N/A	$2,482/$3,000	$2,602/$4,200

close to the rate for a low-level suite. See chapters 2 and 5 for more information on pricing and choosing your cabin.

3 The Cost: What's Included & What's Not

A cruise adds up to a great value (and an even bigger convenience) when you consider that the main ingredients of what you need are included in the **almost-all-inclusive rates.** Accommodations, all meals and most snacks, stops at ports of call, a packed schedule of activities, and free use of resort-quality facilities like gyms and pools, as well as cabaret, jazz performances, dance bands, discos, and more, are all covered in the rate.

When figuring out your budget, though, there are **additional costs** to consider that are not included. Truth is, no cruise is truly all-inclusive, although a handful of the most luxurious and expensive lines (like Radisson Seven Seas, Seabourn, and Cunard) come the closest by including some alcoholic beverages (and sometimes tips) in the cruise rate.

So how much should you expect to spend over and above the cruise rate? Be prepared to shell out at least another $200 per person for a 7-night cruise for tips, bar tabs, shore excursions, and possibly port charges (and easily double or triple that, if, for instance, you have a bottle of wine with dinner every night, go on three $60 shore excursions, and buy some trinkets in the onboard shops). Airfare can run from maybe $100 to over $500 depending on where you're flying from and when you purchase your tickets. Of course, just as at a hotel, you pay extra for items like ship-to-shore phone calls or faxes, E-mails, spa and salon treatments (such as massages, manicures, facials, and haircuts), shopping in ship boutiques and at the ports of call, medical treatments in the ship's infirmary, and, of course, gambling (assuming you lose).

4 Money-Saving Strategies

From early-booking discounts to last-minute deals, from sharing cabins to senior-citizen and frequent-cruiser discounts, there are a lot of ways to save money on your cruise, and in this section I'll fill you in on them.

EARLY BOOKING VS. LAST-MINUTE BOOKING

More than ever before, there are no steadfast rules about pricing—policies differ from line to line, and from week to week, depending on supply and demand. Just a few years ago, booking-early—3 to 9 months before a cruise departed—was the thing to do. For a while cruise lines actually guaranteed early-booking rates would not be undercut by last-minute discounts. Well, seems many cruise lines have quietly backed away from

Cruise Tip: Put Aside Some Money for Crew Gratuities

Almost all cruise lines have the same kind of deal with their staff that restaurants do in the United States: They pay them minimal salaries on the assumption that they'll make most of their pay in **tips.** Generally, each passenger can expect to drop about $70 in tips for a weeklong cruise.

these early-booking guarantees. If there's empty space on a ship as the sailing date nears, lines, of course, would rather sell a cabin for a lower fare than not sell it at all. While booking early will still get you as much as a 50% discount off the brochure rates and give you a better pick of cabins, waiting to book until just a few weeks or a month or two before sailing will often get you an even better rate. Exceptions to this include cruises during ultra-popular times, like holidays (New Year's, Thanksgiving, Easter, and Presidents' week in Feb) and summers in the Caribbean when demand is up because there are fewer ships deployed there.

Of course, you've got to have the flexibility essential for playing the waiting game. Since savings are not offered on every ship, or on every sailing, or on every cabin category, you may have to settle for something that isn't the cruise of your dreams. Another point to consider when booking at the last minute is that if you have to fly to the port of embarkation, you may have to pay an airfare so high that it cancels out your savings on the cruise (and that's assuming you can get a ticket at all; San Juan is particularly difficult to come by at the last minute). If you were planning to use frequent-flier miles, you'll likely discover that frequent-flier seats are all taken on the flights you need. You may have to fly a multileg route instead of a direct one. Moreover, most last-minute deals are completely nonrefundable.

You'll find last-minute deals advertised online, and in the travel section of your Sunday newspaper, especially the *Miami Herald, LA Times,* and *New York Times.* You should also check with a travel agent, or an agency or discounter that specializes in cruises.

PRICE PROTECTION

It's a little-known fact that if the price of your cabin category goes down after you've booked it, some cruise lines, like Princess and Holland America, will agree to make up the difference, in effect guaranteeing you the lowest rates up until the day of sailing. (Keep in mind, there is no law requiring lines to do so; you can't walk into a grocery store with the can of peas you bought a month ago demanding a refund because of a sale on them that started today—same thing applies here.) If a line does reduce rates just before a cruise because there are some empty cabins they'd like to fill, don't expect them to call you and the other people who booked 4 months before at a higher rate and tell you the prices have been reduced. Many agencies, especially the impersonal discounters who work only over the phone, won't be clamoring to refund money to you, and they're not obligated to do so. Here's where a trusted travel agent comes into play; someone who will look for your best interests because they want you to come back again. You and/or your travel agent would need to monitor the prices on a weekly basis and then call the cruise line, which, of course, requires more time and energy than many people want to spend; also keep in mind that most travel agents will lose a part of their commission if you get a refund, so they'll have that much less incentive.

BUDGET CRUISE LINES

Industry-wide discounting and the glut of space has blurred the distinction between the so-called budget cruise line prices and the mainstream cruise line prices. At certain times,

Average Cost of Onboard Extras

Just so you're not shocked when your shipboard account is settled at the end of your trip, here are some average onboard prices.

Laundry	50¢–$6 per item
Self-service laundry	$1–$1.50 per load
Pressing	$1–$4 per item
Massage (25-min. session)	$55–$65 plus tip
Massage (50-min. session)	$84–$99 plus tip
Facial (50-min. session)	$84–$99 plus tip
Men's shampoo and haircut	$25–$29 plus tip
Women's shampoo and set	$26–$45 plus tip
Manicure	$21–$25 plus tip
Pedicure	$24–$40 plus tip
Spa treatments	$10–$242 plus tip
5×7-inch photo purchased from ship's photographer	$6–$7
Scotch and soda at an onboard bar	$3–$4.50
Bottle of domestic beer	$2.50–$3
Bottle of imported beer	$3.50–$5
Bottle of wine to accompany dinner	$10–$300
Bottle of Evian water, 1.5 liters	$2.95
0.5 liters	$1.95
Can of Coca-Cola	$1.50
Ship-to-shore phone call or fax	$4–$15/minute
Sending E-mails	$1–$5/message
Shore excursions	$20–$200
Ship souvenirs (logo T-shirts, key-chains, etc.)	$3–$35
Sunscreen, 6-ounce bottle	$10
Disposable camera	$20

ads in major newspapers and online sites promote 7-night cruises on mainstream lines like Carnival, Royal Caribbean, Celebrity, and Norwegian for rates nearly as low as the bargain-basement prices often offered by Premier, Commodore, Mediterranean Shipping, Regal, and Windjammer Barefoot, budget lines with classic, older, small- to midsize ships. Generally, though, you'll find the budget lines offering 7-night cruises about $50 to $200 lower than equivalent itineraries on the mainstream lines. These ships won't be as plush as the new megas, but if you know what to expect, they can be wonderful experiences and a great value for the money. Bottom line: Compare and contrast the prices (and balance them with your expectations) before you make your decision.

BOOKING AIR-TRAVEL THROUGH THE CRUISE LINE

To get to the port of embarkation (assuming you can't drive there), whether it be Miami, Fort Lauderdale, or San Juan, Puerto Rico, you can either purchase airfare on your own or buy it through your travel agent when booking your cruise. The latter is often referred to as an **air add-on** or air/sea package. (Except during special promotions, air-fare is rarely included in the cruise rates for Caribbean cruises, as it often is on Europe and Asia itineraries.) You can usually find information on these programs in the back of cruise line brochures, along with prices and flights from over 100 U.S. and Canadian cities to the port of embarkation. Aside from the issue of price, there are benefits and disadvantages to booking your airfare through the cruise line.

- **Benefits:** You usually get round-trip transfers between the airport and the ship. A uniformed cruise line employee will be in the airport to direct you to the right bus, and your luggage will be taken from the airport to the ship without you having to lift a finger. The cruise line will know your airline schedule, and in the event of delayed flights and other unavoidable snafus, will be able to do more to make sure you and the other people on your flight get on the ship; if you've booked your air transportation separately, you're on your own.

- **Disadvantages:** Air add-ons may not be the best deal and it might be cheaper to book your own airfare. You probably won't be able to use any frequent-flier miles you may have accumulated. The air add-on could require a circuitous routing—with indirect legs and layovers—before you finally arrive at your port of embarkation.

If you choose to arrange your own air transportation, make sure the airfare is not included as part of your cruise contract (it rarely is with Caribbean itineraries). If it is, you're often granted a deduction (usually around $250 per person) off the cruise fare.

MORE WAYS TO CUT CRUISE COSTS

Here are some more suggestions to save money booking a cruise:

- **Be flexible with dates and itineraries.** Off-season cruises and repositioning cruises (when ships leave one cruise region and sail to another—for instance, to and from summers in Alaska to a winter season in the Caribbean) are often discounted, and two-for-one deals are not uncommon. Keep in mind, since most repositioning cruises require crossing great stretches of ocean, they tend to have fewer stops at ports of call, and your cruise will include long stretches of time at sea.

- **Share a cabin with family or friends.** Many lines offer cabins that can house a total of three or four passengers (sometimes even five)—two in regular beds and two in bunk-style berths that pull down from the ceiling or upper part of the wall. So for families of four or groups of very good friends, if you're willing to be a bit (or a lot) crowded, you can save money by sharing your cabin. The rates for the third and fourth passengers in a cabin, whether adults or children, are typically half that of the normal adult fare, and sometimes less than half. Also, look into sharing a suite; most ships have some. Disney Cruise Line, for example, offers mostly family-style suites comfortably accommodating up to five people and with $1\frac{1}{2}$ bathrooms.

- **Book your cruise with a group.** Some cruise lines offer reduced rates to groups occupying at least eight cabins (some as few as five cabins), with two adults in each cabin (for a total of 16 passengers), making cruise ships a good bet for family reunions and the like. Also, travel agents are especially good at coordinating widely scattered members of a group that plan to travel together, which could save you significant time and frustration.

  Based on two people per cabin, typically the 16th person in the group gets a free cruise, and the entire group can split the savings. In general, discounts for this type of group travel can be significant, but are wholly determined by the cruise line and seasonal demand at the time you're booking.

  Some high-volume cruise agencies might be able to team you up with a "group" of their own devising that they're booking aboard a certain ship. Unlike group travel on land, shipboard groups are not herded about as a community and, of course, have individual cabins. You're only a group in the sense that you're considered one by the booking agents.

• **Read the fine print.** You never know what obscure special deals might apply to you. Carnival, for instance, offers really low rates on the *Carnival Destiny* if you book one of the cabins that's one deck directly above the disco. The brochure calls them "Night Owl Staterooms—if you love to party late into the night." Turns out the dozen, category 6, inside cabins located directly under the disco on the upper deck are on the receiving end of a lot of noise courtesy of the music above. But if you're planning on being there yourself, dancing into the wee hours of the night, you might want to consider these cabins, which are discounted at 50% or more than other, quieter cabins in the same category!

• **Book back-to-back cruises.** Depending on when you go, cruise lines offer discounts to passengers who book what's in essence a double cruise. Technically, you'll be taking two separate cruises, but you'll be on the same ship. On ships that alter their itineraries by the week, you'll be visiting different ports on the second phase of your journey, and you'll sail with a different set of passengers. Policies vary from line to line, but typically a flat discount of up to 50% on your second cruise is offered. For instance, if you combine two or more cruises for a total of 20 days or more, Seabourn offers 10% to 50% savings on one of the cruises. Windstar offers the same deal if you book two cruises back-to-back. Most common are discounts like the one Carnival offers: a $100 per-cabin discount on the total cruise price when two 7-night cruises are combined. Of course, this only represents a discount if you intended to take a long trip anyway.

• **Take advantage of sail-and-stay promotions.** If you had planned to spend a few days' vacation on land before or after your cruise, cruise lines often offer good prices for hotels in the cities of embarkation and debarkation. Since most cruises depart from ports that are tourist attractions in their own right, you might want to explore Miami before you sail, drive to Disney World from Port Canaveral, or spend a few days in San Juan. The cruise lines' package deals usually include hotel stays and transportation from the hotel to the ship (before the cruise) or from the docks to the hotel (after a cruise).

AVOIDING THE SINGLE PENALTY

Since cruise lines base their rates on two paying passengers sharing a cabin, passengers wanting to travel alone, in their own cabin, are usually socked with something called the **single supplement.** Sounds like you're getting a deal, doesn't it? Well, you're not— it's the cruise line that gets the supplementary cost, which is usually between 50% and 100% *in addition to* the standard cruise fare.

The only thing you can do to avoid this penalty is to take advantage of a service offered by some cruise lines—like Carnival, Holland America, and Windjammer Barefoot Cruises (fewer lines are doing this than in the past)—whereby the cruise line will match you with a (same-gender) roommate, through which arrangement the cruise line gets its full fare for the cabin. Keep in mind, you won't be able to get any info about your roommate until you walk through the cabin door (although Holland America lets you specify smoking or nonsmoking; Carnival, on the other hand, doesn't guarantee it).

If you don't want to share a cabin, a handful of ships—Cunard's *QE2* and *Caronia* and Regal's *Regal Empress,* for example—have **cabins designated for singles.** Rates for these cabins are usually 15% to 25% higher than rates for passengers sharing a cabin, though a very few carry no additional charge. Although sizes vary, keep in mind that single cabins are usually small, at 80 to 100 square feet.

SENIOR-CITIZEN DISCOUNTS

The cruise industry offers some discounts to seniors (usually defined as anyone 55 years or older), so don't keep your age a secret, and always ask your travel agent about these types of discounts when you're booking. Carnival, for instance, offers savings of up to $200 per cabin on certain ships and itineraries.

For discounts in general, the best organization to belong to is **AARP (American Association of Retired Persons),** the biggest outfit in the United States for seniors. For more information, contact AARP at 601 E. St. NW, Washington, DC 20049 (☎ **800/ 424-3410** or 202/434-AARP; www.aarp.org).

Tour operators, many of whom are experienced in selling cruise packages to senior citizens, are alert to cruise-industry discounts, and often configure blocks of cabins aboard selected cruise ships that are geared to mature clients. One well-known expert is **Grand Circle Travel,** 347 Congress St., Boston, MA 02210 (☎ **800/221-2610** or 617/350-7500; www.gct.com). Write to them for a free booklet called *101 Tips for the Mature Traveler.*

REPEAT PASSENGER PROGRAMS

If you've been on one cruise (or sometimes two), you're considered a valued "repeater" and are often rewarded for it. You'll get not only special mailings and newsletters from the cruise line, but, at the least, invitations to **private cocktail parties,** 5% to 20% **discounts** on future cruises, **priority check-in** at the terminal, **cabin upgrades,** and maybe even a **free cruise** if you've racked up enough sailings. Carnival, Holland America, and Windstar, for instance, offer some of these goodies.

Repeater programs are the most generous and prevalent on the smaller, upscale ships, because these ships tend to attract wealthy guests with the means to cruise often, and also because the small, high-end ships have varied worldwide itineraries that appeal to cruisers interested in traveling many weeks a year. If you sail a total of 140 days with Seabourn, for instance, you're entitled to a free 14-day cruise. After the 15th Crystal cruise, you get a business-class air upgrade, and if you're booked into a suite on the penthouse deck, you also get a $250 shipboard credit among other perks. After your first cruise with Cunard, you get 10% to 20% savings on future cruises in addition to any early-booking discounts or other deals that may apply.

Often a special host sails on board acting as a concierge for any repeaters on that cruise. In every way possible, guests are treated like very special, valued customers. Repeat cruisers on some upscale ships are admitted into a secret society of sorts, wearing special lapel pins, sometimes hats and windbreakers, and often recognizing one another from past cruises—much like a private club. Commonly, these guests are invited to dine with the captain or another officer one night.

5 Using Travel Agents & Internet Sites

Like never before, there is more than one way to skin a cat when it comes to booking a cruise. Instead of using the services of a traditional **travel agent,** you can also head for your computer and check out what the **online cruise agencies and discounters** are offering; a handful even allow you to actually submit your credit card online and make a reservation without ever having to talk to a soul. And some cruise lines, like Carnival, NCL, Royal Caribbean, and Celebrity, even have their own booking sites (although at press time, they weren't particularly user-friendly).

While most online cruise sellers still require you to actually call them when you're ready to make a booking, the agent on the other end might not know too much more than pricing. They're often just order takers—as many traditional travel agencies and 1-800 agents are—so don't be surprised if they've never even been on a cruise themselves. If you are

Cruise Tip: It Never Hurts to Ask

With a little bit of a poker face and a touch of patience, you can sometimes wrangle free stuff out of your travel agent if you imply that you can't book a cruise unless he or she sweetens the deal. So just ask for a complimentary cabin upgrade, free shore excursions, free wine with dinner on your anniversary, or free or discounted lodging at hotels before or after your cruise. It never hurts to ask.

an experienced cruiser or simply have a very good idea of what you want, this may work perfectly well for you. But unlike buying airfare online, which is a relatively simple thing (you want to go from point A to point B and you choose coach or first-class—end of story), shopping for a cruise is a much more complicated purchase, being that there are hundreds of different ships to choose from, with sometimes dozens of different types of accommodations on each, and that the trip you're planning might *also* entail booking air travel, and synching it all up.

Keep in mind, too, that the quality of the information on the Internet is inconsistent, ranging from great to dated and downright misleading. Plus, since the Internet is a constant work in progress, sites add features on a daily basis and brand new sites pop up all the time. You gotta stay on your toes. Further, not all Web sites are easy to use (including the cruise lines' own sites); sometimes information is buried under layers of commands and dead-ends—you could be at your computer for hours figuring things out. All this said, not all old-fashioned travel agents are easy to work with either; there are good and bad representatives of both.

If you need help and some hand-holding, you need an *experienced* travel agent, someone who not only knows what discounts and special promotions are currently available, but who has sailed on or inspected a variety of ships and is knowledgeable about the industry in general. A good travel agent is the keeper of some specialized information (much like the kind of information I've included in this book, though not in such a small, convenient package!), such as which cabins' views are obstructed by lifeboats, which cabins are near loud areas like discos, children's playrooms, and the engine room, and, in general, what the major differences are between cabin categories, so that you can be assigned a cabin you're happy with.

So, can you avoid both agent and Internet and just call up a cruise line directly to make your own reservation? Well, if you really insist, most lines will take your reservation, but they prefer you use a travel agent, whether the traditional kind or online—that's just how the industry has been set up to work (although with the advent of the Internet, things are changing fast in this area; stay tuned). In the United States, 90% to 95% of all cruise bookings are arranged through travel agents.

WHAT MAKES A GOOD TRAVEL AGENT?

Out of some 30,000 travel agencies in North America, about 3,000 of them sell 75% of all travel in North America, and of these about 40% (or around 1,200) are considered cruise-oriented. As the name implies, **cruise-oriented agencies** specialize in selling cruises. They also usually sell airfare along with a cruise. Some of the largest cruise-only agencies work exclusively from toll-free numbers and/or Web sites and deal with clients mostly over the phone or via E-mail. If you know exactly what you want or, conversely, if you don't have a specific ship or itinerary in mind, are flexible, and like the convenience of booking a cruise by phone, then one of the big cruise-only firms may be your best bet. On the other hand, if you want personalized service, hand-holding, and meeting face-to-face with an agent, you probably won't get it from a huge reservation-center-type agency. For more personalized, one-on-one service, ask friends if they can refer you to a home-based agent

---

Factoid

Many of the most reliable large cruise-oriented travel agencies advertise in *Cruise Travel* **magazine.** Look for the bimonthly mag on your newsstand, or call for a subscription (☎ **800/877-5893;** www.travel.org/CruiseTravel/).

(or look in the Yellow Pages); these types of agents are affiliated with the big national agencies but embrace more of a mom-and-pop style.

Full-service agencies can book all aspects of travel, including cruises. For instance, they can shop around for airfare or put together a tailor-made land-based tour to add on to your cruise vacation—maybe a hotel and sightseeing package in the port of embarkation. Many full-service agencies have extensive knowledge of the cruise industry, just as the cruise-oriented agencies do, and sell large numbers of cruises.

Whether cruise-oriented or full-service, a competent travel agency handles all the details involved in planning a cruise, from sending you the tickets to reserving an early or late dinner seating, arranging a limousine to take you from the airport to the ship, and ordering special extras such as a bottle of champagne for your cabin when you arrive or a tuxedo rental for formal nights. They'll also be there to help out and act as an intermediary should any problems arise with your booking. Because they sell such a high volume of cruises, many agencies, like online cruise sellers, get **special rates** and **additional discounts** directly from the lines and pass the savings on to you.

So how do you know an agency is any good? The best way, of course, is to use an agent who has been referred to you by a reliable friend or acquaintance. Another pretty good initial giveaway is to look at the letters after an agent's name. Most agents dealing in cruises are members of the **Cruise Line International Association (CLIA),** an industry marketing organization. Agents who are CLIA Master Cruise Counselors **(MCC)** or Accredited Cruise Counselors **(ACC)** have spent many hours studying the cruise industry and inspecting ships, and it's safe to assume they really know what they're talking about. Agents with a **CTC** designation after their names are Certified Travel Counselors, and have taken many hours worth of travel-related courses to earn this title. It also can't hurt if an agent is a member of industry organizations, such as the **American Society of Travel Agents (ASTA)** or the **National Association of Cruise Oriented Agents (NACOA).**

RECOMMENDED AGENCIES

Travel agencies come in all shapes and sizes, from small neighborhood stores to huge chain operations. For example, Cruise Holidays, AAA Travel Related Services, American Express Travel Related Services, and the McDonald's of travel agencies, the mega Travel Company, are all large, reputable companies operating nationwide through numerous affiliates. You may notice an agency you've used in the past has changed its name or has become affiliated with another agency. Well, get used it to it: Like banking, telecommunications, and the auto industry, the travel industry—from the cruise lines themselves to travel agencies—is rife with consolidation.

AGENCIES SPECIALIZING IN MAINSTREAM CRUISES

To give you an idea of where to begin, here's a sampling (by no means comprehensive) of both cruise-only and full-service agencies that have solid reputations in selling mainstream cruises such as Princess, Carnival, Royal Caribbean, Celebrity, Holland America, Norwegian Cruise Line, and Premier. A few are affiliated with the big chains; most are not. The agencies listed operate from a combination of walk-in business and toll-free telephone-based business.

Beware of Scams

If you're uneasy about the travel agent you're working with, trying calling your state consumer protection agency, the Better Business Bureau, or the cruise line to check on the agent's credentials. If you ever fail to receive a voucher or ticket on the date it's been promised, place an inquiry immediately. If you're told that your cruise reservation was canceled because of overbooking and that you must pay extra for a confirmed and rescheduled sailing, demand a full refund.

Also, it's not a good sign when an agent, whether brick-and-mortar or online, suggests a particular cruise line without asking you questions first about your tastes. Agents work on commissions from the lines and some might try to shanghai you into cruising with a company that pays them the highest rates, even though that line might not be right for you. Be prepared: Read through the cruise line reviews in chapters 6 through 9 so you'll be able to say to sneaky agents, "But *Frommer's* says . . ."

I can't stress enough that although we're all concerned with getting the best price we can, there's value in knowing and trusting a travel agent you've worked with in the past, who will be there for you if a problem arises. Some agents know very little about cruises beyond knowing, for example, that Carnival and Royal Caribbean are popular. Customer service has a value. You might not want to go to the car dealership with the cheapest advertised prices if your salesperson knows little or nothing about the car you're interested in buying and will not be motivated to help you if it breaks down a week after you buy it. Same thing here.

- **Admiral of the Fleet Cruise Center,** 12920 Bluemound Rd., Elm Grove, WI 53122 (☎ **800/462-3371** or 262/784-2628)
- **Admiral of the Fleet Cruise Center,** 3430 Pacific Ave. SE, Suite A-5, Olympia, WA 98501 (☎ **800/877-7447** or 360/866-7447)
- **The Cruise Company,** 10760 Q St., Omaha, NE 68127 (☎ **800/289-5505** or 402/339-6800)
- **Cruises By Brennco,** 508 E. 112th St., Kansas City, MO 64131 (☎ **800/955-1909** or 816/942-1000)
- **Cruise Value Center,** 6 Edgeboro Rd., East Brunswick, NJ 08816 (☎ **800/231-7447**)
- **Hartford Holidays,** 129 Hillside Ave., Williston Park, NY 11596 (☎ **800/828-4813** or 516/746-6670)
- **Just Cruisin' Plus,** 5640 Nolensville Rd., Nashville, TN 37211 (☎ **800/888-0922** or 615/833-0922)
- **Kelly Cruises,** 1315 W. 22nd St., Suite 105, Oak Brook, IL 60523 (☎ **800/837-7447** or 630/990-1111)
- **Mann Travel** and **Cruises American Express,** 4400 Park Rd., Charlotte, NC 28209 (☎ **800/849-2301** or 704-556-8311)
- **National Leisure Group,** 100 Sylvan Rd., Suite 600, Wobrun, MA 01801 (☎ **800/435-7683** or 617/424-7990)

And lastly, there's the biggest one of all. In 1997, Travel Services International formed **The Travel Company,** 220 Congress Park Dr., Delray Beach, FL, 33445 (☎ **800/242-9000;** www.mytravelco.com), which is now the nation's largest cruise-selling agency, with numerous branches throughout the country. The company has deals with the nation's largest cruise lines (Carnival, Royal Caribbean, and Princess) and is even

---

Cruise Tip: Weigh Value Against Price ————————————

While of course you want the best price, it's important not to make price your only concern. Value—what you get for your money—is just as important as the dollar amount you pay. Keep in mind that the advertised prices you see in newspapers are usually for the lowest-grade cabin on a ship; a better cabin—one with a window and maybe a private veranda—is likely to cost more.

---

partially owned by a Carnival Corporation subsidiary. The Travel Company and its branches, like Cruises Only, prominently advertise in most of the nation's largest travel sections every Sunday. The company has a growing reputation for good last-minute deals in the mainstream cruise market, but has not yet seriously penetrated the premium and luxury cruise markets.

AGENCIES SPECIALIZING IN ULTRA-LUXURY CRUISES

This sampling of reputable agencies, both cruise-only and full-service, specializes in selling ultra-luxury cruises like Cunard, Seabourn, Silversea, Crystal, Radisson Seven Seas, and Windstar.

- **Altair Travel,** 2025 S. Brentwood Blvd., St. Louis, MO 63144 (☎ **314/968-9600**)
- **Bancroft Cruise and Tour,** 162 E. Wisconsin Ave., Oconomowoc, WI 53066 (☎ **800/638-7777** or 262/567-8537)
- **Bee Kalt Travel Service,** 30301 Woodword, Royal Oak, MI 48073 (☎ **800/ 284-5258** or 248/288-9600)
- **Cruises of Distinction,** 2750 S. Woodword Ave., Bloomfield Hills, MI 48304 (☎ **800/634-3445** or 248/332-2020)
- **Cruise Headquarters,** 4225 Executive Sq., Suite 1600, La Jolla, CA 92037 (☎ **800/ 424-6111** or 619/453-1201)
- **Jean Rose/Atlantic Coast Travel,** 140 Intracoastal Pointe Dr., Jupiter Fl 33477 (☎ **800/441-4846** or 561/575-2901)
- **Largay Travel,** 5 F Village St., Southbury, CT 06488 (☎ **800/955-6872** or 203/ 264-6581)
- **Melroy Travel,** 4434 Highland Dr., Salt Lake City, UT 84124 (☎ **800/344-5948** or 801/272-8015)

The 244 members of **Virtuoso** (formerly known as **Allied Percival International** group or API), a consortium based in Fort Worth, Texas, also specialize in upscale vacation travel. To find a branch in your area, call ☎ **800/401-4274** or check out their Web site at www.Virtuoso.com.

ONLINE CRUISE SELLERS & TRAVEL COMPANIES

This is a sampling of reputable Web-based cruise sellers, both cruise-only and travel generalists, that sell cruises along with airfare, tour packages, and car rentals. Most focus on last-minute deals for cruises departing in a few weeks to 2 months. A few allow you to book directly online, submitting your credit card and the works, but most still require you to call them after you've perused the site. Keep in mind, these Web sites are constant works in progress, adding new features all the time.

- **Icruise.com** is a cruise specialist, and is my favorite of the lot (that's why I asked them to provide me with the cruise rates for this book). It's the most user-friendly and extensive online cruise seller that I've found, with a database of about 150 ships, so if you know what you want, you merely type in the ship name, itinerary, date, and cabin number (there's even a nifty deck plan for each ship). Icruise.com's database is connected directly to Commodore, Regal, Premier, and Mediterranean Shipping cruise lines, so with these lines you'll know if the cabin is available within seconds (if not, an alternate similar cabin number will pop up), and then a price appears. *Voilà!* If you like what you see, you fill out a form online, submit your credit card, and press send. For all other lines, while you'll know right away if the cabin of your choice is not available, you'll have to wait up to 24 hours for a confirmation via E-mail, fax, or phone that it is.

- **Cruise.com** is a cruise specialist with a large inventory, but their site is cluttered and not the most user-friendly, and you can only search for cruises by destination and itinerary length, not by ship name. There are links to cruise line Web sites, but overall not a lot of useful content if you're looking for info before you book. To book, you must call an 800-number—there's no direct booking online.

- **Cruise411.com** is also a cruise specialist. Its database allows users to search for a cruise by cruise line and destination. There's a handy feature that lets you compare four cruises side-by-side in a chart. You must call an 800-number to make a booking—there's no direct booking online.

- **mytravelco.com** is a travel generalist; it's the site of The Travel Company, the country's largest cruise-selling agency. It's very user-friendly. You can search for a cruise via ship name or destination. At press time this site allowed users to book certain cruise lines directly online (although this never worked when I tried); while for most other lines users must call the site's 800-number to make a booking.

- **Previewtravel.com and Travelocity.com** share the same cruise info. Both are travel generalists and, at press time, the database only included 9 cruise lines. You cannot search by ship, only by line or destination. This site does have a neat feature allowing users to compare prices, itineraries, and other stats of up to 10 cruises in an easy-to-read chart. Overall, it's easy to use. You can fill out a booking form online, and your reservations will be confirmed within about 24 hours.

- **spurof.com (Spur of the Moment Cruises)** lists lots of last-minute cruise deals. Discounts can be good, but not usually that much better than the other cruise sites listed. You must call an 800-number to make bookings.

- **Moments-notice.com** lists mostly last-minute travel deals, including some cruises. Discounts can be good, but like spurof.com, not that much better than the other cruise sites listed. There's an annual $25 membership fee and you must call an 800-number to make a booking.

BOOKING AIR-TRAVEL (AND MORE) ONLINE

Most cruise passengers book their air travel to the port of embarkation—and sometimes pre- or postcruise hotel stays, too—through their cruise line, lumping it all together into a package with their cruise price. If you decide not to go this route, one of your other options is booking online. You can book domestic or international flights, hotels, and rental-car bookings through the following top Web sites.

✪ **Expedia.com:** Expedia is known as the fastest and most flexible online travel planner for booking flights, hotels, and rental cars. It offers several ways of obtaining the best possible fares: **Flight Price Matcher** service allows your preferred airline to match an available fare with a competitor; a comprehensive **Fare Compare** area shows the differences in fare categories and airlines; and **Fare Calendar** helps you plan your trip around the best possible fares. Its main limitation is that, like many online databases, Expedia focuses on the major airlines and hotel chains, so don't expect to find too many budget airlines or one-of-a-kind B&Bs here.

Personalized features allow you to store your itineraries and receive weekly fare reports on favorite cities. You can also check on the status of flight arrivals and departures, and, through MileageMiner, track all of your frequent flyer accounts.

Expedia also offers vacation packages, cruises, information on specialized travel (like family vacations, casino destinations, and adventure and golf travel). There are also special features for travelers accessing information on mobile devices.

(*Note:* In early 2000, Expedia bought travelscape.com and vacationspot.com, and incorporated these sites into expedia.com.)

- **Travelocity.com and Previewtravel.com:** Travelocity uses the SABRE system to offer reservations and tickets for more than 400 airlines, plus reservations and purchase capabilities for more than 45,000 hotels and 50 car-rental companies. An exclusive feature of the SABRE system is its **Low Fare Search Engine,** which automatically searches for the three lowest-priced itineraries based on a traveler's criteria. Last-minute deals and consolidator fares (provided by Travel Information Software Systems, or TISS) are included in the search. If you book with Travelocity, you can select specific seats for your flights with online seat maps, and also view diagrams of the most popular commercial aircraft. Its hotel finder provides street-level location maps and photos of selected hotels.

  Travelocity features an inviting interface for booking trips, though the wealth of graphics involved can make the site somewhat slow to load, and any adjustment in desired trip planning means you'll need to completely start over.

  This site also has some very cool tools. With the **Fare Watcher** E-mail feature, you can select up to five routes and receive E-mail notices when the fare changes by $25 or more. If you own an alphanumeric pager with national access that can receive E-mail, Travelocity's **Flight Paging** can alert you if your flight is delayed. You can also access real-time departure and arrival information on any flight within the SABRE system.

  Note to AOL Users: You can book flights, hotels, rental cars, and cruises on AOL at keyword: Travel. The booking software is provided by Travelocity/Preview Travel and is similar to the Internet site. Use the AOL "Travelers Advantage" program to earn a 5% rebate on flights, hotel rooms, and car rentals.

- **Trip.com:** Trip.com began as a site geared toward business travelers, but its innovative features and highly personalized approach have broadened its appeal to leisure travelers as well. It is the leading travel site for those using mobile devices to access Internet travel information.

  TRIP.com includes a trip-planning function that provides the average and lowest fare for the route requested, in addition to the current available fare. An on-site "newsstand" features breaking news on airfare sales and other travel specials. Among its most popular features are **Flight TRACKER,** which allows users to track any commercial flight en route to its destination anywhere in the United States while accessing real-time FAA-based flight monitoring data, and **intelliTRIP,** which allows users to identify the best airline, hotel, and rental-car rates in less than 90 seconds.

  In addition, the site offers E-mail notification of flight delays, plus city resource guides, currency converters, and a weekly E-mail newsletter of fare updates, travel tips, and traveler forums.

- **Yahoo Travel (www.travel.yahoo.com):** Yahoo is currently the most popular of the Internet information portals, and its travel site is a comprehensive mix of online booking, daily travel news, and destination information. The **Best Fares** area offers what it promises, and provides feedback on refining your search if you have flexibility in travel dates or times. There is also an active section of Message Boards for discussions on travel in general and specific destinations.

LAST-MINUTE DEALS & OTHER ONLINE BARGAINS

There's nothing airlines hate more than flying with lots of empty seats. The Net has enabled airlines to offer last-minute bargains to entice travelers to fill those seats. Most of these are announced on Tuesday or Wednesday and are valid for travel the following weekend, but some can be booked weeks or months in advance. You can sign up for weekly E-mail alerts at the airlines' sites or check sites that compile lists of these bargains, such as **Smarter Living** or **WebFlyer** (see below). To make it easier, visit a site that will round up all the deals and send them in one convenient weekly E-mail. But last-minute deals aren't the only online bargains; other sites can help you find value even if you haven't waited until the eleventh hour. Increasingly popular are travel auction sites and services that let you name the price you're willing to pay for an air seat or vacation package.

- **Cheaptickets.com:** Cheap Tickets has exclusive deals that aren't available through more mainstream channels. One caveat about the Cheap Tickets site is that it will offer fare quotes for a route, then later show this fare is not valid for your dates of travel—most other Web sites, such as Expedia, consider your dates of travel before showing what fares are available. Despite its problems, Cheap Tickets can be worth the effort because its fares can be lower than those offered by its competitors.

- ❂ **1travel.com:** Here you'll find deals on domestic and international flights, cruises, hotels, and all-inclusive resorts such as Club Med. 1travel.com's **Saving Alert** compiles last-minute air deals so you don't have to scroll through multiple E-mail alerts. A feature called "Drive a little using low-fare airlines" helps map out strategies for using alternate airports to find lower fares. And **Farebeater** searches a database that includes published fares, consolidator bargains, and special deals exclusive to 1travel.com. *Note:* The travel agencies listed by 1travel.com have paid for placement.

- **Bidfortravel.com:** Bid for Travel is another of the travel auction sites, similar to Priceline (see below), which are growing in popularity. In addition to airfares, you can bid on vacation packages and hotels.

- **Go4less.com:** Specializing in last-minute cruise and package deals, Go4less has some excellent offers. The Hot Deals section gives an alphabetical listing by destination of super discounted packages.

- **LastMinuteTravel.com:** Suppliers with excess inventory come to this online agency to distribute unsold airline seats, hotel rooms, cruises, and vacation packages. It's got great deals, but you have to put up with an excess of advertisements and slow-loading graphics.

- **Moments-notice.com:** See description under "Online Cruise Sellers & Travel Companies," above.

- **Priceline (www.travel.priceline.com):** Launched in 1998 and known for its $10-million ad campaign featuring William Shatner, Priceline lets you "name your price" for domestic and international airline tickets and hotel rooms. In other words, you select a route and dates, guarantee with a credit card, and make a bid for what you're willing to pay. If one of the airlines in Priceline's database has a fare lower than your bid, your credit card will automatically be charged for a ticket. Downsides? You have to accept any flight leaving between 6am and 10pm on the dates you selected, and you may have to make a stopover—which are big stumbling blocks if you have to be in Miami by 2pm to catch your cruise. Also, no frequent flyer miles are awarded, and tickets are non-refundable and can't be exchanged for another flight.

- **Smarterliving.com:** Best known for its E-mail dispatch of weekend deals on 20 airlines, Smarter Living also keeps you posted about last-minute bargains on everything from Windjammer Cruises to flights to Iceland.

- **SkyAuction.com:** An auction site with categories for airfare, travel deals, hotels, and much more.
- **Travelzoo.com:** At this Internet portal, over 150 travel companies post special deals. It features a Top 20 list of the best deals on the site, selected by its editorial staff each Wednesday night. This list is also available via an E-mail list, free to those who sign up.
- **WebFlyer.com:** WebFlyer is a comprehensive online resource for frequent flyers and also has an excellent listing of last-minute air deals. Click on "Deal Watch" for a round-up of weekend deals on flights, hotels, and rental cars from domestic and international suppliers.

6 Choosing Your Cabin

Once you have some idea of the cruise line you're interested in, and have tracked down a good rate, whether through an agent or online, you have to make one more big decision: what kind of cabin to choose. In this section I'll give you some tips for doing just that.

THE MONEY QUESTION

When it comes right down to it, choosing a cabin is really a question of money. From an inside, lower-deck cabin with an upper and lower bunk to a balconied suite with a butler, cruise ships can offer a dozen or more different cabin categories, all at different prices. Location, size, amenities, and service can vary greatly.

It's traditionally been a rule of thumb that the higher up you are and the more light gets into your cabin, the more you pay; the lower you go into the bowels of the ship, the cheaper the fare. However, on some of the more modern ships, that old rule doesn't always ring true. On ships launched recently by Carnival, for instance, designers have scattered their most desirable suites on midlevel decks as well as top decks, thereby diminishing the prestige of an upper-deck cabin. For the most part, though, especially on some of the newer ships and smaller ships, where most cabins are virtually identical, cabins on higher decks are still generally more expensive, and outside cabins (with windows) are more expensive than inside cabins (without).

EVALUATING CABIN SIZE

Don't fool yourself, it's a fact of life at sea: Inch for inch, cruise ship cabins are smaller than hotel rooms. Of course, having a private balcony attached to your cabin, as many do these days, will make your living space that much bigger.

A roomy **standard cabin** is about 180 square feet, although some of the smallest are about 85 to 100 square feet. Carnival has some of the more spacious standard cabins at sea, measuring about 185 square feet. Standard cabins on Celebrity and Holland America are also fairly roomy. By way of comparison, equivalent standard cabins on Norwegian and Royal Caribbean lines are quite a bit smaller—try 120 to 160 square feet—and can be cramped. Cabins on the small-ship lines like Windjammer, Clipper, and ACCL are quite snug, too. Older ships, like the *QE2* and *Regal Empress,* have cabins of extreme sizes—many standard cabins are very large (vestiges of the long cruises of ocean liner days) and some are just plain tiny (old third-class cabins and cabins for singles, or merely the result of the ships being repeatedly reconfigured and chopped up).

All the "standard" cabins on the high-end lines are roomy: Windstar's cabins are 188 square feet; Seabourn's *Legend* and *Pride* are 275 square feet and its *Seabourn Goddess* twins are 205 square feet; and the *Seven Seas Navigator*'s are about 246 square feet (not including a 55-sq.-ft. balcony). Across the board, **suites and penthouses** are the most

Typical Outside Cabin Configurations

- Twin beds (can often be pushed together)
- Upper berths for extra passengers fold into walls
- Bathrooms usually have showers only (no tub)
- Usually (but not always) have TVs and radios
- May have portholes or picture windows

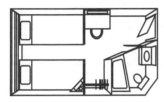 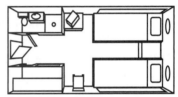

Typical Suite Configurations

- Queen-size or double beds
- Sitting areas (sometimes with sofa beds for extra passengers)
- Large bathrooms, usually with tub
- Refrigerators (sometimes stocked, sometimes not)
- Stereos and TVs with VCRs are common
- Large closets
- Large windows or outside verandas

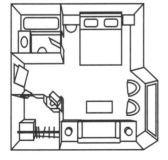 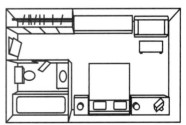

spacious, measuring about 250 square feet on up to over 1,000 square feet, not including private verandas.

How can you avoid dimensional shock when your steward shows you your cabin for the first time? Most cruise lines provide **schematic drawings,** with square footage—and in some cases, measurements of length and width—as part of the standard cruise brochures. Consider measuring off the dimensions on your bedroom floor and imagining your temporary oceangoing home, being sure to block out part of that space for the bathroom and closet. As a rough guideline, within a cabin of around 100 square feet, about a third of the floor space is gobbled up by those functional necessities.

Now, while you're sitting there within the chalk marks (or whatever) thinking "Gee, that's really not a lot of space," remember that, like a bedroom in a large house, your cabin will in all likelihood be a place you use only for sleeping, showering, and changing clothes. Out beyond the door, vast acres of public spaces await, full of diversions. So unless you plan on holing up for most of your cruise, watching movies on your cabin TV and ordering room service, you probably don't need a palatial space.

To help you compare cabin sizes, I've included square footages of most cabins in the cruise ship descriptions in chapters 6 though 9.

THE SCOOP ON INSIDE CABINS VERSUS OUTSIDE CABINS

Whether you really plan to spend time in your cabin is a question that should be taken into account when deciding whether to book an inside cabin or outside cabin (that is, one without windows or one with), or whether to spend the extra money for a cabin with a veranda. If you plan on being up and out to the buffet breakfast and not stopping till the cows come home, you can probably get away with booking an inside cabin and saving yourself a bundle. Inside cabins in general are not as bad or as claustrophobic as they sound. Most cruise lines today design and decorate them to provide an illusion of light and space. These are not the steerage dormitories you saw in *Titanic.* Some, in fact—such as those aboard Celebrity's *Mercury, Galaxy,* and *Century,* as well as Carnival's whole fleet—are quite nice and just as spacious as the outside cabins.

If, on the other hand, you want to lounge around and take it easy, maybe ordering breakfast from room service and eating while the sun streams in—or, better yet, eating out *in* the sun, on your private veranda—then an outside cabin is definitely a worthwhile investment. Remember, though, that if it's a view of the endless sea you crave, be sure when booking that your window doesn't just give you a good view of a lifeboat or some other obstruction. Some cruise line brochures tell you which cabins are obstructed, but in any case, your travel agent or a cruise line's reservation agent can help you determine this.

OTHER CABIN MATTERS TO CONSIDER

Many other matters come into play when booking your cabin. For instance, **cabins on the promenade deck** are often costly and sound just grand, but you may be distracted by passengers walking or talking outside (do keep in mind, there's generally—though not always—double-sided glass in these cabins, allowing you to see out, but no one to see in).

Then there's the matter of translating the cruise line brochures into real English. Increasingly, cruise lines use the terms "deluxe" and "standard" for their cabins. These terms can vary from line to line and are a bit meaningless, except to suggest that deluxe is larger, better located, and has more amenities. Generally, you ask your travel agent for a specific cabin category, even a specific cabin if there's one in particular you'd like. With a few exceptions, your travel agent can tell you what your exact cabin number is when you book the cruise. (Exceptions include passengers booking as part of a

---

Cruise Tip: Book Low-End Cabins on Luxury Ships

Rather than booking upper-end cabins on budget ships, some savvy cruisers book lower-end cabins aboard luxury cruise ships. That way they can enjoy the benefits of sailing on an upscale ship while paying less for the privilege.

---

group, passengers asking the cruise line to match them up with a roommate, and passengers choosing to forgo knowing the cabin they'll occupy in exchange for a lower rate—this is called a "guarantee," where the line guarantees you a cabin, but you won't know which one until the last minute or once on board, or you'll only know if it will be an inside or outside cabin.) Before agreeing to a certain cabin, make sure it suits your particular needs. For instance, are there elevators close by? Convenient, but it can also be noisy. Is your cabin above, below, or adjacent to any noisy public rooms, such as the disco, children's playrooms, or the ship's engines? Is the view out the cabins' windows obstructed by lifeboats or other ship equipment? You can see from the **deck plans** included in the cruise line brochures what's where, and if some cabins in your chosen category are in a questionable spot, be sure to inquire. (See the "Reading a Ship's Deck Plan" diagram for visual reference.)

Here are a few more tips:

- **Keep cabin position in mind if you suffer from seasickness.** If stability is important to you, a midship location is best because it's the area least affected by the vessel's rocking and rolling in stormy seas. In general, the best and most expensive cabins on any vessel are amidships and generally high up, and preferably include a balcony. However, the higher cabins are subject to more motion and swaying. The cheaper cabins are down below in the bow and stern; those toward the stern may suffer from engine vibrations.

- **Inquire about bed sizes if you have particular concerns.** Beds can vary in size from cabin to cabin and from ship to ship, and a king-size bed at sea isn't as large as the one in your bedroom. If you're especially tall, you're often out of luck. Your preference for a twin or queen-size bed is another factor. Most twin-bedded cabins can be converted to make one larger bed by merely pushing the two beds together, but some, such as those whose frames are built into the cabin (as if often the case with small ships) and those with upper and lower berths, cannot.

- **Book early if you want cabins that will be in demand.** The **single-berth cabin** has almost disappeared on ships today, although they exist in older vessels. A single person can, of course, book any cabin he or she so chooses, but if you are not planning on sharing it (the cruise lines can match you with a same-sex single passenger) you'll be charged the double-occupancy rates—that is, the price of two adults, or maybe a bit less. Likewise, cabins with **third** and **fourth berths** (usually bunks or a pull-out couch) are of particular interest to families, so try to book early as they tend to disappear fast. Families who can afford it often book suites or book two cabins side by side, with connecting doors. This is especially desirable for those who are traveling with teenagers.

- **Pay careful attention to bathroom setups (if that's a concern of yours).** If your bathroom is important, always inquire what is offered. Many vessels offer cabins with shower only. Some others feature a shower and a tub; each of the cabin bathrooms on Radisson's *Seven Seas Navigator,* for instance, has a separate shower and a separate tub. In some deluxe categories you even get a tub with a whirlpool. The *Disney Magic* and *Disney Wonder* are winners for the best-bathrooms award: Most of the cabins have 1^1/$_2$ bathrooms—one has a toilet and sink and the other a tub and shower combo.

Reading a Ship's Deck Plan

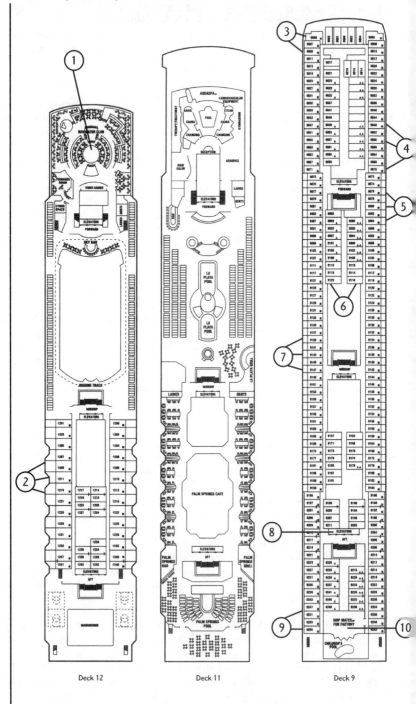

Deck 12

Deck 11

Deck 9

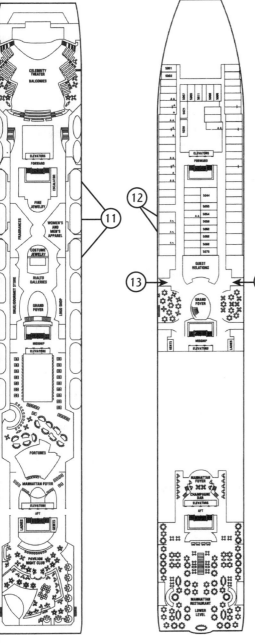

Deck 7

Deck 5

Some Cabin Choice Considerations:

1. **Note the position of the ship's disco** and other loud public areas, and try not to book a cabin that's too close or underneath. This disco is far from any cabins—a big plus.

2. **Cabins on upper decks** can be affected by the motion of the sea. If you're abnormally susceptible to seasickness, keep this in mind.

3. **Ditto for cabins in the bow.**

4. **Outside cabins without verandas** appear as solid blocks of space.

5. **Outside cabins with verandas** are shown with a line dividing the two spaces.

6. **Inside cabins** (without windows) can be a real money-saver.

7. **Cabins amidships** are the least affected by the motion of the sea, especially if they're on a lower deck.

8. **Cabins that adjoin elevator shaftways** might be noisy. (Though proximity makes it easier to get around the ship.)

9. **Cabins in the stern** can be affected by the motion of the sea, and tend to be subject to engine vibration.

10. **Cabins near children's facilities** may not be the quietest places, at least during the day.

11. **Check that lifeboats** don't block the view from your cabin. The ones in this example adjoin public rooms, and so are out of sight.

12. **Cabins for people with disabilities** are ideally located near elevators and close to the ship's entrances (#13).

(Thanks to Celebrity Cruises for use of the Mercury's deck plan.)

Prebooking Your Dinner Table & Arranging Special Diets

In addition to choosing your cabin when booking your cruise, you can also **choose your meal seating** for breakfast, lunch, and dinner, and sometimes even put in a request for the size table you're interested in (tables for 2, 4, 8, 10, etc.). Early seatings allow you to get a jump on the day and, after dinner, get first dibs on shipboard nightlife (or, conversely, promptly hit the sack); late seatings, on the other hand, allow you to sleep later in the mornings and, at dinnertime, linger a little longer over your meal. For a more detailed discussion, see "An Introduction to Shipboard Dining" in chapter 4, "The Cruise Experience."

Also, if for any reason you follow a **special diet**—whether vegetarian, low-salt, low-fat, heart-healthy, kosher, halal, or any other, or if you have certain food allergies—make this known to your travel agent when you book, 30 or more days before the cruise if at all possible. Many ships routinely offer vegetarian meals and health-conscious choices as part of their menus these days, but it can't hurt to arrange things ahead of time. Cruises are not the place to go on an involuntary starvation diet.

- **Addicted to TV? Make sure your cabin has one.** Remember that not all cabins have television sets or VCRs, although the vast majority do have TVs, except for casual, small-ship lines like Windjammer, Clipper, and ACCL, and some of the oldest ships, like Premier's *SeaBreeze*. If these amenities are important to you, always determine their availability in advance (they're listed in the ship reviews in chapters 6 through 9). Remember, too, that you generally aren't going to have the selection aboard ship that you get from your home cable system—at best, you'll have a few channels broadcasting movies, port lectures, and other information of onboard interest, and maybe CNN and ESPN.

A last note: For the best variety, try to book early. The cheapest and the most expensive cabins tend to sell out first.

7 Cancellations & Insurance

What should you do if the cruise you've booked is canceled before it departs? A cruise could be canceled because of shipyard delays if you've booked an inaugural cruise, or because of an impending hurricane, acts of war, the outbreak of an infectious disease, or mechanical breakdowns such as nonfunctioning air-conditioning or an engine fire.

In the event of a cancellation, in this competitive market cruise lines have been making extraordinary efforts to appease disappointed passengers, including rescheduling the cruise and offering big discounts on future cruises—after all, they don't want the bad press they'd get if they screwed hundreds or thousands of passengers. There are, however, no set rules on how a line will compensate you if it cancels a cruise. And, since almost all ships are registered in foreign countries, suing the line is difficult.

If you need to cancel your cruise several months ahead of time, you'll generally get every cent back—most lines provide a full refund if you cancel at least 2 to 3 months before your departure date, although details vary from line to line. Getting closer to the cruise departure date, partial refunds are given up to anywhere from 15 to 7 days before the cruise. After that, no refund is given at all, even for medical reasons.

So what would you do if you needed to cancel a cruise at the last minute because of a sudden illness or other emergency? Or what if you've missed a flight because of bad weather and then missed the ship?

To protect yourself from any of these unpredictable occurrences, you might want to think about purchasing **travel insurance.** There are policies sold through the cruise lines (which vary from line to line) and others sold independently of the cruise lines. Both have pros and cons.

Now, on the other side of the coin, many aggressively commission-driven travel agents and Web-based cruise sellers automatically add insurance coverage to the bill, which may not be in your best interest. Check your cruise contract before paying. You may wind up buying insurance even if you don't want it. And you might not want to bother—it depends on your individual needs. For example, keep in mind that most cancellation policies do not cover cancellations due to work requirements. So if, for instance, a healthy 36-year-old lawyer has a court date moved after booking a cruise, it might be impossible for her to make the cruise. That person is not served well by insurance policies, either independent or the cruise line variety. On the other hand, a 77-year old retiree with a history of medical problems would be well served.

EVALUATING INSURANCE COVERAGE

Like all insurance, travel insurance comes with many optional riders that protect you against eventualities you hope you'll never encounter. Two possibilities are of major concern. The first is the potential expense of an emergency medical evacuation of the ill person from the Caribbean and, if your regular insurance doesn't cover it, the potential cost of major medical treatment while away from home. The second concern is the loss of your prepaid fare if your cruise is interrupted or if you must cancel because of a death in the family or a medical emergency, or if you missed the boat at the pier because of a flight delay.

Most insurance policies reimburse you when your trip is affected by unexpected events, such as airplane crashes or dockworkers' strikes, but not by "acts of God," such as hurricanes and earthquakes.

COVERAGE CHECKLIST

When evaluating travel insurance policies, check to see that they cover the following situations. Some may cover some, others cover others. Buy the insurance that's right for your situation.

- **Trip cancellation.** Caused by you or a member of your immediate family getting sick or dying, not limited to those who cruise. If you're traveling with a nonfamily member, make sure the policy covers you if you need to cancel the cruise because of sickness or a death in your companion's family.
- **Preexisting medical conditions.** The policy should include a preexisting-sickness exclusion rider—critical if you or any family member has a preexisting medical condition.
- **Medical expenses.** Should cover medical expenses on board or in port, and should include any necessary medical evacuation from the ship or a port of call.
- **Emergency air travel home.** If necessary in the event of a personal or family medical emergency or death.
- **Trip delay.** Your policy should have interruption protection should you have problems, such as weather, that prevent you from getting to the cruise on time.
- **Accident coverage.** Including traveling to and from the airplane and/or ship.
- **Baggage protection.** Including loss, damage, or late arrival.
- **Bankruptcy or default of cruise line.**

Additional insurance to protect your **jewelry and valuables** on a cruise usually falls under the riders attached to your homeowner's policy. If you're in any doubt as to whether they're covered, though, check the fine print of your policy, guard your jewels carefully (confining them to your in-cabin safe or the purser's safe when not in use), or just save the aggravation and leave them at home.

Onboard Medical Care

The vast majority of cruise ships have an onboard infirmary staffed by a doctor and a nurse or two. While medical services are not free, you can visit the infirmary for seasickness and cold remedies as well as more serious ailments. A few ships, in fact, have very sophisticated equipment. Princess Cruises' *Grand Princess* and *Ocean Princess,* for instance, have not only a staff of one doctor and five nurses, but also high-tech medical equipment that, via special cameras and a live-video system, link the ships' medical staff with the emergency department at the Cleveland Clinic Florida, in effect offering a real-time second opinion. The only ships that won't have any medical professionals on board are small-ship lines such as American Canadian Caribbean, Windjammer, and the Clipper Cruise Line ships reviewed in this book (since they generally don't sail far from land). Of course, ships big and small have the communication capabilities to contact medical assistance from the closest shore point in the event of an emergency, and in dire circumstances may have helicopters pick up and evacuate a seriously ill passenger. Although the captain does his utmost to get help or head for the nearest port, depending on where the ship is during such an emergency, you can't be sure how long it might take to get reliable care.

In fall of 1999, the *New York Times* ran a huge story on medical care at sea, concluding that it is inconsistent at best, and that doctors were not necessarily certified in the United States and weren't necessarily specialists in important areas like cardiology. Further, many doctors at sea earn far less working on a cruise ship then they would if they practiced on land—which makes you wonder if the cruise lines are getting the best people. The author of the *Times* article did conclude that Holland America and Princess had the best onboard medical facilities (and they pay the doctors a decent wage, too). So, should you be afraid? No, you shouldn't. But do be realistic and don't expect the medical staff and facilities on a cruise ship to be anywhere as extensive as what you'd get in a hospital on land. Always bring with you any medications and any other medical paraphernalia you routinely use.

Note that many policies do not reimburse you if your travel agent goes bankrupt. The bankruptcy of a travel agency poses greater risks than the bankruptcy of a cruise line. Again, using a travel agent you're very familiar with or who has been recommended to you is the safest precaution you can take.

SO WHICH INSURANCE POLICIES ARE THE BEST?

A good travel agent can tell you about policies sold through the cruise lines and ones sold independently of the lines. Even though agents get a commission for selling cruise line policies and non-, most agents and industry insiders believe that non–cruise line policies are the best bet because they are much more comprehensive. Cruise line policies, for instance, do not cover medical expenses due to preexisting conditions and often do not provide coverage if you or a family member gets sick a day or two before the cruise. Cruise line policies also do not cover you if the cruise line goes bankrupt.

Access America, Box 90315, Richmond, VA 23286 (☎ **800/284-8300;** www.accessamerica.com), and **Travel Guard International,** 1145 Clark St., Stevens Point, WI 54481 (☎ **800/826-1300** or 715/345-0505; www.noelgroup.com), are two reputable insurance agencies specializing in travel coverage.

8 Putting Down a Deposit & Reviewing Tickets

You've booked your cruise and now have to leave a deposit to secure the booking. Depending on the policies of the line you selected, the amount will either be fixed at a predetermined amount or represent a percentage of the ticket's total cost. More often than not, within 7 days of making a booking, a fixed $100 deposit is required on a 3- or 4-night cruise, a $250 deposit is required on a 7-night cruise, and a $300-to-$400 deposit is needed for a 10- to 14-night cruise. Upscale lines, because they cost more, may require a larger deposit or a percentage of the cruise price. For instance, Windstar requires a $500 deposit within 7 days of booking and Seabourn requires a 25% deposit within 10 days of making your reservation.

The balance of the cruise price is due anywhere from about 45 to 75 days before you depart; holiday cruises may require final payments even earlier, like 90 days before departure. The payment schedule for groups is different. Booking at the last minute usually requires payment in full at the time of booking.

Payments, whether by check or credit card, are made to your travel agent, who in turn pays the cruise line.

Carefully review your ticket, invoice, itinerary and/or vouchers to confirm that they accurately reflect the departure date, ship, and cabin category you booked. The printout usually lists a specific cabin number; if it doesn't, it designates a cabin category. Your exact cabin location is then assigned to you when you board ship.

The ticket also represents a legal agreement established between you and the cruise line. The fine print should explain what happens if the cruise is canceled or you fail to show up at the pier on time. Especially if you haven't purchased travel insurance, you should check what happens if you're faced with a personal emergency and can't take the cruise or must leave before the cruise's end and fly back home on your own.

3 Things to Know Before You Go

You've bought your ticket and you're getting ready to cruise. Here's the lowdown on what details you need to consider before you go.

1 Passports & Visas

Good news in the convenience category: Visas are not generally required for American, Canadian, and European citizens visiting the Caribbean islands or ports in Mexico (although, depending on the itinerary, you may be asked to fill out tourist cards or other forms in the airplane, airport, or cruise terminal, especially if you're flying to a non-U.S. port to start your cruise). Passports aren't necessarily required either, although it's a good idea to have one. A passport speeds your way through Customs and Immigration and you never know when entry requirements can change. Read through the documents your cruise line sends you with your tickets, and contact the line if you have any questions.

If you find you don't need a passport, you will still need **identification.** Acceptable forms of ID include an ongoing or return ticket plus an original birth certificate (or a copy that has been certified by the U.S. Department of Health) and a photo ID, such as a driver's license or an expired passport. *A driver's license is not acceptable as a sole form of identification.* As you would before any trip abroad, make two photocopies of your documents and ID before leaving home. Take one set with you (keeping it in a different place from your original documents) and keep one at home.

Each particular port of embarkation has its own ritual. You may be asked to turn over your ID (for instance, your passport) and sometimes your airline tickets to cruise line officials at the start of the cruise. They'll facilitate the procedures for group or individual port clearances and immigration formalities throughout the cruise, and return your documents to you at the end of the cruise.

All non-U.S. and non-Canadian citizens must have valid passports, alien-registration cards, and the requisite visas when boarding any cruise ship or aircraft departing from and/or returning to American soil. Noncitizens also need to present an ongoing or return ticket for an airline or cruise ship as proof that you intend to remain on local shores only for a brief stay.

2 Money Matters

Cruise ships operate on a cashless basis. Basically, this means you keep a running tab, signing for virtually everything you want to buy all week

No Vaccinations Required

The Caribbean islands do not generally require inoculations against tropical diseases, although you might want to check out the Centers for Disease Control (CDC) Web site to see what they suggest (www.cdc.gov). In early 2000, for instance, the CDC advised travelers to the rural and southeastern parts of the Dominican Republic to take malaria-prevention medications like chloroquine before traveling there.

long—drinks at the bar, shore excursions, and gift-shop purchases—and paying up at the end of the cruise with cash or a credit card. Very, very convenient, yes—and also very, very easy to spend more than you would if you were doling out wads of cash each time.

Shortly before or after embarkation, a purser or check-in clerk in the terminal or on board will request the imprint of one of your credit cards. On the last day of your cruise, an **itemized account** of all you've charged throughout the cruise is slipped beneath your cabin door. If you agree with the charges, they are automatically billed to your credit-card account. If you'd rather pay in cash or if you dispute any charge, then you need to stop by the ship's cashier or purser's office, where there's usually a long line. Have fun!

At embarkation, larger ships issue you an **identification card** that you show whenever you get back on the ship after spending the day in port and that you use when you sign for something. On the newest ships, this same ID card often serves as your room key. Smaller and older ships may not have either of these ID cards, and still issue regular room keys. (Some lines, such as Windjammer and American Canadian Caribbean Line, rely on the honor system and don't even use room keys.)

The cashless system works just fine on board, but you'll likely need some dough in port. Of course, you can put any shore excursions you sign up for on your room tab, and credit cards are accepted at most port shops (as are traveler's checks), but I do recommend having some real cash on you, ideally in small denominations, for any taxi rides, tips to tour leaders, or purchases you make from craft markets and street-side hawkers.

For the most part, don't worry about **exchanging money** to local currency, since the good ole U.S. dollar is widely accepted in the Caribbean (at least in the tourist-savvy ports of call you're likely to visit) and is the legal currency of the U.S. Virgin Islands, the British Virgin Islands, and Puerto Rico. Exceptions include Guadeloupe, where you'll need to exchange your dollars for some French Francs if you intend to buy anything. If you're running low on dough, there are ATM machines in nearly every cruise port covered in this guide, in some cruise terminals, and on board many of the megaships. (Remember, though, you'll get local currency from machines in the Caribbean.) Expect a hefty fee for using ATMs on board cruise ships (like $5 in addition to what your bank charges you). Many lines, like Carnival and Royal Caribbean, cash traveler's checks at the purser's desk (and sometimes personal checks of up to about $200 if issued in the U.S.); with an American Express card, you can typically cash a check for up to $250. Specific currency information is included in chapter 11, "Caribbean Ports of Call," and chapter 12, "Bermuda & the Panama Canal Route."

3 Packing

One of the beauties of cruising is that you only need to unpack once. Even though you'll be visiting several different countries on a typical weeklong cruise, you check into your cabin on day one, unpack, and settle in. The destinations come to you!

Cruise Tip: Don't Forget Cash When Going Ashore

It's happened to me and it's happened to my friends, so it can happen to you, too: After a few days of living cash-free aboard ship, it doesn't even cross your mind to grab the greenbacks when you're going ashore. You get there and realize you're penniless. It's *soooo* frustrating. Don't let it happen to you.

Just what do you need to pack? To some extent, that depends on the kind of cruise you're taking. But overall, cruise ship life mirrors that on land. Dress codes are being relaxed, and aside from the ultra-deluxe lines and formal nights on the large ships, **casual clothes** are the norm. In fact, instead of having a combination of formal, informal, and casual nights throughout the week as in the past, many lines—Carnival for instance—are just going with the two formal nights and the rest of the week is considered casual. NCL has ditched the concept of formal nights completely.

DAYTIME CLOTHES

Across the board, casual daytime wear means shorts, T-shirts, bathing suits, and sundresses. Remember to bring a cover-up and sandals if you want to go right from your deck chair to lunch in one of the restaurants or to some activity being held in a public room. When in port, the same dress code works, but do respect local customs and err toward modesty (that is, something more than a skimpy bikini top if you're straying from the beach area). You might want to bring a pair of **aquasocks** if you plan on doing any snorkeling or water sports in port (if you don't have them, many cruise lines will charge you about $5 to rent a pair), and some good **walking shoes** to explore the islands as comfortably as possible.

If you plan on hitting the gym, don't forget sneakers and your workout clothes. And it can't hurt to bring along one pair of long casual pants and a long-sleeved sweatshirt, as well as a lightweight raincoat in case the weather turns dicey.

EVENING CLOTHES

Whether you like it or not, it seems cruise ship passengers are dressing down more than ever. It's the American way. Still, formal nights still survive at sea, at least a couple of nights per cruise, and, except on the ultra-casual, small-ship lines (see chapter 9, "Soft-Adventure Lines & Sailing Ships"), you'll want to pack a few dressy duds. Exceptions to this are the ultra-casual Windjammer, Star Clippers, and American Canadian Caribbean lines, where shorts, T-shirts, and sandals can take you through the day and into the evening meals (although most people tend to dress up a tad more for dinner). Windstar and Club Med encourage a "smart casual" look, and have a no-jackets-required rule the entire week. Passengers aboard Clipper go casual during the day but tend to ratchet up to jackets and dresses at dinner.

Most ships have two **formal nights** on a 7-night cruise (usually the second night of the cruise for the captain's cocktail party, and the second-to-last night of the cruise). Imagine what you'd wear to a nice wedding: Men are encouraged to wear dark suits or tuxedos and women cocktail dresses, sequined jackets, or gowns (or recycled bridesmaids

Cruise Tip: Stowing the Crown Jewels

If you want to bring good jewelry, most cabins have personal safes operated by a digital code, credit card, or, once in a while, a lock and key. If your cabin doesn't have a safe (usually it's the older ships that don't), the ship's purser can keep your valuables.

Cruise Tip: Tuxedo Rentals

If you don't own a tux or don't want to bother lugging one along, you can often arrange a rental through the cruise line or your travel agent for about $75. In some cases, a rental offer arrives with your cruise tickets. If you choose this option, your suit will be waiting for you in your cabin when you arrive.

---

dresses!), or other fancy attire. If you just hate dressing up, women can get away with a blouse and skirt or pants. And of course, accessories like jewelry and scarves can dress up an otherwise nondescript outfit.

The other nights are much more casual, and are designated either **semiformal** (or informal) or **casual.** Semiformal calls for suits or sports jackets for men and stylish dresses or pantsuits for women; casual nights call for chinos or dress pants and collared shirts for men, and dresses, skirts, or pantsuits for women.

In spite of the suggested dress codes, which are usually described in the back of a cruise line's brochure, you'll still find a wide variety of outfits being worn. Invariably, one person's "formal" is quite different from another's. Passengers are asked not to wear jeans, baseball caps, shorts, and T-shirts for dinner in the formal dining rooms (although a few always try and succeed—few people are ever turned away at the dining room door because of what they're wearing). At the same time, despite the casual trend in America (casual Fridays and the baseball-cap, fur-coat-wearing Park Avenue set, for instance), you'll find there's a contingent of folks on board who like to get all decked out. I personally find getting dressed up for dinner a few nights a week to be part of the fun; in fact, I like to plunk myself in some heavily trafficked lounge an hour or two before dinner and do some people-watching. It's a veritable fashion show!

SUNDRIES

Like hotels, many ships (especially the newest and the high-end ones) come equipped with hair dryers and supply bathroom amenities such as shampoo, conditioner, lotion, and soap (although you might still want to bring your own products—I find the ones provided often seem watered down). Some lines, like Carnival, do skimp, and provide only soap in cabins and not even hair dryers (except on *Destiny, Triumph,* and *Victory*). With the exception of the *Voyager of the Seas,* Royal Caribbean doesn't have hair dryers on its ships either. If you bring your hair dryer, curling iron, or laptop, you might want to bring an adapter, although the vast majority of ships run on 110 AC current.

No need to pack a **beach towel,** as they're almost always supplied on board (exceptions: Windjammer and ACCL). Bird watchers will want their **binoculars** and manuals, golfers their clubs (although they can always be rented), snorkelers their gear (which can also be rented), and shoppers an extra duffel for their goodies.

If you forget to pack a personal effect or two, don't despair. Even the smallest, no-frills ships have at least one small shop on board, selling items like razor blades, toothbrushes, sunscreen, film, and other items, though at inflated prices. Some also stock bestsellers (and most ships have libraries) but you're probably best off bringing your own books.

Aside from the small ships, most vessels have a **laundry service** on board and some **dry-cleaning** too, with generally about a 24-hour turnaround time; there will be a price list in your cabin. Some ships have **self-service laundry rooms** on board.

4 The Cruise Experience

Cruise ships are like mini-societies, cities at sea, floating summer camps for adults. Evolved from the days when ships were nothing more than utilitarian modes of transport, cruise ships today are attraction-filled destinations themselves, bustling worlds where there are countless things to do and people to meet. Good food and drink are plentiful, entertainment and activities are nonstop, and an undeniable rhythm takes hold for the duration of a cruise.

While the cruise experience varies from ship to ship, the common denominator is choice. You can run from an aerobics class to line-dancing, then to an art auction, and then bingo all before lunch, or choose to do nothing more than sunbathe all day on a quiet corner of deck. Whether you like to do it all or do nothing at all, cruising is a convenient and leisurely way of traveling from one exotic port to another. Unpack once, settle in, and enjoy the ride.

In the pages that follow, I'll give you a taste of cruise life, starting with a little history. . . .

1 The History of Cruising

From rough-hewn dugout canoes crossing rivers to proud clipper ships carrying explorers across vast oceans to steamers transporting throngs of European immigrants to new lives in the United States, the modern-day cruise evolved from a basic and timeless need to get from point A to point B.

THE EARLY DAYS   It wasn't until the late 19th century that British shipping companies realized they could make money not just by transporting travelers, cargo, and immigrants, but by selling a luxurious experience at sea. It's generally accepted that the first cruise ship was the *Ceylon,* a vessel powered by both steam and sail and owned by the Peninsular & Oriental Steam Navigation Company (known today as P&O). In 1881, when already 23 years old, the small, 2,000-ton *Ceylon* was converted to a cruising yacht for carrying wealthy, adventurous guests on world cruises in lavish style. A few years later, in 1887, North of Scotland, Orkney & Shetland Steam Navigation's *St. Sunniva* was launched as the first steamer built expressly for cruising.

The Germans joined the British in the fledgling cruise trade in 1891, when the **Hamburg-American Line** sent their *Augusta Victoria* on a Mediterranean cruise from Hamburg. In 1901, the line completed its luxurious 4,400-gross-ton *Prinzessin Victoria Luise,* the first ship to offer bathrooms in every passenger cabin. These early cruise ships were extravagantly appointed with things you'd never find on a modern cruise ship—statues, frescos, ornate wooden stairways, and even plaster walls—but the onboard activities and entertainment were comparatively few. Besides lavish, very social dinners, about the only pastimes were reading, taking a good hardy walk around the deck, and sitting for musical recitals.

More and more players entered the cruise trade during the early 1900s, spending summers crossing the Atlantic and Pacific and the rest of the year doing pleasure cruises to ports in the Canary Islands, the Caribbean, Scandinavia, and the Mediterranean. Before World War I, though, cruising for pleasure still took a back seat to the more lucrative trade of transporting well-off travelers and immigrants across the Atlantic in three classes of accommodation, and there were only a handful of small ships built for cruising. The competition was fearsome between famous shipping lines such as Cunard, White Star, Hamburg America, French Line, North German Lloyd, Holland America, Red Star Line, and a host of smaller companies, who sought to attract customers by trying to build the fastest, largest, or most luxurious new ships. It was the era of rich wood paneling, chandeliers, grand ballrooms and smoking lounges, and huge gilded suites with antiques, art, and servants' quarters. First-class became plusher, and the second and steerage classes were being upgraded (at least in name) to cabin class and tourist class, to sound more appealing. When these ships did do pleasure cruises, generally only first-class accommodations were sold and the other cabin classes were shut down until the transatlantic schedules were resumed; it wasn't until the late 1960s that the multiclass system was eliminated completely.

THE SHIP YOU ALL KNOW (& A FEW OTHERS)   Soon after Cunard launched its popular 2,165-passenger *Mauretania* and *Lusitania* in 1906, J. Bruce Ismay, son of the White Star Cruise Line's founder, Thomas Ismay, envisioned a trio of the largest and most luxurious vessels in the transatlantic service to appeal to the rich American industrialists now crossing regularly. By 1911 the first of these three sisters, the 2,584-passenger, 46,000-ton *Olympic,* was in service, with the ***Titanic*** (yes, that one) scheduled for an April 1912 maiden voyage. (The third sister, originally planned as the *Gigantic,* was on the drawing boards to follow *Titanic.*)

Touted as the world's greatest ship, the *Olympic*'s maiden voyage in June 1911 was a grand, much-heralded affair. In fact, the launch of *Titanic* the following year was not nearly as anticipated; then, as we all know, tragically, the *Titanic* never made it to New York. The *Olympic* sailed on, doing time as a hospital ship in World War I, and the third of Ismay's planned trio, launched in 1914 as the *Britannic,* had a short life as a hospital ship in the Mediterranean before hitting a land mine and sinking in 1916.

Right up until World War I, the Brits and Germans continued building bigger and bigger ships, exceeding 50,000 tons. During the war, practically any seaworthy ship was requisitioned to carry soldiers, supplies, and weaponry to the troops in Europe. Many grand ships were lost in the war, including Cunard's *Lusitania.*

CRUISING BETWEEN THE WARS   After the First World War, the popularity of cruising increased tremendously because far fewer immigrants were flooding to the west. During the winter months, when transatlantic travel was slow, more and more ships were rerouted to sunnier climes in the Caribbean and Mediterranean for long and expensive cruises geared to the well heeled. Cunard's *Mauretania* and its new running mate, the *Aquitania,* for instance, were yanked off the Atlantic for a millionaire's romp through the Mediterranean, carrying as few as 200 pampered passengers in the lap of luxury. In the 1920s, Cunard introduced five ships—the *Scythia, Samaria, Laconia, Franconia,* and *Carinthia*—which offered a variety of cruising options worldwide, including Bali, Bangkok, Saigon, Athens, and the Holy Land, as well as the Caribbean and Scandinavia. Between the wars, other great lines emerged as well, like Canadian Pacific, whose white-hulled *Empress of France* and *Empress of Britain* (the latter a dual-use ship built for both cruises and crossings) cruised worldwide. The British-owned Anchor Line ran a series of annual cruises to the West Indies from New York aboard its *Caledonia* and *Transylvania.*

As they headed to warmer climates, the traditional black hulls of the North Atlantic trade ships were painted white to help them stay as cool as possible in these pre-air-conditioning years. This became a tradition itself, to the point that nearly all the Caribbean's ships were at one time painted a dazzling white. Today, although they're still the norm, we're seeing something of a reverse trend, with hulls being painted black or blue-black to present a more classic, dignified image and play to the public's nostalgia for the old ocean liner days.

By the 1930s, shipboard activities and amenities were becoming much more sophisticated all around, with morning concerts, horse racing, quoits, shuffleboard, bridge, Ping-Pong, motion pictures, and the first "swimming baths" (as pools were called in the early years) appearing on board. Often no more than burlap or canvas slung over wooden supports, the first permanent outdoor pools appeared in the 1920s on the Italian transatlantic ships the *Roma* and the *Augustus.* In the 1930s, the large outdoor pool on the *Rex* actually included a patch of sand to evoke the Lido Beach of Venice. When the great French liner *Normandie* made its maiden voyage in 1935, it boasted the cruising world's first air-conditioning system in its first-class dining room.

WORLD WAR II   When World War II began, again the great liners were called into service, and many never made it back to civilian life. The *Normandie* burned and capsized at its pier while under conversion in New York to become a troopship. Cunard's *Carinthia* and *Laconia* didn't survive either. A few, however, did complete distinguished wartime service, like the United States Line's *America,* Cunard's *Queen Elizabeth* and *Queen Mary,* and Holland America's *Nieuw Amsterdam.*

THE POSTWAR YEARS   When the war ended and with the economy in great shape, cruising boomed in the 1950s and for the first time became accessible to the growing middle class. More than ever before, cruising was both transportation and a pleasurable vacation experience to boot, with onboard life enhanced by activities like pool games, bingo, art classes, dance lessons, singles' parties, and midnight buffets—all aspects of cruising that still exist today. In the 1950s, New York became one of the biggest and most important cruise ship ports in the world, offering short runs to Bermuda and serving as the home port for longer world cruises.

By the 1960s, though, the new jet airplanes replaced transatlantic ships as the public's transportation of choice, and the boom was over. Increasingly expensive to maintain, many of the great 1950s liners were sent to the scrap yards. The industry seemed doomed.

But, fortunately, not for long. In the early 1960s, two Norwegian cargo and tanker ship operators, Christian and Knut Kloster, decided to get into the passenger-ship business, offering Caribbean cruises aboard the 11,000-ton *Sunward* from a home port in Miami. The rest is history. The vacation cruise ships that soon began to proliferate in the Caribbean did away with the liners' multiclass system and focused solely on offering a fun-in-the-sun party at sea for all. (Cunard's **QE2,** built in 1969 for both crossings and cruising, was one of the last ships built with a multiclass system; today the ship's Queen's Grill restaurant is still reserved for passengers booked in the most expensive cabins only.)

Soon, the Caribbean-cruise trade exploded. **Royal Caribbean Cruise Line** was formed in January 1969, and in the late sixties and early seventies **Royal Viking, Carnival, Princess, Costa,** and **Holland America** joined the lucrative circuit as well. It was in 1968, on board Costa's *Carla C.* (at the time chartered to Princess and doing Mexican Riviera and Panama Canal cruises from Los Angeles), that American writer Jeraldine Saunders was inspired to write the novel ***The Love Boat,*** from which the popular television series was born. Now, millions would be introduced to cruising.

While many traditionalists disdain today's cruise ships, which retain few vestiges of ocean travel's golden age, time does move on. Casual, active, and geared to the masses, today's passenger-ship industry is bigger, bolder, and more successful than ever before, and with over 40 new ships scheduled to debut over the next several years, it's a safe bet that at least some of them are the classic ships of the future.

2 Checking In & Boarding

You're ready to go, packed, at the port, and even on the right pier. Do you remember the name of the ship on which you're sailing? With so many like-sounding ship names these days—dozens of Something-ations and Blah-Blah-of-the-Seas—it can get confusing. Make sure you know where you're going: You don't want to schlep your stuff to the wrong terminal.

As a safety precaution against emergencies at home, distribute your ship's **satellite phone** and fax number and E-mail address (more and more ships have them) to people in charge of your affairs back home, but advise them to contact you only in an emergency. It also can't hurt to leave behind the number of the cruise line's headquarters or reservations department, too.

After you arrive at the docks, head for the terminal; if you need a porter, tip him $1 per bag. It doesn't pay to arrive too early at the pier. Even if your ship has been berthed at port since early in the morning, new passengers are often not allowed on board until about 1pm. The cruise lines enforce this policy stringently to allow enough time for luggage and supplies to be unloaded and loaded, cabins to be vacated by former occupants and cleaned, and paperwork and customs documents to be properly completed.

When you pour out of the buses (or the car, if you drove) that have transported you from the airport to the cruise ship terminal, you'll feel like a celebrity (well, almost) making his or her way from a limo, across a red carpet, and into the Oscars ceremony at some chichi theater. You'll be greeted by an army of smiling cruise line employees directing you to the check-in desks, and a ship photographer just beyond check-in is ready to capture that first moment of your vacation. If you're arriving by air, the treatment begins in the airport, when uniformed ushers (often retirees) stand at the ready holding a sign with your cruise line's or ship's name on it, waiting to direct you and dozens of other giddy passengers to the buses bound for the terminal.

At the terminal, your **luggage** is whisked away from the bus or your car, never to be seen again (just kidding, but it may be a few hours before it's delivered to your cabin). Sometimes it's there by the time you've made it to your cabin, but sometimes it takes a few hours, depending on how big the ship is and just how much luggage needs to be delivered. Anyway, it's a good idea to keep a small bag with you containing a change of clothes, and maybe a swimsuit and a pair of sunglasses, so you don't waste any time heading out on deck, grabbing a deck chair, and starting your vacation.

Before boarding, you need to check in at the terminal, hand over your cruise tickets, show some ID (with a picture), and give an imprint of your credit card to establish your onboard account. On small ships, all of this is done on board. Depending on when you arrive and the crowd situation, you may find yourself waiting in line for as much as an hour or so; usually it's less.

For security reasons, very few cruise lines allow temporary visitors on board the ship. You'll have to say your good-byes on land.

WELCOME TO YOUR CABIN

Once on board, you may be guided to your cabin (there is no need to tip the person who leads you) or most likely you'll be on your own to find it. When you get there, your **cabin steward** will probably stop by to introduce him- or herself, inquire if the configuration of beds is appropriate (that is, do you want separate twin beds or a pushed-together double), and give you his or her extension number so you can call if you need anything. The brochures and **daily programs** in your cabin will answer many questions pertinent to your ship's social and safety rituals.

Cabins have air-conditioning and heating, usually controlled individually; hot and cold running water; life preservers for the number of people occupying the cabin (a legal requirement and essential to your safety at sea—check that they're there); extra blankets and pillows; and usually a safe for storing your valuables, operated either with a credit card, a combination lock, or a key. On ships that don't offer in-cabin safes—usually older ships—you can generally check your valuables at the purser's desk.

Most ships sailing the Caribbean have **North American–style electrical outlets** (twin flat prongs, 110 AC current), although some ships have outlets for both European current (220 AC) and North American. Keep in mind, there's often only one outlet for that curling iron or hair dryer you may bring along with you, and it's usually not in the bathroom, but above the desk or dresser.

With a few notable exceptions, cruise ships have direct-dial **telephones** in cabins, along with instructions on how to use them, and a directory of phone numbers for the departments or services on board. From most cabin phones you can call, via satellite beams, anywhere in the world, but although it's getting cheaper compared to a few years ago, this is still expensive. Charges range from around $3.95 to about $18 a minute, with $9.50 being about average. It's cheaper to call home from a public telephone in port, or to send an E-mail on those ships that are plugged in.

3 An Introduction to Onboard Activities

You can run around like a chicken all day long if you want to, happily going from one activity to another. Most 800-passenger-plus ships offer an extensive schedule of activities from morning till night every day, especially during days at sea, when the ship isn't visiting a port. To keep track of the games, contests, lessons, and classes, check out the ship's **daily schedule of events,** which is placed in your cabin the previous evening, usually while you're at dinner. A **cruise director** and his or her staff are in charge of the festivities and do their best to ensure a good time is had by all. Smaller ships offer activities, too, but often with less hoopla; there may be wine tastings, trivia contests, port talks by the cruise director and captain, and maybe presentations by guest speakers on subjects ranging from history to politics to food. The very small 50- and 100-passenger ships won't even have that.

ONBOARD GAMES

The ships in the Carnival, Royal Caribbean, Norwegian, Princess, Celebrity, Costa, Premier, and Commodore fleets are well known for their wacky poolside contests scheduled for an hour or two each afternoon. You might even say they sometimes go overboard (har har), but you'll certainly be in stitches watching the blind-folded pillow fights, belly-flop contests, the stuff-the-most-Ping-Pong-balls-or-fruit-into-your-bathing-suit contest, and the pool relay races, which require team members to pass bagels to one another with their teeth.

And it's not just the classic party ships that let their hair down. Many other lines indulge their guests in the tomfoolery, too. At its weekly deck parties, Holland America, for example, features a nearly obscene and absolutely hilarious rendition of the pass-the-balloon-from-between-my-knees-to-yours relay race. All ages participate, and you'll want to check your pride at the door before you volunteer for this one.

Game-show simulations, such as the "Newlywed/Not-So-Newlywed" games, are popular. Volunteer yourself or, better yet, listen to fellow passengers blurt out the truth about their personal lives—just like on *Oprah!* The Carnival *Paradise* and *Triumph* actually stage very realistic Jeopardy-like game shows, complete with buzzers, contestant podiums, and digital point-keeping.

If you're a performer at heart, volunteer for the weekly passenger talent show or head to the nightclub one evening and wiggle your way into the hula-hoop or twist competitions. Cerebral types can sign up for trivia quizzes or do puzzles, or join chess, checkers, bridge, or backgammon tournaments.

Winners get more than a good time, too. Prizes like champagne, T-shirts, mugs, or key chains—maybe even a massage from the spa—all make getting involved a worthwhile proposition.

SHIPBOARD CASINOS

For all you high rollers out there, all but the smallest, adventure-oriented ships have casinos. Not surprisingly, the megas have the biggest, flashiest, Vegas-style casinos, bathed in neon, with literally hundreds of **slot machines** and dozens of **blackjack, poker,** and **craps** tables as well as **roulette.** You really will think you're in Vegas or Atlantic City when you're playing in the sprawling, glitzy casinos of Carnival, Royal Caribbean, the newer Princess ships, and Celebrity. Smaller ship lines, like Windstar and Seabourn, have casinos as well, albeit scaled-down ones, with maybe a dozen slots and a couple of blackjack and poker tables. Some of the budget lines, such as Commodore, Regal, and Premier, boast active casino scenes, too. Stakes aboard most ships are relatively low, with maximum bets rarely exceeding $200. Average minimum bets at blackjack and poker tables are generally $5; the minimum at roulette is typically 50¢ or $1.

Gambling is legal once a ship has sailed 12 miles from American shores, but local laws almost always require onboard casinos to close down whenever a ship is in port. Keep this in mind when cruising to Bermuda; ships stay there for 3 whole days and there's no gambling whatsoever during that period.

Children are not allowed in onboard casinos.

Most ships also have a **card room,** which is usually filled with serious bridge or poker players and sometimes supervised by a full-time instructor. Most ships furnish cards for free, although some charge $1 or so per deck.

CLASSES, LESSONS & DEMONSTRATIONS

For the eternal student, there are volumes of learning opportunities aboard most ships. Line, country, and ballroom **dancing lessons** are usually held a few times a week in the

English Comes Second

Some crew members—especially cabin stewards, who come from all over the world—may have limited English-language skills, so you might want to brush up on your nonverbal communication. Crew members have to know a modicum of English to be hired, but sometimes it seems less rather than more, and you might run into some frustrating moments trying to get your point across. Remember, though, these folks are very hard-working employees who are sending most of their wages home to their families, and it won't kill you to speak slower and more simply if need be.

main show lounge and are taught by one of the onboard entertainers. Many cruise lines frequently put on informative **seminars** on subjects like cooking, bartending, arts and crafts, and wine tasting; there is usually a $5-to-$15 charge for the wine tasting and sometimes there's a cost for arts and crafts materials. Celebrity Cruises and Radisson Seven Seas, for instance, frequently features classes on intriguing topics such as **personal investing** or **handwriting analysis.**

The chef might do a food-decorating demonstration and share tips on how to carve flowers and animals out of fruits and vegetables. Demonstrations by the salon and spa staff on hair and skin care are common, too (and a ruse for getting passengers to sign up for the not-so-cheap spa treatments).

INTERNET AT SEA: WHO'S PLUGGED IN

In just the past 2 years, many lines have hustled to add computer rooms and Internet cafes to their ships to satiate Americans' growing desire to stay connected via E-mail to home and work at all times, even on vacation. Some are hooked up to the Internet, too, so guests can surf the day away. Rates for E-mail use are reasonable, averaging roughly $1 to $3 per message (of a reasonable length, usually equivalent to six or seven pages) or at a rate of about 50¢ a minute—loads cheaper than the $4-to-$18 per minute charge of a phone call from ship to shore. These computer centers have supplanted the seemingly archaic business centers aboard many ships, which operated only a few hours day and were equipped with only a couple of computers and printers for letter writing, with no Internet or E-mail capabilities.

Crystal, with its Computer University, was the pioneer in bringing computers to sea. Both the *Harmony* and *Symphony* have well-stocked computer labs with over 20 computer workstations and complimentary training classes to boot. Computer use is free of charge, except for a $5 fee to set up an E-mail account and a charge of $3 every time you send or receive an E-mail up to about seven to eight pages long.

When NCL's *Norwegian Sky* debuted in fall 1999, it came touting its Internet cafe (with rates of 75¢ a minute), and the line has since added some version of the same to the rest of its fleet. By the time Holland America's *Volendam* debuted in late 1999 and sister *Zaandam* in May of 2000, both also came loaded with a state-of-the-art computer room, complete with eight flat-screen models (75¢ per min., with a 5-min. minimum). Holland America subsequently added a computer room to the *Rotterdam,* and plans to retrofit its entire fleet in the near future.

Royal Caribbean's *Voyager of the Seas* stormed onto the scene in late 1999 as well, with a sophisticated computer room with 18 workstations that have not only E-mail and Internet access but Net cams too—small cameras attached to the monitor so users can take pictures of themselves while typing and send out digital postcards to friends back home. The rest of the Royal Caribbean fleet has computer centers open 24 hours with between 10 and 16 machines apiece; the cost of being online is 50¢ a minute. As a topper, Adam Goldstein, a senior VP with Royal Caribbean, said *Voyager*'s sister ship, *Explorer of the Seas,* will have Internet access in the cabins when it debuts in late 2000 (we'll see . . .).

Each of Princess's Grand-Class ships (*Sun Princess, Dawn Princess, Sea Princess, Ocean Princess,* and *Grand Princess*) have small business centers with four to five computers. The cost for using a computer is $30 per hour or $7.50 for every 15 minutes, whether a passenger is sending E-mail, using word processing, or playing Solitaire. Radisson's new *Navigator* has three computers in a nook off of its library, which guests can use to send and receive E-mails (sending is $1 a message, receiving is free). The *Radisson Diamond* also has a pair of computers, with E-mail access at the same rates as *Navigator*.

There are 10 computers on Seabourn's *Seabourn Sun* and one each on the *Pride, Spirit,* and *Legend* (sending E-mails costs $5 for the first five kilobytes of information and $1 for each additional kilobyte; incoming E-mails are free). Cunard's *QE2* and *Caronia* each have 10 spiffy new computers with E-mail access at the same rates Seabourn charges. Star Clippers' *Star Clipper* and *Royal Clipper* each have one computer in their libraries that can be used for E-mail (you buy a $5 or $10 debit card from the purser to use). Windstar's *Wind Surf* has five computers in the library with E-mail access at a cost of $7.50 per for up to 5,000 characters; a company spokeswoman said the line hopes to offer E-mail and Internet access fleet-wide by year-end 2000. At press time, there were even plans to have the Regal Cruise Line's old *Regal Empress* plugged with E-mail access.

So who's not yet plugged in? Surprisingly, at press time Celebrity did not offer Internet or E-mail access except aboard the new *Millennium,* even though the *Century, Galaxy,* and *Mercury* do have small computer centers and have always prided themselves on being high-tech, with their interactive cabin television systems and their affiliation with SONY. A company spokeswoman has said the fleet will be plugged in by year-end 2000.

Costa also does not offer its passengers Internet or E-mail access, and nor do Disney's ships, though at press time a company spokeswoman said they would in the not-so-distant future. Carnival is not hooked up either—their passengers are having too much fun by the pool to think about staying indoors staring at a computer monitor.

ART AUCTIONS

You'll either find them a convenient way to buy some pictures for your living room or find them incredibly annoying and a blatantly tacky way for the cruise lines to make more money. Truth is, art auctions on cruise ships are big business these days on mainstream and ultra-luxury lines, and lots of pieces are sold. Held three or four times a week for an hour or two at a time, the auctions are a way you can leisurely shop for art if you so choose, a luxury you may not have at home. There are often enticements like champagne to attract passengers to the auctions. The "auctioneer" is a salesman for the company that sells the art. From a stage, he briefly discusses a selection of the hundreds of paintings by well-known artists like Peter Max and Erté, lithographs by greats Dalí, Picasso, and Miró, and Disney animation pieces, as well as pieces by artists you've never heard of, all of which are displayed around the auction space. The art, framed or unframed, is duty-free to U.S. citizens and is packed and mailed home for the lucky winner.

ONBOARD SPORTS & FITNESS OPTIONS

If you're into sports, the megaships pack the most punch. In addition to having well-equipped gyms rivaling those on shore, they boast outdoor volleyball, basketball, and paddle tennis courts as well as outdoor jogging tracks and several pools for water polo, volleyball, aqua aerobics, and swimming. And the most mega of the megas, Royal Caribbean's enormous *Voyager of the Seas,* goes entirely off the deep end with, believe it or not, a bona fide ice-skating rink, outdoor rock-climbing wall, and in-line skating track, as well as a full-size basketball court, miniature golf, and lots more.

See "Shipboard Gyms & Spas" later in this chapter for more information.

WATER SPORTS

For water-sports enthusiasts, small ships are the best equipped. Windstar, Radisson Seven Seas, Club Med, and Seabourn have retractable water-sports platforms that, weather-permitting, can be lowered from the stern into calm waters when the ship is anchored, allowing passengers to almost step right from their cabins to snorkel, windsurf, kayak, sail, water-ski, go on banana-boat rides, and swim (all free of charge).

What's in a Name?

So why are the names *Monrovia, Panama,* or the *Bahamas* boldly emblazoned across a ship's bow or stern? It's not where the ship was built, as you might assume, but where the ship is registered or flagged. In fact, the country where your ship is flagged or registered has nothing to do with the cruise line's home base (which is likely Florida, California, Washington, or New York). That's because most flags are based on financial considerations (read: no income tax required or minimum wage enforced) and other matters of convenience to the cruise lines. Truth is, the cruise lines save many millions of dollars a year this way, and investigative reports in the past few years in major newspapers like the *New York Times* have been critical of this arrangement. Like many American-based corporations and manufacturing companies that produce goods in foreign countries where costs are low, the cruise lines want to have their cake and eat it too (spending as little as possible and making as much as they can). Panama and Liberia have liberal rules governing unions and so forth, so you see a lot of cruise ships registered there. Other common flags include the Bahamas, Bermuda, and the Netherlands Antilles. What does this mean to you? Chances are, not a thing. The only time it would is in the very unlikely event that a crime or accident, for instance, is committed on board a ship; in that case, you'd have to contend with the country of registry's laws when seeking justice, restitution, etc.

GOLF

If golf is your bag, more and more cruises are offering the opportunity to tee off, both on board and on shore. For the casual golfer, a few ships—Royal Caribbean's *Voyager, Splendour,* and *Legend of the Seas,* and Princess' *Grand Princess*—have **miniature-golf courses** on board. For the more serious swingers, the new, technologically advanced ships like *Voyager of the Seas,* Celebrity's *Century, Galaxy,* and *Mercury,* Princess's *Grand, Ocean, Sea, Sun,* and *Dawn Princess,* and the *Seabourn Sun* have **golf simulators.** These state-of-the-art virtual-reality machines allow you to play the great courses of the world without ever leaving the ship (for about $15 or $20 per half-hour). Full-size clubs are used and a virtual-reality video screen allows players to watch the electronic path of a ball they've actually hit soar high over the greens or land flat in a sand trap.

Many more lines, including Norwegian, Crystal, Princess, Radisson Seven Seas, and Cunard, have **outdoor golf cages**—areas enclosed in netting where you can swing, putt, and whack at real golf balls any time of the day. Some other lines (like Celebrity) also have golf cages, but they're monopolized by the onboard golf pro using them for private golf lessons—you want to play, you gotta pay.

Some lines are offering **golf lessons** that include instruction and tips by golf pros who sail on board, videotaping lessons and going over techniques with passengers; half-hour lessons are about $30 to $40, and hour-long lessons are $60 to $70. In port, even more ships have **golf excursions** to well-known courses such as Mahogany Run in the Caribbean and Mid-Ocean in Bermuda; packages typically include greens fees, cart, and transportation between the ship and course, and range from $100 to $200 per person. Celebrity, Costa, NCL, Seabourn, and Crystal all offer onboard instruction by golf pros on all or select cruises, as well as golfing excursions in port.

SPORTS FOR COUCH POTATOES

No need for those sports-loving couch potatoes out there to be deprived. NCL's *Norwegian Sky, Norwegian Wind, Norwegian Dream,* and *Norway,* Royal Caribbean's *Voyager* and *Explorer of the Seas,* Carnival's *Destiny, Triumph,* and *Victory,* Disney's *Magic* and *Wonder,* and Princess's *Grand Princess* all have dedicated **sports bars** with large-screen televisions broadcasting ESPN and live NFL games. Each of Holland America's ships has a large-screen TV in one lounge showing sports. During popular sporting events, like the Super Bowl, many lines outfit a public area or bar with televisions for game viewing. If you want to watch the game from the comfort of your cabin, no problem: ESPN is available on cabin TVs on Royal Caribbean, Holland America, Norwegian, Crystal, and Princess ships. For star-struck sports fans, NCL does a series of annual **sports theme cruises,** where pro basketball, football, baseball, and hockey players, as well as past greats, sail on board and mingle with passengers.

4 Introducing Onboard Entertainment

Cruises offer a vast repertoire of exciting entertainment, and, as you'd expect, the biggest ships offer the most variety. From Vegas-style cabaret to magicians, soloists, pianists, dance bands, quartets, jugglers, DJs, puppeteers, and X-rated comedians, you've got choices.

ENTERTAINMENT ON THE MEGASHIPS

Entertainment is a big part of the cruise experience on the biggest 1,200-passenger-plus megaships of Carnival, Royal Caribbean, Celebrity, Costa, Princess, NCL, and Holland America. Not surprisingly, they have an extensive variety of options throughout the day. Afternoons, you can dance the day away on deck with the **live dance band** jamming with calypso music or Bob Marley tunes. Or get your waltzing shoes on and head inside to one of the lounges for some big-band-style dancing; lines like Holland America, Cunard, and NCL often feature a Glenn Miller–style group playing a set or two of 1940s dance tunes.

By about 5pm, before the first-seating dinner (and again at 7pm before the late seating begins), the entertainment choices really kick in. Head to the piano bar for a cocktail or do some predinner dancing to a live jazz or big-band quartet.

About twice a week, after both the early- and the late-dinner seatings, the main show lounge features **Vegas-style musicals,** where a flamboyant troupe of anywhere from 4 to 16 male and female dancers decked out in feather boas, sequins, and top hats slide and kick their way across the stage (and lip sync to the songs' choruses) as a soloist or two belts out show tunes. You'll hear favorites from *Phantom of the Opera, Cats, Hair, Grease, A Chorus Line,* and all the classic Gershwin and Rodgers and Hammerstein greats. If you're the type that hits all the Broadway shows in New York City, these revues certainly won't compare, but the elaborate stage sets and frequent costume changes make these exciting shows the entertainment highlight of the week.

When the Broadway-show stuff isn't scheduled, entertainment other nights might be a **magic show,** complete with sawing in half scantily clad assistants and pulling rabbits from hats, **acrobatic acts** (always a big hit), and **headlining soloists** (some quite good).

But if Broadway isn't your bag and magic doesn't fool you, the **disco** gets going around 9pm or 10pm and goes until 2 or 3am (sometimes later). Shake your booty to the best of seventies, eighties, nineties, and current pop and rock music; often a live band plays until about midnight, when a DJ takes over until the wee hours. There may be a **karaoke session** thrown in for an hour or two.

Active Shore Excursions

While there's lots to do on board most ships, there's a lot you'll want to check out in port, too. With more and more active excursions being offered, you'll get to see the less touristy, natural parts of the islands, all the while getting a good workout. Aside from the tried and true **snorkeling** and **diving** trips, in nearly every Caribbean port there are **biking, hiking, kayaking, horseback riding,** and **river tubing** trips offered, generally running about $50 to $100 per person.

An alternative to the disco or the main show might be a **1950s sock hop** in another lounge or a **jazz trio** in yet another romantic nightspot. Night owls who love a good laugh won't want to miss the **R- and/or X-rated comedian** who does a late-night show at about midnight or 12:30am. Or for a quiet evening, many lines, like Holland America, Celebrity, and Crystal, have cinemas showing **first-run movies.**

Innovative new options are being created all the time. For example, Disney Cruise Line's *Disney Wonder* and *Disney Magic* have some of the most unique entertainment choices at sea, presented in their nostalgic, remarkably well equipped Walt Disney Theatre, where actors disappear into trap doors, fly across the stage, and go through endless exciting costume changes while playing out scenes in musicals inspired by Disney movies. Each ship also has an innovative (and very funny) **improv comedy** act in one of the adults-only lounges.

To prove that not all innovative entertainment has to be big, Celebrity's ships have been featuring **roving a cappella bands** who roam around the ships in the evening, performing wherever people are gathered. Royal Caribbean's *Voyager of the Seas* has street performers like **jugglers** and **magicians** periodically meandering through its four-deck-high Royal Promenade, the ship's main hub of activity.

ENTERTAINMENT ON THE SMALL SHIPS

Ships carrying 100 to 400 passengers have fewer entertainment options, but are no less appealing if you like things mellow. On the high-end lines, there may be a quartet or pianist performing before dinner and maybe afterward a small-scale **Broadway dance revue,** plus dancing in a quiet lounge. The more casual small ships might have taped music or a solo performer on an electric piano before and after dinner; expect a crew and a **passenger talent show** to be scheduled during many cruises, too. While in port, small-ship lines like Windstar, Clipper, Star Clippers, and Windjammer Barefoot Cruises often bring on **local musicians** and/or dancers for an afternoon or evening of entertainment. Some of the more education-oriented lines, like Clipper and Royal Olympic, might schedule informal **lectures** on the nature and history of the ports of call.

5 Shipboard Gyms & Spas

If your idea of a perfect vacation starts with a run on the treadmill and a set of curls, or if a relaxing seaweed facial is more your thing, the newest ships in the Carnival, Celebrity, Royal Caribbean, Princess, and Holland America lines have the biggest and best-equipped spa and fitness facilities. Since the early 1990s, cruise lines have prioritized their spa and fitness areas, moving them out of windowless corners of bottom decks and into prime top-deck positions with oodles of space and lots of glass for soothing views of the ocean. They offer **state-of-the-art workout machines** and a host of **spa treatments** that run from the basic to the bizarre.

GYMS: AN ANTIDOTE TO THE MIDNIGHT BUFFET

The well-equipped fitness centers on the megaships may feature a dozen treadmills and just as many stationary bikes, step machines, upper- and lower-body machines, and free weights. Celebrity's *Century, Galaxy,* and *Mercury,* for instance, have **virtual-reality stationary bikes,** and the *Mercury* even has a machine that simulates in-line skating. As ships get bigger, the options just keep increasing: Royal Caribbean's *Voyager of the Seas* is currently king with its rock-climbing wall and in-line and ice-skating rinks (though use of these will cost you extra). When it comes to big, the huge two-story Nautica gyms on the 2,642-passenger **Carnival** *Destiny, Triumph,* and *Victory* take the cake. There are dozens of exercise machines facing floor-to-ceiling windows and tons of space to work out in; there is even a pair of hot tubs and an aerobics room on the upper level.

The roomy **aerobics studios** on the *Grand Princess, Voyager of the Seas,* and on Holland America's and Carnival's post-1990 ships are like the kind you have at your gym back home, with mirrors and special flooring, and offer at least a couple of aerobics and stretch classes per day. Certified instructors teach the classes, which usually range from the traditional to the trendy—high- and low-impact, funk, step, body sculpting, stretch and tone, and abdominals. That said, I've been noticing there seem to be fewer free classes these days and more spa demonstrations (to entice passengers to book treatments) or personal training sessions (at $75 a pop) monopolizing the aerobics room.

Older ships, usually those built before 1990, often do not devote nearly as much space and resources to sports and fitness. The gyms on ships built pre-1990 are generally going to be smaller and more spartan, but on all but the small, adventure-oriented cruise lines—Windjammer, Star Clippers, Clipper, and ACCL—you'll find at least a couple of treadmills and a stationary bike or step machine or two, plus some free weights. On ships with limited or no gym facilities, aerobics and stretching classes will be held out on deck or in a lounge.

ONBOARD SPAS: TAKING RELAXATION ONE STEP FURTHER

If your idea of a heavenly vacation is spending half of it under a towel being massaged and kneaded with some soothing mystery oil, choose a cruise ship with a well-stocked spa (for my picks, see "Best Fitness Facilities & Spas" in the "Frommer's Favorites" chapter).

On ships of almost all sizes, spas are big business. On big ships built in the past 10 years, they've been given spacious quarters on top decks. The largest spas have 8 or 10 treatment rooms, a sauna and a steam room or two, and full locker rooms with showers. Like the gyms, the spas on ships built pre-1990, though, are generally going to be small; the large spas on 30-year-old-plus *Norway* and *QE2* are exceptions. Even most of the smaller upscale ships have some semblance of a spa and a beauty salon. For instance, Windstar Cruises' *Wind Surf* carries only 300 passengers but boasts an impressive spa, and Radisson's 490-passenger *Seven Seas Navigator* has a respectable spa with six treatment rooms. It's only on the smallest ships—like Windjammer, ACCL, Star Clippers, and Clipper's Caribbean-itinerary vessels—that you won't find spas.

Some of the best spas and fitness facilities at sea are aboard **Celebrity Cruises'** *Millennium, Century, Galaxy,* and *Mercury.* Called the AquaSpa, these spacious health meccas are as pleasing to the eye as they are functional. The *Galaxy*'s resembles a Japanese bathhouse and the *Mercury*'s features a Moroccan motif. The focal point in all four is a huge **thalassotherapy pool,** a bubbling cauldron of warm, soothing seawater that's a great place to relax before a massage.

The soothing ShipShape spas on **Royal Caribbean's** *Explorer, Voyager, Vision, Rhapsody, Grandeur,* and *Enchantment of the Seas* are also some of the most attractive around. The *Voyager*'s spans two decks. Adjacent to the spas are spacious solariums with a pool, deck chairs, floor-to-ceiling windows, and a retractable glass ceiling. These spots are a peaceful place to repose before or after a spa treatment, or any time at all.

Other impressive spas include the 6,000-square-foot Roman Spa on **Norwegian Cruise Line's** *Norway* and the Pompeii Spa on **Costa Cruise Lines'** *CostaVictoria,* which features accoutrements such as tile mosaics, rattan lounge chairs, and a small plunge pool.

THE UBIQUITOUS STEINER

The spas and hair salons on most ships (over 90 of them) are staffed and operated by a firm called Steiner, a London-based company with a hands-down corner on the market. You'll find most of the prices are steep when you factor in the 15% tip (and this coming from a New Yorker). Rates can vary by about $15 per treatment, depending on the ship (although, the length of the treatments are the same). A sampling of treatments and their standard Steiner rates, which increased a whopping 30% to 50% in late 1999, are as follows (rates listed here do not include a tip):

- 50-minute full-body massage: $84 to $99
- 25-minute back and legs massage: $55 to $65
- Manicure: $21 to $25
- Pedicure: $34 to $40 (ridiculous!)
- 55-minute facial: $84 to $99
- Bikini wax: $21 to $25
- 55-minute Ionithermie slimming treatment: $102 to $120

The young women, mostly Brits, who do the massages, facials, manicures, pedicures, reflexology, and other services are professional, charming, and attractive in their matching white-and-light-green frocks. That said, while I'm one of the first in line to sign up, I've found the quality of the treatments to be inconsistent, ranging from really average (like I felt I'd had big dollops of oil and creams wimpily smeared on me with no rhyme or reason) to excellent (when all I wanted was more, more, more). Generally, shipboard massages are pretty good and equivalent to what you'd get from a professional at home (and, of course, like anywhere, it's hit and miss and some masseuses are better than others), but I've found some of the more exotic treatments, as well as pedicures and facials, to be disappointing and certainly not worth the money. I mean, $40 for a mediocre pedicure, are you joking? Likewise, when I ask questions about some of the more exotic treatments (like the Ionithermie facials or slimming/detox treatments, which use electrodes to stimulate cells to release toxins), inquiring what is being done to my leg, head, shoulder, or whatever, the answers often seem to be nothing more than a memorized pat description of the treatment from some brochure and rarely sheds much light. I expect more when I'm paying $90-plus.

There are exceptions of course. A masseur I had on a recent cruise on the *Sovereign of the Seas* was a trained sports therapist and a student of chiropractics—he was excellent.

Steiner isn't shy about pushing its extensive and expensive collection of creams, exfoliants, moisturizers, toners, and masks, either. Get a facial and you'll wind up with an itemized list of four or five products that they recommend you buy to get the same effect at home. The items on these lists can easily add up to over $200 (of course, you can just say no). The shameless promotion of these fancy ointments, just as you're coming out of your semiconscious post-massage trance, certainly jars you back to reality, that's for sure.

They tell me these products have higher amounts of active ingredients than anything that can be bought in the United States, and that's why they cost so much. Oh. A few years ago, to test this explanation, I grudgingly bought a tube of La Therapie cleanser,

---

Sweating for Dollars

Some lines dangle incentives in front of passengers to encourage and reward participation in **onboard fitness programs.** Holland America, Princess, Royal Caribbean, and Celebrity have fitness programs that award participating passengers with points redeemable at the end of the cruise for things like hats and T-shirts.

---

a bottle of toner, and a pot of moisturizer totaling over $200 (for research, mind you). They lasted me about 6 months, and I admit I liked the products. Still, the price has inhibited me from ever doing this again.

MAKING YOUR APPOINTMENT AT THE SPA

Hurry up! Since spas are so popular these days, you'll want to head to the spa reservation desk first thing. No time to unpack or grab lunch; got to head up to that spa pronto. Appointments fill up fast, with people lining up to reserve their spots—on the megaships, snaking lines 20 and 30 deep are not uncommon on the afternoon of embarkation—and if you don't sign up on the first day (second at the latest), there's a good chance the only appointment you can get will be totally undesirable (like during dinner or at some ungodly hour of the morning); worse yet, you might not get one at all.

Treatments range in price from about $10 to over $240, plus the 15% tip you're expected to give (of course, if you're unhappy with the treatment, don't tip), and are charged to your onboard account. Celebrity and Windstar allow you to prebook spa packages with your travel agent, but appointment times cannot be reserved until you board the ship.

---

6 An Introduction to Shipboard Dining

Food, food, food everywhere. From elegant five-course meals served in grand two-story dining rooms with sea views, to intimate Japanese, Italian, and Tex-Mex restaurants, massive midnight buffets, 24-hour pizza, ice-cream, pastry, and coffee shops, and even sushi bars, cruise ships big and small are offering more and more choices. The megas, of course, are nothing short of floating smorgasbords. The latest trend: dinner any way you like it. You can still go for the traditional dinner in the formal dining room, or you can now opt for a casual one in the Lido cafe or an intimate meal in a cozy reservations-only Italian restaurant. If you're feeling really unmotivated, Carnival offers pizza and Caesar salad 24 hours a day and Celebrity even delivers pizza to your cabin! Disney has a hot-dog counter by the pool, NCL's *Norwegian Sky* has nachos and cheese in the sports bar, and Royal Caribbean's *Voyager of the Seas* has an entire 1950s-style diner. Smaller ships have fewer choices, but even they are getting in on the pizza and alternative-restaurant bandwagon—the budget *Regal Empress* makes a mean pizza pie, and all the upscale lines are offering alternatives, too.

With such a spread to choose from, here's a blow-by-blow look at all the delicious choices.

FORMAL DINING

Dinner in the formal dining room is generally served from about 7 to 10pm, with ships carrying fewer than 500 passengers having one open-seating dinner, where guests can stroll in when they want and sit with whomever they choose. On ships carrying more than 400 or 500 passengers there are either one or two seatings in one main dining room or, on the largest ships, two (or even three) main dining rooms with two scheduled seatings—Princess's *Grand Princess,* for instance, has three formal dining rooms serving two seatings and Royal Caribbean's *Explorer* and *Voyager of the Seas* have a whopping three-deck-high dining room doing two seatings. Putting a unique twist on things, the *Disney Magic* and *Disney Wonder* do two seatings in three main themed dining rooms that passengers rotate amongst over the course of the cruise.

If there are two seatings, the early or first one is about 6:30pm (early breakfast is at 7 or 7:30am and lunch about noon) and late or second is about 8:30pm (late breakfast is at 8:30am and lunch at about 1:30pm). **First seatings** are for those who prefer dining early and are ready to leave the dining room once the dishes are cleared; elderly passengers and families with children tend to choose this seating. If you choose **second seating,** you won't have to rush through predinner showering and dressing after an active day at a port of call, and the meal tends to be more leisurely, allowing you to linger over coffee and after-dinner drinks.

You need to reserve either the early or late seating when booking your cruise. Your choice might be confirmed at the pier during check-in or soon after you get to your cabin. If you get assigned to the first seating and you want the second one, tell your maître d', who will probably be at or near his or her station in the dining room during your initial embarkation. Most can accommodate your wishes, if not on the first night of sailing, then on the second night.

Generally, 7-night cruises have 2 nights per week (and 10- to 14-night cruises have 2) designated as **formal nights,** when the dress code in the main dining room calls for dark suits or tuxedos for men and cocktail dresses or fancy pantsuits for women. Other nights are designated informal and/or casual.

From **menus** that offer three to six options for each course, you can choose from a wide array of international fare like escargot, vichyssoise, and veal scaloppini to American favorites, such as poached salmon, prime rib, and pastas. There are also at least one or two **vegetarian choices** as well as **healthier entrees** that are designed to be lower in fat, calories, cholesterol, and sodium.

Tables generally seat between 4 and 10. Don't get your hopes up if you're looking to get a table for two, as there are very few aboard most ships. If dining alone or as a couple is a major priority, the smaller, upscale ships are usually better equipped than the megas to accommodate you in this area. If you *do* want to meet and mingle with other passengers (hey, that's what cruises are for), I suggest trying to get a table that seats at least 6 to 10. You'll be more likely to meet pleasant dining companions and it won't be as potentially boring as a smaller grouping of four. Rotate seats every so often during the week to keep things lively and chat with new people.

Smoking is prohibited in virtually all dining rooms.

DINNER-TABLE DIVORCES

Many cruisers claim their dining companions either made or ruined their cruise. If you get stuck with a couple of yahoos who seem to offend every bone in your body or there just isn't any chemistry, there's no need to suffer in silence. It's best to explain to the maître d' as courteously and as soon as possible that your table assignment simply won't do, and request a change. You will usually be accommodated.

SPECIAL DIETS

If you follow any special diet, inform the cruise line as early as possible, preferably when booking your cruise. **Vegetarian dishes** and **kosher food** are commonly available, and almost all cruise lines now feature a selection of healthier, **lighter meals,** labeled as such on the menu. On all but the most cost-conscious cruise lines, the kitchen usually tries to satisfy reasonable culinary requests.

CASUAL DINING

If you'd rather skip the formality of the main dining room, all but the tiniest ships serve breakfast and lunch (and now, even dinner—see below) in a casual **buffet-style cafe restaurant.** Usually located on the Lido Deck, with indoor and outdoor poolside seating, these restaurants serve an extensive spread of both hot and cold food items. On the megas, nearby may be a **grill** where at lunch you can get hamburgers, hot dogs, and often chicken; sometimes there are specialty stations, offerings **taco fixings** or **Chinese food.** On most ships, **breakfast and lunch buffets** are generally served for a 3- to 4-hour period, so guests can stroll in and out whenever they desire—although Princess Cruises has the Lido cafe open around the clock on its newest ships.

If you're not in the mood for the fuss of formal dining in the evening, either, many ships—including those of the Royal Caribbean, Carnival, Norwegian, Celebrity, Princess, Holland America, and Cunard lines—now offer dinner in the buffet-style cafe restaurant. Most serve dinner buffet-style, but some do a combination of sit-down service and buffet. Wear what you want, stroll in when you please, and, in most cases, sit where you please (most are open seating). After soup and salad, two or three entrees are offered, like prime rib, salmon, or stir-fry, followed by dessert.

If you do want the fine dining and formality, but with fewer fellow diners in tow, you can take advantage of one of the intimate, **reservations-only restaurants** some lines have added in recent years, seating fewer than 100. Crystal's *Crystal Harmony* has an Asian and an Italian restaurant; Radisson's *Radisson Diamond* and *Seven Seas Navigator,* Italian; Disney's *Disney Magic* and *Disney Wonder,* Italian (there's a $5 per person cover charge); Princess's *Grand Princess,* Tex-Mex and Italian ($3.50 per person cover charge); Seabourn's *Seabourn Legend, Spirit, Pride,* and *Sun,* French and Italian; Cunard's *Vistafjord,* Italian; and Holland America Lines' new *Volendam* and *Zaandam,* Italian.

BETWEEN-MEAL SNACKING

Beyond the normal three meals a day is another full schedule of endless eating opportunities. The traditional **midnight buffet extravaganza** is still a highlight on many big ships, offering heaps of elaborately decorated fruits, vegetables, and pastries, as well as real treats like shrimp, and invariably featuring a majestic ice sculpture to top off the festive mood. Sometimes the nighttime feast is focused on a culinary theme, such as Tex-Mex, Caribbean, or chocolate. In recent years, though, because of all the other onboard dining choices and people's healthier eating habits, more and more lines are featuring the classic midnight buffets only once or twice a week, and substituting smaller **snack stations** instead. Some lines (like Celebrity and Disney) have even done away with midnight buffets completely, instead having waiters passing around trays of hors d'oeuvres in the lounges and bars instead (which keeps those drinkers where they belong: at the bar, running up their tabs).

Throughout the day, if hunger pangs get the best of you between lunch and dinner, the megaships have **pizza** available (pizzerias on Carnival's ships, for example, operate 24 hours a day and serve Caesar salad, too) and self-serve **frozen yogurt** and **ice-cream** machines (cheapo Princess doesn't; they only sell Häagen-Dasz). The upscale lines do elegant **afternoon tea service,** offering finger sandwiches, pastries, and cookies along with tea and coffee; the megas, too, offer a couple of trays of cookies or sandwiches midday. Small-ship lines, like Star Clippers, Windstar, Clipper, and Windjammer, serve predinner snacks and hors d'oeuvres in the main lounge or bar area.

Some lines, like Princess and Carnival, also have a **patisserie** and/or **cappuccino bar** on board their ships, but they're not free. Specialty coffees and ultra-rich desserts go for about $1 to $4 each. If you'd rather not leave your cabin, most ships offer **24-hour**

room service from a limited menu, or for suite guests, the same meals served in the dining room can be served in the cabin.

7 Shopping Opportunities on Ship & Shore

SHOPPING ABOARD SHIP

Even the smallest ships have at least a small shop on board selling T-shirts, sweatshirts, and baseball caps bearing the cruise line logo. The big new megaships, though, have the most extensive onboard shopping. Like mini-malls, they may have as many as 10 different stores selling items like **toiletries and sundries** (film, toothpaste, candy, paperback books, and even condoms) as well as totes, T-shirts, mugs, toys, key chains, and other **cruise line logo souvenirs.** You'll find **formal wear** like sequin dresses and jackets, silk dresses and scarves, purses, satin shoes, cummerbunds, ties, and tuxedo shirts, as well as **perfume, cosmetics, jewelry** (costume and the real stuff), and **porcelain figurines.**

A few ships have name-brand stores. The *Carnival Paradise* and the *Norwegian Wind,* for instance, both have Fossil boutiques on board, selling mostly watches. The Disney ships, of course, have shops selling Disney souvenirs, clothing, and toys. And appropriately, the *QE2* recently added a Harrods shop to its hallowed halls, offering lots of those cute stuffed bears, green totes, and biscuits.

All merchandise sold on board while a ship is at sea is tax-free, and to maintain that tax-free status, the shops are closed whenever a ship is in port. Prices can vary, though: Some items sell for less—as much as a third less than on shore—and some items cost substantially more. Some of the best deals are on alcohol. By midcruise, there are often good sales on a selection of T-shirts, tote bags, jewelry, and booze. Things that usually cost you more on board than off are disposal cameras, sunscreen, and candy and snack foods. Prices on clothing and good jewelry vary; some things are quite overpriced.

SHOPPING IN PORT

If you want to shop on shore, see "Best Islands for Serious Shoppers" in the "Frommer's Favorites" chapter, for the best shopping islands.

Before each port of call, the cruise director or shore-excursion manager gives a **port talk** about that place's attractions. Now, it's no secret that many cruise lines have mutually beneficial deals with certain shops in every port, so on the big, mass-market ships especially, a good 75% of the port info disseminated will be about shopping (better bring along your own guidebook—this one!—if you want information on history or culture). The lines often recommend a list of shops in town where they say the merchandise is guaranteed, and if the stone falls out of the new ring you bought at one of them once you get home, the cruise lines say they'll try to help you get a replacement—but don't hold your breath; the whole thing is a bit ambiguous. If you're not an expert on jewelry or whatever else it is you want to buy, it might be safer to shop at these stores, which tend to be of the touristy chain variety. That said, you won't get much of a taste for the local culture in one of them. Browsing at **outdoor markets** and in smaller **craft shops** is a better way to get an idea of the port's local flavor.

Part 2

The Cruise Lines & Their Ships

Detailed, in-depth reviews of all the cruise lines in the Caribbean, with discussions of the experiences they offer and the lowdown on their ships.

Part 2

The Cruise Lines
& Their Ships

The Ratings (and How to Read Them)

Okay, this is it: The point where you get to decide which ship is going to whisk you off for your Caribbean getaway and be your home, entertainment center, and means of transportation for the duration of your trip. As I've said in previous chapters, all ships are not created equal, and finding the one that best matches your style is the key to getting the vacation experience you deserve.

Ship, ships, ships. Some are huge, overwhelming fortresses of activities and entertainment; others are tiny, functional, "get me from here to there" vessels with the feel of a summer camp bunkhouse. Some are high-toned country clubs that happen to float, and others are like a Texas roadhouse on a Saturday night. I've been on more ships than you could shake a stick at, and in this section I'll fill you in on what each one has to offer.

1 Cruise Line Categories

To make your selection easier (and to make sure you're not comparing apples and oranges), I've divided the cruise lines into four distinct categories, given each category a chapter of its own, and rated each line only in comparison with the other lines in its category (see more about this in "How to Read the Ratings," below). The categories are as follows:

THE MAINSTREAM LINES (chapter 6) These are the most prominent players in the industry, the jack-of-all-trades lines with the biggest ships, carrying the most passengers, and providing the most diverse cruise experiences to suit many different tastes, from party-hearty to elegant and refined. (And with all the competition in the industry today, they tend to offer good prices, too.) **Lines reviewed:** Carnival Cruise Lines, Celebrity Cruises, Costa Cruises, Crown Cruise Line, Disney Cruise Line, Holland America Line, Norwegian Cruise Line, Princess Cruises, and Royal Caribbean International.

THE BUDGET/OLD-SHIP LINES (chapter 7) On a limited budget? These lines and their midsize ships offer some great bargains, particularly on shorter sailings of 2, 3, and 4 nights. And for the price, these lines tend to pack in plenty of good times. They don't have spiffy new ships, but for some people, that's a draw in itself: Sailing aboard some of these older vessels is like taking a trip back in time. **Lines reviewed:** Commodore Cruise Line, Mediterranean Shipping Cruises, Premier Cruise Lines, and Regal Cruises.

THE ULTRA-LUXURY LINES (chapter 8)   Got some big bucks to spend on a superluxurious cruise? These are the ships for you. Offering elegant, refined, and doting service, extraordinary dining, spacious cabins, and high-toned entertainment aboard intimately sized, finely appointed vessels, they're the Dom Perignon of cruises. **Lines reviewed:** Crystal Cruises, Cunard, Radisson Seven Seas Cruises, Seabourn Cruise Line, and Windstar Cruises.

SOFT-ADVENTURE LINES & SAILING SHIPS (chapter 9)   And now for something completely different. Maybe you want the kind of really intimate experience that a ship with only 70 to 100 passengers can offer. Or maybe you want to visit small, out-of-the-way ports that the bigger ships ignore. Maybe you prefer a good book and conversation to a large ship's roster of activities. Or maybe you want to *really* sail—on a sail-powered ship. If any of this describes you, head for this chapter, where you'll find lines that operate small, intimate ships offering unusual cruise experiences. **Lines reviewed:** American Canadian Caribbean Line, Clipper Cruise Line, Star Clippers, and Windjammer Barefoot Cruises.

HOW TO READ THE RATINGS

The cruise industry today offers such a profusion of experiences that it makes my head spin. It also makes comparing all lines and ships by the same set of criteria completely impossible.

Think about it: Would you compare a Mercedes Benz to a sport utility vehicle? A jumbo jet to a hang-glider? A Park Avenue high-rise apartment to an A-frame in Aspen? No, you wouldn't. For the same reason, I came to the conclusion that the typical, across-the-board ratings used by most cruise guidebooks are illogical and don't give you, the reader, the kind of comparisons you need to make your decision.

For that reason, I've developed a simple system based on the classic customer-satisfaction survey. In each of these "Frommer's Ratings" I judge the cruise lines on the following important considerations, rating them either *poor, fair, good, excellent,* or *outstanding*.

- Enjoyment Factor
- Entertainment
- Dining
- Service
- Activities
- Overall Value
- Children's Program

Again, though, you can't compare the experiences you'll have aboard an ultra-luxury line like Seabourn, an ultra-casual line like Windjammer Barefoot Cruises, a megaship line like Carnival, and a budget line like Regal. They're different animals, catering to different kinds of travelers seeking different kinds of experiences. For that reason, **I've graded the cruise lines on a curve.** Remember how you used to just *love* it when the teacher did that? It works the same way here as it did in school. You should read the ratings for a line *only in relation to the other lines in the same chapter.* For example, if you see in the "Soft-Adventure Lines & Sailing Ships" chapter that Star Clippers achieves an "outstanding" rating for its dining experience, that means that among the lines in that chapter, Star Clippers has the best cuisine. It may not be up to the level of, say, the ultra-luxurious Seabourn (it's not), but if you're looking for an adventurous cruise that also has great food, this line would be your best bet.

STRUCTURE OF THE CRUISE LINE REVIEWS

Each cruise line's review begins with **The Line in a Nutshell** (a quick word about the line in general) and **The Experience,** which is just what is says: a short summation of the kind of cruise experience you can expect to have aboard that line. Following this, the **ratings** table judges the individual elements of that line's cruise experience compared with the other lines in the same category (see above for ratings details). The text that follows fleshes out the review, providing all the details you need to get a feel for what kind of a vacation the cruise line will give you.

RATING THE INDIVIDUAL SHIPS

The individual ship reviews that follow the general cruise line description get down into the nitty-gritty, giving you all the details on the ships' accommodations, facilities, amenities, comfort level, and upkeep.

People feel very strongly about ships. For centuries, mariners have imbued their vessels with human personalities, and usually referred to them as "her." In fact, an old (really old) seafaring superstition holds that women should never be allowed aboard a ship, because the ship, being a woman herself, will get jealous. Guess that means I've made a lot of ships jealous in my time.

Be that as it may, it's a fact that people bond with the ships they sail aboard. They find themselves in the gift shop, loading up on T-shirts with the ship's name emblazoned on front. They get to port and the first question they ask other cruisers they meet is "Which ship are you sailing on?," and then engage in a friendly comparison, each walking away knowing in his heart that *his* ship is the best. I know people who have sailed the same ship a dozen times or more, and feel as warmly about it as though it were their own summer cottage. That's why, when looking at the reviews, you want to look for a ship that says "you."

In rating the ships, I've used a version of the same Frommer's Ratings system with which I reviewed the lines. It evaluates the ships' cabins, public spaces, cleanliness, decor, gyms/spas, itineraries, and a few other elements on a 1-to-5 scale, which you should read like this:

1	=	Poor	4	=	Excellent
2	=	Fair	5	=	Outstanding
3	=	Good			

In instances where the category doesn't apply to a particular ship (the Windjammer and American Canadian Caribbean ships, for instance, don't have gyms or spas), I've simply noted "not applicable" (N/A). After all, you can't rate what ain't there.

SPECIFICATIONS

I've listed some of the ships' vital statistics—ship size, year built and most recently refurbished, number of cabins, number of officers and crew—to help you compare.

Size is listed in both length of the ship, which is pretty self-explanatory, and in tons. Note that these are not actual measures of weight, but **gross register tons (GRTs),** which is a measure of the interior space used to produce revenue on a ship. One GRT equals 100 cubic feet of enclosed, revenue-generating space. Among the crew/officers statistics, an important one is the **passenger/crew ratio,** which tells you, in theory, how many passengers each crew member is expected to serve.

ITINERARIES

Each cruise line review includes a chart showing itineraries for each ship the line has assigned to Caribbean, Bermuda, or Panama Canal itineraries for 2001. Often, a single ship sails on alternating itineraries—for instance, doing an eastern Caribbean route one week and a western Caribbean route the next, ad infinitum until season's end. When this is the case, I've listed both and noted that they alternate. Consult your travel agent for exact sailing dates.

(continued on page 98)

Ships at a Glance				
Cruise Line	Ship	Type of Cruise	Duration of Cruise (days)	Year Built
ACCL	**Grande Caribe**	Soft Adventure	11	1997
	Grand Mariner	Soft Adventure	11–14	1998
	Niagara Prince	Soft Adventure	6–10	1994
Carnival	**Carnival Destiny**	Mainstream	7	1996
	Carnival Pride	Mainstream	7	2001
	Carnival Spirit	Mainstream	7	2001
	Carnival Triumph	Mainstream	7	1999
	Carnival Victory	Mainstream	7	2000
	Celebration	Mainstream	7	1987
	Ecstasy	Mainstream	3–4	1991
	Fantasy	Mainstream	3–4	1990
	Fascination	Mainstream	7	1994
	Imagination	Mainstream	4–5	1995
	Inspiration	Mainstream	7	1996
	Jubilee	Mainstream	10–11	1986
	Paradise	Mainstream	7	1998
	Sensation	Mainstream	7	1993
	Tropicale	Mainstream	4–5	1982
Celebrity	**Century**	Mainstream	7	1995
	Galaxy	Mainstream	7	1996
	Horizon	Mainstream	10–11	1990
	Infinity	Mainstream	7	2001
	Mercury	Mainstream	7	1997
	Millennium	Mainstream	7	2000
	Constellation	Mainstream	7	2001
	Zenith	Mainstream	7–14	1992
Clipper	**Nantucket Clipper**	Soft Adventure	7	1984
	Yorktown Clipper	Soft Adventure	7–10	1988
Commodore	**Enchanted Capri**	Old/Budget	2–5	1976
	Enchanted Isle	Old/Budget	7	1958
Costa	**CostaAtlantica**	Mainstream	7	2000
	CostaRomantica	Mainstream	7	1993
	CostaVictoria	Mainstream	7	1996

Gross Tonnage	Passenger Capacity (Double Occupancy)	Passenger/Crew Ratio	Alternative Dining	Casino	Children's Activities	Children's Playroom	Gym	Jogging Track	Library	Infirmary	Spa (L=limited facilities)	Swimming Pool(s)	Theater/Cinema	Wheelchair Access (P=partial)
99	100	5.5:1												
99	100	5.5:1												
99	84	5:1												
101,353	2,642	2.6:1	✓	✓	✓	✓	✓	✓	✓	✓	✓	✓	✓	✓
84,000	2,114	2.6:1	✓	✓	✓	✓	✓	✓	✓	✓	✓	✓	✓	✓
84,000	2,114	2.6:1	✓	✓	✓	✓	✓	✓	✓	✓	✓	✓	✓	✓
102,000	2,758	2.6:1	✓	✓	✓	✓	✓	✓	✓	✓	✓	✓	✓	✓
102,000	2,758	2.6:1	✓	✓	✓	✓	✓	✓	✓	✓	✓	✓	✓	✓
47,262	1,486	2.2:1	✓	✓	✓	✓	✓	✓	✓	✓	✓	✓	✓	✓
70,367	2,040	2.2:1	✓	✓	✓	✓	✓	✓	✓	✓	✓	✓	✓	✓
70,367	2,040	2.2:1	✓	✓	✓	✓	✓	✓	✓	✓	✓	✓	✓	✓
70,367	2,040	2.2:1	✓	✓	✓	✓	✓	✓	✓	✓	✓	✓	✓	P
70,367	2,040	2.2:1	✓	✓	✓	✓	✓	✓	✓	✓	✓	✓	✓	✓
70,367	2,040	2.2:1	✓	✓	✓	✓	✓	✓	✓	✓	✓	✓	✓	✓
47,262	1,486	2.2:1	✓	✓	✓	✓	✓	✓	✓	✓	✓	✓	✓	✓
70,367	2,040	2.2:1	✓	✓	✓	✓	✓	✓	✓	✓	✓	✓	✓	✓
70,367	2,040	2.2:1	✓	✓	✓	✓	✓	✓	✓	✓	✓	✓	✓	✓
36,674	1,022	1.9:1	✓	✓	✓	✓	✓	✓	✓	✓	✓	✓	✓	✓
70,606	1,750	2:1	✓	✓	✓	✓	✓	✓	✓	✓	✓	✓	✓	✓
77,713	1,896	2:1	✓	✓	✓	✓	✓	✓	✓	✓	✓	✓	✓	✓
46,811	1,354	2.1:1	✓	✓	✓	✓	✓	✓	✓	✓	✓	✓	✓	✓
91,000	1,950	2:1	✓	✓	✓	✓	✓	✓	✓	✓	✓	✓	✓	✓
77,713	1,896	2:1	✓	✓	✓	✓	✓	✓	✓	✓	✓	✓	✓	✓
91,000	1,950	2:1	✓	✓	✓	✓	✓	✓	✓	✓	✓	✓	✓	✓
91,000	1,950	2:1	✓	✓	✓	✓	✓	✓	✓	✓	✓	✓	✓	✓
47,225	1,374	2.1:1	✓	✓	✓	✓	✓	✓	✓	✓	✓	✓	✓	✓
1,471	102	3.2:1												
2,354	138	3.5:1												
15,410	460	2.4:1		✓						✓		✓	✓	
23,395	725	2.1:1		✓	✓	✓	✓		✓	✓	L	✓	✓	P
84,000	2,112	2.3:1	✓	✓	✓	✓	✓	✓	✓	✓	✓	✓	✓	✓
53,000	1,356	2:1	✓	✓	✓	✓	✓	✓	✓	✓	✓	✓	✓	✓
76,000	1,928	2.4:1	✓	✓	✓	✓	✓	✓	✓	✓	✓	✓	✓	✓

Ships at a Glance				
Cruise Line	Ship	Type of Cruise	Duration of Cruise (days)	Year Built
Crown	Crown Dynasty	Mainstream	7	1993
Crystal	Crystal Harmony	Luxury	7–12	1990
	Crystal Symphony	Luxury	10–11	1995
Cunard	Caronia	Luxury	12–16	1973
	QE2	Luxury	5–16	1969
Disney	Disney Magic	Mainstream	7	1998
	Disney Wonder	Mainstream	3–4	1999
Holland America	Amsterdam	Mainstream	N/A	2000
	Maasdam	Mainstream	10	1993
	Nieuw Amsterdam	Mainstream	14	1983
	Noordam	Mainstream	7–10	1984
	Ryndam	Mainstream	7	1994
	Veendam	Mainstream	7	1996
	Volendam	Mainstream	10	1999
	Westerdam	Mainstream	7	1986
	Zaandam	Mainstream	10	2000
Mediterranean Shipping	Melody	Old/Budget	11	1982
Norwegian	Norway	Mainstream	7	1961
	Norwegian Dream	Mainstream	7	1992
	Norwegian Majesty	Mainstream	7–11	1992
	Norwegian Sea	Mainstream	7	1988
	Norwegian Sky	Mainstream	7	1999
	Norwegian Sun	Mainstream	7	2001
	Norwegian Wind	Mainstream	7	1993
Premier	Big Red Boat I	Old/Budget	3–4	1965
	Big Red Boat II	Old/Budget	7	1966
	Big Red Boat III	Old/Budget	7	1961
	Rembrandt	Old/Budget	7	1959
	SeaBreeze	Old/Budget	7	1958
Princess	Crown Princess	Mainstream	10	1991
	Dawn Princess	Mainstream	7	1995
	Golden Princess	Mainstream	7	2001
	Grand Princess	Mainstream	7	1998

Gross Tonnage	Passenger Capacity (Double Occupancy)	Passenger/Crew Ratio	Alternative Dining	Casino	Children's Activities	Children's Playroom	Gym	Jogging Track	Library	Infirmary	Spa (L=limited)	Swimming Pool(s)	Theater/Cinema	Wheelchair Access (P=partial)
20,000	800	2.6:1	✓	✓	✓	✓	✓	✓	✓	✓	✓	✓	✓	✓
49,400	960	1.7:1	✓	✓	✓	✓	✓	✓	✓	✓	✓	✓	✓	✓
51,044	960	1.7:1	✓	✓	✓	✓	✓	✓	✓	✓	✓	✓	✓	✓
24,492	679	1.7:1	✓	✓			✓	✓	✓	✓	✓	✓	✓	✓
70,327	1,740	1.8:1	✓	✓	✓	✓	✓	✓	✓	✓	✓	✓	✓	✓
83,000	1,760	1.9:1	✓		✓	✓	✓	✓		✓	✓	✓	✓	✓
83,000	1,760	1.9:1	✓		✓	✓	✓	✓		✓	✓	✓	✓	✓
61,000	1,380	2.2:1	✓	✓	✓	✓	✓	✓	✓	✓	✓	✓	✓	✓
55,451	1,266	2.2:1	✓	✓	✓	✓	✓	✓	✓	✓	✓	✓	✓	✓
33,930	1,214	2.2:1	✓	✓	✓	✓	✓	✓	✓	✓	✓	✓	✓	✓
33,930	1,214	2.2:1	✓	✓	✓	✓	✓	✓	✓	✓	✓	✓	✓	✓
55,451	1,266	2.2:1	✓	✓	✓	✓	✓	✓	✓	✓	✓	✓	✓	✓
55,451	1,266	2.2:1	✓	✓	✓	✓	✓	✓	✓	✓	✓	✓	✓	✓
63,000	1,440	2.2:1	✓	✓	✓	✓	✓	✓	✓	✓	✓	✓	✓	✓
53,872	1,494	2.3:1	✓	✓	✓	✓	✓	✓	✓	✓	✓	✓	✓	✓
63,000	1,440	2.2:1	✓	✓	✓	✓	✓	✓	✓	✓	✓	✓	✓	✓
36,000	1,076	2:1		✓	✓	✓	✓	✓	✓	✓	L	✓	✓	P
76,049	2,032	2.3:1	✓	✓	✓	✓	✓	✓	✓	✓	✓	✓	✓	✓
56,760	1,748	2.8:1	✓	✓	✓	✓	✓	✓	✓	✓	✓	✓	✓	✓
38,000	1,460	2.7:1	✓	✓	✓	✓	✓	✓	✓	✓	✓	✓	✓	✓
42,000	1,504	2.4:1	✓	✓	✓	✓	✓		✓	✓	✓	✓	✓	✓
80,000	2,002	2.7:1	✓	✓	✓	✓	✓	✓	✓	✓	✓	✓	✓	✓
80,000	2,002	2.7:1	✓	✓	✓	✓	✓	✓	✓	✓	✓	✓	✓	✓
56,760	1,748	2.8:1	✓	✓	✓	✓	✓	✓	✓	✓	✓	✓	✓	✓
38,772	1,116	2.3:1		✓	✓	✓	✓			✓	L	✓	✓	P
35,000	967	2.3:1		✓	✓	✓				✓	L	✓	✓	
31,793	1,146	2.3:1		✓	✓	✓			✓	✓	L	✓	✓	
38,645	1,074	2:1		✓	✓	✓			✓	✓	✓	✓	✓	
21,010	842	2.1:1		✓	✓	✓	✓		✓	✓	L	✓		
70,000	1,590	2.3:1	✓	✓	✓	✓	✓	✓	✓	✓	✓	✓	✓	✓
77,000	1,950	2.2:1	✓	✓	✓	✓	✓	✓	✓	✓	✓	✓	✓	✓
109,000	2,600	2.2:1	✓	✓	✓	✓	✓	✓	✓	✓	✓	✓	✓	✓
109,000	2,600	2:1	✓	✓	✓	✓	✓	✓	✓	✓	✓	✓	✓	✓

Ships at a Glance				
Cruise Line	Ship	Type of Cruise	Duration of Cruise (days)	Year Built
Princess (cont.)	**Ocean Princess**	Mainstream	7	1999
	Pacific Princess	Mainstream	7	1971
	Sea Princess	Mainstream	7	1998
	Sun Princess	Mainstream	10–11	1997
Radisson Seven Seas	**Radisson Diamond**	Luxury	4–10	1992
	Seven Seas Navigator	Luxury	7–10	1999
	Seven Seas Mariner	Luxury	N/A	2001
Regal	**Regal Empress**	Old/Budget	4–11	1953
Royal Caribbean	**Enchantment of the Seas**	Mainstream	7	1997
	Explorer of the Seas	Mainstream	7	2000
	Grandeur of the Seas	Mainstream	7	1996
	Majesty of the Seas	Mainstream	3–7	1992
	Monarch of the Seas	Mainstream	7	1991
	Nordic Empress	Mainstream	3–7	1990
	Radiance of the Seas	Mainstream	7	2001
	Sovereign of the Seas	Mainstream	3–4	1988
	Splendour of the Seas	Mainstream	10–11	1996
	Vision of the Seas	Mainstream	10–11	1998
	Voyager of the Seas	Mainstream	7	1999
Royal Olympic	**Olympic Explorer**	Educational	N/A	2001
	Olympic Voyager	Educational	9–13	2000
	Stella Solaris	Educational	10–56	1953
Seabourn	**Seabourn Goddess I**	Luxury	7	1984
	Seabourn Goddess II	Luxury	7	1985
	Seabourn Legend	Luxury	5–16	1992
	Seabourn Pride	Luxury	6–10	1988
	Seabourn Sun	Luxury	10–14	1988
Star Clippers	**Royal Clipper**	Sailing Ship	7	2000
	Star Clipper	Sailing Ship	7	1991
Windjammer	**Amazing Grace**	Soft Adventure	13	1955
	Flying Cloud	Sailing Ship	6	1927
	Legacy	Sailing Ship	7	1959
	Mandalay	Sailing Ship	6–13	1923

Gross Tonnage	Passenger Capacity (Double Occupancy)	Passenger/Crew Ratio	Alternative Dining	Casino	Children's Activities	Children's Playroom	Gym	Jogging Track	Library	Infirmary	Spa (L=limited)	Swimming Pool(s)	Theater/Cinema	Wheelchair Access (P=partial)
77,000	1,950	2.2:1	✓	✓	✓	✓	✓	✓	✓	✓	✓	✓	✓	✓
20,000	640	1.8:1		✓			✓	✓	✓	✓	L	✓	✓	✓
77,000	1,950	2.2:1	✓	✓	✓	✓	✓	✓	✓	✓	✓	✓	✓	✓
77,000	1,950	2.2:1	✓	✓	✓	✓	✓	✓	✓	✓	✓	✓	✓	✓
20,295	350	1.8:1	✓	✓			✓	✓	✓	✓	✓	✓	✓	✓
30,000	490	1.5	✓	✓	✓	✓	✓	✓	✓	✓	✓	✓	✓	✓
50,000	708	1.6	✓	✓	✓	✓	✓	✓	✓	✓	✓	✓	✓	✓
22,000	1,068	2.8:1	✓	✓	✓	✓	✓	✓	✓	✓	L	✓	✓	✓
74,140	1,950	3:1	✓	✓	✓	✓	✓	✓	✓	✓	✓	✓	✓	✓
142,000	3,114	2.7:1	✓	✓	✓	✓	✓	✓	✓	✓	✓	✓	✓	✓
74,000	1,950	2.5:1	✓	✓	✓	✓	✓	✓	✓	✓	✓	✓	✓	✓
73,941	2,354	2.9:1	✓	✓	✓	✓	✓	✓	✓	✓	✓	✓	✓	✓
73,941	2,354	2.9:1	✓	✓	✓	✓	✓	✓	✓	✓	✓	✓	✓	✓
48,563	1,600	2.4:1	✓	✓	✓	✓	✓	✓		✓	✓	✓	✓	✓
85,000	2,100	2.7:1	✓	✓	✓	✓	✓	✓	✓	✓	✓	✓	✓	✓
73,192	2,276	2.7:1	✓	✓	✓	✓	✓	✓	✓	✓	✓	✓	✓	✓
69,130	1,804	2.5:1	✓	✓	✓	✓	✓	✓	✓	✓	✓	✓	✓	✓
78,491	2,000	3:1	✓	✓	✓	✓	✓	✓	✓	✓	✓	✓	✓	✓
142,000	3,114	2.7:1	✓	✓	✓	✓	✓	✓	✓	✓	✓	✓	✓	✓
25,000	840	2.3:1		✓			✓	✓	✓	✓	✓	✓	✓	✓
25,000	840	2.3:1		✓			✓	✓	✓	✓	✓	✓	✓	✓
18,000	620	1.9:1		✓			✓	✓	✓	✓	✓	✓	✓	P
4,250	116	1.3:1		✓			✓		✓	✓	✓	✓		
4,250	116	1.3:1		✓			✓		✓	✓	✓	✓		
10,000	204	1.5:1	✓	✓			✓		✓	✓	✓	✓		✓
10,000	204	1.5:1	✓	✓			✓		✓	✓	✓	✓		✓
38,000	758	1.7:1	✓	✓			✓	✓	✓	✓	✓	✓	✓	✓
5,000	224	2.2:1					✓		✓		✓	✓		
2,295	172	2.5:1							✓		L	✓		
1,525	94	2.4:1							✓					
400	74	3:1												
1,165	120	2.8:1			✓									
420	72	2.6:1												

Ships at a Glance				
Cruise Line	Ship	Type of Cruise	Duration of Cruise (days)	Year Built
Windjammer (cont.)	Polynesia	Sailing Ship	6	1938
	Yankee Clipper	Sailing Ship	6	1927
Windstar	Wind Spirit	Luxury	7	1988
	Wind Star	Luxury	7	1986
	Wind Surf	Luxury	7	1990

For those of you who are thinking about taking a non-Caribbean cruise at some point, I've also noted other itineraries sailed by the ships. You can find more details on many of these itineraries in *Frommer's Alaska Cruises* and *Frommer's European Cruises.*

2 Evaluating & Comparing the Listed Cruise Prices

Figuring out the price of a cruise is rarely a simple task—it's like driving in some foreign place without a map. My aim, with the help of Web-based cruise seller Icruise.com, is to give you some direction.

As I discussed in chapter 2, "Booking Your Cruise & Getting the Best Price," rates listed in the cruise line brochures are inflated and, except during holiday periods, you can expect to pay anywhere from 10% to 50% less. The discounts come from the cruise lines when you book 3 to 9 months early and, to make things confusing, also when you book at the last minute on ships that haven't filled up. Travel agencies and online cruise sellers usually offer additional savings, too. They sell so many cruises, they get bulk discounts from the cruise lines and pass the savings on to you.

To give you an accurate look at what you can expect to pay, I've taken an approach not used in other guidebooks. The rates listed in the ship reviews in chapters 6, 7, 8, and 9 and in Appendix A, "Cruise Price Comparisons," come straight from the experts at Icruise.com, rather than from the cruise lines' brochures. While, of course, rates are always subject to the basic principles of supply and demand, the prices that appear in this book are the **actual prices** Icruise.com was offering its customers at press time (May 2000) on cruises departing in late January 2000. Remember, though, they are meant as a guide only and are in no way etched in stone—so the price you pay may be higher or even lower, depending when you book, when you choose to travel, whether there are any special discounts being offered by the lines, and a slew of other factors. Other travel agencies and online sites may also be able to obtain similar rates.

Gross Tonnage	Passenger Capacity (Double Occupancy)	Passenger/Crew Ratio	Alternative Dining	Casino	Children's Activities	Children's Playroom	Gym	Jogging Track	Library	Infirmary	Spa (L=limited facilities)	Swimming Pool(s)	Theater/Cinema	Wheelchair Access (P=partial)
430	126	2.8:1												
327	64	2.2:1												
5,350	148	1.6:1	✓		✓		✓	✓	L	✓				
5,350	148	1.6:1	✓		✓		✓	✓	L	✓				
14,745	312	1.6:1	✓	✓		✓	✓	✓	✓	✓	✓			

PRICES LISTED IN THE REVIEWS

Based on what Icruise.com can offer versus brochure rates, in each ship review I've calculated **per diem prices** (the cruise price divided down to represent the rate paid per person, per day) for the following three basic types of accommodations:

- Lowest-category inside cabin (i.e., one without windows)
- Lowest-category outside cabin (i.e., one with windows)
- Lowest-category suite

Remember that cruise ships generally have several different categories of cabins within each of these three basic divisions, all priced differently, and that the prices I've listed represent the *lowest* categories for inside and outside cabins and suites. If you're interested in booking a roomier, higher-level cabin in any category, you'll find the price will be higher. In general, the cost of a top-level inside cabin will probably be very close to the rate for a low-level outside cabin, and the cost of a top-level outside may be very close to the rate for a low-level suite.

To contact **Icruise,** visit their Web site at **www.icruise.com**. All rates are cruise only (without airfare and other extras), per person, and based on double occupancy. Offers are capacity controlled and may be withdrawn by the cruise lines without notice. Fares reflected may vary depending on sailing date and are shown to provide the average level discount which can be obtained by booking through Icruise.com. Rates include port charges; government fees and taxes are additional. Other restrictions may apply.

COMPARING BROCHURE & ACTUAL PRICES

In "Price Comparisons: Discounted Rates vs. Brochure Rates," in chapter 2, I've listed all the ships reviewed in this book, with their brochure rates noted right next to the discounted rates provided for this book by icruise.com. Take a look—seeing how much you'll probably save can be a real eye-opener, and should entirely do away with that nasty sense of sticker shock most people get when they start looking at cruise line brochure prices.

6 The Mainstream Lines

These are the shopping malls of cruise ships—they're big, bustling, and attract a cross-section of mostly American guests. There's lots to eat, lots to buy on board, and lots of other people sharing the experience with you.

Granted, the term "mainstream" covers a lot of ground, and that's the point. These ships are generalists, attempting to offer a little something for almost everyone—all ages, backgrounds, and interests. You'll find people with no couth and lots of tattoos as well as genteel types with graduate degrees and subscriptions to *Smithsonian*. It's a mixed-bag kind of crowd, there's no doubting that.

Within the mainstream category, the more elegant and refined of the lot are commonly referred to as **premium,** a notch up in the sophistication department from others that are described as **mass-market.** Quality-wise, for the most part they're all on equal footing and, overall, are more alike than they are different. That's why I've lumped them all in the same category.

Since the mainstream category is the most popular, it's the one that's seen the most growth, innovation, and investment in recent years, meaning the ships are, as a general rule, remarkably new—and also remarkably *big*. This is the category where the **megaships** reside, those hulking 1,200- to 3,200-passenger floating resorts that offer the widest variety of activities and entertainment. All the lines in this chapter (but particularly the "Big Three"—Carnival, Royal Caribbean, and Princess) have been pumping billions into building newer, bigger, and fancier ships, offering a wide variety of different cabins—inside (no windows), outside (with windows), suites, and cabins with private balconies and without. They'll have both formal and informal dining options, a wide array of entertainment (heavy on the Vegas-style stuff), computer rooms with E-mail access, and more activities than you can possibly squeeze into one day. Choose from a dizzying number of things to do, from line-dancing lessons, to bingo games, game-show-style contests, singles mixers, port talks, galley tours, spa demos (a ploy of course, to get you to sign up for one of the expensive spa treatments), art auctions, and nutty contests by the pool that pit passengers against each other to try and stuff the most Ping-Pong balls down their bathing suits, or swim across the pool with a bagel in their mouths. Overall, the atmosphere is very social.

Frommer's Ratings at a Glance: The Mainstream Lines

1 = poor   **2** = fair   **3** = good   **4** = excellent   **5** = outstanding

Cruise Line	Enjoyment Factor	Dining	Activities	Children's Program	Entertainment	Service	Overall Value
Carnival	5	3	3	4	4	3	5
Celebrity	5	4	4	3	4	5	5
Costa	4	3	4	2	3	3	4
Crown	4	3	3	2	3	4	4
Disney	5	3	3	5	4	3	4
Holland America	5	3	3	2	3	4	5
Norwegian	4	3	4	3	4	3	5
Princess	4	3	3	3	3	4	4
Royal Caribbean	4	3	3	4	3	3	4

NOTE: Cruise lines have been graded on a curve that compares them only with the other Mainstream lines. See "Cruise Line Categories" in chapter 5 for a detailed explanation of my ratings methodology.

DRESS CODES   Dress-down Fridays have come to sea! The age of black tie and pearls is quickly transforming into cargo shorts and sandals. Maybe there will be a backlash, but for now the mainstream lines are looking the other way when passengers stroll into the main dining rooms wearing jeans. In fact, Norwegian Cruise Line has become the first line to completely do away with formal nights, except in one of their five restaurants on one night of the cruise. The rest of the lines in this chapter still officially have two formal nights a week that call for dark suits or tuxedos for men and cocktail dresses, sequined numbers, or fancy pantsuits for women—and there still are *some* people who like to get all gussied up. The other 5 nights are some combination of semi-formal and casual (mostly casual) and call for slacks and polo shirts for men, and dresses, pantsuits, or skirts and tops for women. Guests are asked not to wear shorts and T-shirts in the formal dining rooms, but you'll see that some people do anyway. Daytime is casual.

Carnival Cruise Lines

3655 NW 87th Ave., Miami, FL 33178-2428. ☎ **800/327-9501** or 305/599-2200. Fax 305/406-4740. www.carnival.com.

THE LINE IN A NUTSHELL Moderately priced, jumbo-size resort ships bathed in neon and glitz. If you like Las Vegas, New Orleans, and Time's Square, Carnival's brand of flamboyant fun is awesome.

THE EXPERIENCE Nobody does it better in the party department than Carnival. It's the Coca-Cola of cruising, the line with the most recognized name in the biz, offering a very casual, down-to-earth, middle-American vacation that's enjoyed by millions. The line is incredibly innovative, continually updating its onboard programs, offering, for instance, sushi on the *Elation, Paradise, Imagination, Inspiration,* and *Jubilee,* 24-hour pizza and Caesar salad fleet-wide, and an entirely smoke-free ship, the *Paradise.*

The line's decor, like its clientele to some degree, has mellowed a bit since its riotous beginnings, yet still each ship is an exciting collage of textures, shapes, and images. Where else but on these floating playlands would you find life-size mannequins of Hollywood stars like Marilyn Monroe and Humphrey Bogart, a San Francisco trolley car, or real oyster-shell wallpaper? The outrageousness of the decor is part of the fun, and the point—Carnival ships provide a fantasyland you can't get at home. Call it whatever you want, but don't call it dull.

Pros

- **Fun theme-park ambiance** and fanciful decor is unmatched.
- **Large standard cabins.** At 188 square feet, Carnival's standard inside and outside cabins are the roomiest in the mainstream category.
- **All ages.** The clientele cuts a broad path across many age groups, from 20-something singles and honeymooners to families with young kids to even grandparents.
- **Exciting entertainment.** Ranges from some of the best head-turning Broadway-style musical reviews at sea to the classic dose of adult comedy and raging discos.

Cons

- **You're never alone.** Not in the hot tubs, on shore excursions, in the pool, while sunbathing, at the gym, at the frozen-yogurt machine. . . .
- **Limited port info.** The information you'll get from port lectures and handouts revolves around shopping; there's next to nothing on history and culture.
- **Too casual.** If you like a little elegance, you'll have to grin and bear the white plastic ice/wine buckets in the cabins and the contingent of guests who insist on wearing their jeans and Birkenstocks to the dining room, disco, and bars in the evening.

Compared with the other Mainstream lines, here's how Carnival rates:					
	Poor	Fair	Good	Excellent	Outstanding
Enjoyment Factor					✓
Dining			✓		
Activities			✓		
Children's Program				✓	
Entertainment				✓	
Service			✓		
Overall Value					✓

CARNIVAL: BIG LINE, BIG FUN

Carnival is the Big Kahuna of the cruise world. It's got the most name recognition, the most ships, the most passengers, and those bubbly commercials with the happy music and dancing fish. The assets of its parent company, Carnival Corporation, are enormous and growing: In addition to its own fleet of 15 ships, Carnival holds majority owner- ship of Cunard, 50% interest in Seabourn and Costa Cruises, full ownership of both Windstar Cruises and Holland America Line, and a 30% stake in U.K.-based tour op- erator Airtours. Whew, that's over 30% of the entire North American cruise industry in Carnival's hands.

The origins of the Miami-based company were as precarious as they were acciden- tal. Company patriarch Ted Arison, a somewhat reclusive billionaire who passed away in 1999, had sold an air-freight business in New York in 1966 and intended to retire to his native Israel to enjoy the fruits of his labor. After he negotiated terms for char- tering a ship in the Mediterranean, he compiled a group of paying passengers, only to discover that the ship's owner could no longer guarantee the vessel's availability. Accord- ing to latter-day legend, a deal was hastily struck whereby Arison's passengers would be carried aboard a ship that was owned by Knut Kloster, a prominent Norwegian ship- ping magnate, and was at the time laid up in Europe. Well, the ship was brought to Miami, and the combination of Arison's marketing skill and Kloster's hardware created an all-new entity that, in 1966, became the corporate forerunner of Norwegian Cruise Line.

After a bitter parting of ways with Kloster, Carnival got its start in 1972 when Arison bought the *Empress of Canada,* known for its formal and somewhat stuffy administra- tion, and reconfigured it into Carnival's first ship, the anything-but-stuffy *Mardi Gras.* After a shaky start—the brightly painted ship, carrying hundreds of travel agents, ran aground just off the coast of Miami on its first cruise—Arison managed to pick up the pieces and create a company that, under the guidance of astute and tough-as-nails com- pany president Bob Dickinson and chairman Micky Arison (Ted's son), eventually evolved into the most influential trendsetter in the cruise ship industry. Fifteen ships later, the rest is truly history.

THE FLEET

One frequently asked question is, "Aren't all Carnival ships alike?" Yes and no. As with many other lines, Carnival's 15 ships (soon to be 20) have gotten bigger and more ex- pensive through the years, and can easily be categorized into three groups. There are four older, 1,000- to 1,500-passenger midsize ships—the *Tropicale, Holiday, Jubilee,* and *Celebration*—built in the early- to mid-1980s at a cost of about $100 million to $170 million a piece. They are cramped and less glamorous than the newer ships, but also less boxy and more like "real" ships to ship buffs. The second group, the eight 2,000- passenger Fantasy-class ships—*Fantasy, Ecstasy, Sensation, Fascination, Imagination, Inspiration, Elation,* and *Paradise* (the last a completely smoke-free ship)—were built between 1990 and 1998 and feature wide-open decks, towering atria, large gyms and spas, and flamboyant, fanciful decor, and cost an average of $300 million each. Amaz- ingly, in the nearly 10-year span between when the first Fantasy-class ship was built and the last one, very little of the design changed (the term "cookie-cutter" comes to mind). The third category of Carnival ships are the newest and biggest: The $400-million 2,642-passenger *Destiny,* built in 1996, and its $415-million sisters *Triumph,* built in 1999, and *Victory,* built in 2000, are the largest and most stunning in the fleet, with super-size versions of everything the Fantasy-class ships have and a somewhat more sophisticated air due to the use of more earth tones and less neon. Two more Destiny

Carnival: To Be Rowdy or Not to Be

"We have lost by design a certain segment of the population—one of rowdiness, anything goes, yelling and screaming in the halls. You can't be everything to everybody and we purposefully backed away from that group."

—Carnival President Bob Dickinson, quoted in
industry newsletter "Cruise Week," late 1999

"Oh gaaaahd, I llluuvvv dis place, it's aaaww[hic!]some. I nevah want to leave."

—Anonymous 30-something passenger aboard the *Paradise* in early 1999
(following which he, his wife, and another couple staggered to their cabins
clutching yard-long beer glasses from Cozumel's Carlos 'N Charlies)

sisters, the **Carnival Conquest** and **Carnival Glory,** are slated to debut in 2002 and 2003, respectively.

As if this wasn't enough, three 84,000-ton Spirit-class vessels are in the works. The 2,112-passenger **Carnival Spirit** and **Carnival Pride** are expected to enter service in early and late 2001, respectively, and a third sister, the **Carnival Legend,** is expected in 2002.

More than any other line in its league, Carnival sticks to the Caribbean and Bahamas, deploying 11 of its ships there year-round. The *Holiday* and *Elation* cruise round-trip from Los Angeles on year-round 3-, 4-, and 7-night cruises to the Mexican Riviera, and are not reviewed in this book.

PASSENGER PROFILE

It's a melting pot alright. On Carnival ships you'll see the whole spectrum, from Gucci and Ralph Lauren to Mötley Crüe T-shirts and tattoos. Carnival attracts a little bit of everything—couples, singles, and families; young, old, and lots in between. You'll see a cross section, and this trend will only grow as Carnival continues to mellow from its early wild and crazy days. While it's one of the best lines to choose if you're single, Carnival's ships certainly aren't overrun by singles (in fact, you'll notice that families and couples seem to be in the majority). Carnival estimates about 30% of passengers are under age 35, another 30% are between 35 and 55, and 40% are over age 55. Half of all passengers are first-time cruisers.

Worried about sharing your Carnival cruise with a bunch of rowdy spring breakers? Well, while you'll still find teen groups on board, especially between March and June, at least there are limits. Per guidelines Carnival implemented in early 1997, no one under 21 is allowed to sail unless sharing a cabin with an adult over 25, with exceptions made for married couples and young people whose parents are lodged in a different cabin. This is a far cry from the old days: I sailed in 1996 when more than 500 graduating high-school seniors practically took over—and ruined—a cruise on the *Celebration.*

Regardless of their age, passengers tend to be young at heart, ready to party, and keyed up for nonstop, round-the-clock activities. Many have visited the casinos of Atlantic City and Las Vegas and the high-rise resorts of Cancún and Jamaica, and of course, are well acquainted with the pleasures of soaks in sardine-can-like hot tubs, sunbathing, piña coladas or buckets of beer before lunch, and late-night dancing.

The typical Carnival passenger likes to dress casual, even at dinner, and a line spokesperson told me Carnival has unofficially relaxed its evening dress codes, turning a blind eye to jeans and T-shirts on all but formal nights. Even on formal nights, it's not

---

Carnival's Vacation Guarantee

Introduced in 1996, Carnival's Vacation Guarantee program continues to make one of the boldest claims in the cruise industry and proves just how confident Carnival is about its product: It stipulates that guests who are dissatisfied with their cruise may disembark at their first non-U.S. port of call and, subject to some restrictions, get a refund for the unused portion of their cruise contract and reimbursement for coach-class air transport back to their ship's home port. To qualify, passengers must inform the ship's purser before their first port of call.

---

uncommon for some passengers to run back to their cabins to change out of their dressier duds and put on their shorts or jeans before heading out to the discos and bars.

DINING

It's no surprise Carnival's on top of the industry's ever-evolving dining trends, offering casual alternative dining in lieu of the main restaurant fleet-wide, as well as **24-hour pizza** and **Caesar salad,** soft ice cream, and even a **sushi bar** on the *Elation, Paradise, Imagination, Inspiration,* and *Jubilee.* The *Triumph* has a Chinese-food station in its buffet restaurant and the *Destiny* has an Italian section serving lasagna and manicotti. There are specialty coffee bars and patisseries on the *Elation, Paradise, Destiny, Triumph,* and *Victory,* selling gourmet goodies for about $2 to $5 a pop, and caviar and champagne combos are now available in certain bars fleet-wide. There's a gala, pull-out-all-the-stops **midnight buffet** once a week and a crêpes buffet following the regular midnight buffet feast at least once a week.

Overall, it's no secret that the quality and presentation of Carnival's food has improved over the years and now is on par with Royal Caribbean, Princess, and Holland America—and, dare I say, not so far from Celebrity's. Servers fleet-wide also have new, classier uniforms. The line recently enhanced its dining-room menus, adding more interesting dishes like honey-basted fillet of salmon, roasted quail, and West Indian pumpkin soup to the dinner menus, in addition to such old, all-American favorites as surf-and-turf and prime rib, plus pasta dishes, grilled salmon and broiled halibut, and Thanksgiving-style turkey served with all the trimmings. At lunch, you'll now find appetizers like sushi and fried calamari, and entrees like focaccia filled with arugula, roasted peppers, and fresh mozzarella, and a linguini dish in a light tomato sauce with julienne of tomatoes and hickory smoked ham. There are also healthier **"Nautica Spa" options** on each menu as well as **vegetarian choices.**

Except for the *Tropicale,* all Carnival ships have two main dining rooms, each with two seatings for each of the day's three meals, with tables seating 4 to 12. Dining is a bustling, social affair, and hundreds of passengers line up early outside the doors, eager to get in (that said, the main dining rooms are often not full because of all the other dining choices). Despite the hectic pace and ambiance, **service** is consistently efficient and friendly, culminating at dessert time, when the lights are dimmed and the flashing neon is turned on to illuminate the waiters doing their nearly nightly song-and-dance routines.

For you wine drinkers, don't expect a sommelier—your waiter handles the wine as well as the water.

In keeping with the popular **alternative dining** trend that has swept the industry, guests aboard all Carnival ships can opt to have any meal in the **buffet-style Lido restaurants** (at no extra charge). For an unstructured and casual dinner, walk in any time between 6 and 9:30pm for tasty entrees like chicken, pasta, steaks, prime rib, swordfish steak, and stir fries. At lunch, buffets in the Lido feature the usual suspects—salads, meats, cheeses, pastas, grilled burgers, and chicken fillets, and several hot choices such as fish-and-chips, roast turkey and mashed potatoes, or stir fry. The buffets also feature specialty stations at lunch, serving up things like pasta or Chinese food or a Cajun fish dish. At times the buffet line gets backed up as passengers wait for bins to be restocked and servers scramble to fill them.

The most visible array of alternative options is aboard Carnival's mammoth *Destiny, Triumph,* and *Victory,* which offer the attractive and dramatic two-level Galaxy and Universe dining rooms, with ocean views from both the main floor and the mezzanine level. Additionally, the casual buffet restaurants on each include a pair of **specialty food stations:** Italian on the *Destiny,* Chinese on *Triumph* and *Victory.*

Pizza (the best at sea), Caesar salad, and garlic bread are available 24 hours a day, and the **self-serve soft ice cream** and frozen-yogurt machines operate throughout the day.

All ships offer **24-hour room service** from a standardized menu of ho-hum staples, and kids can select from **children's menus.**

ACTIVITIES

Never a dull moment—you can run from one activity to the next all day long if you want to. Carnival doesn't skimp in the keeping-busy department. By day, the main pool decks are the heart of the action, and between the blaring band and microphone-wielding social hosts whipping up interest in a pillow-fighting competition or belly-flop contest, you'll barely be able to hear yourself think. Lest things get too out of hand, uniformed security guards watch over the pool deck and bars to make sure things stay safe. On the megas, it's a little quieter up on the second tier of the Sun Deck, and each ship has a quieter pool and sunbathing area at the stern, sans loudspeakers.

Slot machines begin clanging at 8am in the **casinos** when the ships are at sea, and before lunch even starts waiters and waitresses in bright pink and blue uniforms are tempting passengers with trays of fruity **theme cocktails.** There are line-dancing and ballroom classes, trivia contests, facial and hairdo demonstrations, singles and newlywed parties, game shows, shuffleboard, bingo, art auctions, and movies. You can spend some time in the roomy **gyms** on the Fantasy-, Destiny- and Spirit-class ships (gyms are tiny afterthoughts on the four oldest ships) or treat yourself to one of dozens of relaxing treatments in the Steiner-managed **spas.**

Not surprisingly, with this pace, you won't find any focus on quiet times, except in the subdued, handsome-looking **libraries** on each ship. And don't expect enrichment lectures on art or history or any other cerebral topic; Carnival's breed of activities are of the hearty-fun and hands-on variety. On the other hand, the line just introduced its first Internet cafe on the *Triumph,* and promises to have the other ships wired by the end of 2001.

Incidentally, Carnival vessels have based part of their success on recognizing what adults want. Each ship posts a small but obvious sign at the bottom of stairs leading to one of the sun-flooded upper decks (usually near the stack) that reads, ADULTS ONLY, TOP-OPTIONAL SUNBATHING. I've rarely seen many takers, though—the area is usually deserted.

Cruise Trivia

On a typical weeklong Carnival cruise, a heck of a lot of food and drink are consumed. Here's a run-down of the gluttony: 8,000 pizzas, 2,000 steaks, 35,000 shrimp, 5,500 hamburgers, 41,660 eggs, 315 pounds of coffee, 1,800 bagels, 10,000 tomatoes, 10,080 bananas, 1,000 fresh pineapples, 18,200 soft drinks, 2,920 bottles of wine, 24,450 bottles of beer, and 600 bottles of rum. Dang!

CHILDREN'S PROGRAM

Carnival is right up there with the best ships for families—the line estimates that when final counts are in, some 250,000 kids will have sailed on board its ships in 2000. A few hundred children per cruise is pretty normal and there can be as many as 700 to 800 on Christmas and New Year's cruises. On Carnival's post-1990 ships, the kids' facilities are fairly extensive, with the *Victory, Triumph, Destiny, Elation,* and *Paradise* offering the biggest and brightest **playrooms** in the fleet, stocked with computer stations offering the latest educational and entertainment software, a climbing maze, 16-monitor video wall showing movies and cartoons, arts and crafts, and oodles of toys and games. The *Elation, Paradise, Triumph,* and *Ecstasy* even have Macintosh iMac **computers.**

The newly revamped **Camp Carnival program** offers supervised kids' activities all day long from 9am till 10pm for ages 2 through 15 in four different age groups: toddlers 2 to 5, juniors 6 to 8, intermediates 9 to 12, and teens 13 to 15. A new turndown service for kids includes complimentary chocolate-chip cookies on their pillows at bedtime on the first and last night of their cruise. Nine to 12 **counselors** organize the fun and games, which include face painting, computer games, puzzles, fun with Play-Doh, picture bingo, making pirate hats, and pizza parties for toddlers. For juniors, there's Nintendo, computer games, ice-cream parties, story time and library visits, T-shirt coloring, and swimming; for intermediates, there are scavenger hunts, trivia and bingo, Ping-Pong, video-game competitions, arts and crafts, computer games, dance classes, and talent shows. There are even "homework help" sessions available for kids who need to keep up while on vacation. Separate teen discos have been phased out (seems they just weren't popular), but interested teens can join in on karaoke parties, computer games, scavenger hunts, talent shows, card and trivia games, Ping-Pong, disco parties (in the adult disco before it opens at 10pm), and, of course, they can also hang out in the video arcades—the newest ships have **virtual-reality games.** The *Ecstasy* has a neat contraption called the Sticker Star Machine: Like a passport-photo booth, you climb in, insert a few dollars, get your picture taken, choose a border, and *voilà!* A sheet of fun stickers with your face on them is spit out.

As if that's not enough, the entire fleet has a **children's wading pool,** and for bigger kids there's that great signature snaking slide at the main pool.

Mom and dad can really have the evening to themselves on the week's two formal nights, when the counselors supervise **kid's mealtime** in the Lido restaurant between about 6 and 7pm in a special section reserved for the kids. A newly enhanced children's menu, which is printed on the back of a fun coloring/activity book (crayons are provided), features the classic favorites—hot dogs, hamburgers, French fries, chicken nuggets, pepperoni pizza, peanut butter and jelly sandwiches, banana splits, Jell-O, and a daily special. Then, like every night, more supervised children's activities kick in between 7 and 10pm. After that, although Carnival does not offer private baby-sitting, it has **group, slumber-party-style baby-sitting** available from 10pm to 3am each evening in the playroom, and also now offers group baby-sitting between 8am and noon on port days for kids under age 2, for $5 per hour for the first child, $3 per hour for each additional child.

For kids under age 21, there are convenient Fountain Fun Cards that can be purchased for **unlimited soft-drink purchases** (they're $8 for a 3-night cruise to $18 for 7-day voyages).

Cribs are available with prior notice.

ENTERTAINMENT

Even aboard its smaller, older ships, Carnival consistently offers the most lavish entertainment extravaganzas afloat. Aboard the newer megaships, the cruise line has spent

---

Deals for Seniors & a Handy Hotline for Everyone

AARP Discounts: AARP members receive a $200 discount per stateroom on cruises of 10 days or more, $100 on 7-day cruises, and $50 on 3- and 4-day Bahamas cruises.
24-Hour Hotline: For help with unexpected snafus or emergencies, Carnival's got a toll-free travel hotline for guests. Call ☎ 877/885-4856 toll free, or 305/406-4779.

---

millions on stage sets, choreography, and acoustical equipment that leave many other floating theaters in the dust. The show lounges on the *Destiny, Triumph,* and *Victory* are spectacular three-deck extravaganzas and the casinos are so large you'll think you landed in Vegas.

Carnival megaships each carry about 8 to 12 flamboyantly costumed dancers, complete with feathers, sequins, and towering headdresses, for twice-weekly **Vegas-style musicals.** One or two live soloists carry the musical part of the show, while the dancers lip-synch the chorus (sometimes so well that most people don't realize the dancers aren't actually singing). A **12- to 16-piece orchestra** of traditional and digital instruments deftly accompanies the acts each night. While they may not match the most sophisticated productions on Broadway, Carnival shows are pretty sensational.

You'll also find comedians, jugglers, acrobatics, rock-and-roll bands, country-western bands, classical string trios, pianists, and Dorsey- or Glenn Miller–style big bands, all performing, if not simultaneously, at least during the same cruise, and sometimes on the same night. Aboard *Carnival Destiny,* there are multiple **karaoke stations**—one for every table in the Apollo Bar—and teenage dance contests.

Besides the main show lounge, most entertainment happens somewhere along the indoor Main Street–like promenade. Called the "something-or-other Boulevard" or "something-or-other Way," it stretches along one entire side of each ship and is lined with just about the ships' entire repertoire of nightclubs, bars, lounges, patisseries, and the disco and casino. One bar on all the Fantasy- and Destiny-class ships welcome cigar smoking, and fleet-wide, cigars are sold at the pool bar and during midnight buffets.

By day, entertainment includes a Caribbean-style **calypso** or **steel-drum band** performing Bob Marley and other pop songs on a deck poolside, and a pianist or sting trio playing in the atria of the line's newest ships.

SERVICE

It's a fact of life aboard megaliners like Carnival's that service is simply not as attentive as aboard smaller vessels. Service is professional, but can sometimes be too brisk—it's clear your dining-room waiter and cabin steward have a lot of work ahead of them and have little time for much chitchat (though they do all look more sophisticated in the brand-new uniforms the line's been introducing, starting with the *Triumph, Destiny,* and *Paradise*)—and lines can get long at the breakfast and lunch buffets and, at certain times, at the pizza counter. There always seem to be plenty of drink waiters and waitresses roaming the pool decks, though, looking to score some drink orders.

All in all, a Carnival ship is a well-oiled machine, and you'll certainly get what you need—but not much more. When you board the ship, for instance, you're welcomed by a polite and well-meaning staff at the gangway, given a diagram of the ship's layout, and then pointed in the right direction to find your cabin on your own, carry-on luggage in tow. It'll take you a minute to figure where you're going, and longer than that to get to your cabin, due to crowding at the elevators.

There is a **laundry service** on board each ship (for washing and pressing only) that charges by the piece, as well as a handful of **self-service laundry rooms** with irons and coin-operated washing machines and dryers. Dry cleaning is not available.

Carnival Fleet Itineraries

Ship	Home Ports & Season	Itinerary	Other Itineraries
Carnival Destiny	Round-trip from San Juan alternate weekly, year-round.	**7-night E. & S. Carib:** St. Thomas, St. Lucia, Curaçao, and Aruba. **7-night E. & S. Carib:** St. Thomas, Antigua, Guadeloupe, and Aruba.	None
Carnival Triumph	Round-trip from Miami, itineraries alternate weekly, year-round.	**7-night E. Carib:** San Juan, St. Croix, and St. Thomas. **7-night W. Carib:** Playa del Carmen/Cozumel, Grand Cayman, and Ocho Rios (Jamaica).	None
Carnival Victory	Round-trip from Miami, itineraries alternate weekly, year-round.	**7-night E. Carib:** San Juan, St. Croix, and St. Thomas. **7-night W. Carib:** Playa del Carmen/Cozumel, Grand Cayman, and Ocho Rios (Jamaica).	None
Celebration	Round-trip from Galveston, alternating year-round.	**4-night W. Carib:** Playa del Carmen/ Cozumel. **5-night W. Carib:** Playa del Carmen/Cozumel, Calica/Cancún.	None
Ecstasy	Round-trip from Miami, both itineraries offerred weekly, year-round.	**3-night:** Nassau. **4-night:** Key West, and Playa del Carmen/Cozumel.	None
Fantasy	Round-trip from Port Canaveral, both itineraries offered weekly, year-round.	**3-night:** Nassau. **4-night:** Nassau and Freeport.	None
Fascination	Round-trip from San Juan, year-round.	**7-night E. Carib:** St. Thomas, Sint Maarten, Dominica, Barbados, and Martinique.	None
Imagination	Round-trip from Miami, itineraries alternate weekly, year-round.	**4-night W. Carib:** Key West, and Cozumel/Playa del Carmen. **5-night W. Carib:** Grand Cayman, Calica/Cancún or Grand Cayman, and Ocho Rios (Jamaica).	None
Inspiration	Round-trip from New Orleans, year-round.	**7-night W. Carib:** Montego Bay (Jamaica), Grand Cayman, Playa del Carmen/Cozumel.	None
Jubilee	Round-trip from Tampa, itineraries alternate year-round.	**4-night W. Carib:** Key West and Playa del Carmen/Cozumel. **5-night W. Carib:** Grand Cayman and Playa del Carmen/ Cozumel.	Hawaii
Paradise	Round-trip from Miami, itineraries alternate weekly, year-round.	**7-night E. Carib:** San Juan, Nassau, and St. Thomas. **7-night W. Carib:** Cozumel/ Playa del Carmen, Grand Cayman, and Ocho Rios (Jamaica).	None
Sensation	Round-trip from Tampa, year-round.	**7-night E. Carib:** Grand Cayman, Playa del Carmen/Cozumel, and New Orleans.	None
Tropicale	Panama Canal itinerary round-trip from Fort Lauderdale, **Nov 2000–Jan 2001;** 7-night W. Carib round-trip from Fort Lauderdale, beginning Feb 2001.	**10-night Panama Canal:** Aruba; Cartegena (Colombia), partial transit of Panama Canal, Limon (Costa Rica), and Key West. **7-night W. Carib:** Belize, Playa del Carmen/Cozumel, Progreso/Merida, and Key West.	None

Celebration • Jubilee

The Verdict

Fun ships, yes, but these older Carnival ships seem outdated and frumpy compared to their slick, glamorous Fantasy-class sisters.

Jubilee *(photo: Carnival Cruise Lines)*

Specifications

Size (in tons)	47,262	Crew	670 (International)
Number of Cabins	743	Passenger/Crew Ratio	2.2 to 1
Number of Outside Cabins	453	Year Built	
Cabins with Verandas	10	*Celebration*	1987
Number of Passengers	1,486	*Jubilee*	1986
Officers	Italian/ Internat'l	Last Major Refurbishment	1999

Frommer's Ratings (Scale of 1–5)

Cabin Comfort & Amenities	4	Pool, Fitness & Spa Facilities	2
Ship Cleanliness & Maintenance	4	Children's Facilities	3
Public Comfort/Space	3	Itinerary	4
Decor	4	Worth the Money	4

While this pair of mid-1980s sisters can't compare with their new post-1990 sisters in the style and amenities departments, they still successfully offer that wild and crazy brand of Carnival fun. If you like smaller ships (these are half the size of the Destiny-class ships, but they're still not *small* in any normal sense) and don't mind fewer high-tech bells and whistles, you'll find these ships more intimate and easier to explore than a megaship.

The decors of these medium-size twins encompass all the colors of the rainbow, with healthy doses of brass and mirrors, à la the 1980s disco scene. There is no atrium and the Pool Decks can get crowded and cramped at high noon.

Recent refurbishments on the *Jubilee* included replacing hot tubs with new models; installing new carpeting, tile, counters, and equipment for the Funnel Bar & Grill Lido restaurant; and adding a new video-game arcade and a photo gallery. The cramped Lido buffet restaurants on both have been recently remodeled, creating a more open area; teak floor was replaced with tile and carpeting, and a new pizzeria was also installed.

CABINS   Like the standard cabins in the entire Carnival fleet, they're big. Beige with red and black accents, the decor is nothing to write home about, but the identical rooms (save the suites, of course) with their blond wood tones and accoutrements are clean and uncluttered. Like the rest of the fleet, beds can be configured as twins or doubles, and each cabin has piped-in stereo music as well as a wall-mounted TV. The medium-size bathrooms have showers.

The 10 suites on the Veranda Deck of each ship are as large and comfortable as those offered aboard vessels charging a lot more. Each has a whirlpool tub and shower, an L-shaped sofa that converts into a foldaway bed, a safe, minibar, walk-in closet, and sliding glass doors leading to a private balcony.

About a dozen cabins are wheelchair accessible.

Cabins & Rates

Cabins	Per diems from	Bathtub	Fridge	Hair Dryer	Sitting Area	TV
Inside	$94	no	no	no	no	yes
Outside	$111	no	no	no	no	yes
Suite	$328	yes	yes	no	yes	yes

PUBLIC AREAS   You may need to keep on your sunglasses even when you're inside the ship: Public areas explode with color in that original outrageous Carnival way. We're talking lots of red, black, fuchsia, chrome, brass, glass, and neon. There's a bar designed like the inside of a trolley car and the Red Hot Piano Bar is just that—all red. In all, there are seven bars, six entertainment lounges, a casino, disco, library, card room, and video arcade. There's also a children's playroom, beauty salon, boutiques, and a small infirmary with a doctor and nurse on call. Elevators interconnect all eight decks.

POOL, FITNESS & SPA FACILITIES   When the *Celebration* and *Jubilee* were built in the mid-1980s, fitness wasn't the priority it is today, and—as aboard most ships of their age—it shows. But, in late 1999, the tiny gyms were remodeled and expanded to about twice their original size—a welcome improvement. The spas, while small, have recently been upgraded and new massage and locker rooms were added. Each also has a sauna each for men and women, and both ships have small hair salons.

There are three pools, including a small wading pool for children, and two hot tubs.

Carnival Destiny • Triumph • Victory

The Verdict

The biggest and most stunning in the fleet, these three behemoths capture the classic Carnival whimsy with mind-boggling design features, yet have a somewhat mellower color scheme than the line's other, older ships.

Carnival Destiny *(photo: Carnival Cruise Lines)*

Specifications

Size (in tons)		Number of Passengers	
Destiny	101,353	*Destiny*	2,642
Triumph	102,000	*Triumph*	2,758
Victory	102,000	*Victory*	2,758
Number of Cabins		Officers	Italian/Internat'l
Destiny	1,321	Crew	1,000 (Internat'l)
Triumph	1,379	Passenger/Crew Ratio	2.6 to 1
Victory	1,379	Year Built	
Number of Outside Cabins		*Destiny*	1996
Destiny	806	*Triumph*	1999
Triumph	853	*Victory*	2000
Victory	853	Last Major Refurbishment	N/A
Cabins with Verandas			
Destiny	480		
Triumph	508		
Victory	508		

Frommer's Ratings (Scale of 1–5)

Cabin Comfort & Amenities	5	Pool, Fitness & Spa Facilities	5
Ship Cleanliness & Maintenance	4	Children's Facilities	5
Public Comfort/Space	4	Itinerary	4
Decor	5	Worth the Money	5

Late in 1996, Carnival inaugurated the 101,000-ton *Destiny,* then rolled out its 102,000-ton sisters *Triumph* (in July 1999) and *Victory* (in Aug 2000). All three are nearly identical, though the *Triumph* and *Victory* are a tad larger than the *Destiny* (having an additional deck at top) and are reconfigured in a few minor ways. Taller than the Statue of Liberty, the 13-deck-high ships cost a staggering $400 million to $440 million apiece to construct and carry 2,642 passengers based on double occupancy and 3,400 with every berth filled. The *Destiny* was the first cruise ship ever built to exceed 100,000 tons, and its sheer size and spaciousness inspired the cruise industry to build more in this league: Since its debut, Princess launched the 109,000-ton *Grand Princess,* and Royal Caribbean, the massive 142,000-ton *Voyager of the Seas.*

Carnival plans on launching two more *Destiny* sisters, the *Carnival Conquest* and *Glory,* for a total of five. They're scheduled to enter the market in the fall of 2002 and summer of 2003, respectively.

CABINS   It would make sense that Carnival's biggest ships have the biggest cabins. Including the verandas, standard outside cabins are 220 square feet (and some are 260 sq. ft.) compared to the veranda-less Fantasy-class standard cabins, which are already big enough at about 190 square feet. Inside cabins are a bit smaller than the outside ones, measuring 185 square feet (still quite large). More than 60% of the cabins on these ships offer ocean views, and some 60% of them have private balconies and sitting areas. Of the *Destiny*'s 806 outside cabins (and the *Triumph* and *Victory*'s 853), there are some 480 private verandas, and 508 on the *Triumph* and *Victory!* That's compared to a paltry 54 private verandas on the 618 outside cabins on the Fantasy-class ships.

Unlike the rest of Carnival's fleet, the major entertainment and recreation decks on these ships are sandwiched between accommodation decks. This design centrally locates the indoor entertainment and recreation facilities for all guests (a good thing, since these ships are so dang huge) and also allows for unobstructed views from dozens of balconied staterooms and suites.

There are two categories of suites: veranda suites measuring a mammoth 340 square feet and penthouse suites where you can live like the Sultan of Brunei with 430 square feet, which is roomy indeed. Both are located on Deck 7, smack dab in the middle of the ship. Specially designed family staterooms, at a modest 230 square feet (which is comfortable, but not roomy), offer connecting cabins located convenient to children's facilities. In lieu of a private veranda, these family-friendly staterooms feature floor-to-ceiling windows for ocean views. All standard cabins have a TV, safe, hair dryer, desk, dresser, one chair and a stool, and a bath with shower. The *Destiny, Triumph,* and *Victory* are the only ships in the fleet to have hair dryers in the cabins.

A total of 25 cabins on the *Destiny* and 27 on the *Triumph* and *Victory* (all on the Upper, Empress, Veranda, Lido, and Panorama decks) are wheelchair accessible.

Cabins & Rates

Cabins	Per diems from	Bathtub	Fridge	Hair Dryer	Sitting Area	TV
Inside	$87	no	no	yes	no	yes
Outside	$112	no	no	yes	yes	yes
Suite	$244	yes	yes	yes	yes	yes

How Many Passengers?!?!

With most of its cabins' third and fourth berths occupied, the *Carnival Triumph* carried a record number of passengers on an August 1999 cruise: a whopping 3,413 warm bodies (that's about a third more passengers than the ship's double-occupancy capacity of 2,600).

PUBLIC AREAS Carnival interior designer Joe Farcus never had so much public space to play with, and he took full advantage. The ships are dominated by staggering nine-deck atria with casual bars on the ground level, and the three-deck-high showrooms are a sight—the *Destiny*'s was the first of this magnitude on any cruise ship. The ships' mondo casinos span some 9,000 square feet and feature 324 slot machines and 23 table games. A photography studio enables passengers to make appointments for portrait taking; photographs can be digitally enhanced with borders and a variety of photo-related souvenirs are sold. It's ideal for honeymooners.

Many of the ships' 12-plus bars and entertainment venues are located along the bustling main drag of the Promenade Deck. Here you'll find the dazzling, dimly lit, two-level discos, of the likes you'd find in happening metropolises like New York City. The Sports Bar on each ship boasts multiple TV monitors projecting different sporting events simultaneously. Each ship has a wine bar, a cafe in the middle of the action to grab a cappuccino and watch the throngs traipse by, and a piano bar, which aboard the *Triumph* is called the Big Easy and sports thousands of real oyster shells covering its walls (collected from the famous Acme Oyster House in New Orleans). One deck below is an elegant lounge for a drink or a cigar; on the *Triumph* it's called the Oxford Bar and it's a clubby place with dark wood paneling, leather furniture, and gilded picture frames (too bad you can hear the disco music pounding above late at night).

There are a pair of two-story dining rooms as well as a two-story casual buffet restaurant. The ships all have several shopping boutiques, a spacious beauty salon, library, and card room, plus several self-service, coin-operated laundry rooms.

Bottom line: You'll get a workout making your way from room to room on these mammoth ships.

POOL, FITNESS & SPA FACILITIES Facilities are the most generous among the Carnival vessels, with four pools (including a kids' wading pool), seven whirlpools, and a 214-foot, two-deck-high corkscrew-shaped water slide.

The tiered, arena-style decks of the sprawling midships Lido pool area provide optimal viewing of the band and stage, pool games, and all the hubbub that happens in this busy part of the ship. Along with two whirlpools, the *Destiny* has swim-up bars at two of its main pools; the *Triumph* and *Victory* eliminated the swim-up bars in exchange for more deck space, larger pools, and the addition of a wading area a few inches deep surrounding the two pools. The aft pool area on both ships features two whirlpools and a retractable glass roof that covers it all, enabling deck activities and entertainment to continue even in rainy weather. On the *Triumph and Victory,* the big stage adjacent to the main Continent pool is even bigger than the one on *Carnival Destiny,* and has been reconfigured to allow more space for guests at deck parties, and to make the pool deck more open and visually appealing. Another modification is the placement of a small performance stage aft on Lido Deck near the New World pool.

The ships' huge gyms are second in size only to Royal Caribbean's *Voyager of the Seas* (and frankly, Carnival's gyms are much roomier and feel bigger). The two-deck-high, 15,000-square-foot Nautica Spa health-and-fitness center on the *Destiny* and *Triumph* feature more than 30 state-of-the-art exercise machines, including virtual-reality stationary bikes. There's a juice-bar-cum-aerobics room, men's and women's saunas and steam rooms, and a pair of hot tubs. As on all Carnival ships, the spas and locker rooms, while offering all the latest treatments at the latest high prices, are surprisingly drab, and the only place to wait for your masseuse is on a cold, high-school-locker-room bench, wrapped in a towel (no robes are provided).

The well-stocked 1,300-square-foot indoor/outdoor play center has its own pool and is nicely sequestered on a top deck, out of the fray of the main pool deck areas. The ships also have virtual-reality video arcades that promise hours of fun.

Ecstasy • Fantasy • Fascination • Imagination • Inspiration • Paradise • Sensation

Fantasy *(photo: Carnival Cruise Lines)*

The Verdict

These time-tested favorites are the line's original megas, and their whimsical decor and endless entertainment and activity options spell excitement from the get-go.

Specifications

Size (in tons)	70,367	Year Built	
Number of Cabins	1,020	*Ecstasy*	1991
Number of Outside Cabins	618	*Fantasy*	1990
Cabins with Verandas	26	*Fascination*	1994
Number of Passengers	2,040	*Imagination*	1995
Officers	Italian/Internat'l	*Inspiration*	1996
Crew	920 (Internat'l)	*Paradise*	1998
Passenger/Crew Ratio	2.2 to 1	*Sensation*	1993
		Last Major Refurbishment	
		Ecstasy	1999
		All Others	N/A

Frommer's Ratings (Scale of 1–5)

Cabin Comfort & Amenities	5	Pool, Fitness & Spa Facilities	5
Ship Cleanliness & Maintenance	4	Children's Facilities	4
Public Comfort/Space	4	Itinerary	5
Decor	5	Worth the Money	5

These Fun Ships and their grin-inducing risqué names offer a successful combination of hands-on fun and a glamorous, fantasyland decor, with acres of teak decking plus all the diversions, distractions, and entertainment options for which Carnival is famous.

Each of the eight ships was built at a cost of between $225 million and $300 million at the Kvaerner Masa shipyard in Helsinki, Finland, between 1990 and 1998. Each is identical in size, profile, and onboard amenities (with a few exceptions), but each ship's unique personalities shine through the combination of Carnival-style colors, decors, wall hangings, artwork, and themes.

From the first ship of the series, the *Fantasy,* to the last, the *Paradise,* the ships evolved to a mellower state, with muted shades of copper, teal, gold, and deep red replacing the earlier shocking primary reds, yellows, and blues. Following the lead of the *Destiny,* the

You Paid What?

47,000 hotels, 700 airlines, 50 rental car companies. And a few million ways to save money.

Travelocity.com
A Sabre Company

Go Virtually Anywhere.

AOL Keyword: Travel

Travelocity® and Travelocity.com are trademarks of Travelocity.com LP and Sabre® is a trademark of an affiliate of Sabre Inc.
© 2000 Travelocity.com LP. All rights reserved.

Will you have enough stories to tell your grandchildren?

©2000 Yahoo! Inc.

Yahoo! Travel

Do You
YAHOO!
?

Elation and *Paradise* did away with hulking atria statues and instead offer a casual lobby bar in their place, making the area a more useful meeting place and hub.

The decor of the *Fantasy,* with a geometric, urban-metropolis kind of feel, is a tiny bit ragged and tired. Nevertheless, it has all the electric colors you expect from the line, and a full 15 miles of neon tubes to boot, so there's no mistaking that it's a Carnival cruise you're on.

The *Ecstasy* features a city-scene motif, with one lounge built around an antique Rolls Royce and another around neon-bedecked skyscraper sculptures. Recent refurbishments to this ship include a Formalities shop offering tuxedo rentals, fresh flowers, and photography-related things like frames and albums; a patisserie; new beverage stations on the Lido Deck; and a new video-game room.

The *Sensation* avoids an obvious razzle-dazzle in favor of artwork enhanced with ultraviolet lighting, sound, and color, while the *Fascination* borrows heavily from Broadway and Hollywood movie-star legends and features head-turning life-size mannequins of famous legends like John Wayne and Marilyn Monroe.

Aboard the *Imagination,* miles of fiber-optic cable make the mythical and classical artwork glow in ways the Greek, Roman, and Assyrian designers of the originals never would have imagined. Medusas and winged Mercuries adorn the public areas, and the eclectic library contains copies of the columns Bernini added to St. Peter's Basilica in Rome. Although the ship has miles and miles of neon, it's more muted here, the feeling more elegant.

For its inspiration, *Inspiration* turns to styles exemplified by such artists and artisans as Toulouse-Lautrec, Fabergé, Frank Lloyd Wright, and Tiffany. The most striking part of this design is in the Brasserie Café, with its twisting tubes of lavender-colored aluminum illuminated by back-lit stained glass and neon. Designer Joe Farcus saw these tubes as a fanciful interpretation of the flowers and vines adorning Métro stops in Paris. Another Carnival-like touch is the guitar-shaped rock-and-roll dance club.

The *Paradise* is just that if you're a nonsmoker. Launched in 1998, the ship, with design motifs in some rooms based vaguely on the great Atlantic ocean liners, is one of the industry's only two completely smoke-free ships (Renaissance Cruises' R-ships are the others). There is no lighting up anywhere aboard for passengers or crew, not even on the open decks, and Carnival isn't shy about pointing out the penalties dished out if you get caught trying: In addition to a $250 fine, all law-breakers will be asked to disembark the ship at the next port of call and fly home at their own expense. To date, several dozen passengers and a handful of crew members have been discharged. You'll notice that apparently smoking and drinking really do go hand in hand, though, because the bars and discos on the *Paradise* are noticeably less bustling and some are deserted way earlier in the evening than they would ever be on other Carnival ships. As quoted in "Cruise Week," an industry newsletter, Carnival president Bob Dickinson explained why he thought the nonsmoking *Paradise* brings in less bar and casino revenues: "The better the education, the lower the alcohol consumption, the lower the gambling. That's just the way it is—smarter people smoke less, smarter people gamble less." Hmmm, looks like the line will think twice before ever launching a second smoke-free ship for those smarty-pantses!

Anyway, despite a perceived preponderance of brainy teetotalers, the *Paradise* is actually still fun, fun, fun, even if it is a tad mellower than the rest of the fleet. It boasts some novelties like a complimentary sushi bar open late afternoons.

CABINS   As with the entire fleet, standard cabins on the Fantasy-class ships are roomy at 190 square feet and are neat, tidy, and minimalist in design, with stained-oak trim accents and conventional, monochromatic colors like salmon red—subdued compared to the flamboyance of the public areas. The cabins are not big on personality but are functional and well laid out.

Accommodations range from lower-deck 185-square-foot inside cabins with upper and lower berths to large suites with verandas, king-size beds, sitting areas, and balconies. There are 26 demi-suites and 28 suites, all 54 with private verandas. The 28 suites each have a whirlpool tub and shower, an L-shaped sofa that converts into a foldaway bed, a whirlpool bath, a safe, minibar, walk-in closet, and sliding glass doors leading to a private balcony, and is positioned midway between stern and bow, on a middle deck subject to the least tossing and rocking during rough weather.

All cabins, even the least expensive inside ones, have enough storage space to accommodate a reasonably diverse wardrobe and feature safes, TVs, desk and stool, chair, reading lights for each bed, and bathrooms with roomy showers and generous-size mirrored cabinets to store your toiletries.

There are about 20 cabins on each ship for passengers with disabilities.

Cabins & Rates

Cabins	Per diems from	Bathtub	Fridge	Hair Dryer	Sitting Area	TV
Inside	$90	no	no	no	no	yes
Outside	$113	no	no	no	no	yes
Suite	$213	yes	yes	no	yes	yes

PUBLIC AREAS Each ship boasts the same configuration of decks, public lounges, and entertainment venues, including a six-story atrium flanked by glass-sided elevators, plus two big-windowed dining rooms, casinos, at least eight bars, and several whirlpool tubs scattered about the ships, but good luck squeezing in—they're usually packed solid. The cluster of shops on each ship is surprisingly cramped and won't be winning any design awards.

Each has several self-service, coin-operated laundry rooms.

POOL, FITNESS & SPA FACILITIES Although nothing special in the decor department, the 12,000-square-foot Nautica Spas have everything you'll need to stay fit and healthy. Each has a roomy, separate, mirrored aerobics room and a large windowed Pepto Bismol–colored gym with (last time I counted) seven treadmills, five stationary bikes, two rowing machines, two step machines, and dozens of free weights. Each has men's and women's locker rooms and massages rooms (both areas surprisingly drab and institutional feeling), as well as a sauna and steam room, whirlpools, and three swimming pools. The Sun Deck of each ship offers an unobstructed one-eigth-mile jogging track covered with a rubberized surface.

Tropicale

The Verdict

Intimate and classic but also old, small, and obviously outmoded, the *Tropicale* struggles hard to compete with the array of amenities and facilities aboard the line's larger, modern ships.

Tropicale *(photo: Carnival Cruise Line)*

Specifications

Size (in tons)	36,674	Officers	Italian
Number of Cabins	511	Crew	550 (International)
Number of Outside Cabins	324	Passenger/Crew Ratio	1.9 to 1
Cabins with Verandas	12	Year Built	1982
Number of Passengers	1,022	Last Major Refurbishment	1998

Frommer's Ratings (Scale of 1–5)

Cabin Comfort & Amenities	4	Pool, Fitness & Spa Facilities	2
Ship Cleanliness & Maintenance	4	Children's Facilities	3
Public Comfort/Space	4	Itinerary	5
Decor	4	Worth the Money	4

In the fast-paced world of the cruise industry, a vessel that debuts as a star can quickly become yesterday's has-been—but there's always some nostalgic and loyal folks to keep carrying its banner. Such is the case with *Tropicale,* the oldest ship in Carnival's fleet and the one with the best-established pedigree. The first all-new ship ever commissioned by the then-fledgling Carnival Cruise Lines, its construction began in 1978, and delivery to a then-skeptical marketplace occurred 3¹/₂ years later.

In many ways, its debut was a savvy reflection of the waves of things to come: In the year of its construction, its weight of nearly 37,000 tons (bulky and ponderous by cruise ship standards of the day) was considered larger than market conditions would easily bear. Soon enough, though, *Tropicale* was breaking sales records throughout the cruise ship industry, and in the 1980s was the venue for the kind of hard-partying cruises that eventually evolved into the mega-million-dollar Carnival "Fun Ship" image.

In 1998, the *Tropicale* underwent some substantial refurbishments, including putting in a new granite floor, seating, and lighting and sound system in Dance Club disco; new chairs and carpeting in the dining room; and a new video arcade. Still, the ship has long since been surpassed in size, glamour, and stylishness by Carnival's other vessels, and observers get the definite feeling that *Tropicale's* days with the line are numbered. Until it's finally auctioned off somewhere, though, expect a serviceable and amiable if somewhat battered ship that's seen more hard-party action than a houseful of graduating frat boys. Also look for the embryonic beginnings of design features that were later expanded and improved upon during Carnival's adolescent years, including a T-shaped (or whale-tailed) smokestack where fumes are vented high overhead and then off to either side.

Preview: *Carnival Spirit & Pride*

Bigger than Carnival's eight Fantasy-class ships and smaller then its three Destiny-class vessels, the 2,112-passenger, 84,000-ton *Carnival Legend* and *Carnival Spirit* are expected to enter service in early and late 2001, respectively. (A third sister, the *Carnival Legend,* is expected in 2002.) At a cost of approximately $375 million a piece, the 960-foot-long fun ships will have new features for Carnival, including a wedding chapel, conference center, and, in addition to the formal dining room and casual buffet restaurant, an alternative restaurant that will sit high-up between the ship's smokestack and the uppermost section of the ships' atria. The ships will also have more of what makes Carnival tick, including a two-level gym, balconies on over half the cabins, a large children's center, and two consecutive decks of bars, lounges, and nightspots, one with an outdoor wraparound promenade.

CABINS   Like the rest of the Carnival fleet, most cabins are spacious but utilitarian in design. Inside cabins aboard *Tropicale,* however, measure 170 square feet—slightly less than most of their inside equivalents across the rest of the fleet. There are a dozen suites, each with a private veranda. Most beds can be converted into either kings or twins, and a number of cabins have bunk-style third and fourth berths. All cabins have stereos, TVs, and wall safes. For obvious noise reasons, you might want to think twice about booking the cabins that abut the children's playroom, aft on the Empress Deck.

There are 11 cabins configured for passengers with disabilities.

Cabins & Rates						
Cabins	Per diems from	Bathtub	Fridge	Hair Dryer	Sitting Area	TV
Inside	$76	no	no	no	no	yes
Outside	$101	no	no	no	no	yes
Suite	$214	yes	yes	no	yes	yes

PUBLIC AREAS   The dining room lies down at the water line (as opposed to more modern ships, which perch their dining rooms on one of the higher decks) and has no windows. Other than that, you'll find scaled-down versions of many of the features from other Carnival ships, including a corkscrew-shaped water slide and a piano bar whose decorative motif was inspired by the ebony and ivory keys of a piano. The Boiler Room Bar & Grill Lido restaurant, for alternative dining, is brightly painted and fitted with jarringly exposed industrial-looking pipes inspired by the exterior of the Centre Pompidou in Paris. The casino is a cozy, smaller version of the mammoth gaming areas aboard larger Carnival ships. The Exta-Z disco's psychedelic lights shimmer and twirl as the beat goes on.

There is also a library, children's playroom, video-game room, and a volleyball court.

POOL, FITNESS & SPA FACILITIES   The *Tropicale* has scaled-down versions of the facilities aboard Carnival's larger ships. The spa, gym, and hair salon are tiny. There are men's and women's saunas and three outside swimming pools, including one kids' wading pool.

Celebrity Cruises

1050 Caribbean Way, Miami, FL 33132. ☎ **800/327-6700** or 305/539-6000. Fax 800/722-5329. www.celebrity-cruises.com.

THE LINE IN A NUTSHELL Celebrity offers the best of two worlds: If you like elegance without stuffiness, fun without bad taste, and pampering without a high price, Celebrity is king.

THE EXPERIENCE With the most elegant big ships in the industry, Celebrity's entire fleet offers the best of both worlds: a refined cruise experience, yet one that is fun and active.

Each of the line's ships is spacious, glamorous, and comfortable, mixing sleekly modern and vaguely art-deco styles and throwing in an astoundingly cutting-edge art collection to boot. Their genteel service is exceptional: Staff members are exceedingly polite and professional, and contribute greatly to the elegant mood. Dining-wise, Celebrity shines, offering innovative cuisine that's a cut above all the other mainstream lines.

Like all the big-ship lines, Celebrity offers lots for its passengers to do, but its focus on mellower pursuits and innovative programming sets it apart. Niceties such as roving a cappella bands who sidle up to your table to entertain during pre- or after-dinner drinks lend a warmly personal touch, while seminars on personal investing and handwriting analysis offer a little more cerebral meat than the usual fare.

Celebrity gets the "best of" nod in a lot of categories: The AquaSpas on the line's megaships are the best at sea, the art collections are fleet-wide the most compelling, the cigar bars the most plush, and the onboard activities among the most varied. Celebrity pampers suite guests with butler service, and treats all guests to in-cabin pizza delivery.

Pros

- **Spectacular spas and gyms.** Beautiful to look at and well stocked, the spas and gyms on the *Millennium, Century, Galaxy,* and *Mercury* are the best at sea today.
- **Fabulous food.** High-rated cuisine is tops in the mainstream category.
- **Innovative everything.** Its entertainment, art, cigar bars, service, spas, and cuisine are some of the most innovative in the industry.

Cons

- **Sort-of-private verandas.** Most of the huge Sky Suite verandas on the *Century, Galaxy,* and *Mercury* are exposed to the public decks above (keep that robe on!).
- **No E-mail access for passengers.** Hey, what year is this anyway? At press time, the *Millennium* was the only ship in the fleet to be plugged in.

Compared with the other Mainstream lines, here's how Celebrity rates:					
	Poor	Fair	Good	Excellent	Outstanding
Enjoyment Factor					✓
Dining					✓
Activities				✓	
Children's Program			✓		
Entertainment				✓	
Service					✓
Overall Value					✓

CELEBRITY: THE BEST OF TWO WORLDS

Celebrity is one of those rare companies that lives up to its advertising: As the song in its commercial says, it's "simply the best" for moderately priced cruises that feel like they should cost a lot more.

Celebrity's roots go back to the powerful Greek shipping family Chandris, whose patriarch John D. Chandris founded a cargo shipping company in 1915. The family expanded into the cruise business in the 1960s, introducing the down-market Fantasy Cruises in the late 1970s, serving a mostly European market. Fantasy dissolved in 1989 just as the Chandris family pushed into the Caribbean marketplace in a big, big way by creating Celebrity Cruises. The company's rise to prominence was so rapid and so successful that in 1997 it was courted and acquired by the larger and wealthier Royal Caribbean Cruises, Ltd., which now operates Celebrity as a sister line to Royal Caribbean International. So far it's been a fortuitous marriage: Reservations, bookkeeping, maintenance, and provisioning were merged, but Celebrity has maintained its own very fine identity, offering a product that's among the best in the cruise industry.

THE FLEET

With their crisp navy-blue-and-white hulls and rakishly angled funnel decorated with a giant *X* (actually the Greek letter for *ch,* as in *Chandris,* the line's founding family), the profiles of Celebrity's ships rank among the industry's most distinctive. Especially striking are the designs of their raked rear decks—tiered in dramatically rising increments upward and forward, like the terraces in a formal garden—and their bows, steeply pitched toward the water and flowing smoothly up into the ships' superstructures, suggesting both speed and grace.

Unlike Carnival, Royal Caribbean, Princess, and Costa, all of Celebrity's ships were built after 1989. The 1,354-guest *Horizon* and 1,375-guest *Zenith* still look nearly as modern and innovative today as they did when they were introduced, and the megaships that followed, the 1,750-guest *Century* and the 1,870-guest *Galaxy* and *Mercury,* are gems too.

It's hard to believe that something already so good is getting even better, but the new 1,950-passenger *Millennium,* which debuted in June of 2000, is the first of an even more impressive line of Celebrity ships. Two more in this class, the *Infinity* and the not-yet named *Millennium-class III,* are slated to debut in February 2001 and August 2001, with a fourth sister scheduled for April 2002. They'll carry on the Celebrity tradition, featuring innovative spas, cigar bars, and a continued focus on fine dining, plus expanded worldwide itineraries. The ships are being built at the Chantiers de l'Atlantique shipyard in St. Nazaire, France. Following the Alaska season in summer 2001, *Infinity* will move through the Panama Canal and then head to the Southern Caribbean for 7-night round-trips from San Juan, through April 2002. The Millennium-class III will sail 12-night Baltic and/or Mediterranean cruises when it debuts in late summer 2001.

All of the line's ships spend at least half of each year in the Caribbean, and its *Horizon* and *Zenith* sail Bermuda itineraries from New York in the summer and fall.

PASSENGER PROFILE

Celebrity vessels attract a wide range of ages and backgrounds, although the common denominator among passengers is that they want a toned-down, somewhat elegant brand of fun cruise, with lots of activities and a glamorous, exciting atmosphere, yet not *too* wild and nutty. The line focuses on middle- to upper-middle-income cruisers, although a handful of discreetly wealthy patrons might be on any given cruise or, conversely, a small-business owner, school teacher, police officer, construction worker, or restaurant manager. Most of the clientele give the impression of being prosperous but not obscenely rich, well behaved but not above a hearty laugh at the dress-your-husband-up-in-women's-clothes act featured on one recent cruise.

Much of the clientele hails from the East Coast, and most are couples in their thirties on up, with decent numbers of honeymooners and couples celebrating anniversaries, as well as children in summer and during the holidays.

DINING

Celebrity has poured lots of time and money into creating a culinary format that consistently provides well-orchestrated, well-presented, and good-tasting meals. In the mid-1990s, the company signed on as its culinary consultant internationally known chef **Michel Roux,** whose most visible successes were his direction of both Le Gavroche, one of London's best restaurants, and the Waterside Inn (in Bray, Berkshire), which has attracted the attention of well-heeled European foodies—including the queen of England—for many years.

While Celebrity loves touting Michel Roux and its food, and while the stuff is tasty, I must say the meals served in the formal dining room are really not *that* much better than the cuisine being served these days on the newest Carnival, Royal Caribbean, Princess, and Disney ships. And this, I think, is due more to the other lines improving their cuisine over the past few years than to Celebrity's slipping. It could be said that Celebrity's cuisine probably includes more exotic or international fare, like Asian and French, that more experienced palates will appreciate. Overall, though, they are pretty much in the same league now and it would be splitting hairs to argue otherwise.

A dinner menu is likely to feature something along the lines of escargots à la bourguignonne, pheasant mousseline with blueberry vinaigrette, pan-fried salmon with parslied potatoes, *pad Thai* (noodles and veggies in a peanut sauce), tournedos Rossini with foie gras and Madeira sauce, or a well-seasoned slab of prime rib with horseradish and baked potato. To balance such heartiness, at every meal Celebrity offers **lighter "spa" fare,** like a seafood medley in saffron sauce or oven-roasted rack of veal with steamed veggies (calories, fat, cholesterol, and sodium are listed on the back of the menu) and **vegetarian entrees** such as curried Indian vegetables or linguini with shiitake mushrooms and herbs.

The two-story formal dining rooms on the *Century, Galaxy,* and *Mercury* are stunning rooms reminiscent of the grand liners of yesteryear, punctuated by a wide and dramatic staircase leading into the center of the ground floor of the restaurants, and by a floor-to-ceiling wall of glass facing the astern to the ship's wake. The *Millennium* not only has a two-story dining room and a casual buffet restaurant, but also the line's first formal 134-seat **reservations-only restaurant** called The Olympic. In the tradition of the grand old ocean liners, the restaurant features the actual interior wood paneling from the great liner *Olympic,* the *Titanic*'s sister ship, which debuted in 1911, a year before that ill-fated ship was introduced. Here, elegant surroundings are matched with sophisticated service, which includes food being prepared and served table-side. A recommended wine will be suggested for each course from a wine cellar of more than 175 labels.

Aside from the fancier stuff, Celebrity also offers the same usual suspects as its peers. An **alternative casual dining venue** is available in the Lido restaurant. Don't expect great atmosphere (it's a bit bright and spartan on the *Zenith* and *Horizon*), but do expect a simple five-course meal, with a choice of main entrees like salmon, steak, pasta, and chicken. Unlike Carnival and Royal Caribbean, which offer buffet-style alternative restaurants, dinner here is served by waiters between 6:30 and 8:30pm by reservation only. **Lunch buffets** feature all-American favorites like salads and stir fries, grilled hamburgers and hot dogs, fish-and-chips, cheeses and breads, omelets, pizza, smoked salmon, and French onion soup.

A nice touch that appears on all formal nights is a late-night culinary soirée known as **Gourmet Bites,** where a series of upscale canapés and hors d'oeuvres like fish tempura and roasted garlic lemon chicken are served by waiters in the ship's public lounges between midnight and 1am. On other nights, themed **midnight buffets** might offer up Oriental, Italian, Tex-Mex, or tropical smorgasbords, with a spread of fancifully carved fruits.

Once per cruise fleet-wide, there's what the line calls **Elegant Tea,** where white-gloved waiters serve tea with rolling trolleys of finger sandwiches, scones, and desserts. The line's 24-hour **room service** allows passengers to order off the lunch and dinner menus during those hours. Did I mention **pizza?** Not only is it tasty and available throughout the afternoon fleet-wide, but you can also get it delivered to your cabin (in a box and pouch like your local pizzeria) between 3 and 7pm and 10pm and 1am daily.

Wine-wise, Chef Roux's choices are offered in a wide price range to suit every budget. A few of the wines featured on board are produced by French vineyards with which Roux has a direct link and, in some cases, of which he is the owner.

ACTIVITIES

On Celebrity, there's a lot to do and a lot not to do, and the ships offer opportunities for both.

If you like to stay busy, activities during days at sea are fairly standardized across the fleet, and may include one of the fascinating **enrichment lectures** (which are complimentary) often offered by experts on topics such as personal investing and handwriting analysis. There are also the tried-and-true wine tastings, horse racing, bingo, art auctions, trivia games, arts and crafts, spa and salon demos, and line-dancing lessons. Activities are not without a dose of token cruise tomfoolery. Afternoons in the main pool area, silly pool games like the **Mr. Celebrity contest** are held, where cheeky guys strut their stuff around the pool as a panel of bathing-suit-clad female volunteers rate them. During the day, a live pop band plays a couple of sets on the Pool Deck.

If you prefer curling up with a good book in some quiet nook, you'll have no problem finding one. On the *Horizon* and *Zenith,* the aft tiered decks and the forward Marina Deck are perfect places for quiet repose, and on the *Galaxy* and *Mercury,* you can find some peace in the far corners of the Sky Deck and on the aft Penthouse Deck. On the *Millennium,* its uppermost deck aft, near the jogging track, harbors a cluster of deck chairs away from the main-pool fray. Inside there are many hideaways, including Michael's Club, the edges of Rendez-Vous Square, a lounge chair at the spa's thalassotherapy pool (on the *Century, Galaxy, Mercury,* and *Millennium*) and in the Fleet and America's Cup observation lounges (on the *Zenith* and *Horizon*). The *Millennium*'s online computer area has 18 computers with E-mail capabilities for 95¢ per minute. And, while there are small computer rooms on the *Century, Galaxy,* and *Mercury,* they do not provide Internet access or E-mail services, although at press time a company spokeswoman said these services will be offered by year-end 2000.

CHILDREN'S PROGRAM

Although it did not originate that way, Celebrity has evolved into a cruise line that pampers kids as well as adults, during the summer months and holidays (with a limited program available at other times of the year if there are lots of kids on board). Each ship has a **playroom** (called the Ship Mates Fun Factory on the *Millennium* and the Century-class ships and the Children's Playroom on the *Horizon* and *Zenith*), **supervised**

Cruise Tip

If you plan on spending quiet time in your cabin during the day, you might want to avoid booking a cabin near the children's playroom, which on all but the *Millennium* are located next to cabins. Their locations are marked on brochure deck plans.

activities practically all day long, and **private and group baby-sitting.** The *Galaxy, Mercury,* and *Millennium* also have wading pools.

During kid-intensive seasons, **activities** are geared toward four different age groups between the ages of 3 and 17, with the largest facilities on the Century-class ships. Kids ages 3 to 6, dubbed "Ship Mates," can enjoy treasure hunts, clown parties, T-shirt painting, dancing, movies, ship tours, and ice-cream-sundae-making parties. "Cadets," ages 7 to 9, have T-shirt painting, scavenger hunts, board games, arts and crafts, ship tours, and computer games. Your 10-to-12-year-old might want to join the "Ensign" activities, like karaoke, computer games, board games, trivia contests, arts and crafts, movies, and pizza parties. For teens ages 13 to 17 who don't think themselves too cool to participate, the "Admiral T's" group offers talent shows, karaoke, pool games, and trivia contests. On the Century-class ships there are attractive teen discos/hangout rooms. Special activities offered in the summer include **summer-stock theater presentations,** which involve three age groups: the Ship Mates and Cadets sing, dance, and act, and the Ensigns direct and produce the plays. The Young Mariners Club offers kids the chance to get a behind-the-scenes look at the cruise ship, with activities and tours related to the entertainment, food and beverage, and hotel departments. **Junior Olympics** are held poolside and the whole family is encouraged to cheer on the kids who compete in relay races, diving, and basketball-hoop shooting. There are also masquerade parties, where Ship Mates and Cadets make their own masks and then parade around the ship.

On both formal nights of a weeklong cruise (again, only during the summer and holidays), a complimentary **parents' night out program** allows mom and dad to enjoy dinner alone while the kids are invited to a pizza party with the counselors. Every evening, group slumber-party-style **baby-sitting** in the playroom is available from 10pm to 1am for children ages 3 to 12, for $3 per child per hour or $5 per hour for two or more children from the same family. Private in-cabin baby-sitting by a crew member is available on a limited basis for $8 per hour for up to two children.

ENTERTAINMENT

Although entertainment is not a prime reason to sail on a Celebrity ship, the line does offer a nice selection of varied, innovative performances. For instance, they've introduced a **strolling a cappella group** that performs in lounges and public areas fleet-wide in the afternoons and before and after dinner. The four-man troupe of singers, sans instruments, delights passengers with well-known songs old and new, performed in a fun, entertaining style.

Celebrity also offers the popular favorites, like **Broadway-style musicals** led by a sock-it-to-'em soloist or two and a team of lip-synching dancers in full Vegas-esque regalia. On the *Millennium* and the Century-class ships, these shows are performed on some of the best-equipped, highest-tech stages at sea. They've got hydraulic orchestra pits, easily maneuverable sets (which move along tracks in the stage floor), trap doors, turntables, a video wall (showing images that coincide with the performance), and lasers. Showrooms aboard all Celebrity ships have excellent acoustics and sight lines that

Celebrity Art: Take a Walk on the Wild Side

Celebrity's ships—particularly the *Century, Galaxy*, and *Mercury*—contain the most impressive and striking (and sometimes downright weird) art collections at sea, featuring works by Robert Rauschenberg, Damien Hirst, Jasper Johns, David Hockney, Pablo Picasso, Andy Warhol, Sol LeWitt, Helen Frankenthaler, and many others. Public areas on *Mercury* alone contain more than 400 works of art, including paintings, tapestries, cartoonish murals, and stark metal sculptures; some particular standouts include Christian Marclay's record-cover collages, Anish Kapoor's hallucinatory *Mirror,* Lawrence Weiner's puzzling poetic lines painted on walls throughout the ship, Lynn Davis's starkly beautiful iceberg photographs, the benignly endearing photographs of discarded flip-flops or the close-ups of smiling kids, and Art Club 2000's disturbing takeoffs of the 1990s' heroin-chic advertising trend. These compelling works sometimes greet you at unexpected moments, and may even make you pause and reflect—a most rare cruise ship phenomenon.

are among the most panoramic and unobstructed at sea. As for the sound and light spectaculars that are so much a part of the entertainment experience these days, check this statistic: The Celebrity Showroom aboard the *Mercury* has no less than 152 speakers, and a typical evening show uses between 1,000 and 1,100 different lighting cues. How's that for whiz bang?

Other nights in the showroom you'll find magicians, comedians, cabaret acts, and passenger talent shows.

When you tire of Broadway-style entertainment, you'll find all the ships have **cozy lounges** and **piano bars** where you can retreat for a romantic nightcap. In these more intimate lounges, the music of choice is often laid-back jazz or music from the Big Band era, spiced with interpretations of contemporary Celine Dion or Whitney Houston type hits. There's also the elegant and plush **Michael's Club** for a cigar and cordial and some quiet conversation. Each ship has late-night disco dancing, usually until about 3am. You'll also find **karaoke** and **first-run movies** in the theater on the *Millennium* and the Century-class ships.

Each ship has a rather spacious **casino,** and while they may not be as hopping as the ones on Carnival, they're bustling enough to put gamblers in the mood.

Celebrity has over the years had a running association with Sony that was originally thought to be a big selling point, allowing the ships to offer enhanced audio and video enjoyment. What? You didn't hear about that? Or care? Well, neither did most other people, so the PR hoopla has since fizzled out to a large degree. Of greater merit are the half dozen or so Sony personal **computers** that are available for guests to play around with on *Millennium* and the three Century-class ships, although E-mail and Internet access are not yet available.

You'll also enjoy the **interactive system** wired to all cabin TVs. It's pretty cool and very convenient—when it's working; however, it has never functioned completely 100% on the five Celebrity cruises I've taken over the past few years. When it's up to speed, you can order room service from on-screen menus, select the evening's wine in advance of dinner, play casino-style games, or browse in "virtual" shops for a wide selection of merchandise for delivery directly to your home at the end of your cruise. The systems are also touted as allowing guests to check the balance of their onboard account, but this nifty option has never been operational when I've sailed with Celebrity. At press

Celebrity Fleet Itineraries

Ship	Home Ports & Season	Itinerary	Other Itineraries
Century	Round-trip from Fort Lauderdale; itineraries alternate weekly, year-round.	**7-night E. Carib:** San Juan, St. Thomas, St. Maarten, and Nassau. **7-night W. Carib:** Ocho Rios (Jamaica), Grand Cayman, Cozumel, and Key West.	None
Galaxy	Round-trip from San Juan, late Oct to late Apr.	**7-night S. Carib:** St. Croix, St. Lucia, Barbados, Antigua, and St. Thomas.	Alaska Inside Passage
Horizon	Round-trip from Aruba; Nov–Apr; New York–Bermuda itineraries Apr–Oct.	**7-night S. Carib:** St. Thomas, St. Kitts, St. Lucia, and Barbados. **7-night Bermuda:** Hamilton and St. George's.	None
Mercury	Round-trip from Fort Lauderdale, late Oct–Apr.	**7-night W. Carib:** Key West, Calica, Cozumel, and Grand Cayman.	Alaska Inside Passage and Gulf, South America
Millennium	Round-trip from Fort Lauderdale, itineraries alternate weekly Nov–Mar.	**7-night E. Carib:** San Juan, Catalina Island, St. Thomas, and Nassau. **7-night W. Carib:** Key West, Calica, Cozumel, and Grand Cayman.	Europe in summer 2001
Zenith	Caribbean itineraries round-trip from Fort Lauderdale, alternating, Nov–Apr; New York–Bermuda itineraries Apr–Oct.	**10-night E. and S. Carib:** Sint Maarten, St. Lucia, Barbados, Antigua, and St. Thomas. **11-night E. and S. Carib:** Curaçao, La Guaira (Venezuela), Grenada, Barbados, Martinique, and St. Thomas. **7-night Bermuda:** Hamilton and St. George's.	None

time a company spokesman said the interactive cabin TVs on all of Royal Caribbean and Celebrity's new ships would by early 2000 also allow guests to check their stocks.

SERVICE

Overall, service is polite, attentive, cheerful, and especially professional. Waiters have a poised, upscale-hotel air about them, and their manner contributes to the elegant mood. There are very professional sommeliers in the dining room, and waiters are on-hand in the Lido breakfast and lunch buffet restaurants to carry passengers' trays from the buffet line to a table of their choice.

If you occupy a suite on any of the ships, you'll get a tuxedo-clad **personal butler** who serves afternoon tea, complimentary cappuccino and espresso, and complimentary hors d'oeuvres from 6 to 8pm, bringing them right to your cabin. If you ask, he'll handle your laundry, shine your shoes, make sewing repairs, and deliver messages. For instance, on one sailing with my mother, our butler brought her a glass of juice each night, which she needed to take with her medication. Your butler will serve you a full five-course dinner if you'd rather **dine in your cabin** one night, and even help you organize a cocktail party for your cruising friends (you foot the bill for food and drinks, of course), either in your suite or a suitable public area.

Other hedonistic treats bestowed upon suite guests include a bottle of champagne on arrival, personalized stationery, terry-cloth robes, a Celebrity tote bag, oversize bath towels, priority check-in and debarkation, express luggage delivery at embarkation, and, on the *Century, Galaxy, Mercury,* and *Millennium,* complimentary use of the soothing thalassotherapy pool. Suite guests can even get an **in-cabin massage** daily between the hours of 7am and 8pm.

Century • Galaxy • Mercury

The Verdict

Three of the most attractive and all-around appealing megaships at sea. Down-to-earth and casual, this trio also manages to be elegant and exciting.

Mercury *(photo: Matt Hannafin)*

Specifications

Size (in tons)		Number of Passengers	
Century	70,606	*Century*	1,750
Galaxy	77,713	*Galaxy*	1,896
Mercury	77,713	*Mercury*	1,896
Number of Cabins		Officers	Greek
Century	875	Crew	International
Galaxy	948	*Century*	843
Mercury	948	*Galaxy*	900
Number of Outside Cabins		*Mercury*	900
Century	571	Passenger/Crew Ratio	2 to 1
Galaxy	639	Year Built	
Mercury	639	*Century*	1995
Cabins with Verandas		*Galaxy*	1996
Century	61	*Mercury*	1997
Galaxy	220	Last Major Refurbishment	N/A
Mercury	220		

Frommer's Ratings (Scale of 1–5)

Cabin Comfort & Amenities	5	Pool, Fitness & Spa Facilities	5
Ship Cleanliness & Maintenance	4	Children's Facilities	4
Public Comfort/Space	5	Itinerary	4
Decor	5	Worth the Money	5

When it was launched in December 1995, the $320-million *Century* got tremendous publicity, partly because it represented Celebrity's entry into the world of megaships and partly because it was, quite simply, a particularly well conceived and beautiful ship. The *Galaxy* was launched a year later, in December 1996, and the *Mercury* appeared 1 year after that. The three are more or less equivalent in size and amenities (with the primary differences being in the interior decors, arrangement of public rooms, and itineraries), and although colossal by the standards of a decade ago, none attains the mega-bulk of some of the new 100,000-ton-plus behemoths run by such competing lines as Royal Caribbean, Princess, and Carnival.

Of the three ships, the one that's the most dissimilar to its mates is *Century*. Although similar in many ways, it's lighter by 7,000 tons, has a capacity for 120 fewer guests, and has a brighter, glitzier feel, flaunting its high-techness with video monitors, among other things, blended into the decor. It also has a smaller children's playroom and doesn't have a wading pool. The *Galaxy* and *Mercury* are warmer and more reminiscent of classic ocean liners, but with a modern feel. The decor casts a chic and sophisticated mood, with lots of warm wood tones as well as rich, tactile textures and fabrics in deep primaries, from faux zebra-skin to buttery soft leathers, velvets, chrome, and futuristic-looking applications of glass and marble.

It's difficult to say what's most striking on these three ships. The elegant spas and their 15,000-gallon thalassotherapy pools? The twin three- and four-story atria with their serpentine staircases that seem to float without supports and their domed ceilings of painted glass? The distinguished Michael's Club cigar lounges with their leather wingbacks, velvet couches, and hand-rolled stogies? The two-story old-world dining rooms set back in the stern, with grand floor-to-ceiling windows allowing diners to espy the glow of the wake under moonlight? An absolutely intriguing modern-art collection unmatched in the industry?

Take your pick—you won't go wrong.

Cabins & Rates

Cabins	Per diems from	Bathtub	Fridge	Hair Dryer	Sitting Area	TV
Inside	$140	no	no	yes	no	yes*
Outside	$172	no	yes	yes	some	yes*
Suite	$309	yes	yes	yes	yes	yes*

All TVs show CNN and Discovery Channel.

CABINS Simple yet pleasing decor is cheerful and based on light-colored furniture and monochromatic themes of muted purple-blue, green, or pinky red. At 170 to 175 square feet, inside cabins and standard outside ones are larger than the norm (although not as large as Carnival's 190-footers), and suites, which come in four different categories, are particularly spacious and feature marble vanity/desk tops, art-deco–style sconces, and rich inlaid wood floors. Some, such as the Penthouse Suite, offer more living space (1,219 sq. ft., expandable to 1,433 sq. ft. on special request) than you find in many private homes, plus such wonderful touches as a private whirlpool bath on the veranda. Royal Suites run about half that size at 537 square feet (plus 100-ft. balconies), but offer touches like French doors between the bedroom and seating area, both bathtub and shower in the bathroom, and TVs in each room. The *Galaxy* and *Mercury*'s 246-square-foot Sky Suites offer verandas that, at 179 square feet, are among the biggest aboard any ship—bigger, in fact, than those in the more expensive Penthouse and Royal suites on these ships (you might want to keep your robe on, though, as people on the deck above can see down onto part of the Sky Suite verandas). All suite bathrooms have tubs with whirlpools and magnified makeup mirrors.

All cabins are outfitted with built-in vanities/desks, minibars, hair dryers, radios, and safes. Closets and drawer space are roomy and well designed, as are the bathrooms, and all standard cabins have twin beds convertible to doubles.

Cabin TVs are wired with an interactive system that allows guests to order room service from on-screen menus, select wine for dinner, play casino-style games, or go shopping.

Eight of the cabins aboard each ship (one inside and seven outside) were specifically designed for passengers with disabilities.

PUBLIC AREAS   All three ships also are designed so well that it's never hard to find a quiet retreat when you want to be secluded but don't want to be confined in your cabin.

Dinners are served in style in the ships' gorgeous two-deck main dining rooms—the Grand Restaurant aboard the *Century,* the Orion Restaurant aboard the *Galaxy,* and the Manhattan Restaurant aboard the *Mercury,* this last featuring beautiful wooden ceilings with burnished metal joins and a number of allusions to its namesake, including a retractable screen over the aft windows printed with an image of New York's famed Flatiron Building. The raising of this screen during meals always occasions generous oohs and ahhs.

Each vessel also boasts a cozy and rarely packed Michael's Club cigar bar, decorated like the parlor of a London men's club. If you're a dedicated nonsmoker, don't even think of spending time here. Otherwise, puff away at some of the best cigars this side of Havana and wash them down with a fine cognac or a good single-malt Scotch. On the *Century* and *Galaxy,* Michael's Club maintains its wood-paneled clubbiness somewhat better than aboard the *Mercury,* where it wraps around the main atrium and lets onto a very uncozy view of the shopping below. Still, you can't beat the high-backed, buttery-leather chairs and the master cigar-roller who sets up shop in the corner.

For those who don't find that smoky ambiance appealing, Tastings Coffee Bar offers an alternative, with every kind of specialized upscale caffeine you can imagine. There's also the popular Rendez-Vous Square, arranged so that even large groups can achieve a level of privacy and couples can find their own nook as well. Champagne bars appear aboard the *Galaxy* and *Mercury,* and the latter also sports a nice, modern deco–looking martini bar set in the ship's aft atrium, about which my only complaint is the audible clanging of the casino's slot machines, which seems to get trapped and amplified by the atrium's drum shape. Various other bars, both indoor and outdoor, are tucked into nooks and crannies throughout all three ships.

The multitiered, glass-walled nightclubs/discos are spacious, sprawling, and elegant in a clean, modern way, yet designed with lots of cozy nooks for romantic conversation over champagne. Each of the three ships has double-decker theaters with unobstructed views from almost every seat (though avoid those at the cocktail tables at the back of the rear balcony boxes, unless you have a really long neck) and scads of state-of-the-art equipment. Each boasts a cantilevered orchestra pit and a wall of video screens to augment the action on the stage.

Libraries aboard both ships are comfortable, but not as big or well stocked as they could be. The onboard casinos are larger and more comprehensive than those aboard the line's older *Horizon* and *Zenith.*

POOL, FITNESS & SPA FACILITIES   Resort decks aboard these vessels feature a pair of good-size swimming areas rimmed with teak benches for sunning and relaxation. Even when the ships are full, these areas don't seem particularly crowded. Aboard the *Galaxy* and *Mercury,* retractable domes cover one of the swimming pools during inclement weather.

Some of the best spas and fitness facilities at sea are on board these three ships. Called the AquaSpa, these spacious, windowed, 10,000-square-foot health meccas are a feast for the eyes as well as a sanctuary for the body and soul. The gym wraps around one side of the bow like a hook, the large spa straddles the middle, and a very modern and elegant beauty salon faces the ocean on the other side of the bow. You'll feel as though you've booked yourself into an exclusive European spa resort. The focal point of these spas is a 115,000-gallon thalassotherapy pool, a bubbling cauldron of warm, soothing seawater. After a relaxing 15- or 20-minute dip, choose a massage, Rasul treatment (a mud pack and steam bath in one), a facial, or one of the many other pampering treatments offered. As aesthetically pleasing to the eye as they are functional, each of the AquaSpas employs a design theme—a Japanese bathhouse on the *Century* and *Galaxy* and a Moroccan motif on the *Mercury*.

Although managed by Steiner like the spas on most other ships, these spas offer more exotic treatments than most—for example, mud packs, herbal steam baths, and a variety of water-based treatments involving baths, jet massages, and "aquameditation," in which you're caressed by light, whirling showers while lying on a soft mat. Certain procedures are offered in a "partner" arrangement, whereby you and your significant other can apply medicinal muds to each other and share an herbal steam bath while massaging each other with sea salt. The whole shebang ends with a warm shower and the application of an aromatic "potion" to the skin. Sounds exotic, huh? There are also saunas and steam rooms (including the *Mercury*'s impressive Turkish Hammam, with its uniformly heated surfaces and beautiful tile work).

In the generously sized gyms, you can get lost in the landscapes unfolding on the color monitors of the ships' high-tech virtual-reality stationary bikes. (You can even ride through the virtual water traps and make squishy sounds as you come up the other side—fun!) There are also aerobics classes in a separate room, and each of the three ships has an outdoor jogging track on an upper deck, a golf simulator, and one deck that's specifically designed for sports.

Horizon • Zenith

The Verdict

A casually elegant tribute to both the gentility of classic cruising and the fun and glamour of today's exciting megaships, these midsize ships are a very pleasing package.

Horizon (photo: Celebrity Cruises)

Specifications

Size (in tons)		Officers	Greek
Horizon	46,811	Crew	International
Zenith	47,225	*Horizon*	645
Number of Cabins		*Zenith*	628
Horizon	677	Passenger/Crew Ratio	2.1 to 1
Zenith	687	Year Built	
Number of Outside Cabins		*Horizon*	1990
Horizon	529	*Zenith*	1992
Zenith	541	Last Major Refurbishment	
Cabins with Verandas	0	*Horizon*	1998
Number of Passengers		*Zenith*	1999
Horizon	1,354		
Zenith	1,374		

Frommer's Ratings (Scale of 1–5)

Cabin Comfort & Amenities	4	Pool, Fitness & Spa Facilities	4
Ship Cleanliness & Maintenance	4	Children's Facilities	3
Public Comfort/Space	4	Itinerary	4
Decor	4	Worth the Money	5

The design of the twins *Horizon* and *Zenith,* with their signature sterns and bows and the immediately identifiable Chandris *X* on their funnels, has since become the touchstone on which all subsequent Celebrity ships have been based. Like their megaship sisters, these two smaller ships boast classy, modern interiors, fantastic service, and distinctive art collections, and after $4.5-million refurbishments in late 1998 (*Horizon*) and late 1999 (*Zenith*), they also offer such signature Celebrity elements as cigar lounges, patisseries, martini bars, art galleries, a new boutique selling upscale accessories and clothing, and enlarged spa facilities (although they lack the megas' thalassotherapy pools).

Even at peak capacity, the ships' well-designed passageways, hallways, seating arrangements, and traffic patterns create the feeling of more space than a ship of this size would ordinarily provide. An exceptionally wide indoor promenade gives passengers the feeling of strolling along a boulevard within the ship's hull. Art and sculpture decorate the ships, but the works don't equal the premier collection aboard *Century, Galaxy,* and *Mercury.*

Cabins & Rates

Cabins	Per diems from	Bathtub	Fridge	Hair Dryer	Sitting Area	TV
Inside	$130	no	no	yes	no	yes*
Outside	$145	no	no	yes	some	yes*
Suite	$255	yes	yes	yes	yes	yes*

* All TVs show CNN and ESPN.

CABINS   As on the Century-class ships, accommodations offer a generous amount of space, with all inside as well as standard outside cabins measuring 172 square feet. The muted blue, green, or red fabrics and accoutrements are tasteful, subdued, and well maintained.

All cabins on both ships have twin or double beds, with generally roomy bathrooms, and many have upper and lower berths for families or friendly foursomes. Standard cabin amenities include a glass-topped coffee table, a desk, and a nightstand with a solitary lamp that may be inadequate, especially if you're in a double. Eight cabins on *Horizon* and six on *Zenith* are positioned all the way aft, with windows facing the wake. Some passengers who've sailed on the line before request these rooms, preferring this classically romantic view. (Bear in mind, on the *Zenith,* the children's playroom is right in the midst of these cabins; on *Horizon,* it's adjacent to cabins amidships on the Florida deck. So if you're planning on quiet daytimes in your cabin and will sail during school holidays, you might not want to book one of them.)

The 20 roomy suites on each ship measure 270 square feet and are about 25 square feet bigger than most of the suites on the Century-class ships (the only difference being that the *Horizon* and *Zenith* do not have any private verandas). Each suite has a marble bathroom with whirlpool tub, a sitting area, a minibar, and butler service.

The *Horizon* has a pair of Presidential suites measuring 340 square feet and the *Zenith* has two Royal suites at 500 square feet, each with large sitting rooms (and on the *Zenith,* a dining table and chairs), marble bathrooms, walk-in closets, as well as butler service, VCR, CD player, and minibar.

Regardless of category, each accommodation has cabin music, a personal safe, TV, glass-topped coffee table, twin or double bed, and marble-topped vanity. Be careful when booking if views are important to you: Most of the Category 7 outside cabins on the Bermuda (*Horizon*) and Bahamas (*Zenith*) decks have views blocked by lifeboats.

Four cabins are wheelchair accessible.

PUBLIC AREAS   The decor on both is plush and modern rather than classical and conservative, with both a metallic and nautical motif working in concert. There are no multideck atria or flashing lights (except maybe on the dance floor of the disco). Layout differences between the two ships are minimal (*Zenith* has a larger forward observation deck, for instance).

One of the most attractive spaces is the spacious bar/observation lounge on the Marina Deck, called Fleet Bar on the *Zenith* and the America's Cup Club on the *Horizon*. Espousing a nautical motif, both have floor-to-ceiling windows, navy-blue furniture, and honey-brown wood accents. The dining rooms may be the most chrome-intensive places on board (ceiling, railing, chair frames, and pillars), yet they're still comfortable and pleasing enough places to dine, with banquette seating for tables along the sides of the rooms.

There's no really bad seat in the modern, minimalist, two-level Celebrity Show Lounge. Amidships is the Rendezvous Lounge and Rendezvous Bar, where guests, especially on formal nights, can show off their finery and relax with cocktails before heading to the adjacent dining room.

Recent refurbishments on both ships have transformed the space that was once a disco into three different rooms: a library, a card room, and an elegant Michael's Club cigar bar with wingback chairs, leather couches, and even a faux fireplace. Where the library and card room used to be, next to the Rendez-Vous Bar, there's now a martini bar, an art gallery offering the same kind of works you'll see at onboard art auctions, and another boutique. The disco is now part of the enlarged Zodiac Club, with lots of room for dancing and for sitting in cozy clusters. The Plaza Bar has been transformed into the COVA Café, offering specialty coffees and chocolates as well as champagne, wine, and liquors.

POOL, FITNESS & SPA FACILITIES   The *Horizon* and the *Zenith* have ample space dedicated to recreation, including two good-size swimming pools that never seem to be overcrowded, even when the ships are full. The newly renovated top-deck spa and fitness areas on both ships have floor-to-ceiling windows and resemble the spas aboard Celebrity's larger ships, and while they don't offer as many of the more exotic treatments or have the thalassotherapy pool featured on the Century-class ships, they now have expanded and enlarged spa-treatment rooms and a Seraglio steam/mud room (like the Rasul on the larger ships). The gyms have more fitness equipment, and although they're larger than they were, they're still relatively small by modern standards—too small, for instance, to hold fitness classes (they're held instead in one of the nightclubs).

Other recreation facilities and options include a putting green, a golf driving net used for lessons with the pro, and a jogging track. There are no hot tubs on either ship.

Millennium •
Infinity (preview) •
Summit (preview)

The Verdict

New millennium, new *Millennium.*
Celebrity's newest and biggest ship is a total
knockout, offering all the leisure, sports, and
entertainment options of a megaship and an
atmosphere that combines old world elegance
and modern casual style.

Millennium, nearing completion
(photo: Celebrity)

Specifications

Size (in tons)	91,000	Officers	Greek
Number of Cabins	975	Crew	999 (Int'l)
Number of Outside Cabins	780	Passenger/Crew Ratio	2 to 1
Cabins with Verandas	590	Year Built	2000
Number of Passengers	1,950	Last Major Refurbishment	N/A

Frommer's Ratings (Scale of 1–5)

Cabin Comfort & Amenities	4	Pool, Fitness & Spa Facilities	5
Ship Cleanliness & Maintenance	5	Children's Program	4
Public Comfort/Space	5	Itinerary	4/3*
Decor	5	Worth the Money	4

* Itineraries alternate weekly; western Caribbean itinerary is much more interesting than eastern.

The Golden Age of sea travel may have ended about the same time top hats went out
of style, but who's saying we can't have a new, more casual golden age of our own? *The
Millennium* might just be the ship to ring it in. In creating its newest vessel, which debuted in June 2000, Celebrity took the best ideas from *Century, Galaxy,* and *Mercury*
and ratcheted them up, both in terms of scale and number, then added a state-of-the-
art gas-turbine propulsion system that lessens environmental impact and provides a
smoother, quieter ride for passengers. The result? Celebrity's got a winner on its hands.

Millennium's sister ships—*Infinity, Summit,* and a still unnamed fourth vessel—are
set to debut in January 2001, August 2001, and April of 2002, respectively, and will
feature facilities comparable to *Millennium,* but with slightly different themes.

Cabins & Rates

Cabins	Per diems from	Bathtub	Fridge	Hair Dryer	Sitting Area	TV
Inside	$145	no	yes	yes	yes	yes
Outside	$173	no	yes	yes	yes	yes
Suite	$330	yes	yes	yes	yes	yes

CABINS   *Millennium's* cabins fall into the contemporary "light-wood modern" school
of cruise cabin design, with amenities like fridges and TVs smoothly incorporated into
the layout. Standard inside and outside cabins are a roomy 170 square feet, and come
with a small sitting area, convertible lower beds, and (in outsides) panoramic window.
Premium and Deluxe staterooms run from 170 to 191 square feet.

In the suite category, Celebrity offers four levels of accommodation. All have whirlpool bathtubs, 24-hour butler service, TV/VCR combos, and large sitting areas. At the

lowest level are the very pleasant 251-square-foot Sky Suites, with 57-square-foot verandas, while at the top of the food chain, the two massive, 1,432-square-foot Penthouse Suites are the largest in the biz, with everything the other suites have (but better) plus a massive 1,098-square-foot veranda and other extras.

Passengers requiring use of a wheelchair can choose between accommodations in four categories, including suites. There are no cabins specifically designated for singles.

PUBLIC AREAS The Grand Foyer atrium is a real stunner, a rectangular, three-deck area featuring a translucent, inner-illuminated onyx staircase that glows beneath your feet. Off on the port side, guests can ride between decks on oceanview elevators, which give the illusion that you'll keep going right down into the water after you pass the bottommost deck. Overlooking the Foyer, an Internet center has 18 computer stations. Guests can send and receive E-mail or surf the Web (though at a pricey 95 cents per minute) or take a variety of computer classes.

In the ship's bow is the three-deck Celebrity Theater, an elegant room partially illuminated by what look like torches all around. The effect gives the room a warm, flickering glow. Seating on all three levels is unobstructed.

The COVA Cafe is a bustling, bistro-like space for specialty coffees and freshly baked pastries. The Platinum Club is an elegant lounge with martini, champagne, and caviar bars, while one deck below the Rendez-Vous Lounge is a brighter, more modern space for music performances and dancing. For the *real* dancing, head up to the 100% stunning Cosmos nightclub. For the best effect, enter from the outside Sunrise deck, through a foyer dominated by a huge Robert Indiana LOVE sculpture under a painted blue sky.

The main Metropolitan Dining Room is a beautiful two-level space with a huge window in the stern, oversized round windows along both sides, and a central double staircase that provides a dramatic entry. The huge Ocean Grill buffet restaurant offers regular buffet selections, plus pizza, pasta, and ice cream specialty stations. The pizza is yummy.

The *Millennium's* really special dining experience, however, is to be had in the reservations-only Olympic restaurant, whose main attraction is several dozen hand-carved and gilded French walnut wall panels that were originally installed aboard White Star Line's *Olympic.* The room and dining experience Celebrity has created to match this historic paneling is amazing: 134 guests are served by a staff of 10 chefs, 10 servers, 5 sommeliers, and 5 maitre d's. Cuisine is a combination of newer dishes and recipes from the *Olympic.* For atmosphere, a piano/violin duo performs music from the early 20th century.

Other rooms include a sports bar, two-deck library, music library, conference center and cinema, cigar bar, and large casino. The ship's Emporium Shops are the most extensive at sea, with upscale shops like DKNY, Versace, H. Stern, and others, plus a Michel Roux gourmet shop.

For kids, the Shipmates Fun Factory has both indoor and outdoor soft-surface jungle gyms, a wading pool, a ball-jump, a computer room, a movie room, arts-and-crafts area, a video arcade, and more.

POOL, FITNESS & SPA FACILITIES The 25,000-square-foot AquaSpa complex features a range of esoteric hydrotherapy treatment as well as the usual array of massage and beauty procedures. Next door to the spa there's a very large cardio room with 46 exercise machines, free weights, and a large aerobics floor. A nice touch, and maybe a first on a cruise ship, is that all the treadmills look out onto an open deck area that's been planted with grass and flowers. Beautiful!

The large, bubbling Thalassotherapy pool sits outside the spa under a glass roof and is free for all passengers. There are also facilities for basketball, volleyball, quoits, and paddle tennis, plus a jogging track (3 laps equal 1 kilometer), golf simulator, 2 pools, 4 whirlpools, and large open areas for sunning.

Costa Cruises

World Trade Center, 80 SW 8th St., Miami, FL 33130-3097 (mailing address: P.O. Box 01964, Miami, FL 33101-9865). ☎ **800/462-6782** or 305/358-7325. Fax 305/375-0676. www.costacruises.com.

THE LINE IN A NUTSHELL   Costa's Italian-flavored mid- and megasize European-styled ships offer a moderately priced, festive, international experience that you can't find on any other line.

THE EXPERIENCE   With an illustrious history stretching back almost 90 years, Costa has managed to hold onto its heritage with its mantra of "Cruising Italian Style," and that's what primarily distinguishes it from the "all-American" experiences of the competition. Its corporate offices are in both Genoa and Miami, its officers are Italian, and its ships' interiors, food, and activities are still as Italian as you can find. Although on your Caribbean routing you're likely to get a less intense dose of rampant Italianism than you would aboard the line's Mediterranean sailings, and although the line employs far fewer Italian-born stewards and crew members than in years past, the line's strength in the Italian-American market means that you'll still get quite a lot.

Costa holds a somewhat unique position in the industry with a market focus that caters heavily to Europeans while still serving substantial numbers of Americans. Its Caribbean cruises attract mostly Americans (about 80% on any given sailing), and, conversely, its Mediterranean cruises attract mostly Europeans. That said, even in the Caribbean, the passenger mix is much more international than on most other lines.

Pros

- **Italian flavor.** Like no other line in this category, entertainment, cuisine, and service are presented with a festive Italian flair.
- **Great value for the money.** For passengers taking advantage of early-booking discounts, 1-week cruise rates start at just over $100 per person per day for an inside cabin and about $150 per person for an outside cabin.

Cons

- **Few private verandas on *Victoria*.** While the *Atlantica* has hundreds, the *Victoria* has none.
- **Small gyms.** Given its size, the *Victoria*'s gym is relatively tiny.
- **Few large windows.** Compared to its peers, the *Victoria* doesn't have many windows or terribly much natural light in its interiors.

Compared with the other Mainstream lines, here's how Costa rates:					
	Poor	Fair	Good	Excellent	Outstanding
Enjoyment Factor				✓	
Dining			✓		
Activities				✓	
Children's Program		✓			
Entertainment			✓		
Service			✓		
Overall Value				✓	

COSTA: CONTINENTAL FLAVOR IN THE CARIBBEAN

Costa's origins are as Italian as could be. In 1860, Giacomo Costa established an olive-oil refinery and packaging plant in Genoa. After his death in 1916, his sons bought a ship, called *Ravenna,* to transport raw materials and finished products from Sardinia through Genoa to the rest of Europe, thereby marking the founding of Costa Line in 1924. Within a decade or so, the family had acquired an additional half-dozen ships, but their fortune fell with that of their country in the years during and after World War II. At war's end, only one tiny ship remained in the family's fleet, but within 3 years they managed to acquire a dozen more, most of them carrying freight and some carrying European passengers. Costa was the world's largest operator of passenger ships in the early 1960s, before the explosion of the U.S. cruise industry nudged it into fifth place.

In 1968, the Costa family made a major commitment to the U.S. market by establishing Costa Cruises, now a subsidiary of Genoa-based Costa Crociere. The size of both the ships and the fleet grew rapidly. In 1966, most of the line's ships weighed in the range of 20,000 tons or so; by 1993, the *CostaRomantica* topped out at 54,000 tons. Today, the line's newest ship, the 80,000-ton *CostaAtlantica,* is Costa's largest ship.

In the late 1960s, Costa pioneered San Juan as a point of departure for cruises, which bolstered Puerto Rico's early attempts to restore San Juan's colonial core. Around the same time, Costa also became the first cruise line to offer air/sea packages between U.S. cities and San Juan (and soon after, to Florida also).

In 1997, Carnival Corporation and Airtours (a British tour operator in which Carnival has a 30% stake) each bought a 50% interest in Costa, vowing to keep the line just the way it is. And so they have. Today, despite its glossy corporate veneer, the Costa organization is still very much in the family. Key administrative positions affecting the North American market, however, are often filled from the ranks of Italian-born, U.S.-trained executives from outside the family. A good example is CEO Dino Schibuola, whose past experiences include stints at Celebrity Cruises and Athens-based Home Lines.

THE FLEET

The Costa fleet is diverse, from gleaming megas to old, rebuilt liners from the 1960s. Of its current fleet of seven, there are two megaships, the new 2,002-passenger *CostaAtlantica* and the 1,928-passenger *CostaVictoria,* built in 2000 and 1996, respectively; a pair of midsize 1,300-passenger ships, the *CostaRomantica* (built in 1993) and the *CostaClassica* (built in 1991, and to be stretched in late 2000 with 400 additional cabins added); the 800-passenger *CostaAllegra,* built in 1969 and rebuilt in 1992; the 770-passenger *CostaMarina,* built in 1969 and rebuilt in 1990; and the 972-passenger *CostaRiviera,* built in 1963 and rebuilt in 1993. The *CostaAtlantica* and *CostaVictoria* are the only two ships in the fleet deployed in the Caribbean during the 2000/2001 winter season, between November and April, and marketed to North Americans (although about 20% of passengers are Europeans). Summers and the rest of the year, the entire fleet is in the Mediterranean, Northern Europe, and the Baltic. On these sailings, about 80% of cruisers are European.

Costa's first new build since the launch of the *CostaVictoria* in 1996, the 2,112-passenger, 80,000-ton *CostaAtlantica* debuted in July of 2000. In many ways, the ship represents a new chapter for Costa. The *Atlantica* will be the first Costa ship to have a substantial number of private verandas—a whopping 75% of cabins will be outfitted with them.

PASSENGER PROFILE

This line attracts passengers of all ages who want to pay a reasonable price and who deliberately avoid all-American megaships like those of Carnival. Costa passengers are impressed with Italian style, appreciate a sense of cultural adventure and fun, and like the atmosphere of casual elegance and romance at which the Italians excel—for these reasons the line can be a good choice for honeymooners. Italian-Americans are heavily represented aboard every Caribbean cruise.

Costa appeals to retirees and young couples alike, although there are more passengers over 50 than under. There are children on board, but not in overwhelming numbers—typically 5% to 10% of passengers are traveling as families (expect more families on cruises during holidays). While about 80% are from North America, there's usually a contingent of passengers from Europe and South America. You'll also find a substantial number of repeaters as well as passengers celebrating birthdays, anniversaries, or renewed wedding vows.

DINING

Food is well prepared, heavily Italian (and at least continental), and hearty—not exactly memorable, but rather decent, flavorful cuisine.

Lovers of **Italian food** never lack for choices at the six-course dinners, which feature cuisine from a region of Italy. Appetizers might include fried calamari and Parma ham and melon along with soup, salad, and a choice of pasta dishes such as fettuccine, cannelloni, and manicotti. Among the main courses are roast rack of lamb with an herb crust, salmon with dill sauce, and beef tenderloin in puff pastry. Also available on every menu are selections from the **spa menu** such as heart-healthy lasagna, grilled sea bass, and curried vegetables and lentils. And everyone's eyes light up in anticipation of the arrival of desserts with an Italian flair, such as tiramisu, cannelloni siciliani, and chocolate soufflé.

The fare is also appreciated as much for its entertainment as for its gastronomic value: Much emphasis and a few theatrics are placed on tossing a pasta or energetically seasoning a salad while diners look on. Menus are written in both Italian and English and always feature a **pasta of the day.**

No evening on board begins without a theme, and in keeping with the line's Italian origins, three of the seven **theme nights** on a typical cruise focus on Italian food and some aspect of Italian lore, legend, and ambiance. *Festa Italiana* turns the ship into an Italian street festival at sea, where guests are encouraged to wear the colors of the Italian flag and have fun participating in bocce ball, pizza-dough-tossing contests, tarantella dance lessons, Venetian-mask making, and Italian karaoke. On *Notte Mediterranean,* staff members don the native dress of cultures around the Mediterranean and present a red rose to each woman passenger during dessert. Another night is the *Notte Tropical* deck party with a Mediterranean twist, where guests can enjoy ethnic dancing and ice-carving demonstrations. The highlight of many cruises is **Roman Bacchanal Toga Night,** when at least some of the guests don togas (usually a bed sheet fastened around the waist with a belt) along with a good sense of humor. Even the cruise director (who is usually American during Caribbean sailings) is likely to threaten, "No sheet, no eat." So, whether you look good in a toga or not, you'll probably be wearing one at dinner. So traditional are these toga nights that some repeat passengers have actually commissioned couture versions from their tailors in anticipation of their next cruise.

The *CostaVictoria* has two dining rooms and the newest and biggest ship, *CostaAtlantica,* has three. Both ships maintain the typical two-seating policy—lunch is served at noon and 1:30pm and dinner at 6:15 and 8:30pm. Each also has a casual breakfast and lunch

Life on Costa's Private Island

On all eastern Caribbean itineraries, passengers spend 1 day at Costa's private beach, **Catalina Island** (formerly called Serena Cay), a deserted island off the coast of the Dominican Republic. This relaxing patch of paradise not only offers palm tree–fringed beaches and sunbathing, but activities like volleyball, beach Olympics, and snorkeling. There's a band and a beach barbecue to round out the day. A local island vendor rents jet skis and offers banana-boat rides.

buffet restaurant where, 2 nights a week (Tues and Thurs), you can also have an **informal buffet-style dinner** instead of heading to the formal dining room. Both ships boast formal **alternative restaurants,** called "Ristorante Magnifico by Zeffirino" and charging guests a staggering $18.75 per person for the privilege of dining there. (Whoa! Hope this isn't an industry trend!) Based on the famous Zeffirino's restaurant first opened in Genoa in 1939 (now there's one in Las Vegas, too), these intimate restaurants will feature candlelight, flowers, and live soft music.

There are, of course, plenty of places to eat between meals. Juliette's Pâtisserie serves espresso, chocolates, and pastries aboard each ship, and **Romeo's Pizzeria** offers pizza throughout the day and night. Laden with herbs and fresh mozzarella, their pies are considered by many passengers to be the most genuinely addictive food on board. **Buffets,** unfortunately, tend to lack pizzazz, focusing on tried-and-true hot and cold staples. Low-fat, low-salt, low-cholesterol menus are available in the dining room. Unfortunately, as on most lines, cappuccino and espresso count as bar drinks and appear on your bar tab at the end of the cruise.

ACTIVITIES

More than anything else, Costa is known for its lineup of festive activities reflecting its Italian heritage. Nights are given over to Italian and Mediterranean theme nights (see "Dining," above); daytime activities include **Italian language and cooking classes** as well as such traditional cruise staples as jackpot bingo, bridge, arts and crafts, dance classes, shuffleboard, art auctions, horse racing, Ping-Pong, and fun poolside competitions (like who looks most like Al Pacino or sings like Pavarotti). Each ship also has a library and a card room.

Avid duffers can take part in the Costa's "Golf Academy at Sea" program, featuring **private golf lessons** and videotaped golf-swing analysis by a PGA member golf instructor (the 15-min. lesson is $25, a 30-min. lesson is $45, and the hour-long lesson is $80). There is also a putting cage and daily putting tournaments, and the pro will accompany guests who sign up for golfing shore excursions to some of the best courses in the Caribbean, like Mahogany Run in St. Thomas and The Links at Safe Haven in Grand Cayman.

Some Special Deals

Senior Discounts: "Super Senior Discounts" are sometimes available, allowing passengers over age 60 to deduct an additional $100 per cabin from early-booking fares booked 120 days before sailing. **Children's Discounts:** Children under 17 sharing a cabin with two adults can sometimes cruise for as little as $199 per person, excluding port charges. Kids under age 2 sail for free.

Costa Fleet Itineraries			
Ship	Home Ports & Season	Itinerary	Other Itineraries
Costa-Atlantica	Round-trip from Fort Lauderdale; itineraries alternate weekly, Nov–Apr.	**7-night W. Carib:** Key West, Playa del Carmen/Cozumel, Ocho Rios (Jamaica), and Grand Cayman. **7-night E. Carib:** San Juan, St. Thomas, Catalina Island, and Nassau.	Mediter-ranean
Costa-Victoria	Round-trip from Fort Lauderdale; itineraries alternate weekly, Nov–Apr.	**7-night W. Carib:** Key West, Playa del Carmen/Cozumel, Ocho Rios (Jamaica), and Grand Cayman. **7-night E. Carib:** San Juan, St. Thomas, Catalina Island, and Nassau.	Mediter-ranean

A priest conducts **Catholic mass** almost every day in each ship's chapel. For married couples, vow-renewal ceremonies are conducted on board in Port Everglades and St. Thomas.

CHILDREN'S PROGRAM

Compared to other cruise lines, Costa places less emphasis on separating children from adult passengers. In 1999, only 5% to 10% of passengers traveled with their families, so there are not throngs of children on board.

The kids' programs and facilities are not nearly as extensive as those available on other lines such as Disney or Carnival. At least two full-time **youth counselors** are available aboard each Costa ship, with additional staff pressed into service whenever more than a dozen children are on the passenger list. Both ships offer **supervised activities** for kids 3 to 17, divided into two age groups unless enough children are aboard to divide them into three (3 to 5, 6 to 8, and 9 to 12 years). The "Costa Kids Club," for ages 3 to 12, includes such activities as Nintendo, bridge and galley tours, arts and crafts, scavenger hunts, Italian-language lessons, bingo, board games, face painting, movies, kids' karaoke, and "Coketail," pizza, and ice-cream sundae parties. The *Atlantica* and *Victoria* each have a **children's playroom** and a **teen disco.** If there are enough teens on board, the "Costa Teens Club" for ages 13 to 17 offers sports and fitness programs, movie-making sessions (using camcorders), and karaoke.

When ships are at sea in the Caribbean, supervised Kids Club hours are from 9:30 to 11:30am, 2 to 5pm, and 8 to 10pm. The program doesn't usually operate when ships are in port unless parents specifically request it.

Two nights a week there is a complimentary **Parents Nights Out program,** when from 5 to 11pm the kids are entertained and given a special buffet or pizza party while mom and dad get a night out alone.

All other times, **group baby-sitting** for ages 3 and up is available on request every evening from 6:30pm to 11am, unless the vessel is in port, when hours are extended to include morning and afternoon sessions. Group baby-sitting costs $10 per child per night. There is no in-cabin private baby-sitting available.

ENTERTAINMENT

Although the passengers are international and the location is the Caribbean, the main entertainment focus aboard Costa ships is decidedly—you guessed it—Italian.

Preview: Costa's New *CostaAtlantica*

Like her sister ships, the 2,112-passenger *CostaAtlantica,* due to debut just as this book goes to the printer, is a sleek megaship with a European ambiance and stunning decor, but with more cutting-edge features. The ship is a first for Costa in several ways and is a harbinger for things to come. It has balconies on over 75% of its cabins (the *Victoria* has none) and is the first Costa vessel to have a two-story ocean-view spa and fitness center and a retractable glass roof over its main pool. It's also the line's fastest ship, with a maximum speed of 24 knots. The ship's 12 passenger decks are all named after movies by the famous Italian film director Federico Fellini—such as *Ginger & Fred, 8¹/₂, Roma, La Strada, Amarcord,* and *La Dolce Vita.* The Venetian-style cafe is being modeled on the famous 18th-century Caffe Florian in Venice's St. Mark's Square, and will serve specialty coffees and drinks. Among the numerous bars and lounges, the Madame Butterfly Grand Lounge will come complete with geisha waitresses (how exactly is that Italian?) and the walls of the Coral Lounge are covered with, what else, coral. Aside from the grand two-story dining room, there is an alternative, reservations-only restaurant in the Club Atlantica, a two-deck space on top of the ship. Like the "Ristorante Magnifico by Zeffirino" on the *Victoria,* it will charge guests a whooping $18.75 per person for the privilege of dining in the candlelit restaurant.

Entertainment directors program amusements such as concerts, puppet or marionette shows, mime, acrobatics, or cabaret that, although produced with an Italian bent, do not require audiences to actually know the language.

If you're not looking for Las Vegas–style glitter, you'll likely find the entertainment programs amusing—and, it should be noted, completely inoffensive, a remarkable thing these days.

Both ships have state-of-the-art **showrooms**—two-tiered, half-moon-shaped affairs that evoke 18th-century opera houses—as well as **casinos.** The Broadway-style acts in the main showroom are not nearly as elaborate or professional as those on other major cruise lines; however, it seems passengers have a great time no matter who or what is performing (pretty much the same reaction they have to the cuisine). The **discos** are popular places, and there's always a coterie dancing into the wee hours.

Many passengers choose to cruise on special **Italian theme cruises** featuring popular Italian-American entertainers such as Julius La Rosa, Al Martino, and Don Cornell.

SERVICE

While far from pampering, service is more than adequate in both the dining room and cabins. The young, enthusiastic staff members are friendly, alert, hip, and quick-witted. Dining-room staff is composed of charming waiters capable of handling most culinary requests. In recent years, greater numbers of the staff hail from South America, the Philippines, and many other points, although at least two or three in any dining-room crew are likely to be the genuine Italian article.

There are no self-service laundry facilities on any of the Costa ships.

CostaVictoria

The Verdict

A sleek megaship with a European ambiance and stunning decor, the *Victoria* is an all-around beauty for those liking an internationally flavored Caribbean cruise.

CostaVictoria *(photo: Costa Cruises)*

Specifications

Size (in tons)	76,000	Officers	Italian/International
Number of Cabins	964	Crew	800 (International)
Number of Outside Cabins	573	Passenger/Crew Ratio	2.4 to 1
Cabins with Verandas	0	Year Built	1996
Number of Passengers	1,928	Last Major Refurbishment	N/A

Frommer's Ratings (Scale of 1–5)

Cabin Comfort & Amenities	4	Pool, Fitness & Spa Facilities	4
Ship Cleanliness & Maintenance	4	Children's Facilities	3
Public Comfort/Space	4	Itinerary	4
Decor	5	Worth the Money	5

The ship that launched Costa Cruises into the megaship era was inaugurated in the summer of 1996, and until the *Atlantica* came along it was the largest and most technologically sophisticated ship ever launched by the line. Built in Bremerhaven, Germany, with an impressive cruising speed of between 21 and 23 knots, it has a sleek, streamlined, futuristic-looking design with four tiers of glass-fronted observation decks facing the prow. Its mammoth size allows for many spacious and dramatic interior features and many options for dining and after-dark diversions.

As a nod to some of its mega-competitors, the interior is splashier and more colorful than that of any previous Costa vessel. It's also more monumental, with a design that's imposing but, like a well-dressed Italian who knows how to tastefully blend patterns, fabrics, and accessories to create a look right out of fashion magazines, it's also compelling.

Signature design elements include an abundant use of stainless steel, teak, suede, leather, tile mosaics, and Italian marble in swirled patterns of blues and greens. For instance, brilliant royal blue suede covers the tops of card tables and deep, salmon-colored suede is used on the walls of the Concorde Plaza lounge. The Bolero Buffet features teak floors, and a wraparound tile mosaic creates eye-catching walls in the Capriccio Lounge.

The sleek, seven-story Planetarium Atrium—a Costa first—features four glass elevator banks and is punctuated by a thin string of ice-blue neon subtly spiraling toward the glass ceiling dome. Also a new concept in the Costa fleet are the *Victoria*'s two dining rooms, with two seatings and an abundance of seating for couples (ideal for honeymooners).

Cabins & Rates						
Cabins	**Per diems from**	**Bathtub**	**Fridge**	**Hair Dryer**	**Sitting Area**	**TV**
Inside	$103	no	yes	yes	no	yes
Outside	$131	no	yes	yes	no	yes
Suite	$295	yes	yes	yes	yes	yes

CABINS Surprisingly, the cabins on this newer ship are smaller than those on some of the line's older vessels. At 120 to 150 square feet, standard inside and outside cabins certainly won't win any awards for their size (the smallest are like walk-in closets), but their sleek design and decor bring a delicious European touch to the cruise experience. Decorative fabric panels hang on the wall above headboards, matching the bedspreads. Bedside tables and dressers are sleek and art deco. Stainless steel is used for all bathroom sinks, and for dressers and mirrors in the mini-suites. All cabins have TVs, music channels, hair dryers, minibars, and safes. None have verandas. Some 60% of them feature oversize round portholes.

Especially desirable are the 14 mini-suites, which have separate living rooms, reading areas, and tubs with hydro-massage equipment. Each is outfitted with one queen-size bed and two Pullman-style beds. What makes them a bargain is that they contain many of the same amenities and interior design features as the more expensive suites, and their space is very generous at 301 square feet. For those with imperial taste, six full-size suites raise the beam on luxury, with one queen and two Pullman-style beds and generous 430-square-foot proportions that make them feel roomy even if they're bunking four passengers. Furnishings in these suites are made of pear wood, with fabrics by Laura Ashley, who is not even remotely Italian, and whose particular patterns in this case are relatively bold and (thank god) not particularly frilly looking. Some of the suites have floor-to-ceiling windows.

Six inside cabins are specifically outfitted for passengers with disabilities. Cabins on Deck 6A don't benefit from direct elevator access and require that guests climb a half-flight of stairs from the nearest elevator bank.

PUBLIC AREAS Public areas, especially the casino, throb with color and energy. Designed to re-create an Italian piazza, the four-story Concorde Plaza is one of the *Victoria*'s signature public areas. Seating over 300 as the venue for evening dancing and music as well a perfect place for a relaxing drink by day, the Plaza boasts a four-story-high waterfall on one end and, on the other, a wall of windows facing the sea. An elevator bank whizzes guests between floors; glass walls allow sections of cabin hallways to be privy to the attractive plaza below. A granite bar is complemented by stainless steel accoutrements. The observation lounge serves first as a grand arena for socializing and special shipboard events and second as a theater for evening entertainment.

In the Central Hall, an atrium begins in the lobby, rises seven decks, and is topped by a crystal dome that floods the interior with sunlight. Four glass-sided elevators offer passengers a quick panorama of life on board at every level.

Two main dining rooms (the Sinfonia and the Fantasia) operate on the standard two-seatings plan at both lunch and dinner. The multifunction Tavernetta Lounge features the music of a three-piece dance band and wraparound paintings of other ships in the Costa fleet, created by marine artist Stephen Card. Evenings the lounge now doubles as a new alternative restaurant, called "Ristorante Magnifico by Zeffirino," named after a famous restaurant in Genoa. It'll cost you a staggering $18.75 per person for the privilege of dining in the candlelit restaurant. There are also buffets, a grill, a pizzeria, and an ice-cream bar to ensure that no one ever goes hungry between meals.

Gamblers gravitate to the big and brassy Monte Carlo Casino, the boldest, most dramatic, and biggest of any in the Costa fleet. It's linked to the Grand Bar Orpheus, one floor below, by a curving stairway whose glass stair treads are illuminated in patterns that are almost psychedelic. This bar is the preferred spot aboard for sampling an espresso or cappuccino, or—if it's late enough and you feel a bit reckless—a selection of grappas.

Other public rooms include a play area for children, a club for teens, a chapel (not always a feature aboard today's megaships), three conference rooms, an array of boutiques, a card room, a library, and a disco.

POOL, FITNESS & SPA FACILITIES   The *Victoria*'s Pompeii Spa is large and well accessorized, and has its own indoor pool. It's done with richly colored mosaic tiles and Roman columns. You can release your tensions in a steam bath, a sauna, or a Turkish bath, or sit and soak in the spa's Jacuzzi, which is perched artfully within the larger waters of the spa's heated swimming pool. The attractive but smallish workout room shares a glass wall with the spa and pool area and features over a dozen exercise machines. The ceilings are low in the gym—tall people beware.

Out on deck, there's a pair of swimming pools as well as a "misting pool" that cools off overheated sunbathers with fine jets of water. Further decks wrap around the pools and their sunbathing area, providing plenty of space for passengers to stretch out and soak up the rays, even when the ship is fully booked. It looks like a resort on the Italian Riviera with its bright yellow and blue deck chairs and its nautical blue-and-white-striped lounges. There are four Jacuzzis, a tennis court that does double-duty as a half-size basketball court, and a jogging track, four circuits of which equal 1 mile. There's also a beauty salon aboard.

Crown Cruise Line

4000 Hollywood Blvd., Suite 385, South Tower, Hollywood, FL 33021. ☎ **877/276-9621** or 954/967-2100. Fax 954/967-2147. www.crowncruiseline.com.

THE LINE IN A NUTSHELL   An attractive alternative to the megaships, the one and only ship in the recently revived Crown Cruise Line is an immaculate, well-designed, midsize vessel and a bargain way to see Bermuda and the southern Caribbean.

THE EXPERIENCE   The 800-passenger *Crown Dynasty* offers a quality low-key experience that is a far cry from the "party hearty" atmosphere of many other mainstream Caribbean-bound ships. Built in 1993, the ship is bright and modern, with lots of windows, polished woods, and soft hues for what the company calls a "Bermuda decor." Most passengers enjoy mellow pastimes like playing cards and relaxing, snoozing, or reading a book from the comfort of a deck chair. Even announcements, which are few and far between, are only broadcast in public areas to foster a relaxing atmosphere. While most passengers eschew loud, rowdy behavior, they still enjoy a good time, and it's not unusual to see a lively group of couples sipping piña coladas in the hot tubs.

In the summer of 2000, the *Dynasty* became the sixth ship permitted to visit Bermuda on a regular seasonal basis, offering Wednesday departures from Philadelphia and Baltimore from May through October; the rest of the year, the *Dynasty* does weeklong round-trip cruises out of Aruba, departing Saturdays.

Pros

- **One-of-a-kind itineraries.** Both of the ship's routes are unique: Its wintertime southern Caribbean cruises visit all three ABC Islands (Aruba, Bonaire, and Curaçao) and its summertime Bermuda cruises sail from Philadelphia and Baltimore.
- **The price is right.** For the 2000 season, for example, group rates as well as special Florida-resident pricing started as low as $799 per person, including port charges.
- **Shipshape condition.** The *Crown Dynasty*'s sparkling interiors show surprisingly little wear and tear for a ship in service since 1993. Plus, most cabins were spruced up with new carpeting, curtains, and bedspreads during its $5 million refurbishment in 1999.

Cons

- **Chartered flights.** The chartered flights to Aruba that most passengers book along with the cruise have some inconvenient departure times.
- **No alternative restaurant.** Unlike all the mainstream ships, the *Crown* has only one dining room open for dinner, although there are two for breakfast and lunch.
- **Obscured views and too few balconies.** A total of 58 outside cabins (34 on Warwick Deck and 24 on Paget Deck) have either partially or totally obstructed views. Only 10 suites have balconies.

Compared with the other Mainstream lines, here's how Crown rates:					
	Poor	Fair	Good	Excellent	Outstanding
Enjoyment Factor				✓	
Dining			✓		
Activities			✓		
Children's Program		✓			
Entertainment			✓		
Service				✓	
Overall Value				✓	

CROWN: A LOW-PRICED GEM

In early 2000, the newly revived Crown Cruise Line entered the cruise market as the upmarket sister company to the down-market Commodore Cruise Line, which has been around since the late 1960s. Crown's past life started about a decade ago. In 1990, the first Crown Cruise Line was formed and owned by the Grunstad family, operating the newly built *Crown Monarch* and *Crown Jewel* out of Palm Beach, Florida. A couple of years later, Commodore, which was owned by Scandinavian-based EffJohn International, acquired the line. By 1993 though, just before the *Crown Dynasty* debuted, the Crown brand was already dead. EffJohn soon sold the *Jewel* to Singapore-based Star Cruises, leased the *Monarch* to another Singapore-based cruise concern, and chartered the *Dynasty* first to Cunard and then to Norwegian Cruise Line. Now, once again, the *Crown Dynasty* is back with its birth mother and destined to carry on the Crown tradition.

In the summer of 2000, the *Dynasty* became the sixth ship permitted to visit Bermuda on a regular seasonal basis (the island's government limits the number of permits). Unlike the other five ships plying the route, the *Dynasty* is the only one there on weekends. In conjunction with partner Apple Vacations, a tour operator, the ship's weeklong cruises depart Wednesdays from Philadelphia or Baltimore; if passengers don't want to do the full 7-night cruise, they have the option of flying one way and cruising the other, with a 3- or 4-day hotel stay in Bermuda in between.

The rest of the year, the *Dynasty* does weeklong round-trip cruises out of Aruba, departing Saturdays. While it's a great itinerary—few other ships sail out of Aruba—the only downside is getting there. The chartered flights most passengers book along with the cruise have some inconvenient departure times. For example, at press time, the chartered Allegro Air flight from JFK in New York to Aruba departed at an ungodly early 6am on a Saturday morning, while the return flight to JFK didn't depart Aruba until 9:30pm on Saturday night, arriving in NYC around 1am Sunday morning.

THE FLEET

In its short life, the 800-passenger **Crown Dynasty** has been shuttled from one cruise line to another like an unwanted child. Launched in 1993 for Crown Cruise Line, the ship was leased almost immediately to Cunard, where it sailed as the *Cunard Dynasty,* then spent a few years with NCL as the *Norwegian Dynasty* before Commodore Holdings, which runs the budget-minded Commodore Cruise Line, purchased it for $82 million in early 2000, restored its original name, and revived the then-moribund Crown Cruise Line.

Don't think its orphan status over the years means the ship is somehow at fault. Indeed, the *Dynasty* is a lovely midsize ship that offers an easy-on-the-eyes, easy-on-the-wallet cruise experience on several great itineraries.

PASSENGER PROFILE

While many passengers are mature professional couples, including a substantial number of retirees, the wide passenger range includes younger couples in their thirties and forties along with a few 20-something honeymooners. Many have likely cruised before on lines such as Celebrity and Holland America, and it's not uncommon to encounter those who sailed on the *Dynasty* when it was originally with Crown Cruise Line and/or belonged to the Cunard or NCL fleets. On the ship's Caribbean itinerary approximately 90% to 95% of passengers are Americans, with the balance consisting of Dutch, German, French, and South Americans (mostly Venezuelans). Primarily, this is an all-couples cruise and is not recommended for singles. Families with children are also few and far between, except during holiday periods.

Crown Cruise Line Fleet Itineraries			
Ship	Home Ports & Season	Itinerary	Other Itineraries
Crown Dynasty	Bermuda cruises round-trip from Philadelphia or Baltimore, May–Oct; Caribbean cruises round-trip from Aruba, Dec–May.	**7-night Bermuda:** Docks at Royal Naval Dockyard. **7-night S. Carib:** Barbados, St. Lucia, Grenada, Bonaire, and Curaçao.	Eastern Canada

DINING

The ship's one main dining venue—the 420-seat Hamilton Dining Room—serves all three meals daily. Breakfast and lunch are open seating, while there is assigned seating for an early and a late dinner. Passengers seeking a more casual atmosphere opt for the breakfast and lunch buffets in the Dockyard Café, where both indoor and outdoor seating are available. Outdoor tables have panoramic sea views and are especially well positioned for sunrise viewing. Afternoon tea is served daily at 4pm with sandwiches, cakes, and cookies. **Late-night buffets** are available nightly at 11:30pm and feature different themes like Tex-Mex or tropical fruit, with one over-the-top gala buffet each cruise. Specialty coffees are available in the dining room and in the lounges for an additional charge.

While the overall quality of the food is average (dinner entrees could use more spices and/or sauces, if you ask me), choices are plentiful. Dinner menus include a choice of three appetizers, like a baked mushroom and sweet onion tart or smoked salmon plate; three soups, such as a Bahamian chowder or corn-and-potato chowder; three salads; and five entrees, like baked New England cod, prime rib, or regional dishes like a Dutch-inspired beef-and-vegetable pie (on the Caribbean itinerary), plus a vegetarian selection. Four dessert choices, like crème brûlée or baked Alaska, are available along with a cheese or fruit plate. The complimentary **24-hour room-service** menu includes the usual suspects: soup, sandwiches, salads, and pastries, plus coffee, tea, and milk. Wine, cocktails, and soft drinks may also be ordered through room service from 9am to 2am at prevailing bar prices.

On the ship's Bermuda runs, there is a Royal Bermuda Brunch on Sundays.

ACTIVITIES

While many passengers choose not to participate, the activities schedule will keep those who do busy with old faithfuls like jackpot bingo, audience participation shows like Name That Tune and the Not-So-Newlywed Game, shuffleboard and Ping-Pong tournaments, golf-putting contests, line dancing, ice-carving demos, art auctions, morning walkathons, and aerobics classes. Among the more unusual activities on a recent Caribbean cruise was a ventriloquism seminar conducted by one of the entertainers. Special port lecturers are aboard on the ship's Bermuda itineraries.

CHILDREN'S PROGRAM

With so few children aboard most cruises, there is no official children's program, although there is a small supervised playroom, called the Rainbow Room, which accommodates up to 20 kids.

ENTERTAINMENT

While there are none of the lavish productions you find on the megaships, there are nightly performances by an enthusiastic troupe of dancers who perform the standard mix of Broadway show tunes and pop hits, along with performances by comedians and ventriloquists. Nighttime activities include a masquerade party (though on a recent Caribbean cruise only 30 of 550 passengers participated), swing-dance party, fifties and sixties sock hops, karaoke, and predinner piano music. There's also a disco with a DJ in the Port Royal Pub. By day, a steel band plays on-deck poolside.

SERVICE

Both the dining room staff and the cabin attendants aboard the *Dynasty* are warm and accommodating, and their upbeat attitude goes a long way toward enhancing the overall cruise experience. Room service is exceptionally fast day and night—for example, on three occasions during my cruise I ordered continental breakfast to be delivered to my cabin at 7:30am and it always arrived exactly on time.

The ship's small infirmary is staffed by a doctor and a nurse. There is no self-service laundry.

Crown Dynasty

The Verdict

Thumbs-up for a stylish midsize ship with a pair of one-of-a-kind itineraries at amazingly reasonable rates.

Crown Dynasty *(photo: Crown Cruise Line)*

Specifications

Size (in tons)	20,000	Officers	European
Number of Cabins	400	Crew	320 (International)
Number of Outside Cabins	277	Passenger/Crew Ratio	2.6 to 1
Cabins with Verandas	10	Year Built	1993
Number of Passengers	800	Last Major Refurbishment	1999

Frommer's Ratings (Scale of 1–5)

Cabin Comfort & Amenities	3	Pool, Fitness & Spa Facilities	2
Ship Cleanliness & Maintenance	3	Children's Facilities	2
Public Comfort/Space	3	Itinerary	5
Decor	3	Worth the Money	5

The midsize (800-passenger) *Crown Dynasty* is bright and modern, with lots of windows, polished woods, and soft hues that contribute to the quiet, low-key onboard mood. It's a lovely midsize vessel that offers a couple of great itineraries at a great price.

CABINS   The good news: Bright and cheery cabins feature warmly colored carpets, drapes, and bedspreads, and the use of polished light woods adds a Scandinavian flavor. The bad news: The average size of an outside cabin is a compact 140 square feet and inside cabins are a very tight 130 square feet (by comparison, Carnival's standard

TIMBUKTU   KALAMAZOO

AT&T Direct® Service

The easy way to call home from anywhere.

Global connection with the AT&T Network	**AT&T** direct service

For the easy way to call home, take the attached wallet guide.

AT&T Calling Card, AT&T Corporate Card, AT&T Universal Card, MasterCard®, American Express®, Diners Club®, and Discover® cards accepted. Credit card calling subject to availability. Payment terms subject to your credit card agreement. ©2000 AT&T

Make Learning Fun & Easy

With IDG Books Worldwide

Frommer's®

FOR DUMMIES®

WEBSTER'S NEW WORLD™

Betty Crocker's

the Unofficial Guide®

BURPEE®

ARCO®

HOWELL BOOK HOUSE™

WEIGHT WATCHERS®

Available at your local bookstores

Cabins & Rates

Cabins	Per diems from	Bathtub	Fridge	Hair Dryer	Sitting Area	TV
Inside	$137	no	no	yes	no	yes*
Outside	$166	no	no	yes	no	yes*
Suite	$209	no	some	yes	yes	yes*

All TVs show CNN.

cabins are 188 sq. ft.). Bathrooms are also tiny. However, there is ample storage space with two large floor-to-ceiling closets plus two sets of drawers. The amenities also help to make up for the small cabins: all cabins also have a small desk and one armchair, as well as terry bathrobes, hair dryers, safes, and a selection of fancy toiletries. The TVs broadcast CNN and two movie channels.

The only accommodations with both a sitting area and a balcony are the 10 top-of-the line deluxe suites on Deck 7, which range from 312 to 374 square feet, while the 24 junior suites on Decks 6 and 7 have a sitting area (those on Deck 7 have views partially obstructed by lifeboats). All sizes range between 160 and 350 square feet, with the deluxe suites being the largest. Suite guests are treated to the services of a butler in addition to the room steward. All 10 of the balcony suites are named after Bermuda flowers, and potpourri in each suite has been manufactured by the Bermuda Perfume Company from the essence of the flower the suite's named after.

Two inside and two outside cabins are wheelchair accessible.

PUBLIC AREAS   The ship's modest yet elegant five-story atrium, decorated with a generous use of glass, polished wood, and brass, sets the tone for the rest of the ship's public spaces. During the day the atrium is bathed in natural light pouring in through skylights and picture windows. Space and openness are prominent features of the interior design and contribute to the ship's light and airy feel. In keeping with the ship's Bermuda itinerary, decks and public rooms are named after that island's beautiful parishes and popular attractions.

Decorated with warm beige, red, and brownish hues and surrounded by expansive windows with panoramic views, the completely nonsmoking Hamilton Dining Room is a pleasant place to dine. Low partitions strategically positioned around tables give the room an intimate feeling. The bright and airy Dockyard Cafe located in the aft section of Deck 6 seats up to 100 at both inside and outside tables for buffet breakfast and lunch.

With its marble-and-brass bar along with blue-and-gold banquettes and chairs, the 90-seat Queen of Bermuda Bar is the most intimate, and popular, venue for predinner cocktails and after-dinner drinks. A pianist plays tunes there before dinner.

All nightly stage shows are performed in the multilevel Gombey Lounge, which seats a max of 450 people and is warmly decorated with blue and gold accents and furnished with plush barrel chairs and couches. (*Tip:* For evening shows, arrive early to grab seats in the front middle section because the stage view from some seats in the rear are obscured by pillars; other seats in the back are situated at severe angles away from the stage.) Other lounges featuring nightly musical entertainment are the Southampton Club, where a duo performs pop material, and the Port Royal Pub, which serves as the disco (with a DJ). Located on Deck 5 amidships is the modest (though lively) Atlantic Casino, with some 70 slots, four blackjack tables, one roulette table, and a Caribbean stud-poker table. The ship also boasts an exceptionally large library, a card room, and three shops.

POOL, SPA & FITNESS FACILITIES   I use the term "spa" loosely here, given that the small facility has just two massage rooms along with a beauty parlor. There are separate steam rooms and saunas for men and women, plus three hot tubs (a pair poolside and one in the spa). The fitness area has an exercise floor and two treadmills, two stationery bicycles, two stair-steppers, and one rowing machine, plus several pneumatic exercise machines and an assortment of weights. The ship's one medium-size swimming pool is located on the top deck, where there is ample space for sunbathing. You can also venture to one of the ship's tiered aft decks for a quieter spot to repose, or even to the patch of Deck 5 at the bow, called the Observation Deck.

Disney Cruise Line

210 Celebration Place, Suite 400, Celebration, FL 34747-1000. ☎ **800/951-3532** or 407/566-7000. Fax 407/566-7353. www.disney.com/DisneyCruise.

THE LINE IN A NUTSHELL   This pair of floating theme parks is like no other in the industry. Mellow, even elegant interiors allow the line's impressive innovations in dining, entertainment, kids' facilities, and cabin design to take center stage. If you love Disney, you'll love these ships; if not, there are cheaper cruises.

THE EXPERIENCE   The *Disney Magic* and *Disney Wonder* are the famous company's first foray into cruising, and boast a handful of truly innovative, Disney-style features, including a rotating series of restaurants on every cruise, cabins designed for families, Disney-inspired entertainment, and the biggest kids' facilities at sea. It's innovations like these that set Disney's cruises far apart from their closest peers in the Carnival, Royal Caribbean, Celebrity, and Premier lines. In many ways, the experience is more Disney than it is cruise (for instance, there's no casino or library). On the other hand, the ships are surprisingly elegant and well laid out, and the Disneyisms are subtly sprinkled, like fairy dust, throughout their mellow, art deco– and art nouveau–inspired interiors and grand, classic liner–inspired exteriors. Head to toe, the ships are a class act.

In the spirit of Disney's penchant for organization, its 3- and 4-day cruises are designed to be combined with a land-based Disney theme park and hotel package to create a weeklong all-Disney vacation (though you can book the cruises separately). They even whisk you from Disney World to the ship in a fleet of custom Disney buses.

Pros

- **Kids' programs.** Two huge playrooms plus a teen cafe are the largest kids' facilities at sea.
- **Family entertainment.** Endearing, family-oriented Disney musicals are performed on some of the best-equipped and most high-tech stages of any ship today.
- **Family-style cabins.** All cabins have sitting areas with sofa beds to sleep families of at least three, and the majority have 1$\frac{1}{2}$ bathrooms.
- **Dining.** No other ships have diners rotating between three different but equally appealing sit-down restaurants.

Cons

- **Limited adult entertainment.** There is no casino or library.
- **Small gyms.** Considering the ships' large sizes, their gyms are on the small side and border on being cramped.
- **Meager breakfast and lunch buffets.** In relation to the size of the ship, the buffet spread in the Topsider Cafe is limited, and the space is cramped.

Compared with the other Mainstream lines, here's how Disney rates:					
	Poor	Fair	Good	Excellent	Outstanding
Enjoyment Factor					✓
Dining			✓		
Activities			✓		
Children's Program					✓
Entertainment				✓	
Service			✓		
Overall Value				✓	

DISNEY: THE OLD MOUSE & THE SEA

There ain't nothing else like Disney's pair of floating tributes to Mickey, that's for sure. However, the idea of ships catering to families isn't a new one. Back in 1984, Premier pioneered the family cruise niche and was for a number of years the official cruise line of Walt Disney World. Today Premier's *Big Red Boat* is still providing family-friendly (and very inexpensive) 3-, 4-, and 7-night Bahamas cruises, albeit sans Mickey and Goofy (the line has it own set of characters), and has proven that the family-cruise market is indeed a viable one.

So, Disney, the ultimate purveyor of family vacations, got in on the family-fun-at-sea act in the summer of 1998, with the debut of the much ballyhooed (and very late) *Disney Magic,* and sister *Disney Wonder* a year later.

In many ways, Disney Cruise Line marches to the beat of its own drummer (but much less so than they originally intended) and is a unique species within the cruise world. From its ships' blue-black hulls and twin funnels (only one works; the other is ornamental) to its rotating restaurant concept, family suites with two bathrooms, and lack of a casino (and ships' horns that blast the first few notes from "When You Wish Upon a Star"), Disney is different—and therein lies the appeal.

That said, after a slightly rough start Disney has made some substantial adjustments to improve its product. By trial and error, the company has learned that it can indeed learn from the industry and from practices that established lines have perfected. For instance, unlike most other lines operating in the Caribbean and Bahamas, Disney originally bundled its cruise and Orlando packages with airfare, thus making their prices, which aren't ultra-cheap to begin with, seem even higher and harder to compare against similar packages offered by other lines. Disney has since changed its pricing format, and prints airfare separately in its brochures, just like everyone else. It also has lowered its rates, believe it or not, to be more competitive with the handful of other ships doing the 3- and 4-night cruise-and-Orlando packages. In the beginning, Disney also didn't think it needed a cruise director or hotel director (the officer in charge of passenger services, including cabins, restaurants, and bars). It now has both, and attributes a smoother onboard experience to these two key individuals. The line also has added more adult activities like cooking demos, photography workshops, and dancing classes, and has put the *Magic* on a 7-night eastern Caribbean route year-round, while the *Wonder* continues the year-round 3- and 4-night Bahamas routes both ships used to ply. Former Disney Cruise Line president Arthur Rodney was quoted in early 1999 as saying, "We're evolving. Those who traveled on the *Magic* in the beginning wouldn't recognize her today." There you go: You really can teach an old mouse new tricks.

THE FLEET

Both *Disney Magic* and *Disney Wonder* have the same size, layout, and, for the most part, mellow decorative motifs. Inside and out, they represent Disney's attempt to re-create the grandeur of the classic transatlantic liners—an attempt at which, if we allow for their modern, Disneyfied manner, they succeed.

Both ships weigh in at 83,000 gross register tons, measure 964 feet in length (about as long as New York's famous Chrysler Building is tall), and carry 1,750 passengers at the rate of two per cabin, or up to a whopping 3,325 if every third, fourth, and fifth berth in every cabin is filled. An American staff and a crew of 945 service the 875 staterooms.

The Disney touch is evident throughout the ships, although, to the designers' credit, it's not overwhelming or cloying. Both ships have virtually identical layouts, with the main differences being the names of public rooms and the design motif: The *Magic's* is art deco and the *Wonder's* is art nouveau. The main place you'll notice the design difference is the atrium chandeliers: The *Wonder's* is a colorful avant-garde blown-glass

The Disney Cruise/Park Package

In the spirit of Disney's penchant for organization, its "seamless" vacation mantra tends to leave little to chance or whim. To shuttle passengers to and from the Orlando International Airport and Disney's theme parks, Disney's got an army of special buses (with little Mickey silhouettes worked into the upholstery) at the ready. To get passengers in the mood, an orientation video about the cruise is played during the nearly hour-long trip between Orlando and the ship. At Disney's swank new cruise terminal at Port Canaveral, guests who have come from the resorts (guests doing the 7-night parks/cruise combo must do the parks portion first) already have their all-purpose, computerized Key to the World cards, which get them into their cabins, serve as the onboard charge cards, and function as their ID when getting on and off the ship in port. There's no need, then, to actually check in at the terminal—which is a big plus. If you're just doing the cruise (as about 30% of passengers do), you get your Key to the World card when you arrive at the terminal.

Most of Disney's passengers purchase the "seamless" 7-day land/sea packages (as opposed to the cruise only), which include either 3 or 4 days at Disney World resort and 4 or 3 days aboard ship. Costs for a 7-day package for a family of four, with airfare, are roughly equivalent to a weeklong holiday at Walt Disney World in Orlando. Published rates for Disney's cruises and land/sea packages are lower than a year or two ago, though they're still a bit higher than the other Port Canaveral–based vessels of Premier, Carnival, and Royal Caribbean, each of which currently offers short sailings coordinated with vacations at or near central Florida theme parks.

---

creation, while the *Magic*'s is a somewhat more sedate, deco-inspired piece. Overall, the design of both ships is subtle, elegant, and nostalgic. On both, Mickey's big-eared head appears on the pair of giant red funnels, fanciful golden curlicues decorate the pointed blue-black bow, oversize portholes line the main drag on Deck 3, outlines of Mickey and the gang are quietly worked in to the silver-toned grillwork and frieze in the atrium, and an understated bronzy statue is the focus of the three-story atrium (on the *Magic* it's Mickey as the sorcerer's apprentice in *Fantasia,* and on the *Wonder* it's Aerial from *The Little Mermaid*). You'll find the framed story sketches from famous 1930s and 1940s Disney animated movies blended tastefully against the generous caramel-colored wood paneling in the ships' stairways and corridors, and a huge white-gloved Mickey hand holds up the snaking slide at the children's pool while tiny little Mickey hands quietly point to the floors above the banks of elevators.

PASSENGER PROFILE

Just walk around Walt Disney World and you'll see exactly the kind of people Disney attracts to its ships—families, honeymooners, adults without children, and seniors. Just about everybody, actually. There's also a fair number of foreign passengers as well—it seems like *everyone* loves Disney.

DINING

Disney's dining concept sets it apart from the big-ship crowd. While the food is average cruise fare and service varies from efficient to a bit harried and amateur, the neat catch is that there are **three restaurants** that passengers (and their servers) rotate among over the course of the cruise. There is an early and late seating in all three, and like groups are scheduled to rotate together as much as possible (for example, families with young children, adults alone, and families with teens). On one night, in the *Magic*'s elegant 1930s-era Lumiere's restaurant or the *Wonder*'s equally elegant nautical-themed Triton, passengers dine on a beef tenderloin in a green peppercorn sauce or a herb-baked sea bass on a bed of spinach; on another night they enjoy the likes of roasted rum pork or roasted lobster tail in the tropical Parrot Cay restaurant; and on the third they eat in Animator's Palate, a bustling, high-tech, very Disney eatery that starts out completely black and white and over the course of the meal gradually becomes awash in color as the walls and ceiling light up. Here, choices include a Thai linguini with Oriental vegetables and a grilled pork chop with asparagus-corn risotto and wild-mushroom sauce. Desserts are served on cute palate-shaped plates (unfortunately, Disney's removed the fun squeeze bottles filled with strawberry and chocolate toppings for decorating the ice cream).

In all restaurants, a **vegetarian option** is offered, and the **kids' menus** include more healthy fare like fresh fruit with dipping sauce, cream of chicken soup, beef tenderloin, and baked salmon in addition to the hamburger, hot-dog, and macaroni-and-cheese staples. If your kids are big soda drinkers and suck down three or more a day, there's a new **soft-drink package** available for children 12 and under: Unlimited soda refills go for $12 for the 3-night cruise and $16 for the 4-night sailings. A single soda goes for $1.50.

The buffet-style breakfast and lunch spread in the *Magic*'s Topsider and the *Wonder*'s Beach Blanket restaurants offer items like deli meats, cheeses, and a carving station, as well as rice and vegetable dishes. There's a salad bar and a dessert table. Overall, though, compared to other ships this size, the cramped food stations in the casual buffet restaurants have not been smartly designed and offer slim pickins, although seating is plentiful and spills onto attractive wooden tables and chairs out on deck. Options for afternoon noshing poolside include Pinocchio's Pizzeria; Pluto's Dog House for hot dogs, hamburgers, and fries; and Scoops ice-cream bar. There's **24-hour room service** from a limited menu, but there's no midnight buffet (except if you count the spread offered at the late-night deck party held once per cruise); instead, hors d'oeuvres are served to passengers in the bars around midnight. If you're lucky enough to actually snag a table, the 136-passenger, **reservations-only restaurant,** Palo, is a romantic adults-only dining venue serving Italian specialties far away from the fray. If you want to dine here, be sure to book a table as soon as you get aboard the first day—and try to get aboard early, since tables go *fast* (there's a $5 cover charge per person).

The *Magic*'s 7-night itinerary includes all the choices above plus a champagne brunch, afternoon tea, themed dinners, and buffets.

ACTIVITIES

Activities for adults are limited compared to other big-ship lines, but there are indeed some pastimes geared to adults and adults only. Though there is no casino of any kind (nor a library or a card room), each ship has an entertainment complex with three lounges for adults only (see "Entertainment," below), plus the cozy, reservations-only Palo restaurant (see "Dining," above); a sprawling, casual **Promenade Lounge** where live jazz is played; and the **ESPN Skybox bar,** a smallish, brightly lit sports bar with a huge wide-screen TV showing all manner of sports on ESPN.

Despite this, in the first few months after the *Magic* was launched in July 1998, complaints were common about the ship not offering enough activities for adults. To Disney's credit, the company listened and responded by adding more programming. Tapping its land-based Disney Institute program, as well as its parks and hotels, it now offers **adult workshops** on subjects like acting (taught by the actual Beast from the Broadway show, for instance), animation, photography, antiques, and topical subjects

Castaway Cay: A Well-Oiled Machine

Not surprisingly, Castaway Cay, Disney's 1,000-acre private island in the Bahamas and a port of call on all cruises, is a well-oiled machine. Disney has developed only 55 acres of the island, and guests can snorkel, feast on a buffet barbecue, ride bikes along a trail, shop, send postcards, have a massage, or just lounge in a hammock or lie on the beach.

What's its best quality? It's accessible. Unlike the private islands of Holland America, Royal Caribbean, Princess, Costa, and NCL, which require the ships to anchor offshore and shuttle passengers back and forth on tenders, Castaway Cay's dock allows the *Magic* and *Wonder* to pull right up so guests can literally step from the ship right onto the pink cement path that leads to the island of fun. It's a 7-minute walk to the main beach area, or you can hop one of the shuttle trams, which transport passengers to the main beaches and to the adults-only beach and bar, about a mile away.

The ships arrive at the cay in the morning, and passengers are greeted by a host or hostess and given a towel, after which they scatter in all directions—families to one beach (strollers and cargo carts are available here free of charge) lined with lounge chairs and pastel-colored umbrellas; teens to another, where they can swim, lounge, or play volleyball, soccer, or tetherball; and adults 18 and older to a third, the secluded, mile-long alabaster stretch aptly called Serenity Bay, located in the north part of the island, where the emphasis is on rest and relaxation. Guests can have a drink at the nearby Castaway Air Bar, grab some grub at the food area or fruit bar, lie on the beach, go for a swim, or head to a private ocean-view cabana for an open-air 55-minute massage.

To make sure all members of the family are covered, parents can first head to Scuttle's Cove, a **children's activity center** for ages 3 to 12 where activities include arts and crafts, music and theater, and an excavation site where little ones (and big ones) can check out the skeletal remains of a 35-foot female whale. Kids can also go on their own dig, complete with sifting pans, and make plaster molds of what they find. Families who go to the **family beach** can explore the island's 15-acre snorkeling course or rent a kayak, paddle boat, or banana boat. Adult- and child-size bicycles can be rented for $5 for a ride along a 3-mile bike path around the island.

(like Jewish history) at certain times of the year. During the day at sea on the 4-night cruise itinerary, a **master chefs program** features cooking demonstrations and wine tasting by Disney resorts' top chefs and sommeliers. All these activities are complimentary except wine tasting, which costs $15 per person. There are also **adult movies** (no, not *that* kind!), that cruise stalwart the Not-So-Newlywed Game, and a **captain's cocktail party** with complimentary drinks once per cruise. For the *Magic*'s 7-night itinerary, additional things to do include programs based on nautical themes (storytellers tell tales about navigation, shipbuilding, and the culture of the Caribbean), behind-the-scenes Disney (backstage tours, galley demos, and bridge tours), and the Art of Entertaining seminars (cooking demos, invitation design, and party planning).

And, if your idea of staying active is a soothing massage, the ships now offer **in-cabin massages** to guests staying in the concierge-level suites on Deck 8. The 50-minute massage, which you can have on your private cabin veranda or in the cabin itself, go for $105, not including tip.

Disney Fleet Itineraries			
Ship	Home Ports & Season	Itinerary	Other Itineraries
Disney Magic	Round-trip from Port Canaveral, weekly, year-round.	**7-night E. Carib:** St. Maarten, St. Thomas, and Castaway Cay.	None
Disney Wonder	Round-trip from Port Canaveral, itineraries alternate weekly, year-round.	**3- and 4-night Bahamas:** Nassau and Castaway Cay, plus Freeport on 4-nighter.	None

CHILDREN'S PROGRAM

Not surprisingly, with as many as 500, 800, or more kids on any given sailing, Disney's kids' facilities are the most extensive at sea, with at least 50 dedicated **counselors** on-hand to supervise the fun for five age groups. Nearly half a deck and two huge spaces are dedicated to kids. The Oceaneer Club, for ages 3 to 8 (with separate activities for ages 3 to 5 and 6 to 8), is a playroom themed on Captain Hook. Kids can climb and crawl on a giant pirate ship's bow as well as jumbo-size animals, barrels, and a sliding board, and get dressed up from a trunk full of costumes. The far-out Oceaneer Lab offers kids ages 9 to 12 (with separate activities for ages 9 to 10 and 11 to 12) a chance to work on computers, learn fun science with microscopes, and do arts and crafts.

On Disney's **private island,** Castaway Cay (which each itinerary visits for a day), activities like scavenger hunts are scheduled for the kids while adults can head for the adults-only Serenity Bay. (There's also a family beach, if you're not in too dire a need of some serenity.)

For teens, the cool **teen coffee bar,** called Common Grounds, is the place to buy a cappuccino or virgin Margarita, plop down into the big comfy chairs, flip through one of the many magazines in the rack, or pop on one of the headphone sets hooked to a selection of over 70 music CDs. There's nothing close to this on any other ship, and even your way-too-cool teens might be enticed by the atmosphere.

Kids can eat **lunch and dinner with counselors** in the Topsiders and Beach Blanket restaurants all but the first evening of the cruise (these restaurants are not open for dinner).

In mid-1999, private baby-sitting services were dropped on both ships and a new program was adopted: the Flounder's Reef **Nursery** for kids ages 3 months to 3 years. It operates from 2 to 4pm and from 7pm to midnight daily, and the price is $6 per child per hour, and $5 for each additional child in a family. For kids 3 to 12, the Oceaneer Club and Oceaneer Lab playrooms stay open to 12:30am (some nights 1am) for parents who want a night out.

And lastly, how's this for convenience: Parents get a **tuned beeper** when they first check into the kids' program so that they can be contacted in the spa, the cabin, a dance class, or anywhere by counselors if their child needs them for any reason.

ENTERTAINMENT

The ships' fresh, family-oriented entertainment is a standout and unparalleled at sea. In the nostalgic Walt Disney Theatre, on one of the best-equipped stages found aboard any ship, actors disappear into trap doors, fly across the stage, and go through endless exciting costume changes. After-dinner performances by **Broadway-caliber entertainers** in this showroom include "Disney Dreams," a sweet musical medley of Disney classics, taking the audience from *Peter Pan* to *The Lion King;* "Voyage of the Ghost Ship," an adventurous musical with a piratey theme; and "Hercules, A Muse-ical Comedy," a salute to the popular Disney film. While the singing is live, the music isn't. But, believe me, there's so much to enjoy you'll barely notice there's no live orchestra. The *Magic*'s 7-night itinerary will include these three shows plus a new stage show based on magic and illusion.

So what else is there, after the show is over and the kids are in bed? There's an adults-only entertainment area called Beat Street on the *Magic* (on the *Wonder,* it's called Route 66). Offering entertainment for those 18 and older, these isolated sections of the forward part of Deck 3 each boast three themed nightclubs: an elegant and plush piano bar for **romantic music,** jazz, and blues; a 1970s-style bright and whimsical **comedy club** featuring really funny improv skits; and a room styled after an American **roadhouse** and featuring—what else?—rock-and-roll and a large dance floor. These areas (especially the piano bar) can get crowded when the ship is carrying a full load, and there won't be a quiet nook to be found. Two other nightspots include the sprawling Promenade Lounge, where live jazz is featured daily, and the ESPN Skybox sports bar open till midnight.

While adults traveling without children should think twice about booking with Disney during the peak kid season, for Disney fanatics and families not afraid of crowds, the ships offer the classic Disney brand of wholesome fun in an elegant seafaring setting.

SERVICE

Some 50 nationalities come together to serve you, including Americans, just as at the parks. Expect service in the dining rooms to be roughly equivalent to the top-level Disney World restaurants in Orlando—friendly and efficient, but at times a tad amateurish. Overall, things run smoothly, and the ultra-organized check-in facilities at Disney's private Port Canaveral terminal do away with the often long waits you'll encounter embarking other ships.

Services include **laundry** and **dry cleaning** (the ships also have **self-service laundry rooms**), and 1-hour photo processing. Strollers are available at no extra cost. On Castaway Cay, bicycles for kids and adults can be rented for $5 apiece; cargo carts to carry your beach stuff are free.

Disney Magic •
Disney Wonder

The Verdict

The only ships on the planet that successfully re-create the grandeur of the classic transatlantic liners, albeit in a modern, Disneyfied way.

Disney Magic *(photo: Disney Cruise Line)*

Specifications

Size (in tons)	83,000	Crew	945 (International)
Number of Cabins	880	Passenger/Crew Ratio	1.9 to 1
Number of Outside Cabins	640	Year Built	
Cabins with Verandas	280	*Magic*	1998
Number of Passengers	1,750*	*Wonder*	1999
Officers	European/ Norwegian	Last Major Refurbishment	N/A

* Note: Double-occupancy figure. With children's berths filled, capacity can go as high as 3,325.

Frommer's Ratings (Scale of 1–5)

Cabin Comfort & Amenities	5	Pool, Fitness & Spa Facilities	3
Ship Cleanliness & Maintenance	4	Children's Facilities	5
Public Comfort/Space	4	Itinerary	4
Decor	5	Worth the Money	4

These long, proud-looking ships carry 1,750 passengers at the rate of two per cabin, but, since Disney is a family company and its ships were built expressly to carry three, four, and five people in virtually every cabin, the ship could theoretically carry a whopping 3,325 passengers. Zowie! Typically, though, every single bed will not be filled (the ships would be pretty darned crowded if they were!), and getting up past about 2,600 passengers is not common.

Cabins & Rates

Cabins	Per diems from	Bathtub	Fridge	Hair Dryer	Sitting Area	TV
Inside	$134	yes	yes	yes	yes	yes
Outside	$161	yes	yes	yes	yes	yes
Suite	$249	yes	yes	yes	yes	yes

CABINS The Disney ships offer the family-friendliest cabins at sea, with standard accommodations equivalent to the suites or demi-suites on most ships. All of the 875 cabins have at least a sitting area with a sofa bed to sleep families of three, a bunch also have a pull-down wall-bunk to comfortably sleep four, and nearly half have private verandas. At 214 square feet, the ships' standard outside cabins are about 25% larger than the industry standard (but you pay for it: A cruise on the *Magic* or *Wonder* will often cost more than one on Carnival or Royal Caribbean). Family suites, at 304 square feet including the balcony, have private verandas and sleep four or five comfortably. Outside cabins that don't have verandas have jumbo-size porthole windows.

The decor of each cabin is virtually identical, with warm wood-tone paneling and furniture. On both, there's a framed black-and-white 1930s shot of Mr. and Mrs. Walt Disney aboard the fabled ocean liner *Rex,* and on the *Magic,* above each bed is an enlarged piece of sheet music with the notes and lyrics to "When You Wish Upon a Star."

Their best feature? Look no further than the bathrooms to find the pièce de résistance of the ships' staterooms and something found on only a few ships today: The majority of cabins are equipped with *two bathrooms*—a sink and toilet in one and a shower/tub combo and a sink in the other. Both, while compact, have ample shelf space.

All cabins have a minifridge, hair dryer, safe, TV, shower-tub combo, sitting area, and lots of storage space. Sixteen cabins are fitted for wheelchair users.

PUBLIC AREAS The ships' three-story atria are more understated than you might expect—so much so that when I first entered the *Magic*'s I wasn't sure I was even in the main hub of the ship. It's more like a pleasant, upscale hotel lobby than your typical flashy megaship atrium.

The adults-only area includes a comedy club, elegant piano lounge, and a large disco. There's also a family-oriented entertainment lounge called Studio Sea for karaoke, game shows, and dancing for the whole family, and a sports bar, the ESPN Skybox, located near the ship's forward funnel and featuring worldwide sports television coverage. A really neat observation area above the bridge—unfortunately open only while the ship is in port, but who can blame the captain for wanting a little privacy—allows passengers to look down into the bridge and get some idea of how a ship is operated. A 270-seat cinema shows first-run or classic Disney movies. The children's facilities, as you'd expect, are the largest on any ship at sea (see "Children's Program," above, for details).

POOL, FITNESS & SPA FACILITIES The Pool Deck of each ship pretty well sums up the segregated-yet-integrated adults/children scheme of the Disney experience: Toward the stern is Mickey's Kids' Pool in the shape of Mickey's big-eared head, with a great big white-gloved Mickey hand holding up the snaking yellow sliding board; then, separated by a rest-room area and Pinocchio's Pizza, comes Goofy's Family Pool, where adults and children can mingle. Moving forward past this family area, past the stage and the teen cafe and video arcade, you enter the Quiet Cove Adult Pool, with its whirlpools and poolside Signals Bar.

Just beyond the adult pool area is the surprisingly drab, smallish fitness center. Decor aside, the gyms do have a pair of virtual-reality step machines that are pretty cool, a separate aerobics area, and views of the bow and bridge below. The 8,500-square-foot, Steiner-managed Vista Spa & Salon, on the other hand, is much more impressive, with attractive tiled treatment rooms, changing rooms with comfy chaise lounges upholstered in bright tropical fabrics, a sauna, and a steam room. The ships have an outdoor sports deck with basketball and paddle tennis. There's also a jogging track, shuffleboard, and Ping-Pong.

Holland America Line

300 Elliott Ave. W., Seattle, WA 98119. ☎ **800/426-0327** or 206/281-3535. Fax 800/628-4855. www.hollandamerica.com.

THE LINE IN A NUTSHELL   More than any other line today (except Cunard), Holland America has managed to hang on to some of its seafaring history and tradition, offering a moderately priced, classic, casual yet refined cruise experience.

THE EXPERIENCE   Holland America consistently delivers a worthy and solid product for a fair price, and is unique for offering midsize-to-large ships with an old-world elegance that remains low-key and not stuffy. These ships aren't boring, but they're sedate, so it's no surprise that the line attracts mostly passengers in their fifties on up.

The line's well-maintained ships are mostly midsize, creating a cozy atmosphere, and their decors are stylish, sleek, and, for the most part, understated, and their excellent layouts ease passenger movement. The new *Volendam,* however, has ushered in a brighter, more colorful side to HAL while still maintaining its low-key attributes. HAL's two older ships, the *Westerdam* and *Noordam,* are the most humble.

HAL emphasizes tradition, and that's what sets it apart. In the public areas you'll see trophies and memorabilia, and the very names of the vessels hark back to the line's past. For example, the *Rotterdam* is the sixth HAL ship to bear that name.

Pros

- **History and tradition.** The impressive collection of artifacts and artwork on the ships reflect Holland America's important place in seafaring history and lend the ships more of a traditional ocean-liner ambiance than can be found on nearly any other line.
- **Private verandas.** Over 25% of all cabins on the Statendam-class ships and the *Volendam* and *Zaandam* boast private cabin balconies.
- **Great gyms.** I thought the gyms on Statendam-class ships were huge, but those on the *Volendam* and *Zaandam* are even bigger, and are some of the most attractive, roomy, and well-stocked gyms and aerobics areas at sea.

Cons

- **Sleepy nightlife.** While there's always a few stalwarts and a couple of busy-ish nights, if you're big on late-night dancing and bar hopping, you may find yourself partying mostly with the entertainment staff.
- **Homogenous passenger profile.** Although this is changing to a certain degree, passengers tend to be a pretty homogenous group of low-key, 55-plus North American couples who aren't overly adventurous.

Compared with the other Mainstream lines, here's how HAL rates:

	Poor	Fair	Good	Excellent	Outstanding
Enjoyment Factor					✓
Dining			✓		
Activities			✓		
Children's Program		✓			
Entertainment			✓		
Service			✓		
Overall Value					✓

HOLLAND AMERICA: GOING DUTCH

One of the most famous shipping companies in the world, Holland America Line was founded in 1873 as the Nederlandsch-Amerikaansche StoomvAart Maatschappij (Netherlands-American Steamship Company), and because the line provided service between New York City and Rotterdam, Holland, it soon became known as Holland America Line. The company's first ocean liner was the original *Rotterdam,* which took its maiden, 15-day voyage from the Netherlands to New York City in 1872.

By the turn of the century, Holland America owned a fleet of six passenger-cargo ships, and traveled between Holland and Asia (the Dutch East Indies) via the Suez Canal. In the early 1900s, Holland America was one of the major lines transporting thousands of hopeful immigrants from Europe to the United States, and continued a regular schedule of transatlantic crossings up until 1971, when the line turned to offering cruises full time.

During World War II, the company's headquarters moved from Nazi-occupied Holland to Dutch-owned Curaçao, then the site of a strategic oil refinery, and strong links were forged with North American interests after the war. In 1973, Holland America Line changed its name to Holland America Cruises to promote its new focus on cruising; then, in 1974, HAL became linked with Seattle-based tour operator Westours to give the line a presence in Alaska, where it has remained one of the two biggest cruisetour players today.

The line changed its name back to Holland America Line in 1983, seeking to capitalize on its history and seafaring traditions, and began building the large fleet of midsize ships that exists now. In the midst of this building spree, in 1988 HAL acquired Windstar Cruises, expanding its midlevel services into the upper echelons of the cruise experience. To everyone's surprise, both companies were acquired a year later by Carnival Corporation. Many industry observers predicted the company's demise, yet the opposite occurred. Carnival improved entertainment quality and quantity (the line needed both), upgraded HAL's cuisine, and provided the cash and credit to commission four additional vessels, with more to come.

THE FLEET

Of its nine ships, the 1,214-passenger *Noordam* (launched in 1984, and likely to be sold off in the very near future) and the 1,494-passenger *Westerdam* (built in 1986 for Home Lines and purchased by HAL in 1988) are the older, somewhat plainer ships of the HAL fleet. Built in the pre-Carnival days, they lack many of the frills you'll see on the later ships. (In late 2000, the *Nieuw Amsterdam,* sister to *Noordam,* was sold to the new venture, United States Lines, and renamed the *Patriot.* The ship will do year-round Hawaii cruises.) The company's four 1,266-passenger Statendam-class ships—the *Statendam* and *Maasdam* (both inaugurated in 1993), *Ryndam* (1994), and *Veendam* (1996)—are carbon copies of the same attractive, well-crafted design (with a dash of glitz here and there). All were built at the Fincantieri shipyard in Monfalcone, Italy, which is also building several new ships for the line.

In 1997, HAL launched its most sophisticated ship, *Rotterdam VI,* which replaced the 1957-vintage *Rotterdam V* (sold to Premier Cruises and rechristened the *Rembrandt*). The line's new flagship, it spends most of its year outside the Caribbean, and therefore isn't reviewed in this book. I've also not reviewed the *Statendam,* which spends its year in Mexico, Hawaii, and Alaska.

The 1,440-passenger *Volendam* officially debuted in November 1999 and the *Zaandam* in May 2000. The brightest and boldest HAL ships to date, the *Volendam*

Holland America's Theme Cruises

Holland America Line is big on special cruises, most aboard the 1,494-passenger *Westerdam* in the eastern Caribbean. For 2001, the line will continue its extremely popular series of **Big Band cruises,** which feature the smooth sounds of the Glenn Miller Orchestra, Guy Lombardo's Royal Canadians, and the Tommy Dorsey Orchestra. Also on the schedule are 1950s **Sock Hop cruises** featuring performers like Bobby Rydell, The Shirelles, and Little Anthony & The Imperials (passengers are encouraged to bring their poodle skirts and loafers); **Broadway-theme** sailings featuring greats like Carol Channing; **Country Music sailings** with stars like B. J. Thomas and Juice Newton; and a cruise paying tribute to **Frank Sinatra,** with dancing, sing-alongs, and trivia games.

---

and *Zaandam* combine features of the Statendam-class ships with innovations developed first for the *Rotterdam VI,* and are slightly larger than the latter in size (63,000 tons, as opposed to 59,652), and carry more passengers (1,440, against the *Rotterdam*'s 1,316 and the Statendam class's 1,266). Harking back to HAL's Dutch roots, the *Volendam*'s decorative theme is flowers while the *Zaandam*'s theme is music—exemplified by one of the more unusual and inspired atrium decorations I know of: a huge, working pipe organ with mechanical figures of dancing musicians.

At press time, the new sister ship to the *Rotterdam VI,* the 1,380-passenger *Amsterdam,* is scheduled to launch in late 2000. And in late 2002, HAL will join the megaship crowd by introducing the first (and as yet unnamed) vessel in a long line of ships carrying 1,800-passengers double occupancy and measuring about 950 feet long (*Volendam* is roughly 800 ft.).

PASSENGER PROFILE

All in all, HAL stands for good, solid quality with its well-rounded onboard experience. Shipboard ambiance is characterized by an unstuffy lack of pretension, relaxed friendliness, and good value for the money.

Before the line's acquisition by Carnival in 1989, HAL passengers tended overwhelmingly to be older people in their sixties and seventies, but Carnival's influence has moved the demographics toward a somewhat younger market, although any kind of real transformation is slow as molasses in coming and far from complete, if indeed it ever will be—note the fold-down seats in the elevators for an indication of the average passenger age; HAL's passenger rosters typically include some graying, 50-ish members of the baby-boom generation, mixed in with many passengers of their parents' age.

Passengers tend to be better educated than their equivalents aboard a Carnival ship, but a lot less affluent than those aboard a luxury line like Seabourn. They're generally hospitable and amiable, and sensible with their money. They tend to be fairly set in their ways and not adventurous.

The line attracts many groups traveling together, from incentive groups to social clubs on a lark together. If you're a 40-something member of such a group and are worried about finding company aboard, don't abandon hope, particularly if you happen to be a divorcée, widow, or widower: You won't be alone.

DINING

Joining the trend, Holland America recently began offering an **alternative dinner option** in its casual buffet-style breakfast-and-lunch Lido restaurant. It will be available

Holland America's Private Slice of Paradise

Who wants to bother with passengers from those "other" cruise lines anyway! On Half Moon Cay, HAL's 2-mile-long, 2,500-acre private Bahamian island, it'll be just you and the other HAL passengers, all with the freedom to do what you want, whether it's just flopping down on a beach towel to sunbathe, or signing up for windsurfing, snorkeling, or kayaking. The crescent-shaped island is a port of call on most of the line's Caribbean and Panama Canal cruises.

Like the private Bahamian islands Princess, NCL, Royal Caribbean, Disney, and Premier lay claim to, Half Moon Cay is well equipped to make sure you don't have to rough it too much. There are shops, a food pavilion, bars, ice-cream stand, first-aid station, kids' play area, and even a post office selling exclusive Half Moon Cay stamps for your postcards. HAL also offers "Just for Kids" shore excursions, with special excursions for 'tweens and teens. The island is handicapped accessible.

For a special treat, you can get a **massage on the beach** from the Steiner therapists, who set up a pair of blue tents on the sand. The digs are equipped with ceiling fans and (of course) massage tables. Shower facilities also are located nearby. Choose from a 50-minute full-body massage for $79; a 25-minute back, neck, and shoulder massage for $39; a chair massage at $1 per minute (10-min. minimum); or, oddly enough, even a sun-tanning treatment (in which, actually, tanning creams are used).

every night of the cruise except the last night, and feature open seating from 7 to 8:30pm, so guests can dine when they choose. A pianist will entertain guests, tables will be set with linens, and there is waiter service for beverages, entrees, and desserts (other courses are self-serve). The set menu features the basics: Caesar salad, shrimp cocktail, or fresh fruit cup appetizer, French onion soup, freshly baked dinner rolls, and four entree choices, including salmon, sirloin steak, roast chicken, and lasagna, served with a vegetable of the day and a baked potato or rice pilaf. Among the dessert choices are cheesecake or chocolate cake.

Of course, an elegant dinner in the main dining room is still the preferred venue (smoking is permitted in designated sections of dining rooms, although a company spokeswoman says this may change). As its executive chef, HAL employs the renowned Reiner Greubel, formerly of Westin Hotels, New York's Plaza Hotel, and his own Reiner's Restaurant in Seattle. Instead of daring experimentation, he recognizes that some of the world's finest cuisine comes from classics prepared with fresh and high-quality ingredients, and that some sophisticated palates still prefer traditional favorites: osso buco, cassoulet, Alaskan king crab, and Caribbean snapper, for instance. Dinner items might be as straightforward as roast prime rib of beef with baked Idaho potatoes and horseradish cream, or as esoteric as warm hazelnut-crusted Brie with a compote of apples and onions. Children can enjoy tried-and-true staples like pizza, hot dogs, burgers with fries, chicken fingers, and tacos. These dishes are supplemented with chef's specials, such as pasta or fish-and-chips. The wine list comprises about 70% U.S. vintages, with the rest from Europe, Chile, and Australia.

Greubel has also expanded the line's **light and healthy cuisine** with more fresh fish, such as pompano and grouper, and more pasta dishes with vegetable-based sauces.

A major improvement in the cuisine is the **desserts.** Greubel has moved away from grandmother's favorite cakes and heavy, cream-laden desserts in favor of newer, more sophisticated and delicate creations like a tropical trifle with salmon berries, raspberries, pineapple, kiwi, and coconut cream.

Buffets with the inevitable queues are bountiful and frequent. Statendam-class ships and newer have some of the best-planned buffet set-ups at sea—there are separate stations for drinks, salads, and dessert, for instance, which keeps the lines and crowding to a minimum. At lunch, they are supplemented by stations where you can make your own tacos, well-stocked salad bars, a new deli station (on *Volendam, Zaandam,* and *Rotterdam* only), stir-fried dishes made to order, and an ice-cream station where you can get a scoop or two and add your own toppings. **Indonesian dishes** are the theme for lunch once a week, with a special pasta on another day. Daily, there's also pizza and a burger grill.

Breakfasts contain some vestiges of Dutch cuisine, such as Gouda cheese, and Dutch influences also prevail at least once during each cruise in a **Dutch Chocolate Extravaganza,** a Holland-themed midnight buffet where the calories stack up so fast you might as well give up trying to count them. The rest of the week there are regular midnight buffets.

Room service is available 24 hours a day and ranks among the fastest and most efficient at sea. Midmorning bouillon and **afternoon teas** are well-attended events, the latter with waiters passing around teeny sandwiches and cookies in one of the main lounges. Hot canapés are served in some of the bar/lounges during the cocktail hour. During warm-weather cruises, iced tea and lemonade are served on-deck, one of many thoughtful touches provided at frequent intervals by the well-trained staff. All ships but *Westerdam* and *Noordam* have **Java Cafes,** a comfy cluster of seating around a small coffee bar serving complimentary espresso and cappuccinos (HAL is one of the few lines that doesn't charge for such drinks) mornings and afternoons.

The *Rotterdam* was the first in the fleet to have an **alternative, reservations-only restaurant,** and the *Volendam* and *Zaandam* have followed suit. Seating 88 passengers, they are intimate and elegant and the perfect place to forget you're on a big cruise ship (and there's no cover charge either). Serving Italian cuisine, the *Volendam's* Marco Polo Restaurant is covered with small eclectic prints from the likes of Rembrandt, Henry Moore, Matisse, and Picasso, as well as some lesser-known artists. The ship's principal architect, Frans Dingemans, says he designed the room to resemble a European artists' bistro. The food's as tasty as the room is appealing.

At dinner, a choice of six antipasto dishes includes salami and prosciutto with cornichons and marinated roasted vegetables, and a pepper-seared beef tenderloin. Six

E-Mail the Grandkids!

Who'd have expected HAL to be plugged in? On the *Volendam* and *Zaandam* you can surf the Net or send off E-mails from one of the eight new flat-screen computers in the ocean-view computer room, called the Web Site. Located between the library and card room, the room is open 24 hours a day and staffed for much of it. (The *Rotterdam* also has six computers in an Internet center, and the line plans to eventually retrofit all its ships with online capability). It'll cost you 75¢ per minute to go online or use E-mail, with a 5-minute minimum. Guests who want to send E-mails but don't have their own accounts (with America Online, Hotmail, etc.) can set up a "cruisemail" account on board for a charge of $5.95 per E-mail. Here's a tip, though: You can set up a Hotmail account just by going to their site (www.hotmail.com) and registering. It takes about 2 minutes and is totally free, so registering before your cruise will save you some cash.

pasta selections include the likes of fettuccine with rock shrimp, chopped tomato, spinach, garlic and toasted pine nuts, as well as a linguini pasta with Italian sausage, peppers, onions, tomato, and sangiovese wine sauce. Choose from six entrees like a marinated chicken breast in garlic purée and rosemary served on steamed spinach with mushroom risotto, or a grilled veal chop served with sautéed mushrooms. The restaurant is also open for lunch on sea days, serving things like fancy pizzas and a poached salmon salad.

ACTIVITIES

Activities are varied, relatively nontaxing, and fun. Shopping-oriented talks on upcoming ports of call are popular, as are deck games. You can learn how to dance cheek-to-cheek, be taught the fine art of vegetable carving or creative napkin folding, or play bingo or bridge. There are trivia games and Pictionary tournaments. A crew member will take interested passengers on **art tours,** discussing the ship's impressive art collection and giving passengers a handout about the pieces. Of course, you can also just relax all day in a lounge chair with a good book.

Activities pick up a bit at night, when predinner cocktails and **dancing** are a major event of the day. Afterward, you might visit the show lounge and/or the **casino,** attend a "Fabulous Fifties" party or a country-western night, take part in the "Champagne Slot Tournament" or "Night-Owl Pajama Bingo," indulge yourself at the Dutch Chocolate Extravaganza, or take in a movie in the cinema or the ever-popular **crew show,** in which Indonesian and/or Filipino crew members present songs and dances from their homelands.

Fleet-wide, HAL has an incentive-based **fitness program** in which passengers are awarded points every time they take an aerobics class or do some other fitness activity. Points can be redeemed at cruise end for T-shirts, souvenirs, and so on.

On cruises 14 nights and longer and on transatlantic sailings, women traveling alone or those whose escorts have two left feet need not fear for lack of dance partners: A complement of "gentlemen hosts" sail on board and are available for a whirl or two around the dance floor.

CHILDREN'S PROGRAM

Whenever demand warrants it, HAL offers supervised programs for children, called **Club HAL.** The menu of activities is not anywhere as extensive as on lines like Disney, Carnival, Celebrity, Royal Caribbean, and Princess, and HAL never pretends it is. When enough kids are on board, programs are designated for three different age brackets: 5- to 8-year-olds, 9- to 12-year-olds, and teens through 17. However, based on the number of young people aboard, these barriers sometimes blur.

Regardless of the age of the attendees, young people are diverted with pizza-and-soda parties, as well as tours of the bridge, the galley, and other areas below deck. There might also be movies, ice-cream parties, arts and crafts, storytelling sessions, games, karaoke, golf lessons, disco parties, charades, bingo, and Ping-Pong. On the first night of each cruise, parents meet and mingle with staff responsible for the care, counseling, and feeding of their children. Activities are not scheduled while a ship is in port.

There are **playrooms** on all ships, though they're not dedicated spaces (in fact, they're just meeting rooms when not doing kid duty, and so are very drab as children's centers go).

Baby-sitting is sometimes (but not always) available from volunteers among a ship's staff. If a staff member is available—and be warned, their availability is never guaranteed—the cost is usually around $5 per child per hour.

HAL: The Generous Line

Holland America is generous with its complimentary treats (a rarity in today's nickel-and-diming industry), serving hot canapés in some of the bars/lounges during the cocktail hour, offering freshly popped popcorn in the movie theater, doling out espresso and cappuccino at no charge in the Java cafes, and serving iced tea on-deck on all warm-weather cruises. Unlike other lines, there's no cover charge in the small, alternative restaurants on the *Volendam, Zaandam,* and *Rotterdam.* Stewards replenish a bowl of fruit in your cabin daily, and each guest is given a Holland America canvas tote bag. Did I mention the line spends about $4,500 on flowers for each ship every week? That's a cool $2 million a year for the whole fleet. Zowie!

ENTERTAINMENT

While not the line's forte by a long shot, onboard entertainment has improved (and has been geared to a slightly younger crowd) since HAL's acquisition by Carnival, a company that really understands how cabaret shows should be presented. Don't expect the shows to knock your socks off, but hey, at least they're trying. For instance, in late 1998, Holland America augmented its entertainment lineup with the introduction of *Barry Manilow's Copacabana.* This 60-minute, Vegas-style show, which is the biggest and most lavish production ever staged on an HAL ship, is set in 1948 at the famous Copacabana night club, and is being performed on the *Ryndam, Statendam,* and *Volendam.*

Copa aside, each ship features small-scale glittery and shimmery **Broadway-style shows** with live music and laser lights. There are also trios and quartets playing big band–style oldies as well as pianists performing classical stuff in the lounges.

First-run movies are shown an average of three times a day in an onboard cinema, and there's even hot, freshly made popcorn dispensed from a machine near the entrance for those who can't watch a movie without it. There's always a **crew talent show** once per week, as well as an outdoor Caribbean-themed deck party where all sorts of silly games and contests are held. At one of these parties, I once watched dozens of passengers whooping it up in a relay-race contest that had something to do with balloons and blindfolds. It was a riot for participants and voyeurs alike.

On the Statendam-class and newer ships, the **disco** is part of the spacious Crow's Nest observation lounge. Generally, a live four-piece band plays from about 9pm to midnight and a DJ takes over for the next few hours (if anyone stays past midnight, that is). These are attractive areas, and a few nights a week there's likely to be a small coterie of late-night types (and I mean small—you can usually count their number on the fingers of one hand) dancing up a storm; invariably, some of the young dancers from the show troupe hang out as well. On the *Noordam,* the disco is also in a large lounge and sees more action than you might expect a few nights a week. There's usually a fifties sock hop theme one night in the disco to get people in the mood, with twist and hula-hoop contests, for instance. Did I mention karaoke? It's alive and well fleet-wide.

SERVICE

Service is efficient, genteel, and nostalgic. During lunch, a uniformed employee might hold open the door of a buffet, and at dinnertime a steward resembling that vintage Philip Morris pageboy rings a chime at the entrance to the dining room to formally announce the two seatings.

Holland America is one of the few cruise lines that maintains a training school (a land-based facility in Indonesia known within HAL circles as "the SS Jakarta") for the selection and training of its staff. On the ships, the soft-spoken staffers smile more often than

Holland America Fleet Itineraries

Ship	Home Ports & Season	Itinerary	Other Itineraries
Maasdam	Round-trip from Fort Lauderdale, year-round (alternating part of the year; rest of the year is E. Carib. only)	**7-night W. Carib:** Playa del Carmen/Cozumel, Grand Cayman, Ocho Rios (Jamaica), and Half Moon Cay. **7-night E. Carib:** Nassau, San Juan, St. John/St. Thomas, and Half Moon Cay.	Europe, Canada/New England
Noordam	Round-trip from Tampa, Dec–Apr.	**14-night S. Carib:** San Juan, St. John/St. Thomas, Guadeloupe, Barbados, St. Lucia, Isla de Margarita, Bonaire, Aruba, and Grand Cayman.	Mediterranean, Europe
Ryndam	Round-trip from Fort Lauderdale, Oct–Apr.	**7-night W. Carib:** Half Moon Cay, Grand Cayman, Playa del Carmen/Cozumel, and Key West.	Alaska, South America
Veendam	Round-trip from San Juan, Oct–Mar, and Oct–Dec.	**7-night S. Carib:** Dominican Republic, Barbados, Martinique, St. Maarten, and St. John/St. Thomas.	Alaska
Volendam	Round-trip from Fort Lauderdale; itineraries alternate Nov–Apr.	**10-night S. Carib 1:** Bonaire, Isla de Margarita (Venezuela), St. Lucia, St. Kitts, St. John/St. Thomas, and Nassau. **10-night S. Carib 2:** Antigua, St. Lucia, Barbados, Guadeloupe, St. John/St. Thomas, and Nassau.	Alaska
Westerdam	Round-trip from Fort Lauderdale; 7-nighters Oct–Dec 2000, 5-nighters Jan–Apr and Nov–Dec 2001, 8-nighters, Jan–Apr and Oct–Dec 2001.	**7-night E. Carib:** Nassau, San Juan, St. John/St. Thomas, and Half Moon Cay. **5-night E. Carib:** Key West, Half Moon Cay, and Nassau. **8-night E. Carib:** Nassau, San Juan, St. Maarten, St. John/St. Thomas, and Half Moon Cay.	Alaska
Zaandam	Round-trip from Fort Luaderdale; itineraries alternate Nov–Apr.	**10-night S. Carib 1:** Bonaire, Isla de Margarita (Venezuela), St. Lucia, St. Kitts, St. John/St. Thomas, and Nassau. **10-night S. Carib 2:** Antigua, St. Lucia, Barbados, Guadeloupe, St. John/St. Thomas, and Nassau.	Alaska

not as they labor to offer attentive service (though they at times struggle with English). You won't find a staff member rushing toward you every time you raise an eyebrow, but if you're only moderately demanding, you'll certainly get what you want.

Although Holland America proudly touts its no-tipping-required policy, it's more diplomacy on the part of HAL than anything else. In fact, as aboard most other ships, tips are expected; it's just that on Holland America ships you won't be bombarded by guidelines and reminders—you can feel as though you're tipping because you truly enjoyed the service. HAL's no-tipping-required policy includes bar tabs, which, unlike on most lines, do not automatically include a 15% gratuity (if you want, you can tip a bar waiter in cash or hand-write one onto your tab, although some have been known to refuse it).

Onboard services aboard every ship in the fleet include **laundry** and **dry cleaning.** Each ship also maintains several **self-service laundry rooms** with irons.

Maasdam • Ryndam • Veendam

The Verdict

Some of the most attractive midsize ships out there. Functional, appealing public areas are enlivened with just a dash of glitz and collections of mostly European and Oriental art and artifacts and shipping memorabilia.

Ryndam *(photo: Holland America Line)*

Specifications

Size (in tons)	55,451	Passenger/Crew Ratio	2.2 to 1
Number of Cabins	633	Year Built	
Number of Outside Cabins	502	*Maadam*	1993
Cabins with Verandas	150	*Ryndam*	1994
Number of Passengers	1,266	*Veendam*	1996
Officers	Dutch	Last Major Refurbishment	N/A
Crew	588 (Indonesian/ Filipino)		

Frommer's Ratings (Scale of 1–5)

Cabin Comfort & Amenities	4	Pool, Fitness & Spa Facilities	5
Ship Cleanliness & Maintenance	4	Children's Facilities	3
Public Comfort/Space	5	Itinerary	4
Decor	4	Worth the Money	5

These three nearly identical vessels (plus the *Statendam,* which sails in Hawaii, Mexico, and Alaska) represent the most massive investment in hardware Holland America has ever made. Weighing in at 55,000 tons each, they were built within a 3-year span at the Fincantieri shipyard in Monfalcone, Italy, and fall somewhere between midsize and megaships.

The ships all demonstrate an extremely good use of space that pays attention to traffic flows, and each has eight elevators connecting all decks.

Interior components include leather, glass, cabinets, textiles, and furniture from around the world. Touches of marble, teakwood, polished brass, and around $2 million worth of artwork for each vessel evoke the era of the classic ocean liners. Decorative themes usually emphasize the Netherlands' seafaring traditions, and the role of Holland America in opening commerce and trade between Holland and the rest of the world.

Cabins & Rates

Cabins	Per diems from	Bathtub	Fridge	Hair Dryer	Sitting Area	TV
Inside	$141	some	no*	yes	no	yes
Outside	$169	yes	no*	yes	some	yes
Suite	$229	yes	yes	yes	yes	yes

* *Fridges can be requested through your travel agent and placed in cabins for a few dollars extra.*

CABINS   Cabins are roomy, unfussy, uncomplicated, and comfortable. Mini-suites are 284 square feet, larger than those aboard some of the most expensive ships afloat, such as Cunard's *Sea Goddesses*. Full suites are 563 square feet, and the penthouse suite sprawls across a full 1,126 square feet. Most inside cabins are 182 square feet and standard outside cabins, 197 square feet. (All square footage measurements include the cabin's veranda.)

Cabins are outfitted with light-grained furniture, most with beige (read: dull) floral or Indonesian batik-patterned curtains that separate the sleeping area from the sitting area. The same prints are used for bedspreads and curtains, too, and, along with artwork, reflect aspects of Holland's history and aesthetic. Closets and storage space are larger than the norm. Bathrooms are well designed and well lit.

All cabins have twin beds that can be converted to a queen and, in some cases, a king. About 200 cabins can accommodate a third and fourth passenger on a foldaway sofa bed and/or an upper berth.

Outside cabins have picture windows and none are blocked by dangling rows of lifeboats, although those on the Lower Promenade Deck have pedestrian walkways (and, consequently, pedestrians) between you and your view of the sea. Special reflective glass prevents outsiders from spying in during daylight hours. To guarantee privacy at nighttime, you have to close the curtains.

Fresh flowers, white-gloved stewards, and bowls of fresh fruit in the cabins add a warm, hospitable touch. Suites and mini-suites also come stocked with terry bathrobes for use during the cruise.

On each ship, six cabins are wheelchair accessible and specially outfitted for passengers with disabilities. That, plus spacious corridors, wide elevators, and wheelchair-accessible toilets, makes these ships popular with people with disabilities.

PUBLIC AREAS   Joe Farcus, the designer who launched Carnival Cruise Lines' "Fun Ship" theme, played a role in the interior design of these ships, albeit with considerably more reserve and subtlety than he used at Carnival.

For the most part, public areas are subdued, consciously tasteful, and soothing. Some of the most appealing areas are the Sky Decks, which offer a 360° panorama where the only drawback is the roaring wind. One floor below that, almost equivalent views are available from the gorgeous Crow's Nest nightclubs. With floor-to-ceiling windows and its cozy clusters of seating, this romantic venue is perfect for predinner cocktails and then becomes the ships' disco and after-dinner nightclub. Each ship contains an exciting (relatively speaking) three-story atrium—small compared to those aboard Carnival and Royal Caribbean ships, but pleasingly designed with a dose of brass and flash generally centered on an imaginative (sometimes bizarre) sculpture based on some aspect of marine mythology.

Showrooms aboard each ship are stylish, modern tributes to Holland's great artists: Aboard *Maasdam* it's Rembrandt; *Ryndam* is Vermeer (with references to Holland's national flower, the tulip); and *Veendam* is Rubens. Unlike most ships, which have rows of banquettes or theaterlike seats, the showrooms on these ships are uniquely configured with cozy groupings of cushy chairs (that can be moved) and banquettes.

Each vessel's large library also pays homage to some aspect of North European culture. The one aboard *Maasdam* honors Leyden, *Ryndam*'s honors Delft, and *Veendam*'s commemorates Hugo de Groot. Onboard libraries are tranquil and oft-visited retreats. There is also a spacious card room and video arcade, and computer rooms with Internet and E-mail access will soon be added. Nice-size casinos are designed with enough glamour and flashing lights to get gamblers in the mood. Each ship also has a cozy piano bar nestled in a quiet nook, as well as a larger lounge where a live band plays for dancers before dinner.

POOL, FITNESS & SPA FACILITIES   All three ships have a sprawling expanse of teak-covered aft deck surrounding a swimming pool. One deck above that is a second swimming pool plus a wading pool and spacious deck area that can be sheltered from inclement weather with a sliding glass "magrodome" roof. Both areas are well planned and wide open. In the enclosed pool area, there is a dolphin sculpture at one end of the pool and some imaginative, colorful tile designs to spice up the area a bit. Also in this area is the attractive Dolphin Bar, with umbrellas and wicker chairs, and two hot tubs.

These ships have practice tennis courts and an unobstructed track on the Lower Promenade Deck for walking or jogging. The ships' roomy, windowed Ocean Spa gyms are some of most attractive and functional at sea, with a couple of dozen exercise machines, a large separate aerobics area, steam rooms, and saunas. The Steiner-managed spas lack pizzazz, but offer the typical menu of treatments (see chapter 4, "The Cruise Experience," for a discussion of spa options). In good weather, aerobics classes are held on-deck and sometimes in the pool.

Noordam

The Verdict

This midsize 1980s ship is the oldest and coziest in the fleet, offering a comfortable, calm, glitz-free cruise experience and a slice of the past (at least compared to the line's newer ships).

Noordam *(photo: Holland America Line)*

Specifications

Size (in tons)	33,930	Officers	Dutch
Number of Cabins	607	Crew	530 (Indonesian/ Filipino)
Number of Outside Cabins	413	Passenger/Crew Ratio	2.2 to 1
Cabins with Verandas	0	Year Built	1984
Number of Passengers	1,214	Last Major Refurbishment	N/A

Frommer's Ratings (Scale of 1–5)

Cabin Comfort & Amenities	4	Pool, Fitness & Spa Facilities	3
Ship Cleanliness & Maintenance	4	Children's Facilities	2
Public Comfort/Space	3	Itinerary	4
Decor	4	Worth the Money	5

The *Noordam,* now sisterless since the *Nieuw Amsterdam* was sold off in late 2000, is the line's oldest ship and nostalgically evocative of the pre-megaship age of ocean liner cruising (don't be surprised, though, if the line sells her off pretty quickly as the race for more and more new ships continues). Tiered aft decks offer lots of nooks for sunbathing and recall a traditional ship style. In general, outside deck space and interior public rooms are not wide-open, sprawling, flowing spaces as on most newer ships, but are more like clusters attached to one another, creating cozy, intimate areas. Compared to the newer ships, the *Noordam* is pared down in scope and scale, with cabins going at a commensurately pared-down price.

Overall, passengers aboard these ships tend to be more sedate and low-key than those aboard the line's larger ships, and more conscious than usual of getting value for their dollars. That said, HAL guests are certainly not opposed to a good time. When I spent a week on the *Noordam,* I nearly passed out one evening from laughing so hard watching two teams of volunteers participating in a pass-the-balloon-from-my-knees-to-yours relay race at the weekly deck party. It was a big hit!

If you're planning on traveling with children, it's wiser to opt for the larger, newer HAL ships, although the *Noordam* does have children's programs during holidays and on sailings that have a lot of kids on board. At these times, an all-purpose room is converted to a children's playroom.

Cabins & Rates

Cabins	Per diems from	Bathtub	Fridge	Hair Dryer	Sitting Area	TV
Inside	$124	no	no*	no	no	yes
Outside	$152	some	no*	no	some	yes
Suite	$170	yes	yes	no	yes	yes

* Fridges can be requested through your travel agent and placed in cabins for a nominal fee.

CABINS   Standard cabins are a decent size (although smaller than any other HAL ship except the *Westerdam*) and are representative of Holland America's comfortable, low-key style. Standard outside cabins measure 155 to 177 square feet and inside cabins 152 square feet (smaller, for instance, than Carnival's standard 185- to 190-sq.-ft. cabins). Bedding, upholstery, and carpeting are done in earth tones (bordering on drab) and the furniture looks vaguely art deco. Mirrors make the space seem larger than it is, and storage space is more than adequate. Bathrooms are compact and well designed.

Most cabins on the Boat and Navigation decks have views obstructed by lifeboats, and those on the Upper Promenade Deck overlook an unending stream of walkers, joggers, and passersby. Cabins near the stern are subject to more than their share of engine noise and vibration. Many cabins have bathtub/shower combos and all have TVs, music channels, and a fruit bowl. (There are no in-cabin safes, but valuables can be kept at the purser's desk.)

Four cabins in the B Category—deluxe outside double rooms on the Boat Deck— are suitable for people with disabilities. Elevators are wheelchair accessible.

PUBLIC AREAS   The decor sports teakwood, polished rosewood, and discreet colors. Bouquets of fresh flowers are liberally scattered through public areas. A 15-foot-wide teak-covered promenade allows deck chairs, strollers, joggers, and voyeurs to mingle under the open sky. Some passengers consider it the ship's most endearing feature and it's a lovely reminiscence of the classic ocean liner.

The ship has a movie theater, library, and card room.

There are some unfortunate design flaws. For example, showrooms aren't large enough to seat all passengers, so there's standing-room-only in the cabaret theater, with some sight lines blocked. And, in general, the ship's choppy clusters of public areas (which could be considered "cozy," I guess) and decks can leave you disoriented at times. The one-story main-dining rooms, while pleasant, are dull compared to the more glamorous ones on the line's newer ships.

POOL, FITNESS & SPA FACILITIES   The ships have two outside pools on the decks, a wading pool, and one hot tub. You can walk or jog on the broad, unobstructed Upper Promenade Deck. The gym and spa are small, as they are on most ships built in the 1980s and earlier. The gym, located on one of the topmost decks, has windows and is equipped with rowing machines, weight machines, and stationary bicycles. The spa is really just a couple of treatment rooms for massages and facials, plus a steam room and sauna. Aerobics classes are held on the decks or in a public room. A sports deck up top features a pair of practice tennis courts and shuffleboard. There's also a beauty salon/barber shop.

Volendam • Zaandam

The Verdict

These handsome ships mark the beginning of a brighter, hipper Holland America. While still as elegant and genteel as a big ship can get, they've got more pizzazz and style than any other in the fleet.

Volendam *(photo: Holland America Line)*

Specifications

Size (in tons)	63,000	Officers	Dutch/International
Number of Cabins	720	Crew	647 (Indonesian/ Filipino)
Number of Outside Cabins	581	Passenger/Crew Ratio	2.2 to 1
Cabins with Verandas	197	Year Built	1999
Number of Passengers	1,440	Last Major Refurbishment	N/A

Frommer's Ratings (Scale of 1–5)

Cabin Comfort & Amenities	4	Spa Facilities	3
Ship Cleanliness & Maintenance	4	Children's Facilities	3
Public Comfort/Space	4	Itinerary	4
Decor	4	Worth the Money	5
Pool, Fitness Facilities	5		

The *Volendam* and *Zaandam* mark a new face for HAL. Although the line still caters to and attracts an older, mature, mostly 60-plus crowd, these ships are a bold and a sassy step for the very traditional HAL, which is trying to evolve toward a more mainstream product that will appeal to a broader range of ages, especially the younger 40-something boomers. The ships also have the Web Site computer room, for instance, while many lines with much younger crowds don't even offer E-mail access yet, nor the kind of small, alternative restaurants you also find here.

That said, the ships still offer a more traditional ambiance (compared, at least, to Carnival, Princess, and Royal Caribbean). For instance, the *Volendam*'s elegant flower theme—evident in flower-bright colors in certain places, like carpeting and upholstery, and in floral-themed artwork and murals—is subtle but lends a classic air. Each aft staircase landing has a still-life painting of flowers, though the most vividly flower-themed spot is the collection of elaborate delft tulip vases outside the library (ironically, with fake silk tulips). You could even call the gorgeous graduated colors in the show lounge seating florally themed—with colors from magenta to marigold creating a virtual garden in bloom.

CABINS   In a word, roomy! The size of a standard outside cabin is a whopping 194 square feet and the smallest inside is 186 square feet, among the larger standard cabins

Cabins & Rates						
Cabins	Per diems from	Bathtub	Fridge	Hair Dryer	Sitting Area	TV
Inside	$169	no	no	yes	yes	yes
Outside	$205	yes	no	yes	yes	yes
Suite	$276	yes	yes	yes	yes	yes

in the industry. Every single cabin has a sitting area with a small couch. There are 197 cabins with balconies, all part of the suites and mini-suites on the Verandah and Navigation decks. There are 28 suites measuring 563 square feet (including veranda); one gorgeous penthouse suite at 1,126 square feet (including veranda), adorned with one-of-a-kind pieces like a large 19th-century Portuguese porcelain vase and a pair of early-20th-century Louis XVI marble table lamps; and 168 mini-suites, measuring 284 square feet, including veranda.

Cabins on the *Volendam* break from the line's standard beige- and-batik motif, employing more color and a much more modern, daring (for HAL) look with fabrics in salmon-red, burgundy, gold, and bronze with gilt-framed prints on walls of a striped, pale gold fabric. All outside cabins have shower/tub combos in bathrooms with short tubs, while inside cabins have only showers. Overall, bathrooms are roomy and well designed, with adequate storage shelves and counter space. Drawer space is plentiful, and closets are roomy, with great shelves that fold down if you want to adjust the configuration of space. There is also a storage drawer under each bed.

All cabins have sitting areas, TVs with CNN and other channels, and hair dryers. Soaps, shampoos, and lotions come in nostalgic-looking HAL packaging, and a bowl of fruit is replenished daily. Minifridges can be rented for $2 a day. Highly functional bed headboards have not only reading lights, but controls for the programmed radio and every light in the cabin. Suites and mini-suites also come stocked with terry bathrobes for use during the cruise.

There are 21 wheelchair-accessible cabins, and all elevators are accessible.

PUBLIC AREAS   For those who have been aboard the *Rotterdam VI,* the layout of the *Volendam* and *Zaandam* will feel similar. And, like the other HAL ships, both of these vessels have an impressive collection of art and antiques sprinkled throughout their public areas. The booty on *Volendam* is worth about $3 million and includes an authentic Renaissance fountain outside the casino (the ship's most pricey piece), a $20,000 inlaid marble table in the library, and a small earthenware mask dating back to 1200 B.C. and kept in a display case near the Explorer's Lounge. Art tours are offered every cruise.

In general, public areas are very well laid out and easy to navigate. Corridors are broad, and there's no worry of getting lost or disoriented on this well-planned midsize ship. In fact, if you do lose your bearings on the *Volendam,* here's a trick: blue tapestry prints line the underside of the amidships stairwell, while burgundy tapestries line the forward and aft staircases. Surfaces and fabrics on the *Volendam* are an attractive medley of subtle textures and materials, from tapestry walls and ceilings to suede walls woven to resemble rattan, velveteen chairs, marble tabletops, smoky glass, and a red-lacquer piano. (And did I mention the weird red, green, and blue tubelike glass atrium sculpture?)

The warm and almost glowingly cozy Explorer's Lounge is one of my favorite areas, along with the round, pill-like leather seats lining the nearby Sea View lounge and piano bar. The Ocean Bar can get crowded by the bar on busy nights, but if you're seated across the room or near the dance floor, where a live band plays danceable oldies before and after dinner, there's plenty of space. The ship's signature space, the top-deck Crow's Nest observation lounge and disco, is wrapped in floor-to-ceiling windows and bathed in warm colors and soft lines. It's a popular spot for predinner cocktails or a little dancing to today's popular tunes afterwards. The Crow's Nest is also the venue for the line's afternoon tea.

The ship's main showrooms, like those on the Statendam-class ships on up, is a two-story affair with movable clusters of seating on the ground level in front of the stage, so passengers can get comfortable. Just outside the second level of the dining room, which is wrapped in floor-to-ceiling windows, is a place you ladies won't want to miss: a wonderful powder room with ocean views and lots of elbow room for primping, with vanity tables and stools in one room and the toilets and sinks adjacent. For you guys, there's an equally posh adjacent men's room with a marble wall urinal set-up rigged with a continuous waterfall (how soothing is that!).

The Lido buffet restaurants, as on the Statendam-class and newer ships, are efficiently constructed, with separate stations for salads, desserts, and beverages, cutting down on the chance of monstrously long lines. There's even a station for sandwiches made to order on delicious fresh-baked breads. Both ships feature cozy Italian-themed reservations-only alternative restaurants for intimate dining, well-stocked children's playrooms, three-story atria, cinemas, coffee cafes, and computer rooms located between the card room and the spacious and much-used library (which is not as well stocked as you might expect), open 24 hours with Internet and E-mail access. There's a video arcade and a cute but smallish children's room sequestered on a top deck (don't expect tons of kids on these ships, except on holiday cruises).

POOL, FITNESS & SPA FACILITIES   The ship's gym is downright palatial, and you might wonder, like I did on a recent sailing, if there was more equipment on back order or something else coming to fill the space. Hey, no complaints here. Because of its size, it's one of the best gyms at sea. Dozens of state-of-the-art machines are surrounded by floor-to-ceiling windows. The adjacent aerobics room is huge too—nearly as big as the one I go to at home. The spa and hair salon are adequate, but are nothing special compared to the unforgettable gym. The *Volendam*'s three pools are on the Lido Deck and include the main one and a wading pool under a retractable glass roof in a sprawling area that includes the pleasant, cafelike Dolphin Bar, and a smaller and more quiet aft pool on the other side of the Lido buffet restaurant. There are also more-isolated areas for sunbathing above the aft pool on an aft patch of the sports deck, and in little slivers of deck aft on most of the cabin decks. On the Sports Deck is a pair of paddle-tennis courts as well as shuffleboard. Joggers can uses the uninterrupted Lower Promenade Deck for a good workout.

Westerdam

The Verdict

An appealing ship with an ocean-liner-like feel, the *Westerdam* is solid, spacious, and modestly elegant, though an odd layout makes it tricky to find some public rooms.

Westerdam *(photo: Holland America Line)*

Specifications

Size (in tons)	53,872	Officers	Dutch
Number of Cabins	747	Crew	642 (Indonesian/Filipino)
Number of Outside Cabins	495	Passenger/Crew Ratio	2.3 to 1
Cabins with Verandas	0	Year Built	1986
Number of Passengers	1,494	Last Major Refurbishment	1989

Frommer's Ratings (Scale of 1–5)

Cabin Comfort & Amenities	4	Pool, Fitness & Spa Facilities	3
Ship Cleanliness & Maintenance	4	Children's Facilities	2
Public Comfort/Space	4	Itinerary	4
Decor	4	Worth the Money	5

Launched in 1986 as the Home Lines' *Homeric* and bought by HAL 2 years later, the ship was literally sawed in half at a German shipyard in 1989 to allow for the insertion of a 140-foot midsection of cabins and public rooms. The result is a very long ship reminiscent of an old-time ocean liner, with portholes on some decks, a wide wraparound promenade, a truly lovely showroom, and spacious cabins and lounges. Unfortunately, the stretching also produced a traffic problem: Since the dining room and the gym/spa sit basically alone on their respective decks, they can only be accessed from certain elevators and stairs—it can get confusing. That complaint aside, the *Westerdam* is a comfortable, stately vessel that boasts the same great service for which HAL is known. An added perk? Because it's an older ship, HAL generally sells *Westerdam* cruises, like *Noordam* cruises, at a lower price than cruises on its newer vessels.

Cabins & Rates

Cabins	Per diems from	Bathtub	Fridge	Hair Dryer	Sitting Area	TV
Inside	$119	yes	no*	no	no	yes
Outside	$143	some	no*	no	some	yes
Suite	$281	yes	yes	no	yes	yes

* Fridges can be requested through your travel agent and placed in cabins for a nominal fee.

CABINS Many ship cabins employ light woods and fabrics to make them seems bigger than they are, but aboard the *Westerdam* many cabins—especially the deluxe staterooms, are large enough to risk the dignified dark woods with which many are appointed. The cabins are decorated in conservative colors (earth tones and pastels) and batik prints, which aren't exactly uplifting. Some cabins have sofa beds and/or upper berths to accommodate additional guests; all have TVs and music channels. There are no in-cabin safes, and no verandas. Though clean and spacious enough, bathrooms feel old, with tiled showers that show some wear. Try to avoid cabins in the stern on the Lower Promenade Deck, which are right below the disco and casino and can be noisy.

Four cabins, plus all elevators, are wheelchair accessible.

PUBLIC AREAS   Most public rooms are located on the spacious Promenade Deck, including several lounges/bars, a low-key disco, shops, a library, casino, and the Admiral's Lounge showroom, a truly lovely space, which, with the lights dimmed, takes on a rich, dark, burgundy glow and evinces a kind of Weimar feel—you kind of expect Marlene Dietrich to show up onstage. Throughout the ship, artwork reflects the theme of Dutch exploration, with large-scale antique ship models and a salvaged cannon being standout display items.

The main one-story dining room, divided into two sections and located four decks down, is sometimes difficult to find, but rewards persistence with a feeling that's both cozy and spacious. Unlike modern ships, the room is located near the waterline and so has portholes instead of large viewing windows, but as curtains are drawn during dinner on pretty much every ship, it's an inconsequential difference. The ship has two separate buffet areas.

The small children's center is basically a near-empty room, with only the "Club Hal" logo on the door; its also used for meetings when necessary.

POOL, FITNESS & SPA FACILITIES   The ship has two outside pools, one at the stern and the other up top, with a retractable dome for bad weather. Walkers and runners will enjoy the broad Upper Promenade Deck, while tennis players and shuffleboarders can use the mini-courts on the Sports Deck. The small and basic Ocean Spa health club has windows and offers a handful of machines and weights, but can't hold a candle to the facilities on the line's newer ships. Aerobics classes are offered in one of the lounges, on-deck, or in the pool. There's a steam room, sauna, and a couple of massage rooms, plus a beauty salon.

Norwegian Cruise Line

7665 Corporate Center Dr., Miami, FL 33126. ☎ **800/327-7030** or 305/436-4000. Fax 305/436-4126. www.ncl.com.

THE LINE IN A NUTSHELL   NCL offers affordable (sometimes downright cheap) down-to-earth cruises on its diverse fleet of midsize and megasize ships.

THE EXPERIENCE   Unlike many lines that offer a similar product across the board, NCL has a varied fleet, from new to old, midsize to mega, making it difficult to generalize about the line's ships. Its two largest—the *Norwegian Sky* and the *Norway*—both carry about 2,000 passengers each but are as different as night and day, the former being a brand-new megaship and the latter one of the most classic ocean liners afloat. The line's four other vessels carry about 1,500 passengers each. In general, the ships attract a wide variety of cruisers, with some drawn by the line's popular music- or sports-theme cruises, some by the nostalgia of the *Norway,* and others simply by low prices—discounters always seem to have some last-minute space on NCL.

Despite its shortcomings, the line is very innovative in certain areas. In May of 2000, NCL launched its "Freestyle Cruising" concept on the *Sky,* introducing a flexible dining program sure to please. All restaurants on the ship (and fleetwide by year-end 2000) operate with a casual dress code and have open seating between about 5:30pm and midnight every evening. NCL also justifiably touts its music- and sports-theme cruises, which in 1999 included the first "Sports Illustrated Afloat" cruise, an Elvis Cruise that featured a skydiving show by the Flying Elvi, and a blues cruise that featured Bo Diddley, Son Seals, and Johnny Johnson. Sports bars are also a big draw, as are alternative dining choices (a concept popular aboard megaships but much less common aboard medium-size vessels).

Pros

- **Theme cruises.** NCL offers more music- and sports-theme cruises than any other line.
- **Flexible dining.** NCL's new policy lets you dine when you want and dress like you want.
- **Down-to-earth crowd.** NCL attracts a mixed bag of easygoing, easy-to-please, bargain-hunting fun-seekers.

Cons

- **Inconsistent service.** Across the board, service isn't always as sharp as it could be and often seems lackadaisical.

Compared with the other Mainstream lines, here's how NCL rates:					
	Poor	Fair	Good	Excellent	Outstanding
Enjoyment Factor				✓	
Dining			✓		
Activities				✓	
Children's Program			✓		
Entertainment				✓	
Service			✓		
Overall Value					✓

NCL: CRUISE LINE IN SEARCH OF AN IDENTITY

Norwegian Cruise Line was one of the pioneers of the North American cruise market, beginning in the days of the now-defunct Kloster Cruises. In 1966, Knut Knutson, the Norwegian owner of Kloster, had a cruise ship but no marketing system, and Ted Arison, an Israeli, had a great North American marketing system but no ships. Together, they formed Norwegian Caribbean Line, launching 3- and 4-day cruises from Miami to the Bahamas. In 1972, Arison and his entourage split from the company to form Carnival Cruise Lines, now the giant of the industry.

Over the years that followed, NCL had its difficulties, financial and otherwise, but by 1997 the hardest times seemed to be past, and a major program of expansion and marketing was put in place. Are you ready? This gets confusing: In 1996, NCL acquired the former *Crown Odyssey* (which was built in 1988 for Royal Cruise Line, a line bought by NCL a year later and run as a separate brand until 1996) and renamed it *Norwegian Crown* before transferring the ship to Norwegian's sister line, Orient Lines, in April 2000. In 1997, NCL acquired two more ships, the former Majesty Cruise Line *Royal Majesty* (renamed *Norwegian Majesty*) and the former Cunard *Crown Dynasty* (renamed *Norwegian Dynasty*), originally built for Crown Cruise Lines in 1993 and running for a short time in the mid-1990s as Majesty Cruise Line's *Crown Majesty*. In early 2000, Commodore purchased the ship for $86 million, restored the name *Crown Dynasty*, and revived Crown Cruise Line (see review in this chapter). Are you still following all this?

Over the past few years, NCL changed the names of almost all its ships to include the word *Norwegian*, and also "stretched" three of its ships, cutting them in two and inserting a newly constructed midsection. The *Norwegian Dream* and *Norwegian Wind* increased their passenger capacity from around 1,200 to around 1,700, and *Norwegian Majesty* increasing its size from just over 1,000 to 1,462. In May 1998, NCL also purchased Orient Lines and its 800-passenger M/V *Marco Polo*, then, in August 1999, debuted the first new ship in 6 years, the megaship *Norwegian Sky*.

Today, NCL is 100% owned by Singapore-based Star Cruises, a successful company with the moolah to make serious investments in NCL's future. In the spring of 2000 a mostly new management team began crafting yet another "new" NCL, announcing new deployments in Asia and 2- and 5-night Caribbean cruises for the *Norway*, as well as open-seating dining fleetwide by year-end 2000. A new 2,300-passenger ship, originally planned for Star, will now go to NCL for delivery in October of 2002 and is to feature tons of impressive innovations as part of the line's new "Freestyle Cruising" concept, including all open-seating dining, combo tv/computer monitors in all cabins, and self-service coffee- and tea-making facilities in all cabins.

THE FLEET

While at times it's hard to keep track, at press time Norwegian had six ships in its fleet. The brand-new 2,000-passenger **Norwegian Sky** debuted in August of 1999; the 1,750-passenger **Norwegian Wind** and **Norwegian Dream** were built in 1993 and 1992, respectively; the 1,462-passenger **Norwegian Majesty** (formerly Majesty Cruise Line's *Royal Majesty*) was built in 1992 and acquired by NCL in 1997; and the 1,504-passenger **Norwegian Sea** was built in 1988. The classic 2,032-passenger **Norway** was built in 1962 as the *France* and extensively refurbished over the years, and is in a class by itself.

Over the past few years NCL has divested itself of some ships as well. The 1,052-passenger *Norwegian Crown*, which joined NCL in 1996, was transferred to Norwegian's sister line, Orient Lines, in April 2000. The 950-passenger *Leeward*, which joined NCL in 1995, left the fleet in late 1999 when its charter agreement ended. Likewise, the 800-passenger *Norwegian Dynasty* left the fleet in late 1999 when it joined Commodore's revived Crown Cruise Lines.

NCL is looking to the future, too, and has signed letters of intent to build a second 2,000-passenger ship sister to the *Norwegian Sky,* at press time slated to debut in June of 2001 as the *Norwegian Sun.*

PASSENGER PROFILE

NCL as a rule attracts a diverse lot, and in general a younger, more price-conscious, and more active crowd than lines such as Holland America, Celebrity, and Princess. Typical NCL passengers are couples ages 25 to 60, and include a fair number of honeymooners and families with kids during summers and holidays. The atmosphere aboard all NCL vessels is informal and well suited to the party-maker taking a first or second cruise. NCL's recent acquisition by Singapore-based Star Cruises means the line will be shooting for some 25% of the passenger mix to come from the Asia and Australian markets, but you can count on it still catering to a mostly American market, plus a decent number of Europeans.

NCL has pioneered more theme cruises than any other line, so its passenger list is often composed of special-interest groups, including sports fans, older passengers who book big-band cruises to relive the days of Glenn Miller and Benny Goodman, and young professionals attracted to the jazz-, Dixieland-, or blues-theme cruises.

Active vacationers particularly like the line because of its enhanced **sports programs.** For instance, snorkeling and scuba lessons are often held in the ships' pools. Scuba programs, run by independent concessionaires, are aggressively promoted when they're offered. For the more sedentary sports fan, all major weekend games, including NFL playoffs, are broadcast via ESPN and CNN into passengers' cabins and onto the video monitors of each vessel's sports bar, sometimes with multiple screens broadcasting different games in different areas of the bar.

DINING

None of the Norwegian Cruise Line vessels is distinguished for its cuisine, but the way they handle the business of dining these days is pretty darn innovative. In early 2000, after NCL's association with Star Cruises was cemented, management introduced a new flexibility concept called "Freestyle Cruising." The *Sky* was the first to go freestyle, just before this book went to press, making all of its five restaurants open-seating each and every evening, allowing you to dine when and with whom you like, strolling in any time between about 5:30pm and midnight (all must be seated by 10pm). And, you can dress however you like, too: Even jeans and T-shirts are acceptable. Of course, this means you'll now see a guy in jeans and a baseball cap seated next to a lady in a dress and pearls. The plan is to have only one restaurant be formal on the night of the captain's cocktail party. Welcome to the new face of cruising! NCL expects to implement the freestyle concept aboard its other ships by year-end 2000, and I'm sure it won't take long for other lines to follow suit, given how casual even the corporate world is going these days.

Dining room meals on NCL are often focused on specific cuisines, such as French, Italian, Caribbean, Viking (as in Norwegian), or Tex-Mex, and you can usually count on choices like broiled mahimahi, salmon or fillet of flounder, beef Wellington, broiled lobster tail, chicken Parmesan, fettuccine Alfredo, or perhaps a Jamaican jerk pork roast, Wiener schnitzel, or roast prime rib. The wine lists appeal to standard mid-American tastes, and aren't offensively expensive.

All NCL ships have at least one **reservations-only alternative restaurant,** called Le Bistro, which are smaller and more intimate than the main dining rooms and serve continental specialties at no extra cost (except a suggested $5 tip). The food here is better than in the main dining rooms, and includes items like a yummy Caesar salad (made for you right at, or near, your table), a juicy beef tenderloin, and a marvelously

---

Cruise Tip

NCL offers convenient (and cost-saving) **soft-drink packages** for kids if yours like to fill up on Cokes (costs add up otherwise: A can goes for $1.50 a pop, and fountain sodas are $1). For those under age 17, Kids Soda packages offer a personalized soda cup, special straw, and unlimited fountain sodas, and can be purchased once you board ship for $16 on a 7-day cruise, $10 on a 4-day cruise, and $8 on a 3-day cruise. Deluxe "backpack packages" include the soda deal and a backpack full of fun stuff like a baseball cap, T-shirt, sunglasses ($39.50 for a 7-night cruise, $33 for 4-night cruises, and $28 for 3-night cruises).

---

decadent chocolate fondue. Be sure to make your reservations as soon as you get aboard (though there are often tables available for walk-ins).

There is a **light spa cuisine** choice as well as a **vegetarian entree** at lunch and dinner. Fresh fruit is often offered throughout the day from a station near one of the deck restaurants. There are also **children's menus** featuring the popular standards: burgers, hot dogs, grilled cheese sandwiches and french fries, spaghetti and meatballs, ice-cream sundaes, and even something you might not expect: vegetable crudités and cheese dip.

It's generally agreed that the best cuisine in the fleet is served aboard the *Sky,* followed by the *Norway.* The *Sky,* as the new-generation NCL ship, boasts two main dining rooms, two 84-seat alternative restaurants (Le Bistro and Ciao Chow, serving Italian and Asian cuisine), and a large indoor/outdoor casual buffet restaurant. The *Norway* has two main dining rooms, the classic dome-ceilinged Windward and the two-level Leeward, plus a casual outdoor buffet restaurant.

The *Norwegian Dream* and *Norwegian Wind* each have smaller, more intimate dining areas (four for dinner), with seating ranging from 76 in the smallest bistrolike areas to nearly 450 in the largest main dining room. Both ships have a **Sports Bar and Grill,** with indoor/outdoor snacking and drinking, room for almost 150 people, and almost constant background noise from the TVs.

The *Norwegian Sea* has two main dining rooms, the 280-passenger Four Seasons and the larger, 476-passenger Seven Seas. Both are located on the Main Deck. Its Lido restaurant is best for its panoramic views and informal buffets.

All NCL vessels offer daily **midnight buffets** and each also has an ice-cream bar open a few hours a day. Fleet-wide, you can also drool over the popular **Chocoholic Extravaganza** midnight buffet, offering everything from tortes to brownies in a format that's appealing and very fattening. English high tea is offered on 7-night cruises fleet-wide.

All the ships serve **pizza,** and there is a **coffee bar** on the *Norwegian Wind, Dream,* and *Sky* serving specialty coffees as well as other beverages. **Room service** is available 24 hours a day.

ACTIVITIES

Adult activities are one of the line's strongest points. You'll find the most action aboard the *Sky* and *Norway,* but all the ships offer impressive rosters. You can take cha-cha lessons; play bingo, shuffleboard, or basketball; attend an art auction or spa or beauty demonstration; or listen to the live poolside calypso band. There are galley and bridge tours, snorkeling demonstrations in the pool, makeovers, talent shows, wine tasting (for $10 a person), and trivia contests. There are silly **poolside competitions** to keep you laughing all afternoon long. The *Sky* and *Sea* have **Internet cafes** or computer rooms (with E-mail access), and NCL intends to have all the other ships wired by summer 2000.

Private Island Paradise, Norwegian Style

Early in its corporate history, NCL became the first cruise line to develop a private island for the use of its guests when it acquired **Great Stirrup Cay,** a stretch of palm-studded beachfront in the southern Bahamas. Since then, as part of a land rush for hideaway islands with deepwater access, such competitors as Royal Caribbean, Princess, Costa, Holland America, and, most recently and expensively of all, Disney, have each acquired private islands or beachfronts of their own.

Sleepy Great Stirrup Cay suddenly comes alive when an NCL vessel docks, becoming an instant party loaded with lunch, bar, and water-sports facilities. Music is either broadcast or performed live, barbecues are fired up, hammocks are strung between palms, and rum punches are spiced and served. Passengers can ride paddleboats, sail Sunfish, go snorkeling, or do nothing more than sunbathe all day long. Pleasingly, the island is not overdeveloped and manages to retain more of a natural feel than some of the other major lines' islands.

In port, the shore-excursion menu is heavy with active tours, such as snorkeling and diving, mountain biking, and kayaking. Especially popular are the **snorkeling excursions** escorted by certified instructors that are part of NCL's Dive-In program. At least one snorkeling tour is offered on just about every Caribbean port of call. Introductory scuba diving instruction is offered only in St. Thomas. Word to the wise: The Dive-In program is extremely popular and snorkeling excursions get sold out quickly, so be sure to sign up as soon as possible once aboard.

CHILDREN'S PROGRAM

Although the programs are not nearly as extensive or playrooms as well stocked as many other lines, NCL has expanded its Kids Crew program to offer year-round **supervised activities** for children ages 3 to 17. The program divides children into four age groups: junior sailors, ages 3 to 5; first mates, ages 6 to 8; navigators, ages 9 to 12; and teens, ages 13 to 17. During the off-season, activities are offered for three age groups (3 to 5, 6 to 12, and 13 to 17 years). **Activities** vary across the fleet, but may include sports competitions, dances, face painting, treasure hunts, magic shows, arts and crafts, and even a Circus at Sea. Children get their own "Cruise News" detailing the day's events.

Norwegian Dream, Norwegian Wind, Norwegian Majesty, and *Norwegian Sky* have a **playroom** called "Kids Korner" (the *Norway*'s is called "Trolland" and the *Norwegian Sea*'s is called "Porthole"). The facilities on the new *Sky* are the best by far, and include a separate teen center and a wading pool as well as a large, well-stocked playroom. The *Norway*'s facilities are NCL's next best (or at least biggest).

Group baby-sitting is offered every night except the first and last night of the cruise for $12 per child per night for 3 hours between 10pm and 1am. **Private, in-cabin baby-sitting** by a member of the crew is available from noon to 2am aboard all NCL's ships for $8 per hour for the first child and $2 per hour for each additional child (2-hr. minimum).

ENTERTAINMENT

NCL has found a nice balance between theme-related events and general entertainment that keeps everyone happy. The **Vegas-style productions** are expensive, surprisingly lavish, and artistically ambitious, especially on the *Sky* and *Norway*, the biggest ships in the fleet. All the ships contain a fully equipped theater where abridged productions of such

NCL Fleet Itineraries

Ship	Home Ports & Season	Itinerary	Other Itineraries
Norway	All round-trip from Miami, year-round; year-round 2- and 5-nighters beginning April 2001.	**7-night E. Carib:** St. Maarten, St. John/ St. Thomas, and Great Stirrup Cay (Bahamas). **2-night Bahamas:** Great Stirrup Cay. **5-night W. Carib:** Grand Cayman and Cozumel.	None
Norwegian Dream	Round-trip from San Juan through Dec. 2000.	**7-night E. Carib:** St. Lucia, Antigua, St. Kitts, St. Croix, and St. Thomas. **7-night S. Carib:** Aruba, Curaçao, Tortola, and St. Thomas.	Europe, Mediterranean, South America (beginning Dec 2000)
Norwegian Majesty	Bermuda itineraries round-trip from Boston, Apr–Oct. Caribbean cruises round-trip from San Juan, alternating weekly starting Dec. 17, 2000.	**7-night Bermuda:** St. George's. **7-night E. Carib:** St. Lucia, Antigua, St. Kitts, St. Croix, and St. Thomas. **7-night S. Carib:** Aruba, Curaçao, Tortola, and St. Thomas.	None
Norwegian Sea	Round-trip from Miami; itineraries alternate year-round starting Jan 2001.	**3-night Bahamas:** Key West and Nassau. **4-night W. Carib:** Key West and Cozumel.	None
Norwegian Sky	Round-trip from Miami; itineraries alternate weekly, Oct–Mar.	**7-night E. Carib:** Eleuthera, San Juan, St. Thomas, and Great Stirrup Cay. **7-night W. Carib:** Grand Cayman, Ocho Rios (Jamaica), Nassau, and Great Stirrup Cay.	Alaska, Hawaii
Norwegian Wind	Round-trip from Miami, Dec–Mar.	**7-night W. Carib:** Grand Cayman, Roatán (Honduras), Belize, and Cozumel.	Alaska, Hawaii, Asia (Starting Sept. 2001)

shows as *Crazy for You, Grease, 42nd Street, Will Rogers Follies,* and *Dreamgirls* have been presented. NCL also produces its own Vegas-inspired extravaganzas, *Sea Legs Express, Broadway Tonight,* and *Sea Legs Goes Hollywood,* all in the glitzy and glamorous tradition. On a recent *Sky* cruise, I was very impressed with the caliber of singers and dancers, and it appears the quality of NCL's entertainment is definitely on an upswing, putting it on par with Royal Caribbean, Carnival, Princess, and Celebrity. On some nights, the showrooms also feature comedians and juggling acts.

Serious gamblers should only consider the *Sky* and the *Norway* since these two ships boast the fleet's biggest and splashiest **casinos.**

All the ships have bars where you can slip away for a quiet rendezvous, and small tucked-away corners for more intimate entertainment, like **pianists** and **cabaret acts.** Music for dancing is popular aboard all the ships and takes place before or after shows, and each ship has a late-night disco.

NCL pioneered the concept of **theme cruises,** and its program today includes jazz cruises, blues cruises, Dixieland cruises, fifties- and sixties-era music cruises, big-band

Some Special Deals

Children's Discounts: Children under 2 sail free with Norwegian Cruise Line (although they still have to pay port charges).

---

cruises, and country-western cruises. Sometimes well-known headliners are brought on for certain theme cruises. On NCL's popular **"Sports Afloat" cruises,** professional players and Hall of Famers from pro basketball, football, hockey, and baseball sail aboard, signing autographs, conducting demonstrations and contests, and mingling with passengers.

SERVICE

Some passengers, especially first-timers, find the service excellent. Generally, room service and bar service fleet-wide is speedy and efficient. Waiters are attentive and accommodating. If you get too hot while sunbathing, you can even ask one of the waiters to spritz you with his water bottle.

While service isn't bad aboard the other vessels, it's better on the *Sky* because it's a new ship and new ships are often stocked with the best staff in the fleet. Service also seems better on the *Norway,* whose staff appears to be more seasoned and conscious of their ship's long tradition of elegance. With the line's new flexible dining program, additional crew members, mostly waiters and kitchen staff, have been added to each ship. On a recent *Sky* cruise, service in the buffet restaurant was especially efficient, even when the place got packed, as it often did at breakfast. Deck service by the pool is also good, so you'll rarely be kept waiting for a cool drink. If problems occur with service, it's usually in the main dining rooms, where the stress of feeding hundreds of passengers can take its toll.

Norway

The Verdict

It was once one of the grandest liners afloat, but it ain't what it used to be. Still, there's enough left to make the experience refreshingly nostalgic and rewarding. (And who can complain about the low rates!)

Norway *(photo: Heidi Sarna)*

Specifications

Size (in tons)	76,049	Officers	Norwegian
Number of Cabins	1,016	Crew	900 (International)
Number of Outside Cabins	656	Passenger/Crew Ratio	2.3 to 1
Cabins with Verandas	56	Year Built	1961
Number of Passengers	2,032	Last Major Refurbishment	1998

Frommer's Ratings (Scale of 1–5)

Cabin Comfort & Amenities	3	Pool, Fitness & Spa Facilities	4
Ship Cleanliness & Maintenance	4	Children's Facilities	3
Public Comfort/Space	4	Itinerary	4
Decor	3	Worth the Money	5

The last of the 1,035-foot luxury liners, this ever-enduring legend, with its long, sleek hull, is the only vessel of its kind sailing today. Built in 1962 as the SS *France* and stretching the length of $3^1/2$ football fields, the ship was enormous by the standards of the time, and although many megaships rival it in size today, it projects an aura of nostalgia they simply cannot match. The *Norway*'s only true peer in size and age is the *QE2*, which is a much more luxurious, formal ship. As a classic liner in the midmarket range plying the Caribbean, the *Norway* is a singularly unique ship.

Sadly, after many face-lifts over the decades (including a $65 million refurbishment begun in 1990 and a 1996 refit that brought the ship into compliance with international Safety of Life at Sea standards), the ship's interior hardware retains little of its original grandeur, and it has become a misfit of sorts. New carpeting, fabrics, and signs have been installed in the ship's public areas, and in late 1998 a fire sprinkler system (with many of the pipes and hardware exposed, because it was deemed too costly to rip out ceilings to hide them) and a new sports bar were added. Even though so much of the ship's grand history has been stripped away, its classic profile will still please ship buffs, who can revel in being there and knowing what the ship once was. The razor-sharp bow is stunning and a nostalgic reminder of the once-booming transatlantic trade, and, if you look, there are a few places on board where the past is alive. The Club Internationale is nearly as it was 40 years ago when it served as an elegant first-class lounge. Today, it's ultra-high ceiling, pillars, art-deco lighting fixtures, multilevel floor, and original pale golden yellow and teal colors still evoke the grandeur of yesteryear. The Club is a nice place for a cocktail before or after dinner, when live jazz music is featured. It's also the venue for high-tea and the weekly captain's cocktail parties. The windowless, circular Windward dining room (the former first-class dining room when the ship was the *France*) has not changed dramatically over the years and casts a warm, amber glow on diners. Further, some cabins still have their original etched-glass mirrors above dressers, and about 20 cabins on the Viking Deck are original.

Despite these few rooms that have survived, time-warp style, there have been some losses over the years that are just a crying shame. Did I mention that the tacky, modern Dazzles disco, located on one of the lower decks, is built over what was once an indoor pool? While I'm intrigued by the *Norway*'s history, I realize many of you could care less. For you folks, the *Norway*'s variety of activities and affordable price are what's most alluring.

The *Norway* today is famous for its theme cruises, and the ship is credited with pioneering such jaunts to fill the cabins during off-peak periods. Whatever the subject— country music or jazz, basketball or fitness and beauty—these theme cruises, offered throughout the year, appeal to a wide variety of tastes. Owing to its many commodious public rooms and easy flow of traffic, the *Norway* is an ideal venue for these kinds of special cruises.

The ship's huge size limits its access to certain smaller ports, so if your interest is in visiting more remote islands, this isn't the vessel for you. When you do stop at a port of call, the passenger count causes monstrous lines upon disembarkation, which can severely limit your time ashore. Lines can also be long at buffets.

Although menus are similar throughout the fleet, the food preparation and presentation is better on the *Norway*. On most NCL ships, the alternative Le Bistro Restaurant is head and shoulders above the main dining rooms. Not so on the *Norway*, where the meals and service in the main restaurants are quite good. The buffet at the ship's Great Outdoor Restaurant is pretty average, except for the paella cooked up on the grill. The delectably spicy dish, which includes some marvelous jumbo shrimp, sends many passengers scrambling back for seconds.

Cabins & Rates						
Cabins	Per diems from	Bathtub	Fridge	Hair Dryer	Sitting Area	TV
Inside	$115	no	no	no	no	yes*
Outside	$143	some	some	no	some	yes*
Suite	$179	yes	yes	some	yes	yes*

* TVs show ESPN and CNN.

CABINS   As aboard all old ships, there's a vast array of jigsaw-puzzle-like cabin sizes and configurations, some of them quirkily charming because of floor plans that were designed before cruise lines came up with the idea of standardization. The good news is that since the *Norway* is an older ship built for transatlantic journeys, cabins are bigger than average and offer better drawer and closet space. You can choose from 20 cabin categories, ranging from spacious Owner's Suites with private balconies to minuscule inside cells with upper and lower berths. Cabins are spread across 10 decks, and the farther down you go, the cheaper the price.

Cabins are furnished traditionally and plainly, with some art-deco touches. Since the cabin plans are so intricate, you might seek the advice of a good travel agent familiar with the ship in selecting one. Bathroom size and amenities tend to be consistent regardless of your cabin's size. Plumbing fixtures are a bit more solid than the cheaper plastic models installed aboard many newer ships.

Usually the first cabins to sell out are the new 100 or so luxury cabins and suites on the two uppermost glass-enclosed decks. Half have verandas, but the veranda partitions aren't solid and don't ensure privacy. Views from cabins on the Olympic or Fjord decks are obstructed completely or partially by lifeboats.

There are about 100 cabins for singles, a rarity today that's shared only by a few ships (Cunard's *QE2* and *Caronia* among them). Travelers with disabilities should book on the International Deck, near the major public rooms, where 10 cabins are wheelchair accessible.

PUBLIC AREAS   There are 12 passenger decks, and their public areas are the most generously sized of almost any ship. The wide International Deck, where many of the lounges and public rooms are located, makes it easy to move from end to end of the ship, and, in general, the expansive public rooms give everyone plenty of elbow room, something that doesn't exist on the newer ships in NCL's fleet.

Besides the Club Internationale, the two best public rooms on the ship are the sprawling Sports Illustrated Cafe and the Windjammer Bar. The Sports Illustrated room is a very modern (so much so that it seems out of place on this ship), slick bar decorated with memorabilia from sports superstars and dedicated to the late Florence Griffith-Joyner, who died shortly before she was supposed to help celebrate the room's opening. The Windjammer Bar is an intimate, nautically themed bar where a pianist holds forth with nightly melodies and memories, and the occasional guest singer from the audience.

If you want company, the North Cape Lounge on the pool deck accommodates 750 passengers. Two large, very busy dining rooms keep passengers fed and happy during two separate seatings, while the partially open-air Great Outdoor Restaurant in the stern is the venue for buffets.

The vast Monte Carlo Room is a gambler's heaven, with a couple of hundred slot machines and seven blackjack tables. The balconied, two-story Saga Theater has some bad seats, but its sound, lighting, and audiovisual facilities are state of the art, and much of the room is original. Club Internationale, as I say above, is an elegant lounge with very high ceilings and a lovely ambiance harkening back to the ship's early life. There's also a library.

The *Norway* is not an ideal ship for children, given its complex layout and lack of modern kids' activities, but a solid children's program is in place and families shouldn't write this ship off. There is a playroom housed in a space that, back when the ship sailed as the *France,* served as the kennel. Bow wow!

POOL, FITNESS & SPA FACILITIES   The *Norway* has two large outdoor pools, the one near the Lido Bar being the larger, with ample room for sunning. There's also a cushioned, quarter-mile circuit for jogging, and games include paddleball, table tennis, skeet shooting, shuffleboard, and basketball. Snorkeling and diving classes are often available aboard in the pool and offshore during excursions.

The fitness center and separate Roman Spa are excellent, roomy facilities, the former with floor-to-ceiling windows, an indoor pool, exercise equipment, two steam rooms, and two saunas, plus body-jet showers and a whirlpool. There are also golf tees and nets for golf practice, basketball and volleyball courts, facilities for trapshooting, and the most appealing and best-stocked library of any ship in NCL's fleet.

It may be a bit of a hassle to reach the Roman Spa, located deep within the ship, as only two elevators go there from the top decks (you may want to take the stairs rather than wait what seems like a lifetime for the elevators). Once there, however, you'll find one of the best spas at sea, with 16 treatment rooms and the first hydrotherapy baths on any cruise ship.

Sadly, much of the ship's classic teak decking, in places very shabby and worn, at press time was being replaced with a beige, rubberized surface.

Norwegian Dream • Norwegian Wind

The Verdict

These two 1,700-passenger ships are pleasant and affordable ways to see the Caribbean, but their lack of wide-open spaces and clusters of public rooms leading into one another makes them feel either cozy or cramped—take your pick.

Norwegian Wind *(photo: NCL)*

Specifications

Size (in tons)	50,760	Crew	614 (International)
Number of Cabins	874	Passenger/Crew Ratio	2.8 to 1
Number of Outside Cabins	716	Year Built	
Cabins with Verandas	48	*Norwegian Dream*	1992
Number of Passengers	1,748	*Norwegian Wind*	1993
Officers	Norwegian	Last Major Refurbishment	1998

Frommer's Ratings (Scale of 1–5)

Cabin Comfort & Amenities	4	Pool, Fitness & Spa Facilities	4
Ship Cleanliness & Maintenance	4	Children's Facilities	3
Public Comfort/Space	3	Itinerary	4
Decor	4	Worth the Money	4

If your heart isn't dead-set on a cruise aboard a brand-new megaship, you may find NCL's bright and cheerful, mid- to megasize twin ships, the *Dream* or *Wind,* appealing. In 1998, both the *Wind* and *Dream* sailed into the Lloyd Werft shipyard in Bremerhaven, Germany, where they were "stretched" by grafting a 130-foot midsection into each, an operation that raised the ships' tonnage from 41,000 to 50,760 and increased their capacity from the 1,200-passenger range to over 1,700. Improvements made possible by the stretch included the addition of a casual restaurant, a gift shop, lounges, a library, card room, cigar bar, and improved spas, health clubs, and children's facilities.

First-time cruisers like these two vessels. An informal style permeates both, the Norwegian officers are very smooth and charming, and most crew members are efficient and friendly.

Cabins & Rates

Cabins	Per diems from	Bathtub	Fridge	Hair Dryer	Sitting Area	TV
Inside	$133	no	no	yes	no	yes*
Outside	$153	no	no	yes	some	yes*
Suite	$197	yes	yes	yes	yes	yes*

* TVs have ESPN and CNN.

CABINS   Nearly all cabins are outside (716 of 874) and have sitting areas and picture windows. There are 74 cabins with private balconies, all on the Norway and Sun Deck. At 160 square feet, the outside deluxe staterooms are smaller than outside cabins on other mainstream ship lines such as Holland America and Carnival (inside cabins on both are just over 180 sq. ft. for ships built post-1990). The inside cabins are even smaller, ranging in size from 130 to 150 square feet. The *Dream*'s top-of-the-line accommodations are the 12 owner's suites on Sun Deck (Deck 11), which have balconies and a living room, convertible double-bed sofa, separate bedroom, refrigerator, stereo with CD library, plus tub and shower. These babies are 385 square feet, including the balconies. The 10 Superior Deluxe Penthouse suites amidships on Norway Deck have partially obstructed views because of the overhang from the restaurant above. Avoid them.

The accommodations have a pleasant, breezy decor with wood accents and pastels evocative of the West Indies (similar to the decor of Royal Caribbean's cabins). Unfortunately, storage space is minimal. Two people can just barely manage, but when a third or fourth person shares a cabin, it can get truly cramped. Bathrooms are also small. The small sitting area each cabin has is a nice touch; even inside cabins have a small couchette next to the bed. That said, to accommodate this feature, the area around the beds was made smaller and is now rather cramped. Most cabins have twin beds that can be converted to queen size. Cabins on the port side are for nonsmokers. Note that lifeboats block the views of the Category F and G cabins at amidships on the Norway Deck, and early morning joggers might disturb late sleepers who have cabins on the Promenade Deck.

Nearly a dozen cabins are wheelchair accessible, and nearly 40 are equipped for those with hearing impairments, an innovation aboard cruise ships. These cabins have a light panel on the wall facing the bed that signals the doorbell, phone, and any emergency on the ship; there's also a vibrating alarm clock, a fire-alarm light, and a special door-knocker.

PUBLIC AREAS   Both forward and aft, the ships' upper decks cascade down in evenly spaced tiers with slivers of deck open to passengers looking for panoramic views both ahead and behind the moving ship. However, in an attempt to save money, low-grade materials were used in the passageways and stairways, so you know you're not on a luxury yacht (or even on any Carnival, Celebrity, Holland America, or Princess ship).

With three main dining rooms plus a fourth alternative restaurant, the ships avoid the impersonal "banquet-style" dining that other mainstream ships fall into. The largest restaurant has a seating capacity of about 450 as opposed to the 600 to 700 on some ships. The most appealing is the Terraces restaurant, a cozy, three-level venue with floor-to-ceiling windows facing aft over the stern, and evoking a supper club in a 1930s movie. The Four Seasons restaurant is also an attractive spot to dine with great views; it's got tiered seating and curved walls of glass that bubble out over the edges of both the port and starboard sides of the ship. Couples who want a romantic dinner should try and make advance reservations for one of the tables-for-two along the windows.

Most of the public spaces are concentrated on the International and Star decks. The entrances to three of the ships' four restaurants are located on the International Deck, and congestion here is common at dinnertime, when passengers are traipsing through the Coffee Bar, Rendezvous Bar, and card/game room squeezed between the restaurants. Also on this deck is the library, which, with only three glass shelves of books, definitely seems like an afterthought, and never seemed to be open on a recent cruise.

For breakfast and lunch, you'll either miss the sprawling one-stop-shop indoor/outdoor buffet restaurants most megas offers or appreciate the many different choices the *Dream* and *Wind* offer. The Four Seasons restaurant offers the best buffet breakfast, while sit-down breakfasts and lunches are served in the Sun Terrace and The Terraces dining rooms. You can also grab a continental-style breakfast of sweet rolls, cereal, and fruits at the somewhat cramped indoor/outdoor Sports Bar and Grill, located at far aft of the ship on Sports Deck, as well as hamburgers, hot dogs, or salad for lunch. A limited breakfast buffet along with a lunch spread offering pizza, pasta, a salad bar, and desserts is available daily at the outdoor Pizzeria adjacent to the main swimming pool.

The dark, very black and Vegas-like casinos are glitzy, but are on the small side. Some lounges offer music and dancing, while in others you can find lounges with soft music (or no music at all), where you can engage in conversation. Lucky's Bar and the Dazzles disco on the Star Deck see the most late-night action. The sports bars with giant-screen TVs blasting the big game (and with somewhat chintzy, outdated photos of sports celebrities and memorabilia lining the walls) are the most popular bars on the ships. The Observatory Lounge on the Sports Deck, a sequestered ocean-view spot, functions as the disco, but if you're there during the day, keep in mind the basketball/volleyball court is just overhead.

POOL, FITNESS & SPA FACILITIES   With their attractive dark wooden decking and crisp blue-and-white-striped canvas umbrellas, the pool decks have a sort of European beach-resort quality about them. Each ship has two pools, and the larger one, on the Sun Deck, has a swim-up pool bar and two hot tubs. The problem here is that the high walls added to the Sun Deck when the ships were stretched cut off sea views for those lounging poolside and have created a closed-in, somewhat claustrophobic feeling. For the panoramic views of sea and sky, you have to walk up the stairs to the lounge chairs on the Sports Deck, or head to the small pool aft on the International Deck, where semicircular rows of lounges and deck chairs surround an almost purely decorative keyhole-shaped pool at the ships' stern. The ocean views here are good.

For a ship carrying 1,700 passengers (double occupancy), the cramped gym is pretty inadequate. There are four treadmills, four stair-steppers, and five stationery bikes squished into a small room with little space to spare. On a recent cruise, passengers were waiting in line to use machines, and several were out of order the entire cruise. The gym and small spa are also right underneath the basketball/volleyball court, so expect some intense banging when a game is in progress. The spa offers a range of treatments as well as his and hers saunas.

The Sports Deck has Ping-Pong tables and a golf driving range. One deck above, there's a combo basketball/volleyball court, and joggers will appreciate the wraparound Promenade Deck. Snorkeling and water-sports lessons and programs are often offered at the pool.

Norwegian Majesty

The Verdict

Though the *Majesty* really doesn't excel in any one area, considering its low prices it's a classy-enough, understated, informal midsize ship with good food, good service, and enough entertainment and activity options to keep everyone occupied.

Norwegian Majesty *(photo: NCL)*

Specifications

Size (in tons)	38,000	Officers	Norwegian
Number of Cabins	730	Crew	550 (International)
Number of Outside Cabins	481	Passenger/Crew Ratio	2.7 to 1
Cabins with Verandas	0	Year Built	1992
Number of Passengers	1,460	Last Major Refurbishment	1999

Frommer's Ratings (Scale of 1–5)

Cabin Comfort & Amenities	3	Pool, Fitness & Spa Facilities	3
Ship Cleanliness & Maintenance	4	Children's Facilities	3
Public Comfort/Space	4	Itinerary	5
Decor	4	Worth the Money	4

By normal standards, the *Norwegian Majesty* would be classified as a fairly new ship, but the explosive growth in the cruise business over the past decade has made some ships seem dated before their time.

By early 1999, the *Majesty* was beginning to show its age, both in its condition and its lack of pizzazz, so NCL pulled the ship out of service for just over 100 days, sending it to the Lloyd Werft Shipyard in Bremerhaven, Germany, to be stretched (like fleet mates *Dream* and *Wind*) and renovated. In what's become a relatively routine operation in the cruise industry, the ship was literally sawed in half, like a magician's assistant, and a preconstructed midsection was grafted into its middle, measuring just over 100 feet and containing 220 additional cabins, a new second dining room, more pool and deck space, and the alternative Le Bistro restaurant, a signature room on NCL's ships these days. The *Majesty* is now 680 feet long and carries 1,460 people at double occupancy.

In addition to increasing the ship's size, NCL also redid all outside decking, replaced carpets, and redecorated the existing cabins. In short, the old girl got a face-lift, and it's looking pretty good!

Now, the *Norwegian Majesty* is not going to excite fans of the Royal Caribbean, Celebrity, or Princess megaships. Nor will *Majesty* make anyone forget Holland America's or Celebrity's midsize vessels. But it doesn't try. NCL isn't selling *Majesty* as a floating art museum, a Las Vegas at sea, or a night at the Ritz. *Majesty* is what it is:

An understated, informal, midsize ship with good food, good service, and enough entertainment and activity options to keep everyone occupied—and at a great price.

Cabins & Rates						
Cabins	Per diems from	Bathtub	Fridge	Hair Dryer	Sitting Area	TV
Inside	$129	no	no	yes	no	yes**
Outside	$150	no	some	yes	no	yes**
Suite	$207	yes	yes	yes	yes	yes**

*Rates for Bermuda itineraries are higher on average. ** TVs show CNN and ESPN.*

CABINS *Norwegian Majesty* was originally built as a Baltic ferry, but was transformed into a cruise ship (the *Royal Majesty,* for Majesty Cruise Line) before it ever left the shipyard. It was intended for short, 3- and 4-day jaunts from Miami to the Bahamas, Key West, and Cozumel—short itineraries that didn't really require large cabins.

Today, though, *Majesty* does 7-night Bermuda cruises from Boston in summer, and in winter it sails 7-night Caribbean cruises out of San Juan, and on these longer voyages some folks may find the accommodations to be a bit, shall we say, intimate. The ship has 10 price categories, although there are just two cabins in the Penthouse Suite category. The Superior Deluxe Suites (18 of them) are more than adequate, with bathtubs and tile bathrooms, sitting areas, and enough room to move. Most Category A outside staterooms are a barely adequate 145 square feet, but in lower categories it gets even tighter at 106 square feet. All cabins have hair dryers, televisions (with ESPN, CNN, two movie channels, and an in-house station—but you probably won't want to lie around these small cabins watching TV for very long), and safes, and some rooms have refrigerators. Many cabins can accommodate a third and fourth passenger.

Some cabins on Norway and Viking decks have views that are obstructed by lifeboats. On Promenade Deck, you are likely to open your curtain in the morning and come face-to-face with a jogger. The best cabins (other than suites) may be Category A rooms on Majesty Deck, especially the ones in the bow that have windows offering sweeping vistas of the sea ahead.

There are seven cabins equipped for passengers with disabilities.

PUBLIC AREAS *Norwegian Majesty* is among the easiest ships to find your way around, and you are never far from something to do. Public areas aren't glitzy, decorated instead with a pleasant mixture of blues, lavenders, ivories, and lots of teak and brass.

There are two bars and the informal buffet restaurant, Cafe Royale, on Sun Deck. Although many ships put their buffet restaurant in the stern, this ship's cozy cafe is in the bow, with panoramic windows to see what's ahead. The room isn't huge, and can be crowded at mealtimes, with long lines. There is another munching option in the stern: Piazza San Marco, where you can get pizza, hot dogs, and burgers.

There are outdoor tables on Sun Deck, but if you want to stay inside and the Cafe Royale tables are taken, slip down the stairs into the Royal Observatory Lounge, another bow-facing room with great views. It's also the scene of live entertainment nightly, including karaoke. This room is easy to miss, tucked away in the bow on a deck with no other public rooms except the Kids Corner all the way back in the stern.

The rest of the ship's nightlife is on Decks 5 and 6, except for the Frame 52 Disco on Deck 7 aft. The disco is small and not as technically advanced as some, but it serves its purpose and hops until about 3am nightly.

The Palace Theater could be described as intimate; it could also be described as claustrophobic. Either way, the sight lines are not good, with support columns all around the room. The low ceiling prevents dancers from getting too energetic.

The Polo Club just outside the theater is a good place to have a drink before the show or before (or after) dinner. It usually features a pianist/vocalist. On the opposite end of the long, narrow room is the Monte Carlo Casino, which was totally redone when the ship was stretched, and is now darker and moodier, a perfect setting for you and your money to have a parting of the ways.

Down on Deck 5 you can eat, drink, and be merry. Both the Seven Seas and the Four Seasons dining rooms seem quite crowded. Le Bistro, the line's signature alternative restaurant, is a small, intimate room off the corridor that links the two main dining rooms. Next door to Le Bistro is a new coffee bar. Sit on a stool at the bar or carry your drink to a nearby window-side table and watch the world go by inside and out. Shops are forward from the lobby, and there's a new card room, a small video arcade, a library, and a meeting room.

The Rendezvous Lounge piano bar and Royal Fireworks dance lounge, for adult contemporary sounds, abut each other in the bow. Both rooms tend to be underused by passengers who have no other reason to find themselves in that end of the ship.

POOL, FITNESS & SPA FACILITIES   When *Majesty* got a new midsection it got a whole lot of new deck space on Decks 10 and 11 and a second swimming pool, which should relieve some of the overcrowding the original pool used to experience. There's also a splash pool for kids on Deck 8, and you can catch some rays in relative peace and quiet in another area at the stern of Viking Deck (Deck 8).

Joggers and walkers can circle the ship on the wraparound Promenade Deck 7, which is also home to the Bodywave spa and fitness center. These facilities are not extensive by any means. The workout room is basic and has several weight stations and cardiovascular stations, and there's a separate aerobics room across the hall.

Norwegian Sea

The Verdict

While the *Sea* seems tired and dated in many ways, this midsize, middle-aged ship offers an ultra-casual cruise and a great itinerary at a very affordable price.

Norwegian Sea *(photo: NCL)*

Specifications

Size (in tons)	42,000	Officers	Norwegian
Number of Cabins	752	Crew	616 (International)
Number of Outside Cabins	519	Passenger/Crew Ratio	2.4 to 1
Cabins with Verandas	0	Year Built	1988
Number of Passengers	1,504	Last Major Refurbishment	2000

Frommer's Ratings (Scale of 1–5)

Cabin Comfort & Amenities	3	Pool, Fitness & Spa Facilities	2
Ship Cleanliness & Maintenance	3	Children's Facilities	1
Public Comfort/Space	3	Itinerary	5
Decor	3	Worth the Money	4

The *Norwegian Sea* isn't a bad ship, but it's an aging ship, a relic at 12 years old. Too young to be a classic, too old to be contemporary, the ship is just right for the kind of inexpensive, casual, laid-back 3- and 4-night cruises it's now offering year-round out of

Miami, where it competes nicely with the other somewhat dated ships on this route—Carnival's *Ecstasy* and Royal Caribbean International's *Majesty of the Seas*.

In early 2000, the ship got face-lift that included new carpeting and upholstery throughout as well as the addition of an Internet cafe.

Cabins & Rates

Cabins	Per diems from	Bathtub	Fridge	Hair Dryer	Sitting Area	TV
Inside	$128	no	no	yes	no	yes*
Outside	$145	some	some	yes	some	yes*
Suite	$235	yes	yes	yes	yes	yes*

* TVs show CNN and ESPN.

CABINS When NCL built the ship in 1988, it didn't waste space on the cabins. The rooms are small by any measure, although in most cases they do provide adequate drawer and hanging space for two people. Their decor is pleasant, and their soundproofing is great—I heard the couple next door only once. Things get cozy—that's real-estate language for "cramped"—in the standard cabins, especially the inside ones, the cheapest of the bunch. With two fold-down upper bunks and two regular berths, they allow you to cram four people into a space that's adequate for one. But if the choice is going as an anchovy or not going at all, then break out the capers. In general, bathrooms are tiny: I found a new way to turn off the shower without using my hands. It was strictly inadvertent, but it illustrates just how little room there is to maneuver.

There are four owner's suites and three deluxe suites, and these are the best and most spacious accommodations, if you can afford them. They have sitting areas, bathtubs, and mini-refrigerators. Note that many cabins on both the Star and Norway decks have their views either obstructed or partially obstructed by lifeboats.

All cabins have hair dryers and TVs showing ESPN and CNN. Some cabins have personal safes (for those that don't, the purser can put your valuables in a safety-deposit box).

The *Sea* has four cabins equipped for passengers with disabilities.

PUBLIC AREAS This is not a glitzy ship, and some parts of it look the most spartan of anything in the NCL fleet. Nevertheless, the *Norwegian Sea* is seaworthy in every way and sleek in design, and it's been a hit for NCL, especially among Americans, who make up a good percentage of its passenger list and its crew.

A striking two-deck-high lobby has a water-and-crystal sculpture, along with a cascading fountain splashing into a marble-lined pool. I found lots of quiet little nooks in the wide, bright elevator lobbies (not to be confused with the tiny, dark elevators). On some decks there are chairs and tables near the windows in these spaces. You can sit outside Oscar's, the smoky little piano bar off the atrium, retreat to the not-very-well-stocked library, or play a game in the card room just off the large, roomy casino (with its 178 slot machines). Card games are accompanied by the sounds of a Western-themed slot machine that exhorts anyone within 50 yards to "Round 'em up—it's a stampede!"

There's another little bar, Gatsby's, tucked away on Deck 10 aft. It can be a bit drafty, and the chairs, while attractive, aren't conducive to long stays, but it's an intimate little wine-and-cigar space with soft piano music. Right across the deck is Le Bistro, the ship's alternative restaurant, which you have to try at least once (love that chocolate fondue!). The two main restaurants are unremarkable, and the casual dining restaurant, with the most convoluted, exasperating buffet line I've ever seen, can be a pain. The food is better than it looks, though, and the specialty station outside the main buffet—pick-your-own-ingredients omelets for breakfast and soup for lunch—are delightful.

The Cabaret Lounge is the main showroom, and you'd better get there early for a seat without an obstructed view. The Stardust Lounge is a cabaret-style room that offers some alternative entertainment. There's also a disco that heats up late at night; it may be small, but it works.

POOL, FITNESS & SPA FACILITIES   There are many ships to choose from when it comes to fitness and spa programs. This is not one of them. The fitness room is on the small side and has your basic equipment, and the "full-service" spa has two treatment rooms, one each for men and women. There are also his-and-hers saunas.

Outside, it's not always easy to find a deck chair near the pool. Go up one flight to the Sun Deck and it gets easier—the farther from the pool and band, the less crowded it is. And you are never too far from one of the outdoor bars. There are two nice pools on-deck (one is quite large) and a couple of whirlpools.

The Promenade Deck features a quarter-mile jogging and walking track, and adjacent to the spa and gym is a golf driving net. There's also Ping-Pong and shuffleboard, and snorkeling lessons can be arranged.

Norwegian Sky

The Verdict

The line's biggest, best, and snazziest ship to date, the *Sky* has great features like an Internet cafe, five restaurants, a cigar bar, cabin balconies, and a great Sports Deck, complete with a basketball/volleyball court and golf driving nets.

Norwegian Sky *(photo: Norwegian Cruise Line)*

Specifications

Size (in tons)	80,000	Officers	Norwegian
Number of Cabins	1,001	Crew	750 (International)
Number of Outside Cabins	574	Passenger/Crew Ratio	2.7 to 1
Cabins with Verandas	252	Year Built	1999
Number of Passengers	2,002	Last Major Refurbishment	N/A

Frommer's Ratings (Scale of 1–5)

Cabin Comfort & Amenities	3	Pool, Fitness & Spa Facilities	4
Ship Cleanliness & Maintenance	5	Children's Facilities	4
Public Comfort/Space	4	Itinerary	4
Decor	4	Worth the Money	4

The NCL *Sky* marks the line's first entry into the modern megaship world, and despite some flaws, it's an impressive debut. The *Sky* comes loaded with today's must-have features, from cabin balconies to an Internet cafe and a cigar bar—and, most importantly, it has a fabulous dining program, boasting five restaurants, all of which operate under a casual dress code (all the way down to jeans and T-shirts if that's your thing) and an open-seating policy in which you can dine anytime between about 5:30pm and midnight.

The biggest drawback of the ship: the size and storage capacity of its cabins.

Cabins & Rates						
Cabins	**Per diems from**	**Bathtub**	**Fridge**	**Hair Dryer**	**Sitting Area**	**TV**
Inside	$151	no	yes	yes	yes	yes*
Outside	$159	no	yes	yes	yes	yes*
Suite	$231	some	yes	yes	yes	yes*

TVs show CNN and ESPN.

CABINS Can we say "no storage space"? OK, the *Sky*'s cabins are pretty, done up in wood tones and pastels, but they're small and there's nary a place for your knickers. All cabins, even suites, have only a two-panel closet and a small bureau with four slim drawers. Be prepared to use your suitcase to store whatever else doesn't fit. Oh, and watch out for those reading lamps above the beds: Their protruding shades make sitting up impossible.

The 252 suites with balconies measure 202 square feet, including the veranda, and the vast majority of standard outside and inside cabins measure only about 150 square feet (compared to Carnival's standard 188 square feet). Bathrooms are compact, with tubular shower stalls and slivers of shelving. The cabins do have some redeeming qualities, though. Every single one has a small sitting area, and comes accoutered with a mini-fridge (not stocked), hairdryer, robes (flimsy ones, however), TVs, and a desk and chair.

It's worth noting that the ship's hull was originally built a few years back by Costa, who'd planned for the cabins to have portholes and no balconies. Costa sold the hull to NCL after the shipyard went bust, and, unwilling to bring out a megaship without balconies, NCL compromised, working around the existing portholes and adding balconies, resulting in an odd door-and-porthole combo (most ships have sliding glass doors) in the 252 cabins with balconies.

There are six cabins equipped for wheelchairs. The ship offers laundry and dry-cleaning service, but does not have self-service launderettes.

PUBLIC AREAS Like its namesake, the *Sky* is a bright and sun-filled ship due to its abundance of floor-to-ceiling windows. Surrounding the atrium on several levels is a bar, a pianist, and clusters of chairs creating relaxing pockets.

Above all else, the *Sky* excels in the restaurant department. For breakfast, lunch, and dinner, there are two elegant dining rooms (plus a small, cozy third room connecting the two, Horizons), whose elegance belies the jeans- and T-shirt-clad passengers often eating in them. The rooms have lots of tables for two and four. There's also a large indoor/outdoor casual buffet restaurant for all three meals. For lunch and dinner, you can also choose from a pair of 84-seat alternative restaurants: Le Bistro serves continental and Ciao Chow serves Italian and Asian; both are located on the topmost decks for great views. Reservations are required for dinner in both. Ciao Chow lunch buffets are a highlight, with daily themes including authentic, handmade sushi and sashimi, or a create-your-own Oriental soup. The place also serves up the best pizza at sea, with a delectable thin crust, from about noon to 4pm; you can also get it from room service 24 hours a day.

Food aside, other public areas include nearly a dozen bars, including a dark and cozy cigar club with the most comfortable thick leather chairs and couches around, a sports bar, Gatsby's wine bar, Checkers nightclub/disco, two large poolside bars, and a coffee bar associated with the Internet cafe. (The only problem is, it's not very private, being located along the edge of a main corridor between the casino and the show lounge). Most of the balcony seats in the cream-colored Stardust show lounge have obstructed views of the stage.

For kids, the *Sky's* huge children's area includes a sprawling playroom with ridiculously high ceilings, a teen center with a large movie screen and a pair of Foozball games, and a video arcade.

POOL, FITNESS & SPA FACILITIES   The well-stocked gym may be on the small side for a ship of this size, but, like the large adjacent aerobics room, has floor-to-ceiling windows that make it a pleasure to work out in, and a convenient location abutting the main pool deck. Nearby, the attractive spa and beauty salon are ocean-view too, with lovely gilded Buddha statuary dotting the area.

Out on deck, there are a pair of pools with a cluster of four hot tubs between them. There's a fifth hot tub and kids wading pool sequestered at the aft end of the deck above, the Sports Deck. Up there you'll find the combo basketball/volleyball court, a pair of golf driving nets, and shuffleboard. (And if you happen to look on the ship's deck plan and see a batting cage up there too, don't go looking for it: That plan was scrapped at a late date.)

Princess Cruises

10100 Santa Monica Blvd., Los Angeles, CA 90067-4189. ☎ **800/421-0522** or 310/553-1770. Fax 310/284-2845. www.princesscruises.com.

THE LINE IN A NUTSHELL Princess's mostly mega fleet offers a quality, mainstream cruise experience. Its newest ships are stylish, floating resorts with just the right combination of fun, glamour, and gentility for a pleasant and relaxing cruise.

THE EXPERIENCE Although Princess doesn't position any one of its ships in the Caribbean year-round (most spend their summers in Alaska and the Mediterranean), those ships it does bring in for the Caribbean season are its newest and largest. If you were to put Carnival, Royal Caribbean, Celebrity, and Holland America in a big bowl and mix them all together, you'd come up with the Princess's megas. The *Grand, Sea, Sun, Dawn,* and *Ocean Princess* (the Grand-class ships) are less glitzy and frenzied than Carnival and Royal Caribbean; not quite as cutting-edge or witty as Celebrity's *Millennium, Century, Galaxy,* and *Mercury;* and more exciting, youthful, and entertaining than Holland America's near-megas, appealing to a wide cross section of cruisers by offering lots of choice, activities, and touches of big-ship glamour, along with lots of private balconies and plenty of the quiet nooks and calm spaces of smaller, more intimate-size vessels. You'll see: The ships feel smaller than they really are.

Overall, the Princess ships are one notch above their most aggressive mainstream competitors, Carnival and Royal Caribbean. Aboard Princess, you get a lot of bang for your buck, attractively packaged and well executed.

Pros

- **Balconies.** Nearly half of all the cabins on the *Ocean, Sea, Sun,* and *Dawn* have private balconies; on the *Grand Princess,* over half do!
- **Lots of dining choices.** The Grand-class ships have two or three main dining rooms, intimate alternative restaurants, a 24-hour buffet, and an ice-cream stand.

Cons

- **No free ice cream.** It may sound petty, but it's irritating that Princess sells only Häagen-Dazs ice cream—at $1.90 a scoop and $3.75 for a sundae—in lieu of the free self-service frozen yogurt and soft ice cream most other lines offer. (Princess serves the free stuff only in the dining rooms at mealtime.)
- **Average food.** The ships' cuisine is perfectly fine if you're not a gourmet, but if you are, you'll find it's pretty banquet hall–like and not as good as Celebrity's, Carnival's, Disney's, or Holland America's.

Compared with the other Mainstream lines, here's how Princess rates:					
	Poor	Fair	Good	Excellent	Outstanding
Enjoyment Factor				✓	
Dining			✓		
Activities			✓		
Children's Program			✓		
Entertainment			✓		
Service				✓	
Overall Value				✓	

PRINCESS: MELLOW MEGAS

Few other cruise lines (except Carnival) have managed to start so small and grow so rapidly in such a short time, starting as an obscure West Coast cruise outfit and growing into the hyper-modern upper-middle-class giant it is today.

Princess Cruises originated in 1962 when the company's founder, Stanley McDonald, chartered the *Yarmouth* as a floating hotel for the Seattle World's Fair, running trips from California. In 1965, he chartered the long-gone *Princess Patricia* for cruises between Los Angeles, Alaska, and the Pacific coast of Mexico, and named his company after it. Soon, two additional ships, one of them brand-new, were leased from Costa Cruises to meet demand. In 1974, the company was snapped up by British shipping giant P&O Group, which has intensified its efforts to promote Princess vessels and Caribbean itineraries in markets on both sides of the Atlantic.

In the 1970s, Princess gained enormously by associating itself and its ships *Island Princess* and *Pacific Princess* with the TV series **The Love Boat,** which portrayed the cruise experience as an almost foolproof matchmaking machine. The series created a flood of paying customers anxious to experience romance on the high seas, all skippered and shepherded by tactful Gavin MacLeod and his witty crew, or some reasonable facsimile. The series gets enormous credit for promoting cruises in general and Princess in particular, so it's no wonder the company's been unwilling to let the association slip away. To this day, you'll still hear the theme song from the show sung aboard ship, and still see Gavin MacLeod pitching for the line.

The fleet first bulked up in 1988 when Princess received a massive influx of staff, equipment, and hardware through P&O's purchase of Italian-owned, Los Angeles–based Sitmar cruises. As part of this deal, Princess acquired three huge, cutting-edge ships, the *Star Princess* (which has since been commandeered by P&O to sail as its *Arcadia*), and the futuristic-looking *Crown Princess* and *Regal Princess,* identical 70,000-ton twins whose avant-garde design today appears somewhat dated in comparison with the line's newer ships. By 1995, a billion-dollar building spree that's still in high gear began with the launching of the cutting-edge Grand-class ships. The crescendo? The launching in May 1998 of what was to date the largest cruise ship in the world, the 109,000-ton *Grand Princess.*

THE FLEET

Princess's diverse fleet of 10 ships includes five Grand-class megaships all launched since 1995—the 109,000-ton supersize megaship **Grand Princess** (1998) and the three mega-sisters **Ocean Princess** (2000), **Sea Princess** (1998), **Dawn Princess** (1997), and **Sun Princess** (1995)—plus two near-megas, the 1,590-passenger **Regal Princess** (1991) and **Crown Princess** (1990); two slightly smaller ships, the 1,200-passenger **Sky Princess** (1984) and **Royal Princess** (1984); and the small, 640-passenger **Pacific Princess** (1971), one of the original Love Boats. The *Sky, Royal,* and *Regal* do not sail in the Caribbean, and so are not reviewed in this book. In early 1999, Princess announced the sale of one of its original Love Boats—the *Island Princess,* built way back in 1972—to Hyundai Merchant Marine, a Korean conglomerate that once had a short-lived partnership with Carnival Corporation.

At press time, two sisters to the 109,000-ton *Grand Princess* (*Golden Princess* and another that's as yet unnamed) are in the works and scheduled to enter service in April 2001 and January 2002. Plus, another pair of ships has been ordered for delivery in July 2003 and May 2004, to be built by Mitsubishi in Japan, with tonnage at 113,000 apiece.

For 2001, the 6-year-old *Sun Princess* and the oldest of the Princess mega-lot, the nearly 10-year-old, 1,590-passenger *Crown Princess,* will spend half the year doing

10- and 11-night Panama Canal cruises, and the 30-year-old *Pacific Princess,* the oldest and smallest of the fleet, will spend its second summer season in Bermuda.

PASSENGER PROFILE

In the past, most Princess passengers were middle-aged middle Americans, but the new megas are attracting younger, 30- and 40-something cruisers as well as those in their fifties and sixties, and generally a broader cross section of more active types. Overall, the passengers are not as rowdy and boisterous as those aboard Carnival, not as rich as those aboard Seabourn, and not as staid as those aboard Holland America. The *Grand Princess* and *Ocean, Sea, Dawn,* and *Sun Princess* have extensive kids' facilities and are ideal ships for families. The *Grand Princess* lures wedding parties with its wedding chapel, the first ship to have one (now Royal Caribbean's *Voyager of the Seas* and Carnival's new *Spirit* and *Pride* have them as well, but the *Grand* remains the only ship where the captain conducts official marriage ceremonies on board every week). Perfect for a romantic vacation, the ships strike a balance between formal and informal. There's a lot going on, but also plenty of opportunities to do your own thing.

DINING

The newer and bigger the ship, the more dining options. Princess's food, on its newest ships especially, is on a par with Royal Caribbean and Norwegian, and ranges from good to mediocre. The line doesn't seem to focus on food-and-beverage presentations as assiduously as, for example, Celebrity. Service is generally efficient, but not memorable or extraordinary in any way.

On the megas, two or three **main dining rooms** have two seatings at dinner and usually two at breakfast and lunch as well. A choice of four or five entrees at dinner might include prime rib, lobster, king crab legs, turkey with all the Thanksgiving trimmings, halibut in a citrus-caper butter sauce, rack of lamb with Dijon sauce, Cornish hen, and even pan-roasted rabbit with rosemary and sage; there are always **"healthy" choices** and **vegetarian options,** too.

There's also the buffet-style Horizon Court Lido restaurant for more **casual dining** morning, noon, and night. For breakfast, you'll find everything from fresh fruit to cold cuts, from cereal to fish, and from steam-table scrambled eggs to cooked-to-order fried eggs. At lunch, you'll find several salads, fruits, hot and cold dishes, roasts, vegetarian choices, and something new: In the summer of 1999, the entire Princess fleet began offering a **sushi bar** here between 11am and 3pm on days at sea, featuring freshly prepared (and tasty) choices like California rolls and tasty rolls filled with shrimp, crab, avocado, and vegetables. The restaurant's multistation setup keeps lines to a minimum. Evenings, this becomes the Horizon Court Bistro, a casual (no reservations required) sit-down restaurant like you'll find on Carnival and Royal Caribbean. The food is as good as you'll get in the dining room, with a set menu all week enhanced by a few specials.

The Grand-class ships have far and away the most choices beyond the typical dining rooms. Unlike any other ship in the fleet, the *Grand Princess* has two alternative, **reservations-required restaurants** specializing in Italian (with specialty pizzas, antipastos, and six kinds of pasta) and Tex-Mex (with choices like fajitas and tequila chicken). They're a great way to break up the week. Both charge a $3.50-per-person cover. The *Ocean, Sea, Sun,* and *Dawn* have **sit-down pizzerias** with menus of pizza choices for lunch and late dinner. In all these alternative venues, dining is more casual, intimate, and quiet, with tables seating mostly parties of two, four, and six. There's also **24-hour noshing** available in the Horizon Court. Pizza and grilled burgers, chicken fillets, and french fries are served from a **poolside grill** in the afternoons, and there's a

---

Princess Cays: Private Island Paradise

Princess's eastern and western Caribbean itineraries offer an additional advantage for beach buffs: the line's private island, Princess Cays, off the southwestern coast of Eleuthera in the Bahamas. You can swim and snorkel, and make use of Princess's fleet of Hobie Cats, Sunfish, banana boats, kayaks, and paddle wheelers. There's live music, a beach barbecue, and several dozen great tree-shaded hammocks at the far end of the beach for anyone who wants to get away from it all or sleep off too many rum punches. Local vendors set up stands around the island to sell conch shells and crafts like shell anklets and straw bags, and also offer hair braiding (remember, here you need to pay cash). There is also a Princess shop for T-shirts and other clothing as well as other souvenirs of the mug-and-key-chain variety (here you can bill purchases to your cabin account).

While overall the island experience is a pleasure, on a recent visit I found the service at the water-sports shack to be poor. The crew in charge of the jet skis (which passengers were paying a nice chunk of change to rent for a half hour or hour) seemed to have no idea what was going on, and weren't apologetic about it either. Renters had to wait way past their allotted times and were left to their own devices to grab a jet ski when one became available. Let's hope this was an aberration.

Häagen-Dazs **ice-cream parlor** serving the yummy stuff in scoops and sundaes for several dollars a pop (unfortunately, this is in lieu of the free frozen-yogurt and ice-cream machines most megas have operating most of the day).

In the Horizon Court buffet restaurants on board the *Ocean, Sea, Dawn, Sun, Grand, Royal, Crown,* and *Regal* Princesses, a **kids' menu** offers goodies like burgers, hot dogs, fish sticks, chicken fingers, and, of course, the PB&J sandwich. Kids can also enjoy a buffet salad and desserts like chocolate brownies, jumbo cookies, and fruit salad.

There's also **24-hour room service** in the cabins.

ACTIVITIES

The line that wants to be all things to all people is expert at programming activities to please a wide range of tastes, with the Grand-class ships offering the most elaborate and extensive repertoire and the *Crown Princess* and *Pacific Princess* being much more sedate.

Activities fleet-wide include art auctions, bingo, cards, trivia games, aerobics classes, shuffleboard, Ping-Pong, golf putting, first-run movies, dancing lessons, water volleyball, beauty and spa demonstrations, and more. Additionally, the Grand-class ships offer golf via virtual-reality simulators, and the *Grand Princess* has basketball and volleyball, the biggest and best virtual-reality game room at sea, and a **miniature-golf course.** And, of course, you can always relax in your cabin and watch *Love Boat* reruns.

While the pitch of activities isn't as frenzied as aboard Carnival or Royal Caribbean, the Grand-class ships aren't anywhere near sedate, moving Princess closer to its more party-happy competitors than ever before. The **discos** rage most nights with a fairly packed dance floor, and there are always a couple of silly **pool games** each afternoon, like a belly-flop contest or a stuff-the-most-fruit-or-Ping-Pong-balls-into-your-bathing-suit contest.

Princess's "New Waves" program offers passengers the chance to earn **PADI scuba-diving certification,** a rare and worthwhile experience that's not available aboard many other ships. Sign up in advance (by calling the PADI New Waves Dive Line at ☎ 888/919-9819 or through the Web site at www.newwaves.com) or the moment you get aboard, as the course requires that you attend at least 15 hours of classroom and practice sessions. If you opt to pursue this, approach it with the seriousness it deserves, and plan to spend some time studying.

Princess devotes a lot of attention and space to its onboard **libraries.** The *Grand Princess* also has a cozy writing area, a place to pen all those postcards you'll want to send. The Grand-class ships have small and unimpressive business centers with a fax machine and a couple of computers with E-mail capability (for $7.50 per 15 min.), open for limited hours each day.

CHILDREN'S PROGRAM

Supervised activities are offered year-round for ages 2 to 17, and are divided into two groups: "Princess Pelicans," ages 2 to 12, and teens, ages 13 to 17. Princess's newest Caribbean-bound ships, the *Grand, Ocean, Sea, Sun,* and *Dawn,* are well equipped for children and are clearly intended to cater to families as Princess seeks to broaden its appeal and distance itself from its old image as a staid, adults-only line. They've each got a spacious **children's playroom** and a sizable area of fenced-in outside deck dedicated for kids only, with a shallow pool and tricycles. **Teen centers** have computers, video games, and a sound system (and the one on the *Grand Princess* even has a teen's hot tub and private sunbathing deck). Wisely, these areas are placed as separate as possible from the adult passengers.

While in dry dock in early 1999, Princess added a playroom to the *Crown* (it doubles as a meeting room when there aren't many kids on board), but neither the children's area nor the supervised activities on this ship are anywhere near as extensive as aboard the Grand-class ships. The small *Pacific Princess* isn't especially child-friendly, although when there are at least 15 kids on board, some supervised activities are provided. There's no dedicated playroom.

Activities fleet-wide include karaoke, movies, swimming and snorkeling lessons, tours of the galley and bridge, scavenger hunts, arts and crafts, coloring contests, birthday parties, dance marathons (on those ships with teen discos), hula parties complete with grass skirts, and teenage versions of "The Dating Game."

In late 1998, Princess lowered its minimum-age requirement to 6 months (previously a child had to be at least a year old to sail). Princess does not offer private in-cabin baby-sitting at all, but does provide **slumber-party-style group baby-sitting** in the playroom for $4 an hour (10pm to 1am nightly, and 9am to 5pm when in port).

ENTERTAINMENT

The Grand-class ships have a lot going on, and the quality of the overall package ranks way up there. From glittering, well-conceived, and well-executed **Vegas-style production shows** to New York cabaret singers on the main stage; from a wonderfully entertaining **cabaret piano/vocalist** in the Atrium Lounge (a throwaway space for many

---

Love Boat Loans

If you're low on cash, Princess Cruises offers their customers special loan programs that allow you to finance virtually all the costs of your trip, from the cruise price and air travel all the way down to shore excursions and onboard spending. The loans, which are repayable in 24, 36, or 48 months, are approved on an instant basis after you review your credit information on the phone with a participating bank. Princess's loan program is aptly called the Love Boat Loan, and offers rates that can vary from 14.99% to 26.99%, depending on your credit history. To apply, call **MBNA America Bank** ☎ 888/791-6262. The loans are available to U.S. residents only.

Princess Fleet Itineraries

Ship	Home Ports & Season	Itinerary	Other Itineraries
Crown Princess	Round-trip from Fort Lauderdale; itineraries alternate Oct–May.	**10-night Panama Canal 1:** Cartagena (Colombia), Puerto Limón (Costa Rica), Grand Cayman, and Cozumel. **10-night Panama Canal 2:** or Ocho Rios (Jamaica), Puerto Limón, Cartagena, and Aruba.	Mediterranean, Canada, and New England
Dawn Princess	Round-trip from San Juan; itineraries alternate weekly, Oct–Apr.	**7-night S. Carib 1:** Trinidad, Barbados, Antigua, Tortola, and St. Thomas. **7-night S. Carib 2:** St. Thomas, St. Kitts, Martinique, Isla Margarita, and Curaçao.	Alaska
Grand Princess	Both itineraries round-trip from Fort Lauderdale; eastern Caribbean itinerary weekly through spring 2001; eastern and western itineraries alternate weekly beginning summer 2001.	**7-night E. Carib:** St. Thomas, Sint Maarten, and Princess Cays. **7-night W. Carib:** Cozumel, Grand Cayman, Princess Cays, and Costa Maya (100 miles from Cozumel).	None
Ocean Princess	Round-trip from San Juan; itineraries alternate weekly Oct–Apr.	**7-night S. Carib 1:** Aruba, Caracas/ La Guaira (Venezuela), Grenada, Dominica, and St. Thomas. **7-night S. Carib 2:** Barbados, St. Lucia, St. Kitts, Sint Maarten, and St. Thomas.	Alaska
Pacific Princess	Round-trip from New York, Apr–Oct.	**7-night Bermuda:** Hamilton and St. George's.	Mediterranean, Europe, and Africa
Sea Princess	Round-trip from Fort Lauderdale, Oct–Apr.	**7-night W. Carib:** Princess Cays, Ocho Rios (Jamaica), Grand Cayman, and Cozumel.	Alaska
Sun Princess	North- and south-bound between San Juan and Puerto Caldera (Costa Rica); itineraries alternate Oct–Apr.	**10-night Panama Canal:** St. Thomas, Dominica, Barbados, Aruba, Cartagena (Colombia), and Puntarenas (Costa Rica).	Alaska

ships) to a rocking disco, this line offers a terrific blend of musical delights, and you'll always find a cozy spot where some soft piano or jazz music is being performed. You'll also find entertainment like hypnotists, puppeteers, and comedians, plus karaoke for you audience-participation types, and, in the afternoons, a couple of sessions of that ubiquitous cruise favorite, the "Newlywed and Not-So-Newlywed Game."

Among the many bars and lounges on the Grand-class ships is the clubby, old-world Wheelhouse Lounge, with its dark wood details and ship memorabilia. Each of the ships covered in this review also has a **wine bar** selling caviar by the ounce and vintage wine, champagne, and iced vodka by the glass.

The Princess **casinos** are sprawling and exciting places, too, and are bound to keep gamblers entranced (hypnotized?) with their lights and action.

SERVICE

Overall, service is efficient and lines (at least on the Grand-class ships) are short, even in the busy Lido buffet restaurants. Staff and crew aren't the friendliest, nor are they the surliest; they're just well-intentioned, hard-working staff doing their jobs.

Cabin steward service is the most consistent, with dining and bar service sometimes on the slow side (and language barriers with bar servers can be frustrating when you're trying to get your martini just right). In all cabins on the Grand-class ships, bathrobes are provided for use during the cruise.

All of the Princess vessels in the Caribbean offer **laundry** and **dry-cleaning** services, and have their own **self-service Laundromats.**

Crown Princess

The Verdict

In spite of its cramped outdoor deck space, most people will find the *Crown's* newly renovated exterior and interior design appealing and dramatic, and the cruise an overall winner.

Crown Princess *(photo: Princess Cruises)*

Specifications

Size (in tons)	70,000	Officers	Italian
Number of Cabins	795	Crew	696 (International)
Number of Outside Cabins	624	Passenger/Crew Ratio	2.3 to 1
Cabins with Verandas	184	Year Built	1990
Number of Passengers	1,590	Last Major Refurbishment	2000

Frommer's Ratings (Scale of 1–5)

Cabin Comfort & Amenities	4	Pool, Fitness & Spa Facilities	3
Ship Cleanliness & Maintenance	4	Children's Facilities	3
Public Comfort/Space	3	Itinerary	4
Decor	4	Worth the Money	5

Between 1991 and 1995, the *Crown Princess,* along with its identical twin, the *Regal Princess,* were the company's most modern, most dramatic, and most frequently photographed vessels. Their designer, Renzo Piano, is also responsible for such high-profile designs as the Centre Pompidou in Paris and reconstruction plans for the reunited Berlin, projects that were among the most talked about in Europe since the building of the Eiffel Tower in the 1880s.

You'll either adore or dislike the *Crown's* exterior, which its designer has compared to the silhouette of a porpoise moving through the water. (Less generous souls say it reminds them of Darth Vader's helmet, albeit in good-guy white.)

Most cruisers will find the design appealing and dramatic, but its outdoor deck space is insufficient, leading to congestion at deck buffets and around swimming pools whenever the ship is full (which is often). There's no uninterrupted Promenade Deck around the periphery of the ship, either. All in all, aboard the *Crown Princess,* you'll find that there's more of an emphasis on indoor space than on outdoor.

In early 2000, the *Crown's* interior received a major facelift, updating, upgrading and generally bringing the 10-year-old ship very gracefully into the 21st century. The ship now feels much more open and its warm earth tones, cherry wood, and marble have created a look much closer to what you'll find on the Grand-class ships. Chrome columns and shiny surfaces have been replaced by soft wood tones and a more sophisticated air.

Cabins & Rates						
Cabins	Per diems from	Bathtub	Fridge	Hair Dryer	Sitting Area	TV
Inside	$152	no	yes	yes	no	yes*
Outside	$166	no	yes	yes	no	yes*
Suite	$351	yes	yes	yes	yes	yes*

* TVs show CNN, ESPN, TNT, Nickelodeon, and BBC.

CABINS   Of 795 total, 624 are outside cabins, and two whole decks of them have private verandas. Standard cabins are quite spacious at 190 square feet to 210 square feet, and suites with balconies are 587 square feet, including balcony. Decor includes light-grained wood, color schemes of warm beiges and peaches, comfortably upholstered chairs and sofas, and rectangular windows for easy wave-gazing. Bathrooms are compact but comfortable. The 14 suites and 18 mini-suites have balconies, sitting areas, bathtubs, and minifridges.

Note that views from Category F cabins on the Dolphin Deck are partially obstructed by lifeboats, and the Category H outside cabins have only portholes.

All cabins have safes, terry-cloth robes for use during the cruise, and TVs typically broadcasting CNN, ESPN, Nickelodeon, BBC programming, and TNT. Ten cabins are wheelchair accessible.

PUBLIC AREAS   The makeover in early 2000 gave the *Crown* a new, stylish look, replacing the harsher design schemes based on blacks, greens, and chrome with rich autumn-hued fabrics, carpeting, and wall surfaces in burnt oranges, golds, and burgundies. Now you'll find touches of stained glass, marble, cherry-wood paneling, soft lighting, and more classic murals and artwork.

At the ship's core is the three-story Plaza Atrium, with a grand staircase. The lower level houses the lobby and reception area, as well a newly redesigned patisserie and wine bar. The ship's massive casino-cum-bar-cum-observation-deck is strikingly dramatic, framed by polished, rounded, bone-white "ribs" arching from ceiling to floor and glassed in by 270° of panoramic curved glass windows. Situated decks above the other bars, restaurants, and public areas, it feels a million miles from everything else on the ship. In the casino, tables and slot machines lie close to a stage, where a piano player or a band keeps you entertained between hands.

The refurbished Crown Court dining room boasts cozier seating clusters and an elegant new entrance. The ship also now has a casual restaurant open 24 hours a day, as well as a two-level show lounge for nightly Vegas-style entertainment. At midships is Kipling's, an attractive piano bar. If you'd like to escape the hordes, though, seek out the relative calm and soothing premises of the Intermezzo Bar. There's also a library, card room, and a 2,000-square-foot children and teen center on the top, with ocean views to boot.

POOL, FITNESS & SPA FACILITIES   Two pools on the Lido Deck can become crowded when the ship is completely booked. Two hot tubs are adjacent to the pools. There's shuffleboard on the Promenade Deck and Ping-Pong on the Lido Deck.

The *Crown Princess*'s health club/spa lies way down deep in the ship, so you won't have any inspiring views of the waves while you're working out. The gym is on the small side, but there is a separate aerobics room. You'll find a spa with several massage and treatment rooms, as well as steam rooms, saunas, and a tiny beauty salon.

Dawn Princess • Sea Princess • Sun Princess • Ocean Princess

Sun Princess *(photo: Princess Cruises)*

The Verdict

These relaxed, pretty ships are pleasant (though not remarkable) and are great for families and for grownups who like to enjoy the good life without pretension.

Specifications

Size (in tons)	77,000	Passenger/Crew Ratio	2.2 to 1
Number of Cabins	975	Year Built	
Number of Outside Cabins	603	*Dawn Princess*	1995
Cabins with Verandas	410	*Sun Princess*	1997
Number of Passengers	1,950	*Sea Princess*	1998
Officers	Italian	*Ocean Princess*	2000
Crew	900 (Interntl.)	Last Major Refurbishment	N/A

Frommer's Ratings (Scale of 1–5)

Cabin Comfort & Amenities	4	Pool, Fitness & Spa Facilities	4
Ship Cleanliness & Maintenance	4	Children's Facilities	4
Public Comfort/Space	5	Itinerary	5
Decor	5	Worth the Money	5

Love isn't all that's exciting and new at the Love Boat line. Anyone familiar with Princess Cruises from the old TV show or from sailing on the older ships will be thrilled with the four *Ocean, Dawn, Sea,* and *Sun* sisters, and with the huge *Grand Princess.* The ships are pretty but not stunning; glitzy but not gaudy; spacious but not overwhelming—I was surprised at how easy it was to find my way around. By the end of the first day, I had the important landmarks memorized. These ships are a great choice when you want a step up from Carnival, Royal Caribbean, and NCL, but aren't interested in the slightly more chic ambiance of Celebrity.

The decor of these ships is done in a style that's a combo of classic and modern, using materials such as varnished hardwoods, marble, etched glass, granite, and textured fabrics. Their decor doesn't sock you between the eyes with its daring; instead, it's comforting, restrained, and will probably age gracefully. Light color schemes predominate, as opposed to the darker and bolder hues of Carnival and Celebrity, for instance.

The medical centers are arguably the best at sea, each with a staff of two doctors and four nurses. The *Ocean Princess* (along with the *Grand*) even boasts a high-tech "telemedicine" program that on this ship, via a live video and electronic hookup, links the onboard doctors to experts at Cleveland Clinic Florida.

Cabins & Rates

Cabins	Per diems from	Bathtub	Fridge	Hair Dryer	Sitting Area	TV
Inside	$141	no	yes	yes	no	yes*
Outside	$182	no	yes	yes	no	yes*
Suite	$277	yes	yes	yes	yes	yes*

* *TVs show CNN, ESPN, TNT, Nickelodeon, and BBC.*

CABINS   In general, the staterooms are cozy, which is real-estate speak for "cramped." Standard outside cabins are 178 square feet including their balconies (in comparison, Carnival's standard cabins *without* balconies are nearly 190 sq. ft.); the standard outside cabins without balconies are 135 to 173 square feet, and insides are 135 to 148 square feet. On these ships, what you gain in balcony space you lose in room space. More than 400 cabins on each vessel boast private balconies (though at about 3 by 8 feet, they're small), which help keep crowds dispersed (in other words, passengers might spend more time in their cabins/verandas instead of crowding the Pool Deck or some inside public room).

Suites can be as large as a sprawling 754 square feet, again including a veranda. All suites and mini-suites come with white-gloved butlers (in addition to the regular cabin stewards) who will unpack for guests, deliver afternoon tea and canapés before dinner, stock your minibar (it's stocked once on a complimentary basis, including alcohol, and thereafter you're charged for what you drink), arrange shore excursions, and make spa and beauty parlor appointments.

The 32 mini-suites on each ship are gorgeous, measuring 374 to 536 square feet (including balcony), with a separate bedroom area divided from the sitting area with a curtain, with a pull-out sofa, chair and desk, refrigerator, two TVs, walk-in closet, and a separate whirlpool tub and shower in a separate room from the toilet and sink. Closets are on the small side, and hanging and drawer space are limited.

All cabins have TVs broadcasting CNN, ESPN, Discovery Channel, TNT, and other programming, plus refrigerators, safes, hair dryers, and terry bathrobes for use during the cruise. Some 19 cabins on each vessel are wheelchair accessible.

PUBLIC AREAS   These ships shine when it comes to communal areas. All have a decidedly unglitzy decor that relies on lavish amounts of wood, glass, and marble, and feature $2.5 million collections of original paintings and lithographs. You'll notice lots more tropical plants and flower bouquets on these ships than on most, cared for by two full-time florists per ship.

The one-story showrooms offer unobstructed viewing from every seat, and several seats in the back are reserved for passengers with mobility problems. The sound systems are good, and lighting is state of the art. The smaller Vista Lounge also offers shows with good sight lines and comfortable cabaret-style seating. The pair of dining rooms on each ship are broken up by dividers topped with frosted glass. There are no dramatic sweeping staircases for making an entrance; instead, these rooms feel intimate. The elegant, nautical-motif Wheelhouse Bar is done in warm, dark wood tones and features live entertainment; it's the perfect spot for pre- or postdinner drinks.

There's a dark and sensuous disco; a bright, spacious, enticing casino; and lots of little lounges for an intimate rendezvous, such as the Entre Nous and the Atrium Lounge.

If you're hungry, options besides the usual main dining rooms and the buffet include an all-night sit-down restaurant (you can get a full dinner until 4am) and Lago's Pizzeria, a sit-down restaurant open afternoons and nights. Sorry: No take-out or delivery. Pizza is also available by the slice in the Horizon Court between 4 and 7pm daily.

POOL, FITNESS & SPA FACILITIES   The center of the action for any Caribbean cruise is the pool, and these ships have plenty of space to party on the Riviera Deck. There's a lot going on, too, and if you've ever wanted to become a certified diver, this cruise will give you the chance. The New Waves program offers snorkeling and scuba lessons and rental equipment. There's also advanced lessons for divers who are already certified.

In total, there are four adult pools and one kids' wading pool, and hot tubs scattered around the Riviera Deck. In all, there are three spacious decks for sunbathing.

These ships boast some of the best-designed, most appealing health clubs of any of the line's vessels. The spa offers all the requisite massage and spa treatments. The gym is on the small side for ships of this size, but roomier than the one on the *Grand Princess*. A teakwood deck encircles the ship for joggers, walkers, and shuffleboard players, and a computerized golf center called Princess Links simulates the trickiest aspects of some of the world's best and most legendary golf courses.

Fitness classes are available throughout the day in a very roomy aerobics room, where stretching and meditation classes are also offered.

Grand Princess •
Golden Princess (preview)

The Verdict

Second in size only to Royal Caribbean's *Voyager of the Seas,* the huge, well-accoutred *Grand Princess* and its future sister ships are very easy to navigate and never feel as crowded as you'd expect; in fact, much of the *Grand's* interior feels downright intimate and cozy.

Grand Princess *(photo: Princess Cruises)*

Specifications

Size (in tons)	109,000	Officers	Italian/British
Number of Cabins	1,300	Crew	1,100 (Interntnl.)
Number of Outside Cabins	928	Passenger/Crew Ratio	2 to 1
Cabins with Verandas	710	Year Built	1998
Number of Passengers	2,600	Last Major Refurbishment	N/A

Frommer's Ratings (Scale of 1–5)

Cabin Comfort & Amenities	5	Pool, Fitness & Spa Facilities	4
Ship Cleanliness & Maintenance	4	Children's Facilities	4
Public Comfort/Space	5	Itinerary	4
Decor	5	Worth the Money	5

For its first year of life, the 109,000-ton, 2,600-passenger *Grand Princess* was the world's biggest and most expensive ($450 million) cruise ship. With 18 towering decks, the ship is taller than the Statue of Liberty (from pedestal to torch) and too wide to fit through the Panama Canal. In fact, it's so big that the line's *Pacific Princess,* the original Love Boat, could easily fit inside its hull and still have lots of room to spare. The ship is truly a destination in itself, and the ports visited can't help but take a back seat to the onboard life—they're just one among many diversions and activities.

Inside and out, the *Grand Princess* is a marvel not only of size but of design. Its massive white, boxy body with its spoilerlike aft poking up into the air cuts a bizarre, space-age profile and is like nothing else at sea. It's intimidating from afar, but inside the ship is well laid-out, very easy to navigate, and, amazingly, never feels as crowded as you'd expect—in fact, its public areas are generally less crowded than those of many smaller ships, owing to a variety of nooks that create a surprisingly cozy environment.

The ultra-modern ship even manages to offer a few areas with traditional accents. Its tiered aft decks, clubby and dimly lit lounges, and elegant three-story atrium with its classical string quartet recall a grander era of sea travel.

Even the ship's medical center is grand: It boasts a high-tech "telemedicine" program that, via a live video hookup, links the ship's doctors to the emergency room at Cleveland Clinic Florida.

Two sister ships, the *Golden Princess* and another as yet unnamed, are due to debut in April 2001 and January 2002, respectively.

Cabins & Rates						
Cabins	Per diems from	Bathtub	Fridge	Hair Dryer	Sitting Area	TV
Inside	$169	no	yes	yes	no	yes*
Outside	$196	no	yes	yes	no	yes*
Suite	$249	yes	yes	yes	yes	yes*

* TVs show CNN, ESPN, TNT, Nickelodeon, and BBC.

CABINS   The *Grand Princess* has 710 cabins with verandas (only Royal Caribbean's *Voyager of the Seas* has more, with 757). Be forewarned, though: The verandas are tiered, so passengers in levels above may be able to look down on you. Cabins are richly decorated in light hues and earth tones and all have safes, hair dryers, refrigerators, robes for use during the cruise, and TVs broadcasting CNN, ESPN, Nickelodeon, BBC programming, and TNT. Storage is adequate and features more closet shelves than drawer space.

A standard outside cabin (including its balcony) ranges from 215 to 255 square feet; suites are anywhere from 515 to 800 square feet, including the balconies. Cabins with balconies are larger than the equivalent on the *Ocean, Sea, Sun,* and *Dawn Princess* because, since the *Grand Princess* can't fit through the Panama Canal anyway, its balconies are allowed to protrude out farther rather than cutting into actual room space, as they do on the other Grand-class ships.

At 325 square feet (including balcony), the 180 mini-suites on the *Grand Princess* (the entire Dolphin Deck is nothing but mini-suites) are smaller than the 32 mini-suites on the *Ocean, Sea, Dawn,* and *Sun,* but are comfortable and also offer two TVs, a sitting area, chair and desk, balcony, walk-in closet, and mini-fridge, but only one bathroom. There are 26 full suites, ranging in size from 515 to 683 square feet, including balcony. Two penthouse suites have an average square footage of 775 (including balcony) and feature all the above amenities plus two bathrooms (one with the toilet, the other with a separate whirlpool tub and a shower). A pair of Grand Suites even have fireplaces (not real wood-burning ones, of course) and hot tubs. There are two family suites that can sleep up to eight. In addition to the room stewards, all suites and mini-suites come with the service of white-gloved butlers who will unpack for guests, deliver afternoon tea and canapés before dinner, stock your minibar (it's stocked once on a complimentary basis, including alcohol, and thereafter you're charged for what you drink), arrange shore excursions, and make spa and beauty parlor appointments.

The views from many cabins on the Emerald Deck are obstructed by lifeboats. The ship has 28 wheelchair-accessible cabins, more than any other ship afloat. (The Skywalkers disco has a wheelchair lift up to the elevated dance floor, too.)

PUBLIC AREAS   Even sailing with a full load of passengers (as many as 3,100 if all third and fourth berths are filled), you'll wonder where everyone is. The *Grand Princess* is a huge ship with a not-so-huge-ship feeling. Because of its smart layout, private verandas in 710 of its 1,300 cabins, six dining venues, expansive outdoor deck space divided into four main sections, and diversions like a nine-hole miniature-golf course, a golf simulator, gigantic virtual-reality game room, basketball/volleyball/paddle tennis courts, four pools, nine hot tubs, and a business/computer center (where you can send and receive E-mail, among other things), passengers are dispersed rather than concentrated into one or two main areas. There's even an attractive wedding chapel where the captain himself performs about eight bona fide, legal marriages every cruise.

Coupled with this smart layout is the ship's sophisticated decor. Like the *Ocean, Sea, Dawn,* and *Sun Princess,* the *Grand* offers public areas with a contemporary and upscale appeal, done up with caramel-colored wood tones and pleasing color schemes of warm blue, teal, and rust with a touch of brassy details and marble to give the place some pizzazz. Two full-time florists create and care for impressive flower arrangements and a large variety of live plants.

While the decor is soothing, the entertainment is pretty hot. Gamblers will love the sprawling and dazzling Atlantis Casino, one of the largest at sea at 13,500 square feet. Three main entertainment venues include a well-equipped two-story show lounge for Broadway-style musicals performed by 18 dancers and four singers, as well as a second one-level venue for smaller-scale entertainment like hypnotists and singers, and a pleasing travel-themed nightclub called the Explorer's Club, with murals of Egyptian and African scenes and a live band nightly. There's also the clubby, old-world Wheelhouse Lounge as well as a woody sports bar called Snookers.

The Skywalkers disco/observation lounge, sequestered in the far aft reaches of the ship, is raised 150 feet above the ocean in a pod at the back of the ship. The unique spot offers floor-to-ceiling windows with two impressive views: forward, for a look at the ship itself from a bizarre floating-in-space perspective, or back, for a look at the sea and the giant vessel's very impressive wake. The multilevel area has lots of cozy nooks as well as the flashing lights expected from a disco. It's well positioned away from any cabins and there's a funky moving-sidewalk–like walkway that gets you there—it's my favorite disco at sea.

For kids, the sequestered two-story, indoor/outdoor Fun Zone kids' play area has tons of games and toys as well as computers and a ball bin; after Disney, it's one of the best seagoing kids' areas you'll find. On the second (outdoor) level there's a splash pool, tricycles, and a mini-basketball setup, as well as a teen disco and a teens-only private patch of outdoor deck space with lounges and a hot tub.

Grand Princess's three one-story main dining rooms are named for famous artists—da Vinci, Botticelli, and Michelangelo—and decorated with murals and artwork accordingly. They are pleasant and laid out with slightly tiered levels and, by way of some strategically placed waist-high dividers, feel cozy (although the ceilings are a tad on the low side). The Horizon Terrace casual Lido restaurant is designed to feel much smaller than it actually is. With clusters of buffet stations serving a wide variety of food (stir fries, sides of beef, turkey and pork, lots of fruit, salads and cheeses, and lots more), lines are kept to a minimum and you're hardly aware of the enormity of the space. For buffet-style breakfast, lunch, and dinner, this venue is a well-executed operation and is open 24 hours a day.

Besides a long list of daily diversions, the *Grand Princess* has a cavernous and truly amazing virtual-reality arcade, with dozens of machines you can climb onto and do virtual things like hang-gliding, downhill skiing, fly-fishing, and motorcycle riding. Each machine costs a couple of dollars. There's also a theme-park–like digital photo studio where you can choose from over 40 scenes for the backdrop for your pictures.

The ship also has a library, small writing room, card room, and a business center with a few computers, from which E-mails can be sent and received ($7.50 for 15 min. of use).

POOL, FITNESS & SPA FACILITIES   This ship has something like 1.7 acres of open deck space, so it's not hard to find a quiet place to soak in the sun. There are four great swimming pools, including one with a retractable glass roof so it can double as a sort of solarium, another touted as a swim-against-the-current pool (although, truth be told, there really isn't enough room to do laps if others are in the pool, and the jets are kept at a level barely powerful enough to keep a 150-lb. person in place), and a third, aft under the disco, that feels miles from the rest of the ship. The fourth pool is for kids.

A large, almost separate part of the ship, on the forward Sun Deck, is reserved for pampering the body. Surrounding the lap pool and its tiered, amphitheater-style wooden benches is the large Plantation Spa, ocean-view beauty parlor, and the ocean-view gym, which is surprisingly small and cramped for a ship of this size (although there's an unusually large aerobics floor). Unfortunately, the sports decks are just above the spa, and if you're getting a relaxing massage when someone is playing basketball, you'll hear the thump, thump, thump.

Other recreation offerings include a Sports Deck with a jogging track, basketball, and paddle tennis, a fun nine-hole putting green, and computerized simulated golf.

Pacific Princess

The Verdict

Not for the party animals out there, this small and cozy 30-year-old classic liner offers a calm cruise in a pleasant setting.

Pacific Princess *(photo: Princess Cruises)*

Specifications

Size (in tons)	20,000	Officers	British
Number of Cabins	305	Crew	350 (International)
Number of Outside Cabins	238	Passenger/Crew Ratio	1.8 to 1
Cabins with Verandas	0	Year Built	1971
Number of Passengers	640	Last Major Refurbishment	1993

Frommer's Ratings (Scale of 1–5)

Cabin Comfort & Amenities	4	Pool, Fitness & Spa Facilities	3
Ship Cleanliness & Maintenance	4	Children's Facilities	N/A
Public Comfort/Space	4	Itinerary	5
Decor	3	Worth the Money	5

The original star of the *Love Boat* series (along with its recently sold sister, the *Island Princess*), the 30-year-old *Pacific Princess* is an intimate vessel. Although in a different league than its mondo, much flashier mega-sisters, the small, 640-passenger *Pacific* is novel in its own way. Public areas and the Pool Deck are well laid out and the lack of neon and glitz, towering atrium, and sprawling showroom creates a homey, very relaxing ambiance; it's ideal for cruises to the genteel island of Bermuda, where the ship will spend its second season in the summer of 2001. Overall, the ship is well maintained, and public areas are fairly roomy for its size.

Cabins & Rates

Cabins	Per diems from	Bathtub	Fridge	Hair Dryer	Sitting Area	TV
Inside	$86	no	no	no	no	yes
Outside	$114	some	some	no	no	yes
Suite	$274	yes	yes	no	yes	yes

CABINS   Cabins are not huge and none have verandas, as is to be expected on older ships. Standard cabins measure 235 square feet. Color schemes are based on earth tones (which are a bit drab) and the furniture is circa 1970s (a neat retro touch for all you sentimentalists!). All cabins have TVs, plus bathrobes for use during the cruise. There are four suites and nine mini-suites, all on the Promenade Deck (note that many cabins on this deck look out on the Promenade and some have partially obstructed views). The four suites have a sitting area, refrigerator, and bathtub. All but the suites have convertible sofa-style beds and some have third and fourth berths (a tight squeeze in the standard cabins).

There are two cabins that can accommodate wheelchair users, and all four elevators and public bathrooms are accessible.

PUBLIC AREAS   The beauty of such a small ship is its inherent coziness. There are several intimate bars to retreat to as well as a decent-size showroom for after-dinner cabaret and small-scale Vegas-style shows. The ship has a casino with slots and gaming tables, and there's a theater and an ocean-view library. There's a pleasant formal dining room deep down in the ship, and the Sun Deck has a casual buffet-style Lido restaurant featuring a made-to-order omelet/salad bar and lots of indoor and outdoor seating.

The ship isn't especially child-friendly, although some supervised activities are provided when there are at least 15 kids on board. There is no dedicated playroom.

There is an infirmary on board.

POOL, FITNESS & SPA FACILITIES   Outdoor deck space is well planned and fairly spacious considering the size of the ship. There are two pools, one located aft on the Riviera Deck, with nice views of the sea and the ship's wake, and the other, on the Sun Deck adjacent to the Lido restaurant, with a retractable glass roof to ward off bad weather. Each offers ample seating and has a wide-open feel. There's a small gym, a pair of saunas, a couple of massage rooms, and a beauty salon. There's also shuffleboard, Ping-Pong, and a jogging track.

Royal Caribbean International

1050 Caribbean Way, Miami, FL 33132. ☎ **800/327-6700** or 305/539-6000. Fax 800/722-5329. www.royalcaribbean.com.

THE LINE IN A NUTSHELL   These megas provide fun, well-rounded, activity-packed cruises on attractive, glamorous, but not too over-the-top-glitzy ships (there's so much going on you might not notice how small the cabins are).

THE EXPERIENCE   Royal Caribbean International is one of the steadiest and best-conceived cruise companies in the industry, with a fleet of mostly similar ships designed to appeal to a wide range of people—except for the older *Nordic Empress* and *Viking Serenade* (the latter of which does year-round Baja Mexico cruises), the company's vessels are all megas and share such similar attributes as multistory atria and mall-like shopping complexes, two-story dining rooms and showrooms, and wide-open public areas and conversely small cabins. There's lots of activities, a varied and well-executed entertainment repertoire, and enough glamour and glitz to keep things exciting, but not so much that they overwhelm the senses (except for the *Voyager* and *Explorer of the Seas,* which do). Decor-wise, these ships are a shade toned down from the Carnival brood, and while at the end of the day the onboard experience of the two fleets is similar, the Royal Caribbean ships feel and look less in-your-face than their Carnival counterparts.

Activities, daily programs, cuisine, bar service, and cabin service make for a nice package and reasonable prices to boot.

Pros

- **Entertainment.** Repertoire is one of best at sea, with glamorous, well-executed, Vegas-style shows occasionally drawing well-known names.
- **Attractive public rooms.** Well designed, spacious, and glamorous, the lounges, restaurants, and outdoor Pool Decks are inviting: not too flashy and flamboyant, not too staid and soft.

Cons

- **Small cabins.** No two ways to slice it: At just over 100 square feet, many cabins, especially on the pre-1995 ships, are downright small, making them (along with NCL) the smallest in the mainstream category.
- **Lines.** Hey, these are big ships, so there are going to be lines at times, especially in the buffet restaurants and getting on and off the ship in port.
- **High crew-to-passenger ratio.** The number of crew members to passengers hovers around 3 to 1 (most peers are more like 2 or 2.5 to 1).

Compared with the other Mainstream lines, here's how RCI rates:

	Poor	Fair	Good	Excellent	Outstanding
Enjoyment Factor				✓	
Dining			✓		
Activities				✓	
Children's Program				✓	
Entertainment			✓		
Service			✓		
Overall Value				✓	

ROYAL CARIBBEAN: FUN & GAMES, COOL SHIPS

Royal Caribbean was the first company to launch a fleet specializing exclusively in Caribbean ports of call—hence the company name. In the late 1980s, the company expanded its horizons beyond the Caribbean, offering cruises to Europe, Alaska, and the Pacific, in the process tagging the "International" onto its name.

What began in 1969 as a consortium of Norwegian ship owners with big eyes for the North American cruise market has blossomed into an immensely profitable multinational corporation with a staggering volume and a flotilla of state-of-the-art megaships valued in the billions. In 1988, the Pritzker family (creative force behind the Hyatt empire) bought a major stake in the company, and funds from the sale, coupled with all the credit-worthiness of Hyatt, helped finance the line's massive building spree during the 1990s. In 1997, Royal Caribbean acquired the smaller and somewhat fancier Celebrity Cruises. At the time of this writing, the two lines together control 19 relatively young ships with over 40,000 berths, attracting a big chunk of the Caribbean's cruise ship passengers, a figure that will only increase as both lines continue to add new ships.

It was Royal Caribbean that ushered in a new generation of megaships in 1988 with the 73,192-ton *Sovereign of the Seas.* This vessel was the largest passenger ship built in the previous 50 years and was between two and four times as large as any other vessel in the fleet as it then stood. Along with its newer, improved clones, *Monarch* and *Majesty of the Seas,* the *Sovereign* tripled Royal Caribbean's cabin capacity in a mere 4 years. Beyond sheer size, though, the ships were innovative, featuring such now-standard features as soaring, multistory atria with glass-sided elevators, fountains splashing into marble pools, and an observation lounge (the Viking Crown Lounge) perched 10 or 11 stories above sea level, wrapped around the rear smokestack in a style reminiscent of big-windowed airport control towers. Today, the line has again raised the stakes on the whole cruise industry by introducing the absolutely monstrously, amazingly huge 142,000-ton Eagle-class ships, *Voyager of the Seas* and its sister *Explorer of the Seas,* with more still to come.

THE FLEET

Royal Caribbean has 13 ships in its fleet, with another three due before year-end 2002. The most famous are the 142,000-ton (some say it's 137,000 tons), 3,114-passenger *Voyager of the Seas,* the first of Royal Caribbean's three Eagle-class sister ships, which entered service in November of 1999. Sister *Explorer of the Seas* is, at press time, scheduled to make its debut in October 2000. These two can carry as many as 3,838 passengers if every single bed is filled—wow! In addition to these behemoths, six Vision-class ships, built between 1995 and 1998, are similar in design and include the 2,000-passenger *Vision of the Seas* (1998), the 1,950-passenger *Enchantment of the Seas* (1997), the 2,000-passenger *Rhapsody of the Seas* (1997), the 1,950-passenger *Grandeur of the Seas* (1996), the 1,804-passenger *Splendour of the Seas* (1996), and the 1,804-passenger *Legend of the Seas* (1995). The *Rhapsody* and *Legend* do not sail in the Caribbean. The rest of the fleet includes the 2,354-passenger sister ships *Majesty of the Seas* (1992) and *Monarch of the Seas* (1991), 1,600-passenger *Nordic Empress* (1990), 1,512-passenger *Viking Serenade* (1990), and 2,276-passenger *Sovereign of the Seas* (1988).

At press time, construction is already underway on the line's next generation of ships. The first of a pair of 85,000-ton, 2,100-passenger Project Vantage ships, *Radiance of the Seas,* is due in spring 2001, with sister *Brilliance of the Seas* to be introduced in summer 2002. The third super-mondo-megaship Eagle-class sister, the 3,114-passenger *Adventure of the Seas,* is to be introduced in spring of 2002.

Dirty Laundry: Royal Caribbean International Pays for Polluting

In 1998 and 1999, Royal Caribbean pleaded guilty to dumping oil and hazardous chemicals in waters off Florida, Alaska, New York, Los Angeles, St. Thomas, and San Juan in the mid-1990s, and has agreed to pay nearly $30 million in fines. The line has cleaned up its act these days, so to speak, installing new waste treatment systems, increasing training for employees, and hiring an environmental officer for each of its ships.

PASSENGER PROFILE

You'll find all walks of life on a Royal Caribbean cruise. The common denominator: passengers looking for fun and action in an attractive setting. You'll find passengers in their twenties through sixties, with mostly couples (a good number of them honeymooning), but also lots of families (of the nearly 1.5 million passengers who sailed with Royal Caribbean in 1998, about 100,000, or about 7%, were kids) and single friends traveling together in groups. The majority of passengers come from somewhere in North America, with about 25% international (the *Voyager* and *Explorer* especially attract a steady contingent of foreigners). There are books in the library in French, Spanish, and Dutch, and even in-cabin documents like room-service menus are in five languages, including Italian and Portuguese.

A shade more sophisticated than Carnival (at least in terms of ship decor), the line attracts passengers who think Carnival is a bit too glitzy and party-animal-ish. In reality, though, the differences between the two are few. Overall, passengers are active, social, and looking for a good time, no matter what their age.

The line's shorter, 3- and 4-night cruises tend to attract more of the partying crowd, as is the case with most short cruises.

DINING

Falling closer to NCL than to Carnival or Princess, food isn't one of the Royal Caribbean's strong points, but generally it's fine if your expectations aren't incredibly high. Entrees include choices like poached Alaskan salmon, oven-roasted crispy duck served with a rhubarb sauce, prime rib served with a stuffed baked potato, and baked ziti. There's always a **light and healthy option** as well as a **vegetarian option** at lunch and dinner. Spa cuisine might feature roast turkey with sweet potatoes and vegetables or a grilled chicken breast topped with spinach, prosciutto, and fresh mozzarella, and vegetarian entrees might include an eggplant parmigiana or curried vegetables served in a light cilantro-coconut sauce.

The **formal dining rooms** feature two seatings and the **alternative dining option,** held in the Windjammer Cafe on the Pool Deck, offers a casual ambiance and open seating for dinner between 6:30 and 9:30pm 3 nights a week. Decor varies from ship to ship, but is always patterned on a theme inspired by a successful Broadway play or Hollywood film. You can eat breakfast and lunch in the main dining room or in the buffet-style Windjammer Cafe. Lines, unfortunately, can grow long. **Ice cream** and a couple of toppings are available throughout the day from a station in the Windjammer. There's also one gala pull-out-all-the-stops **midnight buffet** per week (and hors d'oeuvres served the other days), as well as **pizza** served afternoons and late night for those after-partying munchies.

A fairly extensive **kids' menu** (which is a fun pastime in and of itself, with word and picture games, and pictures to color in—crayons included!) features the likes of fish

---

Getting the Royal Treatment on a Private Island

Royal Caribbean maintains two private beach resorts, and many of its cruises feature a day at one or the other of them. **CocoCay** (Little Stirrup Cay) in the Bahamas and **Labadee,** an isolated and sun-flooded peninsula along Haiti's north coast, are tropical retreats that the company has transformed into fun-in-the-sun playlands.

At CocoCay, an otherwise uninhabited 140-acre landfall in the Berry Islands of the Bahamas, you'll find lots of beach, hammocks, food, drink, and all the water sports you could fit into a day.

The line organizes fun activities like volleyball, limbo contests, water-balloon toss contests, relay races, and volleyball tournaments. As if the natural attractions weren't enough, Royal Caribbean even built and sank a replica of one of the pirate Bluebeard's schooners to give snorkelers an extra thrill.

The line's other private resort, Labadee, is isolated on a scenic, carefully protected (read: fenced off from the rest of Haiti), 270-acre peninsula, and boasts five separate beaches, each with different characteristics, evoking everything from the gravel and rocks of New England to the sandy atolls and palm trees of the southern Caribbean. If it weren't for local souvenir vendors hawking Haitian paintings, you'd never know you were in poverty-stricken Haiti, so removed does the site seem from the problems of the rest of the country.

On both Labadee and CocoCay, children's activities include beach parties, volleyball, seashell collecting, and sand-castle building.

---

sticks, burritos, oven-fried lemon chicken, spaghetti and meatballs, pizza, and the standard burgers, hot dogs, and fries, plus lots of yummy desserts.

Room service is available 24 hours a day from a fairly routine, limited menu. However, an especially nice feature: During normal lunch and dinner hours, a cabin steward can bring many items served in the restaurant to your cabin.

ACTIVITIES

You'll have no problem keeping yourself occupied on a Royal Caribbean cruise. Of course, if you want to remain glued to a deck chair and do nothing, that's no problem either.

Daytime activities are typical cruise line fare: bingo, shuffleboard, horse racing, line-dancing lessons, napkin folding, spa and beauty demonstrations, art auctions, and outrageous poolside contests sure to draw laughs. The *Voyager, Explorer,* and *Splendour of the Seas* even feature **miniature-golf courses** right on board!

Royal Caribbean ("Official cruise line of the PGA Tour and Senior PGA Tour," whatever that means) has a **golf program,** "Golf, Ahoy!," that lets golfers play the best local course in any of about 10 Caribbean ports of call.

For fitness freaks, or those who just like staying active, the line's **ShipShape fitness program** rewards passengers who participate in aerobics, dance classes, basketball free-throws, Ping-Pong tournaments, early morning walkathons, and any other such activity with prizes like T-shirts and baseball caps.

If **shopping** can be considered an activity, Royal Caribbean beats out Carnival with its impressive selection of boutiques, with boutiquelike storefronts, clustered around the atrium (although surprisingly, many close during lunch on sea days).

CHILDREN'S PROGRAM

Year-round, Royal Caribbean offers **supervised kids' programs** fleet-wide for children ages 3 to 17. The scope of the kids facilities on the *Voyager* and *Explorer* far exceed the

Royal Caribbean Fleet Itineraries

Ship	Home Ports & Season	Itinerary	Other Itineraries
Enchantment of the Seas	Round-trip from Miami, itineraries alternate weekly year-round.	**7-night W. Carib:** Key West, Playa del Carmen/Cozumel, Ocho Rios, and Grand Cayman. **7-night E. Carib:** St. Maarten, St. John/St. Thomas, and Nassau.	None
Explorer of the Seas	Round-trip from Miami, year-round.	**7-night E. Carib:** San Juan, St. Thomas, Nassau, and Labadee.	None
Grandeur of the Seas	Round-trip from San Juan, year-round.	**7-night S. Carib**: Aruba, Curaçao, Sint Maarten, and St. Thomas.	None
Majesty of the Seas	Round-trip from Miami; itineraries alternate year-round.	**3- and 4-night Bahamas:** Nassau, CocoCay, and (on 4-nighter only) Key West.	None
Monarch of the Seas	Round-trip from San Juan, year-round.	**7-night S. Carib:** St. Thomas, Antigua, Barbados, St. Lucia, and St. Maarten.	None
Nordic Empress	Caribbean itineraries round-trip from San Juan, alternating Nov–Apr; Bermuda cruises round-trip from New York.	**3- and 4-night W. Carib:** St. Thomas, St. Maarten, and St. Croix (on 4-nighter only). **7-night Bermuda:** Kings Wharf and Hamilton.	None
Sovereign of the Seas	Round-trip from Port Canaveral; itineraries alternate year-round.	**3- and 4-night Bahamas:** Nassau, CocoCay, and (on 4-nighter only) Key West.	None
Splendour of the Seas	Round-trip from Miami; itineraries alternate Nov–Apr.	**10- and 11-night Carib:** Key West (11-nighter only), Playa del Carmen/ Cozumel, Grand Cayman, Ocho Rios (Jamaica), Aruba, and Curaçao.	South America
Vision of the Seas	Alternating itineraries between San Juan and Acapulco, Nov–Apr.	**10-night Panama Canal:** St. Thomas, Curaçao, and Costa Rica. **11-night Panama Canal:** Costa Rica, Curaçao, Aruba, and St. Thomas.	Alaska, Hawaii
Voyager of the Seas	Round-trip from Miami, year-round.	**7-night W. Carib:** Grand Cayman, Ocho Rios (Jamaica), Cozumel, and Labadee.	None

rest of the fleet, with the kids' areas on the other 11 ships roughly comparable (though those on the Vision-class ships are a slight notch better than the rest and are on par with Carnival's *Elation* and *Paradise*). Male and female youth staff all have college degrees in education, recreation, or a related field. The "Adventure Ocean" program offers fun and games for four age groups: Aquanauts, ages 3 to 5; Explorers, ages 6 to 8; Voyagers, ages 9 to 12; and Navigators, ages 13 to 17. Each ship has a **children's playroom,** a **teen center and disco,** and a **video arcade.** There are children's menus, books, and movies, too. All day long, the fun includes talent shows, karaoke, pizza and ice-cream parties, bingo, scavenger hunts, game shows, volleyball, face painting, and beach parties. The "Adventure Science" program is always a hit and both teaches and tickles kids with scientific experiments that are loads of fun and educational.

Packin' 'Em In

On May 28, 2000, the *Voyager of the Seas* had a record 3,608 guests on board for a 7-night cruise from Miami to the western Caribbean. The ship has 3,114 guest berths at double occupancy, but since many staterooms have third and fourth berths, total capacity can reach as high as 3,838 berths.

Slumber-party-style **group baby-sitting** for children 3 and up is available in the kids' playroom nightly between 10pm and 1am, and from noon until sailing on days the ship is in port. The hourly charge is $4 per child. Private, **in-cabin baby-sitting** by a crew member is available from about 8am to 2am and must be booked at least 24 hours in advance through the purser's desk. The charge is $8 per hour for up to two children in the same family, and $10 per hour for a maximum of three kids in the same family.

ENTERTAINMENT

The line doesn't scrimp in the entertainment department, incorporating sprawling, high-tech cabaret stages into each of its ships' showrooms, some with a wall of video monitors to augment live performances. As in a Las Vegas showroom, entertainment begins before dinner and continues late, late into the night. There are music acts, comedy acts, sock hops, toga parties, talent shows, and that great cruise favorite, **karaoke.**

Practically no one does entertainment as well as Royal Caribbean, and the **Vegas-style shows** are filled with all the razzle-dazzle passengers come to expect. There's usually a mystery "name" entertainer popping up. Don't expect Tony Bennett or Alanis Morissette, but terrific entertainers like Marvin Hamlisch, Maureen McGovern (you've never heard "Ding Dong, the Witch Is Dead" until you've heard Miss McGovern's version), Clint Holmes, and Frankie Avalon are booked occasionally to augment the ships' regular offerings.

Royal Caribbean uses 12- to 16-piece bands for its main showroom, and large-cast revues are among the best you'll find on a ship. Show bands and other lounge acts keep the music playing all over the ship; all are first-rate.

SERVICE

Overall, service in the restaurants and cabins is friendly, accommodating, and efficient, despite some language-barrier problems (sign language often comes in handy). You're likely to be greeted with a smile by someone polishing the brass in a stairwell, a greeting that supervisors encourage on the part of even the lowest-ranking employees. That said, big, bustling ships like Royal Caribbean's are no strangers to crowds, lines, and harried servers not able to get to you exactly when you'd like them to. Them's the breaks on a mega at sea.

Considering the vast armies of personnel required to maintain a line as large as Royal Caribbean, it's a miracle that staffers appear as motivated and enthusiastic as they do.

Laundry and **dry-cleaning** services are available on all the ships, but none have self-service Laundromats.

Enchantment of the Seas •
Grandeur of the Seas •
Splendour of the Seas •
Vision of the Seas

The Verdict

This is what they had in mind when they
called contemporary cruise ships "floating resort hotels." These four ships are glitzy and
exciting without going overboard.

Splendour of the Seas *(photo: RCCL)*

Specifications

Size (in tons)		Number of Passengers	
Enchantment	74,140	*Enchantment*	1,950
Grandeur	74,000	*Grandeur*	1,950
Splendour	69,130	*Splendour*	1,804
Vision	78,491	*Vision*	2,000
Number of Cabins		Officers	Norwegian/Interntl.
Enchantment	975	Crew	(International)
Grandeur	975	*Enchantment*	760
Splendour	902	*Grandeur*	760
Vision	1,000	*Splendour*	720
Number of Outside Cabins		*Vision*	765
Enchantment	575	Passenger/Crew Ratio	
Grandeur	576	*Enchantment*	3 to 1
Splendour	575	*Grandeur*	2.5 to 1
Vision	593	*Splendour*	2.5 to 1
Cabins with Verandas		*Vision*	3 to 1
Enchantment	212	Year Built	
Grandeur	212	*Enchantment*	1997
Splendour	231	*Grandeur*	1996
Vision	229	*Splendour*	1996
		Vision	1998
		Last Major Refurbishment	N/A

Frommer's Ratings (Scale of 1–5)

Cabin Comfort & Amenities	4	Pool, Fitness & Spa Facilities	5
Ship Cleanliness & Maintenance	4	Children's Facilities	4
Public Comfort/Space	5	Itineraries	3
Decor	5	Worth the Money	5

There's a reason Royal Caribbean has given its Vision-class ships names like *Grandeur of
the Seas* and *Enchantment of the Seas*. It's because the ships are, quite simply, grand and
enchanting. From the incredible amounts of glass that give the ships their light (each contains about 2 acres of glass canopies, glass windbreaks, skylights, and floor-to-ceiling windows with sweeping views) to the colorful and whimsical artwork that livens every turn,
the high-tech, high-energy theater and casino to the dizzying number of entertainment
options, these ships are mighty fine. The glitz and glass of the atrium—with sunlight
streaming in and glinting off the chrome, the glassed-in elevators, and the white marble

staircase that winds down to a landing and bandstand—is a sight that stops you in your tracks. It's the first thing passengers see when coming aboard, and it sets the tone for the rest of the cruise.

The six Vision-class vessels (including the *Legend* and *Rhapsody of the Seas*, which globe-trot from Europe to the South Pacific, Mexico, and Alaska) evolved slightly over the 3 years between the first and latest, but for the most part they're a set of bright, cheerful siblings with similar features. The *Vision* and *Grandeur,* whose decors are newer, brighter, and classier, are simply more stunning than the older and somewhat more frayed *Splendour of the Seas.* The *Enchantment of the Seas* has more brassy-looking artwork and flashier, more metallic decorative themes than the *Vision* and *Grandeur.*

Cabins & Rates

Cabins	Per diems from	Bathtub	Fridge	Hair Dryer	Sitting Area	TV
Inside	$136	no	no	no	yes	yes
Outside	$166	no	some	no	yes	yes
Suite	$307	yes	yes	no	yes	yes

CABINS   To be polite, cabins are "compact." Granted, they're noticeably larger than the cramped cubicles that were standard issue aboard the company's older ships (the *Nordic Empress*'s standard outside cabins, for instance, are a tiny 122 sq. ft.), but they're still cramped compared to the competition. Inside cabins measure 138 square feet and outsides 153 square feet (compared to Carnival's 190 sq. ft. for standard cabins). For big, check out the Royal Suite on each of these ships—they measure a mammoth 1,150 square feet. The *Vision*'s even has a grand piano.

In keeping up with the Joneses of today's balcony-loving industry, nearly one-fourth of the cabins aboard each ship have private verandas. About a third can accommodate third and fourth passengers, too. Regardless of the ship you opt for, your cabin will have soft color schemes of pastels that alternate with varnished hardwood trim.

All cabins have adequate storage space, safes, music channels, and TVs offering some 20 channels of video, four different music channels, three more for movies, and three more with satellite programming—tons more than competitors like Norwegian and Carnival, which offer just a few channels. Bathrooms, while not the largest by far, have a nice multilevel built-in shelf in the shower stalls.

Each vessel has between 14 and 17 staterooms equipped for wheelchair users.

PUBLIC AREAS   Warm woods and brass, luxuriant fountains and foliage, glass and crystal, buttery leathers, and carefully chosen artwork and textures highlight the public areas. Some public areas evoke a private Roman villa; others are deliberately glitzier and flashier. Different areas of the ship were designed to evoke different places in America—for example, a wine bar in New York or a gambling hall in Las Vegas.

The layout of the Promenade and Mariner decks—the main indoor public decks on each ship—allows for easy passage. Corridors are wide and bright. Focal points on the six ships are the soaring seven-story atriums known as "Centrum." Each is crowned by a sloped two-deck-high skylight. Glass elevators, à la Hyatt, take passengers up through Centrum into the stunning Viking Crown Lounge, a glass-sided aerie high above the waves. Accessorized with a superb sound-and-light system, it's high on everybody's list of favorite wave-watching and sightseeing spaces, especially during transits of the Panama Canal.

The shopping arcade, Boutiques of the Centrum, is like a shipboard Fifth Avenue or Rodeo Drive, and is much more extensively stocked (and appealing to look at) than Carnival's Fantasy-class shopping complexes, which are cramped and off the beaten track. The Schooner Bar is a casual piano bar with lots of wood and rope, befitting its nautical name, and is a great place for a predinner drink or late-night unwinding. Ditto the Champagne Terrace at the foot of the atrium. Listen and dance to a trio while sipping fine wines or a glass of bubbly.

In deliberate contrast to such massive showcase spaces, each ship contains many hideaway refuges, including an array of cocktail bars, a library, and card rooms. Hundreds of potted plants and more than 3,000 original artworks aboard each ship add humanity and warmth.

The large dining rooms aboard the vessels span two decks and are interconnected with a very grand staircase and flanked with walls of glass nearly 20 feet high. Each has a decor that's contemporary and tasteful (if not reminiscent of a banquet hall), replete with lots of stainless steel, mirrors, and dramatic chandeliers. A pianist plays a massive grand piano throughout dinner service.

Full musical revues are staged in glittery, two-story showrooms, and there's not a bad seat in the house. Each has an orchestra pit that can be raised and lowered hydraulically to provide dramatic effects during cabaret shows.

The ship's casinos are Vegas-style flashy and consciously overaccessorized with hundreds of gambling stations so densely packed that it's sometimes difficult to move and always difficult to hear.

Each ship has a higher-than-expected amount of open deck space. One of the most dramatic is the Sun Deck, which manages to incorporate two swimming pools (one covered by a retractable glass roof), whirlpools, and the Windjammer buffet-style restaurant.

The ships' conference rooms can hold up to 200 people.

Regrettably, there are no self-service Laundromats.

POOL, FITNESS & SPA FACILITIES   The Steiner-managed ShipShape spas on these ships, especially on the *Vision, Rhapsody, Grandeur,* and *Enchantment,* are some of the most attractive around and are truly soothing respites from the hubbub of ship life. They offer a wide selection of treatments, as well as the standard steam rooms and saunas. Adjacent to the spas are spacious solariums, each with a pool, lounge chairs, floor-to-ceiling windows, and a retractable glass ceiling. These spots are a peaceful place to repose before or after a spa treatment, or any time at all. They're bright, comfortable, and each has an inventive design motif, like Roman, Egyptian, or Moorish. Surprisingly, the gyms are small for the ships' size, and in comparison to those on Carnival's, Holland America's, and Celebrity's megaliners.

The main pool area has four whirlpools (two on *Splendour*) and there are two more in the Solarium. There's usually loud music by the pool along with silly contests (of the belly-flop genre), which most passengers seem to love dearly.

There's a jogging track, shuffleboard, and Ping-Pong. And, if you want to swing a few clubs, the *Splendour of the Seas* actually sports a 6,000-square-foot, 18-hole miniature golf course.

Majesty of the Seas •
Monarch of the Seas

Majesty of the Seas *(photo: RCCL)*

The Verdict

These ships are huge, and while they feel somewhat dated compared to their spiffy new Vision-class sisters, they manage to maintain an easygoing elegance, with their light color scheme and spread-out public areas.

Specifications

Size (in tons)	73,941	Crew	825 (International)
Number of Cabins	1,177	Passenger/Crew Ratio	2.9 to 1
Number of Outside Cabins	732	Year Built	
Cabins with Verandas	62	*Majesty*	1992
Number of Passengers	2,354	*Monarch*	1991
Officers	Norwegian/Interntl.	Last Major Refurbishment	N/A

Frommer's Ratings (Scale of 1–5)

Cabin Comfort & Amenities	4	Pool, Fitness & Spa Facilities	3
Ship Cleanliness & Maintenance	4	Children's Facilities	4
Public Comfort/Space	4	Itinerary	3
Decor	4	Worth the Money	5

These mirror-image twins were built at the same Breton shipyard in western France (in 1992 and 1991, respectively) for a cost of $300 million each. Their profiles are clean and distinguished, while inside are 14 passenger decks and 11 passenger elevators, and a dazzling lineup of public spaces. Decor-wise, these ships sport more brass, chrome, and neon than their newer Vision-class sisters (see review above), and smack of the parachute-pants-wearing big-haired eighties, making them seem a bit dated and dull by comparison. All in all, though, they work just fine.

Cabins & Rates

Cabins	Per diems from	Bathtub	Fridge	Hair Dryer	Sitting Area	TV
Inside	$111	no	no	no	no	yes
Outside	$141	some	some	no	some	yes
Suite	$438	yes	yes	no	yes	yes

CABINS The worst feature of the entire fleet—small cabins—is no less prevalent on these two ships. Standard cabins, scattered over nine decks, average a too-snug 120 square feet. Bathrooms aren't much better in the size department. In 62 of the outside cabins, some of the cramped feeling is relieved by verandas. Over 100 cabins have upper and lower berths in order to house four, albeit quite tightly. Suites are larger, of course, and moderately more comfortable than the standard cabins. The Royal Suites and the Owners' Suites are significantly larger.

All cabins have safes, music channels, and TVs with a tremendous selection (see Vision-class ship review, above, for details).

Four cabins on each ship can accommodate wheelchair users.

PUBLIC AREAS   Like the rest of the fleet, the glass-enclosed Viking Crown Lounge sits way up on the topmost deck, some 150 feet above sea level, and is clearly the ships' signature piece. This is a great place for a drink before dinner and the place to go to dance into the wee hours.

A dramatic five-story atrium, with a color scheme that glows in a metallic shade of either bronze or champagne, is the ships' interior focal point. A sweeping staircase curves down onto the ground floor and makes for a grand scene. Public areas—including one of the largest casinos afloat—are wisely clustered aft of the atrium to minimize noise in the forward section of the ships, where most cabins are located. Broadway musicals and Hollywood films inspired the names and decor of most public areas: the Brigadoon dining room, the Ain't Misbehavin' Nightclub, the April in Paris Lounge. Each ship contains a paneled library any passenger would be proud to have at home, a massive two-story showroom with lots of tiered seating, and a host of other bars and cubbyholes scattered throughout, some with modern art-nouveau decors.

Although these are monstrous ships, they're so well designed that passengers don't seem to get lost very often, and only when you find yourself standing in long lines (or taking the stairs instead of the elevators to the Viking Crown Lounge) do you realize just how big they are.

POOL, FITNESS & SPA FACILITIES   Two good-size swimming pools, each ringed with lounge chairs, are located on the Sports Deck. Looking at this space when it's empty, you'd think there's all the room in the world, but when the ship is full, the rows of sunbathers resemble sardines in a tin.

The gyms aboard both ships are fairly spacious, with a wall of windows facing aft. The spas have a handful of massage and treatment rooms offering a wide range of treatments as well as separate saunas for men and women. In size and style, though, they can't hold a flame to the spas on the Vision-class ships. Other sports and fitness facilities include an unobstructed jogging track, a basketball court, shuffleboard, and Ping-Pong.

Nordic Empress

The Verdict

This midsize ship is an appealing, easy-to-navigate package. Public rooms are well laid out and decor is just glittery enough to keep the mood festive.

Nordic Empress *(photo: RCCL)*

Specifications

Size (in tons)	48,563	Officers	Scandinavian
Number of Cabins	800	Crew	671 (International)
Number of Outside Cabins	471	Passenger/Crew Ratio	2.4 to 1
Cabins with Verandas	69	Year Built	1990
Number of Passengers	1,600	Last Major Refurbishment	N/A

Frommer's Ratings (Scale of 1–5)

Cabin Comfort & Amenities	4	Pool, Fitness & Spa Facilities	3
Ship Cleanliness & Maintenance	4	Children's Facilities	4
Public Comfort/Space	4	Itinerary	3
Decor	4	Worth the Money	5

This hefty 48,000-ton vessel looks small when compared to the megaships forming the rest of Royal Caribbean's modern fleet. Originally intended to sail for Admiral Cruises, a now-defunct subsidiary of Royal Caribbean during its early days, the *Nordic Empress* was retained by Royal Caribbean as part of a bid to capture a segment of the 3- and 4-day cruise market. The ship was specifically created for this type of cruise, where passengers tend to hurl themselves into onboard activities, knowing they don't have a languorous week to explore their surroundings, so its designers built in the most bang for the buck. It's an attractive ship and is consistently flooded with sunlight from big windows, which dominate most of the ship's stern. It's got the requisite glass, chrome, and neon, but not so much that it's overwhelming. The ship spends winters doing 3- and 4-night cruises out of San Juan, and summers plying the New York–to–Bermuda run.

Cabins & Rates

Cabins	Per diems from	Bathtub	Fridge	Hair Dryer	Sitting Area	TV
Inside	$110	no	no	no	no	yes
Outside	$158	no	no	no	some	yes
Suite	$434	yes	yes	no	yes	yes

CABINS Again, cabins are small; at not more than an embarrassing 130 square feet (equivalent in size and amenities to those aboard the *Sovereign,* the *Majesty,* and the *Monarch*). Drawer and closet space is limited, and you may find yourself just keeping some things in your suitcase.

Although small, the cabins are carefully designed, which makes them seem more livable. A large number of them are inside, however, and are downright claustrophobic, practically guaranteeing that passengers will spend more time on-deck or in public areas. Upper-end cabins and suites have verandas; outside cabins without them offer rectangular picture windows. Even if you upgrade for one of the smaller suites, you won't gain that much additional elbow room, although amenities are better and locations within the vessel are more convenient. Newlyweds and lovers note: Many cabins have twin beds in an L-configuration that cannot be combined into a queen-size bed.

All cabins have safes, music channels, and TVs with a tremendous selection (see Vision-class ship review, above, for details).

Four cabins are wheelchair accessible.

PUBLIC AREAS Considering the relatively small size of this vessel, the inclusion of a six-deck atrium was an astonishing design choice. Aboard the *Nordic Empress,* light floods into the atrium from above and from big windows flanking five decks on either side. So intent were the designers on creating a razzle-dazzle venue for exciting parties that they sacrificed space that might otherwise have gone toward cabins. Adding to the decor are a splashing fountain ringed with tropical plants and unusual and original artwork based on Nordic themes. Thoughtful layout makes it easy to navigate throughout the ship.

More than aboard any other of the company's ships, the Sun Deck is an important space both daytime and night. Loaded with sunbathers during the day, it's transformed into a starlit dance floor when the sun goes down. Fountains, a gazebo, and sail-like canopies create a cozy, almost clubby ambiance.

The *Nordic Empress* boasts its own version of Royal Caribbean's signature Viking Crown Lounge and disco. Positioned at the ship's stern like all the others and sitting 11 stories above the waterline, this version is two stories high.

With a relatively mellow and un-jarring decor, the ship's spacious three-level casino is a unique place to while away the evening, and offers cozier places to play than on most ships.

The two-story Strike Up the Band Showroom is very Atlantic City and very, very pink. In all, there are five bars, three entertainment lounges, a vibrant disco, a video-game room, a playroom, and a conference center.

POOL, FITNESS & SPA FACILITIES   On the Sun Deck, where virtually everything seems to happen, there are four hot tubs, a generous swimming pool fed by a fountain, a wading pool for children, and enough shady spots to get a break from the sun.

Although the exercise area isn't the largest afloat, it's got floor-to-ceiling windows and enough equipment to satisfy most users. A hot tub is adjacent. There's a sauna, plus massage, and the ship has an unobstructed jogging track.

Sovereign of the Seas

The Verdict

A trendsetter in its heyday, this ship is now somewhat dated, but it still promises and delivers action-packed, ultra-casual (read: shorts and jeans in the dining room at night are common) 3- and 4-night cruises for the whole family.

Sovereign of the Seas *(photo: RCCL)*

Specifications

Size (in tons)	73,192	Officers	Norwegian
Number of Cabins	1,138	Crew	840 (International)
Number of Outside Cabins	722	Passenger/Crew Ratio	2.7 to 1
Cabins with Verandas	0	Year Built	1988
Number of Passengers	2,276	Last Major Refurbishment	1997

Frommer's Ratings (Scale of 1–5)

Cabin Comfort & Amenities	3	Pool, Fitness & Spa Facilities	3
Ship Cleanliness & Maintenance	4	Children's Facilities	4
Public Comfort/Space	3	Itinerary	3
Decor	4	Worth the Money	5

When it was launched in 1988, after costing $185 million to build, *Sovereign of the Seas* was the largest passenger vessel built during the previous 50 years and the largest cruise ship in history. Today, in terms of gross tonnage, it's only slightly more than half the size of its giant fleet mate, *Voyager of the Seas*. Talk about the march of progress.

Like its 1980s contemporaries, the *Sovereign* seems dated in comparison to the swank newcomers in the industry, and has its share of bumps and bruises accumulated from its hectic year-round 3- and 4-night cruise schedule. On a cruise in early 2000, certain areas were not as kept-up as they should have been. For instance the patch of outdoor-dining seating forward of the Lido buffet restaurant was strewn with napkins, straw paper, beer cans, and other litter and none of it was ever picked up during my hour lunching there.

Most travel agents, as well as Royal Caribbean itself, tend to lump this ship in the same category as two later models, *Monarch of the Seas* and *Majesty of the Seas;* however, the *Sovereign* has a slightly different deck layout and weighs a bit less. The ship has no cabin balconies whatsoever or decks devoted exclusively to public rooms; instead, its lounges, restaurants, kids' facilities, and spa/gym are sort of stacked along successive aft decks.

Cabins & Rates						
Cabins	Per diems from	Bathtub	Fridge	Hair Dryer	Sitting Area	TV
Inside	$111	no	no	no	no	yes*
Outside	$136	some	no	no	some	yes*
Suite	$341	yes	yes	no	yes	yes*

* TVs broadcast CNN and ESPN.

CABINS　Light, pastel colors try to make the cabins appear larger than they are, but there's no disguising their paltry 120-square-foot size (put four people in there, which many commonly do, and it's like camping in a pup tent). The 84 Larger Staterooms on Commodore Deck are a roomier 157 square feet, and the dozen top suites range from 382 square feet to 670 square feet; none have balconies.

Overall, cabin decor is spartan and uninspired, relatively clean, but worn. Cabins have limited storage space (remember, though, this ship's itineraries are only 3 and 4 nights long) but do have TVs offering the same extensive programming as on the line's other ships (see Vision-class review above for details). Cabin categories R, A, B, C, D, and F have personal safes; for everyone else, there are lock boxes at the purser's desk. There are nice adjustable reading lamps above each bed. All the cabins on Mariner Deck have obstructed views, and you can see the tops of these same lifeboats from the windows of all cabins on the Commodore Deck.

On a recent cruise, I was in a cabin that had an interconnecting door to the one next to mine, and the soundproofing was poor; I could hear every word said above a whisper (in fact, we and our neighbors actually had to resort to whispering mornings and evenings to avoid disturbing one another). The cabin bathrooms, although relatively roomy and well designed, could also have used a face-lift—the soap dish was about to fall off the wall, water collected on the floor (leaking from the tub, I think) after every shower, and the caulking around the tub was peeling and discolored. There was also a thick layer of dust under the TV and in the crevices of the reading lamps. These kinds of maintenance issues, plus things like incorrect signage—in the cabins and throughout the ship, the small instruction signs above the toilets said PUSH BUTTON TO FLUSH, when really you had to pull it—give an impression of haphazardness to the ship's operation.

Six cabins are fitted for passengers with disabilities.

PUBLIC AREAS　A wide-open, crowd-friendly, five-story atrium interconnects most of the ship's many airy public areas, and there are four huge spaces (including the casino) for after-dinner entertainment, a layout that keeps any one area from getting too crowded. A collection of well-laid-out shops are grouped around the atrium.

Public areas are clustered toward the stern, with cabins mainly in the forward half of the ship, an arrangement that creates the illusion that this mighty vessel is more intimate than it is. The two-story main show lounge, Follies, is roomy and well planned, with lots of cocktail-table and chair clusters for two and a huge stage. Sight lines are good except from parts of the balcony. There are two other large nightclubs for dancing and live music, plus that Royal Caribbean architectural trademark, the Viking Crown Lounge and disco encircling the smokestack 14 stories above sea level. The popular Schooner piano bar is located next to the sprawling, glitzy, chrome-covered, pink-themed casino (whose bells and whistles you can hear from the edge of the Schooner). You'll find these lounges, like the entire ship, populated by people wearing everything from cut-off shorts and flip-flops to nice dresses and suits. It's a real mixed bag.

The children's play area is downright huge, although a bit on the spartan side. It has nine computer monitors. There's even a separate, and also extremely large, teen center and disco, as well as a third space for younger kids and a video arcade with about a dozen machines.

There's a very impressive computer nook on the Main Deck, adjacent to the purser's desk, with 12 new computers equipped with Web cams that allow you to make E-mail postcards of yourself.

POOL, FITNESS & SPA FACILITIES   The deck layout and two good-size swimming pools are stylish and impressive when they're empty, but the staggering number of passengers aboard this ship almost guarantees that they'll fill up, becoming a wall-to-wall carpet of people. Anyone have a shoe horn so I can wedge myself into one of those two hot tubs?

That said, there are many patches of more isolated deck space all over the ship, from the quiet slices of tiered aft deck to two levels of far-forward deck space, many spots sporting a profusion of live plants (there's a full-time plant caretaker on board). Chaise-lounge-flopping sunbathers beware: The beach towels on this ship are hand-towel-size.

The Sports Deck, up high in the stern, has six Ping-Pong tables, a pair of golf putting greens, and, one deck above, basketball.

The half-moon-shaped gym is bright and has floor-to-ceiling windows. The machines—five treadmills, five stationary bikes, five step machines, and a handful of weight machines and free weights—line the perimeter of the room, facing the sea, and the inner part of the room serves as the aerobics space. Not the smartest design move: The adjacent spa as well as the gym are wedged between the sports deck above and the engine room below. My masseuse told me when the ship pulls out of port the massage tables vibrate and the tranquillity of the spa is disrupted.

Voyager of the Seas • Explorer of the Seas (preview)

The Verdict

Vegas-meets-a-theme-park-at-sea, this biggest-in-the-world ship carries its weight well and is a winner if you like your vacations larger than life. But, if you don't like sharing your holiday with thousands of others and don't like walking a mile to get to the other end, think twice.

Voyager of the Seas *(photo: RCCL)*

Specifications

Size (in tons)	142,000	Officers	Scandinavian
Number of Cabins	1,557	Crew	1,176 (Interntl.)
Number of Outside Cabins	939	Passenger/Crew Ratio	2.7 to 1
Cabins with Verandas	757	Year Built	1999
Number of Passengers	3,114	Last Major Refurbishment	N/A

Frommer's Ratings (Scale of 1–5)

Cabin Comfort & Amenities	4	Pool, Fitness & Spa Facilities	5
Ship Cleanliness & Maintenance	4	Children's Facilities	5
Public Comfort/Space	4	Itineraries	4
Decor	4	Worth the Money	5

The *Voyager* is an architectural marvel if there ever was one, and a ship of firsts. Not only is it currently the largest cruise ship in the world (the ship is 50 feet wider than any other passenger ship), it's got features none of the others do. A marvel in size and cost (we're talking $500 million to build this baby), the 3,114-passenger, 142,000-ton *Voyager of the Seas* has 17 decks (14 accessible to passengers), rises over 200 feet above the sea, and contains over 538,000 square feet of carpet and 15,000 chairs. Believe it or not, the ship has a 60 × 40-foot ice-skating rink featuring two performances a night (and skating for passengers at all other times), a rock-climbing wall stuck to the side of the funnel, an outdoor in-line skating track (skates can be rented or you can bring your own), a wedding chapel, and an amazing number of shops. If that's not enough excitement for you, head over to the ship's nine-hole miniature-golf course, driving range, or golf simulator; regulation-size basketball, paddleball, and volleyball courts; or sprawling two-level gym and spa.

Another unique feature, and what really sets this ship apart, is a four-deck-high boulevardlike promenade running down the center of the ship between two multistory atria for some 500 feet, its ground floor lined with shops, bars, restaurants, and entertainment outlets. As at Disney World, evenings performers like clowns, jugglers, and actors dressed as turn-of-the-century cops or 1930s cocktail waitresses or street cleaners stroll about entertaining and interacting with the throngs. It's a great place to people-watch—beat out only by the three decks of inside cabins above the promenade, which have views from bay windows of the "street scene" below. Who needs ocean views? Did I mention there's also a whopping three-story dining room, a three-deck-high showroom (five, if you count the orchestra pit and the domed ceiling), a bar featuring four huge aquariums, a florist shop (you never know when you'll need a dozen roses), and a "peek-a-boo" bridge on Deck 11 that allows guests to gather above and watch the crew steering the ship? Nearly half of all staterooms have balconies and every cabin has a minibar, a hair dryer (a Royal Caribbean first!), and a TV.

The ship even needed it's own specially built multimillion-dollar, 250,000-square-foot terminal in Miami to accommodate it (the terminal's white, sail-like design bears a remarkable resemblance to the Sydney Opera House in Australia).

At press time, sister ship *Explorer of the Seas* was slated to debut in October of 2000. While it will share many of *Voyager*'s bells and whistles, including the Royal Promenade, an ice-skating rink, an in-line skating track, and a rock-climbing wall, it will also have something unique: an atmospheric and marine laboratory, with an interactive environmental classroom. Hmmm, sounds interesting.

The *Voyager* and *Explorer*'s identical sisters, the *Radiance* and *Brilliance of the Seas,* are due to enter service in spring of 2001 and summer of 2002 respectively.

Cabins & Rates

Cabins	Per diems from	Bathtub	Fridge	Hair Dryer	Sitting Area	TV
Inside	$166	no	yes	yes	no	yes
Outside	$209	no	yes	yes	some	yes
Suite	$288	yes	yes	yes	yes	yes

CABINS   A vast improvement from Royal Caribbean's signature small cabins, those on the *Voyager* are more civilized in size, running 188 square feet for a standard ocean-view cabin (including balcony), and 160 square feet for an inside (remember, Carnival standard inside and outside cabins are nearly 190 square feet, without a balcony). Still, bathrooms are on the cramped side, with little storage space and a thin sliver of counter (although there's more space out in the cabin on shelves above the desk). The cylindrical shower stalls, though tight for large-size people, have neat sliding doors that keep the water and warmth in. And here's an amazing fact, of value to every longhaired man or woman out there: *Voyager* is the first Royal Caribbean ship to offer guests hair dryers (they're hidden in a drawer of the vanity and are actually powerful enough to dry hair!).

Of the 1,557 cabins, 939 are ocean-view and 757 have verandas. There's one huge penthouse suite, 10 owner's suites, and 4 Royal Family suites accommodating a total of eight people, with two bedrooms plus a living room with sofa bed and a pair of bathrooms. There are also smaller and cheaper family cabins with sitting areas and sofa beds, which sleep six. The superior and deluxe ocean-view cabins have balconies and sitting areas, many with sofa beds. There are 138 atrium cabins on the second, third, and fourth level of the four-story Royal Promenade, with windows facing the action below (and curtains and soundproofing to keep most of the light and noise out).

In that signature Royal Caribbean way, cabin color schemes are pastel-based and pleasant, but they're nothing innovative. Thoughtfully rounded corners on the beds are appreciated, though, as are the extra-wide corridors, a nice touch considering how much time you'll spend in them trekking to and from your cabin—at the beginning of the week it can feel like forever getting from one end of the ship to the other (I got used to it; you may, too).

All cabins have TVs, high-tech minifridges (via electronically gadgetry, your cabin account is automatically billed when you remove a drink, so be careful what bottles you jiggle!), hair dryers, and safes.

Twenty-six cabins are wheelchair accessible, as are all elevators.

PUBLIC AREAS　Gee, where do I start. Well, there's a lot of 'em, that's for sure. But, like the *Grand Princess,* public spaces are divided into many separate lounges and nooks, making the ship feel smaller than it is.

The four-story-high, shopping-mall-like Royale Promenade is truly a pleasure if you like people-watching, shopping malls, or the international villages in theme parks. It's bustling and open, with strolling performers to keep things lively. It's got an Irish Pub, a sports bar lined with TV monitors, a cafe for pizza or pastries, an ice-cream station with the machine-generated stuff and lots of toppings, a mini-casino, and shops. Above the main street, a string of cabin windows face all the fun below.

In the bars-and-entertainment category, there are some 30 places to grab a drink, including the Viking Crown cluster on the top deck, the tucked-away-behind-a-door, feels-like-a-private-club Connoisseur Club cigar bar, the dark and romantic nautically themed Schooner Bar, and a feels-like-this-is-Manhattan disco called the Vault, with a funky sensor thing on which you place your open palm in order to get in (it gets a bit slimy and sweaty, actually). There's the Aquarium champagne bar with, as the name suggests, aquariums built into the walls and filled with real fish. Cool!

A $500,000 crystal chandelier at the center sets the tone for the ship's surprisingly elegant three-story dining room, among the most stunning and classy in the entire mainstream niche. Each level of the room has its own name and is thought of as a separate restaurant, though the dramatic Georgian-style theme is consistent throughout.

The Island Grill and Windjammer casual buffet restaurants are joined into one large space, but do have separate lines and stations to keep things moving. Although huge, it's a pleasant area, but one thing is missing: outdoor seating. Unlike most casual buffet restaurants, the *Voyager*'s has none. The main pool area, however, is on the same deck, just right outside the entrance.

Just outside of these restaurants is the cozy, ocean-view Portofino, a reservations-only alternative restaurant that provides a welcome getaway if you can get a table.

Did I mention there's a two-story library-cum-computer-room with 18 computer stations and Net cams, too (so you can put your own picture in electronic postcards). There's also a sprawling kids' area that takes up the better part of the aft third of Deck 12, with a huge ocean-view playroom, teen disco, outdoor pool and play area (complete with mini–deck chairs and lounges), and a jumbo arcade (second in size only to the one on the *Grand Princess*) with a pair of good old-fashioned air-hockey tables mixed in among its many high-tech diversions.

POOL, FITNESS & SPA FACILITIES   There's plenty to keep you occupied, that's for sure. The windowed gym is well equipped, though it feels a bit cramped when full; if you don't watch where you swing those barbells, you could club someone. Comparing it to the gyms on some of its megaship competition, it's much better and bigger than the one on the *Grand Princess* but not as user-friendly and wide-open as those on the *Carnival Destiny, Triumph,* and *Victory,* or Holland America's *Volendam* and *Zaandam.* There's a huge aerobics studio—one of the biggest at sea—and the two-level spa complex is also one of the largest and best accoutred out there. There's a peaceful waiting area (which you won't find on the Carnival ships) with New Agey tropical birdsong music piped in overhead. Ahhhh, relaxation—until you get your bill. (The spa's management raised its rates big time in late 1999. See Steiner review in chapter 4.)

While the crowds on board will be dispersed among the ship's myriad venues, on a hot sunny day things get tight out on the main pool deck—let's just say it's tenement-style sunbathing. As aboard the *Carnival Destiny, Triumph,* and *Victory,* deck chairs are squeezed into every level of the multitiered, amphitheaterlike deck. It's a sight to behold from the Sky Bar at the top.

Cheap Cruises, Older Ships: The Budget Lines

In this category you'll find classic ocean liners, some of which have managed to stay around for almost 50 years. These ships have great appeal for ship buffs and nostalgic folks, and have retained varying amounts of their former grandeur—some have aged gracefully, others not so much. For instance, Premier's *Rembrandt* (formerly Holland America's *Rotterdam V*) is the most beautiful and intact relic left, with much of its original furniture, wall finishings, and artwork still impressing passengers (though who knows what time will bring: at press time, Premier was undecided whether or not to rename it the *Big Red Boat IV* in late 2000, paint its hull red, and rejigger its gorgeous interior). The line's *SeaBreeze* and *Big Red Boat,* on the other hand, retain only their classic exterior lines, with most of their interiors stripped of any original features.

Depending on what you like, the age of a ship can be a plus or a minus. If you appreciate relics of the past—prewar buildings over modern ones, antiques instead of IKEA—then you might like these 30-year-old-plus liners: With long, sweeping hulls, tiered decks, wood paneling, and chunky portholes, they offer a nostalgic glimpse back to a lost age of cruising. Decks, doors, railings, and bar tops are made of solid varnished wood, and cabin doors may still operate with a lock and key rather than with a computerized key-card. In comparison to the often cramped cabins on mainstream megas, cabins and closets on these ships are often quite large, owing to the fact that they formerly did long-haul sailings for a clientele traveling with steamer trunks and lots of luggage. Tall sills in most doorways require some high stepping to avoid tripping (old ships are not for wheelchair users), and there's no shortage of exposed cables, fire doors, pipes, ropes, winches, and all manner of hardware. These are ships that look like ships, and for ship buffs, they're charming. For bargain hunters, too, they're often the best deal in town, with rates at times dipping down below $100 per person per day. (Although I must add, owing to the glut of cabin space throughout the industry these days, at times the rates for inside and low-category cabins on Carnival, Royal Caribbean, NCL, and even Celebrity and Princess can drop nearly as low.)

Now, if you're a lover of all things fresh, new, and modern, you might want to pass on a cruise on one of the oldies. The old-timers can't hide the wear and tear accumulated from logging thousands of miles at sea. Repeatedly refurbished and restored through the years (often haphazardly and in the least expensive ways), many are a hodgepodge of design schemes and awkward spaces. Discos, spas, and gyms are often small, dark spaces in lower decks, and carpeting, wall finishes, and outside decks are often worn. All in all, you won't be seeing a lot of flash, but you will be seeing some old ships that might not be around much longer: The future of some of them will depend on compliance with a set of international safety regulations known as the **Safety of Life at Sea (SOLAS),** predominantly concerned with issues like fire prevention. Ships built after 1994 automatically incorporate SOLAS safety features, while ships built before 1994 have been required to add them by a progressive set of deadlines. The most sweeping changes were completed by a 1997 deadline, another series had to be made by 2000, and more must be implemented by 2005 and 2010. The changes required could prove too costly for many of these old-timers and seal their fate forever—so enjoy them while you can.

Note: There are four oldies I could have included in this section, but for various reasons decided to put elsewhere. Cunard's *QE2* is a 32-year-old classic liner that attracts a more upscale clientele than any other old-timer, so look for a review of that ship in chapter 8, "The Ultra-Luxury Lines." NCL's 40-year-old *Norway,* the former *France,* also claims a liner pedigree, but nowhere near as upscale as the *QE2;* to make things easier, I've kept the *Norway* review with the rest of the NCL fleet, in chapter 6, "The Mainstream Lines." Also, for convenience's sake, the review of Princess Cruises' 30-year-old *Pacific Princess* can be found with the rest of its fleet, also in chapter 6. Lastly, because of its bent toward onboard educational and enrichment programs, I've put Royal Olympic Cruises' 48-year-old *Stella Solaris* in chapter 9, "Soft-Adventure Lines & Sailing Ships," alongside its brand new sister, *Olympic Voyager.*

DRESS CODES   Like the mainstream lines, weeklong cruises on these ships generally feature two formal nights, but with the exception of Premier's *Rembrandt,* you won't find too many passengers in tuxedos or fancy sequin dresses. Overall, ships in this category are somewhat more casual, with guests preferring suits or sport coats to tuxes, and pantsuits or sundresses to gowns (although it's not unheard of to see a tux and a shimmery dress). Guests are asked not to wear shorts and T-shirts in the formal dining room—although, as on the mainstream lines, I'm seeing more and more people trying and succeeding. Daytime is casual.

Frommer's Ratings at a Glance: The Budget Lines

1 = poor   2 = fair   3 = good   4 = excellent   5 = outstanding

Cruise Line	Enjoyment Factor	Dining	Activities	Children's Program	Entertainment	Service	Overall Value
Commodore	4	3	4	2*	4	3	4
Mediterranean Shipping	3	3	3	2	3	3	3
Premier	4	3	4	5*	4	4	5
Regal	4	3	3	2	3	3	4

NOTE: Cruise lines have been graded on a curve that compares them only with the other budget/old ship lines. See "Cruise Line Categories" in chapter 5 for a detailed explanation of my ratings methodology.
* Does not apply to all ships in the line's fleet. See individual ship reviews for details.

Commodore Cruise Line

4000 Hollywood Blvd., South Tower 385, Hollywood, FL 33021. ☎ **800/237-5361** or 954/967-2100. Fax 954/967-2147. www.commodorecruise.com.

THE LINE IN A NUTSHELL   These Sputnik-era vessels may show their age, but they offer down-to-earth, fun cruises at rock-bottom rates.

THE EXPERIENCE   Commodore Cruise Line's *Enchanted Isle* and *Enchanted Capri* are, despite several drawbacks, two of the best bargains sailing the Caribbean: The line's low rates are fantastic for first-time cruisers on a budget. Fares are cheaper mainly because the vessels are old and lack most of the newfangled entertainment gadgets that appear on newer ships. But what the line lacks in technology, it makes up for in spunk, its officers and crew working hard to give passengers what they paid for, and then some. The cruises are casual, carefree, and fun, and the ships' small size means passengers begin to recognize each other after only a day or so at sea—sooner than aboard larger ships.

Dubbed the "Happy Ship," *Enchanted Isle* pioneered theme cruises, and the *Isle* and *Capri* still have sock hops and "Remember When" cruises featuring music legends of the 1950s. The *Capri* has an especially active casino scene—in fact, the ship's lease is coheld by Commodore and a land-based casino concern, and you'll always see many casino regulars aboard, particularly on the 2-night cruises. Today, both ships homeport in New Orleans, giving passengers a vastly different embarkation experience than they'd get in Florida. The line attracts most of its passengers from states in this region: Louisiana, Mississippi, Texas, Arkansas, and Alabama.

Pros
- **Bargain of the century.** It's not uncommon to pay as little as $70 per day, which, of course, includes all meals and entertainment.
- **Go-get-'em spirit.** Although they don't have a lot to work with props-wise, cruise directors and entertainers really leap through hoops to give passengers a good time. I give them an A for effort.
- **Roomy cabins.** The majority of cabins on the *Capri* and *Isle* are spacious.

Cons
- **Rough around the edges.** These ships are old, so you'll notice some wear.
- **The low-budget shows.** Though the crew does what it can to get around this point (see "Pros"), you can't help but notice that they aren't given a lot to work with. In the shows, a costume change means the singer changes her hat, and in the dining rooms, ingredients are pretty basic.

Compared with the other Budget lines, here's how Commodore rates:					
	poor	fair	good	excellent	outstanding
Enjoyment Factor				✓	
Dining			✓		
Activities				✓	
Children's Program		✓*			
Entertainment				✓	
Service			✓		
Overall Value				✓	

* Applies only to Enchanted Isle; Enchanted Capri *has no children's program.*

COMMODORE: GOOD CHEAP FUN

Formed in 1966, Commodore has been plugging along quietly ever since. The company doesn't make a lot of waves (figuratively speaking), but where some of its competitors have experienced fits of instability over the past several years, it's continued going strong, giving passengers buckets of fun at a bargain-basement price. They must be doing something right: In early 2000, Commodore Holdings Limited, the line's parent company, purchased NCL's 800-passenger *Norwegian Dynasty* for just over $86 million. The ship became the *Crown Dynasty* and was deployed as the first ship in Commodore's new premium cruise brand, **Crown Cruise Line** (see review in chapter 6). In partnership with Apple Vacations, the ship spends the summer cruising between Philadelphia and Bermuda (a few sailings also depart from Baltimore), and the rest of the year the ship does 7-night southern Caribbean cruises out of Aruba.

THE FLEET

Both of these small, elderly ships sail round-trip out of New Orleans and have had interesting, full lives as other-named ships for other lines. The 43-year-old, 725-passenger *Enchanted Isle* started off in 1958 as the *Argentina* and over the next 30 years sailed for five different owners, including Holland America (where it was the company's *Veendam* for 11 years). Commodore bought the ship in 1990, but even then its adventures weren't over: The ship served as the "Hotel Commodore" in St. Petersburg, Russia, in 1994/95. Perhaps this Russian connection got the company thinking, because in 1998 it leased a 460-passenger vessel that had spent the previous years as a cruise ship for the Soviet Union. Built in 1975 as the *Azerbaydzahn,* the **Enchanted Capri** is a small, attractive, very shippy ship with a split personality: On the one hand, it's loaded with leftovers from its Soviet past (hammers and sickles on the life jackets!), and on the other, it has some garishly decorated public spaces that scream "I'm a Caribbean cruise ship, dammit!" It's a weird mix. MTV apparently thought it was hip enough, though: It held its first MTV Spring Break cruise on the ship in 1999.

PASSENGER PROFILE

Commodore Cruises draws one of the widest spectrums of passengers in the business. Many passengers are first-time cruisers lured by the line's low per diem rates. Nearly all the passengers are American, a few hailing from the Midwest and a handful from California, but since sailings depart from New Orleans, and because so many of the line's marketing efforts are aimed directly at the regions around the Mississippi Delta, the large majority of this line's passengers come from Louisiana, Mississippi, Alabama, Texas, Arkansas, and the Florida Panhandle.

The line draws couples of all ages looking for an inexpensive, fun cruise, as well as many retirees, particularly on Caribbean winter voyages, where they account for about one in four passengers. During school vacations, Commodore draws a lot of families, plus other young white-collar and blue-collar workers lured by the low rates. Group travel makes up a huge percentage of Commodore's business. Budget-minded honeymooners can arrange to have their wedding ceremonies held free of charge out on deck while their ship is docked in New Orleans, or indoors in a lounge for a $50 room fee (a variety of extras, like a pianist or onboard reception packages, including champagne, hors d'oeuvres, and photography, can be purchased through the line).

DINING

This isn't a cruise you choose because of its cuisine. That said, the stuff isn't bad—it's just that it's average. Entrees are the kind of thing you'd cook at home for a Sunday dinner or maybe go out to a local restaurant for: Southern fried chicken, crab cakes, linguini with seafood in a cream sauce, roast prime rib, or perhaps veal Parmesan with pasta. Ingredients and seasoning are run-of-the-mill, but if you keep in mind the low price you're paying for the cruise, you'll grab your fork, dig right in, and leave with a smile on your face.

In the **main dining room,** there are two seatings for each meal. At dinner, you're usually offered a choice of three main dishes, plus a pasta that might also serve as the **vegetarian option.** Desserts include an apple strudel, cheesecake, a cheese plate with fruit, and ice cream with your choice of sauces. More celebratory dinners (such as a final-night farewell party) are likely to include surf-and-turf and a "scaloppini à la française." Menus are coordinated to theme nights, the "Remember When" shindig, or a Mexican/Caribbean deck party.

The Bistro Grill aboard the *Enchanted Isle* offers a buffet-style breakfast and lunch, and since early 2000, a buffet-style barbecue dinner is served here once a week (Tues) as a casual alternative to the main dining room. Grilled steaks are served along with Caesar salad and grilled corn on the cob, and there's a bar where you can get baked potatoes with a variety of toppings. The *Enchanted Capri* has no buffet option—all meals are served in the dining room. Every Commodore cruise features a breakfast specialty from Brennan's Restaurant in New Orleans, such as eggs Sardou, a flavorful version of poached eggs with hollandaise sauce atop creamed spinach and artichoke bottoms. A continental breakfast is available from room service. The *Isle*'s bistro also has an espresso bar, where for about $2, caffeine-loving passengers can order an espresso, cappuccino, or other specialty coffee.

An absolutely incredibly monstrously huge **midnight buffet** is offered nightly and features every noshing option you could want, from meats and pastas through crackers and cheese to fruits, desserts, caviar on some nights, and tray upon tray of chocolates. I found the food here to be better, in general, than is offered at regular meals. Go figure. Expect long lines to get to the buffet tables, because *everybody* on board will be there.

ACTIVITIES

Routine activities include bingo, scavenger hunts, trivia games, and **silly poolside games** of the break-the-balloon-in-your-partner's-lap-with-your-butt and stuff-a-hundred-Ping-Pong-balls-into-your-bathing-suit variety. Shipboard versions of the "Liar's Club," "Family Feud" (or in this case "Passenger Feud"), and Newlywed/Not-So-Newlywed games provide lotsa laughs, as does a first-day icebreaker game called **Afternoon Madness,** in which the passengers, broken into teams, have to produce whatever items the cruise director calls for, and then run up with their numbered team paddles to score the first point. It all starts innocently enough, with easy items such as chewing gum, lipstick, and $5 bills being called out, but it's only a matter of time before the proceedings get more risqué, and before you know it, women are struggling to remove their bras (tastefully, of course) and men are struggling to put them on. Before the game winds down, normally staid gentlemen are prancing around in high heels and lipstick, telling the MC why they should be named "Queen of the Ship." (The winner's reason on my cruise? "Because I want you . . . and your brother, too," said to one of the identical-twin cruise directors.) Say what you will about the declining morals of Western civilization, but after a game like this it's a sure bet that the passengers aboard have safely parted company with their inhibitions and are ready for the cruise ahead.

Commodore Fleet Itineraries			
Ship	Home Ports & Season	Itinerary	Other Itineraries
Enchanted Capri	Round-trip from New Orleans; itineraries alternate weekly year-round.	**2-night Cruises to Nowhere:** At sea. **5-night W. Carib:** Playa del Carmen/ Cozumel and Progreso/Mérida (Mexico).	None
Enchanted Isle	Round-trip from New Orleans, year-round.	**7-night W. Carib:** Playa del Carmen/ Cozumel, Grand Cayman, and Montego Bay (Jamaica).	None

Each ship has a **disco** and **casino** that's open until the wee hours (on the *Capri*'s 2-night sailings, the casino is open 24 hours while the ship is in international waters).

Commodore hosts a number of popular **theme cruises** each year on the *Isle,* featuring 1950s rock-and-roll, rhythm and blues, country, big-band music, and even Scottish music. There are also **singles cruises** from time to time, with activities, mixers, and games geared to solo passengers.

CHILDREN'S PROGRAM

Depending on the number of children on board, Commodore offers **supervised activities** for three age groups: 5 to 10, 11 to 15, and 16 to 20 (oddly enough), including parties, scavenger hunts, dancing, movies, and games. Activities are held in the kids' playroom (on the *Isle* only) or in public areas and outside decks. The *Isle* also features the Commodore Cudley mascot, a huge fuzzy bear that mills around the ship to the delight of young kids. There's even a children's tuck-in package for purchase that includes a visit from Cudley bearing cookies and milk, and a photo album. Baby-sitting may be available from a crew member.

ENTERTAINMENT

Musical acts perform throughout the day and evening, including a Caribbean dance band, a pianist, and an orchestra. Each evening offers at least one show, too, which in the past has included a **comedian/impressionist** and a **"Lullabies of Broadway"** revue performed by the Commodore Showstoppers, four young, eager singers who make up with enthusiasm what they lack in costumes, sets, or props. While the comedian's material may touch on adult themes, his act—like most of the activities and entertainment on board—will likely be designed to cater to the ship's wide passenger demographics.

Each ship offers **karaoke** and **passenger lip-synch shows** some evenings, and has a cinema showing recent films.

SERVICE

Service generally wins nothing but favorable comments. Dining-room wait staff manage beautifully in spite of noisy, overcrowded tables and the sometimes impossible demands made upon them—they'll even bring second helpings, and are always friendly and never reserved. Ditto for bartenders in the lounges and deck-side bars. The cabin staff keep the rooms immaculate.

There is **laundry service** available as well as photo processing.

Enchanted Capri

The Verdict

A weird mix of bright Caribbean decor and fixtures left over from the ship's Soviet days make for an offbeat and almost hip atmosphere; buckets o' fun at a dirt-cheap price make for a hell of a bargain.

Enchanted Capri *(photo: Commodore Cruise Line)*

Specifications

Size (in tons)	15,410	Officers	Ukrainian/ International
Number of Cabins	230	Crew	300 (International)
Number of Outside Cabins	112	Passenger/Crew Ratio	2.4 to 1
Cabins with Verandas	0	Year Built	1976
Number of Passengers	460	Last Major Refurbishment	1998

Frommer's Ratings (Scale of 1–5)

Cabin Comfort & Amenities	3	Food & Beverage	3
Ship Cleanliness & Maintenance	3	Pool, Fitness & Spa Facilities	1
Public Comfort/Space	3	Children's Facilities	N/A
Decor	3	Itinerary	3
Service	3	Worth the Money	5

The time: the early 1990s. The place: Ukraine. Following the breakup of the Soviet Union, the Ukrainians began selling off surplus cruise ships, including a passenger-ferry-turned-cruiser named the *Azerbaydzhan,* which became, briefly, the *Island Holiday* for New SeaEscape Cruises before being leased by Commodore and a southern casino operator and rechristened the *Enchanted Capri.*

The transition makes for a bizarre experience. Aside from some garish decor Commodore added to make the vessel look more Caribbean, the *Capri* is still essentially a Soviet ship. The crew (but not the service staff) is Ukrainian, most signs are in Russian with English subtitles, most of the artwork depicts Azerbaijani folk scenes, the wall-mounted crew telephones would look more at home on a nuclear submarine than on a cruise ship, and the life jackets still sport the Communist hammer and sickle. It's as if we'd said, "We won the cold war, now give us your cruise ships."

The onboard experience, though, is 100% American. The *Capri* is a far cry even from modern mainstream ships—it's small, old, and a bit frumpy—but it's a solid vessel, and its deep draft (the amount of ship below the waterline) makes for a stable ride even on the sometimes choppy Gulf of Mexico. For a bargain-basement price, passengers get good-size cabins, passable if not remarkable meals, and almost nonstop entertainment presided over (at least when I was aboard) by identical-twin cruise directors. No kidding: identical twin brothers!

Cabins & Rates

Cabins	Per diems from	Bathtub	Fridge	Hair Dryer	Sitting Area	TV
Inside	$103	no	no	no	no	no
Outside	$119	no	no	no	no	no
Suite	$153	yes	no	no	yes	no

CABINS As aboard many older ships, a good number of cabins are relatively large, particularly for the price. Also like most older ships, cabin sizes vary widely, ranging from a small 100 to nearly 600 square feet. Some inside cabins are larger than the outsides. For instance, Category 4 outside cabins are 140 square feet, Category 8 inside cabins are just over 160 square feet and Category 6 and 7 insides are 132 square feet—keep this in mind when booking since inside cabins are sold at lower rates. Almost all can comfortably accommodate a third passenger, and some can accommodate a fourth. Even the lowest-priced inside cabins are adequate for two people, although their Partridge Family–looking candy-striped bedspreads might take some getting used to. All have air-conditioning and music channels. At the high end, the two Royal Suites are decorated in more elegant colors and at nearly 600 square feet are bigger than some of my friends' apartments, with large bathrooms, enough storage space for 2 or 5 months let alone 2 or 5 days, couches, chairs, makeup mirrors, and large, full-size refrigerators. I've been told that the ship served as a sometimes troop transport in its Soviet days. If so, this is where the generals stayed.

Bathrooms in all cabins are spacious enough that you won't bump into the furnishings. Each has a shower; suites have bathtubs and bidets.

No cabins are designed specifically for wheelchair passengers, and because of the ship's old-fashioned layout, wheelchair users would have a tough time aboard.

PUBLIC AREAS The *Capri* is a real shippy ship, a classic-style oceangoer with well-trod wooden decks, machinery more in evidence than glitz, and wooden-plank rope ladders lying bound under tarps on-deck—ready, it seems, should the passengers decide to stage a pirate raid on one of the oil tankers the ship passes heading down the Mississippi and into the Gulf of Mexico.

The main hub of social activity is the pool deck and open-air bar, all the way aft. From there forward, two promenades and open areas on the top deck and just behind the bow offer considerable sunning space and wonderful observation perches. The small, mirrored disco—located on the lowest passenger deck and appropriately named The Hideaway—is reached via a hard-to-find stairway near the purser's desk. (When I was aboard, the stairway was identified only with a paper sign that read DISCO, stuck with masking tape to a wall, with an arrow pointing down.)

Next door to the disco, the relatively sizable cinema is straight out of 1970s Moscow, with its period decor and long balcony with only three—count em', three—comfortable swivel chairs sitting all by themselves toward the front. In the half-light, it's easy to imagine Leonid Brezhnev and his staff sitting there, playing hooky from the Kremlin. The cinema can serve as a meeting room for business groups on board.

The center of real action is the casino. Bracketed by the gaudily decorated show lounge and more restrained dining room, it opens as soon as the ship reaches the 3-mile international border and stays open all hours when the ship is at sea.

A pleasant enough piano lounge called the Rendezvous is located in the stern. A library/observation lounge, perched at the top of the ship, has few books and sees almost no visitors. A wide-open deck area just behind the bow and below the bridge offers a great wind-in-your-face observation perch.

There is one extraordinarily tiny, coffinlike elevator.

POOL, FITNESS & SPA FACILITIES The ship's one small pool is perched in the stern and is a daytime hot spot even though it's just plain tiny. (An interesting side note: The pool has small windows built into its walls. On the other side of the windows is the Rendezvous Lounge. These windows would, in theory, allow a very clear underwater view of passengers frantically stuffing their bathing suits full of Ping-Pong balls during the traditional goofy pool games. The windows have other uses as well. One woman, obviously a repeat passenger, told me, "See the windows? That's where my friend Bayard mooned everybody. His wife was so mad.")

The ship has no gym or spa, and none of its decks completely encircle the ship, so joggers and walkers must deal with some stairs if they want to get in a long workout.

Enchanted Isle

The Verdict

Ship buffs and fun-seeking bargain-hunters will appreciate this matronly 43-year-old classic liner turned festive party ship.

Enchanted Isle *(photo: Commodore Cruise Line)*

Specifications

Size (in tons)	23,395	Officers	European/American
Number of Cabins	361	Crew	350 (International)
Number of Outside Cabins	289	Passenger/Crew Ratio	2.1 to 1
Cabins with Verandas	2	Year Built	1958
Number of Passengers	725	Last Major Refurbishment	1997

Frommer's Ratings (Scale of 1–5)

Cabin Comfort & Amenities	3	Food & Beverage	3
Ship Cleanliness & Maintenance	3	Pool, Fitness & Spa Facilities	2
Public Comfort/Space	3	Children's Facilities	2
Decor	3	Itinerary	4
Service	3	Worth the Money	4

This vessel, built in 1958 in the Ingalls Shipyard of Mississippi, has undergone more name changes than any other modern liner, having been known as the *Argentina, Monarch Star, Bermuda Star,* and, in the 1970s and early 1980s, as the *Veendam* for the Holland America Line. Commodore acquired the ship in 1989 and named it the *Enchanted Isle.* For a time in 1994, it docked in St. Petersburg, Russia, and served as a floating hotel—the Hotel Commodore—before returning to the Caribbean. In 1997, cabins were overhauled to allow greater flexibility in the configuration of beds, and verandas were added to some of the suites.

Cabins & Rates						
Cabins	**Per diems from**	**Bathtub**	**Fridge**	**Hair Dryer**	**Sitting Area**	**TV**
Inside	$94	no	no	no	no	yes
Outside	$110	some	no	no	no	yes
Suite	$130	yes	no	no	yes	yes

CABINS   The ship has a large number of outside cabins with views—only 77 of the 361 cabins are insides. There are 11 cabin categories, ranging from six deluxe suites with sitting areas to a pair of deluxe outside cabins with private balconies to somewhat cramped inside cabins with upper and lower berths. Overall, though, many cabins are roomy—the smallest are 120 square feet (not roomy) and the largest are nearly 300 square feet (very roomy).

Cabins show wear and tear, but the maintenance is top-notch, and a 1997 renovation added additional flexibility to the variety of sleeping configurations available in many of them. All cabins have TVs, telephones, air-conditioning, and music channels. There are no in-cabin safes, but passengers can check their valuables at the purser's desk. There's plenty of drawer and closet space (unless there's a fourth passenger, and then it's very tight). Many cabins have single beds that can be converted to double beds. The spotless, tiled bathrooms are large if a bit worn and contain no hair dryers or bathrobes, but a few offer bidets. Electrical outlets are a bit scarce.

If ocean views are important to you, avoid outside cabins on the Navigation Deck, since the primary view here is of lifeboats. The views from cabins 222, 223, and 224 are not obstructed. Cabins on the Boat Deck open onto the public promenade, which cuts down on your privacy (unless you close the curtains).

In the lower-level cabins, passengers complain of noise, as the walls seem to be too thin; engine humming and the workings of the crew can be bothersome. There is also no elevator access to cabins on the lowest deck, but all this inconvenience might be worth it if you're on a budget.

Although the line claims to have two cabins accessible to wheelchair users, this isn't the best ship for people with mobility problems. Some public-room doorways have ledges, but they are fitted with ramps; elevators are accessible to wheelchair users.

PUBLIC AREAS   Although the rather plainly decorated, not-very-bright public rooms are polished daily, they look as though they've hosted untold thousands before you—because they have. Beyond the nicks and dents, if you look hard you can still see vestiges of the ship's early art-deco design.

As is normal on older, many-times reconfigured ships, the public areas are oddly shaped. Those on the Promenade Deck stretch the full length aft to the main pool and buffet area. There's a casino, show lounge, and a handful of bars/lounges where you're sure to find a cozy corner.

There's also a small library (but serious readers should bring their own books), a card/writing room, and a movie theater that's also the disco at night. If you want to slip away, go to the Spyglass Lounge, an observation lounge on the Sun Deck, which most passengers don't seem to discover until near the voyage's end.

The ship has a small video-game room and a children's playroom.

POOL, FITNESS & SPA FACILITIES   Deck space is adequate for the number of passengers. The ship's tiered aft decks offer three levels of sunbathing spots, with the outside swimming pool on the Promenade Deck. On the Sports Deck, there's aerobics, jogging, and shuffleboard. The minuscule, windowless gym, with Nautilus, free weights, cardiovascular equipment, and not much else, can get crowded fast. Way down on the Theatre Deck is a small beauty salon and a massage room.

Mediterranean Shipping Cruises

420 Fifth Ave., New York, NY 10018. ☎ **800/666-9333** or 212/764-4800. Fax 212/764-8593.

THE LINE IN A NUTSHELL   While the line's one Caribbean ship, the *Melody*, isn't the fanciest afloat, it is well laid out and roomy and offers a pair of great, port-packed, and low-priced 11-night itineraries catering to Europeans and North Americans.

THE EXPERIENCE   A relative newcomer to the North American cruise market, Mediterranean Shipping Cruises is an Italian company that sails its three ships mostly in the Mediterranean. Even in the Caribbean, about half of the passengers are European.

The one ship the line position in the Caribbean, the 1,076-passenger *Melody*, once sailed as the Big Red *Star/Ship Atlantic* for Premier Cruise Lines, and before that as the *Atlantic* for Home Lines. It's a generally well-laid-out ship and a pretty good bargain to boot, and if you and your family sailed aboard the ship before, in its Premier days, expect déjà vu: Other than painting the ship's red hull white, MSC made next to no changes to the ship's decor, which was last refurbished in early 1997. The big change that has occurred is that when the *Melody* operated as a Big Red Boat, it was child-oriented. That is no longer the case. This is now a ship for adults, with supervised children's activities provided when demand warrants (even if there are only a few kids on board, there will be supervised activities offered, at least for a few hours a day).

Unlike ships of the other Italian line, Costa, the *Melody* is older, smaller, and less plush, and its product less glossy and well rehearsed. To a point, the Italianness of the line adds a touch of European holiday to your Caribbean jaunt, but by no means should you expect elegance. At its worst, this ship is dowdy and a bit creaky. At its best, it can be fun and filled with Neapolitan flair. Above all, it's affordable.

Pros

- **International flair.** While not as pervasive as Costa's, the ship's Italian flavor and a more international passenger mix create a more exotic onboard experience than you'll find aboard most Caribbean ships.
- **Well-laid-out and spacious public rooms.** It's not difficult to navigate between the two decks housing the entertainment lounges, bars, casino, Lido restaurant, shops, fitness area, and pool.
- Cheapo rates. The 11-night Caribbean cruises start at $995 per person.

Cons

- **Low-brow dining.** The scene in the Galaxy Restaurant tends to be crowded, loud, bright, and generally like a cafeteria.
- **Few windows.** Most of the public areas get very little natural light and can be a bit drab.

Compared with the other Budget lines, here's how MSC rates:					
	poor	fair	good	excellent	outstanding
Enjoyment Factor			✓		
Dining			✓		
Activities			✓		
Children's Program		✓			
Entertainment			✓		
Service			✓		
Overall Value			✓		

MELODY: A CATCHY TUNE (& CHEAP, TOO)

In 1985, one of MSC's corporate predecessors, Flotta Lauro, became infamous as the owner of the *Achille Lauro,* whose passengers endured a much-publicized terrorist attack off the coast of Egypt. Partly because of the bad publicity that ensued, the company changed its name to StarLauro Cruises and then, in 1996, to Mediterranean Shipping Cruises. In 1998, the company expanded from its European base into the rapidly growing Caribbean market, and offers 11-night eastern and western Caribbean itineraries from Fort Lauderdale.

THE FLEET

The 1,056-passenger, 36,500-ton *Melody,* MSC's only Caribbean ship, formerly sailed as the Big Red *Star/Ship Atlantic* for Premier Cruise Line. Aside from a paint job, the line has made virtually no changes to the ship since its purchase.

MSC has two other ships under its flag. The *Monterey,* built in 1952, and the *Rhapsody,* built in 1974, both offer itineraries in the Mediterranean.

PASSENGER PROFILE

Unlike most of the lines reviewed in this book, MSC is an all-Italian entity that's only recently begun marketing in North America. Consequently, you're likely to have a higher percentage of Europeans aboard, although it's safe to say about half of the passengers are from North America. Americans aboard this line tend to be older and a bit more staid than many of the Europeans who fly into Fort Lauderdale as part of inexpensive package trips. European passengers tend to be younger, sometimes with children.

DINING

Lunch and dinner are both served in two seatings (and breakfast in one seating) in the big, well-lit Galaxy Restaurant, down close to the waterline and straddling the entire width of the ship. **Cuisine** is primarily Italian and continental, and might include rolled prosciutto in a gelatin glaze, creamed chicken in puff pastry, a Caesar salad Palmiere, sottadito of lamb with balsamic vinegar and "Pont-neuf" potatoes, and flambéed crêpes "Vesuvio." Appetizers often include a serving of sevruga caviar or pâté Maison. The wine list is mostly made up of well-chosen Italian vintages.

Buffet-style breakfast and lunch are served on the pool deck.

ACTIVITIES

This nearly 20-year-old ship doesn't offer the range of amenities and state-of-the-art distractions you'll find on the big new megaships. There are no golf ranges, computer rooms, water slides, or paddle-tennis and basketball courts. That said, there's still plenty going on to keep passengers busy. There's a **casino** and **disco,** plus activities like bridge, cards, jigsaw puzzles, sunset cocktail parties with dance music, poolside contests, a visit to the small gym or beauty salon, a massage, stretch-and-tone aerobics classes, and movies in the theater.

CHILDREN'S PROGRAM

A low-tech, low-key indoor/outdoor **children's center** offers a modest selection of activities and a kids' wading pool, but in general there are few efforts to segregate children into their own areas. Children's programs are run depending on the number of children aboard, mostly during the holidays and summer. **Baby-sitting** by a crew member can usually be arranged, for about $10 or more an hour.

ENTERTAINMENT

There's at least one singer and a **musical group** that trots out danceable show tunes and favorites from both sides of the Atlantic, plus an occasional **comedian.**

Mediterranean Shipping Fleet Itineraries

Ship	Home Ports & Season	Itinerary	Other Itineraries
Melody	Round-trip from Fort Lauderdale; itineraries alternate between Jan and Apr.	**11-night W. Carib/partial Panama Canal:** Montego Bay (Jamaica), Cartagena (Colombia), Partial transit of Panama Canal, Puerto Limón (Costa Rica), and Key West. **11-night E. Carib:** St. Thomas, Antigua, Grenada, St. Lucia, Guadeloupe, Tortola, and Nassau.	Mediterranean

You won't find any of the tongue-in-cheek "Italian-style" diversions, like toga parties by the pool, that receive such attention at Costa. You're also unlikely to find such bizarre mind-benders as "stuff your bikini with Ping-Pong balls" contests, which pop up aboard some other cruise lines. Expect lots of emphasis on sunbathing, reading, mealtimes, and visits to the ports of call.

SERVICE

Overall, the *Melody* is manned by career staffers, many from Italy, and benefits from that country's superb tradition of attentive service.

There is laundry service available, but no self-service launderettes.

Melody

The Verdict

While not the prettiest thing on the high seas, this well-laid-out ship offers lots to do and relatively roomy spaces in which to do it.

Melody *(photo: Mediterranean Shipping Cruises)*

Specifications

Size (in tons)	36,000	Officers	Italian
Number of Cabins	538	Crew	539 (International)
Number of Outside Cabins	371	Passenger/Crew Ratio	2 to 1
Cabins with Verandas	0	Year Built	1982
Number of Passengers	1,076	Last Major Refurbishment	1997

Frommer's Ratings (Scale of 1–5)

Cabin Comfort & Amenities	3	Food & Beverage	3
Ship Cleanliness & Maintenance	4	Pool, Fitness & Spa Facilities	3
Public Comfort/Space	4	Children's Facilities	2
Decor	3	Itinerary	3
Service	4	Worth the Money	5

This medium-size ship was built in the style of a classic ocean liner, with a layout of decks and public areas originally conceived for long-haul sailings. There's more weight and metal in this ship's design than in more-modern vessels, where lighter materials and structural innovations sometimes create a cookie-cutter similarity. Teakwood decks and heavy doors with the traditional raised sill are commonplace—children often have to experiment to learn to open them. Real round portholes—an increasing rarity in these picture-window days—have been retained in many instances, and provide a nice reminder of traditional ship design.

If you opt for a cruise aboard this ship, remember that many thousands of nautical miles have washed beneath its hull, and that several previous owners used it hard and intensely—not least in its days as Premier's *Big Red Boat,* when it carried throngs of children around the Caribbean. Very few cosmetic or architectural changes have been made since the ship's acquisition by MSC in 1997.

Cabins & Rates						
Cabins	Per diems from	Bathtub	Fridge	Hair Dryer	Sitting Area	TV
Inside	$80	no	no	no	no	yes
Outside	$122	some	no	no	some	yes
Suite	$172	yes	yes	no	yes	yes

CABINS   The relatively roomy cabins aboard *Melody* come in nine different configurations, with the majority of inside and outside cabins no smaller than about 185 square feet. Suites, which can accommodate four or five people and are geared to families, are a bit more plush, with square footage of between 280 and 440 square feet.

Many cabins sleep between two and five occupants with upper berths and, in some cases, sofa beds. This can make shipboard density high if lots of the third, fourth, and fifth berths are occupied. Busy patterned fabrics of curtains and bedding tend to make cabins appear smaller than they are.

Furniture in all cabins is of the durable, indestructible variety. To make it easier for passengers to find their way home, cabin doors are color-coded in blue, yellow, green, or purple, with the interior monochromes matching the color of the doors' exterior. Each cabin has a TV and music channels. Bathrooms are as family-friendly as possible, with angles rounded off to spare you any bumps and bruises.

Four cabins are wheelchair accessible.

PUBLIC AREAS   The decor is cheerful, but definitely feels like vintage early 1980s, with lights twinkling along shiny metallic surfaces and bright but not jarring color schemes. The Galaxy Restaurant is very cafeteria-like, with lots of chrome and flimsy, uncomfortable chairs. The only somber-looking place is the deliberately darkened and artsy-looking jazz pub space, the Blue Riband.

There are four bars aboard, and cabaret and comedy acts are presented at Club Universe. There's also a photo gallery, an unmemorable casino that's set amidships on the Lounge Deck, and a video arcade. There's no library, although some books are available (err on the side of caution: pack your own). The Mercury Theater shows movies from both sides of the Atlantic.

The ship has a kids' recreation center, along with a wading pool, sequestered on the aft Premier Deck. There's also an infirmary.

POOL, FITNESS & SPA FACILITIES   *Melody* has two swimming pools, one kids' wading pool, and three whirlpools, all of which can get quite full. One of the pools is covered by a retractable magrodome roof. The ship's tiered aft decks offer lots of prime spots for sunbathing.

There's a windowless gym with a couple of massage rooms and a beauty salon. There's an unobstructed jogging track on the Sun Deck, plus setups for volleyball, aerobics classes, Ping-Pong, and shuffleboard on the ship's uppermost deck.

Premier Cruise Lines

400 Challenger Rd., Cape Canaveral, FL 32920. ☎ **800/990-7770** or 407/783-5061. Fax 407/784-0954. www.premiercruises.com.

THE LINE IN A NUTSHELL Its ships aren't spring chickens, but Premier's low prices and fleet of diverse oldies has something to please almost everyone, from families with kids to older folks and ship lovers, to anyone looking for a cheap cruise and a unique itinerary. Now if we could only keep up with the name changes, paint jobs, and itinerary switches the company keeps announcing . . .

THE EXPERIENCE The ambiance aboard all of Premier's Caribbean ships is unpretentious and undemanding, making them a good choice for first-time cruisers. The ships range in age from 36 to 43 years old, and while they can't hide their wear and tear, they continue to offer decent cruises. Along with the newly acquired *Big Red Boat II,* the *Big Red Boat I* continues to be geared to families with kids. For ship lovers and nostalgic types, the *Rembrandt* is the best ship in the fleet, the most elegant and spacious and closest to its original grandeur. The *SeaBreeze* and *IslandBreeze/Big Red Boat III* are the least special of the five, but recent refurbishments have improved them and created more of a nautical flavor; their itineraries are some of their best features.

Don't expect glamour or anything approaching cutting-edge technology. A Premier cruise is good value for the money, but keep in mind that you may have to endure elbow-to-elbow people if your ship is full, and amenities that are acceptable but not remarkable. It's all a matter of being realistic about your expectations.

Pros

- *Big Red Boat I* and *II:* **Great for kids.** With their supervised programs for five age groups and spacious indoor/outdoor play area, these two are some of the industry's family-friendliest.
- *Rembrandt:* The *Rembrandt* is the best-preserved classic ocean liner sailing today, with a wealth of art-deco and funky late-fifties-/early-sixties-style decor and furnishings.
- *Sea Breeze* and *Big Red Boats II* and *III:* Unique itineraries.

Cons

- **Crowds.** When the *Big Red Boat I* and *SeaBreeze* are carrying full loads, you'll notice crowded public areas and lines at buffets and getting on and off the ship.
- **Inconsistent service.** As Premier struggles to find its niche, the service on its ships seems to struggle at times, too.

Compared with the other Budget lines, here's how Premier rates:					
	poor	fair	good	excellent	outstanding
Enjoyment Factor				✓	
Dining			✓		
Activities				✓	
Children's Program		✓*			✓**
Entertainment				✓	
Service				✓	
Overall Value					✓

* *SeaBreeze, Big Red Boat III, and Rembrandt.* ** *Big Red Boat I and II.*

PREMIER: FICKLE FLEET OF OLD-TIMERS

Premier was formed in 1997 after Florida-based Cruise Holdings, Inc. decided to merge its Dolphin, Seawind, and Premier Cruise Line brands into one line. The new company started with five ships, and then added a sixth, the *Rembrandt* (recently renamed *Big Red Boat IV*), but in 1999 it signed agreements to charter its *Seawind Crown* and *OceanBreeze* for the foreseeable future, taking them out of the North American market (the *OceanBreeze* was later sold to Imperial Majesty Cruise Line, which operates 2-night cruises from Florida to the Bahamas), then announced plans to acquire another ship, the *Edinburgh Castle,* rename it *Big Red Boat II,* and refit it with extensive facilities for kids. So, at press time, there were five ships plying the Caribbean for the North American market. The Premier ships are old warhorses that have washed about a zillion miles of ocean beneath their bows. They're not opulent, but cruise liners don't come much tougher.

The original Premier Cruise Lines gained fame for its Big Red Boats, which, in association with Disney, spent years ferrying families on 3- and 4-day cruises between Port Canaveral and the oft-visited, heavily touristed ports in the Bahamas. The line's success no doubt influenced Disney to jump into the cruise market with both flashy, Disneyfied feet. Now that the *Disney Magic* is up and running, the product offered aboard today's *Big Red Boat I* and *II* looks downright antiquated by comparison—but, on the other hand, it's offered at a much more down-market price.

Since its Disney days, Premier has struggled to find its niche, with company president Bruce Nierenberg continually trying new things to see what sticks—sometimes they do, sometimes they don't. For instance, in late 1999, the line introduced 3- and 4-night cruises out of Puerto Vallarta and Cancún, Mexico, then promptly canceled the whole program just months later. Later in the year something called "seven-star service" was announced and actually implemented. (How far is this star thing going to go? Will we soon seen 10-star or 27-star service? That's why you see no ratings stars in this book. Not one.)

Are you ready for this year's batch of changes? First of all, the line changed its name back from Premier Cruises to Premier Cruise Lines, then, late in 1999, announced it was changing the names of three of its ships to include the successful brand name "Big Red Boat," appending II, III, and IV to the names to distinguish them. (So for now—or at least for as long as I can hold my breath—Premier's North America–based fleet comprises four Big Red Boats plus the *SeaBreeze.*) Oh, and did I mention, at press time, the plan was to paint their hulls red? At least the hulls of the *Big Red Boat III* (formerly *IslandBreeze*) and the *Big Red Boat II* (formerly the *Edinburg Castle,* which joined the fleet in mid-2000). Whether the venerated *Rembrandt* (formerly Holland America's *Rotterdam V*) also goes under the brush and is renamed Big Red Boat IV is still to be seen, though at press time it looked like a grass-roots letter-writing campaign, among other things, might have succeeded in getting Premier to reverse its original decision and leave it more or less as is. Let's hope this is true. The proposed conversion would be a crime.

Other new programs include the *IslandBreeze/Big Red Boat III* moving to Houston, Texas, in May of 2000 to do year-round Mexico cruises. Despite all the dizzying changes, you have to give Premier a hand for trying!

THE FLEET

All five ships are at least 36 years old, each had long and illustrious careers with various cruise lines before being bought by Premier, and each has gone through more name changes than a struggling cabaret act looking for a lucky break. The 842-passenger,

21,010-ton *SeaBreeze* was built in 1958 as Costa's luxury flagship *Federico C.,* and in 1983 was bought by Premier, extensively refurbished, and renamed the *Royale.* It underwent another refit under Dolphin in 1989 and was renamed the *SeaBreeze.* The 1,116-passenger, 38,772-ton *Big Red Boat I* was built in 1965 as Home Lines' *Oceanic,* then was renamed *Star/Ship Oceanic* under the original Premier. The 967-passenger, 35,000-ton *Big Red Boat II* was built in 1966 as Costa's *Eugenio C.* and later operated as the *EugenioCosta,* before being renamed the *Edinburgh Castle* in 1998 when an outfit called Direct Cruises brought it to New York for an ill-fated stint as a gambling ship for Manhattan Cruises. The 1,146-passenger, 31,793-ton *Big Red Boat III* was built in 1961 as the *Transvaal Castle* (a few years later renamed the *s.a. Vaal*), a passenger/mail ship for the Union-Castle Steamship line. Then it was purchased and rebuilt in 1977 by Carnival and renamed the *Festivale* before joining Dolphin Cruise Line in 1996 and renamed the *IslandBreeze.* The 1,074-passenger, 38,645-ton *Rembrandt* was built in 1959 as Holland America's flagship *Rotterdam V,* and sailed in that capacity until its acquisition by Premier in 1997. Modernization on the other ships has given them a somewhat cheap, though cheerful, look, but *Rembrandt* maintains a solid, dignified poise and has aged quite gracefully without plastic surgery. Let's just hope they don't go and screw it up.

PASSENGER PROFILE

Because of its diverse fleet, Premier attracts a diverse lot. The link between them all? They're budget seekers. All five ships tend to attract a lot of first-timers—or if they've sailed before, it's likely to have been aboard one of the company's corporate predecessors, Dolphin or Seawind, or aboard other budget lines such as Commodore or Regal—as well as a good percentage of the Florida-based family and honeymoon trade. You'll find passengers of all ages, 20- and 30-something to retirees. The *Rembrandt* tends to draw an older clientele attracted to the ship's venerated history and classic-liner ambiance. Passengers have a good time aboard these boats, but it's not the all-night party circuit you'll find on Carnival.

Passenger lists aboard the *Big Red Boat* and the *Big Red Boat II* include lots and lots of kids. The ships also attract a fair number of international guests. Their midweek cruises are likely to be less crowded than weekend cruises, and with noticeably fewer children. Cruises during school holidays—Christmas, Easter, summer vacations—have the highest percentages of children and are the most crowded.

DINING

Food aboard Premier ships is of the hotel-banquet variety and is somewhat limited in selection and presentation. If you don't expect much, you won't be disappointed.

All three vessels have two seatings each for breakfast, lunch, and dinner. Dining options, especially at lunch, are supplemented with offerings from an alfresco on-deck buffet. Late-night hunger pangs can be assuaged at the **midnight buffets,** a standard feature. There are themed dinners, 24-hour room service, a poolside grill, and pizza and ice-cream counters. Afternoon tea is a regular feature, and is most elaborate on the *Rembrandt.*

Dining rooms, especially aboard The *Big Red Boat I* and *SeaBreeze,* can be crowded and noisy. There's often piano music during dinner and special culinary theme nights. Likewise, buffets draw crowds too, and are lavish, although quantity usually wins out over quality. Relatively speaking, the dining ambiance is the most elegant (although still fairly informal) aboard the *Rembrandt.*

Cuisine aboard all the line's ships is filling and sometimes savory, but isn't spectacular. Examples might include baked Alaskan salmon with a dill mousseline sauce, roast prime rib of beef with horseradish sauce, duckling à l'orange, and flaming cherries jubilee. As a change of pace, some meals might, for example, feature Greek dishes such as lamb kebabs, souvlaki, or moussaka. **Vegetarian dishes** are available, and there's always a **light and healthy option** that's lower in salt, fat, and calories.

Children's menus feature popular standards like chicken nuggets, burgers, fish sticks, pizza, spaghetti and meatballs, and, in some cases, tacos.

ACTIVITIES

Among the featured activities might be bingo, bridge, trivia games, horse racing, wine tastings, art auctions, movies, napkin-folding lessons, karaoke, Name That Tune, newlywed and not-so-newlywed games, and singles mixers. Many guests find their days at sea richly overscheduled and a lot more fun than they'd expected.

On the *Rembrandt,* activities are more sedate, but include much of the above plus things like charades, Pictionary, and spa and salon demonstrations. There are gentleman hosts on board to dance with ladies in need of a partner.

All of Premier's vessels have **casinos** and glittery **discos.** Aboard all the ships except The *Big Red Boat,* discos are far enough from cabins that they don't disturb sleeping passengers. Aboard The *Big Red Boat,* think twice before booking stern-side cabins on the Continental Deck, which are directly under that ship's disco. Likewise, on the *BRB III* far-forward cabins on the Empress Deck are right below the disco.

CHILDREN'S PROGRAM

Premier now has two of the most family-friendly ships in the industry. The *Big Red Boat I* and The *Big Red Boat II* both employ over a dozen full-time youth counselors, each of whom has past training in child care, education, nursing, or some related field. Both ships have supervised activities for children in five different age categories (2 to 4, 5 to 7, 8 to 10, 11 to 13, and 14 to 17), running all day long. In certain ports, children even have the option of heading off on their own (chaperoned) shore excursions, allowing parents to pursue their own land or sea activities.

The *Big Red Boat I* contains an accessory-packed area aft on the Premier Deck, with a large **playroom** and outdoor-deck play space with a wading pool (all encircled with a net to keep children from falling overboard), which is the second-best children's recreation center after Disney in the 3- and 4-night cruise market. There's a kid-oriented ice-cream parlor, a video arcade, and a teen center. The newly created kids facilities on The *Big Red Boat II* boast four different playrooms, including a disco/club for teens only and a video arcade.

Group baby-sitting is available for kids at least 2 years of age from 10pm to 2am the following morning. The cost is $5 per hour for the first child and $3 per hour for each additional child.

The *BRB III* also has a playroom and supervised kids' facilities, functioning year-round. On the *SeaBreeze* and *Rembrandt* there are small playrooms and limited children's activities available during the summer and over holidays for ages 3 to 13, but nothing close to what's provided on The *Big Red Boat I* and *II*.

In the past, Premier has had Disney and then Looney Tunes characters and themes aboard ship, but contracts for these have now expired. At press time, Premier said it would soon have its own cast of warm and fuzzy characters running around the ship.

ENTERTAINMENT

Some passengers find Premier's entertainment quite cheerful and upbeat, although few consider it top-tier. Most evenings, there's some kind of **cabaret act,** and a live dance band or a singer performs in one of the bars. The line's **Legends in Concert** shows are

Premier Fleet Itineraries

Ship	Home Ports & Season	Itinerary	Other Itineraries
The Big Red Boat I	Round-trip from Port Canaveral; itineraries alternate year-round.	**3- and 4-night Bahamas:** Nassau and Salt Cay.	None
Big Red Boat II	Round-trip from Tampa, Oct–Apr.	**7-night W. Carib:** Cozumel, Roatán (Honduras), Belize, and Key West.	Eastern Canada
Big Red Boat III (IslandBreeze)	Round-trip from Houston, year-round.	**7-night W. Carib:** Vera Cruz, Cozumel, and Playa del Carmen.	None
Rembrandt	Round-trip from Port Canaveral, Oct–Apr.	**7-night E. Carib:** St. John/St. Thomas, San Juan, Nassau, and Nassau.	Eastern Canada, Alaska
SeaBreeze	Round-trip from Fort Lauderdale, Oct–Apr.	**7-night W. Carib:** Cozumel, Roatán (Honduras), Belize, and Key West.	Eastern Canada

a big hit, with entertainers impersonating the greats like Elvis and Madonna. **Karaoke** is popular across the fleet and so are theme nights (like 1950s nights). Each ship has a movie theater that can also be used for meetings.

Aboard The *Big Red Boat,* entertainment has a distinct and not-always-subtle theme: Families that sail together stay together. So don't expect either sophistication or raunchy humor.

On the *Rembrandt,* dancing and hobnobbing in cozy piano lounges are more the norm. The formal and theme dance nights in the ship's glamorous Ritz Carlton Lounge (with dance bands playing popular country and western, 1950s favorites, and ballroom tunes) bring out the rhythm in everyone. The away-from-it-all Sky Bar is a romantic venue for a taste of caviar, pâté de foie gras, and champagne before dinner (for a charge, of course). The funky Ambassador Lounge is another place to merely hang out, listening to music and sipping a drink. The lovely Smoking Room has a pianist who draws good crowds late in the day and after dinner. There are thoroughly routine Vegas-style performances in the show lounge (originally built as a cinema), and some nights there might be a magician, comedian, or soloist.

SERVICE

While service is not the most polished at sea, considering the low cost of the cruises, it's good, and for the most part the staff is friendly and accommodating. The staff on The *Big Red Boat I* and *II* is very patient and indulgent with children, even in difficult moments, and on the *Rembrandt* many of the officers and crew display a palpable pride in their gracious ship.

As aboard most of the mainstream and upscale lines, Premier's ships stock a nice toiletry set in each cabin bathroom, with shampoo, conditioner, lotion, and soap.

The *Rembrandt* is the only ship with a self-service launderette, although all the rest do offer **laundry service** through the cabin stewards.

The "seven star" service enhancements Premier announced in 1999 and continues to trumpet boil down to complimentary amenities for all passengers, like terry bathrobes passengers can take home with them and nightly pillow sweets including a Godiva chocolate one night, and chocolate-dipped strawberries and petit fors on others. Not bad!

Some Special Discount

Single-Parent Rates: Single parents pay the regular per person rates (no supplement) and kids under 17 pay the third/fourth/fifth passenger rates. **Senior Rates:** Senior citizens (over 55) and their spouses or guests (of whatever age group) receive discounts of 10% off their cruise when booking any nonsuite-category cabin. **Family Discounts:** Children under 2 sail free (but must pay port charges). Also, when a family books three nonsuite cabins for at least 10 guests, the first and second guest in each of the three cabins gets a 10% discount. **Honeymoon/Anniversary Discounts:** Honeymooners and couples celebrating their anniversaries within a week of their cruise get complimentary champagne.

Big Red Boat I •
Big Red Boat II

The Verdict

In the family and kids department, these ships know their stuff. While not new and glamorous like the Disney ships, these old-timers hold their own.

Big Red Boat I *(photo: Premier)*

Specifications

Size (in tons)		Officers	Greek/International
Big Red Boat I	38,772	Crew	(International)
Big Red Boat II	35,000	*Big Red Boat I*	565
Number of Cabins		*Big Red Boat II*	568
Big Red Boat I	574	Passenger/Crew Ratio	
Big Red Boat II	484	*Big Red Boat I*	2.0 to 1
Number of Outside Cabins		*Big Red Boat II*	1.7 to 1
Big Red Boat I	261	Year Built	
Big Red Boat II	265	*Big Red Boat I*	1965
Cabins with Verandas		*Big Red Boat II*	1966
Big Red Boat I	21	Last Major Refurbishment	
Big Red Boat II	0	*Big Red Boat I*	1997
Number of Passengers		*Big Red Boat II*	2000
Big Red Boat I	1,116		
Big Red Boat II	967		

Frommer's Ratings (Scale of 1–5)*

Cabin Comfort & Amenities	3	Pool, Fitness & Spa Facilities	3
Ship Cleanliness & Maintenance	3	Children's Facilities	5
Public Comfort/Space	4	Itinerary	4
Decor	3	Worth the Money	5

Ratings based on Big Red Boat I.

Rule no. 1 when considering a cruise on *The Big Red Boat:* You've either got to have kids of your own or like being around them *a lot.* These are both parents-with-kids kinds of ships.

The Big Red Boat I, a pioneer in family cruising, has been catering to families since the 1980s. Supervised programs are offered for children in five age groups. Aside from its fire-hydrant-red hull, it's a dignified and stately vessel, a worthy example of the way ocean liners used to be built. Note that phrase "used to": This is by no means a modern, state-of-the-art megaship with all the newfangled gadgets. No matter how many coats of red paint get slapped on, there's no denying that it's an elderly ship whose wrinkles show. However, most passengers, both children and adults, seem more concerned with the magic of their first ocean voyage than with architectural niceties.

Ditto for the *Big Red Boat II,* which was built as Costa's *Eugenio C.* in the early 1960s and later operated as the *EugenioCosta,* then as the *Edinburgh Castle* when an outfit called Direct Cruises brought the ship to New York in 1998 for an ill-fated stint as a gambling ship for Manhattan Cruises. That didn't last long and Premier scooped it up and spent several million dollars adding extensive children's facilities and even a computer center with E-mail access—or at least that's what they tell me. The fact is, the *Big Red Boat II* has been plagued by problems during what has, at this writing, been its first month of service. It was unexplainedly late coming into port in New York to begin summer coastal cruises in June 2000, when I took a boat down into the harbor to get a first look at it. After that, things only went downhill. Several preview open-houses for the travel trade were cancelled, and my repeated attempts to get aboard independently met with no luck. When the ship finally did sail, after many delays (and without me), it suffered engine and air conditioning problems that have at this writing reportedly been resolved, but that probably explain the line's apparent initial reluctance to let press and travel agents aboard. With luck, the vessel will be ship-shape by the time you read this, but at this point all I can report is that, from the outside at least, the *BRB II* has a great old ocean liner profile. Inside? That'll have to wait till *Caribbean Cruises 2002.* For now, this review is based almost entirely on *Big Red Boat I,* with a few known facts about *BRB II* sprinkled in.

Cabins & Rates*

Cabins	Per diems from	Bathtub	Fridge	Hair Dryer	Sitting Area	TV
Inside	$91	no	no	no	no	yes
Outside	$141	some	no	no	some	yes
Suite	$213	yes	yes	yes	yes	yes

All rates and info for BRBI only.

CABINS Aboard the *Big Red Boat I,* some of the outside cabins are gratifyingly large, with suites up to 500 square feet, 21 of them with private verandas. There are more inside cabins on this ship than outside ones, and overall quite a variety of sizes and shapes. The smallest inside cabins, Categories J and K, are about 80 square feet, while Category I insides are a bit bigger, many at about 112 square feet. Configured with upper berths and sofa beds, cabins sleep between two and five. Furniture is relatively solid, and the decor is simple. To make it easier for kids to find their way home, cabin doors are color-coded. Bathrooms are family-friendly, with rounded angles. Many of the outside cabins on the Premier Deck have views that are partially blocked by lifeboats.

Because of the density of cabins compared to most other cruise lines, there's lots more activity and noise in hallways, especially during embarkation and disembarkation.

Aboard the *Big Red Boat II,* many of the cabins can accommodate three to six passengers, which explains why the ship carries 967 passengers double occupancy and a whopping 1,659 passengers if all berths are filled. All cabins have TVs and telephones.

Aboard the *BRB I* there is only one cabin designed for passengers with disabilities. Aboard the *BRB II* there are four. These ships are not the best equipped for wheelchair users.

PUBLIC AREAS   The interior design of the *BRB I* is based on shiny metallic surfaces, lots of twinkling lights, and bright but not jarring colors. All told, there are five bars on board (including a couple of somewhat cozy ones, like the Heroes and Legends jazz pub, where adults can hide from the constant barrage of kiddiedom) plus a casino and several lounges where entertainment is offered. The ship's large, banquet-hall-like restaurant, the Seven Continents dining room, can get mighty noisy and isn't the most elegant place you'll ever dine.

POOL, FITNESS & SPA FACILITIES   On the *Big Red Boat I* there are two swimming pools and two whirlpools, plus a kids' wading pool. Both pools can be covered by a retractable glass roof. There's a small windowless gym on the Sun Deck and an equally small beauty salon and massage room down on the Continental Deck. Aerobics classes are offered on an outside deck or in an unused public lounge, and there is shuffleboard, a combo volleyball/basketball/practice tennis court, Ping-Pong, and, on the Sun Deck, an unobstructed jogging track.

Big Red Boat III/ IslandBreeze

The Verdict

While it's certainly not the most polished or cutting edge, this midsize ocean liner offers a wonderful glimpse of the past, and more importantly, a casual, unpretentious Caribbean cruise out of Houston at bargain-basement rates.

Big Red Boat III / IslandBreeze *(photo: Premier)*

Specifications

Size (in tons)	31,793	Officers	International
Number of Cabins	580	Crew	612 (International)
Number of Outside Cabins	230	Passenger/Crew Ratio	1.9 to 1
Cabins with Verandas	8	Year Built	1961
Number of Passengers	1,146	Last Major Refurbishment	1997

Frommer's Ratings (Scale of 1–5)

Cabin Comfort & Amenities	3	Food & Beverage	3
Ship Cleanliness & Maintenance	3	Pool, Fitness & Spa Facilities	3
Public Comfort/Space	3	Children's Facilities	1
Decor	3	Itinerary	4
Service	3	Worth the Money	4

With its long lines and tiered decks, this shippy ship is a classic and retains both vestiges of the past—with its sweeping profile, long tiered foredeck, and a decent amount of its original wood and brass fittings—as well as the glitzy touches and hodgepodge modern design imposed on the ship during its long stint as a Carnival ship. Built in 1961 as a passenger/mail ship called the *Transvaal Castle* for the Union-Castle Steamship line, it was purchased and rebuilt in 1977 by Carnival and renamed the *Festivale,* then joined Dolphin Cruise Line (a line which Premier absorbed in 1997) in 1996 and was renamed the *IslandBreeze.*

As was prevalent during the era it was built, over half of this ship's cabins are inside. And because of its somewhat cluttered layout of public rooms, when the ship is full you'll know it.

Cabins & Rates

Cabins	Per diems from	Bathtub	Fridge	Hair Dryer	Sitting Area	TV
Inside	$113	no	no	no	no	no
Outside	$141	no	no	no	no	no
Suite	$227	yes	no	no	yes	no

CABINS   Cabins come in 11 categories, with more than half being inside cabins (54%). While they of course don't have windows, some (categories G and H) are actually larger than some of the outside doubles. The smallest cabins are tiny, with the J- and K-Category insides hovering around 85 square feet and the H-Category insides in the neighborhood of 115 square feet. The largest suites are 237 square feet. Despite a freshening up in 1997, cabins are pretty much no-frills places to sleep and not much else (hey, you're on a cruise; who wants to be hanging out in the cabin anyway). All cabins have private bathrooms, individually controlled air-conditioning, music channels, and telephones. In February 2000, I was told TVs would be added to each cabin before the ship began its year-round Caribbean cruises out of Houston, but that didn't happen—no big surprise there.

There are no cabins specifically outfitted for passengers who require use of a wheelchair.

PUBLIC AREAS   Most of the ship's Promenade Deck is devoted to bars, lounges, and the casino, as well as a library, boutique, and the kids' playroom on the far aft end. When the ship is carrying a full load, traffic gets easily backed up on this deck, as one public room blends into another. One deck below is the cinema, another gift shop, beauty salon, and tour and purser's desks. No one leaves this ship without spending quality time in both the small buffet-style Capri Bar and Grill, adjacent to the stern-side swimming pool on the Sun Deck, and the Grand Dining Room, a glittering modern dining room that sprawls across the width of the ship on the vessel's Main Deck.

POOL, FITNESS & SPA FACILITIES   It's difficult not to admire the ship's classic ocean-liner-style tiered aft decks, perfect for views of the ship's wake and the open sea. There are two pools on the ship's Sun Deck, the larger near the stern and the second, a smaller wading pool, closer to the bow. There's a third smallish pool a deck below the other two, aft on the Verandah Deck. Adjacent to this pool, just inside, is a humble gym as well as sauna and massage facilities. Sequestered on the aft end of the Promenade Deck is a kids' playroom, a video arcade, and a patch of outdoor deck space for children. There's a tiny beauty salon off of Purser's Square a few decks below.

Rembrandt

The Verdict

The *Rembrandt* is Premier's best ship and the truest and most gorgeous 1950s ocean liner afloat today—and a cruise on it is affordable to boot! (Let's just hope management doesn't go ahead with plans to paint the hull red and redo its interiors.)

Rembrandt *(photo: Premier Cruises)*

Specifications

Size (in tons)	38,645	Officers	Greek
Number of Cabins	575	Crew	550 (International)
Number of Outside Cabins	307	Passenger/Crew Ratio	2 to 1
Cabins with Verandas	0	Year Built	1959
Number of Passengers	1,074	Last Major Refurbishment	1997

Frommer's Ratings (Scale of 1–5)

Cabin Comfort & Amenities	4	Pool, Fitness & Spa Facilities	3
Ship Cleanliness & Maintenance	3	Children's Facilities	2
Public Comfort/Space	4	Itinerary	3
Decor	5	Worth the Money	5

The *Rembrandt,* formerly Holland America's proud flagship, the *Rotterdam V,* is a treasure to savor for those who would like to be transported back to the spacious steamship era. Now over 40 years old, the decor remains amazingly true to its period, and some rooms are simply outstanding, with fine wood and leather paneling, ceramic artwork, mosaic tiles, and lacquer murals. Other rooms are more 1960s funk, but all are well-maintained, museumlike specimens. Furniture is solidly made, unlike so much of what is produced these days, and screams quality. Overall, the ship boasts a truly stunning retro look and instantly transports all who enter back in time. (That said, wear and tear can't be hidden. You'll notice worn carpeting and decks, and some cabins are musty.)

The deck spaces are roomy and varied, with a wonderful teak and rubber-mat circular promenade, wooden deck chairs, and lots of tiered and semiprivate deck areas. This is an ideal ship for whiling away lazy days at sea, either busy as a bee or reclusively sequestered somewhere with a good book. Never one of the 5-day transatlantic greyhounds, the ship is solid and classy (but not opulent), although whether you find it nostalgically beautiful or just out of date depends on you. For me, the ship is something special—and I'm not alone. In late 1998 the hip British magazine *Wallpaper* noted that "Our ship finally [came] in—in the shape of retro-deluxe '50s ocean-liner SS *Rembrandt,* the only vessel of its kind still riding the waves. . . . To sail in the *Rembrandt* it to travel in a time machine."

As noted earlier, Premier has been going back and forth about whether the vessel will be painted red and converted for family cruising. In April 2000, responding to an intense letter-writing campaign against this conversion, Premier president Bruce Nierenberg was quoted in "Cruise Week," an industry newsletter, as saying, "We'll call the ship the *Big Red Rembrandt,* and we'll paint the left side blue and the right side red. . . . Just kidding." He went on to say Premier would retain the ship's art-deco theme in all significant adult public areas. "We will convert the less traditional areas and lounges into kiddy areas," he added. Only time will tell.

Cabins & Rates						
Cabins	Per diems from	Bathtub	Fridge	Hair Dryer	Sitting Area	TV
Inside	$95	no	no	no	no	yes
Outside	$145	some	no	no	some	yes
Suite	$217	yes	no	no	yes	yes

CABINS   Cabins come in a motley assortment of shapes and sizes even within the same category, from spacious 332-square-foot suites to lowly 100-square-foot inside rooms with barely enough space to turn around in. The best-value cabins—and there are lots of them—are the larger ones on Lower Promenade, Main, and A-Deck, with a vast amount of floor space and twins beds set what seems like miles apart. The look is a bit dowdy save for the colorful batik bedspreads and curtains, but you'd need to be carrying two world cruises worth of clothes to fill the three or four illuminated closets and the several sets of drawers.

Bathrooms are definitely old, with exposed plumbing fixtures, but you also get heated towel racks (!) and the best shower pressure on the high seas.

All cabins have TVs, but do not have safes (the purser can keep an eye on your valuables). Views from cabins on the Sun Deck are partially obstructed by lifeboats.

There are no cabins officially designated for wheelchair users, and in many parts of the ship it would be difficult to get around. Not recommended.

PUBLIC AREAS   Because the ship was once a two-class North Atlantic liner, the Upper Promenade and Promenade decks are completely filled with public rooms from stem to stern, with intimate bars, the large Queen's Lounge (one of the least attractive rooms) for the big functions, a beautiful wood and leather-paneled nonsmoking Smoking Room, a proper 620-seat theater with a balcony for live entertainment and movie screenings, a comfy library with windows facing onto the Promenade Deck, a casino, a card room, several shops, and the stunning retro Ambassador Lounge, which is awash in red and nearly museum-quality. The two-tiered Ritz Lounge, with its dramatic curved staircase, large windows facing aft, retro 1960s furniture in plush navy and burnt orange, wood paneling, and a sweeping mural, has no equal for elegance among ships at sea today. A formal white-glove afternoon tea with music takes place in this lounge.

There's a pair of elegant, and very similar, two-deck-high dining rooms with ceramic-tile ceilings and bas-relief terra-cotta figures along the walls. The Lido Terrace restaurant, serving buffet-style breakfast and lunch, has lots of indoor and outdoor seating, but seating can still be at a premium at prime times.

When demand warrants it, a children's playroom is created on the forward Promenade Deck.

There are self-service laundry rooms on board.

POOL, FITNESS & SPA FACILITIES   The ship has an outdoor pool located aft and surrounded by lots of deck space, plus, true to its North Atlantic heritage, a pretty, tiled indoor pool deep down on D-Deck, adjacent to the small, Steiner-run spa. There are separate male and female saunas and massage rooms. The gym is decent, and while not the most high-tech you'll ever set eyes on, is located high up on the Sun Deck with large windows facing aft onto the open deck. Here and one deck above are shuffleboard and practice tennis courts. The wraparound promenade (partially covered) is one of the best afloat and is wide enough to cater to joggers, speed-walkers, and Sunday strollers.

SeaBreeze

The Verdict

While nothing fancy (many cabins are small and none have TVs), the *SeaBreeze* has great lines, classic tiered sundecks, a couple of decent public rooms, a unique Cozumel/Honduras/Belize itinerary, and a really low price tag.

SeaBreeze *(photo: Premier Cruises)*

Specifications

Size (in tons)	21,010	Officers	Greek
Number of Cabins	421	Crew	400 (International)
Number of Outside Cabins	263	Passenger/Crew Ratio	2.1 to 1
Cabins with Verandas	0	Year Built	1958
Number of Passengers	842	Last Major Refurbishment	1997

Frommer's Ratings (Scale of 1–5)

Cabin Comfort & Amenities	3	Pool, Fitness & Spa Facilities	3
Ship Cleanliness & Maintenance	3	Children's Facilities	2
Public Comfort/Space	3	Itinerary	5
Decor	3	Worth the Money	4

When acquired by Dolphin in 1989, this older vessel (built in 1958 as the *Federico C.* by Costa Lines) received a $5.5 million rebuilding and reconfiguration. Additional improvements completed in 1997 greatly improved some cabins with fresh carpeting and bedding in attractive orange and blue nautical motifs. Purser's Square also got a welcome face-lift, with fresh carpeting and new nautical-inspired wall treatments resembling wood paneling. Today, the ship boasts a somewhat classic ocean liner design (at least the hull is sweeping and long, although the stubby stack and twin booms cut an awkward profile), and a decor that looks a lot fresher than you'd expect from such an aged ship. However, renovations over the years have produced a somewhat labyrinthine layout, and despite its face-lifts, you'll still find some tinny metal doors, dented walls, and low ceilings in places.

Cabins & Rates

Cabins	Per diems from	Bathtub	Fridge	Hair Dryer	Sitting Area	TV
Inside	$77	no	no	no	no	no
Outside	$127	no	no	no	no	no
Suite	$198	no	no	no	yes	no

CABINS   Because of the ship's vintage, there's a jigsaw-puzzle-like layout of cabins, in all manner of shapes and sizes. There are 11 different price categories.

Cabins are small—the smallest about 90 square feet—but many have been recently outfitted in cheery navy and burnt orange nautically inspired carpeting, bedding, and drapes, which enliven the small spaces considerably. Furniture is minimal, with small space-saving writing tables that pull out from the dressers or side tables. Most bathrooms are cramped. Many cabins can accommodate three and four guests (and some even five), but keep in mind, five in a cabin won't be a picnic. There are four roomy deluxe suites and three regular suites, the largest at around 300 square feet. There are tiny cabins for singles.

Cabins on the Daphne Deck look onto a busy walkway, and outside cabins on La Bohème Deck (Deck B) overlook a flotilla of hanging lifeboats.

All cabins have music channels. This is the only ship in the fleet that does not have TVs in the cabins.

There are no cabins specifically designed for wheelchair users, and while some public areas are accessible, this ship is not recommended for passengers using wheelchairs.

PUBLIC AREAS Because this ship has been chopped up, renovated, refurbished, and rearranged over the decades, some public areas have assumed somewhat disjointed patterns that require circuitous walks to get from one point to another. Despite this—and despite a close configuration of chairs and tables, especially in the dining room—public areas are cheerful and bright, and mostly decorated with jazzy colors (and, unfortunately, hard-looking metallic ceilings and columns, although some renovation has created more subdued, nautical motifs).

The Agitato disco is dark and way down in the lowest depths of the ship, and transports revelers to another time and place (specifically, your favorite John Travolta *Saturday Night Fever* disco, circa 1977). The attractive Serenade Lounge is a piano bar and has nice dark wooden floors and rattan chairs, and the Prelude Lounge sports dark wooden floors and nautical signal flags decorating the walls. The Carmen show lounge is pleasant and features your classic blue-and-lavender upholstered seating as well as some fairly large windows letting in natural light. The Bacchanalia restaurant is one of the more attractive rooms, but it can get loud and the armless, flimsy chairs are not ideal.

POOL, FITNESS & SPA FACILITIES The ship's tiered aft decks are very attractive and tend to disperse crowds and keep everyone from piling up in one place on sunny days at sea. There is one pool and three hot tubs, as well as a small, windowless gym and a tiny beauty salon and massage room down on the Fidelio Deck. There's a great unobstructed jogging track encircling the Electra Deck, as well as shuffleboard and a basketball net.

Regal Cruises

300 Regal Cruise Way, Palmetto, FL 34221. ☎ **800/270-7245** or 941/721-7300. Fax 941/723-0900. www.regalcruises.com.

THE LINE IN A NUTSHELL   While the line's one ship isn't exactly regal, ship buffs will appreciate the vestiges of classic decor and bargain shoppers will love the price.

THE EXPERIENCE   Regal Cruises offers 1- to 12-night itineraries at rock-bottom prices—like less than $70 per person per day at times. Its shorter cruises are party-hearty while its longer sailings are just the opposite. But if you're on a tight budget and are looking for a small-scale Carnivalesque experience, this is a line to consider.

The 48-year-old *Regal Empress* keeps chugging along, but shows its age despite dedicated efforts to keep it in shape. (What do you expect? It's nearly half a century old!) The most noteworthy refurbishments included a $5.5 million overhaul in 1997 that placed a TV in every cabin, added verandas to some of the suites, and generally spiffed up the interior appearance. Rumor has it that, by year-end 2000, a computer room with E-mail access will be added. Impressive for the old bird! Still, the ship is a blend of the best of yesterday and the worst of today. There's more wood paneling than on most other ships in this chapter, but there's also Astroturf on the outside decks and no shortage of chintzy chrome and mirrors in the public rooms. Quirks and all, though, the *Regal Empress* offers an unpretentious cruise with decent food and entertainment—especially considering its often bargain-basement prices. If you can afford it, book one of the suites or any of the Category 3 superior outside staterooms, and you'll have plenty of space to retire to if the crowds (big ones when the ship is fully booked) get to you.

Pros

- **It's cheap cheap cheap.** Advertised specials commonly tout rates as low as $499 for a 7-night cruise. Hard to beat that.

- **Wood paneling.** Lots of old paneling survives and it's incredibly charming if you appreciate the "old ocean liner" look.

- **Classic nautical lines.** The ship's long, bowed hull and tiered aft decks cut a sharp profile in this age of boxy look-alikes.

Cons

- **Feels crowded.** There aren't that many public rooms, and the outside decks, while tiered, get packed on sunny days at sea. The buffet line gets backed up often.

- **Tired in places.** The sorry-looking shops and cheesy casino, for instance, are reminders that this is, in many ways, a patched together, catch-as-catch-can ship.

Compared with the other Budget lines, here's how Regal rates:					
	poor	fair	good	excellent	outstanding
Enjoyment Factor				✓	
Dining			✓		
Activities			✓		
Children's Program		✓			
Entertainment			✓		
Service			✓		
Overall Value				✓	

REGAL EMPRESS: OLD, CHEAP & CHARMING

In 1993, the owner of two enormous travel agencies, GoGo Tours and Liberty Travel, paired up with another investor and bought the then 40-year-old *Caribe I* for a reasonable price, changing its name and marketing it through Liberty and GoGo's formidable army of sales representatives. The poor ship had its problems at first: It flunked its first two sanitation inspections and required expensive reconfigurations; then, during its first summer of operation, inexperienced crew members battled glitches in an operation schedule that demanded grueling 4-hour turnarounds between cruises. (Today, turnaround time is a reasonable 8 hours, about the equivalent of most competitors.) The company's beginnings were rocky, but some of the most obvious problems have been corrected. Those that remain? Let's just say that the cheap-as-dirt prices do a lot to alleviate complaints. Frankly, this is the perfect line for anyone who's unwilling to spend a lot of money and who doesn't particularly care about glamour. Fares are sometimes so cheap that if you happen to live within driving distance of the ship's home port (Florida's Port Manatee), you might conceivably spend less on a cruise than you would entertaining yourself back home.

Port Manatee is set in the southern boondocks of Tampa Bay, has difficulty attracting any other cruise lines to its bare-bones facilities, and usually devotes its energy to the loading of phosphates. Romantic, huh? So why does Regal dock its ship there? Remember that old saw about "In the land of the blind, the one-eyed man is king"? At Port Manatee, the *Empress* is queen of all it surveys—and port charges are less than at the nearby Port of Tampa. Another reason involves laws that say casinos can't open until ships reach international waters. Since it's quicker to get into the Gulf of Mexico from Port Manatee than it is from Tampa, the casino can open about an hour sooner. (Port Manatee is a 45-minute drive south of the Port of Tampa. Take exit 45 off I-75—it leads onto U.S. Highway 41—and follow the signs.)

During the summer, the *Empress* docks in New York and turns up the proverbial volume, using that city as a base for hard-partying 1- to 3-night "cruises to nowhere" and more sedate excursions up and down the coast of Canada and New England (plus a handful of cruises to Bermuda).

THE FLEET

The 48-year-old, 910-passenger, 22,000-ton **Regal Empress** is Regal Cruises' only ship (see ship review for details). Its name creates some consumer confusion, similar as it is to the larger and better-accessorized *Regal Princess* operated by Princess Cruises. The similarity stops at the name, though. While the *Regal Princess* is a stylish, futuristic-looking megaship, the *Regal Empress* is older, smaller, and much less luxurious.

Built in Scotland in 1953 as a two-class ocean liner called the *Olympia* for Greek Line, the ship made its debut sailing from Glasgow and Liverpool to New York. In 1970, long after air travel killed the transatlantic trade, the ship switched to running cruises, but by 1974 ended up mothballed at a pier in Piraeus, Greece, where it languished until 1983. In 1984, after a major refitting, the ship sailed as the *Caribe I* ("The Happy Ship") for Commodore Cruise Lines. It was sold to Regal in 1993.

PASSENGER PROFILE

Passengers run the gamut from very young to very old, although there are many older passengers because zillions of retirees live in the Clearwater/Tampa/St. Petersburg area. You'll also find hard-drinking, hard-playing passengers determined to get their money's worth aboard this vessel, but the cruises out of Port Manatee tend to be slightly more sedate than the rowdy midsummer party cruises out of New York. On the other end of the spectrum, children under age 2 sail free.

Regal Fleet Itineraries			
Ship	Home Ports & Season	Itinerary	Other Itineraries
Regal Empress	Round-trip from Port Manatee; itineraries alternate from Nov–May.	**3-night W Carib:** Key West. **4-night W. Carib:** Cancún and Playa del Carmen/ Cozumel. **5-night W. Carib:** Progreso and Cozumel or Key West and Cozumel. **6-night W. Carib:** Progreso, Cozumel/ Playa del Carmen, and Cancún. **7-night W. Carib:** Cancún, Playa del Carmen, Cozumel, and Key West. **10-night Panama Canal:** Grand Cayman, San Blas Islands, Puerto Limón (Costa Rica), and San Andrés (Colombia).	South America, New England/ Canada, cruises to nowhere

DINING

Regal emphasizes eating and more eating, just like the more expensive cruise lines, but with fewer of the grace notes and frills. You can enjoy early morning coffee, juices, and pastries; three square meals a day in the dining room; afternoon tea; a midnight buffet; and 24-hour room service from a limited menu.

The *Empress*'s attractive, wood-paneled Caribbean dining room still retains the grandeur of its past and outshines the food served there. There are two seatings for each meal, and the cuisine, while not gourmet in any way, is decent and served professionally. The main entrees, such as grilled Alaskan salmon with dill, prime rib with Yorkshire pudding, chicken marinated in lemon with rosemary, and pork scaloppini, tend to be better than the appetizers, which are mostly ultra-basic and low-brow, like fried chicken fingers and bland soups, although an exception is the classic Waldorf salad with apples, celery, and walnuts. There's one **vegetarian option,** like eggplant parmigana, and a **"calorie counter" choice,** such as a poached fish.

The buffet-style indoor-outdoor **alternative restaurant,** La Trattoria, on the Promenade Deck near the pool, serves up the basics for breakfast, lunch, and dinner, for guests not wanting to cover up their bathing suits and put on shoes to dine in the Caribbean dining room. Besides salads, cheese, fruit, and cold cuts, there are burgers, hot platters, and real tasty pizzas.

ACTIVITIES

You'll find the usual cruise ship activities, just fewer of them. Those you do find include bingo, horse racing, card parties, shuffleboard tournaments, limbo contests, skeet shooting, and live music and dancing by the pool, and there's always a movie playing. You can improve your **golf**-putting skills on an Astroturf green, or try to piece together the enormous communal jigsaw puzzles that are laid out on a prominent table. During days at sea, everyone sunbathes on deck, but the lounge chairs are rather close to one another.

Set near the stern, on the same deck as the restaurant, the ship's casino is hardly the most spectacular afloat, but it might be one of the busiest, especially when the ship is packed.

CHILDREN'S PROGRAM

This ship is not a particularly great choice for kids; however, when at least 10 kids are on board, **youth counselors** supervise children's activities such as crafts lessons and guided ship tours for several age groups. There is a **children's activity room** and a **video**

arcade, but Regal doesn't have the awesome array of children's activities offered by Premier, Disney, Carnival, Royal Caribbean, and Princess.

Baby-sitting can be arranged with an available crew member for a fee (negotiated between the passenger and crew member).

ENTERTAINMENT

Entertainment varies according to what and who is hired to perform in the Grand Lounge showroom or the Mirage, which functions as a movie theater during the day and a disco after 10pm. There's live dance music in the Mermaid Lounge before and after dinner, and there's always **karaoke,** with the ship providing props. Virtually every cruise hosts a cocktail party for repeat passengers, of whom there are many.

SERVICE

Service is better than you might expect from such an inexpensive line, offering creditable amounts of guest pampering. The dining staff is professional and experienced, and the bartenders at the Pool Bar have their job down pat, pouring the drinks and offering lots of pleasant chit-chat.

There is a self-service laundry on the Sun Deck.

Regal Empress

Regal Empress *(photo: Regal Cruises)*

The Verdict

However rough around the edges it may be, this old-timer retains some charming original ocean-liner features.

Specifications

Size (in tons)	22,000	Officers	International
Number of Cabins	455	Crew	386 (International)
Number of Outside Cabins	226	Passenger/Crew Ratio	2.8 to 1
Cabins with Verandas	8	Year Built	1953
Number of Passengers	910	Last Major Refurbishment	1997

Frommer's Ratings (Scale of 1–5)

Cabin Comfort & Amenities	4	Pool, Fitness & Spa Facilities	2
Ship Cleanliness & Maintenance	3	Children's Facilities	2
Public Comfort/Space	3	Itinerary	4
Decor	4	Worth the Money	5

Despite years of hard use by various owners, the *Empress* retains vestiges of its original elegance and good taste—for instance, the library, Caribbean dining room, Commodore lounge, and Pool Bar are all sheathed in wood paneling, and are the most pleasant (and original) public areas on board. Another great old ocean-liner feature is the glass-enclosed promenade, though its virtues would be more appropriate during windy weather in the North Atlantic—during hot days in the Caribbean, you'll wish it was open. Overall, the ship boasts ample amounts of deck space, although when it's full there won't be an inch to spare.

Cabins & Rates

Cabins	Per diems from	Bathtub	Fridge	Hair Dryer	Sitting Area	TV
Inside	$85	no	no	no	no	yes
Outside	$127	no	no	no	no	yes
Suite	$197	yes	yes	yes	yes	yes

CABINS   As with most old ships, the 453 cabins vary widely in size, location, and configuration, with the smallest measuring a cramped 80 square feet and the largest suites a spacious 216 to 410 square feet. The majority of cabins are about 100 to 120 square feet, and a large number are inside cabins without views.

Cabins look their age for the most part. Decor is sparse, but brightly colored matching drapes and bedspreads cheer things up. The 120-square-foot Category-3 superior outside cabins, for instance, are bright and cheerful and feel bigger than they are. In general, walls are white and furniture institutional looking, with touches of wood trim and, more rarely, paneling. Suites E and F, and mini-suites U90 and U91, on the Upper Deck, for instance, contain quite a bit of original wood and are most distinctive, despite awkward shapes. Most doors are solid wood, and unlike the new ships (which all use computerized key-cards) are all operated with lock and key, just like the old days.

In late 1997, eight suites were reconfigured to include private verandas. In all cabins, televisions and safes were added; overall, much of the carpeting, bedding, drapery, and upholstery was replaced, and everything was freshened with new coats of paint.

Overall, bathrooms are small and somewhat cramped; only the largest of the ship's suites have bathtubs.

Most cabins can be configured for up to four occupants through bunk-bed arrangements. Some can be configured to accommodate five. Cabins have enough storage space, and in some cases tons of space, and a reasonable amount of elbow room, at least for a cruise of short duration. Even in the lowest category, an inside cabin might have two lower beds, two closets, and two dressers that can store most of a couple's possessions. About 10 cabins are singles.

One cabin is accessible to wheelchairs, but overall, with its awkward layout and high doorway sills, this ship is not well suited to people with mobility problems.

All cabins have TVs, music channels, and safes. Many outside cabins have portholes, and some have rectangular windows.

PUBLIC AREAS   A hodgepodge of old and new, the *Regal Empress* has managed to hold on to some of its original wooden and brass fittings, but they exist side-by-side with chrome, mirrors, and other shiny surfaces. There are vestiges of the past in the rich wood paneling covering the main stairs and landings and in the purser's lobby. The library, too, is an oasis of clubbiness with its all-over wood paneling, rich carpeting, and well-upholstered chairs. The Caribbean dining room is a gem, too, retaining much of the past with its etched glass, ornate wall sconces, original murals of New York and Rio, wooden paneling, waiters' stations, and columns. Some of the chairs are rickety rattan numbers, while others are beautiful, sturdy wooden jobs upholstered to match nicely with the deep hues in the carpeting.

The cozy Commodore Lounge is also mostly original (at least its deep wood paneling and detailing are) and on either edge of the room offers sunken seating clusters for truly private cocktails and conversation.

The slightly elevated and always bustling Pool Bar on the Sun Deck is the hub of action. It's generously done in deep caramel-colored wood and is surrounded by numerous sturdy bar stools.

The casino is popular, but tired and cheap-looking with its rainbow-painted walls and slots stools. A two-level disco (the Mirage, which doubles as a movie theater during the day) is dark and sultry—your classic metallic hideaway. The Mermaid bar and night-club is modern if uninspired, and pleasant with its bright blue carpeting and upholstery and sizable dance floor. The modern Grand Lounge is nothing special and is the place for cabaret acts, comedians, singing groups, and whatever other after-dinner entertainment is being featured. On the Promenade Deck near the Pool Bar, the La Trattoria buffet-style restaurant, created during the 1997 refurbishment, is nothing more than a somewhat crowded buffet line, but the colored tiles and bright canvas awnings are a nice touch. Seating is outdoors on-deck or more or less inside under a patch of the covered Promenade Deck.

There's also a so-called sports bar with flimsy chairs and cheap framed prints of sport stars on the wall.

At busy times, like before and after dinner, pedestrian traffic is heavy as passengers migrate from one area of the ship to another. When the ship is full, you'll know it.

POOL, FITNESS & SPA FACILITIES   The ship's tiered decks are very attractive and recall a classic liner. There's one small pool aboard—more a spot for sunbathers than a place to really swim—and two adjacent hot tubs, surrounded by deck chairs and tables with nice ocean-blue canvas beach umbrellas. Beige Astroturf covers virtually all of the outside decks, hiding any teak that may be underneath and detracting somewhat from the otherwise appealing areas.

There's a beauty salon and one massage room. You'll find a few exercise machines in a rather bland room on the top deck, but no sauna or showers. Stretch-and-tone classes are led by one of the showroom's dancers.

8 The Ultra-Luxury Lines

These cruise lines are the top-shelf, the best (and most expensive) of the best. Their ships, mostly small and intimate, are the sports cars of cruise ships and cater to discerning travelers who want to be pampered with fine gourmet cuisine and wines and ensconced in spacious suites with marble bathrooms, down pillows, sitting areas, minibars, and walk-in closets. Caviar is served on silver trays and chilled champagne poured into crystal glasses. Elegant dining rooms are dressed in the finest linens, stemware, and china, and guests dress in tuxedos and sparkling dresses and gowns on formal nights and suits and ties on informal nights. (An exception to this is Windstar Cruises, which, though luxurious and upscale, offers a much more casual kind of luxury and a more laid-back decor. Radisson Seven Seas also tends toward the casual, but not to Windstar's degree.) Exquisite French, Italian, and Asian cuisine rivals that of the best shoreside restaurants and is served in high style by doting, gracious waiters who know how to please. A full dinner can even be served to you in your cabin, if you like. Luxuries like these are part of the wonderfully decadent daily routine.

Entertainment and organized activities are more dignified than on other ships—you won't see any raunchy comedy routines or bordering-on-obscene pool games—and are more limited as guests tend to amuse themselves, enjoying cocktails and conversation in a piano bar more than they would a flamboyant Vegas-style routine.

With the exception of the *QE2* and the *Crystal Harmony* (which are larger, but still quite cushy), these high-end ships are small and intimate—usually carrying just a few hundred passengers—and big on service, with almost as many staff as passengers. You're not likely to feel lost in the crowd, and staff will get to know your likes and dislikes early on. The onboard atmosphere is much like a private club, with guests trading traveling tales and meeting for drinks or dinner.

The high-end lines are discounting more than ever, so you may be able to afford something you thought was out of your price range. That said, a high-end cruise still can cost twice as much (or more) as your typical mainstream cruise. Barring specials and low-season rates, expect to pay at least $2,000 per person for a week in the Caribbean, and easily more if you opt for the penthouse suite or choose to cruise during the busiest times of the year. Besides early-booking discounts, many high-end lines give discounts to repeat cruisers and those booking back-to-back cruises, and sometimes offer two-for-one deals and free airfare.

Many extras are often included in the cruise rates. For instance, Radisson's and Seabourn's rates include tips, wine with dinner, one-time stocked minibar, and unlimited soda and bottled water. Seabourn's rates also include some shore excursions and free wine with lunch. Cunard offers unlimited stocked minibars to passengers in top suites.

Most people attracted to these types of cruises are sophisticated, wealthy, relatively social, and used to the finer things in life. While most are well traveled, they tend to stick to the five-star variety.

These ships are not geared to children at all, although every so often one or two show up. In this event, baby-sitting can sometimes be arranged privately with an off-duty crew member.

DRESS CODES   On Seabourn, Cunard, and Crystal, bring the tux and the sequined gown—guests dress for dinner on the two or three formal nights on these cruises. Informal nights call for suits and ties for men and fancy dresses or pantsuits for ladies; sports jackets for men and casual dresses or pantsuits for women are the norm on casual nights. That said, like the rest of the industry, even the high-end lines are relaxing their dress codes, heading closer to lines like Windstar, which espouses a "no jackets required" policy during the entire cruise. Men need only pack dress slacks, chinos, and nice collared shirts (short or long sleeves); women, leave the pantyhose at home—casual dresses and slacks are fine for evenings. The *Seabourn Goddesses* are also now following a no-jackets-required policy, even on formal night. Radisson is somewhere in between, so bring the suits and nice dresses, but no need to lug the tux or fancy full-length gown on board if it's not your style (in fact, on a recent *Seven Seas Navigator* cruise I saw several 60+ passengers in jeans, sneakers, and T-shirts—albeit the $50 kind—at dinner in the formal dining room on casual nights).

Frommer's Cruise Line Ratings at a Glance: The Ultra-Luxury Lines							
1 = poor 2 = fair 3 = good 4 = excellent 5 = outstanding							
Cruise Line	Enjoyment Factor	Dining	Activities	Children's Program	Entertainment	Service	Overall Value
Crystal	5	5	5	3	4	4	5
Cunard	4	4	4	2*	3	4	4
Radisson Seven Seas	4	4	4	N/A	3	4	5
Seabourn	5	5	2	N/A	2	5	5
Windstar	5	4	2	N/A	2	3	4

NOTE: Cruise lines have been graded on a curve that compares them only with the other lines in the Ultra-Luxury category. See "Cruise Line Categories" in chapter 5 for a detailed explanation of my ratings methodology.
* Does not apply to all ships in the line's fleet. See individual ship reviews for details. Lines with N/A rating for children's programs have no program whatsoever.

Crystal Cruises

2121 Ave. of the Stars, Los Angeles, CA 90067. ☎ **800/446-6620** or 310/785-9300. Fax 310/785-3891. www.crystalcruises.com.

THE LINE IN A NUTSHELL Fine-tuned and fashionable, Crystal's pair of dream ships give passengers pampering service and scrumptious cuisine on ships large enough to offer lots of outdoor deck space, generous fitness facilities, four restaurants, and over half a dozen bars and entertainment venues.

THE EXPERIENCE Crystal has the two largest truly upscale ships in the industry. Carrying 960 passengers, they aren't huge, but they're big enough to offer much more than their high-end peers. You won't feel hemmed in and you likely won't be twiddling your thumbs from lack of stimulation. Service is excellent, and the cuisine is very good and on par with Seabourn and Radisson; the line's Asian food is tops. Unlike Seabourn, which tends to be more staid, Crystal's California ethic tends to keep things mingly and chatty. Passengers are social and active, and like dressing for dinner and being seen.

Pros
- **Four restaurants.** Only the megaships offer as many options—and none so sophisticated. There are two alternative restaurants as well as a formal dining room and a casual restaurant that puts on some of the best theme luncheon-buffet spreads at sea.
- **Best Asian food at sea.** The ships' reservations-only Asian restaurants serve up utterly delicious, authentic, fresh Japanese food, including sushi. At least once per cruise they also hold an Asian-theme buffet lunch offering an awesome spread.
- **Fitness choices.** There's a nice-size gym, paddle-tennis court, shuffleboard, Ping-Pong, an uninterrupted jogging circuit, golf-driving nets, and a putting green.
- **Computer learning.** No other ship has such an extensive computer lab, with over 20 computer stations, complimentary training classes during sea days, and quick and easy E-mail access (both outgoing and incoming).

Cons
- **Formality.** If you're not nuts about dressing up fit to kill nearly every night, think twice about a Crystal cruise. Some passengers even get gussied up during the day.
- **Cabin size.** While certainly not tiny or uncomfortable, accommodations are smaller compared to Seabourn and Radisson.
- **Cabin bathroom size.** A generous complement of Neutrogena bath products await, yes, but size-wise, bathrooms are tiny (especially on the *Harmony*) and counter and storage space is limited compared to Radisson and Seabourn.

Compared with the other Ultra-Luxury lines, here's how Crystal rates:

	poor	fair	good	excellent	outstanding
Enjoyment Factor					✓
Dining					✓
Activities					✓
Children's Program			✓		
Entertainment				✓	
Service				✓	
Overall Value					✓

CRYSTAL: SPARKLING & SPACIOUS

Established in 1990, Crystal Cruises has held its own in the high-stakes lottery of the super-upscale cruise market, establishing a unique place there. Its ships are the largest in the high-end sector of the industry, and while not quite as dripping with luxury as its closest competitors—Seabourn and Silversea (a line that doesn't have either of its ships in the Caribbean, and so is not reviewed in this guide)—the Crystal sisters provide a truly refined cruise for discerning guests who appreciate superb service and top-notch cuisine.

Crystal is the North American spin-off of Japan's largest container shipping enterprises, Nippon Yusen Kaisa (NYK). Despite these origins, a passenger aboard Crystal could conceivably spend an entire week at sea and not even be aware that the ship is Japanese-owned, -built, and -funded. More than anything else, Crystal is international, with a strong emphasis on European service. The Japanese exposure is more subtle, and you'll feel it in the excellent Asian cuisine and tasty sake served in the Kyoto alternative restaurant and in the Asian-theme buffets, as well as in the handful of Japanese passengers on board many cruises. (There's a Japanese concierge on board, so don't worry about having to sit through announcements and activities being translated into Japanese.)

THE FLEET

Crystal's fleet comprises two nearly identical 960-passenger ships. The *Crystal Harmony* was built in 1990 and weighs 49,400 tons, and since 1998 has been doing a handful of Caribbean and Panama Canal itineraries each year, in addition to cruising in South America, Alaska, and the South Pacific. The ***Crystal Symphony*** was built in 1995 and weighs 51,044 tons. The *Symphony* is slightly bigger, with a larger atrium and some expanded public rooms (like the casino), and overall embraces a somewhat lighter color scheme. In addition to spending the year cruising in the South Pacific, Asia, the Mediterranean, and Europe, the ships are spending more time in the Caribbean and Panama Canal than ever before. Looks like a trend. In March of 2000, Crystal finally announced its intent to build a third ship in the 50,000-ton range, similar to the *Harmony* and *Symphony* in style but with innovations as well. As far as names go, rumor has it *Crystal Melody* is in the running. Company president Joe Watters said they were shooting for a 2003 debut date.

PASSENGER PROFILE

Few other cruise lines attract as loyal a crop of repeat passengers, many of whom hail from affluent regions of California and most of whom step aboard for a second, third, or fourth cruise with a definite sense of how they want to spend their time on board. There's commonly a small contingent of passengers (about 15% of the mix) from the United Kingdom, Australia, Japan, Mexico, Europe, and South America. Most passengers are well-heeled couples, stylish but not particularly flamboyant, and over 55. A good number of passengers "step up" to Crystal from lines like Princess and Holland America. Passengers tend to be well traveled, although not particularly adventurous.

Many Crystal passengers place great emphasis on the social scene before, during, and after mealtimes, and many enjoy dressing up (sometimes way up) for dinner and adorning themselves with the biggest and best diamonds they own. You'll see no shortage of big rocks and gold Rolexes. The onboard jewelry and clothing boutiques do a brisk business, and it's obvious that women on board have devoted much care and attention to their wardrobes and accessories. On formal nights—at least three of which occur during every 10- or 11-day cruise—the majority of men wear tuxes and many women wear floor-length gowns, although your classic black cocktail dress is just fine. As on most ships, dress codes are much more relaxed during the day.

There are rarely kids on board except during holidays, when you may see 20 to 40.

DINING

One of Crystal's best features is its diverse and high-quality cuisine. Its two themed, reservations-only **alternative restaurants**—Kyoto, a Japanese restaurant on the *Harmony,* and Jade, a pan-Asian restaurant on the *Symphony* (and Prego, an Italian restaurant on both)—are right up there with the best at sea. Personally, my favorite is Kyoto, where the Japanese food is excellent, with completely authentic sushi platters, miso soup, beef teriyaki, and pork dishes. The accoutrements help set the tone, too—chopsticks (and little chopstick rests), sake served in tiny sake cups and decanters, and sushi served on thick blocky glass platters. Only complaint: Sometimes service is a bit harried in the alternative restaurants—nothing another waiter or two wouldn't remedy.

Overall, the galleys aboard these ships cook up a light-textured, thoughtful cuisine with selections like a roasted duck with apricot-sage stuffing served with a Grand Marnier orange sauce, broiled Black Angus sirloin steak, or seared sea scallops and jumbo shrimp served with a light lobster beurre blanc over a bed of pumpkin risotto. At lunch and dinner in the dining room, there's a **low-fat selection,** such as broiled fillet of sea bass served with steamed vegetables (with calories, fat, cholesterol, sodium, carbohydrates, and protein content listed), as well as an **entree salad**—like a mixed grill salad with grilled herb-marinated chicken breast, jumbo shrimp, and filet mignon—if you'd rather skip the main course. **Vegetarian** meals are available.

In a kind of homage to the California wine industry, Crystal offers one of the most sophisticated inventories of **California wines** on the high seas. An extensive selection of **French wines** is also offered, with many bottles in the $20-to-$60 range, and some as high as $800.

The main dining room on both ships is chic and stylish, with white Doric columns, high-backed chairs, and mirrored ceilings with lotus-flower lighting fixtures. Tables are not too close together, and there are well over 20 tables for two, mostly along the side or near the ocean-view windows.

Because of the size of the ship, **dinner is served in two seatings** here. Lunches and breakfasts, however, are open seating in the dining room and the Lido buffet restaurant. Service by the team of ultra-professional, gracious European male waiters is excellent, and there sometimes seem to be more nattily attired staff than passengers. In the main dining room—and to a somewhat lesser degree in the alternative restaurants—table settings are lavish and include fine, heavy crystal and porcelain. Even in the Lido restaurant, waiters are at hand to serve you your salad from the buffet line, prepare your coffee, and then carry your tray to wherever it is you want to sit.

Themed luncheon buffets—Asian, Mediterranean, or a Western barbecue, for instance—are excellent and are generously spread out at lunchtime by the pool and an extra-special gala buffet is put on once per cruise in the lobby/atrium, where the midnight buffet also takes place. No expense or effort is spared to produce elaborate food fests, with heaps of jumbo shrimp, homemade sushi, Greek salads, shish kebabs, beef satay, stir-fry dishes, and more.

If you don't want to stroll much further than your deck chair or if you've slept through lunch, between 11am and 6pm daily you can order something from the Trident Grill on the Pool Deck and have a seat, in your bathing suit if you so desire, at adjacent tables or head back to your deck chair. The Grill serves beef, chicken, and salmon burgers, pizza, tuna melts, hot dogs, fries, fruit, and a special of the day, like a Caesar salad and chicken wrap.

Yet another place for a snack or a specialty coffee is the Bistro, open from 9:30am to 11:30am for a late continental breakfast and then between 11:30am and 6pm for complimentary grazing at the buffet-style spread of cheeses, cold cuts, fruit, cookies, and pastries. For a few dollars, you can also sip an almond mocha, hazelnut latte, espresso, or fruit shake, or a glass of pinot grigio or a nice merlot.

For **afternoon tea,** it's the ultra-chic Palm Court on one of the ship's uppermost decks. A sprawling space with floor-to-ceiling windows and pale-blue and white furniture in leather and rattan, the area gives off an overall light, soft, and ethereal ambiance.

There is, of course, **24-hour room service.**

ACTIVITIES

While not overwhelming, Crystal offers an interesting selection of activities. Count on several **enrichment lectures** throughout a cruise, such as a historian presenting a slide show and speaking about the Panama Canal and how it was built, or a movie critic talking to guests about Hollywood and movies. Most speakers are not celebrities, but well-known personalities do occasionally show up on Crystal cruises. In the past, some notables have included TV patriarch Walter Cronkite, former secretary of state and Iran-contra defendant Caspar Weinberger, Hollywood gossip enthusiast Bill Harris, "Laugh-In" regular Arte Johnson, biographer David McCullough, maritime historian Bill Miller, game-show guru Regis Philbin, *Time* magazine correspondent Christopher Ogden, *Variety* columnist Army Archerd, broadcast journalist Linda Ellerbee, actress Jane Russell, *Wall Street Week* host Robert Stovall, and author and radio personality Garrison Keillor.

Crystal also offers its **Wine & Food Festival** program during many of its cruises (nearly 30 in 2000), where a respected wine expert conducts at least two complimentary tastings and a guest chef from a well-known restaurant, such as Andre Soltner or Jacques Pepin, conducts a pair of cooking demonstrations for guests and then presents the results of those lessons at dinner that night. Guests can ask questions and mingle with these interesting personalities.

There are often **dancing lessons** taught by guest teachers as well, popular when offered. Learn to swing or do the rumba and merengue. Group lessons are complimentary, and sometimes private lessons can be arranged with the instructors for about $50 per hour per couple. Crystal is also big on organizing **bridge and paddle-tennis competitions,** game-show-style contests, and trivia games, as well as providing midafternoon dance music with the resident dance trio or quartet, serving tea to the accompaniment of a harpist, offering interesting arts and crafts like glass-etching, and even presenting guest fashion shows. Commonly, a golf expert sails on board, too, conducting complimentary **group golf lessons** by the driving nets several times per cruise (again, private lessons can be arranged for a fee).

Kudos to the line's **Computer University**—there's nothing else like it at sea! Each ship has a well-stocked computer lab with over 20 computer workstations. On cruises with at least 6 days at sea, complimentary classes are offered on topics like a basic introduction to using the computer, understanding the Internet and the Web, and how to buy a computer. Cruises with fewer sea days also offer guests the opportunity to learn about using E-mail. On all cruises, **E-mail access** is readily available, so passengers can send and receive E-mails via a special personal shipboard address they're given when they get their cruise documents. Computer use is free of charge, but there's an initial $5 fee to set up an E-mail account and a charge of $3 every time you send or receive an E-mail (up to about seven to eight pages long). No other ship offers anything as extensive.

Crystal Fleet Itineraries

Ship	Home Ports & Season	Itinerary	Other Itineraries
Crystal Harmony	Itineraries between Puntarenas and Ft. Lauderdale, Acapulco and Ft. Lauderdale, New Orleans and Acapulco, San Francisco and Acapulco, Acapulco and San Juan, Puntarenas and New Orleans, and San Juan and Puntarenas, Mar–May and Nov–Dec 2001; eastern Caribbean itineraries round-trip from Ft. Lauderdale and between San Juan and Ft. Lauderdale, Dec 2001.	**10-, 11-, and 12-night Panama Canal:** May visit Grand Cayman, Aruba, St. Thomas, St. Maarten, Cartagena, Puerto Quetzal, Antigua, St. Kitts, and Playa del Carmen/Cozumel. **9-, 10-, and 14-night E Carib:** May visit St. Thomas, Key West, Aruba, Isla de Margarita (Venezuela), Antigua, St. Maarten, Tortola, and Barbados.	Alaska, South America, New England
Crystal Symphony	14-night itinerary between Los Angeles and Ft. Lauderdale;15-night itinerary between Los Angeles and San Juan. Both offered Dec–Jan.	**14- and 15-night Panama Canal:** May visit Aruba, St. Thomas, Cartagena, Puntarenas (Costa Rica), Acapulco, and Playa del Carmen/Cozumel.	World cruise, Mediterranean, Europe, Africa

CHILDREN'S PROGRAM

Crystal is a sophisticated cruise line that focuses its attention on adults, so by implication it's generally not a line for kids, few of which you'll ever see aboard. That said, each ship does have a small but bright **children's playroom,** primarily used during holiday and summer cruises (primarily in Alaska) when as many as 20 to 40 kids may be on board. At times like this, **counselors** are on-hand to supervise activities for several hours in the morning and in the afternoon (on a recent Easter-time cruise, six counselors were on board to supervise about 35 kids). **Baby-sitting** can be arranged privately through the concierge, but Crystal is not shy about pointing out that they do not offer a day-care service and parents are expected to make sure their kids are well behaved.

ENTERTAINMENT

Shows in the horseshoe-shaped, rather plain Galaxy Lounge encompass everything from **classical concertos** by accomplished pianists to **comedy.** A troupe of spangle-covered, lip-synching dancers and a pair of lead singers are likely to do a **Vegas-style performance** based on the hits of Cole Porter or a medley of the best works of Rodgers and Hammerstein. Onboard entertainment is good, but certainly not the high point of the cruise. There sure are lots of options, though.

In addition to the Galaxy show lounge, after dinner each night, a second large, attractive lounge is the venue for **ballroom-style dancing** to a live band. There's also a small, separate (and usually empty) **disco** on the *Harmony,* featuring **karaoke** a couple of nights per cruise (on the *Symphony,* the disco is part of the Starlight Club), and a pianist in the dark, paneled, and romantic Avenue Saloon (my favorite room) playing popular show tunes and pop hits from "New York, New York" to "My Funny Valentine" before and after dinner. You can enjoy cigars in the Connoisseurs Club on the *Symphony* and in the *Harmony*'s Vista Lounge. A **movie theater** shows first-run movies several times a day, and cabin TVs feature a wonderfully varied and full menu of movies, listed in the daily schedules under categories such as Comedy, Classics, Arts and Documentaries, Concerts, and regular first-run movies.

Children's Specials

Children 11 and under pay 50% of the minimum fare when accompanied by two guests paying full fare.

Gamblers will have no problem feeling at home in the roomy **casinos,** which are supervised directly by Caesar's Palace Casinos at Sea (the one on the *Symphony* is nearly twice as large as the one on the *Harmony*).

SERVICE

The hallmark of a high-end cruise like Crystal is its service, so the line's staff is better-trained and more attentive than that aboard most other cruise lines, and is typically of an international cast: The dining room and restaurant staffs hail from Italy, Portugal, and other European countries, and have trained in the grand restaurants of Europe and North America; the pool attendant who brings you a fresh towel and a glass of lemonade, as well as the bartender mixing your martini, is likely to be Filipino; and the cabin stewardess who tidies your stateroom is likely to be from Scandinavia or some other European country like Hungary. Overall, the dining/bar staff is best, outshining the room stewardesses, though everyone, even the staff manning the information and concierge desks in the lobby, is endlessly good-natured and very helpful—a rare find, indeed.

(I might note, the Crystal ships are among the few that have not only a small pool for their crew members, but a hot tub too, located at the bow of the ship on Deck 5. It pays to keep the crew happy, I guess!)

In addition to laundry and dry-cleaning services, **self-serve laundry** rooms are available.

Crystal Harmony • Crystal Symphony

The Verdict

These gracious, floating pleasure palaces are small enough to feel intimate and personal yet large enough for a whole range of entertainment, dining, and fitness diversions.

Crystal Harmony *(photo: Crystal Cruises)*

Specifications

Size (in tons)		Number of Passengers	960
Harmony	49,400	Officers	Norwegian/
Symphony	51,044		Japanese/Int'l
Number of Cabins	480	Crew	545 (International)
Number of Outside Cabins		Passenger/Crew Ratio	1.7 to 1
Harmony	461	Year Built	
Symphony	480	*Harmony*	1990
Cabins with Verandas		*Symphony*	1995
Harmony	260	Last Major Refurbishment	N/A
Symphony	276		

Frommer's Ratings (Scale of 1–5)

Cabin Comfort & Amenities	4	Pool, Fitness & Spa Facilities	4
Ship Cleanliness & Maintenance	3	Children's Facilities	2
Public Comfort/Space	5	Itinerary	4
Decor	4	Worth the Money	5

Plush, streamlined, extravagantly comfortable, and not as overwhelmingly large as the megaships being launched by less glamorous lines, these ships compete with the hyper-upscale Seabourn vessels, although Crystal's ships are almost five times as large as Seabourn's, with a broader choice of onboard diversions and distractions. *Harmony* has a few flawed features (like a small casino) that were "corrected" in 1995 with the design of the ship's newer twin, the *Crystal Symphony,* a slightly bigger ship with a larger casino, no inside cabins, and a larger atrium/lobby area. Its two alternative restaurants are on the main entertainment deck with the rest of the action (the *Harmony*'s are on the Lido Deck).

The hub of both ships is the atrium. Impressive and stylish, and less overwhelming than aboard some of the larger mainstream ships, it's where you'll find the concierge, information-and-shore-excursion desk, the Crystal Cove lounge, the ship's chic shops, and the site of the much-awaited midnight buffets (and a luncheon buffet or two), which are presented with fanfare every evening.

In May of 2000, the *Harmony* was put into dry dock for a face-lift. Its Crystal Dining Room was on the receiving end of new carpeting, window dressings, chairs, and a grand new entrance. The atrium was refurbished with new carpeting, drapes, and chairs and the ship's four boutiques were spruced up. All four of the Crystal Penthouses on Deck 10 were given a fresh new set of nearly everything—carpeting, upholstery, Oriental rugs, and entertainment system (including a new 33-inch TV with DVD player).

Cabins & Rates

Cabins	Per diems from	Bathtub	Fridge	Hair Dryer	Sitting Area	TV
Inside	$228	yes	yes	yes	yes	yes
Outside	$349	yes	yes	yes	yes	yes
Suite	$697	yes	yes	yes	yes	yes

* TVs show CNN and ESPN.

CABINS　Despite their high price tag, the majority of Crystal's cabins are smaller than the smallest aboard any of the Seabourn vessels (which measure 205 sq. ft.). About half the accommodations have small verandas, measuring about 6 by 8 feet. The smallest, balconyless cabins aboard *Harmony* begin at 183 square feet and on the *Symphony* at 202 square feet, a size large enough to incorporate a sofa, coffee table, and desk. Outside staterooms without verandas measure 198 to 215 square feet; those with verandas are 246 square feet (including the veranda). The *Harmony* has 19 inside cabins; the *Symphony* has none. Of the cabins without verandas, most have large rectangular windows; on the *Harmony,* 14 have rounded portholes instead. Each of them is positioned near the bow on Deck 5, below the show lounges, and forward of the ship's main dining room. The E Category cabins located amidships on the *Harmony* on Decks 7 and 8, and on the *Symphony* on Deck 8, have views obstructed by lifeboats.

Deck 10 holds the ships' spectacular, attractively styled penthouses; the four best measure nearly 1,000 square feet, including the balconies. The other two categories are about 492 and 360 square feet, including balconies. All have walk-in closets, Jacuzzi bathtubs, and bidets, and the four Crystal Penthouses have full-fledged Jacuzzis in their living rooms, with ocean views to boot!

Overall, color schemes are pastels—pinks, mints, blues, and beiges—and golden-brown wood tones, and are cheerful, breezy, and light. Each cabin has a sitting area; TVs broadcasting CNN, ESPN and lots of other channels; VCR; minibar; hair dryer; and safe. While drawer space is adequate in all cabins, the hanging closets are smaller and tighter than you'd expect on ships of this caliber. Bathrooms have both bathtub (a compact one on the lower category cabins) and shower, and are mostly tiled. They're compact (I'm being generous) on the *Harmony* and don't offer a lot of storage space or convenient towel racks; those on the *Symphony* are larger and better designed. I found the cabins to be not entirely sound-proofed; I could hear our neighbors talking and hear their television quite easily.

PUBLIC AREAS Throughout the ship, you'll find marble features and brass, glass, and hardwood paneling mingling with flowers and potted plants (especially palms). In that classic California style, the color schemes are light and airy throughout with lots of white and very pastel furniture and walls. Passenger throughways are wide and easy to navigate. The atrium/lobby areas on these ships are miniature, more subdued versions of the glittery megaship atria, but are still the most dazzling areas of the ships.

Designed with curved walls and low, vaulted ceilings, the ship's main dining rooms are elegant and spacious and done up in light colors. The chunky silverware and heavy crystal glassware twinkle and shine and mirror a sophisticated land-based restaurant. The Jade and Prego alternative restaurants on the *Symphony* are much more interesting and colorful than the *Harmony*'s plainer, almost ordinary decor.

There are two large entertainment lounges, one for Vegas-style material and another for ballroom dancing to a live band.

The ship has a hushed, somewhat academically charming library that's outfitted with comfortably upholstered chairs and a worthy collection of books, periodicals, and videos. There's also a large theater for movies and slide lectures.

The ship has six-plus bar/entertainment lounges as well as a roaming staff that wanders the public areas throughout the day and much of the night, offering to bring drinks to wherever you happen to be sitting. The dark Avenue Saloon, where polished mahogany, well-maintained leather upholstery, and a live pianist draw passengers in, is one of the prime before- and after-dinner cocktail spots (and my personal favorite, by far).

POOL, FITNESS & SPA FACILITIES These ships offer a lot of outdoor activities and spacious areas in which to do them. There are two outdoor swimming pools separated by a bar, ice-cream bar, and sandwich grill, as well as two hot tubs. One of the pools is refreshingly oversize, stretching almost 40 feet across one of the sundecks; the other can be covered with a retractable glass roof (and the *Harmony*'s has a swim-up bar). The gym and separate aerobics area are positioned for a view over the sea and the adjacent Steiner-managed spa and beauty salon are sizable.

There's also a pair of golf driving nets, a putting green, a large paddle-tennis court, and Ping-Pong tables. Runners and walkers, note: Just under four laps equals 1 mile on the broad, uninterrupted teak Promenade Deck.

The ships' generous tiered after-decks are gorgeous and provide quiet places for an afternoon spent dozing in a deck chair or for quiet repose leaning against the railing and allowing yourself to become entranced by the ship's wake.

Cunard

6100 Blue Lagoon Dr., Miami, FL 33126. ☎ **800/5-CUNARD** or 305/463-3000. Fax 305/269-6950. www.cunardline.com.

THE LINE IN A NUTSHELL   It's been said Cunard is the biggest consumer of caviar on earth—get the picture? Catering to a wealthy, well-traveled clientele, the line offers an onboard experience that's high-brow British all the way.

THE EXPERIENCE   Can you say "history"? Can you say "God Save the Queen"? Cunard, about 160 years old at this writing, is a bona fide cultural icon, a tangible reminder of the days when Britannia really did rule the waves, and that's what sets it apart from the pack. From the formal, British-style service to the decor, which through artwork and memorabilia pays tribute to England and Cunard's long history, the experience is nostalgic and genteel. Activities are relatively mellow, featuring enrichment lectures, ship tours, reading, and movies. Likewise, entertainment features pianists, singers, live dance bands, and lots of conversation and cocktails. Passengers participate at their own pace. Dining is a formal affair, and guests dress the part.

Cunard currently has two ships in its fleet, the classic *QE2* and the *Caronia* (the former *Vistafjord,* only recently renamed). The *QE2* recalls the great ocean-liner days of decades ago—among other reasons, because it was built decades ago (in 1969). Both ships got face-lifts in late 1999. New carpeting and fabrics have perked up the 32-year-old *QE2*, which, while in good shape, can't hide a smattering of water-stained ceilings, mustiness on lower decks, and a hodgepodge of cabin decor. The *Caronia,* too, sports its share of age-related imperfections like warped cabin ceilings and rusty bathroom fixtures, but overall manages to look pretty healthy after its recent sprucing up.

Pros

- **British flavor.** If you're a fan of Britain and things British, sailing Cunard is the next best thing to being there. The onboard ambiance is quiet, sedate, and ever so polite.
- **Service.** Overall, service is highly professional, efficient, and nonintrusive.
- **History.** These ships evoke the past with their decor, staff, and their own proud nautical histories, making for a special, comforting, nostalgic, and educational experience.

Cons

- **Ships show their age.** Although both underwent multimillion-dollar face-lifts in late 1999, they're older ships and can't hide their wrinkles completely.
- **Few verandas.** The *QE2* has only 30 and the *Caronia* just 25.
- **Staid attitude.** If you're not looking for a low-key jaunt, you'll likely be bored.

Compared with the other Ultra-Luxury lines, here's how Cunard rates:					
	poor	fair	good	excellent	outstanding
Enjoyment Factor				✓	
Dining				✓	
Activities				✓	
Children's Program		✓*			
Entertainment			✓		
Service				✓	
Overall Value				✓	

* QE2 *only.*

CUNARD: THE OLD GUARD LIVES ON

Once upon a time, Cunard was the absolute king of the seas, operating ships whose names still carry the ring of luxury, grandeur, and the power of the British Empire: *Mauretania, Berengaria, Queen Mary.* But that was a long time ago, and in recent years the company has had its ups and downs, going through a period of declining revenues, bad relations with travel agents, and general decline, until around 1998 when it finally got its act together to such a degree that it was snatched up as a hot commodity (or maybe a good bargain) by none other than the savvy Carnival Corporation. Almost immediately, grand plans began to be hatched, the biggest being the merging of Cunard with Carnival's ultra-luxurious Seabourn line. Now the transferring and name changing is complete: Cunard's smallest ships—the two *Sea Goddesses* and the *Royal Viking Sun*—have been transferred to Seabourn and renamed the *Seabourn Goddesses* and the *Seabourn Sun,* respectively. This has left Cunard with two ships, the famous *QE2* and the newly renamed *Caronia* (formerly *Vistafjord*), with a third on the way. In March 2000, a letter of intent was signed to build the line's third ship, the super-liner *Queen Mary 2,* at the Alstom Chantiers de L'Atlantique shipyard in France. The liner is expected to be launched in late 2003, and will fly the British flag and be homeported in Southampton, England.

The point to all of this? Creating two distinct upscale brands—Cunard's *QE2* and *Caronia* (and *QM2* down the road) offering old-world, British-style big-ship cruising and Seabourn's ships offering a modern style of cruising on small, intimate ships.

To get ready for the rebranding and the new millennium, the *QE2* went into a monthlong dry dock in late 1999 for an $18-million sprucing up, which included new carpeting throughout the ship as well as curtains, upholstery and some furniture. Much of the attention went to refurbishing the Caronia Restaurant, which now has mahogany paneling, crystal chandeliers, a new music system, etched-glass doors at the entrance, and new carpeting, curtains and chairs. At year-end 1999, the *Vistafjord* underwent a $5 million transformation into the *Caronia,* getting a new paint job (black for the hull, red for the funnel) as well as British-flavored carpeting, a sprinkling of nostalgic Cunard shipping posters (prints) on walls, and a general overhaul of the furnishings throughout its public areas and cabins.

To get to this exciting time in Cunard's life, this resurrection of sorts, the line has had to go through its share of turbulence, doubt, and monumental change. Today, though, the Cunard name continues to carry formidable prestige, the line's operational finesse is on the upswing, and its famous flagship, the *QE2,* remains the most famous passenger ship in the world, and the only ship (until the *QM2* arrives) offering trans-atlantic service on a regular schedule.

THE FLEET

The new Cunard is made up of the 1,740-passenger, 70,327-ton **QE2,** built in 1969, and the 24,492-ton, 677-passenger **Caronia** (the former *Vistafjord*), built in 1973, both of which received face-lifts in late 1999.

This is something of a come-down in numbers from earlier days. In 1983, Cunard bought the Norwegian American Line, in the process acquiring both the *Vistafjord* (now *Caronia*) and the *Sagafjord* (which was subsequently sold in 1996). In 1986, the company obtained its yachtlike *Sea Goddess I* and *Sea Goddess II,* which are now with Seabourn. In 1994, Cunard added another luxury worldwide cruise ship, the *Royal Viking Sun,* which is also now with Seabourn. In the mid-1990s, the line also sold off its most downscale ship, the *Cunard Countess,* and ended its operation of the *Cunard Dynasty* (now sailing as Crown Cruise Lines' Crown Dynasty). Confusing? For Cunard, at least, less might prove to be more, as the company's presentation is now much better focused, allowing them to more easily tell the world what it is they stand for: old-fashioned seagoing elegance.

Cunard has something new on the way, too, dubbed **Project Queen Mary.** For a few years now Cunard has been saying they intend to build a brand-new *Queen Mary* to re-create the grandeur of the old Queen liners. The skinny is that the ship will be similar in profile and ambiance to the *QE2*—with separate dining rooms for different cabin categories, for instance—but overall will be larger (projected to be the biggest passenger ship ever, in fact) and more modern. Sources say the new grand 'ole 150,000-ton liner will cost somewhere in the neighborhood of $700 million to build, and it's projected it will debut in late 2003. Let's see.

PASSENGER PROFILE

Cunard attracts a well-traveled, soft-spoken crowd of older passengers, many of them repeaters, generally in their fifties and up. They're usually the type who would prefer a 4pm tea to a communal soak in a hot tub with a bottle of tequila and a gaggle of strangers. They appreciate Cunard's old-timey virtues. Passengers are typically of an Anglophile bent, and many U.K. folks sail this line—approximately 70% of any given sailing will be Brits. There are mostly couples, but also many widows and widowers, as well as friends and relatives traveling together. Gentlemanly hosts are on board to chat and dance with single ladies.

Cunard probably carries more clients who sail just for the pleasures of sea- and star-gazing than any other line. If you crave solitude and the healing powers of a sojourn at sea, no Cunard staff member will ever disturb your quietude.

DINING

The *QE2* has its own unique dining setup, like no other ship that exists today. **Five reserved-seat restaurants** are assigned according to the cabin accommodation you've chosen. The Queen's Grill, located high on the Boat Deck, is the crème de la crème. The virtually identical 100-seat Princess Grill and Britannia Grill are smaller, tiered, and facing port and starboard, respectively, while the large, high-ceiling Caronia Restaurant has been redesigned in the style of an English country house, with mahogany paneling and crystal chandeliers. The sprawling but nicely partitioned, two-sitting Mauretania Restaurant is reserved for the lowest-priced cabins.

Menu choices are basically the same across all the restaurants, although more is available at the Queen's Grill, which features table-side cooking and carving. Expect to see a traditional American roast beef and an English cut with Yorkshire pudding, grilled Dover sole, medaillons of veal in a marsala sauce, poached salmon with shallots, or sliced breast of duck with raspberry sauce.

Because they serve fewer passengers, presentation is generally more sophisticated in the grill rooms. **Special orders** are no problem in the Queen's Grill, and you can request dishes you might have seen on earlier menus or something you've dreamed up on your own. At dinnertime on its transatlantic crossings, this ship can be one of the most formal afloat, with guests dressed to the nines, especially in the grill rooms. In the Caribbean, though, formality and fanciness are a bit more toned down.

If you want to go more casual, the *QE2*'s large and airy minty-green Lido **buffet-style restaurant** for breakfast, lunch, and dinner has several well-laid-out stations (successfully reducing queues) with lots of variety and attractive presentation. The Pavilion, one deck below, is the venue for a light continental breakfast or a simple hamburger/hot-dog grill lunch.

Vegetarian and health-conscious dishes are available.

The *Caronia*'s elegant Franconia dining room serves the ship's well-dressed passengers good food at one unhurried sitting. There are lots of tables for two in this lovely mint-green-and-ivory, candlelit room. Tivoli, a 40-seat reservations-only restaurant with its own kitchen (and seating both indoors and out), offers an all-Italian dinner menu and wine list and sea views over the stern. Buffets are set up in the indoor/outdoor Lido Cafe and by the pool.

There is 24-hour **room service** aboard both ships.

ACTIVITIES

In addition to cards, trivia games, and reading on both ships, the *QE2* is also well known for its unique agenda of activities. The ship's popular **lecture program** features a wide range of speakers, some well known and others just very good at what they do, on diverse topics such as an author's latest book (which is available for purchase and a signing at the huge library, 'natch), producing a movie, investing in the stock market, foreign affairs, and ocean-liner history.

The *Caronia* also features about a dozen theme cruises every year, with guest lecturers on board ranging from a professor of marine biology to an art historian.

Aboard the *QE2,* a member of the staff will take passengers on the ship's **Heritage Trail,** which details Cunard's 160-year history in original oil paintings, trophies, and collected memorabilia, including a wonderful photo display of the famous passengers who have crossed on Cunard ships.

On both ships, there are regular classes in the **Computer Learning Center,** and the rooms, with 10 computers each, are open for those who already know what they're doing. You can send and receive E-mail through an account you set up aboard ship. Sending an E-mail costs $5; receiving one is free.

Out on the *QE2*'s deck, activities include a **putting green** and **golf driving net,** a combo basketball and paddle-tennis court (basketball on this ship? there's a funny thought), shuffleboard, and an outdoor pool. The *Caronia* has a pool on its gorgeous and expansive classic aft deck, as well as a golf driving net on an upper deck.

The *QE2*'s **library** may very well be the biggest at sea, with one large section of books to borrow and another with books for sale. The *Caronia*'s wood-paneled, Oriental-carpeted library is also impressive. It's even got a nifty a globe of the moon hanging from the ceiling.

Both Cunard vessels have a **casino,** although they're nothing like the electronic, glittering mini-Vegases you find aboard the more high-charged Carnival ships. The one on the *Caronia* is small, but not cramped, with three gaming tables and nearly 30 slots.

CHILDREN'S PROGRAM

While you're not likely to encounter hordes of kids, it's not uncommon to see a handful of them, mostly grandkids, on board for Cunard's Caribbean itineraries, and the Christmas cruise attracts lots of children.

The *QE2* is large enough that exploring it would keep kids entertained and busy even without a lot of organized activities, but there are also **supervised programs** and an excellent nursery and **children's playroom,** with cute tiny furniture and games, staffed by well-trained English-style nannies. Kids will enjoy visits to the pet kennels, just next door, as well as activities like a captain's Coketail party, kids' talent show, a costume party in the Grand Lounge with lots of prizes, magic shows, tea parties, and tours of the ship.

On the *Caronia,* supervised children's programs are offered for children between 7 and 14 when there are at least 15 children on board.

Baby-sitting can be arranged privately with a staff member.

Cunard Fleet Itineraries

Ship	Home Ports & Season	Itinerary	Other Itineraries
Caronia	E. Caribbean itineraries round-trip from Ft. Lauderdale, Nov 2000 –Jan 2001; 14-night Caribbean/ Amazon cruises between Ft. Lauderdale and Manaus, Mar–Apr 2001.	**12- and 16-night E. Carib:** May visit St. Croix, Dominica, Antigua, Barbados, St. Maarten, Grenada, Bonaire, Aruba, Isla de Margarita (Venezuela), Puerto Rico, and Tortola. **14-night Carib/Amazon:** May visit Parintins, Santarém, and Alter do Chao (Brazil), Devil's Island (French Guiana), Barbados, St. Kitts, Dominica, Tortola, Puerto Rico, Guadeloupe, Antigua, and St. Croix.	Transatlantic, Canary Islands, South America, Europe, Eastern Canada, Africa
Queen Elizabeth 2	10-nighter between Miami and Southampton, Oct 2000; 5-night Caribbean round-trip out of Miami, Oct 2000; 6-night Bermuda cruise round-trip from New York, Sept 2001; 16-night Caribbean round-trip out of New York, Dec 2001.	**10-night Bermuda/Transatlantic:** Hamilton. **5-night E Carib:** St. Thomas. **6-night Bermuda:** Hamilton, Royal Naval Dockyard. **16-night E. and S. Carib:** May visit Jamaica, Curaçao, Bonaire, Barbados, St. Thomas, Cape Canaveral (Florida), and Miami.	Transatlantic, Europe, Eastern Canada/New England

ENTERTAINMENT

The *QE2*'s Grand Lounge is not set up for big Vegas-style production shows, but the smaller shows performed there are decent. Throughout the ship are cabaret acts, singers, small bands, large bands, cocktail and classical pianists, a harpist, and even karaoke. There's a great house band for dancing the fox-trot, jitterbug, tango, and waltz in the Queen's Room, a traditional ballroom. (And attention single ladies: There are always gentlemanly hosts sailing on board with whom you can dance and chat.) Throughout the ship there are nearly a dozen bars and entertainment lounges, and the Golden Lion Pub is always a favorite watering hole. The ship's library stocks videos for in-cabin viewing by suite passengers; there's a large movie theater as well, if the big screen serves you better.

The *Caronia* offers the same type of elegant, understated entertainment as her bigger sister, with after-dinner concerts in the bright and cheery Garden Lounge and shows and big-band dancing in the spacious, high-ceilinged Ballroom, which features cozy banquet seating all along its windowed port and starboard sides. Amidships is a proper movie theater for first-run films and special-interest lectures.

SERVICE

Overall, service is efficient and first-class; however, in that British way, it's quiet and not gushing. The *QE2* is a hard to ship to work because of the long distances to and from the galleys, so things can get a bit harried in the ship's two-sitting Mauretania Restaurant.

There are **self-service laundry rooms** on both ships.

Tips on Tipping: Cunard

In early 2000, Cunard introduced a new tipping policy. Instead of passengers tipping in cash at the end of the cruise (as is done with most lines), gratuities will be added to each guests' shipboard account at a rate of $10 to $13 per day, depending on your accommodation. At the end of the cruise, guests can adjust the amount depending on their view of the service.

Caronia

The Verdict

Like the *QE2*, the newly refurbished 28-year-old Caronia is a shippy ship offering a British-flavored experience at sea; unlike the *QE2*, it only carries 679 passengers, creating a more intimate, personal ambiance.

Caronia *(photo: Cunard)*

Specifications

Size (in tons)	24,492	Officers	British/European
Number of Cabins	376	Crew	400 (European)
Number of Outside Cabins	324	Passenger/Crew Ratio	1.7 to 1
Cabins with Verandas	25	Year Built	1973
Number of Passengers	679	Last Major Refurbishment	1999

Frommer's Ratings (Scale of 1–5)

Cabin Comfort & Amenities	3	Pool, Fitness & Spa Facilities	4
Ship Cleanliness & Maintenance	4	Children's Facilities	2
Public Comfort/Space	4	Itinerary	4
Decor	4	Worth the Money	4

Originally completed in 1973 as the combo liner/cruise ship *Vistafjord,* this 679-passenger, 24,492-ton vessel is still very much an ocean liner, known for its sophisticated long-voyage cruises catering to older, well-heeled Americans, Germans, and British. The ship got a $5 million refit in late 1999 that transformed it into the *Caronia,* complete with British registry, a black Cunard hull and red funnel, and Cunard ship names for its public rooms (like the Franconia dining room and White Star Bar). This *Caronia* is the third ship in Cunard's history to bear that name (the first sailed from 1905 to 1931; the second, called the "Green Goddess" because of the color of its hull, from 1948 until 1970) and is intended, like the *QE2,* to provide a traditionally British experience, with British officers (who will serve aboard both ships on an alternating basis) and a 400-member, mostly European staff.

In great shape despite its vintage, the *Caronia* feels like a classic ship in many ways, from its grand aft tiered decks to the sheer of its cabin corridors and sloping cabin floors, the brass clocks on the walls by the elevators and stairwells, and the smattering of black-and-white vintage photos of the old *Caronias* lining the walls.

Cabins & Rates						
Cabins	**Per diems from**	**Bathtub**	**Fridge**	**Hair Dryer**	**Sitting Area**	**TV**
Inside	$181	no	yes	yes	no	yes*
Outside	$197	some	some	yes	some	yes*
Suite	$380	some	yes	yes	yes	yes*

* TVs have VCRs, plus CNN.

CABINS   Most of the 376 cabins are outsides, and all are designed for longer voyages, with spacious floor plans and plentiful stowage. The detailed cabin plans are well worth studying because of the intriguing variety of arrangements. All cabins have light wood accents, TVs with VCRs, two-music channels, phones, safes, minibars, robes, fresh fruit daily, half-bottles of sparkling wine upon embarkation, and a collection of lovely English-made Bronnley shampoos and soaps in the bathrooms. Some cabins in the top categories have generous-size verandas, and two Hollywood-style duplex suites are among the nautical world's best, featuring bedroom with whirlpool bath below and a sitting area with sauna, treadmill, and another whirlpool bath on the upper level, which also leads to a private balcony with another hot tub and an absolutely enormous area of deck that's reserved solely for occupants of the two duplex suites. These suites have lots of huge floor-to-ceiling windows, plenty of closets, and two bathrooms, both with bidets and double sinks.

In general, cabins are in good shape, but if you look closely you'll see uneven and nicked floors, ceilings, and walls, telltale signs of an aging ship. Views are obstructed on the 13 B-Category cabins aft on the Promenade Deck, and in Cabin 14 on the Bridge Deck. While the ship boasts balconies on 25 cabins, 23 are on the Sun Deck, where views are partially obstructed by lifeboats. Cabin 103 on this deck juts out further than most of the others and has a cozy balcony facing aft; the homey bamboo furniture decorating it was picked out by a guest who frequently books that cabin.

Single travelers have more accommodation options aboard this ship (and the *QE2*) than nearly any other afloat, with a choice of 71 dedicated single cabins. Most of these are outside, and half have bathtubs.

As aboard the *QE2,* suite guests (Duplex Penthouses and Category S1 suites) have minibars stocked with two bottles of wine or liquor of their choice (soft drinks, bottled water, and beer are replenished free upon request). In the other cabins and throughout the ship's public rooms, wine, liquors, beer, and soft drinks are available for purchase.

With lots of stairs and multilevel decks, the *Caronia* isn't the best for wheelchair users, although six cabins are equipped to handle them.

PUBLIC AREAS   *Caronia's* public rooms represent understated elegance, with an overall warm linerlike feel and a decor dominated by burgundies and golds and wood paneling (mostly the faux stuff, of course, in these safety-conscious days). The forward circular Garden Lounge, with its lovely semicircular bands of colored lights recessed in the ceiling and abundance of live plants, is the place for proper afternoon tea and after-dinner concerts. The spacious Ballroom offers shows and big-band dancing on a large wooden floor, and intimate banquette seating along the windows invites quiet conversation. Gentleman hosts provide company and act as dance partners for ladies traveling alone. A small but functional casino leads into the new White Star Bar (which replaced the North Cape Bar), a quiet place done up in blue, gold, and dark green along the Starboard side of the ship, filled with nostalgic touches like repros of Cunard advertising posters.

The ship's recent refit gave it a collection of onboard boutiques collectively called the Regent Shops after one of London's most prestigious shopping sections. In a layout similar to the *QE2*'s, a bookshop/souvenir-store was added near the *Caronia*'s wood-paneled library and sells a small collection of Cunard-related and general interest books as well as shippy souvenirs like prints of old-time Cunard posters, T-shirts, and show plates. There's also a very impressive new computer room where a shop used to be, housing some 10 new computers, all rigged with E-mail access.

Amidships is a proper movie theater for first-run films and special-interest lectures, and the aft-facing Piccadilly nightclub doubles as a daytime retreat for readers, who revel in the views over the Veranda Deck pool.

In addition to the lovely mint- and ivory-hued Franconia restaurant with its crystal chandeliers and elegantly set candlelit tables with silver bud vases, the ship has an indoor/outdoor buffet restaurant. The indoor part can get cramped, while the umbrella tables on the aft pool deck are a gorgeous place to lunch. There's also the Tivoli, an alternative Italian dining venue for evenings, with both indoor and outdoor seating. Located above the Piccadilly lounge and sharing the same aft deck views, it's a dark and romantic place for a quiet dinner. By day, Tivoli's tables become card tables.

POOL, FITNESS & SPA FACILITIES   The *Caronia* has a gorgeous set of tiered aft decks. The main and largest one, the Lido Deck, contains the main pool, tables with umbrellas for diners from the adjacent Lido Café, a bar, and plenty more room for lounge chairs and strolling. Besides the Lido Deck, there are lots of other places to stow away with a good book, including the wide teak wraparound promenade beneath the lifeboats (and with several indented nooks that cut the wind), and the slices of tiered aft deck leading down to the Lido. Keep in mind here that the stairs between outside decks are quite steep.

In addition to the pool on the Veranda Deck, a second pool lies deep within the hull in a complex that includes a surprisingly roomy though windowless gym, sauna, and massage facility. Last time I looked, there were four treadmills, four stationary cycles, two step machines, a weight room, and a handful of massage rooms. Note that during departures and docking, the watertight doors leading into the gym are shut and users need to follow a circuitous set of crew stairs to get there.

Queen Elizabeth 2

The Verdict

For the past two decades, this grande dame has been the only game in town for a traditional, regularly scheduled transatlantic crossing, and it gives passengers that same wonderful ocean-liner feel and nostalgic British flavor when at sea en route to Bermuda and the Caribbean.

QE2 *(photo: Cunard)*

Specifications

Size (in tons)	70,327	Officers	British/European
Number of Cabins	931	Crew	1,000 (Internat'l)
Number of Outside Cabins	625	Passenger/Crew Ratio	1.8 to 1
Cabins with Verandas	33	Year Built	1969
Number of Passengers	1,740	Last Major Refurbishment	1999

Frommer's Ratings (Scale of 1–5)

Cabin Comfort & Amenities	3	Pool, Fitness & Spa Facilities	4
Ship Cleanliness & Maintenance	3	Children's Facilities	3
Public Comfort/Space	4	Itinerary	4
Decor	4	Worth the Money	5

The *Queen Elizabeth 2* turned 30 in 1999 and is still doing what it was designed for, providing a fast transatlantic crossing (it remains the only ship doing so on a regular schedule) and undertaking a series of short and long cruises to the Caribbean and Bermuda from both the United States and United Kingdom. Its high speed allows it to get to the Caribbean more quickly than nearly all other ships.

In late 1999, the ship received an $18 million face-lift that covered it in new carpeting throughout, added drapes and upholstery to many public areas, and replaced carpeting, bedspreads, valances, and draperies in every single cabin. Happily, with these renovations and the $65 million worth of refittings made in 1994 and 1996, the *QE2* has entered the millennium in terrific shape, sporting its classic ocean liner's midnight-blue hull (which was stripped of a zillion layers of old paint before a new coat was applied), spotless white superstructure, and the famous Cunard red-orange-and-black funnel.

The ship has an intensely loyal following, with passengers coming back year after year. They'll even book the same cabin and dine in the same restaurant, often even at the same table. There are also those who come once to say they have done it, and may never come again.

Cabins & Rates

Cabins	Per diems from	Bathtub	Fridge	Hair Dryer	Sitting Area	TV
Inside	$191	no	no	no	no	yes*
Outside	$260	some	some	some	some	yes*
Suite	$513	yes	yes	yes	yes	yes*

* TVs show CNN.

CABINS   Being an older ship originally designed for two classes, there's a huge range of cabin accommodations (21 at last count), and layout and decorative variations within a single category. The ship's refit in late 1999 resulted in the addition of two new QS-category Grand Suites (and grand they are): the 777-square-foot Aquitania on Two Deck and the 575-square-foot, wheelchair-accessible Caledonia Suite on Boat Deck, adjacent to the Queens Grill (this far-forward suite was carved out of the radio room and, with its low windows facing right out onto Boat Deck promenade, it feels a bit like an aquarium). Both have marble master bathrooms plus guest bathrooms, a dining area, and large picture windows.

There is a total of 30 high-up cabins with balconies (which were added to the ship over the years), located in a separate penthouse location on the Signal Deck, effectively cut off from the rest of the ship. The amidships Deck 1 and 2 Q3 Grades were the top accommodations when the ship was new, and they remain the preferred choice for traditionalists who want an authentic steamship-type cabin. They have wood paneling, satin-padded walls, a large elliptical window or three elliptical portholes, walk-in closets/dressing rooms, a corner for a standing steamer trunk (we all have one of those, right?), and a large marble bathroom with full-size tub and bidet.

The midprice Princess and Caronia Grade cabins are also roomy for this level, while the lowest priced are deep in the ship and tight, with many inside, including some with upper and lower berths. However, they provide moderately priced accommodations for those who couldn't otherwise afford the ship. During rough weather conditions, the portholes on Five Deck may be sealed by metal covers called "deadlights."

All cabins have TVs showing CNN, lots of movies, and even Cunard history films. Top suites have VCRs. Many outside cabins have sitting rooms, bathtubs, and minifridges. Views from some of the cabins on the Sports and Boat decks are partially obstructed by lifeboats.

Over 100 cabins are designated for singles, and four cabins are specially equipped for wheelchair users, although parts of the ship have small steps and raised doorways.

PUBLIC AREAS Nearly all the public rooms range over two complete decks (Upper and Quarter decks) and offer a great variety of venues for socializing, reading, and special functions. Every public room has been redone several times over, so the decor is now both traditional and up-to-date but not dated, using effects like burled wood paneling, royal-blue carpets, art-deco–style room dividers in the Mauretania Restaurant, a teak deck in the Yacht Club bar, and etched glass and wood partitions in the Golden Lion Pub (where you have an impressive choice of international beers and ale). The Chart Room, a lovely two-part lounge bar, has a harpist alternating with a pianist playing the room's centerpiece: the grand piano from the old *Queen Mary*. The boxy, convention-hall-like theater is not one of the ship's loveliest spaces (not by a long shot), but it's the place for movies and lectures.

The ship's refreshing face-lift in late 1999 added new carpeting and upholstery to many public areas and corridors, including the Golden Lion Pub, Chart Room, Crystal Bar, and casino, which also got new gaming tables and leather stools. The Queens Room, the spot for high tea and after-dinner dancing, now has new furniture and repaneled mahogany walls. The Caronia restaurant also received a face-lift that has transformed it into a sort of warm English-country-house-style dining room with rich mahogany paneling and crystal chandeliers. Quite appropriately, a mini-Harrods shop selling the ubiquitous green totes, stuffed bears, and cookies was added to the ship, joining the intensive cluster of preexisting shops, which sell things from Bally shoes to Wedgwood china, Waterford crystal, maritime antiques, and collectibles like an ornate pair of epaulettes and a porthole.

Cunard's heritage is all over the ship, fortunately. Before the 1994 refit, much of the memorabilia and art that now makes the ship so special and grand apparently had not been deemed fashionable enough to display. Times have changed, though, and the past is in vogue again. Most notable are huge oil paintings located in the central stairway, one of Queen Elizabeth (which the Queen Mother commissioned for the *QE2*'s long-gone older sister, the original *Queen Elizabeth*) and another of Princess Elizabeth and Prince Philip that once hung in the main lounge of the old green-hulled world cruiser *Caronia,* which sailed from 1948 until the early 1970s. The 10-foot lighted scale model of the record-breaking *Mauretania,* the fastest ship on the Atlantic for over two decades, is a showstopper in the same foyer, and nearby is a large oil painting showing the same ship coming down the River Tyne near Newcastle, England, where it was built. The aft stairway is a two-deck gallery of original paintings by two artists (one being Stephen Card) showing Cunard ships from the line's 160-year history.

Cunard's history is also captured in several museum-quality display cases throughout the ship, which hold Cunard memorabilia like table settings, old tickets, brochures, and luggage tags, and a nostalgic collection of photos of VIPs—celebrities, politicians, and heads of state who have sailed on the venerated Cunard ships over the course of the century. There are also trophies and posters on display, as well as historical tidbits about the *QE2*'s life as a troopship during the Falkland Islands War, for instance. To assure that you'll get the most out of the collection, take one of the staff-directed "Heritage Trail" tours that are offered, which include some handouts on the collections.

A medical center staffed by doctors and nurses is available.

There are self-service laundry rooms.

POOL, FITNESS & SPA FACILITIES   The *QE2* has four hot tubs and two pools, one indoors on a lower deck with the spa and gym and the other located on the ship's classic tiered aft decks, which fill up quickly (as do the limited deck chairs) during sunny days at sea. These tiered aft decks are an ideal place to perch for a wonderful view of the sea and the ship's wake. The best location for a deck chair is on the Sun Deck because it's sheltered from the wind by a surrounding glass enclosure and is somewhat off the beaten track.

Steiner runs the spa and fitness facilities (as they do on most ships), and although they're complete in the range of offerings, they are *waaaaaayyy* down in the hull, with the spa on Six Deck and the gymnasium and indoor pool (a rarity these days) on Seven Deck. Think of it this way: You'll get a workout just by walking there. The spa offers a 10-station AquaSpa as well as treatment rooms, sauna, and massage. The gym, positioned alongside the glassed-in pool, has the typical range of treadmills, cycles, and weight machines, and there are aerobics classes and daily forced-march hikes out on deck.

Deck facilities include a putting green and golf driving net, a combo basketball (ha! don't expect this one to get much use!) and paddle-tennis court, and shuffleboard.

Radisson Seven Seas Cruises

600 Corporate Dr., Suite 410, Ft. Lauderdale, FL 33334. ☎ **800/285-1835** or 954/776-6123. Fax 954/772-3763. www.rssc.com.

THE LINE IN A NUTSHELL   Radisson carries passengers in style and extreme comfort. Its brand of luxury is casually elegant and subtle, and its cuisine is near the top.

THE EXPERIENCE   These ships are spacious, and service is supreme. Unlike some high-end ships these days, extras like tips, wine with dinner, stocked minibars (stocked once), and unlimited soft drinks and mineral waters are included in the rates. Both the *Radisson Diamond* and the *Seven Seas Navigator* have all outside cabins, and well over half of them have private balconies; the *Mariner* will have balconies on every single cabin. Cuisine is some of the best at sea, and in addition to their formal restaurants, all three ships have alternative, reservations-only restaurants specializing in northern Italian food. Even if what tickles your fancy isn't on the menu, the chef will prepare it for you. In fact, you can hardly walk anywhere on the ship without staff members asking if there's something they can do for you. These ships tend to be less stuffy, less snooty, and a bit more casual than Seabourn and Cunard. You can chuck your tux for the most part, although on formal nights they certainly aren't uncommon.

Pros

- **Few extra charges.** Unlike some of its peers, Radisson includes tips, wine at dinner, unlimited soft drinks and mineral water, and an initial stocked minibar in its cruise rates. The only charges are for alcoholic beverages and shore excursions.
- **Lots of private verandas.** In fact, at least 75% of cabins have them on all three ships.
- **Great dining.** Cuisine is superb, and both ships have just one open seating for all meals (as opposed to early and late seatings).
- **Large cabins on the *Navigator*.** All of the ship's standard suites measure 301 square feet, including balcony, bigger than Seabourn's and Crystal's.
- **Amazing bathrooms on the *Navigator*.** Bigger and better than those on the high-end Seabourn and Crystal ships, every single cabin bathroom on the *Navigator* has a separate shower stall and a full-size bathtub long enough for normal-size humans.

Cons

- **Few windows on the *Diamond*.** This boxy vessel has much underutilized space, and many key public rooms are somewhat cold and have no windows.
- **Unstable in stormy seas.** Between the *Diamond*'s catamaran-style hull and the *Navigator*'s top-heavy design, these ships aren't the most stable in rough weather.

Compared with the other Ultra-Luxury lines, here's how Radisson rates:					
	poor	fair	good	excellent	outstanding
Enjoyment Factor				✓	
Dining				✓	
Activities				✓	
Children's Program	N/A*				
Entertainment			✓		
Service				✓	
Overall Value					✓

* Radisson has no children's program.

RADISSON: INFORMAL ELEGANCE

With the much-publicized launch of the catamaran-style *Radisson Diamond* in 1992, Minneapolis-based Radisson Hotels Worldwide began a venture that has evolved into Radisson Seven Seas Cruises. It's a line that markets and manages (but in many cases does not own) a mini-armada of widely different, though luxurious, globetrotting ships.

THE FLEET

Radisson Seven Seas operates a diverse five-ship fleet, including the 708-passenger *Seven Seas Mariner,* which, at press time, was to debut in March of 2001 under French registry. The *Mariner* will be the largest ship in the Radisson fleet, besting the 490-passenger, 30,000-ton *Seven Seas Navigator,* which entered service in August 1999, and the 350-passenger, 20,000-ton, 1992-built *Radisson Diamond.* At press time, I expect to see all three spending time in the Caribbean.

From its snub nose to its hydraulically lowered marina in the stern, the boxy-looking *Diamond* is a showstopper, although more for its unusualness than any shiplike beauty. Designed and built by a group of Finnish investors at a price of around $125 million, it is basically a gigantic catamaran, its vast, wide shell supported by a pair of submarinelike hulls supporting a six-deck superstructure that rides 28 feet above the water and is 103 feet wide by 420 feet long. Compare that to Cunard's *QE2,* which is 963 feet long, but only 2 feet wider than the *Diamond.*

The 180-passenger, 8,282-ton *Song of Flower* sails exotic itineraries worldwide, including Europe, the Mediterranean, and the Far East. The 320-passenger, 18,800-ton *Paul Gauguin* spends the year doing 7-night cruises in French Polynesia. The 188-passenger, 9,000-ton *Hanseatic,* a luxurious expedition ship, cruises in the Antarctic.

PASSENGER PROFILE

This line appeals primarily to well-traveled and well-heeled passengers in their fifties and sixties, but younger passengers and honeymooners pepper the mix. These are frequent cruisers, many of whom have sailed on Seabourn and a good number on Holland America. Though they have sophisticated tastes, they also appreciate a somewhat less formal ambiance and don't need napkin-folding classes to entertain them during the day. Still, you'll always find a coterie of women at breakfast or strolling the pool deck in full makeup and coifed do, with coordinating jewelry and shoes matched to bags; many wear chunky gold necklaces and high-heeled sandals with bathing suits, and some of their men have gold Rolexes the size of Texas. That said, even this group doesn't escape the casual trend. On a recent *Navigator* cruise, casual night in the formal dining room attracted a range that included polo shirts and jackets and expensive T-shirts, jeans, and sneakers.

Some passengers traveling independently complain that the *Diamond* is too heavily oriented to conventioneers, as it was almost exclusively after its debut. Even so, most conventioneers are top executives or top producers for their organizations, all of whom fit very well into the ship's passenger demographics. Nevertheless, when a sizable group is on board they might take over the lounge, and other passengers might feel excluded. To avoid this, Radisson tries not to book more than three corporate groups at a time onto any sailing.

DINING

Superb menus are designed for a sophisticated palate, and include some of the best cuisine in the cruise industry. The highest-quality ingredients include the freshest fish at sea, and dishes like sushi. Nice red and white house wines are complimentary at dinner, and there's an extensive menu of vintages from France, California, Washington, and Australia.

On the *Navigator,* elaborate and elegant meals are served in a single, open seating in the Compass Rose dining room by a staff of mostly Europeans (men and a handful of women). Appetizers might include the likes of an oven-roasted pheasant salad or avocado fritters in a spicy sauce, with main entrees including enticing dishes like zucchini-wrapped chicken breast stuffed with olives and tomatoes or herb-crusted roast leg of lamb. Each dinner menu offers a vegetarian option such as a vegetable curry, a light and healthy choice like grilled tuna steak in a leek-and-tomato vinaigrette, and when you've had enough of fancy, there are four standards called **"simplicity dishes"** available daily: spaghetti with tomato sauce, filet mignon, and grilled chicken breast or salmon. The Portofino restaurant is a more intimate venue with tables for two or four, and serves buffet-style breakfast and lunch and a sit-down reservations-only dinner for which the menu includes antipasti choices like marinated salmon rings or Bresaola carpaccio with Parmesan cheese and mushrooms, pasta courses that may feature a jumbo-prawn risotto, and main courses such as a grilled lobster or osso buco. Breakfast includes made-to-order omelets as well as the typical selection of hot and cold breakfast foods, and at lunch pastas and Caesar salads are tossed to order on line. Lunch entrees include dishes like a spicy paella as well as rich homemade soups and a spread of cheeses, cold cuts, salads, and plenty of tropical fruits like mango and papaya. If you don't want to get out of your bathing suit at lunch, there's a poolside sandwich grill with waiters serving guests hamburgers and fries at tables clustered on deck.

On the *Radisson Diamond,* you might start dinner with chilled snow-crab claws or a medley of California rolls, followed by a chilled cantaloupe bisque or Filipino shrimp soup, and then maybe a spinach salad. Main courses might include grilled sea bass with a mango chutney, double-broiled tournedos of beef with a béarnaise-and-peppercorn sauce, or grilled scallops on a bed of leeks. Each evening's menu on the *Diamond* includes a wok special, a **light choice,** and chef's special and sumptuous (though too rich) entrees. The Grand Dining Room has an open seating policy for all meals. The Grill, a splendid and very popular indoor/outdoor setting, offers a variety of beautifully presented foods at breakfast and lunches, focusing on a theme such as Scandinavian, Asian, or seafood. Each evening, the Grill transforms into Don Vito's, one of the liveliest reservations-only **alternative dining venues** you're likely to encounter at sea, with singing waiters belting out "O Sole Mio" and inviting you to join in. It's perhaps the most fun experience you'll have on board. Its fixed multicourse menu changes daily, and might feature farfalle with fresh tomato, eggplant and mozzarella, risotto with pumpkin and truffle flavor, or a veal tenderloin with pine-nut sauce. The room seats only about 55, so don't dawdle in making your reservations.

On both the *Diamond* and *Navigator,* hot hors d'oeuvres are served in the lounges before dinner, and if you take advantage of the **24-hour room service,** a steward will come in and lay a white tablecloth along with silverware and china, whether you've ordered a full-course dinner or just a plate of fruit. Plus you can always get virtually anything on request.

Specialty coffees are complimentary any time.

ACTIVITIES

Days are basically unstructured, with most passengers lazing around the pool deck. During the day, there might be activities (more offered on the *Navigator* because it's bigger) like tap-dancing or line-dancing classes poolside (which don't generally attract hordes of passengers), and passengers are free to hit some balls into the ships' golf nets.

Radisson Fleet Itineraries

Ship	Home Ports & Season	Itinerary	Other Itineraries
Radisson Diamond	6-night itineraries round-trip from San Juan, Nov–Feb; 7- and 9-night between Ft. Lauderdale and Puerto Caldera (Costa Rica), San Juan and Gamboa (Panama), Gamboa and Aruba, Aruba and Puerto Caldera, Aruba and San Juan, Dec–Feb.	**3-, 4-, 6-, and 7-night E. Carib:** May visit Martinique, St. Kitts, Barbados, and St. Thomas. **7- and 9-night Panama Canal:** May visit San Blas Islands (Panama), Cartageña (Colombia), Aruba, Curaçao, and St. Thomas.	Europe & Mediter- ranean
Seven Seas Mariner	Panama Canal cruises sail between Puerto Caldera and Ft. Lauderdale, Mar. Bermuda cruises round-trip from Ft. Lauderdale, Apr and Oct. Caribbean cruises round-trip from Ft. Lauderdale, Nov.	**9-night Panama Canal:** Calica and Cozumel (Mexico), Grand Cayman, Cartageña (Colombia), and Gatun Yacht Club (Panama). **9-night Bermuda:** Charleston (South Carolina), Hamilton, and Nassau. **7- and 10-night W. Carib:** May visit Grand Cayman, Cozumel and Calica, Key West, and New Orleans.	Alaska, Mexican Riviera
Seven Seas Navigator	Panama Canal cruises sail between Ft. Lauderdale and Puntarenas (Costa Rica) or Ft. Lauderdale and Callao (Peru), Jan–Feb. Caribbean cruises sail between Ft. Lauderdale and Palm Beach or round-trip from Ft. Lauderdale, Nov–Dec.	**9-, 10-, and 12-night Panama Canal:** May visit Puerto Armuelles (Panama), Cartageña (Colombia), Aruba, Grand Cayman, Roatan (Honduras), Cozumel, Calica/Cancun, and Key West. **7- and 9-night Carib:** Port calls not yet determined at press time.	Mediter- ranean & Europe, South America

Inside, you'll find pursuits like wine tasting, art auctions, bridge, bingo, and seminars led by guest experts on subjects like handwriting analysis and relationships. Another pastime includes shopping, Fifth Avenue style: the *Navigator*'s two boutiques, for example, tempt the well-heeled with $500 Alfred Dunhill humidors; $18,500 gold, safire-studded Cartier watches; and $700 gold Mont Blanc pens for sale along with sundries and souvenirs.

Because it's smaller than the *Navigator,* the *Diamond* is more of an amuse-yourself ship, where you're provided with a plush setting and a staff that brings you luxurious food and drink whenever they're needed, but after that you're on your own. Arm yourself with a good book and/or interesting companion and you'll be fine. Videotapes and books are available on both ships, 24 hours daily, from the library.

CHILDREN'S PROGRAM

These ships are geared to adults, and mature ones at that. There's no child care and no special activities for children.

ENTERTAINMENT

As on other relatively small ships, entertainment is modest, and most passengers are happy with the low-key offerings such as pianists, singers, or small bands. Entertainment is mainly a few headline crooners and musicians and enrichment lecturers. Evenings, passengers are content cocktailing with new friends.

On the *Navigator,* there's a decent amount of evening entertainment for a ship its size. Small-scale Vegas-style music reviews, typical of larger ships, are featured in the two-story show lounge, and though they're certainly not a high point of the cruises, they add a nice touch to the evenings. A show on a recent cruise included hits from the 1930s and 1940s on up through the 1980s, with a Village People segment thrown in. The crowd seemed to enjoy it; in fact, I couldn't help but admire a 70-plus woman in a wheelchair and connected to an oxygen tank bopping her head happily to the Village People hit "Feel My Body." After-dinner entertainment also includes the smooth tunes of a pianist in the romantic glass-enclosed Galileo's Lounge, and a live duo crooning pop hits in the Stars Lounge (which doubles as the ship's disco).

On the *Diamond,* there isn't enough entertainment to satisfy those who enjoy the facilities and activities aboard large mainstream ships or those who love a Las Vegas ambiance. That isn't what this ship is about, but even if it were, the poor design of the showroom—surely one of the most oddly configured theaters at sea—would only add to the problems: Essentially, it's a stage sunk in a well of balconies with the only good sight lines being on the immediate periphery. For any energetic night owls, the *Diamond* has a **late-night disco** (Windows Lounge, set toward the bow on Deck 8) for anyone still up at midnight (there won't be many).

Each ship also has a **small casino** as well (the *Navigator*'s is bigger, with nearly 50 slots, three blackjack tables, one poker and one craps table, and a roulette wheel).

SERVICE

Service is a major plus on both the *Diamond* and the *Navigator,* and especially on the former it goes a long way toward overcoming the ship's physical limitations. Staff strive to fulfill every passenger request with a smile. You rarely, if ever, hear the word "no." The service is a major plus that goes a long way to overcoming the *Diamond*'s physical limitations (low natural light, plain decor, and so forth).

The *Navigator*'s crew-to-passenger ratio is 1.5 passengers to every crew member (the *Diamond*'s is almost that good)—so high that you could almost expect one staff person to pour your coffee while another stirs in your sugar. Stewardesses ably care for your cabin, although slip-ups are not unheard of. Surprisingly, at check-in on a recent *Diamond* cruise, I found six empty water bottles in our storage drawers and a pair of old sneakers and a chocolate wrapper under the bed. However, stateroom service and the attention generally given it are excellent.

The European wait staff is highly trained and supremely gracious and professional. They're intimately knowledgeable about the menu, and eager to please guests at every turn. Cruise rates include wine with dinner, unlimited sodas and bottled water, and gratuities, although many passengers tip anyway. However, unlike most lines, port charges are not included in the cruise rates, and will run you an extra $200 to $300 per person, depending on the length of the cruise.

Radisson Diamond

The Verdict

The *Radisson Diamond* offers small-ship luxury cruising for well-heeled passengers who enjoy excellent service and fine cuisine without snootiness and without an ultra-formal dress code.

Radisson Diamond *(photo: Radisson)*

Specifications

Size (in tons)	20,295	Officers	International
Number of Cabins	177	Crew	192 (International)
Number of Outside Cabins	177	Passenger/Crew Ratio	1.8 to 1
Cabins with Verandas	121	Year Built	1992
Number of Passengers	350	Last Major Refurbishment	N/A

Frommer's Ratings (Scale of 1–5)

Cabin Comfort & Amenities	4	Pool, Fitness & Spa Facilities	3
Ship Cleanliness & Maintenance	3	Children's Facilities	N/A
Public Comfort/Space	4	Itinerary	4
Decor	3	Worth the Money	5

The *Radisson Diamond* is surprisingly informal for a luxury vessel, and the extraordinarily low density of passengers and the high ratio of crew members to passengers makes you feel like you're on a private yacht. It's as luxurious as Seabourn without the formality and price, and offers ample space—from the dramatic three-deck-high forward lounge to the underwater viewing room in the starboard hull, the ship gives you plenty of legroom and elbow room for stretching. While the ship has its faults—most notably, it has few windows and natural light, and a somewhat plain decor—service and cuisine are top-notch, and passengers will find some of the most carefully crafted interiors (spruced up with a $3 million refurbishment in early 2000, including new carpeting almost everywhere, plus some new artwork and flooring), most upscale amenities, and most superb cuisine afloat. As such, the ship has become a favorite of North America–based big-ticket spenders, many of them repeaters. It has also become a favorite choice for full charters (which must be arranged at least a year in advance) and oceangoing conventions. A company spokeswoman said about a third of *Diamond*'s passengers in a given year are part of meeting/convention groups. The vessel is intimate enough, and its staff is savvy enough, to pull off such combinations of business and pleasure with high style.

So, what's the deal with the vessel's catamaran-style SWATH (Small Waterplane Area Twin Hull) design? It's been touted as providing the utmost in stability because of its stabilizers and pair of pontoons that sit at a depth of only about 5 feet below the water line. (For this reason, the letters before the ship's name are not the more standard MV—motor vessel—or MS—motor ship—but rather SSC, or semisubmersible craft: the SSC *Radisson Diamond*.) Truth is, while the ship is very stable in calm seas and generally rolls less from port to starboard, when seas get choppy or waves are coming at the ship head on, the ship is no more stable than any other. In fact, it's safe to say it's got a *rougher* ride than most in stormy seas, when waves slam against the underside of the raised area between the pontoons, creating a loud and most unpleasant shuddering sensation. My point? I just don't want you to think the ship's unique hull design somehow indemnifies it from getting uncomfortable in certain sea conditions. Chances are, though, that you won't encounter rough seas, since the *Diamond* doesn't travel far between ports—primarily because it's an absolute slowpoke, with a cruising speed that rarely exceeds a maximum of around 12.5 knots, about 40% slower than many other cruise ships.

Cabins & Rates

Cabins	Per diems from	Bathtub	Fridge	Hair Dryer	Sitting Area	TV
Inside	$473	yes	yes	yes	yes	yes*
Outside	$524	yes	yes	yes	yes	yes*
Suite	$924	yes	yes	yes	yes	yes*

* TVs have CNN.

CABINS   The cabins are among the largest and most luxurious in Caribbean waters, and in early 2000 they all received new carpeting as well as new granite bathroom floors. All accommodations are outside suites measuring 243 square feet (in the case of the 121 balcony suites, this includes the balcony); this compares to fleet mate *Navigator's* 301 square-foot standard cabins, including balcony. The 53 cabins without balconies have big, rectangular windows. Views are wide open and unobstructed from every cabin aboard. Despite their size, many of the staterooms are deep and narrow, meaning there's very little room between the foot of the beds and the cabin's wall. About half the cabins on Deck 8 can accommodate a third person on a foldaway couch. Done in a mix of modern and art-deco styling, the decor is subdued, with touches of blond woods, pastel colors, and comfortable settees. In early 2000, two more master suites were created by joining two pairs of Deck 9 staterooms, for a total of four master suites, ranging between 486 and 522 square feet, including balconies (the Deck 9 master suites have two bathrooms). All four were also spruced up with new carpeting, drapes, and furniture.

All cabins have TVs broadcasting CNN and other channels, a VCR, minibar stocked free of charge one time, terry bathrobes, and a safe.

Stateroom bathrooms fall short of superluxury styling: While there are marble-topped vanities, bathtubs with showers, and hair dryers, they're not as opulent as you might expect given the glamour and spaciousness of the cabins, and they certainly can't compare to the awesome bathrooms on the *Navigator*.

Two cabins, newly refurbished, are specially outfitted for people with disabilities.

PUBLIC AREAS   Most public rooms are situated around a central core, making the *Diamond* a very simple ship to negotiate. The ship's most notable space is its single-seating main dining room, one of the loveliest and most romantic at sea. The vast room, buttressed by a two-deck-high wall of glass, is divided into three intimate sections and punctuated by soaring stylized acanthus-leaf columns that lend the room an art-deco feel. Except for the dining room, though, the decor is not as drop-dead gorgeous as you might expect on a luxury vessel.

Since the designers deliberately placed all the passenger accommodations along the perimeter of the ship, most public rooms (including the casino and the main show lounge) are inside, and therefore get little direct sunlight—but since these areas are busy mostly after dark, you don't always notice. Exceptions to this are the main restaurant, which has banks of windows overlooking the ship's stern, and The Grill, where sunlight floods in from the side.

One complete deck, called the Constellation Center, is almost solely devoted to a convention-and-meeting center. It's accessorized with in-house publishing facilities, a pair of computers with E-mail access (at $1 per message sent, no charge for those received), small boardrooms for gatherings of about a dozen participants each, an auditorium that seats 240, and audio and video devices to record the minutes of your meeting.

The Lounge, a three-tier room with a dramatic forward view of the sea, serves as an observation post, cocktail lounge, teatime rendezvous spot, after-dinner dance floor, and late-night disco. On the deck above is "The Club," a quiet, comfortable, and commodious (yet windowless) lounge that features a live pianist before and sometimes after the dinner hour. Usually when passengers want privacy and quiet, they retreat to their suites, but you might also find a secluded spot on an out-of-the way deck chair, in a quiet corner of the cocktail bar, or in an unused conference room. The library has popular videotapes, films, and books. There are plans to add a pizzeria on the pool deck aft.

POOL, FITNESS & SPA FACILITIES   Passengers flock to the outdoor decks on sunny days, and there's always enough deck space and chairs to go around. There are intimate alcoves as well, but many of them are rather too oddly configured to be of much advantage. The only part of the ship that offers great sunbathing is poolside and the nearby flanks of the vessel (or on your private veranda, of course).

The ship lacks a traditional promenade deck, but the perimeter of Deck 11 has been turned into a jogging track (13 laps equal 1 mile) that encloses the ship's Steiner-managed spa and gym, which is stocked with Nautilus machines, treadmills, and stationary bicycles. The spa offers steam and four massage rooms, beauty treatments, and herbal wraps. There are daily aerobics and yoga classes held in the Lounge, on its small wooden stage.

When the waters are dead calm, a floating marina can be lowered from the stern for use as a convenient platform for sailing, swimming, windsurfing, and waterskiing.

Seven Seas Navigator

The Verdict

Awash in autumn hues and deep blues, the warm and appealing 490-passenger *Navigator* is an ideal size for an ultraluxe cruise: small enough to be intimate and large enough to offer plenty of elbow room and more than a few entertainment outlets.

Seven Seas Navigator *(photo: Radisson)*

Specifications

Size (in tons)	30,000	Officers	International
Number of Cabins	245	Crew	325 (International)
Number of Outside Cabins	245	Passenger/Crew Ratio	1.5 to 1
Cabins with Verandas	209	Year Built	1999
Number of Passengers	490	Last Major Refurbishment	N/A

Frommer's Ratings (Scale of 1–5)

Cabin Comfort & Amenities	5	Pool, Fitness & Spa Facilities	4
Ship Cleanliness & Maintenance	4	Children's Facilities	N/A
Public Comfort/Space	4	Itinerary	4
Decor	4	Worth the Money	5

Radisson's fifth and largest ship, the *Navigator* has well laid out cabins and public rooms, and if you've been on either of the Silverseas ships, you'll notice a similar layout in spots (namely the Navigator's Star Lounge and Galileo's Lounge) since the ships were all built in the same yard, Italy's Mariotti, and designed by the same architects. While the *Navigator*'s interior is very attractive, its exterior is somewhat ungainly: The hull was originally built to be a Russian spy ship with a four-deck-high superstructure, but when bought by Radisson to become the basis of the *Navigator,* three additional decks were added, creating a top-heavy profile. (According to a company spokesman, the ship's tendency to heel, which I experienced on a cruise in late 1999, should be remedied during a March 2000 dry dock, when the ship was to be reballasted.)

Cabins & Rates

Cabins	Per diems from	Bathtub	Fridge	Hair Dryer	Sitting Area	TV
Inside	$315	yes	yes	yes	yes	yes*
Outside	$441	yes	yes	yes	yes	yes*
Suite	$815	yes	yes	yes	yes	yes*

* *TVs show CNN.*

CABINS   Elegant suites are cloaked in shades of deep gold, beige, and burnt-orange, with caramel-toned wood furniture and a swath of butterscotch-colored suede just above the beds. Nearly 90% of them have private balconies, a real asset on the ship's scenery-intensive Alaska and Panama Canal itineraries. Only the handful of suites on the two lowest passenger decks have bay windows in lieu of balconies, and the only ones with obstructed views are those on the port side of Deck 6 looking out onto the promenade. The standard suites are a roomy 301 square feet, including a 55-square-foot balcony; the 18 top suites range from 448 square feet to 1,067 square feet, including 47- to 200-square-foot balconies. Passengers in the top suites are treated to butler service in addition to regular service by the staff of all-female room stewardesses. Each cabin has a huge marble bathroom—the best at sea, I might add—with a separate shower stall, long tub, lots of counter space, and wonderful lemon-scented bath products from spa guru Judith Jackson. Every abode also has a wide walk-in closet with a tall built-in dresser, safe, and terry robes, as well as a sitting area with couch, a pair of chairs, desk, vanity table (with an outlet above for a hair dryer or curling iron) and stool, TV/VCR, and minibar stocked with two complimentary bottles of wine or spirits. (*Note:* Since the safe is on top of the dresser, don't do what I did and leave the safe door open, then bend over to rummage through a drawer and then *Bam!,* smack my noggin but good on the way back up. I gave myself quite a lump.)

PUBLIC AREAS   The ship's attractive decor is a marriage of classic and modern design, with contemporary wooden furniture, chairs upholstered in buttery leather, walls covered in suede, and touches of stainless steel, along with silk brocade draperies, dark wood paneling, burled veneer, and marble. The ship has lots of intimate spaces, so you'll never feel overwhelmed like you would on larger ships.

Most of the public rooms are on Decks 6 and 7, just aft of the three-story atrium and main elevator bank (you'll notice the exposed wiring and mechanics of the backside of the elevator shaft could have been better disguised). A well-stocked library and its computer nook, with three computers for E-mail access (only $1 a message), is adjacent to a card room. Across the way, the cozy Navigator Lounge, paneled in mahogany and cherry wood, is a popular place for predinner cocktails (which means it can get tight in there during rush hours). Next door is the Connoisseur Club cigar lounge, a somewhat cold (and often underutilized) wood-paneled room with umber leather chairs.

Radisson's *Seven Seas Mariner* (Preview)

Slated to enter service in March of 2001, the 708-passenger, 50,000-ton *Seven Seas Mariner* will be Radisson's biggest ship to date. It will be an all-suite, all-balcony ship—the first at sea—and will have four restaurants, with the main dining room serving all guests in a single open seating. It's also going to have one of the best computer facilities at sea (second only to the Crystal ships and *Voyager of the Seas*). Called Club.Com, the state-of-the-art computer center will have 12 computer stations set up in a classroom style, with an instructor on-hand 8 hours a day (like Crystal's computer-learning center). There will also be a more casual Internet-cafe area with six more workstations. Wow! Apart from the complimentary computer classes, guests will be able to send and receive E-mails and surf the Internet (both for a nominal fee).

Down the hall is the roomier Stars Lounge, with a long black granite curved bar and clusters of oversize ocean-blue armchairs, where there's a small dance floor and a live duo crooning pop numbers nightly. Even if you don't gamble, the attractive dark-paneled casino with its striking mural of curving, colorful forms is bound to attract your eye.

There are two restaurants, the formal Compass Rose dining room and the more casual Portofino Grill, which serves buffet-style breakfast and lunch and is then transformed every evening into a very cozy, dimly lit, reservations-only restaurant specializing in northern Italian cuisine. In Portofino, you can usually bank on getting a table for two. The Compass Rose, a pleasant, wide-open room done in warm caramel-colored woods, offers a single open-seating at all meals. There's also a casual grill on the pool deck for burgers, grilled chicken sandwiches, fries, and salads at lunchtime; waiters serve bathing-suit-clad passengers at tables clustered around the deck.

Surrounded by windows on three sides, Galileo's Lounge is a gorgeous space in the evening especially (it's my favorite nightspot), when a pianist is on-hand for cocktails and dancing and the golden room glows magically under soft light. When the doors to the deck just outside are opened on a balmy, star-soaked night, the small dance floor spills out, creating a most romantic, dreamy scene. By day, Galileo's is a quiet venue for continental breakfast, high tea, seminars, and meetings, and is a perfect perch to watch the seascape outside float by.

The stage of the twinkling two-story Seven Seas showroom is large enough for the kind of sizable Vegas-style song-and-dance reviews typical of ships much larger (which means you won't find them on Seabourn, or on Radisson's *Diamond* for that matter). While sight lines are good from the tiered rows of banquettes on the first level, views from the sides of the balcony are severely obstructed.

The cheerful windowed Vista observation lounge is used for meetings and is another great scenery-viewing spot. Conveniently, it leads directly out to the huge patch of forward deck space just over the bridge.

POOL, FITNESS & SPA FACILITIES   The ocean-view gym is bright and roomy for a ship of this size. There's even a separate aerobics room offering impressively grueling classes like circuit training and step. (Bring your Italian phrase book, though, as instructions on the machines are not in English.) Although the *Navigator* boasts a pair of golf nets and two Ping-Pong tables, they're situated high on Deck 12 in an ash-plagued nook just behind the smokestacks that's accessible only by using a hard-to-find set of interior crew stairs (it seems the whole thing was an afterthought).

Though surprisingly uninspired decor-wise, the *Navigator*'s six-room Judith Jackson spa, adjacent to the gym, provides some 17 quality treatments, including innovative ones you won't find on other ships, like a relaxing 20-minute hair-and-scalp oil massage for $25, and a 1-hour, four-hand massage (yep, two therapists work simultaneously—talk about Nirvana) for $165. It's wonderful to have a spa vendor other than the ubiquitous Steiner, which operates the spas on virtually every other ship, and though Jackson's prices are about equal to Steiner's (which increased its rates in late 1999), Jackson's operation gets extra points just because its five therapists don't hawk their skin-care products just as clients are coming out of massage-induced trance, the way Steiner does.

At the pool area, a wide set of stairs joins a balcony of deck chairs to a large pool and pair of hot tubs on the deck below. In the afternoons a five-piece band plays soft oldies near the pool bar as waiters bring cold drinks to passengers reclining in the padded chaise lounges.

Seabourn Cruise Line

55 Francisco St., Suite 710, San Francisco, CA 94133. ☎ **800/929-9595** or 415/391-7444. Fax 415/391-8518. www.seabourn.com.

THE LINE IN A NUTSHELL　Seabourn's ships are floating pleasure palaces bathing all who enter in doting service and nearly the finest (if not *the* finest) cuisine at sea.

THE EXPERIENCE　This line is a genuine aristocrat, with perfect manners. Its five small, luxurious ships have unprecedented amounts of onboard space and staff for each passenger (as do the suites aboard the larger *Seabourn Sun*), and all ships have service worthy of the grand hotels of Europe and the kind of hushed, ever-so-polite ambiance that appeals to prosperous, usually older passengers who appreciate the emphasis on their individual pleasures. If you're the type of person who responds to discretion and subdued good taste (and who has the cash to pay for it), Seabourn might be perfect for you. A travel agent faced with a "which ship is for us" query from Henry and Nancy Kissinger would definitely book them on one of Seabourn's small ships. And with the addition of the midsize *Sun* to the fleet, there's now a Seabourn ship for a younger or more casual set looking for sophistication at more tempered levels (and at a more modest cost).

Pros

- **Top-shelf service.** Staff seems to know what you need before you ask, and there's more staff per passenger than most any other line afloat. They're professional, polished, and chomping at the bit to please. On the *Goddesses,* you'll even be served champagne and caviar on the beach when in port.
- **Excellent cuisine.** Rivaling the best land-based restaurants, cuisine is as exquisite as it gets at sea, with creative, flavorful dishes served with an extensive wine list.
- **Remote ports of call.** These small ships are able to visit less-touristed Caribbean ports (like the British Virgin Islands) that larger ships can't or don't visit.
- **Large cabins on *Legend* and *Pride*.** While not as large as those on Radisson's *Seven Seas Navigator,* roomy suites have walk-in closets, bathtubs, quality bath amenities from Neutrogena, personalized stationery, and complimentary stocked minibars.

Cons

- **Few or no private verandas.** Except for *Sun,* which has 145 balconies, there are only six private balconies on the *Legend* and *Pride,* and none on the *Goddesses.*
- **Limited activities on the small ships.** The Seabourn ships have limited organized activities on board (but those they do have are good).

Compared with the other Ultra-Luxury lines, here's how Seabourn rates:

	poor	fair	good	excellent	outstanding
Enjoyment Factor					✓
Dining					✓
Activities		✓			
Children's Program	N/A*				
Entertainment		✓			
Service					✓
Overall Value					✓

* *Seabourn has no children's program.*

SEABOURN: THE CAVIAR OF CRUISE SHIPS

Seabourn was established in 1987 when luxury cruise patriarch Warren Titus and Norwegian shipping mogul Atle Brynestad commissioned a trio of ultra-upscale 10,000-ton vessels from a north German shipyard. Although now co-owned by founder Brynestad and industry giant Carnival Corporation, which bought into the company in 1991, the line maintains strong links with its Norwegian roots, registering each of its ships in the country.

In mid-1998, Carnival Corporation bought Cunard Line, one of Seabourn's primary competitors in the luxury cruise market. Faced with the problem of how to market the two brands, Carnival decided to go with core strengths, maintaining Seabourn's niche in the small-ship Ultra Luxury market and pushing Cunard as the option for cruisers who want the traditional British ocean liner experience. As a result, three of Cunard's small ships—the *Sea Goddess I, Sea Goddess II, and Royal Viking Sun*—were transferred to the Seabourn fleet at year-end 1999 and renamed *Seabourn Goddess I, Seabourn Goddess II,* and *Seabourn Sun.* Together, the two brands, operating under the umbrella banner of Cunard Line Limited, account for almost 50% of the worldwide luxury cruise market.

THE FLEET

The Seabourn fleet now comprises six ships, its three original and three former Cunarders. Of its original 204-passenger, 10,000-ton trio, the **Seabourn Legend,** built in 1992, and the **Seabourn Pride,** built in 1988, spend part of the year in the Caribbean. (The final member of the trio, *Seabourn Spirit,* was built in 1989 and roams along the coast of Africa and Asia most of the year, rarely returning to the western hemisphere at all.) Streamlined, with modern, yacht-inspired designs, these ships manage to look both aggressive and elegant in their bright white paint jobs, and are small enough to venture safely into exotic harbors where megaships cannot go. Seeing one of them moored at St. George's Harbour in Grenada, one of the world's most colorful ports, is an especially beautiful sight. Seabourn's new adoptees are the 116-passenger, 4,260-ton **Seabourn Goddess I** and **Seabourn Goddess II** (built in 1984 and 1985) and the 758-passenger, 37,845-ton **Seabourn Sun,** built in 1988. The *Sun* splits its time between the Mediterranean, Europe, South America, the Pacific, and the Caribbean and Panama Canal.

PASSENGER PROFILE

Most have more than comfortable household incomes (usually in excess of $250,000), many are retired (or maybe never worked to begin with), and many have net worths in the millions, and sometimes much higher. The majority of passengers are couples, and there are always a handful of singles as well, usually widows or widowers. Few seem to come aboard with children or grandchildren in tow. In many ways, the passenger roster looks like the membership of a posh country club, where old money judges new money. Most passengers are North American, and dress expensively though not, of course, flashily. Many passengers are not particularly chatty, giddy, or outgoing. They are likely to have sailed aboard other luxury cruise lines and stayed in five-star hotels. Passengers expect to receive good service in an atmosphere of discreet gentility.

On the larger *Seabourn Sun,* the guest demographic skews to a lower average age and income, but not by much.

The line's history of attracting repeaters passengers is among the highest in the industry; it 1999, it was over 40%.

Goddesses on the Beach

The pièce de résistance of your *Seabourn Goddess* cruise comes at midday near the end of the trip, as you lounge on a quiet beach. As you gaze out toward the anchored ship you'll see the captain, standing at the bow of a bright-red Zodiac and holding a flag, coming swiftly toward the beach, looking like George Washington crossing the Delaware, but in decidedly better weather and absolutely bluer water.

The captain's soldiers—20-something European stewards wearing Hawaiian shirts—hop out carrying a life ring that doubles as a floating serving tray for an open tin of Russian malossol caviar, encircled by little dishes of sour cream, chopped egg, and minced onion. Wade into the gentle surf up to your waist and spoon up a morsel. Stewards move about with bottles of Moët et Chandon champagne and Absolut vodka encased in orchid-filled cylinders of ice.

A buffet spread out under a lean-to features choices such as freshly grilled lobster tails, barbecued spare ribs, carved roast beef, baked potato, salads, and fresh fruit. Passengers feast under umbrellas at tables set with proper china and hotel silver brought ashore by the staff.

It doesn't get any better than this!

DINING

Cuisine is one of Seabourn's strongest points, matching what you'd find in a world-class European resort hotel. The line assumes that most of its passengers are used to getting what they want, usually whenever they want it, so meals are served in a manner that satisfies both appetite and the expectation of high-class service. Fleet-wide, dining is offered in a single seating, and, except for the *Sun*, which assigns passengers to specific tables, the ships have an open seating policy, allowing guests to dine whenever they choose and with whomever they want, within a window of several hours at each mealtime.

While tables seat up to 8 or 10, you usually won't have a problem getting a table for two if that's your wish. Also, tables are spaced far enough apart so you'll never feel crowded.

On the *Legend, Spirit,* and *Pride,* dinner service is high-style and extremely formal. Men are expected to wear jackets and, on most evenings, neckties as well. Two formal evenings are held during the course of any 1-week cruise. Virtually every male present appears in a tuxedo, and staff members almost run at a trot through the elaborate, six-course European service.

On the *Goddesses,* the dress code and ambiance is less formal and stuffy (no-jackets are required, although many will still wear them), but the food and service is no less top-of-the-line. On the *Sun* too, while civility still reigns, the dress code is more relaxed, and on formal nights men in suits needn't feel intimated by their tuxedo-clad peers.

Seabourn cuisine is an eclectic mix. The *Legend, Pride,* and *Spirit* feature old favorites such as beef Wellington, Dover sole, and broiled lobster, as well as ethnic dishes reflecting the itinerary of wherever the ship happens to be at the time. Dishes are prepared to order, **spa menus** are available at every meal, and passengers can make virtually any special request they want. On the *Goddesses* and *Sun,* the dinner menu includes three appetizers such as carpaccio of beef tenderloin, lobster aspic and sautéed crab cakes, three hot or cold soups, a pasta dish (on the *Sun* only), and four entrees such as a baby lamb loin or stuffed quail, plus a Golden Door Spa menu and a **vegetarian dish.**

Complimentary wines are served at lunch and dinner, and every night features a flaming dessert served in individual portions or such choices as chocolate mousse with fresh berries or coconut crème brûlée.

If your mood doesn't call for the dining room, the *Legend, Pride,* and *Spirit* have an **alternative dining option,** the Veranda Café (on the *Sun* it's called the Venezia Restaurant). On the *Goddesses,* all meals are served in the dining room, and one night there's a festive dinner served out on deck by the pool. All the ships have a casual restaurant as well, serving bountiful breakfasts every morning, with omelets made fresh to your specifications. At lunchtime, you'll find salads, sandwich makings, fresh pasta, and maybe jumbo shrimp, smoked salmon, and smoked oysters on the cold side and hot sliced roast beef, duck, and ham on the carving board. On the *Legend, Spirit,* and *Pride,* a **special of the day**—pizza with pineapple topping, chili, or corned beef—will also be available at the Sky Bar overlooking the Lido for those who don't want to change out of their swimsuits. On these ships, dinner is served under the stars on the Lido Deck several evenings a week as well, offering a meal roughly equivalent to whatever's being whipped up in the main dining room. Dinners here are romantic candlelight affairs, and are often based on Italian, French, and seafood themes. In good weather it's a treat to eat at one of the arc of tables located aft overlooking the wake and under a protective canvas awning.

On the *Goddesses* especially, there are wonderful hors d'oeuvres, such as jumbo shrimp, smoked salmon, and the best caviar available practically around the clock in unlimited quantities. Jumbo shrimp and caviar can also be ordered poolside at no charge on the *Legend* and *Pride* (aren't you salivating just reading this?).

Room service is available 24 hours a day on all ships. During normal lunch or dinner hours your private meal can mirror the dining room service, right down to the silver, crystal, and porcelain. The menu is more limited after hours, with burgers, salads, sandwiches, and pastas. And whenever a cruise itinerary calls for a full-day stopover on a remote island, a lavish beach barbecue might be whipped up at midday.

ACTIVITIES

Seabourn's small ships don't offer much in the way of organized activities, and that's what most passengers really love about the line. With no rah-rah, in-your-face cruise directors shouting at them, passengers are just left alone to pursue their own personal peace.

With the exception of the *Sun,* which is bigger and provides more activities, on the rest of the fleet you won't find the bingo, karaoke, and silly poolside contests featured by mass-market lines. The atmosphere is ever-tasteful and unobtrusive. Activities include card games and tournaments, trivia contests, tours of the ship's galley, visits to the cozy library, and watching movies in your cabin. You can also twiddle around on computers; the *Sun* has 10 and the *Spirit, Legend,* and *Pride* each have one (the *Goddesses* do not have any). All have E-mail access, at $5 per message for the first 5K (5000 bytes) and $1 for each additional (there's no charge for incoming E-mails). You'll soon realize that many passengers are aboard to read, quietly converse with their peers, and be ushered from one stylish spot to the next.

One Good Deal & a Tip on Tips

Solo Passenger Rates: Depending on the cruise, single supplements are as low as 110% of the per-person rate for double occupancy of the same standard suite. **Tips:** Gratuities are officially included in the cruise fare, but staff is not prohibited from accepting additional tips.

Seabourn Fleet Itineraries

Ship	Home Ports & Season	Itinerary	Other Itineraries
Seabourn Goddess I and II	Several alternating home ports: round-trip from St. Thomas; between St. Thomas and Barbados; round-trip from Barbados; Nov–Apr.	**4-, 5-, 6-, and 7-night E. Carib:** Ports on alternating itineraries may include Mayreau, Carriacou, and Bequia (Grenadines), St. Lucia, Grenada, Dominica, St. Croix, Virgin Gorda, Antigua, Jost Van Dyke, Guadeloupe, St. Barts, St. Martin, Nevis, Martinique, St. Kitts, and Tobago.	Mediterranean
Seabourn Legend	Round-trip from Ft. Lauderdale, West Palm Beach, and San Juan, and between Ft. Lauderdale and San Juan, San Juan and Barbados, and Barbados and West Palm Beach, Nov–Apr.	**7-, 8, 9, 12, 14-, and 15-night E. and S. Carib:** May visit St. Lucia, Antigua, St. Barts, Dominica, St. Martin, St. John, Grenadines, Nevis, Nassau, Cozumel, St. Croix, Puerto Rico, Dominican Republic, St. Martin, Jost Van Dyke, and Virgin Gorda.	Europe
Seabourn Pride	Round-trip from Ft. Lauderdale and San Juan, and between Ft. Lauderdale and St. Thomas, St. Thomas and New Orleans, New Orleans and San Juan, and San Juan and Ft. Lauderdale Oct–Jan 2000 and 2001.	**6- 11-, 12-, 14-, and 16-night E. Carib:** May visit St. Barts, Puerto Rico, Cozumel, Calica, Jamaica, Dominican Republic, St. John, St. Croix, St. Barts, Virgin Gorda, St. Maarten, St. Kitts, Antigua, Guadeloupe, Dominica, New Orleans, and Key West.	Europe, South America, Eastern Canada/New England
Seabourn Sun	Round-trip from Ft. Lauderdale, Nov–Dec 2000 and 2001	**10-, 13-, and 14-night E. Carib:** May visit St. Barts, Tortola, Barbados, Jamaica, Grand Cayman, Belize, Cozumel, New Orleans, Key West, St. Lucia, Grenada, St. Kitts, Puerto Rico, Dominica, and St. Croix.	World Cruise, Europe, Eastern Canada/New England

That said, you don't have to be sedate, either. The *Legend, Pride, Spirit,* and both *Goddesses* have **retractable water sports marinas** that unfold from the ships' stern, weather and sea conditions permitting, and gracefully usher passengers into the sea for water-skiing, windsurfing, sailing, snorkeling, banana-boat riding, and swimming.

There are few, if any, public announcements to disturb your solitude—a relief when compared to the barrage of noise broadcast aboard many other lines.

On certain cruises there are **guest lecturers,** such as noted chefs, authors, or statesmen, or maybe a wine connoisseur, composer, anthropologist, TV director, or professor, who present lectures and mingle with guests. From time to time the line manages to bring on the likes of Lynn Redgrave, Patricia Neal, Andre Previn, and Frank McCourt. (Note, however, that these programs tend to be more prevalent on European/Mediterranean and Far East itineraries than in the Caribbean.) You can generally count on port lectures from resident travel experts.

Each ship has a small-scale, staid, and rather un-casino-like **casino** with a couple of blackjack tables and a handful of slots. The *Sun*'s casino, as you might expect, is a bit larger and offers gaming for about 50 guests.

CHILDREN'S PROGRAM

These ships are not geared to children, although, except for a ban on children under age 1, there are no restrictions against them. So, you may see a young child occasionally on the *Legend, Pride,* or *Spirit,* though he or she will probably be a very bored child, as the line provides no special programs, no special menus, and no special concessions for them. On the *Sun,* there are youth staff on board during holidays and summers, but the programming is not extensive. Suites on the *Goddesses* are not set up to accommodate third or fourth passengers, making them unsuitable for children.

In a pinch, you may be able to arrange to have an available crew member provide baby-sitting.

ENTERTAINMENT

Entertainment is not Seabourn's strong suit, but if you're happy with a singer, pianist, or duo doing most of the entertaining, you'll be pleased enough. On all the ships, a resident dance band or music duo performs a roster of old favorites, while the mellow piano bar is always a good option. The *Sun* has a lounge for small-scale productions and the *Legend* and *Pride* have small show lounges, but the *Goddesses* have none.

SERVICE

Seabourn maintains the finest service staff of any line afloat. Most are young northern Europeans, many Norwegian, who are recruited after they've gained experience at one of the grand hotels of Europe. They are, overall, charming, competent, sensitive, and discreet—among Seabourn's most valuable assets.

Laundry and dry cleaning are available. There are also complimentary self-service laundry rooms on the *Legend, Pride,* and *Sun.*

All Seabourn ships provide Neutrogena bathroom amenities as well as designer soaps from Hermès, Chanel No. 5, and Tiffany. Cabin minibars fleet-wide (though only suites and deluxe outside cabins on the *Sun*) are stocked with two bottles of wine or spirits of the guests' choice. Soft drinks, beer, and mineral water are complimentary and replenished daily.

Seabourn Goddess I • Seabourn Goddess II

The Verdict

About as good as it gets, with highest marks for the small ship atmosphere, the attentive European service, and the creative menus. Of course, the champagne and caviar served poolside whenever you want it it isn't too shabby either.

Seabourn Goddess *(photo: Seabourn Cruise Line)*

Specifications

Size (in tons)	4,260	Officers	Norwegian
Number of Cabins	58	Crew	89 (Euro/Int'l)
Number of Outside Cabins	58	Passenger/Crew Ratio	1.3 to 1
Cabins with Verandas	0	Year Built	1984/1985
Number of Passengers	116	Last Major Refurbishment	1997

Frommer's Ratings (Scale of 1–5)

Cabin Comfort & Amenities	5	Pool, Fitness & Spa Facilities	3
Ship Cleanliness & Maintenance	4	Children's Facilities	N/A
Public Comfort/Space	5	Itinerary	4
Decor	4	Worth the Money	4

These two ships espouse a casually elegant ethos similar to Windstar (but still, not quite that casual or young), where tuxes, ties, and gowns can be left at home. For both weary workaholics or those used to doing very little, it would be hard to find a more relaxing vacation, better food, or more attentive service while enjoying a variety of small Caribbean ports. Calling at yacht harbors and anchoring off beautiful beaches, these petite ships seem to blend right in with the yachts in the harbor.

While the *Seabourn Goddesses* continue to provide the supreme service and yacht-like elegance they did in their Cunard days, they're now being targeted to a younger crowd in their 30s and 40s—people who want the service and top-notch amenities, but sans over-the-top formality. Despite the marketing, expect the ships to continue drawing a mostly middle-aged 50- to 60-something crowd for at least a while longer.

Cabins & Rates

Cabins	Per diems from	Bathtub	Fridge	Hair Dryer	Sitting Area	TV
Outside	$370	yes	yes	yes	yes	yes
Suite	$433	yes	yes	yes	yes	yes

CABINS   Each of the 58 virtually identical one-room ocean-view suites average 205 square feet. Unlike the layouts on many ships, the bedroom is positioned alongside the cabin's large window and the sitting area is inside. They are located forward and amidships; soundproofing between cabins is good and engine noise minimal. While similar in design, cabins are less roomy than those aboard the larger *Legend, Spirit,* and *Pride,* and the bathrooms are small.

The superb design features includes twin beds convertible to queens, several mirrors, remote control television and VCR, music channels, automated wake-up calls, international direct-dial phones, complimentary stocked minibar and refrigerator, fresh flowers, fresh fruit, terry-cloth robes, hair dryer, and bathrooms with full-size tubs. The 24-hour room service provides a full-course meal setup in your suite at a proper table seating four.

If you can afford it, two units can be interconnected to provide a full 410 square feet of space.

These ships are not recommended for passengers requiring the use of a wheelchair, as doorways leading to staterooms and toilets are not big enough to accommodate them. Persons in wheelchairs also can't go ashore, because the wheelchairs can't be taken on the launches that shuttle passengers to shore in ports where the vessel must anchor offshore.

PUBLIC AREAS   Upon boarding, you immediately notice the elaborate flower arrangements in all public areas and the sophisticated European atmosphere and high-quality furnishings. Public areas are covered with marble, polished hardwoods, and Oriental carpets. So posh are they, and so yacht-like the feel of the vessels, that you expect an English lord to walk through the door at any moment to suggest a cocktail.

The Main Salon and its small bar alcove are the venue for indoor socializing before dinner, and a singer and musical duo often provide light entertainment. The hot and cold hors d'oeuvres may include smoked salmon, jumbo shrimp, and an open tin of malossol caviar.

There's dancing in the Main Salon after dinner, while one deck up a popular, long-serving pianist entertains at the Club Salon piano bar, located next to the diminutive two-blackjack-table casino. There's also a small book and video library, several slot machines, and a purser's foyer with a boutique.

POOL, FITNESS & SPA FACILITIES   The mostly open and partly shaded Lido Deck (deck 3) has deck chairs, a pool, hot tub, and bar (order yourself some caviar and jumbo shrimp while you lounge, at no charge!). A covered deck above has additional deck chairs with more at Sun Deck level. The gym, spa, and beauty salon are high up, looking aft on Deck 5. There's also a jogging track on this level, but it's so small-scale you're likely to get dizzy if you run it at high speeds.

Seabourn Legend • Seabourn Pride

The Verdict

Hands-down, these ships are top of the market and the cream of the crop. They're the most luxurious ships at sea (along with the Silversea ships), designed to let you be as social or as private as you like.

Seabourn Legend *(photo: Seabourn Cruise Line)*

Specifications

Size (in tons)	10,000	Crew	140 (International)
Number of Cabins	100	Passenger/Crew Ratio	1.5 to 1
Number of Outside Cabins	100	Year Built	
Cabins with Verandas	6	*Legend*	1992
Number of Passengers	204	*Pride*	1988
Officers	Norwegian	Last Major Refurbishment	2000

Frommer's Ratings (Scale of 1–5)

Cabin Comfort & Amenities	5	Pool, Fitness & Spa Facilities	3
Ship Cleanliness & Maintenance	4	Children's Facilities	N/A
Public Comfort/Space	5	Itinerary	4
Decor	4	Worth the Money	4

These two understated, beautifully designed ships represent luxury cruising at its very best, going everywhere one would ever want to cruise. Passengers who like to be social and meet others with similar interests will find plenty of opportunities to do so at open-sitting meals, in the intimate public rooms, and out on deck. On the other hand, if you want to get away from it all, you can also be completely private in your spacious suite, at a table for two in the restaurant, or in a quiet corner of the deck.

By year-end 2000, the *Legend, Pride,* and *Spirit* will each replace the current five-foot picture windows in about half the suites with new French balconies (sliding glass doors with railings). While you can't sit or even stand on one like you can with typical cabin balconies, the sliding doors will allow guests to let the fresh air and ocean breezes into their suites.

Cabins & Rates

Cabins	Per diems from	Bathtub	Fridge	Hair Dryer	Sitting Area	TV
Suite	$338	most	yes	yes	yes	yes**
Owner's Suite	$400	yes*	yes	yes	yes	yes**

* The four handicapped-accessible suites have showers only. ** TVs show CNN and ESPN.

CABINS   The great majority of accommodations are handsomely designed "Type A" 277-square-foot one-room suites (remember, an average cabin on Carnival is 190 square feet), varying only in location but priced at four different levels. Suites are popular for entertaining and dining, as the lounge area's coffee table rises to dining table height, and one can order hors d'oeuvres such as caviar and smoked salmon at no extra charge. Closet space is more than adequate for hanging clothes, but drawer space is more limited. The *Pride* has twin sinks in the all-white marble bathrooms; *Legend* has a single sink.

The two Classic Suites measure 400 square feet, and two pairs of Owner's Suites are 530 and 575 square feet. These six have the only (small) verandas on the ships. The Owner's Suites have dining areas and guest powder rooms. Their dark wood furnishings make the overall feeling more like a hotel room than a ship's suite and, as in any cabins positioned near the bow of relatively small ships such as these, they can be somewhat uncomfortable during rough seas. Owner's Suites 05 and 06 have obstructed views. Double Suites, at 554 square feet, are just that: two combined 277-square-foot Seabourn suites with one room given completely over to a lounge.

Everything about a Seabourn cabin has the impeccably maintained feel of an upscale Scandinavian hotel. Each has either a 5-foot-wide rectangular picture window with an electric blind that, with the flick of a switch, can shut out the glare of the mid-afternoon sun, or one of the new floor-to-ceiling sliding glass doors. Each unit contains a fully stocked bar, a walk-in closet, safe, a VCR and TV broadcasting CNN and ESPN among other channels, crystal glasses for every kind of drink, terry-cloth robes, umbrella, and fresh fruit daily. Videotape movies are available from the ship's library, and the purser's office broadcasts films from the ship's own collection. Color schemes are either tastefully ice-blue or champagne-colored, with lots of bleached oak or birch wooden trim, as well as mirrors and a sophisticated bank of spotlights.

There are four wheelchair-accessible suites.

PUBLIC AREAS   An attractive double open spiral staircase links the public areas, which are, overall, a bit duller than you'd expect on ships of this caliber. For the most part, they're spare and almost ordinary-looking. Art and ornamentation are conspicuous by their absence. It's almost as if in its zeal to create conservative decors, management couldn't decide on the appropriate artwork and so omitted it completely. (There are a few exceptions: The *Legend* has an attractive curved ocean-liner-motif mural in its stair foyers.)

The forward-facing observation lounge on Sky Deck offers an attractive, quiet venue all day long for reading, a drink before meals, cards, and afternoon tea. A chart and compass will help you find out where the ship is currently positioned, and a computerized wall map lets you track future cruises.

The aft-facing Club lounge and bar is the ship's principal social center, with music, a small band, a singer and/or pianist, and fancy hot hors d'oeuvres before and after dinner. Next door, behind glass, is the ship's casino, with gaming tables and a separate small room for slot machines. The semi-circular and tiered formal lounge on the deck below is the venue for lectures, pianists, and the captain's parties.

The formal restaurant, located on the lowest deck, is a large low-ceilinged room with an open seating policy. The Veranda Café, open for breakfast, lunch, and (except on formal nights) dinner, is an intimate, well-designed indoor/outdoor facility.

One of the best places for a romantic, moonlit moment is the isolated patch of deck at the far forward bow on Deck 5.

POOL, FITNESS & SPA FACILITIES   The outdoor pool, not much used, is awkwardly situated in a shadowy location aft of the open Deck 7, between the twin engine uptakes, and is flanked by lifeboats that hang from both sides of the ship. A pair of whirlpools are located just forward of the pool. There's a third hot tub perched on the far forward bow of Deck 5. It's isolated and a perfect spot (as is the whole patch of deck here) from which to watch the landscape or a port come into sight or fade away.

A retractable, wood-planked water sports marina opens out from the stern of the ship so passengers can hop into sea kayaks or go windsurfing, water-skiing, or snorkeling right from the ship. An attached steel mesh net creates a saltwater pool when the marina is in use. The gym and Steiner-managed spa are roomy for ships this small, and are located forward of the Lido. There is a separate aerobics area plus two saunas, massage rooms, and a beauty salon.

Seabourn Sun

The Verdict

As Seabourn's largest, the Sun is a somewhat different breed than the rest of the fleet and is designed to lure younger passengers and first-timers who have high-end taste but don't want a small, yacht-like ship.

Seabourn Sun *(photo: Seabourn Cruise Line)*

Specifications

Size (in tons)	38,000	Officers	(Norwegian/Int'l)
Number of Cabins	384	Crew	460 (International)
Number of Outside Cabins	359	Passenger/Crew Ratio	1.7 to 1
Cabins with Verandas	141	Year Built	1988
Number of Passengers	758	Last Major Refurbishment	1999

Frommer's Ratings (Scale of 1–5)

Cabin Comfort & Amenities	3	Pool, Fitness & Spa Facilities	4
Ship Cleanliness & Maintenance	4	Children's Facilities	N/A
Public Comfort/Space	4	Itinerary	4
Decor	3	Worth the Money	4

The last ship to carry the venerated Royal Viking name, the *Royal Viking Sun,* built in 1988 for luxurious long-distance cruising, was Cunard's most elegant ship, especially after the line spent some $11 million to freshen her up in 1995. In late 1999, this mid-size luxury ship underwent a further $15 million refurbishment and re-entered service as the *Seabourn Sun,* now the line's largest ship. While small by today's megaship standards, the *Sun* is significantly larger than Seabourn's other vessels and lacks their intimacy and understatedness, as well as their open-seating dining policy. The *Sun*'s size, though, does ensure a smoother ride in rough seas than the line's smaller ships, and also allows for features like and extensive spa and variety of onboard activities.

Its size also creates a dual level of service. Guests in suites experience the typical kind of over-the-top individual service Seabourn is known for, like butlers and staff who take great pains to address passengers by name. Guests in other stateroom categories, on the other hand, are privy to service that's plenty good but not nearly as doting. The *Sun* is a hybrid through and through—part pleasure palace, part mainstream ship.

Cabins & Rates

Cabins	Per diems from	Bathtub	Fridge	Hair Dryer	Sitting Area	TV
Inside	$305	some	yes	yes	yes	yes*
Outside	$371	some	yes	yes	yes	yes*
Suite	$904	yes	yes	yes	yes	yes*

* *TVs have VCRs and show CNN.*

CABINS   Except for suites, all outside staterooms are 191 square feet, the same size as Carnival's standard cabins and much smaller than the 277 square feet of Seabourn's *Pride, Spirit,* and *Legend.* All cabins are attractively decorated in blue, turquoise, and red, and are accoutered with walk-in closets, TVs with 13 channels of video and three channels of music, VCRs, mini-fridges, safes or lockable drawers, vanity/desks, hair dryers, and fluffy terry robes. All outside cabins have a sitting area with sofa, table, and chair, and almost 40% (141 cabins) have private balconies. Remarkably for a ship this size, only 25 of the cabins are windowless interiors, measuring a tiny 128 to 138 square feet. Nine of these inside cabins have bathtubs with shower and about half the non-suite outsides have tubs with shower; the rest have shower stalls only.

At 724 square feet, the Owner's Suite is spectacular, with bedroom, living room, dining area, glass enclosed ocean view whirlpool, CD player, VCR and two TVs. The Owner's Suite, Penthouse Suites (488 and 362 square feet) and Deluxe Outside staterooms with verandas (category A), have bars stocked with two bottles of liquor or house wine as selected in advance by guests, plus a bottle of chilled champagne, soft drinks, and beer (unlike the rest of the Seabourn fleet, where all cabins get 2 bottles of complimentary booze in the mini fridges).

Light sleepers might want to avoid cabins on the Promenade Deck—it's the ship's jogging track, resulting in early-morning foot thumps from enthusiastic exercisers running by.

Two cabins are arranged for single occupancy and six are designed for passengers with disabilities.

PUBLIC AREAS Connected by a beautiful circular staircase, the Promenade and Norway decks are the heart of the ship and include most of the public rooms. The Norway Deck could well be called the entertainment deck, as it's anchored at either end by lounges, with the Casino, Oak Room, Espresso bar (one of the most popular spots on board), Starlight Theater (mostly movies), Computer Center, Card Room, boutiques, and Library in-between. The aft Midnight Sun Lounge seats 171 in mostly banquettes of dark blue fabrics and black leather, matching the new bar's black granite and mahogany. The handsome Oak Room is a smoking lounge with a gentleman's club decor—leather chairs, wood-paneled walls, sporting prints and a portrait of Norway's king over the fireplace mantle.

One of the *Seabourn Sun*'s loveliest rooms is the Compass Rose, seating about 60 in chair and sofa clusters. It's a long room, anchored at one end by a baby grand piano and open through the center in a kind of interior promenade delightfully decorated in muted sea green, blue, and rose. Its wall of floor-to-ceiling windows frames the sea with excellent views, yet the room has a cozy, intimate feel, reminiscent of Seabourn's smaller ships.

The Dining Room, arranged in three sections and stretching nearly two-thirds the length of the Promenade Deck, is done in tones of burgundy and green. Decorative wood and glass panels create intimate seating in the center section connecting the two larger rooms. All three have excellent sea views. Unlike other mid-size luxury ships, the *Sun*'s Dining Room serves the entire passenger complement in one seating at assigned tables for dinner, with open seating for lunch and breakfast. (Seabourn's small ships have single open-seating for all meals.)

One of the ship's most beautiful dining areas is the 100-seat Venezia, a reservations-only alternative restaurant, done in dark woods, blues, greens, and burgundies and featuring Italian and Continental cuisine from its own galley. Book your reservations here early, as spots go fast. The window-walled Garden Café, an alternative breakfast and lunch buffet restaurant aft on Bridge Deck, includes a teak-floored outdoor al fresco area reminiscent of a French sidewalk café.

High atop the ship on Sky Deck is the magnificent 120-seat Stella Polaris Room, an observation lounge with deep aqua and blue decor that seems to pull one's line of sight from the room out through the curved window wall to a superb 180-degree view of the sea ahead. It's a splendid place for an afternoon read.

POOL, FITNESS & SPA FACILITIES The ship's new Steiner-operated Spa du Soleil, with a spacious glass-enclosed fitness center, is a big plus for the *Sun*. Designed in a classic Roman theme with Mediterranean sculptures, soft colors, and terra-cotta tile, the spa incorporates nine treatment rooms, including five rooms for hydrotherapy spa treatments, a Rasul chamber (for a mud bath intimately shared by two), a Dry Float room (for womb-like flotation while wrapped in seaweed paste and foil, followed by full body massage), and Cleopatra Bath (for a private soak in a sarcophagus-shaped whirlpool, followed by a back and scalp massage plus full facial). Outside is a lap pool with two whirlpools.

Mid-ship on the Bridge Deck is a uniquely shaped outdoor pool with swim-up bar. There's also a whirlpool and plenty of lounge chairs. The Golf Club and Pro Shop includes a sophisticated video course simulator that gives guests a choice of virtual play on 12 famous courses from around the world. Free onboard golf seminars and clinics are also offered, and there's a putting green and driving cage located on the top deck.

Windstar Cruises

300 Elliott Ave. W., Seattle, WA 98119. ☎ **800/258-7245** or 206/281-3535. Fax 206/281-0627. www.windstarcruises.com.

THE LINE IN A NUTSHELL The no-jackets-required policy on board Windstar's sleek vessels defines the line's casually elegant attitude. The ships really do feel like private yachts—they're down-to-earth, yet service and cuisine are first-class.

THE EXPERIENCE Windstar offers a truly unique cruise experience, giving passengers the delicious illusion of adventure on board its fleet of four- and five-masted sailing ships and the ever-pleasant reality of first-class cuisine, service, and itineraries. This is no barefoot, rigging-pulling, paper-plates-in-lap, sleep-on-the-deck kind of cruise, but a refined yet down-to-earth, yacht-like experience for a sophisticated, well-traveled crowd who despise big ships and throngs of tourists.

On board, fine stained teak, brass details, and lots of navy-blue fabrics and carpeting lend a traditional nautical ambiance. While the ships' proud masts and yards of white sails cut an attractive profile, the ships are ultra-state-of-the-art and the sails can be furled or unfurled at the touch of a button. In the Caribbean, at least once per week if at all possible, the captain shuts off the engines and moves by sail only, to give passengers a real taste of the sea. Under full sail, the calm tranquillity is utterly blissful.

Pros

- **Cuisine.** The ambiance, service, and imaginative cuisine created by renowned Los Angeles chef Joachim Splichal is superb. Seating in the restaurants is open, and guests can usually get a table for two.
- **Informal and unregimented days.** This line offers the most casual high-end cruise out there—an approach much loved by passengers who enjoy fine service and cuisine but don't like the formality and stuffiness of the majority of high-end lines.
- **Itineraries.** The *Wind Spirit* visits a Caribbean port every single day of a weeklong cruise, and the *Wind Surf* and *Wind Song* come close, with only one day at sea. Ports visited are wonderfully less touristed than many of those called on by the megaships.

Cons

- **No verandas.** If they're important to you, you're out of luck.
- **Limited activities and entertainment.** This is intentional, but if you need lots of organized hoopla to keep you happy, you won't find much on these ships.

Compared with the other Ultra-Luxury lines, here's how Windstar rates:					
	poor	fair	good	excellent	outstanding
Enjoyment Factor					✓
Dining				✓	
Activities		✓			
Children's Program	N/A*				
Entertainment		✓			
Service			✓		
Overall Value				✓	

* Windstar has no children's program.

WINDSTAR: CASUAL ELEGANCE UNDER SAIL

Launched in 1986, Windstar Cruises combines the best of 19th-century clipper design with the best of modern yacht engineering. As you see a Windstar ship approaching port, with its four or five masts the height of 20-story buildings, you'll think the sea-faring days of Joseph Conrad or Herman Melville have returned. The ships are beautiful, and so is the experience on board—the line's ad slogan, "180 degrees from the ordinary," is right on target.

But Captain Ahab wouldn't know what to do with a Windstar ship. Million-dollar computers control the six triangular sails with their at least 21,489 square feet of Dacron, flying from masts that tower 204 feet above deck. These computers automatically trim the sails and control fin stabilizers, rudder tab, anti-heeling devices, and much, much more. Sails can be retracted in 2 minutes to a diameter of less than a foot.

The catalyst behind the formation of the company was a flamboyant French entrepreneur, Jean Claude Potier, a native Parisian, who, in a 25-year-span, was instrumental in leading the French Line, the Sun Line, and Paquet during their transition into the modern cruise age. The original designs for the ships were developed by Warsila Marine Industries in Helsinki, and they were built at Le Havre, France.

In the late 1980s, Windstar was acquired by Holland America Line, which is itself wholly owned by Carnival Corporation. As such, Windstar is the most adventure-oriented of Carnival's many cruise line divisions, and although not as luxurious as Carnival's most upscale branch, Seabourn, it nonetheless prides itself on a cruise experience that's much, much more upscale than the ones offered aboard any of Carnival's megaships, and is the most high-end, by far, among the competing sailing cruise ships in the Caribbean (Star Clippers and Windjammer are much less snazzy, with food and service nowhere near Windstar's; they're deliberately mid- and down-market, respectively).

THE FLEET

Today, Windstar's fleet consists of four ships, the 148-passenger *Wind Star, Wind Song,* and *Wind Spirit,* all constructed originally for Windstar and built in 1986, 1987, and 1988, and the 312-passenger *Wind Surf,* built in 1990 and sailed until 1997 as the *Club Med I* for Club Med Cruises. The *Wind Surf* is the only one of the ships to have a spa and to offer a substantial number of suites (31). Of the four, only the *Surf* and *Spirit* spend significant time in the Caribbean. The *Wind Star* sails a Belize/Honduras itinerary from Cancún, and the *Wind Song* does a 7-night Costa Rica itinerary out of Puerto Caldera, Costa Rica, on the country's southwestern Pacific coast.

PASSENGER PROFILE

People who expect high-caliber service and very high-quality cuisine but detest the formality of the other high-end ships and the mass-mentality of the megaships are thrilled with Windstar. Most passengers are couples in their 30s to early 60s (pretty evenly distributed across range, with the average about 48), with a smattering of parents with adult children and the occasional single friends traveling together.

The line is not the best choice for first-timers, since it appeals to a specific sensibility, and it's definitely not a good choice for singles or families with children under 15 or 16.

Overall, passengers are sophisticated, well-traveled, and more down-to-earth than passengers on the other high-end lines. Most want something different from the regular cruise experience, eschew the "bigger is better" philosophy of conventional cruising, and want a somewhat more adventurous, port-intensive Caribbean cruise. These cruises are for those seeking a romantic escape and who like to visit islands not often touched by regular cruise ships, including the Grenadines, the Tobago Cays, the British Virgin Islands, and relatively isolated dependencies of Guadeloupe, such as the Iles des Saintes.

About a third of all passengers are repeaters (a figure that represents one of the best recommendations for Windstar) and about 20% are first-timers. There are usually1 to 5 honeymoon couples on board any given sailing.. Windstar caters to corporate groups too. In 2000, for instance, the 14 weeklong cruises on the *Wind Surf* were chartered to corporate groups, and about 20 charters total were scheduled on the line's other three ships.

DINING

The cuisine is among the better prepared aboard ship in the Caribbean and is a high point of the cruise, although it doesn't quite match the caliber of Seabourn or Radisson. It was created by renowned chef/restaurateur **Joachim Splichal,** winner of many culinary awards (including some from the James Beard Society) and owner of Los Angeles's Patina Restaurant and Pinot Bistro. At its best, Splichal's food is inventive and imaginative, as reflected by such appetizers as a corn risotto with wild mushrooms and basil or a "Farinetta" bread and Parmesan griddle cake with roasted chicken and shallots, followed by a seafood strudel of lobster, scallops, mussels, king crab, and shrimp in a lobster sauce, or an artfully presented potato-crusted fish with braised leeks and apple-smoked bacon, or a salmon tournedos with an herb crust served with stewed tomatoes and garlicky broccoli rabe. Irresistible desserts such as banana pie with raspberry sauce and French profiteroles with hot fudge are beyond tempting. A very good wine list includes California and European vintages.

Called the "Sail Light Menu," **healthy choices** and **vegetarian dishes,** designed by light-cooking expert Jeanne Jones, are available for breakfast, lunch, and dinner (fat and calorie content is listed on the menu). The light choices may feature Atlantic Salmon with couscous and fresh vegetables or a Thai country-style chicken with veggies and oriental rice. The vegetarian options may feature a fresh garden stew or a savory polenta with Italian salsa.

The once-a-week **evening barbecues** on the pool deck are wonderful parties under the stars, and an ample and beautifully designed buffet spread offers more than you could possible sample in one evening. The setting is sublime, with tables set with linens and, often, a live Caribbean-style band performing on board for the evening.

Each ship has **two dining rooms,** one casual and breezy and used during breakfast and lunch (The Veranda) and the other a more formal room (The Restaurant) that's the stage for dinner. On the *Wind Spirit,* The Veranda is a sunny, window-lined room whose tables extend from inside onto a covered deck (unfortunately, you do have to go outside on deck to get to the indoor part of the restaurant, so if it's raining you get wet), while The Restaurant is enclosed and accented with nautical touches like teakwood trim and paneling and pillars wrapped decoratively in hemp rope.

At breakfast and lunch, meals can be ordered from a menu or selected from a buffet, so your choices are many. Made-to-taste omelets and a varied and generous spread of fruits are available at breakfast, and luncheons may feature a tasty seafood paella and a hot pasta dish of the day. There is **open seating for meals,** at tables designed for between two and eight diners. You can often get a table for two, but you might have to wait if you go during the rush.

Windstar's official dress code is "no jackets required," which is a big draw for guests. In The Restaurant, guests are asked to dress "casually elegant," which generally means trousers and a nice collared shirts for men and pantsuits or casual dresses for women.

Windstar Fleet Itineraries			
Ship	Home Ports & Season	Itinerary	Other Itineraries
Wind Spirit	Round-trip from St. Thomas, Dec–Apr.	**7-night E. Carib:** St. John, St. Martin, St. Barts, Tortola, Jost Van Dyke, and Virgin Gorda.	Mediterranean, Costa Rica (beginning fall 2001)
Wind Star	Round-trip from Cancún, Dec–Apr.	**7-night Belize:** Roatán (Honduras), Goff's Cay (Belize), Half Moon Cay Reserve (Belize), San Pedro (Belize), and Cozumel.	Mediterranean
Wind Surf	Round-trip from Barbados, Dec–Apr.	**7-night E. Carib:** Tobago, Bequia, Martinique, St. Lucia, Mayreau or Nevis, St. Martin, St. Barts, Iles des Saintes, and St. Lucia.	Mediterranean

The **24-hour room service** includes hot and cold breakfast items (cereals and breads as well as eggs and omelets) and a limited menu that includes sandwiches, fruit, pizza, salads, and other snacks.

ACTIVITIES

Since these ships generally visit a port of call every single day of the cruise and guests spend the day on shore exploring, there are few organized activities offered, and the daily schedules are intentionally unregimented—the way guests prefer it. Weather and conditions permitting, the ships anchor and passengers can enjoy kayaking, sailing, windsurfing, banana boat rides, and swimming from the **water-sports platform** lowered at the stern. There will be a handful of scheduled diversions, such as gaming lessons in the casino and walk-a-mile sessions and stretch classes on deck. Chances are there may be a vegetable-carving or food-decorating demonstration poolside, as well as clothing or jewelry sale items on display by the pool. Brief orientation talks are held before port visits.

The pool deck, with its hot tub, deck chairs, and open-air bar, is conducive to sunbathing, conversations with shipmates, or quiet repose. There's an extensive video library and CD collection from which passengers can borrow for use in their cabins.

The company's **organized island tours** tend to be more creative than usual, and the cruise director/shore excursions manager/jack-of-all trades person or couple are knowledgeable and able to point passengers toward good spots for such independent activities as bird watching, snorkeling, or a nice meal.

CHILDREN'S PROGRAM

As children are not encouraged to sail with Windstar, there are no activities planned for them. There are often a handful of teenagers on board who spend time sunbathing or holed up in their cabins watching movies.

ENTERTAINMENT

For the most part, passengers entertain themselves. There's often a duo on board (a pianist and a vocalist) performing during cocktail hour before and after dinner in the ship's one main lounge. **Local entertainment,** such as steel bands, calypso bands, or a group of limbo dancers, is sometimes brought aboard at a port of call. A very modest **casino** offers slots, blackjack, and Caribbean stud poker. After dinner, passengers often go up to the pool bar for a nightcap under the stars, and sometimes after 10 or 11pm, disco/pop music is played in the lounge if guests are in the dancing mood.

SERVICE

Windstar is a class operation, as reflected in its thoughtful service personnel. The staff smiles hello and makes every effort to learn passengers' names. Dining staff is efficient and first-rate as well, but not in that ultra-professional, military-esque, five-star-hotel, Seabourn kind of way. That's not what Windstar is all about. Officers and crew are helpful, but not gushing. It's common for several married couples to be among the crew.

The line operates under a "tipping not required" policy, although generally guests do tip staff much as on other ships; on Windstar, like Holland America, there's just less pressure to do so.

Wind Spirit • Wind Star

The Verdict

Some of the most romantic, cozy yet roomy small ships out there, these vessels look chic and offer just the right combination of creature comforts and first-class cuisine, along with a casual, laid-back, unstructured ethic.

Wind Spirit *(photo: Windstar Cruises)*

Specifications

Size (in tons)	5,350	Officers	British/Dutch
Number of Cabins	74	Crew	89 (International)
Number of Outside Cabins	74	Passenger/Crew Ratio	1.6 to 1
Cabins with Verandas	0	Year Built	1988/1986
Number of Passengers	148	Last Major Refurbishment	N/A

Frommer's Ratings (Scale of 1–5)

Cabin Comfort & Amenities	5	Pool, Fitness & Spa Facilities	2
Ship Cleanliness & Maintenance	4	Children's Facilities	N/A
Public Comfort/Space	4	Itinerary	5
Decor	4	Worth the Money	5

Despite these ships' high-tech design and a size significantly larger than virtually any private yacht afloat, they nonetheless have some of the grace and lines of a classic clipper ship—from the soaring masts to the needle-shaped bowsprit—with practically none of the associated discomforts. Getting around is usually easy, except that there's no inside access to the breakfast and luncheon restaurant, so during high winds or rain, access via an external set of stairs can be moderately inconvenient.

Cabins & Rates

Cabins	Per diems from	Bathtub	Fridge	Hair Dryer	Sitting Area	TV
Outside	$355	no	yes	yes	no	yes*
Suite	$372	no	yes	yes	yes	yes*

* TVs show CNN.

CABINS   All cabins are very similar and display a subtle nauticalness. They're roomy at 188 square feet, but nowhere near as large as your typical high-end ship suite. Beds can be adapted into either a one-queen-size or two-twin-size format. Each cabin has a VCR and TV showing CNN and lots of movies (and sometimes ESPN), a CD player, a minibar, a pair of large round portholes with brass fittings, bathrobes, fresh fruit, and a compact closet. Teakwood-decked bathrooms, largish for a ship of this size, are better laid out than those aboard many luxury cruise liners, and contain a hair dryer, plenty of towels, and more than adequate storage space. Like the ship's main public rooms, cabins are based on navy-blue fabrics and carpeting, along with wood tones—attractive, but simple, well-constructed and utilitarian. The large desk/bureau is white with dark brown trim and the rest of the cabinetry is a medium wood tone.

Although all the cabins are comfortable, cabins amidships are more stable in rough seas. Note that the ship's engines, when running at full speed, can be a bit noisy.

This line is not recommended for passengers with serious disabilities or those who are wheelchair bound. There are no elevators on board, access to piers is often by tender, and there are raised doorsills.

PUBLIC AREAS   There aren't a lot of public areas on these small ships, but they're more than adequate for ships that spend most of their time in port. The four main rooms include two restaurants, a library, and the vaguely nautical-looking Lounge, with several cozy, somewhat private partitioned-off nooks and clusters of comfy caramel-colored leather chairs surrounding a slightly sunken wooden dance floor. In one corner is a bar and, in another, a piano and music equipment for the onboard entertainment duo. Here passengers congregate for port talks, pre- and post-dinner drinks, dancing, and any local dance performances. The second bar is out on the pool deck, and also attracts passengers before and after dinner for drinks under the stars. Here there's a piano in the corner of the deck (which doesn't get much play), but mostly this is your typical casual pool bar, and the place where cigars can be purchased and smoked.

The wood-paneled library manages to be both nautical and collegiate at the same time. Guests can read, play cards, or check out one of the hundreds of videotapes (CDs are also available from the purser's office nearby). Windstar expects to have both ships wired for E-mail access at about the time this book goes to press.

The yachtily elegant, dimly lit main restaurant is similarly styled with navy carpeting and fabrics combined with wood details and nautical touches. The Veranda breakfast and lunch restaurant is light and airy. Throughout the ship, large non-opening glass windows allow in plenty of light if not air.

POOL, FITNESS & SPA FACILITIES   The swimming pool is tiny, as you might expect aboard such a relatively small-scale ship, and there's an adjacent hot tub. The deck chairs around the pool can get filled during sunny days, but there's always the crescent-shaped slice of deck above and more space outside of the Veranda restaurant. On Deck Four, there's an unobstructed wraparound deck for walkers.

There's a cramped gym in a cabin-size room, and an adjacent co-ed sauna. Massages and a few other types of treatments are available out of a single massage room next to the hair salon on Deck One. (Unlike most ship spas—in fact, unlike Windstar's own *Wind Surf*—such spa services here are not managed by Steiner Leisure Limited. I might add, one of the best massages I've had at sea was on a Windstar ship.)

Wind Surf

The Verdict

An enlarged version of Windstar's 148-passenger triplets, the 312-passenger *Wind Surf* is a sleek, sexy, super-smooth sailing ship, offering an extensive spa and lots of suites along with an intimate yachtlike ambiance.

Wind Surf *(photo: Windstar Cruises)*

Specifications

Size (in tons)	14,745	Officers	English/Dutch
Number of Cabins	156	Crew	163 (International)
Number of Outside Cabins	156	Passenger/Crew Ratio	2 to 1
Cabins with Verandas	0	Year Built	1990
Number of Passengers	312	Last Major Refurbishment	1998

Frommer's Ratings (Scale of 1–5)

Cabin Comfort & Amenities	5	Pool, Fitness & Spa Facilities	5
Ship Cleanliness & Maintenance	4	Children's Facilities	2
Public Comfort/Space	4	Itinerary	4
Decor	4	Worth the Money	5

The newest member of the Windstar fleet of deluxe motor-sailers continues the line's tradition of delivering a top-of-the line cruise experience that's as chic and sophisticated as it is easy-going and unregimented. Previously sailing under the Club Med banner (it originally entered service as the *Club Med I*), the ship was designed by the same French architect who worked on the other three Windstar vessels, and for the most part is an enlarged copy of them. Purchased for $45 million and subsequently renamed, the *Wind Surf* underwent a major $8 million renovation in early 1998, which included an overhaul of all the public areas, the conversion of many cabins (actually reducing the total number of cabins while creating 30 suites), and the addition of a 10,000-square-foot spa complex, an alternative restaurant, and a casino.

As part of the conversion, many areas were gutted and all the grace notes of upscale, high-end life at sea were added to remake what has emerged since then into a very elegant vessel. Despite a passenger capacity more than double her sister ships (312 versus 148), the *Wind Surf* maintains the feel of a private yacht.

Cabins & Rates

Cabins	Per diems from	Bathtub	Fridge	Hair Dryer	Sitting Area	TV
Outside	$355	no	yes	yes	no	yes*
Suite	$372	no	yes	yes	yes	yes*

* TVs show CNN.

CABINS   Cabins are clones of those described in the *Wind Spirit/Wind Star* review, above. The interiors of both suites and standard cabins feature generous use of polished woods (burled maple and teak), bedspreads and curtains in navy blue and beige color schemes (suites are maroon and beige), white laminated cabinetwork, and plentiful storage space. All cabins have ocean views, and both standard cabins (188 square feet) and suites (376 square feet) are well supplied with creature comforts, including terry robes, hair dryers, well-stocked minibars, safes, VCRs and CD players, and satellite TVs with CNN and sometimes ESPN. Bathrooms have teakwood trim, and are artfully designed and more appealing than those aboard many luxury cruise ships. Extra-spacious suites have separate sleeping and living quarters and his-and-hers bathrooms (each with a shower and a toilet).

As part of *Wind Surf*'s metamorphosis in 1998, cabins were completely reconfigured for a reduced passenger capacity of 312 instead of the *Club Med*'s 386. This included repartitioning total cabin space to allow for 30 suites on Deck 3 (its original layout had only one), making the vessel the most suite-heavy of the Windstar fleet.

The ship has two elevators (unlike the other ships in the Windstar fleet, which have none), but still is not recommended for people with serious mobility problems. Access to piers is often by tender, and ramps over doorsills are not adequate.

PUBLIC AREAS   Since the *Wind Surf*'s passenger-space ratio is 30% greater than its sister ships, its two main public spaces—the bright and airy Wind Surf Lounge where passengers gather in the evening for cocktails and to listen to a three- to five-person band play your favorite requests, and the Compass Rose piano bar, popular for after-dinner drinks—are also roomier than comparable public spaces on the other ships. There's also the pool bar for a drink under the stars.

As on the other Windstar ships, breakfast and lunch are served in the glass-enclosed Veranda Cafe topside, while the *Wind Surf* also offers an alternative dinner option that's unique—in addition to the Restaurant, the smaller 90-seat Bistro (adjacent to the Veranda) serves dinner each night.

Also unlike the other Windstar ships, *Wind Surf* has a 2,100-square-foot conference center that lies amidships and just below the water line (a company spokesperson says about 25% of the *Wind Surf*'s total business comes from charter and corporate incentive business; sometimes the whole ship is chartered, sometimes just half or less). Suitable for between 118 and 180 occupants, depending on the arrangement of tables and chairs, it contains technical amenities such as a photocopy machine and audiovisual equipment.

Other public areas include a casino that's nestled into one edge of the Windsurf Lounge, a library (in which the line hopes to install data-port jacks for laptops by year-end 2000), and a gift shop.

POOL, FITNESS & SPA FACILITIES   The *Wind Surf* has the most elaborate fitness and spa facilities in the Windstar fleet (the line's three 148-passenger ships have no spa and only a tiny gym) and in fact outclasses facilities on other similar-size ships. There's a well-stocked windowed gym on the top deck, a "sports" pool for aqua-aerobics and scuba lessons (passengers can get resort certification), and an aerobics room one deck below that's also used for yoga and golf swing practice. The new Steiner-managed WindSpa offers a roster of exercise, massage, and beauty regimens that rival those available at many land-based spas. A staff of 10 doles out aromatherapy plus a variety of massages and other treatments. There's also a sauna and a steam room. Spa packages—geared to both men and women—can be purchased in advance through your travel agent, with appointment times made once you're on board.

Besides the sports pool, there's another pool on the Main Deck as well as two hot tubs. For joggers, a full circuit teak promenade wraps around the Bridge Deck.

9

Soft-Adventure Lines & Sailing Ships

The ships in this chapter are not your average cruise ships. Whether the small, motorized coastal cruisers of American Canadian Caribbean Line and Clipper or the sailing ships of Star Clippers and Windjammer Barefoot Cruises, they're more like private yachts or summer camps at sea. All of them are small and intimate, carrying between 60 and 200 passengers on average, and are often more adventure tour than they are "cruise" as we have come to know it. Leave the jackets, ties, pumps, and pearls at home: These vessels espouse an ultra-casual ethic and take passengers close up to the islands and the sea.

These ships generally visit a port every day, and because most of them have shallow drafts (the amount of the ship that rides below the waterline) they're able to sail adventurous itineraries to small, out-of-the-way ports that the big cruise ships would run aground trying to approach. Also, since all these ships depart from one or another of the Caribbean islands rather than Florida, there's little time spent at sea getting to your first port. (Though, on the other hand, it can be more expensive to fly to these ports of embarkation than to Florida.)

Passengers are generally well-traveled people who are more concerned with learning and exploring than they are about plush amenities and onboard activities of the bingo and horse-racing variety. There may not be TVs in the cabins and you won't find a casino, but you will find fellow passengers who have booked this type of ship because they like to actually get to know the people they're traveling with and learn something about the ports they visit.

Food on board will be basic, hearty, and plentiful, but don't look for room service and midnight buffets, because there aren't any. Don't expect doting service either, but do expect very personal attention, as crew and passengers get friendly fast. You'll have fun, make lots of new friends, and be able to let your hair down.

Of the bunch, **American Canadian Caribbean** offers the most bare-boned experience whose entire focus is on the ports visited—the ships themselves are marvels of maneuverability and exploration-focused design, but they're not what you'd call plush. Their nearest competitor, **Clipper Cruises,** offers a similarly port-intensive experience, but aboard much more comfortable vessels that remind me of Princess ships stripped down to the basics and shrunk to pint size.

Frommer's Cruise Line Ratings at a Glance: The Soft-Adventure Lines

1 = poor   2 = fair   3 = good   4 = excellent   5 = outstanding

Cruise Line	Enjoyment Factor	Dining	Activities	Children's Program	Entertainment	Service	Overall Value
American Canadian Caribbean	4	3	5	N/A*	3	3	3
Clipper	4	4	4	N/A*	3	4	4
Royal Olympic	5	5	5	N/A*	4	5	4
Star Clippers	5	5	4	N/A*	4	4	4
Windjammer	5	3	3	3*	3	3	5

NOTE: Cruise lines have been graded on a curve that compares them only with the other lines in the Soft-Adventure and Sailing Ship category. See "Cruise Line Categories" in chapter 5 for a detailed explanation of my ratings methodology.

* Does not apply to all ships in the line's fleet. See individual ship reviews for details. Lines with N/A rating for children's programs have no program whatsoever.

Of the sailing ships, **Windjammer Barefoot Cruises** is the line flying the skull and crossbones (and dispensing rum out of a real live barrel up on deck, by the bar), while **Star Clippers** is the line carrying Admiral Nelson, off to protect the interests of the crown—in other words, go for Windjammer if you want a total yo-ho-ho barefoot adventure and Star Clippers if you want something a little more refined (though still casual and relaxing).

Royal Olympic is the oddball of the bunch, since its Caribbean ships—the 620-passenger, ocean-liner-style *Stella Solaris* and sleek, 840-passenger *Olympic Voyager*—are both monsters compared with the tiny vessels operated by the rest of the lines. So why's the line here? *Because it doesn't fit anywhere else, that's why!* Honestly, in the Caribbean, Royal Olympic offers a much more intimate, education-oriented experience than any of the other mid-size and large-ship lines, so while the *Solaris* and *Voyager* aren't small ships by any stretch of the imagination, they've got adventure in their heart.

DRESS CODES   Dress code? What's a dress code? Aboard most of the ships in this chapter you can get away with a polo shirt and khakis (or shorts) at pretty much any hour of the day, and on some—Windjammer especially—you could show up to dinner in your bathing suit and not feel out of place. These are monumentally casual ships.

American Canadian Caribbean Line

461 Water St., Warren, RI 02885. ☎ **800/556-7450** or 401/247-0955. Fax 401/247-2350. www.accl-smallships.com.

THE LINE IN A NUTSHELL Small and intimate, these three no-frills, moderate-priced ships travel to offbeat places and attract a well-traveled, down-to-earth older crowd. It's a dose of real Americana—in the vessels themselves, the officers, the passengers, and the crew.

THE EXPERIENCE This trio of innovative and extremely informal small ships offers an unusual cruising experience, focusing on encounters with indigenous peoples and navigating such hinterlands as the cays off the coast of Belize, remote out-islands in the Bahamas, and exotic islands near the Pacific mouth of the Panama Canal.

ACCL offers a bare-bones experience in terms of amenities, services, and meals. It's the only line featuring a BYOB policy. Owing to the ships' tiny size, there are no quiet nooks besides your cabin for you to run and hide—you're in close quarters and constant contact with everyone else. Luckily, the ships attract a generally convivial crowd, many of whom have sailed with ACCL before.

Pros

- **Casual and unpretentious.** If you're looking for a do-it-yourself, cost-effective adventure at sea, these tiny yet innovative vessels are tops.
- **Imaginative itineraries.** One-of-a-kind itineraries are innovative, and the ships' exploratory technical innovations allow a close-up experience of out-of-the-way islands.
- **BYOB policy.** ACCL's BYOB policy provides substantial savings on bar bills. The bus or van that transports passengers from the airport or hotel to the ship stops at a reasonably priced liquor store en route so those interested can stock up.

Cons

- **No frills.** Cabins are tiny, decor is bland, bathrooms are minuscule, there are no beach towels (bring your own), and meals are served family-style.
- **No place to hide.** When the ships are at or near full capacity, they're very, very full. Your cabin is your only sanctuary—and the accordion-style doors (on the *Niagara Prince* and *Grande Caribe* only) and thin cabin walls will make you feel closer to your fellow passengers than you might prefer.
- **Minimal port information.** For a line that's so destination-oriented, ACCL's ships have a surprising lack of books and naturalists/historians to provide background on the islands' history, culture, and nature.

Compared with the other Soft-Adventure lines, here's how ACCL rates:					
	poor	fair	good	excellent	outstanding
Enjoyment Factor				✓	
Dining			✓		
Activities			✓		
Children's Program	N/A*				
Entertainment		✓			
Service		✓			
Overall Value			✓		

* *ACCL offers no children's program.*

ACCL: TINY SHIPS, BIG ADVENTURE

For more than half a century (since 1949), master shipbuilder and ACCL founder/builder/captain/president Luther Blount has been designing and building a variety of vessels, including cargo ferries, dinner boats, and tugboats in his Warren, Rhode Island, shipyard. In 1966, Blount built his first cruise ship, the 20-passenger *Canyon Flyer,* which specialized in cruising New England and Canadian waters. Over the years he has refined the design of his ships, gradually increasing both size and capacity and expanding itineraries while remaining faithful to his original concept that "small is the only way to cruise." Now past age 80, Blount continues to head one of the only family-owned companies in the cruise industry.

Along with building almost 300 ships over the past 50 years, Blount also holds over 20 patents for his innovative designs, which include an extendible **bow ramp** that, combined with an unusually shallow draft of about 6 ¹/₂ feet, makes it possible for the ships to nudge their bows directly onto beaches, silted riverbanks, or virtually anywhere else and disembark passengers directly onto the shore without needing a pier. The ships also feature **retractable pilot houses** that enable them to cruise under low bridges on inland waterways. Each also has a **stern-side swimming platform,** a Blount-designed 24-passenger **glass-bottomed boat,** and Sunfish boats that are launched for short sails during Caribbean and Central American beach breaks. His ships' appeal is evident by the fact that several former ACCL ships have been purchased by other small-ship cruise lines, including Cruise West and Glacier Bay Tours & Cruises/Voyager.

ACCL's innovative Caribbean itineraries are designed to bypass "tourist trap" ports and islands. If you sail this line, you'll sail waters normally traveled only by private yachts and walk on pristine beaches that passengers from few if any mainstream cruise ships have ever explored.

All said, American Canadian Caribbean is a delightfully rare find. It's one of the few cruise entities in the business that designs, builds, maintains, and markets its own ships. Just be sure you know what you're getting into, because these ships, with their spartan, communal, rough-and-ready lifestyle, just aren't for everyone.

THE FLEET

In operation since April 1997, the 100-passenger *Grande Caribe* is the first of ACCL's Grande Class vessels, carrying more passengers and featuring roomier lounges and dining areas than previous ACCL ships. It is identical in size to its sister Grande Class ship, the 100-passenger *Grande Mariner,* which entered service in 1998. The smaller, 84-passenger *Niagara Prince,* built in 1994, rounds out the current ACCL fleet and is the line's most basic (for example, cabin doors are accordion-style).

Note: You may notice in the ships' technical statistics that ACCL ships have a tonnage of 90 compared to similarly sized ships that may be listed at 1,500 to 2,400 GRTs (gross registered tons). So, what's the story here? Some U.S.-flag coastal vessels use a special measurement system which is unrelated to that used by all other oceangoing vessels. In this measurement's absence, you can compare vessel size with some accuracy by looking at the passenger capacity.

PASSENGER PROFILE

These casual ships appeal to an unpretentious, sensible, early-to-bed cruise crowd of mostly senior couples in their sixties through eighties, with the average age being 72. While some are physically fit, there are usually a few walking with canes and using hearing aids. All are attracted by the ships' casual atmosphere—wash-and-wear fabrics, durable windbreakers, and easy-to-care-for sportswear is about as fancy as you'll get aboard this line—and want to escape overrun Caribbean ports such as St. Thomas and flee to isolated beaches and secluded havens to become quietly acquainted with regional cultures or comb the beaches. That said, passengers tend to be less adventurous than those on other small ship lines, so the line doesn't offer harder activities, such as excursions in inflatable Zodiac boats.

Since many passengers are grandparents, common topics for conversations often concern the grandkids, retirement, and experiences during World War II. Besides senior couples, there may be a few mother-daughter traveling companions.

ACCL has one of the most loyal followings of any line, so it's not unusual to have upward of 50% repeaters on a particular cruise. Many passengers have been on other small-ship lines, such as Special Expeditions, Clipper, Glacier Bay/Voyager, and Cruise West, as well as some of the bigger, more luxurious lines like Holland America and Crystal. Travel programs for seniors, such as Elderhostel, are also popular with the typical ACCL passenger.

The ships will not appeal to young couples, singles, honeymooners, or families. Children under age 14 are prohibited, and there are no children's facilities or activities.

A warning: Ceilings throughout ACCL ships are set at about 6 feet 4 inches, so if you're very tall, you might want to consider another line—unless you enjoy stooping, of course.

DINING

Wholesome, all-American food is well prepared and casually presented, but overall is nothing special. The daily menu with selections for all three meals is posted every morning on the blackboard in the dining room.

Early risers will find "eye-opener" coffee available beginning at 6:30am in the lounge, where you'll also find a selection of fruit juices every morning before breakfast. Breakfast combines buffet and table service, with passengers having a choice from the buffet table of hot or cold cereal, yogurt, and fruit. Slices of a variety of melons are placed on tables while waiters deliver a different hot dish every morning, such as scrambled eggs with bacon, Belgian waffles, pancakes, French toast, or cheese omelets.

Lunch is the lightest meal of the day and consists of homemade soup (such as tomato basil, vegetable, or beef orzo) along with a sandwich on freshly baked bread (turkey, ham and cheese, and tuna) plus a salad, chips, fruit, and dessert.

Dinners begin with a salad and fresh bread followed by a main entree like BBQ ribs, roast beef, chicken, or fish, along with vegetables, rice, or potatoes, plus dessert. Since there is only one entree, anyone wanting an **alternative meal** (such as fish instead of beef) can be accommodated only if he or she notifies the kitchen before 10am. **Special dietary needs** can also be met with advance notice.

Since the line has a **BYOB policy,** all alcoholic beverages—which guests can buy at a liquor store en route to the ship from the airport or their hotel—are kept in the lounge; beer and wine are placed in a cooler near the bar and there are separate shelves set aside for bottles. This is a real money-saving system for passengers—a bottle of rum I bought in Panama City, for example, cost less than $4 (about the price of one drink on most ships). To avoid drinking someone else's booze, all bottles and cans are labeled

---

Cruise Tip: Saving Your Soles on ACCL Excursions

ACCL ships don't always select beach stopovers because of their soft and glistening sands. Many expeditions to remote places include stops at gravel- and/or coral-covered beaches, so it's a good idea to pack a pair of nylon or rubber sandals or shoes to wear on the beach and in the water.

Flexible Itineraries & Other Vagaries of Small-Ship Cruising

As is the case with most other small-ship lines, all ACCL itineraries are flexible and may be altered at the discretion of the captain, who might change direction and head for another island because of sea and/or wind conditions. On itineraries featuring the Panama Canal, the time of transit could take place during the day or night (exact time of crossing cannot be determined before departure). While every effort is made to transit during the day, on a recent cruise, the time was changed the day before from a morning to an evening transit, entering the first lock around 7pm and departing the last set of locks around 3am. Needless to say, passengers were disappointed. Although locks are very well lit throughout the night, the rest of the transit was in darkness.

with the passengers' cabin number. Soft drinks, along with tonic and soda water, are provided free of charge at the bar.

Meals are served promptly at 8am, noon, and 6pm every day and are announced by one of the waitresses clanging a cowbell as she passes through the corridors and lounge. Rather than wandering in gradually, everyone typically arrives within a few minutes of hearing the bell. Dining is open seating, communal-style for all meals, as passengers group themselves around circular and rectangular tables primarily seating eight (just one or two tables are set for four). Passengers interact and get to know each other sooner rather than later. Mixing with your fellow passengers at meals is mandatory since there are no tables for two and no room service for private dining in the cabin.

A variety of teas as well as coffee and hot chocolate are available round the clock in the dining room, along with cookies and fresh fruit.

ACTIVITIES

With the exception of a few printed quizzes and an occasional arts-and-crafts and/or napkin-folding class, daytime activities are concentrated in recreational pursuits off the ship during calls at remote islands and beaches. As some of the areas frequented by ACCL ships (especially those off the coast of Belize) are among the richest repositories of underwater life in the Western Hemisphere, there are frequent opportunities for **snorkeling** (with masks and fins provided free of charge) as well as swimming from the ships' **swimming platform** in the stern. During winters in the Caribbean, the ships haul along a Sunfish (mini-sailboat) for passengers to use as well as a 24-passenger **glass-bottom boat,** which is used at some islands to view coral formations and tropical fish.

The amount of time spent at each island varies from a few hours to an entire morning or afternoon. Except for a couple of overnight sailings, most of the time the ship remains anchored at night, as sailing between islands usually takes place during the day.

Some itineraries include visits to villages inhabited by indigenous tribal peoples. For example, Panama cruises include stops at several Kuna Indian villages and an optional excursion by *cayuga* (a native boat resembling a large dugout canoe) to the Embara village in the Darien Jungle. Those with puritan sensibilities are advised that Embara women wear only grass skirts, and men wear loincloths.

During calls at some of the San Blas islands on the Panama itinerary, the cruise director may bring a member of the community aboard ship to discuss native life and culture. With the cruise director acting as translator, Kuna women discuss their daily lives as well as the art of making molas (colorful hand-stitched decorative tapestries), while a Kuna medicine man comes aboard to discuss methods and techniques of treating illness.

ACCL Fleet Itineraries*

Ship	Home Ports & Season	Itinerary	Other Itineraries
Grande Caribe	Between Balboa and Colón (Panama), Dec–Mar.	**11-night Panama/Panama Canal:** Portobelo, San Blas Islands, Contadora, Isla de Rey, Darien, Contadora, Mogo Mogo, Isla Pacheque, and Tobago.	Erie Canal, St. Lawrence Seaway, Intracoastal Waterway, Nova Scotia
Grande Mariner	Virgin Islands itineraries round-trip from St. Thomas, Dec–Jan; eastern Caribbean itineraries between Antigua and either Sint Maarten or Grenada Jan–Mar; Panama itineraries between Balboa and Colón (Panama), Mar–Apr; other one-time itineraries round-trip from Trinidad to Curaçao and from Balboa to Belize City.	**11-night Virgin Islands Carib:** St. John's, Tortola, Virgin Gorda, Prickly Pear, Salt Island, Anegada, Beef Island, Jost Van Dyke, and Norman Islands. **11-night E. Carib:** Il Pineel and Tinatmarre, Anguilla, St. Barts, Saba, St. Kitts, Nevis or Guadeloupe, Dominica, Martinique, St. Lucia, and Grenadines. **12-night S. Carib/Orinoco:** Margarita Island (Venezuela), Island of Tortuga, Los Roques, and Bonaire. **14-night S. Carib:** Bocas del Toro, Bluefield's, Corn Islands, Pearl Islands, Miskitos Islands, Roatán (Honduras), Livingston (Guatemala), Punta Gorda, West Snake Cay, and Goff's Cay.	Erie Canal, St. Lawrence Seaway, Intracoastal Waterway, Nova Scotia
Niagara Prince	Round-trip from Belize City, Dec–Apr.	**10-night Belize:** Goff's Cay, Tobacco Range, Victoria Channel Reef, Moho Cay, Laughing Bird Cay, Placencia, Punta Gorda, Livingston (Guatemala), El Gofete, Casa Guatemala, Castilo San Felipe, West Snake Cay, Punta Icacos, Lime Cay, and Water Cay. **6-night Belize:** Goff's Cay, Tobacco Cay, Victoria Channel Reef, Moho Cay, Lime Cay, Placencia, West Snake Cay, Punta Icacos, and Laughing Bird Cay.	New England, Intracoastal Waterway

* Note: Itineraries can change on short notice, depending on new markets that open and unforeseen changes in conditions at ports of call—it's all part of the adventure.

That said, although ACCL promotes the fact that all of its cruises are accompanied by experts, the line simply does not have the variety or quality of naturalists and historians you'll find on competing lines (Clipper Cruise Line, for instance, plus such non-Caribbean soft-adventure lines as Special Expeditions, Cruise West, and Glacier Bay/Voyager), and there tend to be fewer speakers on ACCL's Caribbean itineraries than on some of its others. In the way of a library, there isn't one, though the ships do each have a few shelves of background material in the lounge. Because no list or recommended background reading is supplied before the cruise, passengers should do their own research and bring guidebooks.

Instead of a daily printed schedule, the agenda of activities and ports of call is posted every morning on a bulletin board, and the cruise director runs through the daily schedule after breakfast.

A Few Good Deals & One Extra Charge

Unlike most other cruise lines, ACCL's brochure rates are very rarely discounted. That said, they do offer a few good deals. **Cabin Shares:** A 15% discount is granted for anyone sharing a cabin with two other passengers. **Back-to-Back and Repeater Deals:** A 10% discount is given if you book two back-to-back cruises, and the line gives passengers an 11th cruise free after their 10th (paid) cruise. **Port Charges:** Expect to pay between $120 and $200 per person in addition to the cruise rates.

Aside from the destination-oriented activities, the main evening event is a **movie** from the ship's video collection shown after dinner on the large-screen TV in the lounge.

CHILDREN'S PROGRAM

The minimum age for children on board is 14 years old, and there are no special facilities even for those who clear that mark. Unless your teenage child or grandchild is particularly self-reliant and enjoys the company of older passengers, he or she probably wouldn't enjoy this line.

ENTERTAINMENT

Amusement is mostly of the do-it-yourself nature, like board games, puzzles, and reading. The BYOB cocktail hour is a time for songfests, piano music, announcements, and an occasional lecture about an upcoming sight or experience. The cruise director might arrange some onboard activities, but they will be low-key. Sometimes **local entertainers,** such as Garifuna dancers in Belize or soca/reggae musicians in the Virgin Islands, will be invited on board for an evening or will perform for passengers in port.

SERVICE

Generally, all of the personable 17- or 18-member staff is made up of Americans, though in the Caribbean/Panama Canal especially, a few may come from Central American countries and/or the Caribbean. Some of the foreign members of the crew speak limited English, but this does not limit their effectiveness in getting their jobs done. As on most small ships, the crew is versatile by necessity, having to double on many jobs that bigger ships have segregated into separate departments. You may see your cabin attendant waiting tables at dinner, or notice one of the laundry workers clearing dishes.

Service is adequate in the dining room, although with just three or four waiters serving 70 passengers it can be slow at times; however, since the day's agenda proceeds at a leisurely pace, nobody is in a hurry to go anywhere. Cabins are made up once a day after breakfast, while towels are changed every other day.

Much of the young American staff hales from the Northeast, many of them from Rhode Island, Luther Blount's home country. For many, serving aboard an ACCL vessel is like a summer job, something akin to working as a camp counselor in Maine, and they probably won't be doing this type of work as a career. What they lack in experience, though, they make up in enthusiasm and friendliness.

There is no laundry service or room service, nor is there an onboard doctor or medical facilities (ships this size are not required to provide them, as they always sail close to land).

Grande Caribe •
Grande Mariner

The Verdict

Functional and no-frills, these ships are best described as well-thought-out vehicles for transporting passengers to remote ports.

Grande Caribe *(photo: ACCL)*

Specifications

Size (in tons)	99	Crew	18 (American/Int'l.)
Number of Cabins	50	Passenger/Crew Ratio	5.5 to 1
Number of Outside Cabins	41	Year Built	
Cabins with Verandas	0	*Grande Caribe*	1997
Number of Passengers	100	*Grande Mariner*	1998
Officers	American	Last Major Refurbishment	N/A

Frommer's Ratings (Scale of 1–5)

Cabin Comfort & Amenities	2	Pool, Fitness & Spa Facilities	N/A
Ship Cleanliness & Maintenance	4	Children's Facilities	N/A
Public Comfort/Space	3	Itinerary	5
Decor	2	Worth the Money	4

Seaworthy, practical, and unfussy, the *Grande Caribe* and *Grande Mariner* are in many ways the culmination of 30 years of ACCL's corporate philosophy. Even better, they're the most comfortable and appealing vessels the line has ever built. Constructed at a cost of between $7.5 million and $8 million each, they were conceived as state-of-the-art replacements for the less technically sophisticated and more bare-bones *Caribbean Prince* and *Mayan Prince,* vessels that ACCL sold to Alaska-based Glacier Bay Tours and Cruises (a.k.a. Voyager Cruise Line), which now operates them in Alaska and in Mexico's Sea of Cortez.

The design of these ships added a much-needed improvement to ACCL's basic, generic package: a lounge/bar on the upper deck that's separate from the rest of the dining room and can accommodate every passenger on board. The space this area opens up aboard these very small ships does a lot to relieve the claustrophobia that's been an unavoidable hallmark of ACCL vessels in the past.

The *Grand Caribe* and *Mariner*'s system of cabin ventilation is also a marked improvement over earlier ACCL vessels, and they're also a lot quieter due to the use of twin-screwed, 1,400-horsepower engines that are mounted on cushioned bearings.

Cabins & Rates

Cabins	Per diems from	Bathtub	Fridge	Hair Dryer	Sitting Area	TV
Inside	$241	no	no	no	no	no
Outside	$261	no	no	no	no	no

CABINS Spartan in design (four bare walls) and amenities (soap and towels only; no TV or radio), the ships' 50 compact, definitely cramped cabins—measuring between about 80 and 120 square feet—are somewhere between cozy and claustrophobic.

However you describe them, there is minimal room for couples to maneuver (watch out for flying elbows!) and no space to stretch out in the minuscule head-style bathrooms (which, in layman's terms, means the toilet and sink are *in* the shower stall). Passengers around 6 feet or taller, beware of the low bridge over the toilet (I banged my head twice). Most cabins also have a small table plus a second mirror with two small shelves.

The cabins on Sun Deck are the only ones equipped with sliding picture windows and regular doors that open onto an outside deck. All other cabins have sealed windows, and all doors lock from the inside only (there are no keys). On the *Grande Caribe,* cabin doors are accordion-style; in the *Grande Mariner,* they're real doors. About a dozen cabins have two lower berths that can be made up into a double bed.

Six windowless units are adjacent to staff quarters on the lowest deck and have sloping outside walls and upper and lower berths. Cabins on the Main Deck closest to the dining room and cabins on the Sun Deck closest to the lounge are susceptible to noise from these two public rooms.

It's a good idea to pack light since storage space is limited to a small rectangular hanging closet plus three drawers and the space under the beds. There are also five hooks affixed to panels on walls for hanging clothes. There's an extra cabinet for storage between beds on *Grande Mariner.*

None of the cabins are wheelchair accessible. There are no elevators, but there is a stair lift for those who may have difficulty walking between decks.

PUBLIC AREAS Made up of three decks, both ships have larger public spaces than the *Niagara Prince,* with their lounges located on the Sun Deck and the dining room and galley situated on the Main Deck. The ships' main public area is the lounge/bar, with wraparound windows that allow it to serve as a viewing area during the day. Furnished with couches and chairs and containing a small collection of magazines and paperback books left behind by past passengers (bring your own books if you like to read), it also hosts the lively BYOB predinner cocktail hour every evening and is a favorite place to escape the confines of the cabin, read, and socialize. The room also serves as an auditorium for occasional lectures and arts-and-crafts classes, has board games and puzzles, and hosts the screening of movies and documentaries on its large-screen TV/VCR.

The other public space is the dining room, next to the galley on the Main Deck. Although it's splitting hairs, the *Mariner* has more polished woods in both the dining room and lounge, giving it a slightly warmer atmosphere than the public areas of the *Caribe.*

As on the other ships in this category, there's no onboard shop, but logo items—caps, T-shirts and so on—are available for purchase from the cruise director.

During the day, many passengers view the passing scene from atop the ship's Sun Deck, which is partially covered by a large awning that offers protection from the intense tropical sun.

POOL, FITNESS & SPA FACILITIES There are no exercise facilities, swimming pools, or spas aboard either of these ships, which seems to suit many of ACCL's older passengers just fine. You can walk around the Sun Deck for fitness (12.5 laps equals 1 mile). The top outside deck has some deck chairs, partially shaded by an awning, for anyone interested in sunbathing.

Niagara Prince

The Verdict

This bare-bones ship—even smaller and more basic than the Caribe and Mariner—offers the down-to-earth cruiser an adventurous, offbeat way to see the Caribbean.

Niagara Prince *(photo: ACCL)*

Specifications

Size (in tons)	99	Officers	American
Number of Cabins	42	Crew	17 (American/Int'l.)
Number of Outside Cabins	40	Passenger/Crew Ratio	5 to 1
Cabins with Verandas	0	Year Built	1994
Number of Passengers	84	Last Major Refurbishment	N/A

Frommer's Ratings (Scale of 1–5)

Cabin Comfort & Amenities	2	Pool, Fitness & Spa Facilities	N/A
Ship Cleanliness & Maintenance	3	Children's Facilities	N/A
Public Comfort/Space	2	Itinerary	5
Decor	2	Worth the Money	4

Overall, the *Niagara Prince* is more cramped than its two fleet mates, with its lounge and dining areas sharing adjoining open spaces (there are separate lounges and dining areas on the other two ships). Many of *Niagara's* remarkable engineering features were designed specifically for usually cold northern waters, not for the smooth Bahamian winter waters. Consequently, although the ship is versatile, you won't find any of the sun-worshipping options (large sundecks, etc.) that are standard issue aboard most Caribbean-bound ships.

Like its siblings, the *Niagara Prince* is equipped with an extendible bow ramp, shallow draft, retractable stern swimming platform, glass-bottom boat, and Sunfish, all of which facilitate a close-to-nature experience at out-of-the-way ports.

Cabins & Rates

Cabins	Per diems from	Bathtub	Fridge	Hair Dryer	Sitting Area	TV
Inside	$176	no	no	no	no	no
Outside	$227	no	no	no	no	no

CABINS In the Luther Blount tradition, cabins aboard this vessel are even smaller and more cramped than those on the *Grande Caribe* and *Mariner*. Ranging from 72 square feet to 96 square feet, cabins are simple and spartan, utterly without frills and decorated in a spare style. Each has individual climate controls and all but two offer some kind of outside view. Cabin doors are accordion-style and lock from the inside (there are no cabin keys—passengers are on the honor system).

If it's at all possible, try for a cabin in the number range of the 50s, 60s, or 70s, all of which offer sliding picture windows. There are only two inside cabins, inexpensive and a tight 80 square feet each. The 40 outside cabins are more or less equivalent, despite slight variations in their configuration of beds. Some single beds can be made up as doubles, and certain cabins can accommodate a third person (good luck!).

No cabins are wheelchair accessible. There are no elevators, but there is a stair lift for those who have difficulty walking between decks.

PUBLIC AREAS   The *Niagara Prince* has only two decks (Sun Deck and Main Deck), with the main public area on the Sun Deck, where the lounge shares the same space with the dining room and galley. Unfortunately, this area seems full-to-overflowing almost all the time. Frankly, the public areas aboard this ship seem to bulge with passengers regardless of the time of day or night you happen to be there—there's just not enough space for everyone to crowd in together. Your favorite perch—simply for lack of anything better—might be along the railing on one of the narrow side decks, or atop one of the two compact open decks stern-side.

POOL, FITNESS & SPA FACILITIES   As aboard the *Caribe* and *Mariner,* there are no exercise facilities, swimming pools, or spas aboard.

Clipper Cruise Line

7711 Bonhomme Ave., St. Louis, MO 63105-1956. ☎ **800/325-0010** or 314/727-2929. Fax 314/727-6576. www.clippercruise.com.

THE LINE IN A NUTSHELL   Not your typical cruise, these down-to-earth, comfortable small ships focus on offbeat ports of call, learning, and mingling with your fellow passengers. It's the ideal small-ship cruise for people who've tried Holland America or Princess but want a more intimate cruise experience.

THE EXPERIENCE   Clipper caters to mature, seasoned, easy-going, relatively affluent and well-traveled older passengers seeking a casual vacation experience. Being small ships, the ambiance is intimate and conducive to easily making new friends. You won't find any glitter, glitz, or Las Vegas gambling here. On the downside, like many of the American-crewed small ships, cruise rates are not cheap.

The line is particularly strong in providing information on the nature, history, and culture of the ports visited, carrying one or more naturalists on every Caribbean sailing and an onboard historian as well on sailings in the Grenadines. A cruise director helps organize the days, answers questions, and assists passengers.

The line's two Caribbean ships, *Nantucket Clipper* and *Yorktown Clipper,* are small and nicely appointed, with comfortable cabins, sizable lounges and dining rooms, and an overall relaxed feel. Like other small ships, they're able to access remote coral reefs of the southern Caribbean and isolated refuges in the British Virgin Islands and Central America, but they also suffer from the problems of small ships, such as stability: When a ship this size hits rough water, you know it (bring the Dramamine).

Pros

- **Interesting ports of call.** Their smallness enables them to visit more remote ports in the BVI and Grenadines, for instance, that most ships can't get close to.
- **Great learning opportunities.** Historians, naturalists, and educators sail with the ship, offering lectures on board and accompanying guests on shore excursions.
- **Informal atmosphere.** No need to dress up here—everything's casual.
- **Young, enthusiastic American crew.** While they may not be the most experienced, they're sweet, engaging, and hardworking, and add a homey feel to the trip.

Cons

- **No stabilizers.** If you hit some choppy waters and you're prone to seasickness, you're in for some unpleasantness.
- **Noisy engines.** If you can help it, don't book a cabin on the lowest deck (Main Deck), where noise from the engines can get quite loud.

Compared with the other Soft-Adventure lines, here's how Clipper rates:					
	poor	fair	good	excellent	outstanding
Enjoyment Factor				✓	
Dining				✓	
Activities				✓	
Children's Program	N/A*				
Entertainment			✓		
Service				✓	
Overall Value				✓	

* *Clipper offers no children's program.*

CLIPPER: CASUAL SHIPS, ENLIGHTENING TRIPS

Based in St. Louis, of all places, Clipper was founded in 1982 by Barney Ebsworth, creator of the INTRAV group of wholesale travel and travel-related companies, which he started in 1959. The line operates differently than most others in that its ships rarely ply the same itineraries for more than a few weeks at a time, instead moving from region to region, with no one place serving as a real home port—it's as if the ships were on a constant trip around the world, boarding passengers to sail different segments of one very long itinerary.

Although Clipper's ships carry a similar number of passengers and visit many of the same out-of-the-way ports of call as those of competitor American Canadian Caribbean, they're of a different breed: Though ACCL's ships have some wonderful exploratory features (such as the ability to nudge right up onto a beach and debark passengers) they're very, very spartan; with Clipper, on the other hand, you may not be able to get off the ship so easily, but they're so comfortable you might not want to.

THE FLEET

The 102-passenger, 1,471-ton *Nantucket Clipper,* which entered service in 1984, and the 138-passenger, 2,354-ton *Yorktown Clipper,* which entered service in 1988, are of slightly different sizes but are otherwise comparable in design, decor, and amenities. Both offer itineraries in the Caribbean.

In 1998, the company bought a third vessel, the 122-passenger, 4,364-ton *Clipper Adventurer.* Built in 1976 and sailed as a Russian expedition/research vessel for many years, the ship was completely reconstructed after its purchase to convert it into a truly beautiful, comfortable, yet hardy and exploratory cruise ship. It has a hardened-steel hull that allows it to sail itineraries in rougher parts of the world than the Caribbean—to the Arctic and Antarctic, for instance. In 1999 the line acquired a fourth ship, the luxurious 120-passenger, 5,200-ton *Clipper Odyssey,* which was built in 1989 and previously sailed as the *Oceanic Odyssey* from Spice Islands Cruises of Bali, Indonesia. The ship sails year-round in the South Pacific and Asia.

PASSENGER PROFILE

The majority of Clipper passengers are well-traveled 50-plus couples who are attracted by the casual intimacy of small ships and by the opportunities Clipper offers for actually learning something about the places its ships visit. Most are well educated though not academic, casual though not sloppily so, and adventurous in the sense that they're up for a little snorkeling and hiking, but are happy to be able to get back to their comfortable cabins afterwards, or have a cool drink in the lounge. As a company spokesperson notes, "We provide a soft adventure for travelers who may shy away from roughing it, and we think of ourselves not as a cruise line, but as a travel company that just happens to have ships."

Clipper attracts a remarkably high number of repeat passengers: 35 to 40 percent on any given cruise have sailed with the line before, and many have also sailed with other small-ship lines such as Special Expeditions and ACCL. On a recent cruise in the Grenadines, repeaters were thanked verbally at the captain's cocktail party, and the list went on for several minutes. Many, many passengers were on board for their second Clipper cruise and many more were taking their third or fourth, but the winner that day was one couple who were on their eighth. If that doesn't say something about customer satisfaction, I don't know what does.

DINING

The fare is all-American, prepared by attendees of the Culinary Institute of America, and incorporates local ingredients whenever practicable. While relatively simple in ingredients and presentation, the cuisine is easily the equal of all but the best served aboard mainstream megaships.

Breakfast is served in both the lounge and dining room, with cereals, fruit, toast, and pastries at the former and a full breakfast menu in the latter. Similarly, you can create your own sandwich in the lounge from an assortment of cold cuts or get a full lunch in the dining room. Set lunches offer a hot luncheon platter (perhaps crab cakes, baby back ribs, or pasta primavera), a lighter, cold entree (cobb salad, chicken Caesar salad, seafood salad, and more), and one or another kind of omelet, and there's always the option of a platter of fresh fruit and cottage cheese.

Dinner is served in a single open seating in the dining room, at tables set up for four to six, and offers four courses with five main entree options: seafood (perhaps herb-marinated halibut, stuffed lobster tail, or Chilean sea bass), a meat entree (such as roast duck, veal marsala, or prime rib), a **vegetarian** entree (such as marinated grilled portobello mushroom, vegetarian lasagna, and 10-vegetable couscous), a pasta entree, and a "starch and vegetables" entree such as steamed vegetables over saffron rice.

Vegetarian options are available as a matter of course, and Clipper can accommodate other dietary preferences or restrictions if you give them ample warning. One woman aboard my recent cruise was allergic to garlic (like a vampire . . .), and the entire staff was made aware of her needs.

Though the onboard dress code is casual at all times, most passengers tend to get a bit more gussied up at dinner, and men may even wear jackets at the captain's welcome-aboard and farewell parties (though you can get away with a nice shirt and slacks if you don't want to pack the fancies).

In the lounge you can get coffee, tea, iced tea, orange and cranberry juice, and lemonade 24 hours a day. Some kind of crunchy snack food (goldfish crackers, cashew nuts, rice crackers, etc.) is also on the bar during the day, the famous (and really delicious) "Clipper Chipper" cookies are set out here as well in the late afternoon, and hors d'oeuvres are served here before dinner. These may include mushroom caps stuffed with escargot or maybe smoked salmon with petit toasts. Weather permitting, there's a **barbecue** on-deck at least once during each weeklong cruise.

As aboard almost all small ships, there is no room service unless you're too ill to attend meals.

ACTIVITIES

By design, these ships don't offer much in the way of typical cruise ship activities; instead, they offer activities designed to focus your attention on the islands and marine environments you're visiting, giving you the opportunity to return home from your vacation not only relaxed, but enriched.

Each day of the Caribbean itineraries is spent in port, with several organized **excursions** offered in each (at extra cost, as is the case with almost all lines). Typically, excursions are accompanied by an appropriate staff member: the onboard historian while visiting St. Kitts's Brimstone Hill Fortress, for instance, or one of the naturalists while snorkeling in St. Lucia's Anse Chastanet marine park (there's always at least one naturalist aboard, and the ships carry two or more naturalists and/or historians on at least 90% of their Caribbean cruises). Throughout the cruise, these same staff members also offer a series of **lectures,** which on a recent trip included talks on reef fish identification, the nature and geology of the Caribbean islands, American Revolution history in the Caribbean, and plant life. Experts may also offer free informal **shore walks** on certain islands, or even conduct a short tutorial on the rules of cricket (a popular sport in these once-British islands), followed by a game that usually bears little resemblance to

Clipper Fleet Itineraries

Ship	Home Ports & Season	Itinerary	Other Itineraries
Nantucket Clipper	Sails between Antigua and St. Martin, Dec–Feb.	**7-night E. Carib:** Antigua, St. Kitts, St. Eustatius, St. Bart's, Anguilla, St. Martin.	U.S. East coast, Eastern Canada, Great Lakes, Hudson River
Yorktown Clipper	7-night S. Carib. between Curaçao and Trinidad, Dec 2000, and March 2001; 7-night E. Carib. between Grenada and St. Kitts, Jan–Feb 2001; 7-night S. Carib./ Orinoco River round-trip from Trinidad, Dec. 2000.	**7-night S. Carib*:** Curaçao, Bonaire, Isla de Margarita, Tobago, and Trinidad. **7-night E. Carib:** Grenada, Union Island, Bequia, St. Lucia, Dominica, Nevis, and St. Kitts. **7-night S. Carib/Orinoco River:** Tobago, Trinidad, Orinoco River (Venezuela).	Costa Rica, Sea of Cortez, Northern California, British Columbia, Southeast Alaska

* Itinerary includes an eighth night on land.

the real sport. Tips for Americans: You do not hold the bat like a baseball bat, and you do not drop it when you run.

Naturally, passengers have the option of skipping all of this and just sitting on deck, lying on the beach (towels are provided by the line), or, in many ports, **snorkeling,** for which gear is provided free to those who need it.

When arriving at some of the more undeveloped islands, passengers will go ashore via inflatable, steel-floored landing boats and will often have to step from these boats into the surf when debarking, so you might want to consider bringing along a pair of aquasocks (unless you just want to tough it out and go barefoot).

Both ships have small display cases of logo items and island crafts that represents all the shopping to be had on board. The cruise director will have items out to be tried on at least once during each sailing, but you can always ask to see something if money's burning a hole in your pocket.

CHILDREN'S PROGRAM

These ships have no facilities or programs of any kind for children. If you want to bring a young niece, nephew, or grandchild, they'll be expected to behave like young adults. Most teenagers would be bored to death aboard a Clipper Cruise. Baby-sitting is not available.

ENTERTAINMENT

By way of entertainment, Clipper's Caribbean itineraries offer blue skies, blue waters, sandy beaches, schools of brightly colored tropical fish, vibrant island cultures, a smattering of fascinating historical sites, and the occasional diving pelican or leaping dolphin. If your response to this is, "That's all?," then this isn't the line for you. As is true of the vast majority of small-ship companies, Clipper offers no casino, no dancing girls, no comedy and/or magic acts—nothing, in fact, that is usually standard-issue on one of the megas (except the occasional second-run movie shown in the lounge). That said, the line does bring aboard local musicians regularly to perform in the evenings. A February 2000 cruise saw passengers entertained by a steel-drum band, an acoustic island-music trio, and a full modern island band, as well as a tropical fashion show for which one of the models was none other than a recent Miss St. Kitts. Royalty!

Aboard either vessel, *the* spot (meaning, essentially, the *only* spot) for a rendezvous with fellow passengers is the Observation Lounge, where you'll find a piano, a bar, and a small library well stocked with books on island history, culture, nature, and geography (as well as a smattering of best-sellers). Passengers socialize here or curl up quietly with a good book.

SERVICE

Service staff aboard Clipper's ships is basically collegiate or postcollegiate Americans having an adventure before getting on with whatever it is they're getting on with. In other words, these aren't the same folks you'll find serving at the Four Seasons. They're amateurs—fresh-faced, willing to work, and happy to help, but don't expect them to bow when you cross the threshold. Not that you'd want them to—which, I think, is the point. As Clipper's demographic base is generally couples over 50, I suspect a nefarious plot on the line's part to staff its ships with young men and women of approximately the same age as passengers' children and grandchildren, but unlike those real offspring, these substitutes *actually do what you tell them to*. What a refreshing change!

There is no room service, nor any laundry facilities or services. In a nod to water conservation and a more detergent-free environment, bathroom towels are changed only on an as-needed basis: If you want fresh towels, you leave the old ones on the bathroom floor; if you don't, you leave them hanging.

Nantucket Clipper • Yorktown Clipper

The Verdict

Like a pair of your favorite walking shoes, these low-frills yet comfortable and convivial small ships carry the well traveled to off-the-beaten-track ports in search of nature, history, and a nice rum punch or two.

Yorktown Clipper *(photo: Clipper Cruise Line)*

Specifications

Size (in tons)		Officers	American
Nantucket Clipper	1,471	Crew	(International)
Yorktown Clipper	2,354	*Nantucket Clipper*	32
Number of Cabins		*Yorktown Clipper*	40
Nantucket Clipper	51	Passenger/Crew Ratio	
Yorktown Clipper	69	*Nantucket Clipper*	3.2 to 1
Number of Outside Cabins		*Yorktown Clipper*	3.5 to 1
Nantucket Clipper	51	Year Built	
Yorktown Clipper	69	*Nantucket Clipper*	1984
Cabins with Verandas	0	*Yorktown Clipper*	1988
Number of Passengers		Last Major Refurbishment	N/A
Nantucket Clipper	102		
Yorktown Clipper	138		

Frommer's Ratings (Scale of 1–5)

Cabin Comfort & Amenities	3	Pool, Fitness & Spa Facilities	N/A
Ship Cleanliness & Maintenance	3	Children's Facilities	N/A
Public Comfort/Space	3	Itinerary	5
Decor	3	Worth the Money	4

The impression I kept coming back to when sitting in the spacious lounges of these ships, or in my cozy cabin, was that someone had taken one of the Holland America or Princess ships and shrunk it to one-tenth its normal size. Though not boasting the multifarious public rooms of those large ships, the four-deck *Yorktown* and *Nantucket Clipper* offer similar clean styling and easy-to-live-with colors, fabrics, and textures, while also offering a small ship's ability to take passengers into shallow-water ports and other out-of-the-way locations—away from the megaship crowds.

Neither ship has an elevator or any cabins designed for passengers with disabilities.

Cabins & Rates						
Cabins	**Per diems from**	**Bathtub**	**Fridge**	**Hair Dryer**	**Sitting Area**	**TV**
Outside	$193	no	no	no	no	no

CABINS   Although smallish (average cabin size on the *Nantucket Clipper* is 106 to 123 square feet; average on the *Yorktown* is 123 to 140), cabins are very pleasantly styled, with blond-wood writing desk, chair, and bed frames, "Not-really-there"-style paintings (better than a bare wall, I guess), and a goodly amount of closet space, plus additional storage under the beds. There are no phones or TVs, but each cabin does have music channels. There are no cabin safes as such, but two drawers in the closet can be locked.

Cabins come in six different categories, differentiated mostly by their location rather than their size. Each has two lower-level beds, permanently fixed in either an L-shaped corner configuration or as two units set parallel to one another (taller passengers—over 6 ft. 2 in.—would be better off with the L-shaped arrangement, as the others are abutted by wall and headboard and are not much longer than 6 ft. 4 in.). No cabins have beds that can be pushed together to form a king- or queen-size, so these ships are off the list for honeymooners or congenitally randy couples. Some cabins contain upper berths that unfold from the wall to accommodate a third person.

All cabins have picture windows except for a few Category 1 cabins on Main Deck, which have portholes. All cabins on each ship's Promenade Deck and a handful at the stern on the Lounge Deck open onto the outdoors (rather than onto an interior corridor), and whereas I normally prefer this simply because it makes me feel closer to nature, here it doesn't seem to matter as the doors open out—meaning you can't really leave the door open to breezes without blocking the deck. It's worth noting that passengers in the Promenade Deck cabins should also be careful when opening their doors from the inside, lest you run the risk of braining one of your poor fellow passengers out taking a walk around the promenade.

Cabin bathrooms are compact, though not nearly so tiny as aboard rival American Canadian Caribbean Line's ships. Toilets are wedged between the shower and sink area and may prove tight for heavier people. Bathrooms have showers but no tubs.

There are no special facilities aboard for travelers with disabilities and no cabins designed specifically for single occupancy.

PUBLIC AREAS   Each ship has four decks and only two public areas: the dining room and the Observation Lounge. The pleasant lounge has big windows, a bar, a small but informative library, a piano (that gets little use), and enough space to comfortably seat everyone on board for lectures and meetings. It's the main hub of onboard activity. The dining room aboard each ship is spacious and comfortable. Other than that, there are no cozy hideaways on board other than your cabin. There is, though, plenty of outdoor deck space for those liking to linger over a sunset or just sit.

POOL, FITNESS & SPA FACILITIES   Neither ship has a swimming pool or any workout machines. For exercise, you can jog or walk around the deck (18 laps = 1 mile). When the ship in anchored in calm waters you can sometimes go swimming and snorkeling right from the ship courtesy of a small platform that's lowered into the water.

Royal Olympic Cruises

1 Rockefeller Plaza, Suite 315, New York, NY 10020. ☎ **800/872-6400** or 212/397-6400. Fax 212/765-9685. www.royalolympiccruises.com.

THE LINE IN A NUTSHELL The *Stella Solaris* and new *Olympic Voyager* are the only ships in the fleet of Greek-owned, Greek-operated Royal Olympic Cruises to spend time in the Caribbean. While they're not adventurous in the same way as the rest of the lines in this chapter, they do offer itineraries that visit smaller, more remote ports, and their onboard program focuses on providing passengers with a real learning experience.

THE EXPERIENCE In cruise service since 1973, the *Stella Solaris* offers a homey, friendly experience and a low-key atmosphere. The *Stella* is not a glamour ship and will not appeal to those seeking partying fun-in-the-sun days and glitzy nights. The typical passengers are early to bed and early to rise folks who'd enjoy a PBS documentary. The 840-passenger *Olympic Voyager,* which debuted in June of 2000, is a brand-new, high-speed ship, but still offers a low-key, casual experience.

The ships' enrichment programs far surpass others in the Caribbean. Theme itineraries are offered throughout the year; many are sold out well in advance. Especially popular are scientific theme cruises built around solar eclipses and the Mayan-themed cruises, which visit Mayan areas and have archaeologists and historians aboard to lead discussions.

Pros

- **Cultural and scientific enrichment programs.** These comprehensive programs are the major factor distinguishing these ships.
- **Swift, superb service.** Dining and cabin service are delivered with a personal touch.
- **Well-organized and diversified shore excursions.** There are from two to four excursions available at every port, with several excursions devoted to the cruise theme and others to snorkeling and/or beach excursions.
- *Voyager* **is one of the fastest ships afloat.** With a max speed of almost 30 knots, this ship can pack in the ports like no other.

Cons

- *Stella* **shows its wrinkles.** While the crew works diligently to keep the decks, public spaces, and cabins clean and polished, there is evidence of deterioration.
- **Lack of age diversity among passengers.** On both the *Stella Solaris* and *Olympic Voyager,* the passenger list consists primarily of retired couples (generally 65 and over) with some single passengers and a handful of families.

Compared with the other Soft-Adventure lines, here's how ROC rates:					
	poor	fair	good	excellent	outstanding
Enjoyment Factor					✓
Dining					✓
Activities					✓
Children's Program	N/A*				
Entertainment				✓	
Service					✓
Overall Value				✓	

* Royal Olympic offers no children's program in the Caribbean.

ROYAL OLYMPIC: SPANAKOPITA, ANYBODY?

Royal Olympic offers Caribbean/Mexico cruisers something different: A little touch of Greece among the palms and white-sand beaches. Formed in 1995 from a merger of Sun Line and Epirotiki Cruises, the line's ships generally stick to the Mediterranean, but two vessels, the 47-year-old *Stella Solaris* and the new *Olympic Voyager,* make the annual trek west, offering Caribbean, Panama Canal, and Mexico/Central America cruises (the latter of which visit Mayan sites throughout the region), plus itineraries combining the Caribbean and South America.

The Sun Line was founded in 1958 by Charalambos Keusseoglou, who at the time was an executive for Homes Lines. The line's first cruise ship was a converted battleship, and the next two were converted from German excursion vessels—the first *Stella Maris* and the first *Stella Solaris.* They turned out to be good cruise ships, allowing the company to establish itself as the leading Greek/Aegean Sea cruise line for the North American market.

Holland America Line took a stake in Sun Line in 1964, but bowed out after a time, to be replaced by the Marriott Hotel group. The company became synonymous with everything Greek—Greek Island cruising and a very warm onboard Greek atmosphere. Sun Line branched out into the western Mediterranean, the Black Sea, the Red Sea, northern Europe, and then eventually, cruises across the Atlantic, in the Caribbean, Orinoco, Amazon, and South America.

Epirotiki Lines, also a Greek family-owned company, got its start back in the 19th century, and beginning in the 1930s started operating Greek Island cruises. After World War II, they took on a number of secondhand ships from Canada and Britain, and even an ex-American yacht, and had them converted to cruising at a slightly lower level than the Sun Line standards.

Swan Hellenic, one of Britain's top cruise travel operators, chartered Epirotiki's *Orpheus* for more than two decades, and Epirotiki also branched out to other regions, with the Potamianos brothers, George and Andreas, in charge.

The two companies joined forces in 1995 as Royal Olympic Cruises, with the Keusseoglou and the Potamianos families still in charge. In early 2000, that changed. An approximately 40% equity interest in Royal Olympic Cruises was purchased by Cyprus-based Louis Cruise Lines, whose parent company, the Louis Organization, is the island's top travel company, owning ships, hotels, travel agencies, and catering businesses. The Keusseoglou family sold their interest in Royal Olympic and the Potamianos family sold a portion of theirs and remains a minority owner. The new chairman of Royal Olympic's board of directors is Harry Haralambopoulos, a former president, CEO, and a director of Celebrity Cruises. Given its expansion plans, the change in ownership seems like the shot in the arm Royal Olympic needs, especially after a period when a number of cruises were canceled due to war in the former Yugoslavia.

Note: Royal Olympic is somewhat of a misfit when it comes to labels and doesn't neatly fit in to any of my cruise categories (Mainstream, Ultra-Luxury, et al). At nearly 50 years old, the line's *Stella Solaris* would fit into my old ships category, but the line's brand new *Olympic Voyager* certainly wouldn't. So, being that both are relatively small ships that focus on learning and getting passengers up close to the islands, I've put ROC in the soft-adventure category.

THE FLEET

Royal Olympic is in the process of upgrading its aging fleet with the construction of two sleek, high-speed, 840-passenger ships. The first, the **Olympic Voyager,** entered service in June 2000 and will sail some Caribbean and Panama Canal itineraries in winter and spring 2001. The new ships join the line's venerable **Stella Solaris,** in service since 1953. Originally a French cargo ship known as the *Cambodge,* it was renamed after being purchased by Greek-owned Sun Line Cruises in 1973. The ship subsequently underwent a complete reconfiguration (only the hull and steam-powered engines were left intact) that transformed it into Sun Line's flagship. With the 1995 merger of Sun Line and Epirotiki, the *Stella* became the flagship of the newly formed Royal Olympic Cruises.

The other six ships in Royal Olympic's fleet—*Olympic Countess, Stella Oceanis, Odysseus, World Renaissance, Triton,* and *Orpheus*—are based year-round in the eastern Mediterranean and specialize in cruises to ports in the Greek islands and along the Turkish coast.

PASSENGER PROFILE

Passengers are primarily senior couples who are experienced travelers and have previously cruised—either on the *Stella Solaris,* to which many are drawn back because of its enrichment programs, or aboard other ships. You'll find very few first-time cruisers aboard, as Royal Olympic is not nearly as well known in the Caribbean as the big boys (Carnival, Royal Caribbean, Princess, et al).

Younger couples may feel out of place unless they're dedicated culture vultures who enjoy hanging out with an older crowd. On a recent cruise, prizes were given to the oldest person in attendance at one of the roundtable discussions (the winner was age 87) and to the youngest (age 29). When the audience was asked how many were under the age of 50, there were only five hands raised out of approximately 300 in attendance. Honeymooners, single passengers, and families are also few and far between.

DINING

With menus designed to accommodate a wide range of tastes, from carnivores to vegetarians, no one ever goes hungry on these ships. Along with the extensive variety of choices, the quality and presentation of the **Greek cuisine** stands out.

Passengers can eat breakfast and lunch in either the Dining Room or Lido Café, and the *Voyager* also offers a poolside pasta bar and a casual grill and pizza bar. Those who choose the Dining Room have the option of a buffet breakfast and/or ordering from a breakfast menu that includes stewed fruits, hot and cold cereals, pancakes, French toast, several egg dishes, meats, assorted cold cuts and cheese, and home-baked rolls, croissants, and muffins. Buffet-style breakfasts in the Lido feature a choice of hot and cold cereals, freshly baked croissants and muffins, eggs, pancakes, waffles, French toast, and plenty of fresh fruits and cheese. A full five-course lunch is served in the dining room, whereas the Lido has a choice of several salads, cold cuts and cheeses, a selection of sandwiches, several meat and fish dishes, and various desserts.

Dinner menus offer three **continental entrees,** plus **vegetarian, spa cuisine** (low cholesterol, reduced salt), and **Pacific Rim cuisine** (flavor and spices of the Orient and the islands). Lunch and dinner menus usually offer a Greek specialty such as *tash kebab* (chunks of tender beef simmered with tomatoes and herbs and served with rice pilaf), *sfyrida all spetsiota* (baked sea bass in tomatoes with potatoes), and *spanakopita* (spinach pie). Following the entree is a choice of four desserts plus a sugar-free dessert and an assortment of domestic and international cheeses and fresh fruit.

The Lido is the place to go for coffee or tea 24 hours a day, an early-riser's coffee and Danish, bouillon midmorning, a cocktail hour before dinner (during which all drinks except wine, champagne, and the drink of the day are half-price), and a buffet of **late-night snacks** from 11pm to midnight. An **afternoon tea** takes place every afternoon.

ACTIVITIES

At the top of the activity list is the provocative series of **lectures** (many with accompanying slide presentations), **roundtable discussions** (with audience participation), and **documentaries** that make up the enrichment program. Extensive reading material in the form of pamphlets, reprints of articles, maps, and diagrams provided at the beginning of the cruise supplement the lectures and discussions. Throughout the cruise, additional printed materials are distributed, and books written by the lecturers are available for sale. Passengers are encouraged to ask questions with the understanding that "there are never any dumb questions." Away from the formal presentations, lecturers are accessible and mingle with the passengers. In port, excursions are offered that complement the cruise theme; for example, on the Mayan regions itinerary, excursions to key Mayan sites are offered from five of the six ports.

Other **cultural and scientific-related activities** offered during the cruise might include classical piano concerts, stargazing sessions at night, and gatherings at sunset "searching for the green flash" (an atmospheric phenomenon that occurs just after sunset).

In addition to its enrichment programs, the ships offer such **leisure activities** as Ping-Pong and shuffleboard tournaments; dance instruction; arts-and-crafts classes; napkin-folding workshops; a perfume seminar and hair, beauty, and massage demonstrations; and daily (sometimes twice daily) snowball jackpot bingo. Those who want to limber up in the mornings can participate in various **exercise sessions,** including group walk-a-mile workouts around the deck, stretching classes, and low-impact aerobics. At various times throughout the cruise are also Trivial Pursuit, blackjack, bridge, and gin-rummy tournaments.

The *Stella Solaris* has **dancing** before dinner and after the show in the Solaris Lounge. It's here that the ship's dance hosts are kept busy as partners for all the women who desire their services. On a recent cruise, a dapper, dashing host known as "Valentino" was in especially high demand. *Voyager* has a modern disco on its top deck.

CHILDREN'S PROGRAM

As a matter of course, very few children sail aboard the ships' Caribbean cruises, and so there are no organized programs or activities for either children or families.

ENTERTAINMENT

Twice nightly, a talented troupe of singers and dancers perform in one of the lounges, joined occasionally by a comedian, a magician, and/or a guest musician. Especially popular performers on a recent "Maya Equinox" cruise were the Riga Dancers, five young, lissome ladies from Latvia who lit up the stage with their colorful costumes and fancy footwork. Cruise director Dave Levesque also occasionally displayed his skill as a stand-up comedian.

Greek-flavored musical entertainment is provided at poolside during lunchtime and some evenings. A Greek violin and piano duo also performs during daily afternoon tea and in the dining room at night, where they often move from table to table playing Greek tunes.

The most exciting night of entertainment on every cruise is **Greek Night,** during which the crew and most of the passengers sport the blue and white colors of the Greek flag. Festivities begin at sunset with an ouzo party in the Lido Café accompanied by bouzouki music, followed by a dinner featuring a five-course, all-Greek meal. The evening culminates with a gala celebration of Greek music and dance in a lounge featuring the ship's various entertainers along with several members of the crew. At the

Royal Olympic Fleet Itineraries

Ship	Home Ports & Season	Itinerary	Other Itineraries
Olympic Voyager	All itineraries round-trip from Ft. Lauderdale, Jan–April 2001.	**17-night S. Carib/Amazon (southbound):** San Juan, Tortola, Barbados, Amazon River, French Guiana, Trinidad, Martinique, St. Thomas, and Boca da Valeria, Manaus, and Santarem (all in Brazil). **12-night S. Carib/Orinoco:** San Juan, Tortola, Orinoco River, Puerto Ordaz (Venezuela), Trinidad, Martinique, and St. Thomas. **11-night W. Carib/Central America:** Montego Bay (Jamaica), Roatan and Puerto Cortes (Honduras), Santo Tomas (Guatemala), Belize City, Playa del Carmen, Cozumel, and Key West.	Mediterranean
Stella Solaris	Panama Canal between Ft. Lauderdale and San Diego, Dec 2000–early Jan 2001; South America cruise round-trip from Fort Lauderdale, Jan–Mar 2001.	**15-night Panama Canal:** Grand Cayman or Jamaica; Balboa (Panama), Puerto Caldera (Costa Rica), and Acapulco, Mazatlan, and Cabo San Lucas (Mexico). **58-night South America circumnavigation.**	Mediterranean

conclusion of the show, passengers are invited to come onstage and join in several spirited Greek dances.

At some ports, **local entertainers** are invited on board to perform. On a recent sailing, a group of schoolchildren came aboard at Puerto Cortés (Honduras) to perform folk dances, and a mariachi band enlivened the evening during the ship's stay at Cozumel.

SERVICE

While many cruise lines have a rapid turnover in personnel, crew members on the *Stella Solaris* have worked on the ship for an average of 14 years and some have been with the ship over 20 years, so it's not uncommon to see them greet repeat passengers like old friends—a greeting the passengers return in kind. Dining-room service is always fast and efficient, with little waiting time between courses. Many of the waiters have worked together for years and it shows in their performance, as everyone carries out his or her duties with clockwork precision. Waiters make a special effort to know passengers' names and are always willing and eager to please. In addition, there is more pampering at meal times than one would expect on a moderately priced cruise; waiters carry passenger trays to tables during buffet breakfasts in the dining room and for breakfast and lunch buffets in the buffet restaurant. Delivery of continental breakfast to cabins is always on time and room service throughout the day and night is fast and efficient. Cabin stewards also deserve kudos for making up rooms in record time.

The *Solaris* and *Voyager* both offer laundry and pressing services, but no dry cleaning or self-service laundries.

Olympic Voyager

The Verdict

A total departure for Royal Olympic, the *Voyager* is a stylish, souped-up, modern cruise ship for people who want great, port-intensive itineraries and a casual yet moderately elegant cruise experience.

Olympic Voyager *(photo: Matt Hannafin)*

Specifications

Size (in tons)	25,000	Officers	Greek
Number of Cabins	418	Crew	360 (Int'l)
Number of Outside Cabins	292	Passenger/Crew Ratio	2.3 to 1
Cabins with Verandas	12	Year Built	2000
Number of Passengers	836	Last Major Refurbishment	N/A

Frommer's Ratings (Scale of 1–5)

Cabin Comfort & Amenities	4	Pool, Fitness & Spa Facilities	2
Ship Cleanliness & Maintenance	5	Children's Program	N/A
Public Comfort/Space	4	Itinerary	5
Decor	4	Worth the Money	4

Able to leap tall buildings in a single bound, the *Voyager* is one of the fastest passenger ships currently sailing, able to reach up to about 30 knots. It's also a departure from ROC's fleet of older ocean liners, the *Voyager* is new, new, new, from its sleek, high-tech hull design and propulsion system to its bright, modern interior, designed by the people behind many of the beautiful rooms on Celebrity's ships. It's also obviously targeted at the North American market—all ship signs are in English, for instance.

Cabins & Rates

Cabins	Per Diems from	Bathtub	Fridge	Hair Dryer	Sitting Area	TV
Inside	$136	no	yes	yes	no	yes
Outside	$173	no	yes	yes	no	yes
Suite	$223	yes	yes	yes	yes	yes

CABINS   Call them "cruise ship modern," and very much in the same smooth style as aboard many modern megaships. All are decorated in warm wood tones countered by stark, appealing white walls hung with abstract paintings. Standard cabins, at about 140 square feet, are not huge but are well laid-out. Each has huge floor-to-ceiling mirrors, plus safes, TVs, small fridges, and a good amount of well-designed storage space—essential on the long itineraries the ship will follow. Bathrooms are smallish but smartly designed. Inside staterooms are comparable with standard outsides, sans natural light.

One place where the *Voyager* is deficient is in the number of veranda cabins—there are only 12, the Deluxe Sky Suites, but what the ship lacks in quantity it makes up in quality and size: Balconies range from 11-by-12 feet in most and all offer lots of privacy. All Sky Suites have a sitting area, teensy bathtub, and great modern art that echoes the pieces elsewhere on the ship. Sixteen Bay Window Suites offer a nice seating area in a bay window that allows views down the length of the ship.

Cabins in the stern on the Venus and Dionysus Decks get some vibration and noise when the ship gets up to speed, but not more so than the average slower ship. Two of these, cabins 3138 and 3151 on Dionysus Deck, are two-room affairs that are perfect for families; the second room, without windows, has a convertible couch that sleeps two.

Four cabins are wheelchair accessible. No cabins are designated for single passengers.

PUBLIC AREAS   In its whole history up till now, Royal Olympic's fleet has consisted exclusively of old, classic-style ocean liners, which generally were built to offer roomy public areas—a must when passengers were cooped up inside during cold Atlantic crossings. Perhaps it was this history that informed the design of *Voyager,* which offers some startlingly spacious interiors for a ship this size. On the other hand, the company's inexperience with building new vessels might also account for such weird choices as having almost invisible deck numbers in the otherwise well-designed stairtowers, which makes it difficult to tell where you are when moving from deck to deck, especially if you get mesmerized by reading the two Greece-themed poems that adorn the walls of the stairtowers.

The main, single-level Selene Dining Room and the Garden Lounge buffet restaurant have tables spaced incredibly far apart, offering great privacy. For even more privacy, you can try and wrangle one of the four tables for two in the Selene, two of them in the stern, flanking the captain's table. They're great, romantic spots, giving a real panorama of the sea. At the opposite end of the dining spectrum, a pizza station near the pool on Helios Deck serves up good personal pies, while the bar next door has Amstel on tap. Bon appetit!

The central area of the Apollon Deck (the main entertainment deck) offers a nice, airy piano bar, two small shops, a card room, and a library with three computer stations and a video map screen showing the ship's geographical position. One wall of this corridor, opposite the Library, has small cubbyhole display cases containing sculptures and other artifacts.

The Anemos Nightclub/Observation Lounge/Disco is perched on the *Voyager's* topmost deck, and is filled with small swiveling chairs that look like they should shoot up on little pistons when you sit in them, but don't. One level below, the Alexander the Great Lounge is a single-level affair where small-scale revues and music and magic acts are staged. The ship's casino is split into two small sections on each side of the small, two-level reception atrium, one side containing 44 slot machines and the other with four poker tables, roulette, and a bar. A comfortable Cigar Room rounds out the public room offerings, with great recliner-like couches and chairs mixed with a faux fireplace and incongruous modern art. There are no facilities whatsoever for children.

POOL, FITNESS & SPA FACILITIES   Honesty is the best policy: This ship was not really designed for hardcore sports and fitness folks. The gym is very small and not terribly pretty. There are only three windows, and those are not well placed, offering views only from the two treadmills and the single step machine. The three exercise bikes actually face *away* from the windows, a bizarre decision that I'll bet will be changed once someone takes time to think about it. There are also four weight machines (two in a separate, grim, windowless area), a small selection of free weights, and a sauna and Turkish bath.

The Jade Spa, next to the gym, is run by the Greek spa company Flair Limited, and offers a range of massage, beauty, and steam, mud, and aquatherapy treatments at prices substantially lower than Steiner's. A beauty salon sits on the port side of the gym/spa area.

Outside, the main area of activity is the open 3-deck stern, with a single small pool flanked by wading pools and showers. A bar, the ship's pizza station, and an outdoor dining area lie just forward of the pool under a huge tent-like awning. Other than this there's a minimum of outdoor deck space—just two small side decks with lounge chairs, and an area circling the nightclub on the top deck, forward. There's no jogging track, nor anywhere where you can get in a good walk.

Stella Solaris

The Verdict

Calling all culture vultures! This warm, hospitable nearly 50-year-old Greek ship certainly isn't the most cutting-edge, but its innovative itineraries and enrichment programs are tops.

Stella Solaris *(photo: Royal Olympic Cruises)*

Specifications

Size (in tons)	18,000	Officers	Greek
Number of Cabins	329	Crew	320 (International)
Number of Outside Cabins	250	Passenger/Crew Ratio	1.9 to 1
Cabins with Verandas	0	Year Built	1953
Number of Passengers	620	Last Major Refurbishment	1997

Frommer's Ratings (Scale of 1–5)

Cabin Comfort & Amenities	4	Food & Beverage	4
Ship Cleanliness & Maintenance	2	Pool, Fitness & Spa Facilities	2
Public Comfort/Space	4	Children's Facilities	N/A
Decor	3	Itinerary	5
Service	5	Worth the Money	5

After almost half a century of service, the *Stella Solaris,* with its classic profile and tiered aft decks, continues to run smoothly, although it shows obvious signs of wear in both the public spaces and cabins. The teak decks are warped and uneven in many places, and wood furnishings and metal moldings in the cabins are chipped and dented. Bathroom fixtures also show signs of age (such as leaky faucets and cracks in porcelain tubs). Many of the carpets in the cabins, corridors, and public areas are stained and worn, and drab upholstery and fabrics in public areas and cabins need replacing.

However, most passengers who choose to sail on the *Stella Solaris* don't seem to mind any of this, and the ship continues to sell out many of its cruises and maintains a strong, loyal following with a repeat-passenger rate averaging around 50% per cruise. I shared a table at dinner with a couple who were warmly welcomed by several of the waiters as we sat down. It turned out they'd been on nine previous cruises aboard the ship and said they immediately felt right at home upon boarding. "This is the only ship we want to sail on anymore," they said. "It seems like family to us." Another passenger noted that "This ship has a heart and soul that you don't find on the big ships." Many passengers praised the quality of the enrichment programs and affirmed that the *Solaris* is their ship of choice because of these programs and the crew's friendly, hospitable attitude.

Cabins & Rates

Cabins	Per diems from	Bathtub	Fridge	Hair Dryer	Sitting Area	TV
Inside	$125	no	no	no	no	no
Outside	$141	yes	no	no	yes	no
Suite	$175	yes	no	yes	yes	yes

CABINS The ship's interior design maximizes space devoted to individual staterooms, which are divided into 11 price categories. Top-of-the-line accommodations are the 34 deluxe suites located on the Boat Deck, which measure a spacious 215 square feet and look out through picture windows onto the classic promenade just outside. The remaining 32 suites are located on Golden Deck and Ruby Deck, as are the 100 deluxe outside cabins, measuring 182 square feet. Other cabin categories range from superior outside to inside. Superior and standard cabins have two beds, and some have the option of upper berths to accommodate three or four people. (The lowest-level inside cabins have bunk beds only.) All standard cabins have showers; suites and deluxe and superior outside cabins have bathtubs. Suites have walk-in closets; other cabins have standard closets and more than ample storage space.

All suites and cabins come with four music channels featuring Greek, classical, easy-listening, and American Armed Services radio news, and are also equipped with individually controlled air-conditioning, telephone, and hair dryers, plus shampoos, sewing kits, and shower caps. All cabins have lockable drawers in which passengers can store valuables. Suites are the only category with TVs, which screen four movies daily plus national news, weather, sports, and financial reports.

No cabin or suite categories have private verandas. None are equipped for wheelchair users (and in fact, the layout of the ship would make it a bad bet all around).

PUBLIC AREAS   The user-friendly interior design of the *Solaris* provides quick and easy access from all cabins to three major public areas situated adjacent to each other amidships on the Solaris Deck.

The classic, all-purpose, 550-seat Solaris Lounge is the ship's largest public space and serves as gathering place, activity hub, and entertainment center, during the day accommodating everything from lectures to dance classes to bingo and in the evening hosting before- and after-dinner dancing and cocktails, as well as nightly cabaret-style shows. Situated at one end of the lounge is the Solaris piano bar, which along with a grand piano has three gaming tables (two blackjack, one roulette). The rest of the casino is made up of 19 slot machines located in a separate room off the Solaris Foyer, near the shore-excursions desk.

Just steps away from the Solaris Lounge is the 320-seat dining room, an expansive, cheerful space surrounded by large picture windows. Just around the corner is the Grill Room, a richly appointed piano bar with leather chairs—it's the ship's best evening watering hole, where the incomparable Octavian, master of the electric piano, performs.

The Lido Café opens directly onto the Pool Deck and, weather permitting, offers passengers the option of eating inside or at one of the tables around the pool.

Other public areas include a 275-seat cinema that hosts lectures and also screens daily movies and occasional documentaries. There is also a combination card room/library where passengers can check out books and board games. Buried deep in the bowels of the ship on Main Deck is the Taverna Disco, which opens for business every night around 11:30 and is decorated like the hold of a pirate ship—very bizarre. Since most passengers are asleep by midnight, it's the least used of all the public areas—except for a few crew members, on my cruise it played to a nearly empty house.

POOL, FITNESS & SPA FACILITIES   The beauty parlor, Daphne Spa, and gym are located next to each other in a small area on Golden Deck, aft. The small gym has only a few exercise machines crammed into one room; the spa offers five massage/treatment rooms plus sauna and steam rooms.

The wide, shaded promenade encircling the Boat Deck provides plenty of space for walkers and joggers, and on days at sea is an ideal place to relax in a deck chair with a good book. On the roomy Lido Deck, there is a single pool just aft of the Lido Bar, but no hot tubs.

Star Clippers

4101 Salzedo Ave., Coral Gables, FL 33146. ☎ **800/442-0553** or 305/442-0550. Fax 305/442-1611. www.star-clippers.com.

THE LINE IN A NUTSHELL With the sails and rigging of classic clipper ships and some of the cushy amenities of modern megas, a cruise on this line's 170- to 228-passenger ships offers adventure with comfort.

THE EXPERIENCE On Star Clippers, you'll have the best of two worlds: On one hand, these cruises espouse an unstructured, let-your-hair-down, hands-on ethic—you can climb the masts (with a harness, of course), pull in the sails, crawl into the bow netting, or chat with the captain on the open-air bridge. On the other hand, the ship offers comfortable, almost cushy public rooms and cabins.

On board, ducking under booms, stepping over coils of rope, leaning against railings just feet above the sea, and watching sailors work the winches are constant reminders that you're on a real working ship. Further, listening to the captain's daily talk about the next port of call, the history of sailing, or some other nautical subject, you'll feel like you're exploring some of the Caribbean's more remote stretches in a ship that belongs there—an exotic ship for an exotic locale. In a sea of look-alike megaships, the *Star Clipper* and new *Royal Clipper* stand out, recalling a romantic, swashbuckling era of ship travel.

Pros

- **Hands-on experience.** You never have to lift a finger if you don't want to, but if you do, you're free to help out.
- **Comfortable amenities.** A pair of pools, a piano bar and deck bar, a bright and pleasant dining room serving tasty food, and a clubby, wood-paneled library balance out the swashbuckling spirit.
- **Rich in atmosphere.** On these ships, it's a real treat to just wallow in the ambiance.
- **Off-beat itineraries.** While not as far-flung as those offered by ACCL or Clipper, Star Clippers' itineraries do take passengers to some of the Caribbean's more remote islands, like the Grenadines and Guadeloupe.

Cons

- **Rolling.** Even though the ships have stabilizers and ballast tanks to reduce rolling, you'll feel the motion if you run into rough seas, as is the case with any small ship.
- **No fitness equipment on *Star Clipper*.** The new *Royal Clipper* will have a fitness center, but on the *Star Clipper* you're out of luck for anything but a massage.

Compared with the other Soft-Adventure lines, here's how Star Clippers rates:					
	poor	fair	good	excellent	outstanding
Enjoyment Factor					✓
Dining					✓
Activities				✓	
Children's Program	N/A*				
Entertainment				✓	
Service				✓	
Overall Value				✓	

* *Star Clippers offers no children's program.*

STAR CLIPPERS: COMFY ADVENTURE

Clipper ships—full-sailed, built for speed, and undeniably romantic—reigned for only a brief time on the high seas before being driven out by steam engines and iron (and then steel) hulls. During their heyday, however, these vessels engendered more romantic myths than any before or since. They helped open the Pacific Coast of California during the gold rush of 1849, carrying much-needed supplies around the tip of South America from Boston and New York. Even after the opening of the Suez Canal in 1869, names like *Cutty Sark, Ariel,* and *Flying Cloud* remained prestigious, and no sailing ship has ever surpassed the record of *Sea Witch,* a vessel that once sailed from Canton, China, to New York in 74 days.

By the early 1990s, despite the nostalgia and sense of reverence that had surrounded every aspect of the clippers' maritime history, nothing that could be technically classified as a clipper ship had been built since the *Cutty Sark* in 1869. In fact, their return to the high seas as viable commercial ventures could only have been realized by a nautical visionary with a passion for ship design and almost unlimited funds. The right combination of these factors emerged in Mikael Krafft, a Swedish-born industrialist and real-estate developer who invested vast amounts of personal energy and more than $80 million in the construction of two modern-day clippers at a Belgian shipyard in 1991 and 1992.

Before this venture, Krafft had sailed a series of high-tech yachts, including a particularly spectacular 128-foot version. To construct his clippers, he procured the original drawings and specifications of Scottish-born Donald McKay (a leading naval architect of 19th-century clipper-ship technology) and employed his own team of naval architects to solve such engineering problems as adapting the square-rigged, four-masted clipper design to modern materials and construction.

In its short history, the line's *Star Flyer* (sister ship to the *Star Clipper,* which sails in the Caribbean) has assembled quite a list of firsts: the first scheduled commercial sail-driven vessel to cross the Atlantic in 90 years; the first ship ever to pass full U.S. Coast Guard certification and safety exams on the first try; and one of the only ships to ever enter the Port of Miami under full sail—a daunting feat, considering the motorized traffic barreling through on all sides. Also impressive is the fact that both the *Flyer* and *Clipper* received the highest rating available by Lloyd's Register—the "+100 A-1-a" rating, which hadn't been awarded to a sailing vessel since 1911. On Star Clippers, you'll be sailing aboard vessels where safety and nautical logistics are more visible and more all-encompassing than aboard most other lines, which generally keep such operations hidden away.

How do their prices and amenities compare to the products of Windjammer Barefoot Cruises and Windstar Cruises, two other companies that run original (if modernized) sailing ships or have replicated the sailing ships of yore? Star Clippers is smack dab in the middle—more luxurious and a bit more expensive than the bare-boned, no-frills Windjammer excursions and less opulent, less formal, and less expensive than Windstar. The onboard atmosphere is quite casual. During the day, polo shirts, shorts, and topsiders are standard issue, and for dinner many passengers simply change into cleaner and better-pressed versions of the same, with perhaps a change from shorts to slacks for most men. Overall, the experience is salty enough to make you feel like a fisherman keeling off the coast of Maine, without the physical hardship of actually being one.

THE FLEET

The awesome new 228-passenger, five-masted, fully-rigged **Royal Clipper** was scheduled to debut just as this book went to press in summer 2000, joining the line's pair of 170-passenger sailing ships. At 439 feet in length, the *Royal Clipper* will be one of the largest sailing ships ever built, and it's the line's most luxurious. The ***Star Clipper,*** built in 1992, spends its winters in the Caribbean, and the *Star Flyer,* built in 1991, operates entirely in the Far East and the Aegean. The twin vessels are at once traditional and radical. With dimensions about 100 feet longer than the average 19th-century clipper, they're also the tallest and among the fastest clipper ships ever built, and are so beautiful that even at full stop they seem to soar.

Part of the ships' success derives from a skillful blend of traditional aesthetics and newfangled materials and technology. Sails, for instance, are made of lightweight Dacron rather than canvas, which rots easily and is so heavy that the amount of sail each of Krafft's ships flies (36,000 sq. ft.) would probably have capsized an original clipper. Further innovations include masts crafted from steel and aluminum alloys instead of tree trunks and a network of electric winches that eliminates the backbreaking labor historically involved in the sails' raising and lowering. Fewer than 10 deckhands can manipulate the ships' sails, as contrasted to the 40 to 55 that were needed to control and maintain sails aboard the 19th-century ships. Other concessions to modern design include a bow thruster and a single propeller that's used to navigate in and out of tricky harbors or during dead calms. When used together, they can spin each craft around on a very tight axis.

As opposed to ships like the *Club Med 2* and Windstar's *Wind Surf,* bulkier cruise ships that just happen to be outfitted with sails, Star Clippers' ships look like they should sail under wind power, and generally rely on sails for about 25% to 35% of their propulsion (the rest of the time, they rely on the engines). Each ship performs superlatively—during the *Star Clipper*'s maiden sail in 1992 off the coast of Corsica, it sustained speeds of 19.4 knots, thrilling its owner and designers, who had predicted maximum speeds of 17 knots. The new *Royal Clipper* was designed to make up to 20 knots under sail (14 max under engine alone). During most cruises, however, the crew tries to keep passengers comfortable and decks relatively horizontal, and so the vessels are kept to speeds of 9 to 14 knots.

PASSENGER PROFILE

While you're likely to find a handful of late-20-something honeymoon-type couples, the majority of passengers are well-traveled couples in their late forties to sixties, all active and intellectually curious professionals such as executives, lawyers, and doctors.

With no more than about 230 passengers aboard the largest ship in the fleet, each cruise seems like a triumph of individuality and intimacy. The line's unusual niche appeals to passengers who might recoil at the lethargy and/or sometimes forced enthusiasm of cruises aboard larger, more typical vessels. About 20% of any passenger roster is composed of people who have never cruised before, perhaps for this very reason. On the flip side, according to a company spokesperson, 80% of passengers have cruised before on big ships, like Holland America or Princess, and appreciate a "premium" soft-adventure cruise like Star Clippers. Overall, the company spokesperson said a whopping 60% of passengers are repeaters.

As the line has matured and increased both its stature and its prestige, many passengers have tended to be repeaters. About half are European, the remainder North American, with a sprinkling of Latin Americans. All tend to be active, sports-conscious, and curious—and, as you might expect, many come from boating or yachting backgrounds. Many are devoted conservationists who appreciate a vessel that relies primarily on wind power rather than diesel fuel, and many have traveled extensively.

Mikael Krafft himself may even be on board, in many cases with his wife and children, traveling as a low-key, highly accessible guest.

DINING

Overall, food is good and presented well, with breakfast and lunch buffets being the best meals of the day. Star Clippers' cuisine has evolved and improved through the years as the line has poured more time and effort into it. In fact, in the spring of 1999, an executive chef was hired to enhance the overall quality of meals fleet-wide, shifting from ship to ship to implement an enhanced menu that now includes four entree choices at each evening meal. All meals are open seating and served in the restaurant to tables of four, six, and eight, and the dress code is always casual. Catering to the European as well as the North American clientele, all buffets include a better-than-average selection of cheeses like brie and smoked Gouda, several types of salad, cold cuts, and fish. At breakfast, in addition to a cold and hot buffet spread, there's an omelet station where a staff member will make your eggs the way you like them. Late-afternoon snacks served at the Tropical Bar include items like tacos, spring rolls, or ice-cream sundaes with fresh coconut and pistachio toppings.

At dinner, five main entrees (a seafood, meat, chef's special, vegetarian, and light dish), appetizers, and dessert courses are offered as well as a soup and salad. Choices include, for example, lobster and shrimp with rice pilaf, beef curry, and pasta dishes. Dinners are sometimes sit-down and sometimes buffet, and can be somewhat chaotic and rushed. When the ship is at full capacity, things can feel a bit frenetic (breakfast and lunch don't get as crowded as passengers tend to eat at staggered times). On the *Star Clipper,* the booths along the sides, seating six, are awkward when couples who don't know each are forever getting up and down to let the others in and out (the *Royal Clipper*'s roomier dining-room layout avoids this). The *Star Clipper*'s dining room has mahogany trim and a series of thin steel columns that pierce the center of many of the dining tables. While from an engineering standpoint the columns were the best way to solve the structural problem inherent in such a large open space, they sometimes slightly block sight lines across the tables.

Waiters and bartenders are efficient and friendly, and dress in costume for several theme nights each week.

There's a worthwhile selection of **wines** on board, with a heavy emphasis on medium-priced French, German, and California selections. Coffee and tea are available from a 24-hour coffee station in the piano bar.

On the *Star Clipper,* room service is available only for guests who are sick and can't make it to the dining room,; on the *Royal Clipper,* those lucky passengers staying in the 14 suites and owner's suites get 24-hour room service.

ACTIVITIES

If you're looking for action, shopping, and dozens of organized tours, you won't find much on these ships and itineraries, and in fact, that's a big part of the line's allure. For the most part, enjoying the experience of being on a sailing ship and socializing with fellow passengers and crew members are the main activities (as it is on most any ship of this size).

The friendliness starts the moment you board, with the captain and hotel director personally greeting passengers and inviting them to have a complimentary cocktail and some hors d'oeuvres. Throughout the cruise, the captain gives informal talks on maritime themes, and at least once a day the cruise director speaks about the upcoming ports

Port Charges Not Included

Port charges are $155 per person in addition to the cruise rates for 7-day Caribbean cruises with Star Clippers.

Star Clipper Fleet Itineraries			
Ship	Home Ports & Season	Itinerary	Other Itineraries
Royal Clipper	Round-trip from Barbados; itineraries alternate weekly, Oct–Apr.	**7-night E. Carib 1:** Martinique, Iles des Saintes, Antigua, St. Kitts, Dominica, and St. Lucia. **7-night E. Carib 2:** Martinique, St. Lucia, Bequia, Tobago Cays, Grenada, and Grenadines.	Mediterranean
Star Clipper	Round-trip from Barbados; itineraries alternate weekly through Oct 22, 2000. From Oct 22, 2000 till Apr 2001, ship sails round-trip from St. Maarten; itineraries alternate weekly.	**7-night E. Carib 1 from Barbados:** Martinique, Iles des Saintes, Antigua, St. Kitts, Dominica, and St. Lucia. **7-night E. Carib. 2 from Barbados:** Martinique, St. Lucia, Bequia, Tobago Cays, Grenada, and Grenadines. **7-night E. Carib 1 from St. Maarten:** St. Barts, Nevis, Guadeloupe, Dominica, Iles des Saintes, and Antigua. **7-night E. Carib 2 from St. Maarten:** Anguilla, Sandy Cay, or Jost Van Dyke, Norman Island, Virgin Gorda, St. Kitts, and St. Barts.	None

and shipboard events. Knot-tying might be the topic of the day, or you might get to participate in a man-overboard drill. Within reason, passengers can lend a hand with deck-side duties, observe the mechanics of navigation, and have a token try at handling the wheel when circumstances and calm weather permit. Each ship maintains an **open-bridge policy,** allowing passengers to wander up to the humble-looking navigation center at any hour of the day or night.

Other activities might include a brief engine-room tour and a **scuba lesson** in the pool (resort certification is available). Of course, sunbathing is a sport in and of itself. Best spot for it? In the bowsprit netting, hanging out over the water. It's sunny, it's a thrill in itself, and it's the perfect place from which to spot dolphins in the sea just feet below you. **Massages** are available on both ships, too (and are a great deal at $28 an hour): On the *Star Clipper,* they're doled out in a spare cabin or a small cabana on deck; on the *Royal,* there's a dedicated massage room.

Port activities are a big part of these cruises. Sailing from one island to another and tending to arrive at the day's port of call sometime after 9am (but usually before around 11am and usually after a brisk early morning sail), the ships anchor offshore and passengers are shuttled back and forth by tender (on many landings, you'll have to walk a few feet in shallow water between the tender and the beach).

Activities in port revolve around beaches and water sports, which are all complimentary. Partly because Mikael Krafft is an avid scuba diver and partly because itineraries focus on waters that teem with marine life, each ship offers (for an extra charge) the option of PADI-approved **scuba diving.** Certified divers will find all the equipment they'll need on board. Even uncertified/inexperienced divers can pay a token fee for training that will grant them resort certification and allow them to make a number of relatively simple dives. There's also **snorkeling** (complimentary equipment is distributed at the start of the cruise), waterskiing, windsurfing, and banana-boat rides offered by the ship's water-sports team in all ports (the ships carry along Zodiac motor boats for this purpose). Being that everything is so laid back, there are no sign-up sheets for these activities, so guests merely hang out and congregate by the gangway or on the beach until it's their turn.

Ships tend to depart from their island ports of call early enough so they can be under full sail during sunset. Trust me on this one: Position yourself at the ship's rail or dawdle over a drink at the deck bar to watch the sun melt into the horizon behind the silhouette of the ships' masts and ropes. It's something you won't forget.

CHILDREN'S PROGRAM

This is not a line for young children, so there are no supervised activities and no baby-sitting is available unless a well-intentioned crew member agrees to volunteer his or her off-duty hours. That said, an experience aboard a sailing ship can be a wonderful educational and adventurous experience, especially for self-reliant children at least 10 years old.

ENTERTAINMENT

Some sort of featured entertainment takes place each night after dinner by the Tropical Bar, which is the main hub of activity on both ships. There's a **crew talent show** one night, and on others a trivia contest or a performance by **local entertainers** (such as a steel-drum band) who come on board for the evening. A keyboard player is on-hand to sing pop songs before and after dinner. Some nights, disco music is put on the sound system and a section of the deck serves as an impromptu dance floor.

A couple of movies a day are available on cabin TVs, if you feel like vegging. Besides this, it's just you, the sea, and the conversation of your fellow passengers.

SERVICE

Service is congenial, low-key, unpretentious, cheerful, and reasonably attentive. During busy times expect efficient but sometimes slightly distracted service in the cramped dining room on the *Star Clipper* (less so on *Royal*) and realize that you'll have to fetch your own ice, bar drinks, and whatever else you might need during your time on-deck.

The crew is international, hailing from places like Poland, Switzerland, Russia, Germany, Romania, Indonesia, and the Philippines, and their presence creates a wonderful international flavor on board. Crew members are friendly and indulgent and usually good-natured about passengers who want to tie knots, raise and lower sails, and keep the deck shipshape. As English is not the mother language of some crew members, though, certain details might get lost in the translation.

Officers typically dine with guests at every meal, and if you'd like to have dinner with the captain, just go up to the bridge one day and ask him.

Star Clipper

The Verdict

With the sails and rigging of a classic clipper ship and the creature comforts of a modern mega, a cruise on the 170-passenger *Star Clipper* offers the best of two worlds and a wonderful way to do the Caribbean.

Star Clipper *(photo: Star Clippers)*

Specifications

Size (in tons)	2,298	Officers	International
Number of Cabins	84	Crew	70 (International)
Number of Outside Cabins	78	Passenger/Crew Ratio	2.5 to 1
Cabins with Verandas	0	Year Built	1992
Number of Passengers	172	Last Major Refurbishment	N/A

Frommer's Ratings (Scale of 1–5)

Cabin Comfort & Amenities	3	Pool, Fitness & Spa Facilities	3
Ship Cleanliness & Maintenance	4	Children's Facilities	N/A
Public Comfort/Space	3	Itinerary	5
Decor	3	Worth the Money	5

Life aboard the *Star Clipper* means life on-deck—since there are few other hideaways, that's where most passengers spend their days. Made from teakwood, these decks were planned with lots of passenger space, although much of them are cluttered with the winches, ropes, and other equipment necessary to operate these working ships. There are lots of nooks and crannies on-deck, and even with a full load the ship rarely feels overly crowded (except at dinner). More sail-trimming activity occurs amidships and near the bow, so if you're looking to avoid all bustle, take yourself off to the stern.

Cabins & Rates

Cabins	Per diems from	Bathtub	Fridge	Hair Dryer	Sitting Area	TV
Inside	$157	no	no	yes	no	no
Outside	$186	no	no	yes	no	yes
Suite	$357	yes	yes	yes	no	yes

CABINS Cabins feel roomy for a ship of this size and were designed with a pleasant nautical motif—blue fabrics and carpeting, portholes, brass-toned lighting fixtures, and a dark wood trim framing the off-white furniture and walls. The majority of cabins have windows, measure from about 120 to 130 square feet, and have two twin beds that can be converted into doubles, a small desk/vanity with stool, and an upholstered seat fitted into the corner. Storage space is more than adequate for a 7-night casual cruise in a warm climate, with both a slim floor-to-ceiling closet and a double-width closet of shelves; there is also storage below the beds, desk, nightstand, and chair. Each cabin has a telephone, hair dryer, and safe, and all but the four smallest windowless inside cabins (measuring a compact 95 sq. ft.) have a color television showing news and a selection of popular movies.

Standard bathrooms are small but functional, with marble walls, a nice mirrored storage cabinet that actually stays closed, and a narrow shower divided from the rest of the bathroom by only the curtain (surprisingly, the rest of the bathroom stays dry when the shower's being used). The sink and shower are fitted with water-saving (but annoying) push valves that release water only when they're compressed. The only real difference between the cabins in Categories 2 and 3 is about a square foot of space. The eight deluxe cabins measure about 150 square feet, open right out onto the main deck, and have minibars and whirlpool bathtubs. Because of their location near the Tropical Bar, though, noise can be a problem (especially if there are late-night revelers at the bar). Take note also: The ship's generator tends to drone on through the night; cabins near the stern on lower decks are the most susceptible to this.

None of the units is a suite, except for one carefully guarded (and oddly configured) owner's suite in the aft of the Clipper Deck that's available to the public only when it's not being set aside for special purposes.

No cabins were designed for wheelchair accessibility. These ships are not recommended for passengers with mobility problems.

PUBLIC AREAS The handful of public rooms include the dining room, a comfy piano bar, the outside Tropical Bar (sheltered from the sun and rain by a canopy), and a cozy, paneled library with a decorative, nonfunctioning fireplace and a good stock of

Preview: Star Clippers' *Royal Clipper*

Clipper's biggest and plushest ship to date, the 5,000-ton, 228-passenger *Royal Clipper,* is scheduled to be launched just as this book goes to press, and will boast more luxurious amenities than the line's older ships, such as a small gym, a spa, and three pools. And with five masts flying 42 sails that together stretch to 56,000 square feet, it will also be powerful, able to achieve 20 knots under sail power only, and 14 knots under engine power. For all its size and power, the *Royal Clipper* will also be well accoutred, with a cool bar/lounge called Captain Nemos, as well as a three-story glass atrium and a three-level restaurant with a rich Edwardian flair, including a grand, spiraling staircase, ornate polished brass railings, mahogany-accented paneling, and nautically-inspired paintings.

Unlike the line's *Star Clipper* and *Star Flyer,* the *Royal* will have a retractable swimming and water-sports platform, plus three pools and a massage-and-fitness area. In the gym, portholes below the waterline will allow you to watch the sea and maybe some fishy creatures swim past as you're working out or having a massage. Pretty novel, isn't it? Similar to the *Star Clipper* and *Flyer,* the ceiling of the piano bar will be the glass bottom of the main swimming pool.

The ship will have 114 cabins, almost all outside, with average outside cabins measuring a roomy 148 square feet. All cabins will have marble bathrooms, brass lighting fixtures, mahogany furniture and detailing, hair dryers, safes, telephones, and TVs. Some 22 cabins have a third berth and there are six inside cabins. Measuring 255 square feet (including balcony), 14 deluxe suites located forward on the Main Deck will have private balconies, sitting areas, minibars, and marble bathrooms with a whirlpool tubs. There will also be two owner's suites on the Main Deck measuring 320 square feet and each boasting a pair of double beds, a sitting area, minibar, and—count 'em—two marble bathrooms.

coffee-table books, tracts on naval history and naval architecture, and a cross-section of general titles. There's even a computer in there with E-mail access (receiving messages is free, and debit cards for sending messages can be purchased from the purser).

The roomy yet cozy piano bar has comfy banquette seating and is a romantic place for a drink. That area and the outdoor Tropical Bar are the ship's hubs of activity.

Throughout, the interior decor is pleasant but unmemorable, mostly white with touches of brass and mahogany or teakwood trim—not as upscale-looking as vessels operated by Windstar, but cozy, appealing, well designed, and shipshape.

POOL, FITNESS & SPA FACILITIES   Each ship has two small pools, meant more for dipping than swimming, one with glass portholes peering from its depths into the piano bar (shave those legs, girls!). The pool near the stern tends to be more languid and is thus the favorite of sunbathers, whereas the one amidships is more active, with more noise and splashing and central to the action. At both, the ship's billowing and moving sails might occasionally block the sun's rays, although this happens amidships much more frequently than it does at the stern.

While there's no gym of any sort, aerobics and stretch classes are frequently held on-deck between the library and Tropical Bar.

Windjammer Barefoot Cruises

1759 Bay Rd., Miami Beach, FL 33139 (P.O. Box 190-120, Miami Beach, FL 33119). ☎ **800/ 327-2601** or 305/672-6453. Fax 305/674-1219. www.windjammer.com.

THE LINE IN A NUTSHELL   Ultra-casual and delightfully carefree, this eclectic fleet of cozy, rebuilt sailing ships (powered by both sails and engines) lures passengers into a fantasy world of pirates-and-rum-punch adventure.

THE EXPERIENCE   When you see that the captain is wearing shorts and shades and is barefoot like the rest of the laid-back crew, you'll realize Windjammer's vessels aren't your typical cruise ships. Their yards of sails, pointy bowsprits, chunky portholes, and generous use of wood create a swashbuckling storybook look, and while passengers don't have to fish for dinner or swab the decks, they are invited to help haul the sails, take a turn at the wheel, sleep out on-deck whenever they please, and depending on the captain's ruling, crawl into the bow net. With few rules and lots of freedom, this is the closest thing you'll get to a real Caribbean adventure.

Making their way to off-the-beaten-track Caribbean ports of call, the ships are ultra-informal, and hokey yet endearing rituals make the trip feel like summer camp for adults. Add in the line's tremendous number of repeat passengers (and a few of its signature "rum swizzles") and you have a casual experience that's downright intimate.

Pros

- **Informal and carefree.** You can wear shorts and T-shirts (and go barefoot) all day—even to dinner and to the bar.
- **Friendly and down-to-earth.** Crew and passengers mix and mingle, and in no time the ships feel like one great big happy family at sea.
- **Adventurous.** With the sails flapping and wooden decks surrounding you, it's no great leap of faith to feel like a pirate lost at sea.
- **Cheap.** Windjammer's per diem rates tend to be lower than those of Star Clipper and significantly lower than Windstar Cruises, and bar drinks are a steal.

Cons

- **Tiny cabins.** No polite way to say it: Cabins are cramped.
- **Mal de mer.** If you're prone to seasickness, these ships may set you off and running; luckily, though, the majority of each day is spent in port.
- **Loose port schedule.** Sailings usually follow the routes described in the brochures, but one destination might be substituted for another if a particularly adverse wind is blowing, or if there's a storm between you and your scheduled destination.

Compared with the other Soft-Adventure lines, here's how Windjammer rates:					
	poor	fair	good	excellent	outstanding
Enjoyment Factor					✓
Dining			✓		
Activities			✓		
Children's Program			✓		
Entertainment			✓		
Service			✓		
Overall Value					✓

* *Children's program is available on the* Legacy *only.*

WINDJAMMER BAREFOOT CRUISES: LETTING IT ALL HANG OUT

When British poet Thomas Beddos wrote, "The anchor heaves, the ship runs free, the sails swell full, to sea, to sea," he might as well have been describing the Windjammer operation. There's no pretense here: On these authentic vessels, which have withstood the test of time and tide, you can taste the salt air as it blows among the riggings and feel the sails stretch to the wind, propelling you toward adventure.

With six sailing ships, Windjammer has the largest fleet of its kind at sea today (the runner-up is reportedly the Norwegian government). From an inspired if unintentional beginning, it has grown into one of the major lines for cruisers who want to forgo the orchestrated regimentation on the giant cruise ships.

The famous and now semi-retired **Captain Mike Burke**—Cap'n Mike, as he's been known for the past half century—founded the company in 1947 with one ship, and for years ran down-and-dirty party cruises popular with singles, purchasing ships rich in history but otherwise destined for the scrap yard and transforming them into one-of-a-kind sailing vessels.

Legend has it that Burke, released from navy submarine duty in 1947, headed for Miami with $600 in back pay, intending to paint the town red. He succeeded. The next morning, he awoke with a blinding hangover and no money, on the deck of a 19-foot sloop moored somewhere in the Bahamas. Mike Burke had apparently bought himself a boat. Using a mostly empty bottle of Scotch, he christened the boat *Hangover,* and the rest is history. He lived aboard to save money, and then started ferrying friends out for weekends of sailing and fishing. Demand escalated, and Burke quit his full-time job to become a one-man cruise line.

After another year, Burke acquired a 150-foot schooner named *Janeen,* which had run aground and was in need of serious repairs, and thus began his life's work as a restorer of tall ships. After refurbishing *Janeen* himself, Burke rechristened her *Polynesia,* hired a crew of four, and began carrying passengers on weeklong cruises. *Polynesia* was followed by *Brigantine Yankee* and the *Polynesia II,* and then by the ships that form the current Windjammer fleet. Some people collect antique cars: Mike Burke collects tall ships. And, in this age of homogenous, cookie-cutter megaships that barrel their way through the Caribbean headed to crowded ports, Burke's tiny, eclectic, and appealingly imperfect ships are a breath of fresh, rustic air.

Burke works on a principle that anyone who's ever bought an old house will understand: Buy them cheap and decrepit, fix them up, and then stand back and admire your handiwork. His six children (including company president Susan) have assisted him in his ventures, renovating the vessels at the line's old shipyard near Miami and at a new yard in Trinidad. Burke says that the saddest thing he's ever seen is a tall ship permanently tethered to a pier, serving as a museum.

Are these cruises fun? No cruise can be all bad when it includes complimentary Bloody Marys in the morning, Rum Swizzles at sunset, and wine (albeit really cheap wine) with dinner. Since service for each meal involves two separate seatings, passengers have plenty of time to enjoy another drink or two while waiting for dindin. The bar operates on a doubloon system—a kind of debit card for drinks.

Swimming pools? There's no need, as the crystal-clear Caribbean is the swimming hole. Shuffleboard? Are you kidding? That's for those other cruise ships. Work the sails? Steering the wheel? Well, no. The crew handles that (although passengers are sometimes invited to lend a hand). This is a barefoot adventure, not a Shanghai special: Your duty is to sit back and live it up, not winch up a topsail whenever the captain barks an order.

This is a T-shirt-and-shorts adventure that's ultra-laid-back: There are no keys for the cabins, rum punch is served in paper cups, daily announcements are written in magic marker on a bulletin board, chances are the purser doubles as the nurse and gift-shop manager, and itineraries are only partially finalized before a ship's departure and are based on wind and tides. Vessels tend to sail during the late afternoon or night, arriving each morning at landfalls, allowing passengers to enjoy the local terrain and diversions. Favored waters include the Grenadines and the Virgin Islands, mini-archipelagos that offer some of the most challenging and beautiful sailing in the hemisphere, as well as esoteric landfalls such as cone-shaped Saba, historic Statia, or mysterious Carriacou, sites almost never visited by larger ships. (The line's one sailless ship, *Amazing Grace,* serves as a supply vessel in addition to carrying passengers, and so maintains a more rigid schedule.)

Just as aboard Star Clippers and Windstar, you won't be tacking into the wind like Erroll Flynn (it's just not practical to rely on wind only if the vessels hope to maintain any kind of schedule), but you can still take joy in the sheer beauty of the sails, and get a thrill when they do catch the wind, stretching taut from the masts. What this means is that you'll always hear a certain amount of engine noise, so if you're hoping for the silence of true sailing, you'll be disappointed. That said, if at all possible, the captain will navigate under sail alone at least for an hour or two.

Windjammer still remains for the most part a let-your-hair-down, party-on scene and a great way to see some of the Caribbean's more offbeat islands, but since Mike Burke's children have taken over control of the company, they've made an effort to offer a somewhat more wholesome, mainstream experience—it's just not the same wild and crazy Windjammer that used to advertise in *Hustler* and promised its passengers they'd get a "bang" out of their vacation. A few years back, the company added an activities mate (a.k.a. cruise director) to organize a few more activities for passengers, and food quality has improved over the past few years. It also began offering a kids' program on the flagship *Legacy* during the summer months for ages 6 to 12. There have been a few behavioral restrictions imposed, too. For instance, you can't climb the masts anymore—the line dislikes being sued by passengers who've had one too many rum swizzles and fallen off—but you're still welcome, *very* welcome, to have that one rum swizzle too many. Just be sure to keep your feet on deck while you're doing it—or, if you're adventurous and if your captain says it's OK, sit out in the bow rigging, as a bunch of us did on the *Legacy* after late champagne one memorable night in 1998.

So has Windjammer gone soft? No more so than the rest of us. As one longtime captain told me, the line has just had to change its approach to keep up with what people want. After all, it's not the seventies anymore. Despite any changes, the rum swizzles still flow freely and the wind still blows through the rigging. What more could a wannabe pirate want? Yo ho ho, y'all.

THE FLEET

Not a ship younger than 40 in the bunch, the Windjammer fleet of six includes **Mandalay,** built in 1923; **Flying Cloud,** built in 1935; **Yankee Clipper,** built in 1927; **Polynesia,** built in 1938; **Amazing Grace,** built in 1955; and **Legacy,** built in 1959.

Mandalay was once one of the most famous and luxurious ships in the world, *Husar IV,* dream boat of financier E. F. Hutton and his wife, Marjorie Merriweather Post. Later, it was commissioned as a research vessel by Columbia University, which sailed it for 1.25 million miles trying to develop theories (since proven correct) about continental drift. It's estimated that by the early 1980s, half the knowledge of the world's ocean floor was gathered by instruments aboard this ship.

Flying Cloud, built in Nantes, France, in 1935, functioned long ago as a training vessel for French cadets. During World War II the ship served as a decoy and spy ship for the Allied Navy. Its moment of glory came when Charles de Gaulle decorated it for sinking two Japanese submarines while it was carrying nitrates from Tahiti. More than any other vessel in the Windjammer fleet, this one actually resembles a pirate ship of old.

Yankee Clipper, once the only armor-plated sailing yacht in the world, was built by arms baron Alfred Krupp, whose armaments influenced the outcome of the Franco-Prussian War of 1870. Hitler once stepped aboard to award the Iron Cross to one of his U-boat commanders. Seized by the United States as war booty after World War II, the ship eventually became George Vanderbilt's private yacht. While the Vanderbilts owned it, *Yankee Clipper* was the fastest two-masted sailing vessel off the California coast, once managing an almost frightening 22 knots under full sail. Burke bought the ship just before it was due to be broken down for scrap, then gutted, redesigned, and rebuilt it, stripping off the armor in the process. Renovations in 1984 added a third mast, additional deck space, and cabin modifications. Although not as light and streamlined as it was originally, it's still a fast and very exciting ship.

Polynesia, built in Holland in 1938, was originally known as the *Argus,* and served as a fishing schooner in the Portuguese Grand Banks fleet. Windjammer bought it in 1975. Its original fishiness has disappeared thanks to a good scrubbing, a complete reconfiguration of the cabins and interior spaces, and the addition of varnished wood. Less stylish-looking than many of its thoroughbred siblings, it nonetheless remains one of the fleet's most consistently popular ships.

Amazing Grace is the sailless, diligent, dogged, and diesel-driven workhorse in the bunch, functioning as the freight-carrying ship that keeps the other members of the fleet supplied and provisioned. Because of its large hold, it's the most stable vessel in the fleet. Though it's a slow-mover, its itineraries are more comprehensive than those of any other ship in the fleet, stopping at each port the others use, as well as at supply depots en route.

In 1997, the line launched its newest and largest ship, *Legacy.* Originally a motored research vessel for the French government, it was designed with a deep keel that gave it additional balance during North Atlantic and North Sea storms. At the time, it was one of several government-owned ships sending weather reports to a central agency in Paris, which used them to predict storm patterns on the French mainland. The advent of global satellites made the vessel obsolete. It was bought by Windjammer in 1988, and, over the course of a decade, over $10 million was poured into a massive reconfiguration conducted at Windjammer's family-managed shipyard in Trinidad. Four steel masts and 11 sails were added, plus accoutrements the vessel needed for 7-day barefoot jaunts through the eastern Caribbean. At 1,165 tons, it's larger than any other vessel in the Windjammer fleet, although still tiny compared to a megaship.

The *Legacy* may represent the first of a new breed for Windjammer, which has thrown around talk of possibly building new 160-passenger-or-so staysail schooners, powered by both sails and engines, at its shipyard in Trinidad.

Which is the line's best ship? Each of them is nearly human, according to crew members, with distinctive personalities to match their distinctive lines. *Mandalay, Yankee Clipper, Flying Cloud,* and *Polynesia* are roughly equivalent in amenities, activities, and onboard atmosphere, and since each has been extensively refurbished, they have more or less equivalent interior decors. As for their capabilities as sailing ships, Captain Stuart Larcombe, who has served aboard them all, told me that the award goes to *Yankee Clipper,* followed by *Mandalay* (but his favorite, all around, was *Fantôme,* which was tragically lost in 1998's Hurricane Hugo. Though no passengers were aboard, 31 crew members lost their lives. Aside from a few battered pieces of wreckage, the *Fantôme* and its crew were never recovered). The *Legacy* is larger, roomier, and more comfortable than its siblings, and tends to rely heavily on its engines to augment the sails. Rather than quibble about differences between these ships, I'd suggest paying less attention to their minor physical differences and more to their different itineraries and varied ports of embarkation. Where exactly is it you want the wind to take you?

Amazing Grace is a different bird, with a quieter onboard atmosphere, and tends to attract a much older clientele. As one bartender on the ship told me, "If we have a young person aboard, they probably made a mistake."

Sometime in the future, Windjammer hopes to refurbish the *Rogue,* a second cargo/passenger ship the company acquired in the 1990s, to sail itineraries much like those followed by the *Grace.*

PASSENGER PROFILE

Unlike some "all things to all people" lines, Windjammer is for a particular kind of informal, fun-loving, and down-to-earth passenger, and though some compare the experience to a continuous fraternity party, I wouldn't go that far. In fact, the passenger and age mix puts the lie to that description. From honeymooning couples in their twenties to grandparents in their seventies, the line attracts a broad range of adventurers who like to have fun and don't want anything resembling a highly regimented vacation. Passengers are pretty evenly divided between men and women, and 15% to 20% overall are single. Passengers aboard the *Amazing Grace* commissary ship, however, tend to be older (60 and over) than those aboard the wind-driven sailing ships.

Many passengers love the experience so much that they return again and again. The record is still held by the late "Pappy" Gomez of Cleveland, Ohio, who sailed with Windjammer more than 160 times, but many, many people have sailed with the line 30 to 50 times. The line's supply officer told me he never steps aboard one of the ships without seeing passengers he's sailed with before.

Young children should probably not go (in fact, the line doesn't accept passengers under 6), nor should anyone prone to seasickness (there's quite a bit of that the first days out) or anyone wanting to be pampered (there's none of that during any day out). These ships are not for people with disabilities, either.

DINING

When it comes to dining, "slide over and pass me the breadbasket" about sums it up. Family-style and informal, there's nothing gourmet about the food; it ranges from mediocre to delicious. All breads and pastries are homemade, and at dinner, after soup and salad are served, passengers can choose from two main entrees, like curried shrimp and roast pork with garlic sauce. Don't be surprised if the waiters ask for a show of hands to see who wants what. Unlimited carafes of cheap red and white wine are complimentary and freely poured into the plastic wineglasses. Tasty breakfasts include all the usual plus items like eggs Benedict, and lunches include items like lobster pizza and apple salad. Both of these meals are served buffet-style. At certain islands, the crew lugs ashore a picnic lunch for an afternoon beach party, and each sailing usually includes an on-deck barbecue one evening. There are two open seatings for dinner.

Online Last-Minute Windjammin' Discounts

In 1999 Windjammer initiated a fantastic "CyberSailors" program of last-minute deals on its Web site (www.windjammer.com). Sign up and the line will send you weekly updates of incredibly discounted cruises, some up to 50% off. The catch? They're really last-minute, with the notices sent not more than 2 weeks before a sailing. Still, if you're able to pick up and go at a moment's notice, you can often get a weeklong Caribbean cruise (without airfare) for around $450.

Many dishes overall are rooted in Caribbean tradition. The chef will accommodate **special diets,** including vegetarian and low-salt. And don't be shy if it's your birthday: The chef will make a cake (free, of course) for you and serve it at dinner.

ACTIVITIES

Windjammer deliberately de-emphasizes the activities that dominate life aboard larger vessels, although it might occasionally host an on-deck crab race. Otherwise, your entertainment is up to you. If the weather's fine and you want to help trim the sails, you might be allowed to lend a hand.

Generally at least once per cruise, on one of the ships' beach visits—to Jost Van Dyke, perhaps—the activities mate might also organize a **hike around the island** or **team games** reminiscent of mid-1960s cocktail-party movies (think Cary Grant and Audrey Hepburn in the nightclub scene in *Charade*). It's the usual embarrassing stuff: Passengers twirl hula-hoops while dressed in snorkel gear; pass cucumbers to each other, clasping them only with their thighs; flop onto slippery foam mats and try to swim out to and around a landmark. Silliness, in other words—but it does make for instant camaraderie. After all, after someone's seen you act this dumb, they've seen it all.

The line still hosts **singles cruises** on *Polynesia* and *Flying Cloud* several times a year. (See the box on theme cruises, below, for more info.)

CHILDREN'S PROGRAM

No children under 6 are allowed aboard any ship in the Windjammer fleet, and children under age 16 must be accompanied by an adult. Sales agents usually prefer that children be at least 10 years old. Aboard most of the ships, teenagers divert themselves the same way adults do, with conversation, shore excursions, reading, and watching the wide blue sea. Otherwise, few concessions are made for their amusement. Baby-sitting is not available. This situation is markedly different aboard *Legacy,* which has a "Junior Jammers" kids program. Here, younger children are divided into roughly compatible age brackets and kept involved for 12 hours a day with a roster of summer-camp-style activities, while the ship's "Teen Cadet Sailing Program" has teens learning about sailing and navigating. There are also introductory scuba classes for 8-to-10 year olds and 11-to-16 year olds.

ENTERTAINMENT

Part entertainment, part education, the captain's "Story Time" held each morning out on deck is the first event of the average day on a Windjammer ship. It's a short talk that's 20% ship business, 40% information about the day's port call, activities, or sailing route, and 40% pure humor (the last trip I took, a joke about a cat and certain part of a woman's anatomy was par for the course). At these morning meetings, the captain will come out and shout "Good morning, everybody!" and the passengers—many of whom have taken these trips before and know the drill—bark back in chorus, "Good morning, Captain SIR!" The Windjammer crowd loves every minute of it.

Stowaways & Other Deals (Plus One Extra Charge)

Stowaways: Rather than fork over a bundle for a hotel the night before your cruise, you can stay aboard your docked ship for a relatively modest $55 per person, double occupancy. **Children's Rates:** A child under 12 sharing a cabin with two adults is charged 50% of the adult fare. **Port Charges:** Six- and 7-night cruises generally run $65 per person. Port charges for 13-day outings cost $150 per person.

Windjammer Fleet Itineraries

Ship	Home Ports & Season	Itinerary	Other Itineraries
Amazing Grace	Round-trip between the Bahamas and Trinidad, year-round.	**13-night E. and S. Carib:** Ports include Antigua, Bequia, Concepción, Cooper Island, Dominica, Grand Bahama, Grand Turk, Grenada, Little Inagua, Iles des Saintes, New Providence, Nevis, Palm Island, Plana Cay, Providenciales, Puerto Plata, Montserrat, St. Barts, St. Kitts, St. Lucia, Sint Maarten, Tobago, Tortola, Trinidad, and Virgin Gorda.	None
Flying Cloud	Round-trip from Tortola; itineraries alternate year-round.	**6-night E. Carib 1:** Salt Island, Cooper Island, Virgin Gorda, and Jost Van Dyke. **6-night E. Carib 2:** Cooper Island, Peter Island, Norman Island, and Virgin Gorda.	None
Legacy	Round-trip from Fajardo (Puerto Rico); itineraries alternate year-round.	**7-night E. Carib 1:** Culebra (Puerto Rico), St. Croix, St. John, St. Thomas, and Jost Van Dyke. **7-night E. Carib 2:** Culebra, St. Croix, Virgin Gorda, St. John's, and Vieques (Puerto Rico).	None
Mandalay	Alternating 13-night itineraries between Grenada and Antigua and 6-night itineraries round-trip from Grenada.	**13-night E. Carib:** Antigua, Bequia, Carriacou, Canouan, Dominica, Grenada, Guadeloupe, Iles des Saintes, Martinique, Mayreau, Nevis, Montserrat, Palm Island, St. Lucia, St. Vincent, and Tobago Cays. **6-night E. Carib:** Grenadines. **6-night S. Carib:** Chimana Segunda, Playa Blanca, Isla de Margarita, and Los Testigos.	None
Polynesia	Round-trip from Sint Maarten; itineraries alternate year-round.	**6-night E. Carib 1:** St. Barts, Anguilla, Tintamarre, Montserrat, and Saba. **6-night E. Carib 2:** Colombier Beach, St. Barts, St. Eustatius, Nevis, and St. Kitts.	None
Yankee Clipper	Round-trip from Grenada; itineraries alternate year-round.	**6-night E. Carib 1:** Carriacou, Palm Island, Bequia, St. Vincent, and Mayreau. **6-night E. Carib 2:** Palm Island, Union Island, Bequia, Canouan, Tobago Cays, and St. Vincent.	None

* Note: Windjammer's ships often adjust their itineraries in mid-cruise to reflect changing wind and weather patterns, as well as any island event of particular interest. Each cruise itinerary is up to the ship's captain, as long as the ship both leaves the port of embarkation and returns at the scheduled time.

In general, social interaction centers around the bars and top sundeck. There's typically a **passenger talent show** 1 night, 1 or 2 nights a week a **local pop band** is brought on board for a few hours of dancing, and there's a weekly barbecue buffet dinner and a **costume party**—a Windjammer tradition that has passengers decked out as cross-dressers, pirates, and other characters. Bring your own get-up or rummage through the pile of shabby costumes the ship hauls out before the party. Either way, it's a ball! Otherwise, there's almost no organized nightlife.

Just about every day is spent in port somewhere and the occasional day at sea might feature a knot-tying demonstration and a bridge tour. The entertainment is the ship itself and the camaraderie between passengers. At about 5pm every day, gallons of complimentary **rum swizzles** are generously offered along with hors d'oeuvres like spicy meatballs, chicken fingers, and cheese and crackers. Guests gather on-deck, often still in their sarongs and shorts, mingling in the fresh sea air with taped music playing in the background. On a recent cruise, a woman sang a silly song she wrote about the cruise and the people she had met, as an officer accompanied her on his flute.

After dinner, head up to the on-deck bar (drinks are cheap: $2 for a Red Stripe or Heineken and $3 for the most expensive cocktail) or grab a deck chair or mat and hit the deck. Generally, the ship stays late in one or two ports so passengers can head ashore to one of the island watering holes.

SERVICE

Service is friendly and efficient, but not doting; matter-of-fact and straightforward rather than obsequious. Unlike more upscale cruise lines, with Windjammer there's no master/servant relationship between passengers and staff—the crew are simply fellow travelers who just happen to steer the ship or serve dinner or drinks when their schedules call for it. They're a good bunch.

The line tends to attract a staff that shares founder Mike Burke's appreciation for the wide-open sea and barely concealed scorn for corporate agendas and staid priorities. Many are from the same Caribbean islands Windjammer's ships visit.

Amazing Grace

The Verdict

If you're looking for a slow and easy (and cheap) tour of the Caribbean and like the novelty of being on a supply ship as it does its rounds, a trip on this somewhat charming tub is bound to create lasting memories.

Amazing Grace *(photo: Windjammer)*

Specifications

Size (in tons)	1,525	Officers	British/American
Number of Cabins	47	Crew	40 (International)
Number of Outside Cabins	46	Passenger/Crew Ratio	2.4 to 1
Cabins with Verandas	0	Year Built	1955
Number of Passengers	94	Last Major Refurbishment	1995

Frommer's Ratings (Scale of 1–5)

Cabin Comfort & Amenities	2	Pool, Fitness & Spa Facilities	N/A
Ship Cleanliness & Maintenance	3	Facilities	N/A
Public Comfort/Space	3	Itinerary	5
Decor	3	Worth the Money	5

Amazing Grace, a dowdy but reliable sea horse, is the closest thing to a banana boat in the cruise industry. Moving its way doggedly and regularly through most of the Caribbean archipelago, it is the only vessel in the Windjammer fleet that does without sails.

Built as the *Pharos* in Dundee, Scotland, in 1955, it mostly carried supplies to isolated lighthouses and North Sea oil rigs, but once or twice it was pressed into service as a weekend cruiser for the queen of England. The vessel was acquired by Windjammer in 1988 and, despite many modernizations, still retains some vestiges of its British past. Today, it's still a freighter servicing remote outposts, albeit in the warm Caribbean rather than the chilly North Sea. If you come aboard expecting to be treated like royalty, however, you'll be sorely disappointed.

Some of the line's least dramatic (but cheapest) cruises are its languid "slow boat to China" odysseys aboard *Grace,* and its itinerary, featuring an amazing number of off-beat ports, is top-notch. The lack of organized activities is a drawback on these long sailings, however, so you'll be forced to create your own. Guests are noticeably more sedentary, definitely older, and less party-oriented than those aboard the line's more raffish sail-powered vessels. Most tend to turn in by 10pm.

Cabins & Rates						
Cabins	Per diems from	Bathtub	Fridge	Hair Dryer	Sitting Area	TV
Inside	$132	no	no	no	no	no
Outside	$111	no	yes	no	yes	no
Suite	$213	no	yes	no	yes	yes

CABINS   Cabins are utterly without frills and very small, but they're still a tad roomier than others in Windjammer's fleet. About half contain the varnished paneling from the ship's original construction; the others are more modern, with almost no nostalgic value. Although there's a sink in each cabin, this is the only ship in the fleet where you'll have to share shower and toilet facilities with other passengers. The honeymoon suite, near the stern, is often rented by non-honeymooners because of its slightly larger size. There are no wheelchair-accessible cabins.

PUBLIC AREAS   You can have a lot of fun aboard this ship, although there's no avoiding reminders that it is indeed a glorified freighter. A bar/lounge faces forward across the bow and another sits in open air on the stern, and there's a TV room. Some of the greatest authenticity preserved from the ship's early days is a piano room and a smoking room/library, which sports etched glass doors and mahogany walls. Because large sections of this vessel (the storage areas) are off-limits to passengers, many people tend to gravitate to the deck areas—including the lovely Promenade Deck—for reading, napping, or whatever.

The dining room has booth-type tables that seat up to eight passengers. There are two open seatings, generally at 6:30pm and 8pm.

POOL, FITNESS & SPA FACILITIES   There's no swimming pool, gym, or fitness facilities. Instead, you'll get your exercise during snorkeling and scuba sessions at the ports of call. Snorkeling gear (mask, fins, snorkel, and carrying bag) rents for $20 per week, and one-tank dives, as offered by an array of outside concessionaires, cost around $50 at each of the ports of call. (Novice divers pay $85 for a "resort course.") Shore outings sometimes include strenuous hiking expeditions. All excursions and scuba expeditions are conducted by outside agencies, not by Windjammer, and passengers are required to sign a liability release before participating.

Flying Cloud • Mandalay • Polynesia • Yankee Clipper

The Verdict

Bound by wood and sails, this oddball group of little ships have led fascinating and long lives and today promise adventure, good times, and offbeat ports for a bargain price.

Yankee Clipper *(photo: Windjammer)*

Specifications

Size (in tons)		Officers	British/American/
Flying Cloud	400		Australian
Mandalay	420	Crew	International
Polynesia	430	*Flying Cloud*	25
Yankee Clipper	327	*Mandalay*	28
Number of Cabins		*Polynesia*	45
Flying Cloud	33	*Yankee Clipper*	29
Mandalay	36	Passenger/Crew Ratio	2.2–3.1 to 1
Polynesia	46	Year Built	
Yankee Clipper	32	*Flying Cloud*	1935
Number of Outside Cabins		*Mandalay*	1923
Flying Cloud	33	*Polynesia*	1938
Mandalay	36	*Yankee Clipper*	1927
Polynesia	46	Last Major Refurbishment	
Yankee Clipper	32	*Flying Cloud*	1991
Cabins with Verandas	0	*Mandalay*	1982
Number of Passengers		*Polynesia*	1990
Flying Cloud	74	*Yankee Clipper*	1984
Mandalay	72		
Polynesia	126		
Yankee Clipper	64		

Frommer's Ratings (Scale of 1–5)

Cabin Comfort & Amenities	2	Pool, Fitness & Spa Facilities	N/A
Ship Cleanliness & Maintenance	3	Children's Facilities	N/A
Public Comfort/Space	3	Itinerary	5
Decor	3	Worth the Money	5

Despite different origins, different histories, and subtle differences in the way they react to the wind and weather, each of these sailing ships shares many things in common with the others, and for adventure and interesting ports of call they're all absolutely top-notch. I've opted to cluster them into one all-encompassing review because of the extent to which each has been rebuilt and reconfigured to the Windjammer ideal. For the ships' individual histories, refer to the pages above.

How to select one or another if you're a first-time Windjammer client? I advise you to select your ship based on its itinerary rather than its aesthetics, taking into account the frequent cruises for singles that are held aboard *Polynesia* and *Flying Cloud*. Other than that, choose the boat you want to float based on your schedule and any special promotions the line might be offering.

Cabins & Rates						
Cabins	Per diems from	Bathtub	Fridge	Hair Dryer	Sitting Area	TV
Outside	$176	no	no	no	no	no
Suite	$196	no	some	no	yes	some

CABINS   There's no getting around it: Cabins are cramped, just as they would have been on a true 19th-century clipper ship. Few retain any glamorous vestiges of their original owners and most are about as functional as they come, although cabins on the *Mandalay* and *Yankee Clipper* are pleasantly rustic because they're wood-paneled. They're adequate enough, though, and it's the adventurous thrill of sailing on one of these ships that you come for, not luxurious cabins.

Each cabin has a minuscule bathroom with a shower, many of which function with a push-button—for every push you get about 10 seconds worth of water (you'll wind up keeping your finger on it the whole time while trying to wash up with one hand). On many vessels, hot water is available only during certain hours of the day, whenever the ships' galleys and laundries aren't using it. Be prepared for toilets that don't always function properly, and retain your sense of humor as they're repaired.

Storage space is limited, but this isn't a serious problem because few passengers bring very much with them. Many cabins have upper and lower berths, some have lower-level twins, and a few have doubles. The *Polynesia* has a couple of dormlike cabins sleeping six in bunks, great for singles (the *Poly* in fact does several special singles cruises annually) or groups of friends traveling together and looking for a bargain.

Some vessels have a limited number of suites that, although not spacious by the standards of larger ships, seem to be of generous proportions when contrasted to standard cabins. There are no wheelchair-accessible cabins on any of these ships.

PUBLIC AREAS   What glamour may have been associated with these ships in the past is long gone, lost to the years or in the gutting and refitting they required before entering Windjammer service. There are patches of rosewood or mahogany, but otherwise the decors are durable, washable, and practical, and appropriate backdrops for passengers so laid-back that few bother to ever change out of their bathing suits, T-shirts, and shorts. Dining rooms are cozy and some feature wood paneling in places; overall, they've been designed with efficiency in mind. *Mandalay*'s is open-air, and is the only dining room in the fleet that isn't air-conditioned (no need to worry about sweating it, though, evening breezes keep it nice and cool). By contrast, the seemingly endless teakwood decks look positively opulent, and many passengers adopt some preferred corner of them as a place to hang out.

POOL, FITNESS & SPA FACILITIES   These ships are too small to offer health clubs or any of the sauna and fitness regimens so heavily promoted aboard larger ships, and none has a swimming pool. You'll get an adequate amount of exercise, however, during snorkeling and scuba sessions conducted at the ports of call. Snorkeling and diving fees/specifications are the same as aboard *Amazing Grace* (see review above).

Legacy

The Verdict

The brightest and most spacious of Windjammer's ships, the *Legacy* is a real winner in my book, with comfortable cabins, good-size private bathrooms, a cheerful dining saloon with large round booths, and a sprawling expanse of outdoor deck space. Even when full, the ship doesn't feel crowded.

Legacy (photo: Windjammer Barefoot Cruises)

Specifications

Size (in tons)	1,165	Officers	American/British/
Number of Cabins	60		Australian
Number of Outside Cabins	40	Crew	43 (International)
Cabins with Verandas	0	Passenger/Crew Ratio	2.8 to 1
Number of Passengers	120	Year Built	1959
		Last Major Refurbishment	1998

Frommer's Ratings (Scale of 1–5)

Cabin Comfort & Amenities	3	Pool, Fitness & Spa Facilities	N/A
Ship Cleanliness & Maintenance	4	Children's Facilities	N/A
Public Comfort/Space	4	Itinerary	5
Decor	3	Worth the Money	5

Legacy is Windjammer's newest acquisition, its biggest and most modern, and the first of a new breed. Built in 1959 as a motorized research vessel, the ship was acquired by Windjammer in 1989, converted into a traditional-style "tall ship," and relaunched in 1997. Roomier and more stable than the rest of the sailing fleet, it sports a lovely profile that makes it the center of attention whenever it sails into port.

Some hard-core Windjammer veterans consider the *Legacy* a wimpy addition to the rough-and-tumble venerated fleet. Equating Windjammer's signature yo-ho-ho pirate adventures with the cramped, bare-bones life aboard its smaller, older ships, stalwart fans wondered whether the comfort available on this new vessel (and the children's program it offers—a Windjammer first) meant the old days were gone forever. It was like seeing a group of 30- or 40-somethings returning to their favorite college-era dive bar and finding it newly sheathed in wood paneling, with brass lamps in place of the neon lights and light jazz on the juke box instead of "Born to Run."

Well, here's the scoop: Though it is indeed the most comfortable of the Windjammer lot, it still embraces that irreverent Windjammer spirit we've come to know and love. It takes only a glance at the carved wooden figurehead on the ship's prow—which depicts none other than Cap'n Mike Burke himself, wearing a tropical-print shirt, beer in one hand and a ship's wheel in the other—to see that this is still very much a laid-back, partying vessel. It's just a cushier one.

Cabins & Rates						
Cabins	Per diems from	Bathtub	Fridge	Hair Dryer	Sitting Area	TV
Outside	$213	no	no	no	no	no
Suite	$229	no	no	no	yes	yes

CABINS   Cabins aboard *Legacy* are a little larger and more comfortable than aboard the line's older ships, but if you're used to sailing aboard large cruise ships they'll probably seem cramped. Berths are either doubles or bunk beds, and if you're in the upper portion of the latter, watch your head: More than one passenger has woken up and knocked himself silly on the metal porthole cover that projects from the wall when open. You might do well to sleep with your feet toward it.

Suites—both the Admiral Suites and Burke's Berth, which is the best in the house—offer windows instead of portholes, plus space for a third occupant. There are a handful of single cabins and a triple-berth option offered as well in the Commodore-class cabins, but it affords a minimum of personal space. Burke's Berth is the only cabin aboard that offers an entertainment center, bar, and vanity. Storage in all cabins is perfectly adequate for this type of T-shirt-and-shorts cruise, with each containing a small closet/drawer unit and having additional space under the bed.

Bathrooms offer an adequate amount of maneuvering space and small, curtained showers, some with a raised lip that contains the runoff but some not, making for a perpetually wet bathroom floor. Although these facilities are small and spartan compared to those offered on larger and glitzier ships, they're still far better than the head-style facilities aboard the other Windjammer sailing ships.

Single cabins are available. As with all the Windjammer ships, the *Legacy* is not a good option for people with disabilities.

PUBLIC AREAS   The top deck, with a large canopied area at its center, is the social focus of the cruise, the space where the rum swizzles are dispensed at sunset, where visiting bands perform at night, and where the captain conducts his daily morning "Story Time" session. The ship's bar is also located on this deck, as is the requisite barrel of rum—a real barrel, from which the bartender siphons off what he needs every day.

The Poop Deck offers the best sunbathing space, although the position of the sails—when they're raised—could force you to move quite often. Passengers lounge on patio-style white plastic recliners or on one of the many blue cushions strewn about, which many passengers also use to sleep out on deck under the stars, something the line fully encourages.

Navigation of the ship is often from the ship's wheel mounted out in open air near the bow. When seas are calm and sailing is easy, the crew offers passengers a chance to steer. Unlike on most larger cruise ships, the *Legacy*'s bow is generally open to passengers, allowing you (if the captain says it's OK) to do your Leonardo DiCaprio "King of the World" bit, or, even better, to climb out on the netting that projects to the tip of the bowsprit, and lounge there while the blue Caribbean Sea splashes and sprays below you. Don't miss this opportunity if it's offered—trust me.

All meals are served in the comfortable aft dining room, fitted with large circular tables (a bummer if you're stuck in the middle, three or four people from freedom) and decorated with faux tropical plants. The only other interior public room is a small and not terribly appealing lounge that offers a TV/video arrangement and a smattering of books and board games. In an entire week aboard, the only person I saw using this room

Windjammer's Theme Cruises: You're Not in Kansas Anymore

Windjammer is not what you'd call a straitlaced cruise line during normal sailings, so it really means something that when the ships are chartered for theme cruises, the level of permissive wackiness actually goes *up*. Don't expect the kind of tame country music or big-band themes that Holland America and NCL have run through like phases of the moon for years. Besides the half dozen or so **singles theme cruises** it schedules every year on *Polynesia,* Windjammer charters its ships occasionally to groups who put together **gay cruises** (there was one scheduled in 1999), **nudist cruises** (there's even been a gay nudist cruise), and **Parrothead cruises,** where fans of Jimmy Buffet do the Margaritaville thing (note that Buffett does not officially endorse these events). Don't worry about getting stuck on one of these cruises if you don't want to: They're special cruises put together and marketed by travel agents. If one of them appeals to you, though, inquire with Windjammer about when the next one is scheduled.

was a 10-year-old boy watching movies. Where was everyone? Out on deck, where they belong.

POOL, FITNESS & SPA FACILITIES   As aboard the rest of the line's ships, there are none. No spa, no gym, no jogging track. Aboard ship, the most exercise you're likely to get is if you volunteer to help hoist the sails. In port, however, you'll have such options as snorkeling, scuba diving, sea kayaking, and hiking to help you work off dessert. Of course, there are silly beach relay races and other games organized by the activities mate to get your heart rate up. Snorkeling and diving fees/specifications are the same as aboard *Amazing Grace* (see review above).

Part 3

The Ports

With information on the ports of embarkation, advice on things you can see and do on your own in 33 Caribbean ports of call plus Bermuda and the Panama Canal, and tips on the best tours.

10 The Ports of Embarkation

11 Caribbean Ports of Call

12 Bermuda & the Panama Canal Route

The Ports of Embarkation 10

The busiest of the ports of embarkation is Miami, followed by Port Everglades in Fort Lauderdale and Port Canaveral at Cape Canaveral. Tampa, on Florida's west coast, is also becoming a major port, especially for cruise ships visiting the eastern coast of Mexico, while New Orleans is popular for ships sailing to Mexico. San Juan, Puerto Rico, is both a major port of embarkation in the Caribbean and a major port of call. (See chapter 11, "Caribbean Ports of Call," for a review.)

All these ports are tourist destinations themselves, so most cruise lines now offer special deals to extend all Caribbean/Bahamian cruise vacations in the port either before or after the cruise. These packages, for 2, 3, or 4 days, often offer hotel and car-rental discounts as well as sightseeing packages. Have your travel agent or cruise specialist check for the best deals.

In this chapter, I'll describe each port of embarkation, tell you how to get to it, and suggest things to see and do there, whether it's hitting the beach, sightseeing, or shopping. I'll also recommend a sampling of restaurants and places to stay. You'll find more detailed information about each destination in *Frommer's Florida, Frommer's Miami & the Keys, Frommer's New Orleans,* and *Frommer's Puerto Rico.*

1 Miami & the Port of Miami

Miami is the cruise capital of the world. More cruise ships, especially supersize ones, berth here than anywhere else on earth, and more than three million cruise ship passengers pass through yearly. Not surprisingly, the city's facilities are extensive and state-of-the-art, and Miami International Airport is only 8 miles away, about a 15-minute drive.

Just across the bridge from the Port of Miami and a few minutes away is **Bayside Marketplace,** downtown Miami's waterfront and restaurant shopping complex, which can be reached via regular shuttle service between each cruise terminal and Bayside's main entrance.

Industry giants Carnival and Royal Caribbean both have long-term, multimillion-dollar agreements with the port, and to accommodate the influx of new cruise ships, Miami spent $76 million on major improvements to terminals 3, 4, and 5, and added a 750-space parking facility. In fact, Terminal 5 (which was created out of the old 5 and half of Terminal 4) is now the new 250,000-square-foot home for Royal Caribbean's *Voyager of the Seas* (and subsequent Eagle-class ships), designed specially to accommodate the hulking ships and about 8,400 passengers at a time. You can't miss it: It has sail-like structures on its roof and a replica of Royal Caribbean's Viking Crown Lounge on top of the terminal as well. The renovated terminals offer enhanced facilities, like 4,000 additional passenger seats between them, a new departure area in each, VIP lounges, and airport-style conveyer belts for luggage coming on and off the ship. The port is even hoping to soon be able to issue airline boarding passes to departing passengers.

Still on the drawing board are plans for a **Maritime Park,** to be built on Watson Island, a tract of land just across the channel from port. Although still in the early planning stages, the complex would likely include two new ship terminals, a convention bureau, and entertainment facilities for passengers.

GETTING TO MIAMI & THE PORT

The Port of Miami is at 1015 N. America Way, in central Miami. It's on Dodge Island, reached via a five-lane bridge from the downtown district. For information, call ☎ 305/371-PORT.

BY PLANE   Miami International Airport is about 8 miles west of downtown Miami and the port. If you've arranged air transportation and/or transfers through the cruise line (see chapter 2, "Booking Your Cruise & Getting the Best Price"), a representative will be at the airport and will direct you to **shuttle buses** that take you to the port. **Taxis** are also available; the fare between the airport and the Port of Miami is about $18. Some leading taxi companies include **Central Taxicab Service** (☎ 305/532-5555), **Diamond Cab Company** (☎ 305/545-5555), and **Metro Taxicab Company** (☎ 305/888-8888).

You can also take a no. 7 **Metrobus** for $1.25 (☎ 305/770-3131) from the airport to downtown Miami (stop is at Miami Dade Community College), which will land you across the street from the bridge that leads to the port (not a good option with luggage). **SuperShuttle** (☎ 305/871-2000) charges about $7 to $14 per person, with two pieces of luggage, for a ride within Dade County, which includes the Port of Miami. Their vans operate 24 hours a day.

BY CAR   The Florida Turnpike, a toll road, and Interstate 95 are the main arteries for those arriving from the north. Coming in from the northwest, take Interstate 75 or U.S. 27 to reach the center of Miami. Parking lots right at street level face the cruise terminals. Parking runs $8 per day. Porters can carry your luggage to the terminals.

BY TRAIN   Amtrak (☎ 800/872-7245) offers three trains daily between New York and Miami, and daily service between Los Angeles and Miami. You'll pull into Amtrak's Miami terminal at 8303 NW 37th Ave. (☎ 305/835-1206).

EXPLORING MIAMI

Miami is no longer just a beach-vacation destination. A sizzling, multicultural mecca, Miami and its beaches offer the best in cutting-edge restaurants, unusual attractions, shopping, and luxury, boutique, kitschy, and charming hotels.

After a relaxing day on the water, take advantage of choice theater or opera, restaurants serving exotic and delicious food, the hopping, star-studded club scene, or the lively cafe culture.

VISITOR INFORMATION   Contact the **Greater Miami Convention and Visitors Bureau,** 701 Brickell Ave., Miami, FL 33131 (☎ 800/283-2707 or 305/539-3000), for the most up-to-date information.

GETTING AROUND   See "Getting to Miami & the Port," above, for **taxi** information. The meter starts at $1.50, and ticks up another $2 each mile and 25¢ for each additional minute, with standard flat-rate charges for frequently traveled routes.

Miami at a Glance

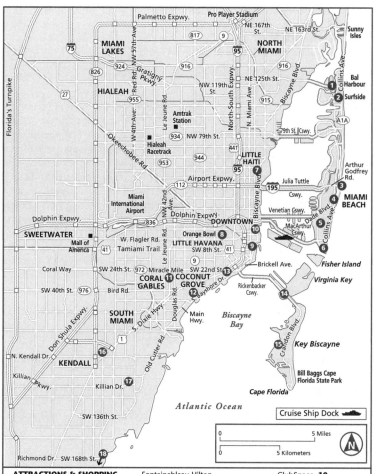

Cruise Ship Dock

	5 Miles
0	
0	5 Kilometers

ATTRACTIONS & SHOPPING

Art Deco district **5**
Bal Harbour Shops **1**
Bass Museum of Art **5**
Bayside Marketplace **10**
CocoWalk and the
Streets of Mayfair **12**
Coral Gables Merrick
House & Gardens **11**
Crandon Park Beach **15**
Dadeland Mall **16**
Lincoln Road shopping **5**
Miami Seaquarium **14**
Miracle Mile **11**
Monkey Jungle **18**
Parrot Jungle and Gardens **17**
Vizcaya Museum & Gardens **13**

ACCOMMODATIONS

The Beach House **2**
Biltmore Hotel **11**
The Delano **5**
The Eden Roc **3**

Fontainebleau Hilton
Resort & Towers **3**
The Hotel **6**
Hotel Astor **5**
Hotel Ocean **5**
Hotel Place St. Michel **11**
Indian Creek Hotel **4**
The Kent **5**
Miami Hotel Inter-Continental **10**
Park Washington Hotels **5**
Sonesta Beach Resort
Key Biscayne **15**
The Tides **5**
Wyndham Grand Bay Hotel **12**

DINING & NIGHTLIFE

Albion's Falabella Bar **5**
Bambu **6**
Bar Room **6**
Bash **5**
Café Nostalgia **8**
Café Tu Tu Tango **12**
Casa Panza Restaurant **8**

ClubSpace **10**
crobar **5**
East Coast Fisheries
& Restaurant **10**
Forge **3**
Groove Jet **4**
Joe's Stone Crab **6**
Joia **6**
Larios on the Beach **6**
Level **5**
Lombardi's **10**
Nemo's **6**
Norman's **11**
Pacific Time **6**
Rose Bar **5**
Rusty Pelican **15**
Soyka **7**
Spris **6**
Tantra **5**
Tiramesu **6**
Tobacco Road **9**
Van Dyke Cafe **6**
Versailles **8**

Bus transportation in Miami is often a nightmare. Call ☎ **305/770-3131** for public transit information. The fare is $1.25.

Metromover (☎ **305/770-3131**), a 4.4-mile elevated line, circles downtown, stopping near important attractions and shopping and business districts. It's fun if you've got time to kill. It runs daily from about 5am to midnight. The fare is 25¢.

HITTING THE BEACH

A 300-foot-wide sand beach runs for about 10 miles from the south of Miami Beach to Haulover Beach Park in the north. (For those of you who like to get an all-around tan, Haulover is a known nude beach, though it's not mandatory that you sunbathe in your birthday suit.) Although most of this stretch is lined with a solid wall of hotels, beach access is plentiful, and you are free to frolic along the entire strip. A wooden boardwalk runs along the hotel side from 21st to 46th streets—about 1¹/₂ miles.

There are lots of **public beaches** here, wide and well maintained, complete with lifeguards, toilet facilities, concession stands, and metered parking (bring lots of quarters). Lifeguard-protected public beaches include 21st Street, at the beginning of the boardwalk; 35th Street, popular with an older crowd; 46th Street, next to the Fontainebleau Hilton; 53rd Street, a narrower, more sedate beach; 64th Street, one of the quietest strips around; and 72nd Street, a local old-timers spot. On the southern tip of the beach is family favorite South Pointe Park, where you can watch the cruise ships. Lummus Park, in the center of the Art Deco district, is the best place for people-watching and model-spotting. The beach between 11th and 13th streets is popular with the gay crowd. Senior citizens prefer the beach from 1st to 15th streets.

To escape the crowds, head up to the 40-acre **Oleta River State Recreation Area** (formerly known as the North Shore State Recreation Area), 3400 NE 163rd St. at Collins and Biscayne (☎ **305/919-1844**). It costs $2 per person to get in, or $4 per car for up to eight people.

In Key Biscayne, **Crandon Park,** 4000 Crandon Blvd. (☎ **305/361-5421**), is one of metropolitan Miami's finest white-sand beaches, stretching for some 3¹/₂ miles. There are lifeguards, and you can rent cabanas with a shower and chairs. Saturday and Sunday the beach can be especially crowded. Parking nearby is $3.50.

SOUTH BEACH & THE ART DECO DISTRICT

Miami's best sight is a part of the city itself. Located at the southern end of Miami Beach, the ✪ **Art Deco district** is filled with outrageous and fanciful 1920s and 1930s architecture that shouldn't be missed. This treasure trove features more than 900 pastel, Pez-colored buildings in the art-deco, Streamline Moderne, and Spanish Mediterranean Revival styles. The district stretches from 6th to 23rd streets, and from the Atlantic Ocean to Lennox Court. **Ocean Drive** boasts many of the premier art-deco hotels.

Also in South Beach is the ✪ **Bass Museum of Art,** 2121 Park Ave. (☎ **305/673-7533**), with a permanent collection of Old Masters, along with textiles, period furnishings, objets d'art, ecclesiastical artifacts, and sculpture. Rotating exhibits include pop art, fashion, and photography, and attract South Beach's fashion-forward lovers of modern art.

CORAL GABLES & COCONUT GROVE

These two Miami neighborhoods are fun to visit for their architecture and ambiance. In **Coral Gables,** the old world meets the new as curving boulevards, sidewalks, plazas, fountains, and arched entrances evoke Seville.

Today the area is an epicurean's Eden boasting some of Miami's most renowned eateries. "The Gables," as the locals say, is also home to the University of Miami and the

Miracle Mile (it's actually half a mile), a 5-block retail mecca stretching from Douglas Road (37th Avenue) to Le Jeune Road (42nd Avenue). You can even visit the boyhood home of George Merrick, the man who originally developed Coral Gables. The **Coral Gables Merrick House & Gardens,** 907 Coral Way (☎ **305/460-5361**), has been restored to its 1920s look and is filled with Merrick memorabilia. The house and garden are open for tours on Wednesday and Saturday between 1 and 4pm.

Coconut Grove, South Florida's oldest settlement, remains a village surrounded by the urban sprawl of Miami. It dates back to the early 1800s when Bahamian seamen first sought to salvage treasure from the wrecked vessels stranded along the Great Florida Reef. Mostly people come here to shop, drink, dine, or simply walk around and explore. But don't miss the ✪ **Vizcaya Museum & Gardens,** 3251 S. Miami Ave. (☎ **305/250-9133**), a spectacular 70-room Italian Renaissance–style villa.

ANIMAL PARKS

Just minutes from the Port of Miami in Key Biscayne, the **Miami Seaquarium,** 4400 Rickenbacker Causeway (☎ **305/361-5705**), is a delight. Performing dolphins such as Flipper, TV's greatest sea mammal, perform along with "Lolita the Killer Whale." You can also see endangered manatees, sea lions, tropical-theme aquariums, and the gruesome shark feeding. It's open daily from 9:30am to 6pm. Admission is $21.95 for adults and $16.95 for children 3 to 9, free for children under 3.

At **Monkey Jungle,** 14805 SW 216th St., Homestead (☎ **305/235-1611**), the trick is that the visitors are caged and nearly 500 monkeys frolic in freedom and make fun of them. The most talented of these free-roaming primates perform shows daily for the amusement of their guests. Beware of monkeys in heat, however, as they may mistake you for a possible object of their affections. The site also contains one of the richest fossil deposits in South Florida, with some 5,000 specimens. It's open daily from 9:30am to 5pm. Admission is $13.50 for adults, $8 for children 4 to 12, and free for children under 3.

In South Miami, **Parrot Jungle and Gardens,** 11000 SW 57th Ave. (☎ **305/669-7030**), is actually a botanical garden, wildlife habitat, and bird sanctuary all rolled into one. Children can enjoy a petting zoo and a playground. It's open daily from 9:30am to 6pm. Admission is $14.95 for adults, $9.95 for children 3 to 10, and free for children under 3.

ORGANIZED TOURS

BY BOAT From September through May **Heritage Tours of Miami II** features jaunts aboard an 85-foot schooner. Tours depart from the Bayside Marketplace at 401 Biscayne Blvd. (☎ **305/442-9697**). The daily 2-hour cruises pass by Villa Vizcaya, Coconut Grove, and Key Biscayne and put you in sight of Miami's spectacular skyline. They leave at 1:30, 4, and 6pm. Tickets cost $15 for adults and $10 for children under 12. On Friday, Saturday, and Sunday evenings, there are 1-hour tours to see the lights of the city at 9, 10, and 11pm.

ON FOOT An **Art-Deco District Walking Tour,** sponsored by the Miami Design Preservation League (☎ **305/672-2014**), leaves every Saturday at 10:30am from the Art Deco Welcome Center at 1001 Ocean Dr., South Beach. The 90-minute tour costs $10.

SHOPPING

Most cruise ship passengers shop right near the Port of Miami at **Bayside Marketplace,** a mall with 150 specialty shops at 401 Biscayne Blvd. Some 20 eateries serve everything from Nicaraguan to Italian food; there's even a Hard Rock Café. Many have outdoor seating right along the bay for picturesque views of the yachts harbored there (unfortunately, sometimes the water here is littered with debris like plastic bottles). You can also watch the street performers, enjoy the pulsating rhythms of live salsa music, or take a boat tour from here.

A free shuttle from the Hotel Inter-Continental in downtown Miami takes you to the **Bal Harbour Shops** at 9700 Collins Ave. They're Miami's version of Rodeo Drive, housing big-name stores from Chanel and Prada to Lacoste to Neiman-Marcus and Florida's largest Saks Fifth Avenue. In addition to shopping, Bal Harbour Shops is an ideal people-watching venue and a favorite hangout for foreigners looking to unload lots of cash before their trip back to their native countries.

In South Beach, **Lincoln Road,** an 8-block pedestrian mall, runs between Washington Avenue and Alton Road, near the northern tier of the Art Deco district. It's filled with popular shops such as the Gap and Banana Republic, interior-design stores, art galleries, and even vintage-clothing outlets, as well as coffeehouses, restaurants, and cafes. Despite the recent influx of commercial anchor stores, Lincoln Road still manages to maintain its funky, arty flair, attracting an eclectic, colorful crowd.

Just a short drive south of downtown, the Dadeland Mall, at the corner of U.S. Highway 1 and SW 88th Street (☎ **305/665-6226**), is the most popular shopping plaza in suburban Dade County. Its tenants include Burdines and Burdines Home Gallery, Lord & Taylor, and Saks Fifth Avenue. The food court offers many quick-bite options from fast food to sweets.

Coconut Grove, centered on Main Highway and Grand Avenue, is the heart of the city's boutique district and features two open-air shopping and entertainment complexes, **CocoWalk** and the **Streets of Mayfair.**

In Coral Gables, **Miracle Mile,** actually a half-mile stretch of SW 22nd Street between Douglas and Le Jeune roads, features more than 150 shops.

For a change of pace from the fast-paced glitz of South Beach or the serene luxury of Coral Gables, head for **Little Havana,** where pre-Castro Cubans commingle with young artists who have begun to set up performance spaces in the area. It's located just west of downtown Miami on SW Eighth Street. In addition to authentic Cuban cuisine, the cafe Cubano culture is alive and well.

ACCOMMODATIONS

Thanks to the network of highways, you can stay virtually anywhere in Greater Miami and still be within 10 to 20 minutes of your cruise ship.

DOWNTOWN   Set across the bay from the cruise ship piers, the **Miami Hotel Inter-Continental,** 100 Chopin Plaza (☎ **800/327-3005** or 305/577-1000), is a bold triangular tower soaring 34 stories.

SOUTH BEACH   The art-deco, comfy-chic ✪ **Hotel Astor,** 956 Washington Ave. (☎ **800/270-4981** or 305/531-8081), originally built in 1936, reopened after a massive renovation in 1995. The Astor is only 2 blocks from the beach, but if that's still too far for you, try the upscale **Hotel Ocean,** 1230–38 Ocean Dr. (☎ **800/783-1725** or 305/672-2579). If you're on a budget, but want a cozy Deco feel, try the **Park Washington Hotels**—Park Washington, Belaire, Taft, and Kenmore—a group of small, low-frills hotels next door to the Astor, at 1020 Washington Ave. (☎ **305/532-1930**). **The Delano,** 1685 Collins Ave. (☎ **800/555-5001** or 305/672-2000), is a sleek, postmodern, and self-consciously hip celebrity hot spot, but it's worth at least a peak. ✪ **The Hotel,** 801 Collins Ave. at the corner of Collins and 8th Street (☎ **305/531-5796**), formerly known as The Tiffany Hotel until the folks behind the little blue box threatened to sue, is a deco gem, not to mention the most fashionable hotel on

South Beach thanks to the whimsical interiors designed by haute couturier Todd Oldham. ✪ **The Tides,** 1300 Ocean Dr. (☎ **800/688-7678** or 305/604-5000), is located right on the beach and features a retro fab yet ultra-modern nautically inspired Deco monument. **The Kent,** 1131 Collins Ave. (☎ **305/531-6771**), like The Tides, is part of Chris Blackwell's Island Outpost chain and attracts a less upwardly mobile yet no less chic crowd of young, hip travelers.

MIAMI BEACH   At the ✪ **Indian Creek Hotel,** 2727 Indian Creek Dr. at 28th Street (☎ **800/491-2772** or 305/531-2727), each room is an homage to the 1930s art-deco age. **The Eden Roc,** 4525 Collins Ave. (☎ **800/327-8337** or 305/531-0000), and the **Fontainebleau Hilton Resort & Towers,** next door at 4441 Collins Ave. (☎ **800/ 548-8886** or 305/538-2000), are both popular, updated 1950s resorts evoking the bygone Rat Pack era, with spas, health clubs, outdoor swimming pools, and beach access. **The Beach House,** 9449 Collins Ave., in Surfside (☎ **305/865-3551**) brings a taste of Nantucket to Miami with soothing hues, comfortable furniture, oceanfront views, and a Ralph Lauren-decorated interior.

COCONUT GROVE   Near Miami's City Hall and the Coconut Grove Marina, the ✪ **Wyndham Grand Bay Hotel,** 2669 S. Bayshore Dr. (☎ **800/327-2788** or 305/ 838-9600), overlooks Biscayne Bay.

CORAL GABLES   The famous ✪ **Biltmore Hotel,** 1200 Anastasia Ave. (☎ **800/ 228-3000** or 305/445-1926), was restored a few years ago, but despite renovations, exudes an old-world, stately glamour and is rumored to be haunted by ghosts of travel days past. There's also the **Hotel Place St. Michel,** 162 Alcazar Ave. (☎ **800/848-HOTEL** or 305/444-1666), a three-story establishment reminiscent of an inn in provincial France.

KEY BISCAYNE   The **Sonesta Beach Resort Key Biscayne,** 350 Ocean Dr. (☎ **800/SONESTA** or 305/361-2021), offers relative isolation from the rest of congested Miami.

DINING

DOWNTOWN   **Lombardi's,** in Bayside Marketplace (☎ **305/381-9580**), is a moderately priced Italian restaurant. **East Coast Fisheries & Restaurant,** 360 W. Flagler at South River Drive (☎ **305/372-1300**), is a no-nonsense retail market and restaurant, offering a terrific variety of the freshest fish available. Further up Biscayne Boulevard near the burgeoning Miami Design District is **Soyka,** 5580 NE Fourth Court (☎ **305/759-3117**), the hip downtown sibling of South Beach's News and Van Dyke cafes.

SOUTH BEACH   Join the celebs and models at **Nemo's,** 100 Collins Ave. (☎ **305/ 532-4550**). Take time to stroll down the pedestrian mall on Lincoln Road, which offers art galleries, specialty shops, and several excellent outdoor cafes such as **Spris,** 731 Lincoln Rd. (☎ **305/673-2020**), the **Van Dyke Cafe,** 846 Lincoln Rd. (☎ **305/ 534-3600**), and **Tiramesu,** 731 Lincoln Rd. (☎ **305/532-4538**). The standout culinary trendsetter on Lincoln Road, however, is **Pacific Time,** 915 Lincoln Rd. (☎ **305/ 534-5979**), where you can enjoy a taste of the Pacific Rim with a deliciously modern South Beach twist. Another Asian-inspired newcomer to Lincoln Road is **Bambu,** 1661 Meridian Ave. (☎ **305/531-4800**), the hot eatery co-owned by actress Cameron Diaz. At the legendary **Joe's Stone Crab,** 227 Biscayne St., between Washington and Collins avenues (☎ **305/673-0365**), about a ton of stone-crab claws are served daily during stone-crab season from October to May, and keep people waiting for up to 2 hours for a table. Even if Gloria Estefan weren't part-owner of **Larios on the Beach,** 820 Ocean

Dr. (☎ **305/532-9577**), the crowds would still flock to this bistro serving old-fashioned Cuban dishes, such as *masitas de puerco* (fried pork chunks).

COCONUT GROVE If you'd like to people-watch while you eat, head for **Café Tu Tu Tango,** 3015 Grand Ave. (☎ **305/529-2222**), on the second floor of CocoWalk. This second-floor restaurant is designed to look like a disheveled artist's loft, complete with original paintings (some half-finished) on easels or hanging from the walls.

CORAL GABLES ✪ **Norman's,** 21 Almeria Ave. (☎ **305/446-6767**), possibly the best restaurant in the entire city of Miami, is run by its namesake, Norman Van Aken, a James Beard award-winning chef and pioneer of New World and Floribbean cuisine.

KEY BISCAYNE The surf and turf is routine at the **Rusty Pelican,** 3201 Rickenbacker Causeway (☎ **305/361-3818**), but it's worth coming for a drink and the spectacular sunset view.

LITTLE HAVANA One reason to visit Little Havana is to enjoy its excellent Hispanic cuisine. **Casa Panza Restaurant,** 1620 SW Eighth St. (☎ **305/643-5343**), a taste of old Seville in Little Havana, is a feast for the senses with flamenco dancers, tempting tapas, and a lively atmosphere that reels in crowds on a nightly basis. At 11pm, everyone, no matter what their religion, is given a candle to pray to La Virgen del Rocio, one of Seville's most revered saints—it's a party with piety! Another place to check out is **Versailles,** 3555 SW Eighth St. (☎ **305/538-8533**), a 24-hour palatial, mirrored diner serving all the Cuban mainstays in large and reasonably priced portions.

MIAMI AFTER DARK

Miami nightlife is as varied as its population. Known as Hollywood-south, Miami's sizzling nightlife is no stranger to A-list celebrities from Leonardo DiCaprio and Al Pacino to Gwyneth Paltrow, Sylvester Stallone, and part-time resident Madonna. Look for the klieg lights to direct you to the hot spots of South Beach. And while the blocks of Washington Avenue, Collins Avenue, and Ocean Drive are the main nightlife thoroughfares, you're more likely to spot a celebrity in a more off-the-beaten-path eatery such as **Tantra,** a grass-floored, Middle Eastern (aphrodisiac-inspired) eatery and late-night hangout at 1445 Pennsylvania Ave. (☎ **305/672-4765**); **Joia,** a popular, chic Italian eatery at 140 Ocean Dr. (☎ **305/674-8855**); or the **Forge,** 432 41st St. (☎ **305/ 538-8533**), an ornately decorated rococo-style steak house boasting one of the finest wine selections around (☎ **305/538-8533**). Another hot spot is the Cameron Diaz– co-owned **Bambu,** 1661 Meridian Ave. (☎ **305/531-4800**), an Asian eatery and celebrity magnet with a chichi private upstairs lounge. Restaurants and bars are open late—usually until 5am. Also popular are the hotel bars such as the Delano's **Rose Bar** and the Rubell-owned **Albion's Falabella Bar,** 1650 James Ave. (☎ **888/665-0008**).

As trends come and go, so do clubs, so before you head out for a decadent night of disco, make sure the place is still in business! As of press time, the clubs at which to see, be seen, and, of course, dance, were **Bar Room,** 320 Lincoln Rd. (☎ **305/604-0480**); **Groove Jet,** 323 23rd St. (☎ **305/532-2002**); **crobar,** 1445 Washington Ave. (☎ **305/531-5027**); **Level,** 1235 Washington Ave. (☎ **305/532-1525**); and **Bash,** 655 Washington Ave. (☎ **305/538-2274**).

But South Beach isn't the only place for nightlife in Miami. Not too far from the Miami River is the city's oldest bar, **Tobacco Road,** 626 S. Miami Ave. (☎ **305/ 0374-1198**), a nitty-gritty place which still attracts some of the city's storied, pre–"Miami Vice" natives. **ClubSpace,** 11th Street at NE Second Ave. (☎ **305/577-1007**), occupies a very large warehouse in Downtown Miami and is vaguely reminiscent of a funky, SoHo-style dance palace. Down in Little Havana is **Café Nostalgia,** 2212 SW Eighth St. (☎ **305/541-2631**), where salsa is not a condiment but a way of life.

Other nocturnal options abound in Coconut Grove and Coral Gables and, slowly but surely, the downtown/Design District areas. Check the *Miami Herald, Miami New Times,* and **miami.citysearch.com** for specific events.

2 Fort Lauderdale & Port Everglades

Port Everglades, in Broward County, is the second-busiest cruise port in the world. It boasts the deepest harbor south of Norfolk along the eastern seaboard, an ultra-modern cruise ship terminal, and an easy access route to the Fort Lauderdale airport, less than a 5-minute drive away. The port lies some 40 miles north of Miami's center.

The port itself is fairly free of congestion. Ten modern cruise terminals offer covered loading zones, drop-off and pickup staging, and curbside baggage handlers. An 11th terminal is underway for completion in late 2001, with plans for a couple more terminals within the next 5 years or so. Terminals are comfortable and safe, with seating areas, snack bars, lots of taxis, clean rest rooms, and plenty of pay phones. Parking lots have recently been expanded to offer a total of 4,500 parking places.

For information about the port, call **Port Everglades Authority** at ☎ **954/ 523-3404.**

GETTING TO FORT LAUDERDALE & THE PORT

BY AIR   Small and extremely user-friendly, the **Fort Lauderdale/Hollywood International Airport** (☎ **954/359-6100**) is less than 2 miles from Port Everglades, making this the easiest airport-to-cruiseport trip in Florida—what could be easier than a 5-minute bus or cab ride? (Port Canaveral, on the other hand, is about an hour's drive from the Orlando airport.) Cruise line **buses** meet incoming flights when they know transfer passengers are on board, so make arrangements for pickup when you book your cruise. Taking a **taxi** to the port costs less than $10.

BY CAR   The port has three passenger entrances: Spangler Boulevard, an extension of State Road 84 East; Eisenhower Boulevard, running south from the 17th Street Causeway (A1A); and Eller Drive, connecting directly with Interstate 595. Interstate 595 runs east-west, with connections to the Fort Lauderdale/Hollywood Airport, Interstate 95, State Road 7 (441), Florida's Turnpike, Sawgrass Expressway, and Interstate 75. Convenient parking is available at the port in two large garages. The 2,500-space Northport Parking Garage, next to the Greater Fort Lauderdale/Broward County Convention Center, serves terminals 1, 2, and 4. The 2,000-space Midport Parking Garage serves terminals 18, 19, 21, 22, 24, 25, and 26. Garages are well lit, security-patrolled, and designed to accommodate RVs and buses. The 24-hour parking fee is about $8.

BY TRAIN   Amtrak (☎ **800/USA-RAIL**) trains from New York to Miami make various stops along the way, including Fort Lauderdale. The local station is at 200 SW 21st Terrace (☎ **954/587-6692** or 305/835-1123). Taxis are lined up to deliver you to Port Everglades for a $10 to $15 fare.

EXPLORING FORT LAUDERDALE

Fort Lauderdale Beach, a 2-mile strip along Florida A1A, gained fame in the 1950s as a spring-break playground, popularized by the movie *Where the Boys Are.* But in the 1980s, partying college kids, who brought the city more mayhem than money, began to be less welcome. Fort Lauderdale tried to attract a more mainstream, affluent crowd in an effort to transform itself into the "Venice of the Americas." The city has largely been successful.

In addition to miles of beautiful wide beaches, Fort Lauderdale has more than 300 miles of navigable natural waterways, in addition to innumerable artificial canals that permit thousands of residents to anchor boats in their backyards. You too can easily get on the water by renting a boat or hailing a private, moderately priced water taxi.

VISITOR INFORMATION   The **Greater Fort Lauderdale Convention & Visitors Bureau,** 1850 Eller Dr., Suite 303, Fort Lauderdale, FL 33316 (☎ **954/765-4466**), is an excellent resource, distributing a comprehensive guide on events and sightseeing in Broward County.

GETTING AROUND   For a taxi, call **Yellow Cab** (☎ **954/565-5400**). Rates start at $2.45 for the first mile and $1.75 for each additional mile. **Broward County Mass Transit** (☎ **954/357-8400**) runs bus service throughout the county. Each ride costs $1.15 for the first transfer and 15¢ for each additional same-day transfer.

HITTING THE BEACH

Backed by an endless row of hotels and popular with visitors and locals alike, the **Fort Lauderdale Beach Promenade** underwent a $20-million renovation not long back, and it looks marvelous. It's located along Atlantic Boulevard (Fla. A1A), between SE 17th Street and Sunrise Boulevard. The fabled strip from *Where the Boys Are* is **Ocean Boulevard,** between Las Olas Boulevard and Sunrise Boulevard. On weekends, parking at the ocean-side meters is difficult to find.

Fort Lauderdale Beach at the Howard Johnson is a perennial local favorite. A jetty bounds the beach on the south side, making it rather private, although the water gets a little choppy. High-school and college students share this area with an older crowd. The beach is at 4660 N. Ocean Dr. in Lauderdale by the Sea.

SEEING THE SIGHTS

The **Museum of Discovery & Science,** 401 SW Second St. (☎ **954/467-6637**), is an excellent interactive science museum with an IMAX theater. Check out the 52-foot-tall "Great Gravity Clock" in the museum's atrium.

The **Museum of Art,** 1 E. Las Olas Blvd. (☎ **954/763-6464**), is a truly terrific small museum of modern and contemporary art.

A guided tour of the **Bonnet House,** 900 N. Birch Rd. (☎ **954/563-5393**), offers a glimpse into the lives of the pioneers of the Fort Lauderdale area. This unique 35-acre plantation-style home and estate survives in the middle of an otherwise highly developed beachfront condominium area. One-hour tours are offered Wednesday through Friday at 10:30am, 11:30am, 12:30pm, and 1:30pm, Saturday and Sunday at 12:30, 1:15, 1:45, and 2:30pm; arrive 15 minutes before the tour. $9 adults, $8 senior citizens, $7 students.

Butterfly World, Tradewinds Park South, 3600 W. Sample Rd., Coconut Creek, west of the Florida Turnpike (☎ **954/977-4400**), cultivates more than 150 species of these colorful and delicate insects. In the park's walk-through, screened-in aviary, visitors can watch newborn butterflies emerge from their cocoons and flutter around as they learn to fly. It's open from 9am to 5pm Monday through Sunday. Admission is $12.95 for adults, $7.95 for kids 4 to 12, free for kids under 4.

ORGANIZED TOURS

BY BOAT   The Mississippi River–style steamer *Jungle Queen,* Bahia Mar Yacht Center, Florida A1A (☎ **954/462-5596**), is one of Fort Lauderdale's best-known attractions. Dinner cruises and 3-hour sightseeing tours take visitors up the New River past Millionaires' Row, Old Fort Lauderdale, the new downtown, and the Port Everglades cruise ship port. Call for prices and departure times.

Fort Lauderdale at a Glance

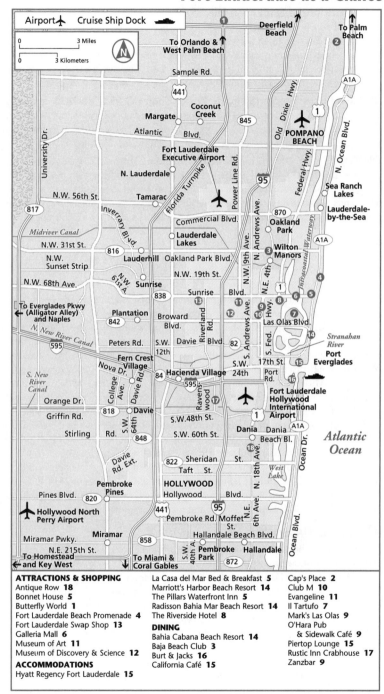

Airport ✈   Cruise Ship Dock 🚢

0 — 3 Miles
0 — 3 Kilometers

Deerfield Beach
To Palm Beach
To Orlando & West Palm Beach
Sample Rd.
441
Margate
Coconut Creek
845
Old Dixie Hwy.
POMPANO BEACH
A1A
1
Atlantic Blvd.
Fort Lauderdale Executive Airport
N. Lauderdale
Power Line Rd.
95
Federal Hwy.
Sea Ranch Lakes
Lauderdale-by-the-Sea
University Dr.
N.W. 56th St.
Tamarac
Florida Turnpike
Intracoastal Waterway
817
Inverrary Blvd.
Midriver Canal
Commercial Blvd.
Lauderdale Lakes
870
Oakland Park
A1A
N.W. 31st St.
816
Lauderhill
Oakland Park Blvd.
N. Andrews Ave.
N.W. 9th Ave.
Wilton Manors
N.W. Sunset Strip
N.W. 19th St.
N.E. 4th Ave.
N.W. 68th Ave.
N.W. 61st Ave.
Sunrise
838
Sunrise Blvd.
To Everglades Pkwy. (Alligator Alley) and Naples
Plantation
842
Broward Blvd.
Riverland Rd.
Hwy.
Las Olas Blvd.
N. New River Canal
Peters Rd.
S.W. Davie Blvd.
82
S. Fed.
Stranahan River
595
S.W. 12th
S. Andrews Ave.
Port Everglades
Fern Crest Village
Nova Dr.
84
Hacienda Village
S.W. 24th
S.W. 17th St.
Port Rd.
S. New River Canal
College Ave.
Davie Rd.
595
Ravenswood
Fort Lauderdale Hollywood International Airport
Orange Dr.
818
Davie
S.W. 64th Ave.
S.W.48th St.
1
Dania
Dania
A1A
Atlantic Ocean
Griffin Rd.
848
S.W. 60th St.
Beach Bl.
Ocean Dr.
Stirling Rd.
Davie Rd. Ext.
822
Sheridan St.
N. 18th Ave.
West Lake
Pembroke Pines
820
Taft St.
HOLLYWOOD
Hollywood Blvd.
Pines Blvd.
441
95
6th Ave.
N.E.
Hollywood North Perry Airport
Pembroke Rd.
Moffet St.
Ocean Blvd.
Miramar Pkwy.
Miramar
858
Hallandale Beach Blvd.
N.E. 215th St.
S.W. 40th A.
Pembroke Park
Hallandale
872
To Homestead and Key West
To Miami & Coral Gables

ATTRACTIONS & SHOPPING
Antique Row **18**
Bonnet House **5**
Butterfly World **1**
Fort Lauderdale Beach Promenade **4**
Fort Lauderdale Swap Shop **13**
Galleria Mall **6**
Museum of Art **11**
Museum of Discovery & Science **12**

ACCOMMODATIONS
Hyatt Regency Fort Lauderdale **15**

La Casa del Mar Bed & Breakfast **5**
Marriott's Harbor Beach Resort **14**
The Pillars Waterfront Inn **5**
Radisson Bahia Mar Beach Resort **14**
The Riverside Hotel **8**

DINING
Bahia Cabana Beach Resort **14**
Baja Beach Club **3**
Burt & Jacks **16**
California Café **15**

Cap's Place **2**
Club M **10**
Evangeline **11**
Il Tartufo **7**
Mark's Las Olas **9**
O'Hara Pub
   & Sidewalk Café **9**
Piertop Lounge **15**
Rustic Inn Crabhouse **17**
Zanzbar **9**

✪ **Water Taxi of Fort Lauderdale,** 651 Seabreeze Blvd. (☎ **954/467-6677**), is a fleet of old port boats that navigate this city of canals. The boats operate taxi service on demand and carry up to 48 passengers each. You can be picked up at your hotel and shuttled to the dozens of restaurants and bars on the route for the rest of the night. The service operates daily from 10am to midnight or 2am. The cost is $7.50 per person per trip, $14 round-trip, $16 for a full day. Opt for the all-day pass—it's worth it.

BY TROLLEY BUS   South Florida Trolley Tours (☎ **954/946-7320**) covers Fort Lauderdale's entire history during a 90-minute air-conditioned trolley tour. Tours cost $12 for adults; children under 12 are free. The trolleys pick up passengers from most major hotels for three tours daily, at 9:30am, 12:05pm, and 2:10pm.

ON FOOT   **The **Old Ft. Lauderdale Museum of History, 231 SW Second Ave. (☎ **954/463-4431**) is open Tuesday to Friday from noon to 5pm, Saturday from 10am to 5pm, and Sunday from noon to 5pm. On occasion, walking tours of the city's historic center are offered. You can also walk along **Riverwalk,** a 10-mile linear park along the New River that connects the cultural heart of Fort Lauderdale to its historic district.

SHOPPING

Not counting the discount "fashion" stores on Hallandale Beach Boulevard, there are three places every visitor to Broward County should know about.

The first is **Antique Row,** a strip of U.S. 1 around North Dania Beach Boulevard (in Dania, about 1 mile south of Fort Lauderdale/Hollywood International Airport) that holds about 200 antique shops. Most shops are closed Sunday.

The **Fort Lauderdale Swap Shop,** 3291 W. Sunrise Blvd. (☎ **954/791-SWAP**), is one of the world's largest flea markets. In addition to endless acres of vendors, there's a mini–amusement park, a 13-screen drive-in movie theater, and even a free circus complete with elephants, horse shows, high-wire acts, and clowns. It's open daily.

Sawgrass Mills, 12801 W. Sunrise Blvd., Sunrise (☎ **954/846-2300**), a behemoth mall shaped like a Florida alligator, covers nearly 2.5 million square feet, including more than 300 shops and kiosks, such as Saks Fifth Avenue, Levi's, Ann Taylor, Waterford Crystal, and hundreds more, offering prices 20% to 60% lower than in the Caribbean. Take Interstate 95 North to 595 West until Flamingo Road, where you'll exit and turn right. Drive 2 miles to Sunrise Boulevard.

Not for bargain hunters, swanky **Las Olas Boulevard** hosts literally hundreds of unusual boutiques. Close to Fort Lauderdale Beach, the **Galleria** mall, 2414 E. Sunrise Blvd., between NE 26th Avenue and Middle River Drive (☎ **954/564-1015**), has Neiman-Marcus, Saks, Lord & Taylor, and many other stores.

ACCOMMODATIONS

Fort Lauderdale Beach has a hotel or motel on nearly every block, and the selection ranges from run-down to luxurious.

✪ **Hyatt Regency Fort Lauderdale** at Pier 66 Marina, 2301 SE 17th St. Causeway (☎ **800/233-1234** or 954/525-6666), is a circular landmark with larger rooms than some equivalently priced hotels in town. Its famous Piertop Lounge, a revolving bar on its roof, is often filled with cruise ship patrons.

Marriott's Harbor Beach Resort, 3030 Holiday Dr. (☎ **800/222-6543** or 954/525-4000), is the only Marriott resort set directly on the beach. Its modest-size bedrooms have water views.

Radisson Bahia Mar Beach Resort, 801 Seabreeze Blvd. (☎ **800/327-8154** or 954/764-2233), is scattered over 42 acres of seacoast. A four-story row of units is adjacent to Florida's largest marina. **The Riverside Hotel,** 620 E. Las Olas Blvd.

(☎ 800/325-3280 or 954/467-0671), which opened in 1936, is a local favorite. Try for a ground-floor room, which has higher ceilings and more space.

La Casa del Mar Bed & Breakfast, 3003 Grand Granada St. (☎ **800/739-0009** or 954/467-2037), a 10-room Spanish-inspired inn, appeals to the bed-and-breakfast fancier and is only a block away from Fort Lauderdale Beach. **The Pillars Waterfront Inn,** 111 N. Birch Rd. (☎ **954/467-9639**), is a small, 23-room inn, the best of its size in the region. The clean and simple accommodations have very comfortable beds. Call the **Fort Lauderdale Convention and Visitors Bureau** (☎ **954/765-4466**) for a copy of *Superior Small Lodgings,* a guide to other accommodations in the area.

A number of chains operate here, including **Best Western** (☎ 800 528-1234), **Days Inn** (☎ 800/325-2525), **Doubletree Hotels** (☎ 800/222-8733), and **Holiday Inn** (☎ 800/465-4329).

DINING

The only restaurant at Port Everglades, ✪ **Burt & Jacks,** at Berth 23 (☎ **954/522-2878**), is a collaboration between actor-director Burt Reynolds and restaurateur Jack Jackson. As you sit at this elegant restaurant, you can watch the cruise ships and other boats pass by. A waiter will arrive with steaks, lobster, veal, pork chops, and more; you choose and your dish will arrive perfectly cooked. Reservations are required and so are jackets for men.

Bahia Cabana Beach Resort, 3001 Harbor Dr. (☎ **954/524-1555**), offers American-style meals three times a day in hearty portions. The hotel's bar, known for its Frozen Rumrunner, is the most charming and laid-back in town.

In the shadow of the Hyatt Pier 66 Hotel, **California Café,** Pier 66, 2301 SE 17th Causeway (☎ **954/728-8255**), serves avant-garde modern cuisine at affordable prices.

Cap's Place, 2765 NE 28th Court, in Lighthouse Point (☎ **954/941-0418**), is a famous old-time seafood joint, offering good food at reasonable prices. The restaurant is on a peninsula; you get a ferry ride over. Dolphin (not the mammal but a local saltwater fish also known as mahimahi) and grouper are popular, and like the other meat and pasta dishes here, can be prepared any way you want.

Evangeline, 211 Hwy. A1A at Las Olas Boulevard (☎ **954/522-7001**), as the name suggests, is a Cajun-style place. At lunch, enjoy an oyster or catfish po' boy, or rabbit gumbo for dinner. You can also try the alligator.

Il Tartufo, 2400 E. Las Olas Blvd. (☎ **954/767-9190**), is the most charming and fun Italian restaurant in Fort Lauderdale. It serves oven-roasted specialties and other Italian standards, plus a selection of fish baked in rock salt.

Mark's Las Olas, 1032 E. Las Olas Blvd. (☎ **954/463-1000**), is the showcase of Miami restaurant mogul Mark Militello. The daily changing menu is continental gourmet and might include Jamaican jerk chicken with fresh coconut salad or a superb sushi-quality tuna.

Zanzbar, 602 E. Las Olas Blvd. (☎ **954/767-3377**), serves the food and wine of South Africa, and not many places can boast that. For a taste of the country, order a sample platter for two that includes ostrich tips, cured beef strips, and savory sausages.

Garlic crabs are the specialty at the **Rustic Inn Crabhouse,** 4331 Ravenswood Rd. (☎ **954/584-1637**), located west of the airport. This riverside dining choice has an open deck over the water.

FORT LAUDERDALE AFTER DARK

From the area's most famous bar, the ✪ **Piertop Lounge,** in the Hyatt Regency at Pier 66 (☎ **954/525-6666**), you'll get a 360° panoramic view of Fort Lauderdale. The bar turns every 66 minutes. There's a dance floor and live music, including blues and jazz.

On weekends it's hard to get into **Club M,** 2037 Hollywood Blvd. (☎ **954/ 925-8396**), one of the area's busiest music bars. Although the small club used to be a local blues showcase, it now features a DJ and live bands on weekends playing blues, rock, and jazz.

O'Hara Pub & Sidewalk Café, 722 E. Las Olas Blvd. (☎ **954/524-1764**), is often packed with a trendy crowd who come to listen to live blues and jazz. Call their jazz hot line (☎ **954/524-2801**) to hear the lineup.

If you want to dance, try the **Baja Beach Club,** 3200 N. Federal Hwy. (☎ **954/ 563-8494**), perhaps the world's only dance club that anchors an entire shopping mall.

With the 1991 completion of the **Broward Center for the Performing Arts,** 201 SW Fifth Ave. (☎ **954/462-0222**), Fort Lauderdale finally got itself the venue it craved for top opera, symphony, dance, and Broadway productions. Look for listings in the *Sun-Sentinel* or the *Miami Herald* for schedules and performers or call the 24-hour **Arts & Entertainment Hotline** (☎ **954/357-5700**).

3 Cape Canaveral & Port Canaveral

Underrated Port Canaveral is Florida's most unusual and multifaceted port, with facilities that are the most up-to-date, stylish, and least congested of any port in Florida. After years of underutilization, the cruise industry is starting to give the port the attention it's due. With the competition between a stronger Premier, an expanded Disney product, Carnival, and Royal Caribbean, Port Canaveral's 3-to-4-day-cruise market continues to remain strong and keeps this port on the map. Cruise lines appreciate the port's proximity to Cape Canaveral's Kennedy Space Center and Walt Disney World at Orlando. Many lines offer pre- or postcruise packages.

The 3,300-acre port covers an area larger than the Port of Miami. Terminal no. 9/ 10, completed in 1995, was built in a modern, dramatic style. Terminal no. 5, built in 1991, looks a bit like a glossy downtown hotel. The new Disney terminal, no. 8, the port's newest, was built in 1998 in an updated, Disneyfied art-deco style. The other terminals are more the traditional, industrial-looking kind. On the drawing boards is a fourth mega cruise ship terminal, no. 6/7. As you head for your cruise ship, look for shrimp- and fishnets drying in the sun. This port is the home base for the region's fishing industry.

GETTING TO CAPE CANAVERAL & THE PORT

Port Canaveral is located at the Cape Canaveral side of the Bennett Causeway on the 528 Bee Line Expressway. For information about the port, call the **Canaveral Port Authority** at ☎ **407/783-7831.**

BY AIR   The nearest airport is the **Orlando International Airport** (☎ **407/ 825-2001**), a 45-mile drive from Port Canaveral via Highway 528 (the Bee Line Expressway). Cruise line representatives will meet you if you've booked air and/or transfers through the line. **Cocoa Beach Shuttle** (☎ **800/633-0427** or 407/784-3831) offers shuttle service between Orlando's airport and Port Canaveral; the trip costs $20 per person each way.

BY CAR   Port Canaveral and Cocoa Beach are about 35 miles southeast of Orlando and 190 miles north of Miami. They're accessible from virtually every interstate highway along the east coast. Most visitors arrive via Route 1, Interstate 95, or Highway 528 (the Bee Line Expressway from Orlando). At the port, park in the North Lots for north terminals nos. 5 and 10 and the South Lots for nos. 2, 3, or 4. Parking costs $7 a day.

Cape Canaveral at a Glance

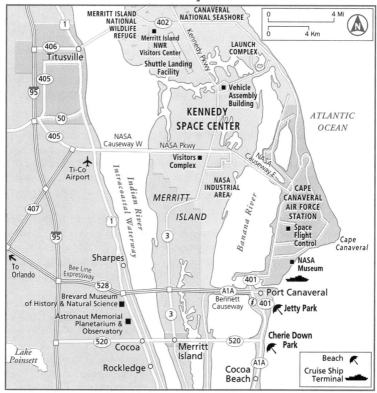

BY TRAIN   **Amtrak** (☎ **800/USA-RAIL**) trains make stops at Kissimmee, Sanford, and Orlando, the closest points to the port, but still about 55 to 60 miles away. You'll have to rent a car or take a taxi to the port. The **Kissimmee railway station** is at 316 Pleasant St. (☎ **407/933-1170;** corner of Dakin Street and Thurman Street). The **Orlando station** is at 1400 Sligh Blvd. (☎ **407/843-7611**), between Columbia and Miller streets.

EXPLORING CAPE CANAVERAL

Most passengers spend only a night or two in Cocoa Beach, visiting the Kennedy Space Center and going to the beach, before rushing to nearby Orlando and Walt Disney World.

VISITOR INFORMATION   Contact the **Cocoa Beach Chamber of Commerce,** 400 Fortenberry Rd., Merritt Island, FL 32952 (☎ **407/459-2200**).

GETTING AROUND   For taxis, call **Comfort Travel** (☎ **800/567-6139,** 407/784-8294, or 407/799-0442). Buses are run by the **Space Coast Area Transit Authority (SCAT)** (☎ **407/633-1878** for information and schedules). A ticket costs $1 for adults, 50¢ for senior citizens, and is free for children under 6. No buses pass close to the port.

✪ TOURING THE JOHN F. KENNEDY SPACE CENTER

Set amid many square miles of marshy wetlands favored by birds, reptiles, and amphibians, the **John F. Kennedy Space Center Visitor Complex** (☎ **407/452-2121**), open

Monday through Friday from 8am to 5:30pm, has played an important role in the minds of people around the world as the cradle of the space age and a symbol of America's technological prowess. Even if you've never really considered yourself a science buff, you'll appreciate the sheer grandeur of the place and the achievements represented by the facilities here. A $120-million renovation of the site, completed in 1999, has sparked it with new life, making it more appealing for visitors than ever. The visitor center stands with an isolated, even eerie, dignity within the municipality of the Space Center.

The sheer scope of the site can be confusing, even baffling, without some guidance from the organization's official caretakers. Parking is free in any of the vast lots nearby. (Remember to note the location of your car!) It's best to make a stop—maps and advice are free—at a highly visible booth, Information Central, within the visitor center. It maintains the same hours (9am to 5:30pm daily except Christmas and some launch days) as the complex itself. Expect to spend a full day on-site to best experience the wealth of options.

The core of the site revolves around the visitor center, site of the **Rocket Garden,** which displays the now-obsolete shells of at least eight space rockets that during their heydays were the hottest things in the world of astrophysics. There are also hundreds of exhibitions and a timeline of photographs detailing humankind's exploration of space. The visitor center is also home to two IMAX theaters that show three separate films, each about 45 minutes long.

Some visitors pressed for time opt to remain entirely within the center, which does not charge admission. But for a more complete insight into the space age, take a bus tour of the complicated subdivisions that rise from the hundreds of acres of marshy flatlands nearby. Self-guided and self-timed, they depart at 15-minute intervals. Each bus is equipped with video screens portraying great moments of the space program's past. Tours make stops at three pivotal points within the complex, the Apollo Saturn V Center, Launch Complex 39, and the International Space Station Center.

The most comprehensive visitor package is the **Crew Pass.** Priced at $26 for adults, and $20 for children aged 4 to 11, free for children under 4, it includes unlimited access to any of the tour buses and entrance to any one of the ongoing IMAX movies. The Maximum Access Badge pass combines the Kennedy Space Center tour with two IMAX movies at $26 for adults and $20 for kids. The tour itself, without access to any of the IMAX theaters, costs $14 for adults and $10 for children under 11. Admission to the visitor center itself is free. Individual IMAX films are $7.50 each per adult, and $5.50 per child under 11. Most major credit cards are accepted throughout the complex.

There's a handful of fast-food, theme-parkish eateries adjacent to the visitor center. Among the cheapest and least formal of the bunch is something called The Launch Pad, serving family-friendly burgers and hot dogs. Better-recommended is Mila's, a fancy diner serving American-style platters, sandwiches, and salads.

ANOTHER SPACE-RELATED ATTRACTION

Six miles west of the Kennedy Space Center is the **U.S. Astronaut Hall of Fame,** State Rd. 405, 6225 Vectorspace Blvd., Titusville (☎ **407/269-6100**), a satellite attraction founded by the astronauts who flew the first *Mercury* and *Gemini* missions into outer space. It contains space-program memorabilia, displayed with a decidedly human and anecdotal touch. It's open daily from 9am to 5pm. Admission is $13.95 for adults, $9.95 for kids 6 to 12, and free for children 5 and under.

Wanna See a Launch?

There are only about a dozen launches from the Kennedy Space Center every year, so chances are you won't catch one. Still, you never know. Call ☎ **407/449-4322** for schedule information; it costs $10 to get on the property. During launch days, some parts of the complex, including Launch Complex 39 and its Observation Gantry, are firmly closed to everyone except NASA insiders.

HITTING THE BEACH

Cocoa Beach, Merritt Island, and the surrounding landscapes are known as "The Space Coast," and most of the beaches there are called "parks." Here are my favorites.

Jetty Park, 400 E. Jetty Rd., near the port, is more like a Florida version of Coney Island than the parks described below. The area has been recently renovated. A massive stone asphalt-topped jetty juts seaward as protection for the mouth of Port Canaveral. You'll see dozens of anglers there waiting for a bite. Parking costs $1 per car.

On the border between Cocoa Beach and Cape Canaveral, **Cherie Down Park,** 8492 Ridgewood Ave., is a relatively tranquil sunning and swimming area. You'll find a boardwalk, as well as showers, picnic shelters, and a public rest room. Parking is $1 per car.

Set in the heart of Cocoa Beach, **Lori Wilson Park,** 1500 N. Atlantic Ave., has children's playgrounds and a boardwalk that extends through about 5 acres of protected grasslands. Parking is $1 per car. Next to it is **Fischer Park,** with public rest rooms and a seasonal scattering of food kiosks. Parking is $2 per car.

The region's best surfing is at **Robert P. Murkshe Memorial Park,** SR A1A and 16th streets, Cocoa Beach, which also has a boardwalk and public rest rooms.

SHOPPING

Cocoa Beach offers a wide array of shopping, but the most unique shopping experience is **Ron Jon Surf Shop,** 4151 N. Atlantic Ave., Cocoa Beach, as you're driving down Florida AIA. The wildly original art-deco building is more interesting than the merchandise, but if you're looking for a surfing souvenir, you'll find it here. The store also rents beach bikes, boogie boards, surfboards, in-line skates, and other fun stuff by the hour, day, or week. It's open 24 hours a day.

ACCOMMODATIONS

Closest to the port and the Kennedy Space Center is the ✪ **Radisson Resort at the Port,** 8701 Astronaut Blvd. (☎ **800/333-3333** or 407/784-0000). The bedrooms are comfortable, but not as wonderful as those at The Inn at Cocoa Beach (see below). Chain hotels in the area include the **Cocoa Beach Hilton,** 1550 N. Atlantic Ave. (A1A) (☎ **800/HILTONS** or 407/799-0003); the **Holiday Inn Cocoa Beach Ocean Front Resort,** 1300 N. Atlantic Ave. (☎ **800/206-2747** or 407/783-2271), more upscale and better designed than the average Holiday Inn; and the **Howard Johnson Express Hotel/Cocoa Beach,** 2082 N. Atlantic Ave. (☎ **800/654-2000** or 321/783-8855).

Between the sea and route AIA and behind Ron Jon Surf Shop, ✪ **The Inn at Cocoa Beach,** 4300 Ocean Beach Blvd. (☎ **800/343-5307** or 407/799-3460), is more of an upscale, personalized inn than a traditional hotel (it even calls itself an oversize bed-and-breakfast). A taxi from Port Canaveral to the inn will cost around $12 to $15. Call **Comfort Taxi** at ☎ **407/799-0442.**

DINING

In the heart of Cocoa Beach, **Bernard's Surf,** 2 S. Atlantic Ave. (☎ 407/783-2401), has been a Florida institution since 1948. Specializing in steaks and seafood, the name "Bernard's Surf" should be followed by "and Turf"—it's a carnivore's paradise. The walls are adorned with pictures of astronauts who have celebrated their safe return to Earth with a filet mignon here.

Near the port is **Flamingo's,** in the Radisson Resort at the port, 8701 Astronaut Blvd. (☎ 407/784-0000). The fish dishes here are the best around the port, made with top-notch ingredients and deftly prepared.

✪ **The Mango Tree,** 118 N. Atlantic Ave. (☎ 407/799-0513), is the most beautiful and sophisticated restaurant in Cocoa Beach. Indian River crab cakes are perfectly flavored, and the sesame-seed-encrusted grouper with a tropical fruit salsa is yummy.

PORT CANAVERAL AFTER DARK

The Pier, 401 Meade Ave. (☎ 407/783-7549), is the largest and busiest entertainment complex in Cocoa Beach, crowded every afternoon and evening with diners, drinkers, and sunset-watchers. Two open-air cafes, four bars, and a pair of restaurants jut 800 feet beyond the shoreline into the waves and surf. At **Marlin's Good Times Bar and Grill,** you can enjoy fish platters, drinks, or sandwiches and a view of the sea that practically engulfs you. One or sometimes two bands play live 6 nights a week.

In Cocoa Beach's Heidelberg restaurant, the smoky and noisy **Heidi's Jazz Club,** 7 N. Orlando Ave. (☎ 407/783-6806), offers jazz and classic blues.

4 Tampa & the Port of Tampa

The Port of Tampa is set amid a complicated network of channels and harbors near the historic Cuban enclave of Ybor City and its deepwater Ybor Channel. The port's position on the western (Gulf) side of Florida makes it the logical departure point for ships headed for westerly ports of call, including the beaches and Mayan ruins of the Yucatán, the aquatic reefs of Central America, and the ports of Venezuela. The port's safe harbors have kept ships secure even during devastating tropical storms.

The bulk of the port's 400,000-plus annual passengers makes their way through the modern **Garrison Seaport cruise terminal** no. 2, which was doubled in size in 1998. The 30-acre site also includes the constantly evolving **Channelside,** a massive complex of restaurants, theaters, and shops inspired by Baltimore's Inner Harbor complex. This hub of waterfront activity and entertainment includes the Florida Aquarium and a multiscreen theater complex.

GETTING TO TAMPA & THE PORT

The **Garrison Seaport Terminal** at the Port of Tampa is located at 1101 Channelside Drive. For information, call ☎ 813/905-5044.

BY AIR **Tampa International Airport** (☎ 813/870-8700) lies 5 miles northwest of downtown Tampa, near the junction of Florida 60 and Memorial Highway. If you haven't arranged transfers with the cruise line, the port is an easy 15-minute taxi ride away; the fare is $10 to $15 via **Central Florida Limo** (☎ 813/396-3730). Travel Ways (☎ 813/643-5533) also runs a bus service, which costs $16 per person from the airport to Garrison Terminal.

BY CAR Tampa lies 200 miles southwest of Jacksonville, 63 miles north of Sarasota, and 254 miles northwest of Miami. It's easily accessible from Interstate 275, Interstate 75, Interstate 4, U.S. 41, U.S. 92, U.S. 301, and many state roads. The port has ample parking with good security, and costs $8 per day.

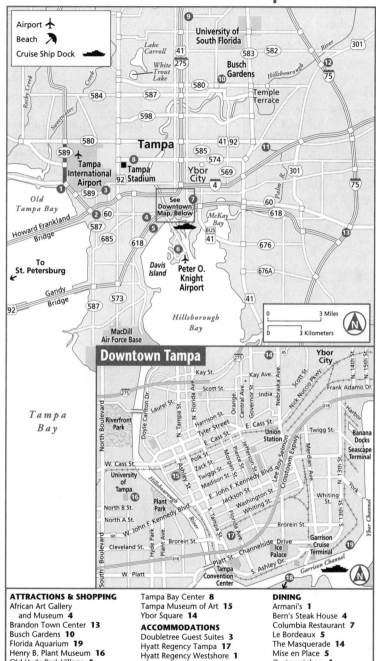

Tampa at a Glance

Legend:
- Airport ✈
- Beach
- Cruise Ship Dock

University of South Florida

Busch Gardens

Temple Terrace

Tampa

Tampa International Airport

Tampa Stadium

Ybor City

Old Tampa Bay

Howard Frankland Bridge

To St. Petersburg

Gandy Bridge

Davis Island

Peter O. Knight Airport

MacDill Air Force Base

Hillsborough Bay

McKay Bay

Lake Carroll
White Trout Lake

0 — 3 Miles
0 — 3 Kilometers

Downtown Tampa

Ybor City

Tampa Bay

Riverfront Park

University of Tampa

Plant Park

Henry B. Plant Museum

Tampa Convention Center

Union Station

Banana Docks

Seascape Terminal

Ice Palace

Garrison Cruise Terminal

Garrison Channel

Ybor Channel

ATTRACTIONS & SHOPPING

African Art Gallery
  and Museum **4**
Brandon Town Center **13**
Busch Gardens **10**
Florida Aquarium **19**
Henry B. Plant Museum **16**
Old Hyde Park Village **5**
Prime Outlets at Ellenton **12**
Shops on Harbour Island **18**

Tampa Bay Center **8**
Tampa Museum of Art **15**
Ybor Square **14**

ACCOMMODATIONS

Doubletree Guest Suites **3**
Hyatt Regency Tampa **17**
Hyatt Regency Westshore **1**
Wyndham Harbour Island **18**
Wyndham Westshore **2**

DINING

Armani's **1**
Bern's Steak House **4**
Columbia Restaurant **7**
Le Bordeaux **5**
The Masquerade **14**
Mise en Place **5**
Oystercatchers **1**
The Skipper Dome/
  Skipper's Smokehouse **9**

383

BY TRAIN Amtrak (☎ 800/USA-RAIL) trains arrive at the Tampa Amtrak Station, 601 Nebraska Ave., Tampa (☎ 813/221-7601). Taxi fare to the port costs $5 to $7.

EXPLORING TAMPA

Tampa is best explored by car, as only the commercial district can be covered on foot. If you want to go to the beach, you'll have to head to neighboring St. Petersburg.

VISITOR INFORMATION Contact the **Tampa/Hillsborough Convention and Visitors Association, Inc. (THCVA),** 400 North Tampa St., Suite 1010, Tampa, FL 33602 (☎ 800/44-TAMPA or 813/223-2752). You can also stop by the **Tampa Bay Visitor Information Center,** 3601 E. Busch Blvd. (☎ 813/985-3601), north of downtown in the Busch Gardens area. The office books organized tours of Tampa and the rest of Florida.

GETTING AROUND Taxis in Tampa do not normally cruise the streets for fares; instead, they line up at public loading places. You can also call **Yellow Cab** (☎ 813/253-0121) or **United Cab** (☎ 813/253-2424 or 813/251-5555).

The **Hillsborough Area Regional Transit/HARTline** (☎ 813/254-HART) provides regularly scheduled bus service between downtown Tampa and the suburbs. Fares are $1.15 for local services and $1.50 for express routes; exact change is required.

✪ BUSCH GARDENS

Yes, admission prices are high, but Busch Gardens remains Tampa Bay's most popular attraction. The 335-acre family entertainment park, at 3000 E. Busch Blvd. (☎ 888/800-5447 or 813/987-5171), features thrill rides, animal habitats, live entertainment, shops, restaurants, and games. The park's zoo ranks among the best in the country, with nearly 3,400 animals.

In 1996, Busch Gardens opened Montu, the world's tallest and longest inverted roller coaster. It's part of **Egypt,** the park's ninth themed area. The area includes a replica of King Tutankhamen's tomb, plus a sand-dig area for kids.

Timbuktu is a replica of an ancient desert trading center, complete with African craftspeople at work. It also features a sandstorm ride, Dolphin theater with daily shows, a boat-swing ride, a roller coaster, and an electronic-games arcade. **Morocco,** a walled city with exotic architecture, has Moroccan craft demonstrations, a sultan's tent with snake charmers, and the Marrakech Theaters. The **Serengeti Plain** is an open area with more than 500 African animals roaming freely in herds. This 80-acre natural grassy veldt can be viewed from the tram ride, the Trans-Veldt Railway, or the Skyride.

Nairobi is home to a natural habitat for various species of gorillas and chimpanzees, a baby-animal nursery, a petting zoo, reptile displays, and Curiosity Caverns, where visitors can observe animals active at night. **Stanleyville,** a prototype African village, has a shopping bazaar and live entertainment, as well as two water rides: the Tanganyika Tidal Wave and Stanley Falls. **The Congo** features white-water raft rides, as well as Kumba, the largest steel roller coaster in the southeastern United States, and Claw Island, a display of rare white Bengal tigers in a natural setting.

Bird Gardens, the original core of Busch Gardens, offers rich foliage, lagoons, and a free-flight aviary holding hundreds of exotic birds, including golden and American bald eagles, hawks, owls, and falcons. This area also features Land of the Dragons, a new children's adventure area.

Crown Colony, a multilevel restaurant overlooking the Serengeti plains, is the home of a team of Clydesdale horses, as well as the Anheuser-Busch hospitality center. Akbar's Adventure Tours, which offers a flight-simulator adventure experience, is located here.

A 1-day ticket costs $45.70 for adults, $36.75 for children ages 3 to 9; kids 2 and under are free. The park is open daily from 9am through 7pm, with extended hours in summer and during holiday periods. To get here, take Interstate 275 northeast of downtown to Busch Boulevard (Exit 33), and go east 2 miles to the entrance on 40th Street (McKinley Avenue). Parking costs $6.

MORE ATTRACTIONS

Only steps from the newly built Garrison Seaport Center, the ✪ **Florida Aquarium** (☎ 813/273-4000) celebrates the role of water in the development and maintenance of Florida's topography and ecosystems, with more than 10,000 aquatic plants and animals. An overriding theme follows a drop of water as it bubbles through Florida limestone and wends its way to the sea.

Thirteen silver minarets and distinctive Moorish architecture make the stunning ✪ **Henry B. Plant Museum,** 401 W. Kennedy Blvd. (☎ 813/254-1891), the focal point of the Tampa skyline. This National Historic Landmark, built in 1891 as the 511-room Tampa Bay Hotel, is filled with European and Oriental furnishings, and decorative arts from the original hotel collection. Definitely a worthwhile trip.

Only about a mile or so from the cruise ship docks, a visit to **Ybor City,** Tampa's historic Latin enclave and one of only three national historic districts in Florida, is a must. Once known as the cigar capital of the world, Ybor offers a charming slice of the past with its Spanish architecture, antique street lamps, wrought-iron balconies, ornate grillwork, and renovated cigar factories. Stroll along Seventh Avenue, the main artery (closed off to traffic at night), where you'll find cigar shops, boutiques, nightclubs, and the famous 100-year-old **Columbia Restaurant,** a classic covered in tiles and lots of historic character, serving up paella, Cuban sandwiches, seafood, and other local favorites. **Walking tours** of Ybor City are available, call the Ybor City Museum, 1818 E. Ninth Ave. (☎ 813/247-6323), for more info.

The **African Art Gallery and Museum,** 1711 W. Kennedy Blvd. (☎ 813/258-0223), features visual art by and about people of African descent. The collection includes ancient African artifacts and modern carvings and furniture.

The permanent collection of the **Tampa Museum of Art,** 600 N. Ashley Dr. (☎ 813/274-8130), is especially strong in ancient Greek, Etruscan, and Roman artifacts, as well as 20th-century art. The museum grounds, fronting the Hillsborough River, contain a sculpture garden and a decorative fountain.

In St. Petersburg, the ✪ **Salvador Dalí Museum,** 1000 Third St. S. (☎ 727/823-3767), contains the largest assemblage of the artist's works outside Spain. The former marine warehouse that houses this widely divergent collection is as starkly modern as the works of art displayed within. It's open Monday to Saturday from 9:30am to 5:30pm (Thurs till 8pm), Sunday from noon to 5:30pm. The entrance fee is $9 for adults, $7 for senior citizens, $5 for students, and free for children under 10.

ORGANIZED TOURS

BY BUS **Swiss Chalet Tours,** 3601 E. Busch Blvd. (☎ 813/985-3601), operates guided tours of Tampa, Ybor City, and the surrounding region. Four-hour (10am to 2pm) tours run on Monday and Thursday, and cost $40 for adults, $35 for children. Seven-hour tours (10am to 5pm) cost $70 for adults and $65 for children. You can also book full-day tours to most Orlando theme parks, including MGM Studios, Walt Disney World, and Sea World, as well as to the Kennedy Space Center, Cypress Gardens, Universal Studios, and Islands of Adventure.

HITTING THE BEACH

You have to start at St. Petersburg, across the bay, for a north-to-south string of interconnected white sandy shores. Most beaches have rest rooms, refreshment stands, and picnic areas. You can either park on the street at meters (usually 25¢ for each half hour) or at one of the four major parking lots, located from north to south at Sand Key Park (in Clearwater), beside Gulf Boulevard (also known as Route 699), just south of the Clearwater Pass Bridge; Redington Shores Beach Park, beside Gulf Boulevard at 182nd Street; Treasure Island Park, on Gulf Boulevard just north of 108th Avenue; and St. Pete Beach Park, beside Gulf Boulevard at 46th Street.

St. Petersburg Municipal Beach lies in the town of Treasure Island. **Clearwater Beach,** with its silky sands, is the place for beach volleyball. Water-sports rentals, lifeguards, rest rooms, showers, and concessions are available. The swimming is excellent, and there's a pier for fishing. Parking is $10 a day in gated lots (or $1.50 an hr.).

If you want to shop as well as tan, consider **Madeira Beach,** midway between St. Petersburg and Clearwater, with a boardwalk, T-shirt emporiums, and ice-cream parlors.

Honeymoon Island isn't great for swimming, but it has its own rugged beauty and a fascinating nature trail. From here, you can catch a ferry to **Caladesi Island State Park,** a 3¹/₂-mile stretch of sand at 3 Causeway Blvd. in Dunedin (☎ 727/469-5942 for information).

You can also go south to **Fort Desoto Park,** 3500 Pinellas Bayway S. (☎ 727/866-2484), consisting of 1,136 acres and 7 miles of waterfront exposed to both the Gulf of Mexico and a brackish channel. There are fishing piers, shaded picnic areas, a bird-and-animal sanctuary, campsites, and a partially ruined fort near the park's southwestern tip. Take Interstate 275 South to the Pinellas Bayway (Exit 4) and follow the signs.

SHOPPING

On and around **Seventh Avenue in Ybor City,** you'll find lots of cigar stores selling handmade stogies as well as a variety of interesting boutiques and shops. At press time, a new shopping complex at 1600 E. Seventh Avenue called Centro Ybor was slated to open in the summer of 2000. It will have six restaurants, 30 new stores, a 20-screen movie theater, and a high-tech entertainment center called GameWorks, sponsored by Steven Spielberg's Dreamworks and Universal Studios.

Upscale stores are located in **Old Hyde Park Village,** an outdoor, European-style market at Swann and Dakota avenues near Bayshore Boulevard (☎ 813/251-3500). **The Shops on Harbour Island,** 601 S. Harbour Island Blvd. (☎ 813/202-1830), are set on an island off the coast of Tampa's commercial heart.

Malls include the **Brandon Town Center,** at the intersection of State Road 60 and Interstate 75, and the city's largest mall, **Tampa Bay Center,** Himes Avenue and Martin Luther King, Jr. Boulevard. You'll find substantial discounts at the **Prime Outlets at Ellenton,** 5461 Factory Shops Blvd., at the junction of Interstate 75 and Highway 301 (☎ 941/723-1150).

ACCOMMODATIONS

TAMPA   Each handsomely furnished accommodation at the **Doubletree Guest Suites,** 11310 N. 30th St. (☎ 800/222-TREE or 813/971-7690), contains two separate rooms, one with a wet bar and small refrigerator.

There are two Tampa Hyatts: the **Hyatt Regency Tampa,** Two Tampa City Center at 211 N. Tampa St. (☎ 800/233-1234 or 813/225-1234), which towers over Tampa's commercial center; and the ✪ **Hyatt Regency Westshore,** 6200 Courtney Campbell Causeway (☎ 800/233-1234 or 813/874-1234), at the Tampa end of the long causeway traversing Tampa Bay. At the Westshore, some Spanish-style townhouses/villas are set about a half mile from the main hotel building.

Three miles south of Tampa International Airport is **Wyndham Westshore,** 4860 W. Kennedy Blvd. (☎ 800/822-4200 or 813/286-4400), Tampa's most stylish modern hotel. The 11-story building is modeled after a butterfly.

Wyndham Harbour Island, 725 S. Harbour Island Blvd. (☎ **800/822-4200** or 813/229-5000), sits on one of Tampa Bay's most elegant residential islands.

ST. PETERSBURG   The ✪ **Don CeSar Beach Resort and Spa,** 3400 Gulf Blvd. (☎ **800/282-1116** or 727/360-1881), is the most famous landmark in town. This pink-sided Moorish/Mediterranean fantasy, listed on the National Register of Historic Places, sits on 7½ acres of beachfront. Guest rooms are first-rate, usually with water views. Also in St. Pete, ✪ **Stouffer Renaissance Vinoy Resort,** 501 Fifth Ave. NE at Beach Drive (☎ **800/HOTELS1** or 813/894-1000), reigns as the grande dame of the region's hotels. Accommodations in the new wing ("The Tower") are slightly larger than those in the hotel's original core.

DINING

On the 14th floor of the Hyatt Regency Westshore Hotel, **Armani's,** 6200 Courtney Campbell Causeway (☎ **813/874-1234**), is a stylish northern Italian restaurant. Jackets are required.

The steaks at ✪ **Bern's Steak House,** 1208 S. Howard Ave. (☎ **813/251-2421**), are close to perfect. You order according to thickness and weight.

Le Bordeaux, 1502 S. Howard Ave. (☎ **813/254-4387**), presents competent French food at reasonable prices. The changing menu often includes bouillabaisse and fillet of beef with Roquefort sauce.

In Ybor City, the nearly 100-year-old ✪ **Columbia Restaurant,** 2117 Seventh Ave. E., between 21st and 22nd streets (☎ **813/248-4961**), occupies an attractive tile-sheathed building that fills an entire city block, about a mile from the cruise docks. The aura is pre-Castro Cuba. The more simple your dish is, the better it's likely to be. Filet mignons, roasted pork, and the black beans, yellow rice, and plantains are flavorful and well prepared. Flamenco shows begin on the dance floor Monday through Saturday at 7:30pm.

At lunch, ✪ **Mise en Place,** 442 W. Kennedy Blvd. (☎ **813/254-5373**), serves an array of delicious sandwiches, as well as savory pastas, risottos, and platters. More formal dinners feature free-range chicken with smoked tomato coulis, and loin of venison with asparagus, tarragon mash, and red-onion balsamic marmalade.

The best fish in Tampa is served at **Oystercatchers,** in the Hyatt Regency Westshore Hotel complex, 6200 Courtney Campbell Causeway (☎ **813/874-1234**). Pick the fish you want from a glass-fronted buffet or enjoy mesquite-grilled steaks, chicken rollatini, and shellfish.

TAMPA AFTER DARK

Nightfall now transforms **Ybor City,** Tampa's century-old Latin Quarter, into a hotbed of music, ethnic food, poetry readings, and after-midnight coffee and dessert. Thousands crowd one of its main arteries, Seventh Avenue, Wednesday through Saturday evenings when its closed to all but pedestrian traffic. **The Masquerade,** 1503 E. Seventh Ave. (☎ **813/247-3319**), set within a 1940s movie palace, is the first of the many nightclubs that pepper the streets here.

Elsewhere, **The Skipper Dome/Skipper's Smokehouse,** 910 Skipper Rd. (☎ **813/971-0666**), is a favorite evening spot, with an all-purpose restaurant and bar (with oysters and fresh shellfish sold by the dozen and half dozen). For live music, head out back to the "Skipper Dome," a sprawling deck sheltered by a canopy of oak trees.

The Tampa/Hillsborough Arts Council maintains **Artsline** (☎ **813/229-ARTS**), a 24-hour information service about current and upcoming cultural events.

5 New Orleans & the Port of New Orleans

There's power and majesty in this historic port, 110 miles upriver from the Gulf of Mexico. By some yardsticks, it's the busiest port in the nation, servicing many vessels much larger than the cruise ships that call New Orleans home. Although the bulk of business conducted here mainly involves the transport of grains, ores, mining byproducts, machinery, and building supplies, the city is poised for increased visibility as home port to a handful of cruise ships. Cruises from here are mainly bound for the western edge of the Caribbean, including the western "Mexican Riviera" and Cancún and Cozumel.

If you're boarding a cruise ship in New Orleans, it's almost certain your access will be through the Julia Street Cruise Ship Terminal on the Julia Street Wharf. Originally developed as part of the 1984 Louisiana World's Exposition, the cruise ship area was inaugurated in 1993, then doubled in size in 1996, and now one of the terminals is being expanded again to accommodate Carnival's *Inspiration*, which will make New Orleans its year-round home port in September of 2000. The docks lie near the commercial heart of town, a 10-minute walk from the edge of the French Quarter, or a short and convenient streetcar ride away.

GETTING TO NEW ORLEANS & ITS PORT

The port is at 1350 Port of New Orleans Place. For information, call the **Port of New Orleans** at ☎ **504/522-2551.**

BY AIR   **New Orleans International Airport** (☎ **504/464-0831**) is about 15 miles northwest of the port. Cruise line representatives meet all passengers who have booked transfers through the line. For those who haven't, a taxi to the port costs about $21 and takes about 20 minutes. **Airport Shuttle** (☎ **504/592-0555**) runs vans at 10- to 12-minute intervals from outside the airport's baggage claim to the port and other points in town. It costs $10 per passenger each way; free for children under 6.

BY CAR   Highways I-10, U.S. 90, U.S. 61, and Louisiana 25 (the Lake Pontchartrain causeway) lead directly to New Orleans. You can park your car in long-term parking at the port, but only for blocks of 1 week. Reserve parking directly with your cruise ship operator. You must present a boarding pass or ticket before parking.

BY TRAIN   Amtrak (☎ **800/USA-RAIL**) trains stop at the **Union Passenger Terminal** at 1001 Loyola Ave., in the central business district. Taxis are outside the passenger terminal's main entrance; the fare to the port is $6.

EXPLORING NEW ORLEANS

In many respects, the **French Quarter** *is* New Orleans, and many visitors never leave its confines. It's the oldest part of the city and still the most popular for sightseeing. But if you venture outside the French Quarter, you'll be able to feel the pulse of the city's commerce, see river activities that keep the city alive, stroll through spacious parks, drive or walk by the impressive homes of the Garden District, and get a firsthand view of the bayou/lake connection that explains why New Orleans grew up here in the first place.

VISITOR INFORMATION   Contact the **Greater New Orleans Convention and Visitors Bureau,** 1520 Sugar Bowl Dr., New Orleans, LA 70112 (☎ **504/566-5011;** www.neworleanscvb.com), for brochures, pamphlets, and information. Once you arrive, stop at the **New Orleans Welcoming Center,** 529 St. Ann St. in the French Quarter (☎ **800/672-6124**).

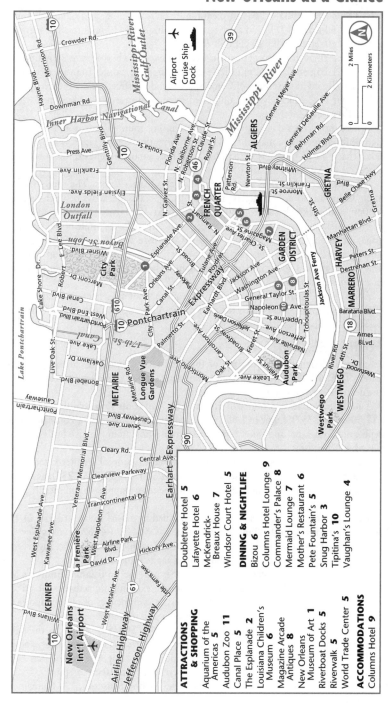

New Orleans at a Glance

Airport
Cruise Ship
Dock

2 Miles

2 Kilometers

**ATTRACTIONS
& SHOPPING**
Aquarium of the
  Americas **5**
Audubon Zoo **11**
Canal Place **5**
The Esplanade **2**
Louisiana Children's
  Museum **6**
Magazine Arcade
  Antiques **8**
New Orleans
  Museum of Art **1**
Riverboat Docks **5**
Riverwalk **5**
World Trade Center **5**

ACCOMMODATIONS
Columns Hotel **9**

Doubletree Hotel **5**
Lafayette Hotel **6**
McKendrick-
  Breaux House **7**
Windsor Court Hotel **5**

DINING & NIGHTLIFE
Bizou **6**
Columns Hotel Lounge **9**
Commander's Palace **8**
Mermaid Lounge **7**
Mother's Restaurant **6**
Pete Fountain's **5**
Snug Harbor **3**
Tipitina's **10**
Vaughan's Lounge **4**

GETTING AROUND   Taxis are plentiful. If you're not near a taxi stand, call **United Cabs** (☎ **504/522-9771**) and a cab will come within 5 to 10 minutes. The meter begins at $2.10, and rises $1.20 per mile thereafter.

Streetcar lines run the length of St. Charles Avenue. They operate 24 hours a day and cost $1.25 per ride (you must have exact change). A transfer from streetcar to bus costs 25¢. Board at the corner of Canal and Carondelet streets in the French Quarter. A VisiTour Pass, which gives you unlimited rides on all streetcar and bus lines, sells for $5 for 1 day, $12 for 3 days.

Where the trolleys don't run, a **city bus** will. For route information, call ☎ **504/248-3900** or pick up a map at the Visitor Information Center (address above). Most buses charge $1.25 (plus 25¢ for a transfer) per ride, although some express buses charge $1.50.

A **Vieux Carré Minibus** takes you to French Quarter sights. The route is posted along Canal and Bourbon streets. The minibus operates weekdays between 5am and 6:30pm and weekends 8am to 6:30pm and costs $1.25.

From Jackson Square (at Decatur Street), you can take a 2¼-mile horse-drawn carriage ride through the French Quarter. **Royal Carriage Tour Co.** (☎ **504/943-8820**) offers group tours for $10 per person in open-topped surreys suitable for up to 10 passengers at a time, daily from 9am to midnight. Private rides for up to four passengers in a Cinderella carriage go for $50 a pop.

A **ferryboat** departs at frequent intervals from the foot of Canal Street, carrying cars ($1) and passengers (free) across the river to the Algiers section of town. A round-trip passage takes about 25 minutes.

SEEING THE SIGHTS

At the well-designed ✪ **Aquarium of the Americas,** 1 Canal St., at the Mississippi River (☎ **504/861-2537**), a 400,000-gallon tank holds a kaleidoscope of species from the deep waters of the nearby Gulf of Mexico.

You'll need at least 3 hours to visit the ✪ **Audubon Zoo,** 6500 Magazine St. (☎ **504/861-2537**), home to 1,500 animals in natural habitats. In a Louisiana swamp replication, alligators and other reptiles slither and hop among native birds and clusters of marsh grasses.

Despite its massive Doric columns and twin staircases, local architects nonetheless refer to **Beauregard-Keyes House,** 1113 Chartres St. (☎ **504/523-7257**), as a "Louisiana raised cottage." Built in 1826, it's one of the most impressive and socially prestigious structures in town.

Incorporating seven historic buildings connected by a brick courtyard, the ✪ **Historic New Orleans Collection,** 533 Royal St. (☎ **504/523-4662**), evokes New Orleans of 200 years ago. The oldest building in the complex escaped the tragic fire of 1794. The others hold exhibitions about Louisiana's culture and history.

Housed in a former granary 4 blocks from the river, the **Louisiana Children's Museum,** 420 Julia St. (☎ **504/523-1357**), divides its exhibits into activities for children over and under the age of 12. The Lab demonstrates principles of physics and math, motion, and inertia. Younger children can play in a simulated supermarket.

Musée Conti Wax Museum, 917 Conti St. (☎ **504/525-2605**), is the bayou equivalent of Madame Tussaud's, featuring pivotal figures in Louisiana history and legend. Look for the replicas of the notorious politico Huey Long, jazz meister Pete Fountain, Andrew Jackson, and Jean Lafitte. It's open daily from 10am to 8pm.

The collections of the **New Orleans Historic Voodoo Museum,** 724 Dumaine St. (☎ **504/523-7685**), celebrate the occult and the mixture of African and Catholic rituals first brought to New Orleans by slaves from Hispaniola. A gift shop and voodoo

The French Quarter

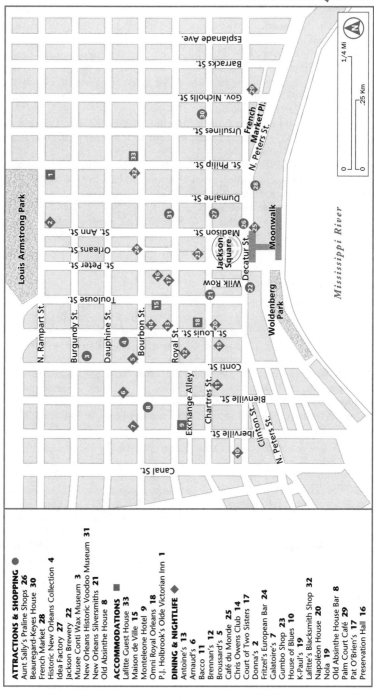

ATTRACTIONS & SHOPPING ●
Aunt Sally's Praline Shops **26**
Beauregard-Keyes House **30**
French Market **28**
Historic New Orleans Collection **4**
Idea Factory **27**
Jackson Brewery **22**
Musee Conti Wax Museum **3**
New Orleans Historic Voodoo Museum **31**
New Orleans Silversmiths **21**
Old Absinthe House **8**

ACCOMMODATIONS ■
Lafitte Guest House **33**
Maison de Ville **15**
Monteleone Hotel **9**
Omni Royal Orleans **18**
P.J. Holbrook's Olde Victorian Inn **1**

DINING & NIGHTLIFE ◆
Antoine's **13**
Arnaud's **6**
Bacco **11**
Brennan's **12**
Broussard's **5**
Café du Monde **25**
Chris Owens Club **14**
Court of Two Sisters **17**
Donna's **2**
Fritzel's European Bar **24**
Galatoire's **7**
Gumbo Shop **23**
House of Blues **10**
K-Paul's **19**
Lafitte's Blacksmith Shop **32**
Napoléon House **20**
Nola **19**
Old Absinthe House Bar **8**
Palm Court Café **29**
Pat O'Brien's **17**
Preservation Hall **16**

parlor are stocked with apothecary ingredients. Staff there can also provide you with psychic services. Admission is $7 for adults, $5.50 for college students and seniors, and $4.50 for high-school kids. It's open daily from 10am to 8pm. A **guided voodoo-and-cemetery walking tour** of the French Quarter departs from the museum daily at 10:30am and 1pm; tour of the undead departs at 8pm. These group tours (and others), as well as private customized tours, are led by a gal calling herself **Bloody Mary** (☎ 504/486-2080), a folk historian and acclaimed storyteller. The walking tours are all $15 and include museum admission.

The collections of the **New Orleans Museum of Art (NOMA),** Lelong Avenue (☎ 504/488-2631), span the centuries, with one floor devoted to ethnographic and non-Western art.

The ✪ **Old Absinthe House/Tony Moran's Restaurant,** 240 Bourbon St. (☎ 504/523-3181), is the oldest bar in New Orleans, built in 1806 by two Spanish partners. Upstairs is a restaurant, Tony Moran's, open only for dinner (closed Sun).

The **World Trade Center of New Orleans,** 2 Canal St. (☎ 504/529-1601), one of the tallest buildings in town, has the ✪ **Viewpoint** observation platform on its 31st floor. Check out the freighters, cruise ships, tug boats, submarines, and aircraft carriers that ply the swift-flowing waters of New Orleans's harbor. A cocktail lounge spins slowly on the 33rd floor.

ORGANIZED TOURS

ON FOOT   Friends of the Cabildo (☎ 504/523-3939) lead 2-hour walking tours of Vieux Carré (the French Quarter). They leave from the Museum Store at 523 St. Ann St. every Tuesday through Sunday at 10am and 1:30pm, and Monday at 1:30pm, except holidays. Donations are expected: $10 per adult, and $8 for seniors over 65 and children ages 13 to 20 (kids under 12 are free).

Magic Walking Tours (☎ 504/588-9693) offers theme tours associated with the city's cemeteries, its Garden District, and its voodoo traditions. Two-hour tours cost $13 per person ($10 for seniors and students).

You can see historic interiors on a **Hidden Treasures Tour** (☎ 504/529-4507); $20 per person by reservation.

BY BOAT   The paddle wheeler *Creole Queen* (☎ 504/524-0814), departs from the Poydras Street Wharf, adjacent to the Riverwalk mall, every day at 10:30am for a 2½-hour waterborne tour. Riverwalk is at the end of Canal Street; the wharf is about 2 blocks east. There's a buffet restaurant and a cocktail lounge on board. Daytime cruises cost $21 with lunch for adults, $14 with lunch for children ($15 and $8, respectively, without lunch). Evening cruises, which sail from 8pm to 10pm, with live jazz and dinner, run $45 for adults and $22 for children ($21 and $13 without dinner).

Another steam-powered stern-wheeler is the *Natchez* (☎ 504/569-1414), departing daily from the Toulouse Street Wharf, next to the French Quarter's Jackson Street Brewery. Cruises begin at 11:30am and 2:30pm and feature live jazz and an optional Creole-style luncheon buffet. The cost with lunch is $21.75 for adults and $13.75 for children 6 to 12 ($15.75 and $7.75 without lunch); free for children under 6. Evening jazz cruises depart at 7pm, and with a buffet dinner cost $45.50 for adults and $22.75 for children ($25.50 and $12.75 without dinner).

The riverboat *John James Audubon* (☎ 504/586-8777) departs from the Canal Street dock and travels the Mississippi between the Audubon Zoo and the aquarium. The cruise costs $14.50 for adults, $7.25 for children.

BY BUS   A 2-hour **Gray Line** bus tour, 1300 World Trade Center of New Orleans (☎ 800/535-7786 or 504/587-0861), offers a fast overview of the city. Tours cost $22 for adults and $10 for children, and require advance booking.

SHOPPING

Shopping here is, in a word, fun. Antique stores are especially well stocked, and gift shops seem to sell more than just a cheap array of T-shirts and souvenir items (although there are plenty of those, too).

Major shopping venues include the triple-tiered mall **Canal Place,** where Canal Street meets the Mississippi Wharves. **The Esplanade,** 1401 W. Esplanade, boasts a constantly busy food court and more than 150 retailers. **The French Market,** whose main entrance is on Decatur Street across from Jackson Square, is big on Louisiana kitsch and cookware. The **Jackson Brewery,** adjacent to Jackson Square, is a transformed suds factory filled with more than 125 retailers. **Riverwalk** is a covered mall that runs along the wharves between Poydras Street and the Convention Center.

You'll find a row of art galleries along **Julia Street,** between the Mississippi River and Camp Street. A jumble of antiques and flea market–style emporiums sit along a 6-block stretch of **Magazine Street,** between Audubon Park and Canal Street. There's also **Magazine Arcade Antiques,** 3017 Magazine St. (☎ **504/895-5451**).

For crafts, try the **Idea Factory,** 838 Chartres St. (☎ **504/524-5195**), where they stock a colorful array of wooden letterboxes, trays, paper-towel holders, and wall brackets. You'll find new and antique silver flatware at **New Orleans Silversmiths,** 600 Chartres St. (☎ **504/522-8333**).

You can see pralines being made at **Aunt Sally's Praline Shops, Inc.,** 810 Decatur St. (☎ **504/944-6090**). They'll ship anything home for you, and sell you items such as cookbooks, packaged Creole food, and Louisiana memorabilia.

ACCOMMODATIONS

Seekers of Southern charm and grace head for the **Columns Hotel,** 3811 St. Charles Ave. (☎ **800/445-9308** or 504/899-9308), a former private residence from 1883 now converted into a small hotel. One of the stateliest remaining examples of belle-époque Italianate architecture, it's listed on the National Register of Historic Places.

Conveniently located near both the embarkation piers for cruise ship passengers and the French Quarter, the **Doubletree Hotel,** 300 Canal St. (☎ **504/581-1300**), is at the edge of the city's business district. Rooms are comfortable and clean.

The ✪ **Omni Royal Orleans,** 621 St. Louis St. (☎ **800/THE-OMNI** in the U.S. and Canada, or 504/529-5333; fax 504/529-7037), is a most elegant hotel located smack in the center of the Quarter. The lobby is a small sea of marble, and the rooms are sizable and comfortable. Truman Capote and William Styron both stayed here.

✪ **Lafayette Hotel,** 600 St. Charles Ave., at Lafayette Square (☎ **800/827-5621** or 504/524-4441), resembles an upscale turn-of-the-century hotel in London. From old-world architecture, French doors, and wrought-iron balconies to marble floors, polished mahogany, and English botanical prints, the ambiance is consistently luxurious.

Lafitte Guest House, 1003 Bourbon St. (☎ **800/331-7971** or 504/581-2678), is a meticulously restored elegant French manor house furnished with splendid antiques. The three-floor brick structure in a residential section of Bourbon Street was built in 1849. Its wrought-iron balconies and Victorian antiques are as alluring as each of its individually decorated bedrooms, which come in various sizes.

In the heart of the French Quarter, you can follow in the footsteps of Tennessee Williams (who often stayed in room no. 9) and head for ✪ **Maison de Ville,** 727 Toulouse St. (☎ **800/634-1600** or 504/561-5858), located on its original 1742 site. It was here that Williams wrote *A Streetcar Named Desire.* Though the hotel is just steps from honky-tonk Bourbon Street, it has an air of Southern gentility.

One of the best guest houses for value is **The McKendrick-Breaux House,** 1474 Magazine St. (☎ **888/570-1700** or 504/586-1700), built at the end of the Civil War by a wealthy plumber and Scottish immigrant. Located in the lower Garden District, it has been completely restored to its original charm. Each room is furnished with antiques, family collectibles, and fresh flowers.

About 7 blocks from the cruise ship terminal is the grande dame of the French Quarter, the atmospheric **Monteleone Hotel,** 214 Royal St. (☎ 800/535-9595 or 504/523-3341). Decor and floor layouts are slightly different in each of the 597 rooms.

Three streets from Bourbon in the French Quarter, ✪ **P. J. Holbrook's Olde Victorian Inn,** 914 N. Rampart St. (☎ 800/725-2446 or 504/522-2446), is a beautifully restored 1840s home, with antiques and reproductions. Some rooms have balconies, and most come with fireplaces. P.J. herself exemplifies Southern hospitality.

Only blocks from the French Quarter, ✪ **Windsor Court Hotel,** 300 Gravier St. (☎ 800/262-2662 or 504/523-6000), rents 224 beautifully furnished bedrooms, all but 50 of which are suites. From its $8-million art collection to the harpist floating celestial music over the afternoon tea drinkers, the Windsor Court provides an experience more like visiting an English country house than sojourning in Louisiana.

DINING

Don't ask what's new at **Antoine's,** 713 St. Louis St. (☎ 504/581-4422), established in 1840. Oysters Rockefeller, first served here in 1899, is still available. Tournedos of beef and ramekins of crawfish cardinal remain perennial favorites, and rightly so. The only radical menu change occurred in the 1990s, when French menu terms were given English translations.

The legendary **Arnaud's,** 813 Bienville St. (☎ 504/523-5433), lies within three interconnected, once-private houses from the 1700s. The five belle-époque dining rooms are lush with Edwardian embellishments. Menu items include shrimp Arnaud, snails *en casserole,* oysters stewed in cream, rack of lamb diablo, roasted duck à l'orange, and classic bananas. The dark balcony around the main dining room is where proper New Orleans gentlemen used to dine with their mistresses while their wives dined below, unawares.

A great New Orleans bistro, **Bacco,** 310 Chartres St. (☎ 504/522-2426), stands adjacent to the De La Poste Hotel, right in the heart of the French Quarter. In an elegant setting of pink Italian marble floors and Venetian chandeliers, you can feast on wood-fired pizzas, regional seafood, and such specialties as porcini roasted duck and crabmeat and pappardelle.

Bizou, 701 St. Charles Ave. (☎ 504/524-4114), is hardly the most glamorous place in New Orleans, but its cuisine, a rejuvenation of Creole and French traditional cookery, has the exuberance of a spring day. Try the crawfish cakes with Creole mustard and baby greens in a Tabasco-infused white butter.

Broussard's, 819 Conti St. (☎ 504/581-3866), has thrived here since 1920. It's a quieter, more dignified version of Antoine's, less heavily patronized by out-of-towners, and more authentic to the "Nawlins" ethic. Dishes include fillets of pompano Napoléon-style (with scallops and a mustard-caper sauce, served in puff pastry with a side order of shrimp).

At the corner of Washington Avenue and Coliseum Street in the Garden District, **Commander's Palace,** 1403 Washington Ave. (☎ 504/899-8221), still reigns as one of the city's finest dining choices. The cuisine is haute Creole. Try anything with shrimp or crawfish, or the Mississippi quail.

✪ **Galatoire's,** 209 Bourbon St. (☎ 504/525-2021), feels like a bistro in turn-of-the-century Paris, and still basks in its legendary reputation. Menu items include trout (*meunière* or *amandine*), remoulade of shrimp, oysters en brochette, a savory Creole-style bouillabaisse, and a good eggplant stuffed with a purée of seafood.

K-Paul's Louisiana Kitchen, 416 Chartres St. (☎ **504/524-7394**), is one of Louisiana's most famous restaurants. There are two dining rooms, one of which takes reservations and another that doesn't (at this one you may be seated at a communal table with other diners). Try fiery gumbos, Cajun popcorn shrimp, roasted rabbit, and the delicious spicy blackened fish (especially tuna). For the rare vegetarian, the breaded, vegetable-stuffed eggplant is just amazing.

Brennan's, 417 Royal St. (☎ **504/525-9711**), is the place for the legendary "Breakfast at Brennan's," a multicourse affair that's changed very little over the years. It includes traditional dishes like eggs Hussarde, eggs Sardou, and trout Nancy (fillet of fresh trout sautéed and topped with lump crabmeat, sprinkled with capers and lemon-butter sauce). Turtle soup is a famous local dish, and Brennan's makes one of the best. Desserts include bananas Foster (sautéed in liqueur, brown sugar, cinnamon, and butter; drenched in rum; set ablaze; and served over vanilla ice cream). It's a little overwhelming. A friend ate there recently and afterward stumbled to the nearest phone, canceled his lunch and dinner reservations, and went back to the hotel for a nap.

The ambiance is more of a draw than the food at the **Court of Two Sisters,** 613 Royal St. (☎ **504/522-7261**), but what an ambiance it is. You enter through a huge courtyard filled with flowers, fountains, and low-hanging willows, with a wishing well at its center. You can dine outside amid the greenery or in the Royal Court Room. The daily jazz brunch buffet features more than 80 dishes (meat, fowl, fish, vegetables, fresh fruits, homemade bread, and pastries) and a strolling jazz band.

The **Gumbo Shop,** 630 St. Peter St. (☎ **504/525-1486**), is a cheap and convenient place to get solid, classic Creole food. The menu reads like a textbook list of traditional local food: red beans and rice, shrimp Creole, crawfish étouffée. The seafood gumbo with okra is a meal in itself, and do try the jambalaya. Other dishes include crawfish and penne pasta, filet mignon, salads, po' boys (from regular ham and cheese to Cajun sausage), and homemade desserts such as Southern pecan pie with ice cream.

If you don't mind facing the world's toughest waitresses, head for **Mother's Restaurant,** 401 Poydras St. (☎ **504/523-9656**), at the corner of Tchoupitoulas. Customers have been flocking to this crowded place since 1938. Homemade biscuits and red-bean omelets are featured at breakfast, giving way at lunch to po' boys. For dinner you can get everything from soft-shell crabs to jambalaya.

Napoléon House, 500 Chartres St. (☎ **504/524-9752**), at the corner of St. Louis Street, would have been the house of the lieutenant himself if some locals' wild plan to bring him here in exile had panned out. A landmark 1797 building, this place is a hangout for drinking and good times, but also serves food. The specialty is Italian muffuletta, with ham, Genoa salami, pastrami, Swiss cheese, and provolone.

At **Nola,** 534 St. Louis St. (☎ **504/522-6652**), Cajun New Orleans mingles gracefully with Hollywood. Try such intriguing dishes as slow-roasted duck with a sweet and spicy glaze, along with a buttermilk corn pudding.

✪ **Café du Monde,** at 800 Decatur St., right on the river (☎ **504/581-2914**), is basically a 24-hour coffee and donuts stop (Okay, coffee and beignets—a square, really yummy French doughnut-type thing, hot and covered in powdered sugar), but it's *the* place for people-watching (if you don't want to wait for a table, you can always get a bag of beignets to go).

NEW ORLEANS AFTER DARK

Life here in "The Big Easy" is conducive to all manner of nighttime entertainment, usually raucous. Visitors reel from club to club in the neighborhoods around Bourbon and St. Louis streets. There's a reason why jazz was born in this town.

Do what most people do: Start at one end of **Bourbon Street** (say, around Iberville), walk down to the other, and then turn around and do it again. Along the way, you'll hear R&B, blues, and jazz pouring out of dozens of bars, be beckoned by touts of the numerous strip clubs, and see one tiny little storefront stall after another sporting hand-lettered signs that say OUR BEER IS CHEAPER THAN NEXT DOOR. It's a scene. Base and immoral? Maybe, but it's loads of fun. Grab yourself a big $2 beer or one of the famous rum-based Hurricanes (preferably in a yard-long plastic cup shaped like a Roswell alien) and join the party.

Preservation Hall, 726 St. Peter St., just off Bourbon (☎ 504/523-8939), is a deliberately shabby little hall with very few places to sit and no air-conditioning. Nonetheless, the place is usually packed with people in to see the house band, a bunch of mostly older musicians who have been at this for *eons*. Don't request "When the Saints Go Marching In" 'cause the band won't play it—even classics get to be old smelly hats when you've played them 45,000 times.

Chris Owens Club, 500 Bourbon St. (☎ 504/523-6400), is a one-woman cabaret act. New Orleans legend and mistress of ceremonies Ms. Owens sings along with whatever band happens to be accompanying her that night. On nights when Owens is indisposed, the venue becomes a dance club.

On a small stage in ✪ **Fritzel's European Bar & Cuisine,** 733 Bourbon St. (☎ 504/561-0432), musicians will improvise, boogie, and generally shake, rattle, and roll. It's one of the better places on Bourbon. Very late at night, musicians from other clubs might hop onstage to jam.

Lafitte's Blacksmith Shop, 941 Bourbon St. (☎ 504/523-0066), is a French Quarter pub housed in an 18th-century Creole blacksmith shop that looks like only faith keeps it standing. Tennessee Williams used to hang out here.

Established in 1933, the quite touristy **Pat O'Brien's,** 718 St. Peter St., just off Bourbon (☎ 504/525-4823), is famous for its twin piano players, raucous high jinx, singers, and gargantuan Hurricanes. There's also an outdoor courtyard.

If you're looking to get away from the Bourbon scene and hear some real brass-band jazz, head up to ✪ **Donna's,** 800 N. Rampart St., at the top of St. Ann Street (☎ 504/596-6914). This joint is often packed, especially for the more famous acts—the Marsalis family has been known to play here from time to time—though when I was there in late 1998 to see a fella named Tuba Fats and his band, the patrons were almost outnumbered by the musicians. There's no better place to hear that authentic sound that made New Orleans famous. Cover varies, but is always reasonable. Owner Donna is often tending bar.

Elsewhere in town, Pete Fountain, the Dixieland clarinet maestro, runs **Pete Fountain's** in the plush third-floor interior of the New Orleans Hilton, 2 Poydras St. (☎ 504/561-0500). If he's not on tour, Fountain usually performs several nights a week.

Jazz, blues, and Dixieland pour out of the nostalgia-laden bar and concert hall **Tipitina's,** 501 Napoleon Ave. (☎ 504/891-8477); there's a second location at 233 Peter's St. (☎ 504/895-8477).

At the **Mermaid Lounge,** 1100 Constance St. (☎ 504/524-4747), in the Warehouse District, anything goes, and music ranges from rockabilly to jazz. It's open Wednesday through Saturday, and sometimes Tuesday night, if the mood strikes. The joint keeps going at least until 2am, but if it's jumping, the owners will keep it open later.

House of Blues, 225 Decatur St. (☎ 504/529-2583), is one of the city's largest live-music venues. You stand and move among the several bars that pepper the club. There's also a restaurant.

Follow the footsteps of Michael Jordan and U2 to the Victorian Lounge at the **Columns Hotel,** 3811 St. Charles Ave. (☎ **504/899-9308**), and try one of the staff's justly celebrated Bloody Marys. A young local crowd is attracted to this bar on the fringe of the Garden District, where a jazz trio entertains on Tuesday nights.

At **Palm Court Café,** 1204 Decatur St. (☎ **504/525-0200**), you'll find an equal appreciation of good jazz and international food.

One block beyond Esplanade, on the periphery of the French Quarter, **Snug Harbor,** 626 Frenchman St. (☎ **504/949-0696**), is a jazz bistro, a classic spot to hear modern jazz in a cozy setting. Sometimes R&B combos and blues are added to the program. There's a full dinner menu as well.

Vaughan's Lounge, 800 Lesseps St. (☎ **504/947-5562**), is a genuine New Orleans joint.

6 San Juan & the Port of San Juan

In addition to being the embarkation port for a number of ships, San Juan is also a major port of call. See chapter 11, "Caribbean Ports of Call," for all information.

11 Caribbean Ports of Call

There are two kinds of cruisers when it comes to ports of call: those who choose a certain cruise because of its itinerary and those who don't. But even if you've been there, done that, and cruise primarily for the onboard ship life, you'll want to know how best to spend the limited time you have in whichever port you happen to land.

Here's the good news: There are no lousy Caribbean islands! Sure, depending on your likes and dislikes, you'll appreciate some more than others. Some of the ports and islands—like Key West, St. Thomas, and Nassau—are much more overrun with tourists than others, but then again, they'll appeal to shoppers with their large variety of stores and bustling main streets. Other islands—Virgin Gorda, St. John's, Jost Van Dyke, and the Grenadines, for instance—are quieter and more natural and will appeal to those of you who'd rather walk along a deserted beach or take a drive along a lonely, winding road in the midst of pristine tropical foliage. Some ports are expensive—like Bermuda, the U.S. Virgin Islands, St. Barts, St. Martin, and Aruba—while others are cheaper, like Cozumel, Jamaica, and the Grenadines.

Choosing what activities to participate in on board the ship is one thing, but when the ship pulls up to a port of call, figuring out how to make the best of your limited time there is another. Should you take an organized tour or go off on your own and wing it? And just what are the best shore excursions? Where are the best beaches? Where's the shopping? Any good restaurants or bars nearby?

I'll answer all those questions and more, as I take you to 33 ports of call, mainly in the Caribbean, but also including the Bahamas, Mexico's Yucatán Peninsula, and Key West. This year I've added coverage of a handful of new islands for the first time: Bonaire, Dominica, Iles des Saintes, Trinidad and Tobago, the Dominican Republic, Nevis, Union Island, and Bequia. (See chapter 12, "Bermuda & the Panama Canal Route," for coverage of Bermuda and the ports along the Panama Canal routes.)

At some ports, your best bet is to just head off **exploring on your own,** but at others, this could take too much time, entail lots of hassles and planning, may cost more, and might not be safe (because of poor roads or driving conditions, for instance). In these cases, the **shore excursions** offered by the cruise lines are the way to go. Under each port review I'll run through a sampling of both the best excursions and the best sights and activities you can see and do on your own.

Shore excursions can be a wonderful and carefree way to get to know the islands, offering everything from **island tours** and **snorkeling and sailing excursions** (often with a rum-punch party theme) to more physically challenging pursuits, like **bicycle tours, hiking, kayaking,** and **horseback riding excursions.** Keep in mind, shore-excursion prices vary from line to line, even for the exact same tour; the prices I've listed are typical and are adult rates. Also note that in some cases the excursions fill up fast, especially on the megaships, so don't dawdle in signing up. When you receive your cruise documents, or at the latest when you board the ship, you'll get a pamphlet with a listing of the excursions offered for your itinerary. Look it over, make your selections, and sign up the first or second day of your cruise. (In some cases, if a tour offered by your ship is booked up, you can try and book it independently once you get to port. The popular *Atlantis* submarine tour, for example (offered at Grand Cayman, Nassau, St. Thomas, and more), usually has an office/agent in the cruise terminals or nearby.) If there's an excursion you absolutely *need* to take and don't want to risk getting left out of, a company called **Port Promotions** in Planation, Florida, is now allowing travel agents and passengers to book shore excursions online at www.portpromotions.com.

As I said, in some cases it's a great idea to go off on your own, so I'll also advise you which islands are good for solo exploring, whether on foot or by taxi, motor scooter, ferry, or otherwise. Remember, though, if you opt to do your own independent touring, you'll be forgoing the narrative a guide gives, and may miss out on some of the historical, cultural, and other nuances of a particular island.

Most cruise ships arrive in port sometime before 10am, though this will vary slightly from line to line and port to port. You rarely have to clear Customs or Immigration, because your ship's purser has your passport or documents and will have done all the paperwork for you. When local officials give the word, you just go ashore. Sometimes you can walk down the gangplank right onto the pier, but if you're on a large cruise ship and the port isn't big enough, your ship will anchor offshore and ferry passengers to land via a small boat called a **tender.** In either case, you might have to wait in line to get ashore, but the waits can be longer if you have to tender in. Once ashore, even if you've come by tender, you aren't stuck there—you can return to the ship at any time for lunch, a nap, or whatever. Tenders run back and forth on a regular basis. They all look pretty much alike, though, so be sure you get on the one that's heading to your ship.

All shore excursions are carefully organized to coincide with your time in port. If you're going it on your own, you can count on finding taxi drivers at the pier when your ship docks. It's a good idea to arrange with the driver to pick you up at a certain time to bring you back to the port. In most ports you can also rent a car, moped/scooter, or bicycle.

With regard to **duty-free shopping,** the savings on duty-free merchandise can range from as little as 5% to as much as 50%. Unless there's a special sale being offered, many products carry comparable price tags from island to island. If you have particular goods

---

Calling Home

Since the prices for calling home from a cruise ship are so sky high (anywhere from $4 to $18 a min.), it's a better idea to call from land, when you're in port. I've included information on where to find phones in all the port reviews. Country codes are as follows: United States and Canada, 1; Australia, 61; New Zealand, 64; the United Kingdom, 44; and Ireland, 353.

Don't Wear the Coral!

You may be eyeing that gorgeous piece of black-coral jewelry, but did you know it's illegal to bring many products made from coral and other marine animals back to the United States? Remember, corals aren't rocks: They're living animals—a single branch of coral contains thousands of tiny coral animals (called polyps). Of course, the shopkeeper selling it won't tell you that, and it may in fact be legal for him to sell it. Nonetheless, you will be in violation of U.S. and international law if you bring these items back to the States. If caught, you could face stiff penalties and have your treasured mementos confiscated.

Sea turtles, too, are highly endangered, and sea horses, while not yet protected by laws, are currently threatened with extinction. The best way to appreciate and protect all of these natural beauties is with an underwater camera on a snorkeling expedition.

---

you're thinking of buying this way, it pays to check prices at your local discount retailer before you leave home, so you'll know whether you're really getting a bargain. (Note that the **U.S. dollar** is widely accepted throughout the islands as well as in Bermuda, so even though I've listed each island's official local currency, there's rarely a need to exchange U.S. dollars. Credit cards and traveler's checks are also widely accepted.)

It's also a good idea to talk with your cruise director or shore-excursion manager before you reach a port if you want to do something special (like find a special restaurant for lunch) or pursue a sport, be it scuba, golf, tennis, horseback riding, or fishing. Keep in mind that they'll most likely just tell you to sign up for one of their organized excursions and won't have the time or ability to help you arrange personal and private tours. This is especially true on the megaships; the small, high-end lines, though, can and will help you in this way. You'll need to reserve spots for many of these activities before you land, because facilities might be filled by land-based vacationers or by passengers from other cruise ships. It goes without saying that if you arrive at a port of call and find the harbor filled with ships, expect the shops, restaurants, and beaches—everything, as a matter of fact—to be crowded. Call from the docks for any reservations.

Most passengers start heading back to the ship around 4pm or not much later than 5pm. By 6pm you're often sailing off to your next destination. In some cases—in Nassau, New Orleans, Key West, and the British Virgin Islands (for the smaller ships), for instance—the ship may leave after midnight so passengers can stay ashore to enjoy the nightlife on the island.

THE CRUISE LINES' PRIVATE ISLANDS

Most of the big lines have a private island or patch of island in the Bahamas that's included as a port of call on many of their Caribbean and Bahamas itineraries. Royal Caribbean, Princess, Disney, Holland America, Norwegian, and Costa all have one of these well-stocked island paradises that are off-limits to anyone but the line's passengers. While completely lacking in any true Caribbean culture, they do offer cruisers a guaranteed beach day with all the trimmings—a long stretch of beach with lounge chairs and strolling waiters selling tropical drinks, as well as water sports, shops, walking paths, hammocks, and casual picnic-style restaurants. On Disney's island, you can even rent bicycles and ride around the island.

1 Antigua

Rolling, rustic Antigua (An-*tee*-gah) in the British Leewards claims to have a different beach for every day of the year. This may be an exaggeration, but its numerous sugary-white, reef-protected beaches are reason enough to visit, even if just for a day. Antigua is also known for its **English Harbour,** home of Nelson's Dockyard National Park, one of the Caribbean's major historical attractions.

Some British traditions (including a passion for cricket) linger on, although the nation became independent in 1981. Some 4,000 years ago, Antigua was home to a people called the Ciboney, who later disappeared completely and mysteriously from the island. When Columbus showed up in 1493 (he named the island after the Santa Maria La Antigua cathedral in Seville, Spain), the Arawaks had already settled on the island. They were joined in the mid-17th century by the English, who eventually won out after many conflicts.

On Antigua you'll find isolated and conservative (but very glamorous) resorts, poorly maintained highways, and some of the most interesting historic naval sites in the British maritime world. Antigua is politically linked to the sparsely inhabited and largely underdeveloped island of Barbuda, about 30 miles north.

Sleepy **St. John's,** the capital, springs to life when cruise ships come to town. It's a large, neatly laid-out town, 6 miles from the airport and less than a mile from Deep Water Harbour Terminal. Protected in the throat of a narrow bay, St. John's is full of cobblestoned sidewalks, weather-beaten wooden houses, corrugated iron roofs, and louvered Caribbean verandas. The streets were built wide to let the trade winds keep them cooler. The port is the focal point of commerce, industry, and government, as well as visitor shopping.

Frommer's Favorite Antigua Experiences

- **Taking a four-wheel-drive island tour:** Drive down rain-forest trails and make a stop at the beach. Sounds fun, huh? (See "Shore Excursions," below.)
- **Visiting Harmony Hall:** The place to go for mouth-watering cuisine, works of art, shopping, refreshing breezes, and some of the island's best people-watching. (See "On Your Own: Beyond Walking Distance," below.)

COMING ASHORE   Most cruise ships dock at Heritage Quay (pronounced *key*) in St. John's, the island's capital. Heritage Quay and Redcliffe Quay (about a 10-minute walk from the dock) are the main shopping centers. Cruise passengers will find duty-free stores, restaurants, taxis, and other services in both quays. On busy port days, ships will also use the Deep Water Harbour Terminal in St. John's. From there, passengers take a short taxi ride to Heritage Quay. Occasionally, smaller vessels drop their anchor at English Harbour; everyone else reaches it via taxi or a shore excursion from St. John's.

Frommer's Ratings: Antigua					
	poor	fair	good	excellent	outstanding
Overall Experience				✓	
Shore Excursions			✓		
Activities Close to Port			✓		
Beach & Water Sports				✓	
Shopping		✓			
Dining/Bars				✓	

Credit-card **phone booths** are located on the dock and throughout both quays and at Deep Water Harbour. Passengers can also head to **Parcel Plus** (☎ 268/562-7587) at 14 Redcliffe St. (in Redcliffe Quay), which offers 10 booths in an air-conditioned setting. You can also check your E-mail from here. The cost is about $8 for a half hour, $11 for 1 hour. **Cable & Wireless** (☎ 268/480-4237) has an office on the corner of Long and Thames streets, where prepaid phone cards can be purchased. Prices start at $4. Phone cards can also be purchased from stores around the quay and from the pilot office at Deep Water Harbour.

CURRENCY The **Eastern Caribbean dollar (EC$)** is used on these islands; however, you'll find that nearly all prices, except those in certain tiny restaurants, are given in U.S. dollars. The exchange rate is EC$2.70 to $1 U.S. (EC$1 is worth about 37¢). It's always a good idea to ask if you're not sure which currency a price tag refers to. The U.S. dollar is readily accepted by most shopkeepers and cab drivers. Unless otherwise specified, rates quoted in this section are given in U.S. dollars.

LANGUAGE The official language is English, spoken with a bit of an island lilt.

INFORMATION Head to the **Antigua and Barbuda Department of Tourism** at Nevis Street and Friendly Alley in St. John's (☎ 268/462-0480). You'll get just the basics from the staff here. Open Monday to Thursday from 8am to 4:30pm and Friday from 8am to 3pm.

CALLING FROM THE U.S. When calling Antigua from the U.S., you need to dial only a "1" before the numbers listed throughout this section.

GETTING AROUND

BY TAXI Taxis meet every cruise ship. They don't have meters, so even though rates are fixed by the government it's always wise to settle on a fare and the currency before taking the ride. One of the best ways to explore the island is by private taxi, since drivers also double as tour guides. Hourly rates are about $20 for up to four people in a cab. The standard tip for a driver is between 10% and 15%.

The rate from St. John's to Nelson's Dockyard, Pigeon Point, and Shirley Heights is about $20. To Half Moon Bay and Harmony Hall from St. John's, a cab costs about $23.

BY BUS The fare for buses is cheap (around $1) but the service is irregular. It is geared to locals rather than tourists. Unless you are a looking for a local adventure or being merely thrifty, buses are not recommended for the average visitor. However, if you want to give it a whirl, the West Bus Station is located near St. John's market. Buses from this locale head to the villages in the southern part of the island and English Harbour.

RENTAL CARS Driving is on the left in this former British colony, and renting a car is not recommended. The roads are narrow and seriously potholed, and there is a definite lack of signage. If you do opt to rent a car, Avis, Dollar, Hertz, and Thrifty have outlets in St. John's. A local permit, which costs $20, is required.

SHORE EXCURSIONS

✪ **Four-Wheel-Drive Island Tour** ($55–$64, 3 hours hours): A tour of the whole island via four-wheel drive will take you along rain-forest trails and to the ruins of forts, sugar mills, and plantation houses, and is a great way to get a feel for Antigua. The tour includes a stop at the beach for some swimming.

Nelson's Dockyard at English Harbour ($37–$39, 3 hours): This is the major excursion on the island. On the way, you get to view some of the island's lush countryside. That still leaves you plenty of time in the day for shopping or hitting the beach.

Map of Antigua showing: Atlantic Ocean, Hodges Bay, Jabberwock Beach, Dickenson Bay, Dutchman's Bay, Cedar Grove, Runaway Bay, Long Island, Deepwater Harbor, Galley Bay, Fort James, V.C. Bird Airport, Hawksbill Beaches, Five Islands, St. John's, Guiana Island, Parham, Pineapple Beach, Long Bay, Indian Town Point, Devil's Bridge, Jennings, Betty's Hope Plantation, Willikies, Megaliths, All Saints, Harmony Hall, Jolly Harbor, Bolans, Potworks Dam, Freetown, Driftwood Beach, Boggy Peak, Fig Tree Dr., Half Moon Bay, Johnson's Point, Urlings, Old Road, Falmouth, Willoughby Bay, Morris Bay, Falmouth Bay, English Harbour, Turner's Beach, Carlisle Bay, Pigeon Point, Nelson's Dockyard National Park, Shirley Heights, Mamora Bay, Rendezvous Bay, Caribbean Sea, 0 5 Miles, 0 5 Kilometers. Legend: Airport, Beach, Mountain, Cruise Ship Dock. N

Catamaran Tour ($39–$49, 3 hours): The boat takes you along the coast of Antigua, making a stop for swimming, sunbathing, and snorkeling.

A Cruise on the *Jolly Roger* ($33–$39 adults, 3 hours): Antigua's famous "pirate ship," the *Jolly Roger,* is one of the island's most popular attractions. You're taken for a fun-filled day of sightseeing and snorkeling, plus dancing on the poop deck and a limbo contest. Lunch (a choice of grilled lobster, chicken, or steak) and drinks are served.

TOURING THROUGH LOCAL OPERATORS

***Jolly Roger* Cruise:** If your ship doesn't offer this excursion, you can book it independently. Call ☎ **268/462-2064** at least a day or two ahead to make a booking. The ship berths at Redcliffe Quay, within walking distance of the cruise ship docks in St. John's. The lunch cruises depart at 10am and return at 2pm.

ON YOUR OWN: WITHIN WALKING DISTANCE

If you don't want to go to **English Harbour,** you can stay in St. John's to shop and explore. All of its minor attractions can be reached on foot from the cruise ship dock. The people in town may impress you, if not the town itself. They're helpful, have a sense of humor, and will guide you in the right direction if you've lost your way.

The Museum of Antigua and Barbuda sells a self-guided walking tour that focuses on the historical buildings of St. John's, particularly the ones in Redcliffe Quay. The tour wraps up in Redcliffe Tavern with a rum punch. The brochure costs $1.

The **market** in the southern part of St. John's is colorful and interesting, especially on Friday and Saturday mornings, when vendors are busy selling their fruits and vegetables, and gossiping. The partially open-air market lies at the lower end of Market Street.

The Anglican **St. John's Cathedral,** on Church Street (between Long and Newgate streets), has had a disastrous history. Originally built in 1681, it was replaced in 1720 by an English brick building, which was destroyed by an earthquake in 1843. The present pitch-pine interior dates from 1846. The church was going through a restoration in 1974 when another earthquake hit. The twin-spired landmark dominates St. John's skyline.

The **Museum of Antigua and Barbuda,** at the corner of Market and Long streets (☎ 268/462-1469), traces the history of the nation from its geological birth to the present day. Housed in the old Court House building dating from 1750, exhibits include a wattle-and-daub house model, African-Caribbean pottery, and utilitarian objects of daily life. It's open Monday to Friday from 8:30am to 4pm, Saturday from 10am to 1pm. Admission is free, but a minimum donation of $2 is requested.

ON YOUR OWN: BEYOND WALKING DISTANCE

One of the major attractions of the eastern Caribbean, **Nelson's Dockyard National Park** (☎ 268/460-1379) sits 11 miles southeast of St. John's on one of the world's safest harbors, and is open daily from 9am to 5pm. (Admission is $5 per person to tour the dockyard; children under 12 are free.) The centerpiece of the national park is the only existing example of a Georgian naval base. English ships used the harbor as a refuge from hurricanes as early as 1671, and Admiral Nelson made it his headquarters from 1784 to 1787. The dockyard played a leading role in the era of privateers, pirates, and great sea battles in the 18th century. The dockyard still plays a pivotal role in Antigua's sailing scene and is the venue for the island's annual Sailing Week. The admission price includes the Dockyard Museum, Dow's Hill Interpretation Center, Shirley Heights, the Blockhouse, and the park.

The restored dockyard is sometimes known as a Caribbean Williamsburg, and in the heart of it is the **Dockyard Museum** (☎ 268/460-8181). Housed in a building from 1855, museum exhibits illustrate the history of the dockyard, from its beginning as a British Navy stronghold to its development as a national park. Nautical memorabilia as well as island artifacts are on display. The museum is open daily from 9am to 5pm.

For a quick bite, head to the **Dockyard Bakery** (☎ 268/460-1474), which features homemade rolls, pastries, and other goodies. It is located right behind the museum.

The park itself is well worth exploring. It's filled with sandy beaches and tropical vegetation, including various species of cactus and mangroves that shelter a migrating colony of African cattle egrets. Nature trails expose the vegetation and coastal scenery. You'll also find archaeological sites that date back to before the Christian era. Tours of the dockyard last 15 to 20 minutes, but tours along nature trails can last anywhere from 30 minutes to 5 hours.

For an eagle's-eye view of English Harbour, take a taxi up to the top of **Shirley Heights,** directly to the east of the dockyard. Still standing are Palladian arches, once part of a barracks. The **Blockhouse** was put up as a stronghold in case of siege. The nearby **Military Cemetery** contains an obelisk monument to the men of the 54th Regiment.

Take a taxi from English Harbour 2¹/₂ miles east to the **Dow's Hill Interpretation Center** (☎ 268/460-2777), which offers a multimedia journey through six periods of the island's history. You'll learn about the Amerindian hunters, the British military, and the struggles connected with slavery. It's open from 9am to 5pm daily, and admission, including the multimedia show, is $5 for adults, free for children under 12. A stone's throw from the center is the **Belvedere,** which provides a panoramic view of the park, and a footpath leads to **Fort Berkley,** a fine specimen of old-time military engineering at the entrance to English Harbour. The path starts just outside the dockyard gate; the fort is about half a mile away.

In Brown's Bay Mill, near Freetown, the partially restored ✪ **Harmony Hall** (☎ **268/460-4120**) 1843 plantation house and sugar mill overlooks Nonsuch Bay, making it an ideal lunch stopover or shopping expedition. The sister establishment to Jamaica's Harmony Hall displays Antigua's best selection of Caribbean arts and crafts and sponsors regular exhibitions. Lunch, served daily from noon to 3pm, features fresh lobster, pasta dishes, and other specialties. You can also take a boat trip to nearby Green Island from here. If you want to go on the boat trip, call before you arrive or send an E-mail to harmony@candw.ag. Harmony Hall is special and worth the effort to reach it.

Go to **Betty's Hope Plantation,** south of Pares village (☎ **268/462-1469**), to see the only operational 18th-century sugar mill in the Caribbean. Restoration work on the former plantation started in the 1980s. On-site are twin mills and a visitor center.

On the way back to your cruise ship from English Harbour, ask your taxi driver to take you along the 20-some-mile circular route down **Fig Tree Drive,** across the main mountain range of Antigua. Although rough and very potholed in places, it's the island's most scenic drive. The drive passes through lush tropical settings and fishing villages along the southern coast. Nearly every hamlet has a little battered church and lots of goats and children running about. There are also the ruins of several old sugar mills. However, don't expect fig trees—*fig* is the Antiguan word for bananas.

SHOPPING

Most shops in St. John's are clustered on St. Mary's Street or High Street, lying within an easy walk of the cruise ship docks. There are many duty-free items for sale here, including English woolens and linens. You can also purchase Antiguan specialties, such as original pottery, local straw work, Antigua rum, hand-printed local designs on fabrics, floppy foldable hats, and shell curios.

Specialty shops in Redcliffe Quay worth exploring include **Jacaranda** on Redcliffe Street (☎ **268/462-1888**), for batik clothing, spices, bath products, and works by Caribbean artists; **The Map Shop** on St. Mary's Street (☎ **268/462-3993**), for old and new map prints, sea charts, and Caribbean literature; and **The Goldsmitty** on Redcliffe Street (☎ **268/462-4601**), for handmade jewels such as black opal and topaz created by Hans Smit.

If you need some additional formal wear during your cruise, visit **Noreen Philips** on Redcliffe Street (☎ **268/462-3127**). Noreen, a former model, designs all the clothing in her shop. There is a fine selection of evening gowns and bags, hats, belts, and costume jewelry, as well as casual outfits. If needed, Noreen can also design something specifically for you in a few hours.

If you are looking for woven goods, stop by the **Workshop for the Blind** on All Saint's Road, by St. John's market (☎ **268/462-0663**). Items such as breadbaskets and straw hats are for sale.

Located at the cruise dock, **Heritage Quay,** Antigua's first shopping-and-entertainment center, is a multimillion-dollar complex featuring some 40 duty-free shops and a vendors' arcade where local artists and craftspeople display their wares. Shops feature artwork, china and crystal, Swiss-made watches, and a great selection of swimwear. Restaurants offer a range of cuisine and views of St. John's Harbour. A food court serves visitors who prefer local specialties in an informal setting.

Redcliffe Quay, near Heritage Quay, was a slave-trading quarter that filled up with grog shops and a variety of merchants after abolition. Now it has been redeveloped and

---

Port Tip: Beach Safety

Be careful if you have your heart set on a deserted beach. You could be the victim of a mugging. Don't bring valuables. Also, readers increasingly complain of beach vendors hustling everything from jewelry to T-shirts. The beaches are open to all, so hotels can't restrain these bothersome peddlers.

---

contains a number of the most interesting shops in town, selling batiks and accessories, casual and dressy clothing, works of art, herbs and spices, and jewelry.

To find a truly authentic Caribbean souvenir, head to **Sofa** (☎ **268/463-0610**), which stands for Sculpture Objets Functional Art, and is housed in a renovated shed in Falmouth Harbour. You'll find an eclectic collection of Caribbean products, including hot sauces, arts and crafts, and items for the home, office, and garden.

BEACHES

On Antigua, it's all about the beaches, and there is certainly an endless supply (tourism folks claim there are 365). All the beaches are public, and there are quite a few that are truly spectacular, including the secluded stretches at Rendezvous Bay and Darkwood Beach. The beach at Galley Bay resort is also stunning. The most well known are Dickenson Bay, Half Moon Bay, and Pigeon Point.

Closest to St. John's is the beach at **Fort Bay,** located about 5 to 10 minutes by taxi from the cruise ship dock (the cab fare is about $7). Both locals and tourists visit this beach, where it is not uncommon to find people playing volleyball or beach cricket.

Further north is **Dickenson Bay** and **Runaway Bay,** where you will get the full resort beach experience—hotels, restaurants, water sports, and more.

One of the island's most attractive beaches can be found on the northwest coast at **Galley Bay** resort. Surfers are fond of this stretch. Also on this part of the coast are four beaches at **Hawksbill,** site of the Hawksbill Beach Resort. For those looking to go au naturel, try the fourth and final beach. It is quite secluded, and clothing is optional.

Good spots on the less-developed southwest coast are the unspoiled **Darkwood Beach** and **Carlisle Bay.** While at Darkwood, stop by O.J.'s (no, not that one!) Beach Bar & Restaurant for a cool drink and a bite to eat. To get there, follow the signposts after the beach. **Carlisle Bay,** where the legendary Curtain Bluff Resort is located, is an ideal spot for swimming.

Pigeon Point is about a 5-minute drive from English Harbour on the southeast coast; try the snorkeling here. Also on the southeast is **Half Moon Bay,** which boasts a loyal following and is known for its pink sands.

One of the better-kept secrets is **Jabberwock Beach** in Hodges Bay on the north coast. It is a favorite with locals. Another quiet and secluded beach is located at **Rendezvous Bay** on the south coast.

Taxis will take you from the cruise ship dock in St. John's to your choice of beach, but remember to make arrangements to be picked up at an agreed-upon time. A typical fare to Pigeon Point (about 25 min.) from St. John's is $20 per car. To Hawksbill and Galley Bay (about 10 min.), the fare is $12. Confirm all fares with the driver before setting out.

GREAT LOCAL RESTAURANTS & BARS

Most cruise passengers dine in St. John's, English Harbour, or Shirley Heights. Reservations usually aren't needed for lunch unless it's a heavy cruise-ship-arrival day. In that case, call from the dock when you come ashore.

The **local beer** of Antigua is Wadadli. The **local rum** is Cavalier.

IN ST. JOHN'S   **Big Banana Holding Company,** on Redcliffe Quay (☎ **268/462-2621**), makes the best pizza on the island in what used to be a slave quarters (you can get a great frothy coconut or banana crush, too, as well as overstuffed baked potatoes, fresh-fruit salad, or lobster salad). **Hemingway's,** on St. Mary's Street (☎ **268/462-2763**), named after Papa himself, has an upper veranda that overlooks Heritage Quay. Tasty salads, sandwiches, burgers, sautéed fillets of fish, pastries, ice cream, and an array of brightly colored tropical drinks are on the menu. **Redcliffe Tavern,** on Redcliffe Quay (☎ **268/461-4557**), is a bustling resorted warehouse that uses machinery from old factories as part of the decor. There is a good selection of lunch entrees, including pineapple stuffed with crab and spicy jerk chicken with plantains, as well as salads, sandwiches, and finger foods.

AT ENGLISH HARBOUR   **Admiral's Inn,** in Nelson's Dockyard (☎ **268/460-1027**), is housed in a 1788 building and features a menu that changes daily but usually features pumpkin soup and a choice of four or five main courses, such as local red snapper, grilled steak, or lobster.

AT SHIRLEY HEIGHTS   **Shirley Heights Lookout** (☎ **268/460-1785**) is the best alternative to the Admiral's Inn. In the 1790s the building was the lookout station for unfriendly ships heading toward English Harbour; today, it offers such favorites as grilled lobster in lime butter and garlic-flavored shrimp. You can order less expensive hamburgers and sandwiches in the pub downstairs. This is the place to be on Thursday and Sunday nights for live music, the island's best barbecue, and to watch the sun sink into the Caribbean.

AT HARMONY HALL   The restaurant at **Harmony Hall** (☎ **268/460-4120**) is worth the trek. Caribbean cuisine with a Mediterranean twist is served in a restored sugar mill that offers sweeping views of Nonsuch Bay.

2 Aruba

Aruba, in the Dutch Leewards, is one of the most popular destinations in the Caribbean. Until its wide white-sand beaches were "discovered" in the 1970s, though, Aruba was an almost forgotten outpost of Holland, mostly valued for its oil refineries and salt factories. Aruba became a self-governed part of the Netherlands in 1986 and has its own royally appointed governor and an elected parliament. Today it's favored for the bizarre lunar landscapes of its desertlike terrain, spectacular beaches, constant sunshine, and gambling.

Just 20 miles long and 6 miles at its widest point, Aruba is shaped more or less like an elongated triangle; one side faces west and is home to the hotels and beaches, and along the southern side are the airport, capital city of Oranjestad, and an oil refinery. It's Aruba's northern half that is wild and woolly—a dry, windswept collage of cacti, rock, and the island's signature divi-divi trees.

The capital, **Oranjestad,** isn't a picture-postcard port, but it has glittering casinos, lots of shopping, and one of the Caribbean's finest stretches of beach. With only 17 inches of rainfall annually, Aruba is dry and sunny almost year-round, and trade winds keep it from becoming unbearably hot. The air is clean and exhilarating, like that of Palm Springs, California. Aruba also lies outside the path of hurricanes that batter islands to the north.

Its population of about 90,000 is culturally diverse, with roots in Holland, Portugal, Spain, Venezuela, India, Pakistan, and Africa.

Frommer's Favorite Aruba Experiences

- **Renting a Jeep or doing a Jeep tour:** There's more to Aruba than a 7-mile strip of oceanfront high-rise hotels and wide white-sand beach, and this is the way to see it. (See "Shore Excursions" and "On Your Own: Touring by Rental Jeep," below.)
- **Taking an *Atlantis* submarine trip:** A real submarine takes you down 150 feet to see the undersea world (see "Shore Excursions," below).

COMING ASHORE Cruise ships arrive at the Aruba Port Authority, a modern terminal with a tourist information booth and the inevitable duty-free shops. From the pier it's just a 5-minute walk to the major shopping districts of downtown Oranjestad. If you opted not to take one of the shore excursions, you can make your way around on your own, allowing some time for Aruba's famous beach (just a 5- to 10-minute taxi ride away) in between luncheon stopovers and shopping. Still a large cargo port, Aruba is now separating its cruise and cargo facilities and beefing up passenger terminal services.

CURRENCY The currency is the **Aruba florin (AFl),** which is divided into 100 cents. Silver coins are in denominations of 5, 10, 25, and 50 cents and 1 and 2¹/₂ florins. The 50-cent piece, the square "yotin," is Aruba's best-known coin. The exchange rate is AFl1.77 to U.S.$1 (1 AFl is worth about 56¢). Unless otherwise stated, prices quoted in this section are in U.S. dollars.

LANGUAGE The official language here is Dutch, but nearly everybody speaks English. The language of the street is often Papiamento, a patois. Spanish is also widely spoken.

INFORMATION For information, go to the **Aruba Tourism Authority,** 172 L. G. Smith Blvd., Oranjestad (☎ **297/8-21019**). It's open Monday to Saturday from 9am to 5pm.

CALLING FROM THE U.S. When calling Aruba from the U.S., you need to dial the international access code (011) before the numbers listed throughout this section.

GETTING AROUND

BY RENTAL CAR It's easy to rent a car or four-wheel-drive vehicle and explore Aruba (I don't recommend renting a scooter or motorcycle, though, unless you plan on keeping to the paved roads only). You won't have much trouble finding your way around, but if you really want to explore Aruba's rough, moonlike hinterland, you need to rent a Jeep. The rental agencies are just outside the airport's main terminal. Try **Budget Rent-a-Car,** 1 Kolibristraat (☎ **800/472-3325** in the U.S., or 297/8-28600); **Hertz,** 142 L. G. Smith Blvd. (☎ **800/654-3001** in the U.S., or 297/8-24545); or **Avis,** 14 Kolibristraat (☎ **800/331-1084** in the U.S., or 297/8-23496).

Frommer's Ratings: Aruba					
	poor	fair	good	excellent	outstanding
Overall Experience					✓
Shore Excursions			✓		
Activities Close to Port				✓	
Beach & Water Sports					✓
Shopping				✓	
Dining/Bars				✓	

California
Lighthouse
☀ *California Point*

Malmok Beach ⟨

Hadikurari
(Fisherman's Hut) ⟨

Palm Beach ⟨

Eagle Beach ⟨   ○ Noord   ■ Altovista Chapel

Manchebo
Beach ⟨   *Bushiribana*

Divi Beach ⟨

Druid Bay   ■ Natural Bridge

                   ○ Casibari

Oranjestad   ○ Ayo

✈ Queen Beatrix Airport

                   ○ Santa Cruz

              ▲▲ Hooiberg

              ■ Caves of
                Canashito   *Spanish
                                Lagoon*

                              **ARIKOK
                              NATIONAL PARK**

*Caribbean
Sea*   ■ Fontein Cave
                                        ■ Boca Prins
                                          Sand Dunes

                                        ■ Guadarikiri Cave

                                                ⟨ Boca Grandi
                         ○ Savaneta

                    Sint Nicolas
                    (San Nicolas)
                                        Seroe
                                        Colorado
              Rodger's Beach ⟨   ○
                         Baby Beach ⟨ *Colorado Point*

*Caribbean
Sea*

| 0 | | 15 Miles |
| 0 | | 15 Kilometers |

Airport ✈ Beach ⟨
Lighthouse ☀ Cruise Ship Dock ⛴

BY TAXI   Taxis don't have meters, but fares are fixed. Tell the driver your destination and ask the fare before getting in. The main office is on Sands Street between the bowling center and Taco Bell. A **dispatch office** is located at Bosabao 41 (☎ **297/8-22116**). A ride from the cruise terminal to most of the beach resorts, including those at Palm Beach, costs about $8 to $16 per car, plus a small tip. A maximum of five passengers is allowed. It's next to impossible to locate a taxi on some parts of the island, so when traveling to a remote area or restaurant, ask the taxi driver to pick you up at a certain time. Some English-speaking drivers are available as guides. A 1-hour tour (and you don't need much more than that) is offered for about $40 for a maximum of four passengers.

BY BUS   Aruba has excellent bus service, with regular daily service from 6am to midnight. The round-trip fare between the beach hotels and Oranjestad is about $2. Try to have exact change. Buses stop across the street from the cruise terminal on L. G. Smith Boulevard and will take you to any of the hotel resorts or the beaches along the West End.

SHORE EXCURSIONS

✪ **Four-Wheel-Drive Backcountry Aruba Tour** ($54, 4 hours): Just like the solo tour described below, but this version does the tour in a convoy of four-passenger sports utility vehicles (with you behind the wheel). A stop is made for lunch and some swimming. If you don't have the gumption to go it alone but you're still looking for some adventure, this is a great alternative.

✪ *Atlantis* **Submarine Journey** ($74 adults, $37 children 4 to 16; 2 hours): One of Aruba's most diverting pastimes, an underwater journey on the submarine *Atlantis* is a great opportunity for nondivers to witness firsthand the underwater life of a coral reef. Passengers submerge to about 150 feet without ever getting wet.

Aruba Bus Tour ($26, 3 hours): This city and countryside air-conditioned bus tour takes passengers along part of Aruba's wild and woolly windward coastline to the Natural Bridge (a rocky "bridge" cut by the sea and wind) and the Casibari rock formations, as well as along Aruba's bustling hotel strip.

ON YOUR OWN: WITHIN WALKING DISTANCE

Bustling **Oranjestad,** the capital and port, attracts shoppers rather than sightseers. The town has a very Caribbean flavor, with both Spanish and Dutch architecture. The main thoroughfare, Lloyd G. (L. G.) Smith Boulevard, runs from the airport along the waterfront and on to Palm Beach, changing its name along the way to J. E. Irausquin Boulevard. Most visitors cross the road heading for **Caya G. F. Betico Croes,** where they find the best shopping.

After a shopping trip, you might return to the harbor, where fishing boats and schooners, many from Venezuela, are moored. Nearly all newcomers to Aruba like to take a picture of **Schooner Harbour.** Colorful boats are docked along the quay, and boat people display their wares in open stalls. The local patois predominates. A little farther along, fresh seafood is sold directly from the boats at the fish market. On the sea side, you'll find **Wilhelmina Park,** named after Queen Wilhelmina of the Netherlands. A tropical garden has been planted here along the water, and there's a sculpture of the Queen Mother.

Aside from shopping, Aruba's major attraction is **Palm Beach,** among the finest beaches in the Caribbean. Most of Aruba's high-rise hotels sit in a Las Vegas–style strip along the pure white sand.

ON YOUR OWN: TOURING BY RENTAL JEEP

The best way to see all of Aruba and its intriguing terrain—a dry, windswept collage of cacti, rock, and the island's signature divi-divi trees—is to ✪ **rent a four-wheel-drive Jeep.** You can rent a convertible Suzuki Samurai or nonconvertible four-wheel drive for about $60 to $75 per day, and share the expense with another couple to cut costs. Car-rental companies, which are located on L. G. Smith Boulevard and Kolibristraat, as well as at the airport, will give you a map highlighting the best routes to reach the attractions.

Here's a good route to follow: Following the system of roads that circle the perimeter of the island, start your journey clockwise from the airport. Head back past the hotel strip and on to the island's northwestern-most point. Here, the **California Lighthouse,** named for a ship that wrecked in the area nearly a century ago, affords sweeping 360° views of the island. (Tour the island counterclockwise and you'll hit the Lighthouse in time to watch the magnificent sunset melt into the sea.)

By the time you reach the Lighthouse, you've already entered Aruba's twilight zone. From here on, your four-wheel-drive adventure will take you into the island's moonlike terrain, past huge heaps of giant boulders and barren rocky coastlines. The smooth, well-maintained road system that links together the hotel strip and Oranjestad transforms itself into a single band of rubble, and the calm, bright turquoise sea turns rough and rowdy.

Reaching the **Alto Vista Chapel,** about 5 miles or so from the Lighthouse, chances are a thin film of red dust has already coated you and the Jeep. But don't let that stop you from having a peek inside the quaint pale-yellow church that sits atop a small hill. From its solitary perch, enjoy breathtaking views.

Farther along on the northern coast, you'll approach the hulking ruins of the **Bushiribana Gold Smelter** amid a desolate stretch of parched landscape. Don't bother stopping for a closer look at its graffitied walls, though; its impact is more powerful from a distance.

Just beyond it is the **Natural Bridge,** one of Aruba's most popular attractions. Over the centuries, the crashing ocean surf and whipping wind crafted this "bridge" out of the vulnerable coral rock. The **Thirst Aid Station** restaurant sits nearby, and with its campy colored lights and used-car-lot metallic fringes strung across the ceiling, you may find it to be an interesting site in itself (it's also one of the few places to grab a couple of cold drinks and a sandwich before hitting the road again).

Just before the Gold Smelter and Natural Bridge, keep a look out for **secluded beach coves.** While some are littered with plastic bottles and debris, just as many are pristine patches of paradise. Often just 50 to 100 feet from the road, the craggy coast opens up to random wedges of protected beach and shallow water, perfect for a dip.

Next, veer off towards the center of the island to check out the bizarre **Ayó and Casibari rock formations.** Somewhat of a mystery even to geologists, it's as though the random piles of massive boulders have been dropped from the sky. If you can handle the gusting winds, climb to the top of the mound for great views. Be sure to look for the ancient **Amerindian drawings** painted on the rocks at Ayó.

In the center of the island, **Hooiberg** is affectionately known as "The Haystack." It's Aruba's most outstanding landmark. On a clear day, you can see Venezuela from atop this 541-foot hill.

Farther east along the desolate northern coast is a series of caves punched into the cliff sides of the area's mesas. Have a look inside the graffiti-covered, bat-inhabited **Guadirikiri, Fontein,** and **Tunnel of Love caves;** rent flashlights for $6 apiece (there's no admission charge).

Heading southeast toward Aruba's behemoth oil refinery is **Baby Beach,** at the island's easternmost point. Like a great big bathtub, this shallow bowl of warm turquoise water is protected by an almost complete circle of rock, and is a great place for a peaceful dip after a sweaty day behind the wheel.

SHOPPING

Aruba is a shopper's paradise. An easy walk from the cruise terminal, Oranjestad's half-mile-long **Caya G. F. Betico Croes** compresses six continents into one main, theme-parklike shopping street. While this is not technically a free port, the duty is only 3.3%, and there's no sales tax. You'll find the usual array of jewelry, liquor, Swiss watches, German and Japanese cameras, English bone china and porcelain, French perfume, British woolens, Indonesian specialties, Madeira embroidery, and Dutch, Swedish, and Danish silver and pewter. Delft blue pottery is an especially good buy, as are Edam and Gouda cheeses from Holland. Stamp collectors can purchase colorful and artistic issues at the post office in Oranjestad.

The **Alhambra Moonlight Shopping Center,** L. G. Smith Boulevard, next to the Alhambra Casino, blends international shops, outdoor marketplaces, cafes, and restaurants, and sells everything from fine jewelry, chocolates, and perfume to imported craft items, leather goods, clothing, and lingerie.

The Seaport Village/Seaport Market, overlooking Oranjestad's harbor, at L. G. Smith Blvd. 82, is Aruba's densest concentration of shopping options, with several bars and cafes, two casinos, and at least 200 purveyors of fashion, gift items, sporting goods, liquors, perfumes, and photographic supplies.

BEACHES

The western and southern shores, known as the **Turquoise Coast,** attract sun seekers to Aruba. An $8 taxi ride from the cruise terminal will get you to **Palm Beach** and **Eagle Beach,** the two best beaches on the island. The latter is closer to Oranjestad. Aruba's beaches are open to the public, so you can spread your towel anywhere along this 7-mile stretch of uninterrupted sugar-white sand, which also includes **Manchebo Beach** or **Druid Bay Beach.** But you will be charged for using the facilities at any of the hotels on this strip.

In total contrast to this leeward side, the northern, or windward, shore is rugged and wild.

SPORTS

WINDSURFING   **Divi Winds Center,** J. E. Irausquin Blvd. 41 (☎ **297/8-23300,** ext. 623), at the Tamarind Aruba Beach Resort, is the island's windsurfing headquarters. Equipment rents for about $15 per hour. The resort is on the tranquil (Caribbean) side of the island, away from the fierce Atlantic waves (still the winds are strong). You can also arrange Sunfish lessons or rent snorkeling gear. The operation has another location at the Hyatt.

GAMBLING

Although most cruise ships have their own casinos, you can also try your luck ashore at roulette, craps, blackjack, Caribbean stud poker, baccarat, and the ubiquitous one-armed bandits. Aruba's gaming establishments are second only to San Juan in the Caribbean. Most casinos here are open day and night, thus drawing both cruise ship passengers and land-based vacationers. They're mainly located in the big hotels on Palm Beach, an $8 to $12 taxi ride from the cruise terminal.

The casino at the **Holiday Inn Aruba Beach Resort,** L. G. Smith Blvd. 230 (☎ **297/8-67777**), wins the prize for all-around gambling action. It keeps its doors open daily from 9am to 4am.

Closer to Oranjestad, the **Crystal Casino** at the Aruba Sonesta Resort & Casino at Seaport Village (☎ **297/8-36000**) is open 24 hours. It evokes European casinos with its luxurious furnishings, ornate moldings, marble, brass, gold leaf, and crystal chandeliers.

Casino Masquerade, at the Radisson Aruba Caribbean Resort & Casino, J. E. Irausquin Blvd. 81 (☎ **297/8-66555**), is the newest casino in Aruba. Located in the center of the high-rise hotel area, it's open daily from 10am to 4am.

The **Casablanca Casino** occupies a large room adjacent to the lobby of the Wyndham Hotel and Resort, J. E. Irausquin Blvd. (☎ **297/8-64466**). **Casino Copacabana,** in the island's most spectacular hotel, Hyatt Regency Aruba, L. G. Smith Blvd. 85 (☎ **297/8-61234**), evokes France's Côte d'Azur. These two are open throughout the day, accommodating cruise ship passengers.

Outdrawing them all, however, is the **Royal Cabaña Casino,** at the La Cabaña All-Suite Beach Resort & Casino, J. E. Irausquin Blvd. 250 (☎ **297/8-79000**), the third largest casino in the Bahamian-Caribbean region. It's known for its three-in-one operation, combining a restaurant, showcase cabaret theater, and nightclub. The casino, the largest on Aruba, has 33 tables and games plus 320 slot machines.

More than just a casino, the **Alhambra,** L. G. Smith Blvd. 47 (☎ **297/8-35000**), offers a collection of boutiques, along with an inner courtyard modeled after an 18th-century Dutch village. The desert setting of Aruba seems appropriate for this Moorish-style building, with its serpentine mahogany columns, repeating arches, and sea-green domes. The casino and its satellites are open daily from 10am until very late at night.

The **Aruba Palm Beach Resort & Casino,** J. E. Irausquin Blvd. 79 (☎ **297/8-23900**), opens its slots at 9am and its other games at 1pm. **Americana Aruba Beach Resort & Casino,** J. E. Irausquin Blvd. 83 (☎ **297/8-64500**), opens daily at noon for slots, blackjack, and roulette; however, other games aren't available until 8pm, when most cruise ships have departed.

GREAT LOCAL RESTAURANTS & BARS

If there are a lot of cruise ships in port, call from a pay phone in the cruise ship terminal to make a reservation. If there aren't many ships around, chances are you can just walk in. All restaurants listed are in Oranjestad.

Boonoonoonoos, Wilhelminastraat 18 (☎ **297/8-31888**), is in an old-fashioned Aruban house on the capital's main shopping street, and features dishes from throughout the Caribbean. ✪ **Chez Mathilde,** Havenstraat 23 (☎ **297/8-34968**), Oranjestad's French restaurant, is expensive, but most agree that it's worth the price, especially those who order the chef's bouillabaisse, made with more than a dozen different sea creatures. **The Paddock,** 13 L. G. Smith Blvd. (☎ **297/8-32334**), is a cafe and bistro with a Dutch aesthetic and ambiance and a menu of sandwiches, salads, fish, and more. **The Waterfront Crabhouse,** Seaport Market, L. G. Smith Boulevard (☎ **297/8-36767**), is a seafood restaurant set at the end of a shopping mall.

3 Bahamas: Nassau & Freeport

Only 36 of the some 700 islands of the Bahamas are inhabited, and only a few of those—Grand Bahama (where Freeport is), New Providence (where Nassau is), Abaco, Eleuthera, Andros, Cat Island, and San Salvador—are known to most travelers. Arawak Indians inhabited the islands until, in 1492, Christopher Columbus first set foot in the New World on the Bahamian island of San Salvador, opening the door to centuries of repression and dominance. The rest, of course, is history and the Caribbean islands were never to be the same again. British settlement of the Bahamas began in 1647 and the islands became a British colony in 1783. In 1973, the Bahamas became an independent commonwealth, and today, of course, they're a major tourist destination, being so close to Miami (Nassau is only 90 miles away).

CURRENCY   The legal tender is the **Bahamian dollar (B$1),** which is on a par with the U.S. dollar. Both U.S. and Bahamian dollars are accepted on an equal basis throughout the Bahamas. There is no restriction on the amount of foreign currency tourists can bring into the country. Most stores accept traveler's checks.

LANGUAGE   The language of the Bahamas is English. Bahamians speak it with a lilt and with more British than American influence. They also pepper their colorful speech with words left from the indigenous Arawak tongue (like *cassava* and *guava*), as well as African words and phrases.

CALLING FROM THE U.S.   When calling Nassau from the United States, you need to dial only a "1" before the numbers listed throughout this section.

NASSAU

Nassau is the capital of the Bahamas, and it has that nation's best shopping, best entertainment, and best beaches. It's big. It's bold. It's one of the busiest cruise ship ports in the world. It's got the old, it's got the new, there's probably something borrowed here, and there's a whole heckuva lot of blue seas. One million visitors a year make their way onto its shores to enjoy its bounty.

With its adjoining **Cable Beach** and **Paradise Island** (linked by bridge to the city), Nassau has luxury resorts set on powdery-soft beaches; all the water sports, golf, and tennis you could want; and so much duty-free shopping that its stores outdraw its museums. Yet historic Nassau hasn't lost its British colonial charms—it just boasts up-to-date tourist facilities to complement them.

Many people come on 3- to 4-day cruises leaving from Miami, Fort Lauderdale, and Port Canaveral. In recent years, the government has spent millions of dollars increasing its facilities, so now about a dozen cruise ships can pull into dock at one time.

Frommer's Favorite Nassau Experiences

- **Dining on fresh conch at Arawak Cay:** The small man-made island across West Bay Street is the place to go for the freshest stuff, washed down with coconut milk laced with gin (see "Great Local Restaurants & Bars," below).
- **Getting your hair braided:** For a new look, get your hair braided in the local style at the Hairbraider's Centre on Prince George Dock (see "On Your Own: Within Walking Distance," below).

COMING ASHORE   The newly expanded cruise ship docks near Rawson Square are at the very center of the city and its main shopping area. The Straw Market, at Market Plaza, is nearby, as is the main shopping artery of Bay Street. The Nassau International Bazaar is at the intersection of Woodes Rogers Walk and Charlotte Street.

Your best bet for making long-distance **phone calls** is the Bahamas Telecommunications Co. phone center on East Street, which runs perpendicular to Rawson Square. Walk about 4 blocks on East Street and it'll be on your right-hand side.

INFORMATION   You can get help from the Information Desk at the **Ministry of Tourism's** office, Bay Street (☎ **242/356-7591**), open Monday to Friday from 9am to 5pm. A smaller information booth can be found at Rawson Square near the dock. For info before you go, call the Tourist Office in the U.S. (☎ **800/327-7678**) or log on to the Web site www.bahamas.com.

GETTING AROUND

Unless you rent a horse and carriage, the only way to really see old Nassau is on foot. All the major attractions and the principal stores are within walking distance. You can even walk to Cable Beach or Paradise Island.

Frommer's Ratings: Nassau					
	poor	fair	good	excellent	outstanding
Overall Experience				✓	
Shore Excursions			✓		
Activities Close to Port				✓	
Beach & Water Sports			✓		
Shopping				✓	
Dining/Bars			✓		

Nassau

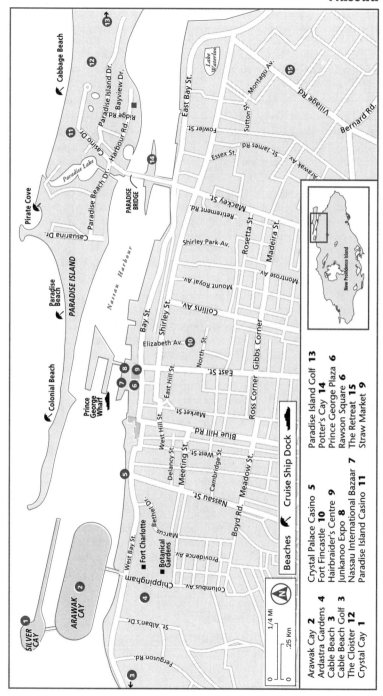

Arawak Cay **2**
Ardastra Gardens **4**
Cable Beach **3**
Cable Beach Golf **3**
The Cloister **12**
Crystal Cay **1**

Crystal Palace Casino **5**
Fort Fincastle **10**
Hairbraider's Centre **9**
Junkanoo Expo **8**
Nassau International Bazaar **7**
Paradise Island Casino **11**

Paradise Island Golf **13**
Potter's Cay **14**
Prince George Plaza **6**
Rawson Square **15**
The Retreat **15**
Straw Market **9**

Beaches ← Cruise Ship Dock ←

New Providence Island

BY TAXI Taxis are practical, at least for longer island trips, and are required to have working meters, so you probably won't be cheated. That said, on a recent trip, my drivers never wanted to use their meters and insisted on flat fees. The official fare is $2 at flag fall and 30¢ for each quarter mile for the first two passengers; additional passengers pay $2. Five-passenger cabs can be hired for $23 to $25 per hour. For a radio taxi, call ☎ **242/323-5111.**

BY MINIBUS The least expensive means of transport is by the medium-size buses called jitneys that the locals take. The fare is 75¢; exact change is required.

BY FERRY Ferries run from the end of Casuarina Drive on Paradise Island across the harbor to Rawson Square for $2 per person. These "water taxis" operate during the day at 20-minute intervals between Paradise Island and Prince George Wharf. The one-way fare is $3 per person.

BY HORSE-DRAWN CARRIAGE The elegant, traditional way to see Nassau is in a horse-drawn surrey. Negotiate with the driver and agree on the price before you get in. The average charge for a 20- to 25-minute tour is $10 per person. The maximum load is three adults plus one or two children under the age of 12. The surreys are available daily from 9am to 4:30pm, except when horses are rested—usually from 1 to 3pm May through October, and from 1 to 2pm November through April. You'll find the surreys at Rawson Square, off Bay Street.

BY MOTOR SCOOTER/MOPED Motor scooters have become a favorite mode of transportation. For a rental, contact **Ursa Investment,** Prince George Wharf (☎ **242/326-8329**). Mopeds cost about $20 per hour or $50 for a full day.

BY RENTAL CAR If you want to rent a car, try **Avis** (☎ **800/331-1212** in the U.S., or 242/326-6380), **Budget** (☎ **800/527-0070** in the U.S., or 242/377-7405), and **Hertz** (☎ **800/654-3131** in the U.S., or 242/377-8684), and remember to drive on the left, British-style.

SHORE EXCURSIONS

There's a lot you can do on your own in Nassau, and it's easy to get around by taxi and on foot. Your ship will probably offer several organized island tours, as well as snorkeling and a range of waterborne sightseeing tours via glass-bottomed boat and submarine and/ or booze cruises aboard a catamaran. Here are some of the best ones.

Heart of Nassau and Ardastra Gardens ($25, 2¹/₂ hours): You're taken along Bay Street, the main shopping district, and later treated to the famous marching flamingo review in the gardens. Other stops include the Queen's Staircase and Fort Charlotte.

Fort Fincastle Tour ($21, 2 hours): This tour takes you to a great view, the Queen's Staircase, and some of the most beautiful homes of Nassau, then across the bridge to view the highlights of Paradise Island, including the Cloisters and its side gardens.

Crystal Cay Tour ($21, 3 hours): The country's most popular attraction has a network of aquariums, an Underwater Observation Tower, landscaped park areas, lounges, and a restaurant. The tour is more expensive if you opt to rent snorkeling equipment. (*Note:* It's almost as easy to go on your own.)

TOURING THROUGH LOCAL OPERATORS

Goombay Guided Walking Tours: These free tours, arranged by the Ministry of Tourism (☎ 242/326-9772), leave from the Tourist Information Booth on Rawson Square. Make an advance reservation, as schedules can vary. Usually the tours leave the booth at 10am and again at 2pm, except on Thursday and Sunday afternoon. These tours last for about 45 minutes and include descriptions of some of the city's most venerable buildings, with commentaries on the history, customs, and traditions of Nassau.

Walking Around Underwater: Hartley's Undersea Walk, East Bay Street (☎ 242/ 393-8234), takes you on a 3¹/₂-hour cruise on the yacht *Pied Piper.* At one point you don a breathing helmet and spend about 20 minutes walking along the ocean bottom through a "garden" of tropical fish, sponges, and other undersea life. Entire families can make this walk. You don't even have to be able to swim. Trips are operated Tuesday to Saturday at 9:30am and 1:30pm.

Day Cruises: Nassau Cruises Ltd., at the Paradise Island Bridge (☎ 242/363-3577), maintains a trio of luxurious three-deck motorized yachts, *Calypso I, Calypso IV,* and *The Islander,* all of which depart from a point just west of the toll booth at the Paradise Island Bridge. Daytime trips leave every day for the secluded beaches of Blue Lagoon Island, a 4-mile sail east of Paradise Island. The day sails leave at 10am and 11:30am and come back from the island at 1:30, 3, and 4:30pm. The day pass is $20 for adults and $10 for children, and pays for the boat ride only. The all-inclusive day pass is $50 for adults and $25 for children (3 to 12), and covers transportation, the boat ride, lunch, two daiquiris for adults, and all nonmotorized water sports.

ON YOUR OWN: WITHIN WALKING DISTANCE

The best way to see some of the major public buildings of Nassau is to take a walk, which gives you not only an overview of the historical monuments, but a feel for the city and its history. Later you can concentrate on specific outlying sights, notably Ardastra Gardens and Coral Island Bahamas.

Begin your stroll around Nassau at **Rawson Square** in the center, home of the Straw Market stalls. I also enjoy the native market on the waterfront, a short walk through the Straw Market. This is where Bahamian fishermen unload a variety of fish and produce—crates of mangoes, oranges, tomatoes, and limes, plus lots of crimson-lipped conch. For a look, it's best to go any Monday-to-Saturday morning before noon.

"Lady, get your hair braided!" You'll be aggressively solicited to have your hair braided in the local style at the ✪ **Hairbraider's Centre,** Prince George Dock. The government sponsors this open-air pavilion where all sorts of braiding experts gather. If you're looking for a new look, here's your chance. If you're not, a polite "no thanks" does the trick.

Potter's Cay, under the Paradise Island Bridge, provides a chance to observe local life as nowhere else. Sloops from the Out Islands pull in here, bringing their fresh catch along with plenty of conch. Freshly grown herbs and vegetables are also sold here, along with limes (the Bahamians' preferred seasoning for fish) and tropical fruits such as *pawpaw* (papaya), pineapple (usually from Eleuthera), and bananas. Little stalls sell conch in several forms: raw, marinated in lime juice, as spicy deep-fried fritters, and in conch salad and conch soup.

The Cloister, in front of the Ocean Club, Ocean Club Drive, Paradise Island (☎ 242/363-3000), is a real 14th-century cloister, built in France by Augustinian monks and reassembled here stone by stone. Huntington Hartford, the A&P stores heir, purchased the cloister from the estate of William Randolph Hearst at San Simeon in California, but the dismantled parts arrived unlabeled and unnumbered on Paradise Island. The deconstructed cloister baffled the experts until artist and sculptor Jean Castre-Manne set about to reassemble it. It took him 2 years, and what you see today presumably bears some similarity to the original. The gardens, extending over the rise to Nassau Harbour, are filled with tropical flowers and classic statuary.

Crystal Cay marine park, on Silver Cay just off West Bay Street, between downtown Nassau and Cable Beach (☎ 242/328-1036), has a network of aquariums, landscaped park areas, lounges, a gift shop, and a restaurant, but its outstanding feature is the Underwater Observation Tower. You descend a spiral staircase to a depth of 20 feet below the surface of the water, where you view coral reefs and abundant sea life in their natural habitat. The tower rises 100 feet above the water to two viewing decks. Graceful stingrays, endangered sea turtles, and Caribbean sharks swim in Shark Tank, which has both an overhead viewing deck and a below-water viewing area. Nature trails with lush tropical foliage, waterfalls, exotic trees, and wildlife further enhance this setting. You can get here via a scenic 10-minute ferry ride from the Prince George Dock.

Fort Fincastle, Elizabeth Avenue (☎ 242/322-2442), which can be reached by climbing the Queen's Staircase, was constructed in 1793 by Lord Dunmore, the royal governor. From here you can take an elevator ride to the top and walk on an observation floor (a 126-foot-high water tower and lighthouse) for a view of the harbor. Although the ruins of the fort can hardly compete with the view, you can walk around on your own or take a guided tour. You don't have to ask for a guide, since very assertive young men wait to show you around. Frankly, there isn't that much to see except some old cannons.

It's quite likely you'll miss the Junkanoo parade beginning at 2am on Boxing Day (Dec 26), but you can relive the Bahamian Junkanoo carnival at the **Junkanoo Expo,** Prince George Wharf (☎ 242/356-2731), in the old Customs Warehouse. All the glitter and glory of Mardi Gras comes alive in this museum, with its fantasy costumes used for the holiday bacchanal.

ON YOUR OWN: BEYOND WALKING DISTANCE

A flock of pink flamingos parading in formation is the main attraction at the lush, 5-acre ✪ **Ardastra Gardens,** Chippingham Road, near Fort Charlotte, about a mile west of downtown Nassau (☎ 242/323-5806). These Marching Flamingos have been trained to obey the drillmaster's oral orders with long-legged precision and discipline. They perform daily at 11am, 2pm, and 4pm. Other exotic wildlife to be seen here are very tame boa constrictors, kinkajous (honey bears) from Central and South America, green-winged macaws, peafowl, blue-and-gold macaws, capuchin monkeys, and more. You can get a good look at the flora of the gardens by walking along the signposted paths, as many of the more interesting and exotic trees bear identification plaques. Guided tours of the gardens and the aviary are given Monday to Saturday at 10:15am and 3:15pm.

A true oasis in Nassau, the 11 acres of unspoiled gardens at **The Retreat,** Village Road (☎ 242/393-1317), are even more intriguing than the Botanical Gardens. They are home to about 200 species of exotic palm trees, as well as the headquarters for the Bahamas National Trust. Half-hour tours of the acres are given Tuesday to Thursday at noon.

GAMBLING

Many cruise ship passengers spend almost their entire time ashore at one of the casinos on Cable Beach or Paradise Island.

All gambling roads eventually lead to the extravagant **Paradise Island Casino,** in the Atlantis, Casino Drive (☎ 242/363-3000). For sheer gloss, glitter, and showbiz extravagance, this mammoth 30,000-square-foot casino, with adjacent attractions, is the place to go. It's the only casino on Paradise Island, and is superior to the Crystal Palace Casino, below. No visit to the Bahamas would be complete without a promenade through the Bird Cage Walk, an assortment of restaurants, bars, and cabaret facilities. Doric columns, a battery of lights, and a mirrored ceiling vie with the British-colonial decor in the enormous gaming room. Some 1,000 slot machines operate 24 hours a day, and from midmorning until early the following morning the 59 gaming tables are all seriously busy.

The glitzy **Crystal Palace Casino,** West Bay Street, Cable Beach (☎ **242/ 327-6200**), screams 1980s with its pink and purple rainbow decor. It's the only casino on New Providence Island and is run by Nassau Marriott Resort. Although some savvy gamblers claim you get better odds in Las Vegas, this 35,000-square-foot casino nevertheless stacks up well against all the major casinos of the Caribbean. The gaming room features 750 slot machines in true Las Vegas style, along with 69 gaming tables. An oval-shaped casino bar extends onto the gambling floor, and a Casino Lounge, with its bar and bandstand, offers live entertainment. Open Sunday to Thursday from 10am to 4am, Friday and Saturday 24 hours.

SHOPPING

In 1992, the Bahamas abolished import duties on 11 categories of luxury goods, including china, crystal, fine linens, jewelry, leather goods, photographic equipment, watches, fragrances, and other merchandise, but even though prices are duty-free, you can still end up spending more on an item in the Bahamas than you would back home. If you're contemplating buying a good Swiss watch or some expensive perfume, it's best to look in your hometown discount outlets before making serious purchases here. While the advertised 30% to 50% reductions off stateside prices might be true in some cases, they're not in most. There are few great bargains here.

The principal shopping area is a stretch of **Bay Street,** the main drag, and its side streets. Here's you'll find chain stores like **Colombian Emeralds, Soloman's Mines,** and **Fendi.** There are also shops in the hotel arcades. In lieu of street numbers along Bay Street, look for signs advertising the various stores.

The crowded aisles of the **Straw Market** in Straw Market Plaza on Bay Street seems to be on every shopper's itinerary. Even those who don't want to buy anything come here to look around. You can watch the Bahamian craftspeople weave and plait straw hats, handbags, dolls, place mats, and other items, including straw shopping bags. You'll also find earrings and other inexpensive items. Most shopkeepers are willing to bargain, though a few won't budge. Give it a shot. Note, though, that some of the items here are not locally made, but imported from Asia. Be careful. The **Bahamas Plait Market,** Wulff Road, and **The Plait Lady,** the Regarno Building, Victoria and Bay streets, are both far superior to the Straw Market, offering good choices for 100% Bahamian-made products. **Island Tings,** Bay Street between East Street and Elizabeth Avenue, and **Seagrape,** West Bay Street, both offer Bahamian arts and crafts, plus jewelry and other items.

The tired-looking **Nassau International Bazaar,** running from Bay Street down to the waterfront near the Prince George Wharf, is composed of some 30 shops selling goods from around the globe. The alleyways here have been cobbled and storefronts are garreted, evoking the villages of old Europe. **Prince George Plaza,** Bay Street, can be crowded with cruise ship passengers. Many fine shops here sell Gucci and other quality merchandise. You can also patronize an open-air rooftop restaurant overlooking the street.

If you've fallen under the junkanoo spell and want to take home some steel drums, stop by **Pyfroms** on Bay Street. If you'd rather listen than play, try **Cody's Music and Video Center** on East Bay Street, corner of Armstrong Street, which specializes in contemporary music of the Bahamas and the Caribbean. The father of owner Cody Carter was mentor to many of the country's first Goombay and junkanoo artists.

Pipe of Peace, on Bay Street between Charlotte and Parliament streets, is called the "world's most complete tobacconist." You can buy both Cuban and Jamaican cigars here. (However, the Cuban cigars can't legally be brought back to the U.S.)

Stamp collectors should stop by the **Bahamas Post Office Philatelic Bureau,** in the General Post Office, at the top of Parliament Street on East Hill Street, for beautiful Bahamian stamps, while **Coin of the Realm,** on Charlotte Street, just off Bay Street, is the place for coin collectors. **The Girls from Brazil** on Bay Street is the best outlet for swimwear in Nassau, and **Mademoiselle, Ltd.,** on Bay Street at Frederick Street, specializes in all kinds of resort wear as well as locally made batik garments by Androsia.

BEACHES

On New Providence Island, sun lovers flock to **Cable Beach,** one of the best-equipped in the Caribbean, with all sorts of water sports and easy access to shops, casinos, bars, and restaurants. The area was named for the telegraph cable laid in 1892 from Jupiter, Florida, to the Bahamas. Cable Beach runs for some 4 miles and is relatively wide. Waters can be rough and reefy, and then turn calm and clear. The beach is about 5 miles from the port and can be reached by taxi (for about a steep $10 a person) or bus no. 10 (for 75¢).

Western Esplanade, which sweeps westward from the British Colonial hotel, is closer and more convenient for those arriving by cruise ship, but is inferior to Cable Beach. It has rest rooms, changing facilities, and a snack bar.

Paradise Beach on Paradise Island is a fine beach and convenient to Nassau—all visitors have to do is walk or drive across the bridge or take a boat from the Prince George Wharf (see "Getting Around," above). Admission to the beach is $3 for adults, $1 for children, including use of a shower and locker. An extra $10 deposit is required for towels. Paradise Island has a number of smaller beaches as well, including **Pirate's Cove Beach** and **Cabbage Beach,** both on the north shore. Bordered by casuarinas, palms, and sea grapes, Cabbage Beach's broad sands stretch for at least 2 miles. It's likely to be crowded with guests of the island's megaresorts. Escapists find something approaching solitude on the northwestern end, accessible only by boat or foot.

SPORTS

GOLF   South Ocean Golf Course, Southwest Bay Road (☎ 242/362-4391), is the best course on New Providence Island and one of the best in the Bahamas. It's located 30 minutes from Nassau on the southwest edge of the island. This 18-hole, 6,706-yard, par-72 beauty has some first-rate holes with a backdrop of trees, shrubs, ravines, and undulating hills. The lofty elevation offers some panoramic water views. It's best to phone ahead in case there's a tournament scheduled. **Cable Beach Golf Course,** Cable Beach, West Bay Road (☎ 242/327-6000), is a spectacular 18-hole, 7,040-yard, par-72 championship golf course, although not as challenging as South Ocean. Under the management of Radisson Cable Beach Hotel, this course is often used by guests of the other nearby hotels. **Paradise Island Golf Club,** Paradise Island Drive (☎ 242/363-3925), is a superb 18-hole championship course at the east end of Paradise Island. The 14th hole of the 6,771-yard, par-72 course has the world's largest sand trap: The entire left side over the hole is white-sand beach.

SCUBA DIVING & SNORKELING   Bahama Divers, East Bay Street (☎ 242/393-5644), offers a half day of snorkeling at offshore reefs, and a half-day scuba trip with preliminary pool instruction for beginners. Participants receive free transportation to the boats. Children must be 8 or older to go snorkeling. Reservations are required, especially during the winter season. **Stuart Cove's Dive South Ocean,** Southwest Bay Street, South Ocean (☎ 800/879-9832 in the U.S., or 242/362-4171), is about 10 minutes from top dive sites, including the coral reefs, wrecks, and an underwater airplane structure used in filming James Bond thrillers. The Porpoise Pen Reefs and steep sea walls are also on the diving agenda. All prices for boat dives include tanks, weights, and belts. A special feature is a series of shark-dive experiences.

GREAT LOCAL RESTAURANTS & BARS

The **local beer** in Bermuda is Kalik. The **local rum** is Bacardi.

✪ **ON ARAWAK CAY**   You'll get all the conch you can possibly eat on Arawak Cay, a small man-made island across West Bay Street. The Bahamian government created the cay to store large tanks of freshwater, of which New Providence Island often runs out. You don't go here to see the water tanks, however, but to join the locals in sampling their favorite food. The conch is cracked before your eyes (not everybody's favorite attraction), and you're given some hot sauce to spice it up. The locals wash it down with their favorite drink, coconut milk laced with gin (an acquired taste, to say the least). This ritual is a local tradition, and you'll feel like a real Bahamian if you participate.

IN NASSAU   **Bahamian Kitchen,** Trinity Place, off Market Street, next to Trinity Church (☎ **242/325-0702**), is one of the best places for good, down-home Bahamian food at modest prices. Specialties include lobster Bahamian style, fried red snapper, and curried chicken. **Café Kokomo,** in the garden of the Parliament Hotel, 18 Parliament St. (☎ **242/322-2836**), serves well-prepared Bahamian seafood in a verdant setting. If you like your dining with a view, there's no better place than the second-floor, open-air terrace of the **Poop Deck,** Nassau Yacht Haven Marina, East Bay Street (☎ **242/ 393-8175**), overlooking the harbor and Paradise Island.

Far removed from the well-trodden tourist path, the **Shoal Restaurant and Lounge,** Nassau Street (☎ **242/323-4400**), is a steadfast local favorite and ranks near the top for authentic flavor.

Green Shutters Restaurant, 48 Parliament St., 2 blocks south of Rawson Square (☎ **242/325-5702**), is an English pub transplanted to the tropics. It offers three imported English beers along with pub-grub favorites such as steak-and-kidney pie, bangers and mash, shepherd's pie, and fish-and-chips. **Gaylord's,** Dowdeswell Street at Bay Street (☎ **242/356-3004**), is the only Indian restaurant in the country, and as such, is now a culinary staple of Nassau, serving a wide range of Punjabi, tandoori, and curry dishes. **Caribe Café Restaurant and Terrace,** in the British Colonial Beach Resort, 1 Bay St. (☎ **242/322-3301**), serves typical faves like beef burgers and freshly made salads.

AT CABLE BEACH   **Café Johnny Canoe,** in the Nassau Beach Hotel, West Bay Street (☎ **242/327-3373**), serves burgers and all kinds of steaks, seafood, and chicken dishes. The best items on the menu are blackened grouper and barbecued fish. **Tequila Pepe's,** in the Radisson Cable Beach Hotel, West Bay Street (☎ **242/327-6000**), serves buffet-style Tex-Mex dishes: fajitas, tacos, burritos, tamales, and chimichangas.

ON PARADISE ISLAND   **The Cave,** at the Atlantis, Casino Drive (☎ **242/ 363-3000**), is a burger-and-salad joint located near the beach of the most lavish hotel and casino complex on Paradise Island. It caters to the bathing-suit-and-flip-flops crowd. To reach the place, you pass beneath a simulated rock-sided tunnel illuminated with flaming torches. **Seagrapes Restaurant,** in the Atlantis, Casino Drive (☎ **242/363-3000**), serves buffet-style tropical food, including Cuban, Caribbean, and Cajun dishes.

FREEPORT/LUCAYA

Bold and brassy Freeport/Lucaya on Grand Bahama Island is the second most popular tourist destination in the Bahamas. Its cosmopolitan glitz and the frenzy of its gambling and shopping scenes might be too much for some visitors, but there's also plenty of sun, surf, and excellent golf, tennis, and water sports. For orientation's sake, note that Freeport is technically the landlocked section of town whereas Lucaya lies right next door, along the waterfront. Though originally intended as two separate developments, they've grown together over the years.

Frommer's Favorite Freeport/Lucaya Experiences

- **Catching a concert at Count Basie Square:** Right in the center of Port Lucaya, a vine-covered bandstand hosts the best live music on the island, performed nightly. And it's free (see "On Your Own: Beyond Walking Distance," below).
- **Visiting the Star Club:** Built in the 1940s, this place has hosted many famous guests over the years, and is now the only 24-hour bar on the island (see "Great Local Restaurants & Bars," below).
- **Taking the Lucaya National Park Tour:** About 12 miles from Lucaya, the park has one of the loveliest, most secluded beaches on Grand Bahama (see "Shore Excursions," below).

COMING ASHORE Unlike some ports of call where you land in the heart of everything, on Grand Bahama Island you're deposited in what cruisers call the middle of nowhere—the west central part of the island. You'll want to take a $10 taxi ride (for two passengers) over to Freeport and its International Bazaar, center of most of the action. As you'll quickly learn after leaving the dreary port area, everything on this island is spread out. Grand Bahama doesn't have the compactness of Nassau.

INFORMATION Information is available from the **Grand Bahama Tourism Board,** International Bazaar in Freeport (☎ **800/823-3136** or 242/352-8044). Another **information booth** is located at Port Lucaya (☎ **242/373-8988**). It's open from 9am to 5:30pm Monday to Saturday. For info before you go, call the **Bahamas Tourism Board** in New York City (☎ **212/758-2777**) or visit their Web site at www.bahamas.com.

CALLING HOME FROM THE BAHAMAS There are long-distance phones in the terminal.

GETTING AROUND

Once you get to Freeport by taxi you can explore the center of town on foot. If you want to make excursions into the West End or East End of the island, you'll either need a car or have to rely on taxis or the highly erratic public transportation.

BY TAXI The government sets the taxi rates. The meter starts at $2, and 30¢ is charged for each additional quarter mile for two passengers. Most taxis wait at the cruise ship dock to pick up passengers, or you can call **Freeport Taxi Company** (☎ **242/352-6666**) or **Grand Bahama Taxi Union** (☎ **242/352-7101**).

Frommer's Ratings: Freeport/Lucaya					
	poor	fair	good	excellent	outstanding
Overall Experience					✓
Shore Excursions			✓		
Activities Close to Port				✓	
Beach & Water Sports			✓		
Shopping				✓	
Dining/Bars			✓		

Freeport/Lucaya

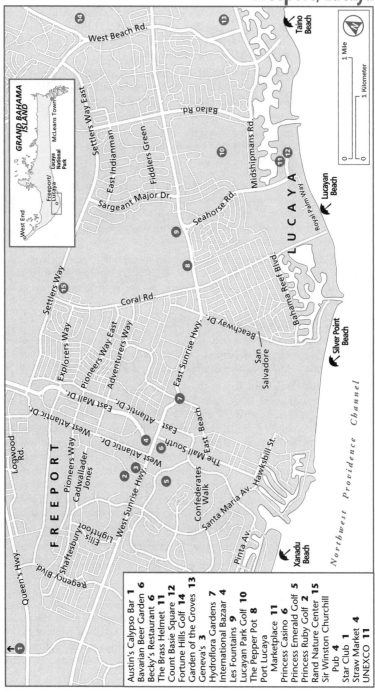

Austin's Calypso Bar **1**
Bavarian Beer Garden **6**
Becky's Restaurant **6**
The Brass Helmet **11**
Count Basie Square **12**
Fortune Hills Golf **14**
Garden of the Groves **13**
Geneva's **3**
Hydroflora Gardens **7**
International Bazaar **4**
Les Fountains **9**
Lucayan Park Golf **10**
The Pepper Pot **8**
Port Lucaya
    Marketplace **11**
Princess Casino **6**
Princess Emerald Golf **5**
Princess Ruby Golf **2**
Rand Nature Center **15**
Sir Winston Churchill
    Pub **4**
Star Club **1**
Straw Market **4**
UNEXCO **11**

BY RENTAL CAR   Roads are generally good on Grand Bahama Island, and it's easy to drive around. For car rentals, try **Avis** (☎ **800/331-2112** in the U.S., or 242/352-7666); **Hertz** (☎ **800/654-3001** in the U.S., or 242/352-9277); or the local **Star Rent-a-Car,** Old Airport Road (☎ **242/352-5953**).

BY MOTOR SCOOTER OR BICYCLE   You can rent them at any of the major hotels such as **Princess Country Club,** West Sunrise Highway (☎ **242/352-6721**). A two-seat scooter requires a $100 deposit and rents for about $40 per day; bicycles require a $50 deposit and cost about $12 for a half day, $20 for a full day.

BY BUS   Public bus service runs from the International Bazaar to downtown Freeport and from the Pub on the Mall to the Lucaya area. The typical fare is 75¢ to $1.

SHORE EXCURSIONS

Because most things to do here are in Freeport, the excursion offerings are weak and you can often manage better on your own. Many cruise ships tout a sightseeing trip where you spend about 30 minutes at the Garden of the Groves and then are led like cattle around the International Bazaar. The latter is better explored on your own. The 3-hour trip costs about $23 per passenger.

Lucaya National Park Tour: Not all lines offer this, but if you see it offered, an excursion to the lush, 40-acre park on Sunrise Highway is a worthwhile and relaxing afternoon. The park, about 12 miles from Lucaya, has one of the loveliest, most secluded beaches on Grand Bahama.

TOURING THROUGH LOCAL OPERATORS

Booze Cruise: Many lines offer booze cruises, but you can also arrange your own with **Superior Watersports** in Freeport (☎ **242/373-7863**), which offers fun cruises on its *Bahama Mama,* a 72-foot catamaran with two semisubmersibles that dive 5 feet.

Swimming with Dolphins: You get to see porpoises up close with **The Dolphin Experience,** operated by the Underwater Explorers Society (UNEXSO), in Port Lucaya opposite Lucayan Beach Casino (☎ **800/992-3483** or 242/373-1250). UNEXSO conducts this unique dolphin/human familiarization program in which participants observe these intelligent, friendly animals close up and hear an interesting lecture by a member of the animal-care staff. This is not a swim-with-the-dolphins type of program, but all ages can step onto a shallow wading platform and interact with the animals. The encounter on shore costs $39. An "Assistant Trainer" program costs $179 and is an all-day interactive experience in which a maximum of four people, aged 16 or older, can learn about dolphins and marine mammals in a behind-the-scenes experience, including swimming with them and feeding them.

ON YOUR OWN: WITHIN WALKING DISTANCE

There's nothing within walking distance of the port; you have to head over to Freeport/Lucaya.

ON YOUR OWN: BEYOND WALKING DISTANCE

The prime attraction is the 11-acre **Garden of the Groves,** at the intersection of Midshipman Road and Magellan Drive (☎ **242/373-5668**). Seven miles east of the International Bazaar, this scenic preserve of waterfalls and flowering shrubs has some 10,000 trees. The **Palmetto Café** (☎ **242/373-5668**) serves snacks and drinks, and a Bahamian straw market sits at the entrance gate.

  Hydroflora Garden, on East Beach at Sunrise Highway (☎ **242/352-6052**), is an artificially created botanical wonder, featuring over 150 specimens of indigenous Bahamian plants. A special section is devoted to bush medicine.

Filled with mangrove, pine, and palm trees, the 40-acre **Lucaya National Park,** Sunrise Highway (for information, contact Rand Nature Centre at ☎ 242/352-5438), is about 12 miles from Lucaya. The park contains one of the loveliest, most secluded beaches on Grand Bahama. A wooden path winding through the trees leads to this long, wide, dune-covered stretch. You can enter two caves, exposed when a portion of ground collapsed. The pools there are composed of 6 feet of freshwater atop a heavier layer of salt water.

Located 2 miles east of Freeport's center, the **Rand Nature Centre,** East Settlers Way (☎ 242/352-5438), is the regional headquarters of the Bahamas National Trust, a nonprofit conservation organization. Forest nature trails highlight native flora and bush medicine in this 100-acre pineland sanctuary. Wild birds abound. Other features include native animal displays, a replica of a Lucayan Indian village, an education center, and a gift shop.

If your ship is in port late, head to ✪ **Count Basie Square** for one of the free nightly concerts. Count Basie had a grand home on Grand Bahama, and in the center of the waterfront restaurant-and-shopping complex of Port Lucaya there's a square named in his honor. There's a vine-covered bandstand where steel bands, small junkanoo groups, and even gospel singers from a local church are likely to perform, their music wafting across the 50-slip marina.

SHOPPING

There's no place for shopping in the Bahamas quite like the **International Bazaar,** at East Mall Drive and East Sunrise Highway. It's one of the world's most unusual shopping marts—Bahamian kitsch in poured concrete and plastic, 10 acres of born-to-shop theme-park tastelessness—but in the nearly 100 shops you're bound to find something that is both a discovery and a bargain. Many items sold in the shops here could run about 40% less than in the United States, but don't count on it. Buses marked INTERNATIONAL BAZAAR take you right to the much-photographed Toril Gate, a Japanese symbol of welcome.

The bazaar blends architecture from 25 countries into several theme areas: the Ginza in Tokyo for Asian goods; the Left Bank of Paris, or a reasonable facsimile, with sidewalk cafes where you can enjoy a café au lait and perhaps a pastry under shade trees; a Continental Pavilion for leather goods, jewelry, lingerie, and gifts at shops with names such as Love Boutique; India House for exotic goods such as taxi horns and silk saris; Africa for carvings or a colorful dashiki; and a Spanish section for Latin-American and Iberian serapes and piñatas.

At the **Straw Market,** beside the International Bazaar, you'll find items with a special Bahamian touch—colorful baskets, hats, handbags, and place mats—all of which make good gifts and souvenirs of your trip.

The **Port Lucaya Marketplace** on Seahorse Road, the first of its kind in the Bahamas, was named after the original settlers of Grand Bahama. This is a shopping-and-dining complex set on 6 acres. Free entertainment, such as steel-drum bands and strolling musicians, adds to a festival atmosphere. The complex rose on the site of a former Bahamian straw market, but the craftspeople and their straw products are back in full force after having been temporarily dislodged. Full advantage is taken of the waterfront location. Many of the restaurants and shops overlook a 50-slip marina, home of a "fantasy" pirate ship featuring lunch and dinner/dancing cruises. A variety of charter vessels are also based at the Port Lucaya Marina, and dockage at the marina is available to visitors coming by boat to shop or dine. A boardwalk along the water makes it easy to watch the frolicking dolphins and join in other activities at the **Underwater Explorers Society (UNEXSO).**

Merchandise in the shops of Port Lucaya ranges from leather to lingerie to wind chimes. Traditional and contemporary fashions are featured for men, women, and children. Some of the better shops are **Coconits by Androsia,** an outlet of the famous batik house of Andros Island; **Jeweler's Warehouse,** a place for bargain hunters looking for good buys on discounted, close-out 14-karat gold and gemstone jewelry; the **UNEXSO Dive Shop,** selling swimsuits, wet suits, underwater cameras, shades, hats, souvenirs, state-of-the-art divers' equipment, and computers; **Colombian Emeralds International,** offering a wide array of precious gemstone jewelry and one of the island's best watch collections; **Sea Treasures,** in the Spanish Section, with gold and silver jewelry inspired by the sea and handcrafted on the island; and **Bahamas Coin and Stamp Ltd.,** Arcade, specializing in Bahamian coin jewelry, ancient Roman coins, and relics from sunken Spanish galleons.

BEACHES

Grand Bahama has some 60 miles of white-sand beaches rimming the blue-green waters of the Atlantic. The mile-long **Xanadu Beach,** at the Xanadu Beach Resort, is the premier beach in the Freeport area. Most beaches are in the Lucaya area, site of the major resort hotels. The resort beaches, with a fairly active program of water sports, tend to be the most crowded in winter.

Other island beaches include **Taíno Beach,** lying to the east of Freeport, plus **Smith's Point** and **Fortune Beach,** the latter one of the finest on Grand Bahama. Another good beach, about a 20-minute ride east of Lucaya, is **Gold Rock Beach,** a favorite picnic spot with the locals, especially on weekends.

SPORTS

GOLF   This island boasts more golf links than any other in the Bahamas. They're all within 7 miles of one another, and you usually don't have to wait to play. All courses are open to the public year-round, and you can rent clubs from any of the pro shops on the island. Go on your own or sign up for an organized golf excursion if your ship offers them. **Fortune Hills Golf & Country Club,** Richmond Park, Lucaya (☎ 242/373-4500), was designed as an 18-hole course, but the back nine were never completed. You can replay the front nine for a total of 6,916 yards from the blue tees. Par is 72. The club is 5 miles east of Freeport. **Lucayan Park Golf & Country Club,** at Lucaya Beach (☎ 242/373-1066), is the best-kept and most manicured course on Grand Bahama. The course was recently made over and is quite beautiful. It's known for its entrance and a hanging boulder sculpture. Greens are fast, and there are a couple of par-5 holes more than 500 yards long. Total distance from the blue tees is 6,824 yards, 6,488 from the white tees. Par is 72. Even if you're not a golfer, sample the food at the club restaurant. It offers everything from lavish champagne brunches to first-rate seafood dishes. **Princess Emerald Course,** The Mall South (☎ 242/352-6721), is one of two courses owned and operated by the Bahamas Princess Resort & Casino. The Emerald Course was the site of the Bahamas National Open some years back. The course has plenty of trees along the fairways, as well as an abundance of water hazards and bunkers. The toughest hole is the ninth, a par-5 with 545 yards from the blue tees to the hole. The championship **Princess Ruby Course,** on West Sunrise Highway (☎ 242/352-6721), was designed by Joe Lee in 1968 and recently hosted the Michelin Long Drive competition. It's a total of 6,750 yards if played from the championship blue tees.

PARASAILING   **Clarion Atlantik Beach Resort,** on Royal Palm Way (☎ 242/373-1444), is the best center on the island for parasailing.

SCUBA DIVING & SNORKELING   One of the premier facilities for diving and snorkeling throughout the Bahamas and Caribbean is the **Underwater Explorers**

Society (UNEXSO), at Lucaya Beach (☎ 242/373-1244). It has daily reef trips, shark dives, wreck dives, and night dives. This is also the only facility in the world where divers can swim alongside dolphins in the open ocean (see "Touring Through Local Operators," above). It offers a popular 3-hour learn-to-dive course every day as well as dives for the experienced and snorkeling trips.

GAMBLING

Even though there are casinos aboard almost all ships, many passengers head immediately for a land-based casino once they hit shore. Most of the day-life/nightlife in Freeport/Lucaya revolves around the **Princess Casino,** the Mall at West Sunrise Highway (☎ 242/352-7811), a glittering, giant, Moroccan-style palace.

GREAT LOCAL RESTAURANTS & BARS

The **local beer** in Bermuda is Kalik. The **local rum** is Bacardi.

If you'd like to see what's left of the Bahamas "the way it was," head for the ✪ **Star Club,** on Bayshore Road (☎ 242/346-6207) in the West End. Built in the 1940s, it was the first hotel on Grand Bahama, and hosted many famous guests over the years. It's been a long time since any guests have checked in, but the place is still going strong and is open daily until at least 2am. Sometimes people leaving the casinos late at night come over here to eat grouper fingers, play pool, or listen to the taped music. The "club" is still run by the family of the late Austin Henry Grant, Jr., a former Bahamian senator and West End legend. You can order Bahamian chicken in the bag, burgers, fish-and-chips, or "fresh sexy" conch prepared as chowder, fritters, and salads. But come here for the good times, not the food. You can also drop in next door at **Austin's Calypso Bar,** a real Grand Bahama dive if there ever was one. Austin Grant, the owner, will tell you about the good ol' days.

Geneva's, Kipling Lane, the Mall at West Sunrise Highway (☎ 242/352-5085), is another place where the food is the way it was before the hordes of tourists invaded. **Les Fountains,** East Sunrise Highway (☎ 242/373-9553), offers a great all-you-can-eat buffet as well as chicken, steak, and lobster, and dishes prepared at the jerk grill outside. **The Pepper Pot,** East Sunrise Highway at Coral Road (☎ 242/373-7655), a 5-minute drive east of the International Bazaar in a tiny shopping mall, serves take-out portions of the best carrot cake on the island, as well as a savory conch chowder, the standard fish and pork chops, chicken souse (an acquired taste), cracked conch, sandwiches and hamburgers, and an array of daily specials. **The Brass Helmet,** in the Port Lucaya Marketplace, directly above UNEXSO Dive Shop (☎ 242/373-2032), serves Bahamian staples, including cracked conch and grouper, plus an array of steaks, lobster, and a variety of pastas. **Becky's Restaurant,** at the International Bazaar, offers authentic Bahamian cuisine prepared in the time-tested style of the Out Islands.

Sir Winston Churchill Pub, East Mall (next to the Straw Market and the International Bazaar; ☎ 242/352-8866), is mainly a pizzeria, and also serves a selection of pastas, salads, and sandwiches. At the International Bazaar, the **Bavarian Beer Garden** features at least a dozen kinds of imported beer, recorded oom-pah-pah music, such German fare as knockwurst, bockwurst, and sauerkraut, and a selection of pizzas.

4 Barbados

No port of call in the southern Caribbean can compete with Barbados when it comes to natural beauty, attractions, and fine dining. With all it offers, you'll think the island is much bigger than it is. But what really puts Barbados on world tourist maps is its seemingly endless stretches of pink-and-white sandy beaches, among the best in the entire Caribbean Basin.

This Atlantic outpost was one of the most staunchly loyal members of the British Commonwealth for over 300 years, and although it gained its independence in 1966, British-isms still remain—the accent is Brit, driving is on the left, and Queen Elizabeth is still officially the head of state.

Originally operated on a plantation economy that made its aristocracy rich, the island is the most easterly in the Caribbean, floating in the mid-Atlantic like a great coral reef and ringed with beige-sand beaches. Cosmopolitan Barbados has the densest population of any island in the Caribbean, a sports tradition that avidly pursues cricket, and a loyal group of return visitors who appreciate its many stylish, medium-size hotels. Overall, service is usually extremely good. Topography varies from rolling hills and savage waves on the eastern (Atlantic) coast to densely populated flatlands, rows of hotels and apartments, and sheltered beaches in the southwest.

The people in Barbados are called *Bajans,* and you'll see this term used everywhere.

Frommer's Favorite Barbados Experiences

- **Renting a car for a Barbados road trip:** Seventeenth–century churches, tropical flowers, snorkeling, great views, and more are just a rental car ride away (see "On Your Own: Beyond Walking Distance," below).
- **Visiting Gun Hill Signal Station:** If you've got less time, hire a taxi or rent a car and go to Gun Hill for panoramic views of the island (see "On Your Own: Beyond Walking Distance," below).
- **Diving deep on a submarine:** Sightseeing submarines make several dives daily (see "Shore Excursions," below).

COMING ASHORE   The cruise ship pier, a short drive from Bridgetown, the capital, is one of the best docking facilities in the southern Caribbean. You can walk right into the modern cruise ship terminal, which has car rentals, taxi services, sightseeing tours, and a tourist information office, plus shops and scads of vendors (see "Shopping," below). You'll also find credit-card telephones, fax facilities, and phone cards and stamps for sale.

If you want to go into Bridgetown, about a mile from the port, instead of to the beach, you can take a hot, dusty walk of at least 30 minutes, or catch a taxi. The one-way fare ranges from $4 on up. There's also a bus running until noon for $1.

Credit-card **phone booths** with AT&T access are located in the cruise ship terminal. Also, in downtown Bridgetown there's a phone center (B.E.T.) on the corner of Hinck Street.

CURRENCY   The **Barbados dollar (BD$)** is the official currency, available in $100, $20, $10, and $5 notes and $1, 25¢, and 10¢ silver coins, plus 5¢ and 1¢ copper coins. The exchange rate is BD$1.98 to $1 U.S. (BD$1 is worth about 51¢). Unless otherwise specified, prices in this section are given in U.S. dollars. Most stores take traveler's checks or U.S. dollars, so don't bother to convert them if you're here for only a day.

Frommer's Ratings: Barbados					
	poor	fair	good	excellent	outstanding
Overall Experience				✓	
Shore Excursions			✓		
Activities Close to Port			✓		
Beach & Water Sports			✓		
Shopping			✓		
Dining/Bars			✓		

Barbados

Airport ✈ Beach ⚓ Church ⊥
Lighthouse ⊥ Cruise Ship Dock 🚢

Atlantic Ocean

Archer's Bay
North Point
River Bay
Stroud Bay
Cuckold Point
Harrison Point ⊥
ST. LUCY
Gay's Cove
Maycock's Bay ⚓ 1B
Fairfield
Pico Teneriffe
Coleton 1C
Half Moon Fort
Morgan Lewis Beach ⚓
Six Men's Bay
Greeland 2
Heywoods ⚓
Beach
ST. PETER
St. Andrew's
Church ⊥
Speightstown
ST. ANDREW
Mullins Beach ⚓
SCOTLAND
Gibbs Beach ⚓
1 Turner's Hall
2A Woods
Chalky
Mount
Cattlewash
Gold Coast
Lower Carlton
Tent Bay
Church Point ⚓
ST. JAMES
Bathsheba
Martin's Bay
FOLKSTONE
2 ST. JOSEPH
Congor Rocks
UNDERWATER PARK ①
3A
Welchman Hall
Hackleton's Cliff
Consett Bay
1A
3
Holetown
Blackmans
ST. JOHN
CULPEPPER
Sunset Crest
4
ISLAND
ST. THOMAS
3B
Ragged Point
Paynes Bay ⚓
Lighthouse ⊥
Lazaretto
2A 2
Three Houses
Kitridge
Prospect
Locust Hall
Point
Paradise Beach ⚓
Warrens
3
Bushy Park
Bottom
Brighton Beach ⚓
5 6
Sandford
Bay
ST. MICHAEL
ST. GEORGE
4
5
Black Rock
4B
ST. PHILIP
Long Bay
2
5
4
Marchfield
7
3
Queen's Park
Deep Water Harbour
Beachy Head
6
CHRISTCHURCH
Crane Beach
🚢 Bridgetown
6
Carlisle Bay
Tom Adams Hwy.
7
Needham's Point ⊥
Hastings
Grantley Adams
Rockley Beach ⚓
St. Lawrence
International Airport ✈
Worthing
Maxwell
7
Sandy Beach ⚓
Oistins
Long Bay
Casuarina Beach ⚓
South
Point ⊥
Silver
Sands Beach

Caribbean Sea

0 _____ 5 Miles
0 _____ 5 Kilometers

Caribbean Islands

Barbados

Flower Forest of Barbados **3**
Francia Plantation **5**
Gun Hill Signal Station **6**
Harrison's Cave **4**
Sam Lord's Castle **7**
St. James Church **1**
Welchman Hall Gully **2**

LANGUAGE   English is spoken with an island lilt.

INFORMATION   The **Barbados Tourism Authority** is on Harbour Road (P.O. Box 242), Bridgetown, Barbados, W.I. (☎ **888/barbados** or 246/427-2623). Its cruise terminal office, which is very well run, is always open when a cruise ship is in port.

CALLING FROM THE U.S.   When calling Barbados from the United States, you need to only dial a "1" before the telephone numbers listed throughout this chapter.

GETTING AROUND

BY TAXI   They're not metered, but their rates are fixed by the government. Even so, drivers may try and get more money out of you, so make sure you settle on the rate before getting in. Taxis are identified by the letter *Z* on their license plates, and you'll find them just outside of the terminal.

BY BUS   Blue-and-yellow public buses fan out from Bridgetown every 20 minutes or so onto the major routes; their destinations are marked on the front. Buses going south and east leave from Fairchild Street, and those going north and west depart from Lower Green and the Princess Alice Highway. Fares are about BD$1.50 (U.S.75¢) and exact change is required; you can use U.S. currency, but you're likely to get change back in local BD$.

Privately owned **minibuses** run shorter distances and travel more frequently. These bright yellow buses display destinations on the bottom-left corner of the windshield. In Bridgetown, board at River Road, Temple Yard, and Probyn Street. Fare is about BD$1.50 (U.S.75¢).

BY RENTAL CAR   While it's a good way to see the island if you've got an adventurous streak and an easygoing attitude, before you decide to rent a car, keep in mind that driving is on the left side of the road and the signs are totally inadequate (boy, could I tell you stories!). There are several car-rental agents at the cruise terminal (be sure you take a look at the car before signing on the dotted line).

SHORE EXCURSIONS

It's not easy to get around Barbados quickly and conveniently, so a shore excursion is a good idea here.

Harrison's Cave ($37–$54 adults and $29–$40 children, 3–4 hours): Most cruise lines offer a tour to Harrison's Cave in the center of the island (see "On Your Own: Beyond Walking Distance," below, for details).

Atlantis **Submarine Adventure** ($83–$89, 2 hours): The *Atlantis* transports passengers through Barbados's undersea world, where you can watch the fishies and other colorful marine life through 28-inch windows.

✪ **Barbados Highlights Bus Tour** ($29–$38, 3 hours): Tours take passengers by bus to Gun Hill Signal Station, St. John's Church, and Sam Lord's Castle Resort (see "On Your Own: Beyond Walking Distance," below, for details).

TOURING THROUGH LOCAL OPERATORS

Island Tours/Eco Tours ($56 per person, 6 to 8 hours): Since most cruise lines don't really offer a comprehensive island tour, many passengers deal with one of the local tour companies. **Bajan Tours,** Glenayre, Locust Hall, St. George (☎ 246/437-9389), offers an island tour that leaves between 8:30am and 9am, and returns to the ship before departure. It covers all the island's highlights. On Friday they conduct a heritage tour, focusing mainly on the island's major plantations and museums. On Tuesday and Wednesday they offer an Eco Tour, which takes in the natural beauty of the island. Call ahead for information and to reserve a spot.

If you can afford it, **touring by taxi** is far more relaxing than the standardized bus tour. Nearly all Bajan taxi drivers are familiar with their island and like to show off their knowledge to visitors. The standard rate is about $20 per hour per taxi (for one to four passengers). You might want to try contacting taxi driver and owner Aaron Francis (☎ **246/431-9059**). He's a gem—friendly, reliable, and knowledgeable.

ON YOUR OWN: WITHIN WALKING DISTANCE

About the only thing you can walk to is the cruise terminal. The modern, pleasant complex has an array of duty-free shops and retail stores, plus many vendors selling arts and crafts, jewelry, liquor, china, crystal, electronics, perfume, and leather goods.

ON YOUR OWN: BEYOND WALKING DISTANCE

I don't recommend wasting too much time in Bridgetown—it's hot, dry, and dusty, and the honking horns of traffic jams only add to its woes. So, unless you want to go shopping, you should spend your time exploring all the beauty the island has to offer instead. The tourist office in the terminal is very helpful if you want to go somewhere on your own.

Welchman Hall Gully, St. Thomas (Highway 2 from Bridgetown; ☎ **246/ 438-6671**), is a lush tropical garden owned by the Barbados National Trust. The gully is 8 miles from the port and features some plants that were here when the English settlers landed in 1627. It can be reached by bus from the terminal.

All cruise ship excursions visit **Harrison's Cave,** Welchman Hall, St. Thomas (☎ **246/438-6640**), Barbados's top tourist attraction. Here you can see a beautiful underground world from aboard an electric tram and trailer. If you'd like to go on your own, a taxi ride takes about 30 minutes and costs just under $20.

A mile from Harrison's Cave is the **Flower Forest,** Richmond Plantation, St. Joseph (☎ **246/433-8152**). This old sugar plantation stands 850 feet above sea level near the western edge of the "Scotland district," in one of the most scenic parts of Barbados. The forest is 12 miles from the cruise terminal; one-way taxi fare is about $15.

A fine home still owned and occupied by descendants of the original owner, the **Francia Plantation,** St. George (☎ **246/429-0474**), stands on a wooded hillside overlooking the St. George Valley. You can explore several rooms. The plantation lies about 20 miles from the port; one-way taxi fare is about $20.

The **Gun Hill Signal Station,** Highway 4 (☎ **246/429-1358**), one of two such stations owned and operated by the Barbados National Trust, is strategically placed on the highland of St. George and commands a wonderful panoramic view from east to west. Built in 1818, the station is 12 miles from the port; the one-way taxi ride costs about $18.

Sam Lord's Castle Resort, Long Bay, St. Philip (☎ **246/423-7350**), was built in 1820 by one of Barbados's most notorious scoundrels, Samuel Hall Lord. Legend says he made his money by luring ships onto the jagged, hard-to-detect rocks of Cobbler's Reef and then "salvaging" the wreckage. You can explore the architecturally acclaimed centerpiece of this luxury resort, which has a private sandy beach. It's a $12 taxi ride from the cruise terminal.

If it's wildlife you want, head for the **Barbados Wildlife Reserve,** in St. Peter Parish on the northern end of the island. It's not exactly Animal Kingdom, but on this 4-acre site you'll see turtles, rabbits, iguanas, peacocks, green monkeys, and a caged python.

Maybe it's the party-life you crave. If so, don't miss the **Mount Gay Rum Tour** in Bridgetown. You'll get a 45-minute soup-to-nuts introduction about rum in an air-conditioned rum shop (they say, of the more than 1,200 rum shops on the island, it's the only one with A/C). The tour costs $6 a person.

SHOPPING

The shopping-mall-size **cruise terminal** contains an array of duty-free shops and retail stores, plus a plethora of vendors selling arts and crafts, jewelry, liquor, china, crystal, electronics, perfume, and leather goods. Check out the clever Christmas tree ornaments made of seashells by local artist Daphne Hunt and her three daughters (they go for $6 to $12 apiece). For rum cake, an island specialty, the family-owned **Calypso Island Bakery** has a shop in the terminal. The shrink-wrapped cakes last up to 6 months and make great gifts! There's also a convenience store in the terminal. In general, though, you'll find a wider selection of stuff to buy and better prices in Bridgetown. Last time I was there, T-shirts in the terminal were going for $15 apiece, a roll of film $5, and a liter of J&B (yellow label) was anywhere from $10.75 to $15.15 (U.S.).

Good duty-free buys include cameras, watches, crystal, gold jewelry, bone china, cosmetics and perfumes, and liquor (including locally produced Barbados rum and liqueurs), along with tobacco products and British-made cashmere sweaters, tweeds, and sportswear. **Cave Shepherd,** Broad Street, Bridgetown, is the largest department store on Barbados and the best place to shop for tax-free merchandise.

Among Barbados handcrafts, you'll find lots of **black-coral jewelry,** but beware: Did you know black coral is endangered and it's illegal to bring it into the United States? I suggest looking, but not buying. Local clay potters turn out different products, some based on designs centuries old. Check out the **Potters House** and **Earthworks,** both on Edghill Heights, in St. Thomas parish. Crafts include wall hangings made from grasses and dried flowers, straw mats, baskets, and bags with raffia embroidery. Bajan leather work includes handbags, belts, and sandals.

Some standout stores include **Articrafts,** on Broad Street in Bridgetown, for Bajan arts and crafts, straw work, handbags, and bamboo items; **Best of Barbados,** in the Southern Palms, St. Lawrence Gap, Christ Church, which sells only products designed and/or made on Barbados (coasters, mats, T-shirts, pottery, dolls and games, cookbooks, and other items); **Colours of De Caribbean,** the Waterfront Marina, Bridgetown, for tropical clothing, jewelry, and decorative objects; **Cotton Days,** Lower Bay Street, St. Michael, for casually elegant one-of-a-kind garments, suitable for cool nights and hot climes; **The Shell Gallery,** Carlton House, St. James, for the best collection of shells in the West Indies, featuring the shell art of Maureen Edghill, the finest artist in the field; and **Walker's Caribbean World,** St. Lawrence Gap, for many locally made items, as well as handcrafts from the Caribbean Basin.

BEACHES

Beaches on the island's western side—the luxury resort area called the **Gold Coast**—are far preferable to those on the surf-pounded Atlantic side. All Barbados beaches are open to the public, even those in front of the big resort hotels and private homes. The government requires that there be access to all beaches, via roads along the property line or through the hotel entrance.

ON THE WEST COAST (GOLD COAST)   Take your pick of the west-coast beaches, which are about a 15-minute, $8 taxi ride from the cruise terminal. **Payne's Bay,** with access from the Coach House or the Bamboo Beach Bar, is a good beach for water sports, especially snorkeling. There's a parking area here. This beach can get rather crowded, but the beautiful bay makes it worth it. Directly south of Payne's Bay, at Fresh Water Bay, is a trio of fine beaches: **Brighton Beach, Brandon's Beach,** and **Paradise Beach.**

Church Point lies north of St. James Church, opening onto Heron Bay, site of the Colony Club Hotel. Although this beach can get crowded, it's one of the most scenic bays in Barbados, and the swimming is ideal. Retreat under some shade trees when you've had enough sun. You can also order drinks at the Colony Club's beach terrace.

Snorkelers in particular seek out the glassy blue waters by **Mullins Beach.** There are some shady areas, and you can park on the main road. Order food and drink at the Mullins Beach Bar.

ON THE SOUTH COAST   Depending on traffic, south-coast beaches are usually easy to reach from the cruise terminal. Figure on about an $8 taxi fare. **Sandy Beach,** reached from the parking lot on the Worthing main road, has tranquil waters opening onto a lagoon. This is a family favorite, with lots of screaming and yelling, especially on weekends. Food and drink are sold here.

Windsurfers are particularly fond of the trade winds that sweep across **Casuarina Beach,** even on the hottest summer days. Access is from Maxwell Coast Road, across the property of Casuarina Beach Hotel. This is one of the wider beaches on Barbados. The hotel has food and drink.

Silver Sands Beach is to the east of the town of Oistins, near the very southernmost point of Barbados, directly east of South Point Lighthouse and near the Silver Rock Hotel. This white sandy beach is a favorite with many Bajans, who probably want to keep it a secret from as many tourists as possible. (Tough luck, Bajans!) Windsurfing is good here, but not as good as at Casuarina Beach. You can buy drinks at Silver Rock Bar.

ON THE SOUTHEAST COAST   The southeast coast is known for its big waves, especially at **Crane Beach,** a white sandy stretch set against a backdrop of cliffs and palms. Prince Andrew owns a house overlooking this spectacular beach, and the Crane Beach Hotel towers above it from the cliffs. Crane Beach often appears in travel-magazine articles about Barbados. It offers excellent body surfing, but this is real ocean swimming, not the calm Caribbean, so be careful. At $17.50 from the cruise pier, the one-way taxi fare is relatively steep, so share a ride with some friends.

SPORTS

GOLF   The 18-hole championship golf course of the west-coast **Sandy Lane Hotel,** St. James (☎ **246/432-1311**), is open to all. Greens fees are $135 in winter and $110 in summer for 18 holes, or $100 in winter and $80 in summer for nine holes. Carts and caddies are available. Make reservations the day before you arrive in Barbados or before you leave home. The course is a 20- to 25-minute taxi ride from the cruise terminal. The one-way fare is about $13.

WINDSURFING   Experts say that Barbados windsurfing is as good as any this side of Hawaii. In fact, it's a very big business between November and April, when thousands of windsurfers from all over the world come here. **Silver Sands** is rated the best spot in the Caribbean for advanced windsurfing (skill rating 5 to 6). **Barbados Windsurfing Club,** at the Silver Sands Hotel in Christ Church (☎ **246/428-6001**), gives lessons and rents boards. To reach the club, take a taxi from the cruise terminal; it's a $10 one-way fare.

GREAT LOCAL RESTAURANTS & BARS

IN BRIDGETOWN OR SOUTH OF BRIDGETOWN   **Brown Sugar,** Aquatic Gap, St. Michael (☎ **246/426-7684**), is an alfresco restaurant in a turn-of-the-century bungalow. The chefs prepare some of the tastiest Bajan specialties on the island. Of the main dishes, Creole-broiled pepper chicken is popular, as are the stuffed crab backs. There's a great lunch buffet for less than $15 per person. **Rusty Pelican,** in downtown Bridgetown overlooking the Careenage, has great atmosphere and Bajan flying fish to boot. Also in town, try **Mustors,** on McGregor Street. It's a favorite with locals and serves authentic Barbadian lunch fare. Wherever you eat, be sure to try a daily Bajan special, a jumbo sandwich, or flying fish. For pub grub, the hopping **Whistling Frog Pub** works (located at Time Out at the Gap Hotel, next to the Turtle Beach resort).

ON THE WEST COAST   The beachside **Lone Star,** north of Old Town near the Royal Pavilion on the island's west side, is a new place serving up great seafood. For pizza cravings, check out **Pizzaz** in Holetown.

5 Bequia

Bequia (meaning "Island of the Cloud" in the original Carib, and inexplicably pronounced *Beck*-wee) is the largest island in the St. Vincent Grenadines, with a population of 5,000. Sun-drenched, windswept, peaceful, and green (though arid), it's a popular stop for small-ship lines such as Clipper, ACCL, Star Clippers, Windjammer, and the more upscale Seabourn and Windstar, which join the many yachts in Admiralty Bay throughout the yachting season.

Very much a tourism-oriented island, Bequia is nevertheless anything but touristy. You'll find a few of the usual cheesy gift shops in the main town, Port Elizabeth, but none of the typical cruise-port giants like Little Switzerland. Instead, the town offers one of the most attractive settings in the Caribbean, with restaurants, cozy bars, a produce market, and craft shops, mostly strung out along the Belmont Walkway, a path that skirts so close to the calm waters of the bay that at high tide you have to skip across rocks to avoid getting your feet wet. Many ships spend the night here or make late departures, allowing passengers to take in the nightlife.

The island's rich seafaring tradition today manifests itself in fishing, sailing, boatbuilding (though most handmade boats you'll see are scale models made for the yachting set), and even whaling, though this is whaling of more of a token, almost ritualistic sort—only about one whale is taken in any given year.

Frommer's Favorite Bequia Experiences

- **Strolling along the Belmont Walkway:** In the evenings this walkway at water's edge makes for a terrifically romantic stroll as you make your way from one nightspot to the next. You might even pick up the company of one of the friendly port dogs, who seem more interested in companionship than panhandling (see "On Your Own: Within Walking Distance," below).
- **Visiting Brother King's Old Hegg Turtle Sanctuary:** Founded in 1995 and dedicated to raising and releasing Hawksbill turtle hatchlings, the sanctuary is run on a shoestring budget and a lot of energy and faith. You'll see hundreds of turtles in the main swimming pool and in their own little cubbyholes, and hear about the sanctuary's conservation efforts (see "On Your Own: Beyond Walking Distance," below). Donations are gladly accepted.

Frommer's Ratings: Bequia					
	poor	fair	good	excellent	outstanding
Overall Experience				✓	
Shore Excursions		✓			
Activities Close to Port				✓	
Beach & Water Sports				✓	
Shopping		✓			
Dining/Bars				✓	

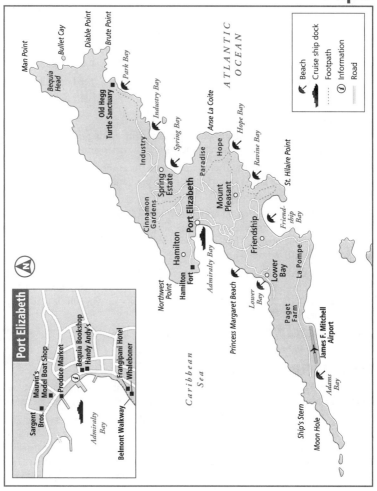

- **Visiting the Lower Bay and Princess Margaret Beach:** South of Port Elizabeth, this stretch of sand is frequently described by cruisers as "the best beach I've ever experienced." It's a little chunk of paradise, backed by waving palms and fronted by yachts bobbing at anchor in the distance (see "Beaches," below).

COMING ASHORE Ships dock right in the center of the island's main town, Port Elizabeth, a stone's throw from the restaurants, bars, and shops that line the waterfront.

CURRENCY The **Eastern Caribbean dollar (EC$)** is used on Bequia; however, U.S. dollars are accepted by all businesses. The exchange rate is EC$2.70 to U.S.$1 (EC$1 is worth about 37¢). It's always a good idea to ask if you're not sure which currency a price tag refers to. Unless otherwise specified, rates quoted in this section are given in U.S. dollars.

LANGUAGE The official and daily-use language is English.

INFORMATION There's a small tourist information booth right on the beach by the cruise dock, but frankly, you can almost see everything there is to do from the same spot. It's a pretty small island. For information before you go, contact the Grenadines Tourist Bureau (☎ 784/458-3286) or the St. Vincent & the Grenadines Department of Tourism (☎ 212/687-4981 in the U.S. or 784/457-1502, www.svgtourism.com).

CALLING FROM THE U.S. To place a call to Bequia you need only dial a "1" before the numbers listed in this section.

GETTING AROUND

Ships dock right in Port Elizabeth, putting you within walking distance of any town sights. The popular Princess Margaret Beach is within walking distance as well.

BY TAXI You'll find plenty of taxis lined up right at the cruise dock to take you around the island. The fare is approximately $15 per hour, or $5 per person per hour for groups of three persons or more.

BY MINIBUS The entire island of Bequia is served by a fleet of small, unofficial **dollar cab** minibuses that cruise regular routes, picking up passengers when flagged down (there are also some obvious "bus stops" scattered around). Tell the driver where you want to go and he'll tell you a price.

BY RENTAL CAR Rentals are available at **Handy Andy's Rentals,** on the Main Road in Port Elizabeth, to the right of the dock if you're facing inland (☎ 784/458-3722; fax 784/457-3402). Day rental of a small golf-cart-type vehicle is $65. A Jeep Wrangler rents for $75.

BY MOTORCYCLE/BICYCLE Handy Andy's (see above) also rents Honda 250XR motorbikes for $45 and Cannondale mountain bikes for $15.

SHORE EXCURSIONS

Bequia is very much a "relax and have a drink" kind of island, rather than one with a lot of definable, tourable attractions. Aside from a standard island tour, most excursions offered are sailing trips around the island and to neighboring Mustique.

Island Tour ($35, 3 hours): The typical island tour is by taxi, meaning you can arrange one easily once you get ashore if your ship doesn't offer one officially. Tours generally visit beautiful Industry Bay on the island's east coast, the Old Hegg Turtle Sanctuary, and a model-boat shop, and at some point stop for a complementary drink in Spring Bay.

Sail & Snorkel Catamaran Trip ($85, 5–6 hours): Your typical booze cruise, though moderation is suggested if you're going to do any snorkeling. The trip sails around Bequia's coast, where you'll see the "Moonhole," a residential community set among odd rock formations, as well as the old whaling station on Petit Nevis, a small island off the coast.

Full-Day Sailing Excursion to Mustique ($85, 7–8 hours): Sail aboard a schooner to exclusive (read: rich people own it) Mustique, just southeast of Bequia, for strolling, shopping, snorkeling, and swimming. Complimentary drinks are included aboard ship.

Half-Day Excursion to Mustique ($65, 3–4 hours): Same excursion as above, but you travel between islands by powerboat rather than sailing ship.

Port Tip: Use Your Ship's Facilities

Since Bequia is an extremely dry island and is very conscious of water conservation, it has few public washrooms, so you'd be well advised to use your ship's bathroom facilities before coming ashore.

ON YOUR OWN: WITHIN WALKING DISTANCE

In theory, almost the entire island of Bequia is within walking distance, but only for serious walkers. I decided to test this theory out by walking from Port Elizabeth first to Hamilton Fort, just north of town, then backtracking through the port and down to the tiny old whaling village of **Paget Farm,** near the airport on Bequia's southern tip. As the crow flies it's not much of a distance, but curving roads and hilly terrain made it a real journey that took about 4 to 5 hours round-trip, with no stops. If your ship is in port late and you're in good shape, it's a great way to see the island (including lovely **Friendship Bay,** on the east coast) and meet some of the local people along the way. Bring water.

For those wanting something less strenuous, strolling around Port Elizabeth itself is close to idyllic. The **Belmont Walkway** runs south from the docks right at the water's edge (meaning at high tide parts of it are actually *under* water), fronting many restaurants, shops, and bars. In the evenings this area is particularly romantic.

Heading north from the docks along the Main Road you'll find a homey **produce market** that also stocks some tourist items. Across the street, **Mauvin's Model Boat Shop** is one of the most visible reminders of the island's boatbuilding tradition, though now the money seems to lie in crafting scale models of real boats for sale to the yachting crowd. Farther along the Main Road, **Sargent Bros. Model Boat Shop** is a larger shop offering the same types of merchandise. The workshop is a little more accessible here, so you can easily see the craftsmen creating their wares (all the work is done by hand; no power tools are employed at all), and see models in various stages of construction. At both shops, the models are amazing, lovingly constructed and signed by the craftsman—and they're not what you'd call cheap: Prices start around $250 for a tiny model, and can go up as high as $10,000 for something really fabulous.

If you continue walking along the Main Road you'll pass through an area with many boating supply stores and a few bars and food stands obviously geared to the local fishing and sailing trades. It's a quiet, pretty walk, even though it may well be the most "industrial" part of the island. Eventually you'll come upon a concrete walkway hanging above the water along the coast. From here the going gets rough—many sections of the walkway have been cracked and heaved drastically off-kilter by hurricanes, and it's patched here and there with planks and other makeshift materials. At the end of the walkway the road starts curving uphill and inland through a quiet residential area, and thus all the way up to **Hamilton Fort,** perched above Admiralty Bay and offering a lovely view of Port Elizabeth, though that's about all it offers—a few tiny fragments of battlements and five plugged canons are all that remain of the old fort. A taxi can take you here as well by another route, if you want to avoid the walk (a good idea unless you're in decent shape and very sure-footed).

ON YOUR OWN: BEYOND WALKING DISTANCE

At Park Beach on the island's northeast coast, 2 miles east of Port Elizabeth, **Brother King's Old Hegg Turtle Sanctuary** offers a chance to see conservation in action. Founded in 1995 by the eponymous King and dedicated to raising and releasing Hawksbill turtle hatchlings, the sanctuary is a real labor of love. A main concrete swimming pool and small plastic kiddy pools allow maturing hatchlings to socialize. Brother King and his assistants are on-hand to tell you about their conservation efforts, and will gladly accept donations to help keep the place going.

Aside from this and the activities in Port Elizabeth, most of the island's other attractions are **beaches,** so turn to that section, below.

SHOPPING

You'll find most shopping worth doing right within walking distance of the docks in Port Elizabeth. Heading south from the pier, one of the first businesses you'll come to is the **Bequia Bookshop** (www.caribbeanbookshop.com), selling books on the island's and region's culture and history, books of poetry and prose by local authors, yachting guides, and a selection of other fiction and nonfiction titles, as well as truly beautiful scrimshaw pocket knives, pendants, money clips, necklaces, and pins, all made from polished camel bone rather than the traditional whale bone. Presumably, camels are not yet endangered.

Sam McDowell, the artist who creates these scrimshaw items, opens his **Banana Patch Studio** for visitors by appointment. Located in the little village of Paget Farm on the southern part of the island, near the airport, the studio displays Sam's scrimshaw and whaling-themed paintings as well as his wife Donna's shellwork. Call or fax ☎ 784/ 458-3865 for an appointment.

There are several generic gift shops farther along, some fronting off the Belmont Walkway, including **Solana's,** for Caribelle batiks, T-shirts, etc., and **The Crab Hole,** for batiks and jewelry.

Heading in the other direction, north from the docks, you'll find the two model-boat shops described above, as well as a couple of open-air souvenir/crafts stalls, a produce market, and **Kennie's Music Shop,** for island sounds on CD and cassette.

BEACHES

Beaches are one of the big draws on Bequia, and are all open to the public. Tops on the list is **Princess Margaret Beach,** a golden-sand stretch lying just south of Port Elizabeth. To get there, take the Belmont Walkway to its end; from there, take the dirt path over the hill. **Lower Bay** beach is a little farther down along the same stretch of coast.

On the northeast coast, the beach at **Industry Bay** is windswept and gorgeous, a scene straight out of a romance novel. Trees on the hills surrounding the bay grow up to a certain height and then level out, growing sideways due to the constant wind off the Atlantic. The small, three-room Crescent Beach Hotel lies along this stretch. Along the southeast coast is **Friendship Bay,** an area that draws many European visitors.

There are no clothing-optional beaches on Bequia. Also, do not under any circumstances pick or eat the small green apples you'll see growing in some spots. These are manchineel, and are extremely poisonous.

SPORTS

Besides walking (see above) and biking (mountain bikes are available to rent from Handy Andy's Rentals right by the cruise dock), the sports here, like the rest of life on the island, center around the water. **Dive Bequia** (☎ 784/458-3504, bobsax@ caribsurf.com) and **Sunsports** (☎ 784/458-3577, www.sunsport@caribsurf.com), both located along Belmont Walkway, right by the docks, specialize in diving and snorkeling. Windsurfing is also available at **De Reef Aquasports,** on the beach in Lower Bay.

GREAT LOCAL RESTAURANTS & BARS

The coastal stretch along the Belmont Walkway is chockablock with restaurants and bars. The local beer of St. Vincent and the Grenadines is Hairoun, which is decent but not up to the level of St. Lucia's Piton. The local rum is Sunset.

De Bistro (☎ 784/457-3428), sporting a sign that reads NEW YORK, LONDON, PARIS, BEQUIA, is a very casual, open-air bar/restaurant located right next to Handy

A Quiet Grenadine Day on Union Island

Some small ships stop for a day at quiet, tranquil (very quiet, very tranquil) Union Island, the southernmost port of entry in the St. Vincent Grenadines. Think of your stop here as a "recovery day" rather than a whiz-bang exciting day in port: There are few facilities (none whatsoever in Chatham Bay, where ships usually tender passengers to land), few people, and few opportunities to do anything more than swim, snorkel, and do a little beachcombing. You'll likely see hundreds of conch-shell pieces along the beach, since a number of local fishermen are based here. (You can always tell if the conch was naturally thrown up on the beach or caught, since those caught have a small gash in the shell—the method the fishermen use to sever the muscle by which the conch beast holds onto its shell home.) Some enterprising fishermen set out the best shells they find on small tables, offering them to tourists for a couple bucks—you miss out on the personal thrill of finding them yourself, but they are some mighty nice shells.

Snorkeling is decent in Chatham Bay, though the waters don't yield the diversity you'll see elsewhere in the eastern Caribbean.

Andy's Rentals, near the dock. It serves the usual casual food: burgers, sandwiches, fish, pasta, and beer.

The ✪ **Frangipani Hotel Restaurant and Bar,** a little farther down the walkway (☎ 784/458-3255), is in a beautiful area right on the water. Lunch served throughout the day includes sandwiches, salads, and seafood platters. Dinner specialties include conch chowder, baked chicken with rice-and-coconut stuffing, and an array of fresh fish. On Thursday nights the bar hosts an excellent steel band. It's a lovely scene, with yachters, locals, cruisers, and a coterie of friendly local dogs all getting to know one another over drinks or settling down for the restaurant's special barbecue.

Farther along, the **Whaleboner Bar & Restaurant** (☎ 784/458-3233) serves a nice thin-crust pizza (with toppings like lobster, shrimp, and generic "fish"), sandwiches, fish-and-chips, and cold beer, either indoors or at tables in their shaded, ocean-view front yard. It's a perfect casual resting-up spot after walking around the island.

The **Gingerbread Restaurant & Bar,** also right along the waterfront (☎ 784/458-3800), has a beautiful balcony dining room, and it's downstairs cafe serves coffee, tea, and Italian ice cream at outside tables. ✪ **Plantation House,** farther along still, is the premier dining spot on the island, serving informal lunches and more formal dinners of the cordon-bleu, roast-breast-of-duck, and conch-chowder variety. Service and cuisine are both first-rate.

Up the Main Road in the opposite direction from the Belmont Walkway, heading left when you walk off the cruise ship dock, you'll find the **New York Sports Bar,** which really needs no explanation.

6 Bonaire

Ever wonder what's going on under all that water you've been cruising on for days? There's no better place to find out than the island of Bonaire—"Divers Paradise," as the slogan on the island's license plates says. Avid divers have known about this unspoiled treasure for years, and consistently rank the island's pristine aquamarine waters, stunning coral reefs, and vibrant marine life among the best in the Caribbean, if not the world, for both diving and snorkeling.

But if diving's not for you, you'll be happy to know the island offers numerous other adventure activities such as mountain biking, kayaking, and windsurfing. If these options still sound too strenuous, why not just marvel at the sun-basking iguanas, fluorescent lora parrots, blue-tailed lizards, wild donkeys, graceful flamingos, and feral goats? As for flora, you're likely to see more cacti in Bonaire than anywhere outside the deserts of Mexico and the Southwest. Sprawling bushes of exotic succulents and permanently windswept divi-divi trees also abound.

If you'd rather just bake in the sun, Bonaire's beaches are intimate and uncrowded. In fact, the entire island is cozy and manageable. In no time at all, you'll feel it's your very own private resort. Shaped like a boomerang, Bonaire is 24 miles long and 3 to 7 miles wide—large enough to require a motorized vehicle if you want to explore, but small enough that you won't get lost.

Relying on your high-school French, you might think Bonaire ("good air") is a French island. It's not. Fifty miles north of Venezuela and 30 miles west of Curaçao, this untrampled refuge is the "B" of the ABC Netherlands Antilles chain (Aruba and Curaçao are the "A" and the "C"). The name "Bonaire" actually comes from the Caiquetio word "bonay," which means "low country." Members of the Arawak tribe who sailed from the coast of Venezuela a thousand years ago, the Caiquetios were Bonaire's first human inhabitants.

Europeans arrived 500 years later in 1499. With the discovery of oil in Venezuela early in the 20th century, Aruba and Curaçao became refining centers, and Bonaire, too, got a piece of the pie. You can see oil storage tanks on the northeast coast. During World War II, the island served as an internment camp for 461 German and Dutch Nazis. Tourism, the island's major industry today, developed after the war, as self-rule was granted (the island remains a Dutch protectorate). The people of Bonaire are a mix of African, Dutch, and South American ancestries. You'll also meet expatriates from the U.S., Britain, and Australia.

Frommer's Favorite Bonaire Experiences

- **Scuba diving:** Diving in Bonaire is said to be easier than anywhere else on Earth. The island's leeward coast has more than 80 dive sites, and whether you're diving from a boat or right from shore, you'll see spectacular coral formations and as many types of fish as anywhere in the Caribbean. If you're not certified to dive, fret not: By taking a half-day resort course, you can see firsthand what divers rave about. And if you'd rather just stick to snorkeling, be assured that abundant marine life is perfectly visible through the crystal-clear water.
- **Mountain biking along the western coast:** Bike along the coast on a road carved through lava and limestone, and bordered with cactus. The road north from the island's capital and main town, Kralendijk (*Crawl*-en-dike), is relatively flat and passes

Frommer's Ratings: Bonaire

	poor	fair	good	excellent	outstanding
Overall Experience			✓		
Shore Excursions				✓	
Activities Close to Port		✓			
Beach & Water Sports					✓
Shopping		✓			
Dining/Bars			✓		

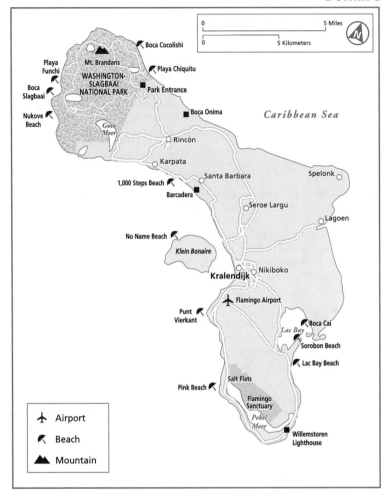

several uncrowded beaches—perfect for cooling off. If you're looking for more of a challenge, pedal uphill to Bonaire's oldest town, Rincon.

- **Exploring Washington-Slagbaai National Park:** This preserve is home to a variety of exotic wildlife and vegetation and offers spectacular coastal views. At times you might think you're in Arizona—with all the towering cacti, iguanas, and thousands of jittery lizards—but the humidity, flamingos, and beaches make it clear you're not.

- **Making new friends at the Donkeys Sanctuary:** Miss your pooch back home? Why not lavish your love on some deserving surrogates? More than 40 wild donkeys, most of them injured or orphaned by cars, call this oasis near the airport home. An entourage of hoofed critters greets you as you enter the gate, then accompanies you around the tidy, brightly colored grounds. The souvenir shop has donkey shirts, donkey bags, and donkey art. After recuperation and rehabilitation, the residents return to their rambling ways in the wild. If you're moved by the animals' unconditional affection, you can adopt one. As a new parent, you'll receive photos and letters from your adoptee twice a year.

A Passion to Preserve

Twenty years ago, the Bonaire Marine Park was established to protect the island's entire coastal waters. Spear fishing is forbidden, divers are prohibited from wearing gloves (they're less likely to touch the ancient and fragile coral that way), anchoring has given way to a system of permanent moorings, and divers must prove they can control their buoyancy in mandatory orientation dives. Don't even think about collecting shells or coral—it's prohibited. The net result of these efforts? One of the healthiest underwater ecosystems on the planet and a veritable environmental showcase.

COMING ASHORE   Cruise ships dock in the port of Kralendijk, the island's capital, commercial center, and largest town (pop. about 2,500). The dock leads to Wilhelmina Park, a pleasant public space named after a former Dutch queen. Queen Beatrix Way, the brick-paved path along the waterfront, is lined with open-air restaurants and bars. Most of the town's shopping is 1 block inland on Kaya Grandi.

Your best bet for making long-distance **phone calls** is the 24-hour central phone-company office (Telbo) on Kaya Libertador Simón Bolívar, next to the tourism office.

CURRENCY   Bonaire's official currency is the Netherlands Antilles florin (NAf), also known as the **guilder.** Each florin is divisible by 100 cents. Don't waste your time exchanging money, though—the U.S. dollar is as widely accepted as the local currency. Change may be a mixture of dollars and florins. The exchange rate is 1.77 florins to $1 U.S. (NAf 1 = 56¢). If you need cash, there are several ATMs along Kaya Grandi.

LANGUAGE   Almost everyone in Bonaire speaks English, which, along with Dutch, is a required course in the local schools. Papiamentu is the local patois and language of the street, a rich blend of Dutch, Spanish, Portuguese, French, English, Caribbean Indian, and several African languages. Given the island's proximity to Venezuela, you're likely to hear Spanish as well.

INFORMATION   The **Tourism Corporation Bonaire** is located at Kaya Libertador Simón Bolívar 12 in Kralendijk (☎ **599/717-8322** or 599/717-8649; fax 599/717-8408; E-mail info@TourismBonaire.com).

CALLING FROM THE U.S.   When calling Bonaire from the United States, you need to dial "011" before the numbers listed throughout this section.

GETTING AROUND

BY RENTAL CAR   Highway signs are in Dutch, and sometimes English, with easy-to-understand international symbols. Driving is on the right, the same as in the States and most of Europe. A valid driver's license is acceptable for renting and driving a car. The island has about 15 car-rental agencies, including **Avis,** at Flamingo Airport (☎ **800/230-4898** in the U.S., or 599/717-5795); **Hertz,** with offices at the airport (☎ **599/717-7221**) and at the Harbour Village Bonaire resort (☎ **800/654-3131** in the U.S., or 599/717-6020); **National,** with offices at Kaya Nikiboko Zuid 114 (☎ **599/717-7907**) and the airport (☎ **888/CAR-RENT** in the U.S., or 599/717-7940); and Flamingo Car Rental, Kaya Grandi 86 (☎ **599/717-5588**). Depending on the season and availability, rates can be as low as $40 per day. If you want a four-wheel-drive vehicle, expect to pay $60 to $65.

BY TAXI   Taxis greet cruise ship passengers at the pier. Although the cars are unmetered, the government establishes rates, and drivers should produce a price list upon request. Most cabs can be hired for a tour of the island, with as many as four passengers allowed to go along for the ride. Negotiate a price before leaving. You can get more information from the **Taxi Central Dispatch** office (☎ 599/717-8100).

BY SCOOTER OR MOPED   If you plan to venture not too far, scooters and mopeds are practical, open-air alternatives. They can be rented from **Hot Shot Scooters,** Kaya Bonaire 4C (☎ 599/717-7166), or **Macho! Scooter Rentals** at the Plaza Resort Bonaire, J. A. Abraham Blvd. 80 (☎ 599/717-2500). Mopeds are about $18 a day; two-seat scooters run about $32.

BY BICYCLE   For getting around town or exploring the nearby coast, try bicycling. The coastal terrain is essentially flat, but the sun can be brutal even before noon. Plan your excursion as early in the day as possible. You can rent a 21-speed mountain bike for $15 to $20 from **Cycle Bonaire,** Kaya L. D. Gerharts 11D (☎ 599/717-7558).

SHORE EXCURSIONS

✪ **Scuba Excursion for Certified Divers** ($69, 3 hours): Dive in the island's famous Bonaire Marine Park.

✪ **Bike Tour** ($64, 3–4 hours): This scenic ride along mostly flat and downhill terrain affords riders views of Bonaire's many species of birds, cacti, and other flora and fauna, including pink flamingos. The ride takes you along the island's northern shoreline.

✪ **Snorkeling** ($39–$69 adults, $24–$39 children, 3 hours): Snorkeling off the coast of Bonaire is some of the best you'll find in the Caribbean. A variety of snorkeling tours include spending time at the uninhabited "No Name Beach," Ebo's Reef, and Karel's Hills, all located offshore from Klein Bonaire.

ON YOUR OWN: WITHIN WALKING DISTANCE

You can walk the length of Kralendijk in an hour or less. Residents readily admit the town is sleepy, but they like it that way, thank you. The tourist office has **walking-tour maps,** but because Bonaire has always been off the beaten track, Kralendijk's highlights are modest and few. You'll probably want to stroll along the seafront with its views and restaurants, and along Kaya Grandi, the island's major shopping district. Just south of the town dock is **Fort Oranje,** a tiny fortress that boasts a cannon dating from the time of Napoléon. The town has some charming Dutch Caribbean architecture—gabled roofs you might see in Amsterdam, but in cheerful Caribbean colors, especially sunny ochre and terra-cotta. If your ship arrives early enough, you can visit the **waterfront produce market.**

ON YOUR OWN: BEYOND WALKING DISTANCE

As a day visitor, you'll probably choose to explore either the northern or southern part of the island. The **coastal road** north of Kralendijk is said to be one of the most beautiful in the Antilles. Turquoise, azure, and cobalt waters stretch to the horizon on your left, while pink-coral and black-volcanic cliffs loom on your right. Towering cacti, intimate coastal coves, strange rock formations, and panoramic vistas add to the beauty. The north also boasts **Washington-Slagbaai National Park,** an impressive, 13,500 acre preserve that occupies the northwestern portion of the island, and **Rincon,** Bonaire's "other" town and oldest settlement.

NORTH OF KRALENDIJK   Soon after leaving Kralendijk on the coast road, across from the Bonaire Caribbean Club, you'll find **Barcadera,** an old cave once used to trap goats. Take the stone steps down to the cave and examine the stalactites.

Just past the Radio Nederland towers is **1,000 Steps beach and dive site.** The view from the top of the steps is particularly lovely: picturesque coves, craggy coastline, and tropical waters of changing hues. Actually, there are only 67 steps, but they're said to feel like a thousand when you're schlepping diving gear.

At the Kaya Karpata intersection, you'll see a mustard-colored building on your right. It's what's left of the aloe-processing facilities of **Landhuis Karpata,** a hundred-year-old former plantation. Here you can learn about the cultivation, harvesting, and processing of aloe, once a major export crop.

Minutes after turning right on Kaya Karpata, you'll arrive in **Rincon,** the original Spanish settlement on the island. The town eventually became the home of African slaves who worked the island's plantations and salt pans. Nestled in a valley away from either coast, Rincon was hidden from marauding pirates, who plagued the Caribbean for decades. Today, the quiet and picturesque village is home to Bonaire's oldest church—a handsome ochre-and-white structure—and to **Prisca's,** an island institution serving the best local ice cream. Prisca, the founder, has passed on, but her daughter keeps the family tradition alive, serving creamy-yet-light homemade ice cream. Try the rum raisin, peanut, pistachio, or *ponche crema* (a little like eggnog). The shop is located in a pistachio-colored building on Kaya Komkomber (that's Papiamentu for "cucumber").

The pride of Bonaire, located on the island's northern tip, is **Washington-Slagbaai National Park,** one of the first national parks in the Caribbean. Formerly two separate plantations that produced aloe and charcoal, and raised goats, it now showcases the island's geology, animals, and vegetation. The park boasts more than 190 species of birds, thousands of kadushi, yatu, and prickly pear cactus, herds of wild goats, foraging donkeys, flocks of flamingos, and what seems like billions of lizards. The scenery includes stark, desertlike hills, quiet beaches, secluded caverns, and wave-crashed cliffs. You can either take the shorter 15-mile route around the park, marked with green arrows, or the longer 22-mile track, marked with yellow arrows. You'll have plenty of opportunities to hike, swim, or snorkel along either way. Admission is $5 per person, and the park is open from 8am to 5pm daily except for major holidays. Guide booklets and maps are available at the gate, where there's also a small museum. The dirt roads can be rugged, so if it's rained recently you may need a jeep.

On your way back to Kralendijk, take the Kaminda Onima, which traces the island's northeastern coast. You'll pass **Onima,** the site of 500-year-old Caiquetio Indian inscriptions. Some of the red and brown drawings depict turtles and rain; others appear to have religious significance. You should be able to recognize snakes, human hands, and suns among the roughly 75 inscriptions.

Before returning to Kralendijk, consider calling on **Sherman Gibbs.** You'll find his monument to the beauty of common objects on Kaminda Tras di Montaña, the road leading back to Kralendijk. Eccentric is one way to describe Mr. Gibbs; genius is another. If you're familiar with the Watts Tower in Los Angeles, you know "junk" can be transformed into something beautiful. Sherman combines old detergent bottles, boat motors, buoys, car seats, and just about anything else that strikes his fancy to create a wondrously happy sanctuary. The wind and old fan blades power his TV. As ingenuous and gentle as his seven iguanas, he's an island treasure.

SOUTH OF KRALENDIJK   Just minutes south of town, dazzlingly bright **salt pyramids** dominate the horizon. These hills, looking more like alpine snowdrifts than sodium mounds, are the product of a process that starts when the tide forces seawater into lakes and ends when evaporation crystallizes the salt.

Farther from the road, abandoned saltworks have been set aside as a **flamingo sanctuary.** Bonaire is one of the world's few nesting places for pink flamingos, a species that until recently was seriously threatened by extinction. Thanks to the reserve, the island's flamingo population during the breeding season now swells to roughly 10,000, rivaling the human population of 14,000. The sanctuary is completely off-limits to the public because the birds are extremely wary of humans and disturbances of any kind. But even from the road you can spot a pink haze on the horizon, and with binoculars you can see the graceful birds feeding in the briny pink and purple waters.

At the island's southern tip, restored **slave huts** stand as mute but damning monuments to the inhumanity of the island's slave era. Each hut, no bigger than a large doghouse, provided rude nighttime shelter for six slaves brought from Africa by the Dutch West Indies Company to cut dyewood, cultivate maize, and harvest solar salt. On Friday afternoons, the slaves trekked 7 hours in the oppressive heat to their homes and families in Rincon for the weekend, returning to the salt pans on Sunday evenings.

Willemstoren Lighthouse, Bonaire's first, was built in 1837. On the eastern side of the island's southern tip, the structure is fully automated today and usually closed to visitors. It's classically picturesque, and the setting implores you to contemplate the power and majesty of the sea. You may notice odd little bundles of driftwood, bleached coral, and rocks in the area. Although they look like something out of *The Blair Witch Project,* they're actually markers constructed by fishermen to designate where they've left their boats.

A few minutes up the east coast, you'll find **Lac Bay,** a lagoon that's every bit as tranquil as the nearby windward sea is furious. The calm, shallow waters and steady breezes make the area ideal for windsurfing, and various fishes come here to hatch their young. Deep inside the lagoon, mangrove trees with Edward Scissorshands roots lunge out of the water; if it weren't for the relentlessly cheerful sun, they might seem sinister. Animal lovers will relish sightings of wild donkeys, goats, and flamingos along the way.

SHOPPING

Don't expect to be caught up in a duty-free frenzy in Bonaire. You'll be able to hit every store in Kralendijk before lunch, and you'll probably find greater selections and prices at other ports. The island is a great place to buy some items, though. Consider top-of-the-line dive watches and underwater cameras. Or how about fine jewelry with fish and other marine themes?

You'll find most shops on Kaya Grandi, the adjacent streets, or in small malls. For Tag-Heuer dive watches, Cuban cigars, Lladró porcelain, Daum crystal, and Kosta Boda glass, try **Littman Jewelers** at Kaya Grandi 33. In the centrally located **Harborside Mall,** Little Holland has silk neckties, Nautica menswear, blue Delft porcelain, and an even more impressive array of Cuban cigars. If you're an aficionado, you'll love the acclimatized **Cedar Cigar Room** with its Montecristos, H. Upmanns, Romeo & Julietas, and Cohibas. **Sparky's,** in the same mall, carries perfume and other cosmetics, including Lancôme, Esteé Lauder, Chanel, Calvin Klein, and Ralph Lauren. **Maharaj Gifthouse,** at Kaya Grandi 21, has jewelry, gifts, and more blue Delft porcelain. **Boolchand's,** at Kaya Grandi 19, has a peculiarly wide range of items, including underwater cameras, electronic goods, watches, sunglasses, and shoes.

Benetton, at Kaya Grandi 49, has smart casual wear at discounts of 20% to 30%. If batik shirts, pareos, bathing suits, or souvenir T-shirts are what you want, you can't go wrong at **Best Buddies,** Kaya Grandi 32, **Boutique Vita,** Kaya Grandi 16, **Bye-Bye Bonaire,** Harborside Mall, or **Island Fashions,** Kaya Grandi 5. Probably the best place for dressier women's clothing, including Hermès scarves, Oscar de la Renta resort wear, and Kenneth Cole shoes, is **The Shop at Harbour Village** at Kaya Gobernador N. Debrot 72. You can also find sunglasses, jewelry, and perfume with Cartier, Fendi, Donna Karan, and Givenchy labels.

A personal favorite is **Cultimara Supermarket** at Kaya L. D. Gerharts 13. On a hot day, nothing beats this behemoth's frozen-food section. The store offers free coffee, a wide assortment of Dutch cheeses and chocolates, straight-from-the-oven breads and pastries, and various products from the Caribbean, Europe, South America, and the United States. And nothing will have greater snob appeal back home than a T-shirt with the Cultimara logo.

BEACHES

Bonaire's intimate and uncrowded beaches, almost all of them on the island's calm-watered west coast, come in a rainbow of colors. The sand at **Pink Beach,** south of Kralendijk near the slave huts, has a pinkish tint when wet. Busy on weekends, the beach is yours alone during the week. North of Kralendijk, **Nukove Beach** is a small white-sand cove carved out of a limestone cliff. A narrow sand channel cuts through an otherwise impenetrable wall of elkhorn coral, giving divers and snorkelers access to the sea. The island's northernmost beach, **Boca Cocolishi** ("seashell bay" in Papiamentu), is another of several beaches in Washington-Slagbaai Park. Algae makes the water here purplish, and the sand, formed by small pieces of coral and mollusk shells, is black. The water's a bit rough for anything more than wading, but it's a perfect spot to picnic. The water's even more treacherous at **Playa Chiquitu,** but the cove, sand dunes, and crashing waves make for an incomparable setting. Two other beaches in the national park are worth mentioning. On one side of **Playa Funchi,** flamingos nest in the lagoon; on the other, there's excellent snorkeling. Nearby **Boca Slagbaai,** once a plantation harbor, is also a favorite place to snorkel and dive. The water at **Lac Bay Beach** is only 1 to 2 feet deep, making it especially popular with families. Across the bay, white-sand **Sorobon Beach** is the island's only nude beach. It's part of the Sorobon Beach Resort, which means as a nonguest you'll have to pay for the privilege of disrobing.

SPORTS

KAYAKING For a peaceful, relaxing time, kayak through the mangroves in Lac Bay. You can proceed at your own pace in the calm waters, taking time to observe hundreds of baby fish and the bizarrely shaped tree roots. Bring protection from the sun and the ravenous mosquitoes. Divers and snorkelers have the added option of towing a light-weight sea kayak behind them as they explore the waters of the leeward coast. Guided trips and kayak rentals are available from **Discover Bonaire,** Kaya Gobernador N. Debrot 79 (☎ **599/717-5252**), and, in Sorobon, from **Jibe City** (☎ **599/717-5233**). A half-day guided tour through the mangroves is about $45, including a guide, kayak, and transportation.

MOUNTAIN BIKING Bonaire has miles of roads, paved and unpaved, flat and hilly. The truly athletic can even follow goat paths. Take a water bottle, a map, and plenty of sunscreen. Discover Bonaire (see above) conducts guided bike tours through the *kunuku* (outback) and Washington-Slagbaai Park.

SCUBA DIVING The leeward coast and the area encircling **Klein Bonaire,** the small, uninhabited island across from Kralendijk, is studded with more than 80 dive sites. Because you'll only have time for one or two dives, put your trust in the dive shop operators. A resort course for beginners, which includes instruction, a skill session, and a boat dive with a dive master, could be the best $120 you'll ever spend; head-to-toe equipment is part of the price. Part of the Harbour Village Bonaire resort, **Great Adventures at Harbour Village,** Kaya Gobernador N. Debrot 72 (☎ **800/868-7477** in the U.S. and Canada, or 599/717-7500), is the island's poshest operation. It's upscale but unpretentious and friendly. If you're looking to feed anemones, tickle fish, or be manicured by cleaner shrimp, reserve a dive with **Dee Scarr's Touch the Sea,** P.O. Box

369 (☎ **303/816-1723** in the U.S., or 599/717-8529). An environmentalist and author, Dee takes two to four certified divers at a time for personalized, "nonstressful" interaction with marine creatures. Make arrangements in advance.

SNORKELING   Bonaire's **Guided Snorkeling Program,** the world's first, includes a slide-show introduction to reef fishes, corals, and sponges, an in-water demonstration of snorkeling skills, and a guided tour of one of several sites. The cost is $25 per person. Equipment rental is about $10 more. You can arrange a tour through any of the dive shops listed above as well as through **Buddy Dive Resort,** Kaya Gobernador N. Debrot 85 (☎ **800/934-DIVE** from the U.S. or 599/717-5080); **Bon Bini Divers,** at the Lions Dive Hotel Bonaire, Kaya Gobernador N. Debrot 90 (☎ **800/327-5424** from the U.S. or 599/717-5424); and **Dive Inn,** Kaya C. E. B. Hellmund (☎ **599/ 717-8761**).

WINDSURFING   Lac Bay's shallow waters, steady breezes, and protection from the stronger-winded east coast assure a safe and enjoyable windsurfing adventure for beginners and pros. There are two equipment-rental centers in Sorobon: **Jibe City** (☎ **599/ 717-5233**) and **Bonaire Windsurf Place** (☎ **599/717-2288**). Boards and sails are $55 per day with discounts if you rent two or more. Special beginner's lessons are $45, including equipment.

GREAT LOCAL RESTAURANTS & BARS

IN KRALENDIJK   Kralendijk offers a variety of culinary options at generally reasonable prices. **Zeezicht Bar and Restaurant,** Kaya Corsou 10 (☎ **599/717-8434**), is a local favorite on the downtown waterfront. Seviche, conch sandwiches, and a gumbo of conch, fish, shrimp, and oysters are on the menu. Mermaids, fishing nets, and pirates adorn the walls. Also on the waterfront, open-air **Shamballa's,** Kaya Grandi 7 (☎ **599/717-8286**), offers Mexican entrees and seafood. **Mi Poron,** Kaya Caracas 1 (☎ **599/717-5199**), is great for traditional Bonairean cuisine.

  Bon Awa, Kaya Nikiboko Zuid 8 (☎ **599/717-5157**), a simpler alternative for local cuisine, has outside tables, killer hot sauce, and outstanding homemade ice cream. Looking for deli picnic sandwiches or pizza? Try **The Sandwich Factory,** Kaya Prinses Marie Plaza (☎ **599/717-7369**). If you're on your way to the national park, ask for free day-old bread to feed the iguanas.

7 British Virgin Islands: Tortola & Virgin Gorda

With small bays and hidden coves that were once havens for pirates, the British Virgin Islands are among the world's loveliest cruising regions. This British colony has some 40 islands in the northeastern corner of the Caribbean about 60 miles east of Puerto Rico, most of them tiny rocks and cays. Only **Tortola, Virgin Gorda,** and **Jost Van Dyke** are of significant size. The other tiny islets have names like Fallen Jerusalem and Ginger. Norman Island is said to have been the prototype for Robert Louis Stevenson's *Treasure Island,* and Blackbeard inspired a famous ditty by marooning 15 pirates and a bottle of rum on the rocky cay known as Deadman Bay. Yo ho ho.

  Columbus came this way in 1493, but the British Virgins apparently made little impression on him. Although the Spanish and Dutch contested it, Tortola was officially annexed by the English in 1672. Today, these islands are a British colony, with their own elected government and a population of about 17,000.

  The vegetation is varied and depends on the rainfall. Palms and mangos grow in profusion in some parts, whereas other places are arid and studded with cacti.

  Smaller cruise lines such as Seabourn, Windstar, and Windjammer Barefoot Cruises call at Tortola and the more scenic Virgin Gorda and Jost Van Dyke. Unlike the rigid programs at St. Thomas and other major docking ports, visits here are less structured, and each cruise line is free to pursue its own policy.

CURRENCY The **U.S. dollar** is the legal currency, much to the surprise of arriving Britishers who find no one willing to accept their pounds.

LANGUAGE English is spoken here.

CALLING FROM THE U.S. When calling the BVIs from the United States, you need only dial a "1" before the numbers listed throughout this section.

TORTOLA

Road Town, the colony's capital, sits about midway along the southern shore of 24-square-mile Tortola. Once a sleepy village, it's become a bustling center since Wickhams Cay, a 70-acre landfill development and marina, brought in a massive yacht-chartering business.

The island's entire **southern coast** is characterized by rugged mountain peaks. On the northern coast are beautiful bays with white sandy beaches, banana trees, mangoes, and clusters of palms.

If your ship isn't scheduled to visit Virgin Gorda but you want to, you can catch a boat, ferry, or launch here and be on the island in no time, since it's only a 12-mile trip.

Frommer's Favorite Tortola Experiences

- **Visiting Bomba's Surfside Shack:** The oldest, most memorable bar on Tortola may not look like much, but it's the best party on the island (see "Great Local Restaurants & Bars," below).
- **Spending a day at Cane Garden Bay:** It's the best beach on the island, with palm trees, sand, and a great local restaurant (shack) for lunch and drinks (see "Beaches," below).
- **Hiking up Sage Mountain:** It's one of the best ways to learn about Tortola's natural character. Organized shore excursions usually include hiking trips to Sage Mountain, the highest point in the entire Virgin Islands (1,780 ft.), beginning with a ride along mountain roads in an open-air safari bus.
- **Take an island tour:** Open-air safari buses take you on a scenic journey around the extremely hilly island (see "Shore Excursions," below). Take the ship's organized tour, or hop in a taxi from the pier and for about $15 per person you get a 2- to 3-hour island tour, including beach stops.

COMING ASHORE Visiting cruise ships anchor at Wickhams Cay 1 in Road Town. You'll be brought ashore by tender. The pier, built in the mid-1990s, is a pleasant 5-minute walk to Main Street. You should have no trouble finding your way around town.

Frommer's Ratings: Tortola					
	poor	fair	good	excellent	outstanding
Overall Experience				✓	
Shore Excursions			✓		
Activities Close to Port			✓		
Beach & Water Sports			✓		
Shopping		✓			
Dining/Bars			✓		

The British Virgin Islands

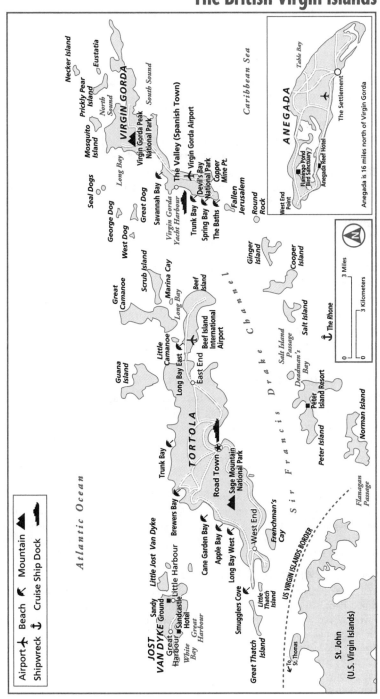

Legend: Airport ✈ · Beach ⚓ · Mountain ▲ · Shipwreck ⚓ · Cruise Ship Dock ⚓

Map labels

Atlantic Ocean

Caribbean Sea

ANEGADA
Table Bay
West End Point
The Settlement
Flamingo Pond Bird Sanctuary
Anegada Reef Hotel
Anegada is 16 miles north of Virgin Gorda

Necker Island
Eustatia
Prickly Pear Island
North Sound
South Sound
VIRGIN GORDA
Mosquito Island
Long Bay
Virgin Gorda Peak National Park
Seal Dogs
George Dog
West Dog
Great Dog
The Valley (Spanish Town)
Virgin Gorda Airport
Savannah Bay
Devil's Bay National Park
Copper Mine Pt.
Virgin Gorda Yacht Harbour
Trunk Bay
Spring Bay
The Baths
Fallen Jerusalem
Round Rock

Scrub Island
Marina Cay
Great Camanoe
Little Camanoe
Long Bay
Beef Island
Beef Island International Airport
Guana Island
Long Bay East
East End
Ginger Island
Cooper Island
Salt Island
Salt Island Passage
Deadman's Bay
Peter Island Resort
Peter Island
Norman Island
The Rhone

D r a k e   C h a n n e l

S i r   F r a n c i s

Flanagan Passage

TORTOLA
Trunk Bay
Brewers Bay
Cane Garden Bay
Apple Bay
Long Bay West
West End
Frenchman's Cay
Road Town
Sage Mountain National Park

JOST VAN DYKE
Sandy Ground
Little Harbour
Sandcastle Hotel
Great Harbour
White Bay
Smugglers Cove
Little Jost Van Dyke
Little Thatch Island
Great Thatch Island

US VIRGIN ISLANDS BORDER
To St. Thomas
St. John (U.S. Virgin Islands)

3 Miles
3 Kilometers
0

INFORMATION   The **B.V.I. Tourist Board Office** (☎ 284/494-3134) is at the center of Road Town near the ferry dock south of Wickhams Cay 1. Pick up a copy of the *Welcome Tourist Guide*. It's open Monday to Friday from 9am to 5pm.

Getting Around

BY TAXI   Open-air and sedan-style taxis meet every arriving cruise ship. To call a taxi in Road Town, call **B.V.I Taxi Assn.** (☎ 284/494-2322) or **Wheatley's** (☎ 284/494-3357). Two other local taxi services, Quality Taxi and the Waterfront Taxi Assn., are within walking distance of the cruise pier.

BY BUS   **Scato's Bus Service** (☎ 284/494-5873) picks up passengers (mostly locals) who hail it down. Fares for a trek across the island are about $1 to $3.

BY RENTAL CAR   I don't recommend driving here, as the roads are bad and driving is on the left. But if you're intent on it, there's a **Hertz** at West End near the Jolly Roger restaurant (☎ 284/495-4405).

Shore Excursions

✪ **Island Tour** ($30–$34, 3¹/₂ hours): Hop on an open-air safari bus and embark on a scenic journey around the island, enjoying some panoramic views and good photo ops, and ending with a stop at Cane Garden Bay Beach for swimming, sunbathing, and just plain old relaxing.

Mount Sage & Cane Garden Bay tour ($34, 4 hours): Start with a hike up Sage Mountain and end with 1¹/₂ hours at Cane Garden Bay beach.

Lambert Beach Resort ($20, 5 hours): After a drive along the lovely north and south coasts you spend an afternoon at the Lambert Beach Resort, where you'll find a bar and Turtle's Restaurant.

Touring Through Local Operators

Bus Tours/Snorkeling/Glass-Bottom Boat Tours: Since the shore excursions here are very modest, you might consider calling **Travel Plan Tours,** Romasco Place, Wickham's Cay, Road Town (☎ 284/494-2872), which will take one to three people on a 3-hour guided tour of the island, a snorkeling excursion, or a glass-bottom boat tour.

Taxi Tours: You can take a 2- to 3-hour taxi tour for about $45 for up to three people. For a taxi in Road Town, call ☎ 284/494-2322.

On Your Own: Within Walking Distance

Besides the handful of shops on Main and Upper Main streets in Road Town, there's also a **Botanic Garden** right in the middle of town, across from the Police Station. The Garden is open daily from 8am to 6pm and features a wide variety of flowers and plants, including a section on medicinal plants.

On Your Own: Beyond Walking Distance

You have mainly nature to look at on Tortola. The big attraction is **Mount Sage National Park,** which rises to 1,780 feet (the highest point in the BVIs and USVIs) and covers 92 acres. It was established in 1964 to protect the remnants of Tortola's original forests not burned or cleared during its plantation era, and is both the oldest national park in the British Virgin Islands and the best present-day example of the territory's native moist forests. You'll find a lush forest of mango, papaya, breadfruit, and coconut trees; many of the plants and trees are labeled, and there are also birchberry, mountain guava, and guavaberry trees here, all of which have edible fruit. This is a great place to enjoy a picnic while overlooking neighboring islets and cays. Any taxi driver can take you to the mountain. Before going, stop at the tourist office (see above) and pick up a brochure with a map and an outline of the park's trails. The two main hikes are the Rain Forest Trail and the Mahogany Forest Trail. For a quiet beach day, head to **Smuggler's Cove,** a picture-perfect, secluded spot with white sand and calm turquoise water.

SHOPPING

Shopping on Tortola is a minor activity compared to other Caribbean ports. Still, you'll find most stores are on Main Street in Road Town. Only British goods are imported without duty, and they are the best buys, especially English china. You'll also find West Indian art, terra-cotta pottery, wicker and rattan home furnishings, Mexican glassware, dhurrie rugs, baskets, and ceramics.

Some good shops to visit include **Pusser's Company Store,** Main Street, Road Town, for Pusser's rum, fine nautical artifacts, and a selection of Pusser's sports and travel clothing and upmarket gift items; and the **Sunny Caribee Herb and Spice Company,** also on Main Street, for Caribbean spices, seasonings, teas, condiments, and handcrafts. You can buy two world-famous specialties here: West Indian Hangover Cure and Arawak Love Potion.

BEACHES

Most of the beaches are a 20-minute taxi ride from the cruise dock. Figure on about $15 per person one-way (some will charge less, like $5 per person if you've got a group), but discuss it with the driver before setting out. You can also ask him to pick you up at a designated time.

The finest beach is at ✪ **Cane Garden Bay,** which compares favorably to the famous Magens Bay Beach on the north shore of St. Thomas. It's on the northwest side of the island, across the mountains from Road Town, but it's worth the effort to get there, and is so special you might take a taxi here in the morning and not head back to your cruise ship until departure time. Plan to have lunch here at **Rhymer's** (☎ **284/495-4639**), where the chef will cook some conch or whelk, or perhaps some barbecue spareribs. The beach bar and restaurant is open daily from 8am to 9pm, serving breakfast, lunch, and dinner, with main courses ranging from $12 to $20. Showers are available. Rhymer's rents towels, as well as Sunfish and Windsurfers.

Surfers like **Apple Bay,** also on the northwest side, but you'll have to watch out for sharks (no joke: on a recent trip a friend saw one while surfing and its dorsal fins were visible from the shore). A hotel here called Sebastians caters to the surfing crowd that visits in January and February, but the beach is ideal year-round. **Brewers Bay,** site of a campground, is on the northwest shore near Cane Garden Bay and is good for beach strolling and swimming. Both snorkelers and surfers come here. **Smugglers Cove** (sometimes known as Lower Belmont Bay) is at the extreme western end of Tortola, opposite the offshore island of Great Thatch and very close to St. John's in the U.S. Virgin Islands. A wide crescent of white sand wrapped around calm, sky-blue water, the soft and sandy bottom grows deep very slowly. Snorkelers also like this beach.

Long Bay Beach is on Beef Island, at the far eastern end of Tortola near the island's airport. To get to this mile-long, typically uncrowded stretch of white sandy beach, cross the Queen Elizabeth Bridge, and then take a left on a dirt road before the airport. From Long Bay you'll have a good view of Little Camanoe, one of the rocky offshore islands around Tortola. Here you'll find Long Bay Beach Resort, which has a nice beach restaurant and bar.

Marina Cay, off Tortola's East End, is known for its good snorkeling beach. I also recommend the beach at **Cooper Island,** across Drake's Channel. Underwater Safaris (see "Sports," below) leads snorkel expeditions to both sites.

SPORTS

HORSEBACK RIDING   Shadow's Ranch, Todman's Estate (☎ 284/494-2262), offers rides through Mount Sage National Park or down to the shores of Cane Garden Bay. Call for details Monday to Saturday from 9am to 4pm. They're located about 15 miles from the cruise dock; taxi fare is $12.

SCUBA DIVING   *Skin Diver* magazine has called the wreckage of the HMS *Rhône,* which sank in 1867 near the western point of Salt Island, the world's most fantastic shipwreck dive. It teems with marine life and coral formations, and was featured in the motion picture *The Deep. Chikuzen* is another intriguing dive site off Tortola, although it's no *Rhône.* It's a 270-foot steel-hulled refrigerator ship that sank off the island's east end in 1981. The hull, still intact under about 80 feet of water, is now home to a vast array of tropical fish, including yellowtail, barracuda, black-tip sharks, octopus, and drum fish. **Baskin in the Sun** (☎ 800/233-7938 in the U.S., or 284/494-2858), a PADI five-star facility on Tortola, is a good choice for divers. It has two different locations: at the Prospect Reef Resort, near Road Town, and at Soper's Hole, on Tortola's West End. Baskin's most popular trip is the supervised "Half-Day Scuba Diving," catering to beginners, but there are trips for more advanced levels as well. Daily excursions are scheduled to the HMS *Rhône,* as well as "Painted Walls" (an underwater canyon formed of brightly colored coral and sponges), and the "Indians" (four pinnacle rocks sticking out of the water, which divers follow 40 feet below the surface). **Underwater Safaris** (☎ 800/537-7032 in the U.S., or 284/494-3235) takes you to all the best sites. It offers a complete PADI and NAUI training facility, and is associated with The Moorings yacht charter company. Underwater Safaris' Road Town office is a 5-minute or about $4 taxi ride from the docks.

GREAT LOCAL RESTAURANTS & BARS

On Cappoon's Bay, ✪ **Bomba's Surfside Shack** (☎ 284/495-4148) is the oldest, most memorable bar on Tortola, sitting on a 20-foot-wide strip of unpromising coastline near the West End. It's the "junk palace" of the island, covered with Day-Glo graffiti and laced with wire and rejected odds and ends of plywood, driftwood, and abandoned rubber tires. Despite its makeshift appearance, the shack's got a sound system that can get a great party going any time of the day. The Sunday and Wednesday night barbecues are about $7 per person. It's open daily from 10am to midnight (or later, depending on business).

Standing on the waterfront across from the ferry dock, **Pusser's Road Town Pub** (☎ 284/494-3897) serves Caribbean fare, English pub grub, and good pizzas. The drink to have here is the famous Pusser's Rum, the same blend of five West Indian rums that the Royal Navy served to its men for more than 300 years. Honestly, it's not the world's greatest rum, but sometimes you just have to do things for the experience. **Capriccio di Mare,** Waterfront Drive (☎ 284/494-5369), is the most authentic-looking Italian cafe in the Virgin Islands, serving fresh pastas with succulent sauces, well-stuffed sandwiches, and the best pizzas on the island. For a great *roti* (curries wrapped in flat bread) sans atmosphere, try **Roti Palace,** in Road Town, which is sparsely furnished and not too attractive. **Callaloo,** at the Prospect Reef Resort (☎ 284/494-3311), sits within a very romantic setting if it's a balmy day and the tropical breezes are blowing. Begin with the conch fritters or shrimp cocktail, and don't pass on the house salad, which has a zesty papaya dressing. Main dishes include fresh fish. At **Pusser's Landing,** Frenchman's Cay, on the West End (☎ 284/495-4554), you can enjoy grilled fish such as mahimahi, West Indian roast chicken, or an English-inspired dish like shepherd's pie. Try the mango soufflé for dessert. **Quito's Gazebo,** on Cane Garden Bay, is owned by local recording star Quito Rhymer. It's a good place for West Indian fish dishes; Quito performs Thursday to Sunday and Tuesday.

VIRGIN GORDA

Instead of visiting Tortola, some small cruise ships put in at lovely Virgin Gorda, famous for its boulder-strewn beach known as **The Baths.** The second-largest island in the colony, it got its name ("Fat Virgin") from Christopher Columbus, who thought the mountain framing it looked like a protruding stomach. At 10 miles long and 2 miles wide, the island is about 12 miles east of Road Town, so it's easy to take a ferry or boat here if your ship only visits Tortola.

The island was a fairly desolate agricultural community until Little Dix Bay Hotel opened here in the early 1960s. Other major hotels followed, but privacy and solitude still reign supreme on Virgin Gorda.

Frommer's Favorite Virgin Gorda Experiences

- **Visiting The Baths:** House-size boulders and clear waters make for excellent swimming and snorkeling in a fabulous setting (see "Beaches," and "Shore Excursions," below).
- **Spending a beach day in Spring Bay or Trunk Bay:** Located near The Baths, Spring Bay has one of the best beaches on the island, with white sand, clear water, and good snorkeling. Trunk Bay, a wide sand beach that can be reached by boat or via a rough path from Spring Bay, is another good bet (see "Beaches," below).
- **Taking an island tour:** Open-air safari buses do a good job of showing guests this beautiful island (see "Shore Excursions," below).

COMING ASHORE   Virgin Gorda doesn't have a pier or landing facilities to suit any of the large ships. Most vessels anchor and send small craft ashore, disembarking passengers at Leverick Bay. Many others dock beside the pier in Road Town on Tortola and then send tenders across the channel to Virgin Gorda. A limited number of taxis are usually available at Leverick Bay.

GETTING AROUND   The best way to see the island is to call Andy Flax at the Fischers Cove Beach Hotel (☎ **284/495-5511**). He runs the **Virgin Gorda Tours Association,** which gives island tours for about $40 per couple. Tours leave twice daily. They will pick you up at the dock if you give them 24-hour notice. Taxis are available in limited numbers at Leverick Bay, and if you can get one, will take visitors to Spanish Town (about 20 min. away) or to The Baths and area beaches for about $5 per person each way.

Frommer's Ratings: Virgin Gorda					
	poor	fair	good	excellent	outstanding
Overall Experience					✓
Shore Excursions			✓		
Activities Close to Port				✓	
Beach & Water Sports				✓	
Shopping		✓			
Dining/Bars			✓		

A Slice of Paradise: Jost Van Dyke

Covering only 4 square miles, mountainous Jost Van Dyke is truly an off-beat, nearly undiscovered retreat—unless you count the small yachts dotting the Great Harbour. There is no cruise pier, so passengers are shuttled ashore via tender. Small-ship lines like Windjammer Barefoot Cruises will sometimes throw an afternoon beach party on the beach at **White Bay,** with the crew lugging ashore a picnic lunch for a leisurely afternoon of eating, drinking, and swimming. If your ship stays late, don't miss a trip to **Foxy's,** a well-known watering hole at the far end of the Great Harbour that's popular with the yachting set as well as locals. It's your classic island beach bar, with music pounding and drinks flowing into the wee hours.

SHORE EXCURSIONS

✪ **The Baths Excursion** ($38, 3–4 hours): All cruise lines stopping at the island offer this trip. (See "Beaches," below, for details.)

✪ **Island Tour** ($42, 3–4 hours): The open-air safari buses do a good job of showing guests this beautiful island. You'll get views of the sea, the entire erratically shaped island, and Tortola and St. Thomas, too, as you head across the island from Leverick Bay via North Sound Road, ascending at least partway up 1,370-foot Gorda Peak. Some tours stop at the base of the mountain, where a local guide walks visitors through the national park there to the peak, from where visitors can mount an observation deck and snap photos. After, visitors reboard their bus for a drive to the quaint capital, called Spanish Town. Tours usually include a stop at Copper Mine Point, where visitors can view the ruins of a 19th-century copper mine.

ON YOUR OWN: WITHIN WALKING DISTANCE

Souvenirs and locally produced artwork are available right in Leverick Bay, where most of the island's shopping is located. The Palm Tree Gallery carries jewelry, artwork, books, postcards, and other souvenirs. The water-sports center in Leverick Bay rents two- and four-person dinghies starting at $40 per half day, and visitors can even hire a water taxi here to visit **Bitter End Yacht Club** in the North Sound area, where guests can have a lobster lunch. The taxis pick up guests at Bitter End for the trip back, with a round-trip fare of $25 per person. Snorkel equipment can be rented for $5 per day at the water-sports center. There's also a local branch of the BVI's famous **Pusser's Company Store,** which includes a gift shop, restaurant, and bar serving the famous Pusser's Rum, a locally produced product.

ON YOUR OWN: BEYOND WALKING DISTANCE

The **Virgin Gorda Yacht Harbour** is a taxi ride away from the Leverick Bay pier, and has several restaurants, shops, a bank, and the local office of the B.V.I. Tourist Board. Stores in the Yacht Harbour area include DIVE BVI, which sells diving equipment and offers diving instructions for all ability levels; Margo's Jewelry Boutique, which sells handcrafted gold and silver items; Virgin Gorda Craft Shop, featuring locally made items; and Wine Cellar, which offers oven-baked French bread and pastries, cookies, and sandwiches. Pelican Pouch Boutique, also in the Yacht Harbour area, sells women's swimwear. A gallery and boutique where Virgin Gorda artists display their works can be found at the Olde Yard Inn.

You might also consider cabbing it to the glamorous **Little Dix Bay** resort, established by Laurence Rockefeller in 1965, to enjoy a lunch buffet at an outdoor pavilion that shows off Virgin Gorda's beautiful hills, bays, and sky.

BEACHES

The major reason cruise ships come to Virgin Gorda is to visit ✪ **The Baths,** where geologists believe ice-age eruptions caused house-size boulders to topple onto one another to form the saltwater grottoes we have today. The pools around The Baths are excellent for swimming and snorkeling (equipment can be rented on the beach), and it's a fun exercise to walk between and among the boulders, which in places are very cavelike. There's a cafe just above the beach, for a quick snack or a cool drink before heading back to the ship. **Devil's Bay** is a great beach near The Baths, and is usually less crowded.

Also near The Baths is ✪ **Spring Bay,** one of the best of the island's beaches, with white sand, clear water, and good snorkeling. Nearby is **The Crawl,** a natural pool formed by rocks that's great for novice snorkelers; a marked path leads there from Spring Bay. ✪ **Trunk Bay** is a wide sand beach that can be reached by boat or via a rough path from Spring Bay. **Savannah Bay** is a sandy stretch north of the yacht harbor, and **Mahoe Bay,** at the Mango Bay Resort, has a gently curving beach and vivid blue water.

Devil's Bay National Park can be reached by a trail from The Baths. The walk to the secluded coral-sand beach takes about 15 minutes through a natural setting of boulders and dry coastal vegetation.

North Sound, on the island's northern edge and accessible via taxi, is another recommended beach. Water-sports facilities are available from the dive center at the Leverick Bay landing.

GREAT LOCAL RESTAURANTS & BARS

At the end of the waterfront shopping plaza in Spanish Town, **Bath and Turtle Pub,** Virgin Gorda Yacht Harbour (☎ 284/495-5239), is the island's most popular bar and pub. You can join the regulars over midmorning guava coladas or peach daiquiris and order fried fish fingers, nachos, very spicy chili, pizzas, Reubens or tuna melts, steak, lobster, and daily seafood specials such as conch fritters. **Valley Inn** (☎ 284/495-5639) serves local specialties, including fried fish, johnnycakes, and curried goat. **Mad Dog** (☎ 284/495-5830) is a hot-dog stop near The Baths that also serves BLTs, beer, and frozen piña coladas.

8 Cozumel & Playa del Carmen

A very popular cruise port, the island of Cozumel has white-sand beaches and fabulous scuba diving, but its greatest draw is its proximity to the ancient Mayan ruins at Tulum and Chichén-Itzá. Some ships also stop at nearby Playa del Carmen on the mainland of the Yucatán Peninsula, as it's easier to visit the ruins from there than from Cozumel. Generally, you can do tours to the ruins from either Cozumel or Playa del Carmen.

CURRENCY   The Mexican currency is the *nuevo peso* (new peso). Its symbol is the "$" sign, but it's hardly the equivalent of the U.S. dollar. The exchange rate is $9.56 pesos to U.S.$1 ($1 peso = 10¢). The main tourist stores gladly accept U.S. dollars, credit cards, and traveler's checks, but if you want to change money, there are lots of banks within a block or so from the Muelle Fiscal pier.

LANGUAGE   Spanish is the tongue of the land, although English is spoken in most places that cater to tourists.

CALLING FROM THE U.S.   When calling from the United States, you need to dial "011" before the numbers listed throughout this section.

MAYAN RUINS ON THE MAINLAND

The largest and most fabled of the Yucatán ruins, **Chichén-Itzá** was founded in A.D. 445 by the Mayans, and then inhabited by the conquering Toltecs of central Mexico. Two centuries later, it was mysteriously abandoned. After lying dormant for two more centuries, the site was resettled and enjoyed prosperity again until the early 13th century, when it was once more relinquished to the surrounding jungle. The area covers 7 square miles, so you can see only a fraction of it on a day trip.

The best known of the ruins is the pyramid **Castillo of Kukulkán,** which is actually an astronomical clock designed to mark the vernal and autumnal equinoxes and the summer and winter solstices. A total of 365 steps, one for each day of the year, ascend to the top platform. During each equinox, light striking the pyramid gives the illusion of a giant snake slithering down the steps to join its gigantic stone head mounted at the base.

The government began restoration on the site in the 1920s. Today it houses a museum, a restaurant, and a few shops. Admission is included in shore excursions.

Eighty miles south of Cancún and about a 1 1/2-hour drive from Playa del Carmen, the walled city of **Tulum** is the single most visited Mayan ruin. It was the only Mayan city built on the coast and the only one inhabited when the Spanish conquistadors arrived in the 1500s. From its dramatic perch atop seaside cliffs, you can see wonderful panoramic views of the Caribbean. Tulum consists of 60 individual structures. As with Chichén-Itzá, its most prominent feature is a pyramid topped with a temple to Kukulkán, the primary Mayan/Olmec god. Other important structures include the Temple of the Frescoes, the Temple of the Descending God, the House of Columns, and the House of the Cenote, which is a well. Entrance is included in shore excursions.

A 35-minute drive northwest of Tulum puts you at **Cobá,** site of one of the most important city-states in the Mayan empire. Cobá flourished from A.D. 400 to 1100 B.C., its population numbering perhaps as many as 40,000. Excavation work began in 1972, but archaeologists estimate that only 5% of this dead city has yet been uncovered. The site lies on four lakes. Its 81 primitive acres provide excellent exploration opportunities for the hiker. Cobá's pyramid, Nohoch Mul, is the tallest in the Yucatán. The price of admission is included in shore excursions.

COZUMEL

The ancient Mayans who lived here for 12 centuries would be shocked by the million cruise passengers who now visit Cozumel each year. Their presence has greatly changed San Miguel, the only town, which now has fast-food eateries and a Hard Rock Café. However, development hasn't touched much of the island's natural beauty. Ashore (away from San Miguel) you will see abundant wildlife, including armadillos, brightly colored tropical birds, and lizards. Offshore, the government has set aside 20 miles of coral reefs as an underwater national park, including the stunning Palancar Reef, the world's second-largest natural coral formation.

Frommer's Ratings: Cozumel					
	poor	fair	good	excellent	outstanding
Overall Experience				✓	
Shore Excursions					✓
Activities Close to Port				✓	
Beach & Water Sports		✓			
Shopping				✓	
Dining/Bars			✓		

The Yucatán's Upper Caribbean Coast

0 25 Miles
0 25 Kilometers

N

Isla Holbox
El Cuyo
Holbox
Río Lagartos Nature Reserve
Isla Contoy
Chiquilá

Isla Mujeres
Punta Sam
CANCÚN
Puerto Juárez
Buenaventura
Isla Cancun

QUINTANA ROO STATE
YUCATÁN STATE
180
Croco-Cun
Jardín Botanico
180 D
180 D
Nuevo Xcan
Puerto Morelos
180
307
Ferry Route
To Valladolid & Chichén Itzá
Punta Bete
Chemax
Xcaret
Playa del Carmen
Pamul
San Gervasio
Xpuha
Ferry Route
Cobá
Puerto Aventuras
San Miguel de Cozumel
Akumal
Yalku Lagoon
Isla de Cozumel
Xelha Lagoon National Park
Chankanaab Nature Park
El Cedral
Tancah
Tulum
Chunyaxche
Muyil
Boca Paila
Caribbean Sea
Chumpón
Vigia Chíco
Punta Allen
Bahia de la Ascensión
Peninsula Vigia Grande
Felipe Carrillo Puerto
Sian Ka'an Biosphere Reserve
To Chetumal

Airport ✈
Reef ⏐⏐⏐⏐⏐
Ruins ◆
Cruise Ship Dock ⛴

Frommer's Favorite Cozumel Experiences

- **Visiting the Mayan ruins at Chichén-Itzá or Tulum:** Chichén-Itzá is the largest and most fabled of the Yucatán ruins—and you get to fly in a small plane to get there! Tulum is perched dramatically above the ocean (and in the middle of "iguana central"—they're everywhere), and tours there often include a stop at the beautiful Xel-Ha Lagoon for some swimming (see "Mayan Ruins on the Mainland," above, and "Shore Excursions," below).
- **Renting a motor scooter:** You can easily see most of the island this way, including its wild and natural side (see "On Your Own: Beyond Walking Distance," below).
- **Signing up for a Jeep trek:** Explore Cozumel's jungles and sandy back roads on a fun self-drive caravan-style adventure, and then stop at a beach for lunch and swimming (see "Shore Excursions," below).

COMING ASHORE   Ships arriving at Muelle Fiscal on Cozumel tender passengers directly to the heart of San Miguel. From the downtown pier, the shops, restaurants, and cafes are just a short walk away. Other ships anchor off the well-accoutred International Pier 3 miles from San Miguel (about a $5 taxi ride from town and about a half-hour walk from the heart of San Miguel). The beaches are close to the International Pier.

You can make **telephone calls** in Cozumel from the Global Communications phone center on the International Pier for $2 a minute, or better yet, from a kiosk inside the terminal for $1.50 a minute (keep in mind, there are often lines). In town, try the **Calling Station,** Avenida Rafael Melgar 27 (☎ 987/2-1417), at the corner of Calle 3 in San Miguel, 3 blocks from Muelle Fiscal.

INFORMATION   The **Tourism Office,** Plaza del Sol (☎ 987/2-0972), distributes the *Vacation Guide to Cozumel* and *Cozumel Island's Restaurant Guide;* both have island maps. It's open Monday to Friday from 8am to 2:30pm.

GETTING AROUND

The town of San Miguel is so small you can walk anywhere you want to go. Essentially, there's only one road in Cozumel—it starts at the northern tip of the island, hugs the western shoreline, and then loops around the southern tip and returns to the capital.

If you're driving in Cozumel, it's helpful to know that the roads parallel to the sea are called avenues, and these have the right of way. The ones running from the sea are called streets, and you have to stop at each street to give way.

BY TAXI   Taxi service is available 24 hours a day. Call ☎ 987/2-0236. Cabs are relatively inexpensive, but since it's customary here to overcharge cruise ship passengers, settle on a fare before getting in—remember, the better you bargain, the cheaper the taxi ride. The average fare from San Miguel to most major resorts and beaches is about $8; between the International terminal and downtown it's about $4. More-distant island rides cost $12 and up.

BY RENTAL CAR   If you want to drive yourself, four-wheel-drive vehicles or open-air Jeeps are the best rental choice. **Budget Rent-a-Car,** Avenida 5A at Calle 2 N. (☎ 800/527-0700 in the U.S., or 987/2-0903), 2 blocks from the pier at Muelle Fiscal, rents both. A four-door economy car rents for about $35 a day, with a Jeep Cherokee going for $45 and up.

BY MOPED   Mopeds are a popular means of getting about despite heavy traffic, hidden stop signs, potholed roads, and a high accident rate. The best and most convenient rentals are at **Auto Rent** (☎ 987/2-0844) in the Hotel Ceiba, a block from the pier at Muelle Fiscal. The cost is about $28 per day. Mexican law requires helmets.

BY FERRY   A number of passenger ferries link Cozumel with Playa del Carmen. The most comfortable are the two big speedboats and water-jet catamaran run by **Aviomar** (☎ **987/2-0477**). They operate Monday to Saturday from 8am to 8pm, Sunday from 9am to 1pm. The trip takes 45 minutes. All the ferries have ticket booths at the main pier. One-way fares range from $4 to $5 per person. You'll get a ferry schedule when you buy your ticket.

SHORE EXCURSIONS

It's easier to see the ruins at Chichén-Itzá, Tulum, and Cobá from Playa del Carmen, since it's on the mainland and therefore closer to the ruins sites. Many ships en route to Cozumel pause in Playa del Carmen to drop off passengers who have signed up for ruins tours. After the tours, passengers either take a ferry back to the ship in Cozumel or, if the tour is by plane, get dropped off at the airport in Cozumel, near downtown. See "Mayan Ruins on the Mainland," above, for details about the ruins. If your ship is not dropping passengers off at Playa del Carmen (many don't), keep in mind shuttling back and forth via ferry or tender will add another hour or two to your schedule. If you're more interested in a lazy, relaxing day (and your ship doesn't go to Playa del Carmen) you may want to just hang out in Cozumel.

✪ **Chichén-Itzá Excursion** ($220–$240, 6–7 hours): Founded in A.D. 445, Chichén-Itzá is the largest and most fabled of the Yucatán ruins—and you can even climb up its tallest pyramid for wonderful views of the ancient city, much of which is still covered in foliage and earth. You'll take a 45-minute flight each way on 10- to 20-seater aircraft. The flight there is almost as interesting as the ruins. This tour may leave from Playa del Carmen. (*Note:* It can get hot. Bring water.)

✪ **The Mayan Ruins of Tulum** ($63–$74 adults, $33–$59 kids, 6–7 hours): Very worthwhile. The ruins of this walled city are all the more spectacular because they're located on a cliff, dramatically perched above the ocean. This tour often includes an hour or two stop at the Xel-Ha Lagoon, a beautiful and natural setting for swimming (in this case, the tour is 7 to 8 hours long and costs another $20 or so). The tour leaves from Playa del Carmen.

✪ **Jeep Trek** ($68–$74, 4–6 hours): Hop in a jeep seating four and explore the natural side of Cozumel, its jungle mangroves and sandy back roads. Much of the roller-coaster-like route is off-road, and the Jeeps travel in a convoy, with one of you driving. Included is a visit to the La Palma ruin where goddess Ixchel is said to still grant wishes (you make them with your eyes closed, facing the sea), and a stop at a lovely secluded beach for swimming and a picnic lunch of tasty Mexican fare.

Horseback-Riding Tours ($71, 3–4 hours): Worthwhile horseback-riding tours offer a chance to see Cozumel's landscape and the fun of riding a horse, and though they tout visits to Mayan ruins, don't get your hopes up—there are really no authentic ruins to speak of on Cozumel; most are reproductions. The tour includes a guide who discusses Mayan culture and customs while exploring the inside of a cave where the Mayans gathered for ceremonial meetings. A bus transports riders to a ranch, where the ride begins.

ON YOUR OWN: WITHIN WALKING DISTANCE

For walkers, the classic grid layout makes getting around the town of San Miguel easy. Directly across from the docks, the main square—**Plaza del Sol** (also called *la plaza* or *el parque*)—is excellent for people-watching. Avenida Rafael Melgar, the principal street along the waterfront, runs along the western shore of the island, site of the best resorts and beaches. Most of the shops and restaurants are on Rafael Melgar, although many well-stocked duty-free shops line the Malecón, the seaside promenade.

Only 3 blocks from Muelle Fiscal on Agenda Rafael Melgar between Calles 4 and 6 N., the **Museo de la Isla de Cozumel** (☎ 987/2-1434) has two floors of exhibits displayed in what was Cozumel's first luxury hotel. Exhibits start in the pre-Hispanic times and continue through the colonial era to the present. Included are many swords and nautical artifacts; one display showcases endangered species. The highlight is a reproduction of a Mayan house. It's open daily from 10am to 6pm; admission is $1.75.

ON YOUR OWN: BEYOND WALKING DISTANCE

You can ✪ **rent a motor scooter** and zip around most of the island, including its wild and natural side. Stop for lunch at a beachside, open-air seafood restaurant for some grilled fish and a cool drink. Scooters can be rented from several outfits, including **Auto Rent** (☎ 987/2-0844) in the Hotel Ceiba, a block from the pier at Muelle Fiscal.

Outside of San Miguel is the **Chankanaab Nature Park,** where a saltwater lagoon, offshore reefs, and underwater caves have been turned into an archaeological park, botanical garden, and wildlife sanctuary. More than 10 countries have contributed seedlings and cuttings. Some 60 species of marine life occupy the lagoon, including sea turtles. Reproductions of Mayan dwellings are scattered throughout the park. There's also a wide white-sand beach with thatch umbrellas and a changing area with lockers and showers. Both scuba divers and snorkelers like examining the sunken ship offshore (there are four dive shops here). The park also has a restaurant and snack stand.

The park is located at Carretera Sur, Kilometer 9 (no phone). It's open daily from 9am to 5pm. Admission is $7; free for children 9 and under. The 10-minute taxi ride from the pier at Muelle Fiscal costs about $5.

Mayan ruins on Cozumel are very minor compared to those on the mainland. **El Cedral** lies 2 miles inland at the turnoff at Kilometer 17.5, east of Playa San Francisco. It's the island's oldest structure, with traces of original Mayan wall paintings. The Spanish tore much of it down, and the U.S. Army nearly finished the job when it built an airfield here in World War II. Little remains now except a Mayan arch and a few small ruins covered in heavy growth. Guides at the site will show you around for a fee.

Another meager ruin is at **San Gervasio,** reached by driving west across the island to the army air base, and then turning right and continuing north 4 miles to San Gervasio. This was once a ceremonial center and capital of Cozumel. The Mayans dedicated the area to Ixchel, the fertility goddess. The ruins cost $3.50 to visit, plus $1 for entrance to the access road. Guides will show people what's left, including several broken columns and lintels, for $12. It's open daily from 8am to 5pm.

SHOPPING

You can walk from the pier at Muelle Fiscal to the best shops in San Miguel. Because of the influx of cruise ship passengers, prices are relatively high here, but you can and should bargain. Silver jewelry is big business here, and it's generally sold by weight. You can find some nice pieces, but again, don't expect to pay peanuts for it. There are wall-to-wall shops along the waterfront in San Miguel, including **Viva Mexico,** for all manner of souvenirs. Also, shops line the perimeter of Plaza del Sol, adjacent to the downtown cruise pier, and there are several shopping arcades accessible from the plaza, including the pleasant, tree-lined **Plaza Confetti. Agencia Publicaciones Gracia,** Avenida 5A, a block from Muelle Fiscal, is Cozumel's best source for English-language books, guidebooks, newspapers, and magazines. **Casablanca,** Avenida Rafael Melgar 33 (located in front of the International Pier), has a fine selection of Mexican jewelry and loose stones, plus a well-chosen collection of Mexican crafts. **Gordon Gilchrist,** Studio 1, Avenida 25 S. 981 at Calle 15 S., produces Cozumel's finest etchings of local Mayan sites. **Rachat & Romero,** Avenida Rafael Melgar 101 has a wide variety of loose stones, which they can mount while you wait. **Ultra Femme,** Avenida Rafael Melgar 341, is one of the most important jewelers in Cozumel, and the exclusive distributor of Rolex watches on the Mexican Riviera. **Unicornio,** 5 Avenida Sur 2 (2 blocks from Muelle Fiscal), has Mexican handcrafts.

If you're docking at the International Pier, there are a bunch of nice shops in the terminal, selling everything from Mexican blankets to jewelry, T-shirts, and handcrafts of all kinds. Again, prices aren't cheap—a roll of film went for $9 at the terminal last time I was there.

BEACHES

Cozumel's best powdery white-sand beach, **Playa San Francisco,** stretches for some 3 miles along the southwestern shoreline. It was once one of the most idyllic beaches in Mexico, but resort development is threatening to destroy its old character. You can rent equipment for water sports here, or have lunch at one of the many *palapa* restaurants and bars on the shoreline. There's no admission to the beach, and it's about a $10 taxi ride south of San Miguel's downtown pier. If you land at the International Pier, you're practically at the beach already.

Many of your fellow cruisers have heard of the fine **Playa del Sol,** about a mile south of Playa del San Francisco, so it's likely to be overcrowded.

Playa Bonita (sometimes called "Punta Chiqueros") is one of the least crowded beaches, but it lies on the east (windward) side of the island and is difficult to reach unless you rent a vehicle or throw yourself on the mercy of a taxi driver. It sits in a moon-shaped cove sheltered from the Caribbean Sea by an offshore reef. Waves are only moderate, the sand's powdery, and the water's clear.

You may want to consider **Parque Chankanaab,** a parklike beach area lined with thatched umbrellas and contoured plastic chaise lounges. While the water is rough here and not ideal for swimming, the beach and scenery are very nice and the place is popular with locals. Admission is $7, and you can swim with dolphins (for a fee, of course) or rent snorkeling equipment. There's also a restaurant and bar. This beach is about a 15-minute, $8 taxi ride from the downtown pier.

If you don't want to go far, there are two hotel beaches a stone's throw north of the International Pier (facing the water, they're on the right) that welcome day visitors. **Le Ceiba** charges $5 per person for the day and includes one tropical drink, and the **Crown Paradise sol Caribe** wants $22 per person for the day (9am to 5pm), including a drink and lunch.

SPORTS

SCUBA DIVING   Jacques Cousteau did much to extol the glory of Cozumel for scuba divers. Here he discovered black coral in profusion, plus hundreds of species of rainbow-hued tropical fish. Underwater visibility can reach 250 feet. All this gives Cozumel some of the best diving in the Caribbean. Cruisers might want to confine their adventures to the finest spot, **Palancar Reef.** Lying about a mile offshore, this fabulous water world features gigantic elephant-ear sponges and black and red coral, as well as deep caves, canyons, and tunnels. It's a favorite of divers from all over the world. The best scuba outfitter is **Aqua Safari,** Avenida Rafael Melgar at Calle 5, next to the Vista del Mar Hotel (☎ **987/2-0101**). A worthwhile competitor is **Diving Adventures,** Calle 51 Sur no. 2, near the corner of Avenida Rafael Melgar (☎ **987/2-3009**).

SNORKELING   Shallow reefs at Playa San Francisco or Chankanaab Bay are among the best spots. You'll see a world of sea creatures parading by, everything from parrot fish to conch. The best outfitter is **Cozumel Snorkeling Center,** Calle Primera Sur (☎ **987/2-0539**), which offers a 3-hour snorkeling tour, including all equipment and refreshments. They can also arrange parasailing here. You can also just rent snorkeling equipment at Chankanaab.

GREAT LOCAL RESTAURANTS & BARS

The **local beer** is Sol. On a hot day, a quart bottle of the stuff is manna from heaven.

Right in front of the in-town cruise dock, ✪ **Café del Puerto,** Avenida Rafael Melgar 3, is a local favorite. The kitchen bridges the gap between Mexico and Europe with dishes like a superbly prepared mustard steak flambé, succulent lobster, and Yucatán chicken wrapped in banana leaves. Also on the main drag in town is **Lobster's Cove** and **Palmeras,** just across from the downtown pier, both offering tasty seafood and Mexican dishes. Just north of the ferry pier, **Carlos 'n Charlie's,** Avenida Rafael Melgar 11, is Mexico's equivalent of the Hard Rock Café, but much wilder (especially on Friday nights!). Sawdust litters the floor (to sop up the beer), music blares, and tourists pound back yard-long glasses of beers like they're going out of style. Many a cruise passenger has stumbled back from Carlos 'n Charlie's, clutching their yard-long glasses as though they were the Holy Grail—proof that they've been to Mexico. People come here for good times and the spicy, tasty ribs. You can dine surprisingly well on Yucatán specialties, and the best chicken and beef fajitas in Cozumel. Another party spot is the **Hard Rock Cozumel** itself, at Avenida Rafael Melgar 2A, which serves the hard stuff as well as burgers and grilled beef or chicken fajitas. Yet another is the **Fat Tuesday,** at the end of the International Pier, where you'll find lots of crew members on their day or night off (you can even hear their revelry from the ship). Join the fun and guzzle a 16-ounce margarita for $5 a pop or a 24-ounce version for $7. A half block from the pier, **Las Palmeras,** Avenida Rafael Melgar, is ideal for casual eating. If you arrive in time, it serves one of the best breakfasts in town; for lunch, they offer tempting seafood dishes or Mexican specialties.

El Capi Navegante, Avenida 10A Sur 312 at Calles 3 and 4 (5 blocks from Muelle Fiscal), offers the freshest fish in San Miguel with a great lobster soufflé. **La Choza,** Calle Rosada Salas 198 at Avenida 10A Sur (2 blocks from the Muelle Fiscal pier), offers real local cooking that's a favorite of the town's savvy foodies.

PLAYA DEL CARMEN

Some cruise ships spend a day at Cozumel and then another at Playa del Carmen, but most drop off passengers here for tours to Tulum and Chichén-Itzá, and then head on to spend the day tied up at Cozumel.

The famed white-sand beach here was relatively untouched by tourists not many years ago, but today the pleasure-seeking hordes have replaced the Indian families who used to gather coconuts for copra (dried coconut meat). If you can tolerate the crowds, snorkeling is excellent over the offshore reefs. Turtle watching is another local pastime.

Frommer's Ratings: Playa del Carmen

	poor	fair	good	excellent	outstanding
Overall Experience				✓	
Shore Excursions					✓
Activities Close to Port			✓		
Beach & Water Sports			✓		
Shopping		✓			
Dining/Bars			✓		

Avenida Juárez in Playa del Carmen is the principal business zone for the Tulum-Cancún corridor. Part of Avenida 5 running parallel to the beach has been closed to traffic, forming a good promenade. Most visitors at some point head for **Rincón del Sol,** a tree-filled courtyard built in the colonial Mexican style. It has the best collection of handcraft shops in the area, some of which offer goods of excellent quality, not the junky souvenirs peddled elsewhere.

Frommer's Favorite Playa del Carmen Experiences

- **Having beer and nachos on the beach:** Hang out on the beach for great views of the anchored ships a mile or so out at sea and the tourists coming in off the tenders. A couple of casual beachside restaurants provide all the beer, quesadillas, and nachos you'll need.
- **Taking a tour of Tulum or Chichén-Itzá:** Both of the tours described in the Cozumel section (see above) are also offered here.

COMING ASHORE   Some cruise ships dock at anchor or at the pier of Cozumel, and then send passengers over to Playa del Carmen by tender. Others dock at the new Puerto Calica Cruise Pier, which is 8 miles south of Playa del Carmen. Taxis meet each arriving ship, and drivers transport visitors into the center of Playa del Carmen.

GETTING AROUND

BY TAXI   Taxis are readily available to take you anywhere, but you can walk to the center of town, to the beach, and to most major shops.

BY RENTAL CAR   If you decide to rent a car for the day, try **National,** Hotel Molcas, 1A Avenida Sur 5A (☎ **987/3-0360**), or **Dollar,** Hotel Diamond at Playacar (☎ **987/3-0340**). Cars at either agency usually come with unlimited mileage and most forms of insurance included, and rent for between $50 and $80 a day.

SHORE EXCURSIONS

Most visitors head for the Mayan ruins the moment they reach shore (see "Shore Excursions" in the Cozumel section, above).

Xcaret Ecological Park ($39 adults, $24 kids): Lying 4 miles south of Playa del Carmen on the coast, Xcaret (pronounced "Ish-car-*et*") is a 250-acre ecological theme park where many visitors spend their entire day. It's a great place. Mayan ruins are scattered about the lushly landscaped acres. Visitors can put on life jackets for an underwater river ride, which takes them through currents running throughout a series of caves. You can also snorkel through these flooded caves (this I highly recommend!). There's also a botanical garden and a dive shop. Xcaret is open Monday to Saturday from 8:30am to 8:30pm, Sunday from 8am to 5pm. Buses from Playa del Carmen come here frequently; a taxi costs about $5 one-way. If you sign up for an organized excursion, a shuttle will transport you between ship and park.

ON YOUR OWN: WITHIN WALKING DISTANCE

You can walk to the center of town, to the beach, and to the small shopping district.

ON YOUR OWN: BEYOND WALKING DISTANCE

Other than the beach, there's no major attraction in Playa del Carmen except **Xcaret** (see above). Xcaret is open Monday to Saturday from 8:30am to 8:30pm, Sunday from 8am to 5pm. The easiest way to get there is to sign up for your ship's organized excursion, which includes transportation. Even if you come independently of a tour, general admission is a steep $39 for adults, $24 for children 5 to 11 (free for kids 4 and under). For information, call ☎ **988/3-0654.** Buses from Playa del Carmen come here frequently; a taxi costs about $5 one-way.

GREAT LOCAL RESTAURANTS & BARS

El Chino, Calle 4, Avenida 15 (☎ **987/3-0015**), is a pristine restaurant known locally for its regional Yucatán specialties as well as standard dishes from throughout Mexico. ✪ **Máscaras,** Avenida Juárez (☎ **987/3-1053**), serves great pastas, brick-oven pizzas, and other Italian dishes. The four-cheese pizza is justifiably the most popular. **El Tacolote,** Avenida Juárez (☎ **987/3-1363**), specializes in fresh seafood and the best grilled meats in town, brought to your table fresh from the broiler on a charcoal pan to keep the food warm.

9 Curaçao

As you sail into the harbor of Willemstad, be sure to look for the quaint "floating bridge," the **Queen Emma pontoon bridge,** which swings aside to open the narrow channel (a man actually drives the bridge in and out of place). Bordering the harbor are those much-photographed, picture-postcard pastel rows of gabled Dutch houses. Welcome to Curaçao, the largest and most populous of the Netherlands Antilles, just 35 miles north of the Venezuelan coast.

Curaçao was first discovered by the Spanish around 1499, but in 1634 the Dutch came and prospered. In 1915, when the Royal Dutch/Shell Company built one of the world's largest oil refineries to process crude from Venezuela, workers from 50 countries poured in to the island. Today, Curaçao remains a melting pot, although it still retains a Dutch flavor. A tropical Holland in miniature, this island has the most interesting architecture in the West Indies. Its Dutch-colonial structures give Willemstad a storybook look, but the rest of the desertlike island seems like the American Southwest, with three-pronged cacti, spiny-leafed aloes, and divi-divi trees bent by trade winds.

Since much of this island's surface is an arid desert, its canny Dutch settlers ruled out farming and developed Curaçao into one of the Dutch Empire's busiest trading posts. Until the post–World War II collapse of the oil refineries, Curaçao was a thriving mercantile society with a capital (Willemstad) that somewhat resembled Amsterdam and a population with a curious mixture of bloodlines (including African, Dutch, Venezuelan, and Pakistani). Tourism began to develop during the 1980s, and many new hotels have been built since.

Frommer's Favorite Curaçao Experiences

- **Visiting Christoffel National Park:** Hike up the 1,230-foot-high St. Christoffelberg, passing cacti, iguanas, wild goats, many species of birds, and ancient Arawak paintings along the way. There's also 20 miles of roads, so you can see the park by car (see "On Your Own: Beyond Walking Distance," below).
- **Gazing into the mirrored waters of Hato Cave:** Stalagmites and stalactites are mirrored in a mystical underground lake in these caves, whose limestone formations were

Frommer's Ratings: Curaçao					
	poor	fair	good	excellent	outstanding
Overall Experience				✓	
Shore Excursions			✓		
Activities Close to Port				✓	
Beach & Water Sports		✓			
Shopping			✓		
Dining/Bars			✓		

Westpunt
Noordpunt
Playa Abao
Westpunt
Boca Tabla
Knip Bay
Christoffel National Park
Playa Lagun
St. Christoffelberg
Santa Cruz
Caribbean Sea
Santa Marta Bay
Soto
Barber
San Juan Bay
St. Willibrordus
Daaibooi
Curaçao International Airport
Boca St. Marie
Boca Hato
Hato Caves
St. Michiel
Julianadorp
Brienvengat
Blauwbaai
Piscadera Bay
Emmastad
Santa Catarina
St. Anna Bay
Santa Rosa
Caribbean Sea
St. Joris Bay
Willemstad
Seaquarium
Montagne
Jan Thiel Bay
Spanish Water
Santa Barbara Beach
Curaçao Underwater Marine Park
Ostpunt

0   5 Miles
0   5 Kilometers
N

Airport ✈ Beach 🏖 Mountain ▲ Cruise Ship Dock 🚢

created by water seeping through the coral (see "On Your Own: Beyond Walking Distance," below).

- **Take the Hato Caves/Curaçao Liqueur Tour:** This is a neat combination. A short bus ride gets you to the caves, and then to a plantation house and the liqueur factory for a tour (see "Shore Excursions," below).

COMING ASHORE   Cruise ships dock at the new $9-million megapier, just beyond the Queen Emma pontoon bridge, which leads to the duty-free shopping sector and the famous floating market. It's a 5- to 10-minute walk from here to the center of Willemstad, or you can take a taxi from the stand. Rumor has it that a private developer plans to build a shopping/entertainment complex in the adjacent historic fort. The town itself is easy to navigate on foot. Most of it can be explored in 2 or 3 hours, leaving plenty of time for beaches or water sports. Although the ship terminal has a duty-free shop, save your serious shopping for Willemstad.

There's a **phone center** at the cruise terminal, which is just beyond the Queen Emma pontoon bridge.

CURRENCY   The official currency is the **Netherlands Antillean florin (NAf),** also called a guilder, which is divided into 100 cents. The exchange rate is 1.78 NAf to U.S.$1 (1 NAf = .56¢). Canadian and U.S. dollars are accepted for purchases, so there's no need to change money. Unless otherwise noted, prices in this section are given in U.S. dollars.

LANGUAGE   Dutch, Spanish, and English are spoken on Curaçao, along with Papiamento, a patois that combines the three major tongues with Amerindian and African dialects.

INFORMATION   For visitor information, go to the **Curaçao Tourist Board,** Pietermaai (☎ 599/9-4616000). It's open Monday to Friday from 9am to 5pm. For information before you go, call the **Tourism Department** in New York at ☎ 800/445-8266 or 212/683-7660 or log on to the Web site at www.Curacao-tourism.com.

CALLING FROM THE U.S.   When calling Curaçao from the United States, you need to dial "011" before the numbers listed throughout this section.

GETTING AROUND

BY TAXI   Taxis don't have meters, so settle on a fare before getting in. Drivers are supposed to carry an official tariff sheet. Generally, there's no need to tip. The best place to get a taxi is on the Otrabands side of the floating bridge or call ☎ **599/9-8690747.** A fleet of DAF yellow buses operates from Wilhelmina Plein, near the shopping center, and runs to most parts of Curaçao. You can hail a bus at any designated bus stop. Up to four passengers can share the price of an island tour by taxi, which costs about $30 per hour.

BY RENTAL CAR   Driving is on the right on paved roads. If you want to rent a car, try **Avis** (☎ **800/331-2112** or 599/9-681163), **Budget** (☎ **800/527-0700** or 599/9-683420), or **Hertz** (☎ **800/654-3001** or 599/9-868118).

SHORE EXCURSIONS

Many excursions aren't really worth the price here—you can easily see the town on your own and hop a taxi to the few attractions on the island outside of Willemstad (see "Touring Through Local Operators," below).

✪ **Hato Caves/Curaçao Liqueur Tour** ($30, 3 hours): After a short bus ride to the caves and a walking tour through the grottoes, stalactites, and petroglyphs, the tour takes passengers to an old plantation house for a look around, and then to Curaçao Liqueur Factory for a tour and a sample of the popular liqueur, which is made from Laraha orange peels.

Countryside Bus Tour ($31, 2–3 hours): This excursion takes you via bus to sights like the Westpunt, Mount Christoffel, the towering cacti, and the rolling hills topped by *landhuizen* (plantation houses) built more than 3 centuries ago. You'll also stop at a beach, the Curaçao Seaquarium, and Chobolobo, an old colonial mansion where the original Curaçao liqueur is still distilled.

ON YOUR OWN: WITHIN WALKING DISTANCE

Willemstad is the major attraction here, and you can see it on foot. After 10 years of restoration, the town's historic center and the island's natural harbor, Schottegat, have been inscribed on UNESCO's World Heritage List. Be sure and watch the Queen Emma pontoon bridge move (it is motorized and a "driver" actually drives it to the side of the harbor every so often so ships and boats can pass through the channel). It's really neat.

A **statue of Pedro Luis Brion** dominates the square known as Brionplein, at the Otrabanda end of the Queen Emma pontoon bridge. Born in Curaçao in 1782, Brion became the island's favorite son and best-known war hero. He was an admiral of the fleet under Simón Bolívar and fought for the independence of Venezuela and Colombia.

Fort Amsterdam, site of the Governor's Palace and the 1769 Dutch Reformed church, has the task of guarding the waterfront. The church still has a British cannonball embedded in it. The arches leading to the fort were tunneled under the official residence of the governor. A corner of the fort stands at the intersection of Breedestraat and Handelskade, the starting point for a plunge into the island's major shopping district.

A few minutes' walk from the pontoon bridge, at the north end of Handelskade, is the **Floating Market,** where scores of schooners tie up alongside the canal. Boats arrive here from Venezuela and Colombia, and from other West Indian islands, to sell tropical fruits and vegetables, as well as handcrafts. The modern market under its vast concrete cap has not diminished the fun of watching the activity here. Either arrive early or stay late to view these marine merchants setting up or storing their wares.

Between the I. H. (Sha) Capriles Kade and Fort Amsterdam, at the corner of Columbusstraat and Hanchi Snog, is the **Mikve Israel-Emanuel Synagogue.** Dating from 1651, the Jewish congregation here is the oldest in the New World.

Next door, the **Jewish Cultural Historical Museum,** Kuiperstraat 26–28 (☎ 599/ 9-4611633), is housed in two buildings dating from 1728. They were the rabbi's residence and the *mikvah* (bath) for religious purification purposes.

You can walk from the Queen Emma pontoon bridge to the **Curaçao Museum,** Van Leeuwenhoekstraat (☎ 599/9-4626051). The building, constructed in 1853 by the Royal Dutch Army as a military hospital, has been carefully restored and furnished with paintings, objets d'art, and antique furniture, and houses a large collection from the Caiquetio tribes. On the museum grounds is an art gallery for temporary exhibitions of both local and international art.

ON YOUR OWN: BEYOND WALKING DISTANCE

Cacti, bromeliads, rare orchids, iguanas, donkeys, wild goats, and many species of birds thrive in the 4,500-acre ✪ **Christoffel National Park,** located about a 45-minute taxi or car ride from the capital near the northwestern tip of Curaçao. The park rises from flat, arid countryside to 1,230-foot-high St. Christoffelberg, the tallest point in the Dutch Leewards. Along the way are ancient Arawak paintings and the Piedra di Monton, a rock heap piled by African slaves who cleared this former plantation. Legend says slaves could climb to the top of the rock pile, jump off, and fly back home across the Atlantic. If they had ever tasted a grain of salt, however, they would crash to their deaths. The park has 20 miles of one-way trail-like roads. The shortest is about 5 miles long, but takes about 40 minutes to drive because of its rough terrain. One of several hiking trails goes to the top of St. Christoffelberg. It takes about 1 1/2 hours to walk to the summit (come early in the morning before it gets hot). There's also a museum in an old storehouse left over from plantation days. Guided tours of the park are available. The park is open Monday to Saturday from 8am to 4pm and on Sunday from 6am to 3pm. Admission is $10 per person.

The **Curaçao Seaquarium,** off Dr. Martin Luther King Boulevard (☎ 599/ 9-4616666), displays more than 400 species of fish, crabs, anemones, and other invertebrates, sponges, and coral. A rustic boardwalk connects the hexagonal buildings, which sit on a point near the site where the *Oranje Nassau* broke up on the rocks and sank in 1906. The Seaquarium also has Curaçao's only full-facility, white-sand, palm-shaded beach. In the "shark and animal encounter," divers, snorkelers, and experienced swimmers are able to feed, film, and photograph sharks, stingrays, lobsters, tarpons, parrot fish, and other marine life in a controlled environment. Nonswimmers can see the underwater life from a 46-foot semisubmersible observatory.

Stalagmites and stalactites are mirrored in a mystical underground lake in ✪ **Hato Caves,** F. D. Rosseveltweg (☎ 599/9-8680379). Long ago, geological forces uplifted this limestone terrace, which was originally a coral reef. The limestone formations were created over thousands of years by water seeping through the coral. After crossing the lake, you enter two caverns known as "The Cathedral" and La Ventana or "The Window." Displayed here are samples of ancient Indian petroglyphs. Professional local guides take visitors through the caves every hour. The caves are open daily from 10am to 4pm. Admission is $7.25 for adults, $5.75 for children 4 to 11 (free for kids 3 and under).

SHOPPING

Curaçao is a shopper's paradise, with some 200 stores lining such streets as Heerenstraat and Breedestraat in the 5-block district called the **Punda.** Many shops occupy the town's old Dutch houses.

The island is famous for its 5-pound "wheelers" of **Gouda or Edam cheese.** Look for good buys in wooden shoes, French perfumes, Dutch blue Delft souvenirs, finely woven Italian silks, Japanese and German cameras, jewelry, silver, Swiss watches, linens, leather goods, liquor, and island-made rum and liqueurs, especially Curaçao liqueur, some of which has a distinctive blue color. Some stores also offer good buys on intricate lacework imported from everywhere between Portugal and China. If you're a street shopper and want something colorful, consider a carving or flamboyant painting from Haiti or the Dominican Republic. Both are hawked by street vendors at any of the main plazas.

Suggested shops include **Bamali,** Breedestraat 2, for Indonesian-influenced clothing (mostly for women); **Gandelman Jewelers,** Breedestraat 35, Punda, for a large selection of fine jewelry as well as Curaçaoan gold pieces; and **Curaçao Creations,** Schrijnwerkerstraat 14, for Curaçao handcrafts.

BEACHES

Curaçao's beaches are not as good as Aruba's 7-mile strip of sand, but it does have some 38 of them, ranging from hotel sand patches to secluded coves. The seawater remains an almost-constant 76°F year-round, with good underwater visibility. **Taxi** drivers waiting at the cruise dock will take you to any of the beaches, but you'll have to negotiate a fare. To be on the safe side, arrange to have your driver pick you up at a certain time and take you back to the cruise dock.

The **Curaçao Seaquarium** has the island's only full-facility, white-sand, palm-shaded beach, but you'll have to pay the full aquarium admission to get in (see "On Your Own: Beyond Walking Distance," above). The rest of the beaches on this island are public.

A good beach on the eastern side of the island is **Santa Barbara Beach,** on land owned by a mining company between the open sea and the island's primary water-sports and recreational area, known as Spanish Water. You'll also find Table Mountain, a remarkable landmark, and an old phosphate mine. The natural beach has pure-white sand and calm water. A buoy line protects swimmers from boats, and there are rest rooms, changing rooms, a snack bar, and a terrace. You can rent water bicycles and small motorboats. It's open daily from 8am to 6pm. The beach has access to the Curaçao Underwater Park.

Daaibooi is a good beach about 30 minutes from town, in the Willibrordus area on the west side of Curaçao. It's free, but there are no changing facilities.

Blauwbaai (Blue Bay) is the largest and most frequented beach on Curaçao, with enough white sand for everybody. Along with showers and changing facilities, there are plenty of shady places to retreat from the noonday sun. To reach it, take the road that goes past the Holiday Beach Hotel & Casino, heading in the direction of Juliandorp. Follow the sign that tells you to bear left for Blauwbaai and the fishing village of San Michiel.

Westpunt is known for its gigantic cliffs and the Sunday divers who jump from them into the ocean below. This public beach is on the northwestern tip of the island. **Knip Bay,** just south of Westpunt, has beautiful turquoise waters. On weekends, live music and dancing make the beach a lively place. Changing facilities and refreshments are available. **Playa Abao,** with crystal turquoise water, is situated at the northern tip of the island.

Warning: Beware of stepping on the hard spines of sea urchins, which are sometimes found in these waters. While not fatal, their spines can cause several days of real discomfort. For temporary first aid, try the local remedies of vinegar or lime juice.

GREAT LOCAL RESTAURANTS & BARS

Curaçao's **local beer** is the very Dutch Amstel. The **local drink** is Curaçao liqueur, some of which has a distinctive blue color.

De Taveerne, Landhuis Groot Vavelaar, Silena (☎ 599/9-7370669), is actually two restaurants: a French restaurant at street level and a less formal brasserie serving inexpensive international food on its second floor. If you're hot, dusty, and in a hurry, your best bet might be to order a platter of food in the brasserie. **Golden Star,** Socratesstraat 2, at the corner of Dr. Hugenholtzweg and Dr. Maalweg, southeast of Willemstad (☎ 599/9-4654795), is the best place to go on the island for *criollo,* or local food. It's inland from the coast road leading southeast from St. Anna Bay, 8 minutes by taxi from the cruise dock. **La Pergola,** in the Waterfront Arches, Waterfort Straat (☎ 599/9-4613482), is an Italian restaurant where the menu items change virtually every day. **Rijstaffel Restaurant Indonesia and Holland Club Bar,** Mercuriusstraat 13, Salinja (☎ 599/9-4612999), is the best place on the island to sample the Indonesian *rijstaffel,* the traditional "rice table" with all the zesty side dishes. You must ask a taxi to take you to this villa in the suburbs near Salinja, near the Princess Beach Resort & Casino southeast of Willemstad.

10 Dominica

First things first. It's pronounced "Dome-ee-*nee*-ka," not "Doe-*min*-i-ka." And it has nothing to do with the Dominican Republic. The Commonwealth of Dominica is an independent country, and English, not Spanish, is the official language. The only Spanish commonly understood in Dominica is *mal encaminado a Santo Domingo* ("accidentally sent to the Dominican Republic"), the phrase stamped on the many letters that make it to their proper destination only after an erroneous but common detour.

To be sure, Dominica has some rough edges. The island is poor, so don't expect luxury or up-to-the-minute technology around every corner, and not everything manmade is as beautiful as nature's handiwork. Balancing this, though, is the fact that Dominica is the most lush and mountainous island in the Caribbean. Twenty-nine miles long and 16 miles wide, and lying between the French islands of Guadeloupe and Martinique, smack-dab in the center of the arc formed by the Antilles, it's blessed with astonishing natural wonders—crystal-pure rivers (one for every day of the year, they say), dramatic waterfalls, volcanic lakes (one gurgles and boils from the heat and tumult in the earth below), and foliage as gargantuan as any H. G. Wells ever imagined on Venus. Volcanic coral reefs, every bit as biologically complex as the rain forests on shore, ring the island, and a bit farther from land, whales mate and calve.

The island's people—primarily descendants of the West Africans brought over to work the plantations, plus some descendants of Europeans and Indians—are another great natural resource. Friendly and proud of their national independence, Dominica's 71,000 citizens remain for the most part unchanged by tourism, a still-developing industry here. One portion of the island's population has immeasurable ethnological significance: Concentrated in a territory in the northeast, Dominica's approximately 3,000 Carib Indians are the last remaining members of the people who dominated the region when Europeans arrived.

Frommer's Favorite Dominica Experiences

- **Hiking to the Emerald Pool:** A 15-minute walk through gorgeous forest brings you to this primeval pool, where you can swim or just take in the beauty of the picture-perfect waterfall, the moss-covered boulders, and the sunlight streaming through branches high overhead. (See "Shore Excursions," below.)
- **Paddling up the Indian River:** Minutes from Portsmouth, the gentle Indian River drains into the Caribbean from its source in the foothills of the island's tallest mountain, 4,747-foot high Morne Diablotin. As a boatman paddles you up the twisting river, you'll pass through swampland that features giant palms and mango trees with serpentine roots. (See "Shore Excursions," below.)
- **Experiencing Carib culture:** Along a rugged portion of Dominica's northeastern coast, the 3,700-acre Carib Territory is home to the world's last surviving Carib Indians. The Caribs today live like most other rural islanders—growing bananas and coconuts, fishing, and operating small shops. But the sturdy baskets of dyed and woven *larouma* reeds and the wooden canoes carved from the trunks of massive *gommier* trees are evidence of the people's links to the past. A traditional big house, called the Karbet, serves as a cultural and entertainment center. If you're lucky, you'll witness a performance of the Karifuna Cultural Group, whose youthful members are dedicated to the regeneration of Carib spirit and culture. (See "Shore Excursions," below.)
- **Exploring Fort Shirley and the rest of Cabrits National Park:** On Dominica's northwestern coast, right by the cruise ship port of Portsmouth, the 260-acre Cabrits National Park combines stunning mountain scenery, tropical deciduous forest and swampland, volcanic-sand beaches, coral reefs, and the romance of an 18th-century fort. (See "On Your Own: Within Walking Distance," below.)

COMING ASHORE   Dominica has two cruise ship ports. The largest and most frequented is in the heart of **Roseau,** the country's capital and largest town. The other is near the northwestern town of **Portsmouth.** Banks, restaurants, a market, a tourism office, and the excellent Dominica Museum line the road opposite Roseau's harbor. Portsmouth's port boasts a tourist-welcoming center (with an auditorium for speakers and films), shops, and instant access to Fort Shirley and Cabrits National Park.

Frommer's Ratings: Dominica					
	poor	fair	good	excellent	outstanding
Overall Experience			✓		
Shore Excursions				✓	
Activities Close to Port			✓		
Beach & Water Sports		✓			
Shopping			✓		
Dining/Bars			✓		

Dominica

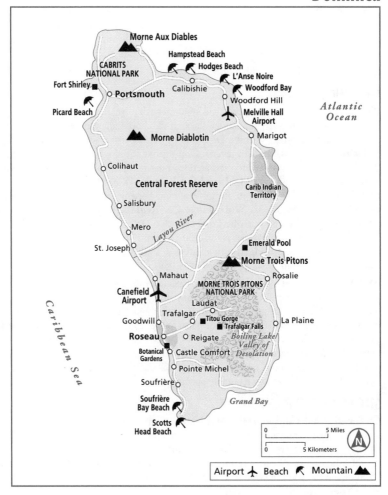

Morne Aux Diables

Hampstead Beach

Hodges Beach

CABRITS
NATIONAL PARK

L'Anse Noire

Fort Shirley

Calibishie

Woodford Bay

Portsmouth

Woodford Hill

Picard Beach

Melville Hall
Airport

*Atlantic
Ocean*

Morne Diablotin

Marigot

Colihaut

Central Forest Reserve

Carib Indian
Territory

Salisbury

Mero

Layou River

St. Joseph

Emerald Pool

Morne Trois Pitons

Caribbean Sea

Mahaut

Rosalie

Canefield
Airport

MORNE TROIS PITONS
NATIONAL PARK

Laudat

Trafalgar

Titou Gorge

La Plaine

Goodwill

Trafalgar Falls

Roseau

Reigate

*Boiling Lake
Valley of
Desolation*

Botanical
Gardens

Castle Comfort

Pointe Michel

Soufrière

Soufrière
Bay Beach

Grand Bay

Scotts
Head Beach

0		5 Miles
0		5 Kilometers

Airport ✈ Beach 🏖 Mountain ▲▲

CURRENCY Dominica's official currency is the Eastern Caribbean dollar (EC$). The exchange rate is roughly 2.7 EC dollars to U.S.$1. U.S. dollars are accepted almost everywhere, but you're likely to receive change in the local currency. Several ATMs in Roseau, including one at the port, dispense both U.S. and EC dollars. Credit cards are widely accepted.

LANGUAGE English is Dominica's official language. Almost everyone speaks Creole as well, a patois that combines elements of French, English, and African languages. Dominica's Creole is the same as that spoken on the neighboring French islands of Guadeloupe and Martinique.

INFORMATION Dominica's **Division of Tourism** operates branches at the Roseau and Portsmouth cruise ship berths (the Roseau office is located a block from the waterfront at the old post office building on Dame M. E. Charles Boulevard). For information before you leave home, call the Dominica Tourist Office at ☎ **212/949-1711**

or log on to www.dominica.dm/travel.htm. Several island businesses, including restaurants, tour operators, and other service providers, have joined forces to create another site, www.delphis.dm/home.htm, which has scores of links and helpful information.

CALLING FROM THE U.S.   When calling Dominica from the United States, you need only dial a "1" before the numbers listed throughout this chapter.

GETTING AROUND

BY RENTAL CAR   Dominica's road system is extensive and well maintained, but driving is on the left side, and passage through the mountains can be harrowing. You need a valid driver's license and a Dominican driver's permit, which costs about $12 and is available through rental agencies. Don't get annoyed when other drivers sound their horns; honking usually indicates an oncoming vehicle (especially at sharp curves) or is meant as a friendly greeting. **Island Car Rentals** (☎ **888/696-4202** in the U.S., or 767/448-2886) has offices in both Roseau and Portsmouth. So does **Valley Rent-a-Car** (☎ **767/448-3233**). **Wide Range Car Rentals,** in Roseau only (☎ **767/448-2198**), specializes in four-wheel-drive vehicles. Daily rates range from $35 to $75. You can also try **Avis,** which has an office in Roseau (☎ **800/882-8471** in the U.S., or 767/448-2481), and **Budget,** with a bureau at Canefield Airport, outside of Roseau (☎ **800/992-2776** in the U.S., or 767/449-2080).

BY TAXI   Taxis and public minivans are designated by license plates that begin with the letters *H* or *HA*. Fleets of both await cruise ship passengers at the Roseau and Portsmouth docks. Drivers are generally knowledgeable about sites and history, and the standard sightseeing rate is $18 per hour for up to four people. The vehicles are unmetered, so negotiate a price in advance and make sure everyone's talking about the same currency. You can get more information from the **Dominica Taxi Association** (☎ 767/449-8533). **Mally's Tour and Taxi Service** (☎ 767/448-3114) and **Julius John's** (☎ 767/449-1968) are two reputable operators.

SHORE EXCURSIONS

✪ **Trafalgar Falls and Emerald Pool Nature Tour** ($40, 4 hours): Drive to Morne Bruce for a panoramic view of Roseau and learn about local flora and fauna at the Botanical Gardens. Proceed to a lookout point for a majestic view of Trafalgar Falls. After refreshment at a nearby restaurant, drive to the Emerald Pool, where after a 15-minute walk, you can swim in a natural pool surrounded by moss-covered boulders at the base of a picture-perfect waterfall.

Roseau and Indian River Tour ($40, 5 hours): Drive through Roseau and fishing villages along the island's western coast to the town of Portsmouth. Embark on wooden canoes for a guided tour of the Indian River. Ferns, lianas, and reeds cluster between the trees, forming a cool green tunnel of foliage. You'll spot herons, bananaquits, and the occasional iguana. Land crabs shuffle between the roots, and fish occasionally pop out of the water. The relaxing trip features informative commentary by your boatman and a brief stop at a rain-forest refreshment stand, where you can also pick up a fish or bird fashioned origami-style from reed.

Carib Indian Territory ($51, 5 hours): Drive to the Carib Territory, where the tribe's chief will acquaint you with Carib history. Attend a performance by the Karifuna Cultural Group and view local crafts.

Champagne Scuba Dive ($51, 3 hours, equipment included): Certified divers can dive the reef named for the bubbles produced by an underwater geothermal vent. Observe corals, fishes, and other marine life.

D'Auchamps Gardens and Museum ($36, 3 hours): Walk through an impressive collection of exotic plants and flowers and learn about their uses and origins. Along a marked trail through this old coffee estate you'll see cacao, avocado, breadfruit, and citrus trees as well as heliconias, orchids, and other spectacular blooms from around the world. View Trafalgar Falls and a variety of birds. Learn about Dominica's history at the recently completed museum.

TOURING THROUGH LOCAL OPERATORS

Dominica has several excellent tour operators who know the island's many features and intricate terrain like the backs of their hands. One truly outstanding and highly recommended operation is **Ken's Hinterland Adventure Tours,** 10 Old St., Roseau (☎ 767/448-4850; www.kenshinterlandtours.com). Ken's offers a wide variety of tours, some that focus on botany, natural history, bird watching, or whale watching; others feature more vigorous activities like river hiking, waterfall stalking, or mountain climbing. **Dominica Tours** (☎ 767/448-2638) is a good alternative. For trips through the Carib Territory, you might want to make arrangements with **NICE (Native Indigenous Carib Excursions)** (☎ 767/448-2489). You can't miss with the firsthand knowledge of Carib traditions offered by NICE's operator, former Carib chief Irvince Auguiste.

ON YOUR OWN: WITHIN WALKING DISTANCE

IN ROSEAU The French, in the early 18th century, chose to build their largest settlement at what is now **Roseau** because the area has the largest expanse of flat land on the leeward coast and is well supplied with freshwater from the nearby Roseau River. The town's name comes from the river reeds (*roseaux* in French) that grow profusely around the estuary. As you come ashore, you'll see the **Dominica Museum,** which faces the bay front. Housed in an old market house dating from 1810, the museum's permanent exhibit provides a clear and interesting overview of the island's geology, history, archaeology, economy, and culture. The displays on pre-Columbian peoples, the slave trade, and the Fighting Maroons—slaves who resisted their white overlords and established their own communities—are particularly informative The museum is open Monday to Friday from 9am to 4pm, Saturday from 9am to noon; admission is $2.

Directly behind the museum is the **Old Market Square.** Vendors of vegetables, fruits, and other merchandise have crowded this cobbled square for centuries, and over the years the location has also witnessed slave auctions, executions, and political meetings and rallies. Today it offers primarily handcrafts and souvenirs. The **Public Market Place** at the mouth of the Roseau River, to your left as you leave the ship, is the Old Market Square's successor as the town's center of commercial activity. It's most colorful on Saturday mornings, when farmers and country vendors from the hills artfully display their fruits, vegetables, root crops, and flowers across the courtyards, sidewalks, and stalls of the marketplace.

It took more than 100 years to build the **Roseau Cathedral** of Our Lady of Fair Heaven, on Virgin Lane, which was completed in 1916. Made of cut volcanic stone, its style is Gothic-Romanesque revival. The original funds to build the church were raised from levies on French planters, and Caribs erected the first wooden ceiling frame. Convicts on Devil's Island built the pulpit, and one of the stained-glass windows is dedicated to Christopher Columbus. The **Methodist Church** stands next door to the Cathedral on land that once belonged to Catholics who later converted to Methodism. The Protestant church's location so close to the cathedral on once-Catholic land caused discomfort in the late 1800s that culminated in a street riot. Things are calmer today.

On the eastern edge of Roseau, the **Botanical Gardens** lie at the base of Morne Bruce, the mountain overlooking the town. The gardens were established at the end of the 19th century to encourage the diversification of crops and to provide farmers with correctly propagated seedlings. London's Kew Gardens provided exotic plants collected from every corner of the tropical world, and experiments conducted to see what would grow in Dominica revealed that everything does. Hurricane David in 1979 destroyed many of the garden's oldest trees. One arboreal victim, an African baobab, still lies on the bus it crushed, a monument to the power of the storm. At the garden's aviary you can see sisserou and jacko parrots, part of a captive-breeding program to repopulate these endangered species.

IN PORTSMOUTH   The cruise ship dock at Portsmouth leads directly to 260-acre **Cabrits National Park,** which combines stunning mountain scenery, tropical deciduous forest and swampland, volcanic sand beaches, coral reefs, and the romance of an 18th-century **Fort Shirley** overlooking the town of Portsmouth and Prince Rupert's Bay. Previous visitors to the area include Christopher Columbus, Sir Francis Drake, Admiral Horatio Nelson, and John Smith, who stopped here on his way to Virginia, where he founded Jamestown. Fort Shirley and more than 50 other major structures comprise one of the West Indies' most impressive and historic military complexes.

ON YOUR OWN: BEYOND WALKING DISTANCE

Approximately 15 to 20 minutes from Roseau, **Trafalgar Falls** is actually two separate falls fancifully referred to as the mother and the father falls. The cascading white torrents dazzle in the sunlight before pummeling black lava boulders below. The surrounding foliage comes in innumerable shades of green. To reach the brisk water of the natural pool at the base of the falls, you'll have to step gingerly along slippery rocks, and the nonballetic are dissuaded from attempting the climb. The constant mist that tingles the entire area beats any spa treatment. The rainbows are perpetual.

Titou Gorge, near the village of Laudat, offers an exhilarating swimming experience. Wending through the narrow volcanic gorge, you struggle against the cool current, which becomes stronger and stronger until you feel like a salmon swimming upstream to spawn. The sheer black walls enclosing you loom 20 feet above. At first, they seem sinister. But worn smooth by the water, they're ultimately womblike rather than menacing. Rock outcrops and a small cave provide interludes from the water flow, and eventually you reach the thundering waterfall that feeds the torrent.

Emerald Pool sits deep in the rain forest not far from the center of the island. After walking 15 minutes along a level trail shaded by majestic trees, you reach a 50-foot waterfall that crashes into the pool named for the moss-covered boulders enclosing it. Splash in the refreshing water. Float on your back to see the thick rain-forest canopy and bright blue sky above you.

About 4 miles from Portsmouth, in the midst of orange, grapefruit, and banana groves, the **Syndicate Nature Trail** provides an excellent introduction to tropical rain forests. The easy loop trail meanders through a stunningly rich ecosystem that features exotic trees such as the *lwoyé kaka* and the *chantannyé*.

Hard-core masochists have an easy choice—the forced march through the **Valley of Desolation** to **Boiling Lake.** Experienced guides say this all-day hike is like spending hours on a maximally resistant Stairmaster; one ex-Marine drill sergeant, a master of understatement, referred to it as "arduous." No joke, the trek *is* part of the Dominican army's basic training (of course, *you* won't have to carry one of your colleagues along the way). Why would any sane person endure this hell? To breathe in the harsh, sulfuric fumes that have killed all but the hardiest vegetation? Because the idea of baking a potato in the steam rising from the earth is irresistible? Maybe to feel the thrill that comes with the risk that you might break through the thin crust that separates you from hot lava? Or could it be the final destination, the 70-foot-wide cauldron of bubbling, slate-blue water of unknown depth. Don't even think of taking a dip in this flooded fumarole: The water temperature ranges from 180° to 197° Fahrenheit. Can we sign you up?

SHOPPING

In addition to the usual duty-free items—jewelry, watches, perfumes, and other luxury goods—Dominica offers handcrafts and art not obtainable anywhere else, most notably **Carib Indian baskets** made of dyed *larouma* reeds and *balizier* (heliconia) leaves. Designs for these items originated in Venezuela's Orinoco River valley and have been handed down from generation to generation since long before the time of Columbus. Dominican designs and materials are similar to those made today in the Orinoco River valley—amazing considering that there's been no interaction for more than 500 years. The Carib basket you buy, therefore, is more than a souvenir—it's a link to the pre-Columbian Caribbean. You can buy Carib crafts directly from the craftspeople in the **Carib Territory** or at various outlets in Roseau. A small, 12-inch model will cost about $10, and you can get a bell-shaped model about 22 inches high for $30 or $35. Floor mats made from *vertiver* grass are another Dominican specialty.

Here are some other great places for local crafts. At **Tropicrafts,** at the corner of Queen Mary Street and Turkey Lane in Roseau, you can watch local women weave grass mats with designs as varied and complex as those you made as a child with your Spirograph. The large store also stocks Carib baskets, locally made soaps and toiletries, rums, jellies, condiments, wood carvings, and masks made from the trunks of giant *fougère* ferns. The **Rainforest Shop,** at 12 Old St. in Roseau, is dedicated to the preservation of Dominica's ecosystem and offers colorful hand-painted items made from recycled materials such as oil drums, coconut shells, and newspapers. **The Crazy Banana,** at 17 Castle St., features Dominican arts and crafts, including straw and ceramic items, as well as jewelry and Cuban cigars. For unique and sometimes whimsical objects, try **Balisier's** at 35 Great George St. Local artist Hilroy Fingal transforms throwaway items like aluminum cans, perfume bottles, rocks, and coconut shells into things of beauty. His aesthetic is a little like Keith Haring's and every bit as fun. **Caribana,** at 31 Cork St., is one of the island's oldest craft shops. It offers items as varied as furniture, home accessories, jewelry, books, and skin-care products. It also serves as a showcase for local painters and sculptors and as a gathering place for the local arts community. **Frontline Cooperative,** at 78 Queen Mary St., specializes in books about Caribbean peoples, issues, and cooking.

BEACHES

If your sole focus is beaches, you'll find Dominica so-so. Much of the seacoast is rocky, and many sandy beaches have darker, volcanic sand. But there are golden sand beaches as well, primarily on the northern coast. Head for **Woodford Bay, L'Ance Tortue, Pointe Baptiste,** or **Hampstead Beach;** all have white sand, palm trees, and azure waters protected by reefs or windswept headlands.

SPORTS

FISHING   Dominica is a prime destination for anglers looking to catch marlin, wahoo, yellowfin tuna, or dorado. The island's numerous rivers flow into the Caribbean, providing an abundance of bait fish like bonito, jacks, and small tuna that attract bigger deepwater species. You can drop your line in the water a mere 15 minutes from the dock. **Rainbow Sportfishing** (☎ 767/448-8650) operates a 32-foot Sea Ray while **Game Fishing (Dominica)** (☎ 888/CASTAWAYS in the U.S., or 767/449-6244) has two boats, a 34-foot Luhrs and a 28-foot Pacemaker. Prices start at $50 per person (four-passenger minimum).

SCUBA DIVING Dominica's lush, beautiful scenery above water is echoed underwater in the surrounding Caribbean and Atlantic. Although the island is drained by hundreds of rivers and streams, the jagged volcanic underseascape prevents runoff sediment from clouding the water. Visibility ranges from 60 to more than 100 feet. Most local dive operations surpass international standards set by PADI, NAUI, and SSI, and small, uncrowded excursions are the norm. **Dive Dominica** (☎ 888/262-6611 in the U.S., or 767/448-2188) is perhaps the island's best operator. Single-tank boat dives run about $50. First-time dives with instruction run about $100 to $125.

SNORKELING Dominica offers almost 30 top-notch snorkeling areas. Snorkelers can join a dive-boat party, participate in special snorkel excursions, or explore the coast in a sea kayak, periodically jumping overboard for a look below. The calm water on the island's leeward side is perfect for viewing the riotous colors of sponges, corals, and the 190-plus fish species native to the area. Offshore snorkeling and equipment rental can be arranged through any of the dive operators listed above. Prices start at approximately $25.

GREAT LOCAL RESTAURANTS & BARS

Seafood, local root vegetables referred to as "provisions," and Creole recipes are among the highlights of Dominican cuisine. Crapaud (mountain chicken in English—it's really mountain frog) is the national delicacy. For a **local beer,** try Kubuli; for a **local rum,** try Soca.

IN ROSEAU Try **La Robe Créole,** 3 Victoria St. (☎ 767/448-2896), which gets top marks for its callaloo soup (made from the spinachlike leaves of the local vegetable, *dasheen,* and coconut), lobster and conch crepes, and mango chutney. The decor features heavy stone walls, solid ladder-back chairs, and colorful madras tablecloths. **Guiyave,** 15 Cork St. (☎ 767/448-2930), an airy restaurant on the second floor of a pistachio-colored wood-frame house, features steamed fish, conch, octopus, and spareribs. Take a table on the veranda and cool off with one of the fresh-squeezed juices. How about soursop, tamarind, sorrel, cherry, or strawberry? The downstairs take-out counter offers chicken patties, spicy rotis, and delectable tarts and cakes. **The Sutton Grille,** 25 Old St. (☎ 767/449-8700), in the Sutton Place Hotel, boasts an airy dining area ensconced in 100-year-old stone walls. You can choose a table a few steps up from the bustle of downtown Roseau or one set back from the action. The menu, a veritable primer of Creole and other West Indian cookery, also offers a generous sprinkling of international and vegetarian dishes.

IN PORTSMOUTH If you disembark in Portsmouth, get a table at the **Coconut Beach Restaurant** at Picard Beach (☎ 767/445-5393). It overlooks the Caribbean and the twin peaks of Cabrits National Park across Prince Rupert's Bay. The fresh seafood and Creole dishes taste even better with the tang of salt in the air. The **Purple Turtle** (☎ 767/445-5296) is closer to the dock and features lobster and crayfish as well as lighter fare such as rotis, sandwiches, and salads.

11 Dominican Republic

Called the "the fairest land under heaven" by some because of its sugar-white beaches and mountainous terrain, the Dominican Republic has, despite a persistent reputation for high crime, poverty, and social unrest, become one of the fastest-growing destinations in the Caribbean. Despite social and political drawbacks, the island still manages to intrigue visitors with its natural beauty and rich colonial heritage, so much so that many return again and again.

Nestled amid Cuba, Jamaica, and Puerto Rico, the island of Hispaniola (Little Spain) consists of Haiti, on the westernmost third of the island, and the Dominican Republic, which has a lush landmass equal to that of Vermont and New Hampshire combined. In the Dominican interior, the fertile Valley of Cibao (rich sugarcane country) ends its upward sweep at Pico Duarte, formerly Pico Trujillo, the highest mountain peak in the West Indies, which soars to 10,417 feet. Puerto Rico sits 54 miles off the Republic's east coast across the Mona Passage, prompting many poverty-stricken Dominicans to risk their lives crossing the channel in hopes of slipping into Puerto Rico and then illegally into the continental United States.

Columbus sighted Hispaniola's coral-edged Caribbean coastline on his first voyage to the New World and pronounced, "There is no more beautiful island in the world." The first permanent European settlement in the New World was founded here on November 7, 1493, and the settlement's ruins still remain near Montecristi in the northeast part of the island. Natives called the island Quisqueya, "Mother Earth," before the Spanish arrived to butcher them.

Much of what Columbus first saw still remains in a natural, unspoiled condition, but that may change: The country is building and expanding rapidly. In the heart of the Caribbean archipelago, the country has an 870-mile coastline, about a third of which is devoted to beaches (the best are in Puerto Plata and La Romana), and near-perfect weather year-round. So, why did it take so long for the Dominican Republic to be discovered by visitors? The answer is largely political. The country has been steeped in misery and bloodshed almost from its beginning, a situation that climaxed with the infamous reign of Rafael Trujillo (1930 to 1961) and the civil wars that followed.

Today the Dominican Republic is being rebuilt and restored, and it offers visitors a chance to enjoy the sun and sea as well as to learn about the history and politics of a developing society. Just exercise caution: Muggings are common (particularly in Santo Domingo); travelers should avoid unmarked taxis at all costs, and be wary of the hustlers in tourist areas.

Frommer's Favorite Dominican Republic Experiences

- **Exploring the Colonial City.** On your own or as part of a shore excursion, this historic section offers a series of firsts for the New World—the first university, hospital, cathedral, and more. The cobblestone streets and restored buildings offer a welcome respite from the bustle of this modern capital (see, "Shore Excursions" and "On Your Own: Within Walking Distance," below).
- **Hitting the beach:** White-sand beaches, blue waters, hotels, restaurants, outdoor cafes, nightclubs, and shops can be found in the seaside resorts of Boca Chica and Juan Dolio. It is worth the trek (see "Shore Excursions" and "Beaches," below).

Frommer's Ratings: Dominican Republic					
	poor	fair	good	excellent	outstanding
Overall Experience		✓			
Shore Excursions			✓		
Activities Close to Port		✓			
Beaches & Water Sports			✓		
Shopping		✓			
Dining/Bars			✓		

COMING ASHORE   Ships dock at San Souci, about 3 miles from downtown Santo Domingo. At the terminal are telephones, a bank, a tourist information stand, and shops. The easiest way to get to the city is by taxi. It costs about $10 to go to the Colonial City from the port. Cruise ships also dock at Catalina Island in La Romana, home to one of the Caribbean's most famous resorts, Casa de Campo. Cruise lines offer excursions to the resort and its environs, including Altos de Chavon, a replica of a 16th-century Mediterranean village that boasts an amphitheater, restaurants, cobblestone streets, and artisans' workshops.

At press time, the Dominican Republic was scheduled to start construction in Samana on a project that would create a marina, hotels, villas, shops, residential and commercial areas, and two or three slips for cruise ships.

Credit-card phones are located at the terminal and throughout the city. Prepaid calling cards are available in stores and in Codetel (the country's main phone company) offices in Santo Domingo.

CURRENCY   The **Dominican peso.** The exchange rate is about 15 pesos to U.S.$1 (RD$1 = U.S.7¢). U.S. dollars are accepted by cab drivers and some shopkeepers.

LANGUAGE   The official language is Spanish, but English is also spoken in tourist areas. Knowing a few key Spanish phrases is helpful.

INFORMATION   Located on the corner of Avenida Mexico and Avenida 30 de Marzo is the city's **main tourist office** (☎ **800/OSECTUR** or 809/221-4660). The office is open during the week from 9am to 5pm. The staff will give you just the basics. For info before you go, call the Dominican Republic tourist office in the U.S. at ☎ **888/374-6361** or 212/588-1015 or log on at www.domincana.com.do.

CALLING FROM THE U.S.   When calling Dominican Republic from the United States, you need to dial only a "1" before the numbers listed throughout this section.

GETTING AROUND

BY TAXI   Taxis aren't metered, and you should settle on the fare before you take the ride. The average fare within Santo Domingo is about $6. A cab to Boca Chica and Juan Dolio costs between $20 and $25 one-way. Avoid unmarked taxis. Another option for getting around Santo Domingo is **moto conchos,** which are motorcycle taxis that offer cheaper fares.

BY BUS   Private companies such as **Caribe Tours** (☎ 809/221-4422) and **Metro Expreso** (☎ 809/566-7126) operate scheduled service on various routes in air-conditioned buses. The fares are inexpensive (ranging from $3 to $6). Public buses, called **guaguas,** are also cheap (about $1) but are generally crowded, and service is erratic.

RENTAL CARS   Driving here is not for the faint of heart. In Santo Domingo, tailgating is an art form. The main highways are relatively smooth, but the secondary ones have potholes. If you dare, Budget, Hertz, National, and Thrifty have outlets here.

SHORE EXCURSIONS

✪ **Colonial City Walking Tour** ($24, 2¹/₂ hours): The tour will take you to the first cathedral in the New World, the earliest fort in the New World, and the oldest street in the New World. There is a stop at the Amber Museum as well as a cigar shop.

Columbus Lighthouse, Amber Museum, and Cathedral Tour ($20, 3 hours): Explore the lighthouse, stop to see amber, and visit the cathedral where Columbus was originally buried.

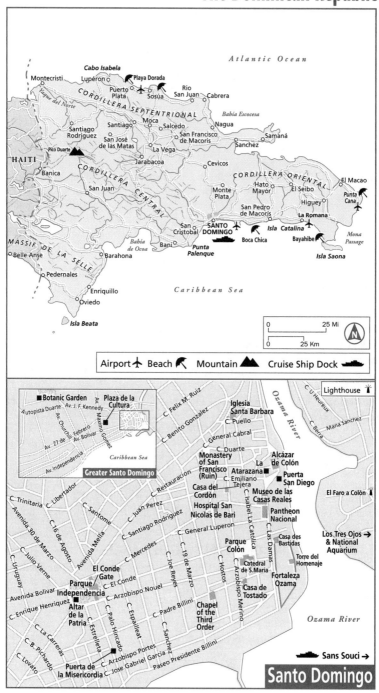

The Dominican Republic

Atlantic Ocean

Cabo Isabela
Montecristi Lupéron Playa Dorada
Puerto Sosúa Rio
Plata San Juan Cabrera
CORDILLERA SEPTENTRIONAL
Bahía Escocesa
Santiago Moca Salcedo Nagua
Rodríguez Santiago San Francisco Samaná
San José de Macoris Sanchez
de las Matas La Vega
HAITI Jarabacoa Cevicos
Pico Duarte CORDILLERA CENTRAL CORDILLERA ORIENTAL El Macao
Banica Monte Hato El Seibo Punta
Plata Mayor Higuey Cana
San Juan San Pedro La Romana
de Macoris
MASSIF DE LA SELLE San SANTO Isla Catalina Mona
Belle Anse Cristobal DOMINGO Boca Chica Bayahibe Passage
Bahía Bani Punta
de Ocoa Palenque Isla Saona
Barahona
Pedernales

Vaque del Norte

Caribbean Sea

Enriquillo
Oviedo
Isla Beata

0   25 Mi
0   25 Km

Airport ✈ Beach ⚓ Mountain ▲▲ Cruise Ship Dock ⛴

Santo Domingo

Lighthouse

■ Botanic Garden Plaza de la
Cultura
Autopista Duarte Av. J. F. Kennedy
Av. Churchill Av. Maximo Gomez
Av. 27 de Febrero Av. Bolivar
Caribbean Sea
Av. Independencia
Greater Santo Domingo

Ozama River C. U Heureux
Mana Sanchez
C. Felix M. Ruiz
C. Benito Gonzalez Iglesia
Santa Barbara
C. Puello
C. General Cabral
C. Duarte
Monastery Alcázar
of San de Colón
Francisco La
(Ruin) Atarazana ■ Puerta
C. Emiliano San Diego
Casa del Tejera
Cordón Museo de las El Faro a Colón ⚓
Casas Reales
Hospital San Pantheon
Nicolas de Bari Nacional
Casa des Los Tres Ojos →
Bastidas & National
Parque Aquarium
Colón
Torre del
El Conde Catedral Homenaje
Gate de S.Maria Fortaleza
El Conde Ozama
Parque Arzobispo Nouel Casa de
Independencia Tostado
Altar Padre Billini
de la Chapel Ozama River
Patria of the
Third
Order
⛴ Sans Souci →
Puerta de
la Misericordia Paseo Presidente Billini

C. Trinitaria C. Libertador
Avenida 30 de Marzo C. Santome
C. 16 de Agosto C. Juan Perez
Avenida Mella C. Santiago Rodriguez
Avenida Bolivar C. Mercedes
C. Julio Verne C. 19 de Marzo
C. Uruguay Joe Reyes
C. Enrique Henriquez C. Hostos
C. La Carrera C. Estrelleta
C. B. Pichardo C. Palo Hincado
C. Lovato C. Arzobispo Portes
C. Jose Gabriel Garcia C. Sanchez
Arzobispo Merino
C. Espaillat
Isabel La Católica
Las Damas
General Luperon
Restauracion

479

❂ **Juan Dolio Beach Tour** ($40, 6 hours): You spend the day at a resort's beach with access to its pool, snorkeling equipment, and clubhouse facilities. A buffet lunch and drinks are included.

ON YOUR OWN: WITHIN WALKING DISTANCE

Heading to the beach or discovering the capital's rich history are the best bets for folks visiting by cruise ship. Visitors should head to the **Colonial City** (Zona Colonial), home to the oldest cathedral, monastery, and university in the New World. The heart of the Colonial District is **Calle Las Damas,** the oldest street in the New World. It is named after the ladies of the viceroy's court who would promenade along the street in the afternoons. **Calle El Conde** is the main shopping thoroughfare. The Colonial City is best explored on foot.

Alcazar de Colon (Columbus's Palace), on Calle Las Damas (☎ **809/687-5361**), was built for Diego, the son of Christopher Columbus, in 1510. Diego was appointed the first viceroy of the Indies, and the palace served as the center of the Spanish court. Inside, visitors will find furnishings and paintings from that era. The restoration of the palace, which overlooks the Ozama River, first started in 1955 and was completed in the 1990s. Admission is $1, and it's open Monday and Wednesday to Friday from 9am to 5pm, Sat from 9am to 4pm, and Sunday from 9am to 1pm.

The **Cathedral of Santa Maria de la Encarnacion,** on Calle Arzobispo Merino (☎ **809/689-1920**), was built in stages from 1510 to 1540, although its bell tower was never completed. Pope Paul III declared it the first cathedral in the New World in 1542. A marble mausoleum inside the Spanish Renaissance-style building held the remains of Christopher Columbus until they were transferred to the Columbus Lighthouse Memorial in 1992. The facade is made of gold coral limestone. Admission is free, and it is open Monday to Saturday from 9am to 4pm.

Next to the cathedral is **Parque Colon** (Columbus Square), which features a larger-than-life bronze statue of the discoverer.

Las Ruinas del Monasterio de San Francisco (The Ruins of the San Francisco Monastery), between Calle Hostos and Calle Emiliano Tejera (☎ **809/682-3780**), has survived hurricanes, earthquakes, the French artillery, and a pillaging by Sir Francis Drake. It was constructed in the early 16th century and is considered—surprise!—the oldest monastery in the New World.

Fortaleza Ozama, on Calle Las Damas, overlooks the Ozama River and is considered the earliest military edifice built in the New World. Inside is **La Torre del Homenaje** (The Tower of Homage) (☎ **809/687-4722**), which served as a prison and fortress well into the 20th century. The fort is open daily from 9am to 5pm, and admission is $1.

ON YOUR OWN: BEYOND WALKING DISTANCE

Outside of the Colonial City is **Faro a Colon** (Columbus's Lighthouse), on Boulevar al Faro (☎ **809/591-1492**). The structure, constructed in the shape of a cross, commemorates the 500th anniversary of Christopher Columbus's arrival in the Americas in 1492 and allegedly houses the discoverer's remains (many other institutions also make this claim), as well as museums and exhibition halls devoted to Columbus. Admission is $2, and it is open Tuesday to Sunday from 10am to 5pm. You'll have to take a cab to get here.

If you're with the kids, visit the **National Aquarium,** on Avenida Espana (☎ **809/ 592-1509**), which features saltwater and freshwater marine life, including turtles and sharks. Admission is $1, and the aquarium is open Tuesday to Sunday from 9am to 6pm.

Los Tres Ojos (The Three Eyes), on Avenida Las Americas, are three subterranean lagoons that are surrounded by stalagmites and lush greenery. The site is open daily and there is no admission charge. It's located about 15 minutes from Santo Domingo.

Diehard baseball fans will recognize **San Pedro de Macoris,** known as the birthplace of many famous baseball players, including Sammy Sosa and Pedro Martinez. The city is about a 45-minute drive from Santo Domingo, and many tourists head to the local stadium to watch a game and check out future major leaguers.

SHOPPING

The duty-free shopping is below the standard of many other islands, but the Dominican Republic does have plenty of good buys. The main shopping areas are on La Atarazana, Avenida Mella, and Calle El Conde in the Colonial City. The best items to take home include amber or *larimar* (the Dominican turquoise) pieces, coffee, rum, cigars, paintings, woodcarvings, and rocking chairs

The city's marketplace, **Mercado Modelo,** is located on Avenida Mella, and is brimming with stalls selling crafts, paintings, produce, spices, and coffee, among other things. Bargaining is the norm here.

Stop by **Ambar Marie** on Caonabo, **Ambar Nacionale** on Calle Restauracion, and **Ambar Tres** on La Atarazana for amber and larimar. **The Santo Domingo Cigar Club** in the Renaissance Jaragua Hotel, on Avenida George Washington, has the finest selection of cigars in the city. Works of art by Dominicans and Haitians can be found at **Galería de Arte Nader** at Lupero and Duarte. Stop by a local **grocery store** to purchase Café Santo Domingo or Mama Ines/Montana Verde coffee.

BEACHES

The Dominican Republic is known for its great beaches, but you won't find them in Santo Domingo. The main beach areas are **Boca Chica** and **Juan Dolio.** Take a cab: Boca Chica is about 35 minutes east of Santo Domingo; Juan Dolio, about 45 minutes east. Hotels, restaurants, and bars—as well as pesky vendors hawking their wares— are part of the scene. Both seaside resorts offer white-sand beaches, and waters that are calm and shallow, making them ideal for swimming.

While at Boca Chica, stop by **Neptuno's Club,** on Avenida Duarte (☎ 809/ 523-4703), for a bite to eat. The open-air restaurant serves a variety of seafood dishes.

GREAT LOCAL RESTAURANTS & BARS

Most cruise ship passengers head to the Colonial City or along the Malecon for lunch. There should be a restaurant to suit every visitor's palate, with cuisines ranging from Italian to Japanese to Mexican. The most popular **local beers** are Presidente and Bohemia. The **local rums** are Brugal and Bermudez.

ON THE MALECON The Malecon is the city's main thoroughfare, which runs along the waterfront. **Vesuvio,** on Avenida George Washington (☎ **809/221-3333**), is the city's best-known Italian restaurant, having opened its doors in 1954. Red snapper, sea bass, and a variety of homemade pastas are on the menu, as well as Dominican specialties. Pizzeria Vesuvio is located next door.

IN THE COLONIAL CITY **Pate Palo Brasserie,** on La Atarazana (☎ 809/687-8089), claims to be the oldest pub in the New World. The high ceilings, stone walls, and gracious wait staff create a charming atmosphere. The international menu features seafood and pasta dishes. **La Bricciola,** on Calle Arzobispo Merino (☎ 809/688-5055), is a restored colonial building that serves delectable Italian cuisine, including lobster medaillons; mushrooms and shrimp; and veal scaloppini with prosciutto, mushrooms, and mozzarella.

For local flavor, **El Conuco,** on Casimiro de Moya (☎ **809/221-3231**), is the place to go. The restaurant, located close to the Colonial City, resembles a hut on a Dominican farm, and serves country-style cooking. There is a great selection of local dishes, including stews, chicken entrees, and the catch of the day.

IN MODERN SANTO DOMINGO   Meson de la Caba, on Avenida Mirador del Sur (☎ **809/533-2818**), is literally an underground experience. Patrons descend a spiral staircase to dine in a natural cave that is 50 feet below the ground. The restaurant is known for its steak and seafood entrees as well as its live entertainment.

12 Grand Cayman

Grand Cayman is the largest of the Cayman Islands, a British colony 480 miles due south of Miami (Cayman Brac and Little Cayman are the others). It's the top of an underwater mountain, whose side—known as the Cayman Wall—plummets straight down for 500 feet before becoming a steep slope that falls away for 6,000 feet to the ocean floor.

Despite its "grand" name, the place is only 22 miles long and 8 miles across at its widest point. Flat and prosperous, this tiny nation depends on Britain for its economic survival and attracts millionaire expatriates from all over because of its lenient tax and banking laws. Relatively unattractive, these islands are covered with scrubland and swamp, but boast more than their share of upscale, expensive private homes and condos. Until recently, Grand Cayman enjoyed one of the most closely knit social fabrics in the Caribbean, but with recent prosperity, some of this is beginning to unravel. More hotels have begun lining the sands of the nation's most famous sunspot, **Seven Mile Beach,** and the island attracts more than its share of scuba divers and snorkelers.

Grand Cayman is also popular because of its laid-back civility (so civil that ships aren't allowed to visit on Sunday). **George Town** is the colony's capital and its commercial hub.

Frommer's Favorite Grand Cayman Experiences

• **Swimming with stingrays:** At Stingray City, you can hop into the water with dozens of these weird-looking but gentle sea creatures, which swim right into your arms, like dogs (see "Shore Excursions," below).

• **Taking in the scene on Seven Mile Beach:** Grand Cayman's famed stretch of sand is known for its array of water sports and its translucent aquamarine waters (see "Beaches," below).

COMING ASHORE   Cruise ships anchor off George Town and ferry their passengers to a pier on Harbour Drive. Located in the heart of the shopping district, the landing

Frommer's Ratings: Grand Cayman					
	poor	fair	good	excellent	outstanding
Overall Experience					✓
Shore Excursions					✓
Activities Close to Port			✓		
Beaches & Water Sports					✓
Shopping			✓		
Dining/Bars		✓			

Grand Cayman

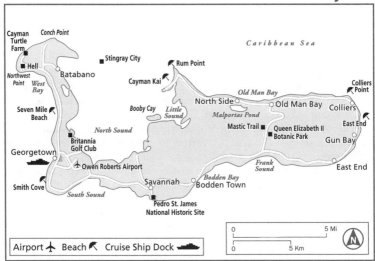

point couldn't be more convenient. There's a tourist information booth at the pier, and taxis line up to meet cruise ship passengers.

There is a **phone center** for credit card calls on Shedden Road, right in downtown.

CURRENCY   The legal tender is the **Cayman Islands dollar (CI).** The exchange rate is CI.83 to U.S.$1 (CI1 is worth about $1.20). Canadian, U.S., and British currencies are accepted throughout the Cayman Islands. Many restaurants quote prices in Cayman Islands dollars, which can lead you to think that food is cheaper than it is. Unless otherwise noted, prices in this section are given in U.S. dollars.

LANGUAGE   English is the official language of the islands.

INFORMATION   The **Department of Tourism** is in the Pavilion Building, Cricket Square (P.O. Box 67), George Town, Grand Cayman, BWI (☎ **800/346-3313** or 345/949-0623). It's open Monday to Friday from 9am to 5pm. To get info before you go, call the **Grand Caymans Tourism Board** in New York City at ☎ **212/682-5582** or visit their Web site at www.caymanislands.ky.

CALLING FROM THE U.S.   When calling Grand Cayman from the U.S., you need to only dial a "1" before the numbers listed throughout this section.

GETTING AROUND

BY TAXI   Taxi fares are fixed; typical one-way fares range from $12 to $20. **Cayman Cab Team** (☎ **345/947-4491**) and **Holiday Inn Taxi Stand** (☎ **345/945-4491**) offer 24-hour service.

BY RENTAL CAR   The roads are good by Caribbean standards, so driving around is relatively easy, as long as you remember to drive on the left side of the road. Reserve a car in advance with **Cico Avis** (☎ **800/331-1084** in the U.S., or 345/949-2468), **Budget** (☎ **800/527-0700** in the U.S., or 345/949-5605), or **Ace Hertz** (☎ **800/654-3131** in the U.S., or 345/949-7861).

BY MOTOR SCOOTER OR BICYCLE   The terrain is relatively flat, so motor scooters and bicycles are another way to get around. **Soto Scooters Ltd.,** Seven Mile Beach (☎ **345/945-4652**), at Coconut Place, offers Honda Elite scooters for about $30 daily, and bicycles for $15 daily.

SHORE EXCURSIONS

Nearly all the shore excursions here are underwater adventures, which you can book on your own or through your cruise ship.

✪ **Stingray City** ($39–$49, 2–3 hours): The waters off Grand Cayman are home to Stingray City, one of the world's most unusual underwater attractions. Set in the very shallow, sun-flooded waters of North Sound, about 2 miles east of the island's northwestern tip, the site was discovered in the mid-1980s when local fishermen cleaned their catch and dumped the offal overboard. They noticed scores of stingrays (which usually eat marine crabs) feeding on the debris, a phenomenon that quickly attracted local divers and marine zoologists. Today, anywhere from 30 to 100 relatively tame stingrays hover in the waters around the site for their daily handouts from hordes of snorkelers (often hundreds of cruise passengers at a time, so don't be surprised if they're not hungry). Stingrays are terribly gentle creatures, but they possess viciously barbed stingers capable of inflicting painful damage to anyone mistreating them. Never try to grab one by the tail. As long as you don't, you can feed and pet these velvet-skinned creatures without incident. Some tours include a quick island tour, including a stop at the Cayman Turtle Farm and a town called Hell (to look at some interesting rock formations and, of course, buy a T-shirt with all manner of Hell logos). The island tour and Stingray City excursion usually runs about 3 hours.

Atlantis **Submarine Excursion** ($76, 1¹/₂ hours): A 45-minute ride in the submarine is usually offered. The "*Atlantis* Expedition" dive visits the Cayman Wall; the "*Atlantis* Discovery" lasts 40 minutes and introduces viewers to the marine life of the Caymans.

Island Tour via Bicycle ($60, 3 hours): A great way to really get a feel for an island—and get some exercise—is via bicycle. You pick up your touring mountain bike at the Beach Club Colony Hotel and then ride along the coastline for views of Seven Mile Beach, then journey inland en route to the north side of the island to ride along the coast again.

TOURING THROUGH LOCAL OPERATORS

Stingray City: If the tours on your ship get booked, about half a dozen entrepreneurs lead expeditions to Stingray City, and there are usually a few tour agents waiting around the terminal in George Town. One well-known outfit is **Treasure Island Divers** (☎ **800/872-7552** from the U.S. or 345/949-4456), which charges snorkelers $30.

Taxi Tours: If you want to see the island, you can grab a taxi in port and take a tour. Taxis should cost about $40 per hour and can hold up to five people, and a 3-hour tour covers all the sights in a leisurely fashion. Make sure to stop in the town called Hell and send a postcard home.

ON YOUR OWN: WITHIN WALKING DISTANCE

In George Town, **Cayman Islands National Museum,** Harbour Drive (☎ **345/949-8368**), is housed in a veranda-fronted building that once served as the island's courthouse and is very worthwhile. Exhibits include Caymanian artifacts collected by Ira Thompson (beginning in the 1930s), and other items portraying the natural, social, and cultural history of the Caymans. There's a gift shop, theater, and cafe (a $5 donation is requested).

ON YOUR OWN: BEYOND WALKING DISTANCE

The only green-sea-turtle farm of its kind in the world, **Cayman Turtle Farm,** Northwest Point (☎ **345/949-3894**), is the island's most popular land-based tourist attraction. Once a multitude of turtles lived in the waters surrounding the Cayman Islands, but today these creatures are an endangered species. The turtle farm's purpose is two-fold: to provide the local market with edible turtle meat and to replenish the waters with hatchlings and yearling turtles. You can look into 100 circular concrete tanks containing turtles ranging in size from 6 ounces to 600 pounds, or sample turtle dishes at a snack bar and restaurant.

On 60 acres of rugged wooded land, **Queen Elizabeth II Botanical Park,** off Frank Sound Road, North Side (☎ **345/947-9462**), offers visitors a 1-hour walk along an 8-mile trail through wetlands, swamps, dry thicket, and mahogany trees. You might spot hickatees (the freshwater turtles found only on the Caymans and in Cuba), the rare Grand Cayman parrot, or the anole lizard with a cobalt-blue throat pouch. There are six rest stations along the trail, plus a visitor center and a canteen. There's also a heritage garden, a floral garden, and a lake.

The **Mastic Trail,** west of Frank Sound Road (☎ **345/949-1996**), is a restored 200-year-old footpath through a two-million-year-old woodland area in the heart of the island. Named for the majestic mastic tree, the trail showcases the reserve's natural attractions, including a native mangrove swamp, traditional agriculture, and an ancient woodland area. You can follow the 2-mile trail on your own, but I recommend taking a 3-hour guided tour. Call to make a reservation first. The trail, adjacent to the Botanical Park, is about a 45-minute drive from George Town.

SHOPPING

There's duty-free shopping here for silver, china, crystal, Irish linens, and British woolen goods, but I've found most prices to be similar to those in the United States. You'll also find cigar shops and international chains like Coach, the leather-goods store. Don't purchase turtle or black-coral products (which you'll see everywhere), since it is illegal to bring them into the United States or most other Western nations.

Some standout shops include **Artifacts Ltd.,** Harbour Drive (on the harbor front, across from the landing dock), for back issues of Cayman stamps; **The Jewelry Centre,** Fort Street, one of the largest jewelry stores in the Caymans; and the **Kennedy Gallery,** West Shore Centre, specializing in watercolors by local artists.

BEACHES

Grand Cayman's ✪ **Seven Mile Beach,** which begins north of George Town, an easy taxi ride from the cruise dock, has sparkling white sands with a backdrop of Australian pines. The beach is really about 5¹/₂ miles long, but the label of "seven mile" has stuck. It's lined with condominiums and plush resorts, and is known for its array of water sports and its translucent aquamarine waters. The average water temperature is a balmy 80°F.

SPORTS

GOLF   The major course on Grand Cayman is at the **Britannia Golf Club,** next to the Hyatt Regency on West Bay Road (☎ **345/949-8020**). The course was designed by Jack Nicklaus and is unique in that it incorporates three different courses in one: a nine-hole championship layout, an 18-hole executive set-up, and an 18-hole Cayman course. Nonguests of the club can reserve no more than 24 hours in advance.

SCUBA DIVING & SNORKELING   Coral reefs and other formations encircling the island are filled with marine life. It's easy to dive close to shore, so boats aren't necessary, but plenty of boats and scuba facilities are available, as well as many dive shops renting scuba gear to certified divers. The best dive operation is **Bob Soto's Diving Ltd.,** P.O. Box 1801, Grand Cayman, BWI (☎ **800/262-7686** or 809/949-2022 for reservations, or 345/949-2022), with full-service dive shops at Treasure Island, the

SCUBA Centre on North Church Street, and Soto's Coconut in the Coconut Place Shopping Centre. There are full-day resort courses as well as dives for experienced people daily on the west, north, and south walls, plus shore diving from the SCUBA Centre. The staff is helpful and highly professional.

GREAT LOCAL RESTAURANTS & BARS

A favorite **local beer** is Stingray, and a favorite **local rum** is Tortuga.

Abank's by the Sea, on Harbour Drive, is less than a half mile's walk south of the pier. It's a great open-air seaside cafe for a sandwich, chicken fingers, and a couple of cool Stingray beers. **Cracked Conch by the Sea,** West Bay Road, near Turtle Bay Farm (☎ 345/945-5217), serves some of the island's freshest seafood, including a succulent turtle steak and the inevitable conch, plus an array of meat dishes, including beef, jerk pork, and spicy combinations of chicken. The **Crow's Nest Restaurant,** South Sound, on the southwesternmost tip of the island, a 4-minute drive from George Town (☎ 345/949-9366), is one of those places that evokes the Caribbean "the way it used to be." There's no pretense here—you get good, honest Caribbean cookery, including grilled seafood, at great prices. Many dishes are spicy, especially their signature appetizer, fiery coconut shrimp.

The **Hog Sty Bay Café and Pub,** North Church Street, near the beginning of West Bay Road (☎ 345/949-6163), enjoys a loyal clientele, and is divided into an amusingly decorated pub and a Caribbean-inspired dining room open to a view of the harbor. In the pub, you can order such British staples as fish-and-chips or cottage pie. **Island Taste,** South Church Street (☎ 345/949-4945), caters more to large appetites than to picky gourmets, and offers great value for the money. Most of the menu is devoted to seafood dishes, such as mahimahi, turtle steak, and spiny lobster. **Ottmar's Restaurant and Lounge,** West Bay Road, side entrance of the Grand Pavilion Hotel (☎ 345/945-5879), is one of the island's top restaurants, offering such dishes as Bavarian cucumber soup, bouillabaisse, French pepper steak, and Wiener schnitzel. My favorite is chicken Trinidad, stuffed with grapes, nuts, and apples rolled in coconut flakes, sautéed golden brown, and served in orange-butter sauce.

13 Grenada

The southernmost nation of the British Windwards, Grenada (Gre-*nay*-dah) is one of the lushest in the Caribbean. Called the "Spice Island," its extravagant fertility—a result of the gentle climate and volcanic soil—produces more spices than anywhere else in the world: cloves, cinnamon, mace, cocoa, tonka beans, ginger, and a third of the world's supply of nutmeg. The beaches are white and sandy, and the populace (a mixture of English expatriates and islanders of African descent) is friendly. Once a British Crown Colony but now independent, the island nation also incorporates two smaller islands: Carriacou and Petit Martinique, neither of which has many tourist facilities.

St. George's, the country's capital, is one of the most colorful ports in the West Indies. Nearly landlocked in the deep crater of a long-dead volcano, and flanked by old forts, it reminds many visitors of Portofino, Italy. Here you'll see some of the most charming Georgian colonial buildings in the Caribbean, many with red tile roofs (the tiles were brought by European trade ships as ballast) and pastel walls. Churches dot the hillside of the harbor. Frangipani and flamboyant trees add even more color.

Crisscrossed by nature trails, Grenada's interior is a jungle of palms, oleander, bougainvillea, purple and red hibiscus, crimson anthurium, bananas, breadfruit, birdsong, ferns, and palms. The island's lush tropical scenery and natural bounty attract visitors who want to snorkel, sail, fish, hike on jungle paths, or loll the day away on the 2-mile-long, white-sand **Grand Anse Beach,** one of the best in the Caribbean.

Grenada

0 | 5 Miles
0 | 5 Kilometers

Levera Beach and National Park

Sauteurs

Victoria

Caribbean Sea

▲ Mt. St. Catherine

Gouyave (Charlottetown)

■ Douglaston Estate

Pearl's Beach

Grand Roy

Grand Etang National Park

Grenville

▲ Mt. Qua Qua

Grenville Bay

Annandale Falls ■

▲ Mt. Sinai

Marquis

Beaulieu

Constantine

St. George's

St. David's

Grand Anse Beach

Morne Rouge Bay

Woburn

Point Salines ✈

L'Anse aux Epines

Atlantic Ocean

Pink Gin Beach

La Sagesse Beach

Airport ✈ Beach 𝄢 Mountain ▲▲ Cruise Ship Dock ⛴

Frommer's Favorite Grenada Experiences

- **Picnicking at Annandale Falls:** A 50-foot cascade is the perfect backdrop for a picnic among tropical flora—and you can swim in the falls afterward (see "On Your Own: Beyond Walking Distance," below).
- **Hiking to the Seven Sisters Waterfall:** A hearty walk along a muddy path that winds through the thick, pristine jungle is a blast. At the end of the approximately mile-long trail there's a set of beautiful waterfalls. You can even jump from the tops of two of them into the pools below (see "Shore Excursions," below).
- **Visiting Levera National Park:** With beaches, coral reefs, a mangrove swamp, a lake, and a bird sanctuary, this is a paradise for hikers, swimmers, and snorkelers alike (see "On Your Own: Beyond Walking Distance," below).
- **Taking the rainforest and Grand Etang Lake tour:** Take a bus to an extinct volcanic crater some 1,900 feet above sea level. On the way, drive through rain forests and stop at a spice estate (see "Shore Excursions," below).

COMING ASHORE Ships either dock at a pier right in St. George's or anchor in the much-photographed harbor and send their passengers to the pier by tender. A tourist information center at the pier dispenses island data. The Carenage (St. George's main street) is only a short walk away from the pier; a taxi into the center of town costs about $3. To get to Grand Anse, you can take a regular taxi or a water taxi (see "Getting Around," below).

You'll find a pair of **credit-card phones** for international calls inside the small cruise terminal and two more just outside of it. There are six more London-style red phone booths midway around the Carenage, less than a half mile from the terminal.

CURRENCY   The official currency is the **Eastern Caribbean dollar (EC$).** The exchange rate is EC$2.70 to U.S.$1 (EC$1 = 37¢). Always determine which dollars—EC or U.S.—you're talking about when discussing a price.

LANGUAGE   English is commonly spoken on this island. Creole English, a mixture of African, English, and French, is spoken informally by the majority.

INFORMATION   Go to the **Grenada Board of Tourism,** on the Carenage in St. George's (☎ **800/927-9554** or 473/440-2279), for maps and general information. Open Monday to Friday from 8am to 4pm. To get information before you go, contact the **Grenada Tourism Board** in New York City at ☎ **212/687-9554** or log on to the Web site at www.grenada.com.

CALLING FROM THE U.S.   When calling Grenada from the United States, you need to only dial a "1" before the numbers listed throughout this section.

GETTING AROUND

St. George's can easily be explored on foot, although parts of the town are steep as it rises up from the harbor.

BY TAXI   Taxi fares are set by the government. Most cruisers take a cab from the pier to somewhere near St. George's. You can also tap most taxi drivers as a guide for a day's sightseeing. The charge is about $15 per hour, but be sure to negotiate a price before setting out. From the pier to Grand Anse Beach is about $10 per carload.

BY MINIVAN   Minivans, used mostly by locals, charge EC$1 to EC$6 (U.S.40¢ to U.S.$2.20), and the most popular run is between St. George's and Grand Anse Beach. Most minivans depart from Market Square or from the Esplanade area of St. George's.

BY WATER TAXI   An ideal way to get around the harbor and to Grand Anse Beach—the round-trip fare is about $4. A water taxi can take you from one end of the Carenage to the other for another $2.

BY RENTAL CAR   I don't recommend driving here, as the roads are very narrow and windy.

SHORE EXCURSIONS

Because of Grenada's lush landscape, I recommend spending at least 3 hours touring its interior, one of the most scenic in the West Indies.

✪ **Rain Forest/Grand Etang Lake Tour** ($33–$37, 3 hours): This is a great way to experience Grenada's lush, cool, dripping-wet tropical interior. Via bus, you travel past

Frommer's Ratings: Grenada					
	poor	fair	good	excellent	outstanding
Overall Experience					✓
Shore Excursions			✓		
Activities Close to Port				✓	
Beaches & Water Sports			✓		
Shopping			✓		
Dining/Bars			✓		

the red-tiled roofs of St. George's en route to the bright blue Grand Etang Lake within an extinct volcanic crater some 1,900 feet above sea level. On the way, you drive through rain forests and stop at a spice estate. Some tours include a visit to the Annandale Falls.

✪ **Hike to Seven Sisters Waterfalls** ($35, 4 hours): After a mile-or-so walk along a muddy path in the lush Grand Etang rain forest, cascading waterfalls and natural pools emerge and passengers are free to take a swim or a hop off a waterfall's edge. It's gorgeous and lots of fun. Don't forget to wear your bathing suit and maybe a pair of Teva-type sandals.

Island Bus Tour ($33, 3 hours): Typical scenic island tours take you through the highlights of the interior and along the coast, including Grand Anse Beach. Along the way you get to see the most luxuriant part of Grenada's rain forest, a nutmeg-processing station, a sugar factory, and many small hamlets. Many cruise lines also book you on a tour ($27, 2 hours) that explores St. George's historical sites and forts before taking you to some of the island's natural highlights, including a private garden where some 500 species of island plants and flowers are cultivated.

Party Cruises ($33, 3 hours): Party cruises are popular here, with no shortage of rum and reggae music. Two large party boats, the *Rhum Runner* and *Rhum Runner II,* designed for 120 and 250 passengers respectively, operate out of St. George's harbor, making three trips daily. The cost includes rum punch, sodas, a beach stop, and sometimes snorkeling.

ON YOUR OWN: WITHIN WALKING DISTANCE

In St. George's, you can visit the **Grenada National Museum,** at the corner of Young and Monckton streets (☎ **473/440-3725**), set in the foundations of an old French army barracks and prison built in 1704. This small but interesting museum houses finds from archaeological digs, including ancient petroglyphs, plus a rum still, native fauna, and memorabilia depicting Grenada's history, including the island's first telegraph. There are also two bathtubs worth seeing—the wooden barrel used by the fort's prisoners and the carved marble tub used by Joséphine Bonaparte during her adolescence on Martinique. The most comprehensive exhibit illuminates the native culture of Grenada. The museum is open 9am to 4:30pm Monday through Friday, and 10am to 1pm Saturdays; admission is $2.

If you're up for a good walk, walk around the historical Carenage from the cruise terminal and head up to **Fort George,** built in 1705 by the French and originally called Fort Royal. (You can pick up a rudimentary walking-tour map from the cruise terminal to help you find interesting sites along the way.) While the fort ruins and the 200- to 300-year-old canons are worth taking a peek at, it's the 360° panoramic views of the entire harbor area—including your ship, the sea, and many of the red-tile-roofed buildings dotting the island—that are most spectacular. Don't forget your camera! Before or after a visit to the fort, be sure to walk along **Church Street** (which leads right to the fort) as far as St. Johns or Juille Street. Along the way, you'll see lots of quaint 18th- and 19th-century architecture framed by brilliant flowering plants: **St. Andrew's Presbyterian Church** built in 1831 with the help of the Freemasons, **St. George's Anglican Church** built in 1825 by the British, the **Houses of Parliament,** and the **Roman Catholic Cathedral** rebuilt in 1884 (the tower dates back to 1818). Along the way you notice examples of Grenada's **Sedan Porches,** originally open-ended porches used as porte cocheres to keep residents dry when going between house and carriage.

ON YOUR OWN: BEYOND WALKING DISTANCE

You can take a taxi up Richmond Hill to **Fort Frederick,** which the French began in 1779. The British, having retaken the island in 1783 under provision of the Treaty of Versailles, completed it in 1791. From its battlements you have a panoramic view of the harbor and the yacht marina.

Don't miss the mountains northeast of St. George's. If you don't have much time, ✪ **Annandale Falls,** a tropical wonderland where a 50-foot-high cascade drops into a basin, is just a 15-minute drive away, on the outskirts of the Grand Etang Forest Reserve. The overall beauty is almost Tahitian. You can have a picnic surrounded by liana vines, elephant ears, and other tropical flora and spices. Annandale Falls Centre offers gift items, handcrafts, and samples of the indigenous spices of Grenada. Nearby, an improved trail leads to the falls, where you can enjoy a refreshing swim. If you've got more time, the even better **Seven Sisters Waterfalls** is further into Grand Etang, an approximately 30-minute drive and then a mile or so hike along a muddy trail. It's well worth the trip and you'll really get a feel for the power and beauty of the tropical forest here. The falls themselves are lovely and you can even climb to the top and jump off into the pool below; be careful, though: It's awfully slippery on those rocks. You may want to skip the jumping and just enjoy a relaxing swim in the cool water after the sweaty hike.

Opened in 1994, 450-acre park ✪ **Levera National Park** has several white sandy beaches for swimming and snorkeling, although the surf is rough. Offshore are coral reefs and sea-grass beds. Inland, the park contains a mangrove swamp, a lake, and a bird sanctuary—perhaps you'll see a rare tropical parrot. It's a hiker's paradise. The interpretation center (☎ **473/442-1018**) is open Monday to Friday from 8am to 4pm, Saturday from 10am to 4pm, and Sunday from 9am to 5pm. The park, about 15 miles from the harbor, can be reached by taxi, bus, or water taxi.

SHOPPING

The local stores sell luxury-item imports, mainly from England, at prices that are not quite duty-free. This is no grand Caribbean merchandise mart, so if you're cruising on to such islands as Aruba, Sint Maarten, or St. Thomas, you might want to postpone serious purchases. On the other hand, you can find some fine local handcrafts, gifts, and art here.

Spice vendors besiege you wherever you go, including just outside of the cruise terminal. If you're finished shopping, a polite no-thank-you usually works ("I just bought some from another vendor" always works for me). But you really should take at least a few samples home with you. The spices here are fresher and better than any you're likely to find in your local supermarket, so nearly everybody comes home with a handwoven basket full of them. Nutmeg products are especially popular. The Grenadians use every part of the nutmeg: They make the outer fruit into either a tasty liqueur or a rich jam, and ground the orange membrane around the nut into a different spice called mace. You'll also see the outer shells used as gravel to cover trails and even parking lots. **Arawak Islands,** Upper Belmont Road, has at least nine different fragrances distilled from such island plants as frangipani, wild lilies, cinnamon, nutmeg, and cloves. You'll also find an all-natural insect repellent that some clients insist is the most effective (and safest) they're ever used. There's also great hot sauce to be found (I only wish I would have bought more than one bottle on my last trip!).

Some worthwhile shops include **Art Fabrik,** Young Street, for batik shirts, shifts, shorts, skirts, T-shirts, and the like; **Creation Arts & Crafts,** the Carenage, for off-island handicrafts (from Venezuela, Sint Maarten, and Cuba); **Sea Change Bookstore,** the Carenage, for recent British and American newspapers; **Spice Island Perfumes,** the

Carenage, for perfumes made from the natural extracts of local herbs and spices; and **Tikal,** Young Street, for handcrafts from Grenada and around the world. You'll find that ubiquitous Caribbean chain store, Colombia Emeralds, midway along the Carenage.

BEACHES

Grenada's ✪ **Grand Anse Beach,** with its 2 miles of sugar-white sands, is one of the best beaches in the Caribbean. It's long and nice and wide. The water is calm and the views of St. George's make the scene complete. There are several restaurants beachside, including CotBam (see "Great Local Restaurants & Bars," below), and you can also join a banana-boat ride or rent a Sunfish sail boat. From the port, it's about a 10-minute, $10 taxi ride, although you can also take a water taxi from the pier for only $4 round-trip.

SPORTS

SCUBA DIVING & SNORKELING   Grenada offers an underwater world rich in submarine gardens, exotic fish, and coral formations. Visibility is often up to 120 feet. Off the coast is the wreck of the nearly 600-foot ocean liner *Bianca C.* Novice divers should stick to the west coast; the more experienced might search out the sights along the rougher Atlantic side. **Daddy Vic's Watersports,** directly on the beach in the Grenada Renaissance, Grand Anse Beach (☎ **473/444-4371,** ext. 638), is the premier scuba-diving outfit. It also offers snorkeling trips, as well as Windsurfer and Sunfish rentals, parasailing, and waterskiing. It can arrange to pick you up at the pier in a courtesy bus and bring you back to the cruise ship later. Canadian-run **Grand Anse Aquatics,** at Coyaba Beach Resort on Grand Anse Beach (☎ **473/444-4129**), gives Daddy Vic's serious competition, offering both scuba-diving and snorkeling jaunts to reefs and shipwrecks teeming with marine life. Diving instruction is available. (*Warning:* Grenada doesn't have a decompression chamber. In the event of an emergency, divers must be taken to the facilities on Barbados.)

GREAT LOCAL RESTAURANTS & BARS

A favorite **local beer** is Carib; a favorite **local rum** is Clarkecourt.

Your last chance to enjoy food from old-time island recipes, many now fading from cultural memory, is at ✪ **Betty Mascoll's Morne Fendue,** at St. Patrick's (☎ **473/442-9330**), 25 miles north of St. George's. This plantation house was built in 1912 of chiseled river rocks held together by a mixture of lime and molasses. Mrs. Mascoll was born that same year and has lived here ever since, continuing her long tradition of hospitality. You dine as an upper-class family did in the 1920s. Lunch is likely to include a yam-and-sweet-potato casserole or curried chicken with lots of island-grown spices. The most famous dish is Betty's legendary pepper-pot stew, which includes pork and oxtail, tenderized by the juice of grated cassava. Mrs. Mascoll and her loyal, veteran staff need time to prepare, so it's imperative to call ahead. They serve a fixed-price lunch Monday to Saturday from 12:30 to 3pm.

Mamma's, Lagoon Road (☎ **473/440-1459**), captures the authentic taste of Grenada. Meals include such dishes as callaloo soup with coconut cream, shredded cold crab with lime juice, freshwater crayfish, fried conch, and rotis made of curry and yellow chickpeas. **The Nutmeg,** the Carenage, located right on the harbor over the Sea Change Shop (☎ **473/440-2539**), is a casual hangout for the yachting set and a favorite with expatriates and visitors. The menu is extensive.

Cool breezes that blow in off the port, making **Pierone,** at the extreme northern end of the Carenage (☎ **473/440-9747**), a great spot for a midday pick-me-up, with or without alcohol. Menu items include such West Indian dishes as *lambi* (conch) chowder, sandwiches, and the most popular dish on the menu, lobster pando, a form of ragoût. Pubby **Rudolf's,** the Carenage (☎ 473/440-2241), serves the best steaks in the capital. Conch is prepared in several different ways, as are shrimp and octopus. Flying fish and mahimahi deserve the most praise.

Midway along the Grand Anse Beach is the **CotBam** bar and restaurant, overlooking the beach. They serve local specialties like curries and seafood as well as great fruity drinks like piña coladas. Just steps from the cruise terminal is the **007 Bar,** a pleasant dive built on a barge in the harbor and offering good views along with drinks, seafood, and snacks.

14 Guadeloupe

Take the things you love about France—sophistication, great food, and an appreciation of the good things in life—add the best of the Caribbean—nice beaches, a relaxed pace, and warm, friendly people—and combine with efficiency and modern convenience. Voilà!: Guadeloupe. And once you leave the crowded, narrow streets of Pointe-à-Pitre, the commercial center and main port, you'll see that the island is more developed and modern than many others.

Guadeloupe's Creole cuisine, a mélange of French culinary expertise, African cooking, and Caribbean ingredients, is reason enough to get off the ship, regardless of how much you're enjoying the food on board. And if shopping's your favorite sport, you'll have ample opportunity to stock up on French perfumes, clothes, and other luxury products. For the more adventurous, there's a volcano, scuba diving, surfing, and hiking to spectacular mountain waterfalls. Of course, you can always work on your tan at one of the island's many beaches. Or maybe you just want to sit at a sidewalk cafe, sip your espresso with a copy of *Le Monde,* and watch the world go by.

Guadeloupe, the political entity, is an overseas region of France that includes the islands of St.-Barthélemy (St. Barts), St. Martin, Les Saintes, La Désirade, Marie-Galante, and Guadeloupe itself. The name *Guadeloupe,* however, usually refers to two contiguous islands—**Basse-Terre** and **Grande-Terre**—separated by a narrow seawater channel, the Rivière Salée. Nestled between Antigua and Dominica, these two islands are shaped like a 530-square-mile butterfly. The eastern wing, the limestone island of Grande-Terre, is known for its white-sand beaches, rolling hills, sugarcane fields, and resort areas. Pointe-à-Pitre, your port of debarkation, is here. The butterfly's larger, volcanic western wing, Basse-Terre, is dominated by the National Park of Guadeloupe, a mountainous rain forest replete with waterfalls and La Soufrière, a brooding, still occasionally troublesome volcano. The capital of Guadeloupe, also called Basse-Terre, is on this western wing. Almost half of Guadeloupe's population of 410,000 is under the age of 20. About 80% of Guadeloupeans are descended from African slaves, with people of European and East Indian ancestry making up most of the remaining 20%.

Frommer's Ratings: Guadeloupe					
	poor	fair	good	excellent	outstanding
Overall Experience				✓	
Shore Excursions				✓	
Activities Close to Port					✓
Beaches & Water Sports				✓	
Shopping				✓	
Dining/Bars					✓

Guadeloupe

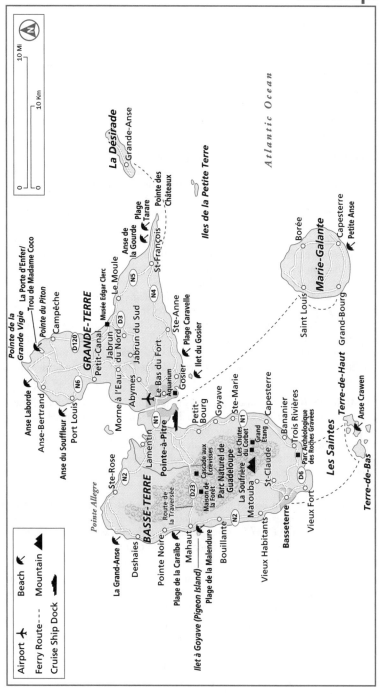

Hunter-gatherers from what is today Venezuela inhabited Guadeloupe more than a thousand years before the birth of Christ. By the 9th century, the peaceful Arawaks had been assimilated by the more aggressive Carib Indians, who still inhabited the island when Christopher Columbus landed on Basse-Terre on November 3, 1493. The Caribs called the island Karukera ("island of beautiful waters"). To honor Nuestra Señora de Guadalupe, the patron saint of Spain's Extremadura region, Columbus named the island Guadeloupe. The Spanish never showed an interest in the inhospitable island, concentrating instead on territories with more immediate value. France, eager to establish a toehold in the Caribbean, eventually filled the vacuum. Today, sugar and rum are the island's main exports.

Frommer's Favorite Guadeloupe Experiences

- **Climbing a volcano:** Draped in thousands of banana trees and other lush foliage, La Soufrière rises 4,800 feet above the surrounding sea and dominates the island of Basse-Terre. You can drive to a parking area at La Savane à Mulets, then hike the final 1,500 feet (two arduous hours) right to the mouth of the volcano. (See "On Your Own: Beyond Walking Distance," below.)

- **Touring the dramatic Atlantic coast of Grande-Terre:** Drive out to Grande-Terre's eastern extreme, La Pointe des Châteaux, to watch the Atlantic and Caribbean vent their fury on the rocky shore. Continue up the coast to La Porte d'Enfer and La Pointe de la Grande Vigie for splendid views of limestone cliffs and sparkling aquamarine waters. (See "On Your Own: Beyond Walking Distance," below.)

- **Soaking up the French-Caribbean ambiance:** It's simple but satisfying. Walk the streets of Pointe-à-Pitre or whatever other town you choose. Browse through the stores, and maybe buy some perfume or "thigh-reducing cream" from one of the upscale pharmacies (look for the neon green cross). Pick up a newspaper—it could even be the English-language *International Herald-Tribune*—find a shady table at a sidewalk cafe, order a cold, fresh-fruit juice, and luxuriate in your blessed life.

COMING ASHORE   Cruise ships dock at the modern Centre Saint-John Perse, adjacent to downtown Pointe-à-Pitre, Grande-Terre's main city. The terminal has phones, shops, restaurants, cafes, and a small tourist office.

Phone booths marked TÉLÉCOM require a "télécarte," a discount prepaid phone card that you can buy at post offices and other outlets marked TÉLÉCARTE EN VENTE ICI. Many phones also accept credit cards for long-distance calls. There are phones in the cruise terminal.

CURRENCY   As elsewhere in France, you'll need **French francs.** There are 100 centimes to 1 franc. The exchange rate is roughly 6.4 francs to U.S.1 (1 franc = U.S.15¢). There are numerous ATMs (*distributeur de billets*) in downtown Pointe-à-Pitre that dispense francs. You'll have no trouble using your credit cards.

LANGUAGE   French is the official language, but you'll often hear islanders speaking a local Creole among themselves. Don't expect to get too far with only English unless you're at one of the larger hotels or busier tourist areas. Any attempt you make to speak French will be appreciated, so bring a phrase book.

INFORMATION   The **main tourist office (Office du Tourisme)** in Pointe-à-Pitre is at 5 Square de la Banque, a 5-minute walk from the port (☎ **590/82-09-30**). The building, a beautiful colonial mansion, is open Monday to Friday from 8am to 5pm, Saturday until noon. If you want information before you leave home, contact the **Guadeloupe Tourist Office** in New Jersey at ☎ **732/302-1223** or log on to the Web site, www.frenchcaribbean.com.

Insider's Tip

The little trolley that meets cruise ship passengers at the port is supposed to provide hassle-free transportation around Pointe-à-Pitre. Unfortunately, it's no match for the city's traffic and narrow roads. Unless you enjoy traffic jams, walk. It's a better way to browse, shop, and visit the museums.

CALLING FROM THE U.S.   When calling Guadeloupe from the United States, you need to dial the international access code (011) before the numbers listed in this section.

GETTING AROUND

BY TAXI   Metered taxis await cruise passengers at the Pointe-à-Pitre pier. Rates are regulated, but they can be expensive, especially on Sundays and holidays, when fares are 40% higher. Taxis can be hired for private tours, but you'll have a hard time finding a driver who speaks English. Negotiate a price before setting out, and make sure all terms are clear to avoid an unpleasant scene later. One recommended driver is **Alain Narcisse,** an enthusiastic, knowledgeable, and English-speaking guide who offers tours of Grande-Terre, northern Basse-Terre, and southern Basse-Terre. He's often booked, so make arrangements in advance by calling ☎ **590/35-27-29** or 590/83-24-79.

BY MOTOR SCOOTER   Motorbikes are available in Pointe-à-Pitre at **Vespa Sun** (☎ **590/91-30-36**) and **Moto Guadeloupe** (☎ **590/82-12-50**). Expect to pay about $30 a day, including insurance and a deposit of roughly $150 (credit cards are accepted).

BY BUS   Buses are inexpensive, comfortable, and efficient. Almost all play zouk, an upbeat local music (at reasonable decibel levels), and some have videos. Signs (ARRÊT-BUS) indicate bus stops, but you can wave down a driver anywhere along the road. Pay the driver or the conductor as you get off. The fare from Pointe-à-Pitre to Gosier is just over $1.

BY RENTAL CAR   With a valid driver's license, you can rent a car; almost all have standard transmissions. Reserve a car before leaving home, especially during the high season. **Hertz** (☎ **800/654-3001** or 590/21-09-35), **Avis** (☎ **800/230-4898** or 590/82-02-71), **National** (☎ **888/CAR-RENT**), and **Budget** (☎ **800/527-0700**) all have offices on the island. Guadeloupe's road system is one of the best in the Caribbean, and traffic regulations and road signs are the same as elsewhere in France. Driving is on the right. Be forewarned that Guadeloupeans are skillful but aggressive drivers; don't tarry in the passing lane.

SHORE EXCURSIONS

Carbet Falls ($40, 4 hours): After driving through the banana plantations and rain forests of Basse-Terre's south side, you'll hike 30 minutes to picturesque Carbet Falls, where you're free to swim in the refreshing water. Wear sturdy walking shoes.

Pigeon Island ($50, 4¹/₂ hours): You'll first pass through Guadeloupe's National Park, a lush and mountainous tropical rain forest, on the Route de la Traversée. At Pigeon Island you'll board a glass-bottom boat for a 90-minute ride around a beautiful coral reef now designated the Cousteau Underwater Reserve. Marvel at the numerous fishes, corals, and other marine life.

ON YOUR OWN: WITHIN WALKING DISTANCE

Pointe-à-Pitre's narrow streets and congested sidewalks are bustling with activity, and its markets are among the Caribbean's most colorful. The largest, **Marché St. Antoine,** at the corner of Rues Frébault and Peynier, is well known for its playful, sassy vendors, who sell tropical produce and spices in madras bags. **Marché de la Darse,** on the waterfront at the foot of Place de la Banque, offers exotic fruits, vegetables, and souvenirs. The **Place Gourbeyre Flower Market,** next to the cathedral, is ablaze with tropical blooms, including *roses de porcelaine* and alpinias. Lined with royal palms, scarlet flamboyants, and travelers palms, the renovated Place de la Victoire commemorates Victor Hugues' defeat of the English in 1794. It's the largest public space in town and is bordered with restaurants and cafes. The nearby **Cathedral of St-Pierre and St-Paul,** built in 1871, has an iron framework designed to withstand earthquakes and hurricanes (three churches destroyed by successive earthquakes form its foundation). The **Musée Municipal Saint-John Perse,** near the corner of Rues Achille-René Boisneuf and Nozières, (☎ 590/90-01-92) chronicles the life of native son Alexis Léger, who won the Nobel Prize for Literature under the *nom de plume* "Saint-John Perse" in 1960. The museum is housed in one of the city's most beautifully restored colonial mansions, an urban chalet that features ornate friezes, voluted consoles, and wrought-iron galleries. Open windows allow breezes into the main parlor, which is furnished with bourgeois furniture of the time. In addition to many of the poet's personal effects, the museum boasts photographs documenting Guadeloupean life from the turn of the century through the 1930s; you can buy postcards of some of them in the museum gift shop for about $2.50. It's open Monday to Friday from 9am to 5pm, Saturday until noon.

The **Musée Schoelcher,** 24 Rue Peynier (☎ 590/82-08-04), tells the story of Victor Schoelcher, the key figure in the move to abolish slavery in Guadeloupe. The powerful exhibit, housed in a renovated mansion, includes a slave-ship model, a miniature guillotine, china from Bordeaux with scenes from Uncle Tom's Cabin, and racist caricatures published in Parisian journals. Particularly moving is an 1845 census document that lists slaves as nothing more than plantation animals. It's open Monday to Friday from 9am to 5pm; admission is about $1.50.

ON YOUR OWN: BEYOND WALKING DISTANCE

Guadeloupe is too large to tour in 1 day. You'll have to choose among Grande-Terre, northern Basse-Terre, and southern Basse-Terre.

GRANDE-TERRE

The **Aquarium de la Guadeloupe,** near the Bas du Fort Marina just east of Pointe-à-Pitre (☎ 590/90-92-38), is compact but has an impressive collection of exotic fish, corals, and sponges from the Caribbean and the Pacific. Come face-to-face with hugging sea horses, sleeping nurse sharks, and graceful sea turtles. Don't miss the polka-dot grouper known as *mérou de Grace Kelly.* Explanatory markers are in both French and English. The souvenir shop sells hand-painted folk art, jewelry, and fish- and sea-themed trinkets and T-shirts. It's open daily from 9am to 7pm; admission is $6 for adults, $3 for children under 12.

Along the northern coasts of Grande-Terre and Basse-Terre, **La Réserve Naturelle du Grand Cul-de-Sac Marin** is one of the Caribbean's largest marine reserves. It features mangroves, swamp forests, marine herbaceous habitats, and coral reefs. Fishing, boating, snorkeling, and swimming are permitted.

BASSE-TERRE

Basse-Terre's greatest attraction is the **Parc National de la Guadeloupe,** 74,000 acres of tropical rain forests, mountains, waterfalls, and ponds. UNESCO designated the park a World Biosphere Reserve in 1992. Its 200 miles of well-marked trails make it one of the best places for hiking in the entire Caribbean. Pick up information and maps at park entrances. Thirty minutes from Pointe-à-Pitre, **La Maison de la Forêt** (Forest House) on the Route de la Traversée, which bisects the park, is the starting point for easy walking tours of the surrounding mountainous rain forest. English-language trail guides describe the plant and animal life. Nearby, the **Cascade aux Ecrevisses** (Crayfish Falls), a slippery 10-minute walk from the roadside, is nice for a cooling dip. To the south, the steep hike to the three falls of **Les Chutes du Carbet** (Carbet Falls) is among Guadeloupe's most beautiful excursions (one of the falls drops 65 feet, the second 360 feet, and the third 410 feet). The middle fall, the most dramatic, is the easiest to reach. On the way up, you'll pass Le **Grand Etang** (Great Pond), a volcanic lake surrounded by tree-size ferns, giant vining philodendrons, wild bananas, orchids, anthuriums, and pineapples.

The park's single greatest feature is the still-simmering volcano **La Soufrière.** Ashes, mud, billowing smoke, and tremors in 1975 proved that the volcano is still active. Rising to 4,800 feet, it's flanked by banana plantations and lush vegetation. You can smell sulfurous fumes and feel the heat through the soil as steam spews from the fumaroles. The summit is like another planet: Steam rises from two active craters, large rocks form improbable shapes, and roars from the earth make it difficult to hear your companions. Go with an experienced guide. On your way down, don't miss La Maison du Volcan, the volcanology museum in St-Claude.

Gardeners should save a couple of hours to visit the **Domaine de Valombreuse** (☎ 590/ 95-50-50), a 6-acre floral park with exotic birds, spice gardens, and 300 species of tropical flowers. Created in 1990 and close to the town of Petit Bourg, the park also has a riverside restaurant and a superior gift shop. It's open daily from 9am to 6pm; admission is $6.

Parc Archéologique des Roches Gravées, on Basse-Terre's southern coast in the town of Trois-Rivières (☎ 590/92-91-88), has the West Indies' largest collection of Arawak Indian petroglyphs. The animal and human images etched on boulders date from between A.D. 300 and A.D. 400. Paths and stone stairways meander through the tranquil grounds, which include avocado, banana, cocoa, coffee, guava, and papaya trees. Explanatory brochures are in French and English. It's open daily from 8:30am to 5pm; admission is $1.50.

SHOPPING

Parlez-vous Chanel? Hermès? Saint Laurent? Baccarat? If you do, you'll find that Guadeloupe has good buys on almost anything French—scarves, perfumes, cosmetics, crystal, and other luxury goods—and many stores offer 20% discounts on items purchased with foreign currency, traveler's checks, or credit cards. You can also find local handcrafted items, madras cloth, spices, and rum at any of the local markets.

Right at Pointe-à-Pitre's port, the **Centre Saint-John Perse** has about 20 shops that frequently offer lower prices than can be found elsewhere in town. L'Artisan Parfumeur sells French and American perfumes as well as tropical scents. Suzanne Moulin features original African-inspired jewelry and crafts. Jean-Louis Padel specializes in gold jewelry. If you're looking for beach and resort wear, stop by Vanilla Boutique and Brasil Tropique. For something a little more provocative, look through the delicate lingerie at Soph't.

Rue Frébault, directly in front of the port, is one of the best shopping streets for duty-free items. **Rosébleu,** 5 Rue Frébault, offers china, crystal, and silver from Christoffle, Kosta Boda, and other high-end manufacturers. **Phoenicia,** 8 Rue Frébault and 121 bis Rue Frébault, has large selections of French perfumes and cosmetics. For men's and women's fashions, as well as for cosmetics and perfumes, browse through **Vendôme,** 8–10 Rue Frébault. Across the street at the intersection of Rues Frébault and Delgrès,

Geneviève Lethu is a French version of Williams-Sonoma, with everything for preparing and serving food. If you find yourself overdosing on froufrou, duck into **Tati,** France's answer to K-mart. It's at the intersection of Rues Frébault and Abbé Grégoire. This venerable old department-store chain, famous for its anti-fashion pink-plaid shopping bags, is great for inexpensive basics.

The French Antilles are where the *beguine* began, so if you're in the market for French Antillean music or French-language books there are a couple of large book and music stores across from each other on Rue Schoelcher: **Librairie Antillaise** at no. 41 and **Librairie Général** at no. 46. Each has a small selection of English-language books as well. CDs by local zouk musicians make great gifts and are the perfect way to relive your vacation once you're back home. Combining African rhythms and drums with a range of traditional Caribbean influences, Kassav' is the best-known zouk band.

Want to see a French shopping mall? The **Destrellan Commercial Center** in Baie-Mahault (just across the Rivière Salée on Basse-Terre) is the island's biggest. For shopaholics, it warrants a special trip. The 70 boutiques include Roger Albert, Martinique's famous parfumerie, a huge supermarket, and the Galerie de l'Artisanat, which showcases the work of the island's best artisans. Here you can buy dolls, lace-trimmed blouses, madras skirts, honeys, and preserved fruit.

BEACHES

Beaches on Grande-Terre's southern coast have soft white sand. Those on the Atlantic coast have wilder water and are less crowded. The convenient **Bas du Fort/Gosier hotel area** has mostly man-made strips of sand with rows of beach chairs, water-sports shops, and beach bars. Changing facilities and chairs are available for a nominal fee. The tiny, uninhabited **Ilet Gosier,** across Gosier Bay, is a quieter option popular with those who want to bare it all. You can take a fishing boat to the island from Gosier's waterfront. The wide strip of white sand at **Ste-Anne,** about 30 minutes from Pointe-à-Pitre, is lined with shops and food stands. **Plage Tarare,** just before the tip of Pointe des Châteaux, is the most popular nude beach. On Basse-Terre, the **Plage de Grande Anse** is a long expanse of ochre sand. A pleasant walk north from Deshaies, it offers changing facilities, water sports, boutiques, and outdoor snack bars. Farther south, the gray expanse of **Plage de Malendure** is alive with restaurants, bars, and open-air boutiques. It's the departure point for snorkeling and scuba trips to the Cousteau Reserve off Pigeon Island.

GREAT LOCAL RESTAURANTS & BARS

Many restaurants change their hours from time to time and from season to season. Call in advance for reservations and exact hours. Most, but not all, restaurants accept major credit cards. There are no **local beers** made on the island anymore, but locals drink Lorraine, made on the island of Martinique. Similarly, the **local rum,** Bielle, isn't made on Guadeloupe but on the offshore island of Marie-Galante.

ON GRANDE-TERRE

Chez Violetta-La Créole, Perinette, in Gosier (☎ 590/84-10-34), was established by the late Violetta Chaville, the island's legendary high priestess of Creole cookery. Her brother continues the family tradition, serving stuffed crabs, cod fritters, and conch fricasée. It's open daily from noon to 3:30pm.

ON BASSE-TERRE

In Deshaies, Lucienne Salcède's family has run **Le Karacoli** (☎ 590/28-41-17), one of Guadeloupe's best seaside restaurants, for almost 30 years. Sit on the beachfront terrace in the shadow of almond and palm trees and let the waves hypnotize you. In the distance, the island of Montserrat is visible. Try a rum aperitif or two, then bliss out on cod fritters, stuffed christophine, and avocado féroce before moving on to Creole lobster or conch. It's open daily from noon to 2pm; reservations are imperative on weekends.

Ice cream gets the final word. **Chez Monia** at 4 Rue Victor Hugues, off of Rue Nozières in Pointe-à-Pitre, serves ice cream that is pure heaven in the midday heat. Flavors (*aromes*) include pear, lemon, kiwi, guava, and champagne. Three scoops in a homemade waffle cone is about $2. Street vendors also offer superior ice cream, usually flavored with fresh vanilla and coconut, straight from their hand-cranked machines.

15 Jamaica

A favorite of North American honeymooners, Jamaica is a mountainous island rising from the sea 90 miles south of Cuba and about 100 miles west of Haiti. It's the third largest of the Caribbean islands, with some 4,400 square miles of predominantly green terrain, a mountain ridge peaking at 7,400 feet above sea level, and, on the north coast, many beautiful white-sand beaches rimming the clear blue sea.

One of the most densely populated nations in the Caribbean, with a vivid sense of its own identity (among other things, it's one of the most successful black democracies in the world), Jamaica has a history rooted in the plantation economy and some of the most turbulent and impassioned politics in the Western Hemisphere.

Most cruise ships dock at **Ocho Rios** on the lush northern coast, although others are increasingly going to the city of **Montego Bay** ("Mo Bay"), 67 miles to the west. Both ports offer comparable attractions and some of the same shopping possibilities. Don't try to do both ports in 1 day, however, since the 4-hour round-trip ride leaves time for only superficial visits to each.

CURRENCY   The unit of currency is the **Jamaican dollar,** designated by the same symbol as the U.S. dollar ($). For clarity, I use the symbol **J$** to denote prices in Jamaican dollars. There is no fixed rate of exchange. The exchange rate is J$38.80 to U.S.$1 (J$1 = U.S.3¢). Visitors can pay in U.S. dollars, but *be careful!* Always find out if a price is being quoted in Jamaican or U.S. dollars.

LANGUAGE   The official language is English, but most Jamaicans speak a richly nuanced patois that's primarily derived from English but includes elements of African, Spanish, Arawak, French, Chinese, Portuguese, and East Indian languages.

INFORMATION   In Ocho Rios, you'll find **tourist board offices** at the Ocean Village Shopping Centre in Ocho Rios (☎ 876/974-2582); open Monday to Friday from 9am to 5pm. There's also a small information stand right at the dock. In Montego Bay, it's at Cornwall Beach, St. James (☎ 876/952-4425). It's open Monday to Friday from 9am to 5pm. To get info before you go, call the **Jamaica Tourist Office** in New York (☎ 800/233-4582 or 212/856-9727; www.jamaica-travel.com).

CALLING FROM THE U.S.   When calling Jamaica from the United States, you need only dial a "1" before the numbers listed throughout this section.

OCHO RIOS

Once a small banana and fishing port, Ocho Rios is now Jamaica's cruise-ship capital, welcoming about two ships per day during high season. The bay is dominated on one side by a defunct bauxite-loading terminal (some say it loaded sugar or gypsum) and on the other by resort hotels with palm tree–fringed beaches.

Ocho Rios area has some of the Caribbean's most fabled resorts and Dunn's River is just a 5-minute taxi ride away, but the town itself is not much to see, though there are a few outdoor local markets within walking distance. Don't expect to shop in the markets without a lot of hassle and a lot of very pushy hawking of merchandise, some of which is likely to be *ganja,* locally grown marijuana. (Remember, although it may be readily available, it's still illegal.) That said, in recent years the government has made an effort to keep things saner. There's an army of blue-uniformed "resort patrol" officers on bikes helping to keep order. At the terminal is an information desk, bathrooms, a telephone center for faxing and postage, and an army of official taxis ready to take you where you want to go. If you want a taxi, it's safest to take one from the pier, and look for the JTB decal (for Jamaican Tourist Board), which insure they're licensed and trained.

Frommer's Favorite Ocho Rios Experiences

- **Tubing on the White River:** The River Tubing Safari excursion offered by most cruise lines is just a downright fantastic experience (see "Shore Excursions," below).
- **Riding horseback through the surf:** An excursion by horseback includes a stint along the beach and through the surf (see "Shore Excursions," below).
- **Riding a mountain bike to Dunn's River Falls:** This excursion takes you to the top of a mountain, where you hop on your mountain bike and soar downhill to the falls (see "Shore Excursions," below).

COMING ASHORE Most cruise ships dock at the port of Ocho Rios, near Dunn's River Falls. Only a mile away is one of the most important shopping areas, Ocean Village Shopping Centre; next door, on the second floor, is the main office of the Jamaican Tourist Board. To help you find your way to this shopping center from the cruise ship pier, the route is marked and called the "turtle walk."

There's a telephone center in the cruise terminal.

GETTING AROUND

BY TAXI Taxis are your best means of transport, but always agree on a fare before you get in. Your best and safest bet is to get a taxi from the pier; there will be lots of them waiting. Taxis licensed by the government display JTB decals, indicating they're official Jamaican Tourist Board taxis. All others are gypsy cabs, which you should avoid. Taxi dispatchers are at the pier and fixed rates are posted. Otherwise, if you're getting into a taxi from somewhere else on the island, always agree to the price before getting in.

BY RENTAL CAR I don't recommend renting a car here.

SHORE EXCURSIONS

Dunn's River Falls Tour ($44, 4 hours): These falls cascade 600 feet to the beach and are the most visited attraction in Jamaica, which means they're hopelessly overcrowded when a lot of cruise ships are in port (the hordes thin out in the afternoon, though, so

Frommer's Ratings: Ocho Rios					
	poor	fair	good	excellent	outstanding
Overall Experience				✓	
Shore Excursions					✓
Activities Close to Port				✓	
Beaches & Water Sports			✓		
Shopping		✓			
Dining/Bars			✓		

Jamaica

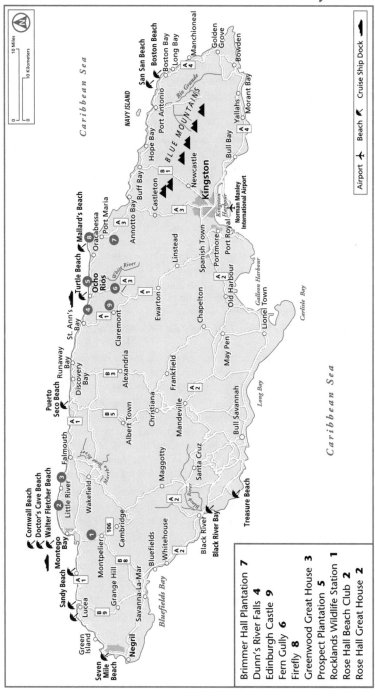

Brimmer Hall Plantation **7**
Dunn's River Falls **4**
Edinburgh Castle **9**
Fern Gully **6**
Firefly **8**
Greenwood Great House **3**
Prospect Plantation **5**
Rocklands Wildlife Station **1**
Rose Hall Beach Club **2**
Rose Hall Great House **2**

Airport ✈   Beach ⟋   Cruise Ship Dock ⟋

consider hopping a taxi there yourself later in the day). Tourists are allowed to climb the falls, and it's a ball to slip and slide your way up with the hundreds of others, forming a human chain of sorts. Don't forget your waterproof camera and your aquasocks (most lines will rent you aquasocks for an extra $5). This tour also visits Shaw Park Botanical Gardens, Fern Gully, and other local attractions, with time allocated for shopping. Wear a bathing suit under your clothes.

✪ **River Tubing Safari** ($59, 6 hours): This is one of the best excursions I've ever taken. After a scenic 30-minute-or-so van ride deep into the pristine jungles of Jamaica, the group of 20 or so passengers and a couple of guides get into the White River, sit back into big black inner tubes (they have wooden boards covering the bottom so your butt doesn't scrape the bottom of the river or any rocks you may run into), and begin the 3-mile glide downriver, passing by gorgeous, towering bamboo trees and other lush foliage. It's sometimes peaceful and sometimes exhilarating—especially when you hit the rapids!

✪ **Chukka Cove Horseback-Riding Excursion** ($79, 4 hours): Riders will love this trip, where after a 45-minute ride from the stables through fields you'll gallop along the beach and take your horse bareback into the surf for a thrilling ride through this beautiful sea. *Tip:* Take the morning ride and your horse is bound to be more energetic. (Also, if you book directly with **Chukka Cove,** ☎ **876-972-2506,** the same tour, including transportation there and back, runs $60. The Chukka folks also offer a 3¹/₂-hour mountain-biking tour; after being driven up picturesque Lillyfield Mountain, you glide down the 7-mile route drinking in the scenery along the way.)

✪ **Dunn's River Falls Mountain-Biking Trek** ($61–$69, 4 hours): After you're driven up to the summit of 1,500-foot-high Murphy Hill, above Ocho Rios, hop on your mountain bike, strap on your helmet, and enjoy a mostly downhill ride through the natural limestone and ferns, passing the eight springs that form Dunn's River Falls. Once at the bottom, you'll have time to climb the falls before heading back to the ship.

Countryside/Plantation Bus Tour ($54, 5 hours): This tour includes a drive through the Jamaican countryside to Brimmer Hall Plantation, a working plantation property with a Great House and tropical crops, such as bananas and pimiento. On the way back, you pass the estates once occupied by Noël Coward and Ian Fleming. Often a stop at Dunn's River Falls is tacked on to the end of the tour. Another variation on this tour ($40, 4–5 hours) stops at the Prospect Plantation instead of Brimmer Hall.

Snorkeling Excursion ($31, 2 hours): A coral reef near the cruise pier is one of the best places in the area for snorkeling, with panoramic underwater visibility. You can also take a 1-hour cruise on a glass-bottom boat for a look at underwater Jamaica.

Martha Brae River Rafting ($50, 5 hours): This tour, in 30-foot, two-seat bamboo rafts, is traditionally one of the most heavily booked tours from both Ocho Rios or Montego Bay. However, most people find it disappointing. I'd recommend the tubing and bicycling excursions instead.

ON YOUR OWN: WITHIN WALKING DISTANCE

Aside from some markets (see "Shopping," below), there's little to do close to the docks.

Insider Tip

If you step inside of the small cruise "terminal" in Ocho Rios you'll find a shop called **Cruise Booze,** which sets up a tasting station where you can sample a ton of different rums, including a 150-proof white rum.

ON YOUR OWN: BEYOND WALKING DISTANCE

South of Ocho Rios, **Fern Gully** was originally a riverbed. Today, the main A3 road winds up some 700 feet through a rain forest filled with wild ferns, hardwood trees, and lianas. For the botanist, there are hundreds of varieties of ferns, and for the less plant-minded, roadside stands sell fruits and vegetables, carved-wood souvenirs, and basketwork. The road runs for about 4 miles.

Near Lydford, southwest of Ocho Rios, are the remains of **Edinburgh Castle.** This was the lair of one of Jamaica's most infamous murderers, a Scot named Lewis Hutchinson who used to shoot passersby and toss their bodies into a deep pit. The authorities got wind of his activities, and although he tried to escape by canoe, he was captured by the navy and hanged. Rather proud of his achievements (evidence of at least 43 murders was found), he left £100 and instructions for a memorial to be built. It never was, but the 1763 castle ruins remain. To get to Lydford, take the A3 south until you reach a small intersection directly north of Walkers Wood, and then follow the signposts west.

If you're here on a Thursday, the 1817 **Brimmer Hall Estate,** Port Maria, St. Mary's (☎ 876/974-2244), 21 miles east of Ocho Rios, is an ideal place to spend part of the day. Brimmer Hall is a working plantation where you're driven around in a tractor-drawn jitney to see the tropical fruit trees and coffee plants. Knowledgeable guides tell you about the processes necessary to produce the fine fruits of the island. Afterward, you can relax beside the pool and sample a wide variety of drinks, including an interesting one called "Wow!" The Plantation Tour Eating House offers typical Jamaican dishes for lunch. There's also a souvenir shop with a good selection of ceramics, art, straw goods, woodcarvings, rums, liqueurs, and cigars.

A mile from the center of Ocho Rios, at an elevation of 420 feet, **Coyaba River Garden and Museum,** Shaw Park Road (☎ 876/974-6235), was built on the grounds of the former Shaw Park plantation. The Spanish-style museum displays artifacts from the Arawak, Spanish, and English settlements in the area. The gardens are filled with native flora, a cut-stone courtyard, and fountains.

At the 600-foot **Dunn's River Falls,** on the A3 (☎ 876/974-2857), you can relax on the beach, splash in the waters at the bottom of the falls, or climb with a guide to the top and drop into the cool pools higher up between the cascades of water. The beach restaurant provides snacks and drinks, and dressing rooms are available. If you're planning to climb the falls, wear aquasocks or sneakers to protect your feet from the sharp rocks and to prevent slipping. At the prettiest part of Dunn's River Falls, known as the Laughing Waters, scenes were shot for the James Bond classics *Dr. No* and *Live and Let Die.*

Three miles east of Ocho Rios along the A3, adjoining the 18-hole Prospect Mini Golf Course, working **Prospect Plantation** (☎ 876/994-1058) is often a shore-excursion stop. On your leisurely ride by covered jitney you'll readily see why this section of Jamaica is called "the garden parish of the island." You'll see pimiento (allspice), banana, cassava, sugarcane, coffee, cocoa, coconut, pineapple, and the famous leucaena "Tree of Life," plus Jamaica's first hydroelectric plant. Horseback riding is available on three scenic trails. The rides vary from 1 to 2¼ hours; you'll need to book a horse 1 hour in advance.

Firefly, Grants Pen, 20 miles east of Ocho Rios above Oracabessa (☎ 876/997-7201), was the home of Sir Noël Coward and his longtime companion, Graham Payn, who, as executor of Coward's estate, donated it to the Jamaica National Heritage Trust. The recently restored house is as it was on the day Sir Noël died in 1973.

Port Tip

Some so-called **duty-free prices** are indeed lower than stateside prices, but then the Jamaican government hits you with a 10% "General Consumption Tax."

SHOPPING

In general, the shopping is better at Montego Bay than here, but if you're not going to Montego, wander around the Ocho Rios **crafts markets.** Literally hundreds of Jamaicans pour into Ocho Rios hoping to peddle something, often something homemade, to cruise ship passengers. Prepare yourself for aggressive selling and fierce haggling. Every vendor asks too much for an item at first, which gives them the leeway to negotiate the price. Shopping in Ocho Rios may not be the most fun you've ever had. You might want to skip it.

There are a handful of main shopping plazas in town, including the **Ocho Rios Craft Park,** a complex of some 150 stalls, **Soni's Plaza,** and the **Taj Mahel.** Word has it Ocho Rios will debut a new craft market near Soni's by late 2000. An eager seller will weave a hat or a basket while you wait, or you can buy from the mixture of ready-made hats, hampers, handbags, place mats, and lampshades. **Coconut Grove Shopping Plaza** is a collection of low-slung shops linked by walkways and shrubs. The merchandise consists mainly of local craft items. **Island Plaza** shopping complex is right in the heart of Ocho Rios. You can find some of the best Jamaican art here, all paintings by local artists. You can also purchase local handmade crafts (be prepared to do some haggling), carvings, ceramics, even kitchenware, and the inevitable T-shirts.

To find local handcrafts or art without the hassle of the markets, head for **Beautiful Memories,** 9 Island Plaza, which has a limited but representative sampling of Jamaican art, as well as local crafts, pottery, woodwork, and hand-embroidered items.

If you'd like to flee the hustle and bustle of the Ocho Rios bazaars, take a taxi to **Harmony Hall,** Tower Isle, on the A3, 4 miles east of Ocho Rios. One of Jamaica's Great Houses, the restored house is now a gallery selling paintings and other works by Jamaican artists. The arts and crafts here are high-quality—not the usual junky assortment you might find at the beach.

BEACHES

Many visitors to Ocho Rios head for the beach. The most overcrowded is **Mallards Beach** at the Jamaica Grand Hotel, shared by hotel guests and cruise ship passengers. Locals may steer you to the good and less-crowded **Turtle Beach,** southwest of Mallards. You might also want to check out the big **James Bond Beach** in Oracabessa, at the east end of Ocho Rios.

SPORTS

GOLF   Super Club's Runaway Golf Course, at Runaway Beach near Ocho Rios on the north coast (☎ **876/973-2561**), is one of the better courses in the area, although it's nowhere near the courses at Montego Bay. Cruise ship passengers should call ahead and book playing times. The charge is about $60 for 18 holes in winter. Players can rent carts and clubs. **Sandals Golf & Country Club,** at Ocho Rios (☎ **876/975-0119**), is also open to the public. The course lies about 700 feet above sea level. To get there from the center of Ocho Rios, travel along the main bypass for 2 miles until Mile End Road; turn right at the Texaco station there, and drive for 5 miles.

GREAT LOCAL RESTAURANTS & BARS

A favorite **local beer** is Red Stripe; a favorite **local rum** is Appleton.

Ocho Rios Jerk Centre, on DaCosta Drive, serves up lip-smacking jerk pork and chicken. Don't expect anything fancy. Just come for platters of meat. For a special lunch out, **Almond Tree Restaurant,** 87 Main St., in the Hibiscus Lodge Hotel, 3 blocks from the Ocho Rios Mall (☎ **876/974-2813**), is a two-tiered patio restaurant overlooking the Caribbean, with a tree growing through its roof. Lobster thermidor is the most delectable item on the menu. **Evita's Italian Restaurant,** Eden Bower Road, 5 minutes south of Ocho Rios (☎ **876/974-2333**), is run by a flamboyant Italian and is the premier Italian restaurant in Ocho Rios. It serves pastas and excellent fish dishes as well as unique ones like jerk spaghetti and pasta Viagra (don't ask). Lunch with drinks runs about $15. **Little Pub Restaurant,** 59 Main St. (☎ **876/974-2324**), is an indoor-outdoor pub serving such items as grilled kingfish, stewed snapper, barbecued chicken, and the inevitable and overpriced lobster. The cooking is competent and the atmosphere very casual. **Parkway Restaurant,** 60 DaCosta Dr. (☎ **876/974-2667**), couldn't be plainer or less pretentious, but it's always packed. Hungry diners are fed Jamaican-style chicken, curried goat, sirloin steak, fillet of red snapper, and to top it off, banana cream pie. Lobster and fresh fish are usually featured also. The food is straightforward, honest, and affordable.

When you're seated at the beautifully laid tables at the **Plantation Inn Restaurant,** in the Plantation Inn, Main Street (☎ **876/974-5601**), you'll think you've arrived at Tara in *Gone With the Wind.* Jamaican specialties help spice up the continental cuisine in this romantic restaurant.

There are probably more great rum bars on Jamaica than churches. Among the best is **Bibi Bips** in Ocho Rios.

MONTEGO BAY

Montego Bay is sometimes less of a hassle than the port at Ocho Rios, and has better beaches, shopping, and restaurants, as well as some of the best golf courses in the Caribbean, superior even to those on Puerto Rico and the Bahamas. Like Ocho Rios, Montego Bay has its crime, traffic, and annoyance, but there's much more to see and do here.

There's little of interest in the town of Montego Bay itself except shopping, although the good stuff in the environs is easily reached by taxi or shore excursion. Getting around from place to place is one of the major difficulties here, as it is in Barbados. Whatever you want to visit seems to be in yet another direction.

Frommer's Favorite Montego Bay Experiences

In addition to these, my favorite shore excursions from Ocho Rios are also offered from Montego Bay.

- **Visiting Rocklands Wildlife Station:** This is the place to go if you want to have a Jamaican doctor bird perch on your finger or feed small doves and finches from your hand (see "On Your Own: Beyond Walking Distance," below).

Frommer's Ratings: Montego Bay					
	poor	fair	good	excellent	outstanding
Overall Experience				✓	
Shore Excursions					✓
Activities Close to Port				✓	
Beaches & Water Sports			✓		
Shopping			✓		
Dining/Bars			✓		

• **Spend a day at the Rose Hall Beach Club:** With a secluded beach, crystal-clear water, a full restaurant, two beach bars, live entertainment, and more, it's well worth the $8 admission (see "Beaches," below).

COMING ASHORE Montego Bay has a modern cruise dock with lots of conveniences, including duty-free stores, telephones, tourist information, and plenty of taxis to meet all ships.

GETTING AROUND

BY TAXI If you don't book a shore excursion, a taxi is the way to get around. See "Getting Around" under "Ocho Rios," above, for taxi information, as the same conditions apply to Mo Bay.

BY MOTOR SCOOTER **Montego Honda/Bike Rentals,** 21 Gloucester Ave. (☎ 876/952-4984), rents Hondas for about $35 a day, plus a $300 deposit.

SHORE EXCURSIONS

Also see "Shore Excursions" under "Ocho Rios," above.

Croydon Plantation Tour ($55, 4–5 hours): Twenty-five miles from Montego Bay, the plantation can be visited on a half-day tour on Tuesday, Wednesday, and Friday. Included in the price are round-trip transportation from the dock, a tour of the plantation, a tasting of varieties of pineapple and other tropical fruits in season, and a barbecued chicken lunch.

ON YOUR OWN: WITHIN WALKING DISTANCE

Nothing really. You'll have to take a taxi to the town for shopping or sign up for an excursion.

ON YOUR OWN: BEYOND WALKING DISTANCE

These attractions can be reached by taxi from the cruise dock.

Charging a steep admission, the most famous Great House in Jamaica is the legendary ✪ **Rose Hall Great House,** Rose Hall Highway (☎ 876/953-2323), located 9 miles east of Montego Bay along the coast road. The house was built about 2 centuries ago by John Palmer, and gained notoriety from the doings of "Infamous Annie" Palmer, wife of the builder's grandnephew, who supposedly dabbled in witchcraft and took slaves as lovers, killing them when they bored her. Annie also was said to have murdered several of her husbands while they slept, and eventually suffered the same fate herself. The house, now privately owned by U.S.-based philanthropists, has been restored. **Annie's Pub** sits on the ground floor.

On a hillside perch 14 miles east of Montego Bay and 7 miles west of Falmouth, **Greenwood Great House,** on the A1 (☎ 876/953-1077), is even more interesting to some than Rose Hall. Erected in the early 19th century, the Georgian-style building was from 1780 to 1800 the residence of Richard Barrett, a relative of Elizabeth Barrett Browning. On display are the family's library, portraits of the family, and rare musical instruments.

It's a unique experience to have a Jamaican doctor bird perch on your finger to drink syrup, or to feed small doves and finches from your hand, or simply to watch dozens of birds flying in for the evening at **Rocklands Wildlife Station,** Anchovy, St. James (☎ 876/952-2009). Lisa Salmon, known as the "Bird Lady of Anchovy," established this sanctuary. It's perfect for nature lovers and bird watchers, but don't take children 5 and under, as they tend to worry the birds. Rocklands is about a mile outside Anchovy on the road from Montego Bay. It's open daily from 2:30 to 5pm, and charges an admission of J$300 (U.S.$8.55).

SHOPPING

The main shopping areas are at **Montego Freeport,** within easy walking distance of the pier; **City Centre,** where most of the duty-free shops are, aside from those at the large hotels; and **Holiday Village Shopping Centre.**

Old Fort Craft Park, a shopping complex with nearly 200 vendors licensed by the Jamaica Tourist Board, fronts Howard Cooke Boulevard up from Gloucester Avenue in the heart of Montego Bay, on the site of Fort Montego. With a varied assortment of handcrafts, this is browsing country. You'll see a selection of wall hangings, handwoven straw items, and hand-carved wood sculptures, and you can even get your hair braided. Vendors can be extremely aggressive, so be prepared for some major hassles, as well as some serious negotiation. Persistent bargaining on your part will lead to substantial discounts.

You can find the best selection of handmade Jamaican souvenirs at the **Crafts Market,** near Harbour Street in downtown Montego Bay. Straw hats and bags, wooden platters, straw baskets, musical instruments, beads, carved objects, and toys are all available here. That "jipijapa" hat will come in handy if you're going to be out in the island sun.

One of the newer and more intriguing places for shopping is a mall, **Half Moon Plaza,** set on the coastal road about 8 miles east of the commercial center of Montego Bay. This upscale minimall caters to the shopping and gastronomic needs of residents of one of the region's most elegant hotels, the Half Moon Club. Also on the premises are a bank and about 25 shops arranged around a central courtyard and purveying a wide choice of carefully selected merchandise.

Ambiente Art Gallery, 9 Fort St., stocks local artwork. At **Blue Mountain Gems Workshop,** at the Holiday Village Shopping Centre, you can take a tour of the workshops to see the process from raw stone to the finished product available for purchase later. **Caribatik Island Fabrics,** Rock Wharf on the Luminous Lagoon, Falmouth (2 miles east of Falmouth on the north coast road), is the private living and work domain of Keith Chandler, who creates a full range of batik fabrics, scarves, garments, and wall hangings, some patterned after such themes as Jamaica's "doctor bird." **Klass Kraft Leather Sandals,** 44 Fort St., offers sandals and leather accessories made on location by a team of Jamaican craftspeople. **Things Jamaican,** 44 Fort St., stocks Jamaican rums and liqueurs, jerk products, sculpture, handwoven Jamaican baskets, and more.

BEACHES

Cornwall Beach is a long stretch of white-sand beach with dressing cabanas. Daily admission is about $2 for adults, $1 for children. A bar and cafeteria offer refreshment.

Doctor's Cave Beach, on Gloucester Avenue across from the Doctor's Cave Beach Hotel, helped launch Mo Bay as a resort in the 1940s. Admission to the beach is about $2 for adults, half price for children up to 12. Dressing rooms, chairs, umbrellas, and rafts are available.

One of the premier beaches of Jamaica, **Walter Fletcher Beach** in the heart of Mo Bay, is noted for its tranquil waters, which make it a particular favorite for families with children. Changing rooms are available, and lifeguards are on duty. There's also a restaurant for lunch. The beach is open daily, with an admission price of about $1 for adults, half price for children.

You may want to skip the public beaches and head for the ✪ **Rose Hall Beach Club** (☎ **876/953-2323**), lying on the main road 11 miles east of Montego Bay. It sits on half a mile of secure, secluded, white sandy beach, with crystal-clear water. The club offers a full restaurant, two beach bars, a covered pavilion, an open-air dance area, showers, rest rooms, and changing facilities, plus beach volleyball courts, various beach games, and a full water-sports activities program. There's also live entertainment. Admission fees are about $8 for adults, $5 for children. The club is open daily from 10am to 6pm.

SPORTS

GOLF   Wyndham Rose Hall Golf & Beach Resort, Rose Hall (☎ 876/953-2650), has a noted course with an unusual and challenging seaside and mountain layout. The 300-foot-high 13th tee offers a rare panoramic view of the sea and the roof of the hotel, and the 15th green is next to a 40-foot waterfall, once featured in a James Bond movie. A fully stocked pro shop, a clubhouse, and a professional staff are among the amenities.

The excellent, regal course at the **Tryall** (☎ 876/956-5660), 12 miles from Montego Bay, has often been the site of major golf tournaments, including the Jamaica Classic Annual and the Johnnie Walker Tournament.

Half Moon, at Rose Hall (☎ 876/953-2560), features a championship course—designed by Robert Trent Jones, Sr.—that opened in 1961. The course has manicured and diversely shaped greens.

Ironshore Golf & Country Club, Ironshore, St. James, Montego Bay (☎ 876/953-2800), a well-known, par-72, 18-hole golf course, is privately owned but open to the public.

HORSEBACK RIDING   The best horseback riding is offered by the helpful staff at the **Rocky Point Riding Stables,** at the Half Moon Club, Rose Hall, Montego Bay (☎ 876/953-2286). The stables, built in the colonial Caribbean style in 1992, are the most beautiful in Jamaica.

RAFTING   Mountain Valley Rafting, 31 Gloucester Ave. (☎ 876/956-0020), offers excursions on the Great River. They depart from the Lethe Plantation, about 10 miles south of Montego Bay. Bamboo rafts are designed for two, with a raised dais to sit on. In some cases, a small child can accompany two adults on the same raft, although caution should be exercised. Ask about pickup by taxi at the end of the run. A half-day experience includes transportation to and from the pier, an hour's rafting, lunch, a garden tour of the Lethe property, and a taste of Jamaican liqueur.

GREAT LOCAL RESTAURANTS & BARS

The **Pork Pit,** 27 Gloucester Ave., near Walter Fletcher Beach (☎ 876/952-1046), is the best place to go for the famous Jamaican jerk pork and jerk chicken. Many beachgoers come over here for a big lunch. Picnic tables encircle the building, and everything is open-air and informal. Order half a pound of jerk meat with a baked yam or baked potato and a bottle of Red Stripe beer. Prices are very reasonable.

The **Georgian House,** 2 Orange St. (☎ 876/952-0632), brings grand cuisine and an elegant setting to the heart of town. The lunch menu is primarily Jamaican. **The Native Restaurant,** Gloucester Ave. (☎ 876/979-2769), continues to win converts with such appetizers as jerk reggae chicken, ackee and saltfish (an acquired taste), smoked marlin, and steamed fish. Boonoonoonŏos, billed as "A Taste of Jamaica," is a big platter with a little bit of everything, including meats and several kinds of fish and vegetables. **Pier 1,** Howard Cooke Boulevard (☎ 876/952-2452), features—among other dishes—fresh lobster, Jamaican soups such as conch chowder or red pea, the juiciest hamburgers in town, and an excellent steak sandwich with mushrooms.

16 Key West

No other port of call offers such a sweeping choice of fine dining, easy-to-reach attractions, street entertainment, and roguish bars as does this heavy-drinking, fun-loving town at the very end of the fabled Florida Keys. It's America's southernmost city at Mile Marker 0, where U.S. Route 1 begins, but it feels more like a colorful Caribbean outpost.

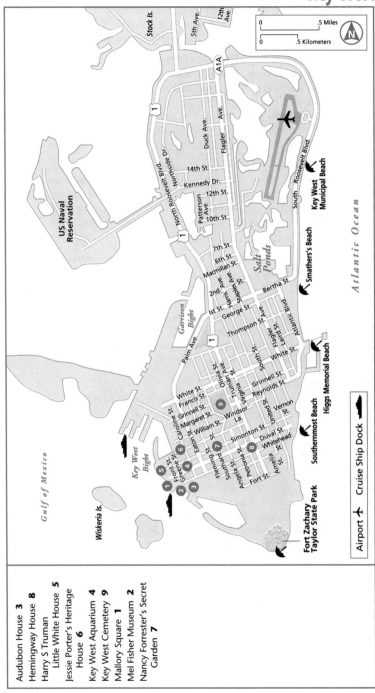

Key West

0 .5 Miles
0 .5 Kilometers

Stock Is.

5th Ave.
12th Ave.

A1A

US Naval
Reservation

North Roosevelt Blvd.
Northside Dr.

Duck Ave.
Flagler Ave.

14th St.
Kennedy Dr.
12th St.
Patterson Ave.
10th St.

South Roosevelt Blvd.

Key West
Municipal Beach

Atlantic Ocean

Salt Ponds

7th St.
6th St.
Macmillan St.
2nd Ave.
1st Ave.
Harris Ave.
Staples Ave.
Bertha St.

Smathers's Beach

Garrison Bight

1st St.
George St.
Thompson St.
Flagler St.
Laird St.
Atlantic Blvd.

Palm Ave.

White St.

Higgs Memorial Beach

Gulf of Mexico

White St.
Francis St.
Olivia St.
Truman Ave.
South St.
Virginia St.
Grinnell St.
Reynolds St.
Vernon St.

Grinnell St.
Margaret St.
Caroline St.
Front St.
Greene St.
Eaton St.
William St.
Windsor La.

9

Southernmost Beach

Key West Bight

Wisteria Is.

5
1 2 3 4
6

Fleming St.
Southard St.
Angela St.
Petronia St.
Amelia St.
Fort St.
Simonton St.
United St.
Duval St.
Whitehead St.

7

8

Cruise Ship Dock

Fort Zachary
Taylor State Park

Airport ✈ Cruise Ship Dock

Audubon House **3**
Hemingway House **8**
Harry S Truman
  Little White House **5**
Jessie Porter's Heritage
  House **6**
Key West Aquarium **4**
Key West Cemetery **9**
Mallory Square **1**
Mel Fisher Museum **2**
Nancy Forrester's Secret
  Garden **7**

You have only a day, so flee the busy cruise docks and touristy Duval Street for a walk through hidden and more secluded byways, such as Olivia or William streets. Or you might want to spend your day playing golf or going diving or snorkeling.

Frommer's Favorite Key West Experiences

• **Viewing the sunset from Mallory Dock:** More than just a sunset, it's a daily carnival. If your ship is in port late enough, don't miss it (see "On Your Own: Within Walking Distance," below).

• **Taking a catamaran party cruise:** The popular Fury catamarans take passengers snorkeling and then back to shore, with music, booze, and a good time (see "Shore Excursions," below).

COMING ASHORE Ships dock at Mallory Square, Old Town's most important plaza, or at nearby Truman Annex, a 5-minute stroll away. Both are on the Gulf of Mexico side of the island. Except for esoteric pockets, virtually everything is at your doorstep, including the two main arteries, Duval Street and Whitehead Street, each filled with shops, bars, restaurants, and the town's most important attractions.

CURRENCY U.S. dollars are used here.

LANGUAGE Speak English here. You're in the U.S. of A., remember.

INFORMATION The Greater Key West Chamber of Commerce, 402 Wall St. (☎ 305/294-5988), lies near the cruise ship docks. This helpful agency answers questions about local activities, distributes free maps, and assists in arranging tours and fishing trips. Ask for *Pelican Path,* a free walking guide that documents the history and architecture of Old Town, and *Solares Hill's Walking and Biking Guide to Old Key West,* which contains a bunch of walking tours. To get info before you go, call the **Tourism Board** at ☎ 800/733-5397 or log on to the Web site at www.seekeys.com.

GETTING AROUND

The island is only 4 miles long and 2 miles wide, so getting around is easy. Hundreds of people who live here own bicycles instead of cars. The most popular sights, including the Hemingway House and the Harry S Truman Little White House, are within walking distance of the cruise docks, so you're hardly dependent on public transportation unless you want to go to the beaches on the island's Atlantic side.

BY TAXI Island taxis operate around the clock, but are small and not suited for sightseeing tours. They will, however, take you to the beach and arrange to pick you up at a certain time. You can call one of four different services: **Florida Keys Taxi** (☎ 305/294-2227), **Maxi-Taxi Sun Cab System** (☎ 305/294-2222), **Pink Cabs** (☎ 305/296-6666), or **Island Transportation Services** (☎ 305/296-1800). Prices are uniform; the meter starts at about $1.40, and adds 35¢ per quarter mile.

Frommer's Ratings: Key West					
	poor	fair	good	excellent	outstanding
Overall Experience				✓	
Shore Excursions				✓	
Activities Close to Port					✓
Beaches & Water Sports		✓			
Shopping			✓		
Dining/Bars				✓	

BY TRAM   The tram/trolley-car tours are the best way to see Key West in a short time. In fact, the **Conch Tour Train** (☎ 305/294-5161) is Key West's most famous tourist attraction. It's a narrated 90-minute tour, going up and down all the most interesting streets and commenting on 60 local sites, giving you lots of lore about the town. The depot is located at Mallory Square near the cruise ship docks. Trains depart every 30 minutes. The trip is nonstop, unlike tours on the Old Town Trolley (see below), which allow you to get on and off. Most ships sell this as an excursion, but you can also do it on your own; departures are daily from 9am to 4:30pm and cost about $17 for adults, $8 for children ages 4 to 12 (3 and under free).

Old Town Trolley is less popular than the Conch Tour Train, but appeals to visitors who want more flexibility since it lets you get off and explore a particular attraction, and then reboard another of its trains later. Professional guides spin tall tales about Key West throughout the 90-minute route. The trolleys operate 7 days a week from 9am to 4:30pm, with departures every 30 minutes from convenient spots throughout town. You can board the trolley near the cruise docks (look for signposts). Call ☎ **305/296-6688** for more information. Tours cost about $18 for adults, $9 for children ages 4 to 12, free for children under 4.

BY MOTOR SCOOTER OR BICYCLE   One of the largest and best places to rent a bicycle or motorbike is **Keys Moped and Scooter Rental,** 523 Truman Ave., about a block off Duval Street (☎ **305/294-0399**). Cruise ship passengers might opt for a 3-hour motor-scooter rental for about $12, or all day for $14. One-speed, big-wheeled "beach-cruiser" bicycles with soft seats and big baskets for toting beachwear rent for about $4 for 8 hours.

BY BUS   The cheapest way to see the island is by bus, which costs only about 75¢ for adults, and 35¢ for senior citizens and children 6 years and older (kids 5 and under ride free).

BY RENTAL CAR   Walking or cycling is better than renting a car here, but if you do rent, try **Hertz,** 3491 S. Roosevelt Blvd. (☎ **800/654-3131** or 305/294-1039), **Tropical Rent-a-Car,** 1300 Duval St. (☎ **305/294-8136**), or **Enterprise Rent-a-Car,** 3031 N. Roosevelt Blvd. (☎ **800/325-8007** or 305/292-0222). If you're visiting in winter, make reservations at least a week in advance.

SHORE EXCURSIONS

In Key West, it's definitely not necessary to take an organized excursion since everything is so accessible by foot or tram. If you like the services of a guide, most lines offer walking tours. Also, the trams and trolleys have running narratives about Key West history and culture.

✪ **Catamaran Party Cruises** ($38, 3 hours): The popular Fury catamarans take passenger to a reef for some snorkeling and then finish the trip back to shore with music, booze, and a good time.

Guided Bike Tour ($25, 2 hours): Get the lowdown on Key West's multifaceted history and quirky culture while peddling along a 2¹/₂-mile route.

TOURING THROUGH LOCAL OPERATORS

Glass-Bottomed Boat Tours: The MV *Discovery* (☎ **305/293-0099**), a 78-foot motor craft, has 20 large viewing windows (angled at 45°) set below the water line. Passengers can view reef life from safety and comfort below deck. Two-hour tours depart daily at 10:30am, 1:30, and 6pm from Land's End Village & Marina at the western end of Margaret Street, a 6-block walk from the cruise ship docks. The cost is about $20.

ON YOUR OWN: WITHIN WALKING DISTANCE

If the lines aren't too long, you'll want to see the Harry S Truman Little White House and the Hemingway House, but don't feel obligated. If you want to see and capture the real-life mood and charm of Key West in a short time, leave the most-visited attractions to your fellow cruise ship passengers and head for the ones below marked with a star. Each of the sights below is an easy walk from the docks.

Audubon House, 205 Whitehead St., at Greene Street (☎ 305/294-2116), is dedicated to the 1832 Key West sojourn of the famous naturalist John James Audubon. The ornithologist didn't live in this three-story building, but it's filled with his engravings. The main reason to visit is to see how wealthy sailors lived in Key West in the 19th century, and the lush tropical gardens surrounding the house are worth the price of admission.

Harry S Truman Little White House, 111 Front St. (☎ 305/294-9911), the president's former vacation home, is part of the 103-acre Truman Annex near the cruise ship docks. The small house, which takes less than an hour to visit, affords a glimpse of a president at play.

There may be long lines at the **Hemingway House,** 907 Whitehead St. (☎ 305/294-1575), where "Papa" lived with his second wife, Pauline. Here, in the studio annex, Hemingway wrote *For Whom the Bell Tolls* and *A Farewell to Arms,* among others. Hemingway had some 50 polydactyl (many-toed) cats, whose descendants still live on the grounds.

Jessie Porter Newton, known as "Miss Jessie" to her friends, was the grande dame of Key West, inviting the celebrities of her day to her house, including Tennessee Williams and her girlhood friend Gloria Swanson, as well as family friend Robert Frost, who stayed in a cottage out back. Today, you can cross her once-hallowed grounds, look at the antique-filled rooms, and inspect her mementos and the exotic treasures collected by six generations of the Porter family at ✪ **Jessie Porter's Heritage House and Robert Frost Cottage,** 410 Caroline St. (☎ 305/296-3575).

On the waterfront at Mallory Square, the **Key West Aquarium,** 1 Whitehead St. (☎ 305/296-2051), in operation since 1932, was the first tourist attraction built in the Florida Keys. The aquarium's special feature is a "touch tank," where you can feel a horseshoe crab, sea squirt, sea urchin, starfish, and, of course, a conch, the town's mascot and symbol. It's worth taking a tour, as the guides are both knowledgeable and entertaining, and you'll get to pet a shark, if that's your idea of a good time.

The ✪ **Key West Cemetery** (☎ 305/296-2175), 21 prime acres in the heart of the historic district, is the island's foremost offbeat attraction. The main entrance is at Margaret Street and Passover Lane. Stone-encased caskets rest on top of the earth because graves dug into the ground would hit the water table. There's also a touch of humor here: One gravestone proclaims "I Told You I Was Sick," and another says, "At Least I Know Where He Is Sleeping Tonight."

Treasure hunter Mel Fisher, who passed away not long ago, used to wear heavy gold necklaces, which he liked to say were worth a king's ransom. He wasn't exaggerating. After long and risky dives, Fisher and his associates plucked more than $400 million in gold and silver from the shipwrecked Spanish galleons *Santa Margarita* and *Nuestra Señora de Atocha,* which were lost on hurricane-tossed seas some 350 years ago. Now this extraordinary long-lost Spanish jewelry, doubloons, and silver and gold bullion are displayed at the ✪ **Mel Fisher Maritime Heritage Society Museum,** 200 Greene St. (☎ 305/294-2633), a true treasure trove near the docks.

Nancy Forrester's Secret Garden, 1 Free School Lane, off Simonton between Southard and Fleming streets (☎ 305/294-0015), is the most lavish and verdant garden in town. Some 130 to 150 species of palms, palmettos, climbing vines, and ground covers are planted here, creating a blanket of lush, tropical magic. It's a 20-minute walk from the docks, near Key West's highest point, Solares Hill. Pick up a sandwich at a deli and picnic at tables in the garden.

If your ship leaves late enough, you can take in a unique local celebration: ✪ **viewing the sunset from Mallory Dock.** Sunset-watching is good fun all over the world, but in Key West it's been turned into a carnival-like, almost pagan celebration—a "blazing festival of joy," some call it. People from all over the world begin to crowd Mallory Square even before the sun starts to fall, bringing the place alive with entertainment—everything from a string band to a unicyclist wriggling free of a straitjacket. A juggler might delight the crowd with a machete and a flaming stick. The main entertainment, however, is that massive fireball falling out of view, which is always greeted with hysterical applause.

ON YOUR OWN: BEYOND WALKING DISTANCE

Nothin'. That's the beauty of Key West: Everything worthwhile is accessible by foot.

SHOPPING

Shopping by cruise ship passengers has become a local joke in Key West. Within a 12-block radius of Old Town, you'll find mostly tawdry and outrageously overpriced merchandise—but if you're in the market for some Key West kitsch, this is the neighborhood for you.

Among the less-kitschy alternatives, a few stand out much farther along Duval Street, the main drag leading to the Atlantic, and on hidden back streets. You reach all these stores from the cruise ship docks in a 15-to-20-minute stroll.

Cavanaugh's, 520 Front St., is a treasure trove of merchandise from all over the world—it's like wandering through the souks in the dusty back alleys of North Africa. **Haitian Art Company,** 600 Frances St., claims to inventory the largest collection of Haitian paintings in the United States. Prices range from $15 to $5,000. **Key West Aloe, Inc.,** 524 Front St. or 540 Greene St., is aloe, aloe, and more aloe; the shop's inventory includes shaving cream, aftershave lotion, sunburn ointments, and fragrances for men and women based on such tropical essences as hibiscus, frangipani, and white ginger. **Key West Hand Print Fashions and Fabrics,** 201 Simonton St., sells bold, tropical prints—handprinted scarves with coordinated handbags and rack after rack of busily patterned sundresses and cocktail dresses that will make you look jaunty on the deck of an ocean liner. **Key West Island Bookstore,** 513 Fleming St., is well stocked in books on Key West and has Florida's largest collection of works by and about Hemingway. In the rear is a rare-book section where you may want to browse, if not buy. **Michael,** 400C Duval St., stocks coins from sunken wrecks and the Middle East, mounted in various settings.

BEACHES

Beaches are not too compelling here. Most are man-made, often with imported Bahamian or mainland Florida sand. Those mentioned below are free and open to the public daily from 7am to 11pm. There are few facilities, except locals hawking beach umbrellas, food, and drinks.

Fort Zachary Taylor State Beach is the best and the closest to the cruise ship docks, a 12-minute walk away. This 51-acre man-made beach is adjacent to the ruins of Fort Taylor, once known as Fort Forgotten because it was buried under tons of sand. The beach is fine for sunbathing and picnicking and is suitable for snorkeling, but rocks make it difficult to swim. To get there, go through the gates leading into Truman Annex. Watering holes near one end of the beach include the raffish Green Parrot Bar and a booze-and-burger joint called Gato Gordo.

Higgs Memorial Beach lies a 25-minute walk from the harbor near the end of White Street, one of the main east-west arteries. You'll find lots of sand, picnic tables sheltered from the sun, and fewer of your fellow cruise ship passengers. **Smathers Beach,** named in honor of one of Florida's most colorful former senators, is the longest (about 1 1/2 miles), most isolated, and least accessorized beach in town. Unfortunately, it's about a $10 one-way taxi ride from the cruise docks. The beach borders South Roosevelt Boulevard. There's no shade here.

In the 1950s, **Southernmost Beach** drew Tennessee Williams, but today it's more likely to fill up with visitors from the lackluster motels nearby. Except for a nearby restaurant, facilities are nonexistent. The beach lies at the foot of Duval Street on the Atlantic side, across the island from the cruise ship docks. It takes about 20 minutes to walk there along Duval Street from the docks. The beach boasts some white sand, but is not good for swimming. Nevertheless, it's one of the island's most frequented.

SPORTS

FISHING As Hemingway, an avid fisherman, would attest, the waters off the Florida Keys are some of the world's finest fishing grounds. You can follow in his wake aboard the 40-foot *Linda D III* and *Linda D IV* (☎ **800/299-9798** in the U.S., or 305/296-9798), which offer the best deep-sea fishing here. Arrangements should be made a week or so before you are due in port.

GOLF Redesigned in 1982 by architect Rees Jones, the **Key West Resort Golf Course,** 6450 E. Junior College Rd. (☎ **305/294-5232**), lies 6 miles from the cruise docks, near the southern tip of neighboring Stock Island. It features a challenging terrain of coral rock, sand traps, mangrove swamp, and pines. The course is a 10- to 15-minute, $15 taxi ride from the dock each way.

SCUBA DIVING The largest dive outfitter is **Captain's Corner,** 0 Duval Street, opposite the Pier House Hotel a block from the dock (☎ **305/296-8865**). The five-star PADI operation has 11 instructors, a 60-foot dive boat (used by Timothy "James Bond" Dalton during the filming of *License to Kill*), and a well-trained staff. To reach the departure point, make a left along the docks, and then walk for about a block to the northern tip of Duval Street.

GREAT LOCAL RESTAURANTS & BARS

RESTAURANTS All the restaurants listed below are within an easy 5- to 15-minute walk of the docks. Several "raw bars" near the dock area offer seafood, including oysters and clams, although the king here is conch—served grilled, ground in burgers, made into a chowder, fried in batter as fritters, or served raw in a conch salad. Even if you don't have lunch, at least sample the local favorites: a slice of Key lime pie with a Cuban coffee. The pie's unique flavor is achieved from the juice and minced rind of the local, piquant Key lime.

Cruise ship passengers on a return visit to Key West often ask for "The Rose Tattoo," a historic old restaurant named for the Tennessee Williams film partially shot on the island. The restaurant is now the **Bagatelle,** 115 Duval St., at Front Street (☎ **305/296-6609**), one of Key West's finest. Look for daily specials or stick to the chef's better dishes, such as conch ceviche (thinly sliced raw conch marinated in lime juice and herbs). **Blue Heaven,** 729 Thomas St. (☎ **305/296-8666**), is a dive that serves some of the best food in town. Some of its finest food is fresh local fish, most often grouper or red snapper, and the hot and spicy jerk chicken is as fine as that served in Jamaica. **Camille's,** 703 1/2 Duval St., between Angela and Petronia streets (☎ **305/296-4811**), is an unpretentious, hip cafe that serves the best breakfast in town and has the best lunch value. Try a sandwich made from the catch of the day served on fresh bread. Its Key lime pie is the island's best. **El Siboney,** 900 Catherine St. (☎ **305/296-4184**), is the place for time-tested Cuban favorites like *ropa vieja,* roast pork with garlic and tart sour oranges, and paella Valenciana (minimum of two).

Half Shell Raw Bar, Land's End Marina, at the foot of Margaret Street (☎ **305/294-7496**), is Key West's original raw bar, offering fresh fish, oysters, and shrimp direct from its own fish market. To be honest, though, I prefer the food at **Turtle Kraals Wildlife Bar & Grill,** Land's End Village, at the foot of Margaret Street (☎ **305/294-2640**). Try the tender Florida lobster, spicy conch chowder, or perfectly cooked fresh fish (often dolphinfish with pineapple salsa or baked stuffed grouper with mango crabmeat stuffing).

Pepe's Café & Steak House, 806 Caroline St., between William and Margaret streets (☎ **305/294-7192**), is the oldest eating house in the Florida Keys, established in 1909. Diners eat under slow-moving paddle fans at tables or dark pine booths with high backs. Cruise ship passengers enjoy the "in between" menu served daily from noon to 4:30pm. You get to choose from zesty homemade chili, perfectly baked oysters, fish sandwiches, and Pepe's deservedly famous steak sandwiches.

If something cool would go down better than a full meal, check out **Flamingo Crossing,** 1105 Duval St., at Virginia Street (☎ **305/296-6124**), which serves the best ice cream in the Florida Keys.

BARS Key West is a bar town. Most places recommended below offer fast food to go with their drinks. The food isn't the best on the island, but usually arrives shortly after you order it, which suits most rushed cruise ship passengers just fine. A favorite **local beer** is Hog's Breath; a favorite **local rum** is Key West Gold (even though it's not actually made on the island).

Heavily patronized by cruise ship passengers, **Captain Tony's Saloon,** 428 Green St. (☎ **305/294-1838**), is the oldest active bar in Florida, and has it ever grown tacky. The 1851 building was the original Sloppy Joe's, a rough-and-tumble fisherman's saloon. Hemingway drank here from 1933 to 1937, and Jimmy Buffett got his start here before opening his own bar and going on to musical glory. The name refers to Capt. Tony Tarracino, a former Key West mayor and rugged man of the sea who owned the place until 1988.

Sloppy Joe's, 201 Duval St. (☎ **305/294-5717**), is the most touristy bar in Key West, visited by almost all cruise ship passengers, even those who don't normally go to bars. It aggressively plays up its association with Hemingway, although the bar stood on Greene Street back then (see "Captain Tony's," above). Marine flags decorate the ceiling, and its ambiance and decor evoke a Havana bar from the 1930s.

Jimmy Buffett's Margaritaville, 500 Duval St. (☎ **305/292-1435**), is the third most popular Key West bar with cruise ship passengers, after Captain Tony's and Sloppy Joe's. Buffett is the hometown boy done good, and his cafe, naturally, is decorated with pictures of himself. And, yes, it sells T-shirts and Margaritaville memorabilia in a shop off the dining room. His margaritas are without competition, but then they'd have to be, wouldn't they?

Open-air and very laid-back, the **Hog's Breath Saloon,** 400 Front St. (☎ **305/296-HOGG**), near the cruise docks, has been a Key West tradition since 1976. Drinking is a sport here, especially among the fishermen who come in after a day chasing the big one. Live entertainment is offered from 1pm to 2am.

For a real local hangout within an easy walk of the cruise ship docks, head to ✪ **Schooner Wharf,** 202 William St., Key West Bight (☎ **305/292-9520**), the most robust and hard-drinking bar in Key West, drawing primarily a young crowd, many of whom cater to the tourist industry or work on the town's fleet of fishing boats.

17 Les Saintes

You want charming? The eight islets of Les Saintes (pronounced "lay sant") are irresistibly charming: pastel-colored gingerbread houses with tropical gardens, sugarloaf hills that slope down to miniature beaches, and picturesque bays with pelicans, sailboats, and turquoise water. Only two of the islands in this French archipelago off the southern coast of Guadeloupe are inhabited: Terre-de-Bas and its more populous neighbor, Terre-de-Haut (more populous, in this case, meaning about 1,500 inhabitants). Terre-de-Haut (pronounced "tear d'oh"), with only one village—the straightforwardly named Le Bourg ("town")—is the destination of most visitors. Some say it's what Saint-Tropez was like before Brigitte Bardot. For a U.S. point of reference, think Fire Island, Provincetown, Martha's Vineyard, or Sausalito with a French-Caribbean twist. Nautical and quaint are the watchwords.

But Les Saintes, also known as Iles des Saintes, isn't a fantasy park built to look enchanting. Although tourism is important to the island's economy, most people still make their living from the sea. Les Saintois, as the locals are called, are widely regarded as the best fishermen in the Antilles, and it's this underlying saltiness that keeps the place from being cloyingly sweet.

Frommer's Favorite Les Saintes Experiences

- **Meandering around Fort Napoléon:** The French built this impressive stone fortification after they regained Les Saintes in 1815, and today it houses engaging, detailed exhibits covering the entire history of the islands. (See "On Your Own: Within Walking Distance," below.)
- **Trekking to the top of Le Chameau:** The highest point on Terre-de-Haut, Le Chameau is located in the southern part of the island and offers a tough (though shaded) 30- to 60-minute climb, for which you're rewarded with spectacular views of the entire archipelago, Guadeloupe, and Dominica. (See "On Your Own: Within Walking Distance," below.)
- **Sunbathing on picture-perfect Pompierre beach:** No beach on Terre-de-Haut is nicer than Plage de Pompierre, located only a 15-minute walk from the dock. Because the bay is a nature preserve, fishing and anchoring are prohibited. (See "Beaches," below.)
- **Climbing along the Trace des Crêtes:** This trail across the center of Terre-de-Haut offers remarkable views of beaches, cliffs, the island's toylike airport, and neighboring islands. (See "On Your Own: Within Walking Distance," below.)

COMING ASHORE   Cruise ships dock at Le Bourg in Terre-de-Haut. The village has two main streets, both lined with cafes, restaurants, and souvenir shops.

Frommer's Ratings: Les Saintes

	poor	fair	good	excellent	outstanding
Overall Experience				✓	
Shore Excursions		✓			
Activities Close to Port					✓
Beaches & Water Sports			✓		
Shopping		✓			
Dining/Bars			✓		

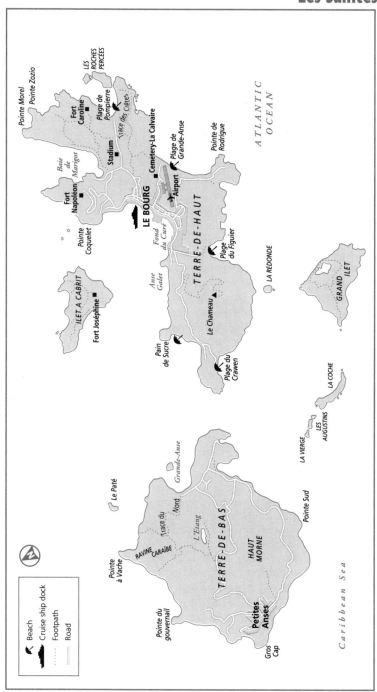

Beach

Cruise ship dock

Footpath

Road

Pointe Morel

Pointe Zozio

LES ROCHES PERCÉES

Fort Caroline

Plage de Pompierre

Plage des Crêtes

Cemetery-La Calvaire

Plage de Grande-Anse

Pointe de Rodrigue

ATLANTIC OCEAN

Stadium

Baie de Marigot

Fort Napoléon

LE BOURG

Airport

Pointe Coquelet

Fond du Curé

TERRE-DE-HAUT

Plage du Figuier

LA REDONDE

GRAND ILET

ILET A CABRIT

Anse Galet

Fort Joséphine

Le Chameau

Pain de Sucre

Plage du Crawen

LA COCHE

LES AUGUSTINS

LA VIERGE

Grande-Anse

Le Paté

Plage du Nord

L'Etang

Pointe Sud

RAVINE CARAÏBE

TERRE-DE-BAS

HAUT MORNE

Pointe à Vache

Caribbean Sea

Pointe du gouvernail

Petites Anses

Gros Cap

Tormented by Love? Have a Pastry

As you disembark from your ship, local women will offer to sell you Les Saintes' signature sweet, tartlets known as *tourments d'amour* (love's torments). Legend has it that young maidens would bake these flaky-crusted, coconut-filled treats to present to their betrotheds as they returned from lengthy fishing expeditions. From time to time, the cruel and heartless sea would claim the life of a beloved, leaving a teary-eyed damsel at the dock with nothing but her pain and pastry. Is it the suffering that makes the tourments d'amour so tasty?

Telephones at the dock require a "télécarte," a prepaid phone card sold at the post office (a 10-minute walk from the dock; take a right) and other outlets marked TÉLÉCARTE EN VENTE ICI. Some phones now accept U.S. calling cards or major credit cards for long-distance calls.

CURRENCY   Les Saintes is part of the larger archipelago of Guadeloupe, an overseas region of France. You'll need **French francs** here. There are 100 centimes to 1 franc. The exchange rate is roughly 6.4 francs to U.S.1 (1 franc = U.S.15¢). An ATM next to the tourism office dispenses them happily.

LANGUAGE   The official language is French. Some islanders speak a local Creole with each other. Few feel comfortable with English, though, so take the opportunity to practice your high-school French. Most everyone is helpful and friendly if you smile and make an effort.

INFORMATION   If you take a right on the main road after you leave the ship, you'll see signs for the tourism office (Office du Tourisme). It's less than a 5-minute walk. Most information is in French, but the maps are helpful even if you don't savvy the lingo. For info before you go, call the **Tourism Board** in the United States at ☎ **410/286-8310** or log on to the Web site at www.frenchcaribbean.com.

CALLING FROM THE U.S.   When calling Les Saintes from the U.S., you need to dial "011" before the numbers listed throughout this section.

GETTING AROUND

If you're reasonably fit, there's no reason you can't walk wherever you want to go. If you're the type who runs 5 miles a day, you can hike up Le Chameau, traipse around Fort Napoléon, head over to Plage de Pompierre, and complete the Trace des Crêtes, with time for a meal or swim before returning to the ship.

There are also a handful of minivans that serve as taxis. Each seats 6 to 8 passengers. You'll find them parked directly in front of the cruise ship dock. Cruise passengers who sign up for shore excursions are transported in similar vans.

BY SCOOTER   Terre-de-Haut is less than 4 miles long and less than 2 miles wide. Aside from tourist vans and the occasional private car, four-wheeled vehicles are rare (at last count, there were less than three dozen). Scooters rule the roads. Scores of them await you just off the dock along Le Bourg's main road. Expect to pay about $36 for a two-seater for the day. A $500 deposit (credit cards accepted) is required.

BY BICYCLE   You can rent bicycles for roughly $15 along Le Bourg's main road. The island is hilly, though. You'd do better to rent a scooter or walk.

SHORE EXCURSIONS

Don't expect any. This is a wander-around-at-your-own pace kind of place.

ON YOUR OWN: WITHIN WALKING DISTANCE

Everything is within walking distance of the dock.

The French built the impressive stone **Fort Napoléon** after they regained Les Saintes in 1815. Sitting atop a hill overlooking the bay, it was completed in 1867. Today it houses engaging, detailed exhibits covering the entire history of the islands—life before Columbus, European expansion into the New World, early French settlements, the Battle of Les Saintes, and the development of the fishing industry. You can wander through barracks, prison cells, and the grounds, which feature an impressive array of cacti and other succulents. If you're lucky, you'll spot iguanas (with names like Victor Hugo and Voltaire), harmless snakes, and turtle doves. Pick up the English-language brochure that describes the vegetation when you purchase your admission ticket (20 francs; about $3). For 5 francs (less than a dollar), you can rent a cassette that provides excellent English commentary as you walk through the museum. The fort is open from 9am till noon, so make it your first destination.

On your way to Fort Napoléon, visit **Jerome Hoff,** a fourth-generation Santois of Alsatian ancestry who paints religious icons in a heartfelt and slightly disturbing style. He has the wild-eyed air of a John the Baptist, but he's a gentle man, retired now, who loves nothing more than talking about his 50 years of singing in the church choir. You can't miss his modest home and studio—they're surrounded by numerous quirky signs that feature colorful saints and passionate prayers. You'll pass **Le Bourg's** stone church on your way to the tourist office. It's humble but worth a moment of your time.

If you're up for some hiking, the **Trace des Crêtes** trail traces the spine of one of Terre-de-Haut's hills just north of the airport and offers remarkable views of beaches, cliffs, and neighboring islands. Although clearly marked, the path is rocky and challenging—you have an advantage if you're part goat. Wear sunscreen and bring water.

Be sure to stop for a few minutes at the **cemetery** next to the airport. You'll notice several graves adorned with conch shells, which signify a sea-related death. On Saturday nights, refrigerator-size speakers are brought in, makeshift food stands are set up, and the cemetery becomes a huge open-air disco. In the same vicinity, **Le Calvaire** is a giant Christ statue at the summit of a hill; numerous steps ascend to great panoramas.

Chameau means camel in French, and with a bit of imagination you can see that **Le Chameau,** the highest point on Terre-de-Haut, looks like the hump of a dromedary. The concrete road to the 1,000-foot summit is off-limits to all motorized vehicles, and, mercifully, it's shaded much of the way. After 30 to 60 minutes of arduous climbing, you're rewarded with spectacular views of the entire archipelago, Guadeloupe, and Dominica. **Tour Vigie,** a military lookout dating from the time of Napoléon, crowns the mountain; unfortunately it's usually locked.

SHOPPING

Little boutiques that sell beachwear, T-shirts, jewelry, and knickknacks line the streets. Stop by **Pascal Foy's Kaz an Nou** Gallery behind the church. You can watch him make Cases Creoles, miniature carved wooden house facades in candy colors. They're becoming collector's items. **Galerie Martine Cotton,** at the foot of the dock, features the work of an artist originally from Brittany who celebrates the natural beauty and fishing traditions of Les Saintes. Beyond the town hall (mairie), **Ultramarine** is a tiny cottage where you can buy unusual dolls, clothes, T-shirts, and handcrafted items from France, Haiti, and Africa. **Galerie Marchande Seaside,** a group of shops around a patio, is just up the street after you turn right from the pier. Art, gifts, antiques, jewelry, lace, beachwear, and ice cream are available.

Insider's Tip

Don't leave anything unattended while swimming at Plage de Pompierre. Savvy goats hide out in the scrub behind the beach, patiently scoping out the action. Once you go into the water, they'll make a bee line for your unattended picnic basket and treat themselves to anything edible. They're especially fond of those tourments d'amour you just bought at the dock. Who's crying now?

BEACHES

Beaches with golden sand are tucked away in almost all of the island's coves. Calm, crescent-shaped **Plage de Pompierre** (sometimes spelled Pont Pierre) is shaded by sea-grape bushes and almond and palm trees. A 15-minute walk from the dock, it boasts soft white sand, shade from coconut palms, and quiet seclusion. The gentle water in the cliff-encircled cove is a stunning aquamarine. Because the bay is a nature preserve, fishing and anchoring are prohibited. It's the island's most popular sunbathing spot, so your best bet is to go early or late.

Secluded on the western coast, **Anse Crawen** is the legal nudist beach, which is not to say you won't see nude bodies on other beaches; they're usually found next to the signs that forbid nude bathing—liberté, égalité, nudité! **Grande Anse,** near the airfield, is large, but there's no shade, and the rough surf has a strong undertow. Although swimming is discouraged, the cliffs at either end of the beach and the powerful breakers make for a dramatic seascape. The usually deserted **Figuier,** on the southern coast, has excellent snorkeling.

SPORTS

FISHING   Going out to sea with a local fisherman is something you won't soon forget. Most of the local sailors will be delighted to take you out, if you can communicate well enough to negotiate a price. Most fishermen operate from the harbor where cruise ships dock. You'll find most of them to the right of the dock; just follow the waterfront to the fishing boats.

WATER SPORTS   For scuba diving and snorkeling, go to **Centre Nautique des Saintes,** at the Plage de la Colline west of town past the market, or **UCPA,** on the other side of Fort Napoléon hill in Marigot Bay. Both also rent sea kayaks and windsurfing equipment.

GREAT LOCAL RESTAURANTS & BARS

Virtually every restaurant in Terre-de-Haut offers seafood that couldn't be fresher, and many feature Creole dishes. A local favorite is smoked kingfish (*tazard*). **L'Auberge Les Petits Saints aux Anarcadiers** is a hillside veranda restaurant overlooking the bay. The inn, on the Route de Rodrigue, was once the mayor's residence. It boasts a tropical garden and countless antiques. The terrace restaurant at the **Hôtel Bois Joli,** on the island's western tip, offers a view of Pain de Sucre, Les Saintes' petite version of Rio de Janeiro's Sugarloaf Mountain, and is fringed with palm trees. For pasta, pizza, or salad, try **La Saladerie's** seaside terrace on the way to Fort Napoléon. **Le Génois,** yet another waterfront option (100 feet from the dock; turn left), is popular with yachties, who can dock right at the restaurant. The salads here are named after legendary sailboats, while the pizzas pay tribute to local beaches. **Café de la Marine** (on the bay and main street) serves thin-crusted pizzas and seafood. One of the island's best bakeries (*boulangeries*), **Le Fouril de Jimmy,** is on the same square as the town hall, across from the tourist office. If you stop in at the right time, you can get a crusty baguette hot from the oven.

18 Martinique

One of the most exotic French-speaking destinations in the Caribbean, Martinique was the site of a settlement demolished by volcanic activity (St. Pierre, now only a pale shadow of a once-thriving city). Like Guadeloupe and St. Barts, Martinique is legally and culturally French, although many Creole customs and traditions continue to flourish. The Creole cuisine is full of flavor and flair, and the island has lots of tropical charm.

When you arrive at **Fort-de-France,** Martinique's capital, you would never guess that this is one of the most beautiful islands in the Caribbean, but past the port are miles of white-sand beaches along an irregular coastline. Martinique offers some of the most stunning natural wonders in the region.

About 50 miles at its longest and 21 miles at its widest, Martinique is mountainous, especially in the rain-forested northern region where the volcano **Mount Pelée** rises to a height of 4,656 feet. Hibiscus, poinsettias, bougainvillea, and coconut palms grow in lush profusion, and fruit—breadfruit, mangoes, pineapples, avocados, bananas, papayas, and custard apples—fairly drips from the trees.

Frommer's Favorite Martinique Experiences

- **Visiting the Church of Balata:** This colonial-era church was designed as a replica of the Sacred Heart Basilica in Paris.
- **Snorkeling at Anse du Four:** A quaint fishing village with a beautiful sheltered bay, the reef here begins just offshore and overflows with colorful sponge, fish, and other marine animals. The spot is perfect for beginning snorkelers, while deeper sections provide diving opportunities for the more experienced.
- **Touring St-Pierre, site of a volcano eruption:** Mount Pelée erupted in 1902, killing 30,000 people. Today, you can see ruins of the church, the theater, and some other buildings, and tour a volcano museum (see "On Your Own: Beyond Walking Distance," below).
- **Visiting the village of Trois-Ilets:** Tour where Joséphine, the wife of Napoleon I, was born in 1763. There's part of her home, a museum, and a botanical garden (see "On Your Own: Beyond Walking Distance," below).

COMING ASHORE Cruise ships now dock at the recently built International Pier, which has docking quays for two large-size vessels. As Martinique is a very popular Caribbean port of call, ships also dock at the main harbor, located on the north side of bay, a few minutes' drive from the center of Fort-de-France. Between the two, the International Pier is more convenient as it's adjacent to La Savane, the heart of Fort-de-France and the downtown area. The pier's proximity to La Savane allows passengers to reach the area quickly by foot and avoid a $10 (or more) cab ride or a fairly long, hot walk

Frommer's Ratings: Martinique					
	poor	fair	good	excellent	outstanding
Overall Experience				✓	
Shore Excursions			✓		
Activities Close to Port			✓		
Beaches & Water Sports				✓	
Shopping			✓		
Dining/Bars			✓		

from the main harbor. Smaller ships also anchor in the bay and ferry passengers to and from shore via tender.

CURRENCY   The **French franc (F)** is the legal tender here. The exchange rate is 6.29F to U.S.$1 (1F = U.S.16¢). If you're going off on your own or plan to visit the countryside, you might want to exchange some money. A money-exchange service, **Change Caraibes** (☎ **0596/60-28-40**), is at rue Ernest-Deproge 4. It's open Monday to Friday from 7:30am to noon and 2:30 to 4pm.

LANGUAGE   French is the official language, but English is spoken in most hotels, restaurants, and tourist facilities.

INFORMATION   The address of the **Office Departmental du Tourisme** (Martinique Tourist Board) is Rue Ernest Deproge, Fort-de-France, 97200 Martinique (☎ **0596/63-79-60**). For info before you go, call the Martinique tourism office in the U.S. at ☎ **800/391-4909** or log on to the Web site at www.martinique.org.

CALLING FROM THE U.S.   When calling Martinique from the U.S., you need to dial "011" before the numbers listed throughout this section.

GETTING AROUND

BY TAXI   Travel by taxi is popular but expensive. Most of the cabs aren't metered, so you have to agree on the price of the ride before getting in. Night fares, in effect from 8pm to 6am, come with a 40% surcharge. For a radio taxi, call ☎ **0596/63-63-62.** If you want to rent a taxi for the day, it's better to have a party of at least three or four people to keep costs down. Taxis are generally available at the cruise pier. Taxi drivers charge approximately U.S.$40 per hour, and passengers should always agree on a fare before stepping into the cab. Check with your ship's port lecturer to determine the current taxi rate. Most taxi drivers do not speak English.

BY BUS   There are collective taxi vans that seat eight and sport A TC sign; they're generally crowded and not the most comfortable. They are widely used by tourists, particularly those who speak some French. The collectives serve Fort-de-France's outlying areas, discharging passengers en route.

BY RENTAL CAR   The scattered nature of Martinique's geography makes renting a car especially tempting. Call **Avis,** rue Ernest-Deproge 4 (☎ **800/331-1212** in the U.S., or 0596/51-17-70); **Budget,** rue Félix-Eboué 12 (☎ **800/527-0700** in the U.S., or 0596/63-69-00); or **Hertz,** rue Ernest-Deproge 24, at Lamentin Airport (☎ **800/ 654-3001** or 0596/60-64-64). Most car-rental rates are about $70 a day, including unlimited mileage. Prices are usually lower if you reserve a car from North America at least two business days before your arrival.

BY FERRY   Take the blue ferry operated by Somatour for $6 per person, round-trip, to reach Pointe du Bout. The schedule is posted at the ferry dock. Pointe du Bout features some of Martinique's best beaches (all beaches here are public). The Méridien Beach Hotel and the Bakoua Resort are good choices as cruise passengers are welcome here and water sports, restaurants, and beach chairs are available.

SHORE EXCURSIONS

Golf at the Country Club of Martinique ($115, 6 hours): The 18-hole, par-71 course here, designed by Robert Trent Jones, is both challenging and picturesque, totaling 6,640 yards of twisting fairways and fast greens. Transportation, greens fees (for 18 holes), and a golf cart are included; lunch is not.

St. Pierre and Rain Forest Drive ($59, 4 hours): Drive through Martinique's lush rain forest and explore the remains of St. Pierre, destroyed by Mount Pelée's eruption in

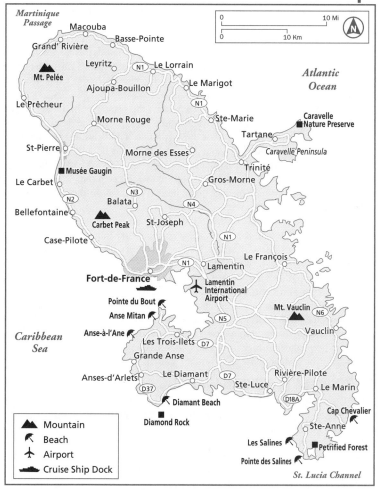

Martinique Passage

Macouba
Basse-Pointe
Grand' Rivière
Leyritz
Le Lorrain
N1
Mt. Pelée
Ajoupa-Bouillon
Le Marigot
Le Prêcheur
N1
Morne Rouge
Ste-Marie
Caravelle Nature Preserve
Tartane
St-Pierre
Morne des Esses
Caravelle Peninsula
Trinité
Musée Gaugin
Gros-Morne
Le Carbet
N3
N2
Balata
N4
Bellefontaine
Carbet Peak
St-Joseph
Case-Pilote
N1
N1
Le François
Lamentin
Fort-de-France
Lamentin International Airport
Pointe du Bout
Mt. Vauclin
N6
Anse Mitan
Vauclin
Anse-à-l'Ane
N5
Les Trois-Ilets
D7
Grande Anse
Anses-d'Arlets
Le Diamant
D7
Rivière-Pilote
D37
Ste-Luce
Le Marin
Diamant Beach
D18A
Cap Chevalier
Diamond Rock
Ste-Anne
Les Salines
Petrified Forest
Pointe des Salines
St. Lucia Channel

Atlantic Ocean

Caribbean Sea

▲▲ Mountain
⌃ Beach
✈ Airport
⛴ Cruise Ship Dock

1902. Passengers stop at the Butterfly Farm, set in a botanical park among the ruins of the island's first sugar plantation, then continue to St. Pierre to visit the ruins. On the drive back to Fort-de-France you'll also visit the Church of Balata, a replica of Paris's Sacred Heart Basilica.

Martinique Snorkeling ($49, 2½ hours): The reef at Anse du Four offers excellent snorkeling opportunities for experts as well as novices. The reef is filled with marine animals, including French grunts, blackbar soldierfish, and silversides. Snorkeling equipment is provided, as are professional instruction, supervision, and transportation.

ON YOUR OWN: WITHIN WALKING DISTANCE

Fort-de-France is a bustling, cosmopolitan town with an unmistakable French air and a little of the flair of the Côte d'Azur—you might say it's a combination of New Orleans and the French Riviera. Narrow streets, pastel buildings, and ornate iron grillwork balconies overflowing with flowers are commonplace. Narrow streets climb up to houses on the steep hills. Almost a third of the island's year-round population of 360,000 lives in the capital, so it's not a small town.

At the center of the town lies **La Savane,** a broad garden with many palms and mangoes bordered by shops and cafes. In this grand square stands a statue of Joséphine, "Napoléon's little Creole," carved in white marble by Vital Debray. The statue has seen its share of troubles, having been beheaded in 1991 after Joséphine's role in reinstating slavery in Martinique was brought to light.

A statue in front of the Palais de Justice portrays the island's second main historical figure (after Joséphine), Victor Schoelcher, who worked to free the slaves more than a century ago—you'll see his name a lot in Martinique. The **Bibliothèque Schoelcher** (Schoelcher Library), rue de la Liberté 21, also honors this popular hero. This elaborate structure was first displayed at the Paris Exposition in 1889. The Romanesque portal in red and blue, the Egyptian lotus-petal columns, and even the turquoise tiles were taken apart and reassembled piece by piece here. It's located on the northwest corner of La Savane, and is open Monday to Saturday.

St. Louis Roman Catholic Cathedral, on rue Victor-Schoelcher, was built in 1875. The religious centerpiece of the island, it's an extraordinary iron building, which someone once likened to a Catholic railway station. A number of the island's former governors are buried beneath the choir loft.

Guarding the port is **Fort St-Louis,** built in the Vauban style on a rocky promontory. In addition, **Fort Tartenson** and **Fort Desaix** stand on hills overlooking the port as well.

Musée Départemental de la Martinique, rue de la Liberté 9, is the one place on Martinique that preserves its pre-Columbian past, with relics left from the early Arawak and Carib settlers. The museum faces La Savane and is open Monday to Friday from 8:30am to 5pm, and Saturday from 9am to noon. Admission is 15F ($2.50) for adults, 10F ($1.65) for students, and 5F (85¢) for children.

ON YOUR OWN: BEYOND WALKING DISTANCE

Sacré-Coeur de Balata Cathedral, overlooking Fort-de-France at Balata, is a copy of the basilica looking down from Montmartre in Paris—and this one is just as incongruous, maybe more so. To get there, take the route de la Trace (Route N3). Balata is 6 miles north of Fort-de-France.

A few minutes' taxi ride from Fort-de-France on Route N3, the **Jardin de Balata** (Balata Garden) is a tropical botanical park created by Jean-Phillippe Thoze on land near his grandmother's house. He has restored the house, furnishing it with antiques and engravings depicting life in other days, and with bouquets and baskets of fruit renewed daily. The garden contains a profusion of flowers, shrubs, and trees. Balata is open daily.

The major goal of all shore excursions, **St-Pierre** was the cultural and economic capital of Martinique until May 7, 1902. That very morning, locals read in their daily newspaper that "Montagne Pelée does not present any more risk to the population than Vesuvius does to the Neapolitans." Then at 8am, the southwest side of **Mount Pelée** exploded in fire and lava. By 8:02am, all but one of St-Pierre's 30,000 inhabitants were dead. St-Pierre never recovered its past splendor. Ruins of the church, the theater, and some other buildings can be seen along the coast.

One of the best ways to get an overview of St-Pierre is to ride a rubber-wheeled "train," the **CV Paris Express,** which departs from the Musée Volcanologique (see below). Tours run Monday to Friday from 10:30am to 1pm and 2:30 to 7pm. In theory, tours depart about once an hour, but actually they leave only when there are enough people to justify a trip.

Musée Volcanologique, rue Victor-Hugo, St-Pierre, was created by American volcanologist Franck Alvard Perret, who turned the museum over to the city in 1933. In pictures and relics excavated from the debris, you can trace the story of what happened to St-Pierre. Dug from the lava is a clock that stopped at the exact moment the volcano erupted. The museum is open daily from 9am to 5pm.

North of Fort-de-France, **Le Carbet** is where Columbus landed in 1502, the first French settlers arrived in 1635, and the painter Paul Gauguin lived for 4 months in 1887 before going on to do his most famous work on Tahiti. Today, the town makes for an idyllic excursion. The landscape looks pretty much as it did when Gauguin depicted the beach in his *Bord de Mer.* **Centre d'Art Musée Paul-Gauguin,** Anse Turin, housed in a five-room building near the beach, commemorates the French artist's stay, with books, prints, letters, and other memorabilia. Of special interest are faïence mosaics made of pieces of colored volcanic rock excavated from nearby archaeological digs. There are also changing exhibits of works by local artists. The museum is open daily from 9am to 5:30pm.

If you're driving yourself around or taking a taxi tour, you will find no better goal than **Hotel Plantation de Leyritz** near Basse-Pointe (☎ **0596/78-53-92**), one of the best restored plantations on Martinique and a good place for an authentic (and expensive) Creole lunch. It occupies the site of a plantation established around 1700 by Bordeaux-born Michel de Leyritz. Sprawled over flat, partially wooded terrain a half-hour's drive from the nearest beach (Anse à Zerot, in Sainte-Marie), it was the site of the "swimming pool summit meeting" in 1974 between Presidents Gerald Ford and Valéry Giscard d'Estaing. Part of the acreage still functions as a working banana plantation. The resort includes 16 acres of tropical gardens. At the core is a stone-sided 18th-century Great House.

Marie-Joséphe-Rose Tascher de la Pagerié was born in the charming little village of **Trois-Ilets** in 1763. As Joséphine, she was to become the wife of Napoléon I and empress of France from 1804 to 1809. She'd been previously married to Alexandre de Beauharnais, who had actually wanted to wed either of her two more attractive sisters. Six years older than Napoléon, she pretended that she'd lost her birth certificate so he wouldn't find out her true age. Although many historians call her ruthless and selfish, she is still revered by some on Martinique as uncommonly gracious. Others, however, blame Napoléon's "reinvention" of slavery on her influence.

To reach her birthplace in Trois-Ilets (pronounced Twaz-ee-*lay*), take a taxi from the pier through lush countryside 20 miles south of Fort-de-France. In la Pagerié, a small museum, **Musée de la Pagerié** (☎ **0596/68-33-06**), sits in the former estate kitchen (the plantation house was destroyed in a hurricane) and displays mementos relating to Joséphine. You'll see a passionate love letter from Napoléon, along with her childhood bed. Here in this room Joséphine gossiped with her slaves and played the guitar. Still remaining are the partially restored ruins of the Pagerié sugar mill and the church where she was christened (the latter is in the village itself). A botanical garden, the **Parc des Floralies,** is adjacent to the golf course Golf de l'Impératrice-Joséphine (see "Sports," below).

Grand'riviere is an old fishing village located on Martinique's isolated north coast. The town is framed by the green cliffs of Mount Pelée, and ringed with palm and breadfruit trees. Many of the town's old customs are still maintained, and visitors can watch village fishermen pull their boats onto the beach as they return with their catch.

Situated on the west side of Route de la Trace (or simply, "The Trace"), a central highland road that winds through Martinique's rain forest, are the **Absalon Mineral Springs.** Near the springs is a hiking trail that begins with a steep climb through the rain forest to a lightly wooded crest along a stream.

Martinique has two casinos located in hotels: the **Casino Trois-Ilets** is in the Le Méridien Hotel on Pointe du Bout, and **La Bateliere** is in La Bateliere Hotel in the Schoelcher region. Both are open from 9pm to 3am.

SHOPPING

Your best buys on Martinique are **French luxury imports,** such as perfumes, fashions, Vuitton luggage, Lalique crystal, or Limoges dinnerware. Sometimes prices are as much as 30% to 40% below those in the United States, but don't count on it. Some luxury goods—including jewelry—are subject to a value-added tax as high as 14%.

If you pay in dollars, store owners supposedly give you a 20% discount; however, their exchange rates are almost invariably far less favorable than those offered by the local banks, so your real savings is only 5% to 11%. Actually, you're better off shopping in the smaller stores, where prices are 8% to 12% less on comparable items, and paying in francs.

The main shopping street in Fort-de-France is **rue Victor-Hugo.** The other two leading shopping streets are **rue Schoelcher** and **rue St-Louis.**

Facing the tourist office and alongside **quai d'Esnambuc** is an open market where you can purchase local handcrafts and souvenirs, many of them tacky. Far more interesting and impressive is the display of vegetables and fruit at the open-air stalls along **rue Isambert.** Gourmet chefs can find all sorts of spices in the open-air markets, and such goodies as tinned pâté or canned quail in the local *supermarchés.*

Shops on every street sell bolts of the ubiquitous, colorful, and inexpensive local fabric, madras. So-called haute couture and resort wear are sold in many boutiques dotting downtown Fort-de-France.

Cadet-Daniel, rue Antoine-Siger 72, competes with **Roger Albert,** rue Victor-Hugo 7–9, to offer the best buys in French china and crystal. Before buying, do some comparison shopping.

Centre des Métiers d'Art, rue Ernest-Deproge, adjacent to the tourist office, is the best and most visible arts-and-crafts store in Martinique. You'll find both valuable and worthless local handmade artifacts for sale, including bamboo, ceramics, painted fabrics, and patchwork quilts suitable for hanging. The owner of **La Belle Matadore,** Immeuble Vermeil-Marina, Pointe du Bout (midway between the La Pagerié Hôtel and the Méridien Hotel), has carefully researched the history and traditions of the island's jewelry, and virtually all the merchandise sold here derives from models developed during slave days by the *matadores* (prostitutes), midwives, and slaves.

Martinique rum is considered by aficionados to be the world's finest (in *A Moveable Feast,* Hemingway lauded it as the perfect antidote to a rainy day), and **La Case à Rhum,** in the Galerie Marchande, rue de la Liberté 5, offers all the brands. They offer samples in small cups to prospective buyers.

Set on the Route de Lamentin, midway between Fort-de-France and the Lamentin airport, **La Galleria** is, by anyone's estimate, the most upscale and elegant shopping complex on Martinique. On the premises are more than 60 different vendors, from France and the Caribbean. There's also a handful of cafes and restaurants, as well as an outlet or two selling the pastries and sweets for which Martinique is known.

BEACHES

The beaches south of Fort-de-France are white and sandy, but those to the north are mostly gray sand. Outstanding in the south is the $1^{1}/_{2}$-mile **Plage des Salines,** near Ste-Anne, with palm trees and a long stretch of white sand, and the $2^{1}/_{2}$-mile **Diamant,** with the landmark Diamond Rock offshore. The water here is pretty rough, but the beach offers a terrific view of the 600-foot high Diamond Rock, which the British fortified and used as a battlement in their 1804 fight with the French for control of the island. Swimming on the Atlantic coast is for experts only, except at **Cap Chevalier** and **Presqu'ile de la Caravelle Nature Preserve.**

Pointe du Bout is a narrow peninsula across the bay from Fort-de-France, accessible by ferry (see "Getting Around," above). It's the most lavish resort area of Martinique, with at least four of the island's largest hotels, an impressive marina, a golf course, about a dozen tennis courts, swimming pools, facilities for horseback riding and all kinds of water sports, a handful of restaurants, a gambling casino, and boutiques. The area's clean white-sand beaches were created by developers. The sandy beaches to the south at **Anse Mitan,** however, have always been there welcoming visitors, including many snorkelers.

SPORTS

HIKING   Personnel of the **Parc Naturel Régional de la Martinique** organize inexpensive guided excursions for small groups of tourists year-round. Contact them at the Excollège Agricole de Tivoli, B.P. 437, 97200 Fort-de-France (☎ **0596/64-42-59**). This should be done 2 or 3 days before your ship arrives in Martinique. **Presqu'ile de la Caravelle Nature Preserve,** a well-protected peninsula jutting into the Atlantic Ocean, has safe beaches and well-marked trails through tropical wetlands to the ruins of historic Château Debuc.

SCUBA DIVING & SNORKELING   Divers come here to explore the Diamond Rock caves and walls and the ships sunk at St-Pierre during the 1902 volcanic eruption. Snorkeling equipment is also available at dive centers. Across the bay from Fort-de-France, in the Hotel Méridien, **Espace Plongée** (☎ **0596/66-00-00**) is a major scuba center and the best in Pointe du Bout. They welcome anyone who shows up. Dive trips leave from the Méridien Hotel's pier. Cruise ship passengers should opt for the morning dives, as afternoon dives may not allow enough time to get back to the ship. The dive shop on the Méridien's beach stocks everything from weight belts and tanks to partial wet suits and underwater cameras.

GREAT LOCAL RESTAURANTS & BARS

A favorite **local beer** is Lorraine; a couple favorite **local rums** are Clement and Saint Jame's.

IN FORT-DE-FRANCE   A La Bonne Viande, 11 rue Lamartine (☎ **0596/63-56-93**), is an atmospheric, charming restaurant in the center of town, serving specialties that include tournedos Rossini with foie gras and T-bones with béarnaise sauce. **Le Planteur,** 1 rue de la Liberté, on the southern edge of La Savane, right in the heart of town (☎ **0596/63-17-45**), serves fresh and flavorful menu items such as cassoulet of minced conch. **La Lafayette,** 5 rue de la Liberte (☎ **0596/63-24-09**), is located in downtown Fort-de-France in the hotel of the same name. The flower-laden restaurant features French-Creole selections and a view of La Savane and the bay.

AT POINTE DU BOUT   Pignon sur Mer, Anse-à-l'Ane, a 12-minute drive from Pointe du Bout (☎ **0596/68-38-37**), is a simple, unpretentious Creole restaurant serving island-inspired dishes that might include delices du Pignon, a platter of shellfish, or whatever grilled fish or shellfish was hauled in that day. **La Villa Créole,** Anse Mitan (☎ **0596/66-05-53**), is a 3- or 4-minute drive from the hotels of Pointe du Bout and serves reasonably priced set-price menus that offer a selection of such staples as accras de morue (beignets of codfish), boudin creole (blood sausage), and un féroce (a local form of pâté concocted from fresh avocados, pulverized codfish, and manioc flour). **La Belle Epoque,** Route de Didier (☎ **0596/64-01-09**), is a small, elegant eatery located on a terrace of a late 19th-century house. The restaurant serves light, creative dishes. **Diamant Creole,** 7 boulevard de Verdun, (☎ **0596/73-18-25**), is a small red-and-white house built in 1927 with a dance studio on the ground floor and a seven-table restaurant upstairs. It serves classic Creole dishes with an updated flair, plus local favorites like soups and vegetables.

19 Puerto Rico

When most people think of Puerto Rico, they think of Old San Juan, that beautiful old cobblestoned city stretched over a hilly peninsula surrounded by the sea. Old San Juan is, of course, the main tourist haunt, but there is more to the island. The Commonwealth of Puerto Rico, under the jurisdiction of the United States, is home to over three million Spanish-speaking people. It's the most urbanized island of the Caribbean, with lots of traffic, glittering casinos, its share of crime, and a more-or-less comfortable mix of Latin culture with imports from the U.S. mainland. The island's interior is filled with ancient volcanic mountains and jungly tropical forests, and its coastline is ringed with sandy beaches. In addition to the main island, the Commonwealth includes a trio of small offshore islands: Culebra, Mona, and Vieques. Vieques has the most tourist facilities of the three.

San Juan, Puerto Rico's 16th-century capital, is the Caribbean's most historic port, with some 500 years of history reflected in its restored Spanish colonial architecture. Its shopping is topped by St. Thomas and Sint Maarten, but overall its historic sights, attractions, gambling, and diversions make it number-one in the Caribbean. You'll find some of the Caribbean's best restaurants and hotels here, as well, and it even has a glitzy beach strip, the Condado.

The Port of San Juan is the busiest ocean terminal in the West Indies, and second only to Miami for the North America cruise trade. Metropolitan San Juan includes the old walled city and the city center, which contains the Capitol building, on San Juan Island; Santurce, on a larger peninsula, reached by causeway bridges from San Juan Island (the lagoon-front section here is called Miramar); Condado, the narrow peninsula that stretches from San Juan Island to Santurce; Hato Rey, the business center; Río Piedras, site of the University of Puerto Rico; and Bayamón, an industrial and residential quarter.

The Condado strip of beachfront hotels, restaurants, casinos, and nightclubs is separated from Miramar by a lagoon. Isla Verde, another resort area, is near the airport, which is separated from the rest of San Juan by an isthmus.

Frommer's Favorite San Juan Experiences

- **Taking a walking tour of 500-year-old Old San Juan:** Its cobblestoned, narrow streets and Spanish colonial architecture are stunning (see "Shore Excursions," and "On Your Own: A Walking Tour of Old San Juan," below).
- **Taking a hike through El Yunque Rain Forest:** The forest is home to 240 species of tropical trees, flowers, and wildlife, including millions of tiny coqui tree frogs (see "Shore Excursions," below).

Frommer's Ratings: San Juan

	poor	fair	good	excellent	outstanding
Overall Experience					✓
Shore Excursions		✓			
Activities Close to Port					✓
Beaches & Water Sports			✓		
Shopping				✓	
Dining/Bars			✓		

Puerto Rico

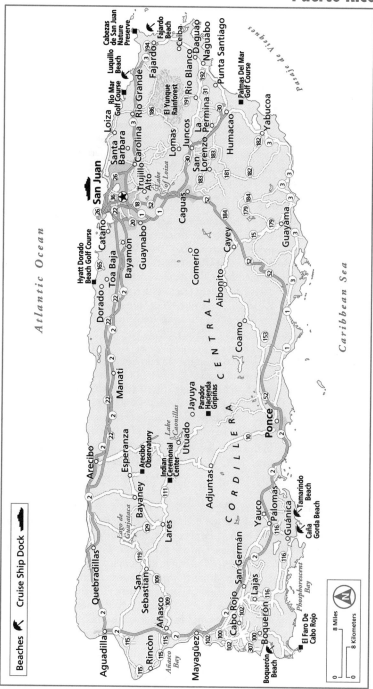

San Juan as a Port of Embarkation

Since a number of cruise ships use San Juan as their port of embarkation and debarkation, you might have the opportunity to spend a night or two here before or after your cruise. If so, here's some information on planning your trip and some picks of the best hotels and nightlife.

GETTING TO SAN JUAN & THE PORT

Visitors from overseas arrive at **Luis Muñoz Marín International Airport** (☎ 787/ **791-1014**), situated on the city's easternmost side. It's about 7¹/₂ miles from the port. Taxis will be lined up outside the airport. The fixed fare is about $8 to Isla Verde, $12 to Condado, and $16 to Old San Juan (including the port). The ride to the port takes about 30 minutes, depending on traffic conditions.

ACCOMMODATIONS

NEAR THE DOCKS   Gran Hotel El Convento, 100 Cristo St. (☎ 800/468-2779 or 787/723-9020), is Puerto Rico's most famous hotel; its third to fifth floors offer large rooms, many with views of the Old Town. **Wyndham Old San Juan Hotel & Casino,** 100 Brumbaugh St. (☎ 800/996-3426 or 787/721-5100), is right on the waterfront and the cruise docks. Bedrooms are tasteful and comfortable, and Old San Juan is at your doorstep. **Gallery Inn at Galería San Juan,** Calle Norzagaray 204–206 (☎ 787/722-1808), is a former 1700s Spanish aristocrat's home set on a hilltop with a sweeping view of the sea. It has comfortable and tasteful rooms (although lacking air-conditioning). There's also an on-site artists' studio here. The **Caribe Hilton,** Calle Los Rosales, Puerto de Tierra (☎ 800/HILTONS in the U.S. or Canada, or 787/721-0303), is near the old Fort San Jerónimo. You can walk to the 16th-century fort or spend the day on a tour of Old San Juan, and then come back and enjoy the beach and swimming cove. **Radisson Normandie,** Avenida Muñoz-Rivera at the corner of Calle Los Rosales (☎ 800/333-3333 in the U.S., or 787/729-2929) was built in the shape of the famous French ocean liner *Normandie,* and lies only 5 minutes from Old San Juan in a beachside setting.

IN CONDADO   In this area filled with high-rise hotels, restaurants, and nightclubs, your best bets are the ✪ **Condado Plaza Hotel & Casino,** 999 Ashford

COMING ASHORE   Cruise ships dock on the historic south shore of Old San Juan, within the sheltered channel that was hotly contested by European powers during the island's early colonial days. Each of the piers is within a relatively short walk of the Plaza de la Marina, the Wyndham Hotel, Old San Juan's main bus station, and most of the historic and commercial treasures of Old San Juan. During periods of heavy volume— usually Saturday and Sunday in midwinter, when as many as 10 cruise ships might dock in San Juan on the same day—additional, less convenient piers are activated. They include the Frontier Pier, at the western edge of the Condado, near the Caribe Hilton Hotel, and the Pan American Dock, in Isla Grande, across the San Antonio Channel from Old San Juan. Unless they're up for a long walk, passengers berthing at either of these docks need some kind of motorized transit (usually a taxi or a van supplied by the cruise line as part of the shore-excursion program) to get to the Old Town. For information about the port, contact the **Port of San Juan,** P.O. 362829, San Juan, PR 00936-2829 (☎ **787/723-2260**).

Ave. (☎ 800/468-8588 in the U.S., or 787/721-1000), and the **San Juan Marriott Resort & Stellaris Casino,** 1309 Ashford Ave. (☎ 800/981-8546 in the U.S., or 787/722-7000). **Aleli by the Sea,** 1125 Sea View St. (☎ 787/725-5313), is a simple but charming small hotel by the sea. Rooms are nothing fancy, but they're clean and the sound of the surf just outside your window and the reasonable rates are big draws (try half what the big hotels charge; an ocean-view room goes for $90 a night).

IN ISLA VERDE   Closer to the airport than the other sections of San Juan, and right on the beach, your best bets are ✪ **El San Juan Hotel & Casino,** 6063 Isla Verde Ave. (☎ 800/468-2818 in the U.S., or 787/791-1000), **The Ritz-Carlton,** 6961 State Rd., no. 187 on Isla Verde (☎ 800/241-3333 in the U.S., or 787/253-1700), and **San Juan Grand Beach Hotel & Casino,** 187 Isla Verde Ave. (☎ 800/443-2009 in the U.S., or 787/791-6100).

SAN JUAN AFTER DARK

If you want to dance the night away, the **Babylon,** in the El San Juan Hotel & Casino, 6063 Isla Verde Ave. (☎ 787/791-1000), attracts a rich and beautiful crowd, as well as a gaggle of onlookers. For action in the Old Town, head for **Laser,** Calle del Cruz 251 (☎ 787/725-7581), near the corner of Calle Fortaleza. Salsa and merengue are often featured.

On the Condado, **Millennium,** in the Condado Plaza Hotel, 999 Ashford Ave. (☎ 787/722-1900), also draws disco devotees. It has a cigar bar on the side. If you just want a drink, **Fiesta Bar,** in the Condado Plaza Hotel & Casino, 999 Ashford Ave. (☎ 787/721-1000), attracts locals and visitors. **Palm Court,** in the El San Juan Hotel & Casino, 6063 Isla Verde Ave. (☎ 787/791-1000), is the most beautiful bar and dance spot on the island.

Stylish and charming, **Violeta's,** Calle Fortaleza 56 (☎ 787/723-6804), occupies the ground floor of a 200-year-old beamed house 2 blocks from the landmark Gran Hotel El Convento (see above). An open courtyard in back provides additional seating. Margaritas are the drink of choice.

There are **phones** for credit-card calls just outside of the Tourism Information Center at Paseo de la Princesa near Pier 1 in Old San Juan.

CURRENCY   The **U.S. dollar** is the coin of the realm. Canadian currency is accepted by some big hotels in San Juan, but reluctantly.

LANGUAGE   Most people in the tourist industry speak English, although Spanish is the native tongue.

INFORMATION   For additional advice and maps, contact the **Tourist Information Center at La Casita,** Paseo de la Princesa near Pier 1 in Old San Juan (☎ **787/721-2400**). For info before you go, contact the tourism board at ☎ **800/223-6530** or log on to the Web site at www.prtourism.com.

CALLING FROM THE U.S.   When calling Puerto Rico from the United States, you need to dial only a "1" before the numbers listed throughout this section.

GETTING AROUND

Driving is a hassle in congested San Juan. You can walk most of the Old Town on foot or take a free trolley. You can also take buses or taxis to the beaches in the Condado.

BY TAXI   Taxis are operated by the **Public Service Commission** (PSC), and are metered in San Juan—or should be. The initial charge is $1, plus 10¢ for each one-tenth of a mile and 50¢ for every suitcase. A minimum fare is $3. Taxi companies are listed in the yellow pages of the phone book under "Taxis," or you can call the PSC (☎ 787/756-1919) to request information or report any irregularities.

BY TROLLEY   When you tire of walking around Old San Juan, you can board one of its free trolleys. Departure points are the Marina and La Puntilla, but you can get on any place along the route. Relax and enjoy the sights as the trolleys rumble through the old, narrow streets.

BY BUS   The Metropolitan Bus Authority operates buses in the greater San Juan area. Bus stops are marked by upright metal signs or yellow posts reading PARADA. Bus terminals in San Juan are in the dock area and at Plaza de Colón. A typical fare is about 25¢ to 50¢. For route and schedule information, call ☎ **787/250-6064.**

BY RENTAL CAR   The major car-rental companies include **Avis** (☎ **800/331-1212** or 787/791-2500), **Budget** (☎ **800/527-0700** or 787/791-3685), and **Hertz** (☎**800/654-3001** or 787/791-0840).

SHORE EXCURSIONS

In Old San Juan, there's really no need to bother with organized shore excursions, since it's easy enough to get around on your own. But if you prefer a guide to narrate or want to explore the island's El Yunque rain forest, an organized tour is a good idea.

San Juan City and Shopping Tour ($22, 3 hours): In Old San Juan you'll visit the massive El Morro Fortress (built in 1539) and a few other sites. Then after some shopping, move on to the modern city of San Juan.

Juan Carlos and His Flamenco Rumba Show ($43, 1 hour): At the Club Tropicoro at the El San Juan Hotel and Casino, enjoy dance performances of the mambo, rumba, samba, conga, and flamenco.

El Yunque Rain Forest and Bacardi Rum Tour ($32, 4–5 hours): By minibus, travel along the northeastern part of the island and take a short hike in the 28,000-acre El Yunque rain forest, home to hundreds of species of plants and animals. Afterward, tour the Bacardi Rum Plant, which produces something on the order of 100,000 gallons of the stuff daily. (And yes, you get free samples.)

TOURING THROUGH LOCAL OPERATORS

Rain Forest and Bacardi Rum Tour: If your ship doesn't offer it, **Castillo Watersports & Tours,** 2413 Calle Laurel, Punta La Marias, Santurce (☎ **787/791-6195** or 787/726-5752), has tours departing in the morning.

ON YOUR OWN: A WALKING TOUR OF OLD SAN JUAN

The streets are narrow and teeming with traffic, but a walking tour through Old San Juan (in Spanish, *El Viejo San Juan*) is a stroll through 5 centuries of history. The throngs thin out by late afternoon, so you might want to linger to enjoy the charming beauty of Old San Juan sans crowds. Within this 7-square-block landmark area in the city's westernmost part are many of Puerto Rico's chief historic attractions.

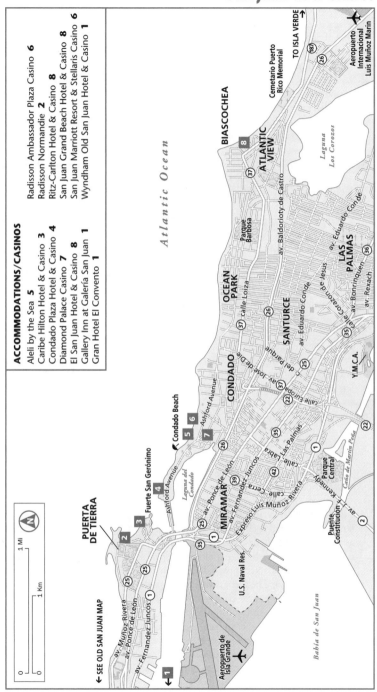

San Juan at a Glance

ACCOMMODATIONS/CASINOS

Aleli by the Sea **5**
Caribe Hilton Hotel & Casino **3**
Condado Plaza Hotel & Casino **4**
Diamond Palace Casino **7**
El San Juan Hotel & Casino **8**
Gallery Inn at Galería San Juan **1**
Gran Hotel El Convento **1**

Radisson Ambassador Plaza Casino **6**
Radisson Normandie **2**
Ritz-Carlton Hotel & Casino **8**
San Juan Grand Beach Hotel & Casino **8**
San Juan Marriott Resort & Stellaris Casino **6**
Wyndham Old San Juan Hotel & Casino **1**

Atlantic Ocean

BIASCOCHEA

TO ISLA VERDE

Cementerio Puerto Rico Memorial

Aeropuerto Internacional Luis Muñoz Marín

ATLANTIC VIEW

Laguna Los Corozos

Parque Barbosa

calle Loíza

av. Baldorioty de Castro

OCEAN PARK

LAS PALMAS

av. Eduardo Conde

av. Borinquen

av. Rexach

SANTURCE

av. Eduardo Conde

calle Corazón de Jesús

Y.M.C.A.

CONDADO

Ashford Avenue

Condado Beach

av. José de Diego

Calle Europa

c. del Parque

calle Las Palmas

av. Ponce de León

Fuerte San Gerónimo

Ashford Avenue

Laguna del Condado

PUERTA DE TIERRA

MIRAMAR

av. Fernández Juncos

Expreso Luis Muñoz Rivera

calle Labra

calle Tierra

av. Kennedy

Parque Central

Puente Constitución

Caño de Martín Peña

U.S. Naval Res.

av. Muñoz Rivera
av. Ponce de León
av. Fernández Juncos

SEE OLD SAN JUAN MAP

Aeropuerto de Isla Grande

Bahía de San Juan

N

1 Mi
1 Km

Begin your walk near the post office, amid the taxis, buses, and urban congestion of:

1. **Plaza de la Marina,** a sloping, many-angled plaza situated at the eastern edge of one of San Juan's showcase promenades—*El Paseo de la Princesa.*

Walk westward along paseo de la Princesa, past heroic statues and manicured trees, until you reach:

2. **La Princesa,** the gray-and-white building on your right, which for centuries served as one of the most feared prisons in the Caribbean. Today it houses a museum and the offices of the Puerto Rico Tourism Company.

Continue walking westward to the base of the heroic fountain near the edge of the sea. Turn to your right and follow the seaside promenade as it parallels the edge of the:

3. **City Walls,** once part of one of the most impregnable fortresses in the New World and even today an engineering marvel. At the top of the walls you'll see balconied buildings that have served for centuries as hospitals and residences of the island's governors.

Continue walking between the sea and the base of the city walls until the walkway goes through the walls at the (*Note:* At press time, most of the seaside promenade here was closed for constuction, but should reopen by mid-2001. Rejoin the walking tour at the San Juan Gate.):

4. **San Juan Gate,** at Calle San Juan and Recinto del Oeste. This is actually more of a tunnel than a gate. Now that you're inside the once-dreaded fortification, turn immediately right and walk uphill along Calle Recinto del Oeste. The wrought-iron gates at the street's end lead to:

5. **La Fortaleza and Mansion Ejecutiva,** the centuries-old residence of the Puerto Rican governor, located on Calle La Fortaleza.

Now retrace your steps along Calle Recinto del Oeste, walking first downhill and then uphill for about a block until you reach a street called las Monjas. Fork left until you see a panoramic view and a contemporary statue marking the center of:

6. **Plazuela de la Rogativa,** the small plaza of the religious procession.

Continue your promenade westward, passing between a pair of urn-capped gateposts. You'll be walking parallel to the city walls. The boulevard will fork (bear to the right); continue climbing the steeply inclined cobble-covered ramp to its top. The views from this part of the walk are awesome. Walk westward across the field toward the neoclassical gateway of a fortress believed impregnable for centuries, the:

7. **Castillo de San Felipe del Morro ("El Morro"),** whose treasury and strategic position were the envy of both Europe and the Caribbean. Here, Spanish Puerto Rico struggled to defend itself against the navies of Great Britain, France, and Holland, as well as the hundreds of pirate ships that wreaked havoc throughout the colonial Caribbean. First built in 1540 and added to in 1787, the fortress walls were designed as part of a network of defenses that made San Juan *La Ciudad Murada* (the Walled City). The fortress sits grandly on a gently sloping, grassy hill, offering some excellent photo ops.

After your visit, with El Morro behind you, retrace your steps through the sunlit, treeless field to the point you stood at when you first sighted the fortress. Walk down the Calle del Morro past the:

8. **Antiguo Manicomio Insular,** originally built in 1854 as an insane asylum. It now houses the Puerto Rican Academy of Fine Arts. Further on, the stately neoclassical building (painted buff with fern-green trim) on your right is the:

9. **Asilo de Beneficencia** ("Home for the Poor"), which dates from the 1840s.

Old San Juan Walking Tour

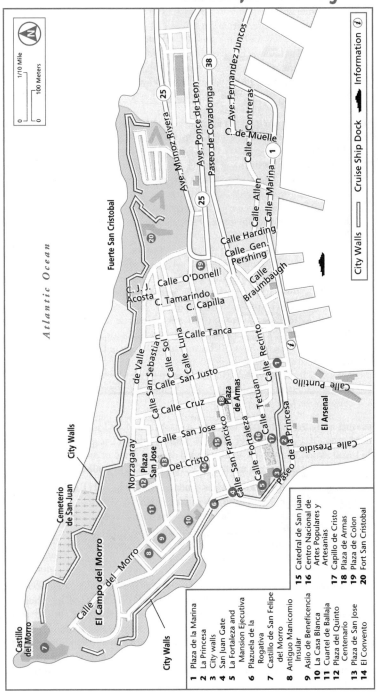

Atlantic Ocean

Castillo del Morro

El Campo del Morro

Cemeterio de San Juan

City Walls

City Walls

Calle del Morro

Norzagaray

Fuerte San Cristobal

C. J. J. Acosta   Calle O'Donell

C. Tamarindo   C. Capilla

Calle Tanca

de Valle   Calle San Sebastian

Calle Sol

Calle Luna

Calle San Justo

Calle Cruz

Calle San Jose

Plaza de Armas

Del Cristo

Plaza San Jose

Calle San Francisco

Calle Fortaleza

Calle Tetuan

Calle Recinto

Calle Puntilla

Calle Presidio

El Arsenal

Calle de la Princesa

Paseo de la Princesa

Calle Harding

Calle Gen. Pershing

Calle Braumbaugh

Calle Allen

Calle Marina

Calle Contreras

C. de Muelle

Ave. Muñoz Rivera

Ave. Ponce de Leon

Paseo de Covadonga

Ave. Fernandez Juncos

25   25   38   1

1   9   20

North

0   1/10 Mile
0   100 Meters

Legend

1 Plaza de la Marina
2 La Princesa
3 City walls
4 San Juan Gate
5 La Fortaleza and Mansion Ejecutiva
6 Plazuela de la Rogativa
7 Castillo de San Felipe del Morro
8 Antiguo Manicomio Insular
9 Asilo de Beneficencia
10 La Casa Blanca
11 Cuartel de Ballaja
12 Plaza del Quinto Centenario
13 Plaza de San Jose
14 El Convento
15 Catedral de San Juan
16 Centro Nacional de Artes Populares y Artesanias
17 Capillo de Cristo
18 Plaza de Armas
19 Plaza de Colon
20 Fort San Cristobal

City Walls ▬▬ Cruise Ship Dock ◀ Information

i Information

Continue walking uphill to the small, formal, sloping plaza at the street's top. On the righthand side, within a trio of buildings, is:

10. La Casa Blanca, built by the son-in-law of Juan Ponce de León to be the great explorer's island home (he never actually lived here, though). Today, this "White House" accommodates a small museum and has beautiful gardens.

Exit by the compound's front entrance and walk downhill, retracing your steps for a half block, and then head toward the massive and monumental tangerine-colored building on your right, the:

11. Cuartel de Ballajá. The military barracks of Ballajá evokes the most austere and massive monasteries of Old Spain. On the building's second floor is the **Museum of the Americas.**

After your visit, exit through the barracks's surprisingly narrow back (eastern) door, where you'll immediately spot one of the most dramatic modern plazas in Puerto Rico, the:

12. Plaza del Quinto Centenario, a terraced tribute to the European colonization of the New World, and one of the most elaborate and symbolic formal piazzas in Puerto Rico.

Now, walk a short block to the southeast to reach the ancient borders of the:

13. Plaza de San José, dominated by a heroic statue of Juan Ponce de León, cast from English cannon captured during a naval battle in 1797. Around the square's periphery are three important sites: the **Museo de Pablo Casals,** where exhibits honor the life and work of the Spanish-born cellist who adopted Puerto Rico as his final home; **Casa de los Contrafuertes** (House of the Buttresses); and **Iglesia de San José,** where the conquistador's coat-of-arms hangs above the altar. Established by the Dominicans in 1523, this church is one of the oldest places of Christian worship in the New World.

Exiting from the plaza's southwestern corner, walk downhill along one of the capital's oldest and best-known streets, **Calle del Cristo.** Two blocks later, at the corner of las Monjas, is:

14. El Convento, originally a convent in the 17th century, but now for many decades one of the few hotels in the old city. Recently restored, it's better than ever. Across the street from El Convento lies the island's most famous church and spiritual centerpiece, the:

15. Catedral de San Juan. Now walk 2 more blocks southward along Calle del Cristo, through one of the most attractive shopping districts in the Caribbean. After passing Calle La Fortaleza, look on your left for the:

16. Centro Nacional de Artes Populares y Artesanias, a popular arts-and-crafts center run by the Institute of Puerto Rican Culture.

Continue to the southernmost tip of Calle del Cristo (just a few steps away) to the wrought-iron gates that surround a chapel no bigger than a newspaper kiosk, the:

17. Capilla de Cristo. Its silver altar is dedicated to the "Christ of Miracles."

Retrace your steps about a block along the Calle del Cristo, walking north. Turn right along Calle La Fortaleza. One block later, go left onto Calle de San José, which leads to the site of the capital's most symmetrical and beautiful square, the:

18. Plaza de Armas, a broad and open plaza designed along Iberian lines during the 19th century. Two important buildings flanking this square are the neoclassic **Intendencia** (which houses certain offices of the U.S. State Department) and **San Juan's City Hall** (Alcaldía).

You can either end your tour here, or forge ahead to two important sites on the east side of Old San Juan. To continue, leave the square eastward along the Calle San Francisco. Eventually you'll come to:

19. **Plaza de Colón,** with its stone column topped with a statue of Christopher Columbus. On the south side of the square is the Tapía Theater, which has been restored to its original 19th-century elegance.

Then continue along Calle San Francisco to its intersection with Calle de Valle, and follow the signs to:

20. **Fort San Cristóbal,** built as part of the string of fortifications protecting one of Spain's most valuable colonies. Today, like its twin, El Morro, it is maintained by the National Park Service and can be visited throughout the day.

When you're through with this walking tour, be sure to just meander about Old San Juan's charming side streets; there are some quaint bars and restaurants that are perfect for a drink or some lunch.

GAMBLING

Casinos are one of the island's biggest draws. Most are open daily from noon to 4pm and again from 8pm to 4am.

The 18,500-square-foot **Casino at the Ritz-Carlton,** 6961 State Rd., no. 187, Isla Verde (☎ **787/253-1700**), is the largest in Puerto Rico. It combines the elegant decor of the 1940s with tropical fabrics and patterns. This is one of the plushest entertainment complexes in the Caribbean. You expect to see Joan Crawford arrive beautifully gowned and on the arm of Clark Gable.

The **San Juan Grand Beach Hotel & Casino,** 187 Isla Verde Avenue in Isla Verde (☎ **800/443-2009** in the U.S., or 787/791-6100), is a 10,000-square-foot gaming facility and an elegant rendezvous. One of its Murano chandeliers is longer than a bowling alley. The casino offers 207 slot machines, 16 blackjack tables, three dice tables, four roulette wheels, and a mini–baccarat table.

You can also try your luck at any of the following:

- **The Caribe Hilton,** Calle Los Rosales (☎ 787/721-0303)
- **The Wyndham Old San Juan Hotel & Casino,** 100 Brumbaugh St. (☎ 787/721-5100)
- **El San Juan Hotel and Casino,** 6063 Isla Verde Ave., Carolina (☎ 787/ 791-1000)
- **The Condado Plaza Hotel & Casino,** 999 Ashford Ave. (☎ 787/721-1000)
- **The Radisson Ambassador Plaza Hotel & Casino,** 1369 Ashford Ave. (☎ 787/ 721-7300)
- **The Diamond Palace Hotel & Casino,** 55 Condado Ave. (☎ 787/721-0810)
- **The Stellaris Casino** at the San Juan Marriott Resort, 1309 Ashford Ave. (☎ 787/722-7000)
- **The Crowne Plaza Hotel and Casino,** Route 187, Kilometer 1.5, Isla Verde (☎ 787/253-2929)

BEACHES

Beaches on Puerto Rico are open to the public, although you will be charged for use of *balneario* facilities, such as lockers and showers. Public beaches shut down on Mondays; if Monday is a holiday, the beaches are open for the holiday but closed the next day. Beach hours are from 9am to 5pm in winter, to 6pm in the off-season.

Bordering some of the Caribbean's finest resort hotels, the **Condado** and **Isla Verde** beaches are the most popular in town. Both are good for snorkeling and have rental equipment for water sports. **Condado Beach** is the single most famous beach strip in the Caribbean, despite the fact it's not the best beach and can be crowded in winter. Its long bands of white sand border some of the Caribbean's finest resort hotels. Locals prefer to head east of El Condado to the beaches of **Isla Verde,** which are less rocky and better sheltered from the waves. You can reach the beaches of **Ocean Park** and **Park Barboa,** on San Juan's north shore, by bus.

Luquillo Beach, lying about 30 miles east of San Juan, is edged by a vast coconut grove. This crescent-shaped beach is not only the best in Puerto Rico, but one of the finest in the entire Caribbean. Coral reefs protect the crystal-clear lagoon from the fierce Atlantic. There are changing rooms, lockers, showers, and picnic facilities. However, the beach isn't as well maintained as it used to be.

Dorado Beach, Cerromar Beach, and **Palmas del Mar** are the chief centers for those seeking the golf, tennis, and beach life. Sometimes they're overcrowded, especially on Saturday and Sunday, but at other times they're practically deserted. If you find a secluded beach, be careful: Solitude is nice, but so is safety in numbers.

SPORTS

DEEP-SEA FISHING   It's said in deep-sea-fishing circles that **Capt. Mike Benitez,** who has chartered out of San Juan for more than 40 years, sets the standard by which to judge other captains. Benitez Fishing Charters can be contacted directly at P.O. Box 5141, Puerto de Tierra, San Juan, PR 00906 (☎ **787/723-2292**). The captain offers a 45-foot air-conditioned deluxe Hateras, the *Sea Born.* Fishing tours for parties of up to six cost around $450 for a half-day excursion, and $750 for a full day, with beverages and all equipment included. In the waters just off Palmas del Mar, the resort complex on the southeast coast of Puerto Rico, **Capt. Bill Burleson,** P.O. Box 8270, Humacao, PR 00792 (☎ **787/850-7442**), operates charters on his fully customized 46-foot sportfishing boat, *Karolette.* Burleson prefers to take fishing groups to Grappler Banks, 18 nautical miles away. It costs $570 for a maximum of six people for 4 hours, $720 for 6 hours, and $960 for 9 hours. He'll give you a discount if you pay in cash. He also offers snorkeling expeditions to Isla de Vieques and other locations.

GOLF   Puerto Rico may be a golfer's dream, but you'll need to sign up for the ship's excursion or rent a car to reach the major courses, which lie 45 minutes to $1\frac{1}{2}$ hours from San Juan. With 72 holes, the **Hyatt Resorts Puerto Rico at Dorado** (☎ **787/796-1234**) offers the greatest concentration of golf in the Caribbean, including the 18-hole Robert Trent Jones, Sr., courses at the Hyatt Regency Cerromar and the Hyatt Dorado Beach, and the par-72 East course at Dorado Beach, with the famous par-5, 5,540-yard 14th hole. The **Golf Club,** at Palmas del Mar in Humacao (☎ **787/852-6000,** ext. 54), is 45 miles east of San Juan. The par-72, 6,803-yard course was designed by Gary Player. **Rio Mar Golf Course,** at Palmer (☎ **787/888-8815**), is a 45-minute drive from San Juan along Route 187, on the northeast coast. The greens fees at this 6,145-yard course are less expensive after 2pm.

SCUBA DIVING   Puerto Rico offers excellent diving, but most of it is not within easy reach of San Juan. **Caribe Aquatic Adventures,** P.O. Box 9024278, San Juan Station, San Juan, PR 00902 (☎ **787/724-1882**), will take you to sites in San Juan. Its dive shop is located in the rear lobby of the Radisson Normandie Hotel. Diving ranges from $45 to $125 for a full-day excursion to Fajardo and $80 for snorkelers.

WINDSURFING, JET-SKIING & SNORKELING   The best place for windsurfing and snorkeling on the island's north shore is along the well-maintained beachfront of the Hyatt Dorado Beach Hotel, near the 10th hole of the hotel's famous east golf course. Here, **Penfield Island Adventures** (☎ 787/796-1234, ext. 3768, or 787/796-2188) offers 90-minute windsurfing lessons and board rentals. Boards designed specifically for beginners and children are available. The school benefits from the north shore's strong, steady winds and an experienced crew of instructors. You can also rent Waverunners (jet skis) and Sunfish sailboats.

SHOPPING

U.S. citizens don't pay duty on items bought in Puerto Rico and brought back to the mainland United States. You can find great bargains in San Juan; prices are often lower than those in St. Thomas. The streets of the **Old Town,** such as Calle San Francisco and Calle del Cristo, are the major venues. Most stores in Old San Juan are closed on Sunday. Local handcrafts can be good buys, including *santos* (hand-carved wooden religious figures), needlework, straw work, ceramics, hammocks, guayabera shirts for men, papier-mâché fruit and vegetables, and paintings and sculptures by Puerto Rican artists.

The biggest and most up-to-date shopping plaza in the Caribbean Basin is **Plaza Las Americas,** which lies in the financial district of Hato Rey, right off the Las Americas Expressway. The complex, with its fountains and advanced architecture, has more than 200 shops, most of them upmarket.

El Alcazar, Calle San José 103, is the largest emporium of antique furniture, silver, and art objects in the Caribbean. The best way to sift through the massive inventory is to begin at the address listed above, on Calle San José between Calle Luna and Calle Sol, and ask the owners, Sharon and Robert Bartos, to guide you to the other three buildings, all stuffed with important art and antiques.

Set in a 200-year-old colonial building, **Puerto Rican Arts & Crafts,** Calle Fortaleza 204, is one of the premier outlets on the island for authentic handcrafts. Of particular interest are papier-mâché carnival masks from the town of Ponce; their grotesque and colorful features were designed to chase away evil spirits.

José E. Alegria & Associates, Calle del Cristo 152–154, is half antique shop, half old-fashioned arcade lined with gift shops and boutiques. **Galería Botello,** Calle del Cristo 208, is a living tribute to the late Angel Botello, one of Puerto Rico's most outstanding artists. Once his home, today the space displays his paintings and sculptures, and also offers a large collection of Puerto Rican antique santos. **Haitian Souvenirs,** Calle San Francisco 206, specializes in Haitian art and artifacts. Its walls are covered with primitive Haitian landscapes, portraits, and crowd scenes, most costing from $35 to $350.

San Juan is also home to some great outlet shops. At **London Fog,** Calle del Cristo 156, and the **Polo Ralph Lauren Factory Store,** Calle del Cristo 201, you can get the famous raincoats and the famous fashions at prices that are often 30% to 40% less than on the U.S. mainland.

GREAT LOCAL BARS & RESTAURANTS IN OLD SAN JUAN

A favorite **local beer** is Medalla; a favorite **local rum** is the famous Bacardi (pronounced Bah-carrrr-*di*), in all its various varieties.

Al Dente, Calle Recinto Sur 309 (☎ 787/723-7303), is a relaxed, trattorialike place serving reasonably priced dishes like brochettes of fresh tuna laced with pepper and Mediterranean herbs. ✪ **Amadeus,** Calle San Sebastián 106, across from the Iglesia de San José (☎ 787/722-8635), offers Caribbean cuisine with a nouvelle twist. **El Patio de Sam,** Calle San Sebastián 102, across from the Iglesia de San José (☎ 787/723-1149), is a popular gathering spot for American expatriates, newspeople, and shopkeepers. It's known for having the best burgers in San Juan. Speaking of burgers, the **Hard Rock Café** is at Calle Recinto Sur 253 (☎ 787/724-7625).

La Bombonera, Calle San Francisco 259 (☎ 787/722-0658), offers exceptional food at affordable prices. For decades a rendezvous for the island's literati and Old San Juan families, the food is authentically Puerto Rican, homemade, and inexpensive. **La Mallorquina,** Calle San Justo 207 (☎ 787/722-3261), was founded in 1848, and its chef specializes in the most typical Puerto Rican rice dish: *asopao.* You can have it with either chicken, shrimp, or lobster and shrimp. The nuevo Latino cuisine at ✪ **Parrot Club,** 363 Calle Fortaleza (☎ 787/725-7370), blends traditional Puerto Rican cookery with Spanish, Taíno, and African influences.

20 St. Barthélemy (St. Barts)

Part of the French department of Guadeloupe, lying 15 miles from St. Maarten, sexy St. Barthélemy (also called **St. Barts** or **St. Barths**) is a small, hilly island with a population of 3,500 people of European and African descent who live on 13 square miles of verdant and dramatically hilly terrain bordered by pleasant white-sand beaches. St. Barts is sophistication in the tropics, an expensive and exclusive stamping ground of the rich and famous, with a distinctive seafaring tradition and a decidedly French flavor—chic, rich, and very Parisian, with a touch of Normandy and even Sweden in its personality. It's quite the European playground, disguised as a Caribbean island.

Forget such things as historical sights or ambitious water sports here. Come instead for white sandy beaches, fine French cuisine, relaxation in ultimate comfort, and the scene. Generally, only small cruise ships can visit this little French pocket of posh.

The island's capital and only town is **Gustavia,** named after a Swedish king. Set in a sheltered harbor, it looks like a little dollhouse-scale port.

Frommer's Favorite St. Barts Experiences

- **Hanging out at the Le Select cafe:** The most popular gathering place in Gustavia is *the* place to get a taste of local life (see "Great Local Restaurants & Bars," below).
- **Heading to the beaches:** There are several utterly gorgeous ones on St. Barts (see "Beaches," below).
- **Touring the Island in a Mini-Moke:** You'll feel totally cool zipping around the island's undulating, hilly roads in one of these open-air vehicles, which are half golf cart and half jeep.

COMING ASHORE   Cruise ships anchor right off Gustavia; tenders then ferry passengers to the heart of town. There are usually shaded refreshment stands on shore. A short walk will get you into Gustavia's restaurant and shopping district.

CURRENCY   The official monetary unit is the **French franc (F),** but most stores and restaurants prefer U.S. dollars. The exchange rate is 6.29F to U.S.$1 (1 F = U.S.16¢). I've used this rate to convert currency throughout this section.

Frommer's Ratings: St. Barts					
	poor	fair	good	excellent	outstanding
Overall Experience				✓	
Shore Excursions			✓		
Activities Close to Port				✓	
Beaches & Water Sports				✓	
Shopping				✓	
Dining/Bars			✓		

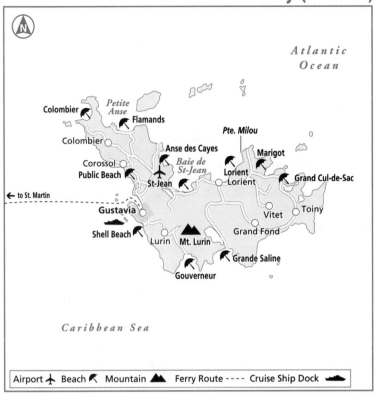

Atlantic Ocean

Colombier

Petite Anse

Flamands

Colombier

Corossol

Public Beach

← to St. Martin

Anse des Cayes

Baie de St-Jean

St-Jean

Pte. Milou

Marigot

Lorient

Lorient

Grand Cul-de-Sac

Gustavia

Shell Beach

Lurin

Mt. Lurin

Vitet

Grand Fond

Toiny

Grande Saline

Gouverneur

Caribbean Sea

Airport ✈ Beach ⌐ Mountain ▲▲ Ferry Route - - - - Cruise Ship Dock ⬛

LANGUAGE   St. Barts is technically part of France, so the official language is French. However, nearly everyone speaks English.

INFORMATION   Go to the **Office du Tourisme** in the Town Hall, quai du Général-de-Gaulle, in Gustavia (☎ 590/27-87-27). It's open Monday to Friday from 9am to 5pm. For info before you go, call the tourist board office in the U.S. at ☎ 410/286-8310 or log on to the Web site at www.frenchcaribbean.com.

CALLING FROM THE U.S.   When calling St. Barts from the United States, you need to dial "011" before the numbers listed throughout this section.

GETTING AROUND

BY TAXI   Taxis meet all cruise ships and aren't very expensive, since no destination is all that far. Dial ☎ 590/27-66-31 for taxi service. The fare is about 25F ($4) for rides up to 5 minutes; each additional 3 minutes is another 20F ($3.20).

BY MINI-MOKE OR SAMURAI   If you're a confident driver, renting one of these open-sided Mini-Mokes or manual-transmission Suzuki Samurais is great fun and the only way to zip around the jagged (and picturesque) hills of this 8-square-mile island in style. It'll cost about $40 a day. Try **Budget** (☎ 800/527-0700 or 590/27-66-30); **Hertz** (☎ 800/654-3001), which operates through a local dealership, Henry's Car Rental; and **Avis** (☎ 800/331-1084 or 590/27-71-43), whose local name is St. Barts Centre-Auto.

BY MOTOR SCOOTER   You can rent motorbikes and scooters from **Rent Some Fun,** rue Gambetta in Gustavia (☎ **590/27-70-59**). The approximately $30 daily rental fee covers both bike and helmet; a $200 deposit is required.

SHORE EXCURSIONS

Many passengers prefer to spend their time ashore walking around and exploring Gustavia, which should take no more than 2 hours.

Minibus Island Tour ($25, 1¹/₂ hours): The duration is so short because there are almost no attractions other than the island's natural beauty and beaches. The minibus goes through the port, and then past the village of St-Jean to an overlook in Salinos, where you can take in the view. On the windward side of the island, you'll notice the different architecture required to withstand the heavy breezes. Next you'll head to Grand Cul-de-Sac for a view of the lagoon, and then have a brief stop at La Savone. You'll be brought back to the ship via Corossol, a tiny fishing village where the locals make straw from lantana palms.

ON YOUR OWN

All the big attractions—beaches, shopping, and people-watching—are covered elsewhere in this section.

SHOPPING

You don't pay any duty on St. Barts, so it's a good place to buy liquor and French perfumes at some of the lowest prices in the Caribbean. In fact, perfume and champagne are cheaper here than in metropolitan France. You'll also find good buys in sportswear, crystal, porcelain, watches, and other luxuries. The only trouble is that selections here are limited.

If you're in the market for **island crafts,** try to find those convertible-brim, fine straw hats St. Bartians like to wear. *Vogue* once featured them in its fashion pages. There are also some interesting block-printed cotton resort clothes on the island.

La Boutique Couleur des Îles, rue du Général-de-Gaulle 8, sells shirts and blouses for about $30 to $50 with hand-embroidered references to the flora and fauna of St. Barts. **Laurent Eiffel,** rue du Général-de-Gaulle, sells imitations of designer items that usually cost 10 times as much. Look for belts, bags, and accessories modeled after Versace, Prada, Hermès, Gucci, and Chanel. **St. Barts Style,** rue Lafayette, near the corner of rue du Port, stocks brightly hued beachwear by Jams World and Vicidomine. **Le Comptoir du Cigare,** rue du Général-de-Gaulle 6, caters to the villa-and-yacht crowd. Its cigars hail from Cuba and the Dominican Republic; connoisseur-quality rums come from Martinique, Cuba, and Haiti. (Remember that Cuban cigars cannot legally be brought into the U.S., so you must smoke them abroad.)

Diamond Genesis/Kornérupine, rue du Général-de-Gaulle 12, Les Suites du Roi-Oskar-II, is one of the few shops on the island where jewelry is handcrafted on the premises (and sells for between $20 and $60,000). **La Maison de Free Mousse,** Carré d'Or, quai de la République, is the most unusual gift shop on St. Barts, with wood carvings and handcrafts from throughout Europe, Asia, and South America.

BEACHES

There are 14 white-sand beaches on St. Barts. My favorites (Gouverneur, Saline, Marigot, and Colombier) are pretty secluded, but few beaches here are ever crowded, even during winter. All are public and free, and easily accessible by taxi from the cruise pier. You can also make arrangements to be picked up at a scheduled time. Nude bathing is officially prohibited, but topless sunbathing is quite common.

Gouverneur on the south is gorgeous and offers some waves, but wear lots of sunscreen—there's no shade. Get there by driving or taking a taxi through Gustavia and up to Lurin. Turn at the Santa Fe Restaurant (see "Great Local Restaurants & Bars," below), and head down a narrow road. To get to the beach **Saline,** to the east of Gouverneur, drive up the road from the commercial center in St-Jean. A short walk over the sand dune and you're there. Like Gouverneur, it offers some waves but no shade.

Marigot, also on the north shore, is narrow but good for swimming and snorkeling. **Colombier** is difficult to get to, but well worth the effort for swimmers and snorkelers. You'll have to take a boat or a rugged goat path from Petite Anse past Flamands, a 30-minute walk. You can pack a lunch and eat in the shade.

The most famous beach is **St-Jean,** which is actually two beaches divided by the Eden Rock promontory. It offers water sports, beach restaurants, and a few hotels, as well as some shady areas. **Flamands,** to the west, is a very wide beach with a few small hotels and some lantana palms.

If you want a beach with hotels, restaurants, and water sports, the **Grand Cul-de-Sac** area on the northeast shore fits the bill. There's a narrow beach here protected by a reef.

SPORTS

SCUBA DIVING   Marine Service, quai du Yacht-Club in Gustavia (☎ **590/27-70-34**), operates from a one-story building on the water at the edge of a marina, across the harbor from the more congested part of Gustavia. The outfit is familiar with at least 15 unusual dive sites scattered at various points offshore, including The Grouper, a remote reef west of St. Barts, close to the uninhabited cay known as Ile Forchue. Almost as important are the reefs near Roche Rouge, off the opposite (i.e., eastern) edge of St. Barts. The island has only one relatively safe wreck dive, to the rusting hulk of *Kayali,* a trawler that sank offshore in 1994. It's recommended only for experienced divers.

WATERSKIING   Marine Service (see above) can also arrange waterskiing, offered daily from 9am to 1pm and again from 4:40pm to sundown. Because of the shape of the coastline, skiers must remain at least 80 yards from shore on the windward side of the island and 110 yards off the leeward side.

WINDSURFING   Try St. Barth Wind School near the Tom Beach Hotel on Plage de St-Jean. It's open daily from 9am to 5pm.

GREAT LOCAL RESTAURANTS & BARS

IN GUSTAVIA   The most popular gathering place in Gustavia is ✪ **Le Select,** rue de la France (☎ **590/27-86-87**), apparently named after its more famous granddaddy in the Montparnasse section of Paris. It's utterly simple. A game of dominoes might be under way as you walk in. Tables are placed outside on the gravel in an open-air cafe garden near the port. The outdoor grill promises a "cheeseburger in Paradise." Jimmy Buffett might show up here, or perhaps Mick Jagger. If you want to spread a rumor and have it travel fast across the island, start it here. The place is open Monday to Saturday from 10am to 11pm.

L'Iguane, Carré d'Or, quai de la République (☎ **590/27-88-46**), offers an international menu that includes sushi, American breakfasts, and California-style sandwiches and salads.

AT MORNE LURIN   Santa Fe Restaurant, Morne Lurin (☎ **590/27-61-04**), is a burger house and sports bar that's carved out a niche for itself among the island's English-speaking clientele. It features wide-screen TVs that present American sports events.

IN GRANDE SALINE   Le Tamarin, Plage de Saline (☎ **590/27-72-12**), is an informal bistro isolated amid rocky hills and forests east of Gustavia. Menu items are mostly light, including gazpacho, a *pavé* of Cajun-style tuna with Creole sauce and baby vegetables, and chicken roasted with lemon and ginger.

IN GRAND CUL-DE-SAC   Lunching at **Club Lafayette,** Grand Cul-de-Sac (☎ **590/27-62-51**), located in a cove on the eastern end of the island, is like taking a meal at your own private, very expensive beach club. The menu includes such items as warm foie gras served with apples, and one of the best meal-size lobster salads on the island. **West Indies Café,** in El Sereno Beach Hotel, Grand Cul-de-Sac, 4 miles east of Gustavia (☎ **590/27-64-80**), incorporates aspects of a Parisian cabaret with simple but well-prepared meals such as fish tartare, eggplant mousse, grilled lobster, and grilled tuna and snapper.

21 St. Croix

Though it's now part of the U.S. Virgin Islands, and though seven different flags have flown over St. Croix in its history, it's the 2^1/$_2$ centuries of Danish influence that is most visible in the island's architecture, while the island's population is descended from African and European origins. Some families have been on the island for 10 generations, with roots dating back to colonial times. Today, St. Croix competes with St. Thomas for the Yankee cruise ship dollar. Although it gets nowhere near the number of visitors, St. Croix is more tranquil and less congested than its smaller sibling. The major attraction here is **Buck Island National Park,** a national offshore treasure.

St. Croix boasts some fine beaches as well, including Sandy Point, Sprat Hall, and Rainbow Beach. At the east end of the island (which, incidentally, is the easternmost possession of the U.S.), the terrain is rocky and arid. The west end is lusher, with a rain forest of mango and mahogany, tree ferns, and dangling lianas. Rolling hills and upland pastures make up much of the area between the two extremes, while African tulips are just one of the many tropical flowers that add a splash of color to the landscape. St. Croix's most prominent landmarks are the ruins of the sugarcane plantations that once covered the islands.

Although large cruise ships moor at **Frederiksted,** most of the action is in **Christiansted,** located on a coral-bound bay about midway along the north shore and featuring more sights and better restaurants and shopping. The town is being handsomely restored, and the entire harbor-front area is a national historic site.

Frommer's Favorite St. Croix Experiences

- **Visiting Buck Island Reef National Monument:** Within this 800-acre preserve, the only underwater national monument in the United States, you can snorkel over a series of unqiue underwater trails and experience some of the best-preserved coral reefs in the Caribbean. A snorkeling instructor guides the excursion.

Frommer's Ratings: St. Croix					
	poor	fair	good	excellent	outstanding
Overall Experience				✓	
Shore Excursions				✓	
Activities Close to Port				✓	
Beaches & Water Sports				✓	
Shopping					✓
Dining/Bars			✓		

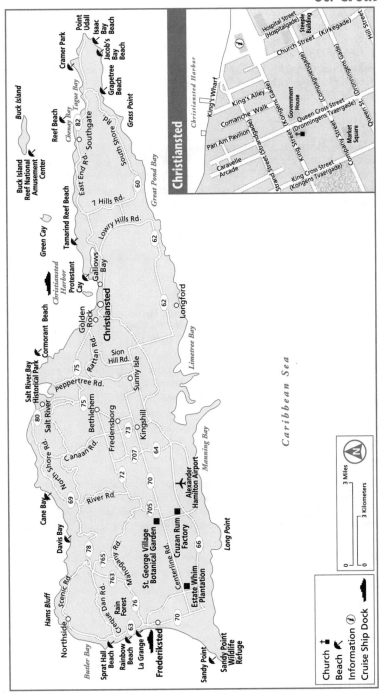

St. Croix

Christiansted

Christiansted Harbor

Hospital Street (Hospitalgade)
Steeple Building
Church Street (Kirkegade)
Hill Street

King's Wharf
King's Alley
Comanche Walk
Government House
Pan Am Pavilion
Strand Street (Strandgade)
King Street (Kongens Gade)
Queen Cross Street (Dronningens Tvaergade)
Queen Cross Street (Dronningens Gade)
Queen St. (Dronningens Gade)
Caravelle Arcade
Market Square
Company Street (Compagniesgade)
King Cross Street (Kongens Tvaergade)

Point Udall
Isaac Bay Beach
Jacob's Bay Beach
Cramer Park
Grapetree Beach
Grass Point
Buck Island
Buck Island Reef National Amusement Center
Reef Beach
Chenay Bay
Tague Bay
82
Southgate
East End Rd.
South Shore Rd.
Great Pond Bay
Green Cay
Tamarind Reef Beach
60
7 Hills Rd.
Lowry Hills Rd.
62
Christiansted Harbor
Protestant Cay
Gallows Bay
Cormorant Beach
Golden Rock
Christiansted
62
Longford
Limetree Bay
Salt River Bay Historical Park
Sion Hill Rd.
Sunny Isle
75
Rattan Rd.
Peppertree Rd.
80
Salt River
75
Bethlehem
Fredensborg
Kingshill
Manning Bay
North Shore Rd.
Canaan Rd.
73
64
707
72
70
Alexander Hamilton Airport
Cane Bay
69
River Rd.
705
Davis Bay
78
St. George Village Botanical Garden
Cruzan Rum Factory
Long Point
765
Mahogany Rd.
Caribbean Sea
Hams Bluff
Scenic Rd.
763
Crèque Dan Rd.
Rain Forest
76
Cemerline Rd.
66
Estate Whim Plantation
Northside
Butler Bay
63
Sprat Hall Beach
Rainbow Beach
La Grange
Frederiksted
70
Sandy Point
Sandy Point Wildlife Refuge

3 Miles
3 Kilometers
0
0

Church †
Beach
Information *i*
Cruise Ship Dock

545

- **Biking along the coast:** On this tour, you pass through Frederiksted, then past ruins and through forests and rolling grasslands (see "Shore Excursions," below).
- **Gambling:** Try your luck at St. Croix's first casino, which opened in early 2000 at the new Divi Carina Bay Hotel.
- **Strolling through Christiansted:** Because of its well-preserved 18th- and 19th-century Danish architecture (particularly Fort Christiansvaern), Christiansted has been designated a National Historic Site. In the late 1700s, it was a crown colony of Denmark and one of the Caribbean's major ports, and today many street signs are still in Danish.

COMING ASHORE   Only cruise ships with fewer than 200 passengers can land directly at the dock at Christiansted. Others moor at a 1,500-foot pier at Frederiksted, a sleepy town that springs to life only when the ships arrive. Both piers have information centers and telephones. I suggest you spend as little time as possible in Frederiksted and head immediately for Christiansted, some 17 miles away. It's easy to explore either Frederiksted or Christiansted on foot (the only way, really), although you might want to consider one of the shore excursions outlined below to see more of the island, especially its underwater treasures.

There are 10 **phone booths** at the end of the pier.

CURRENCY   The **U.S. dollar** is the official currency.

LANGUAGE   English is spoken here.

INFORMATION   The **U.S. Virgin Islands Division of Tourism** has offices in Christiansted at Queen Cross Street (☎ **340/773-0495**), and at the Customs House Building, Strand Street in Frederiksted (☎ **340/772-0357**). Open Monday to Friday from 9am to 5pm. To get info before you go, contact the tourism board office in the U.S. at ☎ **800/372-USVI** or www.visitstcroix.com. To get up-to-the-minute info on St. Croix, from taxi and bus rates to maps and info on restaurants and the island's history and culture, pick up a free copy of the pink *St. Croix This Week*. (It's a lot more than just ads!)

CALLING FROM THE U.S.   When calling St. Croix from the United States, you need to dial only a "1" before the numbers listed throughout this section.

GETTING AROUND

BY TAXI   Taxis are unmetered, so agree on the rate before you get in. The **St. Croix Taxicab Association** (☎ **340/778-1088**) offers door-to-door service. Taxi tours are a great way to explore the island. For one or two passengers, the cost is about $50 for 2 hours or $70 for 3 hours. I don't recommend renting a car. It costs $20 to take a taxi from Christiansted to Frederiksted.

BY BUS   Air-conditioned buses run daily between Christiansted and Frederiksted about every 40 minutes between 5:30am and 9pm. The fare is $1. For more information, call ☎ **340/778-0898.**

SHORE EXCURSIONS

Although it's possible to get around St. Croix on your own, you also have the option of joining some of the most varied organized shore excursions in the Caribbean, including snorkeling and sailing trips, island tours, golf, catamaran party tours, hikes, and bicycle excursions.

Buck Island National Park Tour/Snorkeling ($50, 4–5 hours): The premier tour in St. Croix takes you to a tropical underwater wonderland of blue water and colorful coral reefs. Transportation is provided from the Frederiksted pier to Christiansted, where a powerboat takes you over to Buck Island. An experienced guide provides snorkel lessons.

Island Tour ($31, 4 hours): For a taste of the whole island, this tour includes a visit to the Whim Great House sugar plantation, Christiansted, and other major sites.

St. Croix Bike Tour ($49, 3 hours): Bike along the coast of St. Croix, passing through the town of Frederiksted before heading out on the Northside Road, past ruins and through forests and rolling grasslands.

Hiking Tour ($40, 2 hours): Hike through the 225-acre Butler Bay preserve and enjoy bird watching and a good hearty walk.

Golf at Carambola ($74–$105): One of the Caribbean's most famous courses is another excursion destination. Your cruise line will probably offer an excursion here, or you can do it on your own (see "Sports," below).

TOURING THROUGH LOCAL OPERATORS

Horseback Tour: On this tour, run by Paul and Jill's Equestrian Stables, Sprat Hall Plantation, Route 58 (☎ **340/772-2880**), you'll pass ruins of abandoned 18th-century plantations and sugar mills and climb the hills of St. Croix's western end. Tour guides give running commentaries on island fauna and history and on riding techniques. The stables, owned by Paul Wojcie and his wife, Jill Hurd (a daughter of the establishment's original founders), are set on the sprawling grounds of the island's oldest plantation, and are known throughout the Caribbean for the quality of the horses and the scenic trail rides through the forests. Beginners and experienced riders alike are welcome. Make reservations at least a day in advance.

St. Thomas Hydrofoil or Seaplane Trip: If you want to go to St. Thomas for the day, you can make the 40-mile trip via hydrofoil from Christiansted to Charlotte Amalie in little over an hour for $90 round-trip. A seaplane shuttle between the two is also available for $110 round-trip. Contact **Seaborne Seaplanes** at 34 Strand St. in Christiansted (☎ **340/773-6442**).

ON YOUR OWN: WITHIN WALKING DISTANCE

IN FREDERIKSTED   Frederiksted is nothing great, but if you decide to hang around you should begin your tour at russet-colored **Fort Frederik,** next to the cruise ship pier. Some historians claim it was the first fort to sound a foreign salute to the U.S. flag, in 1776. The structure, at the northern end of Frederiksted, has been restored to its 1840 look. You can explore the courtyard and stables, and examine an exhibit area in what was once the Garrison Room. Admission is free. It's open Monday to Saturday from 8am to 5pm.

IN CHRISTIANSTED   Begin your visit at the **visitor bureau** (☎ **340/773-0495**), a yellow building with a cedar-capped roof near the harbor front. It was built as the Old Scalehouse in 1856 to replace a similar, older structure that burned down. In its heyday, all taxable goods leaving and entering the harbor were weighed here. The scales could once accurately weigh barrels of sugar and molasses weighing up to 1,600 pounds.

Another major attraction is the **Steeple Building** (☎ **340/773-1460**), or Church of Lord God of Sabaoth, which was completed in 1753 as St. Croix's first Lutheran church. It, too, stands near the harbor front; get there via Hospital Street. The building was deconsecrated in 1831 and has served at various times as a bakery, a hospital, and a school. Admission is $2, which also includes admission to Fort Christiansvaern (see below). It's open daily from 8am to 5pm.

Overlooking the harbor, **Fort Christiansvaern** (☎ **340/773-1460**) is the best pre-served colonial fortification in the Virgin Islands. The National Park Service maintains the fort as a historic monument. Its original star-shaped design was at the vanguard of the most advanced military planning of its era. It's open Monday to Thursday from 8am to 5pm, Friday and Saturday from 9am to 5pm. Admission is included in the ticket to the Steeple Building (see above).

ON YOUR OWN: BEYOND WALKING DISTANCE

The only known site where Columbus landed in what is now U.S. territory was at Salt River, on the island's northern shore. To mark the 500th anniversary of his arrival, President George Bush signed a bill creating the 912-acre ✪ **Salt River Bay National Historical Park and Ecological Preserve.** The landmass includes the site of the original Carib village explored by Columbus and his men, along with the only ceremonial ball court ever discovered in the Lesser Antilles.

At the Carib settlement, the men of Columbus liberated several Taíno women and children held as slaves. On the way back to their vessels, the Spaniards faced a canoe filled with hostile Caribs, armed with poison arrows. One Spanish soldier was killed, and perhaps six Caribs were either slain or captured. This is the first documented case of hostility between invading Europeans and the native Americans. Sailing away, Columbus named this part of St. Croix "Cape of the Arrows."

The park today is in a natural state. It has the largest mangrove forest in the Virgin Islands, sheltering many endangered animals and plants, plus an underwater canyon attracting scuba divers from around the world. **The St. Croix Environmental Association,** 3 Arawak Building, Gallows Bay, conducts tours of the area. Call them at ☎ **340/773-1989** for details.

The **Cruzan Rum Factory,** West Airport Road, Route 64 (☎ **340/692-2280**), distills the famous Virgin Islands rum, which residents consider to be the finest in the world. Guided tours depart from the visitor pavilion; call for reservations and information.

The **Estate Whim Plantation Museum,** Centerline Road, about 2 miles east of Frederiksted (☎ **340/772-0598**), restored by the St. Croix Landmarks Society, is composed of only three rooms and is unique among the many old sugar plantations dotting the island. Its 3-foot-thick walls are made of stone, coral, and molasses. Also on the museum's premises is a woodworking shop, the estate's original kitchen, a museum store, a servant's quarters, and tools from the 18th century. The ruins include remains of the plantation's sugar-processing plant, complete with a restored windmill.

Note: The **St. George Village Botanical Garden of St. Croix** (☎ **340/692-2874**), the much loved and popular Eden of tropical trees, shrubs, vines, and flowers 4 miles east of Frederiksted, was unfortunately wiped out by Hurricane Lenny in late 1999. At press time, it had not been rebuilt.

SHOPPING

Americans get a break here, since they can bring home $1,200 worth of merchandise from the U.S. Virgin Islands without paying duty, as opposed to a paltry $400 from most other Caribbean ports. And liquor here is duty-free.

A major redevelopment of the waterfront at Christiansted, following the hurricanes of 1995, was **King's Alley Complex,** a pink-sided compound filled with the densest concentration of shopping options on St. Croix.

Worthwhile specialty shops include **Skirt Tails,** Pam Am Pavilion, one of the most colorful and popular boutiques on the island, specializing in hand-painted batiks for both men and women; **The White House,** King's Alley Walk, which stocks women's clothing ranging from dressy to casual and breezy—but all, everything, in white; **Elegant Illusions Copy Jewelry,** 55 King St., which sells credible copies of the baroque and antique jewelry your great-grandmother might have worn, priced from $9 to $1,000; **Larimar,** The Boardwalk/King's Walk, which specializes in larimar—a pale-blue pectolyte prized for its sky-blue color—in various gold settings; **Estate Mount Washington Antiques,** 2 Estate Mount Washington, which is the best treasure trove of colonial West Indian furniture and "flotsam" in the Virgin Islands; **Folk Art Traders,** 1B Queen Cross St., which deals in Caribbean art and folk-art treasures, such as carnival masks, pottery, ceramics, original paintings, and hand-wrought jewelry; and **Many Hands,** in the Pan Am Pavilion, Strand Street, which sells Virgin Islands handcrafts, spices and teas, handmade jewelry, and more.

The Royal Poinciana, 1111 Strand St., looks like an antique apothecary, but is actually the most interesting gift shop on St. Croix. You'll find such Caribbean-inspired items as hot sauces ("fire water"), seasoning blends for gumbos, island herbal teas, Antillean coffees, and a scented array of soaps, toiletries, lotions, and shampoos.

BEACHES

Beaches are the biggest attraction on St. Croix. The drawback is that getting to them from Christiansted or Frederiksted isn't always easy. Taxis will take you, but they can be expensive. In Christiansted, take a ferry to the **Hotel on the Cay,** a palm-shaded island in the harbor.

Most convenient for passengers arriving at Frederiksted is **Sandy Point,** the largest beach in all the U.S. Virgin Islands. Its waters are shallow and calm, perfect for swimming. Sandy Point is the nesting ground for the endangered leatherback and green sea turtles who lay their eggs every year between early April and early June.

Cramer Park, at the northeastern end of the island, is a special public park operated by the Department of Agriculture. Lined with sea-grape trees, the beach has a picnic area, a restaurant, and a bar.

I highly recommend **Cane Bay** and **Davis Bay.** They're both the type of beaches you'd expect to find on a Caribbean island—palms, white sand, and good swimming and snorkeling. Cane Bay attracts snorkelers and divers with its rolling waves, coral gardens, and drop-off wall. It's near Route 80 on the north shore. Davis Beach draws bodysurfers. There are no changing facilities here. It's off the South Shore Road (Route 60), in the vicinity of the Carambola Beach Resort.

Windsurfers like **Reef Beach,** which opens onto Teague Bay along Route 82, East End Road, a half-hour ride from Christiansted. You can order food at Duggan's Reef. On Route 63, a short ride north of Frederiksted, **Rainbow Beach** invites with its white sand and ideal snorkeling conditions. **La Grange** is another good beach in the vicinity, also on Route 63, about 5 minutes north of Frederiksted. You can rent lounge chairs here, and there's a bar nearby.

At the **Cormorant Beach Club,** about 5 miles west of Christiansted, palm trees shade some 1,200 feet of white sands. A living reef lies just off the shore, making snorkeling ideal. **Grapetree Beach** offers a similar amount of clean white sand on the eastern tip of the island. Follow the South Shore Road (Route 60) to reach it. Water sports are popular here.

SPORTS

GOLF St. Croix has the best golfing in the U.S. Virgins. In fact, guests staying on St. John and St. Thomas often fly over for a day's round on the island's two 18-hole and one nine-hole golf courses. The **Carambola Golf Course,** on the northeast side of St. Croix (☎ 340/778-5638), was designed by Robert Trent Jones, Sr., who called it "the loveliest course I ever designed." The course, formerly the site of "Shell's Wonderful World of Golf," has been likened to a botanical garden. Golfing authorities consider its collection of par-3 holes to be the best in the tropics. Carambola's course record of 65 was set by Jim Levine in 1993. The **Buccaneer,** 2 miles east of Christiansted (☎ 340/773-2100, ext. 738), is a challenging 5,810-yard, 18-hole course with panoramic vistas. Players can knock the ball over rolling hills right to the edge of the Caribbean. A final course is the **Reef,** at Teague Bay on the east end of the island (☎ 340/773-8844), a 3,100-yard, nine-hole course. The longest hole is a 579-yard par 5.

SCUBA DIVING   Divers love St. Croix's sponge life, beautiful black-coral trees, and steep drop-offs near the shoreline. This island is home to the largest living reef in the Caribbean. Its fabled north-shore wall begins in 25 to 30 feet of water and drops—sometimes almost straight down—to 13,200 feet. There are 22 moored diving sites. Favorites among them include the historic **Salt River Canyon,** the coral gardens of **Scotch Banks,** and **Eagle Ray,** filled with cruising rays. **Pavilions** is yet another good dive site, with a pristine virgin coral reef. The best site of all, however, is **Buck Island,** an underwater wonderland with a visibility of more than 100 feet and an underwater nature trail. All the minor and major agencies offer scuba and snorkeling tours to Buck Island. **Dive St. Croix,** 59 King's Wharf (☎ 800/523-DIVE in the U.S., or 340/773-2628; fax 340/773-7400), operates the 38-foot dive boat *Reliance.* The staff offers complete instruction, from beginners' courses through full certification. **S.C.O.R.E./V.I. Divers Ltd.,** in the Pan Am Pavilion on Christiansted's waterfront (☎ 800/544-5911 in the U.S., or 340/773-6045), is the oldest and one of the best dive operations on the island. *Rodales Scuba Diving* magazine rated its staff as among the top 10 worldwide. This full-service PADI five-star facility offers daily two-tank boat dives, as well as guided snorkeling trips to Green Cay.

GREAT LOCAL RESTAURANTS & BARS

A couple favorite **local beers** are Carib and Blackbeard's (made on St. Thomas); a favorite **local rum** is Cruzan.

IN CHRISTIANSTED   Annabelle's Tea Room, 51–ABC Company St. (☎ 340/773-3990), occupies a quiet courtyard and serves an assortment of sandwiches, salads, soups, and platters. **Harvey's,** 11B Company St. (☎ 340/773-3433), features the thoroughly zesty cooking of island matriarch Sarah Harvey. Main dishes are the type of food she was raised on: barbecue chicken, barbecue spareribs (barbecue is big here), boiled fillet of snapper, and even lobster when they can get it. **Indies,** 55–56 Company St. (☎ 340/692-9440), serves what may be the finest and freshest meal on St. Croix. The swordfish with fresh artichokes, shiitake mushrooms, and thyme has a savory flavor, as does the baked wahoo with lobster curry and fresh chutney and coconut.

  Paradise Café, Queen Cross St. at 53B Company St. (across from Government House; ☎ 340/773-2985), serves New York deli–style sandwiches throughout the day—everything from a Reuben to a tuna melt. Of course, burgers are always featured. **St. Croix Chop House & Brew Pub,** King's Alley Walk (☎ 340/713-9820), boasts one of the best harbor views in Christiansted, and serves beer, burgers, and sandwiches at street level and a two-fisted menu upstairs that includes garlic-stuffed fillet steak and such fish as wahoo and marlin. **Tutto Bene,** 2 Company St. (☎ 340/773-5229), serves a full range of delectable pastas, plus fish, veggie frittatas, a chicken pesto sandwich, spinach lasagna, and more.

IN FREDERIKSTED   Le St. Tropez, Limetree Court, 67 King St. (☎ 340/772-3000), is the most popular bistro in Frederiksted, offering crêpes, quiches, soups, or salads at lunch in the sunlit courtyard. At night it's Mediterranean cuisine. **Pier 69,**

69 King St. (☎ **340/772-0069**), looks like a combination of a 1950s living room and a nautical bar, and is a hangout for Christiansted's counterculture and a place for sandwiches and salads.

AROUND THE ISLAND **Duggan's Reef,** East End Road, Teague Bay (☎ **340/773-9800**), is the most popular restaurant on St. Croix. At lunch, a simple array of salads, crêpes, and sandwiches is offered. At dinner, specialties include Duggan's Caribbean lobster pasta and Irish whiskey lobster. **Sprat Hall Beach Restaurant,** Route 63, 1 mile north of Frederiksted (☎ **340/772-5855**), serves local dishes like conch chowder, pumpkin fritters, tannia soup, and the fried fish of the day. These local dishes have an authentic island flavor, perhaps more than anywhere else on St. Croix.

22 St. Kitts & Nevis

Linked politically if not physically—they form one nation, though they're separated by 2 miles of ocean—St. Kitts and Nevis lie somewhat off the beaten tourist track, south of St. Martin and north of Guadeloupe. Formerly possessions of Britain, the two islands were given self-government in 1967, and in 1983 became a totally independent nation known as the Federation of St. Kitts and Nevis. It's a stormy marriage, however: Nevis's 1998 referendum for separation from its larger partner failed by the slimmest of margins.

CURRENCY The local currency is the **Eastern Caribbean dollar (EC$).** The exchange rate is EC$2.70 to U.S.$1 (EC$1 = U.S.37¢). Many shops and restaurants quote prices in U.S. dollars. Always determine which currency locals are talking about. I have used U.S.-dollar prices in this section.

LANGUAGE English is the language of the island.

CALLING FROM THE U.S. When calling St. Kitts or Nevis from the United States, you need to dial only a "1" before the numbers listed throughout this section.

ST. KITTS

St. Kitts—or St. Christopher, a name hardly anyone uses—is by far the more populous of the two islands, with some 35,000 people. It was the first English settlement in the Leeward Islands, and during the plantation age its 68 square miles enjoyed one of the richest sugarcane economies in the Caribbean. Of course, the plantation age depended on slave labor for cultivation, and today, though the bulk of the island's revenue still comes from the nationalized sugar industry, the back-breaking and low-paying work of sugar harvesting is shunned by most of St. Kitts's citizens (in their place, Guayanese workers come in for the harvesting season). Cane fields climb the slopes of a volcanic mountain range, and you'll see ruins of old mills and plantation houses as you drive around the island.

Frommer's Ratings: St. Kitts					
	poor	fair	good	excellent	outstanding
Overall Experience			✓		
Shore Excursions			✓		
Activities Close to Port	✓				
Beaches & Water Sports			✓		
Shopping		✓			
Dining/Bars			✓		

St. Kitts is lush and fertile, dotted with rain forests and waterfalls, but it's also extremely poor and has suffered catastrophically in recent years, being hit with several successive hurricanes. In the aftermath of 1998's Hurricane Georges, the country's U.N. Mission released a statement which said, in part, "Initial reports indicate that all productive sectors including sugar and non-sugar agriculture and manufacturing have come to a standstill. Thousands of people are expected to be out of work." A year later, Hurricane Lenny pounded the ravaged country once again, exacerbating its problems. Despite efforts at wooing tourism to bring in badly needed cash, the country lags behind in amenities and infrastructure.

The island is crowned by the 3,792-foot Mount Liamuiga, a crater that, thankfully, has remained dormant (unlike the one at Montserrat). Its most impressive landmark is the **Brimstone Hill fortress,** one of the Caribbean's most impressive. **Basseterre,** the capital city, is full of old-time Caribbean architecture and a few worthwhile landmarks, but overall has little to hold the interest of visitors.

Frommer's Favorite St. Kitts Experiences

- **Visiting Brimstone Hill Fortress:** Begun by the British in 1690 and subsequently changing hands from British to French and back to British again, it's one of the most impressive forts in the Caribbean, with battlement after battlement leading up to a spectacular view of the sea. (See "Shore Excursions," and "On Your Own: Beyond Walking Distance," below.)
- **Hiking Mount Liamuiga:** The hike up this dormant volcano will take you through a rain forest and along deep ravines up to the rim of the crater at a cool 2,625 feet (see "On Your Own: Beyond Walking Distance," below).

COMING ASHORE   In April 1997, the government of St. Kitts and Nevis attempted to replace the older, drab-looking industrial piers of Basseterre by building Port Zante, a pier stretching from the center of town into deep waters offshore, but fate apparently had other plans, and whacked Port Zante hard with successive hurricanes. At press time, Zante sits unused in the middle of several acres of halted construction, and in a November 1999 address on the effects of Hurricane Lenny, Prime Minister Denzil L. Douglas said "It is safe to say at this point that my government will require a huge degree of persuading before we decide to restart this project in its original design and format. I do not wish here to repeat what informed opinion in the engineering field is, but I am mindful at this stage of the particular maxim 'not all errors can be corrected.'" Expect to arrive at those same old industrial piers for the foreseeable future.

INFORMATION   You can get local tourist information at the **St. Kitts/Nevis Department of Tourism,** Pelican Mall, Bay Road, in Basseterre (☎ **800/582-6208** or 869/465-4040). Open Monday to Friday from 9am to 5pm. For info before you go, contact the tourism board office in the U.S. at ☎ **212/535-1234** or www.stkitts-nevis.com.

GETTING AROUND

BY TAXI   Taxis wait at the docks in Basseterre and in the Circus, a public area near the docks at the intersection of Bank and Fort streets. Since most taxi drivers are also guides, this is the best means of getting around the island. Taxis aren't metered, so before heading out you must agree on the price, and ask if the rates quoted are in U.S. dollars or Eastern Caribbean dollars.

BY RENTAL CAR   I don't recommend renting a car.

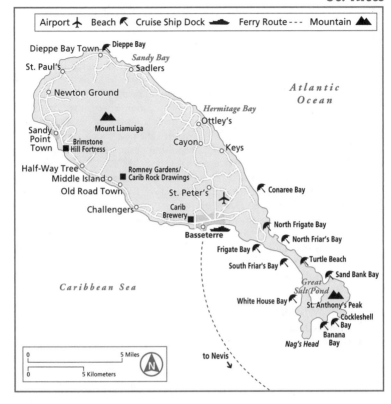

Airport ✈ Beach ⚑ Cruise Ship Dock ⛴ Ferry Route - - - Mountain ▲▲

Dieppe Bay Town • Dieppe Bay
St. Paul's *Sandy Bay*
  Sadlers
Newton Ground
  Atlantic Ocean
  Hermitage Bay
Mount Liamuiga Ottley's
Sandy Point Town
Brimstone Hill Fortress Cayon Keys
Half-Way Tree Romney Gardens/Carib Rock Drawings
Middle Island St. Peter's Conaree Bay
Old Road Town
Challengers Carib Brewery
Basseterre North Frigate Bay
  North Friar's Bay
Frigate Bay Turtle Beach
South Friar's Bay Sand Bank Bay
Caribbean Sea *Great Salt Pond*
White House Bay St. Anthony's Peak
  Cockleshell Bay
  Banana Bay
Nag's Head
0 — 5 Miles
0 — 5 Kilometers
to Nevis

Shore Excursions

✪ **Brimstone Hill Tour** ($28, 2¹/₂ hours): Visit this inspiring 17th-century citadel, which, at some 800 feet above sea level, gives you a panoramic view of the coastline and the island. Tours typically include a visit to the beautiful Romney Gardens, which lie between Basseterre and the fort. You can check out the lush greenery, say "hi" to the cows that graze just across the hill, or shop at Carabelle Boutique, which has its shop on the site.

Rain Forest Adventure Hike ($41, 4 hours): Departing from Romney Gardens, about 5 miles from Basseterre, you'll hike along a loop of trail through lush rain forest. With luck, you'll catch sight of some of St. Kitts's resident monkey population.

Beach Horseback Ride ($38, 1–2 hours): Cruise ship passengers ride well-trained horses along the Atlantic coastline, where trade winds ensure a cool trip.

Sail & Snorkel Catamaran Trip ($46, 3–4 hours): A sailing catamaran takes you to secluded Smittens Bay for snorkeling among the diverse reef fish and coral formations. Complimentary rum punch is served aboard the boat on your return trip.

Touring Through Local Operators

Taxi Tours: Taxi drivers will take you on a 3-hour tour of the island for about $60. Lunch can also be arranged at one of the local inns. Good choices are **Golden Lemon**

at Dieppe Bay (☎ 869/465-7260) or **Rawlins Plantation,** Mount Pleasant (☎ 869/ 465-6221).

ON YOUR OWN: WITHIN WALKING DISTANCE

The capital city of Basseterre, where the docks are located, has typical British colonial architecture and some quaint buildings, as well as shops and a market where the locals display fruits and flowers—but even this description might be overstating the place's appeal. Truth is, it's a very poor town, with few attractions aimed at visitors. Chickens roam the streets, pecking around right outside the headquarters of the government, and it says something (though I'm not sure what) that the most visible component of the town's "skyline" is a Kentucky Fried Chicken. Most businesses are entirely for the local populace (furniture shops, clothing stores, and the like) and there are few charming spots—wherever you go, you're reminded that this is a poor nation that's been dealt a bad hand by mother nature over the past several years, getting beaten down again by hurricanes every time it starts to stand up.

Independence Square, a stone's throw from the docks along Bank Street, is pretty, with its central fountain and old church, but there's no good reason to linger unless it's to sit in the shade and toss back a bottle of the local soda, a refreshing (if sweet) grapefruit-based concoction called Ting.

St. George's Anglican Church, on Cayon Street (walk stright up Church Street or Fort Street from the dock), is the oldest church in town and is worth a look.

ON YOUR OWN: BEYOND WALKING DISTANCE

The **Brimstone Hill Fortress** (☎ 869/465-6211), 9 miles west of Basseterre, is the major stop on any tour of St. Kitts. This historic monument, among the largest and best preserved in the Caribbean, is a complex of bastions, barracks, and other structures ingeniously adapted to the top and upper slopes of a steep, 800-foot hill. The name of the place derives from the odor of sulfer released by nearby undersea vents.

The structure dates from 1690, when the British fortified the hill to help recapture Fort Charles below from the French. In 1782, an invading force of 8,000 French troops bombarded the fortress for a month before its small British garrison, supplemented by local militia, surrendered. When the British took the island back the next year, they proceeded to enlarge the fort into "The Gibraltar of the West Indies." In all, the fort took 104 years to complete.

Today the fortress is the centerpiece of a national park featuring nature trails and a diverse range of plant and animal life, including green vervet monkeys. It's also a photographer's paradise, with views of mountains, fields, and the Caribbean Sea. On a clear day you can see six neighboring islands. From below, the fort presents a dramatic picture, poised among diabolical-looking spires and outcroppings of lava rock.

Visitors will enjoy the self-directed tours among the many ruined or restored structures, including the barrack rooms at Fort George. The gift shop sells prints of rare maps and paintings of the Caribbean. Admission is $5 for adults, $2.50 for children. The park is open daily from 9:30am to 5:30pm.

Mount Liamuiga, in the northwest of the island, was dubbed "Mount Misery" long ago. This dormant volcano sputtered its last gasp around 1692. Today, it's a major goal for hikers. A round-trip to the usually cloud-covered peak takes about 4 hours—2$\frac{1}{2}$ hours going up, 1$\frac{1}{2}$ coming down. Hikers usually make the ascent from Belmont Estate near St. Paul on the north end of St. Kitts. The trail winds through a rain forest and travels along deep ravines up to the rim of the crater at a cool 2,625 feet. Many hikers climb—or crawl—down a steep, slippery trail to a tiny lake in the caldera, some 400 feet below the rim.

You can reach the rim without a guide, but it's absolutely necessary to have one to go into the crater. **Greg's Safaris** (☎ 869/465-4121) offers guided hikes to the crater for about $60 per person (a minimum of four hikers required), including breakfast and a picnic at the crater's rim. The same outfit also offers half-day rain-forest explorations, also with a picnic, for $35 per person.

SHOPPING

Basseterre is not a shopping town, despite the handout maps you'll likely receive when you arrive, which show a listing of shops that would put St. Thomas's Charlotte Amalie to shame—that is, until you look closer and see entries like "R. Gumbs Electrical," "TDC/Finco Finance Co.," and "Horsford Furniture Store." Turns out they just listed *every* business on every street in town, no matter whether it's of interest to visitors or not. Strength in numbers, I suppose.

The closest thing to high-quality shopping is at **Pelican Shopping Mall,** with over a dozen shops, as well as banking services, a restaurant, and a philatelic bureau where collectors can buy St. Kitts stamps and everyone else can mail letters. Here too, though, don't expect much (and whose idea was it to build a covered mall in the sunny Caribbean, anyway?).

At Romney Manor—now more appropriately named Romney Gardens since most of the manor itself burned down in 1996—you'll find **Caribelle Batik** (☎ 869/465-6253) one of the island's most visible boutiques. Inside, artisans demonstrate their Indonesian-style handprinting amid rack after rack of brightly colored clothes. Brimstone Hill and rain-forest hike shore excursions typically include a stop here. If you're coming on your own, look for signs indicating a turnoff along the coast road, about 5 miles north of Basseterre.

BEACHES

The narrow peninsula in the southeast contains the island's salt ponds and also boasts the best white-sand beaches. You'll find the best swimming at **Conaree Beach,** 3 miles from Basseterre; **Frigate Bay,** with its talcum-powder fine sand; the twin beaches of **Banana Bay** and **Cockleshell Bay,** at the southeast corner of the island; and **Friar's Bay,** a peninsula beach opening onto both the Atlantic and the Caribbean. All beaches, even those that border hotels, are open to the public. However, you must usually pay a fee to use a hotel's beach facilities.

SPORTS

GOLF   The **Royal St. Kitts Golf Course,** Frigate Bay (☎ 869/465-8339), is an 18-hole, par-72 championship course featuring seven beautiful ponds. It's bounded on the south by the Caribbean Sea and on the north by the Atlantic Ocean.

SCUBA DIVING & SNORKELING   One of the best diving spots is **Nagshead,** at the southern tip of St. Kitts. This is an excellent shallow-water dive for certified divers starting at 10 feet and extending to 70 feet. You'll see a variety of tropical fish, eaglerays, and lobster here. Another good site is **Booby Shoals,** between Cow 'n' Calf Rocks and Booby Island. Booby Shoals has abundant sea life, including nurse sharks, lobster, and stingrays. Dives here are up to 30 feet in depth, and are good for both certified and beginning divers. **Pro-Divers,** at Turtle Beach (☎ 869/465-3223), arranges scuba-diving and snorkeling expeditions.

GREAT LOCAL RESTAURANTS & BARS

The favorite **local beer** is Carib, brewed right on the northern edge of Basseterre. There's a local cane sugar drink called CSR (Cane Spirit Rothschild), but it's pretty foul.

If you're looking for that unspoiled, casual beach restaurant, try **The Anchorage,** Frigate Bay (☎ 869/465-8235), for a rum drink, hamburgers, or a dozen kinds of sandwiches along with fresh fish. **Ballahoo Restaurant** (☎ 869/465-4197), located in Basseterre's most picturesque intersection, The Circus, right by the cruise dock, serves some of the best chili and baby back ribs in town. Seafood platters, such as chili shrimp or fresh lobster, are served with a coconut salad and rice.

NEVIS

Nevis, though smaller than St. Kitts and lacking a major historical site like Brimstone Hill Fortress, is nevertheless far more appealing and upbeat—perhaps because it hasn't been hit so hard by the hurricanes that have devastated its sister island. It's capital city, Charlestown, has a lovely mixture of port-town exuberance and small-town charm.

Nevis lies 2 miles south of St. Kitts, and when viewed from there appears to be a perfect cone, rising gradually to a height of 3,232 feet. In 1493, Columbus first sighted the island, naming it Las Nieves, Spanish for "snows," because its peak reminded him of the Pyrenees. Settled by the British in 1628, the island became a prosperous sugar-growing island as well as the most popular spa island of the 18th century, when people flocked in from other West Indian islands to visit its hot mineral springs.

Nevis's two most famous historical residents were **Admiral Horatio Nelson,** who married a local woman here in 1787, and **Alexander Hamilton,** who was born here and went on to find fame as a drafter of the American Federalist Papers, as George Washington's secretary of the treasury, and as Aaron Burr's unfortunate dueling partner.

Frommer's Favorite Nevis Experiences

- **Wandering around Charlestown:** The capital city is a fine place to wander around on your own, visiting Alexander Hamilton's birthplace, the small but appealing Nelson Museum, and the 17th-century Jewish cemetery, poking your head into some of the small shops, or greeting the goats and chickens that wander past, evidently taking their own walking tours. (See "On Your Own: Within Walking Distance," below.)
- **Taking some downtime on Pinney's Beach:** It's a little less crowded now that Hurricane Lenny took out the Four Seasons Resort, but Pinney's hasn't otherwise lost any of its charm. Lounge back, have a beer, take a swim in the reef-protected waters, do a little snorkeling, or engage in some beachcombing. Talk about relaxation. (See "Beaches," below.)

COMING ASHORE   Only small ships call on Nevis, docking right in the center of Charlestown and/or dropping anchor off the coast of beautiful Pinney's Bay Beach.

INFORMATION   There's a small tourist board office on Main Street, near the docks. If you want to collect additional information ahead of time, contact the tourism board office in the U.S. at ☎ 212/535-1234 or www.stkitts-nevis.com.

Frommer's Ratings: Nevis					
	poor	fair	good	excellent	outstanding
Overall Experience				✓	
Shore Excursions	✓				
Activities Close to Port				✓	
Beaches & Water Sports			✓		
Shopping		✓			
Dining/Bars		✓			

Nevis

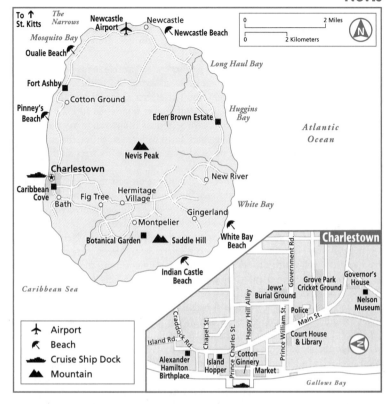

GETTING AROUND

BY TAXI The entirety of Charlestown is accessible on foot, but if you want to visit Pinney's Beach or elsewhere on the island, you can hop a taxi in Charlestown. The cost to Pinney's is about $5.55. Taxi drivers double as guides on Nevis, so if you want to take a general tour of the island, negotiate a price with your driver.

BY RENTAL CAR Driving is on the left side in Nevis and most of the worthwhile sites are within walking distance, so I don't recommend renting a car here.

SHORE EXCURSIONS

Aside from island tours you can arrange through taxi drivers and excursions to Pinney's Beach that are part and parcel of some cruise lines' visits to the island, there are no organized shore excursions offered here.

ON YOUR OWN: WITHIN WALKING DISTANCE

If your ship docks in Charlestown, you're dead center of a perfect walking-tour opportunity. Charlestown is a lovely little place, laid back in somewhat the same manner as St. John, but with some of the really rural character of sister island St. Kitts.

If you head left from the docks and walk a little ways (maybe a quarter mile) along Main Street, you'll come to the **Alexander Hamilton Birthplace,** where the road curves just before the turnoff to Island Road. It's a lovely little two-level house set right on the coastline. On the first floor is a small museum and gift shop (admission $2), but in all honesty you'll do just as well to skip it and just appreciate the outside, spending a moment to read the historic plaque. Far be it for me to take a couple dollars out of the island's economy, though, so if you're feeling philanthropic, drop your two bucks and then head on for the rest of your walk.

Backtracking along Main Street you'll pass several serviceable shops (see "Shopping," below). Keep walking through the center of town, saying "hi" to the occasional mama goat and kids you'll pass, then turn left onto Government Road. One block up on the left you'll find the **Jews' Burial Ground,** with graves from 1684 to 1768. Stones left atop the graves attest to the visitors who have been there before you to pay their respects. When I was there the dead were being entertained with reggae music coming from the doorway of a shop across the street, while a breeze stirred the few trees on the property. All in all, not a bad resting spot.

Backtrack to Main Street, turn left, and continue on past the Grove Park Cricket Ground, bearing left when the road forks. Head up the hill (where you'll see an abandoned hotel and several buildings standing alone on the hill to your right), then turn at the first right, which will bring you back *behind* those buildings, the first of which is the inaccessible Government House and the second of which is the **Nelson Museum.** A very small, very homemade kind of place, it's nevertheless a very interesting and evocative spot, and well worth the $2 admission. The museum traces the history of Admiral Horatio Nelson's career enforcing England's Navigation Acts in the Caribbean, and also houses artifacts from Nevis's Carib, Arawak, and Aceramic peoples, as well as a small display on Nevis today. The timeline of Nelson's Caribbean career includes ship models, ceramic and bronze Nelson figures, paintings of his battles and other scenes, a scrap from the Union Jack under which the admiral was standing when he was shot, a miniature of his casket, and an actual ticket to his funeral, with wax seal. A tiny birdcage with wood enclosing box bears the inscription, "In a number of letters written to Fanny Nisbet [Nelson's wife], Nelson mentioned his search for a traveling birdcage. This bird cage, though not the one Nelson finally procured, is from that period."

The museum's display also includes a number of wonderful clay replicas, including one of the old "Coolie Man's Store," by local artist Gustage "Bush Tea" Williams.

Once back outside, amble slowly off in the same direction you were going (right from the gate). Keep bearing right and you'll eventually be back on Main Street, in plenty of time to do a little shopping or stop into one of the local bars or restaurants.

ON YOUR OWN: BEYOND WALKING DISTANCE

Besides Pinney's Beach (see "Beaches," below), there are few other obvious attractions on the island outside of Charlestown. On the east coast, about 1 1/2 miles from New River, the **Eden Brown Estate** is said to be haunted. Once it was the home of a wealthy planter whose daughter's husband-to-be was killed in a duel at the prenuptial feast. The mansion was then closed and left to the ravages of nature. A solid gray stone still stands. Only the most adventurous, they say, come here on a moonlit night (so it's a good thing you have an excuse—your ship is bound to sail before sunset).

SHOPPING

Nevis is not a shopping hub on the order of St. Thomas or even the much more laid-back St. John. In fact, it's no kind of shopping hub at all. Still, there are a few shops worth poking your head into, all of them along Main Street, right in the port area.

Island Hopper, on Main, one block north of Prince Charles Street, is the best shop for visitors in town, stocking a huge selection of batik clothing. The **Nevis Handcraft Cooperative Society,** at the corner of Main and Prince Charles streets, is pretty sparse, but does carry some folklorically bottled hot sauces and guava jellies, as well as some low-quality craft items. **Pemberton Gift Shop,** across Main Street from Island Hopper, is also sparse, but has a selection of T-shirts, gift items, and a shelf of CSR (Cane Spirit Rothschild), a local cane sugar liquor which, truth to tell, is pretty foul, but cheap enough if you're dead set on exploring all the islands' alcoholic output. **Jerveren's Fashions,** in the Cotton Ginnery complex right at the pier, has a decent selection of T-shirts and gifts.

For stamp collectors, the **Nevis Philatelic Bureau** at the Head Post Office, on Market Street next to the public market (1 block south and 1 block east of the docks) has a range of Nevis stamps.

BEACHES

The name to know on Nevis is **Pinney's Beach,** located north of Charlestown. Though not quite the bustling spot it was before Hurricane Lenny did a number on the adjoining Four Season's Resort (not to mention the backing palm trees, which have seen better days), it's still a lovely spot for swimming, snorkeling, beach-combing, or just sitting back and watching the pelicans dive-bomb into the surf. Sunshine's Bar and Grill, "Home of the Killer Bee," sits right on the beach, offering beer and other refreshments along with the aforementioned Bees.

GREAT LOCAL RESTAURANTS & BARS

Eddy's, on Main Steet in Charlestown (☎ 869/496-5958), on an upper floor and offering a balcony's-eye view of the slowly bustling town below, is the best place in town. **Muriel's Cuisine,** on Upper Happyhill Alley (☎ 869/469-5920), is in the back of a concrete building whose front houses the Limetree shop. It serves typical local West Indian food. **Cotton House Restaurant and Bar,** on the second floor of the Cotton House complex, right by the cruise dock, is nothing fancy, but makes for a pleasant place to grab a snack and a beer in the shade.

23 St. Lucia

In a turbulent history shared by many of its Caribbean neighbors, St. Lucia (pronounced *Loo*-sha), second largest of the Windward Islands at about 240 square miles, changed hands often during the colonial period, being British seven times and French seven times. Today, though, it's an independent state that's become one of the most popular destinations in the Caribbean, with some of the finest resorts. The heaviest development is concentrated in the northwest, between the capital of Castries and the northern end of the island, where there's a string of white-sand beaches. The interior boasts relatively unspoiled green-mantled mountains and gentle valleys, as well as the volcanic Mount Soufrière. Two dramatic peaks (the Pitons), rise along the southwest coast.

Frommer's Ratings: St. Lucia					
	poor	fair	good	excellent	outstanding
Overall Experience				✓	
Shore Excursions				✓	
Activities Close to Port			✓		
Beaches & Water Sports				✓	
Shopping		✓			
Dining/Bars			✓		

Castries, the capital, has grown up around an extinct volcanic crater that's now a large harbor surrounded by hills. Because of devastating fires, the town today has touches of modernity, with glass-and-concrete buildings, but there's still an old-fashioned Saturday-morning market on Jeremie Street. The country women dress in traditional cotton head-dress to sell their luscious fruits and vegetables, while weather-beaten men sit close by playing *warrie,* a fast game played with pebbles on a carved board, or fleet games of dominoes with tiles the color of cherries.

Frommer's Favorite St. Lucia Experiences

- **Riding a catamaran along the coast:** See the lush coast of St. Lucia and the mighty Pitons via catamaran, and then ride a minibus to visit a volcano, the Diamond Baths, and sulfur springs (see "Shore Excursions," below).
- **Exploring a banana plantation:** Bananas are St. Lucia's leading export (see "On Your Own: Beyond Walking Distance," below).
- **Hiking up to Fort Rodney in Rodney Bay:** The beautiful Pigeon Island on Rodney Bay offers the chance to hike up to Fort Rodney, an 18th-century English base that was used as an American signal station during World War II. From the top you can catch site of Martinique. (See "On Your Own: Beyond Walking Distance," below.)

COMING ASHORE   Most cruise ships arrive at the fairly new pier at Pointe Seraphine, within walking distance from the center of Castries. Unlike piers on other islands, this one contains St. Lucia's best shopping. You'll find a money exchange, a small visitor information bureau, and a cable and wireless office. Phone cards are sold for use at specially labeled phones.

If Pointe Seraphine is too crowded, your ship might dock at Port Castries (also called Port Careenage). There's now a shopping terminal here called La Place Careenage, but if you still want to shop in Pointe Seraphine, a water taxi ($1) runs between the two all day. A taxi will cost you around $4. You can also walk between the two. Some smaller vessels, such as Seabourn's, anchor off Soufrière and carry you ashore by tender.

There are **telephones** right outside the port gate at Port Careenage, the town's cargo dock, and at the pier at Pointe Seraphine.

CURRENCY   The official monetary unit is the **Eastern Caribbean dollar (EC$)**. The exchange rate is EC$2.70 to U.S.$1 (EC$1 = U.S.37¢). Most of the prices quoted in this section are in U.S. dollars, which are accepted by nearly all hotels, restaurants, and shops.

LANGUAGE   English is the official language.

INFORMATION   The **St. Lucia Tourist Board** is at Point Seraphine in Castries (☎ **758/452-4094**). It's open Monday to Friday from 9am to 5pm. For info before you go, contact the tourism board office in the U.S. at ☎ **800/456-3984** or 212/867-2950 or www.sluonestop.com.

CALLING FROM THE U.S.   When calling St. Lucia from the United States, you need to dial only a "1" before the numbers listed throughout this section.

GETTING AROUND

BY TAXI   Most taxi drivers have been trained to serve as guides. Their cars are unmetered, but the government fixes tariffs for all standard trips. Be sure to determine if the driver is quoting a rate in U.S. or EC dollars. For touring, expect to pay about $5 per person per hour with a minimum of four passengers; with fewer, it's still $20 an hour. You can hire a taxi to go to Soufrière on your own, too. A taxi for four will cost about $120 for a 3- to 4-hour tour, including a beach stop, photo ops, shopping,

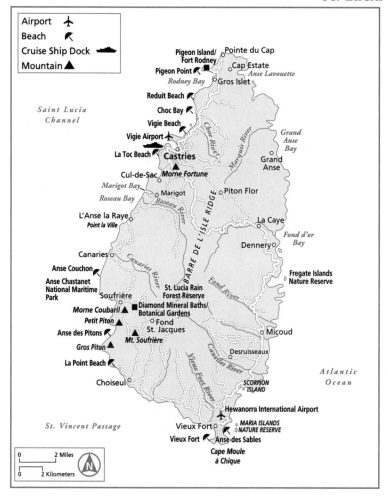

Legend:
- Airport ✈
- Beach 🏖
- Cruise Ship Dock ⛴
- Mountain ▲

Saint Lucia Channel

Pigeon Island/ Fort Rodney
Pointe du Cap
Pigeon Point
Cap Estate
Anse Lavouette
Rodney Bay
Gros Islet
Reduit Beach
Choc Bay
Vigie Beach
Choc River
Marquis River
Grand Anse Bay
Vigie Airport
La Toc Beach
Castries
Morne Fortune
Grand Anse
Cul-de-Sac
Marigot
Piton Flor
Marigot Bay
Roseau Bay
Roseau River
L'Anse la Raye
Point la Ville
La Caye
Fond d'or Bay
Dennery
Canaries
Canaries River
BARRE DE L'ISLE RIDGE
Anse Couchon
Anse Chastanet National Maritime Park
Soufrière
St. Lucia Rain Forest Reserve
Morne Coubaril ▲
Diamond Mineral Baths/ Botanical Gardens
Fond River
Fregate Islands Nature Reserve
Petit Piton ▲
Fond
St. Jacques
Anse des Pitons
Mt. Soufrière ▲
Micoud
Gros Piton
La Point Beach
Desruisseaux
Vieux Fort River
Canelles River
Atlantic Ocean
Choiseul
SCORPION ISLAND
St. Vincent Passage
Hewanorra International Airport
Vieux Fort
MARIA ISLANDS NATURE RESERVE
Vieux Fort
Anse des Sables
Cape Moule á Chique

0 ___ 2 Miles
0 ___ 2 Kilometers

and sightseeing. Avoid any driver who is not in uniform (which is really just a light-cotton tropical shirt).

BY RENTAL CAR   Driving is on the left, and is not recommended.

SHORE EXCURSIONS

Because of the difficult terrain, shore excursions are the best means of seeing this beautiful island in a day or less. In addition to the sampling below, most ships typically offer plantation tours, island bus tours, and snorkeling cruises.

✪ **Island Tour by Land and Sea** ($69 to $82, 8 hours): A picturesque journey from Castries via catamaran to the Piton peaks takes you along St. Lucia's verdant coast, docking at La Soufrière, where passengers board minibuses and visit the volcano, the Diamond Baths (see "On Your Own: Beyond Walking Distance," below), and sulfur springs. Lunch is included at a restaurant in Soufrière or on the boat.

✪ **Mountain Ridge Bike Tour** ($75, 3¹/₂ hours): From Castries, travel by bus to the top of Morne Fortune where your bike ride begins. You'll pedal through hilltop roads with dramatic views of the harbor on one side and a stunning mountain range on the other. The ride goes past banana plantations, through rural neighborhoods, and through lush valleys.

Morne Coubaril Plantation Tour ($46, 4 hours): By minibus, ride along the island's west coast, between the sea and the rain forest, with views of the Pitons. At the Morne Coubaril Estate, tour the working family plantation, and watch how coconuts, coffee, and cocoa are processed.

Pigeon Island Hike and Beach Swim ($44, 4 hours): A steep walk up to the fort on Pigeon Island where St. Lucians last defeated the French. From the summit, you'll have great views of the Pitons, and sometimes you'll even be able to see Martinique. After the hike, there's a pleasant swim in the island's gin-clear waters and complimentary refreshment in the Captain's Cellar, a rustic pub located in an old fort's Soldier's Mess. Outside are wonderful views of the crashing surf on the Atlantic coast.

Anse Chastanet Snorkel Trip ($18, 3 hours): Travel by jeep to St. Lucia's Anse Chastanet National Marine Park, where you snorkel among an amazing variety of reef fish.

ON YOUR OWN: WITHIN WALKING DISTANCE

First, a tip: In the duty-free marketplaces right at Castries's dock, a guy doles out portable massages for $5 for 5 minutes (this could save you a bundle on those expensive Steiner massages on board!).

The principal streets of Castries are William Peter Boulevard and Bridge Street. A Roman Catholic cathedral stands on Columbus Square, which has a few restored buildings. Also take a gander there at the enormous 400-year-old "rain" tree, also called a "noname" tree. **Government House** is a late Victorian structure.

Beyond Government House lies **Morne Fortune,** which means "Hill of Good Luck." Actually, no one's had much luck here, certainly not the French and British that battled for **Fort Charlotte.** The fort changed nationalities many times. You can visit the 18th-century barracks, complete with a military cemetery, a small museum, the Old Powder Magazine, and the "Four Apostles Battery"—four grim muzzle-loading cannons. The view of the harbor of Castries is panoramic. You can also see north to Pigeon Island or south to the Pitons. To reach Morne Fortune, head east on Bridge Street.

Definitely don't miss a walk through town. People are very friendly, and Jeremie Street is chockablock with variety stores of the most authentic local kind, selling everything from spices to housewares. Castries's very colorful **Central Market** right near the dock is also worth a visit. The airplane-hangar-size emporium sells local food, trinkets, and produce. Buy some banana ketchup or local cinnamon sticks to take home.

ON YOUR OWN: BEYOND WALKING DISTANCE

Bananas are St. Lucia's leading export, so if you're being taken around the island by a taxi driver, ask him to take you to one of the huge plantations. I suggest a look at one of the three biggest: the **Cul-de-Sac,** just north of Marigot Bay; **La Caya,** in Dennery on the east coast; and the **Roseau Estate,** south of Marigot Bay.

St. Lucia's first national park, **Pigeon Island National Landmark,** was originally an island but is now joined to the northwest shore of the mainland by a very environmentally unfriendly causeway. The 44-acre island got its name from the red-neck pigeon, or *ramier,* which once made this island home. It's ideal for picnics and nature walks, and is covered with lemongrass that spread from original plantings made by British light opera singer Josset, who leased the island for 30 years and grew the grass to provide thatch for her cottage's roof. Every few years the grass catches fire and immolates much of the island before it can be put out, due to the volatile oils it contains.

The island's Interpretation Centre is equipped with artifacts and a multimedia display of local history, ranging from the Amerindian occupation of A.D. 1000 to the Battle of Saints, when Admiral Rodney's fleet set out from Pigeon Island and defeated Admiral De Grasse in 1782. Right below the interpretation center is the Captain's Cellar pub.

From the interpretation center you can walk up the winding and moderately steep path to a lookout from which you can see Martinique. In 1780, Admiral Rodney said of this spot, ". . . This is the post the Governor of Martinique has set his eye on and if possessed by the enemy would deprive us of the best anchorage place in these islands, from which Martinique is always attackable." Remember that when planning your own assault. From the pinnacle you get a wonderful view, and the cannons that ring the space are a nice place to pose for "I was there" pictures.

On Pigeon Island's west coast are two white-sand beaches. There's also a restaurant, **Jambe de Bois** ("Leg of Wood"), named after a peg-legged pirate who once used the island as a hideout.

The park is open daily from 9am to 5pm. For more information, call the **St. Lucia National Trust** (☎ **758/452-5005**). The best way to get here is to take a taxi and arrange to be picked up in time to return to the ship.

La Soufrière, a little fishing port and St. Lucia's second largest settlement, is dominated by the dramatic ✪ **Pitons,** two pointed peaks called Petit Piton and Gros Piton, which rise to 2,460 and 2,619 feet, respectively, right from the sea. Formed by lava and once actively volcanic, these mountains are now clothed in green vegetation, with waves crashing around their bases. Their sheer rise from the water makes them such visible landmarks that they've become the very symbol of St. Lucia.

Near the town of Soufrière lies the famous "drive-in" volcano, ✪ **La Soufrière,** a rocky lunar landscape of bubbling mud and craters seething with fuming sulfur. You literally ride into an old crater and walk between the sulfur springs and pools of hissing steam. The fumes are said to have medicinal properties. A local guide is usually waiting nearby; if you do hire a guide, agree—then doubly agree—on what the fee will be.

Nearby are the **Diamond Mineral Baths** (☎ **758/452-4759**), surrounded by a tropical arboretum. They were constructed in 1784 by order of Louis XVI, whose doctors told him that these waters were similar in mineral content to the waters at Aix-les-Bains. Their purpose was to help French soldiers fighting in the West Indies recuperate. Later destroyed, they were rebuilt after World War II. The water's average temperature is 106°F. You'll also find another fine attraction here: a waterfall that changes colors (from yellow to black to green to gray) several times a day. For about EC$7 ($2.60), you can bathe and benefit from the recuperative effects yourself.

SHOPPING

Many stores sell duty-free goods; they also deliver tobacco products and liquor to the cruise dock. Keep in mind, you are only allowed to purchase one bottle of liquor here (in St. Thomas, you can buy five). You'll find some good but not remarkable buys in bone china, jewelry, perfume, watches, liquor, and crystal. Souvenir items include designer bags and mats, local pottery, and straw hats—again, nothing remarkable. *A tip:* If local vendors know your cruise also calls in St. Thomas, they may be more amenable to bargaining.

Built for cruise ship passengers, **Pointe Seraphine** has the best collection of shops on the island. You must present your cruise pass when making purchases here. Liquor and tobacco will be delivered to the ship.

Gablewoods Mall, on Gros Islet Highway, 2 miles north of Castries, contains three restaurants and one of the densest concentrations of stores on St. Lucia. Since this mall is near some lovely beaches (and to Sandals St. Lucia), it's possible to plan a day that combines shopping and sunbathing.

At **Caribelle Batik,** Howelton House, Old Victoria Road, The Morne, just a 5-minute taxi ride from Castries, you can watch St. Lucian artists creating intricate patterns and colors through the ancient art of batik. **Eudovic Art Studio,** Goodlands, Morne Fortune, sells wood carvings by Vincent Joseph Eudovic, a native of St. Lucia, and some of his pupils. Take a taxi from the cruise pier. **Choiseul Art & Craft Center,** La Fargue, Choiseul (southwest of Castries), is a government-funded retail outlet and training school that perpetuates the tradition of handmade Amerindian pottery and basketware. Some of the best basket weaving on the island is done here, using techniques practiced only in St. Lucia, St. Vincent, and Dominica. Look for place mats, handbags, woodcarvings (including bas-reliefs crafted from screw pine), and pottery.

BEACHES

If you don't take a shore excursion, you might want to spend your time on one of St. Lucia's famous beaches. A taxi to **Marigot Beach,** for instance, south of Castries Harbour, costs around $20. I prefer the calmer shores along the western coast, since the rough surf on the windward Atlantic side makes swimming potentially dangerous.

Leading beaches include **Pigeon Island,** off the northern shore, with white sand and picnic facilities; **Vigie Beach,** north of Castries Harbour, with fine sands; and **Reduit Beach,** with its fine brown sands, which lies between Choc Bay and Pigeon Point. For a novelty, you might try the black-volcanic-sand beach at Soufrière.

Just north of Soufrière is that beach connoisseur's delight, **Anse Chastanet** (☎ 758/459-7000), with its white sands set at the foothills of lush, green mountains. While here, you might want to patronize the facilities of the Anse Chastanet Hotel.

All beaches are open to the public, even those along hotel properties, but you must pay to use a hotel's beach equipment.

SPORTS

HORSEBACK RIDING   You can go horseback riding at **Cas-En-Bas and Cap Estate Stables,** north of Castries. To make arrangements, call René Trim at ☎ 758/450-8273. Ask about a picnic trip to the Atlantic side of the island, with a barbecue lunch and drinks included. Departures are at 8:30am, 10am, 2pm, and 4pm. Nonriders can also join the excursion; they are transported to the site in a van and pay half price.

SCUBA DIVING   In Soufrière, **Scuba St. Lucia,** in the Anse Chastanet Hotel (☎ 758/459-7000), at the southern end of Anse Chastanet's quarter-mile secluded beach, is a five-star PADI dive center. It offers great diving and comprehensive facilities. Some of the most spectacular coral reefs of St. Lucia—many only 10 to 20 feet below the surface—provide shelter for sea creatures just a short distance offshore. **Rosemond Trench Divers, Ltd.,** at the Marigot Beach Club, Marigot Bay (☎ 758/451-4761), will take both novices and experienced divers to shallow reefs or to some of the most challenging trenches in the Caribbean.

WATER SPORTS   The best center for all water sports except diving is **St. Lucian Watersports,** on Reduit Beach at the Rex St. Lucian Hotel (☎ 758/452-8351).

GREAT LOCAL RESTAURANTS & BARS

A really, really great **local beer** is Piton—very refreshing on a hot day, like Corona but better. A favorite **local rum** is Bounty.

IN CASTRIES At the **Green Parrot,** Red Tape Lane, Morne Fortune, about 1¹/₂ miles east of the town center (☎ 758/452-3399), there's an emphasis on St. Lucian specialties and homegrown produce. It's trained cruise ship chefs in the use of local products when preparing meals. Try the *christophine au gratin* (a Caribbean squash with cheese) or the Creole soup made with callaloo and pumpkin. One of the newest restaurants on the block is **Café Panache,** located next to the Central Library in Castries, near Derek Walcott Square. It's situated in a century-old family home of Sir Arthur Lewis, St. Lucia's first (and probably only) Nobel Prize winner for economics. The menu features a combo of local, French, and American cuisine. **Jimmie's,** Vigie Cove Marina (☎ 758/452-5142), is known for its fresh-fish menu and tasty Creole cookery. Constructed in the 19th century as a Great House, **San Antoine,** Morne Fortune (☎ 758/452-4660), lies up the Morne hill. You might begin with the classic callaloo soup, and then follow with fettuccine Alfredo, or perhaps fresh fish *en papillote* (baked in parchment). The view and ambiance are more stunning than the cuisine. If you're an aficionado of true local cooking, some of the most authentic varieties can be sampled at the tiny restaurants in the Central Market, which serve plates piled high with local dishes (cow-heel soup anyone?).

AT MARIGOT BAY **Café Paradis,** at the Marigot Beach Club (take a ferry across Marigot Bay; ☎ 758/451-4974), is a culinary showplace, the proud domain of a French-trained chef who was eager to escape to the Caribbean. To reach the place, you'll have to take a ferryboat across Marigot Bay. It runs from the Moorings Marigot Bay Resort about every 10 minutes throughout the day and evening. **Hurricane Hole,** in the Moorings, Marigot Bay (☎ 758/451-4357), is the cozy restaurant of the Marigot Bay Resort, which charters yachts to clients from around the hemisphere. The menu is geared to surf-and-turf fans.

IN THE SOUFRIÈRE AREA **Chez Camilla Guest House & Restaurant,** 7 Bridge St., 1 block inland from the waterfront (☎ 758/459-5379), which is the only really good place to eat in the village of Soufrière itself, serves sandwiches, cold salads, omelets, and burgers at lunch. **Dasheene Restaurant & Bar,** in the Ladera Resort, between Gros and Petit Piton (☎ 758/459-7323), serves the most refined and certainly the most creative cuisine in St. Lucia. The chef has a special flair for seafood pasta or marinated sirloin steak. Best bet is the catch of the day, likely to be kingfish or red snapper, grilled to perfection. South of Soufrière is a restaurant with a fabulous view, Dasheene. It's perched atop a 1,000-foot ridge and framed by the rising twin peaks of the Pitons. Everything is local, including the furniture. The menu includes yummy dishes like dumpling and callaloo soup, fresh pumpkin risotto with red pepper coulis, and a banana-stuffed pork with ginger and coconut sauce.

IN RODNEY BAY **The Lime,** Rodney Bay, north of Reduit Beach (☎ 758/452-0761), is a casual local place specializing in stuffed crab backs and fish steak Creole, and it also serves shrimp, steaks, lamb and pork chops, and rotis (Caribbean burritos). **The Mortar & Pestle,** in the Harmony Marina Suites, Rodney Bay Lagoon (☎ 758/452-8711), offers indoor-outdoor dining with a view of the boats moored at the nearby marina. For something truly regional, try the Barbados souse, with marinated pieces of lean cooked pork, or the frogs' legs from Dominica.

24 Sint Maarten & St. Martin

Legend has it that a gin-drinking Dutchman and a wine-guzzling Frenchman walked around this island one day in 1648 to claim territory for their countries. The Frenchman covered the most ground, but the canny Dutchman got the more valuable real estate. Whether the story is true or not, this island, measuring only 37 square miles, is today the smallest territory in the world shared by two sovereign states. The Dutch side is known as Sint Maarten; the French side, St. Martin. Once you've cleared customs on either side, the only way you'll know you're crossing from Holland into France is by the BIENVENUE FRANÇAISE signs marking the boundary. Coexistence between the two nations is very peaceful.

Most cruise ships land at **Philipsburg,** capital of the Dutch side, although smaller ships can maneuver into the harbor of **Marigot** on the French side. Don't come to either side to escape the crowds. The 100% duty-free shopping has turned the island into somewhat of a shopper's paradise (more so on the Dutch side), and Philipsburg especially is nearly always bustling with cruise ship passengers.

Although the boom was severely slowed by the hurricanes of 1995, the island quickly rebuilt, and today its 36 white-sand beaches remain unspoiled, if somewhat rearranged by Mother Nature, and the clear turquoise waters are as enticing as ever.

SINT MAARTEN

Founded in 1763 by Comdr. John Phillips, a Scot in Dutch employ, Sint Maarten's capital, **Philipsburg,** curves along the shores of Great Bay. The main thoroughfare is busy Front Street, which stretches for about a mile and is lined with stores selling international merchandise. More shops lie along the little lanes, known as *steegijes,* that connect Front Street with Back Street, another shoppers' mart.

Frommer's Favorite Sint Maarten Experiences

- **Joining the America's Cup sailing regatta:** What an opportunity! You get to race against actual former contenders from the famed America's Cup race (see "Shore Excursions," below).
- **Heading to the beach at Orient Bay:** On the French side, colorful open-air restaurants line this very European beach and its striped umbrellas (see "Shore Excursions," below).

COMING ASHORE Most vessels land at Philipsburg, docking about a mile southwest of town at A. C. Wathey Pier at Point Blanche. Some passengers walk the distance, but taxis do await all cruise ships. There are almost no facilities at A. C. Wathey Pier except for a few phones. Some ships anchor in the mouth of the harbor, and then take passengers by tender to Little Pier in the heart of town.

There are a few AT&T **credit-card phones** at Philipsburg's A.C. Wathey Pier.

CURRENCY The legal tender in Dutch Sint Maarten is the **Netherlands Antilles guilder (NAf).** The exchange rate is 1.77 NAf to U.S.$1 (1 NAf = U.S.56¢). However, U.S. dollars are also accepted here. Prices in this section are usually given in U.S. currency.

LANGUAGE Although the official language is Dutch, most people also speak English.

Frommer's Ratings: Sint Maarten

	poor	fair	good	excellent	outstanding
Overall Experience				✓	
Shore Excursions			✓		
Activities Close to Port				✓	
Beaches & Water Sports			✓		
Shopping					✓
Dining/Bars			✓		

Sint Maarten & St. Martin

INFORMATION For Dutch Sint Maarten, go to the **Tourist Information Bureau,** in the Imperial Building at 23 Walter Nisbeth Rd. (☎ 599/54-22337). It's open Monday to Friday from 8am to 5pm. For info before you go, contact the tourist board office in the U.S. at ☎800/786-2278 or 212/953-2084 or www.st-maarten.com.

CALLING FROM THE U.S. When calling St. Martin from the United States, you need to dial "011" before the numbers listed in this section.

GETTING AROUND

TAXIS Taxis are unmetered, but Dutch Sint Maarten law requires drivers to list fares to major destinations on the island. There are minimum fares for two passengers, and each additional passenger pays another $2. Call a cab at ☎ 599/54-54317.

MINIBUSES The privately owned and operated minibuses are a reasonable way to get around, if you don't mind some inconveniences and possible overcrowding. They run daily from 7am to midnight and serve most major locations on Sint Maarten. Fares range from about $1 to $2. The most popular run is from Philipsburg to Marigot on the French side.

BY RENTAL CAR Rental cars are a practical way to see both the Dutch and the French sides of the island. **Budget** (☎ 800/527-0700 in the U.S., or 599/54-54030), **Hertz** (☎ 800/654-3131 in the U.S., or 599/54-54314), and **Avis** (☎ 800/331-1212 in the U.S., or 599/54-52847) all have agencies here. If you're calling in advance, you might try **Auto Europe** (☎ **800/223-5555**). Rates begin at about $50 per day with unlimited mileage for a subcompact car. Drive on the right-hand side of the road on both sides of the island.

SHORE EXCURSIONS

The beaches and shopping are some of the biggest attractions here. Other typical excursions include snorkeling cruises and island tours.

✪ **America's Cup Sailing Regatta** ($71, 3 hours): Sail on one of the actual former contenders of the America's Cup race, and compete in an actual race. This is a hands-on tour where you'll be grinding winches, trimming sails, and ducking under booms. It's great fun.

Island Tour ($20, 3 hours): By minibus, you'll see both sides, stopping for panoramic views. There's usually a stopover in Marigot for sightseeing and shopping.

Ilet Pinel Snorkeling Tour ($29, 3 hours): After a scenic bus ride to Cul-de-Sac on the French side, take a tender to Ilet Pinel for snorkeling (equipment is included in the price).

Butterfly Farm and Marigot ($28–$38, 3¹/₂ hours): After a scenic drive through both the French and Dutch sides of the island, visit a butterfly farm, where a guide points out the different species. End the tour with a short stop in Marigot.

Orient Bay Excursion ($43, 4–5 hours): You'll be driven to the beach in Orient Bay, with the driver narrating the sights along the way. Spend a couple of hours at this wide, colorful beach, often called "the French Riviera of the Caribbean." The excursion includes beach chairs and lunch.

ON YOUR OWN

This is a shopping/beaching/gambling kind of port, and all those attractions are covered in the other sections of this review.

GAMBLING

In the absence of natural wonders or man-made attractions, the biggest onshore lure for cruise ship passengers are the casinos on the Dutch side. They open anywhere between 11am and 1pm daily and operate into the wee hours of the night.

Most of the casinos are in the big hotels. **Casino Royale,** at the Maho Beach Hotel on Maho Bay (☎ **599/54-52115**), which opened in 1975, has six roulette wheels, three craps tables, 16 blackjack tables, and three Caribbean stud-poker tables. It also offers baccarat, mini-baccarat, and more than 250 slot machines. There's no admission, and a snack buffet is complimentary.

Another popular casino is at the **Pelican Resort and Casino** on Simpson Bay (☎ **599/54-42503**), built to a Swiss design incorporating a panoramic view of the water. This Las Vegas–style casino has two craps tables, three roulette tables, nine blackjack tables, two stud-poker tables, and 120 slot machines.

The Roman-themed **Coliseum Casino,** on Front Street in Philipsburg (☎ **599/54-32102**), tries hard to attract gaming enthusiasts, especially "high rollers," and has the highest table limits ($1,000 maximum) on Sint Maarten. Upon the management's approval, the Coliseum also offers credit lines for clients with a good credit rating at any U.S. casino.

SHOPPING

The main shopping area is in the center of Philipsburg. Most stores are on the two leading streets, **Front Street** (*Voorstraat* in Dutch), which is closer to the bay, and **Back**

Street (*Achterstraat*), which runs parallel to Front. You'll find all the usual suspects—Little Switzerland and a host of jewelry/gift/luxury item shops—as well as some standout local shops. In general, the price marked on the merchandise in the major retail outlets is what you're supposed to pay. At small, personally run shops, however, some polite bargaining might be in order.

Old Street Shopping Center, with entrances on Front Street and Back Street, features more than two dozen shops and boutiques, including branches of such famous stores as Colombian Emeralds. Dining facilities include the Philipsburg Grill and Ribs Co. and Pizza Hut.

The **Guavaberry Company,** 10 Front St., sells the rare "island folk liqueur" of Sint Maarten, which for centuries was made in private homes but is now available to everyone. Sold in square bottles, the liqueur is aged and has a fruity, woody, almost bittersweet flavor. It's made from rum that's given a unique flavor by rare local berries usually grown in the hills in the center of the island. You can blend it with coconut for a unique guavaberry colada or pour a splash into a glass of icy champagne. Don't confuse guavaberries with guavas—they're very different. Stop in at their shop and free-tasting house.

The **Shipwreck Shop,** Front Street, stocks West Indian hammocks, beach towels, sea salt, cane sugar, spices, baskets, handcrafts, jewelry, T-shirts, postcards, books, and much more.

BEACHES

Sint Maarten has 36 beautiful white-sand beaches, so it's comparatively easy to find one for yourself. But if it's too secluded, be careful: There have been reports of robberies on some remote beaches. Don't carry valuables.

You can often use the changing facilities at some of the bigger resorts for a small fee. Nudists should head for the French side, but the Dutch side is getting more liberal about such things.

On the west side of the island, **Mullet Bay Beach** is shaded by palm trees, but can get crowded on weekends. You can arrange water-sports equipment rentals through the Mullet Bay Resort.

Great Bay Beach is best if you'd like to stay near Front Street in Philipsburg. This mile-long beach is sandy, but since it borders the busy capital it may not be as clean as some of the more remote beaches. Immediately to the west, at the foot of Fort Amsterdam, **Little Bay Beach** looks like a Caribbean postcard, but it, too, can be overrun with visitors.

Stretching the length of Simpson Bay Village, white sand **Simpson Bay Beach,** is shaped like a half moon. It lies west of Philipsburg, just east of the airport. You can rent water-sports equipment here.

West of the airport, **Maho Bay Beach,** at the Maho Beach Hotel and Casino, is ideal in many ways, if you don't mind the planes passing overhead. Palms provide shade, and food and drink can be purchased at the hotel.

The sands are pearly white at **Oyster Pond Beach,** near the Oyster Pond Hotel northeast of Philipsburg. Bodysurfers like the rolling waves here. Nearby **Dawn Beach** is noted for its underwater tropical beauty, with reefs lying offshore.

Beyond the sprawling Mullet Beach Resort on the Dutch side, **Cupecoy Bay Beach** lies just north of the Dutch-French border on the western side of the island. It's a string of three white-sand beaches set against a backdrop of caves and sandstone cliffs that provide morning shade. The beach doesn't have facilities, but is nonetheless popular. One section of the beach is "clothing optional."

SPORTS

GOLF The **Mullet Bay Resort** (☎ 599/54-52801, ext. 1850) has an 18-hole course designed by Joseph Lee that's one of the most challenging in the Caribbean. Mullet Pond and Simpson Bay lagoon provide both beauty and hazards.

HORSEBACK RIDING At **Crazy Acres,** Dr. J. H. Dela Fuente Street, Cole Bay (☎ 599/54-42793), riding expeditions invariably end on an isolated beach where horses and riders can enjoy a cool postride romp in the water. Two experienced escorts accompany a maximum of eight people on the 2¹/₂-hour outings. Riders of all experience levels are welcome. Wear a bathing suit under your riding clothes. Reservations should be made at least 2 days in advance.

SCUBA DIVING Underwater visibility runs from 75 to 125 feet in the island's crystal-clear bays and countless coves. The biggest attraction for scuba divers is the 1801 British man-of-war HMS *Proselyte,* which came to a watery grave on a reef a mile off the coast. The PADI-instructed program at **Pelican Watersports,** Pelican Resort & Casino, Simpson Bay (☎ 599/54-42604), features the most knowledgeable guides on the island, each one familiar with Sint Maarten dive sites. Divers are taken out in custom-built 28- and 35-foot boats. Many say that this is the best reef diving in the Caribbean.

GREAT LOCAL RESTAURANTS & BARS

A favorite **local beer** (on both the Dutch and French sides of the island) is Red White and Blue; a favorite **local rum liqueur** is Guavaberry (see "Shopping," above, for the Guavaberry Company's store in Philipsburg).

    ✪ **Cheri's Café,** 45 Cinnamon Grove, Shopping Centre, Maho Beach (☎ 599/54-53361), is the island's hot spot, once voted best bar in the West Indies by *Caribbean Travel and Life* readers. You can get really fresh grilled fish, 16-ounce steaks, and juicy burgers. Some come for the inexpensive food, others for the potent drinks.

    Antoine's, 119 Front St., Philipsburg (☎ 599/54-22964), offers sophistication, style, and cuisine that mainly consists of old continental favorites, almost equally divided between meat and fish dishes. **Chesterfields,** Great Bay Marina, Philipsburg (☎ 599/54-23484), serves platters of fish, grilled steaks and other meats, sandwiches, and salads at lunchtime. **Crocodile Express Café,** Casino Balcony, at the Pelican Resort & Casino, Simpson Bay (☎ 599/54-42503, ext. 1127), serves hearty deli fare, including well-stuffed sandwiches. **Da Livio Ristorante,** 159 Front St. (at the bottom of Front Street), Philipsburg (☎ 599/54-23363), is the finest Italian dining in Sint Maarten. A favorite dish is homemade manicotti della casa, filled with ricotta, spinach, and a zesty tomato sauce. **The Greenhouse,** Bobby's Marina (off Front Street), Philipsburg (☎ 599/54-22941), is a breezy, open-air restaurant serving lunches that include the catch of the day, a wide selection of burgers, and conch chowder.

ST. MARTIN

The St. Martin side of the island is decidedly French. The tricolor flies over Marigot's *gendarmerie,* towns have names like Colombier and Orléans, and the streets are called "rue de la Whatever."

    French St. Martin is governed from Guadeloupe and has direct representation in the French government in Paris. **Marigot,** the principal town, has none of Philipsburg's frenzied pace and cruise ship crowds. In fact, it looks like a French village transplanted to the Caribbean. Not only is there shopping, but some excellent French Creole restaurants as well.

Frommer's Favorite St. Martin Experiences

• **Joining the America's Cup Regatta or heading to Orient Bay:** Both these excursions listed under "Sint Maarten," above, are also available on the French side.

• **Trekking up to the ramparts of Fort St. Louis:** It's a 10- or 15-minute walk from the heart of Marigot to the top, where you're treated to panoramic views of Marigot and beyond (see "On Your Own," below).

• **Having lunch at Madame Claude's Petit Club:** At the oldest restaurant in Marigot you can savor the rich flavors of the Creole and French cuisine served on the restaurant's cozy, colorfully painted upstairs terrace (see "Great Local Restaurants & Bars," below).

COMING ASHORE   Medium-size vessels can dock at the pier at Port-Royale, at the bottom of the Boulevard de France in the heart of Marigot. When you disembark, you'll see a rather lavish marina, the headquarters of the island's tourist office, and arcades of shops nearby. The pier can accommodate only one ship at a time, so if a cruise ship is already docked, any second ship must anchor and send tenders ashore. Large ships generally dock on the Dutch side of the island, but if they call here, passengers must tender in.

CURRENCY   French St. Martin uses the **French franc (F),** although U.S. dollars seem to be preferred. The exchange rate is 6.29F to U.S.$1 (1F = U.S.16¢). Canadians should convert their money into U.S. dollars, not into francs.

LANGUAGE   Although the official language is French, most people also speak English.

INFORMATION   For French St. Martin, go to the **Tourist Information office,** right in front of the pier at Port-Royale in Marigot (☎ 590/87-5721). It's open Monday to Friday from 8:30am to 1pm and 2:30 to 5:30pm. For info before you go, contact the French St. Martin Tourism Board in the U.S. at ☎ 212/475-8970 or www.st-martin.org.

CALLING FROM THE U.S.   When calling St. Martin from the United States, you need to dial "011" before the numbers listed in this section.

GETTING AROUND

TAXIS   Taxis are the most common means of transport. A **Taxi Service & Information Center** operates at the port of Marigot (☎ 590/87-56-54). It also books 2-hour sightseeing trips around the island. Always agree on the rate before getting into an unmetered cab.

BY MINIVAN   Local drivers operate a diverse armada of privately owned minivans and minibuses. There's a departure every hour between Marigot and the Dutch side.

Frommer's Ratings: St. Martin					
	poor	fair	good	excellent	outstanding
Overall Experience				✓	
Shore Excursions			✓		
Activities Close to Port				✓	
Beaches & Water Sports				✓	
Shopping				✓	
Dining/Bars				✓	

Because it's sometimes difficult for a newcomer to identify the buses, it's best to ask a local. It's about $1 or $2 per ride.

BY RENTAL CAR   Rental cars are a practical way to see the island. **Budget** (☎ **800/527-0700** in the U.S., or 590/87-38-22), **Hertz** (☎ **800/654-3001** in the U.S., or 590/87-73-01), and **Avis** (☎ **800/331-1212** in the U.S., or 590/87-50-60) all have agencies here. Rates begin at $35 per day with unlimited mileage. Drive on the right-hand side of the road.

SHORE EXCURSIONS

All the same excursions offered in Dutch Sint Maarten (see above) are also offered here.

ON YOUR OWN

All of Marigot's shopping is within walking distance, as well as several restaurants and cafes. Don't miss out on a short hike up to Fort St. Louis for lovely, panoramic views of much of the island.

Beyond walking distance, we're mostly talking beaches (see below).

BEACHES

Top rating on the French side goes to **Baie Longue,** a long, beautiful beach that's rarely overcrowded. Chic and very expensive La Samanna, a deluxe hotel, opens onto this beachfront, which is one of the few on the island that grew rather than diminished in size during the 1995 hurricanes. Unfortunately, the storms created unexpected holes offshore, which makes swimming here more hazardous than before. The beach lies to the north of Cupecoy Beach, by the Lowlands road.

If you continue north, you reach the approach to **Baie Rouge,** another long and popular stretch of sand and jagged coral. Snorkelers are drawn to the rock formations at both ends of this beach, many of which were exposed through erosion caused by the 1995 storms. There are no changing facilities, but that doesn't matter for some, who get their suntan *au naturel.*

Orient Beach is one of the Caribbean's most famous clothing-optional beaches. Colorful canvas umbrellas create a European feel, and there are charming beachside cafes for lunch.

On the north side of the island, to the west of Espérance airport, **Grand-Case Beach** is small but select. Despite the many tons of storm debris left in 1995 by the hurricanes, the sands are once again white and clean.

SHOPPING

Many day-trippers come over to Marigot just to look at the collection of French boutiques and shopping arcades. Because it's a duty-free port, the shopping here is some of the best in the Caribbean. Whether you're seeking jewelry, perfume, or St-Tropez bikinis, you'll find it in one of the boutiques along rue de la République and rue de la Liberté. There's a wide selection of **European merchandise,** much of it geared to the luxury trade. Crystal, perfumes, jewelry, and fashions are sometimes 25% to 50% less expensive than in the United States and Canada. You'll also find fine liqueurs, cognacs, and cigars.

Prices are often quoted in U.S. dollars, and salespeople frequently speak English. U.S. dollars, credit and charge cards, and traveler's checks are usually accepted.

At harbor side in Marigot, there's a frisky **morning market** with vendors selling spices, fruit, shells, local handcrafts, and T-shirts galore. Mornings are even more alive at **Port La Royale,** the bustling center of everything. Schooners unload produce from the neighboring islands, boats board guests for picnics on deserted beaches, and a brigantine sets out on a sightseeing sail. The owners of a dozen different little dining spots get ready for the lunch crowd. The largest shopping arcade on the French side is here, with many boutiques that often come and go rapidly.

Galerie Périgourdine, another cluster of boutiques, faces the post office. Here you might pick up some designer wear for both men and women, including items from the collection of Ted Lapidus.

Worthwhile specialty shops include **Gingerbread & Mahogany Gallery,** 4–14 Marina Royale (in a narrow alleyway at the marina), which deals in Haitian art by both "old masters" and talented amateurs; **Havane,** Port La Royale, which offers exclusive collections of French clothing for men, in both casual and high-fashion designs; **La Romana,** 12 rue de la République, which sells chic women's clothing, focusing on Italian styles; and **Oro de Sol Jewelers,** rue de la République, which stocks high-fashion jewelry studded with precious stones, plus gold watches by Cartier, Chopard, Ebel, Patek Philippe, and Bulgari.

Local artist **Roland Richardson,** a gifted impressionist painter known for his landscape, portraiture, and colorful still-life paintings, has an art gallery on the waterfront.

SPORTS

GENERAL WATER SPORTS   Most of St. Martin's large beachfront hotels maintain facilities for jet skiing, waterskiing, and parasailing, often from makeshift kiosks on the beaches. Two independent operators that function from side-by-side positions on Orient Bay, close to the cluster of hotels near the Esmeralda Hotel, are **Kon Tiki Watersports** (☎ 590/87-46-89) and **Bikini Beach Watersports** (☎ 590/87-43-25).

SCUBA DIVING   Scuba diving is excellent around French St. Martin, with reef, wreck, cave, and drift dives ranging from 20 to 70 feet. Dive sites include Ilet Pinel for shallow diving; Green Key, a barrier reef; Flat Island for sheltered coves and geologic faults; and Tintamarre, known for its shipwreck. The island's premier dive operation is **Marine Time,** whose offices are in the same building as L'Aventure, Chemin du Port, 97150 Marigot (☎ 590/87-20-28). Operated by England-born Philip Baumann and his Mauritius-born colleague, Corine Mazurier, this outfit offers morning and afternoon dives in deep and shallow water, to wrecks and over reefs.

SNORKELING   The island's tiny coves and calm offshore waters make it a snorkeler's heaven. The waters off the northeastern shore are protected as a regional underwater nature reserve, **Reserve Sous-Marine Régionale.** This area includes Flat Island (also known as Tintamarre), Ilet Pinel, Green Key, and Petite Clef. The use of harpoons and spears is strictly forbidden. Snorkeling can be enjoyed individually or on sailing trips. You can rent equipment at almost any hotel on the beach.

WINDSURFING   Because of prevailing winds and calmer, more protected waters, most windsurfers gravitate to the island's easternmost edge, most notably Coconut Grove Beach, Orient Beach, and, to a lesser extent, Dawn Beach. The best of the several outfits that specialize in windsurfing is **Tropical Wave,** Coconut Grove, Le Galion Beach, Baie de l'Embouchure (☎ 590/87-37-25), set midway between Orient Beach and Oyster Pond, amid a sunblasted, scrub-covered, isolated landscape. The combination of wind and calm waters here is considered almost ideal.

GREAT LOCAL RESTAURANTS & BARS

As on the Dutch side, a favorite **local beer** is Red White and Blue, while a favorite **local rum liqueur** is Guavaberry.

Madame Claude herself is running the show at the ✪ **Petit Club,** the oldest restaurant in Marigot, located on the main street in the heart of town. Savor the rich flavors of the Creole and French cuisine—like spicy conch stew or fresh fish Creole style— served on the restaurant's cozy, bright-yellow upstairs terrace. **La Brasserie de Marigot,** rue du Général-de-Gaulle 11 (☎ **0590/87-94-43**), is where the real French eat, a great choice for good food at good prices. Meals include pot-au-feu, duck breast with peaches, fillet of beef with mushroom sauce, and even chicken on a spit and steak tartare. **La Maison sur le Port,** Boulevard de France (☎ **0590/87-56-38**), is a grand, Parisian, and upscale choice, with cookery that's grounded firmly in France, but with Caribbean twists and flavors. At lunch, you can choose from a number of salads as well as fish and meat courses.

25 St. Thomas & St. John

Vacationers discovered St. Thomas right after World War II, and they've been flock- ing here in increasing numbers ever since. Today, the island is one of the busiest ports in the Caribbean, often hosting more than 10 cruise ships a day during the peak win- ter season. **Charlotte Amalie,** its capital, has become the Caribbean's major shopping center.

Tourism and U.S. government programs have raised the standard of living here to one of the highest in the Caribbean. The island, 12 miles long and 3 miles wide, is now the most developed of the U.S. Virgins. Condominium apartments have grown up over the debris of bulldozed shacks.

In stark contrast to this busy scene, more than half of nearby St. John, the smallest of the U.S. Virgin Islands, is pristinely preserved in the gorgeous **Virgin Islands Na- tional Park.** The wildlife here is admired by ornithologists and zoologists around the world. A rocky coastline, forming crescent-shaped bays and white-sand beaches, rings the whole island. Panoramic views and ruins of 18th-century Danish plantations dot St. John's miles of serpentine hiking trails. Island guides can point out mysterious geo- metric petroglyphs incised into boulders and cliffs; of unknown age and origin, the fig- ures have never been deciphered.

Most cruise ships dock in Charlotte Amalie on St. Thomas, but a few anchor directly off St. John. Many of those that stop only at St. Thomas offer excursions to St. John. If yours doesn't, it's easy to get to St. John on your own.

CURRENCY The U.S. dollar is the local currency.

LANGUAGE It's English.

INFORMATION The **U.S. Virgin Islands Division of Tourism** has offices at Tolbod Gade (☎ **340/774-8784**), open Monday to Friday from 8am to 5pm and Sat- urday from 8am to noon. Here you can pick up *St. Thomas This Week,* which includes maps of St. Thomas and St. John. There's also an office at the Havensight Mall.

CALLING FROM THE U.S. When calling St. Thomas from the United States, you need to dial only a "1" before the numbers listed in this section.

ST. THOMAS

With a population of some 50,000 and a large number of American expatriates and tem- porary sun-seekers in residence, tiny St. Thomas isn't exactly a tranquil tropical retreat. You won't have any beaches to yourself. Shops, bars, and restaurants (including a lot of fast-food joints) abound here, and most of the locals make their living by the tour- ist trade. Most native Virgin Islanders are the descendants of slaves brought from Africa. In fact, Charlotte Amalie was one of the major slave-trading centers in the Caribbean.

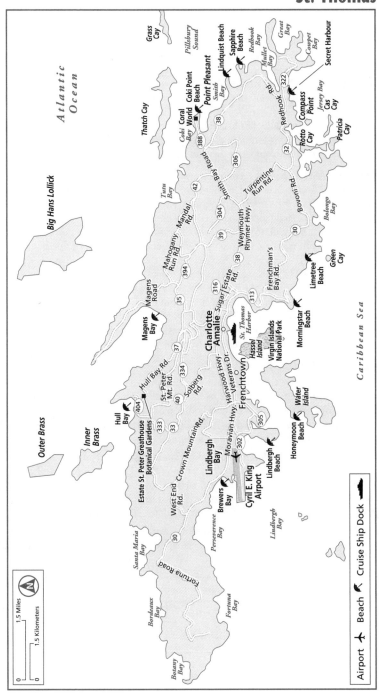

Airport ✈   Beach 🏊   Cruise Ship Dock ⚓

Frommer's Favorite St. Thomas Experiences

- **Biking around the island:** You'll get great views and a great workout, too (see "Shore Excursions," below).
- **Kayaking among the island's mangroves:** You'll learn about the local lagoon eco-system and get some exercise to boot (see "Shore Excursions," below).
- **Visiting the colorful village of Frenchtown:** Have lunch in a village settled by French-speaking citizenry uprooted when the Swedes invaded and took over in St. Barts (see "On Your Own: Beyond Walking Distance," below).
- **Taking a nature walk:** The lush Estate St. Peter Greathouse Botanical Gardens has 200 varieties of plants and trees, plus a rain forest, an orchid jungle, a monkey habitat, and more (see "On Your Own: Beyond Walking Distance," below).

COMING ASHORE   Most cruise ships anchor at Havensight Mall, at the eastern end of Charlotte Amalie Harbor, 1 1/2 miles from the town center. The mall has a tourist information office, restaurants, a bookstore, a bank, a U.S. postal van, phones that accept long-distance credit cards, and a generous number of duty-free shops. Many people make the long, hot walk to the center of Charlotte Amalie, but it's not a scenic route in any way—you may just want to opt for one of the open-air taxis for about $3 per person.

If Havensight Mall is clogged with cruise ships, your ship will dock at the Crown Point Marina, to the west of Charlotte Amalie. A taxi is your best bet—the 30-minute walk into Charlotte Amalie feels longer on a hot day, and isn't terribly picturesque. A taxi ride into town from Crown Point Marina costs about $4.

There are a few AT&T **credit-card phones** at Havensight Mall, at the eastern end of Charlotte Amalie Harbor, 1 1/2 miles from the town center.

GETTING AROUND

BY TAXI   Taxis are the chief means of transport here. They're unmetered, so agree with the driver on a fare before you get in. The official fare for sightseeing is about $30 for two passengers for 2 hours; each additional passenger pays another $12. For 24-hour radio-dispatch service, call ☎ **340/774-7457.** Many taxis transport 8 to 12 passengers in vans to multiple destinations for a lower price.

BY BUS   Comfortable and often air-conditioned, government-run Vitran buses serve Charlotte Amalie and the countryside as far away as Red Hook, a jumping-off point for St. John. You rarely have to wait more than 30 minutes during the day. A one-way ride costs about 75¢ within Charlotte Amalie, $1 to outer neighborhoods, and $3 for rides as far as Red Hook. For routes, stops, and schedules, call ☎ **340/774-5678.**

BY TAXI VAN   Less structured and more erratic are "taxi vans," privately owned vans, minibuses, or open-sided trucks operated by local entrepreneurs. They make un-

Frommer's Ratings: St. Thomas					
	poor	fair	good	excellent	outstanding
Overall Experience				✓	
Shore Excursions				✓	
Activities Close to Port				✓	
Beaches & Water Sports				✓	
Shopping					✓
Dining/Bars			✓		

scheduled stops along major traffic arteries and charge the same fares as the Vitran buses. If you look like you want to go somewhere, one will likely stop for you. They may or may not have their final destinations written on a cardboard sign displayed on the windshield.

BY RENTAL CAR I don't recommend renting a car here.

SHORE EXCURSIONS

In addition to the excursions below, there are plenty of organized snorkeling trips, booze cruises, and island tours offered.

✪ **Island Mountain Bike Adventure** ($59, 3½ hours): For great views of the island and a decent bout of exercise, too, this bike tour starts after a short minivan ride to an elevated part of the island. With a few exceptions, most of the ride is downhill, but you'll definitely work up a sweat. The tour ends at a beach, where there's time for some swimming and relaxing.

✪ **Kayaking the Marine Sanctuary** ($54, 2½ hours): Kayak from the mouth of the marine sanctuary at Holmberg's Marina and spend nearly an hour paddling among the mangroves, while a naturalist explains the mangrove and lagoon ecosystem. At the middle, there's about half an hour to snorkel or walk along the coral beach at Bovoni Point before kayaking back to the starting point.

Island Tour by Minibus and Tram ($30, 3 hours): First drive along the impressive Skyline Drive for panoramic views of St. John and the ship harbor, and then up to the 1,400-foot-high Mountain Top for awesome views of Magens Bay as well as the British Virgin Islands. Then hop in the Paradise Point Tramway for a 15-minute ride to the top of Paradise Point, some 700 feet above the sea.

Atlantis Submarine Odyssey ($70–$74, 2 hours): Descend about 90 feet into the ocean in this air-conditioned submarine for views of exotic fish and sea life.

Virgin Islands Seaplane Exploration ($68, 1½ hours): For great views of these islands, their beaches, old sugar plantations, and lush foliage, there's no better vantage point than from above.

ON YOUR OWN: WITHIN WALKING DISTANCE

The color and charm of a slightly seedy Caribbean waterfront come vividly to life in **Charlotte Amalie.** In days of yore, seafarers from all over the globe flocked to this old-world Danish town. Confederate sailors used the port during the Civil War.

The old warehouses once used for storing pirates' loot still stand and, for the most part, house today's shops. In fact, the main streets (called "Gades" here in honor of their Danish heritage) are now a virtual shopping mall and are usually packed with visitors. Sandwiched among the shops are a few historic buildings, most of which can be covered on foot in about 2 hours.

Before starting your tour, stop off in the so-called **Grand Hotel,** near Emancipation Park. No longer a hotel, it has a restaurant, bar, shops, and a visitor center. Also, from **Hotel 1829** a street farther up, there are views of the harbor below from its wood-paneled pub/restaurant, a great place for a drink or some lunch.

Stray behind the seafront shopping strip (Main Street) of Charlotte Amalie and you'll find pockets of 19th-century houses and, high on the steep sloping Crystal Gade, the truly charming, cozy, brick-and-stone **St. Thomas Synagogue,** built in 1833 by Sephardic Jews. There's a great view from here as well.

Dating from 1672, **Fort Christian** rises from the harbor to dominate the center of town. Named after the Danish king Christian V, the structure has been everything from a governor's residence to a jail. Many pirates were hanged in its courtyard. Some of the cells have been turned into the rather minor **Virgin Islands Museum,** displaying Indian artifacts of only the most passing interest. Admission is free. The fort is open Monday to Friday from 8am to 5pm.

Seven Arches Museum, Government Hill (☎ 340/774-9295), is a 2-century-old Danish house completely restored to its original condition and furnished with antiques. You can walk through the yellow ballast arches and visit the great room with its view of the busy harbor.

The Paradise Point Tramway (☎ 340/774-9809) affords visitors a dramatic view of Charlotte Amalie Harbor at a peak height of 697 feet. The tramways transport customers from the Havensight area to Paradise Point, where riders disembark to visit shops and a popular restaurant and bar.

ON YOUR OWN: BEYOND WALKING DISTANCE

Coral World Marine Park & Underwater Observatory, 6450 Coki Point, off Route 38, 20 minutes from downtown Charlotte Amalie (☎ 340/775-1555), is the number-one attraction in St. Thomas. The 3^1/$_2$-acre complex features a three-story underwater observation tower 100 feet offshore. Through windows you'll see sponges, fish, coral, and other underwater life in their natural state. In the Marine Gardens Aquarium, salt-water tanks display everything from sea horses to sea urchins. An 80,000-gallon reef tank features exotic Caribbean marine life. Another tank is devoted to sea predators, including circling sharks. The entrance is hidden behind a waterfall.

West of Charlotte Amalie, **Frenchtown** was settled by a French-speaking citizenry uprooted when the Swedes invaded and took over in St. Barts. They were known for wearing *cha-chas,* or straw hats. Many of the people who live here today are the direct descendants of those long-ago residents. This colorful fishing village contains several interesting restaurants and taverns. To get there, take a taxi down Veterans Drive (Route 30) west and turn left at the sign to the Admirals Inn.

The lush **Estate St. Peter Greathouse Botanical Gardens,** at the corner of St. Peter Mountain Road (Route 40) and Barrett Hill Road (☎ 340/774-4999), decorates 11 acres on the volcanic peaks of the island's northern rim. It's the creation of Howard Lawson DeWolfe, a Mayflower descendant who, with his wife, Sylvie, bought the estate in 1987 and set about transforming it into a tropical paradise. It's filled with self-guided nature walks that acquaint you with some 200 varieties of plants and trees, including an umbrella plant from Madagascar. There's also a rain forest, an orchid jungle, a monkey habitat, waterfalls, and reflecting ponds. From a panoramic deck you can see some 20 of the Virgin Islands. The house itself is worth a visit, its interior filled with local art.

SHOPPING

St. Thomas is famous for its shopping. As at St. Croix, American shoppers can bring home $1,200 worth of merchandise without paying duty. You'll sometimes find well-known brand names at savings of up to 40% off stateside prices—but you'll often have to plow through a lot of junk to find the bargains.

Many cruise ship passengers shop at the **Havensight Mall,** where they disembark, but the major shopping goes on along the harbor of Charlotte Amalie. **Main Street** (or Dronningens Gade, its old Danish name) is the main shopping area. Just north of Main Street is merchandise-loaded **Back Street,** or Vimmelskaft. Many shops are also spread along the **Waterfront Highway** (also called Kyst Vejen). Running between these major streets is a series of side streets, walkways, and alleys, all filled with shops. All the usual suspects sell all the usual jewelry, watches, perfume, gift items, etc., but there are a number of other interesting shops.

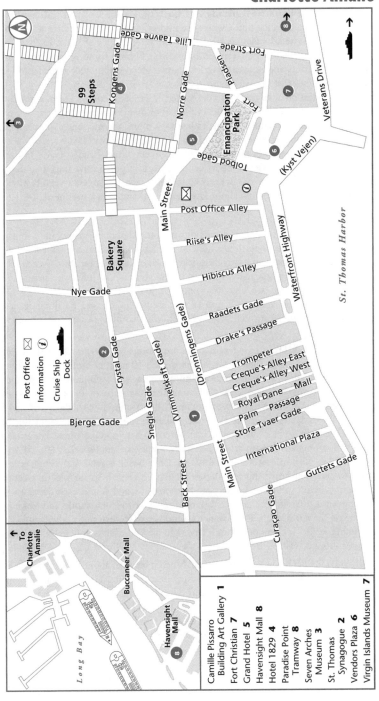

Charlotte Amalie

Lille Taavne Gade
Fort Strade
Kongens Gade
99 Steps
Norre Gade
pladsen
Fort
Emancipation Park
Tolbod Gade
(Kyst Vejen)
Veterans Drive

Main Street
Post Office Alley
Riise's Alley
Bakery Square
Hibiscus Alley
Nye Gade
Raadets Gade
Drake's Passage
Waterfront Highway
St. Thomas Harbor

Post Office
Information
Cruise Ship Dock

Crystal Gade
(Vimmelskaft Gade)
(Dronningens Gade)
Trompeter
Creque's Alley East
Creque's Alley West
Royal Dane   Mall
Palm   Passage
Store Tvaer Gade
Snegle Gade
Bjerge Gade
Main Street
International Plaza
Back Street
Guttets Gade
Curaçao Gade

To Charlotte Amalie
Buccaneer Mall
Havensight Mall
Long Bay

Camille Pissarro
Building Art Gallery **1**
Fort Christian **7**
Grand Hotel **5**
Havensight Mall **8**
Hotel 1829 **4**
Paradise Point
Tramway **8**
Seven Arches
Museum **3**
St. Thomas
Synagogue **2**
Vendors Plaza **6**
Virgin Islands Museum **7**

The **Camille Pissarro Building Art Gallery,** Caribbean Cultural Centre, 14 Dronningens Gade, is the house where the impressionist painter Pissarro was born on July 10, 1830. The art gallery is reached by climbing a flight of stairs. In three high-ceilinged and airy rooms, you'll see all the available Pissarro paintings relating to the islands. Many prints and note cards of local artists are available, too, as well as original batiks, alive in vibrant colors.

Street vendors ply their trades in a designated area called **Vendors Plaza,** at the corner of Veterans Drive and Tolbod Gade. Hundreds of them converge under oversize parasols there Monday to Saturday from 7:30am to 5:30pm, and on Sunday if a cruise ship is expected. Food vendors set up on sidewalks outside Vendors Plaza.

Just for fun, you'll want to have a peak in **Lover's Lane,** Raadets Gade 33 (beside Veterans Drive, on the second floor), with its stock of provocative lingerie, inflatable men and women, massage aids of every conceivable type, the largest inventory of vibrators in the Virgin Islands, and all the lace, leather, or latex you'll ever need.

BEACHES

Instead of looking at the minor attractions or going shopping, many cruise ship passengers prefer to spend their time ashore on a beach. St. Thomas has some good ones, and you can reach them all relatively quickly in a taxi (arrange for the driver to return and pick you up at a designated time). If you're going to St. John, you may want to do your beaching there (see "Beaches," under St. John, below).

All the beaches in the U.S. Virgin Islands are public, but some still charge a fee. Mind your belongings at the beach, as St. Thomas has pickpockets and thieves who target visitors.

THE NORTH SIDE Lying across the mountains 3 miles north of the capital, **Magens Bay** was once hailed as one of the world's 10 most beautiful beaches, but its reputation has faded. Though still beautiful, it isn't as well maintained as it should be and is often overcrowded, especially when many cruise ships are in port. It's less than a mile long and lies between two mountains. Admission is $1 for adults and 25¢ for children under 12. Changing facilities are available, and you can rent snorkeling gear and lounge chairs. There's no public transportation here, so take a taxi. The gates are open daily from 6am to 6pm (you'll need insect repellent after 4pm).

Located in the northeast near Coral World, **Coki Beach** is good, but it, too, becomes overcrowded when cruise ships are in port. Snorkelers come here often, as do pickpockets—protect your valuables. Lockers can be rented at Coral World, next door. An East End bus runs to Smith Bay and lets you off at the gate to Coral World and Coki.

Also on the north side is **Renaissance Grand Beach Resort,** one of the island's most beautiful beaches. It opens onto Smith Bay, right off Route 38, near Coral World. Many water sports are available here.

THE SOUTH SIDE On the south side, **Morningstar** lies about 2 miles east of Charlotte Amalie at Marriott's Frenchman's Reef Beach Resort. You can wear your most daring swimwear here, and you can also rent sailboats, snorkeling equipment, and lounge chairs. The beach can be easily reached via a cliff-front elevator at the Marriott.

Limetree Beach, at the Bolongo Bay Beach Club, lures those who love a serene spread of sand. You can feed hibiscus blossoms to iguanas and rent snorkeling gear and lounge chairs. There's no public transportation, but it's easy to get here by taxi from Charlotte Amalie.

One of the most popular, **Brewer's Beach** lies in the southwest near the University of the Virgin Islands. It can be reached by the public bus marked FORTUNA heading west from Charlotte Amalie. **Lindberg Beach,** near the airport, also lies on the Fortuna bus route heading west from Charlotte Amalie.

THE EAST END   Small and special, **Secret Harbour** sits near a collection of condos. With its white sand and coconut palms, it's a veritable cliché of Caribbean charm. No public transportation stops here, but it's an easy taxi ride east of Charlotte Amalie heading toward Red Hook.

Sapphire Beach is one of the finest on St. Thomas, set against the backdrop of the Doubletree Sapphire Beach Resort & Marina complex, where you can lunch or order drinks. Windsurfers like this beach a lot. You can also rent snorkeling gear and lounge chairs here. A large reef lies close to the shore, and there are great views of offshore cays and St. John. To get to this beach, you can take the East End bus from Charlotte Amalie, going via Red Hook. Ask to be let off at the entrance to Sapphire Bay; it's not too far to walk from there to the water.

SPORTS

GOLF   Designed by Tom and George Fazio, **Mahogany Run** on the north shore, Mahogany Run Road (☎ **800/253-7103** or 340/777-6006), is one of the most beautiful courses in the West Indies. This 18-hole, par-70 course rises and drops like a roller coaster on its journey to the sea. Cliffs and crashing sea waves are the ultimate hazards at the 13th and 14th holes. The golf course is an $8 taxi ride from the cruise dock.

SCUBA DIVING & SNORKELING   The waters off the U.S. Virgin Islands are rated as one of the "most beautiful areas in the world" by *Skin Diver* magazine. Thirty spectacular reefs lie just off St. Thomas alone. **Dive In!**, in the Doubletree Sapphire Beach Resort & Marina, Smith Bay Road, Route 36 (☎ **800/524-2090**), offers professional instruction, daily beach and boat dives, custom dive packages, underwater photography and videotapes, and snorkeling trips.

GREAT LOCAL RESTAURANTS & BARS

IN CHARLOTTE AMALIE   **Beni Iguana's Sushi Bar,** in the Grand Hotel Court, just behind Emancipation Park in downtown (☎ **340/777-8744**), is the only Japanese restaurant on St. Thomas. **Greenhouse,** Veterans Drive (☎ **340/774-7998**), attracts cruise ship passengers with daily specialties, including much American fare and some Jamaican-inspired dishes. The **Hard Rock Café,** 5144 International Plaza (on the second floor of a pink-sided mall), the Waterfront, Queen's Quarter (☎ **340/777-5555**), has the best burgers in town, but people mainly come for the good times. ○ **Virgilio's,** 18 Dronningens Gade, entrance on a narrow alleyway running between Main and Back streets (☎ **340/776-4920**), is the best northern Italian restaurant in the Virgin Islands. The lobster ravioli here is the best there is.

IN FRENCHTOWN   At **Alexander's,** rue de St. Barthélemy, west of town (☎ **340/ 776-4211**), there's a heavy emphasis on seafood—the menu even includes conch schnitzel on occasion. Other dishes include a mouthwatering Wiener schnitzel and homemade pâté. ○ **Craig & Sally's,** 22 Honduras (☎ **340/777-9949**), serves dishes that, according to the owner, are not "for the faint of heart, but for the adventurous soul"—roast pork with clams, filet mignon with macadamia-nut sauce, and grilled swordfish with a sauce of fresh herbs and tomatoes.

ON THE NORTH COAST   **Eunice's Terrace,** 66–67 Smith Bay, Route 38, just east of the Coral World turnoff (☎ **340/775-3975**), is one of the island's best-known West Indian restaurants, and oozes with local color. The place made news around the world on January 5, 1997, when Bill and Hillary Clinton showed up unexpectedly for lunch. Surrounded by secret-service men, they shared a conch appetizer, then Mrs. Clinton went for the vegetable plate while the president opted for the catch of the day, which he reportedly loved.

ON SAPPHIRE BEACH   Seagrape, in the Doubletree Sapphire Beach Resort & Marina, Rte. 6, Smith Bay Rd. (☎ **340/775-6100**), is counted among the finest dining rooms along the east coast of St. Thomas. The lunch menu includes the grilled catch of the day and freshly made salads.

NEAR THE SUB BASE   Victor's New Hide Out, 103 Sub Base, off Route 30 (☎ **340/776-9379**), has some of the best local dishes on the island, but first you have to find it—this hilltop perch is truly a place to hide out. Take a taxi. Its dishes have sophisticated flair and zest, as opposed to the more down-home cookery found at Eunice's Terrace (see above).

ST. JOHN

St. John lies about 3 miles east of St. Thomas across Pillsbury Sound. The island, the smallest and least populated of the U.S. Virgins, is about 7 miles long and 3 miles wide, with a total land area of some 20 square miles. When held under Danish control, it was slated for big development, but a slave rebellion and a decline of the sugarcane plantations ended that idea. Since 1956, more than half its land mass, as well as its shoreline waters, have been set aside as the **Virgin Islands National Park.** Miles of winding hiking trails lead to panoramic views and the ruins of 18th-century Danish plantations. Mysterious geometric petroglyphs incised into boulders and cliffs can be pointed out by island guides; of unknown age and origin, the figures have never been deciphered. Since St. John is easy to reach from St. Thomas, many cruise ship passengers spend their entire day here.

Frommer's Favorite St. John Experiences

- **Touring the island in an open-air safari bus:** The views are spectacular from the island's coastal road, and you'll visit the ruins of a plantation and one of St. John's excellent beaches (see "Shore Excursions," below).
- **Beaching yourself in Trunk Bay:** Although it can get somewhat crowded, it's a gorgeous beach and there's some decent snorkeling, too (see "Beaches," below).

**COMING ASHORE   **Cruise ships cannot dock at either of the piers in St. John. Instead, they moor off the coast of Cruz Bay, sending in tenders to the National Park Service Dock, the larger of the two piers. Most cruise ships docking at St. Thomas offer shore excursions to St. John's pristine acres and beaches.

If your ship docks on St. Thomas and you don't take a shore excursion to St. John, you can get here from Charlotte Amalie by ferry. Ferries leave the Charlotte Amalie waterfront for St. John's Cruz Bay at 1- to 2-hour intervals, from 9am until the last departure around 5:30pm. The last boat leaves Cruz Bay for Charlotte Amalie at 3:45pm. The ride takes about 45 minutes and costs $7 each way. Call ☎ **340/776-6282** for more information.

Frommer's Ratings: St. John					
	poor	fair	good	excellent	outstanding
Overall Experience				✓	
Shore Excursions			✓		
Activities Close to Port				✓	
Beaches & Water Sports				✓	
Shopping		✓			
Dining/Bars		✓			

St. John

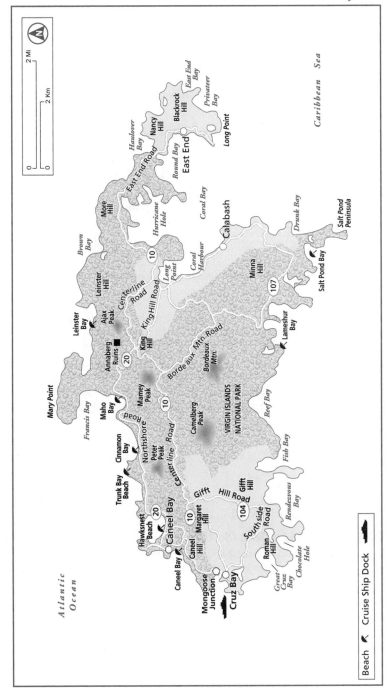

Another ferry leaves from the Red Hook pier on St. Thomas's eastern tip more or less every half hour, starting at 6:30am. It's a 30-minute drive from Charlotte Amalie's port to the pier at Red Hook; the ferry trip to Cruz Bay on St. John takes another 20 minutes each way. The one-way fare is $3 for adults, $1 for children under 11. Schedules can change without notice, so call in advance (☎ 340/776-6282). You can take a Vitran bus from a point near Market Square directly to Red Hook for $1 per person each way, or negotiate a price with a taxi driver.

GETTING AROUND

BY TAXI   The most popular way to get around is by surrey-style taxi. Typical fares from Cruz Bay are $3 to Trunk Bay, $3.50 to Cinnamon Bay, or $7 to Mahoe Bay. For more information, call ☎ 340/693-7530.

BY RENTAL CAR   The extensive Virgin Islands National Park has kept the island's roads undeveloped and uncluttered, with some of the most panoramic vistas anywhere. Renting a vehicle is the best way to see these views, especially if you like to linger at particularly beautiful spots. Open-sided Jeep-like vehicles are the most fun of the limited rentals here. There's sometimes a shortage of cars during the busy midwinter season, so try to reserve early. Remember to drive on the left (even though steering wheels are on the left, too—go figure).

The two largest car-rental agencies on St. John are located on St. John: **Avis** (☎ 800/331-1212 or 340/776-6374) charges between $75 and $85 per day, and **Hertz** (☎ 800/654-3001 or 340/693-7580), $60 to $85 per day. Gasoline is seldom included in the price of a rental, and your car is likely to come with just enough fuel to get you to one of the island's two gas stations. Because of the distance between stations, it's never a good idea to drive around St. John with less than half a tank of gas.

BY BICYCLE   Bicycles are available for rent from the **Cinnamon Bay Watersports Center** on Cinnamon Bay Beach (☎ 340/776-6330). St. John's steep hills and off-road trails can challenge the best of riders, but cyclists in search of more moderate rides can visit the ruins at Annaberg or the beaches at Maho, Francis, Leinster, or Watermelon Bay.

SHORE EXCURSIONS

Island Tour ($39, 4–5 hours): Since most ships tie up in St. Thomas, tours of St. John first require a ferry or tender ride to Cruz Bay in St. John. Then you board open-air safari buses for a tour that includes a stop at the ruins of a working plantation, the Annaberg Ruins, as well as a stop at a beach, like Trunk Bay. The views from the coastal road of the islands and sea beyond are spectacular.

TOURING THROUGH LOCAL OPERATORS

Taxi Tours: Taxi tours of about 2 hours cost from $30 for one or two passengers, or about $12 per person for three or more riders, and are one of the best ways of seeing St. John. Almost any taxi at Cruz Bay can take you on these tours, or you can call ☎ 340/693-7530.

ON YOUR OWN: WITHIN WALKING DISTANCE

Most cruise ship passengers dart through Cruz Bay, a cute little West Indian village with interesting bars, restaurants, boutiques, and pastel-painted houses. You can browse through **Wharfside Village,** a complex of courtyards, alleys, and shady patios with a mishmash of boutiques, restaurants, fast-food joints, and bars.

Located at the public library, **Elaine Ione Sprauve Museum** (☎ 340/776-6359) isn't big, but it does contain some local artifacts, and will teach you about some of the history of the island. It's open Monday to Friday from 9am to 5pm. Admission is free.

ON YOUR OWN: BEYOND WALKING DISTANCE

Two-thirds of St. John is national-park land. If you want to explore the **Virgin Islands National Park,** stop off first at the visitor center (☎ **340/776-6201**), right on the dock at St. Cruz. Here you'll see some exhibits and learn more about what you can see and do in the park.

Established in 1956, the park totals 12,624 acres, including submerged land and water adjacent to St. John. You can explore the park on the more than 20 miles of biking trails, or rent your own car, Jeep, or Mini-Moke. Make sure you drive on the left. If you want to hike, stop at the office of the park ranger, adjacent to the pier, to watch an 18-minute video about the park. Also pick up maps and instructions before setting out on any of the clearly marked hiking trails. You can take a taxi for about $5 to the starting point of whatever trail you select.

Within the park, try to see the **Annaberg Ruins,** Leinster Bay Road, where the Danes founded a thriving plantation and sugar mill in 1718. You'll find tidal pools, forest lands, hilltops, wild scenery, and the ruins of several Danish plantations. It's located off North Shore Road east of Trunk Bay on the north shore. On certain days of the week (dates vary), guided walks of the area are given by park rangers. Check with the park's visitor center.

SHOPPING

Compared to St. Thomas, there's not a lot of shopping on St. John, but the boutiques and shops at Cruz Bay are generally more interesting. Most of them are clustered at **Mongoose Junction,** in a woodsy area beside the roadway, about a 5-minute walk from the ferry dock.

IN MONGOOSE JUNCTION   Bamboula has an unusual and appealing collection of gifts from the Caribbean, Haiti, India, Indonesia, and Central Africa. **The Canvas Factory** produces its own handmade, rugged, and colorful canvas bags. **Donald Schnell Studio** deals in handmade pottery, sculpture, and blown glass. The **Fabric Mill** features silk-screened and batik fabrics from around the world. **R and I Patton Goldsmithing** has a large selection of island-designed jewelry in sterling silver, gold, and precious stones.

IN CRUZ BAY   As you wait at Cruz Bay for the ferry back to St. Thomas, you can browse through the shops of Wharfside Village. **Pusser's of the West Indies** is located here, offering a large collection of classically designed, old-world travel and adventure clothing, along with unusual accessories and Pusser's famous (though not terribly good) rum. A good, cheap gift item is packets of Pusser's coasters, on which is writ the recipe for that classic Caribbean rum specialty, the Painkiller.

BEACHES

For a true beach lover, missing the great white sweep of **Trunk Bay** would be like touring Europe and skipping Paris. Trouble is, the word is out. This gorgeous beach is usually overcrowded, and there are pickpockets lurking about. The beach has lifeguards and offers rentals, such as snorkeling gear. The underwater trail near the shore attracts beginning snorkelers in particular. Both taxis and "safari buses" to Trunk Bay meet the ferry as it docks at Cruz Bay.

Caneel Bay, the stamping ground of the rich and famous, has seven perfect beaches on its 170 acres—but only one open to the public. That's **Hawksnest Beach,** a little gem of white sand beloved by St. Johnians. The beach is a bit narrow and windy, but beautiful. Close to the road you'll find barbecue grills. Safari buses and taxis from Cruz Bay will take you along North Shore Road.

The campgrounds of **Cinnamon Bay** and **Maho Bay** have their own beaches, where forest rangers sometimes have to remind visitors to put their swimsuits back on. Snorkelers find good reefs here. Changing rooms and showers are available.

Salt Pond Bay is known to locals but often missed by visitors. The bay here is tranquil, but there are no facilities. The Ram Head Trail begins here and winds for a mile to a panoramic belvedere overlooking the bay.

SPORTS

HIKING   The network of trails in Virgin Islands National Park is the big thing here. The visitor center at Cruz Bay gives away free trail maps of the park. Since you don't have time to get lost—you don't want the ship to leave without you!—it's best to set out with someone who knows his or her way around. Both **Maho Bay** (☎ 340/776-6226) and **Cinnamon Bay** (☎ 340/776-6330) conduct nature walks.

KAYAKING & WINDSURFING   The most complete line of water sports available on St. John is offered at the **Cinnamon Bay Watersports Center** on Cinnamon Bay Beach (☎ 340/776-6330). The windsurfing here is some of the best anywhere, for both the beginner and the expert. You can also rent kayaks or a 12- or 14-foot Hobie monohull sailboat.

SCUBA DIVING & SNORKELING   Ask about scuba packages at **Low Key Watersports,** Wharfside Village (☎ 800/835-7718 or 340/693-8999). All wreck dives are two-tank/two-location dives. Snorkel tours are also available. The center uses its own custom-built dive boats and also specializes in water-sports gear, including masks, fins, snorkels, and dive skins. It can arrange day-sailing charters, kayaking tours, and deep-sea sportfishing. **Cruz Bay Watersports,** P.O. Box 252, Palm Plaza, St. John, USVI 00831 (☎ 800/835-7730 or 340/776-6234), is a PADI and NAUI five-star diving center. Snorkel tours are available daily.

GREAT LOCAL RESTAURANTS & BARS

Pusser's, Wharfside Village, Cruz Bay (near the ferry dock; ☎ 340/693-8489), is actually three bars, all serving the famous Pusser's rum and menu choices that include jerk tuna fillet, jerk chicken with a tomato basil sauce over penne, and spaghetti with lobster cooked in rum, wine, lemon juice, and garlic. **The Fish Trap,** in the Raintree Inn, Cruz Bay (☎ 340/693-9994), is known for its wide selection of fresh fish, but also caters to vegetarians and the burger crowd. The Italian food at ✪ **Paradiso,** Mongoose Junction (☎ 340/693-8899), is the best on the island—the chicken picante Willie—a spicy, creamy picante sauce over crispy chicken with linguini and ratatouille—was featured in *Bon Appétit.*

26 Trinidad & Tobago

The southernmost islands in the Caribbean chain, Trinidad and tiny Tobago, which together form a single nation, manage to encompass nearly every facet of Caribbean life. Like night and day, one is industrial and the other very natural. Located less than 10 miles east of Venezuela's coast, Trinidad is large (the biggest and most heavily populated Caribbean island) and diverse, with an industrial, cosmopolitan capital city, Port of Spain, and an outgoing, vibrant culture that combines African, East Indian, European, Chinese, and Syrian influences. Little-sister Tobago is the more natural of the two, with rain-forested mountains to spectacular secluded beaches.

Trinidad and Tobago won independence from Britain in 1962 and became a republic in 1976, but some British influences, including the residents' love of cricket, remain.

Trinidad grew rich from oil, and the islands are still the Western Hemisphere's largest oil exporters.

Trinidad's music is another local treasure. The calypso, steel-pan, and soca styles originated here have influenced musical trends worldwide. Trinidad's rhythmic, soulful music is a main feature of Carnaval, the Caribbean-wide bacchanalian celebration held across the islands each year on the Monday and Tuesday before Lent. Of all the Carnaval celebrations across the Caribbean islands, Trinidad's is the king.

Trinidad's residents are charming, friendly, and love to talk. With a literacy rate of 97%, the populace is full of well-informed conversationalists. You'll find Trinis (as residents call themselves) happy to socialize with visitors and discuss just about anything.

CURRENCY   The unit of currency is the **Trinidad & Tobago dollar (TT),** sometimes designated by the same symbol as the U.S. dollar ($) and sometimes just by TT. The exchange rate is TT$6.30 to U.S.$1 (TT$1 = U.S.16¢). Vacationers can pay in U.S. dollars, but ask for price quotes in Trinidad *and* U.S. dollars, and try to get change in U.S. dollars. Local ATM machines mainly dispense TT notes.

LANGUAGE   The official language is English, but like many of their Caribbean neighbors, Trinis speak English with a distinct patois. Hindi, Creole, and Spanish are also spoken amongst various ethnic groups.

CALLING FROM THE U.S.   When calling Trinidad and Tobago from the United States, you need to dial "011" before the numbers listed in this section.

TRINIDAD

Trinidad is the one of the most industrialized countries in the Caribbean, and it shows—if you're looking for a sleepy, quiet Caribbean retreat, go to Tobago instead. Trinidad's capital and commercial center, **Port of Spain,** is an energetic, bustling metropolis of 300,000. There are few distinct attractions—Port of Spain isn't necessarily a tourist city—but the central shopping area at the south end of Frederick Street is a colorfully crowded mix of outdoor shopping arcades and air-conditioned mini-malls.

Independence Square, in the heart of Port of Spain, is the place to get a taxi, find a bank, and get good, cheap food. There are mosques, shrines, and temples here and also several travel agencies in the area. Locals gather at Woodford Square to hear impromptu public speakers or attend outdoor meetings.

While Port of Spain is interesting and not threatening by day, it's unsafe at night, and strolling around is not recommended. Panhandlers are likely to approach visitors at times. The cruise-ship complex has a customs hall, shops, car-rental agencies, and a waiting fleet of taxis.

Frommer's Favorite Trinidad Experiences

- **Visiting the Asa Wright Nature Center:** This 200-acre preserve, located in Trinidad's rain forest in the northern hills, features intertwined hiking trails and a bird sanctuary and conservation center. (See "On Your Own: Beyond Walking Distance," below.)
- **Touring the Caroni Bird Sanctuary:** This ecological wonder features dense mangroves, remote canals, and shallow lagoons that are the breeding grounds for spectacular scarlet ibis. Visitors tour the sanctuary in guided boats. (See "Shore Excursions," below.)
- **Trying a drink with Angostura bitters:** This local specialty contains citrus-tree bark and is made from *a secret recipe.*

COMING ASHORE   Cruise ships visiting Trinidad dock at Port of Spain's 4-acre cruise terminal, built in the early 1990s to accommodate the island's growing cruise traffic. The complex includes a telephone and communications center, a shopping mall, and a branch of the Trinidad and Tobago Tourist Development Authority. Arriving passengers are usually greeted by steel-pan musicians and colorfully dressed dancers. Outside the terminal, there's a craft market with T-shirts, straw items, and other souvenirs.

There is a **telephone** and communications center in the terminal complex.

INFORMATION   At the terminal in Port of Spain, there's the **Tourism and Industrial Development Corporation of Trinidad and Tobago (TIDCO)** at 10-14 Phillips St., open Monday to Friday from 8am to 4:30pm. For info before you, contact the tourism board office in the U.S. at ☎ **888/595-4868** or www.visittnt.com.

Frommer's Ratings: Trinidad					
	poor	fair	good	excellent	outstanding
Overall Experience		✓			
Shore Excursions		✓			
Activities Close to Port	✓				
Beaches & Water Sports		✓			
Shopping		✓			
Dining/Bars			✓		

GETTING AROUND

BY TAXI   Taxis are available at the cruise terminal. The Port Authority posts cab fares on a board by the main entrance (the cars don't have meters). Always establish a fare before loading into the taxi and shoving off. Private cabs can be relatively expensive, but maxi-taxis (minivans operating regular routes within specific zones) are lower priced.

BY BUS/VAN   Maxi-taxis in Trinidad have a yellow stripe. There are also route taxis, shared cabs that travel along a prescribed route and charge TT$2 to TT$3 (U.S.32¢ to U.S.48¢) to drop you at any spot along the route.

BY RENTAL CAR   Driving is on the left. Trinidad has a fairly wide network of roads, and roads in town are generally well marked, but traffic is frequently heavy. There are a few small rental-car companies in Trinidad, but it's probably not necessary to rent a car for a 1-day port call here.

SHORE EXCURSIONS

Caroni Bird Sanctuary ($44, 3 hours): This sanctuary is a pristine network of lush mangroves, quiet canals, and shallow lagoons and is considered a world-class bird-watching preserve. Following a 30-minute drive from the cruise pier, passengers embark for the tour in flat-bottomed boats, which glide through calm-watered canals and lagoons. Guides will point out unique flora and fauna during the ride. Heron, osprey, and scarlet ibis are among the bird species native to this area.

ON YOUR OWN: WITHIN WALKING DISTANCE

Except for the **craft market** right outside the terminal, and a small restaurant across the street, there isn't much to see close to the cruise pier.

ON YOUR OWN: BEYOND WALKING DISTANCE

Among Port of Spain's chief centers of activity, **Independence Square** isn't really a square at all, but parallel streets running east and west and connected at one end by a pedestrian mall. The scene here resembles a Middle Eastern bazaar, with a dense thicket of pushcarts, honking cabs, produce hawkers, and inquisitive shoppers moving constantly to the irresistible beat of soca, reggae, and calypso music blaring from nearby stores and sidewalk stands. Some parts of the square have become run-down in recent years, and some locals consider the area less than safe. Visitors should keep an eye out for pickpockets and petty thieves. **Woodford Square,** laid out by Ralph Woodford, Trinidad's early 19th-century British governor, is among the most attractive areas in Port of Spain, full of large, leafy trees surrounding a rich lawn with landscaped walkways. This area has traditionally served as a center for political debates, discussions, and rallies. The **Cathedral of the Holy Trinity,** built in 1818 by Woodford, lies on the south side of Woodford Square. The church's carved roof is designed as a replica of Westminster Hall in London. Inside of the church is a memorial statue of Woodford.

On the square's western border is **Red House,** an imposing Renaissance-style edifice built in 1906. Red house is indeed red-colored and today houses Trinidad's parliament. The building was badly damaged in 1990 when militants took the prime minister and parliament members hostage. A little farther outside of the city center is **Queen's Park Savannah,** originally part of a 200-acre sugar plantation but now a public park and racetrack with 80 acres of open land and walkways with great shade trees. A depression at the park's northwest section, known as the Hollows, has flower beds, rock gardens, and small ponds. The area has become a popular picnic spot.

There are a number of notable sights along the park's outer edge, including the **Magnificent Seven,** a row of seven colonial buildings constructed in the late 19th and early 20th centuries. The buildings include Queen's Royal College, White Hall, the prime minister's office, and Stollmeyer's Castle, designed to resemble a Scottish castle complete with turrets.

Beyond the northern edge of Queen's Park Savannah lies the **Emperor Valley Zoo,** containing local animals, including tropical toucans and macaws, porcupine, monkeys, and various snakes. But the zoo really emphasizes colorful tropical plants, in evidence all around the zoo's grounds.

The 70-acre **botanical gardens** are east of the zoo. Laid out in 1820, the gardens are landscaped with great trees and attractive walkways. Among the flowering trees here is the wild poinsettia, whose bright red blossom is the national flower. The President's House, built in 1875 as the governor's residence, is adjacent to the gardens.

Near Spring Hill Estate, 30 miles northeast of Port of Spain beside Blanchisseuse Road, the **Asa Wright Nature Center** (☎ 868/667-4655) is known to bird watchers throughout the world. Within its 196 acres, set at an elevation of 1,200 feet in Trinidad's rain-forested mountains, you can see hummingbirds, toucans, bellbirds, manakins, several varieties of tanagers, and the rare oilbird. Hiking trails line the grounds, and guided tours are available. Call for a schedule.

SHOPPING

Shopping in the Port of Spain area means crafts, fabrics, and fashions made by local artists, an array of spices, and colorful artwork. Most of the shopping opportunities lie in the area around Independence Square, particularly Frederick and Queen streets. Art lovers will find a handful of galleries and studios featuring the work of local and regional artists. **Art Creators,** at Seventh Street and St. Ann's Road in the Aldegonda Park section, is a serious gallery offering year-around exhibits from both aspiring and established artists. **Aquarela Galleries,** at 1A Dere St., exhibits the work of recognized and up-and-coming Trini artists and also publishes high-end art books. If you're in the mood for distinctive gift and apparel shopping, hire a cab to the **Hotel Normandie,** 10 Nook Ave. in the St. Ann's section, where the shops feature clothing and jewelry by some of the country's top designers. Officially known as The Village Market, the hotel's shopping plaza features **Greer's Textile Designs,** a boutique carrying colorful batiks and pricey jewelry from designer Jillian Bishop. Also here is **Interiors,** which features all manner of unusual gifts. For craft creations outside of the cruise terminal area, try the **Trinidad and Tobago Blind Welfare Assn.,** at 118 Duke St., which features accessories and gifts of rattan, banana leaves, and other natural substances. All of the products are made by blind craftsmen. **The Trinidad and Tobago Handicraft Cooperative,** at King's Wharf, sells small steel pans, hammocks, and other locally produced items. **Art Potters Ltd.,** located at the cruise terminal, is a pottery specialist.

Music is another of Trinidad's signature products, and the latest soca and reggae styles can be purchased at **Rhyner's Record Shop** at 54 Prince St. in Port of Spain. There's also **Crosby Records,** located in the St. James area.

BEACHES

Unlike its tiny cousin Tobago, Trinidad proper isn't teeming with beautiful beaches. The most popular one is **Maracas Bay,** a scenic, 40-minute drive from Port of Spain. The drive takes vacationers over mountains and through a lush rain forest. As you near the beach, the coastal road descends from a stunning cliff side. The beach itself is wide and sandy, with a small fishing village on one side and the richly dense mountains in the background. There's a lifeguard, changing rooms and showers, and areas for picnics. There's also a small snack stand selling "shark and bake" sandwiches (a local favorite made with fresh slabs of shark and fried bread).

SPORTS

GOLF   The oldest and best-known golf course on the island is 18-hole **St. Andrews Golf Club** in the suburb of Maraval (☎ 868/629-2314). The course, also known as

Moka Golf Course, was established in the late 19th century. Trinidad also has a nine-hole public course, **Chaguaramas Public Golf Club,** and courses in Pointe a Pierre and La Brea.

DEEP-SEA FISHING   The Bocas Islands off Trinidad are well known for excellent deep-sea fishing. **Classic Tours** (☎ 868/628-7053) arranges sportfishing excursions to the area.

GREAT LOCAL RESTAURANTS & BARS

A favorite **local beer** is Stag; a favorite **local rum** is Vat 19 Old Oak.

Trinidad is home to some of the most diverse culinary styles in the entire Caribbean, a result of its African, Chinese, English, French, Indian, Portuguese, Spanish, and Syrian influences. **Rafters,** at 6A Warner St. (☎ 868/628-9258), is an old rum house that still sports brick walls and hand-finished ceilings, and today offers sandwiches, chili, and chicken in its bar. There's also an elegant dining room for more formal meals, and the menu features house specialties. **La Chateau de Poisson,** at 38 Ariapita Ave., is a quality French-Creole restaurant housed in a charming colonial house. There's a lunchtime buffet (11:30am to 2:30pm) priced around TT$50 (U.S.$8). **Solimar,** at 6 Nook Ave. near the Normandie Hotel (☎ 868/624-6267), features a changing menu of international dishes engineered by owner Joe Brown, a peripatetic Englishman who's a former chef for the Hilton hotel chain. Nightclubs, pubs, and bars run late into the night and almost always feature the island's buoyant musical styles. **Cricket Wicket** at 149 Tragarete Rd., is an after-hours bar with various bands performing on weekends.

TOBAGO

Tobago is the antithesis of its larger cousin, Trinidad, as peaceful, calm, and easygoing as Trinidad is loud, crowded, and frenetic. The island is filled with magical white sandy beaches, languid palm trees, and clear blue waters, and you'll find lots of spots for diving and snorkeling. There are also magnificent rain forests and hundreds of tiny streams and waterways carved into a steep crest of mountains rising 2,000 feet and snaking down the island's center. The bird life and nature trails here are impressive.

Frommer's Favorite Tobago Experiences

- **Visiting Pigeon Point Beach:** One of the most beautiful and distinctive spots in the Caribbean, Pigeon Point is an oasis of white sand, aqua water, and tall palm trees.
- **Snorkeling at Buccoo Reef:** The spot is a must-visit for its exotic fish and impressive underwater coral, which can also be observed via glass-bottom boat.
- **Checking out Nylon Pool:** Named for its crystal-clear water, this small lagoon is located near Buccoo Reef and is filled with tropical fish. It's great for wading and swimming.

COMING ASHORE   Cruise passengers arrive at a small but orderly cruise terminal in central Scarborough, the island's main town. There's usually a fleet of taxis ready to

Frommer's Ratings: Tobago					
	poor	fair	good	excellent	outstanding
Overall Experience				✓	
Shore Excursions			✓		
Activities Close to Port	✓				
Beaches & Water Sports				✓	
Shopping		✓			
Dining/Bars		✓			

go just outside of the cruise terminal, and cab rates are posted inside the terminal at the main entrance. There's even a detailed taxi rate chart posted inside the cruise terminal. Larger ships must anchor offshore and transfer passengers to the terminal via tenders.

There are a number of phones inside the terminal, although last time I was there they weren't taking my AT&T phone card and I had to buy a local phone card.

INFORMATION   There is no official information booth at the small terminal in Scarborough. For info before you go, contact the tourism board office in the U.S. at ☎ **888/595-4868** or www.visittnt.com.

Getting Around

BY TAXI   Taxi is the preferred mode of travel for tourists here; the island is small enough that any location worth visiting can be reached this way. Distances can be deceiving, though, because some of the roads are in very bad shape and others wind along the coast and twist through the mountains. There is no road that completely circles the island. Taxis are normally available at the cruise terminal; rates are posted on a board by the main entrance. It pays to agree on a fare before climbing in.

BY RENTAL CAR   There's really no need for a cruise passenger to rent a car on Tobago.

Shore Excursions

Pigeon Point Beach Trip ($49, 5¹/₂ hours, including lunch): Via taxi, you head toward Tobago's most popular beach, where you'll find a restaurant, bar, rest rooms, and small cabanas (huts) lining the beach. You have your pick of water sports, including snorkeling and banana-boat rides (for a fee, of course).

Tobago Island Explorer ($59, 7¹/₂ hours, including lunch): Passengers depart the cruise terminal via bus for a trip that starts at Fort King George and the Tobago Museum. After a tour of the museum, the excursion continues along the Windward Coast Road to the Richmond Greathouse for a guided tour. Continuing to the Speyside lookout, a photo stop is made before the tour proceeds to Jemma's Seafood Kitchen for a tasty lunch.

On Your Own: Within Walking Distance

The well-restored, British-built **Fort King George,** dating from 1777, overlooks Scarborough's east side. There's no admission charge to enter the grounds. The fort offers a great view of Tobago's Atlantic coast, and other historic buildings here include St. Andrew's church (built in 1819) and the Courthouse (built in 1825). Scarborough's botanical gardens are situated between the main highway and town center, but it's not much more than a glorified public park with a few marked trees.

Other than this, there aren't many attractions within walking distance of the cruise terminal in Tobago and even the terminal shops are small and limited. It's best to put aside the shopping excursions for another port and enjoy Tobago's relaxed atmosphere and fine beaches.

Shopping

There simply isn't much shopping for tourists here, beyond the shops inside the cruise terminal and sporadic craft merchants at the popular beaches at Fort King George.

Beaches

Pigeon Point, near the southern tip of Tobago on the Caribbean side, is the best beach on an island filled with great beaches. **Store Bay,** south of Pigeon Point, has white sands and good year-around swimming (there's a lifeguard, too). Here you'll find vendors hawking local wares and glass-bottom-boat tours departing to Buccoo Reef. Despite

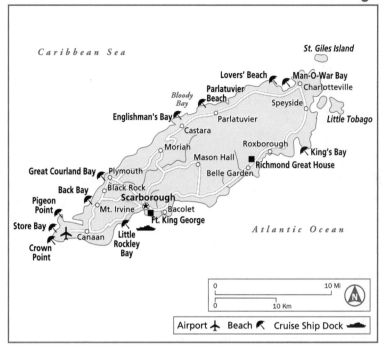

their names, **Parlatuvier** and **Bloody Bay,** on Tobago's Caribbean (west) coast, are tranquil, secluded, and beautiful.

SPORTS

GOLF   There's an 18-hole championship golf course, **Mount Irvine Golf Course** at the Mount Irvine Hotel (☎ **868/639-8871**), about 5 miles from Pigeon Point. It's among the most scenic courses in the Caribbean, and overlooks the sea from gently rolling hills. The clubhouse sits on a promontory and offers great views.

SCUBA DIVING   Tobago is virtually surrounded by shallow-water reefs filled with colorful marine life easily visible through the clear water. The island's reefs offer all kinds of diving experiences, from beginner-level dives at Buccoo Reef to drift diving for experienced divers at Grouper Ground. **Dive Tobago,** at Pigeon Point (☎ **868/639-0202**), is the island's oldest dive operation, offering resort courses and rentals and catering to both beginners and experienced divers.

GREAT LOCAL RESTAURANTS & BARS

There are several moderately priced (U.S.$15 to U.S.$25 per person) restaurants in Tobago, including **The Old Donkey Cart House,** on Bacolet Street in Scarborough (☎ **868/639-3551**), housed in a restored colonial home that once served as Tobago's first guest house. Today it's a bistro serving French wines, light snacks and salads, and specialties like armadillo and opossum (called *manicou*).

The beach at Store Bay is lined with a row of cheap-food stands offering rotis (chicken or beef wrapped in Indian turnovers and flavored with curry), shark-and-bake, crab and dumplings, and fish lunches. **Chrystal's,** on the corner of Store Bay and Milford Road, is another local favorite for flying fish, shark-and-bake, and fruit juices.

12 Bermuda & the Panama Canal Route

After the Caribbean, the island nation of **Bermuda,** sitting out in the Atlantic roughly parallel to South Carolina (or Casablanca, if you're measuring from the east), is the other major cruise destination from the eastern seaboard. Most cruise ships bound for here depart from New York or Boston.

Transiting the **Panama Canal** is spectacular in itself, but on typical Canal itineraries you get more: on the eastern side, visits to the rain forests of Costa Rica, the Mayan ruins of Guatemala, and the Kuna culture of the San Blas Islands; on the western side, the beauty of the Mexican Riviera.

1 Bermuda

Although Bermuda was discovered by the Spanish in the early 16th century, it was the British who first settled here in 1609 when the *Sea Venture,* en route to Virginia's Jamestown colony, was wrecked on the island's reefs. No lives were lost, and the crew and passengers built two new ships and continued on to Virginia, but three crew members stayed behind and became the island's first permanent settlers. Bermuda became a crown colony in 1620 and remains one today. Still very British, the ubiquitous Bermuda shorts are worn by many, horse-drawn carriages trot about, driving is on the left, and the island is divided up into parishes. It's a genteel, sane, and orderly place and even prohibits rental cars and limits the number of regularly visiting cruise ships to six.

Not to say things aren't bustling during the week in **Hamilton** and **St. George's** when the ships are in town, but a calm and controlled atmosphere reigns as visitors fan out across the island. There are many powdery soft beaches easily accessible by taxi or motor scooter; **Horseshoe Bay** and **Elbow Beach** are popular and the many unnamed slivers of silky beach tucked into the jagged coastline are worth discovering. There are more **golf courses** per square mile than any other place in the world. For shoppers, Front and Queen streets in Hamilton offer dozens of shops and department stores, most specializing in English items like porcelain, crystal, wool clothing, and linens. For history buffs, the nearly 300-year-old St. Peter's Church and several museums are within walking distance of the pier in St. George's, and Fort St. Catherine is just about a mile away. The exhibits at the Maritime Museum, which is built into the ruins of Bermuda's oldest fort at the Royal Naval Dockyard, are impressive and varied.

Bermuda

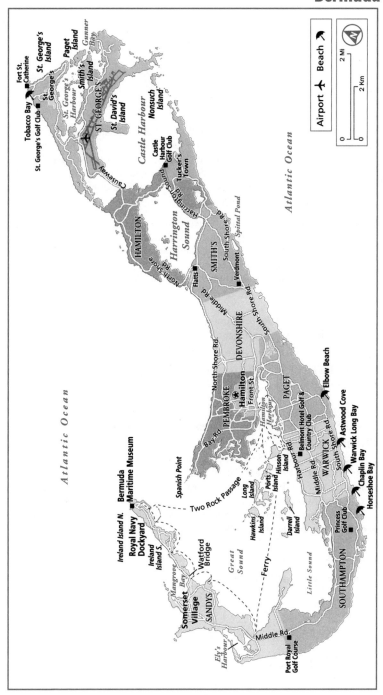

Airport ✈   Beach 🏄

2 Mi
2 Km

Atlantic Ocean

Atlantic Ocean

St. George's Island
Paget Island
Gunner Bay
Fort St. Catherine
St. George's Island
Smith's Island
Tobacco Bay
St. George's
St. George's Golf Club
St. George's Harbour
ST. GEORGE'S
St. David's Island
Nonsuch Island
Castle Harbour
Castle Harbour Golf Club
Tucker's Town
(Causeway)
Harrington Sound Rd
Spital Pond
HAMILTON
Harrington Sound
North Shore Rd
SMITH'S
South Shore Rd
South Shore Rd
Flatts
Verdmont
Middle Rd
DEVONSHIRE
South Shore Rd
North Shore Rd
Elbow Beach
North Shore Rd
Astwood Cove
★ Hamilton
Front St.
PEMBROKE
Hamilton Harbour
PAGET
Belmont Hotel Golf & Country Club
Bay Rd
Harbour Rd
WARWICK
Warwick Long Bay
Middle Rd
Chaplin Bay
Spanish Point
Ports Island
Hinson Island
South Shore Rd
Horseshoe Bay
Two Rock Passage
Long Island
Darrell Island
Princess Golf Club
Hawkins Island
SOUTHAMPTON
Bermuda Maritime Museum
Ireland Island N.
Royal Navy Dockyard
Ireland Island S.
Great Sound
Little Sound
Ferry
Watford Bridge
Mangrove Bay
Somerset Village
SANDYS
Ely's Harbour
Middle Rd
Port Royal Golf Course

Cruise ships have been sailing to Bermuda for over a century, making it one of the earliest cruise destinations. The Quebec Steamship Company, which eventually evolved into the Furness Bermuda Line, began its New York–to–Bermuda service in 1874 with the small steamers *Canima* and *Bermuda* and then added two new ships, the *Orinoco* in 1881 and the *Trinidad* in 1893, plus the liner *Pretoria,* acquired from the Union Line in 1897.

Unlike most Caribbean itineraries, on which ships visit ports for a day at most, the majority of Bermuda-bound ships spend several whole days at the island. Bermuda has carefully managed the number of cruise ships visiting to maintain a semblance of order and keep the island from getting overrun with too many tourists (and to protect its hotel trade). Today, the government allows six cruise ships—five on weekdays and the other on weekends, sailing from New York, Boston, and Philadelphia—to visit the island on a regular basis during its season, late April through October, when the temperatures hover around 75° and extended rainfall is rare.

Frommer's Favorite Bermuda Experiences

- **Hopping a local ferry in Hamilton:** For a few bucks you get a scenic ride to the Royal Naval Dockyard on the island's far west end, where you can tour the historic fortress ruins and excellent museums.
- **Renting a motor scooter and touring the island independently:** Bermuda's roads are well maintained (but can get crowded at rush hour), the island is scenic, and its beaches are easy to find.
- **Having lunch at Waterloo House:** The elegant patio restaurant at the Waterloo House, within walking distance of the cruise ship docks in Hamilton, offers idyllic views of the boats and yachts in Hamilton Harbour.

SHIPS VISITING BERMUDA   For 2001, the six ships sailing regular Bermuda routes are Celebrity's *Zenith* and *Horizon,* Princess's *Pacific Princess,* and Royal Caribbean's *Nordic Empress,* all sailing from New York; Norwegian's *Norwegian Majesty,* sailing from Boston; and Crown Cruise Line's *Crown Dynasty,* sailing from Philadelphia. See cruise line reviews in chapters 6 and 7 for details on all ships and itineraries.

COMING ASHORE   Cruise ships tie up at three harbors in Bermuda; most are at the docks smack dab in the middle of Hamilton or St. George's in the east end, and less often at the Royal Naval Dockyard in the west end. Exploring, especially from Hamilton and St. George's, couldn't be easier as the ships pull right to the docks (no need to tender back and forth).

There are several **credit-card phones** in the terminal in Hamilton, and a bank of phones just off the pier in St. George's.

Frommer's Ratings: Bermuda

	poor	fair	good	excellent	outstanding
Overall Experience					✓
Shore Excursions			✓		
Activities Close to Port				✓	
Beaches & Water Sports					✓
Shopping					✓
Dining/Bars			✓		

CURRENCY   The legal tender in Bermuda is the Bermuda dollar (BD$) and it's pegged to the U.S. dollar on an equal basis—BD$1 equals U.S.$1. There's no need to exchange any U.S. money for Bermudian.

LANGUAGE   English is the official language.

INFORMATION   Bermuda's **Visitor Service Bureau** has several branches, including one at the ferry terminal in Hamilton (☎ **441/295-1480**) and one in King's Square in St. George's (☎ **441/297-1642**).

CALLING FROM THE U.S.   When calling Bermuda from the U.S., you need to dial only a "1" before the numbers listed throughout this section.

GETTING AROUND

BY TAXI   Taxis are regulated by meter and are clean, new, and plentiful at all three cruise piers—but boy are they expensive! Expect to pay at least $4 for the first mile and $1.40 for each additional mile; fares go up 25% between 10pm and 6am as well as on Sundays and holidays. If you want to go touring, the hourly rates for a taxi are $37.50; the minimum is 3 hours. When a taxi has a blue flag on its hood (locals call it the "bonnet"), drivers are qualified to serve as tour guides (and they don't charge extra for the tour). There are several authorized taxi companies on the island, including **Radio Cab** (☎ **441/295-4141**), **C.O.O.P** (☎ **441/292-4476**), and **Sandys** (☎ **441/234-2344**). Taxi fares add up and you can pay $20 or $30 before you know it; if you can, split a taxi (most are minivans) among four people.

BY BUS   Buses are a good option in Bermuda; they're cheap, clean, and go everywhere. Some, however, don't run on Sundays and holidays. Bermuda is divided into 14 zones of about 2 miles each. The regular cash fare for up to three zones is $2.50, or $4 for more than three zones. If you use tokens, these fares are 25¢ less. You must have exact change or tokens to use the buses. You can purchase tokens at the Central Bus Terminal on Washington Street in Hamilton. You can also purchase day passes. For more information on bus service, call ☎ **340/292-3854.**

BY MOTOR SCOOTER   A popular way to travel, there are motor scooters everywhere. Roads are well-maintained on Bermuda, but remember that driving is on the left. Rental fees are pretty standard across the island. Mopeds go for about $35 for the first day and $60 for 2 days; scooters go for about $45 for 1 day. You need a major credit card, and you must buy a one-time insurance policy costing $15. You can rent from **Astwood Cycles** (☎ **441/292-2245**), along Front Street in Hamilton, adjacent to the cruise ship terminal; **Eve's Cycles** (☎ **441/236-6247**), which sets up shop near the cruise terminal in Hamilton; or **Oleander Cycles** (☎ **441/295-0919**) on Gorham Road in Hamilton.

BY FERRY   It's an interesting and efficient way to get around, and you get some sightseeing done in the process. The government-run ferries crisscross Great Sound between Hamilton and Somerset (where the Royal Naval Dockyard is located), charging only $3.75 one-way. Service also goes between Hamilton and Paget and Warwick, across the harbor. Buy tickets and get schedules at the Ferry Terminal (adjacent to the cruise ship docks) or Central Bus Terminal in Hamilton. Or call for information at ☎ **441/ 295-4506.**

BY HORSE-DRAWN CARRIAGE   Before 1946, this was the only way to get around. Now it's the quaint way. Drivers congregate along Front Street in Hamilton, adjacent to the No. 1 cruise ship terminal. A single carriage accommodating one to four passengers and drawn by one horse costs $20 for 30 minutes. Another 30 minutes is another $20. For longer rides, the fee is negotiable. Unless you make special arrangements for a night ride, you aren't likely to find any carriages after 4:30pm. For more information, contact **Terceira's Stables** at ☎ **441/236-3014.**

BY RENTAL CAR   There are no rental cars permitted on the island.

SHORE EXCURSIONS

Bermuda is truly an island made for independent exploring, offering a great combination of history, beaches, and shopping. Take your pick. Hamilton and St. George's are conducive to walking tours, and the beaches and golf courses are easily accessible by taxi, bus, or motor scooter.

Guided Walking Tour of St. George's ($21, 1 hour): Learn about Bermuda's history, including its churches, art galleries, libraries, and private gardens.

West End Highlights ($40, 3 hours): This minibus tour takes you from Hamilton to the Royal Naval Dockyard; en route you'll sight-see and then explore the many exhibits at the Dockyard's museums.

Snorkeling Trip ($42, 3 hours): From Hamilton, board a boat and motor out to a snorkeling spot hear the West End as the captain talks to passengers about Bermuda history and customs. Then, after an hour or so of snorkeling, the fun begins: The music is turned on, the dancing starts, and the bar opens as the boat heads back to port.

Glass-Bottomed Boat Cruise ($30, 2 hours): See the coral reefs and colorful fish living in Bermuda's waters, then view one of Bermuda's famous shipwrecks and enjoy a rum swizzle from a fully stocked bar.

Golf Excursion (about $66 to $160, half-day): Well-known courses visited on these excursions include Mid Ocean Golf Club, among the best in world; Castle Harbour Golf Club; Riddells Bay Golf & Country Club, a veritable golfing institution built in 1922; Port Royal Golf Course; and St. George's Golf Club, Bermuda's newest course, designed by Robert Trent Jones. Excursions include tee times for 18 holes at one of these challenging courses as well as carts. A taxi to and from the courses may be extra and club rental is about $30 extra. The golf excursions are often sold directly through an onboard golf pro who organizes lessons on the ship, too.

ON YOUR OWN: A WALKING TOUR OF HAMILTON

Hamilton has been the capital of Bermuda since 1815, when it replaced St. George's, and was once known as the "Show Window of the British Empire." Today, it's the economic hub of the island. Following is a walking tour that introduces you to all that's noteworthy in Hamilton.

   Start at the harbor front at the:

1. **Visitors Service Bureau/Ferry Terminal.** Pick up some free maps and brochures of the island here.

   From the bureau, you'll emerge onto **Front Street,** Hamilton's main street and shopping area. Before 1946, there were no cars here, but today its busy traffic includes small autos, buses, mopeds, bicycles, and horse-drawn carriages.

   Walk directly south of the Ferry Terminal toward the water, taking a short side street between the Visitors Service Bureau and the large Bank of Bermuda. You'll come to:

2. **Albouy's Point,** a small grassy park with benches and trees that open onto a panoramic vista of the boat- and ship-filled slip. Nearby is the Royal Bermuda Yacht Club, an elite rendezvous for both the Bermudian and the American yachting set since the 1930s.

Walking Tour—The City of Hamilton

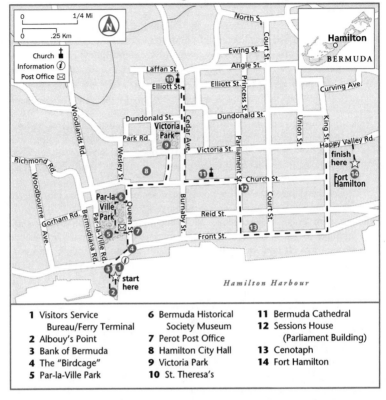

1 Visitors Service Bureau/Ferry Terminal	**6** Bermuda Historical Society Museum	**11** Bermuda Cathedral
2 Albouy's Point	**7** Perot Post Office	**12** Sessions House (Parliament Building)
3 Bank of Bermuda	**8** Hamilton City Hall	**13** Cenotaph
4 The "Birdcage"	**9** Victoria Park	**14** Fort Hamilton
5 Par-la-Ville Park	**10** St. Theresa's	

After taking in the view, walk directly north, crossing Point Pleasant Road, to the:

3. **Bank of Bermuda,** open Monday to Friday from 9:30am to 3pm. Here is Bermuda's most extensive coin collection—there's at least one sample of every coin minted in the United Kingdom since the reign of King James I in the early 17th century. You'll also see Bermuda's famous money, called "hog money." In use since the early 1600s, the hog coin is stamped on one side with the ill-fated *Sea Venture* and on the other side with a wild hog, the main source of food for the early settlers.

Now, head east along Front Street to the point where it intersects with Queen Street. Here is:

4. **The Birdcage,** the perch in the middle of the intersection from which police direct traffic. It's the most photographed sight in Bermuda. If the bobby directing traffic is a man, he'll likely be wearing Bermuda shorts.

Next, continue north along Queen Street until you reach:

5. **Par-la-Ville Park,** which was once a private garden attached to the townhouse of William B. Perot, the first postmaster of Bermuda, who designed the gardens in the 19th century. He collected rare and exotic plants from all over the globe, including the Indian rubber tree, which was seeded in 1847.

Also opening onto Queen Street at the entrance to the park is the:

6. **Bermuda Historical Society Museum,** 13 Queen St., which is also the Bermuda library. Here you'll find items like cedar furniture, collections of antique silver and china, hog money, a 1775 letter from George Washington, and other things.

Next door is the:

7. **Perot Post Office,** which was run by William Perot from 1818 to 1862. It's said that he'd go down to collect mail from the clipper ships, but would put it under his top hat to maintain his dignity. As he strolled through town, he'd greet friends by tipping his hat, and thereby deliver the mail, too. He started printing stamps in 1848 and today they're extremely valuable (only 11 are known to exist).

Continue onto Queen Street, and then turn right onto Church Street to reach:

8. **Hamilton City Hall,** 17 Church St., which dates from 1960 and is crowned by a white tower. The bronze weathervane on top is a replica of the *Sea Venture.*

In the back of Hamilton City Hall, opening onto Victoria Street, lies:

9. **Victoria Park,** a cool, refreshing 4-acre oasis frequented by office workers on their lunch breaks. It has a sunken garden, ornamental shrubbery, and a Victorian bandstand.

Cedar Avenue is the eastern boundary of Victoria Park. If you follow it north for 2 blocks, you'll reach:

10. **St. Theresa's,** a Roman Catholic cathedral that's open daily from 8am to 7pm and for Sunday services. Dating from 1927, its architecture was inspired by the Spanish Mission style. It's one of a half-dozen Roman Catholic churches in Bermuda. Its gold-and-silver chalice was a gift from Pope Paul VI when he visited the island in 1986.

After seeing the cathedral, retrace your steps south along Cedar Avenue until you reach Victoria Street. Cedar now becomes Burnaby Street; continue south on this street until you come to Church Street and then turn left, until you see:

11. **Bermuda Cathedral,** or the Cathedral of the Most Holy Trinity, as it is sometimes called. This neo-Gothic church is the seat of the Anglican Church of Bermuda.

When you leave the cathedral, continue east along Church Street to:

12. **Sessions House (Parliament Building),** on Parliament Street, between Reid and Church streets. It's open to the public Monday to Friday from 9am to 12:30pm and 2 to 5pm. On Fridays you can see Bermuda's political process in action, with the speaker wearing a full wig and a black robe. Bermuda has the third oldest parliament in the world, after Iceland's and England's.

Continue walking south along Parliament Street until you approach Front Street, where you should turn left toward the:

13. **Cenotaph,** a memorial to Bermuda's dead in both world wars.

From here, continue east along Front Street until you reach King Street, and then head north to Happy Valley Road. Go right until you see the entrance (on your right) to:

14. **Fort Hamilton,** an imposing old fortress on the eastern outskirts of Hamilton. The Duke of Wellington ordered its construction to protect Hamilton Harbour. It offers panoramic views of the city and harbor, although with its moat and 18-ton guns, the fort was outdated before it was even completed.

ON YOUR OWN: A WALKING TOUR OF ST. GEORGE'S

St. George's was the second English town to be established in the new world, after Jamestown in Virginia. King's Square, also called Market Square or the King's Parade, is the center of life here, and it's just steps from where the cruise ships dock. From here you can begin the following walking tour, which takes you to all the major sights in this most quaint and historical of towns.

1. **King's Square** is about 200 years old, and it's not as historic as St. George's itself. This was formerly a marshy part of the harbor—at least when the shipwrecked

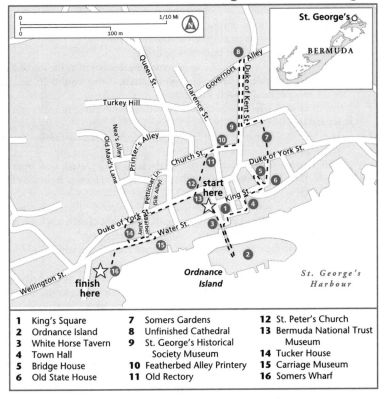

1	King's Square	**7**	Somers Gardens	**12**	St. Peter's Church
2	Ordnance Island	**8**	Unfinished Cathedral	**13**	Bermuda National Trust
3	White Horse Tavern	**9**	St. George's Historical		Museum
4	Town Hall		Society Museum	**14**	Tucker House
5	Bridge House	**10**	Featherbed Alley Printery	**15**	Carriage Museum
6	Old State House	**11**	Old Rectory	**16**	Somers Wharf

passengers and crew of the *Sea Venture* first saw it. On the square, notice a replica of the pillory and stocks that were formerly used to punish criminals (and in many cases, the innocent).

From the square, head south across the small bridge to:

2. **Ordnance Island,** jutting into St. George's Harbour. The British once stored gunpowder and cannons here, but today the island houses the *Deliverance,* a replica of the vessel that carried the shipwrecked *Sea Venture* passengers on to Virginia. Alongside the ship is a ducking stool, a contraption used in 17th-century witch trials.

Retrace your steps across the bridge to King's Square. On the waterside stands the:

3. **White Horse Tavern,** a restaurant jutting out into St. George's Harbour (consider it for lunch or a drink). It was once the home of John Davenport, who came to Bermuda in 1815 to open a dry-goods store. Turns out Davenport was a bit of a miser: Upon his death, some 75,000 English pounds' worth of gold and silver were discovered stashed away in his cellar.

Across the square stands the:

4. **Town Hall,** the meeting place of the corporation governing St. George's. Inside, a multimedia audiovisual presentation is shown several times a day.

From King's Square, head east along King Street, cutting north on Bridge Street. There you'll come to the:

5. **Bridge House,** 1 Bridge St. Constructed shortly after 1700, this was once the home of several governors of Bermuda. Furnished with 18th- and 19th-century antiques, it's now home to an art gallery and souvenir shop.

   Return to King Street and continue east to the:

6. **Old State House,** which actually opens onto Princess Street, at the top of King Street. This is the oldest stone building in Bermuda, dating from 1620, and was once the home of the Bermuda Parliament.

   Continue your stroll down Princess Street until you come to Duke of York Street and the entrance to:

7. **Somers Gardens.** The heart of Sir George Somers, the admiral of the *Sea Venture,* is buried there.

   Walk through Somers Gardens and up the steps to the North Gate onto the Blockade Alley. If you look up the hill, you'll see what is known as the "the folly of St. George's," the:

8. **Unfinished Cathedral,** which was intended to replace St. Peter's (see below). Work began in 1874, but eventually came to an end; the church was beset by financial difficulties and a schism in the Anglican congregation.

   After viewing the ruins, turn left onto Duke of Kent Street, which leads down to the:

9. **St. George's Historical Society Museum,** at the intersection of Featherbed Alley and Duke of Kent Street. An example of 18th-century architecture, the house has a collection of Bermudian historical artifacts and cedar furniture.

   Around the corner on Featherbed Alley is the:

10. **Featherbed Alley Printery,** which has a working replica of the type of printing press invented by Johannes Gutenberg in Germany in the 1450s.

    Go up Featherbed Alley and straight onto Church Street. At the junction with Broad Lane, look to your right to see the:

11. **Old Rectory,** at the head of Broad Alley, behind St. Peter's Church. Now a private home administered by the National Trust, it was built in 1705 by a reformed pirate. It's open on Wednesday only, from noon to 5pm.

    Next, go through the back of the churchyard entrance, opposite Broad Alley, to reach:

12. **St. Peter's Church.** The church's main entrance is on Duke of York Street. This is believed to be the oldest Anglican place of worship in the western hemisphere. In the churchyard, some headstones date back some 300 years. The present church was built in 1713.

    Across the street is the:

13. **Bermuda National Trust Museum.** Once the Globe Hotel, headquarters of Major Norman Walker, the Confederate representative in Bermuda, today it houses relics from the island's involvement in the American Civil War (from Bermuda's perspective).

    As you continue west along Duke of York Street, you'll reach **Barber's Lane,** which honors Joseph Hayne Rainey, a former slave from South Carolina who was a barber in St. George's before eventually returning to the States to be elected the first black member of the U.S. House of Representatives. Nearby is **Petticoat Lane,** also known as Silk Alley. The name dates from the 1834 emancipation, when two former slave women who'd always wanted silk petticoats like their former mistresses finally got some—and then paraded up and down the lane to show off their new finery.

    Continue until you reach:

Bermuda Welcome Wagon

If you plan to see all Bermuda's attractions on your own, the Heritage Passport, recently introduced for cruise passengers, grants admission to eight cultural attractions (museums, historic homes, and the like) over a 4-day period for $35. The passport is available from the visitor service bureaus.

The Bermuda Department of Tourism also recently kicked off a meet-and-greet program with island hoteliers to welcome cruise passengers to Bermuda and introduce them to their properties. Bermuda is anxious to have cruise passengers come back to do land-based vacations.

14. **Tucker House,** which opens onto Water Street. This was the former home of a prominent Bermudian family, and now houses an excellent collection of antiques.

    Diagonally across from the Tucker House is the:

15. **Carriage Museum,** 22 Water St. Here are some of the most interesting carriages used in Bermuda until 1946, when the automobile arrived.

    End your tour across the street at:

16. **Somers Wharf,** a multimillion-dollar waterfront restoration project that includes shops, restaurants, and taverns.

ON YOUR OWN: SANDYS PARISH

If your ship docks at the **Royal Naval Dockyard** on the west end, you can walk to the sprawling complex there. Constructed by convict labor, this 19th-century fortress was used by the British Navy until 1951 as a strategic dockyard. Today, it's a major tourist attraction and its centerpiece is the **Bermuda Maritime Museum,** the most important and extensive museum on the island. Exhibits are housed in six large halls within the complex, and the displays all relate to Bermuda's long connection with the sea, from Spanish exploration to 20th-century ocean liners. You can have a look at maps, ship models, and artifacts like gold bars, pottery, jewelry, and silver coins recovered from the 16th- and 17th-century shipwrecks, like the *Sea Venture.* A visit is a must.

ON YOUR OWN: BEYOND WALKING DISTANCE

A mile or two from King's Square in St. George's, overlooking the beach where the shipwrecked crew of the *Sea Venture* came ashore in 1609, is **Fort St. Catherine,** which you'll want to see. Completed in 1614 and reconstructed several times after, it was named for the patron saint of wheelwrights and carpenters. The fortress houses a museum, with several worthwhile exhibits.

The **Bermuda Railway Trail,** in Sandys Parish, stretches for 21 miles. It was created along the course of the old Bermuda Railway, which served the island from 1931 to 1948, until the automobile was introduced. Armed with a copy of the *Bermuda Railway Trail Guide,* available at the various visitor centers, you can set out on your own expedition via foot or bicycle (most of the moped/scooter rental agencies rent bicycles as well). Most of the trail winds along a car-free route.

SHOPPING

You'll get quality and lots of British items, but don't expect great deals. Nothing in Bermuda is cheap, but keep your eyes peeled for sales, especially at the department stores.

IN HAMILTON Hamilton offers the best and widest shopping choices on the island. **Front and Queen streets** have dozens of shops and department stores, most specializing in English items such as porcelain, crystal, wool clothing, and linens. **Trimingham's** and **H. A. & E. Smith,** two popular department stores on Front Street, as well as other nearby boutiques, sell Waterford, Baccarat, Kosta-Boda, Orrefors, and Galway crystal vases, wine glasses, bowls, and curios; Lalique porcelain figurines; Wedgwood, Royal Doulton, Royal Copenhagen, Spode, Aynsley, and Royal Worcester fine bone china dinnerware, vases, bowls, and curios; Shetland, lamb's wool, and cashmere sweaters and skirts from Scotland and England; and Burberry's rainwear.

Archie Brown on Front Street and the **Scottish Wool Shop** on Queen Street specialize in sweaters, woolens, and tartans of all kinds. **A.S. Cooper & Sons** on Front Street is the island's oldest and largest china and glassware store—it has it all. The **Irish Linen Shop** on the corner of Queen and Front streets sells pure Irish linen tablecloths and hand towels. For antique prints, engravings, and magazine illustrations, check out **Pegasus,** across from the Hamilton Princess Hotel on Pitts Bay Road. Many other stores along and adjacent to Front Street sell clothing, arts and crafts, and souvenirs.

IN ST. GEORGE'S You'll find many shops selling the same types of items as in Hamilton, including branches of famous Front Street stores. You'll find it all on **King's Square,** the **Somers Wharf** complex, and **Water Street.** But if you're a hard-core shopper, don't miss out on Hamilton, which is Bermuda's shopping mecca.

SPORTS

GOLF Bermuda has more courses per square mile than any other place in the world. They're all easily accessible via taxi, and your ship will likely have organized excursions to them if you'd rather not go it alone. The following are all 18-hole courses. The par-70, 5,777-yard course at the **Belmont Hotel Golf & Country Club,** Warwick Parish (☎ 441/236-6400), was designed in 1923 by Emmett Devereux, a Scotsman. It's been challenging golfers ever since, especially its par-5 11th hole, a severe dogleg left with a blind tee shot. **Castle Harbour Golf Club,** Hamilton Parish (☎ 441/298-6959), is a par-71, 6,440-yard course designed by the noted golf architect Charles Banks and known for its challenging tee shots. This is one of the more expensive courses to play on. The par-71, 6,565-yard **Port Royal Golf Course,** Southampton Parish (☎ 441/238-9430), was designed by Robert Trent Jones and lies along an ocean terrain. It's a public course and ranks among the very best on the island—as a matter of fact, it's rated among the best in the *world.* Jack Nicklaus likes to play here. **Southampton Princess Golf Club,** Hamilton Parish (☎ 441/239-6952), is a par-54, 2,684-yard course with elevated tees, strategically placed bunkers, and an array of water hazards to challenge even the most experienced golfers. **St. George's Golf Club,** St. George's Parish (☎ 441/297-8067), is one of the island's newest and best. This par-62, 4,043-yard course, designed by Robert Trent Jones, is within walking distance of historic St. George's.

SCUBA DIVING To see some of Bermuda's shipwrecks, **Blue Water Divers Co., Ltd.,** Robinson's Marina, Southampton (☎ 441/234-1034), is Bermuda's oldest and largest full-service scuba-diving operation. All equipment is provided; reservations are necessary.

BEACHES

Bermuda is known for its beaches, and there are many powdery soft beaches (not really pink as they're touted—or maybe I'm just color-blind) easily accessible by taxi or motor scooter. **Horseshoe Bay** in Southampton Parish and **Elbow Beach** in Paget

Parish are very popular and often crowded public beaches, and the many unnamed slivers of silky beach tucked into the jagged coastline are worth discovering. Hotel beaches are generally private. (Elbow Beach charges $4 for visitors; the adjacent Elbow Beach Hotel offers facilities and rentals. Horseshoe Bay is a free public beach and has a place to get snacks.)

Also consider these public beaches: **Astwood Cove** (Warwick Parish) is remote and rarely overcrowded—ditto for **Chaplin Bay** (Warwick and Southampton Parishes); **Warwick Long Bay** (Warwick Parish) is popular and set against a backdrop of scrubland and low grasses; and **Tobacco Bay Beach** (St. George's Parish), is popular and the most frequented beach on St. George's Island.

GREAT LOCAL BARS & RESTAURANTS

You don't go to Bermuda for its cuisine, but there are some tasty local specialties, such as fish chowder laced with rum and sherry peppers (yum!!), as well as spiny Bermuda lobster, mussel pie, and wahoo steak.

IN HAMILTON Try the **Waterloo House,** Pitts Bay Road (☎ 441/295-4480), at the elegant Relais Châteaux hotel, within walking distance of the ship docks. Lunch is served on the outdoor patio overlooking the colorful and idyllic harbor, and many snazzy-looking businesspeople lunch here. The fish chowder is great. The **Lobster Pot & Boat House Bar,** 6 Bermudian Rd. (☎ 441/292-6898), serves a great baked fish and lobster dish. The **Hog Penney,** 5 Burnaby Hill (☎ 441/292-2534), is Bermuda's most famous pub and a great choice for lunch. With its dark paneled walls and classic pub ambiance, you'll think you're in merry olde England. The fresh fish-and-chips is a good choice, along with a cool pint of ale.

IN ST. GEORGE'S Don't miss a meal at the **Black Horse Tavern,** 101 St. David's Rd. (☎ 441/297-1991), for an authentic taste of Bermuda—or so the locals maintain. Order curried conch stew or fish chowder, among many other options. The **White Horse Tavern,** King's Square (☎ 441/297-1838), is the oldest in St. George's and a favorite casual hangout with tourists. There's a terrace with great views of the square and all the hubbub below. Have a beer and a burger.

2 The Panama Canal

The Panama Canal is an awesome feat of engineering and human effort. Construction began in 1880 and wasn't completed until 1914, at the expense of thousands of lives, and the vast majority of the original structure and equipment is still in use. Transiting the canal, which links the Atlantic Ocean with the Pacific, is a thrill for anyone even vaguely interested in engineering or history.

Transiting the canal takes 1 day, generally about 8 hours from start to finish, and it's a fascinating procedure (it often costs ships about $100,000 to pass through; the fee is based on a ship's weight). Your ship will line up in the morning, mostly with cargo ships, to await its turn through the canal. The route is about 50 miles long and includes passage through three main locks, which, through gravity alone, raise ships over Central America and down again on the other side. Between the locks, ships pass through artificially created lakes like the massive **Gatun Lake,** 85 feet above sea level.

While transiting, your ship will feature a running narration of history and facts about the canal by an expert on board for the day.

Cruises that include a canal crossing are generally 10 to 14 nights long, with popular routes between Florida and Acapulco, visiting a handful of Caribbean islands along the way. A few ports in Central America are also visited, including Panama's San Blas

Panama Canal Area

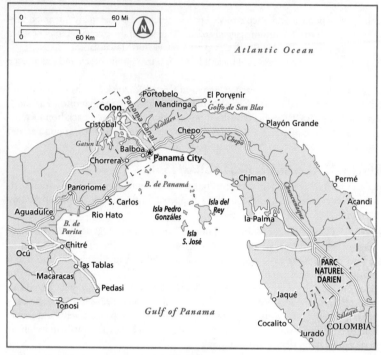

Islands, Costa Rica's Puerto Caldera, and Guatemala's Puerto Quetzal, in addition to other ports along the coast of Mexico.

SHIPS TRANSITING THE PANAMA CANAL For 2001, ships will be sailing itineraries that include transits of the Panama Canal: American Canadian Caribbean's *Grande Caribe*, Carnival's *Jubilee*, Celebrity's *Zenith*, Crystal's *Harmony* and *Symphony*, Cunard's *QE2*, Holland America's *Maasdam* and *Nieuw Amsterdam*, Mediterranean Shipping's *Melody*, Norwegian's *Norwegian Majesty*, Princess's *Crown Princess* and *Sun Princess*, Radisson's *Radisson Diamond* and *Seven Seas Navigator*, Regal's *Regal Empress*, Royal Caribbean's *Vision of the Seas*, Royal Olympic's *Stella Solaris*, and Seabourn's *Seabourn Legend* and *Seabourn Pride*. See the cruise line reviews in chapters 6 through 9 for details.

PORTS ALONG THE CANAL ROUTE

The **San Blas Islands** are a beautiful archipelago and home to the Kuna Indians, whose women are well known for their colorful, hand-embroidered stitching. If you get a chance to go ashore, the tiny women, dressed in their traditional *molas* (brightly and intricately embroidered blouses), sell all manner of embroidered molas in square blocks and strips (and don't underestimate their chutzpah—these gals will only bargain so far). The molas make great pillow covers or wall hangings, and cost about $5 to $10 each. When your ship anchors offshore at the islands, be prepared for throngs of Kunas to emerge from the far-off distance, paddling their dugout canoes (a few have motors) up to the ship, where they will spend the entire day calling for money or anything else ship passengers toss overboard. The Kuna seem to enjoy diving overboard to retrieve fruit or coins thrown to them, but of course, it's a sad sight, too, watching entire families so

---

Canal Changes Hands

In compliance with a treaty signed between the United States and Panama in 1977, at the stroke of midnight on December 31, 1999, canal operations were passed from U.S. into Panamanian hands. I'm glad to report that the transition went smoothly. In fact, Panama is pursuing a handful of development projects to keep the canal a major tourism draw. Not only are they intent on hosting as many ships as possible, Panama tourism officials are bent on adding all kinds of additional attractions to lure cruisers. Take the planned Colon Zoo, for example. It's a $45-million private initiative that is to include a duty-free mall, dining and amusements, a 150-room Radisson hotel, and cruise berths. Some dozen shore excursions offered will focus on local history, culture, and nature.

---

desperate and needy. (Makes you feel damn guilty for rolling in on that fancy cruise ship of yours.)

In **Costa Rica,** many ships call at Puerto Caldera on the Pacific side or Puerto Limón on the Atlantic side. While there's nothing to see from either cargo port, both are great jumping-off points for tours that all visiting ships offer of the country's lush, beautiful rain forests, which are alive with some 850 species of birds, 200 species of mammals, 9,000 species of flowering plants, and about 35,000 species of insects. After a scenic bus ride, tours will take you on a nature walk through the forest.

In **Guatemala,** most Panama Canal–bound ships call at Puerto Quetzal, on the Pacific coast; a few may call at Santo Tomas on the Caribbean side. Both are used as gateways to Guatemala's spectacular Mayan ruins at Tikal. They're the country's most famous attractions and considered the most spectacular yet discovered anywhere in the world, with over 3,000 temples, pyramids, and other buildings of the ancient civilization nestled in thick jungle. Much of it is still uncovered. The setting is surreal. Some of the ruins date as far back as A.D. 300. Excursions here are neither cheap nor easy, but the journey is well worth the effort. A tour involves buses, walking, and a 1-hour flight; expect to pay about $350-plus. Excursions to the less-spectacular Mayan sites in Honduras are also offered from Puerto Quetzal, as are several overland tours of Guatemala's interior.

Part 4

Appendixes

With information on end-of-cruise concerns such as tipping, disem-barking, and retrieving your luggage, plus an index by ship name.

Appendix A: Wrapping Up Your Cruise— Debarkation Concerns

Hardly anybody likes to get off the ship at the end of their cruise, but it's part of the deal. To make matters easier, here's a discussion of a few matters you'll have to take care of before heading back to home sweet home.

1 Tipping

Like waiters and waitresses in the United States, the cruise industry pays its staff low wages, with the understanding that the bulk of their salaries will come from tips. No matter which cabin you occupied or what price you paid for it, if service is satisfactory, you'll be expected to tip a recommended amount (of course, you can always tip more), which comes to about $70 per person (adult or child) for a weeklong cruise. Only some upscale ships, including Radisson's *Radisson Diamond,* forbid tipping altogether.

Tipping is so formally integrated into the cruise experience that it's almost ritualistic, and cruise lines aren't shy about reminding you. Each line has clear **guidelines for gratuities,** which are usually printed in the daily schedule or announced toward the end of the cruise. Likewise, cabin stewards usually leave **little white envelopes** (marked for cabin attendants, dining stewards, and waiters) along with suggested tipping percentages and amounts where you'll be sure not to miss them. Other lines, usually the small, offbeat lines like Windjammer Barefoot Cruises, prefer that a single tip be delivered to a central source; the pooled funds are then equitably distributed to the crew.

Even on lines like Holland America and Windstar, which promote their "tipping not required" policies, tipping really is expected and the policy is more a way to be diplomatic than to discourage tipping. Granted, if you received truly lousy service, reflect that in the tip you leave as you would at a restaurant shoreside.

Suggested tipping amounts vary slightly with the line and its degree of luxury. As a rule of thumb, however, each passenger should expect to tip about $3.50 per person per day for the **cabin steward** and the **dining room waiter** and about $2 for the dining-room **busboy.** (As a generous tipper and one-time waitress, if service has been good, I generally throw in another $5 or $10 for each at the end of the week, but this, of course, is not mandatory.) Like at any good hotel, feel free to distribute additional tips to anyone else who made your life particularly pleasant during your time on board.

Wine stewards and **bartenders** are usually rewarded with a 15% surcharge that's added onto a bill every time you sign it; of course, you may want to tip more if you're a barfly. Some lines suggest you tip the **maître d'** about $5 per person for the week and slip another couple of bucks to the **chief housekeeper;** it's your choice (if I've never even met these people, I don't feel obligated to tip them). Some maître d's will appreciate a discreet tip if they've gone to the trouble of reassigning you to a new table at dinner; some will not accept tips for this.

Tip **masseurs and masseuses, hair stylists,** and **manicurists** immediately after they work on you; 15% is standard. Tips can be paid in cash or charged to your onboard account (and the Steiner spa-and-salon people will do this for you unless you indicate otherwise; don't feel pressured into giving a tip if your treatment was not satisfactory).

WHEN DO YOU DISTRIBUTE YOUR TIPS?

It's good form to tip your dining stewards during the cruise's final dinner, instead of waiting until breakfast the next morning, when stewards might be assigned other stations or be unavailable. Incidentally, you are expected to tip your waiter and busboy for each night of your cruise, even if you did not dine in the main restaurant an evening or two.

SPECIAL TIPPING SITUATIONS

In case you didn't know, tipping the captain or one of the captain's officers is a no-no (they're on full salary, and are—or are expected to be—above all that). If you found someone among the staff to be outstandingly able and helpful, be sure to say so on the **comment card** that's left in your cabin toward the end of your cruise. If you're feeling especially ambitious and kind-hearted, write a brief letter praising this person's performance and send it to the cruise line's director of passenger services.

2 Disembarking

You knew it would finally get to this.

It's a good idea to begin packing before dinner of the final night aboard, and be sure to fill out the **luggage tags** given to you, which might be color-coded, and attach them securely to each piece (if you need more than they leave for you, there are always extras at the purser's desk). You'll be requested to leave your luggage outside your cabin door before you retire for the cruise's final night (by midnight or so), and in the wee hours a crew of deck hands will pick it up and spirit it away. The luggage will be tossed into big rolling carts (like the airlines use) somewhere below deck, and at disembarkation, you'll find your baggage waiting for you at the terminal, organized by the colored or numbered tags you attached to it.

If you've neglected to place any baggage outside your door before the designated deadline, you'll have to lug it off the ship yourself. If you leave something behind, the cruise line might eventually return it to you (if it's ever turned in, of course), but not without a prolonged hassle.

Cruise Tip: Don't Pack Your Booze

Don't pack newly purchased bottles of liquor in the luggage you leave out for the crew to carry off the ship, thinking it's only going 100 yards between your cabin and the terminal before you see it again. A friend absent-mindedly did this and the next morning found her bag sitting in the terminal in a pool of rum. Big mess!

Ships normally arrive in port on the final day of the cruise between 6 and 8am, and need at least 90 minutes to unload baggage and complete dockage formalities. That means no one disembarks much before 9am, and it can sometimes take until 10am before you're allowed to leave the ship.

When disembarkation is announced, get ready for the chaos. No matter how you slice it, departures just aren't graceful, and are, frankly, a blunt return to reality. The staff is distracted and busily preparing for the new group of passengers boarding a few hours later (the friendly bartender you chatted with every night or the perky social hostess may not have much time for you now); the crew has only about 5 hours to prepare the ship for the next departure.

Since guests are generally asked to vacate their cabins by about 8am so stewards can begin cleaning them for the arriving guests, pooped people by the hundreds, surrounded by their bags, fill virtually every available inch of every public area (stairs and floors not excluded), waiting to hear the numbers they've been assigned so they can finally depart. Remember, **patience is a virtue.**

It's no surprise that this whole process goes much more smoothly on smaller ships with fewer passengers.

Disembarking through the cruise ship terminal is the equivalent of departing from an international flight. You need to claim your luggage and then pass through customs before exiting the terminal. This normally entails handing the immigration officer your filled-out customs declaration form as you breeze past, without even coming to a full stop. There are generally **porters** available in the terminals, but you might have to haul your luggage through customs before you can get to them. It's customary to pay them at least $1 per bag. Alternatively, there may be **wheeled carts** available (for free or no more than $1.50 each) to help you push your possessions out the door.

3 Customs

Customs officers are most interested in expensive, big-ticket items like cameras, jewelry, china, or silverware. They don't care much about your souvenir items unless you've bought so many that they couldn't possibly be intended for your personal use, or they're concealing illegal substances.

U.S. CUSTOMS

The U.S. government generously allows U.S. citizens $1,200 worth of duty-free imports every 30 days from the U.S. Virgin Islands; those who exceed their exemption are taxed at a 5% rate, rather than the normal 10%. The limit is $400 for your regular international destinations such as the French islands of Guadeloupe and Martinique. The limit is $600 if you return directly from the following islands and countries: Antigua and Barbuda, Aruba, the Bahamas, Barbados, Belize, Costa Rica, Dominica, the Dominican Republic, Grenada, Guatemala, Haiti, Honduras, Jamaica, Montserrat, the Netherland Antilles (Curaçao, Bonaire, St. Maarten, Saba, and St. Eustatius), Panama, St. Kitts and Nevis, St. Lucia, St. Vincent and the Grenadines, Trinidad and Tobago, and the British Virgin Islands. If, for instance, your cruise stops in the U.S. Virgin Islands and the Bahamas, your total limit is $1,200 and no more than $600 of that amount can be from the Bahamas. If you visit only Puerto Rico, you don't have to go through customs at all, since it's an American commonwealth.

U.S. citizens or returning residents at least 21 years of age who are traveling directly or indirectly from the U.S. Virgin Islands are allowed to bring in free of duty 1,000 cigarettes. Duty-free limitations on articles from other countries are generally 1 liter of alcohol, 200 cigarettes (one carton), and 100 cigars (not Cuban). Unsolicited gifts can be mailed to friends and relatives on the U.S. mainland at the rate of $200 per day from the U.S. Virgin Islands or $100 per day from other islands. Unsolicited gifts of any value can be mailed from Puerto Rico. Most meat or meat products, fruit, plants, vegetables, or plant-derived products will be seized by U.S. Customs agents unless they're accompanied by an import license from a U.S. government agency.

Joint Customs declarations are possible for members of a family traveling together. For instance, if you're a husband and wife with two children, your exemptions in the U.S. Virgin Islands become duty-free up to $4,800!

Collect receipts for all purchases made abroad. Sometimes merchants suggest making up a false receipt to undervalue your purchase, but be aware that you could be involved in a "sting" operation—the merchant might be an informer to U.S. Customs. You must also declare on your Customs form all gifts received during your stay abroad.

I've found clearing customs in Florida to be a painless and speedy process, with Customs officials rarely asking for anything more than your filled-out Customs declaration form as they nod you through the door. Of course, better safe than sorry. It's prudent to carry proof that you purchased expensive cameras or jewelry on the U.S. mainland. If you purchased such an item during an earlier trip abroad, you should carry proof that you have previously paid customs duty on the item.

To be on the safe side, if you use any medication containing controlled substances or requiring injection, carry an original prescription or note from your doctor.

For more specifics, request the free *Know Before You Go* pamphlet from the U.S. Customs Service, P.O. Box 7407, Washington, DC 20044 (☎ **202/927-6724;** www.customs.ustreas.gov).

CANADIAN CUSTOMS

Canada allows its citizens a $500 exemption if they are out of the country for at least 7 days, and they are permitted to bring back duty-free 200 cigarettes, 200 grams of tobacco, 40 Imperial ounces of liquor, and 50 cigars. In addition, they are allowed to mail gifts valued at $60 (Canadian) or less to Canada from abroad, provided the gifts are unsolicited and aren't alcohol or tobacco. It's a good idea to enclose a gift card and write on the package: "Unsolicited gift, under $60 value." All valuables, such as expensive cameras you already own, should be declared with their serial numbers on the Y-38 Form before departure from Canada.

For more information, write for the *I Declare* booklet, issued by **Revenue Canada,** 2265 St. Laurent Blvd., Ottawa, ON, KIG 4K3, or call them at ☎ **800/461-9999** or 613/993-0534.

BRITISH CUSTOMS

If you return from the Caribbean either directly to the United Kingdom or arrive via a port in another European Union (EU) country where you and your baggage did not pass through Customs controls, you must go through U.K. Customs and declare any goods in excess of the allowances. These are 200 cigarettes, 100 cigarillos, 50 cigars, or 250 grams of tobacco; 2 liters of still table wine and 1 liter of spirits or strong liqueurs (over 22% alcohol by volume), or 2 liters of fortified or sparkling wine or other liqueurs; 60cc/ml of perfume; 250cc/ml of toilet water; and £145 worth of all other goods, including gifts and souvenirs. (No one under 17 years of age is entitled to a tobacco or alcohol allowance.) Only go through the green "nothing to declare" line if you're sure you have no more than the Customs allowances and no prohibited or restricted goods.

For further information, contact **HM Customs and Excise Office,** Dorset House, Stamford Street, London SE1 9PY (☎ **0171/202-4227**).

Index by Ship Name

continues

Index by Ship Name (continued)

NOTES

FROMMER'S® COMPLETE TRAVEL GUIDES

FROMMER'S® DOLLAR-A-DAY GUIDES

FROMMER'S® PORTABLE GUIDES

FROMMER'S® NATIONAL PARK GUIDES

Family Vacations in the
   National Parks
Grand Canyon

National Parks of the
   American West
Rocky Mountain

Yellowstone & Grand Teton
Yosemite & Sequoia/
   Kings Canyon
Zion & Bryce Canyon

FROMMER'S® MEMORABLE WALKS

Chicago
London

New York
Paris

San Francisco
Washington D.C.

FROMMER'S® GREAT OUTDOOR GUIDES

New England
Northern California

Southern California & Baja
Southern New England

Washington & Oregon

FROMMER'S® BORN TO SHOP GUIDES

Born to Shop: China
Born to Shop: France

Born to Shop: Italy
Born to Shop: London

Born to Shop: New York
Born to Shop: Paris

FROMMER'S® IRREVERENT GUIDES

Amsterdam
Boston
Chicago
Las Vegas

London
Los Angeles
Manhattan
New Orleans

Paris
San Francisco
Seattle & Portland
Vancouver

Walt Disney World
Washington, D.C.

FROMMER'S® BEST-LOVED DRIVING TOURS

America
Britain
California

Florida
France
Germany

Ireland
Italy
New England

Scotland
Spain
Western Europe

THE UNOFFICIAL GUIDES®

Bed & Breakfasts in
   California
 Bed & Breakfasts in
   New England
Bed & Breakfasts in
   the Northwest
Beyond Disney
Branson, Missouri
California with Kids
Chicago

Cruises
Disneyland
Florida with Kids
Golf Vacations in the
   Eastern U.S.
The Great Smoky &
   Blue Ridge
   Mountains
Inside Disney

Hawaii
Las Vegas
London
Miami & the Keys
Mini Las Vegas
Mini-Mickey
New Orleans
New York City
Paris

Safaris
San Francisco
Skiing in the West
Walt Disney World
Walt Disney World
   for Grown-ups
Walt Disney World
   for Kids
Washington, D.C.

SPECIAL-INTEREST TITLES

Frommer's Britain's Best Bed & Breakfasts and
   Country Inns
Frommer's Britain's Best Bike Rides
The Civil War Trust's Official Guide
   to the Civil War Discovery Trail
Frommer's Caribbean Hideaways
Frommer's Food Lover's Companion to France
Frommer's Food Lover's Companion to Italy
Frommer's Gay & Lesbian Europe
Frommer's Exploring America by RV
Hanging Out in Europe
Israel Past & Present

Mad Monks' Guide to California
Mad Monks' Guide to New York City
Frommer's The Moon
Frommer's New York City with Kids
The New York Times' Unforgettable
   Weekends
Places Rated Almanac
Retirement Places Rated
Frommer's Road Atlas Britain
Frommer's Road Atlas Europe
Frommer's Washington, D.C., with Kids
Frommer's What the Airlines Never Tell You

*Ask for Current Specials
and a FREE
CruiseOne Magazine.*

MAXIMUM
CRUISE SAVINGS

**Whether it's your 1st cruise or
your 1st cruise this year,
CruiseOne is your passport to
the perfect cruise! Ask us
about special rates for
singles, couples, families or
groups on cruise
lines worldwide.**

Mention
This Ad For
Free Booking
Bonus

*With Over Four Hundred Offices
Nationwide — See What The CruiseOne
Advantage Can Do For You!*

Call Our National Toll Free Number

**And Be Connected To A CruiseOne
Independent Cruise Specialist**

1-877-785-6542

CRUISEONE.
#1 In Cruising, Nationwide

CLIA

nacoa

Visit us at our www.cruiseone.com
Limited Franchises Available 800-892-3928

![icruise.com — the cruise portal]

149 Ships

20,000 Sailings

100,000 Low Prices

One more reason to book with us!

Take $100 off per cabin any Norwegian Cruise Line cruise of seven or more days

Just visit www.icruise.com, select any of Norwegian Cruise Lines ships, book a 7 or more day cruise and enter promotion code #1065 in the " special requests" area.

Details: all rates are subject to change and availability. This promotion is not combinable with any other promotion. Promotion code must be entered at time of reservation in order to receive discount.